Susan E. D'Ambrosio
Extension x77732

Clinical Personality Assessment

Oxford Textbooks in
Clinical Psychology

Clinical Personality Assessment

Practical Approaches

Edited by

JAMES N. BUTCHER

New York   Oxford
OXFORD UNIVERSITY PRESS
1995

Oxford University Press

Oxford   New York   Toronto
Delhi   Bombay   Calcutta   Madras   Karachi
Kuala Lumpur   Singapore   Hong Kong   Tokyo
Nairobi   Dar es Salaam   Cape Town
Melbourne   Auckland   Madrid
and associated companies in
Berlin   Ibadan

Published by Oxford University Press, Inc.,
198 Madison Avenue, New York, New York 10016-4314

Oxford is a registered trademark of Oxford University Press

Library of Congress Cataloging-in-Publication Data
Clinical personality assessment : practical approaches
edited by James N. Butcher.
p.   cm.—(Oxford textbooks in clinical psychology : v. 2)
Includes bibliographical references and index.
ISBN 0-19-508569-8
1. Personality assessment.
2. Clinical psychology—Methodology.
I. Butcher, James Neal, 1933-   .
II. Series.
[DNLM: 1. Personality Assessment.
2. Mental Disorders—diagnosis. WM 141 F767   1994]
BF698.4.F68   1994   155.2′8–dc20
DNLM/DLC   for Library of Congress   94-12405

9 8 7 6 5 4 3 2

Printed in the United States of America
on acid-free paper

Preface

Throughout my career in psychology I have been interested in and committed to the field of personality assessment. Although much of my own contribution to the assessment literature has centered around one instrument, the MMPI/MMPI-2/MMPI-A, I have always been intrigued with other potential sources of information that can add to our understanding of personality structure and process. Like many other assessment psychologists, I have tended to focus on one approach to assessment and ignore other approaches to understanding personality. For some time now I have wanted to develop a book that would cross special-interest areas and assessment strategies and focus on practical ideas in psychological assessment for practitioners and researchers.

The direct impetus for this book came from discussions with my colleagues at the first annual meeting of the board for a new series by Oxford University Press called Oxford Textbooks in Clinical Psychology, which was held at the annual convention of the American Psychological Association in 1992. The board members strongly encouraged me to develop this book as a "marker variable" for the Oxford series. I would like to express my appreciation for their encouragement and their ideas about

this book. They certainly deserve prominent mention as an influential force in this book's development: Bruce Bongar, Larry Beutler, Gerry Koocher, John Norcross, and Diane Willis. Their continued encouragement and support throughout this project have been invaluable. Also invaluable to the success of this volume has been the input of Joan Bossert, editor at Oxford University Press. Her vision, encouragement, and sage editorial savvy have been extremely valuable in developing the idea for the book, obtaining timely reviews, and in shepherding the chapters through the process that magically turns sometimes rough renderings into quality text.

I would also like to express my appreciation to the following psychologists who reviewed chapters for this book. I appreciated their promptness as well as the thoroughness with which they approached the task. Their reviews were very valuable to us in developing particular chapters:

Yossef S. Ben-Porath
Alan L. Berman
Philip S. Erdberg
Kenneth Feigenbaum
Bonnie Greenberg

John R. Graham
Eileen Palace
Kenneth S. Pope
Janet L. Sonne
Shirley Feldman-Summers
Paul B. Wood

I would also like to thank two of my secretaries, Elizabeth Pukenis and Linda Fresquez, for their assistance in typing parts of the manuscript and in managing the frequent mailings to contributors. Special thanks go to Linda Fresquez for her advice and assistance in organizing the Index of Psychological Tests that is printed in the Appendix and to Betty Gatewood for editorial suggestions.

Finally, I would like to express my gratitude to the contributors to the volume who make this book a novel and valuable source of ideas and practical guides for assessment psychologists. I especially appreciate the tolerance and goodwill shown by the contributors toward my compulsion for deadlines and textual alterations.

James N. Butcher

Contents

Part II. Special Populations in Personality Assessment

Part III. The Meaning of Personality Test Results

Part IV. Sources of Personality Information

Part V. Problems in Personality Assessment

Contributors

MARVIN W. ACKLIN is a Diplomate in Clinical Psychology, ABPP, involved in the full-time independent practice of clinical and forensic psychology in Honolulu. He is a fellow of the Society for Personality Assessment and is listed in the National Register. A graduate of Georgia State University (1984), he did his internship at Northwestern University Medical School in Chicago. He subsequently taught psychotherapy and psychological assessment at Loyola University of Chicago. After relocating to Hawaii in 1988, he was chief psychologist and director of clinical training at the Queen's Medical Center in Honolulu. Dr. Acklin has published on the Rorschach test and on early memories and serves on several editorial boards. He lives on Windward Oahu with his wife, Denise, and their four children. His hobbies include surfing, paddling, and rough-water swimming.

JANE ANSLEY, PH.D., received her doctorate in clinical health psychology from the University of Miami (Florida) in 1992. She is currently a postdoctoral fellow in clinical neuropsychology in the University of Miami School of Medicine, Department of Neurology. She has published scientific papers addressing cognitive performance in the aged and neuropsychological aspects of Parkinson's disease. Her current research addresses personality and psychosocial aspects of epilepsy and cerebrovascular disease.

RUTH A. BAER, PH.D., is associate professor in the Department of Psychology at the University of Kentucky where she is Associate Director of the Clinical Training Program. She has an active private practice in clinical psychology and has published a number of papers on the detection of dissimulation on the MMPI-2 and has similar research interests for the MMPI-A.

JOSEPH A. BANKEN, PH.D., is assistant professor of psychiatry and adjunct assistant professor of psychology at Texas Tech University in Lubbock, Texas. He is also director of research at the Southwest Institute for Addictive Diseases, a substance-abuse treatment program affiliated with the Texas Tech University Health Sciences Center, School of Medicine, Department of Psychiatry. He is a Diplomate of the American Academy of Psychologists Treating Addictions. Dr. Banken earned a Ph.D. in 1988 from the University of Southern Mississippi. He completed the clinical psychology residency program at Wilford Hall USAF Medical Center in San Antonio, Texas, and served as an Air Force clinical psychologist from 1988 to 1990. Dr. Banken has published articles in various areas of psychological testing. He continues current research on the MMPI-2 and psychological assessment measures in adult substance-abusing and psychiatric populations.

DAVID H. BARLOW received his Ph.D. from the University of Vermont in 1969 and has published over 200 articles and chapters and sixteen books, mostly in the areas of anxiety disorders, sexual problems, and clinical research methodology. Currently he is distinguished professor in the Department of Psychology at the University at Albany, State University of New York, and director of the Phobia and Anxiety Disorders Clinic at the University at Albany, SUNY. This clinic is supported by over $1.5 million in external funds per year to investigate the nature and treatment of anxiety and related disorders. Dr. Barlow's books include Barlow, D. H., Hayes, S. C., & Nelson, R. O. (1984), *The Scientist Practitioner: Research and Accountability in Clinical and Educational Settings.* NY: Pergamon Press; Barlow, D. H. & Hersen, M. (1984). *Single Case Experimental Designs: Strategies for Studying Behavioral Change, 2nd edition.* NY: Pergamon Press; *Anxiety and its disorders: The nature and treatment of anxiety and panic.* NY: Guilford Publications (1988), and most recently Barlow, D. H. (1993, Ed.), *Clinical handbook of psychological disorders, 2nd edition.* NY: Guilford Publications.

YOSSEF S. BEN-PORATH, PH.D., is assistant professor in the Department of Psychology at Kent State University. Dr. Ben-Porath completed his training in clinical psychology at the University of Minnesota in 1989. Dr. Ben-Porath was part of the MMPI research group that developed the new MMPI-2 Content Scales and was extensively involved in the adolescent MMPI project. He also maintains an active clinical practice in forensic psychology.

DAVID T. R. BERRY, PH.D., is associate professor in the Department of Psychology at the University of Kentucky, where he is director of the clinical training program. His interests in the topic of malingering stem from his forensic neuropsychology practice, and he has published a number of papers on the topic.

LARRY E. BEUTLER, PH.D., is professor and Director of the Counseling/Clinical/School Psychology Program at the University of California, Santa Barbara. He obtained his Ph.D. from the University of Nebraska in 1970 and subsequently served on the faculties of Duke University Medical School, Stephen F. Austin State University, Baylor University College of Medicine, and the University of Arizona. Dr. Beutler is a Diplomate of the American Board of Professional Psychology (ABPP) and a past international president of the Society for Psychotherapy Research (SPR).

Dr. Beutler currently is the editor of the *Journal of Consulting and Clinical Psychology.* He is a fellow of the American Psychological Association, The American Psychological Society, and the International Fellowship of Eclectic Psychotherapists. He is the author of approximately 200 scientific papers and chapters, and is the author, editor, or coauthor of ten books on psychotherapy and psychopathology. His current research involves developing and testing a decisional model for matching specific psychotherapy procedures and formats with identified patient qualities.

ARNOLD R. BRUHN, PH.D., has worked with early childhood memories and the assessment of autobiographical memory since the early 1970s. He began his career as an assistant professor of psychology at the George Washington University Medical Center. He formulated the cognitive-perceptual theory of personality in conjunction with his work on autobiographical memories and has written many professional papers on the subject.

Dr. Bruhn holds a Ph.D. in clinical psychology from Duke University and interned at Duke University Medical Center. He is a fellow of the Society for Personality Assessment and is listed in Marquis' *Who's Who in the World, Who's Who in Science and Technology,* and *Who's Who of Emerging Leaders in America.* Currently, he maintains a private practice in Bethesda, Maryland, and lectures on the assessment of autobiographical memories and their use in psychotherapy.

JAMES N. BUTCHER, PH.D., is professor of psychology in the Department of Psychology at the University of Minnesota. He received an M.A. in experimental psychology in 1962 and a Ph.D. in clinical psychology in 1964 from the University of North Carolina at Chapel Hill. He was awarded Doctor Honoris Causa from the Free University of Brussels, 1990. He is a member of the University of Minnesota Press's MMPI Consultative Committee. He is currently the editor of *Psychological Assessment* and serves as consulting editor for numerous other journals in psychology and psychiatry. He is a fellow of the American Psychological Association and the Society for Personality Assessment.

JANET F. CARLSON is assistant professor in the Counseling and Psychological Services Department at the State University of New York at Oswego. She earned her M.A and Ph.D. in clinical psychology from Fordham University after earning her undergraduate degree with honors from Union College. She is a licensed psychologist and certified school psychologist in New York State. She has held full-time teaching positions and has taught courses on numerous topics including assessment and personality at Fordham University, Fairfield University, and Le Moyne College. She has written a variety of published works, including journal articles, book chapters, and test reviews.

Before teaching, Carlson worked as a psychologist in clinical and school settings. Since beginning her teaching career, she has served as a consultant to school systems, including the New York City Board of Education's Office of Research, Evaluation, and Assessment.

MICHELE M. CARTER, PH.D., is currently a research fellow at the Center for Stress and Anxiety Disorders in Albany, NY, and adjunct professor of Psychology at the State University of New York at Albany. At the Center, Dr. Carter is currently project director of the Couples Treatment of Agoraphobia grant funded by the

National Institute of Mental Health and was awarded an NIMH Minority Supplement Grant. He received his M.A. and Ph.D. in clinical psychology from Vanderbilt University, where he was a Dorothy Danforth-Compton Fellow. Dr. Carter's interests are in the nature and treatment of panic disorder with agoraphobia and depression. He has published several chapters and articles and has made numerous presentations on these topics. He is also currently involved in evaluating therapist training in panic control treatment and the effectiveness of training on treatment outcome.

CHERYL A. COLECCHI, PH.D., is a research associate and post-doctoral fellow in the Sleep Disorders Center at the Virginia Commonwealth University/Medical College of Virginia. She obtained her undergraduate education at the University of Massachusetts and received a Ph.D. in counseling psychology from Virginia Commonwealth University. Her current areas of interest include the treatment of insomnia, anxiety disorders, and depression, and women's issues.

NORMAN S. ENDLER, PH.D., F.R.S.C., is Professor at York University, Toronto, Canada, and Senior Research Associate at the Clarke Institute of Psychiatry. His areas of interest include anxiety, stress and coping, depression, ECT, social interaction processes, and the interaction model of personality. Among his eight books is *Electroconvulsive Therapy: The Myths and the Realities*, coauthored with E. Persad, 1988. He has written a description of ECT in *Holiday of Darkness: A Psychologist's Personal Journey Out of His Depression*, which has recently been revised and reissued (Toronto: Wall & Emerson, 1990). Dr. Endler and his colleagues have coauthored the Endler Multidimension Anxiety Scales (1990) and the Coping Inventory for Stressful Situations (CISS) with Dr. James D.A. Parker. Dr. Endler has received the award of merit of the Ontario Psychological Association and is a fellow of the Royal Society of Canada. During 1987–89, Professor Endler was a Killam Research Fellow, Canada council. Recently Dr. Endler coedited *Depression: New Directions in*

Theory, Research and Practice with D. D. McCann. During 1993–94 Dr. Endler is a visiting scholar at Wolfson College, Oxford University.

JOHN E. EXNER, JR. received his Ph.D. from Cornell University in 1958. During nearly thirty years he taught at four universities, during which time he was primarily responsible for designing and initiating the doctoral programs in psychology at Bowling Green State University and Long Island University in 1984. Dr. Exner also founded Rorschach Workshops in 1968 and continues to serve as its executive director. He is a Diplomate in Clinical Psychology and the recipient of the Distinguished Contributions Award from the Society for Personality Assessment. He is the author of eleven books concerning the Rorschach and more than sixty articles that focus on issues in personality assessment.

STEPHEN E. FINN is the director of the Center for Therapeutic Assessment in Austin, Texas, and adjunct assistant professor of psychology at the University of Texas at Austin. He practices, writes, does research, and teaches about psychological assessment.

CARL B. GACONO, PH.D., is a clinical and forensic psychologist in both public and private practice. Formerly the director of the Assessment Center at Atascadero State Hospital, he currently directs the substance abuse treatment program at the Federal Correctional Institute, Fort Worth, Texas, and is a clinical instructor at the University of California, San Francisco, Department of Psychiatry. He is a member of the Society for Personality Assessment.

Dr. Gacono is involved in ongoing research with the Rorschach test and psychopathy and has written numerous articles that have appeared in psychiatric and psychological journals. He is coauthor of *Rorschach Assessment of Aggressive and Psychopathic Personality*. He is sought as an expert in the areas of sexual homicide, psychopathy, criminal personality, and forensic Rorschach research.

CARLTON S. GASS, PH.D., received his doctorate in clinical psychology from the University of Louisville in 1985. He received postdoctoral training in clinical neuropsychology at the University of Miami School of Medicine and is the director of the Neuropsychology Laboratory at the Veterans Affairs Medical Center in Miami, Florida. He currently chairs the VA Psychology Service Research Committee and is actively involved in training psychology interns and postdoctoral students in clinical neuropsychology. Dr. Gass has served as a consulting editor for *Psychological Assessment* and has published numerous scientific papers concerning the evaluation of personality and emotional functioning in neurologically impaired individuals.

KURT F. GEISINGER is Dean of Arts and Sciences and professor of psychology at the State University of New York at Oswego. He earned his Ph.D. from Pennsylvania State University with a specialization in educational and psychological measurement after earning an M.A. in industrial psychology from the University of Georgia and his undergraduate degree with honors from Davidson College. From 1977 to 1992, he was a faculty member within the Department of Psychology at Fordham University, where he also chaired the psychology department and directed the psychometrics doctoral program.

He has published in a variety of journals and is currently on the editorial boards of *Psychological Assessment, Educational and Psychological Measurement, Educational Measurement: Issues and Practice,* and *Educational Research Quarterly,* and he edited the volume *Psychological Testing in Hispanics.* Dr. Geisinger has served on or chaired committees for Divisions 5 and 15 of the American Psychological Association and the Joint Committee on Testing Practices. He consults frequently on testing and measurement issues and has served as an expert witness in more than twenty legal cases, primarily involving test bias.

BERNADETTE GRAY-LITTLE is professor and chair, Department of Psychology at the University of North Carolina. She received her Ph.D. in psychology from St. Louis University. Her postdoctoral research in cross-cultural psychology was made possible by a fellowship from the Fulbright Foundation for study in Denmark. Dr. Gray-Little has also been a Social Science Research Council Fellow and a recipient of a Ford Foundation Senior Scholar Fellowship through the National Research Council. She has served as a consultant to the United States Postal Service, VISTA, and the Health Care Financing Administration.

Dr. Gray-Little has served on the Board of Educational Affairs and Board of Directors of Division 12, both of the American Psychological Association, and on the Board of Directors of the Council of University Directors of Clinical Psychology. She is coauthor (with J. P. Lowman and D. Galinsky) of the book *Predicting Achievement: A Ten Year Follow-up of Black and White Adolescents*. She is associate editor of the *American Psychologist* and has been consulting editor for several journals.

ROGER L. GREENE, PH.D., is professor, chair, and director of clinical training at Pacific Graduate School of Psychology, Palo Alto, CA. He was in the Department of Psychology at Texas Tech University from 1974 to 1992 and had a joint appointment in the Department of Psychiatry at Texas Tech University Health Sciences Center from 1982 to 1992, where he was involved in substance-abuse treatment and research through the Southwest Institute for Addictive Diseases. Dr. Greene is the author of several books and numerous articles on the MMPI/MMPI-2.

ALLAN R. HARKNESS received his B.S. in psychology from Carroll College. His initial graduate studies were in physiological psychology at Ohio University in Athens, Ohio. After a period of fashioning stainless-steel electrodes, operating a microtome, and learning stereotaxic surgery, all in the service of studying osmoregulation in rats, he yearned for work on primates. He began studying human judgment processes with Hal Arkes. After completing an M.S. in experimental psychology at Ohio, he went to the University of Minnesota. While in graduate school at Minnesota, he met and married Claire (Dzur) Harkness, who received her Ph.D. from the Institute of Child Development. They have two children, Alexander and Maxwell.

Dr. Harkness completed his Ph.D. in clinical psychology at Minnesota in 1989 under Auke Tellegen. He was a lecturer in psychology at the University of Wisconsin in Madison before taking his current position as assistant Professor of psychology at the University of Tulsa. He is actively interested in a number of the areas Paul Meehl once listed as psychology's noble traditions: psychodynamics, psychometrics, descriptive psychopathology, and behavior genetics. He maintains a limited individual psychotherapy practice.

T. MARK HARWOOD is a second-year doctoral student in the Counseling/Clinical/School Psychology Program at the University of California, Santa Barbara. He obtained his M.S. from San Diego State University in 1990 and held faculty positions with SDSU before his doctoral study at UCSB. Mr. Harwood is an active member of the Phi Kappa Phi honor society, San Diego chapter, and the California Association of Marriage and Family Therapists (CAMFT).

Mr. Harwood has a diverse teaching background ranging from special education and gifted and talented education at the elementary school level to graduate school instructor at university level. He thoroughly enjoys teaching and aspires to a professorship upon completion of his Ph.D. Presently, Mr. Harwood is a member of Dr. Beutler's research staff.

ROBERT HOGAN, PH.D., is McFarlin Professor and chair of psychology at the University of Tulsa, formerly professor of psychology and social relations at The Johns Hopkins University, and recipient of a number of research and teaching awards. Dr. Hogan is editor of the *Handbook of Personality and Personality Assessment* and the author of the *Hogan Personality Inventory*. He received his Ph.D. at the University of California, Berkeley, and specializes in personality assessment. He was the first editor of the *Personality Processes and Individual Differences* section of the American Psychological Association's *Journal of Personality and Social Psy-*

chology and is the author of over eighty journal articles, chapters, and books. In industrial psychology, Dr. Hogan is widely credited with demonstrating how careful attention to personality factors can influence organizational effectiveness in areas ranging from organizational climate and leadership to selection and team performance. Dr. Hogan has also used personality measures to study occupational success in jobs ranging from entry-level police officers to senior executives in various organizations nationwide. His recent work has focused on managerial and supervisory success and derailment; he is the author of the chapter on personality assessment in the 1991 *Handbook of Industrial-Organizational Psychology*. Dr. Hogan is a fellow of the American Psychological Association.

JAN H. KAMPHUIS is a graduate student in clinical psychology at the University of Texas at Austin. He studied economics and psychology at the Rijks Universiteit Groningen in the Netherlands and received his undergraduate degree in 1989. His primary research interests are psychodiagnostic assessment and anxiety disorders.

ERIC KLINGER is professor of psychology at the University of Minnesota, Morris and Minneapolis, and has taught at the University of Wisconsin and the Ruhr University of Bochum, Germany. He received his A.B. at Harvard and his Ph.D. at the University of Chicago, with a clinical internship at Hines and West Side Veterans Administration Medical Centers. His research interests have centered on motivational and emotional influences on the flow of thought and other cognitive processing. This focus led him to develop theory and assessment tools for both motivation and inner experience, as well as extensions into areas as diverse as daydreaming, mood disorders, and treatment for alcoholism.

DEBI KROLL-MENSING is a 1992 Ph.D. graduate from the clinical psychology program at the University of Minnesota. Her unpublished dissertation is entitled "Differentiating Anxiety and Depression: An Experience Sampling Analysis"; it describes the use of the technique of experience sampling in research exploring anxiety and depressive mood states. Currently, Dr. Kroll-Mensing is the clinical director of Services for Teens at Risk, an outpatient mental health clinic of the University of Minnesota Hospital and Clinics. Additionally, she serves as a part-time clinical faculty member for the Adolescent Health Training Program under the Pediatrics Department of the University of Minnesota.

PAUL M. LERNER, ED.D., is in the private practice of psychoanalysis, psychoanalytic psychotherapy, and psychological testing in Asheville, North Carolina. A graduate of the Toronto Psychoanalytic Institute, he is a member of the Canadian Psychoanalytic Society and the International Psychoanalytic Society. After completing his doctorate at the University of Illinois, he was a postdoctoral fellow in clinical psychology at the Menninger Foundation. He is currently president of the Society for Personality Assessment. For his 1991 book, *Psychoanalytic Theory and the Rorschach*, he received a distinguished writing award from the Menninger Foundation. He has also coedited three books on the Rorschach as well as published numerous articles on psychological testing, psychopathology, and psychoanalytic theory. He is a contributing writer to Amtrak Express, the in-train magazine for Amtrak, and several baseball publications.

MARTIN LEICHTMAN is chief psychologist in the Children's Division of the Menninger Clinic. He received his doctorate in clinical psychology from Clark University, is a graduate of the Topeka Institute for Psychoanalysis, and holds a Diplomate in Clinical Psychology from the American Board of Professional Psychology. He serves on the faculties of the Karl Menninger School of Mental Health Sciences and the Topeka Institute for Psychoanalysis.

MARK H. LICHT received his Ph.D. in clinical psychology from the University of Illinois at Urbana-Champaign in 1980. He has held the position of visiting instructor and researcher at the Department of Psychology, University of Illinois, and is currently associate professor of psychology at Florida State University in Tallahassee. Dr. Licht has served as consultant for various mental health organizations including the Illinois Department of Mental Health and Developmental Disabilities and the Florida Department of Health and Rehabilitative Services. His research and publications have been primarily in the areas of assessment and treatment of chronically institutionalized mental patients. Dr. Licht currently serves on the Board of Editors of *Psychological Bulletin* and has served as consulting editor for several other professional journals. He is a member of the American Psychological Society, American Psychological Association, Association for Clinical Psychosocial Research, and American Association of Applied and Preventive Psychology.

MARCO J. MARIOTTO, PH.D., is Professor of Psychology at the University of Houston and Adjunct Professor of Behavioral Science at the University of Texas Health Sciences Center at Houston. He received his Ph.D. in clinical psychology in 1974 from the University of Illinois at Urbana-Champaign. He was previously a member of the faculty of the Department of Psychological Sciences at Purdue University. Besides his academic appointments, Dr. Mariotto is a clinical and research consultant to federal, state, and local health and mental health units and organizations and maintains an active private practice in clinical and forensic psychology.

Dr. Mariotto's major scholarly interests are in the development, evaluation, and utilization of clinical assessment and measurement procedures. He has served on the editorial board or as a consulting editor for the major journals in the assessment and mental health fields and has written numerous publications and presentations in this area.

EDWIN L. MEGARGEE, PH.D., is professor of psychology and director of clinical training at Florida State University. A Certified Correctional Health Professional, he received his Ph.D. in clinical psychology from the University of California, Berkeley, in 1963. The author of over 100 books, chapters, and journal articles on personality assessment and the classification of criminal offenders, he has served as a consultant to mental health and criminal justice agencies in the United States and Britain, including the Federal Bureau of Prisons and the U.S. Secret Service. He has received awards for Distinguished Achievement from the American Association of Correctional Psychologists and for Significant Research on the MMPI from the University of Minnesota.

J. REID MELOY, PH.D., is a Diplomate in forensic psychology of the American Board of Professional Psychology. He was formerly chief of the Forensic Mental Health Division for San Diego County, California, and now devotes most of this time to a private civil and criminal forensic practice, research, writing, and teaching. He is assistant clinical professor of psychiatry at the University of California, San Diego, School of Medicine and an adjunct professor at the University of San Diego School of Law. He is also a fellow of the Society for Personality Assessment.

Dr. Meloy has published over fifty papers published in scientific journals and two books: *The Psychopathic Mind* (Aronson, 1988) and *Violent Attachments* (Aronson, 1992). He is coauthor of *Rorschach Assessment of Aggressive and Psychopathic Personalities* (LEA, 1994).

CHARLES M. MORIN, PH.D., is associate professor of psychiatry and psychology at Virginia Commonwealth University. He is also director of the Sleep Disorders Center at the Medical College of Virginia. He obtained his undergraduate education at Laval University in Quebec, Canada, and received his Ph.D. in clinical psychology from Nova University, Florida. He completed a residency training at the University of Mississippi Medical Center and was a postdoctoral fellow in sleep disorders medicine at the Medical College of Virginia. Dr. Morin is actively involved in clinical and research activities in the areas of sleep disorders, anxiety, benzodiazepine discontinuation, and aging.

SUMIE OKAZAKI is presently a doctoral candidate in clinical psychology at UCLA. She received a B.S. from the University of Michigan (1988) and an M.A. in clinical psychology from UCLA (1990). She works as a graduate researcher at the National Research Center on Asian American Mental Health. Her research involves examining the relationship between acculturative stress, self-concept, and psychopathology among Asian-Americans.

JAMES D. A. PARKER, PH.D., is a research fellow at the Clarke Institute of Psychiatry, University of Toronto. His areas of interest include anxiety and coping, health psychology, and the history of modern personality psychology. He is an active researcher in the personality area with over fifty publications in various journals and books.

GORDON L. PAUL, PH.D., is Cullen Distinguished Professor of Psychology at the University of Houston and a practicing licensed psychologist. He was previously on the faculty of the University of Illinois at Urbana-Champaign, where he twice received the Award for Excellence in Graduate Training. He has been a supervisory clinical psychologist in both outpatient and inpatient settings since 1965. Dr. Paul was also the Director of Psychosocial Rehabilitation Units and of the Clinical-Research Unit at the Adolf Meyer Mental Health Center, Decatur, Illinois. He is a member of or advisor to numerous regional, state, and national review and policy-making groups concerned with clinical research, assessment, and treatment. He has served on the editorial boards of seven major journals and as a frequent consulting editor for eighteen. His research has led to many awards and recognitions for methodological contributions and for cost-effective assessment and treatment procedures. Dr. Paul is a fellow of several professional associations and a member of advocacy groups on behalf of those who suffer from severe emotional, behavioral, and mental problems and disabilities.

KENNETH S. POPE, PH.D., received advanced degrees from Harvard and Yale and is a Diplomate in clinical psychology and a fellow of the American Psychological Association (APA) and the American Psychological Society (APS). Having previously served as clinical director and psychology director in both private hospital and community mental health center settings, he is currently in independent practice. He previously taught courses in psychological and neuropsychological assessment, abnormal psychology, and related areas at the University of California, Los Angeles, where he served as a psychotherapy supervisor in the UCLA Psychology Clinic. He served as chair of the Ethics Committees of the APA and the American Board of Professional Psychology. His books include *Ethics in Psychotherapy and Counseling* (with M.J.T. Vasquez; Jossey-Bass, 1991), *The MMPI, MMPI-2, and MMPI-A In court: A Practical Guide for Expert Witnesses and Attorneys* (with J. N. Butcher and J. Seelen; American Psychological Association, 1993), and *Sexual Feelings in Psychotherapy: Explorations for Therapists and Therapists-in-Training* (with J. L. Sonne and J. Holroyd; American Psychological Association, 1993).

ERIC C. REHEISER is a research assistant and computer analyst associated with the Center for Research in Behavioral Medicine and Health Psychology at the University of South Florida.

LEE M. RITTERBAND is a graduate student in the doctoral program in clinical psychology and a research assistant at the Center for Research in Behavioral Medicine and Health Psychology at the University of South Florida.

DAMON ROBINSON is a doctoral candidate in counseling psychology at the University of Kentucky. She is currently completing an internship at the Department of Veterans Affairs Medical Center in Cincinnati, Ohio. Her clinical and research interests are in psychotherapeutic issues with women, trauma, and grief.

CYNTHIA J. SANDERSON, PH.D., is assistant professor of psychology in psychiatry at The New York Hospital—Cornell Medical Center—Westchester Division in White Plains, NY. She received her doctorate in clinical psychology from the University of Kentucky in 1987. She completed an internship and postdoctoral fellowship at the Westchester Division of The New

York Hospital and was appointed to the faculty in 1988. Dr. Sanderson has codeveloped, with Charles Swenson, M.D., a day hospital treatment program for patients with severe personality disorders that integrates psychodynamic and cognitive-behavioral theory and techniques. Her clinical and personality strengths to psychotherapy outcome and the role of social supports in preventing relapse in patients with borderline personality disorder.

CHARLES D. SPIELBERGER is Distinguished research professor of Psychology and director of the Center for Research in Behavioral Medicine and Health Psychology at the University of South Florida, where he has been a faculty member since 1972.

KATHLEEN P. STAFFORD earned her Ph.D. in clinical psychology from Kent State University and is a Diplomate in Forensic Psychology of the American Board of Professional Psychology. She is Adjunct Assistant Professor of Psychology at Kent State University and at Northeastern Ohio Universities College of Medicine. She is Vice-President of the American Academy of Forensic Psychology and Chair of the Outreach Training Committee for the American Psychology-Law Society (APA Division 41). She directs a regional court clinic in northeastern Ohio and maintains a private consulting practice in forensic psychology. She also conducts training workshops on forensic issues in Ohio and for the American Academy of Forensic Psychology.

ZIGFRIDS T. STELMACHERS is chief clinical psychologist at the Hennepin County Medical Center, Minneapolis, director of its Crisis Intervention Center, and clinical professor at the University of Minnesota. He is a National Diplomate in clinical psychology and a fellow of the American Psychological Association. He has served on the board of directors of the American Association of Suicidology and serves as one of its regional certification coordinators. Dr. Stelmachers established and directed the first suicide prevention center in Minnesota and has been active in providing community consultation and education as well as formal courses and lectures on topics related to crisis intervention, victimization, suicide, violence, and program evaluation.

STANLEY SUE is Professor of psychology at UCLA and director of the National Research Center on Asian American Mental Health, an NIMH-funded research center. He received a B.S. from the University of Oregon (1966) and a Ph.D. in psychology from UCLA (1971). Before the faculty appointment at UCLA, where he was also associate dean of the Graduate Division, he served for ten years on the psychology faculty at the University of Washington and from 1980 to 1981 was Director of Clinical-community Psychology Training at the National Asian American Psychology Training Center in San Francisco, an APA-approved internship program.

Dr. Sue's research has been devoted to the study of psychopathology among, and delivery of mental health services to, culturally diverse groups. His work has documented the difficulties that ethnic minority groups experience in receiving adequate mental health services and has offered directions for providing culturally appropriate forms of treatment.

SUMNER J. SYDEMAN is a graduate student in the doctoral program in clinical psychology and a research assistant at the Center for Research in Behavioral Medicine and Health Psychology at the University of South Florida.

KAREN K. UNGER is a registered nurse associated with St. Joseph's Hospital, Tampa, Florida, and a research assistant at the Center for Research in Behavioral Medicine and Health Psychology at the University of South Florida.

ROBERTO J. VELASQUEZ is associate professor in the Department of Counseling and School Psychology and adjunct professor in the Department of Psychology at San Diego State University. He is also executive director of Behavioral Health Group (BHG), one of the largest Latino-based mental health organizations in San Diego, California. In addition, Dr. Velasquez maintains a private practice that specializes in the psychological testing and assessment of Latino clients. He has written numerous publications on the use of the MMPI with Latinos including "An Atlas of MMPI Group Profiles on Mexican Americans" (1984). He is presently preparing "The Handbook of Hispanic American MMPI (MMPI-2) Research and Application." His other research interests include mental health and migration, PTSD in ethnic minority veterans, and use of the DSM-III-R (and DSM-IV) with ethnic minority clients. Dr. Velasquez has also served as a consultant on test development and test translation to several test publishers including National Computer Systems (NCS).

IRVING B. WEINER, PH.D., is professor of psychiatry and behavioral medicine at the University of South Florida and director of psychological services at TGH-University Psychiatry Center in Tampa. He is an ABPP Diplomate in clinical psychology and a fellow of the American Psychological Association. For many years he has been concerned both as a scholar and as a practitioner with psychodiagnostic assessment and forensic issues. He is a past president of the Society for Personality Assessment and a recipient of the Society's Distinguished Contribution Award. He served as editor of the *Journal of Personality Assessment* from 1985 to 1993 and is currently the editor of *Rorschachiana: Yearbook of the International Rorschach Society*. His books include *Psychodiagnosis in Schizophrenia* (1966), *Rorschach Handbook of Clinical and Research Applications* (1971), *Clinical Methods in Psychology* (1976, 1983), *Rorschach Assessment of Children and Adolescents* (1982), and *Handbook of Forensic Psychology* (1987).

MARTHA W. WETTER, PH.D., is assistant professor in the Department of Psychology at the University of Kentucky. She maintains a private practice in clinical psychology, which frequently includes forensic cases. She has published several papers on the topic of detection of malingering on the MMPI-2.

THOMAS A. WIDIGER is professor of psychology at the University of Kentucky. He received his Ph.D. in clinical psychology from Miami University (Ohio) and completed his internship at Cornell University Medical College (Westchester). He has published extensively in the area of personality disorder classification and assessment and is on the editorial board of numerous journals. During the past five years he has been serving as the research coordinator for the American Psychiatric Association's fourth edition of the *Diagnostic and Statistical Manual of Mental Disorders* (DSM-IV). He also served on the DSM-IV Task Force and Personality Disoorders Work Group. In addition, he has an active clinical practice that emphasizes in particular the assessment and treatment of maladaptive personality traits.

JUDITH WORELL received her Ph.D. in clinical psychology at Ohio State University. She is currently professor and chair of the Department of Educational and Counseling Psychology at the University of Kentucky. She is the current editor of *Psychology of Women Quarterly*, and is a member of numerous other editorial boards. She was the 1990 recipient of the APA Committee on Women award as Distinguished Leader for Women in Psychology and the Kentucky Psychological Association award for Distinguished Psychologist. Her most recent book is *Feminist Perspectives in Therapy: An Empowerment Model for Women* (Wiley). Her research interests focus on gender in close relationships and feminist identity development.

I
AN INTRODUCTION TO CLINICAL PERSONALITY ASSESSMENT

1

Clinical Personality Assessment: An Overview

James N. Butcher

People have been making personality assessment decisions and personality appraisals since the beginning of human interactions. As an adaptive human activity, effective personality appraisal has clear survival value for our species (Buss, 1991). If our cave-dwelling ancestors happened to chose a hunting partner with the "wrong" personality, the outcome could be tragic. Or if groups from antiquity failed to evaluate whether potential leaders possessed essential personal qualities, their own survival could be threatened. Personality assessments in antiquity were probably based on diverse, if not particularly valid or reliable, sources of information. Early writings, for example, mention such factors as dreams, signs from the gods, oracular speculation, spies, traitors, direct observation, pedigree, physiognomic characteristics, and the interview as important sources of information about people. Even "tests" were employed to evaluate personality characteristics. Hathaway (1965) described an early personality screening situation from the Old Testament:

> For example, Gideon had collected too large an army, and now the Lord saw that the Israelites would give Him scant credit if so many men overran the Midianites camped in the valley.

The Lord suggested two screening items for Gideon. The first of these items had face validity: Gideon proclaimed that all who were afraid could go home. More than two of every three did so. The second was subtle: Those who fought the Midianites were the few who drank from their cupped hands instead of lying down to drink. Altogether it was a battle decided by psychological devices, and 300 men literally scared the demoralized Midianites into headlong flight. (p. 457)

The field of personality assessment as an organized scientific discipline is less than a century old; however, great strides have been made in the science of personality assessment and toward developing the practice of employing effective, practical procedures for evaluating personality in applied settings. Over the past two decades, personality assessment has been rapidly expanding both in terms of developing new measures and in the yield of annual research on testing. The sheer number of research articles and journals devoted to personality assessment methods makes the task of keeping current difficult in more than a few techniques. In fact, many researchers and practitioners tend to narrow their focus and rely exclusively on relatively few techniques in their assessment

Many reasons can be found for the increased rate of research publication and clinical application of personality assessment methods. First, personality assessment devices are often used as criterion measures for psychological research into abnormal behavior and psychological processes. Second, clinical assessment, the activity that accounts for the greatest use of personality tests today, appears to be becoming a more respected and engaging task for clinical practitioners today than it was a few years ago, when it was often considered a much less attractive clinical practice than was, for example, psychotherapy. A third reason for the increased interest in personality assessment can be seen in the broadened acceptance of psychological assessment in forensic settings. Psychological tests are more frequently requested and admitted as evidence in court today than they were even a decade ago (see Pope, Butcher, & Seelen, 1993). A fourth reason is that psychological assessment in industrial applications, both in terms of conducting fitness-for-duty evaluations and for personnel screening have expanded greatly in recent years.

In developing this book, I wanted to bring together in a single volume several important and diverse perspectives on personality assessment to illustrate the broad range of views and methods of study that are prominent today. In choosing contributors, I considered it important to provide comprehensive chapters dealing with important issues in the field to focus on general theoretical issues as well as specific assessment techniques. I wanted to illustrate a number of diverse personality assessment approaches. And finally, as is evident throughout this volume, I considered it important to try to bring a pragmatic focus to the field of personality assessment. Contributors were encouraged to present their ideas within a practical framework.

IMPORTANT CONSIDERATIONS IN PERSONALITY ASSESSMENT

We will begin our survey of personality assessment psychology by exploring several defining issues that are important to the field. The discussion in Chapter 2, by John Exner, who has been a leader in the field of personality assessment for decades, sets the stage for the book by exploring the rationale for personality assessment and documenting the importance of clinical assessment to contemporary applied psychology. Exner provides an illustration of his view that many psychologists may be failing in their responsibility to properly assess their clients in clinical practice. Exner's presentation is followed by an exploration, from the vantage point of a clinical practitioner, of the importance of selecting appropriate tests for the assessment battery. Marvin Acklin, in Chapter 3, describes the process by which clinicians choose assessment strategies and illustrates the importance of using diverse procedures in the psychological test battery.

The most widely held strategy in personality assessment has been to view enduring personality characteristics — traits — as the point of departure. The trait assessment approach is well defined by Allan Harkness and Robert Hogan in Chapter 4. They present a theoretical analysis of trait assessment and provide practical examples of how psychologists can obtain an understanding of traits, which are viewed as more than simple constructs. Harkness and Hogan present a model for understanding personality by evaluating the physiological substrata underlying personality traits. Their approach introduces the reader to the view that traits are in part likely to be based on genetic inheritance. Charles Spielberger and his associates, in Chapter 5, present an informative discussion of the importance of considering states as well as traits in personality assessment and provide a practical guide to evaluating traits as "vital signs" for understanding emotional states.

One of the most important clinical tasks that practitioners are asked to perform in many clinical settings is that of conducting pretreatment planning evaluations — an activity that is often given less attention than it deserves. In Chapter 6 Larry Beutler and Mark Harwood explore a number of important issues concerning this major goal of psychological assessment and provide important new insights into personality assessment in pretreatment planning.

The introductory section of this volume closes with two chapters that discuss issues in modern test processing and effective, ethical management of test results. A chapter on how personality assessment can be enhanced by appropriate use of objective, computer-based test interpretation strategies is presented in Chapter 7 by James Butcher. Computerized personality assessment has a long and distinguished history in applied psychology (Rome, Swenson, Mataya, McCarthy, Pearson, Keating, & Hathaway, 1962) going back to the early 1960s. Many practitioners use one or more computer-derived personality test interpretation programs in developing their personality assessment study of clients. (See Schlosser & Moreland, 1993, for an extensive introduction to computer-based assessment.) In Chapter 7, the clinical use of computerized reports is illustrated and cautions concerning their use provided.

Finally, the care and documentation of psychological test results are discussed. Regardless of one's basic approach to personality assessment, careful accumulation and analysis of information are important considerations in any psychological assessment. In this regard, the discussion by Irving Weiner (Chapter 8) provides the practitioner with important background information and a clear rationale for employing meticulous safeguards in conducting personality evaluations in order to avoid potential legal or ethical problems.

BACKGROUND VARIABLES IN PERSONALITY ASSESSMENT

By its very nature the field of personality assessment is concerned with individual differences and is enveloped in human diversity. In order to understand the behavior and personality of individuals, it is imperative that many "status" variables be given careful consideration. Background factors such as age, gender, and ethnicity are important, since personality is in many respects a function of the environment or groups to which a person belongs. People may share certain characteristics of groups with which they are affiliated. In the assessment of individuals it is important to consider influences that may come from belonging to a group that has been treated differently by our social institutions than others have. Women, for example, may experience situations or activities differently because of the roles in which they may have been cast and in their lack of access to equal opportunities in society. In Chapter 12, Judith Worell and Damon Robinson provide an insightful discussion of issues that are important to consider in the clinical assessment of women.

Similarly, being a member of an ethnic minority group in the United States places a person at considerable risk for discrimination and diminished opportunity. Those who are cast in less dominant societal roles by fact of birth may be at risk for developing problems or adjustment difficulties that are not shared by the majority classes. In order to fully explore the potential problems associated with being a minority-group member in contemporary society, several contributors were asked to provide different perspectives on issues involved in the psychological assessment of minority clients. Sumie Okazaki and Stanley Sue (Chapter 9) contribute an informative discussion of possible factors involved in the assessment of ethnic Asian minorities that need to be considered in cross-ethnic psychological evaluations. Their work with Asian-American clients has made a substantial contribution to clinical as well as to cross-cultural psychology. Roberto Velasquez (Chapter 10) provides an interesting and valuable perspective on factors involved in understanding problems of Hispanic clients, and Bernadette Gray-Little (Chapter 11) examines ways of assessing psychopathology in minority clients.

There are other important individual-difference variables that require careful consideration in personality evaluation. Two "extrapersonality" variables that are important to refining personality evaluation are the focus of separate chapters in this section. In Chapter 13, Charles Morin and Cheryl Colecci examine factors important to consider in assessing older adults; and Carlton Gass and Jane Ansley, in Chapter 14, examine personality factors in the context of organic brain impairment.

THE MEANING OF PERSONALITY TEST RESULTS

Personality test results do not always mean what we think they mean. Under some conditions test scores may not impart the information that we expect. For example, a given test score on a particular scale might not reflect the same level of the measured characteristic in two different samples because the base rates for the characteristic in the two groups are different. Or the scale might not assess the attributes in question because the test is vulnerable to measurement distortion because individuals in the particular setting may tend to dissimulate — claim extreme problems when they do not have them or deny problems when they do. Several contributors were invited to address the important question of what test scores mean.

The initial chapter in this section by Kurt Geisinger and Janet Carlson (Chapter 15) addresses the importance of standards and norms in interpreting psychological test scores. Following this informative presentation is an insightful discussion by Steve Finn and Jan Kamphuis (Chapter 16) on the need for practitioners to consider the relative frequency of phenomena (base rates) in particular settings in order to interpret psychological test scores appropriately. Finally, this section includes a discussion about malingering on psychological tests by David Berry, Martha Wetter, and Ruth Baer (Chapter 17) that highlights the importance of incorporating validity scales in personality assessment evaluations.

SOURCES OF PERSONALITY INFORMATION

Human personality is infinitely varied and highly complex. Personality theorists have viewed personality from very different angles and have assayed different "chunks" of what we know as personality in their efforts to understand these complex human characteristics. The complexity of personality has prompted psychologists to approach the task of assessment through highly diverse means. Differing theories of personality and varying conceptions of how personality is structured have led to rather different assumptions about what data are important to understanding personality. For example, psychodynamic theorists have viewed personality as a complex and intricate system of drives and forces that cannot be understood without extensive personal historical information. The means of understanding the connections between personal history and personality can come from many sources, such as analyses of early memories (see Chapter 20 by Arnold R. Bruhn) or through the individual's response to intentionally ambiguous stimulus material such as the Rorschach ink blots (discussed in Chapter 2 by John Exner and Chapter 22 by Paul Lerner). In his chapter, for example, Lerner uses projective responses to provide clues into how individuals adapt to their environment. The use of projective techniques for providing information about the individual has a long tradition in personality psychology, and Lerner provides the reader with a very insightful approach to understanding the process of human adaptation.

Other perspectives in personality have been oriented more toward "surface" behaviors. For example, a learning- or behavioral-based viewpoint may not involve such historic assumptions as the psychodynamic view but may rely more on overt, observable behaviors.

Most researchers and practitioners are familiar with the "standard" sources of personality information that have been developed to appraise personality today — personality inventories, projective methods, and the clinical interview. In the fourth section of this book we will examine several other sources of personality information that may yield valuable personality information in clinical assessment. The initial article in this section, by Martin Leichtman (Chapter 18), is devoted to clinical observation and reaffirms the importance of clinical observations in a diagnostic study. Leichtman presents a rationale and highlights the importance of information the clinician can obtain in direct observation and accurate recording of his/her impressions about clients. Another, somewhat different, approach to observation is taken by Eric Klinger and Debi Kroll-Mensing (Chapter

19). Their approach employs methodically obtained self-observations that are recorded in a systematic manner. This technique, referred to as the *ideothetic approach*, provides the clinician or researcher with important information about cognitions the subject experiences and reports periodically.

Many practitioners, in the course of their clinical interview or psychological treatment, obtain the earliest memories that clients report and view these pieces of information as particularly important if not central to understanding the personality dynamics of the subject. In Chapter 20, Arnold Bruhn provides a detailed account of one systematic approach to obtaining and organizing the earliest memories patients can recall. His approach to this potentially valuable information will provide practitioners with a clear means of interpreting their clients' early memories.

Traditional personality questionnaires, such as the MMPI, that have been developed by empirical methods are usually interpreted empirically—that is, with reference to the specific criterion research that has accumulated on the scales. Chapter 21, by James Butcher, provides a discussion of a somewhat different approach to personality inventory interpretation (the view that item responses are communications between the patient and the clinician), which proves to be as valid as traditional empirical scales but may have potentially greater utility as a source of personality information about clients in the clinical assessment. This approach to assessment assumes that the patient discloses personal information about his or her problems through the content of the self-report. The potential contribution of the content approach to personality assessment is discussed and illustrated, and practical limitations are considered.

PROBLEM AREAS IN PERSONALITY ASSESSMENT

Psychological assessments are undertaken in many different settings and for many different purposes. The same psychological tests might be employed to evaluate clients in forensic settings, for example, to assist the court in determining custody of minor children in family disputes; in mental health settings to determine the nature and extent of psychological problems in pretreatment planning; or in the workplace to determine if an applicant for a job as a police officer is emotionally stable and mature enough to entrust with a weapon. In this book, a broad range of chapters were assembled to provide the reader with illustrations of a number of different applications. Authors and topics were selected both to cover many problem areas and to consider assessment from a practical point of view. Space limitations, of course, prevent a full exploration of all the areas that might touch on assessment. It is hoped that the topics chosen will illustrate both the diversity and the effectiveness of the assessment techniques involved. In all cases, chapters were invited that would address problem-oriented assessment, and they were written by noted psychologists with substantial expertise in the assessment area in question.

We begin our survey of problem-oriented assessment topics with an exploration of human coping strategies and failures to cope. In Chapter 23, Norman Endler and James Parker provide a comprehensive evaluation of practical steps that practitioners might take in assessing a patient's ability to cope with stressful events. Next, the chapter by Michele Carter and David Barlow (Chapter 24) explores several strategies for assessing the extremely anxious patient. Then we turn to a chapter that takes up the difficult question of what steps a clinician might take in assessing a client's suicidal potential. This chapter (Chapter 25), written by Zigfrids Stelmachers, who founded and directed one of the earliest crisis intervention—suicide prevention services, provides practical wisdom for assessing and managing clients who are at high risk for suicide.

The next three chapters in the book are interrelated in that they deal with personality disorders and aggression. The first chapter, by Thomas Widiger and Cynthia Sanderson (Chapter 26), provides an informative discussion of effective procedures for assessing personality-disordered individuals. Next, Edwin Megargee (Chapter 27) develops a conceptual framework for understanding and assessing aggression and potential violence in patients. And in Chapter 28, Reed Meloy and Carl Gacono provide an informative account of practical procedures for assessing the intriguing disorder known as psychopathic personality.

The next two chapters in the final section of the book deal with the assessment of severe mental disorders. In Chapter 29, Kathy Stafford and Yossef Ben-Porath provide an informative and clear discussion of factors relevant to determining if a person meets the legal definitions of insanity. Such determinations are important to forensic assessment; psychologists' evaluations often determine whether individuals will be deemed incapable of standing trial, whether they were likely to have been insane at the time they committed a crime, or whether they are incapable of managing their own affairs and should be committed to a psychiatric institution. The article by Marco Mariotto, Gordon Paul, and Mark Licht (Chapter 30) explores the most effective strategies for assessing persons who are living in institutions for the chronically mentally ill.

One of the most frequent psychological adjustment problems in society today involves the use and misuse of alcohol and drugs. In many instances, persons who are being seen in mental health or medical settings for problems other than substance abuse also have a hidden problem with addictive substances. Consequently, psychologists frequently find themselves involved in the determination of potential substance abuse in addition to whatever other problems clients are experiencing. Because of the importance of substance abuse assessment problems in many settings, Roger L. Greene and Joseph A. Banken (Chapter 31) address a number of objective assessment strategies for detecting and appraising alcohol and drug problems.

The final chapter in the book deals with a difficult problem that unfortunately is much too frequent in contemporary psychological practice today. A complex set of problems occur when psychotherapists step over the boundaries of sound psychological practice and become sexually involved with their clients. Clients who have been abused by a therapist require special attention in subsequent mental health contacts. The need to assess individuals whose faith in mental health professionals has been violated might pose particular difficulties for assessment in further mental health contacts.

Moreover, therapists who have violated their clients' trust and have become sexually involved with clients may find themselves in the very difficult circumstance of losing their certification or license to practice. After revoking a license, many state licensing boards have to consider these errant therapists for recertification after a period of time or after the person has undergone a successful rehabilitation. The decision to recertify or relicense a therapist who has lost his or her ability to practice is often a difficult and complicated decision, one that involves several seemingly opposing purposes. For example, the licensing body has a clear responsibility to consider the need to protect the public from future potential harm. On the other hand, there may be a legal requirement to consider the possibility that the offending psychologist or psychiatrist may now be successfully rehabilitated and may deserve society's trust to resume practice. In situations such as this, licensing boards often turn to other psychologists to conduct an evaluation of the professional to determine whether he or she has sufficiently changed to be able to resume practice in some capacity. Psychologists who are asked to conduct such evaluations are usually aware that the subject of the evaluation (i.e., the mental health professional) is likely to be experienced in psychological assessment methods himself or herself and might be able to "manage" test responses in a favorable manner. Kenneth Pope, who has consulted widely and published substantially in this area, provides a very insightful approach to this difficult assessment task (see Chapter 32).

INDEX OF ASSESSMENT PROCEDURES

A great variety of personality assessment instruments and procedures are discussed in this volume. Because it is unlikely that readers will be familiar with all of them, each contributor was asked to provide a brief description of the tests they discuss in their chapter. These assessment procedures have been summarized and are described in the Appendix.

A FINAL WORD

When an editor invites authors to contribute chapters to a compendium such as this, it is somewhat analogous to working a complex puzzle. Each of the component parts must mesh together to form an integrated picture. At the beginning of this project, the contributions appearing here were sought to fill an important niche in the overall plan. The vastness of the field of personality assessment today does not permit all noted authorities and all perspectives to be equally represented. Some selectivity was required given the limitations of space. The reader will, of course, be the final judge as to how the many parts blend into an integral picture. As for me, I believe that the final pieces matched the initial plan quite well. A primary goal of this volume was to provide a practical and comprehensive overview of the field of personality assessment. I believe that the contributions included here provide the reader with

a substantial compendium of assessment resources with diverse and interesting elements. I hope that clinicians and clinicians-in-training who are new to the field of personality assessment will be tantalized by the views and strategies presented here and will travel these paths further when this book is set aside.

REFERENCES

Buss, D. (1991). Evolutionary personality psychology. *Annual Review of Psychology, 42,* 459–492.

Hathaway, S. R. (1965). Personality inventories. In B. Wolman (Ed.), *Handbook of clinical psychology* (pp. 451–476). New York: McGraw-Hill.

Pope, K., Butcher, J. N., & Seelen, J. (1993). *The MMPI/MMPI-2/MMPI-A in court: Assessment, testimony, and cross-examination for expert witnesses and attorneys.* Washington, DC: American Psychological Association.

Rome, H. P., Swenson, W. M., Mataya, P., McCarthy, C. E., Pearson, J. S., Keating, F. R., & Hathaway, S. R. (1962). Symposium on automation technics in personality assessment. *Proceedings of the Staff Meetings of the Mayo Clinic, 37,* 61–82.

Schlosser, B., and Moreland, K. L. (1993). *Taming technology: Issues, strategies, and resources for the mental health practitioner.* Washington, DC: American Psychological Association.

2

Why Use Personality Tests? A Brief Historical View

John E. Exner, Jr.

Interest in people and their individuality has existed for centuries, but the notion of personality as a subject for psychological study is less than one hundred years old. Allport (1937) noted that a movement called "the psychology of personality" gained interest only after 1920, yielding numerous but conflicting theories and plentiful but piecemeal research. The works of Freud had, of course, received considerable attention beginning in the late 1800s, but they failed to attract those attempting to address the challenge of defining personality. Allport can probably be credited with bringing the issue into sharper focus. He reviewed some fifty definitions or descriptions of personality and neatly drew these into a logical conception by defining personality as the dynamic organization, within the individual, of those psychophysical forces that determine his (or her) unique adjustments to his (or her) environment.

In formulating this definition, Allport also noted that the uniqueness of each person creates havoc for science in its search for ways to account for the uniformity of behaviors. He put forth a very compelling challenge, namely, that psychology can only achieve its true purpose when it can deal with the issue of individuality. Allport also offered a strong caution about research orientations that might tend to dismember the total person in ways that would present only fragments of information about whole people, and then attempt to extend that information in ways that would neglect individual differences.

Shortly after Allport's classic *Personality* appeared, Henry Murray (1938) published another classic, *Explorations in Personality*. He did not attempt to define personality as Allport had done. Instead, he approached the issue of individuality from a different direction. He highlighted individual uniqueness by explicating the particular and sensitive integration of various characteristics within each person. To do so, he neatly illustrated how information derived from many sources, including psychological tests, could be used to develop a special picture of a person. Both Murray and Allport strove to distinguish between the idiographic and nomothetic approaches to the study of people. Each argued for an integration of both, that is, for an approach that would not simply judge a person against others but would contrast the unique features of one person against those of others.

The arguments put forth by Allport and Murray stimulated much thinking about the objectives of the psychological study of people and in effect created a challenge to those interested in testing or assessment. Subsequently, the idea of assessing personality and/or psychopathology began to be of greater interest to psychologists than had been the case previously. Although the practice of psychological assessment in the United States usually is dated to Lightner Witmer in 1896, most attempts to use tests to understand people did not include much personality testing. People calling themselves clinical psychologists did considerable testing, but their efforts focused mainly on issues of intelligence, aptitude, achievement, interest, and so on, and the term *personality* was often used interchangably with psychopathology. A few, such as Robert Woodworth, attempted to devise methods to detect psychopathology during World War I, and some of those efforts did persist into the 1920s and 1930s with the development of inventories designed to measure some traitlike features such as introversion, extraversion, neuroticism, and the like, but none were used extensively in the clinical setting. Issues of individuality were typically addressed by using data drawn from histories and interviews.

The interest in understanding people as individuals, as advocated by Allport and Murray, increased notably during the late 1930s and grew at an almost incredible pace during World War II, with the huge expansion of clinical services provided by the military and by the Veterans Administration. Concurrently the clinical test battery approach was advocated by many, but it was probably best articulated by the Rapaport group at the Menninger Foundation during the mid-1940s, leading to the procedure that came to be called psychodiagnosis.

The objective of psychodiagnosis was much more than identifying a diagnostic label. It was a multitest procedure designed to study the person as a unique entity. Implicit in the process was the premise that information about the subject concerning assets, liabilities, conflicts, and so on, would contribute in some significant way to the therapeutic well-being of the subject. In other words, the findings contributed to a treatment plan. The notion underlying psychodiagnosis has always been that people behave in

ways that are organized and recognizable. That is the basic tenet on which all of psychology is founded. Thus, the objective of the psychodiagnostic procedure was to detect those elements within the individual that routinely promoted various behaviors, including the presenting symptoms.

Throughout the 1940s and 1950s, clinical psychologists became well recognized and highly regarded for their psychodiagnostic expertise and their input to staff conferences concerning patients in which issues of diagnosis and/or treatment were discussed. Unfortunately, those interested in the study of personality gradually began to take either of two positions. One, more empirically oriented, argued for the study of traits and their relationship to behavior. The second group agreed with many of the basic concepts of trait theorists but also strongly argued that characterization of traits could not simply be defined in terms of their presence or absence. They preferred to think of personality as a unitary entity and argued that a trait is a descriptive, nonexplanatory concept that, following from Allport and Murray, must be weighed in terms of its strength or importance within the individual. Conversely, those arguing for the study of traits maintained that the unitary personality might ultimately evolve through the study of individual characteristics, and that, more important, the approach would be clearly empirical.

The disagreement about how best to approach issues of personality and individual differences was made more complex during the early 1950s, when a falling-out occurred between those who argued strongly in favor of a so-called objective testing approach and a second group that became closely aligned with what was known as the projective psychology movement. The former argued for a more nomothetic approach to the study of personality, while the latter defined itself as more oriented toward understanding the unique individual. Unfortunately, no one profited from this schism, and it was not uncommon in those days for members of one group to avoid those in the other. In other words, the emphasis on psychodiagnosis, or personality assessment as it began to be called, did persist, but with far less uniformity than had been the case previously.

During the late 1950s another force became prominent among some clinicians. It was the advent of radical behaviorism, which brought with it the notion of the black box, and the message that there is no such thing as personality, or even if there is, it cannot be measured through psychological testing. This movement created a new group of clinicians who not only avoided personality assessment but campaigned very actively against it, favoring instead the tactics of observation and counting critical incidents as ways of determining targets for intervention. Thus, by the early 1960s the once reasonably homogeneous specialty of personality assessment had fragmented considerably and had begun to come under serious attack.

This divergence probably had its greatest impact during the mid-1960s and through most of the 1970s as training programs in clinical psychology changed considerably. Students often objected to the laborious training time required to learn about test batteries and their applications. Their objections were often reinforced by many in the academic community from both clinical and nonclinical faculties who held that the specialty of psychodiagnosis, or personality assessment, had only limited value. As curricular changes occurred, many reduced training in personality assessment. It is sad but true to note that for at least a decade these altered programs produced huge numbers of graduates who knew little about assessment and less about personality, and yet tended to glory in their newly acquired therapeutic expertise. The assumption was that psychological tests could only be regarded as creating specimens or samples of performance of restricted functions. In other words, the samples might be conceived as representing something such as problem-solving capacity, but many other characteristics of personality that might also contribute to that activity could not be measured reliably or validly. Another argument was that structural features of personality, if they exist, cannot be measured in ways that truly evaluate their full weight in different situations.

The changes in curricula did not necessarily lead to less personality testing. In fact, several studies published in the 1980s indicate that the use of psychological testing remained at almost the same level during this controversial period, but unfortunately those data may simply reflect the fact that psychological testing had become ingrained as a part of many of the routine procedures used with patients, especially inpatients. It is also sad to note that many clinicians continued to use assessment routines that had become little more than a byproduct of intellectual laziness. These are routines that hark back to the days when patients were subject to hours of testing and interviewing, and the clinicians took many days to write lengthy reports that often neglected much of the data they had collected. But the main force that led to a reduction of training in personality assessment procedures clearly came from the increased emphasis on therapeutic training and the variety of therapeutic methods that might be employed in different situations.

The reduced interest in personality testing was probably increased by an element outside psychology: the important changes that were ongoing in psychiatry. Beginning in the late 1960s or early 1970s training programs in psychiatry began to deemphasize the tactics of individual therapy and instead to emphasize pharmacological issues as a basis for or adjunct to intervention. As psychiatry gradually changed its emphasis, clinical psychology often paused in its own search for identity to condemn this so-called medical model.

The medical model, of course, is strongly embedded in the DSM manuals that search out a listing of characteristics or traits that are determined to be equivalent with a particular syndrome or diagnosis. Thus, many in contemporary psychiatry now tend to perceive the role of the psychologist as being more competitive and the procedures of assessment as being of little use unless they contribute to some DSM designation.

Unfortunately, a lengthy period has followed in which psychologists have neglected opportunities to educate colleagues from psychiatry concerning their potential assessment skills and the way in which those skills can contribute to more precise treatment planning and ultimately to the well-being of the patient. Even in the area of personality assessment, many scientific issues have been cast aside. There has been a notable decline in basic research on personality and personality theory. In effect, the very people who might be best able to investigate the worth of personality assessment have often turned to different areas of research.

The new clinical psychology focuses on treatments, and it has been a confusing and wondrous experience to note the remarkable accumulation of fads about treatment that have appeared during the past two decades, most probably with the objective of enticing new clients or explaining treatment failures. New propositions about such entities as borderlines, anorexia, bulimia, obsessive-compulsive disorders, panic disorders, multiple personalities, anxiety reactions, antisocial personalities, posttraumatic stress disorders, and the like, have created a cadre of specialists in those disorders. These specialists often suggest that their credentials provide an implicit promise of cure, or at least a clear understanding of the problem. Unfortunately, personality assessment has played an almost negligible role in contributing to these propositions, and research on these disorders struggles to reach even a mediocre level. Stated simply, people who purport to specialize in the treatment of these disorders have little interest in personality assessment, for by their logic, they already know what is wrong with the prospective patient and have the methodology readily available for treatment. This unreasonable logic neglects the individual as a unique entity. Even more important, it is based on the naive assumption that symptom presentation dictates a specific form of treatment. In effect, it is an extension of the medical model to which many professional psychologists seem to object so strenuously.

This situation has been clouded further by the fact that many psychologists who practice intervention seem to be motivated by the general premise that it is more important to entice the subject to become a paying client, or a client for whom someone else will pay, rather than to be concerned with what is really wrong with the

subject and/or what is really best for the subject. Unfortunately, a substantial number of clinical psychologists today perceive themselves to be therapists and have settled on one or at most two procedures that they feel comfortable employing with each perspective patient, and they apparently are not very interested in assessment.

In preparation for this brief overview of personality testing, the names of five hundred psychologists were randomly selected from the directory of the National Register of Health Service Providers. This random selection was done to attempt to learn more about the interest in, or practice of, personality assessment by those working in the field, especially those in private practice. To that end, the random selection was restricted to those whose addresses appeared to be residential or office, that is, none were selected whose addresses included a university, hospital, or obvious state, city, or county mental health installation. A brief twelve-item questionnaire was created and sent together with a stamped return envelope. A reproduction of this rather simple questionnaire is shown below as Table 2.1.

A total of 318 (64 percent) of the questionnaires were returned. Although the return is less than desirable, the data are quite striking and seem to send a message to those invested in personality assessment, and especially to those attempting to struggle with the managed-care industry.

Seventy-nine of the 318 respondents (25 percent) indicate that they never use personality testing. Fifty-one of the 79 indicate that they do not find them useful and/or believe that they are invalid. Twenty of the 79 indicate that they are not sufficiently trained in their use. Only six of the 79 indicate that clients object to their use.

The remaining 239 respondents indicate that they do use personality testing, but only 179 of the 239 (75 percent) indicate that they use the results in planning treatment. Of these 179, 154 always use a sentence-completion blank, and the remaining 25 respondents indicate that they often use a SCB.

Of the 239 who do use personality tests, 123 use the MMPI at times (sometimes = 44; often = 42; always = 37). Of the respondents who do

TABLE 2.1. Assessment Practices Questionnaire

Your name has been randomly selected from the Directory of the National Register for Health Service Providers. We are conducting a brief survey concerning the use of various personality tests as they may be used as a basis for planning intervention strategies. A stamped, addressed envelope is provided for your response. Please circle or check the appropriate letter for you response. We appreciate the few minutes required to complete these items.

Please circle or check the letter indicating your highest degree.
    (a) Ph.D.   (b) Psy.D.   (c) Ed.D.   (d) Other

If you maintain a private practice, what percentage of your professional time does your private practice encompass?

    (a) one-quarter time or less (b) less than one-half time but more than one-quarter time (c) about half time (d) more than half time but less than full time (d) full time

1. Do you, or someone who you assign, administer personality testing to clients you are considering to accept or have accepted for treatment either prior to the first treatment session or prior to the third session?
    (a) never   (b) occasionally   (c) often   (d) always

IF YOU HAVE ANSWERED QUESTION 1 AS (A) NEVER, PLEASE ANSWER QUESTION 1a BUT DISREGARD THE REMAINING QUESTIONS, AND PLEASE RETURN THE QUESTIONNAIRE IN THE ENCLOSED ENVELOPE.

1a. Please indicate from the following why you do not administer personality testing to your clients (circle more than one if applicable).
    (a) I do not find them useful
    (b) I do not believe they are valid
    (c) I am not sufficiently trained in their use
    (d) I find that clients object to them

IF YOU HAVE ANSWERED QUESTION 1 AS (B), (C), OR (D) PLEASE DISREGARD QUESTION 1a BUT ANSWER THE REMAINING QUESTIONS AND RETURN THE QUESTIONNAIRE IN THE ENCLOSED ENVELOPE.

2. Do you use the test results to plan your approach to intervention, such as deciding on long-term versus short-term tactics, deciding to use a supportive versus an uncovering or cognitive approach, etc.
    (a) never   (b) occasionally   (c) often   (d) always
3. Do you use the test results to formulate a diagnosis?
    (a) never   (b) occasionally   (c) often   (d) always
4. Do you use a version of the MMPI as a part of the assessment routine?
    (a) never   (b) occasionally   (c) often   (d) always
5. If you have answered (b), (c), or (d) to question 4, which version do you use most?
    (a) Original MMPI   (b) MMPI-2   (c) MMPI-A
6. Do you use a sentence completion blank as a part of the assessment routine?
    (a) never   (b) occasionally   (c) often   (d) always
7. Do you use the Rorschach as a part of the assessment routine?
    (a) never   (b) occasionally   (c) often   (d) always
8. If you answered (b), (c), or (d) to question 7, which approach to the Rorschach do you use?
    (a) Beck   (b) Comprehensive System   (c) Klopfer   (d) Piotrowski   (e) Other
9. Do you use the TAT or some other kind of apperception test as a part of the assessment routine?
    (a) never   (b) occasionally   (c) often   (d) always
10. Do you use any of the Millon inventories as a part of the assessment routine?
    (a) never   (b) occasionally   (c) often   (d) always

test, 102 use the Rorschach at times (sometimes = 25; often = 42; always = 35). Interestingly, the 77 who use the Rorschach often or always also use the MMPI often or always, and 64 of the 79 who use the MMPI often or always also use the Rorschach often or always. These seem to be the people who are invested in the use of personality assessment for purposes of treatment planning, but collectively, they constitute a relatively small proportion of the total group, only about 43 percent of those who do testing for treatment planning and only about 32 percent of all respondents who do use personality tests.

There is no way to know about the testing practices of the 182 nonresponders, but an ominous guess seems reasonable. In some respects, this lackadaisical approach to treatment planning is an unethical disservice to clients; psychologists can and should do much better. The fault is not with the lack of reliable or valid tests. During the past five decades several very useful personality tests have been developed or refined. This is not to suggest that psychology has reached the ultimate in precision in assessing personality or detecting the often subtly unique features that mark people and differentiate them from one another. Nonetheless, currently available personality tests are reasonably sophisticated, and findings from them can be used logically and empirically to generate realistic intervention plans if the data are used wisely and in the context of a cost-benefit analysis that will require the least investment by the subject.

A simple illustration may be useful. It is taken from two real-life cases and seems to affirm the importance of reviewing patients' individual differences in planning the treatment of those who may have the same presenting symptomatology. The illustration involves two women, both between the ages of twenty-seven and thirty-two, who complain of frequent and disruptive bouts of anxiety and frequent panic attacks. They live in markedly disparate parts of the United States, and each was assessed by a psychologist not known to the other.

The woman in Case 1 is separated after four years of marriage, while the Case 2 subject is single. Both have completed at least two years of college. The Case 1 subject currently works as a secretary in an accounting firm. The Case 2 subject works as a costume designer for a theatrical company. If either woman appeared before a consulting psychiatrist, there is a good likelihood that she would be prescribed some kind of antianxiety medication. If either appeared before a psychologist specializing in anxiety or panic reactions, she would probably be subjected to some form of tension reduction treatment and stress management control. The question is whether either form of intervention might be altered if the subjects were evaluated more thoroughly with regard to individual differences and unique personality characteristics. Both subjects were referred for personality assessment by their therapists, and bulk of the testing included the administration of a sentence completion blank, the MMPI-2, and the Rorschach.

The psychologist responsible for the Case 1 assessment reports that the results indicate that subject is quite defensive in spite of the fact that she has considerable resources and that her capacities for control and tolerance for stress are usually as robust as those of most adults. However, these features currently are less effective because of some situationally related stress, which probably has to do with her recent separation. The effects of the stress are relatively modest, but they have created a state of psychological overload. This overload appears to have created a potential for impulsiveness that is more likely to manifest itself in her emotional displays than in her thinking. Much of her stress appears related to an experience of emotional loss and probably translates as feelings of loneliness or neglect. As a result, many of her psychological operations are more complex than usual, and although she appears to have a longstanding confusion about her feelings, this confusion has become intensified.

It is also noted that she is an intensely self-centered person who greatly overestimates her self-worth. One by-product of this tendency is to focus much more on herself than on others. As a result, her interpersonal relationships are usually more tenuous and less mature. Thus, emotional losses or rejections are likely to have a greater impact on her because she perceives them as insults to her over-glorified sense of personal worth. Actually, her self-concept is based much more on imagination than on real experience. Nonetheless, it is important for her to defend her inflated sense of self, and because of this she usually externalizes responsibility, especially for negative events, and tends to avoid or deny unpleasantness.

She also has a strong passive-dependent orientation. She seems prone to seek relationships that are both supportive and nurturing. Unfortunately, this increases her vulnerability to the manipulations of others. It seems likely that she has some awareness of this, and she seems considerably less secure about her interpersonal relations than are most people. She attempts to conceal or contend with these feelings of insecurity by using an intellectual, somewhat authoritarian approach to many issues. Although she is open to social interaction, she is cautious and sometimes even reluctant to initiate interpersonal exchanges, especially those that may require tact and sophistication. She is especially defensive about relationships that may create unwanted demands on her or pose hazards to her control of the situation.

She is an intuitive person who is influenced greatly by her feelings when required to contend with demands for coping or decision making. Typically, she merges her feelings together with her thinking. She prefers to test out her decisions through trial-and-error activity and probably is not very reluctant to display her feelings. In fact, she may often convey the impression of being excessively emotional or even impulsive.

Her thinking is usually clear, but her current stress state tends to interfere with her abilities to concentrate or attend to specific events. Often, when in stressful situations, she creates a self-imposed form of helplessness in which she relies heavily on others to make decisions. She has no major problems in reality testing and seems as prone as most adults to make conventional responses when the circumstances of the situation clearly define expected or acceptable answers. In effect, she is a somewhat hysteroid-like person who is currently foundering and having

much difficulty with her sometimes very intense feelings.

The report concerning the subject in Case 2 indicates that she is a very conservative and cautious person who seems quite insecure about herself and her ability to deal effectively with her world. She is especially reluctant to deal with complexity and has developed a basic orientation toward coping or decision making that causes her to attempt to keep things on a very simple and easily managed level. Although this coping style is not necessarily detrimental, it does serve to reinforce her notion that she is not very capable.

She is a very ideational person who prefers to stop and think things through before reaching a decision or initiating behaviors. Actually, she commits much of her thinking to the development of fantasy, which she uses frequently and often abusively to avoid the stresses of reality. Although her capacities for control are quite adequate, she is vulnerable to disorganization under stress because she really has fewer resources readily available than do most adults. She is quite conservative about processing new information and seems especially fearful of her feelings in decision-making situations. As a result, she tries to avoid emotionally provocative situations whenever possible. In fact, she often goes to the extreme of emotionally isolating herself from close relations with others to avoid the quandaries of dealing directly with her feelings.

Overall, she is a somewhat psychologically impoverished, relatively fragile, and somewhat schizoidish individual. She seems forced to defend herself in an overly complicated world by assuming a passive or submissive interpersonal role. Although she is interested in people, her conceptions of them are based much more on her fantasy life than her real experience. Thus, although she is open to closeness, she seems bewildered about how best this might be achieved and concerned about what sacrifices she might be called upon to make in return. The result is a person who tends to live on the periphery of her environment, seemingly aware of what goes on but unable to partake in deep or mature relationships.

The psychologist reporting on the findings

for Case 1 issues a convincing argument that the findings clearly point to a need for some form of supportive intervention to assist in working through the current stressful situation created by the separation. The findings also stress the importance of her strong passive-dependent orientation in planning for a supportive routine. The report also emphasizes the tendency of the subject to externalize cause, and the volatility sometimes manifest in the overt expression of her feelings as potential targets for intervention, but cautions that these issues probably will not be open to treatment unless a longer-term form of intervention, ideally a developmental model of treatment, can evolve from the supportive intervention. The report notes that she has several assets that can be used to facilitate treatment. She has considerable resources. She has a relatively consistent coping style. She makes a serious effort to process information, and ordinarily she does not distort perceptual inputs. Her thinking is reasonably clear and she obviously has no negative sets toward her environment.

The psychologist writing the assessment report concerning the Case 2 subject argues convincingly that most of her symptoms have evolved because she seems to live a very fragile existence, depending on others with whom she is not really close and not being able to predict how effective or ineffective her avoidance style may be in her everyday living. When she is viewed as a unique person, optimal intervention objectives seem easily identified, but an actual intervention strategy is more difficult to define than for Case 1. First, she must be approached very cautiously. It seems clear that this woman suffers enormously from many developmental problems. She is not sure who or what she is and seems equally confused about others. Her resources are more limited than would be expected and her abusive use of fantasy serves only to sustain her impoverished plight. She is the type of person who, if confronted with the need for some long-term form of treatment, is likely to bolt because the prospect could be too threatening. Thus, it may be more appropriate to broach the treatment issue in a more specific but open-ended way, possibly by suggesting a focus on broadening social skills and contending with feelings more directly to ease some of her symptoms. It also seems logical to caution the therapist about her avoidant and oversimplifying orientation and her abuse of fantasy. Both will clearly cause problems in treatment but the former will tend to interfere most, especially when complex issues are addressed.

If the same therapist were to treat both of these clients, using essentially similar treatment tactics with both, it is likely that he or she might succeed with one but not the other. Stated differently, the intervention methodology that might work well for one of these subjects could not be expected to work for the other. Even though their presenting symptoms are similar, they are very different psychological people and only an extreme optimist could believe that a singular form of treatment would profit both. One seems in need of some sort of supportive treatment that might evolve into longer-term developmental treatment. The second clearly requires a more developmentally oriented form of intervention.

Although anecdotal, these cases illustrate the importance of personality assessment in understanding the individual more thoroughly and planning treatment more realistically. Some have argued that personality testing is time-consuming and that the same information will ultimately be revealed as treatment progresses. Actually, the procedures involved usually take no more than a few hours if done by those competently trained in assessment. What person would submit himself or herself to surgery or some other form of medical intervention without first being assured that all available tests had been completed and that the attending physician was thoroughly aware of the issues involved and had considered all treatment alternatives? Do people seeking mental health attention deserve any less?

It is true that many issues concerning the assessment of personality remain open to inquiry. Research about personality and personality assessment has slowed, mainly because practicing clinical psychologists have shunned those who may be in the best position to study the predictive value of personality assessment, that is, those involved mainly in research. Thus, unfortunately, assessment as a speciality is almost da-taless in terms of predicting response to specific intervention models. Some data do exist, scattered here and there, but the accumulated findings fall far short of offering a convincing need for assessment in most or all cases. It is also obvious that personality assessment can also be used to evaluate treatment outcome, but that is a far less common practice than it should be, and data concerning this process is almost non-existent.

If personality assessment is to be respected and successful into the next century, its purpose should be clearer and more empirically defined than it has been as yet. Students should be taught to select assessment procedures wisely and in the context of the purpose for which the assessment is designed. If an emphasis on treatment planning is provided, the procedures will make more sense—not only to students but to colleagues in psychology and psychiatry—and this will reaffirm the expertise and integrity of the special skills available from the well-trained clinician.

REFERENCES

Allport, G. W. (1937) *Personality: A psychological interpretation.* New York: Holt, Rinehart & Winston.

Murray, H. A. (1938) *Explorations in personality.* New York: Oxford University Press.

3

How to Select Personality Tests for a Test Battery

Marvin W. Acklin

Using psychological tests, whether with one other test (e.g., the MMPI-2 and the Rorschach) or in batteries of tests (Rapaport, Gill, & Schafer, 1968), is not only common practice but has achieved the status of a normative assumption in assessment training and clinical practice. The use of tests together, with the goal of a comprehensive personality assessment, could perhaps be called paradigmatic in clinical psychology for the past forty years. The "focal" use of psychological tests, that is, the use of single tests to answer specific questions (e.g., the use of group intelligence tests), has been a relatively minor, but never absent, subtheme in clinical practice. Recent developments in clinical practice, including the explosion of applications for psychological evaluation; the advent of managed care; shorter "treatment episodes"; the technologization and manualization of psychological treatment; a concern with empirical, problem-focused outcomes; and broader theoretical shifts, including the decline of psychoanalytic theory and the triumph of descriptive diagnosis as represented in the DSMs, currently call the comprehensive "battery" paradigm in assessment into question (Sweeney, Clarkin, & Fitzgibbon, 1987).

These changes cannot be divorced from changes in the broader cultural ethos of psychological evaluation and psychotherapy. Many, if not most, of the assumptions of assessment and treatment have shifted dramatically from those that formed the origins of the test battery in the 1940s (Acklin, 1993b). Managed care and the broader economic assumptions it embodies are a serious challenge to personality assessment as traditionally practiced. The purpose of this chapter is to review the basic conceptual and practical considerations that inform the choice and use of psychological test instruments.

Two important traditions in clinical psychology of the 1940s contributed significantly to the "assumptive world" (Frank, 1974) of assessment practice. These influences derived from two primary innovators and their respective clinical settings and followers: David Rapaport and the Menninger school of psychological evaluation, and Henry Murray and the Harvard Psychological Clinic. These enormously influential traditions, and some of the features of their ethos, will be examined.

David Rapaport's contribution to clinical psychology has been enormous. He and his colleagues at the Menninger Clinic in Topeka, Kansas, made innovations in the practice of psychological evaluation and its relations to clinical theory that remain vital today. For those influenced by Rapaport, the test battery is designed to assess various levels of personality functioning with the goal of providing a "verbal model of the person in adaptive distress (Rapaport, Gill, & Schafer, 1968, p. 15)." The influence of Henry Murray has been similarly influential with its focus on the "study of lives." This strongly idiographic approach toward personality views the whole person and his or her unique adaptation to the world. Both of these traditions naturally lend themselves to comprehensive evaluation goals, with test reports that are likely to be lengthy and extensive.

The Menninger school and the Harvard Psychological Clinic were inevitably influenced by the cultural ethos of the World War II and postwar era. This included the hegemony of humanistic and psychoanalytic approaches to personality theory and treatment, personological traditions that emphasize a comprehensive and holistic view of individuals in their "life-world" (demonstrating a strong affinity with Murray's psychobiography and the humanities), and the nearly complete absence of economic intrusion into the sanctity of the diagnostic and therapeutic setting. Within this framework of assumptions, psychodiagnostic assessment flowered into the full-blown art and science of what we now call personality assessment (represented today in the Society for Personality Assessment and the *Journal of Personality Assessment*). Though the assumptions of personality assessment have never been without their critics (e.g., Mischel, 1973a, 1973b), it is safe to say that these assumptions have become normative for clinical practice. Needless to say, many of these assumptions are currently under challenge.

The ethos of clinical assessment practice today reflects changes that are pervasive, including the rise of operationalism and empiricism, the pervasive impact of behaviorism and the pragmatic prediction of behavior, the preference for theoretical conceptualization based closely on experience, the decline of traditional psychoanalytic metapsychology, and the growing dominance of fiscal imperatives.

Despite these changes in context, clinical psychologists themselves and the practice of psychological assessment continue to reflect the influence of the Menninger and Harvard traditions. Recent surveys have consistently noted that tests are used in common and that a common or "standard battery" of tests has been the norm (Archer, Maruish, Imhof, & Piotrowski, 1991; Lees-Haley, 1992; Lubin, Larsen, & Matarazzo, 1984; Lubin, Larsen, Matarazzo, & Seever, 1986; Piotrowski & Keller, 1989; Piotrowski & Keller, 1992). This "remarkable stability" in test practice (Watkins, 1991), regardless of setting, is deeply rooted in training and practice. While the continuing popularity of the "standard battery" may be due to strict adherence to tradition, it is more likely due to successful adaptation of traditional test measures to changing circumstances in psychiatric diagnosis and clinical decision making (Lovitt, 1988).

Neither can one doubt the cultural shifts that shape and challenge assessment and treatment practice today. In general, the literature in the field of personality assessment has neither reflected nor addressed these changes. A recent, prescient article (Sweeney, Clarkin, & Fitzgibbon, 1987), however, reflects the dramatic, changing economic and clinical realities that govern practice. Recent changes present an opportunity for reexamining and reevaluating the conceptual and practical assumptions that inform the clinician's decision making in choosing tests.

CHOOSING PSYCHOLOGICAL TESTS

The role of the specialist in psychological evaluation rests upon a foundation of extensive training, including basic statistics, psychometrics, interviewing, and normal and abnormal psychology; didactic and supervised experiential training in the administration, scoring, and interpretation of psychological tests; and thorough acquaintance with professional practice standards (American Psychological Association, 1985), ethical guidelines (American Psychological Association, 1992; Berndt, 1983), and applicable state statutes regulating professional practice. While credentialing in the area of psychological evaluation is currently under discussion (the diplomate in clinical psychology awarded by the American Board of Professional Psychology has traditionally included an evaluation work sample), competent practice in the field is probably best viewed as an advanced postdoctoral specialization. Knowledge of the literature in the field is an obvious prerequisite for competent practice (Weiner, 1989). Further, because of changing standards, ongoing research, and the continual emergence of new assessment tools (e.g., the MMPI-2), awareness of the literature and continuing education in the field are necessary.

The choice of psychological tests is not, of course, an end in itself. Rather, it is probably best viewed in the context of the request for consultation in which the evaluator's expertise and professional judgement are being called for. Thus test choice is really a tactical decision in the overall assessment strategy.

Upon receiving a request to perform a psychological evaluation, the well-trained clinician may activate a preestablished and well-routinized set of procedural schemas without reflecting on his or her assumptions. One could initially ask, "Why test at all?" Of course, many critics of testing have assailed the empirical/psychometric foundations of testing, the American preoccupation with testing, and the presumed cultural biases of testing. But examining the "Why test?" question is worthwhile on a strictly procedural basis. What does testing have to offer that interviews or other procedures (e.g., behavioral assessment) do not? What role does psychological assessment have in clinical decision making?

The referral question plays the determinative role here. (See illustration in Appendix A.) "Why test?" (Levine, 1981) is directly linked to the question "What question is intended to be answered?" Related but no less important questions are "Who is the intended beneficiary of the evaluation?" "Who is the audience who will be recipient of the information conveyed by the report?" and "Who is to be evaluated?" Finally, "What are the potential or probable consequences of the evaluation?" Contemporary psychological testing occurs in numerous, diverse contexts. The parameters of assessment may dif-

fer significantly depending on the context and the client. Examiners may be asked to assess intellectual capacity or readiness for work, to rule out thought disorder or learning disability, to assess competency or mental status at the time of a criminal offense, or to provide diagnostic and treatment recommendations for a traditional psychodynamic psychotherapy case. Without clarification of the procedural, content, and ethical dimensions that follow upon these questions, the examiner runs the risk of malpractice.

Well-constructed psychological tests used in an appropriate fashion by qualified examiners provide "essentially an objective and standardized measure of a sample of behavior" (Anastasi, 1988).[1] Using extensive data derived from the Menninger Psychotherapy Project, Appelbaum reported that test-based statements of diagnostic understanding, treatment recommendations, and treatment outcome were superior to interview-based predictions (Appelbaum, 1977). As yet, the field of psychological testing has not developed empirical standards for integrating and weighing test results in the statistical prediction of psychiatric diagnoses (Galluci, 1990). Thus, the competent examiner is at pains to provide an a priori conceptual rationale — theoretical or pragmatic — for combining tests and their results. In Anastasi's terms, the use of tests in combination provides diverse samples of behavior. In the Menninger tradition (Rapaport, Gill, & Schafer, 1968), in the selection of tests, "the leading idea was to obtain material reflecting different aspects and levels of the person's psychic make-up" (p. 48); to assess various levels or domains of personality functioning (p. 47); and to "mass diagnostic indicators" (p. 51). In contrast to interview techniques, the varied task orientations of the testing situation place demands on various aspects of ego functioning (Miller, 1987). The use of test norms allows for comparison of performance between identified groups of individuals classified by demographic or clinical criteria. While empirical research has yet to demonstrate the undisputed superiority of testing in the validity of psychiatric diagnosis, the role of testing in assessing level of intellectual functioning, specific academic skills or abilities, the presence of functional disability in cases of brain injury, presence of thought disturbance, or elicitation of the internalized, "representational world" of the examinee is indisputable.

Several practical questions, then, are embedded in the request for assessment: What is the context of the referral? Who has requested the psychological evaluation? What is the nature of the problem? To what end will the information provided be put? Who is the client? Who is the examinee? (See Appendix B.) Obviously the age and the functional capacity of the person to be examined will play a major role in the choice of tests. Is there a concern about cultural factors in determining a test's validity? (Williams, 1987). What is the nature of the problem? What time and resource considerations are involved, including the cost of the evaluation and who will pay for it? Is there a concern about malingering or simulation? (Dalby, 1988; Schretlen, 1988; Wasyliw, Grossman, Haywood, & Cavanaugh, 1988). To answer the questions at hand, should the evaluation be "focal," using selected tests, or is a more comprehensive (and hence longer and more costly) evaluation needed? In short, the referral question ("what") and the capacities of the examinee and examiner ("who") are central questions in determining the assessment strategy ("how"), including the choice of test instrumentation. A referral question may be so focused that a single standardized test or a single test scale may be sufficient (Korchin, 1976). Answers to these questions will govern the choice of instrument and the assessment strategy and tactics the evaluator will use.

Although the evaluator may have a preliminary rationale for the instruments to be used in an evaluation, the issue does not end here. Interviewing the client or patient may reveal functional deficits that may alter the original choice of tests, for example, discovering that the client or patient is visually impaired, incapable of attending or concentrating, or is functionally illiterate. Not infrequently, pretesting may be of value, for example, administering a brief reading comprehension test before administering the MMPI-2 or neuropsychological tests that require verbal fluency. The examiner may decide to add or drop a test in the middle of the evaluation session based on information or impressions that emerge during the testing process. Finally, tests may be added or dropped after the evaluation session, as a result of inspecting the quality of the test data (for example, noting issues that may require further inquiry). A test may also be dropped from the battery after it has been administered because of doubtful validity (e.g., the patient may have been too distressed or psychotic during the test administration for the results to be interpretively useful).

Practical considerations are not the only issues that bear on the choice of test instruments, however. A second, broad set of considerations, which may best be described as conceptual and utilitarian, are relevant to the evaluator. The battery approach of the Menninger tradition naturally assumes that no single test is sufficient to assess complex human processes. By careful combination of test instruments, the evaluator is able to highlight factors relevant to the referral questions. The question of how to combine and integrate tests may be based on either theoretical or strictly utilitarian premises. The Rapaport school identified a standard battery, the basic components of which have changed little. Their rationale in combining tests this way was driven by both theoretical commitments (largely those of psychoanalytic ego psychology) and practical considerations related to their own treatment setting. In a manner that has largely characterized all subsequent practice, Rapaport noted that his rationale for test combination represented a "systematic linkage of the test-responding process to a theory of personality, thought organization, and psychopathology" (Rapaport, Gill, & Schafer, 1968, p. 19). The "levels of analysis" approach implies a view of personality functioning that is hierarchically organized along the lines of covert versus overt and conscious versus unconscious determination. The fifty-year period following Rapaport's writings on test theory and practice has seen the eclipse of traditional psychoanalytic theory and a shift toward empirical constructs derived from general psychology. Universal adherence to clinical theory is no longer a given in American clinical psychology. It is, furthermore, unlikely that Rapaport and his colleagues could have foreseen the explosion of psychological test applications in business, employment, educational, legal, and clinical situations that characterize the current scene. Strictly pragmatic considerations may rule in a given evaluation situation in which tests may be combined on the basis of the specific referral questions to be addressed. In this case, theoretical commitments will have given way to situational or pragmatic considerations in test choice.

The legacy of the "levels" or "domains" approach continues to be notable. Assessment of various part-processes—for example, thinking, affect organization and management, self-concept, and interpersonal relations—may drive test selection. The evaluator must resort to a multimethod assessment methodology that combines assessment strategies and integrates nomothetic and idiographic data in the generation of test inferences. The use of both nomothetic and idiographic measures generates normative information and provides for a fleshing out of the individual uniqueness favored in personology. Here philosophy-of-science questions come to bear: Is psychological testing based on a social or natural science model, or is it a fundamentally meaning-creating, hermeneutical enterprise?

Tests may be chosen based on whether they are direct "self-report," that is, representing a fixed response format as in the MMPI-2 or other "objective" personality tests, or whether the response format is indirect, as in the projective techniques such as the Rorschach. It may well be that contemporary adherence to the battery model represents less a continuing adherence to the theoretical rationale and principles of ego psychology than pragmatism in assessing salient aspects of personality functioning using a multimethod assessment methodology.

Professional psychological evaluators are usually pragmatists. Tests may be chosen on the basis of their reliability (stability), validity (effectiveness), and utility (efficiency). The most obvious effectiveness and utility questions are "Does the test do what it is supposed to do?" and "How efficiently does it do it?" While the psychometric qualities of a test are crucial with respect to effectiveness and utility, other things being equal, a test that does what it is supposed to do in the shortest time and at the lowest cost is likely to become and remain popular. It is unlikely that tests that do not satisfy the criterion of effectiveness and utility, regardless of their other merits, will survive in the test marketplace.

In summary, the choice of psychological tests is a complex matter that has philosophical, sociological, clinical, and pragmatic considerations. The current parameters that shape psychological assessment practice have shifted dramatically since the foundations of the discipline in the 1940s. The changed reimbursement climate, wherein insurance companies and in the future perhaps the federal government determine what services are paid for, will undoubtedly dictate a shift in the assumptions of assessment practice (see Appendix C). In the current milieu and in the future, evaluators will be at pains to demonstrate the efficiency, effectiveness, and value of testing in the diagnosis, treatment, disposition, and follow-up phases of intervention. Outcome measures are likely to increase in importance. It is likely in this context that the old battles over incremental validity will be reexamined—essentially the question of what testing actually contributes to the clinical enterprise. Just as physicians are being pressured to order specific diagnostic tests rather than broad batteries, psychodiagnosticians will increasingly turn to focal testing or more refined applications of the standard battery, the use of issue-specific tests and measures that are amenable to outcome study. Quality assurance and demonstration of "medical necessity" will probably be in greater demand than before.

The art and science of psychological evaluation will face challenges similar to those psychotherapy has faced. The contribution of psychological evaluation to the many contexts that rely upon it is not likely to diminish. The solitary clinician, the bewildered patient, and the vigilant third party payer will collectively benefit from the incremental information furnished by well-designed psychometric instruments (Charles A. Peterson, personal communication, June 26, 1993). Although the field has felt and will continue to feel the impact of technology and operationalization, the well-trained evaluator will always employ a broad range of instruments, and a humble awareness of their merits and limits, in understanding people in distress.

ACKNOWLEDGMENT

Special thanks to Evelynne Raposo for bibliographic assistance and to Charles A. Peterson, Ph.D., for his sturdy friendship, reliable object constancy, and broad erudition.

NOTE

1. APA *Standards for Educational and Psychological Testing* note that "the term 'test' usually refers to measures of either the constructed-performance or structured-behavior-sample type, in which test takers are expected or instructed to try their best. Instruments for identifying interests and personality characteristics through self-report are typically and properly entitled 'inventories,' 'questionnaires,' or 'checklists' rather than tests. In textual material, such as in the Standards, these self-report instruments may be called tests in order to simplify the language. They are called tests here to indicate that the standards also apply to these instruments" (1985, pp. 4–5).

REFERENCES

Acklin, M. W. (1993a). Integrating the Rorschach and the MMPI in clinical assessment: Conceptual and methodological issues. *Journal of Personality Assessment, 60,* 125–131.

Acklin, M. W. (1993b, March 20). *An overview of managed care and its impact on assessment and treatment planning.* Presentation at the midwinter meetings of the Society for Personality Assessment, San Francisco.

American Psychological Association. (1985). *Standards for educational and psychological testing.* Washington, DC: Author.

American Psychological Association. (1992). *Ethical principles for psychologists.* Washington, DC: Author.

Anastasi, A. (1988). *Psychological testing* (6th ed.). New York: Macmillan.

Appelbaum, S. (1977). *The anatomy of change: A Menninger Foundation report of testing the effects of psychotherapy.* New York: Plenum.

Archer, R. P., Maruish, M., Imhof, E. A., & Piotrowski, C. (1991). Psychological test usage with adolescent clients: 1990 survey findings. *Professional Psychology: Research & Practice. 22,* 247–252.

Berndt, D. J. (1983). Ethical and professional considerations in psychological assessment. *Professional Psychology, 14,* 580–587.

Bond, L., Camara, W., & VandenBos, G. (1989). Psychological test standards and clinical practice. *Hospital and Community Psychiatry, 40,* 687–688.

Dalby, J. T. (1988). Detecting faking in the pre-trial assessment. *American Journal of Forensic Psychology, 6,* 49–55.

Frank, J. *Persuasion and healing: A comparative study of psychotherapy.* New York: Schocken Books.

Galluci, N. T. (1990). On the synthesis of information from psychological tests. *Psychological Reports, 67,* 1243–1260.

Korchin, S. (1976). *Modern clinical psychology.* New York: Basic Books.

Lees-Haley, P. (1992). Psychodiagnostic test usage by forensic psychologists. *American Journal of Forensic Psychology, 10,* 25–30.

Levine, D. (1981). Why and when to test: The social context of psychological testing. In A. Rabin (Ed.), *Assessment with projective techniques: A concise introduction.* New York: Springer.

Lovitt, R. (1988). Current practice of psychological assessment: Response to Sweeney, Clarkin, & Fitzgibbon. *Professional Psychology: Research and Practice, 19,* 516–521.

Lubin, B., Larsen, R. M., & Matarazzo, J. D. (1984). Patterns of psychological test usage in the United States: 1935–1982. *American Psychologist, 39,* 451–454.

Lubin, B., Larsen, R. M., Matarazzo, J. D. & Seever, M. F. (1985a). Selected characteristics of psychologists and psychological assessment in five settings: 1959–1982. *Professional Psychology: Research & Practice, 17,* 155–157.

Lubin, B., Larsen, R. M., Matarazzo, J. D. & Seever, M. F. (1985b). Psychological test usage patterns in five professional settings. *American Psychologist, 40,* 857–861.

Miller, S. B. (1987). A comparison of methods of inquiry: Testing and interviewing contributions to the diagnostic process. *Bulletin of the Menninger Clinic, 51,* 505–518.

Mischel, W. (1973a). Facing the issues. *Journal of Abnormal Psychology, 82,* 541–542.

Mischel, W. (1973b). On the empirical dilemmas of psychodynamic approaches. *Journal of Abnormal Psychology, 82,* 335–344.

Piotrowski, C., & Keller, J. W. (1989). Psychological testing in outpatient mental health facilities: A national study. *Professional Psychology: Research & Practice, 20,* 423–425.

Piotrowski, C., & Keller, J. W. (1992). Psychological testing in applied settings: A literature review from 1982 to 1992. *The Journal of Training and Practice in Professional Psychology, 6,* 74–82.

Rapaport, D., Gill, M., & Schafer, R. (1968). *Diagnostic psychological testing* (Robert Holt, Ed.). New York: International Universities Press.

Schretlen, D. J. (1988). The use of psychological tests to identify malingered symptoms of mental disorder. *Clinical Psychology Review, 8,* 451–476.

Sue, D., & Sue, S. (1987). Cultural factors in clinical assessment of Asian Americans. *Journal of Consulting and Clinical Psychology, 55,* 479–487.

Sweeney, J. A., Clarkin, J. F., & Fitzgibbon, M. (1987). Current practice of psychological assessment. *Professional Psychology: Research & Practice, 18,* 377–380.

Wasyliw, O. E., Grossman, L. S., Haywood, T. W., & Cavanaugh, J. L. (1988). The detection of malingering in criminal forensic groups: MMPI validity scales. *Journal of Personality Assessment, 52,* 321–333.

Watkins, C. E. (1991). What have surveys taught us about the teaching and practice of psychological assessment. *Journal of Personality Assessment, 56,* 426–437.

Weiner, I. B. (1989). On competence and ethicality in psychodiagnostic assessment. *Journal of Personality Assessment, 53,* 827–831.

Williams, C. L. (1987). Issues surrounding psychological testing of minority patients. *Hospital and Community Psychiatry, 38,* 184–189.

APPENDIX A

Case Example: Mrs. B.

The following case study is presented to illustrate the relationship between a clinical problem, referral questions, and the choice of psychological tests. A pragmatic orientation prevails here with a secondary interest in theoretical integration along the lines of psychoanalytic ego psychology.

Mrs. B., a twenty-seven-year-old married Caucasian female with two years of junior college education, was referred for psychological evaluation by the doctoral-level social worker who was seeing her in brief outpatient psychotherapy. He was using hypnotherapy in working on early-life sexual abuse issues when she began to experience "seizures." She had had a history of seizures since age nine, but had not had a seizure for a number of years previously. The client was subsequently examined by a neurologist, who administered an EEG, and a psychiatrist, who performed a clinical interview. In fact, the client was actually observed having a seizure by both the psychiatrist and the neurologist. The EEG turned out to be within normal limits. Neither the psychiatrist nor the neurologist was convinced that the seizures indicated genuine epilepsy. Because of the diagnostic uncertainty and concerns about liability and cost containment, the case was referred for a complete neuropsychological and personality assessment to rule out neuropsychological factors; to provide a picture of Mrs. B.'s personality structure, organization, and style; to provide insight into the etiology of the seizures; and to provide treatment recommendations. The members of the treatment team were eager to have a diagnostic consultant address their uncertainties about the case.

With respect to observations and background, Mrs. B. was observed to be a friendly, loud, somewhat brassy woman, who greeted the examiner with a complete absence of social anxiety or inhibition. Her manner was blunt, bordering on vulgar, when discussing otherwise sensitive issues related to sexuality. She indicated that she thought she had been abused by an older man when she was about nine years old. She said that she was sexually precocious at an early age as a result and had involved herself in multiple, somewhat indiscriminate, sexual pairings. She described her current marriage as "perfect." She was cooperative with the request for psychological evaluation.

Following the clinical interview and a

telephone consultation with her therapist, a battery of psychological tests were chosen and administered in order to address the referral questions, including the Wisconsin Card Sorting Test (WCST), the Halstead Category Test, Trailmaking Test, Parts A and B, Wechsler Memory Scale—Revised (WMS-R), California Verbal Learning Test (CVLT), Rey-Osterreith Complex Figure, Wechsler Adult Intelligence Scale—Revised (WAIS-R), Human Figure Drawings, Minnesota Multiphasic Personality Inventory (MMPI), the Rorschach, Thematic Apperception Test (TAT), Incomplete Sentences, Early Memory Questionnaire, and Personality Adjective Checklist (PACL).

Tests were chosen for inclusion into the battery according to the following rationale.

• The Wisconsin Card Sorting Test, Halstead Category Test, and Trails, Part A and B were chosen for their contribution to an assessment of the integrity of Mrs. B's cerebral hemispheres, especially the frontal areas.

• The Wechsler Memory Scale—Revised, California Verbal Learning Test, and Rey-Osterreith were chosen to assess general memory functioning in various modalities, to determine her learning style and use of memory strategies.

• The Wechsler Adult Intelligence Scale—Revised was chosen to provide an overview of her level of cognitive development and capacity for adaptation, as well as specific skills and cognitive style. The test provides an unusually rich opportunity for observation across a broad range of verbal and nonverbal tasks, with provision of information related to efficiency, frustration tolerance, short- and long-term memory, and self-efficacy. Finally, the test provides information of a general neuropsychological nature relevant to lateralization as well as information that can be subsumed into an ego psychological interpretive framework.

• Human Figure Drawings, including a self-drawing and inquiries, were given to provide a gross assessment of object relations, level of social perception, and body image problems.

• The MMPI was given to provide a self-report of psychiatric symptomatology (e.g., depression, anxiety, somatization), to provide general information about validity and impression management, and to illuminate Mrs. B's personality type. The test's numerous scales provide multiple opportunities for hypothesis generation and development. The test is easily administered, computer scored, and readily interpreted.

• The Rorschach test was given to provide information about Mrs. B.'s level of personality organization, level of object relations, capacities for and style of affect management, cognitive and affective style, accuracy of perception and thinking, and self-perception. The test was administered according to Exner's Comprehensive System, hand scored, and a computer program utilized to compute the structural summary.

• The TAT was given to assess the richness of Mrs. B's thought processes and imagination in her construction of narratives. Levels of social causation, empathy, relationship themes, and affect tone are assessed using the TAT.

• Incomplete Sentences is a minor self-administered test that provides a sampling of attitudes and beliefs. It allows the evaluator to roughly estimate level of ego development and capacity for cognitive and social complexity, and to sample thematic material related to various content areas.

• The Early Memory Questionnaire is extremely useful in assessing the perceptions and themes that organize Mrs. B.'s current predicament, revealed through the metaphor of her earliest childhood recollection. The EM can be scored for self-perception, perception of others, activity or passivity, levels of empathy, and perception of environment.

• The Personality Adjective Checklist (PACL) is a self-report checklist of 153 adjectives. They were endorsed by Mrs. B. as descriptive of her personality. The test is easily administered and computer scored, providing a personality description according to Millon's taxonomy.

APPENDIX B

Some relevant questions that inform the choice of psychological tests in clinical assessment are listed below. Obviously the choice of psychological tests is inseparable from, and only a part of, the overall assessment/consultation strategy.

 ➤ Who is the client for the consultation?

What are the referral questions?

For what purposes is the evaluation being undertaken?

In what domain is the evaluation being conducted (educational, business/industry, clinical, or legal)?

Who is the person to be evaluated? What is this person's age, educational level, and functional capacities (mental, physical, emotional status)?

Who is the intended (or unintended) audience for the findings?

How will the findings be communicated?

Is the case likely to end up in court?

What time parameters bear on the assessment? How much time is available or needed?

Who is paying for the evaluation?

What tests are specifically appropriate to the referral questions?

What tests are currently available in the evaluator's supply?

Which tests demonstrate the best psychometric characteristics?

Which tests will be of most value in obtaining the desired information in the shortest amount of time?

What group of tests will create an appropriate mix of idiographic/nomothetic and objective/projective data?

Is malingering or deception likely to be of concern?

APPENDIX C

Questions typically asked by managed care agents in relation to psychological treatment and assessment are listed below:

What is the medical necessity for the treatment?

What specific symptoms are present?

For how long will the patient be treated (how many sessions)?

What is the focus of treatment?

What are the discharge plans?

What kinds of follow-up will be offered to avoid the reemergence of symptoms?

How will the psychological assessment information contribute to the treatment plan?

What tests will be used? Why?

How long will the evaluation take?

4

The Theory and Measurement of Traits: Two Views

Allan R. Harkness
Robert Hogan

When people use the single word "trait," they can mean many different things, and this is a great source of confusion, real disagreement, and pseudocontroversy in personality assessment. The authors of this chapter have rather different views regarding the meaning of traits, and the chapter sketches two broad perspectives on traits and their measurement. These viewpoints are presented in order to encourage discussion of fundamental issues in personality assessment. First, we will present a variant of the constructive-realist approach to psychological theory construction, using a trait called Constraint. Then we present the socioanalytic position on traits.

TRAITS FROM A CONSTRUCTIVE-REALIST POSITION: THE CONSTRAINT EXAMPLE

"Traits exist in people; constructs (here usually about traits) exist in the minds and magazines of psychologists. People have constructs too, but that is outside the present scope" (Jane Loevinger, 1957).

Consider a hypothetical patient, a portrait synthesized from bits of direct patient contacts and supervisee reports, a constructed, yet perhaps prototypic patient. Mr. X makes an appointment with you and then tells you that he does not really need to be there, but that his wife will divorce him if he does not get some help. It becomes clear that he wants to avoid a divorce but not because of any personal attachment to his wife or sense of responsibility to his children. He wishes to avoid divorce because his wife controls resources that he desires. In the spirit of bragging about his sexual conquests (the patient's viewpoint on sex is indistinguishable from his descriptions of deer hunting), it becomes clear that since early adolescence he has had multiple sexual partners, and under the cover of "drinking with the boys," he is deceiving his wife. He enjoys physical risk taking, an appetite not sated by hard runs on dirt bikes, off-road vehicles, and high-speed spins on public roads. Because he admits no problems, the interview seems stymied until you appear to collude with him (by a knowing smile at the right moment) in seeing his wife as "making a mountain out of a molehill." On this new basis he warms to explaining the various areas that this "nit-picking" wife complains about: gambling away his earnings, not maintaining a steady income (he is a salesman, and it sounds to you like he makes a good initial impression but often fails to follow through), failing to keep regular hours, acquiring traffic tickets, and abusing drugs and alcohol.

As the end of the first meeting nears, you wish you had a firm assessment basis for your intuitions, but you feel the need to put right the misalliance. Further, you feel obligated to try either to establish a reasonable basis for working with this patient or to end the consultation. Your intervention takes the form of a friendly confrontation along with a capsule summary of your honest clinical impression to this point: "You said you did not feel you need to be here, and I believe you were being totally honest when you said that. That would create an impossible basis for us to work together, and I might then be in the dishonest position of being a stage prop to convince your wife that change within you is occurring when in fact it is not. I believe that you have probably suffered greatly in your life, more than you have told me, because you take too many risks and because you don't set and follow prudent rules for yourself. Although you don't want to hear this, there is part of you that knows it is true: you have not lived up to your abilities because frequently you have not stopped yourself when you should have. In the future, or even now, should you decide you really want to change yourself and become more controlled, I would really like to work with you. But I suspect that may be different work than you had in mind. . . ."

A viewpoint on traits, and a particular trait, Constraint (Tellegen, 1982; Watson & Clark, 1993), offers a lens through which the foregoing clinical picture comes into focus: Patient X is at a very low trait level of Constraint. Constructive-realism, a theoretical position on traits and their measurement developed by Loevinger (1957), was named and further elucidated by Messick (1981). As elaborated by Messick, constructive-realism is a general viewpoint on psychological theory construction, and it is not limited to modeling dispositional traits. Constructive realism builds on the earlier ideas of Allport (1937; see also Funder, 1991), Eysenck (1967) and Cattell (1946), and benefits from further clarification and development by Tellegen

(1985, 1988, 1991). All of these writers have at least one thing in common: they do not consider traits to be a convenient fiction; for them, traits have an existence beyond the cognitive activity of the observer. Nevertheless, the constructive-realist accepts that we can only know traits through the mediation of theory, in this case, through constructs that are elements in a larger theory of mind and measurement. Thus the constructive-realist both accepts the limits of human knowers yet rejects the solipsism of social constructionism.

The constructive-realist approach to traits makes a distinction between traits (real structures in subjects), constructs (cognitive theoretical ingredients in the mind of a psychologist that are models of the traits), and trait indicators (test and nontest behaviors stochastically and conditionally linked to the real but latent traits). Some theories are better than others because the linked constructs of the better theories have more verisimilitude or truth-likeness (Meehl, 1978, see p. 818). We deduce that these better theories have more truth-likeness because they lead to predictions that pay off in generative research programs (see, e.g., Urbach, 1974), and because of better fit to the larger pastiche of scientific endeavor. This motivation gives constructive-realist measurement a different focus than measurement from an instrumentalist perspective (where goals are explicitly prediction and control). Constructive-realists seek accurate measurement of well-understood latent traits leading to accurate test interpretation. The basic spirit of constructive-realist measurement is "first understand nature well and then good prediction will follow (if events are predictable!)."

Coordinated with this position are a series of definitions and distinctions regarding traits and trait-related concepts.

Tellegen's Trait Term Distinctions: Dimensions, Levels, Indicators

Tellegen (1988) defines a trait as "a psychological (therefore organismic) structure underlying a relatively enduring behavioral disposition, i.e., a tendency to respond in certain ways under certain circumstances. In the case of a *personality trait* some of the behaviors expressing the disposition have substantial adaptational implications" (p. 622). There are other causes besides traits that could lead to enduring behavioral dispositions, but one important cause of such dispositions is a real, enduring internal structure. Such enduring internal structures are a node in a complex causal chain. These enduring internal structures result from the interaction of sequences of environments with the unfolding genetic blueprint of the individual. They then exert a causal influence on subsequent behavior.

Having defined trait, Tellegen (1988) then offered further distinctions:

> *Trait level* is a quantitative individual-differences variable, or parameter, representing a person's standing on a *trait dimension*. The more purely a set of measures reflect variations among persons in trait level on a given trait, the more they will covary across persons and the less discrepant they will be within persons. Measures thought to reflect trait levels for a given trait . . . are called *trait indicators*. Covariation among such measures in a population is often the basis for inferring a trait dimension, often as the first step toward inferences about a trait structure.
>
> A trait dimension, then, though not itself an organismic structure but a population concept representing a statistical structure, can be linked to organismic structure (Tellegen, 1988, p. 622).

One can also distinguish between potential behavioral indicators of a trait and the measurement instruments (what Tellegen has called the trait indicators).

To take a constructive-realist trait approach in the case of Constraint is to offer the researchable, testable, and refutable conjecture that real, enduring internal structural differences between persons create this trait dimension of adaptive relevance. In viewing Mr. X, a constructive-realist trait approach to Constraint suggests that there is something structural (organismic) about him that yields a disposition to (a) not avoid risky situations; (b) fail to be constrained by traditional morality; (c) not plan

ahead, even when it is clearly desirable; and (d) ignore rules even when they are reasonable and constrain individual conduct for the sake of social existence.

Tellegen defines a trait as the (at this point conjectured but unspecified) underlying structure that causes a disposition. This recalls an earlier distinction; MacCorquodale and Meehl (1948) described *intervening variables* and *hypothetical constructs*. Intervening variables are, for example, mathematical summary statements that have no real existence, whereas a hypothetical construct has "thinginess";[1] according to MacCorquodale and Meehl, a hypothetical construct exists apart from the theory. To illustrate, if a car dealer counted the number of Buicks and Cadillacs sold each year, the variable "Buicks sold" has a direct and none too latent referent: real Buicks that left the lot. "Buicks sold" has a reality status that would qualify as a hypothetical construct. On the other hand, suppose this dealer found that over a period of years, the best predictor of net profit was 1.0 times the number of Buicks sold plus 4.3 times the number of Cadillacs sold. He calls this weighted linear composite "Z." Now Z has a somewhat reduced reality status compared with "Buicks sold." Another dealer, for example, might have different weights. Z, although it has real referents, does not have the same ontological status, that same "thinginess" as a count of steel, plastic, and rubber Buicks. Z is an intervening variable, a convenient mathematical predictor.

In the Constraint example, the hypothetical construct models the underlying structure within patient X that gives rise to his disinhibited disposition. The structure has a degree of "thinginess" that the disposition does not. The disposition is an intervening variable; it is a series of as yet unrealized conditional probabilities of the form

$$p(\text{output behavior}|\text{input class})$$

where the upright solidus "|" of the conditional means "given that the following is realized." The disposition is detectable, but it does not exist in the same ontological sense as the structure giving rise to it. As an analogy, the underlying atomic structure of a piece of glass has an ontological "thinginess" that causes or gives rise to the disposition "breakability," which is potentially realizable. Breakability of the glass can readily be demonstrated (but you do not have to break every piece of glass to have confidence in the disposition—this being a foundering point on which operationism died [Leahy, 1980]). Yet the disposition of breakability does not have the "thinginess" of the underlying atomic structure that gives rise to it.

If people vary on the underlying conjectured structures that cause the disposition (and hence vary along these conditional probabilities) then there is a trait dimension, in this case a trait dimension of Constraint. Mr. X could presumably be contrasted with Patient Y, who is overcontrolled, risk-avoidant, and paralyzed by fear of doing wrong. Patients X and Y are at two different levels of the disposition, and the inference is that there is something structurally, organismically different about X and Y that accounts for the dispositional difference.

What is the structure? Tellegen and Waller (in press) note, "One could conjecture that underlying this dimension is a general inhibition system varying in strength across individuals, and elaborate this notion into a psychobiological construct such as the Behavioral Inhibition System" (Gray, 1982). Thus we see that the conjectured structure is at two Comteian levels: (a) the psychological, with a general inhibition system, and (b) at a psychobiological level. Watson and Clark (1993) offer an integrative psychological and biological model of Disinhibition versus Constraint. Depue and Spoont (1986) and Spoont (1992) have postulated biological mechanisms, and they comment specifically on the role of serotonergic systems in differing trait levels of Constraint versus disinhibition.

Drawing upon these models, the first author believes that the treatment of Patient X would take the form of using cortical controls to override a subcortical regulatory process that causes problems. This is exactly the situation faced by the overweight dieter, and unfortunately, the long-run prognosis is probably similar.

The Nature of Structural Variation

How can we understand the variation in psychological or psychobiological structures? A current best guess is that there is a mixture of both quantitative and qualitative variation. Thus variation might take the form of common, nomothetic traits, where there are highly similar structures across persons with quantitative variation in that common structure. Think of the analogy of a series of eyeballs (common structure) with different degrees of bulging yielding different degrees of myopia. In the case of Constraint, such a conjecture would entail persons sharing a common general inhibition system which differs parametrically across persons in activating thresholds, strength, capacity to override other systems, and so on.

Qualitative variation may occur as well. One might conjecture a small number of fundamentally different structures (see Meehl, 1992). For many traits, nature no doubt provides a mixture of the above models. The distribution of intelligence appears to be a compound of near-normal variation due to multifactorial determination overlaid by an elevation of the left tail due to single big-cause (e.g., chromosomal nondisjunction, PKU) retardations.

One can argue that biology is fundamentally typal and that there are a finite number of structural types; this is the strategy of beginning at the bottom of a hierarchical cluster analysis, where k = N, that is, there are as many types as people. In this view, continuous dimensions are merely platonic ideals that distort nature but nevertheless provide the only usable summary when the number of types is so high that it appears infinite to the human perceiver. In the case of Constraint, much of the variation looks dimensional, with a unimodal distribution pattern common to phenotypes that result from the net influence of many independent causal events.

On the other hand, the tails of Constraint seem to be elevated. The existence of personality disorders, and hence clinically significant base rates at the *extremes* of Constraint, at the very places where the Gaussian curve predicts few cases, suggests that there may be big causal events that can push one to the low-Constraint extreme (e.g., Pick's disease) or the high-Constrait extreme (e.g., Freud's hypothesis about an active role in an early sexual trauma as the cause of obsessive-compulsive features). These hypotheses about single big causes are proximal; they occur in the lifetime of the individual.

One can also advance more distal, evolutionary explanations of the elevated tails of Constraint. The population distribution of Constraint could have resulted from frequency-dependent selection (see, e.g., Barash, 1982). For example, when it is at a low frequency in a population, low Constraint may be selected for. But as the frequency of disinhibited individuals increases, the selection pressure against them may rise. Thus selection pressure depends on frequency. The net population distribution can then settle toward a frequency equilibrium involving an optimal mixture of types, thus maintaining variation in the population. In the case of Constraint, war and other environmental conditions requiring risk-taking, such as forced migrations, may shift the equilibrium point.

The variation of Constraint structure is then considered to consist primarily of parametric variation in the general inhibition system resulting from the independent action of many tiny causes (thus statistically favoring the average) with a possible overlay of a number of big causes (proximal or distal) that create elevations in the extremes.

This account of structures within individuals has not addressed the other structural issue, the covariance structure of trait dimensions in a population. That is the question of how the trait dimension of Constraint covaries with, or is discriminable from, other personality trait dimensions. Such issues are addressed in Watson, Clark, and Harkness (1994); in brief, Constraint appears to be a major higher-order feature in the hierarchy of traits.

Physical Monism and Reductionism

The perspective presented here is not dualism but physical monism: the mind is "the brain in action." Simply, all psychological events require a physiological substrate. Your perception of this page as you read, your indignation, indifference, or agreement with the arguments presented here, all depend on physical events. One needs only to spend an hour on a neurology ward with persons who lack functions we take for granted (e.g., recognizing part of one's own body, being able to think of five words that start with the letter p, knowing what a key is for) to understand physical monism.

Physical monism leads to interesting insights. For example, the distinction between talk therapy and chemotherapy begins to break down. Talk can only work if it has neurochemical effects. Seen in this light, talk therapy is exquisitely specific chemotherapy: the eighth cranial nerve (auditory) is just the first in a sequence of pharmacists filling narrowly targeted prescriptions. Systemic medications may reach where talk cannot, however. For our purposes, physical monism suggests that psychological studies of behavioral dispositions cannot be divorced from research into the physical basis of traits.

Traits Versus States

The endurance of structures defines a continuum from states to traits. Structures that endure over months, years, or decades show the endurance required of a trait. Structures that create psychological events lasting instants, seconds, minutes, hours, or weeks have the endurance that characterizes states. A generalized inhibition system, with parameters and thresholds that endure for months, years, or decades would meet the requirements of this trait model. In the constructive-realist approach, this trait-state distinction informs researchers working at the physiological level of the type of structures and processes that they should be looking for.

In situations where there are both environmental fluctuation and some enduring internal structures promoting stable dispositions, data collected in shorter time samples should reflect greater environmental influence (note that laboratory experiments typically sample an instant of time), whereas data collected in longer time samples (e.g., life course data, summaries of how one tends to be) should reflect stable structures because external fluctuations average out.

What Creates, Develops, and Maintains Traits?

A person's genetic blueprint and the sequences of environments that constitute a life history jointly create, develop, and maintain the structures that give rise to dispositions. Quantitative behavioral genetics offers methodological tools for analyzing the processes of that joint determinism. Constraint variation has been studied using combined twin and adoption methods (Tellegen, Lykken, Bouchard et al., 1988), leading to the estimate that nearly 60 percent of the observed variation in a Constraint scale is due to genetic variation.[2] One of the most fascinating findings of this study is the estimate that virtually all of the environmental contribution to Constraint variation is unshared—not shared with family members. Suppose Mr. X had a brother, and both of these boys were exposed to a very low-Constraint role-model father (who set them apart from other families). For Mr. X, this role model creates the type of shared environmental variation that should (under a social learning theory model) increase within family resemblances. On the other hand, supposing Mr. X went for an exciting motorcycle ride and his brother did not. This is the type of unshared environmental variation that does not increase within family resemblances. The analyses suggest that unshared, not shared, environmental influences shape Constraint levels.

However, this description of the distinction between shared and unshared environmental variation is somewhat misleading. The model estimates the *effects* of environment that tend to make family members similar (shared) or dissimilar (unshared). Suppose the low-Constraint role-model father made his young sons wait in the car while he stole tools from an open garage. Suppose Mr. X admired his father's courage and skill and was amused by the funny faces the father made as he hauled out the heavy loot. On the other hand, suppose Mr. X's brother was

frightened and disgusted by his father's act and swore never to do such a thing. The role model is now a source of unshared environmental variation.

The surprising lack of power of shared environmental influences, and the finding that formative environmental influences on personality tend to be unshared, has not yet had the impact on personality theories that it should if it continues to replicate. The full ramifications of such findings for social learning theories, which place a heavy emphasis on the standardizing effects of shared environments (e.g., common role models, common socioeconomic status, common family and cultural influences, etc.), are yet to be explored.

A number of powerful processes may be at work to channel development along particular paths, that is, to develop and maintain traits (Buss, 1987). Waddington (1957) suggested the label *homeorhesis* to indicate processes that tend to keep a particular developmental trajectory on its path (as opposed to homeo*stasis*, which would indicate processes producing stasis rather than trajectory). Correlations between genotypes and environments would constitute powerful homeorhetic processes. Scarr and McCartney (1983) have suggested a developmental sequence for different types of genotype-environment covariation (Plomin, DeFries, & Loehlin, 1977). Thus at the earliest stages of development, *passive* genotype-environment correlations predominate: if Mr. X as a child had shared a very low-Constraint phenotype with his parents because they happen to share a low-Constraint genotype (a linkage that would create a correlation across a population), then he may have experienced poor parental occupational performance, permissiveness juxtaposed with cruel impulsive punishments, sexual boundary crossing, drug and alcohol excesses, all before Mr. X as a child began to exercise choices. If parents are extremely bad, the state may intervene to try to break passive genotype-environment correlations.

As Mr. X matures, his low-Constraint behavior will elicit responses, thus possibly generating *reactive* or evocative genotype-environment correlation. If, for example, he had often misbehaved in schools and this resulted in repeated punishment, this may, for young Mr. X, have resembled in vivo desensitization: "Hm, sitting in the principal's office isn't so bad—I don't have to hear all that boring stuff in class."

With further development come greater *active* genotype-environment correlations, as a child begins to exercise choice. What environments does he seek out or create? Young Mr. X may have found low-risk, predictable, safe environments populated by rule followers nearly aversive. Instead, young Mr. X may have been drawn to fast dirt bikes and a social world populated by acquaintances whose motto could be the test-pilot phrase "push the envelope."

The blend of passive, reactive, and actively chosen and created environments with a degree of match to existing dispositions creates a powerful fabric of homeorhetic processes. But it also contains opportunities for interventions. The interventions need to be chronic rather than acute, however, and prognosis is conditioned by the fact that change must combat powerful homeorhetic processes.

This concludes the introduction to the first viewpoint on traits. It should be clear that research supporting a constructive-realist viewpoint on traits must be multidisciplinary, drawing broadly on all the social and natural sciences. This approach demands the coordination of behavioral and brain sciences and attacks the notion that personality research can function independently, as a purely pencil and paper science. Having described the nature of traits, we now turn to the constructive-realist viewpoint on their measurement.

Measurement: Exploratory Versus Structured Test Construction

The research agenda of constructive-realism leads to both refinements of measurement and refinements of constructs—hence the title of Loevinger's (1957) classic paper, "Objective Tests As Instruments of Psychological Theory." Tellegen and Waller (in press) distinguish between *exploratory* and *structured* test construc-

tion, and the distinction turns on the readiness of the constructs.

In exploratory test construction, construct evolution is an explicit goal of the research program. Sequences of item creation, data collection, structural data analysis, and then theory adjustment lead back to further item creation to begin the cycle again. Such a research program, which treats the homogeneity of indicators across persons as a signal that "there might be something there," leads to an evolving theoretical picture of a trait. Increasing verisimilitude leads to greater precision in the next round, as well as converging connections with other lines of research.

Constraint, considered as a trait dimension, grew out of Tellegen's (1982) exploratory Multidimensional Personality Questionnaire (MPQ) construction program. Constraint is a superfactor of the MPQ; that is, its variance is composed of the covariance of lower-order factors and is therefore both homogeneous and multidimensional. On this basis one might assume that a generalized inhibition system (hence homogeneity) influences subsystems further downstream (hence multidimensionality) of the (a) verbal-acoustic propositional moral system (i.e., superego; see Malmquist and Meehl, 1978) reflected in Traditionalism; (b) anticipatory anxiety involved in risk assays in Harmavoidance; and (c) executive planning and foresight (Control). Thus the theoretical model of Constraint is explicitly hierarchical, and this is linked to the measurement model. In Tellegen's MPQ, primary factors of Traditionalism, Harmavoidance, and Control are heavily weighted in forming the superfactor of Constraint.

Once test constructors are sufficiently confident that a construct is worth pursuing, *structured* test construction becomes possible. Here, the construct serves as a starting point for scale construction, which can proceed deductively from the construct to the items (Burisch, 1984). In a structured construction program, Watson and Clark (1993) built a Disinhibition versus Constraint scale. The scale can be scored as part of their General Temperament Survey (GTS) or as part of Clark's Schedule for Nonadaptive and Adaptive Personality (SNAP). Watson and Clark (1993, p. 511) consider seven facets as clear markers of Constraint: Impulsivity, Irresponsibility, Risk Taking, Planfulness, Norm Rejection, Danger Seeking, and Disorganization.

Questionnaire Assessment as Quantified Communication

Objective personality assessment can be crudely divided into performance tests and summary questionnaires. In performance tests, one seeks a sample of what is usually nontest behavior. For example, in assaying a person's cynicism, we might pose in true-or-false format the assertion "most people will cheat someone if they are certain they will not be caught." This can be viewed an as attempt to solicit cynicism on the spot. If, on the other hand, we pose in true-or-false format the assertion "I tend to believe most people are motivated primarily by selfishness," then we are asking for a self-summary of average performance. The remainder of this section focuses on summary questionnaires.

Summary questionnaire assessment views the process as quantified communication (the fascinating volume edited by Angleitner and Wiggins [1986] contains many chapters written in the spirit of this position). The reader who understands norms, reliability, and construct validity research is familiar with the quantified aspect of questionnaires, but the communication aspect deserves further explanation. Forty years of evidence that the obvious items do the work (e.g., Duff, 1965; Holden & Jackson, 1979; Wrobel & Lachar, 1982) supports Allport's claim that the quickest way to learn about a person's personality is to ask him (or her). In the communication viewpoint on assessment, the questionnaire directly solicits summaries of the extratest conditional probabilities (estimates of the history of realized conditionals and projections for them) that constitute the dispositions that result from traits. But there is a problem with this viewpoint.

The problem is a too-simple view of communication as pure information exchange. Research with other species (Dawkins & Krebs, 1978; Caryl, 1982) and with humans (Brown & Levinson, 1987; Ervin-Tripp, 1976; C. Harkness, 1990) shows that signals are often used for pragmatic purposes (e.g., manipulation in the service of intraspecific competition) as well as for the transfer of information (emphasizing the cooperative function of signals). Whiten and Byrne (1988) developed a taxonomy of primate deception. In one example, based on observations of guenons, or African long-tailed monkeys, one threatens another with aggressive calls, and several others join in. The target of the attack looks off as if it sees a predator and then gives a social alarm call. The aggressor guenons then take to the trees, abandoning the alarm giver. In this case the information transfer (the message that there is something to be alarmed about) was a lie in the service of a pragmatic purpose, that of ending the aggressive attack.

Therefore, in personality assessment, we need to form the best possible alliance with our test takers so that pragmatic functions are maximally aligned with the information transfer function. If Mr. X decided to work at changing his Constraint status, this might lead him to his best attempt to exchange information with minimal pragmatic spin.

However, because of the ubiquitous tension between the pragmatic and information-transfer functions of communication, quality clinical personality assessment entails not only detecting and quantifying what the person is saying about his or her trait dimension status, but also detecting and quantifying how he or she has approached the test (Ben-Porath and Waller, 1992; Butcher, Dahlstrom, Graham, Tellegen, & Kaemmer, 1989). To this end, the MMPI-2 uses scales such as VRIN and TRIN (developed originally in Tellegen's MPQ, 1982), L, F, Fb, and K to detect the patients' approaches to the test. During arms negotiations in the cold war, Ronald Reagan was fond of saying "Trust, but verify." The strategy advocated here is "Develop trust, but verify." That is, try to make information transfer pragmatic for the subject, but evaluate the degree to which this has been accomplished.

Ability differences between persons further

limit this process. Some people understand trait concepts better than others, with measurable validity differences (Herfkens, Harkness, & Sherman, 1992; Stone, Stone, & Gueutal, 1990). A further example of ability differences is found in Zevon and Tellegen's report (1982) of a follow-up investigation that led to the detection of two alexithymic subjects generating unusual data in a mood study. Again, the answer is more assessment, not less.

The quantified communications model of summary questionnaires understands that all personality information runs through a subject's verbal-propositional network (a PET scan would probably reveal a glowing left hemisphere in most respondents!). This means that the information-processing rules of this network will be part of the measurement model. As an example, Freud (1900/1953) described *secondary revision*, a process by which dream reports become better stories, that is, they gain better narrative structure with repeated retellings. There is some evidence that secondary revision operates in personality questionnaires, with increasing homogeneity as people respond to increasing numbers of obvious items on a single trait test (Knowles, 1988). However, the effect is apparently not large, and the mixing of items in multiscale tests tends to disarm the effect (Wolfe & Johnson, 1993). Nevertheless, the possibility that the verbal propositional network can improve a story suggests that homogeneity (a good story) in questionnaire responses must never be the sole basis for trait inference and serves as a caution that research in the constructive-realist tradition must always be multidisciplinary.

Assessment itself can be therapeutic (e.g., Finn & Tonsager, 1992). Quality assessment feedback can provide thematic coherence to a patient who previously only saw diverse, seemingly unconnected problems. Like brands of psychotherapy that substitute reflection for action, quality assessment can provide a normatively based view of self on adaptively important trait dimensions. From the communications viewpoint, this is accomplished by providing a novel synthesis of information that the patient already had.

Rational Selection of Constraint

Harkness, McNulty, & Ben-Porath (1993) carried out a structured program to build a Constraint scale using the MMPI-2 item pool. They developed a technique called *replicated rational selection*, a method specifically designed for structured test construction from fixed item pools like the MMPI-2. This method uses lay people's replicated judgments of the links between items and constructs.

Sixty-seven[3] lay subjects were trained in convergent (what Constraint facets are like) and discriminant (what Constraint facets are not like) aspects of Constraint. They were then asked to search the MMPI-2 item pool for items that matched the constructs they had studied. For example, 100 percent of the item selectors picked as a Harmavoidance item "I have never done anything dangerous for the thrill of it." Only about 7 percent of the item selectors decided the MMPI-2 item "I like mechanics magazines" was relevant to Harmavoidance. An initial Constraint scale was formed from items chosen by a plurality of lay item selectors. Psychologists then further reduced the item pool with additional rational selection (the experts could remove but not add items).

The result was a Constraint scale with internal consistencies in large clinical and normal samples ranging from .68 to .75. Harkness, McNulty, and Ben-Porath (1993) found that the correlation between MMPI-2-measured Constraint and Tellegen's MPQ-measured Constraint was .57 in a sample of 838 college students. This is quite similar in magnitude to the correlation reported by Watson and Clark (1993) between their structurally constructed GTS measure of Disinhibition (scoring direction reversed from Constraint) and Tellegen's MPQ-measured Constraint ($-.56$ in a sample of 252 college students).

The MMPI-2-based measure of Constraint allows us to assess a clinically relevant trait within an instrument that examines how the patient approached the test. Across our patients, Constraint measures permit us to tap features that color the expression of all pathology (it is wise to worry about a truly low-Constraint patient who has developed a depression yielding desperation). We also need measurement within as well as across our patients. If Mr. X were willing to align with us for change, to dare to make, as Reich (1949) prescribed, features of his own character ego-dystonic, then measures of Constraint would allow for tracking of the process.

Summary of a Constructive-Realist Approach to a Personality Trait

To summarize the first view, constructive-realism is an approach to psychological theory construction. One class of such theory construction involves hypothesizing the existence of real but latent physiological systems that account for differential dispositions across persons. Such an approach requires the joint involvement of behavioral and brain sciences; personality cannot be a purely pencil-and-paper discipline. In this view, enduring physiological systems create stable life patterns that leave a trail, a record in the verbal propositional network of the individual and of observers in the surrounding social matrix.

Quantified psychological assessment involves communication. However, communication is not the simple exchange of information. Frequently communication is pragmatic, that is, the sender attempts (not necessarily consciously) to get the receiver to do something. Clear working alliances between patient and assessor offer the best hope of aligning the information-transfer and pragmatic functions of communication. Assessment is frequently therapeutic in that it can provide a novel synthesis of information that was already in the possession of the patient. This application of constructive-realism to dispositional personality theorizing was illustrated with Constraint, and the discussion of a hypothetical low-Constraint patient. This completes an introduction to one viewpoint on traits and measurement. Here is another.

SOCIOANALYTIC VIEW OF TRAITS

Socioanalytic theory attempts to combine the most valid insights of Freud and psychoanalysis with the most valid insights of G. H. Mead and symbolic interactionism. The essential features of the model can be summarized as follows:

1. Human nature/personality can be best understood in the context of human evolution.
2. People evolved as group-living, culture-using animals; thus, people always live in groups and every group is organized by status.
3. People are primarily motivated by a small number of unconscious biological needs. Our evolutionary history suggests that people primarily need status and social acceptance, because they confer preferential opportunities for reproductive success.
4. Social interaction largely concerns negotiating for status and acceptance. Social interaction is, therefore, an exchange process, and that which is exchanged is status and acceptance.
5. In order to have an interaction people must have parts to play. The part that we most often play is defined by our identity.
6. Interaction is structured by identities and efforts to gain—or avoid losing—status and social acceptance.
7. There is an inherent tension here because status is achieved at the expense of acceptance, and acceptance is gained largely at the expense of status.

The socioanalytic perspective on traits begins by drawing a distinction between the actor's and the observer's view of personality. Personality from the observer's perspective concerns his or her view of another person's personality. These views normally reflect recurring stylistic and distinctive features of an actor's social behavior. Trait words are terms we use to describe the unique or distinctive aspects of another person's behavior.

Traits are inherently evaluative because they are tokens in the exchange process. Each person has a reputation among those with whom he or she interacts. The reputation is coded in terms of trait words and is a rough index of how the person is doing in his or her pursuit of status and social acceptance.

There is also a relatively well-defined structure to trait words. The ordinary trait vocabulary can be organized in terms of about five broad dimensions, and this claim is known as "Big Five" theory or the Five-Factor Model. The five dimensions are known as Adjustment, Extraversion, Prudence/Constraint, Likeability-/Agreeableness, and Intellectance (sounding smart and sophisticated).

Because these five dimensions are found in every language in which they have been searched for, they may reflect universal categories of interpersonal evaluation. That is, people may be prewired to think about and describe others in terms of these categories, and for good reason—the categories describe behavior patterns that affect the degree to which a person will contribute to or detract from the maintenance and functioning of a social group. And although Allport and other worthies in the history of personality theory have dismissed reputations as trivial, reputations are actually useful and important. They contain valuable information on the basis of which we can forecast a person's future behavior. Because reputations are an evaluative summary of a person's past behavior, they are an important guide to future behavior.

Personality from the viewpoint of the observer concerns an actor's reputation. Personality from the perspective of the actor concerns the structures inside an actor that explain or account for the manner in which the actor is described by others. Personality from an observer's perspective is a topic that can be studied empirically, because it is public and observable. Personality from an actor's perspective presents a major challenge to scientific study. We can't see inside other people and must therefore rely on their reports to tell us what is happening inside. From the socioanalytic perspective, there

is no way in principle to verify independently the validity of their reports.

Personality Assessment from a Socioanalytic Perspective

The concept of an operational definition has passed out of fashion in modern psychology; nonetheless, there was some wisdom in Bridgman's original suggestion that we can gain insight into the meaning of our concepts if we think carefully about the specific details of our measurement procedures. Personality assessment consists primarily of presenting a person with a test stimulus—an inkblot, a picture, a question—and asking the person to respond. The response is assigned a score of some sort, the process is repeated several times, and the response scores are aggregated to arrive at a final score. Most of our attention is directed either at the relationships between the various response scores or at the relationship between the aggregated score and scores derived from other sources. We spend very little time thinking about the processes underlying the person's response to an individual test stimulus because, following Allport, we think we know. We call the response a "self-report" and that's the end of it.

From a socioanalytic perspective, to call item endorsements self-reports is to beg the question, to take a pretheoretical view of the process, and to decontextualize personality assessment. In the conventional view, a respondent reads the item "I like fast cars." He searches his memory for experiences with fast cars, evaluates the experiences, and then responds to the item.

There are at least two problems with this model. First, memory doesn't work the way the model assumes it does. Memory is not like a stored videotape that we play back from time to time. Rather, we construct our memory, and the dynamics of that construction process are largely what personality is about.

But second, consider what is actually going on. According to socioanalytic theory, we spend our lives moving from one interaction to another. What are the ingredients of an interaction? At least two persons with parts to play and a pretext or agenda for the interaction. In an assessment situation we have all the ingredients for an interaction. Why would we not assume that what is going on during an assessment is what goes on in any social interaction—i.e., two persons use their identities to negotiate for status and acceptance, knowing that, at the end of the interaction, some accounting will take place.

From a socioanalytic perspective, the dynamics of item endorsement are identical to a move in any other social game. Over time, a respondent has developed a view of himself that he hopes others will believe. This view, he or she has found over thousands of social encounters, is the one that generates the maximum respect and acceptance from those with whom he or she routinely deals. If, like Mr. X in the preceding section, a person's identity is that of a rake, a hell-raiser, and a party timer, he or she uses the items on the inventory to tell us about that identity. Exactly why he has chosen that identity is another question. But it is his identity and we can depend on him to maintain it in this and in future contexts until it stops working for him and he is able to develop an alternative. But the point here is that from a socioanalytic perspective, item endorsements are self-presentations and not self-reports.

DIFFERENCES AND SIMILARITIES BETWEEN THE TWO VIEWS

Two Differences

The socioanalytic approach concentrates primarily on the psychological level. Socioanalytic explanations tend to be in terms of a person's goals, values, intentions, strategies, identity, and/or temperament. The constructive-realist approach is reductive and seeks explanations of psychological phenomena at the physiological level. For this reason, constructive-realist trait research must be multidisciplinary.

The two approaches also differ in the degree to which they include nonsocial phenomena in

defining personality. In socioanalytic theory, social exchange defines the domain of personality. In the constructive-realist approach to traits, physiological systems create life patterns, some of which have social relevance and some of which do not. Tellegen's (1982) factor of Absorption, with its connection to hypnotic susceptibility, is an example of an important trait that frequently has little social impact.

Two Similarities

Both views are interested in the distal and proximal *causes* of enduring behavioral dispositions. Socioanalytic theory is interested in causes that act over long time periods (the selection pressures of human evolution) and causes that act over a short period of time (forces that create and maintain identity in the context of social exchange). The constructive-realist position on traits is also concerned with distal causes (for example, the frequency-dependent selection theory of Constraint variation) and proximal causes (for example, the study of behavior genetics and homeorhetic processes).

Both views are guarded about the interpretation of questionnaire item responses—both viewpoints recognize that the test taker is trying to accomplish something with his or her test responses. Thus both views criticize the notion that test responses represent a simple exchange of facts, and both views warn practicing clinicians to be skeptical and seek corroboration.

NOTES

1. "Thinginess" is a term the first author once heard Paul Meehl use in a lecture.

2. Twin studies have yielded higher estimates of heritabilities of personality traits than adoption methods, possibly because twin studies with zero degree relatives (monozygotic twins) can detect genetic effects not shown in first degree (or higher) relatives.

3. The sixty-seven subjects are a subset of a total of 114 replicated rational selection subjects of Harkness, McNulty, and Ben-Porath (1993). The smaller

subset is made up of those selectors who worked on elements of Constraint.

ACKNOWLEDGMENTS

We appreciate the comments of Claire Harkness and Auke Tellegen on drafts of sections of this chapter.

REFERENCES

Allport, G. W. (1937). *Personality: A psychological interpretation.* New York: Holt.

Barash, D. P. (1982). *Sociobiology and behavior* (2nd ed.). New York: Elsevier.

Ben-Porath, Y. S., & Waller, N. G. (1992). "Normal" personality inventories in clinical assessment: General requirements and the potential for using the NEO personality inventory. *Psychological Assessment, 4,* 14–19.

Brown, P. & Levinson, S. C. (1987). *Politeness: Some universals in language usage.* New York: Cambridge University Press.

Burisch, M. (1984). Approaches to personality inventory construction. *American Psychologist, 39,* 214–227.

Butcher, J. N., Dahlstrom, W. G., Graham, J. R., Tellegen, A., & Kaemmer, B. (1989). *Minnesota Multiphasic Personality Inventory-2 (MMPI-2). Manual for administration and scoring.* Minneapolis: University of Minnesota Press.

Buss, D. M. (1987). Selection, evocation, and manipulation. *Journal of Personality and Social Psychology, 53,* 1214–1221.

Caryl, P. (1982). Animal signals: A reply to Hinde. *Animal Behavior, 30,* 240–244.

Cattell, R. B. (1946). *Description and measurement of personality.* Yonkers, NY: World Book.

Dawkins, R., & Krebs, J. (1978). Animal signals: Information or manipulation? In J. Krebs & N. Davies (Eds.), *Behavioral ecology.* Oxford: Blackwell Scientific Publications.

Depue, R. A., & Spoont, M. R. (1986). Conceptualizing a serotonin trait: A behavioral dimension of constraint. *Annals of the New York Academy of Sciences, 487,* 47–62.

Duff, F. L. (1965). Item subtlety in personality inventory scales. *Journal of Consulting Psychology, 29,* 565–570.

Ervin-Tripp, S. (1976). "Is Sybil there?" The structure of some American English directives. *Language in Society, 5,* 25–66.

Eysenck, H. J. (1967). *The biological basis of personality.* Springfield, IL: Thomas.

Finn, S. E., & Tonsager, M. E. (1992). Therapeutic effects of providing MMPI-2 test feedback to college students awaiting therapy. *Psychological Assessment, 4,* 278–287.

Freud, S. (1900). *The interpretation of dreams.* In J. Strachey (Transl. & Ed.), *The standard edition of the complete psychological works of Sigmund Freud,* Vols. 4 and 5, 1953. London: Hogarth Press.

Funder, D. C. (1991). Global traits: A neo-Allportian Approach to personality. *Psychological Science, 2,* 31–39.

Gray, J. A. (1982). *The neuropsychology of anxiety: An enquiry into the function of the septo-hippocampal system.* Oxford: Oxford University Press.

Harkness, A. R., McNulty, J. L., & Ben-Porath, Y. S. (1993, August). *The Personality Psychopathology Five (PSY-5): Constructs and preliminary MMPI-2 Scales.* Paper presented at the 101st Annual Convention of the American Psychological Association, Toronto.

Harkness, C. (1990). Competition for Resources and the Origins of Manipulative Language. In J. P. Dillard (ed.) *Seeking compliance: The production of interpersonal influence messages.* Scottsdale, AZ: Gorsuch Scarisbrick, Publishers.

Herfkens, K., Harkness, A. R., & Sherman, A. (1992, April). *Who can rate? Assessment of psychological-mindedness via trait knowledge.* Paper presented at the meeting of the Southwestern Psychological Association, Austin, TX.

Hogan, R. (1983). A socioanalytic theory of personality. In M. M. Page (Ed.), *1982 Nebraska symposium on motivation.* Lincoln: University of Nebraska Press.

Holden, R. R., & Jackson, D. N. (1979). Item subtlety and face validity in personality assessment. *Journal of Consulting and Clinical Psychology, 47,* 459–468.

Knowles, E. S. (1988). Item context effects on personality scales: Measuring changes the measure. *Journal of Personality and Social Psychology, 55,* 312–320.

Leahy, T. H. (1980). The myth of operationism. *Journal of Mind and Behavior, 1,* 127–143.

Loevinger, J. (1957). Objective tests as instruments of psychological theory. *Psychological Reports, 3,* 635–694 (Monograph no. 9).

MacCorquodale, K., & Meehl, P. E. (1948). On a

distinction between hypothetical constructs and intervening variables. *Psychological Review, 55,* 95–107.

Malmquist, C. P., & Meehl, P. E. (1978). Barabbas: A study in guilt-ridden homicide. *The International Review of Psycho-Analysis, 5,* 149–174.

Meehl, P. E. (1978). Theoretical risks and tabular asterisks: Sir Karl, Sir Ronald, and the slow progress of soft psychology. *Journal of Consulting and Clinical Psychology, 46,* 806–834.

Meehl, P. E. (1992). Factors and taxa, traits and types, differences of degree and differences in kind. *Journal of Personality, 60,* 117–174.

Messick, S. (1981). Constructs and their vicissitudes in educational and psychological measurement. *Psychological Bulletin, 89,* 575–588.

Plomin, R., DeFries, J. C., & Loehlin, J. C. (1977). Genotype-environment interaction and correlation in the analysis of human behavior. *Psychological Bulletin, 84,* 309–322.

Reich, W. (1949). *Character analysis* (3rd ed.). New York: Orgone Institute Press.

Scarr, S. & McCartney, K. (1983). How people make their own environments: A theory of genotype → environment effects. *Child Development, 54,* 424–435.

Spoont, M. R. (1992). Modulatory role of serotonin in neural information processing: Implications for human psychopathology. *Psychological Bulletin, 112,* 330–350.

Stone, E., Stone, D., & Gueutal, H. (1990). Influence of cognitive ability on responses to questionnaire measures: Measurement precision and missing response problems. *Journal of Applied Psychology, 75,* 418–427.

Tellegen, A. (1982). *Brief manual for the differential personality questionnaire.* Unpublished manuscript, University of Minnesota, Minneapolis. [Since renamed the Multidimensional Personality Questionnaire].

Tellegen, A. (1985). Structures of mood and personality and their relevance to assessing anxiety, with an emphasis on self-report. In A. H. Tuma & J. D. Maser (eds.), *Anxiety and the anxiety disorders.* Hillsdale, NJ: Erlbaum.

Tellegen, A. (1988). The analysis of consistency in personality assessment. *Journal of Personality, 56,* 621–663.

Tellegen, A. (1991). Personality traits: Issues of definition, evidence, and assessment. In W. M. Grove & D. Cicchetti (eds.), *Thinking clearly about psychology: Volume 2: Personality and psychopathology.* Minneapolis: University of Minnesota Press.

Tellegen, A., Lykken, D. T., Bouchard, T. J. Jr., Wilcox, K. J., Segal, N. L., & Rich, S. (1988). Personality similarity in twins reared apart and together. *Journal of Personality and Social Psychology, 54,* 1031–1039.

Tellegen, A. & Waller, N. G. (in press). Exploring personality through test construction: Development of the multidimensional personality questionnaire. In S. Briggs and J. M. Cheek (Eds.), *Personality measures: Development and evaluation* (Vol. 1). Greenwich, CN: JAI Press.

Urbach, P. (1974). Progress and degeneration in the 'IQ debate' (I). *British Journal for the Philosophy of Science, 25,* 99–135.

Waddington, C. II. (1957). *The strategy of the genes.* London: Allen & Unwin.

Watson, D. & Clark, L. A. (1993). Behavioral disinhibition versus constraint: A dispositional perspective. In D. M. Wegner & J. W. Pennebaker (Eds.), *Handbook of mental control.* New York: Prentice-Hall.

Watson, D., Clark, L. A., & Harkness, A. R. (1994). Structures of personality and their relevance to psychopathology. *Journal of Abnormal Psychology, 103,* 18–31.

Whiten, A. & Byrne, R. (1988). Tactical deception in primates. *Behavioral and Brain Sciences, 11,* 233–274.

Wolfe, R., & Johnson, S. (1993). *Serial position and reliability of personality items.* Unpublished manuscript, SUNY, Geneseo, NY.

Wrobel, T. A., & Lachar, D. (1982). Validity of the Wiener subtle and obvious scales for the MMPI: Another example of the importance of inventory-item content. *Journal of Consulting and Clinical Psychology, 50,* 469–470.

Zevon, M. A., & Tellegen, A. (1982). The structure of mood change: An idiographic/nomothetic analysis. *Journal of Personality and Social Psychology, 43,* 111–122.

5

Assessment of Emotional States and Personality Traits: Measuring Psychological Vital Signs

Charles D. Spielberger
Lee M. Ritterband
Sumner J. Sydeman
Eric C. Reheiser
Karen K. Unger

Practical considerations in clinical assessment must be founded on comprehensive theories of personality and psychopathology that identify the major personality traits and syndromes and how these traits are linked to emotions and behavior. Traditionally, personality assessment has focused on measuring individual differences in traits such as extraversion, need for achievement, neuroticism, anxiety, and numerous other characteristics that are considered to be important determinants of human behavior. In contrast, the assessment of emotional states has been relatively neglected.

In the preceding chapter, Harkness and Hogan present a comprehensive analysis of the theory and measurement of personality traits. Although anger and anxiety as personality traits are also discussed in this chapter, the primary focus is on assessing the intensity of these emotions as they influence motivation, coping behavior, and mental health. We will argue that emotions are the critical vital signs of psychological health and well-being, and that measuring the intensity, duration, and frequency of emotional reactions must be an essential, practical consideration in the clinical assessment of personality.

EMOTION AND PERSONALITY

Charles Darwin (1872/1965) considered fear (anxiety) and rage (anger) to be universal characteristics of both humans and animals. Darwin believed that these emotions had evolved over countless generations through a process of natural selection because they facilitated successful adaptation and survival. Early psychological studies of human emotion, using the introspective reports of trained observers, endeavored to discover the qualitative feeling-states ("mental elements") that made up different emotions (Titchner, 1897; Wundt, 1896). Unfortunately, this phenomenological approach generated findings that were obviously artificial and unrelated to other behaviors (Plutchik, 1962; Young, 1943). Distrust of verbal reports was further intensified by psychoanalytic formulations that emphasized the distortions in mood and thought that were produced by unconscious mental processes. Moreover, self-reports of emotional states came to be viewed with extreme suspicion because they were unverifiable and easily falsified (Duffy, 1941).

With the advent of behaviorism, psychological research on emotion shifted from the investigation of subjective feelings to the evaluation of physiological and behavioral variables that could be more objectively measured. The epistemology and methodology of behaviorism, especially the strong bias against measuring experience that was not directly observable, required investigators to evaluate the impact of carefully defined and objectively manipulated antecedent (stimulus) conditions on precisely measured physiological and behavioral responses.

Beginning in the 1960s, stimulated by a renaissance in cognitive psychology, the unique importance of the experiential component of emotions has been increasingly recognized. Most authorities now regard emotions as complex psychobiological states or conditions consisting of specific feeling qualities and widespread bodily changes (Spielberger, 1966). Differences in personality traits resulting from past experience are also acknowledged as influencing emotional states because they may dispose an individual to respond to similar stimulus objects and circumstances in radically different ways (Lazarus, Deese, & Osler, 1952). It is now generally accepted that an individual's appraisal of a particular event or situation as stressful will greatly influence his or her emotional reactions to that circumstance (Lazarus & Opton, 1966; Lazarus & Folkman, 1984).

In the present context, emotions are defined much as this term is currently used in common language, i.e., to refer to complex, qualitatively different psychobiological states or conditions that have both phenomenological and physiological properties. The quality and intensity of the feelings experienced during emotional arousal seem to be the most unique and distinctive features of a particular emotion. Therefore, accurate assessment of emotional phenomena requires not only distinguishing between qualitatively different emotional states but also evaluating the intensity of such states as they fluctuate over time.

The nature of anxiety and anger as emotional states and as personality traits or dispositions, and the assessment procedures that are employed in their measurement, are briefly reviewed in this chapter. Conceptual ambiguities

in the constructs of anger, hostility, and aggression, and instruments that have been developed to assess the experience, expression, and control of anger are then described. The critical importance of measuring depression in diagnosis and treatment is also considered. The chapter concludes with a discussion of the assessment of anxiety, anger, and depression as emotional vital signs of psychological well-being that should be carefully assessed and continuously monitored in counseling, psychotherapy, and behavioral interventions as well as in diagnostic evaluations and studies of treatment outcome.

THE NATURE AND ASSESSMENT OF ANXIETY

Freud (1924) defined anxiety as "something felt," a specific unpleasant emotional state or condition that included experiential, physiological, and behavioral components. Fear, which Freud equated with *objective* anxiety, implied an emotional reaction that was proportional in intensity to a real danger in the external world. In contrast, Freud used the term *neurotic* anxiety to describe emotional reactions that were greater in intensity than would be expected on the basis of the objective danger; the source of the danger was the individual's own unacceptable (repressed) sexual or aggressive impulses. He regarded neurotic anxiety as the "fundamental phenomenon and the central problem of neurosis" (Freud, 1936, p. 85).

In his book *The Problem of Anxiety*, Freud (1936) conceptualized anxiety as a signal indicating the presence of a danger situation. The perceived presence of danger, whether from external sources or one's own repressed thoughts and feelings, evokes this unpleasant emotional state which then serves to warn the individual that some form of adjustment is necessary. In his emphasis on the adaptive utility of anxiety in motivating behavior that helps an individual either to avoid or to cope more effectively with danger, Freud's "danger signal" theory is quite consistent with Darwin's evolutionary perspective.

Conceptual advances over the past fifty years

have clarified the nature of anxiety as a psycho-biological construct and stimulated the development of a number of scales to measure anxiety. Cattell and Scheier (1963), who pioneered the application of multivariate techniques to assessing anxiety, included a variety of self-report and physiological measures in their factor analytic studies; relatively independent "state" and "trait" anxiety factors have consistently emerged from this research (Cattell, 1966). Physiological measures that fluctuate over time, such as pulse rate and blood pressure, had strong loadings on the state anxiety factor but only slight loadings on trait anxiety. In contrast, most self-report psychometric scales were found to be relatively stable over time. Those scales that were relatively stable when measured under different conditions had strong loadings on the trait anxiety factor. Although state and trait anxiety are usually positively correlated, they are logically quite different constructs.

State anxiety (S-Anxiety) refers to an unpleasant emotional state or condition that is comparable to the conceptions of fear and objective anxiety as originally formulated by Darwin (1872/1965) and Freud (1936). Anxiety states consist of consciously perceived feelings of tension, apprehension, nervousness, and worry, and associated activation or arousal of the autonomic nervous system (Spielberger, 1972). These emotional states vary in intensity and fluctuate over time as a function of perceived physical or psychological danger. Trait anxiety (T-Anxiety) is conceptualized in terms of relatively stable individual differences in anxiety proneness. Persons high in T-Anxiety, compared with those who are low in this trait, tend to perceive a wider range of situations as dangerous or threatening and respond to perceived threats with more frequent and more intense elevations in S-Anxiety (Reheiser, 1991).

A variety of questionnaires, rating scales, and psychometric tests are currently employed to measure anxiety in research and clinical practice. Self-report psychometric questionnaires are by far the most valid and popular procedures for assessing T-Anxiety. These include the Taylor (1953) Manifest Anxiety Scale (MAS) and the Anxiety Scale Questionnaire (ASQ), which

Cattell and Scheier (1963) developed to assess anxiety in clinical situations. The Hamilton (1959) Rating Scale, which is widely used for evaluating symptoms of anxiety observed in clinical interviews or psychotherapy sessions, has been used to assess both S-Anxiety and T-Anxiety. Projective techniques such as the Rorschach and the Thematic Apperception Test are also used extensively in the clinical evaluation of anxiety, but these measures do not clearly distinguish between S-Anxiety and T-Anxiety. Furthermore, Rorschach indicators of anxiety appear to be confounded with psychological defenses (Auerbach & Spielberger, 1972).

In early studies of the effects of experimentally induced stress, S-Anxiety was measured by assessing physiological changes associated with activation (arousal) of the autonomic nervous system. For example, a marked increase in heart rate was found for college students who were told they would receive strong electric shocks, but never shocked (Hodges & Spielberger, 1966). Although a number of different physiological measures have been used as indicants of S-Anxiety (see Lader, 1975; Levitt, 1980; Martin, 1973; McReynolds, 1968; Borkovec, Weerts, & Bernstein, 1977), the galvanic skin response and changes in heart rate appear to be the most popular. However, the utility of physiological measures in assessing S-Anxiety has been critically questioned (Hodges, 1976).

The Affect Adjective Check List (AACL) developed by Zuckerman (1960; Zuckerman & Lubin, 1965) was the first instrument designed to assess both S-Anxiety and T-Anxiety. In assessing S-Anxiety, subjects are instructed to check those adjectives that describe how they feel "today"; they are asked to report how they "generally" feel in measuring T-Anxiety. Evidence of the validity of the AACL-Today Form as a measure of S-Anxiety is impressive, but the instructions and format for this scale make it relatively insensitive for assessing momentary changes in the intensity of anxiety as an emotional state. When a person encounters or escapes from a danger situation, the intensity of S-Anxiety can change rapidly from moment to moment. Moreover, checking or not checking a particular adjective, e.g., "tense," does not distinguish between feeling "somewhat" and "very" tense. The concurrent validity of the AACL General Form as a sensitive measure of T-Anxiety is also questionable, as reflected in relatively small correlations with other trait anxiety measures.

Measuring State and Trait Anxiety

The State-Trait Anxiety Inventory (STAI) was developed by Spielberger, Gorsuch, and Lushene (1970) to provide reliable, relatively brief, self-report scales for assessing both state and trait anxiety. Freud's (1936) "danger signal" theory and Cattell's concepts of state and trait anxiety (Cattell, 1966; Cattell & Scheier, 1958, 1961, 1963), as refined and elaborated by Spielberger (1966, 1972, 1976, 1977, 1979, 1983), provided the conceptual framework that guided the STAI test-construction process. The state-trait distinction in anxiety research has been subsequently validated in numerous studies (e.g., Gaudry, Spielberger, & Vagg, 1975). Representative STAI S-Anxiety present and absent items are the following:

Anxiety present: I am tense; I am worried.
Anxiety absent: I feel calm; I feel secure.

In responding to the S-Anxiety items, subjects report how they feel "right now, at this moment" by rating the *intensity* of their anxiety feelings on the following four-point scale: (1) not at all; (2) somewhat; (3) moderately so; (4) very much so. The STAI T-Anxiety Scale instructs subjects to report how they "generally" feel by rating themselves on the following four-point *frequency* scale: (1) almost never; (2) sometimes; (3) often; (4) almost always. The following representative T-Anxiety items reflect the presence or absence of trait anxiety:

Anxiety present: I worry too much over something that doesn't matter; I feel nervous and restless.
Anxiety absent: I am content; I feel pleasant.

Evidence of construct validity of the STAI S-Anxiety Scale is reflected in findings for patients undergoing surgery whose S-Anxiety scores are substantially higher the day before surgery than five to seven days following successful surgery (Auerbach, Wadsworth, Dunn, Taulbee, & Spielberger, 1973). Similarly, the S-Anxiety scores of college students are significantly higher when they are tested during an examination, and significantly lower after relaxation training, than when they are tested in a regular class period (Spielberger, 1983).

Correlations of scores on the STAI T-Anxiety scale with the ASQ and the MAS range from .73 to .85, indicating a high degree of concurrent validity. Since correlations among these scales approach the scale reliabilities, the three inventories can be considered as more or less equivalent T-Anxiety measures. However, a major advantage of the STAI T-Anxiety scale, is that it is made up of only twenty items compared with the forty-three-item ASQ and the fifty-item MAS, and thus requires only about half as much time to administer. An even more important advantage of the revised STAI-Y is that this form of the inventory is less contaminated with feelings of depression and anger than the MAS and the ASQ.

Evidence of the construct validity of the T-Anxiety scale is reflected in findings that various neuropsychiatric patient (NP) groups have substantially higher mean scores compared with normal subjects (Spielberger, 1983). General medical and surgical (GMS) patients with psychiatric complications also have higher T-Anxiety scores than do GMS patients without such complications, indicating that the T-Anxiety scale can help to identify nonpsychiatric patients with emotional problems. Lower T-Anxiety scores of patients with character disorders, for whom the absence of anxiety is an important defining condition, provide further evidence of the discriminant validity of the STAI.

Insights gained in more than a decade of research with the STAI stimulated a major revision of the inventory (Spielberger, 1983). The primary goal of this revision was to develop "purer" measures of state and trait anxiety in order to provide a firmer basis for differentiating between patients suffering from anxiety and depressive disorders. In the construction and standardization of the revised STAI (STAI-Y), 30 percent of the items were replaced, and more than 5000 additional subjects were tested. Detailed information on the psychometric properties of the STAI-Y are reported in the Test Manual (Spielberger, 1983).

A valid measure of state anxiety should reflect the influence of unique situational factors at the time of testing. Consequently, as would be expected, test-retest stability coefficients for the STAI-Y S-Anxiety scale are relatively low, with a median of only .33. Since anxiety states vary in intensity as a function of perceived stress, measures of internal consistency, such as alpha coefficients (Cronbach, 1951), provide a more meaningful index of the reliability of S-Anxiety measures than do test-retest correlations. Alpha coefficients for the STAI-Y S-Anxiety Scale are .90 or higher for large, independent samples of high school and college students, working adults, and military recruits, with a median alpha of .93.

Since its introduction more than a quarter century ago (Spielberger & Gorsuch, 1966), the STAI has been translated and adapted in forty-eight different languages and dialects (Spielberger, 1989). Norms for high school and college students, working adults, military personnel, prison inmates, and psychiatric, medical, and surgical patients are reported in the revised STAI-Y Test Manual (Spielberger, 1983). The State-Trait Anxiety Inventory for Children (STAIC) is widely used in research and clinical practice with children who have emotional or physical problems. Extensive norms are available for fourth-, fifth-, and sixth-grade students (Spielberger, 1973). Over the past twenty years, the STAI and STAIC have been used to measure anxiety in more than 6000 studies.

STATE-TRAIT ANGER AND DEPRESSION

The maladaptive effects of anger are important contributors to the etiology of depression, the psychoneuroses, and schizophrenia. While much has been written about the negative impact of anger and hostility on physical health and psychological well-being, definitions of these constructs are ambiguous and sometimes contradictory (Biaggio, Supplee, & Curtis, 1981). Given the substantial overlap in prevailing conceptual definitions of anger, hostility, and aggression, and the variety of operational procedures used to assess these constructs, we refer to them collectively as the AHA! Syndrome (Spielberger, Johnson, Russell, Crane, Jacobs, & Worden, 1985). The following working definitions of the components of the AHA! Syndrome have been proposed by Spielberger, Jacobs, Russell, and Crane (1983):

> The concept of anger usually refers to an emotional state that consists of feelings that vary in intensity, from mild irritation or annoyance to intense fury and rage. Although hostility usually involves angry feelings, this concept has the connotation of a complex set of attitudes that motivate aggressive behaviors directed toward destroying objects or injuring other people.... While anger and hostility refer to feelings and attitudes, the concept of aggression generally implies destructive or punitive behavior directed towards other persons or objects. (p. 16)

Anger as an emotional state is clearly at the core of the AHA! Syndrome, and different aspects of anger are typically emphasized in various definitions of hostility and aggression. In the 1950s, a number of self-report psychometric scales were developed to measure hostility (e.g., Buss, 1957; Buss & Durkee, 1957; Cook & Medley, 1954; Schultz, 1954; Siegel, 1956). A rational-empirical strategy was employed in developing the Buss-Durkee Hostility Inventory (BDHI), which is generally considered the most carefully constructed measure of hostility. The BDHI was recently revised and is much improved (Buss & Perry, 1992).

Physiological and behavioral facets of anger and a variety of manifestations of hostility and aggression have been investigated in numerous studies. In contrast, the phenomenology of anger, i.e., angry feelings, has been largely ignored in psychological research. Moreover, most psychometric measures of anger and hostility confound angry feelings with the mode and direction of anger expression. By the 1970s, however, the importance of distinguishing between anger and hostility was recognized, as was reflected by the appearance of three anger measures in the psychological literature: the Reaction Inventory (RI), the Anger Inventory (AI), and the Anger Self-Report (ASR). The RI was developed by Evans and Stangeland (1971) to assess the degree to which anger was evoked in a number of specific situations. Similar in conception and format to the RI, Novaco's (1975) AI consists of statements that describe anger-provoking incidents. The ASR was designed by Zelin, Adler, and Myerson (1972) to assess both "awareness of anger" and different modes of anger expression.

Two common problems with existing measures of anger and hostility are that, in varying degrees, these measures: (1) fail to take the state-trait distinction into account; and (2) tend to confound the experience and expression of anger with situational determinants of angry reactions. The ASR Awareness subscale comes closest to examining the extent to which subjects experience angry feelings, but this instrument does not assess the intensity of these feelings at a particular time. Although a number of BDHI items inquire about how often anger is experienced or expressed, most BDHI items evaluate hostile attitudes (e.g., resentment, negativism, suspicion) rather than angry feelings. In a series of studies, Biaggio (1980) and her colleagues (Biaggio & Maiuro, 1985; Biaggio et al., 1981) examined and compared the reliability, concurrent and predictive validity, and the correlates of the BDHI and the RI, ASR, and AI anger scales. On the basis of their research findings, these investigators concluded that the empirical evidence for the validity of the four anger and hostility measures was both fragmentary and limited.

Measuring State and Trait Anger

A coherent theoretical framework that distinguishes between anger, hostility, and aggression as psychological concepts, and that takes the state-trait distinction into account, is essential for guiding the construction and validation of psychometric measures of anger and hostility. The State-Trait Anger Scale (STAS), which is analogous in conception and similar in format to the STAI (Spielberger, 1983; Spielberger et al., 1970), was developed to assess the intensity of anger as an emotional state, and individual differences in anger proneness as a personality trait (Spielberger et al., 1983). In constructing the STAS, state anger (S-Anger) was defined as a psychobiological state or condition consisting of subjective feelings of anger that vary in intensity from mild irritation or annoyance to intense fury and rage, with concomitant activation or arousal of the autonomic nervous system. It was further assumed that S-Anger fluctuates over time as a function of perceived affronts, injustice, and/or frustration. Trait anger (T-Anger) was defined in terms of individual differences in the *frequency* with which S-Anger was experienced over time. Assuming that persons high in T-Anger, compared with those low in this trait, perceive a wider range of situations as anger-provoking (e.g., annoying, irritating, frustrating), high T-Anger individuals are likely to experience both more frequent and more intense elevations in S-Anger whenever annoying or frustrating conditions are encountered.

Factor analyses of the STAS S-Anger items indicated only a single underlying factor for both males and females (Spielberger et al., 1983), suggesting that this scale measures a unitary emotional state that varies in intensity. In contrast, factor analyses of the STAS T-Anger items identified two correlated factors, which were labeled Angry Temperament (T-Anger/T) and Angry Reaction (T-Anger/R). The T-Anger/T items describe individual differences in the disposition to express anger, without specifying any provoking circumstance (e.g., "I am a hot-headed person"). The T-Anger/R items describe angry reactions in situations that involve frustration and/or negative evaluations (e.g., "It makes me furious when I am criticized in front of others"). Crane (1981) found that the T-Anger scores of hypertensive patients were significantly higher than those of medical and surgical patients with normal blood pressure, and that this difference was due entirely to the substantially higher T-Anger/R scores of the hypertensives.

No difference was found in the T-Anger/T scores of the hypertensives and controls.

Deffenbacher (1992) and his colleagues used the STAS T-Anger Scale in a series of studies to assess the correlates and consequences of trait anger. Individuals with high T-Anger scores reported experiencing more intense and more frequent day-to-day anger across a wide range of provocative situations. They also experienced anger-related physiological symptoms two to four times more often than low T-Anger subjects. When provoked, the high T-Anger individuals manifested stronger general tendencies to both express and suppress anger, and more dysfunctional physical and verbal antagonism. Negative events such as failure appeared to have a more devastating (catastrophizing) impact on the high T-Anger individuals (Story & Deffenbacher, 1985), who also reported experiencing higher levels of anxiety than persons low in T-Anger.

Anger Expression: Anger-In and Anger-Out

As anger research has progressed, the importance of distinguishing between the experience and the expression of anger has been clearly demonstrated (Spielberger et al., 1985). Distinguishing between "anger-in" and "anger-out" as the major modes of anger expression has long been recognized in psychophysiological investigations of the effects of anger on the cardiovascular system. In the classic studies of anger expression, Funkenstein and his coworkers (Funkenstein, King, & Drolette, 1954), exposed healthy college students to anger-inducing laboratory conditions. Those who became angry and directed their anger toward the investigator or the laboratory situation were subsequently classified as anger-out; those who suppressed their anger and/or directed it at themselves were classified as anger-in. The increase in pulse rate was three times greater for students classified as anger-in than for the anger-out group.

Consistent with the procedures used by Funkenstein et al. (1954), individuals are generally classified as anger-in if they suppress their anger or direct it inward toward the ego or self (Averill,

1982; Tavris, 1982). When held in or suppressed, anger is subjectively experienced as an emotional state (S-Anger), which varies in intensity and fluctuates over time as a function of the provoking circumstances. Anger directed outward involves both the experience of S-Anger and its manifestation in some form of aggressive behavior. Anger-out can be expressed in physical acts such as slamming doors, destroying objects, and assaulting or injuring other persons, or in verbal behavior such as criticism, threats, insults, or the extreme use of profanity. These physical and verbal manifestations of anger may be directed toward the source of provocation or expressed indirectly toward persons or objects associated with, or symbolic of, the provoking agent.

Harburg and his associates have reported impressive evidence that demonstrates that anger-in and anger-out have different effects on the cardiovascular system (Harburg, Blakelock, & Roeper, 1979; Harburg, Erfurt, Hauenstein, Chape, Schull, Schork, 1973; Harburg & Hauenstein, 1980; Harburg, Schull, Erfurt, & Schork, 1970). Gentry (1972) and his colleagues (Gentry, Chesney, Hall, & Harburg, 1981; Gentry, Chesney, Gary, Hall, & Harburg, 1982) subsequently corroborated and extended Harburg's findings. It should be noted, however, that Harburg and Gentry classified individuals as anger-in who did not report feeling angry, along with those who indicated that they experienced and suppressed their angry feelings. Very different personality dynamics have been attributed to "impunitive" persons, who do not experience anger in anger-provoking situations, and "intrapunitive" persons, who turn anger in and often blame themselves for the anger that is directed toward them by others (Rosenzweig, 1976, 1978).

From the foregoing review, it may be noted that anger expression has been implicitly defined as constituting a single dimension (e.g., Funkenstein et al., 1954; Harburg et al., 1973; Gentry et al., 1982), varying from extreme suppression or inhibition of anger (anger-in) to the expression of anger in assaultive or destructive behavior (anger-out). As a first step in constructing a unidimensional, bipolar scale to assess anger expression, Spielberger et al. (1985) formulated working definitions of anger-in and anger-out. Anger-in was defined in terms of how often an individual experiences but holds in (suppresses) angry feelings. Anger-out was defined on the basis of the frequency that an individual expresses angry feelings in verbally or physically aggressive behavior. Consistent with these working definitions, the content of the items for the Anger Expression (AX) Scale ranged from strong inhibition or suppression of angry feelings (AX/In) to extreme expression of anger toward other persons or objects in the environment (AX/Out). Examples of AX Scale items are:

> AX/In: I boil inside, but I don't show it; I keep things in.
> AX/Out: I lose my temper; I strike out at whatever infuriates me.

The rating scale format for the AX Scale was the same as that used with the STAS T-Anger scale, but the instructions differed markedly from those used in assessing T-Anger. Rather than asking subjects to indicate how they generally feel, they are instructed to report "how often you generally react or behave in the manner described *when you feel angry or furious*" by rating themselves on the following standard four-point frequency scale: (1) almost never; (2) sometimes; (3) often; (4) almost always.

Contrary to our effort to construct a unidimensional bipolar scale, factor analyses of the AX items identified two independent factors that were labeled Anger/In and Anger/Out. Given the strength and clarity of the Anger/In and Anger/Out factors, the striking similarity (invariance) of these factors for males and females, and the large samples on which the factor analyses were based, the test-construction strategy for the AX Scale was modified to identify homogeneous subsets of items for measuring anger-in and anger-out as independent dimensions.

The selection of the items for the AX Anger-In (AX/In) and Anger-Out (AX/Out) subscales was based on the results of further factor analyses and subscale item-remainder correlations (Spielberger et al., 1985). The AX/In subscale

items had uniformly high loadings for both sexes on the Anger/In factor and negligible loadings on Anger/Out; median loadings of the eight Anger-In items on the Anger/In and Anger/Out factors were .665 and −.045, respectively. Similarly, the median loadings for the eight Anger-Out items were .59 on the Anger/Out factor and −.01 on the Anger/In factor. The internal consistency of the AX/In and AX/Out subscales was also adequate; alpha coefficients for these brief eight-item measures varied from .73 to .84. Jacobs et al. (1988) have reported test-retest stability coefficients for the AX subscale ranging from .64 to .86. Essentially zero correlations between the AX/In and AX/Out subscales have been reported for large samples of high school and college students (Johnson, 1984; Knight, Chisholm, Paulin, & Waal-Manning, 1988; Pollans, 1983; Spielberger, 1988). Thus, the anger-in and anger-out factors are factorially orthogonal, and the AX/In and AX/Out subscales are empirically independent, indicating that these scales assess two independent anger-expression dimensions.

In a study of the relationship between anger expression and blood pressure (BP), Johnson (1984) administered the AX Scale to 1114 high school students. Measures of systolic (SBP) and diastolic (DBP) blood pressure were obtained during the same class period in which these students responded to the AX Scale. The correlations of AX/In scores with SBP and DBP were positive, curvilinear, and highly significant for both sexes. Inverse correlations of AX/Out scores with BP were significant but quite small. Height, weight, dietary factors (salt intake), racial differences, and family history of hypertension and cardiovascular disorders also correlated significantly with BP. However, after partialing out the influence of these variables, AX/In scores were still positively and significantly associated with elevated SBP and DBP. Moreover, multiple regression analyses indicated that AX/In scores were better predictors of blood pressure than any other measure, i.e., the AX/In scores were first to enter stepwise multiple discriminant function equations for both sexes.

Three items included in the AX Scale to measure the middle range of the anger-in/anger-out dimension ("Control my temper;" "Keep my cool;" "Calm down faster") had substantial loadings in early studies on both the Anger/In and Anger/Out factors (Spielberger et al., 1985). In subsequent research, these items coalesced to form the nucleus of an anger control factor (Spielberger, 1988), stimulating further work to construct additional anger-control items, which resulted in the development of an eight-item Anger Control (AX/Con) subscale, which correlated negatively with AX/Out ($r = -.59$ for males; $-.58$ for females) in a large sample of university students (Spielberger, Krasner, & Solomon, 1988). The correlations of the AX/In and AX/Out subscales were essentially zero for both sexes.

State-Trait Anger Expression Inventory

The STAS and the AX Scale were recently combined to form the State-Trait Anger Expression Inventory (STAXI), which measures the experience, expression, and control of anger (Spielberger, 1988). Fuqua, Leonard, Masters, Smith, Campbell, and Fischer (1991) administered the forty-four-item STAXI to a large sample of college students and factored their responses to the individual items. The first six factors identified by Fuqua et al. (1991), in the order that they emerged, were: S-Anger, Anger/Con, Anger/In, Anger/Out, T-Anger/T and T-Anger/R. Thus, six of the seven factors corresponded with the anger components measured by the STAXI subscales, and almost all of the STAXI subscale items had salient loadings on the appropriate anger factors and negligible loadings on the other factors. These findings provide strong confirmation that the STAXI subscales measure relatively independent components of the experience, expression, and control of anger.

A seventh factor identified by Fuqua et al. (1991) was defined by secondary but nevertheless salient loadings of .30 or higher for three of the ten STAXI S-Anger items (Feel like . . . breaking things, banging on the table, hitting someone). While these items also had salient loadings on the original S-Anger factor, the findings of Fuqua et al. suggested a second S-Anger factor. The content of the three items with strong loadings on Factor 7 appear to describe high levels of S-Anger that might reflect a strong instigation to express anger in aggressive behavior. This possibility is currently being investigated.

The STAXI has proved useful for assessing anger in both normal and abnormal individuals (Deffenbacher, 1992; Moses, 1992), and in evaluating the components of anger in a variety of disorders, including alcoholism, hypertension, coronary heart disease, and cancer (Spielberger, 1988). Norms for the STAXI for male and female high school and college students, working adults, general medical and surgical patients, prison inmates, and military recruits are reported in the Test Manual (Spielberger, 1988). Guidelines for interpreting high scores on the STAXI subscales are provided in Table 5.1. Individuals with low scores (below the 25th percentile) on the STAXI T-Anger, AX/In, and AX/Out scales generally experience, express, or suppress relatively little anger. Individuals with high anger scores (above the 75th percentile) and low AX/Con scores tend to experience and/or express angry feelings to a degree that may interfere with optimal functioning. The angry feelings of these individuals are also likely to contribute to difficulties in interpersonal relationships or dispose them to develop psychological and/or physical disorders.

Although the contributions of anger and hostility to the etiology of hypertension have been recognized for more than a half-century (Alexander, 1948), empirical verification of this relationship was difficult to obtain because valid measures of anger and hostility were lacking. With the development of better measures of the experience, expression, and control of anger, the critical role of anger in hypertension and cardiovascular disorders has now been clearly demonstrated (Booth-Kewley & Friedman, 1987; Hartfield, 1985; Janisse, Edguer, & Dyck, 1986; Williams, Haney, Lee, Kong, Blumenthal, & Whalen, 1980). Consistent with these findings, high scores on the STAXI AX/In subscale are associated with elevated blood pressure in high school students (Johnson, 1984). Very high scores on both the AX/In and AX/Out

TABLE 5.1. Guidelines for Interpreting High STAXI Scores

Scale	Characteristics of persons with high scores
S-Anger	Individuals with high scores were experiencing relatively intense angry feelings at the time the test was administered. If S-Anger is elevated relative to T-Anger, the individual's angry feelings are likely to be situationally determined. Elevations in S-Anger are more likely to reflect chronic anger if T-Anger and AX/In scores are also high.
T-Anger	High T-Anger individuals frequently experience angry feelings, especially when they feel they are treated unfairly by others. Whether persons high in T-Anger suppress, express, or control their anger can be inferred from their scores on the AX/In, AX/Out, and AX/Con scales.
T-Anger/T	Persons with high T-Anger/T scores are quick-tempered and readily express their anger with little provocation. Such individuals are often impulsive and lacking in anger control. High T-Anger/T individuals who have high AX/Con scores may be strongly authoritarian and use anger to intimidate others.
T-Anger/R	Persons with high T-Anger/R scores are highly sensitive to criticism, perceived affronts, and negative evaluation by others. They frequently experience intense feelings of anger under such circumstances.
AX/In	Persons with high AX/In scores frequently experience intense angry feelings but tend to suppress these feelings rather than to express them either physically or in verbal behavior. Persons with high AX/In scores who also have high AX/Out scores may express their anger in some situations, while suppressing it in others.
AX/Out	Persons with high AX/Out scores frequently experience anger, which they express in aggressive behavior. Anger-out may be expressed in physical acts such as assaulting other persons or slamming doors, or verbally in the form of criticism, sarcasm, insults, threats, and the extreme use of profanity.
AX/Con	Persons with high scores on the AX/Con scale tend to invest a great deal of energy in monitoring and preventing the expression of anger. While controlling anger is certainly desirable, the overcontrol of anger may result in passivity and withdrawal. Persons with high AX/Con and high T-Anger scores may also experience anxiety and depression.

scales (above the 90 percentile) may place an individual at risk for coronary artery disease and heart attacks. Interestingly, chronic pain patients have very low anger scores but tend to be extremely high in T-Anxiety (Curtis, Kinder, Kalichman, & Spana, 1988).

Measuring Depression: The Beck Depression Inventory

Schuyler and Katz (1973) estimate that more than 12 percent of the adult population experience an episode of depression of sufficient severity to warrant treatment. Depression is also a prominent factor in 75 percent of all psychiatric hospitalizations (Secunda, Katz, Freidman, & Schuyler, 1973). Moreover, assessing the extent of depression is critically important because the risk of suicide can be reduced if the ideation

associated with depressive symptoms is recognized (Beck, Resnik, & Lettieri, 1974).

Depressed persons typically experience high levels of anxiety and intense anger that is turned inward, resulting in feelings of low self-esteem and hopelessness. While negative mood and feelings of sadness and despair are the most prominent symptoms of depression, there are also other factors, such as complicated psychological defenses, which make the dynamics of depression extremely complex. In addition to feeling intensely anxious, depressed persons frequently experience anger, blame themselves for their angry thoughts, and thus feel even worse (Beck, Rush, Shaw, & Emery, 1979). It should be noted, however, that experiencing angry feelings may actually indicate improvement in a depressed person, who might otherwise repress or deny such feelings because they typically invoke guilt and shame (Beck et al., 1979). Given the psychological defenses of depressed persons, the emergence of angry feelings might not be reported in therapy; however, these feelings could be detected using an S-Anger scale.

Depressed patients differ from patients with phobias and anxiety neuroses in feeling helpless, hopeless, and worthless; in suicidal ideation; and especially in psychomotor retardation (Barlow, 1985, 1988; Barlow, Di Nardo, Vermilyea, B., Vermilyea, J., & Blanchard, 1986; Benshoof, 1987; Roth & Mountjoy, 1982). The Beck Depression Inventory (BDI) was designed to assess symptoms that contribute to differentiating between patients suffering primarily from depression and those with other disorders (Beck, 1976). The BDI is easy to administer and interpret, provides a rapid assessment of the severity of depression, and facilitates identification of suicidal ideation that requires prompt intervention (Beck, 1967, 1976). Individual BDI items help the therapist to focus on particular symptoms while also providing information about the patient's negative cognitions. According to Beck et al. (1979), the BDI provides "a useful tool for eliciting problems from patients who have difficulty in focusing on distressing symptoms or life situations. We have found that almost any of the items in the Inventory may provide a point of entry into the patient's distorted or dysfunctional constructs" (p. 168).

CLINICAL ASSESSMENT OF EMOTIONAL VITAL SIGNS

As the mainsprings for motivating behavior, emotions have a significant impact on health and personal effectiveness. Therefore, in evaluating psychological well-being, it is essential to monitor emotional states, just as physicians routinely measure pulse rate, blood pressure, and temperature in medical examinations. These physical vital signs are not only indicators of general physical health, but they also tell us how well the body's cardiovascular, neuroendocrine, and immune systems are functioning at a particular time. When a physician detects an abnormal pulse during a physical examination, it signals a potentially significant problem in the

functioning of the cardiovascular system. In addition to the many physical conditions that can give rise to an abnormal pulse, the heart beats much faster when a person is experiencing intense anxiety and somewhat faster when an individual is angry. There is also substantial evidence that individuals who experience angry feelings that are suppressed rather than expressed have higher blood pressure (Johnson, 1984).

While intense anxiety and anger are analogous to elevations in pulse rate and blood pressure, the presence of a fever, as indicated by abnormally high body temperature, is roughly analogous to depression. Perhaps the most stable physical vital sign is a body temperature of 98.6°F for most healthy people. Elevations in temperature that define a fever are interpreted by physicians as a strong indication of the presence of an infection or metabolic problem that requires immediate attention (Guyton, 1977). Similarly, symptoms of depression indicate the presence of pervasive unresolved conflicts that result in an emotional fever. Just as fevers can usually be reduced by antipyretics (e.g., aspirin, acetaminophen) in patients with colds or the flu, depressed moods can also be decreased by pharmacological intervention. However, the emotional conflicts that contribute to clinical depression are not likely to be relieved by either drugs or simple behavioral interventions, because there is a higher threshold for seeking psychological treatment than for using medication to alleviate pain or fever. Consequently, the problems that cause the emotional fever of depression are more likely to persist to a point of crisis before help is sought.

Anxiety, Anger, and Depression as Emotional Vital Signs

The emotional vital signs that are most critical to an individual's well-being are anxiety, anger, and depression. Variations in the intensity and duration of these psychological states provide essential information about a person's mental health and can point to recent events as well as long-standing conflicts that have particular meaning and impact on an individual's life. Since more than 50 percent of the dropouts in therapy occur between the first and fifth interviews (Garfield & Bergin, 1986), assessing and providing meaningful feedback on readings of emotional vital signs during treatment will enhance patients' awareness and understanding of their feelings. Helping them to cope more effectively with these feelings early in treatment will also minimize dropouts.

According to de la Torre (1979), dealing with transitory feelings of anxiety (S-Anxiety) should be a major priority in *all* forms of short-term psychotherapy, including crisis intervention and dynamic treatments that focus on specific problems of the patient or client. Moreover, diverse manifestations of anxiety in various physical and psychological disorders generally require different forms of treatment (Suinn & Deffenbacher, 1988). As de la Torre (1979) has noted:

> The ubiquitousness of anxiety among psychiatric patients demands a careful assessment and diagnosis. The transitory anxiety in a well-compensated individual differs considerably from the intense anxiety that heralds psychotic decompensation. Both situations require different kinds of interventions and will have different prognostic outcomes (p. 379).

Recent research findings suggest that problems with anger are equally ubiquitous. In a series of studies, Deffenbacher (1992) and his associates (Deffenbacher, Demm, & Brandon, 1986; Deffenbacher & Stark, 1990; Hazaleus & Deffenbacher, 1986; Hogg & Deffenbacher, 1986) found that persons high in trait anger experienced heightened S-Anger and physiological arousal on a daily basis across a wide range of situations. Treatments designed to assist clients to learn how to reduce their anger by engaging in self-initiated relaxation exercises helped them to function more effectively and to use problem-solving techniques and social skills that were previously disrupted by their angry feelings.

Careful assessment of the experience, expression, and control of anger is not only essential for understanding problems that are rooted in anger; it is also a necessary first step in treatment planning (Sharkin, 1988). Determining the situations that provoke anger and helping patients to employ adaptive strategies that can be used effectively in such circumstances required detailed knowledge of levels of state and trait anger and modes of anger expression. Research with the STAXI and its subscales provides encouraging evidence of the utility of this inventory for assessing anger in diagnoses and treatment planning and in the evaluation of treatment process and outcome. In a recent comprehensive evaluation and critique of the STAXI, which was described as a "specific, sensitive, psychometric instrument," James Moses (1992) concluded that "there is great potential for its use to significantly further our understanding of important stress-based and stress-influenced syndromes and to help in identifying effective means by which such disorders may be reversed and prevented" (1992, p. 52).

The clinical assessment of emotional vital signs can provide essential information for diagnosis, treatment planning, and monitoring the treatment process. Since management of anxiety, anger, and depression during treatment is a major concern of most psychotherapists and counselors, the continuous valid assessment of these emotions can facilitate the treatment process (Deffenbacher et al., 1986; Novaco, 1979). Consequently, Barlow (1988) emphasizes the importance of utilizing measures that differentiate between depression and anxiety during the course of treatment. Although less attention has been given to the assessment of anger, Deffenbacher's (1992) research clearly demonstrates that anger can be readily measured and that it is important to do so.

Assessing Emotional Vital Signs During Diagnosis and Treatment

Most clients or patients who enter treatment experience a combination of intense emotions and a variety of psychological defense mechanisms that determine the nature of their symptoms. In order to evaluate a patient's problems, a comprehensive assessment involves an initial interview and the administration of a battery of psychological tests such as the Rorschach and the MMPI (Butcher, 1990). Including measures of emotional vital signs that can be rapidly administered and scored in the assessment battery would provide information that could be used to give as timely feedback to the client.

Ideally, the assessment of emotional vital signs should be done before the initial interview so that feedback and crisis-oriented intervention could be given immediately if needed. The availability of computers provides an efficient procedure for administering and scoring tests to assess emotional vital signs while the patient awaits the initial interview. The assessment of vital signs at the beginning of the intake procedure makes it possible to help the client to better understand the problems that are signaled by these feelings. Providing feedback on emotional vital signs also facilitates the treatment process by helping the client learn to cope with these feelings early in treatment.

The BDI and scales to measure S-Anxiety and S-Anger can be rapidly and easily administered and scored, either by computer or manually, while the patient is waiting to be seen. If a patient is depressed or experiencing intense anxiety or anger, it is imperative for the examiner to deal immediately and directly with these feelings. Intense emotional feelings can greatly interfere with judgment and reality testing and can result in injuries to the patient or others. Feedback concerning patients' emotional vital signs, as revealed by assessing anger, anxiety, and depression, can help them to recognize and report relationships between their thoughts and feelings and the events that give rise to them, and thus facilitate the therapeutic process.

Detection of depressive affect and ideation is even more important than the assessment of anxiety and anger because there is always some danger of suicide. Administering the BDI makes it easier for a client to report suicidal cognitions, rather than the therapist's relying on the client's spontaneous reports or responses to direct questions during a clinical interview. Since not all clients report suicidal ideation when responding to the BDI, the presence of high levels of S-Anxiety or S-Anger when pursued may lead to

the detection of such thoughts that might otherwise be defended against.

The therapeutic process can also be facilitated by taking emotional vital signs at the beginning of each treatment session. This can be conveniently done, either by computer or manually, simply by having patients report ten minutes before each session. With such information available at the beginning of a session, the therapist will be alerted to special problems that require immediate attention before proceeding with the regular course of treatment. Dealing with elevations in a client's emotional vital signs should take precedence over regular therapeutic procedures because these signs indicate more immediate needs that must be confronted before working on routine problems. Charting sequential levels of S-Anxiety, S-Anger, and depression over the course of treatment, and providing patients with feedback about these emotional vital signs, can also help to identify significant problem areas and thereby facilitate the patients' understanding of how specific problems influence their emotions.

The BDI is currently utilized by therapists and researchers as a session-to-session measure of depression (Beck, 1979; Burns, 1980; Moras, Telfer, & Barlow, 1993). Information obtained from the BDI provides the therapist with an index of the progression of depression and can lead to subsequent changes in the direction of treatment (DeRubeis & Beck, 1988). The continual assessment of anxiety and anger as emotional vital signs can also provide objective information in regard to the effectiveness of the treatment process. However, periodically obtaining measures of personality traits will provide better evidence of treatment effectiveness, since a decrease in T-Anger, T-Anxiety, and depression should follow periods of reduced scores on state measures of these emotional conditions.

SUMMARY

The critical importance of measuring psychological vital signs in diagnosis and treatment was examined in this chapter. The nature and assessment of anxiety, anger, and depression as emotional states and personality dispositions was reviewed, and a number of psychometric instruments of demonstrated utility for assessing these psychological vital signs were described. Measuring and providing patients with feedback about their emotional vital signs can contribute to effective crisis intervention and may facilitate treatment by linking intense feelings to the events and experiences that give rise to them. It was concluded that anxiety, anger, and depression as indicators of psychological well-being should be carefully assessed in diagnostic eval uations and then continuously monitored in counseling, psychotherapy, and behavioral in terventions.

REFERENCES

Alexander, F. G. (1948). Emotional factors in hyper tension. In F. Alexander & T. M. French (Eds.), *Studies in psychosomatic medicine: An approach to the cause and treatment of vegetative distur bances*. New York: Ronald Press. (Originally pub lished 1939)

Auerbach, S. M., & Spielberger, C. D. (1972). The assessment of state and trait anxiety with the Ror schach test. *Journal of Personality Assessment, 36*, 314–335.

Auerbach, S. M., Wadsworth, A. D., Dunn, T. M., Taulbee, E. S., & Spielberger, C. D. (1973). Emotional reactions to surgery. *Journal of Con sulting and Clinical Psychology, 40*, 33–38.

Averill, J. R. (1982). *Anger and aggression: An essay on emotion*. New York: Springer-Verlag.

Barlow, D. H. (1988). *Anxiety and its disorders*. New York: Guilford Press.

Barlow, D. H. (1985). The dimensions of anxiety dis orders. In A. H. Tuma & J. D. Maser (Eds.), *Anx iety and the anxiety disorders* (pp. 479–500). Hills dale, NJ: Erlbaum

Barlow, D. H., DiNardo, D. A., Vermilyea, B. B., Vermilyea, J. A., & Blanchard, G. B. (1986). Co morbidity and depression among the anxiety dis orders: Issues in diagnosis and classification. *Jour nal of Nervous and Mental Disease, 174*, 63–72.

Beck, A. T. (1967). *Depression: Clinical, experimen tal, and theoretical aspects*. New York: Hoeber.

Beck, A. T. (1976). *Cognitive therapy and the emo tional disorders*. New York: International Univer sities Press.

Beck, A. T., Resnik, H. L. P., & Lettieri, D. (Eds.).

(1974). *The prediction of suicide*. Bowie, MD: Charles Press.

Beck, A. T., Rush, A. J., Shaw, B. F., & Emery, G. (1979). *Cognitive therapy of depression*. New York: Guilford Press.

Benshoof, B. G. (1987). *A comparison of anxiety and depression symptomatology in the anxiety and af fective disorders*. Unpublished doctoral disserta tion, State University of New York, Albany.

Biaggio, M. K. (1980). Assessment of anger arousal. *Journal of Personality Assessment, 44*, 289–298.

Biaggio, M. K., & Maiuro, R. D. (1985). Recent ad vances in anger assessment. In C. D. Spielberger & J. N. Butcher (Eds.), *Advances in personality assessment* (Vol. 5). Hillsdale, NJ: Erlbaum.

Biaggio, M. K., Supplee, K., & Curtis, N. (1981). Reliability and validity of four anger scales. *Jour nal of Personality Assessment, 45*, 639–648.

Booth-Kewley, S., & Friedman, H. S. (1987). Psy chological predictors of heart disease: A quanti tative review. *Psychological Bulletin, 101* 343– 362.

Borkovec, T. D., Weerts, T. C., & Bernstein, D. A. (1977). Assessment of anxiety. In A. R. Ciminero, K. S. Calhoun, & H. E. Adams (Eds.), *Handbook of behavioral assessment* (pp. 367–428). New York: Wiley.

Burns, D. D. (1980) *Feeling good*. New York: Wil liam Morrow.

Buss, A. H. (1961). *The psychology of aggression*. New York: Wiley.

Buss, A. H., & Durkee, A. (1957). An inventory for assessing different kinds of hostility. *Journal of Consulting Psychology, 21*, 343–349.

Buss, A. H., & Perry, M. (1992). The aggression ques tionnaire. *Journal of Personality and Social Psy chology, 63*, 452–459.

Butcher, J. N. (1990). *The MMPI 2 in psychological treatment*. New York: Oxford University Press.

Cattell, R. B. (1966). Patterns of change: Measure ment in relation to state-dimension, trait change, lability, and process concepts. *Handbook of mul tivariate experimental psychology*. Chicago: Rand McNally.

Cattell, R. B., & Scheier, I. H. (1958). The nature of anxiety: A review of thirteen multivariate analyses comprising 814 variables. *Psychological Reports, 4*, 351.

Cattell, R. B., & Scheier, I. H. (1961). *The meaning and measurement of neuroticism and anxiety* (pp. 57, 182). New York: Ronald Press.

Cattell, R. B., & Scheier, I. H. (1963). *Handbook for the IPAT Anxiety Scale* (2nd ed.). Champaign, IL: Institute for Personality and Ability Testing.

Cook, W. W., & Medley, D. M. (1954). Proposed hostility and pharisaic-virtue scales for the MMPI. *The Journal of Applied Psychology, 38,* 414–418.

Crane, R. S. (1981). The role of anger, hostility, and aggression in essential hypertension. (Doctoral dissertation, University of South Florida, Tampa, FL, 1981). *Dissertation Abstracts International, 42,* 2982B.

Cronbach, L. J. (1951). Coefficient alpha and the internal structure of tests. *Psychometrika, 16,* 297–335.

Curtis, G., Kinder, B., Kalichman, S., & Spana, R. (1988). Affective differences among subgroups of chronic pain patients. *Anxiety Research: An International Journal, 1,* 65–73.

Darwin, C. (1965). *The expression of emotions in man and animals.* Chicago: University of Chicago Press. (Originally published 1872)

Deffenbacher, J. L. (1992). Trait anger: Theory, findings, and implications. In C. D. Spielberger & J. N. Butcher (Eds.), *Advances in personality assessment* (Vol. 9, pp. 177–201). Hillsdale, NJ: Erlbaum.

Deffenbacher, J. L., Demm, P. M., & Brandon, A. D. (1986). High general anger: Correlates and treatment. *Behaviour Research and Therapy, 24,* 480–489.

Deffenbacher, J. L., & Stark, R. S. (1990). *Relaxation and cognitive-relaxation treatments of general anger.* Manuscript submitted for publication, Department of Psychology, Colorado State University, Fort Collins, CO.

de la Torre, J. (1979). Anxiety states and short-term psychotherapy. In W. E. Fann, I. Karacan, A. D. Polorny, & R. L. Williams (Eds.), *Phenomenology and treatment of anxiety* (pp. 377–388). Jamaica, NY: Spectrum.

DeRubeis, R. J., & Beck, A. T. (1988). Cognitive therapy. In K. S. Dobson (Ed.), *Handbook of cognitive-behavioral therapies* (pp. 273–306). New York: Guilford Press.

Duffy, F. (1941). An explanation of "emotional" phenomena without the use of the concept "emotion." *Journal of General Psychology, 25,* 283–293.

Evans, D. R., & Stangeland, M. (1971). Development of the reaction inventory to measure anger. *Psychological Reports, 29,* 412–414.

Freud, S. (1924). *Collected papers* (Vol. 1). London: Hogarth Press.

Freud, S. (1936). *The problem of anxiety.* New York: Norton.

Funkenstein, D. H., King, S. H., & Drolette, M. E. (1954). The direction of anger during a laboratory stress-inducing situation. *Psychosomatic Medicine, 16,* 404–413.

Fuqua, D. R., Leonard, E., Masters, M. A., Smith, R. J., Campbell, J. L., & Fischer, P. C. (1991). A structural analysis of the *State-Trait Anger Expression Inventory* (STAXI). *Educational and Psychological Measurement, 51,* 439–446.

Garfield, S. L., & Bergin, A. E. (Eds.). (1986). *Handbook of psychotherapy and behavior change* (3rd ed.). New York: Wiley.

Gaudry, E., Spielberger, C. D., & Vagg, P. R. (1975). Validation of the state-trait distinction in anxiety research. *Multivariate Behavior Research, 10,* 331–341.

Gentry, W. D. (1972). Biracial aggression: 1. Effect of verbal attack and sex of victim. *Journal of Social Psychology, 88,* 75–82.

Gentry, W. D., Chesney, A. P., Gary, H. G., Hall, R. P., & Harburg, E. (1982). Habitual anger-coping styles: I. Effect on mean blood pressure and risk for essential hypertension. *Psychosomatic Medicine, 44,* 195–202.

Gentry, W. D., Chesney, A. P., Hall, R. P., & Harburg, E. (1981). Effect of habitual anger-coping pattern on blood pressure in black/white, high/low stress area respondents. *Psychosomatic Medicine, 43,* 88.

Guyton, A. C. (1977). *Basic human physiology: Normal function and mechanism of disease.* Philadelphia: W. B. Saunders.

Hamilton, M. (1959). The assessment of anxiety states by rating. *British Journal of Medical Psychology, 32,* 50.

Harburg, E., Blakelock, E. H., & Roeper, P. J. (1979). Resentful and reflective coping with arbitrary authority and blood pressure: Detroit. *Psychosomatic Medicine, 3,* 189–202.

Harburg, E., Erfurt, J. C., Hauenstein, L. S., Chape, C., Schull, W. J., & Schork, M. A. (1973). Socioecological stress, suppressed hostility, skin color, and black-white male blood pressure: Detroit. *Psychosomatic Medicine, 35,* 276–296.

Harburg, E., & Hauenstein, L. (1980). Parity and blood pressure among four race-stress groups of females in Detroit. *American Journal of Epidemiology, 111,* 356–366.

Harburg, E., Schull, W. J., Erfurt, J. C., & Schork, M. A. (1970). A family set method for estimating heredity and stress-I. *Journal of Chronic Disease, 23,* 69–81.

Hartfield, M. T. (1985). Appraisals of anger situations and subsequent coping responses in hypertensive and normotensive adults: A comparison. (Doctoral dissertation, University of California, 1985). *Dissertation Abstracts International, 46,* 4452B.

Hazaleus, S. L., & Deffenbacher, J. L. (1986). Relaxation and cognitive treatments of anger. *Journal of Consulting and Clinical Psychology, 54,* 222–226.

Hodges, W. F. (1976). The psychophysiology of anxiety. In M. Zuckerman & C. D. Spielberger (Eds.), *Emotions and anxiety: New concepts, methods, and applications* (pp. 175–194). Hillsdale, NJ: Erlbaum.

Hodges, W. F., & Spielberger, C. D. (1966). The effects of threat of shock on heart rate for subjects who differ in manifest anxiety and fear of shock. *Psychophysiology, 2,* 287–294.

Hogg, J. A., & Deffenbacher, J. L. (1986). Irrational beliefs, depression and anger in college students. *Journal of College Student Personnel, 27,* 349–353.

Jacobs, G. A., Latham, L. E., & Brown, M. S. (1988). Test-retest reliability of the State-Trait Personality Inventory and the Anger Expression Scale. *Anxiety Research, 1,* 263–265.

Janisse, M. P., Edguer, N., & Dyck, D. G. (1986). Type A behavior, anger expression, and reactions to anger imagery. *Motivation and Emotion, 10,* 371–385.

Johnson, E. H. (1984). *Anger and anxiety as determinants of elevated blood pressure in adolescents.* Unpublished doctoral dissertation, University of South Florida, Tampa.

Knight, R. G., Chisholm, B. J., Paulin, J. M., & Waal-Manning, H. J. (1988). The Spielberger Anger Expression Scale: Some psychometric data. *Journal of Clinical Psychology, 27,* 279–281.

Lader, M. (1975). Psychophysiological parameters and methods. In L. Levi (Ed.), *Emotions: Their parameters and measurement* (pp. 341–367). New York: Raven Press.

Lazarus, R. S., Deese, J., & Osler, S. F. (1952). The effects of psychological stress upon performance. *Psychological Bulletin, 49,* 293–317.

Lazarus, R. S., & Folkman, S. (1984). *Stress, appraisal, and coping.* New York: Springer.

Lazarus, R. S., & Opton, E. M., Jr. (1966). The study of psychological stress. In C. D. Spielberger (Ed.), *Anxiety and behavior* (pp. 225–262). New York: Academic Press.

Levitt, E. E. (1980). *The psychology of anxiety* (2nd ed.). Hillsdale, NJ: Erlbaum.

Martin, I. (1973). Somatic reactivity: Methodology. In H. J. Eysenck (Ed.), *Handbook of abnormal psychology* (2nd ed., pp. 417–456). San Diego: Knapp.

McReynolds, P. (1968). The assessment of anxiety: A survey of available techniques. In P. McReynolds (Ed.), *Advances in psychological assessment* (Vol. 1, pp. 244–264). Palo Alto: Science and Behavior Books.

Moras, K., Telfer, L. A., & Barlow, D. H. (1993). Efficacy and specific effects data on new treatments: A case study strategy with mixed anxiety-depression. *Journal of Consulting and Clinical Psychology, 61,* 412–420.

Moses, J. A. (1992). *State-Trait Anger Expression Inventory,* research edition. In D. J. Keyser & R. C. Sweetland (Eds.), *Test critiques* (Vol. IX, pp. 510–525). Austin, TX: PRO-ED.

Novaco, R. W. (1975). *Anger control: The development and evaluation of an experimental treatment.* Lexington, MA: Lexington Books/D.C. Heath.

Novaco, R. W. (1979). The cognitive regulation of anger and stress. In P. C. Kendall & S. D. Hollon (Eds.), *Cognitive behavioral interventions, theory, research, and procedures* (pp. 241–285). New York: Academic Press.

Plutchik, R. (1962). *The emotions.* New York: Random House.

Pollans, C. H. (1983). *The psychometric properties and factor structure of the Anger Expression (AX) Scale.* Unpublished master's thesis, University of South Florida, Tampa.

Reheiser, E. C. (1991). *The interactions of state anxiety and trait anxiety: As evoked by stressful episodic imagery.* Unpublished honors thesis, University of South Florida, Tampa.

Rosenzweig, S. (1976). Aggressive behavior and the Rosenzweig picture frustration study. *Journal of Clinical Psychology, 32,* 885–891.

Rosenzweig, S. (1978). *The Rosenzweig Picture Frustration (P-F) Study: Basic manual and adult form supplement.* St. Louis: Rana.

Roth, M. S., & Mountjoy, C. Q. (1982). The distinction between anxiety states and depressive disorders. In E. S. Paykel (Ed.), *Handbook of affective disorders.* Edinburgh: Churchill Livingstone.

Schultz, S. D. (1954). A differentiation of several forms of hostility by scales empirically constructed from significant items on the MMPI. *Dissertation Abstracts, 17,* 717–720.

Schuyler, D., & Katz, M. M. (1973). *The depressive illnesses: A major public health problem.* Washington, DC: U.S. Government Printing Office.

Secunda, S. K., Katz, M. M., Friedman, R. J., & Schuyler, D. (1973). *Special report: 1973—The depressive disorders*. Washington, DC: U.S. Government Printing Office.

Sharkin, B. S. (1988). Treatment of client anger in counseling. *Journal of Counseling and Development, 66*, 361–365.

Siegel, S. (1956). The relationship of hostility to authoritarianism. *Journal of Abnormal and Social Psychology, 52*, 368–373.

Spielberger, C. D. (1966). Theory and research on anxiety. In C. D. Spielberger (Ed.), *Anxiety and behavior* (pp. 3–20). New York: Academic Press.

Spielberger, C. D. (1972). Anxiety as an emotional state. In C. D. Spielberger (Ed.), *Anxiety: Current trends in theory and research* (Vol. 1, pp. 24–49). New York: Academic Press.

Spielberger, C. D. (1973). *Manual for the State-Trait Anxiety Inventory for Children*. Palo Alto: Consulting Psychologists Press.

Spielberger, C. D. (1976). Stress and anxiety and cardiovascular disease. *Journal of the South Carolina Medical Association* (Suppl. 15), *72*, 15–22.

Spielberger, C. D. (1977). Anxiety: Theory and research. In B. B. Wolman (Ed.), *International encyclopedia of neurology, psychiatry, psychoanalysis, and psychology*. New York: Human Sciences Press.

Spielberger, C. D. (1979). *Understanding stress and anxiety*. London: Harper & Row.

Spielberger, C. D. (1980). *Preliminary manual for the State-Trait Anger Scale (STAS)*. Tampa, FL: University of South Florida, Human Resources Institute.

Spielberger, C. D. (1983). *Manual for the State-Trait Anxiety Inventory: STAI(Form Y)*. Palo Alto: Consulting Psychologists Press.

Spielberger, C. D. (1988). *Manual for the State-Trait Anger Expression Inventory (STAXI)*. Odessa, FL: Psychological Assessment Resources, Inc. (PAR).

Spielberger, C. D. (1989). *State-Trait Anxiety Inventory: A comprehensive bibliography* (2nd ed.). Palo Alto: Consulting Psychologists Press.

Spielberger, C. D., & Gorsuch, R. L. (1966). The development of the State-Trait Anxiety Inventory. In C. D. Spielberger & R. L. Gorsuch, *Mediating processes in verbal conditioning*. Final report to the National Institutes of Health, U.S. Public Health Service on Grants MH–7229, MH–7446, and HD–947.

Spielberger, C. D., Gorsuch, R. L., & Lushene, R. D. (1970). *STAI: Manual for the State-Trait Anxiety Inventory*. Palo Alto: Consulting Psychologists Press.

Spielberger, C. D., Jacobs, G., Russell, S., & Crane, R. (1983). Assessment of anger: The State-Trait Anger Scale. In J. N. Butcher & C. D. Spielberger (Eds.), *Advances in personality assessment* (Vol. 2, pp. 159–187). Hillsdale, NJ: Erlbaum.

Spielberger, C. D., Johnson, E. H., Russell, S. F., Crane, R. J., Jacobs, G. A., & Worden, T. J. (1985). The experience and expression of anger: Construction and validation of an anger expression scale. In M. A. Chesney & R. H. Rosenman (Eds.), *Anger and hostility in cardiovascular and behavioral disorders* (pp. 5–30). New York: Hemisphere/McGraw-Hill.

Spielberger, C. D., Krasner, S. S., & Solomon, E. P. (1988). The experience, expression and control of anger. In M. P. Janisse (Ed.), *Health psychology: Individual differences and stress* (pp. 89–108). New York: Springer-Verlag.

Story, D., & Deffenbacher, J. L. (1985, April). *General anger and personality*. Paper presented at the meeting of the Rocky Mountain Psychological Association, Tucson, AZ.

Suinn, R. M., & Deffenbacher, J. C. (1988). Anxiety management training. *The Counseling Psychologist, 16*, 31–49.

Tavris, C. (1982). *Anger, the misunderstood emotion*. New York: Simon & Schuster.

Taylor, J. A. (1953). A personality scale of manifest anxiety. *Journal of Abnormal Social Psychology, 48*, 285.

Titchener, E. B. (1897). *An outline of psychology*. New York: Macmillan.

Williams, R. B., Haney, T. L., Lee, K. L., Kong, Y., Blumenthal, J., & Whalen, R. E. (1980). Type A behavior, hostility, and coronary atherosclerosis. *Psychosomatic Medicine, 42*, 539–549.

Wundt, W. (1896). *Outlines of psychology*. New York: Dustav E. Stechert.

Young, P. T. (1943). *Emotion in man and animal*. New York: Wiley.

Zelin, M. L., Adler, G., & Myerson, P. G. (1972). Anger self-report: An objective questionnaire for the measurement of aggression. *Journal of Consulting and Clinical Psychology, 39*, 340.

Zuckerman, M. (1960). Development of an Affect Adjective Check List for the measurement of anxiety. *Journal of Consulting Psychology, 26*, 291.

Zuckerman, M., & Lubin, B. (1965). *Manual for the Multiple Affect Adjective Checklist*. San Diego: Educational and Industrial Testing Service.

6

How to Assess Clients in Pretreatment Planning

Larry E. Beutler
T. Mark Harwood

The first and most central question facing the clinician who is assessing a client is, "What purpose will this evaluation serve?" A focused and meaningful evaluation requires that one keep the ultimate uses of the report in mind. It is our experience that clinicians frequently fail to obtain a clear understanding of the referral question and may respond out of habit to certain inferred questions, thus providing results and information that is routine and overly general.

In a related way, much debate has occurred between those who believe that standard procedures and reports can be applied to the process of psychological assessment and those who maintain that each assessment should be specifically tailored to each client's needs and each referent's requests (Clarkin & Hurt, 1988; Sweeney, Clarkin, & Fitzgibbon, 1987). The epitome of the standard assessment approach is embodied in computer-generated reports. This approach utilizes a uniform set of one or more instruments, assesses a uniform set of dimensions, and applies standard descriptive statements to the evaluation of all patients. While this approach is satisfactory as a screening procedure, we believe that even if the same procedures are being used in different cases, an individually focused approach to interpreting and

reporting the results makes better sense than a standard report in those instances when the clinician is asked to provide consultation to someone else.

Psychological assessment is a method for obtaining answers to questions. Without explicitly defining the questions in advance, the conclusions that one reaches and the report that one creates may be needlessly complex, general, uninformative, or inaccurate. Hence, the first task of the clinician is to determine what questions are being asked. Asking the referent for clarification of the question being asked is an obvious first step when the clinician is functioning as a consultant to another professional. In this role, the questions asked by a referring professional usually fall within five categories: (1) What *diagnosis* fits this person's current presentation? (2) What is the *prognosis* for this person's condition? (3) How impaired is this person's *current functioning?* (4) What *treatment* will be most likely to yield positive effects? and (5) What factors are contributing to or *causing* this client's disturbance?

While the report is tailored to the specific question or questions asked, there is some degree of consistency to the nature of the information that is needed in order to answer all of these questions. That is, there are common domains of patient functioning that must be addressed in order adequately to answer any of the questions that might be posed by a referent. These common areas include: (1) an assessment of current level, strengths, and limitations of intellectual, memory, and other cognitive functions; (2) an evaluation of mood, affect, and level of emotional control; (3) a determination of events, conflicts, and needs that trigger the problematic responses for which the patient is seeking help; and (4) a narrative formulation of the patient's resources and deficits. This latter domain entails providing a conceptual formulation of the patient that is distilled from the information available from the other domains of functioning. This formulation usually includes a description of the nature of the patient's interaction with the environments that both evoke and alleviate the problem behaviors, including levels of motivation for treatment, styles of coping with external and internal stressors, and a description of common interpersonal themes or patterns that characterize the patient's functioning.

While an integration of descriptive and inferred information on these domains of functioning provides a common framework for responding to referral questions, different questions require more or less attention to one or more of the different domains. For example, to answer a question that asks if the patient's behavior is characteristic of a central nervous system disorder (a diagnosis question), the clinician will need to focus more on an assessment of cognitive functions (short- and long-term memory, concept formation, sensory and perceptual functions, etc.) than would be required if the clinician were responding to a question about the severity of the patient's depression (a question of current functional level). Likewise, a question regarding whether or not cognitive therapy would be helpful (a treatment question) would require the clinician to formulate an opinion regarding the patient's motivation level and coping styles to a greater extent than a question asking if a history of child abuse was related to current levels of anxiety and social disturbance (a question of etiology).

Unfortunately, the questions actually asked on written referral forms are seldom as clearly framed as one would like. Often, these written questions are much more specific than the ones really motivating the referral and if responded to naively may cause the clinician to omit information the referent really desires and needs. For example, instead of asking for a diagnosis, the referring professional may ask for an MMPI or a Rorschach. At other times, the questions asked may be too broad to direct the clinician's inquiry. Thus, instead of asking for the desired treatment recommendations directly, the referent may ask for personality testing.

In each of these cases, the referring professional may be using a shorthand method of attempting to get information from the consultant. Unless the consultant can decode the question, however, a response to the referent's shorthand will not be found to be helpful. Each cryptically written request for consultation hides some assumptions and specific but unstated questions that the referring clinician is attempting to address. For example, the referent who makes a written request for "neuropsychological testing" may be seeking confirmation of organic etiology in order to allow the patient to receive insurance compensation, or he/she may be trying to predict whether the symptoms are likely to dissipate enough over time to allow the patient to go back to work. Obviously, the responding clinician will want either to undertake a different form of evaluation or to write the report differently in these two instances.

Unless the clinician is very familiar with the referent's habits, he or she must clarify what decisions are being contemplated and what types of questions and dilemmas are facing the referent in order to have prompted this referral. Reframing requests in terms of questions that reflect one of the five aforementioned categories is desirable in order to provide the most reliable and useful information for the referent.

In the final analysis, all questions that are asked of the consulting clinician have implications for treatment and prognosis. This is true even when the clinician is functioning as an intake evaluator for an individual who has come to him or her as a patient for treatment. To the degree that this is true, the questions asked of a consulting clinician fall within the same categories as those that clinicians ask themselves when evaluating a potential psychotherapy client. That is, to the clinician-therapist, the questions that must be first addressed when a patient requests assistance is whether treatment is needed, and if so what treatment is likely to produce the most positive effects. A treatment-related question invokes one or more additional and more specific questions. For example, in the case of an intake evaluation of a person who is seeking treatment, all of the following related questions must be addressed:

1. Should this person be treated?
2. What are the long-term objectives of treatment?
3. Where should this person be treated?
4. Over what period of time and with what frequency should treatment occur?
5. Should the treatment be medical/pharmacological, psychological, or both?
6. Should others be included in the client's treatment (group or family or couple intervention)?
7. What type of relationship should the treating clinician provide?
8. How should the client be prepared for treatment?
9. What should the mediating goals of treatment be?
10. What strategy will have the greatest likelihood of succeeding with this person?
11. What specific procedures and techniques are indicated or contraindicated to implement this strategy?
12. How should treatment procedures and goals be changed over time?

Obviously, the methods of responding to these questions range in complexity and preference. Moreover, a description of ways to assess all of the dimensions on which answers to the myriad of specific questions that can be asked is well beyond the scope of this chapter. However, we will attempt to define some of the most important and frequently useful dimensions that should be considered by the clinician in attempting to outline a treatment plan and will explore some of the implications of these dimensions for selecting among alternative treatments with a specific focus on questions of applying psychotherapeutic strategies.

A PROBLEM-SOLVING APPROACH TO PRETREATMENT PLANNING

Pretreatment planning entails an evaluation that is specifically crafted to meet the patients' needs and/or the referents' requests. Thus, assessment must be focused, meaningful, and attentive to expected changes over time. The complexity of treatment must also be acknowledged. Beutler and Clarkin (1990) suggest that there are four domains in which the clinician makes decisions. The first of these is in the selection of the dimensions of patient functioning that are to be assessed. These variables must be carefully selected to ensure relevance to the questions asked and to possess both concurrent and predictive validity. These *patient predisposing variables* provide the window through which one views subsequent treatment decisions. Hence, these subsequent treatment decisions are only as good as the dimensions and the methods of assessing them that are chosen at this first level.

Empirically and psychometrically sound assessment of relevant patient characteristics serves as the basis for recommending three subsequent and sequentially defined levels of treatment: the *context* in which treatment will be offered, the nature of the *relationship* that will be fostered, and the *specific strategies and techniques* that will be applied by the psychotherapist or counselor. Thus, when initially considering the nature of the referral, one must carefully select procedures that provide information on characteristics that *predispose* the patient to respond differentially to aspects of each of these three domains.

1. The *patient predisposing variables* that are relevant to the most frequently asked questions of treatment planning include such aspects of the patient and the patient's problems as formal diagnosis, probable etiology, target problems, demographic characteristics, personality and response dispositions, relevant environmental circumstances, and nature of available support systems.

2. The *context* of treatment refers to the setting in which treatment will be offered (e.g., inpatient or outpatient), the relative use of medical and psychosocial modalities, the format through which treatment will be conducted (e.g., individual, couples, group), and the intensity of treatment to be offered (i.e., the duration and frequency).

3. Determining the nature of the *relationship* that will optimize treatment outcomes requires a consideration of several factors. These include the assignment of the therapist to fit the patient (i.e., patient-therapist matching), the use and nature of role-induction procedures, and methods for enhancing the therapist's influence or role.

4. The *strategies and techniques* of psychotherapy are those goals and activities of the therapist that initiate and direct the processes of change. Assuming that psychotherapy has been selected as the treatment of choice, decisions at this level entail the microscopic determination of the objectives and mediating goals of treatment, the selection of a strategy of change, and the selection of specific techniques through which this strategy will be implemented in order to achieve optimal treatment results.

Obviously, the determination of what patient predisposing dimensions to evaluate will limit the degree to which one can assign selectively treatment context variables, relationship variables, and specific interventions. The areas deemed to be indicated for assessment, the purpose of the evaluations, the intended use of results, and the historical information obtained will affect the decisions made at each subsequent level and will ultimately come to bear on how one develops the treatment plan. That is, both the needs of the client and the requests of the referent determine the specific instruments and techniques used in selecting components of a treatment plan.

Information gathered at one point in time is insufficient for treatment planning; assessment must be a continual process reflecting the mercurial nature of patient dimensions and dependent therapy focus. Only after a concise, comprehensive, and relevant clinical picture has been rendered may patients be assigned to the therapist and type of therapy, with the duration, frequency, and setting that will achieve optimal results. Again, assessment should be an ongoing process with adjustments in treatment made whenever indicated.

The reader should have gathered that careful pretreatment planning is an important practice that is intended to benefit patients by providing maximal efficiency and results; however, pretreatment planning is a necessary endeavor for other reasons as well. Four closely related observations have converged, highlighting the need to engage in selective, focused, targeted, and efficient selection of patient dimensions for all psychotherapeutic endeavors:

1. There is a growing recognition that conventional diagnosis is not sufficient in and of itself for establishing a focused plan of treatment.

2. There is a virtually endless list of patient variables (personality traits and states as well as demographic, philosophical, and environmental variables) that have been touted as important for enhancing treatment efficacy (i.e., quality of therapeutic alliance, patient-therapist compatibility, patient and therapist investment in therapy and outcome, nature of support systems, etc.).

3. There is a burgeoning array of treatments, at least some of which have proven to be differentially efficacious for various presenting problems (e.g., pharmacotherapy for certain depressive states versus in-vivo exposure for phobic avoidance; cognitive-behavioral versus insight approaches for patients with different personal styles).

4. There are increasing pressures from insurance companies, managed health care systems, and the present state of the economy to limit the cost of and access to services. This means reduced coverage for what eventually come to be considered as unnecessary or ineffective treatments. Health services have become less able to tolerate the inefficiencies and ineffectiveness that has characterized a large portion of psychiatric and psychological practice. Assuming that the health care enterprise will continue to consider patients as being entitled to necessary and effective services, clinicians must carefully direct their assessment efforts to dimensions and qualities that are relevant to assigning efficient and effective treatment planning, and must do so in a way that conserves time and resources.

The therapist practices under a premise that fosters imprecise clinical reasoning when patients are treated without consideration of the accumulation of factors that affect treatment efficacy. The blind application of therapies and other interventions solely as a function of the therapist's proclivities and familiarity, without regard to the suitability of the patient's unique characteristics and problems to those procedures, is wrong—wrong for the patient because substandard services are provided and wrong for mental health professionals because it wastes precious resources and is professionally irresponsible (Clarkin & Hurt, 1988). One could argue that such practice violates ethical considerations by increasing the likelihood of delivering varying degrees of inappropriate or ineffec-

tive treatment. This is not to say that pretreatment planning guarantees that the best treatment or results will be delivered or recommended in the individual case; however, decisions based on patient and treatment qualities that have established relationships to outcomes increases the likelihood of positive results.

Normatively and empirically developed assessment instruments have proven invaluable in deriving useful information for the skilled administrator. Clinical psychologists, by virtue of their expertise in using formal assessment instruments, are wonderfully poised to respond to the pressures for improving efficient treatment assignment. Assurance of reliable and valid measurement (both formal and informal) provides a sound basis for confidence in the inferences made when responding to questions of diagnosis, prognosis, and subsequent treatment decisions.

In sum, careful consideration of a small number of carefully selected and validated patient dimensions can provide the clinician with more valuable and comprehensive information on which to select appropriate treatment components than a plethora of ill-defined opinions based on nonempirical theories. The derivation of valid information both from formal and informal pretreatment assessment procedures is an endeavor that will greatly aid achieving maximum compatibility of patient with treatment.

The following section describes a small number of patient variables that appear to bear a significant relationship to decisions that are invoked at one or more of the levels of treatment selection. In this section, we will identify the domains of treatment decision making to which these variables are most closely related. However, we will provide only an introduction to how these variables may be used in subsequent decisions about treatment context, defining the appropriate means of developing the therapeutic relationship, and selecting treatment strategies and techniques. Further clarification of the relationships between patient predisposing characteristics and subsequent decisions will be reserved for separate discussions of each of the sequential levels of treatment decision making.

Patient Predisposing Variables

Patient predisposing variables are defined as those qualities that characterize the patient and his or her environment at the time they enter treatment. Beutler and Clarkin (1990) suggest that these qualities can be clustered into three basic groups: (1) those related to diagnosis and symptoms; (2) those related to qualities of personal response styles; and (3) those related to the patient's environment. Elements of the treatment plan that most directly relate to diagnostic considerations include the setting, modality, and intensity of treatment; elements that relate to personal response patterns, including the fine nuances of psychotherapeutic interventions; and elements that relate to environmental qualities, including the format and focus of interventions.

More specifically:

• a careful examination of problem severity and available support systems can help the clinician decide whether treatment is warranted or not;
• an examination of diagnosis and problem severity can be used to determine if restrictive or nonrestrictive treatment settings are indicated;
• information on diagnosis, expectations, and severity can also suggest how treatment should balance psychosocial and medical aspects;
• data on problem complexity, patient expectations, and subjective distress or severity can indicate the probable value of short versus long-term intervention;
• an understanding of the complexity of the problem can also be used to delineate whether treatment should be symptom- or conflict-focused;
• an assessment of the patient's coping style can suggest the probable value of cognitive, behavioral, or affectively oriented procedures;
• and information on interpersonal resistance propensities can provide guidance as to the degree of therapist directiveness to be used.

In practice, treatment recommendations are more complex than these simple relationships would suggest. Each of the patient predisposing variables interacts with the others. Acknowledging this complexity will ensure that the clinician considers the patient from a comprehensive multifactorial perspective rather than a narrow and simplistic diagnostic one. Beutler and Clarkin observe that any rigid adherence to decisions made on the basis of any single dimension, including diagnosis, is likely to be ill informed, incomplete, and overly simplistic. Thus, no matter how empirically valid, any proposed relationships among patient predisposing variables and treatment assignment are still far from direct and are to be seen as means of ranking interventions in terms of probable success, not rigid decisions to be mindlessly applied.

While we cannot do justice to the complexity of clinical decisions in the brief space allotted to us here, in the following paragraphs we will describe some of the specific patient qualities that fall within each of the three broad categories of predisposing patient variables. We will also review some of the mediating effects that treatments exert on the relationships among these variables and treatment outcomes. As long as the reader is aware that our consideration of these variables as representing independent classes is an oversimplification performed in the service of clarity, the conclusions and recommendations should be informative for the clinician who attempts to translate assessment results into meaningful answers to meaningful questions.

Diagnostic Variables

The first group of patient predisposing variables that merit evaluation in treatment planning are made up of diagnostically based symptom clusters. Included here are syndromes and specific problems that bear attention. An assessment of these symptoms requires a determination of cognitive level and activity, an evaluation of moods and affects, and a descriptive formulation of problematic interpersonal and social behaviors. The assignment of a formal diagnosis implies the existence of a given pattern of signs and symptoms and reflects on treatment assignment from two perspectives.

First, these diagnostic and problem identifiers serve as markers for change. In other words, they provide a baseline measurement by which to judge progress in treatment. Second, formal diagnoses serve as shorthand indicators of severity and chronicity of the problem and for interrelated symptom clusters. These diagnoses serve as relatively specific indicators assigning aspects of the treatment context.

At the very least, earning a diagnosis suggests that the condition is one deserving of treatment. For example, a pattern of intellectual deficits accompanying a diagnosis of mental retardation is likely to result in a very different decision about whether treatment will be valuable than a similar pattern of cognitive deficits that coexists with a diagnosis of acute intoxication, dementia secondary to depression, or dissociative disorder. Beyond this, diagnoses that suggest the presence of a chronic condition indicate the need for long-term or continuing treatment, whereas transient disturbances suggest that short-term and supportive treatments are indicated. Likewise, the diagnosis of decompensated conditions, such as dementia of the Alzheimer's type, bipolar disorder, and schizophrenia, suggest the need for selecting a controlled environment in which to see the patient.

In many instances, diagnosis provides some guidelines for the selection and application of pharmacological interventions. For example, a diagnosis of major depression may inform the clinician to consider one class of medications while a diagnosis of schizophrenia may lead the clinician to consider another. However, diagnoses tell us little about aspects of the patient's personal characteristics, sociodemographic background, willingness to cooperate in treatment, and other aspects of personality that are so central to selecting among psychotherapeutic goals and procedures (e.g., Barlow & Waddell, 1985; Beutler, 1989). An evaluation that extends diagnostic considerations to the domain of nondiagnostic variables (personal characteristics of the patient and his or her environment) will elicit more complete and necessary information for these latter decisions. Only by extending the evaluation to a consideration of these nondiagnostic areas will one be able to make and im-

plement decisions about the selection of a therapist, enhancing and facilitating patient motivation, and selecting specific psychotherapy strategies and techniques.

To complement the role of diagnosis in treatment planning, nondiagnostic characteristics of the person as well as characteristics of the environment must be assessed. Collectively, the variables in these three general classes provide the foundation for selectively matching treatment to patient needs.

Nondiagnostic Patient Variables

Patients enter treatment with preconceived notions regarding therapy, possible treatments, and the nature of expected outcomes that either enhance or abate their levels of treatment motivation. The task of assigning treatments differentially involves identifying those differences that correspond with variations in the situational and interpersonal demands and characteristics of treatment settings, therapists, and procedures. Some of these differences represent enduring traits that are identified as characteristic of the person, while others are more transient or statelike and are usually characterized as situationally responsive. This distinction, while somewhat arbitrary, is an important one and provides a convenient framework for identifying those variables of each type that may be or appear to be important to treatment planning. In the following paragraphs, we will review some of the most obvious or important patient traits and response states that we believe should be considered when questions of treatment planning in psychological assessment are addressed.

Statelike Qualities

While there are many qualities of problems that vary as a function of specific situations and circumstances, in this section we will describe two that appear to be of major importance to the differential assignment of treatment: patient expectations and subjective distress.

Patient expectations. Patients enter treatment with preconceived and motivational notions regarding therapy, possible treatments, and the nature of expected outcomes. These same patients carry with them "social role expectations" that extend beyond the therapeutic relationship but are nonetheless influential in how they will respond to certain interventions. An assessment and understanding of these expectations allows the practitioner to modify treatment and increase patient-therapist compatibility (Garfield, 1986).

It is important that patient expectations either be met or changed to correspond with treatment format, structure, and duration in order to facilitate and enhance both therapeutic engagement and outcome. Treatment outcome is likely to be unsatisfactory when a patient's expectations do not match his or her treatment experiences. Evidence for this conclusion is to be found among the many studies on therapist-patient matching as well as those on pretreatment preparation. This literature (e.g., Lorion & Felner, 1986; Beutler, 1981; Beutler & Bergan, 1991) suggests that the likelihood of positive outcome increases when therapist attributes and therapeutic processes are consistent with the patient's global beliefs about psychotherapy, or when patient beliefs are brought into line with therapy demand characteristics.

A patient's life history (e.g., social and demographic variables) creates a unique phenomenal life view that shapes his or her beliefs about self and others. In a more limited way, life events predispose the development of certain attitudes and beliefs about therapeutic processes, therapists, and therapy efficacy. As applied to the specific domain of psychotherapy, these expectations are changeable but are apparently correlated with how long patients will stay in treatment, their motivation for change, and the effectiveness of therapy itself. These expectations may be thought of as belonging to three general domains: treatment expectations, social role expectations, and changes in treatment expectations.

Treatment expectations include assumptions about the therapist (e.g., attributes, credibility, and expertness), therapeutic process (e.g., philosophies that govern therapy, beliefs regarding confidentiality and the issues that should be ad-

dressed in therapy), and the nature of outcomes. As already stated, these assumptions are motivational. That is, they initially determine a person's willingness to enter therapy and also provide the inclination toward effective involvement in the therapeutic process.

Social-role expectations are concealed in the patient's history of social roles and functions. A broad review of the patient's background, historical experiences, and social relationships is necessary to distill these types of expectations as they color the view of the psychotherapeutic process. It is important that the therapist have a familiarity with the response variations and outlooks likely to be associated with different sexual, age, ethnic, religious, socioeconomic, and educational backgrounds to help in ferreting out social role expectations. Nuclear family dynamics (structure, overt and covert rules, and attitudes) must also be discussed to understand patients' development of attitudes toward themselves and others.

Therapeutic involvement (as indicated by expressed motivation, compliance, commitment, and retention in treatment) will usually be enhanced if patients' preferences for therapist sex, age, and ethnicity are met and if they share some level of common cultural experiences. While these similarities may be implicated indirectly in treatment efficacy, they seem quite certainly to be implicated in the process of entering and staying in treatment (Bergin & Garfield, 1986). Because of the importance of congruence between patients' expected and experienced exposure to certain therapist attributes, therapeutic roles, and processes, when patients' expectations and preferences are disparate with treatment, the therapist has several choices in applying treatment. He or she may choose to modify treatment, refer the patient to someone else, shape or change the patient's expectations to be more consistent with what happens in therapy, or hope that the patient will come to adopt more compatible roles and expectations with time and experience.

As this would suggest, the relationship between therapist and patient backgrounds, expectations, and beliefs is important in determining the nature of the therapeutic relationship. Similarity of ethnic and social backgrounds increases the likelihood that the level of necessary correspondence exists between the views of patients and therapists about therapy and therapeutic process. Thus, whenever possible, it is advantageous to consider patient and therapist compatibility during treatment planning and to assign patients to therapists accordingly. At the same time, patients apparently look to therapists for different perspectives on aspects of interpersonal relationships, suggesting that some disparity of attitudes toward making and maintaining intimacy and friendships may also bear on therapist compatibility. When patient and therapist backgrounds and interpersonal attitudes "fit" or correspond, fewer treatment modifications may be necessary, thereby increasing the possibility of positive therapeutic outcome (Beutler, Crago, & Arizmendi, 1986).

It should be remembered that patient expectations are statelike. That is, they are dynamic and constantly changing with the confirming and disconfirming effect of each new experience. This requires the therapist to constantly assess the patient's expectations and alter interventions accordingly. While initially setting treatment formats and anticipated length to fit patient expectations is important for retaining patients in treatment, ongoing adaptation of the treatment to fit changing preferences and modified expectations will be likely to enhance treatment outcome. Therefore, therapists are well advised to give careful and close attention to the expressed wishes and desires of those whom they serve (Beutler & Clarkin, 1990).

Subjective distress and arousal. A long history of research on cognitive efficiency and coping suggests that arousal and distress can both motivate change and impair effective functioning, depending on their level. While mild to moderate distress appears to activate, orient one's response, and motivate engagement in activities that may alleviate distress, either very low or very high levels may impair the ability or willingness to attend, introduce either rigidity or inconsistency to problem-solving efforts, and result in ineffective engagement. Levels of distress reflect the patient's success in warding off stress. In this sense, they have been taken as indicators of a

person's ability to cope (Beutler & Clarkin, 1990). That is, a patient's distress level indicates how well coping methods work to keep him or her protected from anxiety. At extreme levels, distress may impair functioning, at low levels it may retard progress, and at moderate levels, it may provide focus and motivation to support and initiate change.

A patient's expectations and distress interact to produce his or her unique level of therapeutic motivation and compliance with treatment demands. In turn, the patient's motivation and compliance level set limitations on the type and degree of psychotherapeutic intervention accepted. Acceptance may be enhanced by the establishment of clear expectations, the encouragement of overtly explicit commitments to comply, and the provision of reasonable incentives.

It is also important to consider the patient's mood, intellectual level, orientation within the environment, cognitive efficiency, cognitive control of imaginal processes, affect and affective control, and intensity of experienced conflict during the assessment of subjective distress and problem severity. Evaluation of these dimensions informs decisions regarding the format and duration of treatment and directs the clinician in selecting the immediate goals of treatment and the intervention strategies to be used. The higher the distress, the more protection and support are required, both in selecting the setting and the frequency of treatment and in determining the methods of intervention to be used.

Traitlike Qualities

"Personality is a description of recurrent but dynamic patterns that are enacted in the face of new and often threatening experience rather than as a collection of static qualities" (Beutler & Clarkin, 1990, p. 66). The things we define as "personality" are usually restricted to those that are traitlike. That is, they endure across situations and are perceived as existing within the person rather than as being primarily determined by the situation. Beutler (1990) and Beutler and Clarkin (1990) have reviewed the many such dimensions that have been considered and have extracted those that seem to be most closely related to the selection of psychotherapy strategies and to the efficacy of specific psychotherapeutic interventions.

Among the many traitlike characteristics of patients that have been proposed to determine the efficacy of different interventions, problem complexity, interpersonal resistance or reactance, and coping ability are the most frequently studied. As with most of the variables and dimensions in this chapter, these three patient traits are interactive and reciprocal; however, convenience and clarity require that we treat them as separate aspects of response.

Problem complexity. One of the ways that patient problems are most distinctive in their relationship to the selection of psychotherapeutic goals is in their level of complexity. Some problems are primarily manifest in a single symptom cluster or in a well-defined set of evoking circumstances, while others cross environments, are made up of varied and often unrelated symptoms, and appear to represent complex recurrences or themes that characterize the person's life. Often the only similarity one can find in the events that evoke these recurrent themes is very abstract, suggesting that a symbolic rather than an objective similarity among situations provokes the onset of problems.

Another way of thinking about problem complexity is to view some problems as being statelike and others as traitlike in their manifestation. This distinction can be clarified by comparing the nature of complex problems to the concept of subjective distress discussed earlier. Subjective distress is a statelike quality and serves as an index of degree of acute impairment. In contrast, complex problems are more stable and less situation-specific than is level of arousal or distress. Indeed, complex problems are manifest by the traditional "neurotiform" behaviors characterized by symbolic (unconscious or preconscious) repetitive and unpleasant reenactments of previously cathected conflictual themes.

On the other hand, noncomplex problems are habitual, unidimensional, and transient in nature. These problems probably result from inadequate or faulty learning histories and are maintained by subjectively felt situational reward. Though more state- than traitlike, introducing the concept here emphasizes the importance of this distinction in selecting the long-term goals and objectives of treatment.

Comprehending how the symptoms developed and are maintained will provide clues to the nature and degree of problem complexity. A careful evaluation of patient predisposing variables will indicate if relatively enduring, repetitive, and symbolic manifestations of characterological struggles are at work or if transient, situation-specific, and unidimensional habitual patterns of behavior are present. This determination will provide a focus for symptomatic, conflictual, or combined therapeutic interventions.

Designating some problems as noncomplex in nature and others as dynamic efforts to resolve an unconscious struggle does not mean that treating one is any less difficult than treating the other. However, it does suggest that different paths to change may be necessary for these two types of problem presentation. Generally, complex problems indicate that outcomes should partially be judged by the resolution of thematic patterns rather than simply by symptom change. In contrast, the success of treating noncomplex problems can legitimately be assessed on the basis of symptom rather than life-style measures and criteria. Thus, intensive, long-term treatments are often indicated for complex problems (Freebury, 1984; Thorpe, 1987) while symptom-focused and short-term therapies are advocated for noncomplex problems.

To the degree that a patient presents with problems that have both complex and secondary reactive qualities, as occurs frequently, the treatment indicated may combine multiple goals. Beutler and Clarkin (1990) point out that since symptom-focused treatments are more rapid, cost efficient, and easy to apply, a convenient rule of thumb is to treat all problems as situational or noncomplex initially and until it becomes obvious that the problem supersedes situations and represents a recurrent interpersonal theme-of-life pattern.

Interpersonal reactance. Interpersonal reactance may be defined as one's sensitivity and resistance to the influence of others. As with problem complexity, this concept has both state- and traitlike features. While a person's tendency to resist influence may largely depend on the environmental circumstance and the relationship that he or she has with the one who is exerting the influence, most researchers (Brehm, 1986; Dowd & Pace, 1989; Shoham-Salomon, 1991) also emphasize that tolerance for external influence varies from person to person in a consistent and stable fashion.

Reactance is a concept extracted from the social psychology literature that has striking applications and parallels in clinical literature. In its clearest form, reactance represents not just a defense against, but an oppositional reaction to, authority. In psychotherapy it is parallel in meaning to the interpersonal (though not the intrapsychic) aspects of the concept of resistance (e.g., Barlow & Waddell, 1985). Essentially, reactance and therapeutic resistance as used here are measured by the degree to which one is disposed, by nature of personal traits, to engage in activities that resist the control of others, including a potential therapist.

Having a low tolerance for being controlled by others is a special problem for patients in psychotherapy since psychotherapy is inherently an experience that threatens one's sense of self-control. Mental health treatment often operates paradoxically by creating temporary dependence on the therapist in the service of encouraging ultimate disengagement and lasting independence.

Interpersonal reactance may prevent one from gratifying needs for nurturance, support, attachment, and social or interpersonal regard. Thus the balance between the need for attachment and the need for independence and autonomy may be disrupted in those who are highly reactant. Hence, whatever homeostasis is maintained through the adoption of defenses against the anxiety of either attachment or separation needs is likely to be unstable and excessive in these people. In the psychotherapy relationship itself, this instability may be manifest by withdrawal from treatment, failure to comply with treatment expectations, and resistance to improvement.

General patient reactance is best assessed via observing a patient's response to the demand characteristics of the therapy environment. Once this is observed, the therapist is well advised to counterbalance the patient's level of reactance with procedures that deemphasize the therapist's power and efforts to change the patient. The use of nondirective, supportive, self-management, and paradoxical interventions are examples of procedures that may serve this function. The appropriate adjustments in therapeutic strategy and specific interventions can be made by attending both to the traitlike and in-session or statelike aspects of patient reactance/resistance.

The careful reader will have noticed the interactive role of defensive behavior and interpersonal reactance. The patient's configuration of interpersonal, ritualized defensive styles of response provides the targets of conflict-oriented treatment strategies — the thematic focus.

Coping styles. Each person has his or her own unique configuration of defenses that can be partially described by a listing of specific defense mechanisms. These defense mechanisms have traditionally been considered to lie outside of conscious awareness. In addition, however, it is also apparent that people select and adopt certain behaviors in a conscious and thoughtful effort to adapt to stress and to avoid discomfort. Coping styles are the collection of conscious and unconscious methods a person uses both to manage anxiety or threat and to compensate for problems in everyday functioning.

Aside from threats from the environment, these constellations of behavior reflect dominant and relatively consistent behaviors that collectively constitute efforts to avoid either recognizing or confronting the contradictions in one's internal experience — opposing wishes, injunctions, contradictory values, unwanted impulses, and discordant beliefs — or even disconfirming information about valued beliefs and self-views (Beutler & Clarkin, 1990).

While much theory and research have been devoted to describing and distinguishing among various coping styles, most of this literature agrees that at least a good share of the variation among people in this characteristic can be defined as existing along a continuum ranging from internalizing to externalizing. Internalizing coping styles consist of the specific defense mechanisms of self-criticism, sensitization, and compartmentalization, while those associated with externalization include acting out, projection, and direct avoidance of threat (Miller & Eisenberg, 1988).

Patients with different styles of coping with threat will often require different treatments. An accumulating body of research has suggested that coping styles have particular implications for whether a therapist uses strategies that are designed to change cognitions and behaviors or to facilitate insight and awareness. We will see how this occurs as we describe the selection of specific strategies.

Environmental Variables

The third major category of patient predisposing variables are those that exist independently of the patient and that provide either sources of stress or of support. These are environmental variables and represent both the stressors and resources in the patient's present environment (e.g., personal support systems, work/school environments, family patterns, the setting or relationship in which dominant conflicts occur, and the social forces that apply pressure and support). These environmental qualities are important considerations that have etiologic and/or mediating/exacerbating significance for the development of a patient's symptoms and problems (e.g., Flaherty & Richman, 1986; Cohen & Sokolovsky, 1978; Horowitz, 1987).

Identification and evaluation of environmental characteristics of the patient's environment bear most directly on the selection of treatment context (mode/format, duration/frequency, and setting). Consideration of the patient's salient environment(s) can also help generate hypotheses about how circumstances and conditions may interact with other treatment-relevant variables to influence the treatment plan. That is, treatment settings and relationships constitute

environments that exist with varying degrees of similarity to the patient's usual environment. Assessment of the immediate family and family history can help provide insight into etiology and maintaining pathology as well as guidelines for what to avoid and what to recommend as a treatment setting to provide a corrective experience for the patient. A thorough history of common environments and social systems (sociodemographics) may also be relevant to predicting the likely compatibility of patient and therapist.

The relationship between diagnosable symptoms and types of family contextual stressors needs careful clinical assessment in the process of planning treatments. For example, some family members may manifest or directly contribute to a diagnosable condition in other family members, while others may discourage pathological or maladaptive responses. An assessment of a patient's family and social support systems will indicate how and if the symptomatic and non-symptomatic family members should be included as an integral part of the treatment plan. Moreover, expanding and enhancing sources of social support is critical in planning for long-term maintenance of gains.

Even diagnostically similar patients require distinctly different treatments, dependent in part on the nature of the family support system and the multicausality of psychological difficulties (e.g., Schulberg & McClelland, 1987). Beutler and Clarkin (1990) have emphasized this point in suggesting that "a functional analysis of similar symptoms will often reveal quite different causal patterns and every patient's unique strengths and family environment will serve as enabling or restraining conditions upon which to predict differential treatment responses" (p. 38).

Treatment context variables, relationship variables, and therapeutic interventions have been mentioned throughout this chapter. However, the roles of the several patient predisposing variables that we advocate assessing in order to answer treatment questions in psychological assessment can be further illustrated by brief but separate discussion of these domains of treatment decision making. This discussion may further clarify the relevance of patient assessment in treatment planning.

TREATMENT CONTEXT

Treatment Setting

Treatment settings range from inpatient to outpatient and differ in the degree to which the situation is monitored or unstructured. Most patients seeking psychological intervention present problems that are amenable to treatment in relatively unrestrictive settings, i.e., in the psychologist's office or in the natural environment in which the problems occur. However, patients exhibiting acute and serious symptoms, such as suicidal behavior or psychotic symptoms, require restrictive settings such as hospitals. Information obtained from the patient predisposing dimension determines the optimal setting (providing the most appropriate treatment with the least restriction).

The presence of a life-threatening condition, as represented both in the identification of the diagnosis and the availability of external supports, is an indicator for restrictive and structured treatment settings. When supports are available in the environment and when the condition is not life-threatening, decompensating, and endangering, less restrictive treatment options may be advantageously made available.

For example, Frances, Clarkin, and Perry (1984) observe that acute suicidal intent, self-destructive behaviors, or any condition that results in an inability to effectively manage independent living (e.g., schizophrenia, Alzheimer's disease, dementia, psychosis, severe major depression) would constitute indicators that might necessitate placement in restrictive settings. These authors propose that nonrestrictive settings are indicated for individuals who do not pose a threat to self or others and who maintain an acceptable level of general functioning. Most anxiety states, nonpsychotic depressions, simple phobias, dysfunctional family problems, and personality disorders are examples of indicators for nonrestrictive treatment settings.

Treatment Mode/Format

Treatment modes may be psychosocial (e.g., individual, group, marital and family therapy formats) and/or medical/somatic (e.g., chemotherapy, surgical procedures, or electroconvulsive therapy). Some patients may require a single treatment format while others may respond best to various format combinations. The nature and complexity of the presenting problem are the major determinants in the selection of treatment mode and format.

Psychosocial treatment formats are indicated for problems requiring behavioral, psychodynamic, and/or person-centered treatment strategies. Family/marital and group treatment formats fall under this rubric as well. Individual treatment formats are usually called for to alleviate complex (neurotiform) and noncomplex problems. Phobic avoidance, anxiety/panic disorders, depression, and personality disorders are examples of problems that may respond well to various individual treatment formats. Group therapy may be indicated for patients experiencing interpersonal conflicts. Support groups are specifically indicated for clients who can benefit from contact other persons with similar difficulties. Family/marital therapy is appropriate when the dyad or family unit is dysfunctional due to pathogenic interpersonal interactions. Family/marital therapy may be necessary when the dysfunction perpetuates undesirable symptoms or behaviors, e.g., when problematic alcohol consumption is the result of internalized negative affect.

Psychosocial treatments are usually contraindicated for problems typified by organicity, schizophrenia, or severe psychoses; however, psychosocial treatment formats may be quite helpful to family members or significant others who are responsible for the care of these severely impaired persons. Group therapy would be contraindicated when the patient does not possess adequate ego strength to withstand the powerful group dynamic. Of course, family/marital therapy is usually contraindicated whenever the presenting problem is not the result of, or maintained by, interactions between members in the dyad or unit.

Medical/somatic treatment formats are indicated for conditions requiring psychotropic medication, electroconvulsive therapy (ECT), and invasive procedures (i.e., injections, surgeries). An ECT format is often advocated for elderly patients with severe depression and delusions (Murphy & Macdonald, 1992). Psychotherapeutic drug formats may be indicated for various diagnoses, such as certain depressions, psychoses, anxiety disorders, and mania. Formats requiring invasive procedures are indicated less often; however, high surgical success rates with certain aberrant neuroanatomical anomalies (e.g., severe forms of epilepsy) may warrant such a format.

Medical treatment formats are contraindicated for problems in which the potential side effects or risks involved in drug therapy, ECT, or surgical procedures outweigh the potential benefits to the patient. For example, pharmacokinetic and pharmacodynamic unpredictability warrants careful consideration in matters where psychotropics are in question (e.g., many antidepressants induce postural hypotension, a potentially disastrous side effect in the elderly). The severity of the presenting problem(s), an awareness of various alternative medical and/or psychosocial treatments, and an evaluation of the indications or contraindications involved informs the course of action regarding medical-/somatic interventions from a patient cost-benefit perspective.

In certain cases, combined psychosocial and medical treatments are particularly effective. For example, a diagnosis of severe major depression may require pharmacotherapy or ECT to alleviate immediate symptoms (Murphy & Macdonald, 1992) and cognitive-behavioral interventions to produce greater improvement and reduce the probability of the depression recurring (Hollon & Beck, 1979).

Treatment Intensity

Treatment duration and frequency (i.e., the components of treatment intensity) are dictated by problem severity, problem complexity, and patient resources (Beutler & Clarkin, 1990;

Frances, Clarkin, & Perry, 1984). While there are no hard-and-fast rules regarding how patients will respond to various treatment intensities, research and accepted theory have provided some broad guidelines in the selection of treatment intensity.

Neurotiform or complex problems generally require long-term intensive treatments. Indicators for long-term intensive therapies include chronic conditions, such as bipolar disorder and schizophrenia (Beutler & Clarkin, 1990); recurring conditions, such as depression; and disorders of the self, such as narcissistic personality disorders (Kohut & Wolf, 1978). The patient's willingness to remain in therapy (Beutler & Clarkin, 1990) and income adequate to shoulder the cost are necessary conditions for long-term intensive treatments.

Short-term symptom-focused treatments are usually indicated for habitual patterns or noncomplex problems. Additional indicators for short-term treatments include minority status, low SES/formal education level (Baekeland & Lundwall, 1975; Garfield, 1986b) and the presence of somatic and externalized symptoms (Dubrin & Zastowny, 1988).

RELATIONSHIP VARIABLES

Relationship variables (demographic and interpersonal) either enhance or hinder the establishment and maintenance of the therapeutic alliance. Patient and therapist compatibility (among attributes and expectations) must be assessed, and treatment should be modified accordingly. It is the responsibility of the clinician to identify potential problems stemming from background or expectation incompatibility and to take the appropriate palliative steps. Attention to relationship variables will reduce interferences caused by incompatibilities, help the therapist overcome patient resistances, and enlist the client as an active participant in therapy.

The therapeutic relationship may be enhanced in many ways. Patient-therapist matching is one relationship-enhancing endeavor that requires the consideration of demographic similarity and interpersonal response patterns (i.e., interpersonal striving, personal beliefs, and attributions).

Important demographic characteristics include gender (Jones, Krupnick, & Kerig, 1987), age (Luborsky, Crits-Christoph, Alexander, Margolis, & Cohen, 1983), ethnicity (Jones, 1978), and socioeconomic background (Carkhuff & Pierce, 1967). These studies indicate that patient-therapist demographic similarity enhances perceptions and feelings regarding therapists and increases the likelihood that the therapeutic relationship and outcome will be perceived favorably.

Interpersonal response patterns may be conceptualized as enduring dispositions to action (Beutler & Clarkin, 1990). Observable behaviors, attitudes, beliefs, needs/striving, and habits make up one's repertoire of interpersonal response patterns. The response patterns of both therapist and patient interact to influence the therapeutic process. Dissimilarities among any aspects of patient-therapist response patterns are potential sources of conflict that may create barriers in the therapeutic process (Luborsky, 1984).

Practitioners should be aware of the patients with whom they work well and the patients they should refer to others. Dissimilarity in any single demographic or interpersonal response characteristic does not preclude successful therapeutic outcome; however, dissimilarities among several characteristics may prove problematic. Therapists should be aware of any potential conflicts and adjust themselves accordingly. When several dissimilarities between therapist and patient exist, it may be necessary to refer the patient elsewhere.

Role induction procedures can enhance the therapeutic relationship while enlisting the patient as an active participant in the therapeutic process. Role induction prepares the client for treatment; i.e., therapists educate clients in terms of therapeutic roles and outcomes before actual treatment per se. Patients may be educated with direct written or verbal information, pretherapy modeling (Truax & Carkhuff, 1967; Truax & Wargo, 1969), or therapeutic contracting (Beck, Rush, Shaw, & Emery, 1979).

Direct written or verbal information about the nature of therapy and the expected roles of patients can facilitate symptomatic change, strengthen the therapeutic alliance, and influence the establishment of positive feelings about treatment (Turkat, 1979; Mayerson, 1984; Zwick & Attkisson, 1985). Of course, written and/or verbal fluency is a must for these procedures to be effective.

Pretherapy modeling helps to develop skills that facilitate treatment response. Videotapes (Truax & Carkhuff, 1967; Truax & Wargo, 1969) and films (Mayerson, 1984, Wilson, 1985) have been used to model appropriate treatment behaviors and representative sessions with positive results. That is, dropout rates decreased and therapeutic involvement and outcome was enhanced.

Therapeutic contracting is a role induction method involving agreements between the client and therapist regarding treatment. The content contained in therapeutic contracts varies; however, some important ingredients have been identified (Beutler & Clarkin, 1990); i.e., contracts should contain (1) explicit time limits for treatment (or contract renewals and progress evaluations); (2) treatment goals; (3) therapist and patient roles; and (4) consequences of failing to comply with the terms of the contract.

STRATEGIES AND TECHNIQUES

The selection of appropriate psychotherapeutic strategies and techniques should take place after evaluating patient predisposing variables, considering treatment contextual elements (implications and ramifications), and developing a working relationship.

Wide-ranging, complex problems (neurotiform) require conflict-oriented treatments of great breadth and intensity (duration and frequency). Psychotherapeutic procedures target unconscious motivations and wishes when treating neurotiform problems. Simple, unidimensional problems indicate symptom-focused, narrow-breadth, short-term treatments. Overt behaviors are the major targets for psychotherapeutic interventions when unidimensional problems are treated.

The presence of neurotiform problems indicates a need to achieve the resolution of internal conflicts. "Recurrent symptom patterns that have long since departed from their original and adaptive form, that are evoked in environments that bear little relationship to the originally evoking situations, or which exist with little evidence of specific, external reinforcers, represent complex symptom patterns indicative of underlying conflict" (Beutler & Clarkin, 1990, p. 226). Complex problems require therapeutic interventions and strategies with conflict-oriented foci; i.e., psychodynamic or other insight-oriented intensive therapies.

Patients presenting with unidimensional (noncomplex) problems require therapies that focus on symptomatic change. Identifying characteristics of noncomplex problems include isolated symptoms (i.e., environment-specific and environment-reinforced) that are easily traced or related to their original adaptive form and etiology. Unidimensional problems often respond well to cognitive-behavioral short-term therapies.

In sum, the goals and strategies/interventions of treatment may be conflict- or symptom-focused depending on the complexity of the presenting problem(s). The specific nature of the intended therapeutic outcome and strategies/interventions depends on the unique circumstances and complaints surrounding the problem(s). Specific treatment activities and techniques may be chosen to accommodate the patient's defensive style. The quality of therapeutic transactions should be monitored and present patient reactance levels should partially govern the selection and use of techniques.

Levels of patient arousal and activity can be therapeutically managed to maximize positive treatment results. This technique facilitates successful outcome with both conflictual (complex) or symptomatic (noncomplex) problems by encouraging self-observation, cognitive reorganization, and disconfirmation of pathognomic beliefs. Therapeutic arousal may be introduced through confrontation, empty-chair techniques, directed fantasies, analysis of transference and defenses, interpretation, silence, and questions. Therapeutic arousal may be decreased with breathing control procedures, attention to somatic sensations, cognitive control strategies, reflection, reassurance, advice and teaching, relaxation and distraction, and managed exposure (e.g., Rapee, 1987).

Optimal levels of therapeutic arousal depend on patient reactance level (which varies across time, situations, and patients); however, some general indicators and contraindicators in the regulation of arousal level have been identified (Blau, 1988). Patients who exhibit high levels of resistance (reactance) to therapist interventions require the use of relatively unintrusive therapeutic techniques, such as encouragement, empathic reflection, unconditional positive regard, and restatement. Patients who are moderately secure in therapy and exhibiting intermediate levels of reactance will generally benefit from moderately intrusive interventions, such as structuring, direct questions, exploring feelings, setting limits, and providing guidance and advice. Intensive probing interventions, such as analysis of resistance and transference, confrontation of behaviors and fears, dream analysis, guided fantasy, and magnification of patient or therapist gestures, are indicated only with patients who are very secure with the therapist.

Coping style (one's conscious and unconscious pattern of defense against internal conflicts) must also be considered when selecting appropriate therapeutically arousing interventions. To date, a plethora of studies in diverse populations have suggested that this may be among the more powerful predictors of differential response to various types or models of psychotherapy. For example, Sloane and colleagues (Sloane, Staples, Cristol, Yorkston, & Whipple, 1975) were among the first to observe, in a post hoc analysis, that patients whose MMPI profiles were weighted toward indicators of behavioral acting out, impulsivity, and aggression were more likely to respond to behavior therapies than to psychoanalytic ones. In contrast, those whose MMPIs were marked by anxiety, self-criticism, and social withdrawal were found to be more responsive to psychoanalytic than behavioral therapies. Beutler and Mitchell (1981) found a similar interaction effect in a correlational study of therapists who held experiential, dynamic, and behavioral allegiances. Such findings led Beutler (1983) to propose that patients who were characterized by "externalizing" coping styles and those who were characterized by "internalizing" coping styles were likely to show a differential response to insight-oriented and behavior-change therapies.

In more systematic studies of this proposition among groups of anxious and depressed patients, Beutler and his colleagues (Beutler, Engle, Mohr, Daldrup, Bergan, Meredith, & Merry, 1991; Beutler, Machado, Engle, & Mohr, 1993; Beutler, Mohr, Grawe, Engle, & MacDonald, 1991; Calvert, Beutler, & Crago, 1988) conducted a series of prospective and comparison studies of this proposition with consistent findings in support of the hypothesis. These findings complement those obtained in controlled clinical trials research conducted in other laboratories and with other populations (e.g., Cooney, Kadden, Litt, & Getter, 1991; Kadden, Cooney, Getter, & Litt, 1990). Collectively, these studies suggest that patient coping style may be an important variable to consider when assigning one to various types of psychotherapy.

SUMMARY

Questions regarding diagnosis, prognosis, current level of functioning, most effective treatment, and causation/maintenance are answerable through an evaluation of relevant patient predisposing variables.

In matters of conventional diagnosis, the clinician must determine the degree to which signs and symptoms fit a defined syndrome. The *Diagnostic and Statistical Manual of Mental Disorders* (DSM-IV) provides a fairly comprehensive guide for conventional diagnostic classification. Clinical skill and experience in the selection and use of formal and informal diagnostic measures facilitates this determination.

Questions about prognosis ordinarily require an evaluation of problem chronicity, personality/defensive style, problem complexity, and environmental circumstances. In some cases an exploration of available and acceptable environmental/behavioral patient alternatives may be necessary. An assessment of the appropriate patient predetermining variables will elicit the information needed to answer these types of questions.

A patient's current level of functioning may be assessed in a variety of ways; however, only a few will be relevant to the specific situation or problem prompting the assessment. Generally, an evaluation for present level of functioning involves formal and informal measures of cognitive ability and/or a determination of problem severity. In some cases, diagnosis, personality, and problem complexity may be relevant in light of the presenting problem and/or patient circumstances.

Treatment questions are best answered through a comprehensive evaluation of the relevant patient predisposing variables; e.g., diagnosis, personality/defensive style, coping ability, problem complexity, problem severity, environmental circumstances, and level of functional impairment. A comprehensive, meaningful, and clear clinical picture must be rendered before treatment questions can be answered competently.

Questions regarding causation (i.e., etiology and maintenance) may require an assessment of environmental circumstances, prior treatment history, family and personal history, current relationships, personality, and medical status and history. The patient's unique circumstances and diagnosis coupled with the specificity of the referral question will determine the patient variables that must be explored in order to answer these question types.

The questions confronting clinicians during referral or treatment planning may be answered through an assessment of patient predisposing variables. Referral questions, once properly specified, may be answered competently by focusing on the appropriate patient variables. In matters of treatment planning, a comprehensive treatment model (an integration of the information gathered from the patient predisposing dimension) facilitates the sequential consideration of the remaining treatment variables and the hierarchical selection of appropriate interventions.

Patients are unique, and their problems, defensive styles, treatment expectations, and environmental conditions are unique as well. Idiosyncratic patient qualities and novel circumstances represent unique psychotherapeutic needs that necessarily require treatment plans crafted to fit the individual. Each patient must be evaluated comprehensively and frequently for therapy to be effective and efficient. Indeed, every patient predisposing variable has treatment ramifications, and it is professionally irresponsible to treat patients without consideration of these therapeutically relevant variables.

ACKNOWLEDGMENT

Work on this chapter was partially supported by NIAAA grant no. RO1–AA 08970 to the first author.

REFERENCES

Baekeland, F., & Lundwall, M. A. (1975). Dropping out of treatment: A critical review. *Psychological Bulletin, 82*, 738–783.

Barlow, D. H., & Waddell, M. T. (1985) Agoraphobia. In D. H. Barlow (Ed.), *Clinical handbook of psychological disorders: A step-by-step treatment manual* (pp. 1–68). New York: Guilford Press.

Beck, A. T., Rush, A. J., Shaw, B. F., & Emery, G. (1979). *Cognitive Therapy of Depression.* New York: Guilford Press.

Beutler, L. E. (1983). *Eclectic psychotherapy: A systematic approach.* Elmsford, NY: Pergamon.

Beutler, L. E. (1989). Differential treatment selection: The role of diagnosis in psychotherapy. *Psychotherapy, 26*, 271–281.

Beutler, L. E., & Bergan, J. (1991). Value change in counseling and psychotherapy: A search for scientific credibility. *Journal of Counseling Psychology, 38*, 16–24.

Beutler, L. E., & Clarkin, J. (1990). *Systematic treatment selection: Toward targeted therapeutic interventions.* New York: Brunner/Mazel.

Beutler, L. E., Crago, M., & Arizmendi, T. G. (1986). Therapist variables in psychotherapy process and outcome. In S. L. Garfield & A. E. Bergin (Eds.), *Handbook of psychotherapy and behavior change* (3rd ed., pp. 257–310). New York: Wiley.

Beutler, L. E., Engle, D., Mohr, D., Daldrup, R. J., Bergan, J., Meredith, K., & Merry, W. (1991). Predictors of differential and self directed psychotherapeutic procedures. *Journal of Consulting and Clinical Psychology, 59*, 333–340.

Beutler, L. E., Machado, P. P. P., Engle, D., & Mohr, D. (1993). Differential patient X treatment maintenance of treatment effects among cognitive, experiential, and self-directed psychotherapies. *Journal of Psychotherapy Integration, 3*, 15–31.

Beutler, L. E., & Mitchell, R. (1981). Psychotherapy outcome in depressed and impulsive patients as a function of analytic and experiential treatment procedures. *Psychiatry, 44*, 297–306.

Beutler, L. E., Mohr, D. C., Grawe, K., Engle, D., & MacDonald, R. (1991). Looking for differential effects: Cross-cultural predictors of differential psychotherapy efficacy. *Journal of Psychotherapy Integration, 1*, 121–142.

Blau, T. H. (1988). *Psychotherapy tradecraft: The technique and style of doing therapy.* New York: Brunner/Mazel.

Calvert, S. J., Beutler, L. E., & Crago, M. (1988). Psychotherapy outcome as a function of therapist-patient matching on selected variables. *Journal of Social and Clinical Psychology, 6*, 104–117.

Carkhuff, R. R., & Pierce, R. (1967). Differential aspects of therapist race and social class upon patient depth of self-exploration in the initial clinical interview. *Journal of Consulting Psychology, 31*, 632–634.

Clarkin, J. D., & Hurt, S. W. (1988). Psychological assessment: Tests and rating scales. In J. A. Talbot, R. E. Hales, & S. C. Yudofsky (eds.), *Textbook of psychiatry.* Washington, DC: American Psychiatric Press.

Cooney, N. L., Kadden, R. M., Litt, M. D., & Getter, H. (1991). Matching alcoholics to coping skills or interactional therapies: Two-year follow-up results. *Journal of Consulting and Clinical Psychology, 59*, 598–601.

Dubrin, J. R., & Zastowny, T. R. (1988). Predicting early attrition from psychotherapy: An analysis of a large private-practice cohort. *Psychotherapy, 25*, 393–408.

Frances, A., Clarkin, J., & Perry, S. (1984). *Differential therapeutics in psychiatry.* New York: Brunner/Mazel.

Freebury, M. B. (1984). The prescription of psychotherapy. *Canadian Journal of Psychiatry, 29*, 499–503.

Garfield, S. L. (1986). Research on client variables in psychotherapy. In S. L. Garfield & A. E. Bergin (Eds.), *Handbook of psychotherapy and behavior change* (3rd ed., pp. 213–256). New York: Wiley.

Hollon, S. D., & Beck, A. T. (1979). Cognitive therapy of depression. In P. E. Kendall & S. D. Hollon (Eds.), *Cognitive-behavioral interventions: Theory, research, procedures* (pp. 153–202). New York: Academic Press.

Jones, E. E. (1978). Effects of race on psychotherapy process and outcome: An exploratory investigation. *Psychotherapy: Theory, Research and Practice, 15*, 226–236.

Jones, E. E., Krupnick, J. L., & Kerig, P. K. (1987). Some gender effects in brief psychotherapy. *Psychotherapy, 24*, 336–352.

Kadden, R. M., Cooney, N. L., Getter, H., & Litt, M. D. (1990). Matching alcoholics to coping skills or interactional therapies: Posttreatment results. *Journal of Consulting and Clinical Psychology, 57*, 698–704.

Kohut, H., & Wolf, E. S. (1978). The disorders of the self and their treatment: An outline. *International Journal of Psychoanalysis, 59*, 413–425.

Lorion, R. P., & Felner, R. D. (1986). Research on psychotherapy with the disadvantaged. In S. L. Garfield & A. E. Bergin (Eds.), *Handbook of psychotherapy and behavior change* (3rd ed., pp. 739–776). New York: John Wiley.

Luborsky, L. (1984). *Principles of psychoanalytic psychotherapy: A manual for supportive-expressive treatment.* New York: Basic Books.

Luborsky, L., Crits-Christoph, P., Alexander, L., Margolis, M., & Cohen, M. (1983). Two helping alliance methods for predicting outcomes of psychotherapy: A counting signs vs. a global rating method. *Journal of Nervous and Mental Disease, 171*, 480–491.

Mayerson, N. H. (1984). Preparing clients for group

therapy: A critical review and theoretical formulation. *Clinical Psychology Review, 4*, 191–213.

Miller, P. A., & Eisenberg, N. (1988). The relation of empathy to aggressive and externalizing/antisocial behavior. *Psychological Bulletin, 103*, 324–344.

Murphy, E., & Macdonald, A. (1992). Affective disorders in old age. *Handbook of Affective Disorders*, 601–618.

Rapee, R. (1987). The psychological treatment of panic attacks: Theoretical conceptualization and review of evidence. *Clinical Psychology Review, 7*, 427–438.

Schulberg, H. C., & McClelland, M. (1987). Depression and physical illness: The prevalence, causation, and diagnosis of comorbidity. *Clinical Psychology Review, 7*, 145–167.

Sloane, R. B., Staples, F. R., Cristol, A. H., Yorkston, N. J., & Whipple, K. (1975). *Psychotherapy versus behavior therapy.* Cambridge MA: Harvard University Press.

Thorpe, S. A. (1987). An approach to treatment planning. *Psychotherapy, 24*, 729–735.

Truax, C. B., & Carkhuff, R. R. (1967). *Toward effective counseling and psychotherapy: Training and practice.* Chicago: Aldine.

Truax, C. B., & Wargo, D. G. (1969). Effects of vicarious therapy pretraining and alternate sessions on outcome in group psychotherapy with outpatients. *Journal of Consulting and Clinical Psychology, 33*, 440–447.

Turkat, D. M. (1979). Psychotherapy preparatory communications: Influences upon patient role expectations. *Dissertation Abstracts International, 39*, 4059B.

Wilson, D. O. (1985). The effects of systematic client preparation, severity, and treatment setting on dropout rate in short-term psychotherapy. *Journal of Social and Clinical Psychology, 3*, 62–70.

Zwick, R., & Attkisson, C. C. (1985). Effectiveness of a client pretherapy orientation videotape. *Journal of Counseling Psychology, 32*, 514–524.

7

How to Use Computer-Based Reports

James N. Butcher

Over three decades have now passed since the first computer was programmed to interpret a psychological test, the original version of the MMPI, at the Mayo Clinic (Rome, Swenson, Mataya, McCarthy, Pearson, Keating, & Hathaway, 1962). Today computers have become an indispensable partner in psychological assessment in health care, forensic, mental health, and other settings. Computers can be used to aid the psychological practitioner in a number of ways in performing clinical evaluations. For example, they can be used to administer test items, to rapidly score and profile test results, and even to interpret test scores and generate a complex, sophisticated report that describes and classifies problems. Moreover, the use of the computer, with its extensive memory and rapid combination capability, allows the psychologist to synthesize vast amounts of information and provide interpretations related to very complex tasks such as determining prognosis and treatment planning.

This chapter will address several facets of using computer-based psychological test reports. First, the rationale and value of using computer-based reports will be explored. Then important factors to consider in selecting a computer testing service will be described and illustrated. Next, the clinical use of one computer-based test report, the Minnesota Report for the MMPI-2, will be described. In this example, the use of the MMPI-2 in providing test feedback to clients in psychological treatment will be illustrated. After this practical case example is described, the use of computer reports in forensic testimony will be explored. Finally, this chapter concludes with an examination of several possible problems with computer-based psychological test reports.

VALUES OF USING COMPUTER-BASED PSYCHOLOGICAL TESTS IN CLINICAL ASSESSMENT

Several reasons can be found for the widespread use of computer-based objective test interpretation in clinical assessment. First, computer-based interpretation systems can usually provide a more comprehensive and objective summary of relevant test-based hypotheses than the clinical practitioner has the time and resources to develop. In interpreting profiles, a computer will attend to all relevant scores and not ignore or fail to consider important information, as sometimes happens when human beings face a large array of complicated information. Computer-assisted test interpretations are usually more thorough and better documented than those typically derived by clinical assessment procedures.

Second, use of computer-based test results avoids or minimizes subjectivity in selecting and emphasizing interpretive material. Biasing factors, such as halo effects, can creep into less structured procedures such as the clinical interview. The computer can carry out the "look-up and combining function" involved in test interpretation in an unbiased manner compared with most human interpreters.

Third, computer-based psychological test results can be obtained quite rapidly, thereby being available for the clinician to use in early clinical sessions. One can often have a summary of test results within minutes of the time the client has completed the testing. The summary information, as we will discuss later, can actually be used in the initial clinical contact with the client instead of a week or two later, as was common for psychological test evaluations in the precomputer era.

Fourth, computer interpretation systems are considered to be almost completely reliable; that is, always produce the same results on the same set of scores.

Finally, a broad range of computer-based assessment services are available for the practitioner to incorporate into his or her practice. Generally, the practitioner can have a great deal of confidence in most commercially available test scoring and interpretation programs, since the testing industry usually maintains high standards for computerized assessment. In his review of computerized psychological assessment programs, Bloom (1992) concluded that "The very high level of professional vigilance over test administration and interpretation software undoubtedly accounts for the fact that computerized assessment programs have received such high marks" (p. 172).

SELECTION OF A TEST SCORING AND INTERPRETATION SERVICE

Many factors will determine which of the commercially available computer scoring and interpretation services best fit one's assessment needs. Foremost in the decision, of course, will be whether a particular test interpretation company provides the range and quality of test scoring and interpretation services that are needed. Testing services are usually dedicated to particular tests and not others. There are no test interpretation companies that offer all tests that a practitioner might wish to use in his or her practice. Some services have limited publication or distribution arrangements and are unable to provide scoring of some tests due to copyright restrictions. For example, a company might not have permission to computer score the scales contained on a test yet it might offer computer-based interpretive reports. In such cases, the tests must be scored manually and the scale scores entered into the computer to obtain interpretations. It is important for the practitioner to assure that the testing company has the type of data-processing option that the practitioner needs. Inquiries need to be made about the exact nature of the test scoring and processing options provided.

The methods of computer test data processing that practitioners can employ are varied. The following are several possible data-entry methods that the practitioner might consider in deciding which computer service option best fits his or her practice requirements:

Mail-in service. The oldest type of scoring and interpretation service commercially available is the mail-in test-processing option. For the most part, this service is provided to practitioners who have limited in-house computer facilities or who may process large numbers of tests in batches. The tests in this scoring option are usually administered to clients in a paper-and-pencil format. The answer sheets are then mailed to the testing service for processing.

In-office computer processing. If the practitioner has a computer available for test processing, there are several test processing options to consider. First, a computer program to administer the items on-line might be available. In this situation, the client is presented the items on a TV screen and endorses them by typing his or her answers on the computer keyboard. A second scoring option involves administering the items using the paper-and-pencil form and key-entering the items into the computer—a procedure that usually takes a clerical assistant about ten minutes for key-entering an inventory the length of the MMPI-2. A third approach to response processing involves administering the items using the paper-and-pencil version of the test with an optically readable answer form. The practitioner or a staff member would process the answer sheet by using an optical scanner, a type of copier that reads blackened marks directly into a computer. The optical scanner usually costs an additional three or four thousand dollars in addition to the cost of the computer. However, this procedure is considered to be quite cost effective if about eight or more tests are administered in a week.

Data telephone transmission. The in-office computer can also be used to connect to the test-scoring service by modem. The test answers, once they are read into a computer file, can be transmitted by data phone to the test interpretation service for processing. The results are usually returned immediately by computer.

Fax processing option. This approach to test scoring is becoming popular now that many offices have fax machines. In using the fax machine as a test-processing option, the practitioner does not need a computer. This option is relatively simple: the practitioner simply administers the test using the paper-and-pencil format and faxes the answer sheet to the test-scoring company for processing. In terms of simplicity, this procedure is similar to the older mail-in service option described above except that there is usually immediate turnaround of the report.

Several questions to consider in selecting a computer-based test interpretation service to process psychological tests are outlined in Table 7.1.

This chapter will focus on practical considerations in using one type of computer-based psychological test interpretive report that is widely used in clinical evaluation settings. The case illustration, to be described below, will involve the MMPI-2 since the MMPI and its derivatives have been the most widely used clinical instrument in most settings (Lubin, Larsen, & Matarazzo, 1984; Piotrowski & Keller, 1989)

TABLE 7.1. Questions to Consider in Evaluating the Adequacy of Computerized Psychological Testing Services

- Does the test on which the computer interpretation system is based have an adequate network of established validity research?
- Do the system developers have the requisite experience with the particular test(s) to provide reliable, valid information?
- Is there a sufficient amount of documentation available on the system of interest? Is there a published user's guide to explain the test and system variables?
- Is the system flexible enough to incorporate new information as it becomes available? How frequently is the system revised to incorporate new empirical data on the test?
- Was the interpretation system developed following the APA guidelines for computer-based tests?
- Do the reports contain a sufficient evaluation of potentially invalidating response conditions?
- How closely does the system conform to empirically validated test correlates? Is it possible to determine from the outputs whether the reports are consistent with interpretive strategies and information from published resources on the test?
- Does the company providing computer interpretation services have a qualified technical staff to deal with questions or problems?
- Are the reports sufficiently annotated to indicate appropriate cautions?

and have the most extensive history of computer adaptation for a psychological test. The idea of computer-based MMPI-2 (MMPI) interpretation is based on the view that tests can more effectively be interpreted in an actuarial manner than through clinical interpretation strategies (See Meehl, 1954). A report made up of objectively applied personality and clinical symptom descriptions that have been established for the test scales or patterns can be more accurately combined by machine than reports derived by clinical means. For the most part, computer-generated clinical reports can be viewed as predetermined or "canned" statements that are applied to individuals who obtain particular psychological test scores. The statements or paragraphs contained in the computerized report, which is often in narrative form, are stored in computer memory and automatically retrieved to match a case when it meets particular scale elevations, profile types, or scale indices. The behavioral correlate information for MMPI-2 scales and code types can be found in a number of sources (see Butcher & Williams, 1992; Graham, 1990; Butcher, Graham, Williams, & Ben-Porath, 1990; Gilberstadt & Duker, 1963; Lewandowski & Graham, 1972; and Marks, Seeman, & Haller, 1975). Computer interpretation requires that test scores be used to access appropriate specific symptoms, behaviors, etc., that are stored in the computer.

The actuarial combination of data from the MMPI-2 scales has been well established. However, empirical research has not provided correlates for all possible scale combinations. Consequently, no MMPI or MMPI-2 interpretation system is fully actuarial. Rather, some interpretations will be based on expert conclusions about the meaning of and the interpretation strategy for single scale scores. The term "automated clinician" more accurately describes the computer-based interpretive systems available, since they are based to some extent on clinical judgment as well as pure actuarial data (Fowler, 1969). The validity of an automated test report will depend on the extent of replicable personality information available on the psychological test on which the interpretive system is based. The validity of the computerized system will also depend on how closely the developer of the system has conformed to the actuarial data and whether clearly replicated correlates have been used to develop descriptors.

There is some debate about how computer-based reports are to be incorporated in the clinical assessment (Fowler & Butcher, 1986; Garb, 1992; Matarazzo, 1986; Rubenzer, 1991). It is important that computerized interpretive reports be used in conjunction with other clinical information about the patient obtained from other sources. Automated MMPI-2 clinical reports are designed for use by professionals who are knowledgeable in the interpretive background of the MMPI-2.

CLINICAL USE OF A COMPUTERIZED MMPI-2 REPORT

In this section, the use of a computer-based test report in pretreatment planning will be illustrated. The MMPI-2 has been used extensively in assessing patients in pretreatment psychological evaluation. Potential therapy patients are administered the MMPI-2 early in the treatment process or before therapy begins. The therapist, or in some cases the clinician evaluating the client in pretreatment planning, may also conduct a test feedback session with the client. In the test feedback session, the individual's test-taking attitudes and their implication for appraising treatment motivation and readiness for therapy can be discussed. The extent and character of the individual's problems, symptoms, etc., can be described. Finally, recommendations and predictions about prognosis for resolving problems can be explored with potential strategies for problem resolution suggested. This approach to providing MMPI-2 feedback in pretreatment planning has been discussed in more detail by Butcher (1990).

Before presenting MMPI-2 results to clients, several factors need to be taken into account. First, the current psychological status of the client receiving the feedback information needs to be appraised. In providing test information, the clinician needs to assess the capacity of the client to understand and utilize the information. For example, the process requires that the client have sufficient reality contact and a "receptive" attitude toward the session in order to be able to understand and integrate the test information accurately. The client's level of intellectual functioning and educational background also need to be considered. For example, if the client is intelligent and well educated, more specific and detailed information can be discussed than if the individual is less well educated or less capable intellectually. The presentation should be varied to suit the individual's general fund of information. The type of setting in which the test was given is an important variable to take into account. Published sources such as Butcher and Williams (1992), Graham (1993), and Greene (1991) contain information about relevant MMPI-2 scale descriptors for varied groups.

Steps in Providing Test Feedback to Clients

The following suggestions (Butcher, 1990) might serve as a useful strategy for providing test feedback to clients in pretreatment planning:

Step one. It is usually useful to establish the credibility and objectivity of the MMPI-2 in the patient's mind by providing some historical information about the instrument: for example, the fact that the test has been used for over fifty years; that it is the most widely used psychological test in the United States today (see Lubin, Larsen, & Matarazzo, 1984; Piotrowski & Keller, 1989); and that it is the most widely used personality instrument around the world, with over 150 translations and broad use in over 45 countries.

Step two. Briefly describe how the scales were developed and highlight the extent of empirical validation research among diverse groups of clients. It is usually helpful to have the client look at his or her own profiles as the test scales are being described.

Step three. Briefly describe how the validity indicators work on the MMPI-2 to provide a picture of the person's approach to the testing—whether they were defensive and inaccessible or were exaggerating their symptoms. Focus on how the client might have presented himself or herself and how he or she is viewing the problem situation at this time. The individual's motivation for being understood can be explored through their approach to the validity measures.

Step four. Explain the likely meanings of their highest ranging clinical scores in terms of prevailing attitudes, symptoms, problem areas, etc. Avoid using psychological jargon by translating technical words into language the person can understand.

Step five. Discuss any clinically significant scale elevations on the MMPI-2 Content Scales (See Butcher et al., 1990). These measures are especially useful in providing test feedback to clients since they represent "messages" or communication from the client to the therapist. The Content Scales are viewed as direct disclosures of problems, attitudes, beliefs, or symptoms that the client has endorsed. The meanings of these scale elevations are usually intuitively apparent to the client since he or she has openly endorsed them.

Step six. Allow the client to ask questions about his or her scores, and clear up any points of concern he or she might have about the interpretations. If the client has become fixated on an inconsequential, trivial, or incorrect point, the clinician has an opportunity to correct it at this point.

Step seven. Discuss how the client feels the test characterizes his or her problems. One way of promoting this discussion is to ask the client to summarize the feedback that has been given to him or her. The clinician can then evaluate whether there are elements of the test interpretation that were particularly surprising to or that were misunderstood by the client. The exchange of information during the feedback session often provides excellent material to incorporate into treatment as well as giving the therapist further information about the client's openness to insight and amenability to changing behavior.

MMPI-2 Feedback as an Intervention

What effect does test feedback have on the patient's behavior and adjustment? Finn and Tonsager (1992) recently showed that the test feedback process itself can be a powerful clinical intervention. They conducted a clinical study in which one group of patients from a therapy waiting list (N = 32) was provided MMPI-2 test feedback according to a model developed by Finn (1990). The second group of patients (N 29) from the waiting list was administered the MMPI-2 but not given test feedback. The results of the study were very informative: individuals who were provided feedback on their MMPI-2, compared with the control group, showed a significant decline in reported symptoms and an increase in measured self-esteem. Finn and Tonsager reported:

This study provides support for the therapeutic impact of sharing MMPI-2 test results verbally with college age clients. Clients who completed an MMPI-2 and later heard their MMPI-2 test results reported a significant increase in their self-esteem immediately following the feedback session, an increase that continued to grow over the 2-week follow-up period. In addition, after hearing their MMPI-2 test results, clients showed a significant decrease in their symptomatic distress, and distress continued to decline during the subsequent 2-week period. Last, compared with clients receiving attention only from the examiner, clients who completed the MMPI-2 and received a feedback session showed more hopefulness about their problems immediately following the feedback session, and this persisted at the final follow-up. (p. 284)

The results of this study suggest that psychological test results can be effectively used as a direct therapeutic intervention. We now turn to a discussion of a case in which the MMPI-2 was administered and used in the pretreatment planning evaluation.

Case History

The patient, a forty-six-year old department-store sales manager, was initially referred to the medical clinic by her supervisor because she had been absent for work on numerous occasions in recent months. In the medical examination she told the doctor that she would like to get treatment for her severe headaches and fatigue that she felt were causing her to miss a lot of work. She also complained about an "inability to sleep and general restlessness." She indicated to the doctor that she had been going through a lot of stress lately after a break-up of a long-term relationship. In her medical examination, the doctor began to suspect that many of her symptoms were psychological and referred her to see the staff psychologist.

In the psychological examination she was interviewed by the clinical psychologist and administered the MMPI-2 after the initial session. The patient had been divorced by her husband five years earlier after he discovered that she had

been having an affair with a prominent man in the community. Her husband had been given custody of their two teenage children, who were now grown and living independently. The patient did not seek custody at the time of the divorce. She has had no relationship with her former husband during the past five years and sees the two children only every few months.

During the hour-and-thirty-minute session with the psychologist, the patient said that she was undergoing a great deal of stress in recent months over the breakup of a long-time relationship with a man whom she had been seeing for several years. She expressed considerable anger over the breakup of the relationship and reported that she was experiencing many physical problems and lately was having difficulty at times making it to work when she felt weak or tired. She also indicated that she had been drinking more since the breakup; however, she did not feel that alcohol was a big problem for her. A follow-up session was planned for two days later.

MMPI-2 Profiles and Report

The MMPI-2 validity scale pattern is shown in Figure 7.1, the clinical and supplemental profile in Figure 7.2, and the MMPI-2 content scale profile in Figure 7.3. The computer-based narrative report is shown in Figure 7.4.

Follow-up Interview and Test Feedback Session

The second interview with the psychologist began with the psychologist asking the client if anything important to her situation had occurred since her last visit to the clinic. He also asked whether she had any questions about the previous session before discussing the results of the testing.

In structuring the feedback session, the psychologist was aware (from the MMPI-2 Report) of the possibility that she might be reluctant to accept personality-test feedback as a result of her general mistrust and tendency to blame others

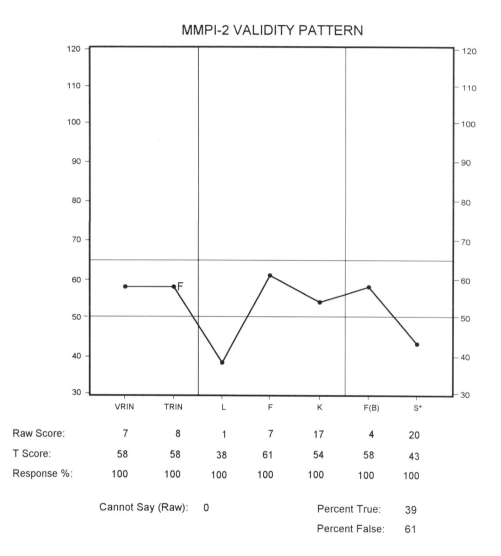

	VRIN	TRIN	L	F	K	F(B)	S*
Raw Score:	7	8	1	7	17	4	20
T Score:	58	58	38	61	54	58	43
Response %:	100	100	100	100	100	100	100

Cannot Say (Raw): 0

Percent True: 39
Percent False: 61

*Experimental

FIGURE 7.1. MMPI-2 validity scale profile for a 46-year-old department store manager.

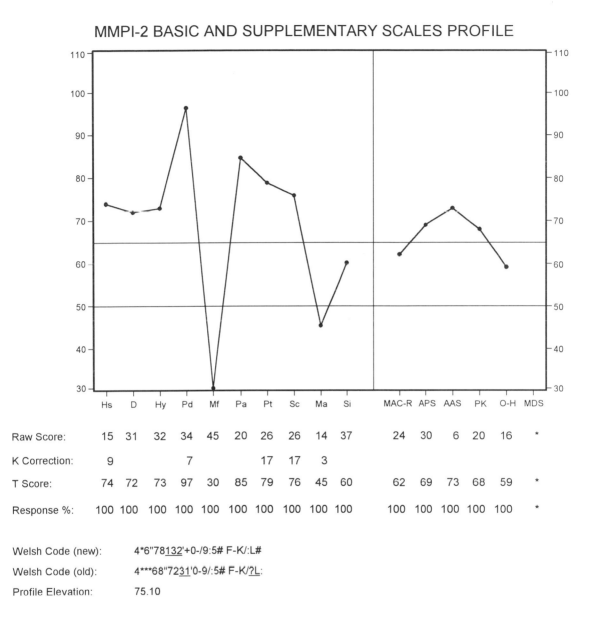

MMPI-2 BASIC AND SUPPLEMENTARY SCALES PROFILE

	Hs	D	Hy	Pd	Mf	Pa	Pt	Sc	Ma	Si		MAC-R	APS	AAS	PK	O-H	MDS
Raw Score:	15	31	32	34	45	20	26	26	14	37		24	30	6	20	16	*
K Correction:	9			7			17	17	3								
T Score:	74	72	73	97	30	85	79	76	45	60		62	69	73	68	59	*
Response %:	100	100	100	100	100	100	100	100	100	100		100	100	100	100	100	*

Welsh Code (new):	4*6"78132'+0-/9:5# F-K/:L#
Welsh Code (old):	4***68"7231'0-9/:5# F-K/?L:
Profile Elevation:	75.10

*MDS scores are reported only for clients who indicate that they are married or separated.

FIGURE 7.2. MMPI 2 clinical and supplemental scale profile for a 46-year-old department store manager.

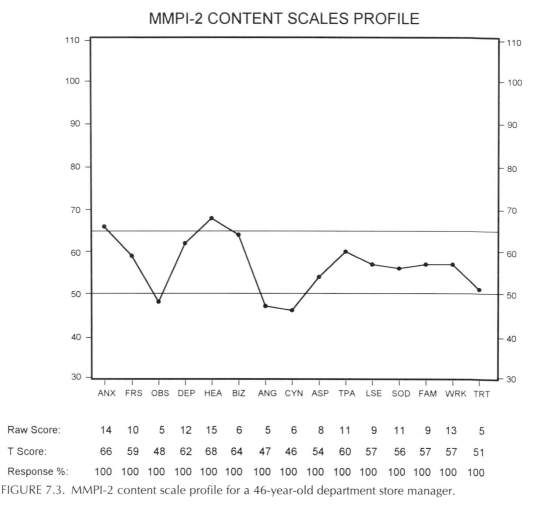

MMPI-2 CONTENT SCALES PROFILE

	ANX	FRS	OBS	DEP	HEA	BIZ	ANG	CYN	ASP	TPA	LSE	SOD	FAM	WRK	TRT
Raw Score:	14	10	5	12	15	6	5	6	8	11	9	11	9	13	5
T Score:	66	59	48	62	68	64	47	46	54	60	57	56	57	57	51
Response %:	100	100	100	100	100	100	100	100	100	100	100	100	100	100	100

FIGURE 7.3. MMPI-2 content scale profile for a 46-year-old department store manager.

for her problems (see Figure 7.4). He wanted to provide her with important personality information without raising her defensiveness to the point that she would be unable to accept the feedback. He began the test feedback session by reminding her of the initial reasons for the psychological evaluation. He next provided her with background as to the reasons for administering the MMPI-2 and what he had hoped that the test would be able to add to an understanding of her situation. First, the practitioner discussed her general cooperativeness with the evaluation by referring to the validity scale elevations in the profile shown in Figure 7.1. Her

PROFILE VALIDITY

Her MMPI-2 clinical profile is probably valid. The client's responses to the MMPI-2 validity items suggest that she cooperated with the evaluation enough to provide useful interpretive information. The resulting clinical profile is an adequate indication of her present personality functioning.

SYMPTOMATIC PATTERNS

The behavioral correlates included in the narrative report are likely to provide a good description of the client's current personality functioning. The clinical scale prototype used in the report, which incorporates correlates of Pd and Pa, is based on scores with high profile definition. Individuals with this MMPI-2 clinical profile tend to show an extreme pattern of chronic psychological maladjustment. The client appears to be very immature and alienated, tending to manipulate others for her own gratification. She also seems quite self-indulgent, hedonistic, and narcissistic, with a grandiose conception of her capabilities. She may be quite aggressive with others, tends to be very impulsive, and acts out her problems. She rationalizes her difficulties and denies responsibility for her actions, preferring instead to blame other people. She tends to be very hostile, resentful, and irritable.

In addition, the following description is suggested by the content of the client's item responses. She is rather high-strung and believes that she feels things more, or more intensely, than others do. She feels quite lonely and misunderstood at times.

PROFILE FREQUENCY

Profile interpretation can be greatly facilitated by examining the relative frequency of clinical scale patterns in various settings. The client's high-point clinical scale score (Pd) occurs in 9.5% of the MMPI-2 normative sample of women. However, only 4.7% of the sample have Pd scale peak scores at or above a T score of 65, and only 2.9% have well-defined Pd spikes. This elevated MMPI-2 profile configuration (4-6/6-4) is very rare in samples of normals, occurring in less than 1% of the MMPI-2 normative sample of women.

The relative frequency of her high-point Pd profile in medical settings is useful information for clinical interpretation. In the NCS medical sample, this high-point clinical scale score (Pd) occurs in 6.8% of the women. Additionally, 5.2% of these women have the Pd spike equal to or above a T score of 65, and 2.9% have a well-defined Pd peak at or above a T score of 65. This elevated MMPI-2 profile configuration (4-6/6-4) is found in 1.3% of the women in the NCS medical sample.

She scored relatively high on APS and AAS, suggesting the possibility of a drug- or alcohol-abuse problem. The base rate data on her profile type among residents in alcohol and drug programs should also be evaluated. This MMPI-2 profile configuration contains the most frequent high point, the Pd score, among alcohol- and drug-abusing populations. Over 26% of the women in substance-abuse treatment programs have this pattern (McKenna & Butcher, 1987).

PROFILE STABILITY

The relative scale elevation of the highest scales in her clinical profile reflects high profile definition. If she is retested at a later date, the peak scores on this test are likely to retain their relative salience in her retest profile pattern. Her high-point score on Pd is likely to remain stable over time. Short-term test-retest studies have shown a correlation of 0.79 for this high-point score.

FIGURE 7.4. The narrative section from the Minnesota Report on the MMPI-2 for a 46-year-old department store manager.

INTERPERSONAL RELATIONS

She has a great deal of difficulty in her social relationships. She feels that others do not understand her and do not give her enough sympathy. She is somewhat aloof, cold, nongiving, and uncompromising, attempting to advance herself at the expense of others. Rocky interpersonal relationships are the norm among individuals with this profile. Marital breakup is relatively common.

She is somewhat shy, with some social concerns and inhibitions. She is a bit hypersensitive about what others think of her and is occasionally concerned about her relationships with others. She appears to be somewhat inhibited in personal relationships and social situations, and she may have some difficulty expressing her feelings toward others.

DIAGNOSTIC CONSIDERATIONS

An individual with this profile is usually viewed as having a severe Personality Disorder, such as an Antisocial or Paranoid Personality. The possibility of a Paranoid Disorder should also be considered, however.

She appears to have a number of personality characteristics that have been associated with substance abuse or substance use problems. Her scores on the addiction proneness indicators suggest that there is a possibility of her developing an addictive disorder. Further evaluation for the likelihood of a substance use or abuse disorder is indicated. In her responses to the MMPI-2, she has acknowledged some problems with excessive use or abuse of addictive substances.

TREATMENT CONSIDERATIONS

Individuals with this profile tend not to seek psychological treatment on their own and are usually not good candidates for psychotherapy. They resist psychological interpretation, argue, and tend to rationalize and blame others for their problems. They also tend to leave therapy prematurely and blame the therapist for their own failings.

MMPI-2	Adult Clinical Interpretive Report
ID 39	Page 5

Her acknowledged problems with alcohol or drug use should be addressed in therapy.

NOTE: This MMPI-2 interpretation can serve as a useful source of hypotheses about clients. This report is based on objectively derived scale indices and scale interpretations that have been developed in diverse groups of patients. The personality descriptions, inferences, and recommendations contained herein need to be verified by other sources of clinical information because individual clients may not fully match the prototype. The information in this report should most appropriately be used by a trained, qualified test interpreter. The information contained in this report should be considered confidential.

FIGURE 7.4. (continued)

validity scale scores suggested that she appeared to be very open to the evaluation and did not seem to be engaging in problem denial. She reported a number of problems in a straightforward manner. The psychologist also told her that some of the test information might not seem appropriate to her (because of her tendency to externalize blame), and she was encouraged to ask questions if she did not see the relevance to her.

Next, using the clinical and content scale profiles, he explained how the MMPI-2 scores provided summaries of her present feelings, symptoms, and attitudes. Her clinical scale scores (particularly the elevations on the Pd and Pa scales shown in Figure 7.2) reflected a great deal of anger and hurt on her part. She seemed to be feeling mistrustful of others and showed a tendency to blame others for her own problems. The MMPI-2 scales reflect immaturity in behavior and relationships that have probably persisted for some time. The psychologist pointed out that she was clearly experiencing a great deal of physical distress and tension at this time and that perhaps many of the problems centered around relationship difficulties.

One of the greatest problems she seemed to be experiencing, although she tended to minimize it in the initial interview, was that of alcohol abuse. The MMPI-2 substance-abuse indicators (as well as her acknowledged pattern of alcohol use, reported in the initial session) suggested a strong likelihood that alcohol abuse was a much more significant problem than she had been willing to discuss before. The remainder of the interview was oriented toward highlighting her major problems and encouraging her to enter an alcohol treatment program. She acknowledged that her life had been going downhill for some months and that her most recent relationship was one that seemed to center on using (and abusing) alcohol; also, her alcohol abuse had been increasing as the relationship broke up. At the end of the session she acknowledged that she had received a DWI citation a year before and had lost her driving privileges for six months. She reported that one of the reasons that she missed some work was that she was unable to drive and relied on her friend to drive

her. Although she acknowledged being usually somewhat mistrustful and "private," she was currently feeling "pretty bad about life" and felt that she needed help for her problems, which she felt were getting worse.

Several possible treatment options were discussed with her. There were a number of inpatient programs that could be recommended, and it was also possible to obtain alcohol problem treatment on an outpatient basis under some conditions. Because of her involvement with alcohol, however, it was strongly recommended that she consider a four-week inpatient treatment program. She was initially very reluctant to agree to inpatient treatment since she felt the absence from work would be detrimental to her job. She asked about the possibility of an outpatient program that would allow her to work during the days. She agreed to returning for a third session to discuss various alcohol treatment program options that were open to her. She was encouraged to discuss the possibility of a leave of absence with her employer before the next session.

In the follow-up session the practitioner initially inquired about her present thinking about the treatment program for her. She reported that her discussion with her employer had been very encouraging and she felt that her supervisor was very supportive of her. Her supervisor (an abstinent alcoholic himself) was very understanding of her situation and urged her to take a leave of absence to participate in the inpatient program as he had done several years before. He gave her assurances that she was a valuable employee and that her job would not be threatened by her absence. She used the session to discuss other possible problems she might encounter by being in an inpatient program. She ended the session with a clear plan to initiate inpatient treatment on Monday.

FORENSIC USE OF COMPUTER-BASED REPORTS

It is becoming more and more important for psychologists to employ clinical procedures that will hold up under rigorous cross-examination in court, because more cases today are becoming the subject of litigation. Psychologists testifying in court might consider using computer-based test reports that provide results in an objective manner, reducing the possibility of subjectivity and bias in interpretation (Pope, Butcher, & Seelen, 1993). Computerized psychological test reports can lend considerable objectivity and credibility to a forensic psychological study. The use of a computer to analyze test-score patterns can remove subjective bias from the interpretation process.

The value of using objective psychological measures in court testimony was described by Ziskin (1981):

> I would recommend for forensic purposes the utilization of one of the automated MMPI services. One obvious advantage is the minimizing or eliminating of the possibility of scoring errors or errors in transposition of scores. Also, these systems are capable of generating more information about an individual than the individual clinician is usually capable of simply by virtue of their ability to deal with greater amounts of information. Another advantage is the reduction of the problems of examiner effects, such as biases entering into the collection, recording, and interpretation of the data (p. 9).

Points to Consider

Several issues concerning the use of computer-based personality test evaluations in forensic assessments need to be addressed. Pope et al. (1993) pointed out that when forensic testimony involves the use of computer-based testing it is very important to be able to establish the chain of custody for the test protocol in question to document that the computer-based report is actually the report for the client in the case. The forensic psychologist should be prepared to explain how the answer sheet was obtained and show that the computer-based results are actually those for the client in question. There have been cases in which the MMPI was excluded from evidence because the psychologist was unable to establish that the test interpretation was

actually the one that the client completed. For example, allowing the client to take the test somewhere other than in the clinician's office may well lead to exclusion of the results from testimony.

It is also important to assure that the particular interpretation in the computer-based report is an appropriate match for the patient's test scores. In cross-examination, an attorney might ask questions about how the psychologist knows that the computer report actually fits the client. As noted earlier, computer-based psychological tests are usually prototypes. Therefore, some of the report descriptions might not apply for a particular case. The psychologist should be prepared, on cross-examination, to deal with descriptive statements in the report that are considered not appropriate for the particular client.

Psychologists who use computer-based MMPI-2 reports in court typically are able to establish the objectivity and utility of the instrument for understanding the client's problems and personality with the test. Most people have found that the MMPI (MMPI-2) is relatively easy to explain to lay people such as juries or to judges. Moreover, judges and juries are often found to be interested in the idea that computers can be programmed to provide an objective appraisal of the test.

CAUTIONS OR QUESTIONS IN USING COMPUTERIZED PSYCHOLOGICAL REPORTS

Some problems or pitfalls can occur with the use of computerized psychological evaluations. Computer-based test users need to be vigilant about possible problems that can enter into blind reliance on computer-based personality assessment and implement remedies to avoid potential problems. In order to have an effective practice, the clinician must be alert to and avoid the following potential problems that could arise with computer-based testing.

Computerized assessments can promote an overly passive attitude toward clinical evaluation. Professionals who allow the computer to do all the work of gathering and summarizing clinical data may fail to pay sufficient attention to the patient in the assessment process to gain a thorough understanding of the client's problems. A great deal can be learned about a patient by carefully observing and keeping in close touch with the test data, and in thoughtfully summarizing the results. Having computerized results should not be considered a substitute for clinical observation and astute integration of a broad range of pertinent information.

Computerized assessments can introduce a mystical aura into the assessment process. Clinicians who become overly enthralled with the marvels of computer-based test results may have difficulty questioning whether interpretations are appropriate or sufficiently tied to research. There is nothing magical or mysterious about a computer-based psychological test report. Computer or automated test results should be qualitatively no different from what a well-trained expert with the test could do if he or she had sufficient time and the available resource information about the test. Essentially, the same sources of information are available and typically used by computer interpretation system developers and by clinicians. The main difference is that the computer system development is usually more extensive and comprehensive than the clinician is able to develop on a single case with limited time available.

The computer may lend an unwarranted impression of scientific precision to test interpretation through the use of impressive-looking printouts. Computerized psychological test results can lure individuals into feeling satisfied that they are finding out the most important and most accurate information about patients. However, the results provided by computers can be trivial, irrelevant, meaningless, or downright wrong. Keep in mind that one could program computers to generate nonsense syllables or horoscopes that have no empirical foundation or predictive value. Any report based on weak or meaningless data will be equally weak and meaningless.

Computer interpretations may not be specific enough to provide differential descriptions of clients. Most clinical psychology students are aware of the phenomenon known as the "P. T. Barnum effect," that is, using general statements in personality description that are so vague and nonspecific that they apply to virtually anyone. O'Dell (1972) conducted a study showing that Barnum-type interpretations in a computer report would be accepted by people as accurate information about them even though the descriptions apply to all people. Although they may sound insightful and descriptive, reports that include a large number of P. T. Barnum-type statements are not very useful in making clinical decisions. Computerized-test users need to be on the alert for Barnum-type statements in the report and avoid making important clinical decisions based on them.

Some information included in a computer-based assessment report may not match every patient. Personality test reports are basically prototypal descriptions. That is, they are generic summaries that are developed for a particular set of scores, configuration, or profile type. Some of the prototypal information that is printed out may not be relevant or appropriate for a particular case. For example, some correlates for a particular scale pattern that are reported in research articles or textbooks on the test might not apply for all cases that have the test pattern. It is up to the clinician to determine if the test hypotheses from the report are relevant and appropriate for the case. Any interpretations or hypotheses that are not appropriate, based on what we know about the client from other sources of information, should be ignored in the conclusions of the report (see the discussion in Pope et al., 1993).

It is also important for the practitioner to assure that the particular interpretation in the computer-based report is an appropriate prototypal match between the patient's scores on the test and the statements generated by the computer. The closer the match between the client's scores and those of the prototype pattern on which the personality descriptions are based, the more appropriate will be the report.

Failure to maintain control over computer-based reports can lead to problems. Practitioners need to assure that computer-derived test reports are appropriately controlled and are not misused (Pope et al., 1993). Computer-based psychological reports, as usually noted on the narrative, were developed for professional use. This generally implies that the consumer has a background in psychopathology and psychological measurements and is knowledgeable about the particular test in use. Computer printouts that become a part of a patient's file should be properly labeled to prevent them from being mistaken for the final report on the patient.

Computerized test reports are *raw test data*, not final products. One important point to consider is that computer-based reports do not usually "stand alone" as a psychological report. The computer printout, if kept in a patient's file, should contain annotation as to how the information was used in the final report (Butcher & Williams, 1992) to assure that future users of the file will not mistake the computer-based hypotheses for the clinician's final report. It is up to the clinician conducting the evaluation to assure that the information is properly labeled.

Relative Accuracy of Computer-Based Systems

An important point to consider in determining whether to use a computer-based interpretive report is that two different computer interpretation services providing interpretations of the same test might actually produce somewhat different results for the same protocol. Theoretically, any computer-based interpretation of a test should be quite similar to any other since they are based on the same correlate research literature. Interpretation of test scores can vary, however. Computer interpretation systems that are based closely on research-validated indexes tend to have similar outputs. However, research has shown that test interpretation services may differ with respect to their amount of information and the accuracy of the interpretations (Eyde, Fishburne, & Kowal, 1991). Practitioners using an automated interpretation system should be familiar with the issues of computerized test interpretation generally and the va-

lidity research on the particular system used (See Eyde, 1993; Eyde et al., 1991; Moreland, 1987).

Are Computer-Based Psychological Assessments Ethical and Appropriate?

Computer interpretation is accepted by the psychological profession as an appropriate means of evaluating test data on clients (see the American Psychological Association Guidelines for Computer-Based Assessment, 1986):

> A long history of research on statistical and clinical prediction has established that a well-designed statistical treatment of test results and ancillary information will yield more valid assessments than will an individual professional using the same information. (APA Guidelines for Computer Based Assessment, p. 9)

Who Can Purchase and Use Computerized Reports?

Are the test reports available only to qualified psychologists, or can other professionals, such as physicians or social workers, buy the services? The question of who can purchase and use computerized psychological test reports is frequently asked. The American Psychological Association (1986) has established guidelines for determining user qualifications for psychological test interpretation services. Psychological tests are grouped into different categories based on the purpose and use of the test. Recommendation for test-user qualifications differ according to the different types of tests involved. For example, clinical-personality tests (such as the MMPI-2) and computerized reports on them are considered B1 level instruments and are available to fellows, members, and associate members of the American Psychological Association as well as to psychologists, physicians, and marriage and family therapists who are licensed by the regulatory board of the state in which they practice.

SUMMARY

Computerized psychological testing, originally developed in the 1960s, has evolved substantially over the past three decades. Computer-based psychological test reports can add significantly to the practitioner's clinical evaluations in terms of providing valuable, thorough, accurate information that is processed in a timely manner. Many reasons account for the widespread use of computerized reports in clinical practice today: computer-based test interpretations are an objective and comprehensive means of interpreting psychological tests; they can be rapidly processed and made available early in the treatment session; and they have a high degree of reliability.

This chapter provided a discussion of how clinicians can incorporate computer-based information into their clinical practice. A case example was included to illustrate the types of information available and the ways it can be incorporated into treatment planning. The use of computer-based interpretive reports in forensic settings was also discussed and some guidelines for their use in court testimony were provided.

Several possible pitfalls that can accompany the use of computer-based psychological tests were discussed. It is important for practitioners to be aware of and to avoid the potential problems that can occur with the incorporation of automated assessment into clinical practice. Ways of avoiding problems were discussed in order to provide the practitioner with assurance that computer-derived information from psychological tests can be readily incorporated into a clinical practice, making it more appropriate and effective without experiencing the difficulties described here.

REFERENCES

American Psychological Association (1986). *American Psychological Association guidelines for computer-based tests and interpretations.* Washington, DC: Author.

Bloom, B. L. (1992). Computer assisted psychological intervention: A review and commentary. *Clinical Psychology Review, 12,* 169–198.

Butcher, J. N. (1990). *Use of the MMPI-2 in treatment planning.* New York: Oxford University Press.

Butcher, J. N., & Williams, C. L. (1992). *MMPI-2 and MMPI-A: Essentials of clinical interpretation.* Minneapolis: University of Minnesota Press.

Butcher, J. N., Graham, J. R., Williams, C. L., & Ben-Porath, Y. S. (1990). *Development and use of the MMPI-2 content scales.* Minneapolis: University of Minnesota Press.

Eyde, L. (1993). Tips for clinicians using computer based test interpretations (CBTIs). In B. Schlosser & K. Moreland (Eds.), *Taming technology: Issues, strategies and resources for the mental health practitioner* (pp. 97–99). Washington, DC: American Psychological Association.

Eyde, L., Kowal, D., & Fishburne, F. J. (1991). In T. B. Gutkin & S. L. Wise (Eds.), *The computer and the decision making process* (pp. 75–123). Hillsdale, NJ: LEA Press.

Finn, S. E. (1990, June). *A model for providing test feedback with the MMPI and MMPI-2.* Paper presented at the 25th Annual Symposium on Recent Developments in the Use of the MMPI (MMPI-2), Minneapolis.

Finn, S., & Tonsager, M. (1992). Therapeutic effects of providing MMPI-2 test feedback to college students awaiting therapy. *Psychological Assessment, 4,* 278–287.

Fowler, R. D. (1969). Automated interpretation of personality test data. In J. N. Butcher (Ed.), *MMPI: Research developments and clinical applications* (pp. 105–125). New York: McGraw-Hill.

Fowler, R. D., & Butcher, J. N. (1986). Critique of Matarazzo's views on computerized testing: All sigma and no meaning. *American Psychologist, 41,* 94–96.

Garb, H. (1992). The debate over the use of computer-based test reports. *The Clinical Psychologist, 45,* 95–100.

Gilberstadt, H., & Duker, J. (1963). *A handbook of clinical and actuarial MMPI interpretations.* Philadelphia: Saunders.

Graham, J. R. (1993). *MMPI-2: Assessing personality and psychopathology* (2nd ed.). New York: Oxford University Press.

Greene, R. (1991). *The MMPI-2/MMPI: An interpretive manual.* Needham Heights. MA: Allyn & Bacon.

Lewandowski, D., & Graham, J. R. (1972). Empirical correlates of frequently occurring two-point code types: A replicated study. *Journal of Clinical Psychology, 39,* 467–472.

Lubin, B., Larsen, R., & Matarazzo, J. D. (1984). Patterns of psychological test usage in the United States: 1935–1982. *American Psychologist, 39,* 451–454.

Marks, P. A., Seeman, W., & Haller (1975). *The actuarial use of the MMPI with adolescents and adults.* Baltimore: Williams & Wilkins.

Matarazzo, J. (1986). Computerized clinical psychological test interpretations: Unvalidated plus all mean and no sigma. *American Psychologist, 41,* 14–24.

Meehl, P. E. (1954). *Clinical versus statistical prediction: A theoretical analysis and a review of the evidence.* Minneapolis: University of Minnesota Press.

Moreland, K. (1987). Computerized psychological assessment. What's available. In J. N. Butcher (Ed.), *Computerized psychological assessment* (pp. 26–49). New York: Basic Books.

O'Dell, J. (1972). P. T. Barnum explores the computer. *Journal of Consulting and Clinical Psychology, 38,* 270–273.

Piotrowski, C., & Keller, J. W. (1989). Psychological testing in outpatient mental health facilities: A national study. *Professional Psychology: Research and Practice, 20,* 423–425.

Rubenzer, S. (1991). Computerized testing and clinical judgment: Cause for concern. *The Clinical Psychologist, 44,* 63–66.

Pope, K., Butcher, J. N., & Seelen, J. (1993). *The MMPI/MMPI-2/MMPI-A in court: Assessment, testimony, and cross-examination for expert witnesses and attorneys.* Washington, DC: American Psychological Association.

Rome, H. P., Swenson, W. M., Mataya, P., McCarthy, C. E., Pearson, J. S., Keating, F. R., & Hathaway, S. R. (1962). Symposium on automation technics in personality assessment. *Proceedings of the Staff Meetings of the Mayo Clinic, 37,* 61–82.

Ziskin, J. (1981). The use of the MMPI in forensic settings. In J. N. Butcher, W. G. Dahlstrom, M. D. Gynther, & S. Schofield (Eds.), *Clinical notes on the MMPI.* (Whole No. 9). Nutley, NJ: Hoffman-LaRoche Laboratories/NCS.

8

How to Anticipate Ethical and Legal Challenges in Personality Assessments

Irving B. Weiner

Personality assessors rarely intend to break the law or violate the ethical standards of their profession. Likewise, few among us wish to look insensitive in our consulting rooms or foolish in the courtroom. At times, however, practitioners painfully discover that their best intentions and wishes have been compromised by insufficient attention to steps they should have taken but did not. This chapter addresses in pragmatic fashion how personality assessors can anticipate ethical and legal issues and, by taking arms against them in advance, avoid a sea of troubles.

For purposes of discussion, the process of personality assessment in clinical practice can be divided into five phases: (1) accepting a referral; (2) selecting the test battery; (3) conducting the psychological evaluation; (4) preparing and presenting a report; and (5) managing case records. With respect to each of these phases of the assessment process, psychologists can minimize potential ethical and legal hazards by keeping the following three guidelines in mind:

1. Whatever you do, imagine that a knowledgeable and unfriendly critic is looking over your shoulder.
2. Whatever you say, imagine that it will be taken in the most unfavorable light possible and used against you.
3. Whatever you write, imagine that it will be read aloud, sarcastically, in a court of law.

Some may feel that such guidelines bespeak an unseemly paranoia. Colleagues who have encountered the kinds of unpleasant situations to be illustrated in this chapter will surely think otherwise. However, to put a less pathological construction than paranoia on how clinicians should conduct their practice, let it be said that it at least behooves one to be hypervigilant. With hypervigilance in mind, a final general principle that should go without saying will be said anyway: Psychologists who want to anticipate ethical and legal issues in the practice of personality assessment should be thoroughly familiar with the Ethical Principles and Code of Conduct set forth by the American Psychological Association (1992) and with applicable statutory law and professional regulations in the state where they work. Recommended reading in this regard also includes contributions by Pope (1991) and by the Committee on Ethical Guidelines for Forensic Psychologists (1991).

By way of further introduction, let it be noted

that the general principles promulgated by the American Psychological Association call for psychologists to be knowledgeable and responsible professionals who respect the rights and dignity of others, show concern for the welfare of their clients and colleagues, and present themselves fairly and honestly to their communities. These features of being a competent clinician and a decent person usually suffice to carry personality assessors with propriety through the several phases of conducting a psychological evaluation. In each phase, however, there are certain steps that can be taken to avoid subsequent ethical and legal jeopardy.

ACCEPTING A REFERRAL

From an ethical and legal perspective, the most important consideration in accepting a referral for diagnostic consultation is knowing who the client is. The client in personality assessment is generally defined as the person or entity who will receive a report of the findings, pay for the services rendered, and command the clinician's primary allegiance. A patient who comes in self-referred to be evaluated and who expects to receive the psychologist's conclusions and recommendations and pay the bill can usually be identified as the client with little difficulty. Often, however, there are other circumstances involved in the delivery of assessment services that can make clienthood a complex matter to unravel.

Frequently, for example, people being examined share their clienthood with other parties or agencies to whom the clinician also has some responsibility. In the case of a minor, there are typically parents who will be paying the bill and rightfully expecting to receive feedback concerning the results of the evaluation. In the case of a patient referred for consultation, other professionals or a clinical unit who will not be paying for the service will nevertheless be the primary recipient of the psychologist's report. In the case of third-party payers of one kind or another, there will be others who pay the bill but ordinarily receive only limited information concerning the outcome of the evaluation, such as

the date of testing, the measures used, and a DSM-IV diagnosis. In each of these instances, the examiner will have dual or even multiple obligations to meet the expectations and entitlements of both the person being tested and the other parties to the case.

Moreover, the examination may occur not in response to a *clinical* referral, but instead following what can be called an *administrative* referral. A clinical referral is made by someone who is concerned about a patient's welfare and trying to be helpful to him or her. An administrative referral is made by someone on behalf of an entity that wants guidance in making a judgment about the person being evaluated; what is learned from the examination may or may not be helpful to the examinee, and the entity is concerned mainly with its own welfare, not the welfare of the person being examined. Common types of administrative referrals include social service requests to evaluate people on disability to see if they are capable of returning to work; court-requested evaluations of defendants to determine if they are competent to stand trial; school-requested evaluations of misbehaving students to assist in deciding whether they should be suspended or expelled; and prison-requested evaluation of inmates to assess their suitability for parole.

In contrast to the usual situation in a clinical referral, subjects examined in response to an administrative referral are involuntary. If an entity exercising control over them had not requested an examination, they would not be in the psychologist's office; they could refuse to be examined or go through the motions of participation without being cooperative, but doing so would probably be viewed negatively by the referring source and work to their disadvantage in any decisions made about them. Unlike self-referred and clinically referred patients, furthermore, administratively referred subjects are not, strictly speaking, the examiner's clients. The client is the entity who wants to have the person examined. It is the entity who will receive the report, and the examiner has no obligation to provide feedback to the subject or to advise the referral source concerning kinds of feedback that might be helpful to him or her.

Yet administratively referred patients are often responsible for paying for the psychological services, which is an aspect of clienthood, and examiners do have an obligation to treat administratively referred subjects with respect, to assess them in a competent fashion, and to report the implications of their test responses accurately and without bias. These and other aspects of clienthood are elaborated in the American Psychological Association publication *Who Is the Client?* (Monahan, 1980).

To safeguard against an inadvertent violation of anyone's rights or an accidental failure to meet anyone's appropriate expectations, personality assessors should determine in advance who their client is and what obligations they will have to whom. Three questions in particular should be asked before testing is begun: Who is requesting the evaluation and why? Who is to be informed of the results of the examination? Who will be paying the psychologist's fees? With answers to these questions clearly in hand, diagnostic consultants are well positioned to avoid four potential sources of ethical and legal unpleasantness: (1) assessing irrelevant or unasked questions; (2) using inappropriate or inadequate measures; (3) giving too little feedback to the person being examined or too much information to other interested parties, and vice versa; and (4) getting into disputes over unexpected or unpaid bills.

SELECTING THE TEST BATTERY

Clinicians preparing to conduct a psychodiagnostic assessment typically select tests that they feel comfortable using and find helpful in answering referral questions. To anticipate possible ethical and legal issues, however, and especially in forensic cases, assessors need to be guided by four considerations that extend beyond their personal preferences.

First, the test battery should be limited to measures that are warranted by the referral question. Clinicians concerned about ethical and legal issues need to recognize when they should exercise restraint by keeping favorite tests on the sidelines. If the referral question concerns neu-

ropsychological impairment, for example, examiners should have a very good reason for including a Rorschach in the test battery, such as an explicit request for comment concerning possible accompanying depression or paranoia. Otherwise, how could they justify administering and billing for a test that makes virtually no contribution to identifying neuropsychological disorder? Likewise, examiners who include a WAIS-R in a battery intended to answer questions about personality style and adequacy of adjustment should be prepared to provide a convincing argument for the utility of the WAIS-R for these purposes, given that there is very little empirical evidence to this effect.

Second, the battery should consist of widely used and well-known measures. This guideline is not intended in general to discourage the development of new tests or the utilization of perfectly respectable measures that happen not to have become widely used or well known. However, a case with forensic implications is not the place for psychological assessors to rely on experimental or esoteric measures or even to include them in their test battery. When there is a possibility of having to testify about their data, assessors can spare themselves potential grief by limiting their battery to tests that judges, juries, and attorneys are likely to recognize by name or that can at least be demonstrated to represent standard professional practice.

If for some reason psychologists decide to include highly specialized or rarely employed measures in their test battery, they should be prepared to make a good case for having done so—a case that goes beyond saying "I sometimes get some interesting information from this test" (which may give the unintended impression that most other professionals do not get much information from it, or else it would be more widely used). Assessors who cannot fully justify the composition of their test battery are at risk for having their credibility challenged, either on the basis of their being cavalier about their work (throwing in measures on a whim) or on the basis of their not conforming to standard practices in conducting a psychodiagnostic evaluation. Published surveys of the relative frequency with which various tests are used in clinical practice can help assessors to select batteries with this consideration in mind (Archer, Maruish, Imhof, & Piotrowski, 1991; Craig & Horowitz, 1990; Piotrowski & Lubin, 1990; Watkins, 1991).

Third, psychological assessors seeking to minimize ethical and legal hazards should limit their test batteries to measures that have a solid psychometric base. Like the previous guideline, this recommendation is not intended to be prejudicial toward measures of uncertain or undetermined psychometric status that clinicians find useful to them in their work. However, if they anticipate that a case will go to court, assessors will be well advised to exclude from their battery any measures for which it would be difficult to expound on their reliability, validity, and normative data.

Avoiding psychometrically suspect measures in cases where ethical and legal matters may become at issue does not mean just excluding them from one's report. Sometimes assessors are tempted to administer a broad battery that includes some personal favorites and some "interesting" but empirically soft measures, and then to prepare a written report or give oral testimony based only on those tests in the battery that do rest on a solid psychometric foundation. Surrendering to such temptation can buy one a ticket to trouble. Should the slightest hint emerge that more tests were administered than are being testified to, what can happen next to an expert witness is not a pretty sight to see. After having said "yes" when asked if other tests not mentioned in the report were also given, the assessor must not only discuss and defend these other tests (which were probably kept out of the report because they would be difficult to discuss and defend), but he or she must also explain why the information about these tests was excluded from the original report or testimony. Few expert witnesses can survive this kind of situation without substantial loss of credibility and respect.

Fourth, assessors should use tests with which they are familiar. The expert witness who cannot cite at least some chapter and verse from literature concerning the measures in the test battery is risking an unpleasant turn on the witness stand: "So, Doctor, you really don't know much at all about the tests you have used, do you?" Aside from being exposed by such a question as not having done their homework, assessors who use tests with which they are not well acquainted are also treading some shaky ethical ground. As the present author has elaborated elsewhere (Weiner, 1989), practicing one's profession ethically requires one to maintain competence in doing so. Psychological assessors who do not keep up with developments in the field, who have not learned new methods that are demonstrably better than older methods, who lack familiarity with revised norms that have superseded previous norms, and who are generally ignorant of contemporary research findings and refinements in interpretation are failing to maintain their competence as psychodiagnostic consultants. Lacking competence, they will be hard put to discharge their responsibility to their clients in an ethical fashion.

CONDUCTING THE PSYCHOLOGICAL EVALUATION

To adequately trained and conscientious psychologists there is little that needs to be said about conducting psychological evaluations in ways that will readily pass ethical and legal muster. Knowing and following standardized instructions for test administration and treating patients with dignity and respect should suffice to prepare examiners adequately for any questions that might later be raised concerning the propriety of their procedures. However, two considerations that may sometimes be overlooked in the press of doing business merit mention.

First, assessors who employ technicians to administer tests should always meet and talk with their testees and will also do well to administer at least a portion of the battery themselves. The clinical reasons for proceeding in this way are obvious. Blind interpretation has its place, for research and teaching purposes and when expert consultants are retained specifically to comment on test protocols produced by individuals to whom they have no obligation. However, when psychologists accept a referral to "see" someone for a psychodiagnostic evaluation, they need to do just that—see them. The information that skilled professionals can glean from observing how people look, talk, dress, and comport themselves, as well as from their behavior while they are taking the tests, adds a valuable dimension to the evaluation process. A technician's observations can be helpful, but they are rarely a satisfactory replacement for firsthand observation by the person who will be preparing the report.

From an ethical perspective, patients who are billed for a psychological examination by someone they saw only briefly or not at all in the process of being examined may rightly believe that they have received shabby treatment. Feeling shortchanged, they may not only decline to pay the bill but may also complain to a third-party payer or regulatory agency that they did not receive the services for which they were charged. In addition to exposing themselves to this kind of ethical jeopardy, psychological assessors who do not see their patients are vulnerable to criticism in the courtroom. Well-prepared attorneys know that they have nothing to lose by asking, "Which of these tests did you actually administer yourself, Doctor?" If assessors have to answer that they did little or none of the actual testing, no amount of explanation can completely eliminate the impression that they are not very committed or conscientious in their clinical work, or that they do not know as much as they should about the person who was examined, or both. Such undesirable ethical and forensic outcomes can be anticipated and avoided by the simple expedient of taking an active role in the evaluation of all referred patients.

Second, assessors should make sure that their test forms will stand up to inspection and give every possible indication that the tests were administered, scored, and evaluated in a careful, proper, and thoroughly professional manner. Standard recording forms should be used for each test, and all of the information requested by the forms should be entered. Examiners who have their own preferred ways of recording test responses and scores that they think are superior to standard published forms should consider ex-

ercising their preferences only when they have no reason to anticipate ethical or legal inquiry concerning their examination. Whenever ethical or legal issues do arise, idiosyncratic deviations from standard practice expose examiners to questions about why they proceeded as they did. No matter how adequately examiners believe that they can answer such questions, and thereby successfully defend their methods, the very fact of their having to defend nonstandard methods can raise doubts in others' minds about the appropriateness of the procedures that were used and the reliability of the results that were obtained.

As for entering all of the requested data, completed test forms convey thoroughness and competence. WAIS-R forms in which the age-adjusted scale scores are omitted look naked to the trained eye, for example, as do other frequently used forms when spaces for inserting numbers or drawing profiles have been left blank. Whether experienced examiners feel they need to fill in test forms completely in order to interpret the data is beside the point. To spare themselves embarrassment when their test data are inspected in an ethical or legal context, psychological assessors should collect and prepare raw test data in a manner that is beyond reproach.

A seemingly pedestrian but often critical aspect of having adequate test forms for appropriate parties to inspect is having legible forms. Examiners should ensure that whatever they have written down can be read by others, should it become necessary. Having legible records signifies a sense of professional responsibility and an openness to sharing information as appropriate; examiners whose records cannot be read by other people in their absence or, worse yet, cannot be read by themselves once they pass out of immediate memory, are at risk for appearing careless and indifferent to their clients' welfare. Psychologists whose handwriting is difficult to read should consider copying their test protocols over or having them typed; should they do so, however, the original record in the examiner's handwriting should be preserved to document who took the record and the accuracy of the transcription.

PREPARING AND PRESENTING A REPORT

The present author has delineated elsewhere some basic guidelines for writing forensic reports (Weiner, 1987), and numerous other psychologists have offered good advice in the preparation and presentation of testimony in the courtroom (Brodsky, 1991; Melton, Petrila, Poythress, & Slobogin, 1987; Shapiro, 1991; Singer & Nievod, 1987). The following brief comments on writing and presenting reports are not intended to cover the same ground as these previous contributions or to provide a comprehensive overview of report writing. Instead, for the purposes of the present chapter, they offer three specific suggestions in communicating assessment results that can help psychological examiners gain respect for their efforts and minimize the impact of subsequent ethical or legal challenges.

First, reports of psychological evaluations should focus explicitly on what the tests show and distinguish test findings from general inferences about the person who was tested. Test reports that consist only of general inferences (e.g., "This person appears to have a schizophrenic disorder") leave the reader uncertain about what led the psychologist to the conclusions drawn and how the test findings contributed to them, if at all. Easier to follow and more convincing are reports that describe the implications of the test findings for particular psychological characteristics (e.g., "Mr. A's responses to the Rorschach demonstrated a marked propensity for illogical thinking and considerable difficulty perceiving events in his life in a realistic manner"); identify specific findings that have special diagnostic or prognostic significance (e.g., "On both the MMPI and the Rorschach Mr. A showed abnormal elevations on indices associated with the presence of a schizophrenic disorder"); and only in conclusion draw general inferences about the person based on the test findings and, as appropriate, other available information as well (e.g., "On the basis of these test findings, and in light of Mr. A's family history of schizophrenia, it appears likely that his recent adjustment difficulties are associated with the onset of a schizophrenic disorder").

As counterpoint to specifying the basis for a positive finding of disorder, examiners should be similarly denotative but also circumspect in reporting negative findings. Most important, whether the referral question concerns schizophrenia, suicidal risk, psychopathy, neuropsychological impairment, or any other issue of adjustive capacity, assessors will be well advised to avoid ruling out the possibility of disorder or handicap, no matter how free from indices of disorder or handicap the test findings appear to be.

Psychometrically, this caution against ruling out possibilities reflects the fact that all of our tests and all of our test batteries produce some frequency of false negative results. Professionally, unqualified assertions that a condition is not present, like any absolute statements concerning probablistic events, expose psychological assessors to potential embarrassment. Having overstated a negative case, they can easily be made to admit some lack of certainty that a person they examined does not have a particular condition and some possibility that a person with this condition may not always show it on psychological tests — which leaves them looking reckless in their judgments and perhaps not fully believable.

To present negative findings with scientific accuracy and professional caution, examiners, as just illustrated, should precede their general inferences by noting what the tests indicate and then couching their conclusions in relative rather than absolute terms. In the case of the hypothetical Mr. A, referred for evaluation of possible schizophrenia, a report of negative findings might parallel the above example with the following statements: "The tests do not contain any evidence of illogical thinking or impaired reality testing; Mr. A did not elevate on any of the commonly used MMPI or Rorschach indices of schizophrenia; accordingly, although the possibility of schizophrenia cannot be ruled out on the basis of these findings, they make it unlikely that his adjustment difficulties are attributable to schizophrenic disorder." Presenting negative findings in this way protects examiners not only against unwarranted overstatement, but also against professional embarrassment and possible liability if subsequent events should document an instance of false negative findings.

Second, in a similar vein, reports should concentrate on describing what people *are probably like* and comment only cautiously on what they *have probably done* or *are likely to do.* Specific and unqualified predictions from psychological test findings to behavior put examiners in a precarious position where their conclusions will be difficult to justify. Typically, however, behavioral predictions are exactly what is being asked and expected of the clinician. In such cases, as an alternative to formulating specific hypotheses about an individual's probable past or future behavior, examiners should consider limiting their comments to comparisons between the firm findings in the case (i.e., test indications of what the person is probably or almost certainly like) and relevant knowledge concerning the behavior of people in general. This approach gives to other parties the opportunity to draw informed conclusions about the implications of the test findings.

To illustrate this approach, suppose that the subject is a girl with no Texture (T) in her Rorschach, and the question is whether she should be removed from a home where there is alleged abuse or neglect. The examiner could say, "This is a child who has been inadequately nurtured by her parents, and she is likely to have social adjustment difficulties in the future if she continues in her present home." Given the absence of T in the Rorschach, this may well be an accurate statement. It would not be an easy statement to defend on the witness stand, however: "Please tell the court, Doctor, how many hours you have spent in this girl's home observing her parents' care of her and what evidence you have actually seen with your own eyes that she is not being nurtured by them." The best way to handle this type of situation is to avoid getting into it in the first place, and the approach being suggested here would do so in the following way.

For purposes of the example, let us say that this child's Rorschach is not only lacking in T but also has no Cooperative Movement (COP), an elevated Isolation Index (ISOL), and little or

no pure Human content (H). The examiner might then include two kinds of comments in the report. With respect to test indications of what the person is like, the report could say, "This is a child who does not easily become attached to people, who does not anticipate being able to form close and mutually supportive relationships with others, who does not see many people as playing an important part in her life, and who feels uncomfortable in dealing with interpersonal situations." With respect to findings about people in general, the report could go on to say, "Children with this pattern of test responses are often found not to have had the benefit of early life experiences that foster a sense of attachment to other people; this pattern is frequently found in foster children, abandoned children, and children in intact families whose parents have been distant from them; such children are often found to have persistent difficulties in social relationships as they grow up."

These kinds of statements, which can be supported by empirical evidence, leave to the psychologist's readers or listeners the opportunity to put two and two together and thereby draw inferences concerning events in the particular child's life. Challenged by an attorney—"Are you saying that this child has been abused or neglected by her parents?"—the psychologist can respond as follows: "No, I'm not saying that, because I don't have any direct evidence to that effect. What I am saying is that this girl's test responses demonstrate difficulties in feeling close and relating comfortably to other people, and that such difficulties are frequently found in children who have been abused or neglected by their parents." Presentations made in this way usually serve effectively to get across the point that examiners are trying to make without putting them at risk for appearing to have drawn conclusions that go beyond their data.

Third, reports should avoid painting subjects in a negative light. Especially in cases of administrative referral, reports of psychological evaluation may be read by many people who are not mental health professionals, including health care managers, employers, and examinees themselves. Many kinds of comments that have traditionally seemed appropriate for entry into clinical records may strike nonprofessional readers, especially examinees, as harsh, critical, judgmental, and pejorative, and examinees who feel they have been unfairly disadvantaged by what a psychologist has said about them may seek recourse by challenging the propriety of the examiner's conduct. There are ways in which examiners can readily say what needs to be said about subjects who are disturbed or impaired without seeming to lack sympathy and understanding, if they watch their words carefully.

For example, in describing a resistive person who was extremely difficult to evaluate, an assessor can say, "Mr. B was uncooperative and invalidated some of the tests by refusing to respond to many items." Or, describing the same person, the assessor can say, "Apparently because of his considerable anxiety about being evaluated, Mr. B found it difficult to comply with the examination procedures and was unable to respond to many of the test items." An unhappy client or an independent observer could well find the first of these comments prejudicial, but it is unlikely that anyone, no matter how disappointed with the results of the examination or its influence on subsequent events, could find fault with the second comment.

Similarly, examiners need to appreciate that too often psychological reports describe subjects' weaknesses and shortcomings without mentioning their personal strengths and assets. Assessors tend to focus on what is wrong with people they examine for good reason, because that is typically what they are being asked to assess. Not uncommonly, in fact, beginning assessors, schooled in tests addressed to differential diagnosis and normed on patient groups, will ask for help in knowing where to look for evidence of personality strengths and assets. Where they should look is at those test data that we typically label "negative findings" and pass over, because they do not identify any adjustment difficulty or deviation from normative expectation. In the service of preparing a balanced report, features of the test data that do not suggest psychological impairment can often be turned from negative into positive findings and described as probable strengths or assets.

For example, subjects who do not show evidence of thought disorder or impaired reality testing can be described as people who appear capable of thinking coherently and logically and perceiving their experience realistically. Those who do not give evidence of being markedly anxious or depressed can be described as relatively free from anxiety and depression. Those whose responses do not suggest social withdrawal or discomfort can be described as people who are outgoing or gregarious and feel comfortable in interpersonal relationships. And so on. Psychologists who take care to speak positively as well as negatively about the people they examine, and to express what is negative in a sympathetic and understanding manner, will minimize the likelihood of facing allegations of malpractice from clients who feel they have been damaged by improper professional conduct.

MANAGING CASE RECORDS

By far the most important ethical and legal consideration in managing case records is maintaining their confidentiality. Confidentiality has been widely discussed and extensively taught over the years, and clear guidelines for its maintenance are specified in the APA Ethics Code and elsewhere.

Less widely discussed but also important in anticipating ethical and legal issues in psychological assessment is careful attention to how case records are compiled and stored. As one aspect of managing their case records carefully, psychological examiners should regard them as they do any other personal property that may be inspected by strangers, sometimes unexpectedly. Records that are complete, orderly, and in reasonably pristine form reflect well on the competence and conscientiousness of the assessor; those that are disorganized and dog-eared suggest that examiners are paying insufficient attention to the rights and dignity of their clients.

Examiners must also take care to maintain the availability of their case records for an adequate period of time. Long after the fact of a psychological examination, clients and those concerned about them have a right to expect that the records will be available if needed for any purpose. This expectation is justified, and the obligation of examiners in this regard may be specified in statutory regulations concerning the practice of psychology. In Florida, for example, the Rules of the Department of Professional Regulation prescribe that complete psychological records must be maintained for at least three years following an examination and a summary of the records for an additional twelve years.

Moreover, the ethical obligations of examiners to maintain records extends not only as long as they are in practice but well beyond. The APA Ethical Standards specify that psychologists should plan in advance to preserve the confidentiality and the availability of their records even after they discontinue practice, and even in the event of their incapacity or death. Accordingly, psychological assessors are obliged to make provisions for the maintenance of their case records in future times when they will no longer be capable themselves of sharing this information with appropriate parties.

In summary, then, psychologists who conduct personality evaluations can protect themselves against ethical and legal recriminations by establishing clearly the identity of the client when they accept a referral; selecting for their test battery measures that are commonly used, well substantiated, and familiar to them; conducting the evaluation in standard ways and recording the data carefully; writing and presenting their reports in an appropriately denotative and circumspect manner; and maintaining the confidentiality and availability of their records for an appropriate period of time.

REFERENCES

American Psychological Association (1992). Ethical principles of psychologists and code of conduct. *American Psychologist, 47*, 1597–1611.

Archer, R. P., Maruish, M., Imhof, E. A., & Piotrowski, C. (1991). Psychological test usage with adolescent clients: 1990 survey findings. *Professional Psychology, 22*, 247–252.

Brodsky, S. L. (1991). *Testifying in court.* Washington, DC: American Psychological Association.

Committee on Ethical Guidelines for Forensic Psychologists (1991). Speciality guidelines for forensic psychologists. *Law and Human Behavior, 15*, 655–665.

Craig, R. J., & Horowitz, M. (1990). Current utilization of psychological tests at diagnostic practicum sites. *Clinical Psychologist, 43*, 29–36.

Melton, G. B., Petrila, J., Poythress, N. G., & Slobogin, C. (1987). *Psychological evaluations for the courts.* New York: Guilford Press.

Monahan, J. (Ed.) (1980). *Who is the client?* Washington, DC: American Psychological Association.

Piotrowski, C., & Lubin, B. (1990). Assessment practices of health psychologists: Survey of APA Division 38 clinicians. *Professional Psychology, 21*, 99–106.

Pope, K. S. (1991). Ethical and legal issues in clinical practice. In M. Hersen, A. E. Kazdin, & A. S. Bellack (Eds.), *The clinical psychology handbook* (2nd ed., pp. 115–127). New York: Pergamon.

Shapiro, D. L. (1991). *Forensic psychological assessment.* Boston: Allyn & Bacon.

Singer, M. T., & Nievod, A. (1987). Consulting and testifying in court. In I. B. Weiner & A. K. Hess (Eds.) *Handbook of forensic psychology* (pp. 529–556). New York: Wiley.

Watkins, C. E., Jr. (1991). What have surveys taught us about the teaching and practice of psychological assessment? *Journal of Personality Assessment, 56*, 426–437.

Weiner, I. B. (1987). Writing forensic reports. In I. B. Weiner & A. K. Hess (Eds.), *Handbook of forensic psychology* (pp. 511–528). New York: Wiley.

Weiner, I. B. (1989). On competence and ethicality in psychodiagnostic assessment. *Journal of Personality Assessment, 53*, 827–831.

II
SPECIAL POPULATIONS IN PERSONALITY ASSESSMENT

9

Cultural Considerations in Psychological Assessment of Asian-Americans

Sumie Okazaki
Stanley Sue

Clinicians and researchers conducting personality assessment of a culturally different client are faced with the formidable task of evaluating the contribution of cultural factors to an individual's personality structure and functioning. With Asian-Americans, the difficulty of the task is magnified due to the heterogeneity of the population (culturally, linguistically, historically, and so forth), lack of existing norms for this population even for the most extensively used assessment tools such as the MMPI (Greene, 1987), and lack of guidelines for conceptualizing individual and group differences on measures of personality.

In the United States, the term "Asian" is used to designate persons from more than twenty culturally and linguistically distinct ethnic groups. The 1990 Census (U.S. Department of Commerce, Bureau of the Census, 1991) showed the Asian or Pacific Islander population to number 7.3 million, or 2.9 percent of the U.S. population; it is the fastest-growing ethnic group in the U.S., showing a 108 percent increase from the 1980 census figure. Some of the ethnic groups within this population are Chinese, Filipino, Japanese, Asian Indian, Korean, and Vietnamese. Because of premigration traumas, the

Southeast Asian groups (Vietnamese, Cambodian, Lao, Thai, and Hmong) are at very high risk for psychopathology, particularly depression and posttraumatic stress disorder (Asian Community Mental Health Services, 1987; Westermeyer, Vang, & Neider, 1983). With the exception of Japanese-Americans, most Asian ethnic groups consist primarily of foreign-born persons (U.S. Department of Commerce, Bureau of the Census, 1988).

Given such a diverse population, the purpose of this chapter is to render a guideline for practical considerations in conducting a personality assessment of persons of Asian descent. To this end, the chapter will be organized into three main sections: (1) a summary of methodological and conceptual issues; (2) a review of existing research on Asian personality and the measures often used; and (3) guidelines for assessment. Due to gaps in research on personality assessment of Asian-Americans, some of our discussion will to some extent be based on the literature from ethnic minority research and personality research on Asians overseas. To place our comments in perspective, methodological and conceptual problems in cross-cultural assessment need to be presented.

METHODOLOGICAL AND CONCEPTUAL ISSUES: PROBLEMS OF EQUIVALENCE

Brislin (1993) outlined three areas in which equivalence of psychological concepts are discussed in cross-cultural research: (1) translation equivalence; (2) conceptual equivalence; and (3) metric equivalence. Translation equivalence exists when the descriptors and measures of psychological concepts can be translated well across languages. To test the translation equivalence of a measure that was developed in a particular culture, it is first translated by a bilingual to another language, then "back translated" from the second language to the first by an independent bilingual translator. The two versions of the measure in the original language are then compared to discern which words or concepts seem to survive the translation procedures, with the assumption that the concepts that do survive are translation equivalent. This procedure can be used to discover which psychological concepts appear to be culture-specific or culture-common.

Conceptual equivalence refers to functional aspects of the construct that serve the same purpose in different cultures, although the specific behavior or thoughts used to measure the construct may be different. For example, one aspect of good decision making in Western cultures is the ability to make a personal decision without being unduly influenced by others, whereas good decision making may be understood in Asian cultures as the ability to make a decision that is best for the group. These two different behaviors pertaining to making decisions may be conceptually equivalent.

Metric equivalence refers to the analysis of the same concept and the same measure across cultures, with the assumption that the scale of the measure can be directly compared. For example, one may consider whether a score of 100 on a certain personality scale may be a metric equivalent of a score of 100 on the translated version of the same personality scale.

Potential problems in translation, conceptual, and metric equivalence exist when assessment instruments developed in one cultural group are applied to a different cultural group. Some researchers sensitive to the problems of equivalence even go so far as to refrain from making any inference from the results of quantitative comparisons of a given measure between subjects from two different cultures (e.g., Hui, 1988). In the next section, evaluating existing research on the Asian or American personality, the relevance of the three types of equivalence will be highlighted.

A REVIEW

One useful way to organize the cross-cultural literature on personality and measures is to consider whether the measures were derived from the Western or the Eastern perspective and whether the measures were used in a different culture. Cross-cultural psychology has made distinctions between etic and emic approaches: the etic perspective refers to assumptions of universality or culture-free-ness of the construct, whereas the emic perspective refers to examination of the construct from the indigenous, culture-specific point of view. Thus, studies that apply Western-derived measures to non-Western populations are based on the imposed etic perspective, and those that strive to construct measures that are purported to be a part of the Eastern personality are based on the emic perspective. Cross-cultural studies of personality have largely adopted an imposed etic or pseudo-etic approach (Berry, 1980), and this is certainly true of personality research involving Asians and Asian-Americans. Imposed etic approaches to assessment do not necessarily mean that the measures are invalid when used across cultures. However, given the problems in equivalence, one cannot assume a priori that the measures are cross-culturally valid.

The Etic Perspective

MMPI Studies

Developed in the United States, the Minnesota Multiphasic Personality Inventory (MMPI) has been used with Asians and Asian-Americans. The MMPI is perhaps the most extensively studied personality instrument across cultures (Butcher, 1985), with available translated versions estimated to be 125 (Lonner, 1990). Although some have warned against its use with ethnic minorities in the U.S. because of the lack of norms among minority populations (Colligan, Osbourne, Swenson, & Offord, 1983) or because of interpretive bias (Dana, 1988), a review by Greene (1987) of MMPI studies on majority and minority groups in the U.S. found no consistent main effects of majority- or minority-group status on the MMPI scales. It is also of note that it has not been empirically determined whether assertions made about cultural differences on the original MMPI apply to the restandardized version of the MMPI (MMPI-2).

With Asian-American populations, there are very few studies to date on which to base our discussion. Marsella, Sanborn, Kameoka, Shizuru, and Brennan (1975) used scale 2 of the MMPI with a normal sample of Chinese- and Japanese-Americans in a larger study to validate depression measures. The researchers found that scale 2 was significantly more elevated among Japanese and Chinese males than among Caucasian males. No ethnic differences were found among females.

S. Sue and D. W. Sue (1974) compared the MMPI profiles of Asian-American and non-Asian college students using student psychological services. Sue and Sue found that although the profiles for Asians were similar to those of non-Asians, many of the scales (L, F, 1, 2, 4, 6, 7, 8, and 0) were more elevated for Asian males than for non-Asian males and that some the scales (L, F, and 0) were also more elevated for Asian than for non-Asian females. Using the critical items for somatic complaints and family problems, the researchers also found that Asian students, regardless of gender, endorsed higher distress on somatic and family problems than did the non-Asian students. This study suggests that there may be some gender and ethnic differences in the MMPI profiles.

However, when Tsushima and Onorato (1982) compared the MMPI scores of white and Japanese-American medical and neurological

patients in Hawaii, they found no significant ethnic differences in the T scores of validity or clinical scales when diagnoses were matched across ethnic groups. Significant gender effect was found across the two ethnic groups such that males scored higher than females on some of the scales (1, 2, 3, 4, 5, 7, 8, and 9) and females scored higher than males on scale 0. The researcher suggested that their results, in contrast to those of the earlier study by Sue and Sue (1974), may be due to their matching the ethnic groups on diagnostic classifications.

In all three available studies of MMPI comparisons between Asian-Americans and whites, the samples were limited (either college students or medical patients), and sample sizes tended to be small. Thus, the generalizability of the results to Asian-American populations is not known. Because all three studies were conducted on Asian-American subjects in the United States, the MMPI was administered in English in all cases and no translations were performed. However, the question of translation equivalence still remains, as it is not clear whether Asian-American subjects in the studies were as proficient in the English language as the non-Asian comparison subjects. There is some evidence to suggest that Asian-Americans who have lived in the United States for several generations still experience some difficulty with English language mastery (Watanabe, 1973). Because of this, the results can only indicate a possible cultural contribution to the elevation on some of the MMPI scales.

More systematic investigations of the MMPI with Asian populations overseas have been carried out in Hong Kong and in China. Cheung and Song (1989) reviewed twenty-six studies of the Chinese-language version of the MMPI on Chinese psychiatric populations. They found that the translation equivalence of the Chinese MMPI had been established through numerous back translations and modification of items (Song, 1991). Thus questions about the cross-cultural validity of the instrument were directed to its conceptual and metric equivalence. The cumulative results of the studies demonstrated that the Chinese version adequately differentiated between Chinese psychiatric patients and normal controls. Three scales (F, 2, and 8) were elevated among the normal Chinese subjects, yet Chinese psychiatric patients were elevated even higher than the baseline norm, often in the range of three standard deviations above the American norm for normal subjects. The patterns of profile elevations on the Chinese MMPI for major mental disorders (e.g., schizophrenia, mania, depression, and neurotic disorders) were comparable to the profile patterns of American subjects. Based on the review, Cheung and Song recommended the clinical application of the Chinese version of the MMPI to Chinese, with a cautionary note on interpreting moderate elevations on scales F, 2, and 8. Because of the significant sample size of the Chinese MMPI studies, metric equivalence could be addressed. Specifically, Cheung and Song suggested allowing for an adjustment of one additional standard deviation on the F, 2, and 8 scales when predicting psychopathology among Chinese.

Cattell's 16PF Studies

Early studies conducted in Hawaii on ethnic differences between Asian-Americans' and whites' personality characteristics tended to use personality tests not now commonly used in clinical assessment. Meredith (1966) administered Cattell's 16PF (Cattell, Eber, & Tatsuoka, 1970) to Japanese-American and white college students and found that the Japanese-American males in his sample tended to appear more submissive, different, reserved, serious, regulated, tense, affected by feelings, and socially precise, compared with their white counterparts. The Japanese-American females appeared more suspicious, group-dependent, submissive, different, reserved, and apprehensive.

Golden (1978) also administered Cattell's 16PF to Japanese-American and white American college students. The results indicated that while the second-order factor pattern for white respondents was almost identical to that reported by Cattell (1970), the Japanese-American respondents' pattern was significantly different from that of the white Americans. Of note, Cattell's Anxiety factor failed to appear as a factor in the analysis of responses by the Japanese-Americans. As the Japanese-American sample were all third-generation Japanese in Hawaii, a group that would be considered highly assimilated to the American culture, the failure to replicate the second-order factor structure of the 16PF with this population raised a question of the cultural utility of this measure. In these two studies with Japanese-Americans, translation, conceptual, and metric equivalence of the 16PF were not addressed, and the interpretation of cultural differences assumed an etic perspective.

OPI Studies

The Omnibus Personality Inventory (OPI; Heist & Yonge, 1968) has also been a popular measure of personality among personality studies of Asian-American college students. The studies using the OPI also tended to interpret elevation on the scales of this self-report measure as signs of maladjustment. That is, the findings have typically been interpreted as showing that Asian-American students appeared more isolated, lonely, nervous, anxious, and less autonomous than white students.

D. W. Sue and colleagues (D. W. Sue & Frank, 1973; D. W. Sue & Kirk, 1973) collected data from entering college students, including responses on the OPI. The sample was made up of 205 Chinese-Americans, 95 Japanese-Americans, and 2,027 white Americans. The researchers found that Asians appeared to be less oriented to theoretical and abstract ideas and concepts than whites on the scale designed to measure intellectual disposition. Asians also tended to endorse items that reflected their dislike for uncertainty, ambiguity, and novel situations in favor of more structured ones, compared with whites. Asians were also found to more strongly endorse conformity, obedience to authority, and less independence. Other ethnic differences showed that Asians tended to report less social extraversion, more feelings of isolation and loneliness, and higher likelihood of being uncomfortable and anxious.

S. Sue and Zane (1985) also used the OPI as a measure of psychological well-being, along with other measures of happiness, satisfaction, and self-esteem. In a study of the relation between academic achievement and socioemotional adjustment, they documented that although both American-born and recent-immigrant Chinese-American students performed significantly higher than the average university student on measures of academic achievement, recent immigrants exhibited socioemotional difficulties, as evidenced by reports of greater unhappiness, anxiety, and less personal integration (feelings of hostility, loneliness, and rejection) on the OPI. Sue and Zane suggested that for some Chinese-American students, particularly recent immigrants, high academic achievement may come at certain academic and psychological costs. The recent immigrant students, for example, were studying longer hours, taking fewer courses, and restricting career alternatives. Sue and Zane speculated that the hardships that accompany immigration and survival in a competitive university setting with less than perfect English skills may exert psychological stress.

Abe and Zane (1990) showed that the ethnic differences among foreign-born Asian-, U.S.-born Asian-, and white American college students in psychological adjustment remain, even after possible confounding variables (demographics, response set, and personality style) were controlled in the analysis. In the study, levels of psychological maladjustment were measured using the Personal Integration subscale of the OPI. The items from the Personal Integration subscale were factor analyzed to yield two factors, interpersonal distress and intrapersonal distress, and foreign-born Asian-American subjects reported significantly greater levels of distress on both factors than did U.S.-born Asian-Americans or white American students.

Critique of the Studies using the Etic Perspective

Chin (1983) argued that ethnic differences on personality measures have often been interpreted with a Western bias that works negatively against Asian-Americans. For example, whereas lower scores on the OPI scales of Social Introversion or Personal Integration may be interpreted as signs of introversion, self-abasement, and lack of self-confidence, an Asian perspective may view the same test results as positive signs of filial piety, modesty, and respect for authority. D. Sue and S. Sue (1987) also argued the importance of distinguishing between the personality and cultural sources of such manifest behavior. For example, on items designed to measure nonassertiveness, it is difficult to distinguish those who endorse the items because of cultural emphasis on maintaining interpersonal harmony from those who endorse the same items because of personality characteristics such as insecurity, lack of confidence, or passive aggressiveness. These arguments point to unresolved issues regarding the conceptual equivalence of many of the scales previously used to study the personality of Asian Americans, such as the 16PF or the OPI.

Use of Projective Tests

Draguns (1990) argued that cross-cultural research on projective measures of personality (such as the inkblot tests or the Thematic Apperception Test) have not been pursued because of premature assumptions that such instruments are too rooted in the Western culture. However, DeVos (1976) asserted that projective tests can be useful diagnostic tools transculturally because these tests are constructed to measure what DeVos considered to be cultural universals (organic basis for mental illness that is manifest in cognitive processes, social and cognitive maturational processes, and universality of altered states of consciousness). It may be true that the stimuli in the projective tests (e.g., inkblots) may be less culturally bound; however, the interpretations of the projective tests may be even more biased by the clinician's cultural background.

An example of a cross-cultural study of personality characteristics in the clinical population using projective testing is a study by Suzuki, Peters, Weibender, and Gilespie (1987) that compared American and Japanese schizophrenics on Rorschach responses. The Rorschach responses were scored and interpreted using the Klopfer system. The researchers found significant differences between the two groups on eight of the thirty variables of the Rorschach (e.g., D percent, FM, CF, etc.). The authors hypothesized that the areas in which ethnic differences appeared (which were interpreted as reflecting differences in thought processes, emotionality, coping mechanisms, and conformity) may be the aspects of schizophrenia that are more amenable to cultural and social shaping than those areas that may be more biologically driven. However, the authors acknowledged that in the absence of norms for these Rorschach variables in the normal Japanese population, it was difficult to discern whether the differences truly reflected cultural differences.

Chin (1983) found that on the Thematic Apperception Test, Chinese-Americans tended to have themes related to shame and authority figures that were qualitatively different from those of non-Asians. Different interpretations of such themes are possible; they may reflect conflict over authority, or they may reflect cultural ideals and adaptive solutions to conflicts. With respect to the Rorschach inkblot tests, Chin also asserted that the cultural value placed on a holistic approach in Asian cultures may be associated with more Whole responses, and that the Chinese culture has a vastly different meaning attached to certain colors such as red or white from the Western connotation of such colors. Clearly, conceptual equivalence problems are also salient in the use of projective tests.

The Emic Perspective

One criticism of etic approaches to the assessment of Asian-Americans is that Western personality theories underlying assessment measures may not be consistent with the culture or cultural explanations of Asian-Americans. There have been recent cross-cultural efforts to

assess the personality of Asians from emic or combined emic-etic points of view.

In a large-scale empirical study, Yang and Bond (1990) explored whether the Chinese hold implicit personality theories that are different from the Big Five dimensions of personality derived from U.S. studies of personality. The Big Five refers to five orthogonal factors—Extraversion, Agreeableness, Conscientiousness, Emotional Stability, and Culture—that have repeatedly been found to underlie personality attributes in research spanning more than half a century, primarily in the U.S. (Wiggins & Picus, 1989). The authors argued that past studies of non-American cultures' personality perception have used either only the personality descriptors taken from the English language or only the personality descriptors that exist in the target culture's language, and that such methodological approaches have made equivalence of the resulting personality dimensions difficult to determine.

Yang and Bond (1990) combined both emic and etic approaches in studying person perception among the Chinese. They carefully selected 150 personality-trait adjectives in the Chinese language that represented a spectrum in social desirability and in semantic categories (other-oriented, thing-oriented, and self-oriented). In addition, the authors selected twenty sets of bipolar adjectives from Cattell's (1947) reduced personality sphere set to represent the Big Five. More than 2,000 Chinese university students rated two target persons out of the six (father, mother, teacher, neighbor, friend, and self) on the 150 adjectives and 20 bipolar adjective sets.

Through factor analysis, Yang and Bond (1990) identified five bipolar factors that may be regarded as the basic emic dimensions of Chinese personality perception: Social orientation—Self-centeredness; Competence—Impotence; Expressiveness—Conservatism; Self-control—Impulsiveness; and Optimism—Neuroticism. The authors then examined the degree of overlap between these indigenous Chinese Big Five Factors with the imported American Big Five. They concluded that overall, the imported factors can be combined to reasonably identify four of the five indigenous factors (all but the Optimism factor), although there is a one-to-one correspondence for only two factors, Social Orientation (with Agreeableness) and Optimism (with Emotional Stability).

Given that indigenous Chinese personality factors do not correspond well with the Western personality factors (Yang & Bond, 1990), the Multi-Trait Personality Inventory (MTPI) was developed by Chinese scholars (Cheung, Conger, Hau, Lew, & Lau, 1992) specifically to address the inadequacy of the imposed etic approach in dealing with functional and conceptual equivalence in personality assessment. The MTPI was developed from an emic perspective of the Chinese culture to identify which of the indigenous Chinese personality dimensions stay stable across four major Chinese populations (mainland China, Taiwan, Hong Kong, and the U.S.) The MTPI consists of 122 items that represent attitudes, beliefs, typical behaviors, and affective reactions; each item is rated on a six-point bipolar scale with the poles being antonyms, logical opposites, or psychological opposites. The measure has nineteen item clusters, which can be classified into five factors (Outgoing vs. Withdrawn; Self-Serving vs. Principled; Conforming vs. Nonconforming; Unstable vs. Stable; Strict vs. Accepting). The common personality characteristics across the four Chinese groups reflected all Chinese perceiving themselves as neither extraverted nor introverted, neither obedient nor rebellious, neither moody nor imperturbable, and neither competitive nor cooperative; however, all Chinese perceived themselves as trusting, principled, tolerant, responsible, self-controlled, and opposed to permissive sex. Such personality traits appear consistent with the Confucian values indigenous to Chinese culture. There were some peripheral differences in personality traits among the four groups. Importantly, the Chinese group in the U.S. were found to have the greatest median standard deviation in the overall distribution of item variances, probably reflecting the heterogeneous origin of the Chinese-American populations.

Preliminary efforts to develop culture-specific measures of overseas Asian personality point to the importance of understanding the cultural roots of Asian-American personality that may be otherwise misinterpreted in assessment. However, the applicability of such personality measures to Asian-Americans is undetermined. One factor that distinguishes Asian-Americans from overseas Asian populations is their experience of being socialized to various degrees in two cultures, and it is this topic to which we next turn our attention.

Measures of Acculturation and Value Orientation

Recent research has produced some measures designed specifically to be sensitive to various levels of acculturation among Asian-Americans rather than to measure the Asian-American personality per se. These measures are relatively new or in stages of development and have not been used extensively with either normal or clinical populations. The measures will be described here because they illustrate important issues regarding the assessment of cultural characteristics of Asian-American clients.

The Suinn-Lew Asian Self-Identity Acculturation Scale (SL-ASIA) was developed for the assessment of acculturation of Asian-Americans (Suinn, Rickard-Figueroa, Lew, & Virgil, 1987). The measure is a twenty-one-item multiple-choice questionnaire modeled after the Acculturation Rating Scale for Mexican Americans (ARSMA) (Cuellar, Harris, & Jasso, 1980). The scale has good reliability (.88 to .91), and a recent concurrent validity study demonstrated that the SL-ASIA scores were significantly correlated with demographic information hypothesized to be associated with levels of Asian-American identity (Suinn, Ahuna, & Khoo, 1992). The scale has a five-factor structure; reading/writing/cultural preference, ethnic interaction, affinity for ethnic identity and pride, generational identity, and food preferences.

There has also been an effort in Asian-American psychology to capture the cultural and ethnic differences in interpersonal dynamics. One such construct proposed and assessed by Zane

(1991) is loss of face. Loss of face is defined as the threat to or loss of one's social integrity, and it has been identified as a salient interpersonal dynamic factor in Asian social relations (Sue & Morishima, 1982). The construct is conceptualized as involving face-threatening behavior in the domains of social status, ethical behavior, social propriety, and self-discipline. Sensitivity to loss of face is considered as a personality or dispositional variable unrelated to psychological maladjustment. The Loss of Face (LOF) scale is a twenty-one-item self-report scale designed to assess the degree to which one is sensitive to loss of face. Each item is measured on a seven-point scale of degree of agreement with each statement. Psychometric studies show good internal consistency (alpha = .83) and show concurrent and discriminant validity with measures of other-directedness, private and public self-consciousness, social anxiety, extraversion, and acting. In a preliminary study, Zane (1991) found a significant ethnic difference between Asian ($M = 91.8$) and white ($M = 80.4$) college students, even when controlled for ethnic differences on social anxiety, acting, other-directedness, social desirability, and acculturation.

The INDividualism-COLlectivism (IND-COL) Scale (Hui, 1988) was developed to measure the construct of collectivism as a personality construct. The measure was developed simultaneously in Chinese and English with a rigorous set of reliability and validation studies. The scale consists of sixty-three items that make up six subscales, each subscale pertaining to collectivist orientation toward a specific target person. The subscales are Spouse, Parent, Kin, Neighbor, Friend, and Coworker, and the sum of all subscales constitutes the General Collectivism Index (GCI). The INDCOL Scale appears to differentiate people within both Chinese and American cultures on the degree to which one holds collectivist, group-oriented tendencies in various interpersonal relationships.

These measures demonstrate promising efforts to understand what may underlie cultural influences on the personality of Asian-Americans. Further research on the relation between these measures and those commonly used in personality assessment may be helpful in examining the gaps in cultural equivalence of personality assessment.

PRACTICAL CONSIDERATIONS

The primary objective of personality assessment is to understand and predict the behavior and personality characteristics of the person. To this end, we must ask, what information is useful? And how should one approach the task? How does a clinician consider translation, conceptual, and metric equivalence issues for each case? The general approach to the assessment of ethnic minority persons must consist of a framework for considering the role of culture in the assessment.

Lessons from Minority Psychology: A Cultural Framework for Assessment

Dissatisfied with the existing conceptualization of culture and cultural equivalence in cognitive-ability testing of African-Americans, Helms (1992) proposed the "culturalist" perspective to examine racial differences. She maintained that racial and ethnic-group comparison studies typically have used race or ethnicity and culture synonymously, and most studies did not attempt to define culture operationally. She asserted that for African-Americans, cognitive-ability tests measure acculturation and knowledge of white culture. Specifically, she asserted that "knowledge of a person's racial group membership reveals nothing about the amount or type of culture the person has absorbed" (p. 1091). The "culturalist" perspective advocates specification and measurement of race-related psychological characteristics (e.g., behaviors, beliefs, and values) that are thought to describe and differentiate racial groups. Helms also argued that there are many dimensions often overlooked in considering cultural equivalence (i.e., functional, conceptual, linguistic, psychometric, testing condition, contextual, and sampling).

Jones and Thorne (1987) also asserted that ethnic minorities cannot easily be compared with members of the dominant cultural group using established assessment measures and techniques. They asserted that established personality inventories (e.g., the MMPI) may be adapted for use with ethnic minorities if rigorous efforts to address equivalence issues are undertaken. However, they also pointed to the practical difficulty in re-norming such measures for ethnic groups in the United States, given within-group heterogeneity and the ever-changing sociocultural context. In addition, education and socioeconomic status often mediate an ethnic minority person's cultural experience, such that established assessment measures may be more valid for those who have achieved middle-class status.

The above discussion of the assessment of ethnic minority persons is useful in conducting the assessment of Asian-Americans. The culturalist perspective stresses the importance of addressing the cultural equivalence issues. In addition, one must consider which source of within-group heterogeneity in the Asian-American population may be relevant in personality assessment. Although there exist cultural commonalities in psychological characteristics and world views among Asian-Americans (Ho, 1982), one important dimension on which they can vary enormously is the level to which they have been exposed to and have acculturated to the American culture. An Asian-American person's performance on Western-derived personality measures may reflect the degree of his or her acculturation (particularly through exposure to American education).

Guidelines

Consideration of equivalence issues in the assessment of Asian-American clients becomes a complex task, as there exist enormous individual differences in the degree to which a given Asian-American person identifies with and can be placed in the American and Asian cultures. Depending on the level of the individual's acculturation and cultural identification, translation, conceptual, and metric equivalence take on varying degrees of importance. Thus, a clinician must first assess the individual's cultural context.

Assessment of Cultural Context

Extensive and detailed historical and background information on the client will be helpful in placing the person, and thus the personality assessment responses, in his or her culture or sociocultural context. Level of acculturation can be assessed formally or informally. For example, a measure specifically designed to assess acculturation level, such as SL-ASIA (Suinn et al., 1987), may be administered as a preliminary or a screening instrument. However, it is strongly recommended that the tester assess the level of acculturation and identification with Asian and American culture with an interview. In assessing the degree of acculturation, it is important first to obtain information regarding the client's generational status (i.e., first generation immigrated to the U.S., second generation born in the U.S. with immigrant parents, and so forth) and the degree to which the client identifies with the American and Asian cultures.

Lee (1982) suggested four general indicators that assess a client's acculturation and adaptation: years in the U.S., country of origin, professional affiliation, and age at the time of immigration. Further, Lee stated that a useful way to understand Chinese-American clients is to understand the client system in three domains: (1) physical and manifest features; (2) psychological features, dynamics, and structures; and (3) social, cultural, and ecological features. Under physical and manifest features, important information that must be inquired about includes language(s) and dialect(s) spoken and degree of fluency, physical health status and medical history, medications used (including herbs and Chinese medicines), work and job roles, help-seeking behaviors and patterns, and other significant demographic data (e.g., immigration status, age, sex, birth order, male and female siblings, educational background in the U.S. and elsewhere, marital status, income, years in the U.S., country of origin). Psychological features that must be assessed include rate and process of adaptation and acculturation, perceived problems and solutions, attitudes toward Western medicine and help, degree and kind of interruptions to the individual's life cycle, and perception of past successes and failures in problem solving and coping. Finally, under social, cultural, and ecological features, Lee suggested assessing the individual's migration and relocation process and history, work hours and work environment, and extent of contact with the social and human services network. These suggestions are applicable to other Asian-American clients as well.

The assessment of acculturation level is important for another reason. The notion of acculturative stress (Berry & Annis, 1974) asserts that certain sets of stress behavior often occur during acculturation, such as lowered mental health status (e.g., anxiety and depression), feelings of marginality and alienation, heightened psychosomatic symptom level, and identity confusion. This assertion is supported by empirical documentation within the Asian-American population of higher levels of depression among foreign-born and immigrant groups (Kuo, 1984; S. Sue & Zane, 1985). Further, Aldwin and Greenberger (1987) found evidence among Korean-American college students that the students' perception of their parents' adherence to traditional Korean values was most strongly associated with higher levels of depression among the students. Such findings suggest that the value orientation of the individual and the family must also be evaluated. A clinician must be aware of the possible stress reactions among Asian-Americans who are undergoing acculturation that may elevate the clinical picture. If the client is an immigrant, it is especially useful to find out reasons for immigration, language use, degree of culture shock experienced, postimmigration adjustment, and discrepancy between pre- and postimmigration life patterns (Kim, 1985).

Testing Procedures

Establishing translation equivalence in the testing procedure poses a particular difficulty with Asian-American clients. The technical aspects of the translation problem are somewhat easier to solve if the client is non-English-speaking, since interviews and measures must be translated appropriately by qualified translators. However, it is important not to assume that translation equivalence is not an issue for English-speaking Asian-American clients. Bilingual clients may be limited in the range of their vocabulary or their ability to express internal psychological experiences in the English language, and they may require assistance from a translator or the assessing clinician in responding to various measures.

Ideally, a testing clinician would like to be able to select appropriate measures depending on the level of acculturation of the Asian-American client. However, there is a notable lack of normative data for Asian-Americans (not to mention the diverse ethnic groups that make up this population) on most personality assessment tools. Many of the measures on which some data exist (e.g., OPI, 16PF) are not widely used in clinical evaluations, and efforts to develop measures of indigenous psychological characteristics of Asian cultures have only begun. Jones and Thorne (1987) suggested that the established measures that are widely used in personality testing may be more valid for those who have achieved middle-class status, and such a principle appears to be applicable to Asian-Americans who are acculturated and have had extensive exposure to the American educational system. The best course of action, then, is not to rely on any single measure of personality but to use multiple sources for information. In the absence of widely used measures with established norms for different Asian groups, it is wise to use assessment data to generate hypotheses that can be supported or not supported by other measures or information. The use of translated measures may be needed.

An important aspect of the testing procedure is the client's nonverbal behavior. Foo and Kaser-Boyd (1993) suggested that a traditional Chinese client who is not familiar with psychology or testing may bring a certain "mental set" to testing. The mental set may include skepticism about psychology and Western medicine, a fatalistic world view (i.e., suffering is part of fate), and a reluctance to disclose one's troubles to strangers. Further, such a mental set may result in the client's being polite and overly cooperative, not openly confronting or challenging the clinician, yet minimally self-disclosing. The test material may look overly constricted, and the communication may be highly indirect.

Interpreting the Results

When the testing clinician is not familiar with the client's culture, it is imperative to contact an ethnic consultant about the assessment results regarding the conceptual equivalence of the measure and the client's responses. For some instruments (e.g., the MMPI), research has suggested using different interpretive norms for Asians living in Asia (see Cheung & Song, 1989). However, for Asian-Americans who are somewhat acculturated, it is not clear which norm (Asian or American) should be used, thus obscuring metric equivalence. In using instruments with no Asian norm, the clinician must be more conservative and cautious in interpreting the results of less acculturated individuals whose scores deviate from the American norm. However, one must also be aware of the danger in underestimating pathology for a culturally different client by over-attributing bizarre behavior or thought patterns to that person's culture (Lopez, 1989).

It is also important for the testing clinician to be aware of possible biases in making clinical observations and judgments of those who are culturally different. Li-Repac (1980) conducted a study with a small number of white and Chinese-American therapists who were asked to rate the psychological functioning of Chinese and white clients interviewed on videotapes. The study found that there were significant differences between the two therapist groups on ratings of the same clients. The white therapists tended to rate the Chinese-American clients as more depressed and inhibited and having less capacity for meaningful interpersonal relationships. The Chinese-American therapists judged the white clients to be more severely disturbed and have more psychopathology than did the white therapists. Thus cultural stereotyping may

have a subtle but important role in the clinical evaluation of a client who is culturally different.

Finally, as Chin (1983) asserted, personality assessment should emphasize the *uniqueness* of the individual and the *diversity* of Asian-American groups, which differ in cultural views and values, as well as the sociocultural milieu. One must be careful not to adhere rigidly to Western standards of mental health (e.g., independence and autonomy, emotional expressiveness, open communication styles) or assume that acculturation to American culture is the sole definition of adaptive personality functioning, but instead consider what is socially and culturally functional for the given individual.

Final Comments

In reviewing the existing literature and guidelines for conducting personality assessment with Asian-Americans, it becomes clear that much research is needed in order to delineate the extent of reliability, validity, and utility of various personality assessment measures and techniques. One useful area of future research would be to investigate the relation between acculturation and normative personality characteristics. Montgomery and Orozco (1985) used acculturation (as measured by the Acculturation Rating Scale for Mexican Americans, ARSMA) as the moderator variable in Hispanic-Americans' performance on the MMPI. As the SL-ASIA was modeled after the ARSMA, it may be potentially used as a moderator to help interpret the MMPI profiles once the relation between the two scales has been examined.

ACKNOWLEDGMENT

This project was supported by NIMH grant No. R01 MH44331.

REFERENCES

Abe, J. S., & Zane, N. W. S. (1990). Psychological maladjustment among Asian and White American college students: Controlling for confounds. *Journal of Counseling Psychology, 37,* 437–444.

Aldwin, C., & Greenberger, E. (1987). Cultural differences in the predictors of depression. *American Journal of Community Psychology, 15,* 789–813.

Asian Community Mental Health Services (1987). *California Southeast Asian mental health needs assessment.* Oakland, CA: Asian Community Mental Health Services.

Berry, J. W. (1980). Introduction to methodology. In H. C. Triandis & J. W. Berry (Eds.), *Handbook of cross-cultural psychology: Vol. 2. Methodology* (pp. 1–28). Boston: Allyn & Bacon.

Berry, J. W., & Annis, R. C. (1974). Acculturative stress: The role of ecology, culture, and differentiation. *Journal of Cross-cultural Psychology, 5,* 382–406.

Brislin, R. W. (1993). *Understanding culture's influence on behavior,* New York: Harcourt Brace Jovanovich.

Butcher, J. N. (1985). Current developments in MMPI use: An international perspective. In C. D. Spielberger & J. N. Butcher (Eds.), *Advances in personality assessment* (Vol. 4, pp. 83–94). Hillsdale, NJ: Erlbaum.

Cattell, R. B. (1947). Confirmation and clarification of primary personality traits. *Psychometrika, 42,* 402–421.

Cattell, R. B., Eber, H. W., & Tatsuoka, M. (1970). *Handbook for the Sixteen Personality Factors Questionnaire (16PF).* Champaign, IL: IPAT.

Cheung, F. M., & Song, W. (1989). A review on the clinical applications for the Chinese MMPI. *Psychological Assessment, 1,* 230–237.

Cheung, P. C., Conger, A. J., Hau, K., Lew, W. J. F., & Lau, S. (1992). Development of the Multi-Trait Personality Inventory (MTPI): Comparison among four Chinese populations. *Journal of Personality Assessment, 59,* 528–551.

Chin, J. L. (1983). Diagnostic considerations in working with Asian Americans. *American Journal of Orthopsychiatry, 7,* 263–278.

Colligan, R. C., Osborne, D., Swenson, W. M., & Offord, K. P. (1983). *The MMPI: A contemporary normative study.* New York: Praeger.

Cuellar, I., Harris, L., & Jasso, R. (1980). An acculturation scale for Mexican American normal and clinical populations. *Hispanic Journal of Behavioral Sciences, 2,* 199–217.

Dana, R. H. (1988). Culturally diverse groups and MMPI interpretations. *Professional Psychology: Research and Practice, 19,* 490–495.

DeVos, G. A. (1976). The interrelationship of social

and psychological structures in transcultural psychology. In W. P. Lebra (Ed.), *Culture-bound syndromes, ethnopsychiatry, and alternate therapies* (pp. 278–298). Honolulu: University Press of Hawaii.

Draguns, J. G. (1990). Applications of cross-cultural psychology in the field of mental health. In R. W. Brislin (Ed.), *Applied cross-cultural psychology.* Newbury Park, CA: Sage.

Foo, L., & Kaser-Boyd, N. (1993, March). *Psychological assessment with ethnic Chinese: Variables in the testing process.* Paper presented at the annual meeting of the Society for Personality Assessment, San Francisco.

Golden, C. J. (1978). Cross-cultural second order factor structures of the 16PF. *Journal of Personality Assessment, 42,* 167–170.

Greene, R. L. (1987). Ethnicity and MMPI performance: A review. *Journal of Consulting and Clinical Psychology, 55,* 497–512.

Helms, J. E. (1992). Why is there no study of cultural equivalence in standardized cognitive ability testing? *American Psychologist, 9,* 1083–1101.

Heist, P., & Yonge, G. (1968). *Omnibus Personality Inventory.* New York: Psychological Corporation.

Ho, D. Y. F. (1982). Asian concepts in behavioral science. *Psychologia, 25,* 228–235.

Hui, C. H. (1988). Measurement of Individualism-Collectivism. *Journal of Research in Personality, 22,* 17–36.

Jones, E. E., & Thorne, A. (1987). Rediscovery of the subject: Intercultural approaches to clinical assessment. *Journal of Consulting and Clinical Psychology, 55,* 488–495.

Kim, S. C. (1985). Family therapy for Asian Americans: A strategic-structural framework. *Psychotherapy, 22,* 342–348.

Kuo, W. H. (1984). Prevalence of depression among Asian Americans. *Journal of Nervous and Mental Disease, 172,* 449–457.

Lee, E. (1982). A social systems approach to assessment and treatment for Chinese American families. In M. McGoldrick, J. K. Pearce, & J. Giordano (Eds.), *Ethnicity and family therapy.* New York: Guilford Press.

Li-Repac, D. (1980). Cultural influences on clinical perception: A comparison between Caucasian and Chinese-American therapists. *Journal of Cross-Cultural Psychology, 11,* 327–342.

Lonner, W. J. (1990). An overview of cross-cultural testing and assessment. In R. W. Brislin (Ed.), *Applied cross-cultural psychology* (pp. 56–76). Newbury Park, CA: Sage.

Lopez, S. R. (1989). Patient variable biases in clinical judgment: Conceptual overview and methodological considerations. *Psychological Bulletin, 106,* 184–204.

Marsella, A., Sanborn, K., Kameoka, V., Shizuru, L., & Brennan, J. (1975). Cross-validation of self-report measures of depression among normal populations of Japanese, Chinese, and Caucasian ancestry. *Journal of Clinical Psychology, 31,* 281–287.

Meredith, G. M. (1966). Amae and acculturation among Japanese-American college students in Hawaii. *Journal of Social Psychology, 70,* 171–180.

Montgomery, G. T., & Orozco, S. (1985). Mexican Americans' performance on the MMPI as a function of level of acculturation. *Journal of Clinical Psychology, 41,* 203–212.

Song, W. (1991). Use and evaluation of a modified MMPI in China. *International Journal of Mental Health, 20,* 81–93.

Sue, D., & Sue, S. (1987). Cultural factors in the clinical assessment of Asian Americans. *Journal of Consulting and Clinical Psychology, 55,* 479–487.

Sue, D. W., & Frank, A. C. (1973). A typological approach to the psychological study of Chinese and Japanese American college males. *Journal of Social Issues, 29,* 129–148.

Sue, D. W., & Kirk, B. A. (1973). Differential characteristics of Japanese-American and Chinese-American college students. *Journal of Counseling Psychology, 20,* 142–148.

Sue, S., & Sue, D. W. (1974). MMPI comparisons between Asian-American and non-Asian students utilizing a student health psychiatric clinic. *Journal of Counseling Psychology, 21,* 423–427.

Sue, S., & Zane, N. W. S. (1985). Academic achievement and sociemotional adjustment among Chinese university students. *Journal of Counseling Psychology, 32,* 570–579.

Suinn, R. M., Ahuna, C., & Khoo, G. (1992). The Suinn-Lew Asian Self-Identity Acculturation Scale: Concurrent and factorial validation. *Educational and Psychological Measurement, 52,* 1–6.

Suinn, R., Rikard-Figueroa, K., Lew, S., & Virgil, P. (1987). The Suinn-Lew Asian Self-Identity Acculturation Scale: An initial report. *Educational and Psychological Measurement, 47,* 401–407.

Suzuki, A., Peters, L., Weisbender, L., & Gillespie, J. (1987). Characteristics of American and Japanese schizophrenic patients elicited by the Rorschach technique and demographic data. *International Journal of Social Psychiatry, 33,* 50–55.

Tsushima, W. T., & Onorato, V. A. (1982). Comparison of MMPI scores of White and Japanese-American medical patients. *Journal of Consulting and Clinical Psychology, 50,* 150–151.

U.S. Department of Commerce, Bureau of the Census (1988). *Asian and Pacific Islander population in the United States: 1980.* Report PC80–2–IE. Washington, DC: U.S. Government Printing Office.

U.S. Department of Commerce, Bureau of the Census (1991). *Race and Hispanic Origin.* 1990 Census Profile, No. 2. Washington, DC: U.S. Government Printing Office.

Watanabe, C. (1973). Self-expressions and the Asian-American experience. *Personnel and Guidance Journal, 51,* 390–396.

Westermeyer, J., Vang, T. F., & Neider, J. (1983). A comparison of refugees using and not using a psychiatric service: An analysis of DSM-III criteria and self-rating scales in cross-cultural context. *Journal of Operational Psychology, 14,* 36–41.

Wiggins, J. S., & Picus, A. L. (1989). Conceptions of personality disorders and dimensions of personality. *Psychological Assessment: A Journal of Consulting and Clinical Psychology, 1,* 305–316.

Yang, K., & Bond, M. H. (1990). Exploring implicit personality theories with indigenous or imported constructs: The Chinese case. *Journal of Personality and Social Psychology, 58,* 1087–1095.

Zane, N. W. S. (1991, August). *An empirical examination of loss of face among Asian Americans.* Paper presented at the 99th annual convention of the American Psychological Association, San Francisco.

10
Personality Assessment of Hispanic Clients

Roberto J. Velásquez

The key to the successful treatment of Hispanic-Americans, in a variety of clinical, mental health, or psychiatric settings (e.g., inpatient and outpatient psychiatric facilities, state hospitals, correctional institutions, substance-abuse treatment programs, and community mental health centers), lies in the effective, accurate, and valid assessment of Hispanic clients in these settings (Chavez & Gonzales-Singh, 1980; Dana, 1993; Malgady, Rogler, & Constantino, 1987; Padilla & Ruiz, 1973, 1975; Rivera & Cespedes, 1983; Velasquez, 1984a; Velasquez & Callahan, 1992). The assessment or evaluation, whether conducted in English or Spanish, or by a Hispanic or non-Hispanic psychologist, serves as the foundation for the understanding and appreciation of a Hispanic client's unique problems or concerns.

In addition, the evaluation, if conducted effectively, can be a potent first step in the culturally sensitive treatment of a Hispanic client. That is, if conducted appropriately, the psychological assessment of a Hispanic client should lead the psychologist to make competent and well-informed decisions that are anchored in the Hispanic client's experience, culture, and world view. At the same time, the evaluation should help the psychologist make sound and

practical decisions about the Hispanic client's treatment (e.g., identify and/or describe mental illness, assist in diagnostic decision making, aid in treatment planning/selection, and evaluate treatment outcome).

Malgady, Rogler, and Constantino (1987), in discussing the need to assess Hispanics in clinical settings, observed that a Hispanic client's "early contacts with a mental health agency are likely to be diagnostic in nature, whether the assessment performed is formal or informal, brief or intensive" (p. 228). They also observed that "the procedure might include a mental status examination . . . psychological tests might be administered . . . and then a social history is taken to place test and interview data in proper [cultural] context. At the end of this process, a diagnosis is formulated, a disposition is rendered, and a treatment plan is developed" (pp. 228–229). Padilla and Ruiz (1975) argued that "a [Hispanic] client's [assessment] performance . . . is extremely important since it is used to determine whether treatment will be offered; and if so, what type" (p. 107). Finally, Rivera and Cespedes (1983) noted that "valid psychological evaluations of . . . Hispanics are important . . . and it may be that without these [assessments] many [Hispanic] clients will be overlooked [by the mental health system] or misunderstood [by the psychologist]" (p. 68).

Over the past two decades, the assessment of Hispanics has received widespread, and overdue, attention in the literature. This is evidenced by the number of articles that have discussed some of the most salient issues in the psychological assessment of Hispanics (e.g., Butcher & Clark, 1979; Butcher & Garcia, 1978; Cervantes & Acosta, 1992; Dahlstrom, 1986; Fabrega, 1990; Frank, 1993; French, 1993; Creene, 1987, 1991; Kinzie & Manson, 1987; Padilla & Ruiz, 1973, 1975; Velasquez, 1984b, 1992, 1993; Velasquez & Callahan, 1992; Williams, 1987; Ziskin, 1981). This is also evidenced by the number of empirical investigations that have examined the performance of Hispanics on a particular psychological assessment instrument. For example, between 1970 and 1993, a remarkable ninety studies were conducted on Hispanics with the Minnesota Multiphasic Personality Inventory (MMPI; MMPI-2).

In addition, researchers have paid significant attention to other relevant issues, including the prevalence of mental disorders among Hispanics, the relationship between Hispanics' acculturation and psychological impairment, bilingualism and the expression of psychopathology, and the psychiatric diagnosis and treatment of mental disorders among Hispanics (e.g., Bamford, 1991; Bradford & Munoz, 1993; Canino, 1982; Cuellar, 1982; Cuellar, Martinez, Jimenez, & Gonzalez, 1983; Cuellar & Roberts, 1984; Flaskerud, 1986; Griffith, 1983; Jenkins, 1988; Jones, Gray, & Parson, 1983; Lopez, Boccellari, & Hall, 1988; Lopez & Hernandez, 1987; Gomez, Ruiz, & Rumbaut, 1985; Marcos, Alpert, Urcuyo, & Kesselman, 1973; Meadow, 1982; Pina, 1985; Price & Cuellar, 1981).

Yet, despite the immense growth of interest in this topic, there remain many lingering questions concerning the psychological assessment or evaluation of Hispanic clients. For example, "What are some of the common misconceptions surrounding the assessment of Hispanic clients?" "What is the current status of assessment research on Hispanics?" "What are some of the practical problems found in the assessment of Hispanics?" and "What are some practical suggestions, or recommendations, for assessing Hispanic clients?"

The purpose of this chapter is to provide some answers to these questions. More important, the author attempts to provide some practical guidelines for the effective, and culturally sensitive, assessment of Hispanic clients. While this chapter does not purport to present all of the answers or knowledge that is necessary to effectively assess Hispanics, it does provide some much-needed practical information that may lessen some of the problems (e.g., misdiagnosis, barriers in communication, etc.) that are often encountered in the assessment and treatment of Hispanic clients. For example, this author believes that the long-standing failure to provide adequate treatment services to Hispanic clients, in a variety of clinical settings, stems from the many errors and faulty assumptions that psychologists often make in the assessment or evaluation of Hispanics. This also stems from the lack of basic "hands-on" information available to psychologists in the professional literature.

Based on the above-mentioned questions, this chapter is divided into four major sections. The first section presents some of the common misconceptions held by psychologists about the assessment of Hispanics. For example, many psychologists are still under the false impression that the psychological assessment of Hispanics in clinical settings is identical to, or parallels, the assessment of Hispanics in educational settings. The second section discusses the current status of assessment research on Hispanics. For example, while there has been an explosion of research on Hispanics over the past decade, the body of research is dominated by investigations on one particular instrument, the MMPI. That is, there is a marked absence of research on other instruments that may be more useful in the assessment of Hispanic clients (e.g., the Rorschach or TAT). The third section presents some of the practical problems found in the assessment of Hispanics. These include poor or inappropriate referrals, improper test selection, poor test administration, and misinterpretation of test data. The final section offers some practical suggestions for psychologists who routinely assess Hispanic clients in clinical practice. For example, psychologists are advised to view the psychological assessment of Hispanic clients as an integral part of treatment. Too often, psychologists make a distinction between assessment and treatment when working with Hispanic clients. That is, they separate the two as if they were independent or mutually exclusive processes. In fact, this author believes that the assessment phase is the first part of any treatment with any client, irrespective of ethnicity, culture, or race.

COMMON MISCONCEPTIONS CONCERNING THE ASSESSMENT OF HISPANICS

In 1984, this author conducted a survey of psychologists in clinical practice. The purpose of this survey was twofold: (1) to determine psychologists' specific assessment/testing practices with regard to Hispanics; and (2) to identify some of the common misconceptions regarding the psychological assessment of Hispanic clients (Velasquez, 1984b). The results of the survey indicated that, in addition to traditional interview techniques, psychological assessment instruments such as the MMPI, Rorschach, and Thematic Apperception Test (TAT) were routinely administered to Hispanic clients in a variety of psychiatric settings. This trend was found to be generally consistent with trends found in the profession (e.g., Lubin, Larsen, & Matarazzo, 1984; Lubin, Larsen, Matarazzo, & Seever, 1985; Piotrowsky & Keller, 1989).

While such a trend was not surprising, what was surprising were some of the respondents' beliefs, or misconceptions, about the assessment of Hispanic clients. That is, psychologists presented false or unsubstantiated impressions about the assessment or evaluation of Hispanics. Below are five of the most common misconceptions.

Misconception 1: *Hispanic clients are more difficult to assess or evaluate because they are not psychologically minded.* This assumption, which echoes long-standing stereotypes of His-

panics, is based on the belief that Hispanic clients are not socialized or familiar with traditional mental health services, compared with the majority of the population. It is also based on the belief that Hispanic clients are not able to communicate to psychologists in the language or terminology that is used in clinical practice, or that Hispanic clients are somehow not able to be insightful about their emotional or psychological functioning. In the author's experience, Hispanic clients are not deficient in communication skills. To the contrary, Hispanic clients are some of the most verbal and articulate clients seen in clinical practice, if they are allowed to communicate in an environment that is not oppressive or prejudicial.

Misconception 2: *Problems in the clinical assessment of Hispanic clients are similar to those found in the intelligence/educational testing of Hispanics.* This assumption is based on the belief that the issues (e.g., test bias, test invalidity, etc.) found in the intelligence testing of Hispanics (usually in educational settings) are identical or parallel to those found in the assessment or evaluation of Hispanics in clinical settings. For example, one respondent noted that "I would never use any assessment instruments on Hispanics because they are just as biased as intelligence tests." This assumption is unwarranted, since the assessment of psychopathology or mental illness is theoretically different from the assessment of intellectual or cognitive functioning in all clients irrespective of ethnicity or race. That is, intelligence is generally a static construct while mental illness is subject to dramatic changes based on a combination of numerous biopsychosocial factors.

Misconception 3: *Psychological assessment devices, whether projective or objective, often misdiagnose or misclassify Hispanic clients.* This assumption is based on the belief that somehow psychological tests are inherently biased, or that a test makes the ultimate decision about the diagnosis of a Hispanic client. While there continues to be a vigorous debate about etic versus emic issues in the assessment of ethnic minorities including Hispanics (see Dana, 1993), and about appropriate test norms (see Cervantes & Acosta, 1992; Padilla & Ruiz, 1973, 1975), psychological assessment instruments alone do not misclassify or misdiagnose a client. In the author's opinion, it is the psychologist who is most responsible for the misdiagnosis of a Hispanic client. For example, if the psychologist depends on only one instrument (e.g., the TAT) or on a computerized interpretation of a particular test (e.g., the MMPI/MMPI-2), then he or she is more likely to make diagnostic errors.

Misconception 4: *Issues in the psychological assessment of Hispanic clients are identical to those found in other ethnic minority groups, most notably African-Americans.* This assumption is based on the belief that the inherent issues in the assessment of Hispanics are identical to those encountered in the assessment of African-Americans. Furthermore, this assumption presupposes that because of a "shared minority status," or because Hispanics and African-Americans share similar historical experiences and sociodemographic characteristics (e.g., poverty, undereducation, high unemployment, etc.), that Hispanics should perform similarly on any type of assessment procedure, or that the emotional problems experienced by Hispanics are the same as those experienced by African-Americans or other minority groups.

An obvious example of this misconception is seen in the type of assessment research frequently conducted on Hispanics. The prototypic approach, borrowed from research on African-Americans, has been to compare the performance of Hispanics to that of whites on a particular measure or test instrument (e.g., Dahlstrom, 1986; Greene, 1987, 1991; Velasquez, 1984a, 1992; Velasquez & Callahan, 1992). While differences are usually, and expectedly, found, the findings often have little or no relevance to clinical practice. This is clearly an incorrect assumption since from the onset, the assessment of Hispanics must consider issues that reflect the heterogeneity of this population (e.g., language use, nationality, immigrant status, acculturation, etc.), and not that of other ethnic minority groups.

Misconception 5: *Only Hispanic psychologists can effectively assess and treat Hispanic clients.* This assumption is based on the belief that somehow "Hispanic psychologists have it in

with Hispanic clients" because both are from the same ethnic group. This is also based on the belief held by many non-Hispanic psychologists that it is better, and easier, simply to refer a Hispanic client to a Hispanic psychologist for assessment and treatment.

While it can be advantageous to have the psychologist and client from the same cultural or ethnic group, it can also be problematic since a Hispanic psychologist can often lose objectivity in the assessment process. For example, this author once supervised an Argentinian-born intern who felt overly confident about her assessment skills when working with Hispanic clients. She was assigned to assess a Chicano or Mexican-American client from the inner city of San Diego. Much to her surprise, she encountered more difficulty in working with this client than in working with non-Chicano clients because of her inability to understand the unique dialect or historical experiences of Chicanos in this country. Also, she wrongly assumed that Argentinians are exactly the same as Chicanos with respect to values and folk beliefs. In this author's experience, the assessment of Hispanic clients can be as well accomplished by a non-Hispanic psychologist as a Hispanic psychologist, if he or she is willing to learn the cultural, social, linguistic, and psychological nuances that define or govern the world view of Hispanic clients.

RESEARCH ON THE PSYCHOLOGICAL ASSESSMENT OF HISPANICS

While the purpose of this chapter is discuss some of the practical issues in the evaluation of Hispanic clients, it is essential to present an overview of assessment research on Hispanics. This is of critical importance, since many erroneous impressions concerning the psychological assessment of Hispanic clients are based on psychologists' limited knowledge of research on Hispanics. For example, it is still quite common to hear psychologists make the following inaccurate generalizations or comments regarding the literature on Hispanics: "Research on Hispanics did not begin until the 1970s," "There are only a handful of studies on the psycholog-

TABLE 10.1. Comparison of Hispanic Research on Five Popular Assessment Instruments by Decade

	Decade					
Instrument	1940–49	1950–59	1960–69	1970–79	1980–89	1990–93
MMPI/MMPI-2 (n = 97)	1	0	6	16	53	21
TAT (n = 12)	0	0	3	1	7	1
Rorschach (n = 11)	1	2	2	1	5	0
BDI (n = 2)	—	—	0	0	2	
MCMI (n = 0)	—	—	—	0	0	0
Total (N = 122)	2	2	11	18	67	22

Note: MMPI = Minnesota Multiphasic Personality Inventory; TAT = Thematic Apperception Test; BDI = Beck Depression Inventory; MCMI = Millon Clinical Multiaxial Inventory.

ical assessment of Hispanics," "The Rorschach is the most frequently used instrument in research on Hispanics," or "Hispanics have never been included in the norming or standardization of a test instrument."

A review of Table 10.1 indicates that contrary to popular belief, there is a rapidly growing body of research on Hispanics. This is especially evidenced by the number of studies conducted between 1980 and 1993. In fact, over 70 percent of all investigations on Hispanics were conducted within this period. At the same time, the table suggests that while the MMPI, TAT, and Rorschach are routinely used in research on Hispanics, it is the MMPI that has received most of the attention. The table also notes a marked absence of research on other popular or established assessment instruments, including the Beck Depression Inventory (BDI), the Personality Assessment Inventory (PAI), and the Millon Clinical Multiaxial Inventory (MCMI-/MCMI-2).

The popularity of the MMPI in research on Hispanics is best described by Williams (1987) who noted that "the MMPI has . . . characteristics that make it attractive for cross-cultural use. It has been translated into more than 100 languages [including Spanish] . . . . [Also] the MMPI is easily administered and scored and has

a large data base for research" (p. 186). The popularity of the MMPI in research on Hispanics also suggests a long-standing affinity with the quantification of psychopathology via objective instruments with ethnic minority clients (Velasquez & Callahan, 1992).

Yet despite this burgeoning body of research, there remain two principal problems with the literature that ultimately have an impact on the assessment of Hispanic clients. First, over 90 percent of all research investigations used only one instrument in the study of Hispanic clients, as if to suggest that this does, or should, occur in clinical practice. Second, most studies continue to focus on ethnic or cultural differences between Hispanics and whites (e.g., Dolan, Roberts, Robinowitz, & Atkins, 1983; Johnson & Sikes, 1965; McCreary & Padilla, 1977; McGill, 1980; Plemons, 1977; Tulchin & Levy, 1945; Velasquez & Callahan, 1990; Whitworth, 1988) rather than the high variation among Hispanics. This type of research, while clarifying some obvious and not so obvious differences between Hispanics and whites, has unfortunately reinforced the idea among professionals that they should always look for differences when assessing Hispanics.

While it is beyond the scope of this chapter to discuss every study on Hispanics (see Appendix A for a complete listing of all studies with the MMPI, Rorschach, and TAT), it is worthwhile to note some of the key events in the history of assessment research on Hispanics. For example, it is a little-known fact that the first documented study on Hispanics dates from 1945, when Tulchin and Levy compared the Rorschach performance of Spanish- and English-born refugee children; or that Hispanics, for the first time ever, were included in the norming and restandardization of the new MMPI, the MMPI-2 (Butcher, Dahlstrom, Graham, Tellegen, & Kaemmer, 1989). The table, while obviously slanted toward the MMPI, nonetheless offers a perspective on the strengths and limitations of assessment research on Hispanics.

Given the current status of research on Hispanics, as noted in Table 10.2, there remain many questions that deserve clarification. These include: "Are instruments such as the Rorschach, TAT, or MMPI valid for use with Hispanics?" "Under what conditions should psychological assessment instruments be used with Hispanics?" "Are norms on Hispanics sufficient grounds to proclaim a particular instrument as valid or credible in the assessment of Hispanics?" "Does the translation of a particular instrument (e.g., MMPI or MMPI-2) into Spanish make the instrument useful in the assessment of diverse subgroups of Hispanics (e.g., Puerto Ricans, Chicanos, or Cuban Americans) who may vary with respect to language or dialect?" and, "Can interpretive guidelines be developed for use on diverse Hispanic clients?"

PRACTICAL PROBLEMS IN THE ASSESSMENT OF HISPANICS

While it is evident that a variety of assessment techniques (e.g., interviews, rating scales, and test instruments), are routinely applied to Hispanics, as to non-Hispanics, there remain several practical problems that psychologists must be aware of in order to work effectively with these clients (Chavez & Gonzales-Singh, 1980).

This section presents four of the most common problems.

Practical Problem 1: *Poor, Inappropriate, or Insensitive Referrals*

The first practical problem in the assessment of Hispanics relates to the types of assessment referrals made to psychologists by colleagues and other mental health professionals (e.g., psychiatrists, social workers, and counselors).

These referrals often pose questions that are difficult or impossible to answer within the context of an evaluation. Questions that are problematic or culturally insensitive include: "Is this Hispanic client adjusted to the norms of this society?" "Is this Hispanic client eligible for treatment in the United States?" "Why should this Hispanic client receive mental health services?" or, "Are the problems or complaints exhibited by this client similar to those exhibited by non-Hispanic clients?"

These poor or inappropriate referrals often place well-meaning psychologists in a sort of "no-win" or cognitive-dissonant situation, since they have to make vital decisions that are based on vague, cryptic, or value-laden referral questions. At the same time, these types of referrals increase the probability of psychologists' making significant assessment errors, which in turn ultimately impede the effective treatment of Hispanic clients.

In the author's opinion, assessment referrals of Hispanic clients should be context-bound, focused, or targeted to the issues unique to Hispanics, in specific clinical settings. The referrals should not be general or vague, but should instead guide the psychologist in determining the depth of assessment that is most appropriate for Hispanic clients. For example, asking the psychologist to determine the effects of immigration on the current psychological adjustment of a Hispanic client, or asking the psychologist to assess the impact of acculturation on a Hispanic client's beliefs or perceptions about the origin of a particular problem or mental disorder are useful and appropriate questions for psychological assessment.

TABLE 10.2. Key Events in Hispanic Assessment Research: A Historical Perspective

Year	Key event
1945	Tulchin & Levy conducted the first documented "assessment" study on Hispanic Americans. They compared the Rorschach responses of Spanish- and English-born refugee children who had experienced war. More important, this study became the model or prototype of subsequent investigations on Hispanics (i.e., comparing Hispanics with Whites on a specific test instrument).
1949	Altus & Clark conducted the first MMPI study on Hispanics. They used the Hs, D, and Hy scales of the MMPI as an index of adjustment in Hispanic and white soldiers.
1955	Kaplan was the first to examine the relationship between acculturation and test performance. Kaplan compared Hispanic, Mormon, Navaho, and Zuñi veterans on the Rorschach and found that acculturation accounts for some changes in personality.
1958	First Spanish-language version of the MMPI was published. This version was primarily designed for use in Costa Rica and Central America (see Butcher & Pancheri, 1976).
1959	Second Spanish-language version of the MMPI was published. This version was primarily designed for use in Puerto Rico (see Butcher & Pancheri, 1976).
1961	Swickard & Spilka conducted the first assessment study on U.S.-born Hispanic children. They used the MMPI Lie scale as a screening measure in a study on adolescent offenders.
1963	Penn, for the first time, examined differences between Hispanics and whites on the complete MMPI.
1963	Field, Maldonado-Sierra, & Coelho conducted the first TAT study on Hispanics. They compared several subgroups of Puerto Rican adolescents on the TAT.
1965	Johnson & Sikes compared the TAT responses of Hispanic and white nonpsychotic inpatients in a VA hospital. This was also the first study to compare the test performance of Hispanics to another ethnic minority group, African-Americans.
1966	Karno, in a case study, discussed the MMPI performance of a client, "Mrs. Martinez." This is the first "assessment case study" presented in the literature.
1967	The Puerto Rican version of the MMPI was adapted for use in Mexico and Latin America. This version is known as the "Nuñez version" of the MMPI (see Butcher & Pancheri, 1976). This version is known to have been used extensively with U.S.-born Hispanics between 1967 and 1984.
1968	Kiev, in a case study, discussed the Rorschach and MMPI performance of a client, "Antonio Gomez." This remains the only attempt at integrating data on two different assessment instruments.
1969	Glatt, for the first time ever, evaluated the equivalence of the Spanish-language version of the MMPI to the English version. Glatt administered the MMPI to bilingual subjects in both English and Spanish. On the Spanish version, subjects scored significantly higher on the L, F, K, Hs, D, Hy, Mf, Pa, and Sc scales, than on the English version. Unfortunately, Glatt never mentioned the ethnicity or nationality of the subjects, except that most were U.S.-born University of Minnesota freshmen.
1973	Padilla & Ruiz published the first of a series of two landmark literature reviews on the assessment of Hispanics in mental health settings. A major contribution of this review was publicizing the marked absence of research on Hispanics.
1975	Padilla & Ruiz published their second literature review on the assessment of Hispanics. This review, published in the *Journal of Personality Assessment*, raised the issues of test bias, clinical interpretation, and test standardization, as they pertain to Hispanics.
1978	Butcher & Garcia discussed pertinent issues in the translation and adaptation of assessment instruments from English to Spanish. They focused on translating the MMPI from English to Spanish.

TABLE 10.2. (continued)

Year	Key event
1984	"MMPI Version Hispana" is published. This version was specifically designed for Spanish-speaking Hispanics in the U.S.
1984	Velásquez published the first interpretive guide for a specific test instrument. Entitled "An Atlas of MMPI Group Profiles on Mexican Americans," this remains the only culturally based interpretive guide.
1986	Dahlstrom published the first comprehensive review of Hispanic MMPI research in "MMPI Patterns of American Minorities" (Dahlstrom, Lachar, & Dahlstrom, 1986).
1989	Hispanics, for the first time, are included in the standardization of the MMPI or MMPI-2 (see Butcher, Dahlstrom, Graham, Tellegen, & Kaemmer, 1989).
1993	The Spanish-language version of the MMPI-2 is published.
1993	Frank published the first-ever review of research on the Rorschach and Hispanics.

Practical Problem 2: *Inappropriate Selection of Assessment Techniques*

The second practical problem in the assessment of Hispanic clients relates to the inappropriate selection of assessment techniques in the evaluation of Hispanic clients. For example, psychologists may select particular techniques, whether interview protocols, rating scales, or test instruments, based on their popularity or the psychologist's preference for a specific technique(s). This is frequently evidenced in the manner in which many psychologists apply psychological test instruments to Hispanic clients. For example, if a psychologist believes that the MMPI or MMPI-2 is useful with all Hispanic clients irrespective of their presenting problems, then he or she is most likely to depend on such an instrument excessively and erroneously in the evaluation of all Hispanic clients.

Also, many referrals require that the psychologist administer a particular set of instruments or techniques irrespective of whether the instruments are valid or applicable in a particular setting. When conducting disability evaluations with Hispanics, for example, this author has frequently encountered the ethical dilemma of having to administer instruments that are ordered or stipulated by the referring party that may or may not assist in making professional decisions about a Hispanic client's eligibility for such services. More specifically, this author has encountered numerous situations in which a Hispanic client who is obviously Spanish-speaking is required to be administered a battery of assessment instruments in English.

In the author's opinion, the psychologist must always be cognizant of the strengths (including validity) and limitations of assessment techniques that are applied to Hispanic clients. At the same time, the psychologist must take on the responsibility of determining whether any assessment techniques that are applied to Hispanics are useful in the treatment of such clients. Thus, it is paramount that psychologists always be open to challenging possible misdiagnosis of Hispanic clients, and that they ultimately determine, based on sound professional and cultural judgment, what is most appropriate in the assessment of Hispanic clients.

Practical Problem 3: *Poor or Inappropriate Administration of Assessment Techniques*

The third practical problem in the assessment of Hispanic clients relates to the poor or inappropriate administration of assessment techniques. For example, it is common to find psychologists who stray from standardized procedures when assessing Hispanic clients. This may include deviating from prescribed procedures on a particular technique or measure, simultaneously translating the assessment technique during the actual evaluation, or administering assessment techniques that have been exclusively translated by the psychologist but that may or may not have appropriate validity or reliability.

For example, this author knows of several psychologists who have developed their own personal translations of the MMPI, which they use in their work with Hispanics. While there is no doubt that these psychologists apply such techniques in good faith and in the belief or conviction that they are truly helping Hispanic clients, these approaches are very dangerous since they have not been determined to be valid or reliable with Hispanics. In the author's opinion, psychologists should always be aware of that the procedures or steps used in the assessment process ultimately affect the relative worth of the assessment data obtained on Hispanic clients.

Practical Problem 4: *Poor or Inadequate Interpretation of Assessment Data*

The fourth and final practical problem in the evaluation of Hispanic clients relates to the misinterpretation of Hispanic clients' assessment data. Of all problems, this is perhaps the one that is the most difficult to remedy or solve, since interpretation of assessment data is based on many factors, including the psychologist's training and clinical experiences, theoretical orientation, familiarity, competence, and comfort with specific techniques or instruments, and cultural competence or wisdom.

In addition, while there have been tremendous gains in the assessment of Hispanics, especially over the past decade, there remains a paucity of information or guidance on the interpretation of assessment data with regard to Hispanics (Chavez & Gonzales-Singh, 1980; Velasquez & Callahan, 1992). Chavez and Gonzales-Singh (1980) noted that "misinterpretation may be described as the inappropriate use of test results to describe or explain certain of the assessed person's [characteristics]. Poor definition of traits . . . and culture-bound criteria

against which tests are validated lead to inappropriate inferences" (p. 163).

In the author's opinion, the interpretation of any assessment techniques applied to Hispanics, whether objective (e.g., paper-and-pencil tests) or subjective, should always involve the element of inference- or hypothesis-testing, from the beginning to the end of the assessment process. That is, psychologists should never view the interpretation of a Hispanic client's assessment performance in singular or unidimensional terms.

PRACTICAL RECOMMENDATIONS FOR ASSESSING HISPANIC CLIENTS

The following practical recommendations, based on the author's experience, are suggested for psychologists who assess Hispanic clients on a routine basis.

1. Psychologists must recognize that the psychological assessment or evaluation of Hispanic clients does not occur in a vacuum or independent of the client's sociohistorical background. Too often, well-intentioned psychologists fail in the assessment of Hispanics by not acknowledging the client's unique experiences that define his or her world view. These experiences include sex roles, socialization processes, acculturative stress, language barriers, immigration, and prejudice and discrimination. For example, the experiences of a third-generation Chicano born and raised in an urban barrio are quite different from those of a Cuban or Central American refugee. From the outset, psychologists must recognize such important background variables.

2. Psychologists must recognize that the psychological assessment of Hispanic clients occurs within the context of a helping relationship between the assessor and assessee. That is, psychologists are more likely to establish

credibility, trust, and openness (i.e., self-disclosure) if the assessment relationship is viewed as comparable to a therapeutic relationship. Thus, a Hispanic client is more likely to participate or cooperate fully in the assessment process if he or she feels that the assessment is based on trust and mutual respect.

3. Psychologists must recognize that the assessment of Hispanic clients is not a simple process that is mechanical or linear, or based on a specific formula (e.g., conduct a mental status examination, obtain a social history, administer a series of tests, and reach a diagnostic conclusion). Instead, the process is complex and requires that the psychologist be flexible, patient, and sensitive to alternative modes of assessment that are anchored in Hispanic culture. This includes assessing the belief systems that Hispanic clients possess concerning the origin and resolution of mental illness.

4. Psychologists must recognize that the psychological assessment of Hispanic clients, like non-Hispanics, should have an educational component that allows the client to feel that he or she can benefit from the ultimate goal of assessment, which is treatment. This is especially critical in Hispanic clients who have had limited or negative experiences in formal treatment or psychotherapy. Too often, psychologists present the evaluation process to Hispanic clients in a rather secretive manner that implies an adversarial relationship between the psychologist and client.

5. Psychologists must recognize the diversity or heterogeneity among Hispanic clients. The long-standing image that "all Hispanic clients are recent immigrants, monolingual, poorly educated, and of low socioeconomic status" is no longer true. Too often, psychologists depend on such a stereotype to make diagnostic and treatment decisions concerning Hispanic clients. Other stereotypes that are often voiced by psychologists include the belief that Hispanic clients are not interested in treatment, that they are best treated with psychotropic medications rather than psychotherapy, or that they are not motivated to change their lives within the context of therapy.

6. Psychologists must recognize that many Hispanic clients have had negative experiences with prior assessment or testing. For example, it is common to work with clients who feel vulnerable or fearful about the assessment process because they were once misdiagnosed in academic settings. For these clients, it is important that the psychologist be open to discussing any reservations held by the client before the assessment or evaluation.

7. Psychologists must always recognize the role of sociocultural or moderator variables in the assessment of Hispanic clients (Dana, 1993). These include age, gender, language, nationality, acculturation, socioeconomic status, sex roles, folk beliefs, community standards, and ecological environment. For example, language or dialect is a powerful factor in defining and understanding the phenomenology of a Hispanic client's problems or concerns. Malgady et al. (1987) observed that "when the fact that bilingualism and language . . . is acknowledged, the following questions arise: In which language, English or Spanish, do bilinguals express greater psychopathology? And, of course, which language conveys the true nature and extent of pathology?" (p. 231).

8. Psychologists should develop individualized culturally based frameworks for assessing Hispanic clients. These frameworks, which are very personalized and unique to each psychologist's experiences with Hispanic culture, should emphasize steps for

FIGURE 10.1 Flowchart for conducting assessment evaluations on Hispanics.

Clarify the referral question(s)

↓

Review previous treatment or evaluation data

↓

Clarify the client's problems or concerns

↓

Determine the client's ethnic identity, nationality, or country of origin

↓

Determine the client's preferred language

↓

Assess the client's level of acculturation

↓

Assess the client's beliefs about the problem

↓

Conduct a comprehensive interview with emphasis on family and community

↓

Assess the client's strengths and motivations

↓

Select appropriate assessment instruments

↓

Administer assessment instruments

↓

Interpret all assessment data from the client's cultural perspective

↓

Review all concerns with a "cultural consultant"

↓

Prepare the final assessment report

gaining a clear and precise understanding of a Hispanic client's problems or concerns. Obviously, the framework should be anchored or grounded in Hispanic culture and should emphasize the clinical necessities of this particular group. Figure 10.1 presents the author's own framework.

CONCLUSION

It is evident from the discussion in this chapter that the psychological assessment of Hispanics, in terms of research and clinical practice, is still in its infancy. While there have been significant

gains in the literature, there remain many more issues that need to be explored. The challenge for psychologists in the 1990s is to: (1) resolve the etic-emic issue regarding the assessment of Hispanics; (2) develop culturally and contextually bound methods of administering and interpreting traditional assessment techniques; (3) determine the role of sociocultural or moderator variables in the assessment and treatment of Hispanics; (4) create new, and as of yet undiscovered, assessment techniques that maximize the role and contribution of culture and minimize outdated cultural stereotypes; and (5) devise educational and training opportunities for psychologists who are invested in the effective assessment and treatment of Hispanic clients.

ACKNOWLEDGMENT

The author extends his appreciation to Ms. Carolyn Lopez and Mr. Wendell Callahan for their assistance in the preparation of Appendix A.

REFERENCES

Altus, W. D., & Clark, J. H. (1949). The effect of adjustment patterns upon the intercorrelation of intelligence subtest variables. *Journal of Social Psychology, 30,* 39–48.

Bamford, K. W. (1991). Bilingual issues in mental health assessment and treatment. *Hispanic Journal of Behavioral Sciences, 13,* 377–390.

Bradford, D. T., & Munoz, A. (1993). Translation in bilingual psychotherapy. *Professional Psychology: Research and Practice, 24,* 52–61.

Butcher, J. N., Dahlstrom, W. G., Graham, J. R., Tellegen, A., & Kaemmer, B. (1989). *Manual for the restandardized Minnesota Multiphasic Personality Inventory: MMPI-2. An administrative and interpretive guide.* Minneapolis: University of Minnesota Press.

Butcher, J. N., & Garcia, R. E. (1978). Cross-national application of psychological tests. *Personnel and Guidance Journal, 56,* 472–475.

Butcher, J. N., & Pancheri, P. (1976). Developments in the use of the MMPI in several countries. In J. N. Butcher & P. Pancheri, *A handbook of cross-national MMPI research.* Minneapolis: University of Minnesota Press.

Campos, L. P. (1989). Adverse impact, unfairness, and bias in the psychological screening of Hispanic peace officers. *Hispanic Journal of Behavioral Sciences, 11,* 122–135.

Canino, G. (1982). The Hispanic woman: Sociocultural influences on diagnoses and treatment. In R. M. Becerra, M. Karno, & J. I. Escobar (Eds.), *Mental health and Hispanic Americans: Clinical perspectives* (pp. 117–138). New York: Grune & Stratton.

Cervantes, R. C., & Acosta, F. X. (1992). Psychological testing for Hispanic Americans. *Applied and Preventive Psychology, 1,* 209–219.

Chavez, E. L., & Gonzales-Singh, E. (1980). Hispanic assessment: A case study. *Professional Psychology: Research and Practice, 11,* 163–168.

Clark, S. A., Velasquez, R. J., Callahan, W. J., & Lopez, C. (1993). MMPI-ER differences among Hispanic worker's compensation applicants by psychiatric diagnosis. *Journal of Applied Rehabilitation Counseling, 24,* 15–18.

Cuellar, I. (1982). The diagnosis and evaluation of schizophrenic disorders among Mexican Americans. In R. M. Becerra, M. Karno, & J. I. Escobar (Eds.), *Mental health and Hispanic Americans: Clinical perspectives* (pp. 61–81). San Diego: Grune & Stratton.

Cuellar, I., Harris, L. C., & Jasso, R. (1980). An acculturation rating scale for Mexican American normal and clinical populations. *Hispanic Journal of Behavioral Sciences, 2,* 199–217.

Cuellar, I., Martinez, C., Jimenez, R., & Gonzalez, R. (1983). Clinical psychiatric case presentation: Culturally responsive diagnostic formulation and treatment in an Hispanic client. *Hispanic Journal of Behavioral Sciences, 5,* 93–103.

Cuellar, I., & Roberts, R. E. (1984). Psychological disorders among Chicanos. In J. L. Martinez & R. H. Mendoza (Eds.), *Chicano Psychology* (2nd. ed., pp. 133–159). San Diego: Academic Press.

Dahlstrom, L. E. (1986). MMPI findings on other American minority groups. In W. G. Dahlstrom, D. Lachar, & L. E. Dahlstrom (Eds.), *MMPI patterns of ethnic minorities* (pp. 50–86). Minneapolis: University of Minnesota Press.

Dana, R. H. (1988). Culturally diverse groups and MMPI interpretation. *Professional Psychology: Research and Practice, 19,* 490–495.

Dana, R. H., & Whatley, P. R. (1991). When does a difference make a difference?: MMPI scores and African Americans. *Journal of Clinical Psychology, 47,* 400–406.

Dolan, M. P., Roberts, R., Robinowitz, R., & Atkins, H. G. (1983). Personality differences among Black, White, and Hispanic-American male heroin addicts on MMPI content scales. *Journal of Clinical Psychology, 39,* 807–813.

Flaskerud, J. H. (1986). Diagnostic and treatment differences among five ethnic groups. *Psychological Reports, 58,* 219–235.

Frank, G. (1993). The use of the Rorschach with Hispanic Americans. *Psychological Reports, 72,* 276–278.

French, L. A. (1993). Adapting projective tests for minority children. *Psychological Reports, 72,* 15–18

Glatt, K. M. (1969). An evaluation of the French, Spanish, and German translations of the MMPI. *Acta Psychologica, 29,* 65–84.

Gomez, R., Ruiz, P., & Rumbaut, R. D. (1985). Hispanic patients: A linguo-cultural minority. *Hispanic Journal of Behavioral Sciences, 7,* 177–186.

Greene, R. L. (1987). Ethnicity and MMPI performance: A review. *Journal of Consulting and Clinical Psychology, 55,* 497–412.

Greene, R. L. (1991). Specific groups: Adolescents, the aged, Blacks, and other ethnic groups. In R. L. Greene, *The MMPI-2/MMPI: An interpretive manual* (pp. 331–354). Needham Heights, MA: Allyn & Bacon.

Griffith, J. (1983). Relationship between acculturation and psychological impairment in adult Mexican Americans. *Hispanic Journal of Behavioral Sciences, 5,* 431–459.

Gynther, M. D. (1989). MMPI comparisons of Blacks and Whites: A review and commentary. *Journal of Clinical Psychology, 45,* 878–883.

Jenkins, J. H. (1988). Ethnopsychiatric interpretations of schizophrenic illness: The problem of nervios within Mexican American families. *Culture, Medicine, and Psychiatry, 12,* 301–329.

Johnson, D. L., & Sikes, M. P. (1965). Rorschach and TAT responses of Negro, Mexican-American, and Anglo psychiatric patients. *Journal of Projective Techniques, 29,* 183–188.

Jones, B. E., Gray, B. A., & Parson, E. B. (1983). Manic-depressive illness among poor urban Hispanics. *American Journal of Psychiatry, 140,* 1208–1210.

Kaplan, B. (1955). Reflections of the acculturation process in the Rorschach test. *Journal of Projective Techniques, 19,* 30–35.

Karno, M. (1966). The enigma of ethnicity in a psychiatric clinic. *Archives of General Psychiatry, 14,* 516–520.

Kiev, A. (1968). *Curanderismo: Mexican-American folk psychiatry.* New York: Free Press.

Kinzie, J. D., & Manson, S. M. (1987). The use of self-rating scales in cross-cultural psychiatry. *Hospital and Community Psychiatry, 38,* 190–196.

Lopez, A., Boccellari, A., & Hall, K. (1988). Posttraumatic stress disorder in a Central American refugee. *Hospital and Community Psychiatry, 39,* 1309–1311.

Lopez, S., & Hernandez, P. (1987). When culture is considered in the evaluation and treatment of Hispanic patients. *Psychotherapy, 24,* 120–126.

Lubin, B., Larsen, R. M., & Matarazzo, J. D. (1984). Patterns of psychological test usage in the United States: 1935–1982. *American Psychologist, 39,* 451–454.

Lubin, B., Larsen, R. M., Matarazzo, J. D., & Seever, M. (1985). Psychological test usage patterns in five professional settings. *American Psychologist, 40,* 857–861.

McCready, C., & Padilla, E. (1977). MMPI differences among Black, Mexican-American, and White male offenders. *Journal of Clinical Psychology, 33,* 171–177.

McGill, J. C. (1980). MMPI score differences among Anglo, Black, and Mexican-American welfare recipients. *Journal of Clinical Psychology, 36,* 147–151.

Malgady, R. G., Rogler, L. H., & Constantino, G. (1987). Ethnocultural and linguistic bias in mental health evaluation of Hispanics. *American Psychologist, 42,* 228–234.

Marcos, L. R., Alpert, M., Urcuyo, L., & Kesselman, M. (1973). The effect of interview language on the evaluation of psychopathology in Spanish-American schizophrenic patients. *American Journal of Psychiatry, 130,* 549–553.

Meadow, A. (1982). Psychopathology, psychotherapy, and the Mexican-American patient. In E. E. Jones & S. J. Korchin (Eds.), *Minority mental health* (pp. 331–361). New York: Praeger.

Padilla, A. M., and Ruiz, R. A. (1973). *Latino mental health: A review of literature* (DHEW Pub. No. ADM: 74–113). Washington, DC: U.S. Government Printing Office.

Padilla, A. M., & Ruiz, R. A. (1975). Personality assessment and test interpretation of Mexican Americans: A critique. *Journal of Personality Assessment, 39,* 103–109.

Penn, M. P. (1963). *A cross-cultural comparison using MMPI profiles from college students.* Unpublished master's thesis, University of Arizona, Tucson.

Pina, G. (1985). Diagnosis and treatment of posttraumatic stress disorder in Hispanic Vietnam veterans. In S. Sonnenberg, A. S. Blank, & J. A. Talbott (Eds.), *The trauma of war: Stress and recovery in Vietnam veterans* (pp. 390–402). Washington, DC: American Psychiatric Press.

Piotrowski, C., & Keller, J. W. (1989). Psychological testing in outpatient mental health facilities: A national study. *Professional Psychology: Research and Practice, 20,* 423–425.

Plemons, A. G. (1977). A comparison of MMPI scores of Anglo- and Mexican-American psychiatric patients. *Journal of Consulting and Clinical Psychology, 45,* 149–150.

Price, C. S., & Cuellar, I. (1981). Effects of language and related variables on the expression of psychopathology in Mexican American psychiatric patients. *Hispanic Journal of Behavioral Sciences, 3,* 145–160.

Pritchard, D. A., & Rosenblatt, A. (1980). Racial bias in the MMPI: A methodological review. *Journal* of Consulting and Clinical Psychology, 48, 263–267.

Rivera, O. A., & Cespedes, R. (1983). Rehabilitation counseling with disabled Hispanics. Journal of Applied Rehabilitation Counseling, 14, 65–71.

Swickard, D. L., & Spilka, B. (1961). Hostility expression among delinquents of minority and majority groups. Journal of Consulting Psychology, 25, 216–220.

Tulchin, S. H., & Levy, D. M. (1945). Rorschach test differences in a group of Spanish and English refugee children. American Journal of Orthopsychiatry, 15, 361–368.

Velásquez, R. J. (1984a). An atlas of MMPI group profiles on Mexican Americans (Occasional Paper No. 19). Los Angeles: Spanish Speaking Mental Health Research Center.

Velásquez, R. J. (1984b). Use of psychological tests with Hispanics: A survey of psychologists. Unpublished manuscript, Arizona State University, Tempe.

Velásquez, R. J. (1992). Hispanic American MMPI research (1949–1992). A comprehensive bibliography. Psychological Reports, 70, 743–754.

Velásquez, R. J. (1993). Hispanic American MMPI research: A review. Unpublished manuscript, San Diego State University, San Diego, CA.

Velásquez, R. J., & Callahan, W. J. (1990). MMPI comparison of Hispanic- and White-American veterans seeking treatment for alcoholism. Psychological Reports, 67, 95–98.

Velásquez, R. J., & Callahan, W. J. (1992). Psychological testing of Hispanic Americans in clinical settings: Overview and issues. In K. Geisinger (Ed.), Psychological testing of Hispanics (pp. 253–265). Washington, DC: American Psychological Association.

Velásquez, R. J., Callahan, W. J., & Young, R. (1993). Hispanic-White comparisons: Does psychiatric diagnosis make a difference?. Journal of Clinical Psychology, 49, 528–534.

Whitworth, R. H. (1988). Anglo- and Mexican-American performance on the MMPI administered in Spanish or English. Journal of Clinical Psychology, 44, 891–899.

Williams, C. L. (1987). Issues surrounding psychological testing of minority patients. Hospital and Community Psychiatry, 38, 184–189.

Ziskin, J. (1981). Challenging assessment of ethnic minority group members. In J. Ziskin, Coping with psychiatric and psychological testimony (pp. 289–305). Venice, CA: Law and Psychology Press.

APPENDIX A
HISPANIC ASSESSMENT RESEARCH: A COMPREHENSIVE BIBLIOGRAPHY OF MMPI, RORSCHACH, AND TAT RESEARCH

Studies Utilizing the MMPI

MMPI Research in Substance Abuse Treatment Settings

Cannon, D. S., Bell, W. E., Penk, W. E., & Finkelstein, A. S. (1990). MMPI differences between alcoholics and drug abusers. Psychological Assessment: A Journal of Consulting and Clinical Psychology, 2, 51–55.

Cavior, N., Kurtzberg, R. L., & Lipton, D. S. (1967). The development and validation of a heroin addiction scale with the MMPI. International Journal of the Addictions, 2, 129–137.

Dolan, M. P., Roberts, W. R., Robinowitz, R., & Atkins, H. G. (1983). Personality differences among Black, White, and Hispanic-American male heroin addicts on MMPI content scales. Journal of Clinical Psychology, 39, 807–813.

Herl, D. (1976). Personality characteristics in a sample of heroin addict methadone maintenance applicants. British Journal of Addiction, 71, 253–259.

Jacobs, R. (1976). A study of drinking behavior and personality characteristics of three ethnic groups (Doctoral dissertation, California School of Professional Psychology, Los Angeles, 1976). Dissertation Abstracts International, 36, 5796B.

Kwant, F., Rice, J. A., & Hays, J. R. (1976). Use of heroin addiction scale to differentiate addicts from rehabilitation clients. Psychological Reports, 38, 547–553.

Martinez de Gandell, M. D. (1982). Personality profiles and psychological orientations of employed and unemployed rehabilitated male heroin addicts: A comparison study (Doctoral dissertation, Ohio State University, 1981). Dissertation Abstracts International, 45, 4588A.

Page, R. D., & Bozlee, S. (1982). A cross-cultural MMPI comparison of alcoholics. Psychological Reports, 50, 639–646.

Penk, W. E., Robinowitz, R., Bell, W., Shattner, H. H., Black, J., & Flores, E. (1983). A comparison of Hispanic-American, Black, and White combat veterans seeking treatment for substance abuse (heroin). Paper presented at the 18th Annual Symposium on Recent Developments in the Use of the MMPI, Minneapolis.

Penk, W. E., Robinowitz, R., Roberts, W. R., Dolan, M. P., & Atkins, H. G. (1981). MMPI differences of male Hispanic-American, Black, and White heroin addicts. *Journal of Consulting and Clinical Psychology*, 49, 488–490.

Shaffer, J. N., Nurco, D. N., Hanlon, T. E., Kinlock, T. W., Duzynski, K. R., & Stephenson, P. (1988). MMPI–168 profiles of male narcotic addicts by ethnic group and city. *Journal of Clinical Psychology*, 44, 292–298.

Velásquez, R. J., & Callahan, W. J. (1990). MMPI comparisons of Hispanic- and White-American veterans seeking treatment for alcoholism. *Psychological Reports*, 67, 95–98.

Venn, J. (1988). MMPI profiles of Native-, Mexican-, and Caucasian-American male alcoholics. *Psychological Reports*, 62, 427–432.

Weisman, C. P., Anglin, M. D., & Fisher, D. G. (1989). MMPI profiles of narcotics addicts: II. Ethnic and criminal history effects. *International Journal of the Addictions*, 24, 881–896.

Woychowski, B. C. (1987). MMPI differences and interaction effects caused by race, sex, and stress experience levels of narcotic dependent patients receiving methadone maintenance treatment (Doctoral dissertation, Florida Institute of Technology, 1987). *Dissertation Abstracts International*, 48, 1825B.

MMPI Research in Correctional/Prison Settings

Bernstein, I. H., Teng, G., Granneman, B. D., & Garbin, D. G. (1987). Invariance in the MMPI's component structure. *Journal of Personality Assessment*, 51, 522–531.

Bohn, M. J., & Traub, G. S. (1986). Alienation of monolingual Hispanics in a federal correctional institution. *Psychological Reports*, 59, 560–562.

Fisher, G. (1967). The performance of male prisoners on the Marlowe-Crowne Social Desireability Scale: II. Difference as a function of race and crime. *Journal of Clinical Psychology*, 23, 473–475.

Gaba, R. J. (1988). *Profile constellations of males accused of sexually abusing children*. Unpublished master's thesis, Mount St. Mary's College, Los Angeles.

Gaba, R. J. (1990). *Hispanic sex offenders: Assessment with the MMPI-168*. Paper presented at the annual meeting of the California State Psychological Association, San Francisco.

Holland, T. R. (1979). Ethnic group differences in MMPI profile pattern and functional structure among adult offenders. *Journal of Personality Assessment*, 43, 72–77.

McCreary, C., & Padilla, E. (1977). MMPI differences among Black, Mexican-American, and White male offenders. *Journal of Clinical Psychology*, 33, 171–177.

Ojeda, S. (1980). *A cross-cultural comparison of MMPI scores of Chicano and Anglo abusive mothers*. Unpublished master's thesis, San Jose State University, San Jose, CA.

Ray, J. B., Solomon, G. S., Doncaster, M. G., & Mellina, R. (1983). First offender adult shoplifters: A preliminary profile. *Journal of Clinical Psychology*, 39, 769–770.

Swickard, D. L., & Spilka, B. (1961). Hostility expression among delinquents of minority and majority groups. *Journal of Consulting Psychology*, 25, 216–220.

Traub, G. S., & Bohn, M. J. (1985). Note on the reliability of the MMPI with Spanish-speaking inmates in the federal prison system. *Psychological Reports*, 56, 373–374.

Velásquez, R. J. (1990a). *MMPI content scale scores of Hispanic American sex offenders: A technical note*. Unpublished paper, San Diego State University, San Diego, CA.

Velásquez, R. J., Callahan, W. J., & Carrillo, R. (1989). MMPI profiles of Hispanic-American inpatient and outpatient sex offenders. *Psychological Reports*, 65, 1055–1058.

Velásquez, R. J., & Carrillo, R. (1990b). *Endorsement of MMPI critical items by Hispanic sex offenders*. Unpublished paper, San Diego State University, San Diego, CA.

MMPI Research in Clinical/Psychiatric Settings

Adams, P. L., & Horovitz, J. H. (1980). Psychopathology and fatherlessness in poor boys. *Child Psychiatry and Human Development*, 10, 135–143.

Arsuaga, E. N., Higgins, J. C., & Sifre, P. A. (1986). Separation of brain-damaged from psychiatric patients with the combined use of an ability and personality test: A validation study with a Puerto Rican population. *Journal of Clinical Psychology*, 42, 328–331.

Fox, D., & Sunlight, C. (1985). *The validity of MMPI critical items in different ethnic groups*. Paper presented at the 20th Annual Symposium on Recent Developments in the Use of the MMPI, Honolulu, HI.

Frye, T. F. (1973). *An evaluative actuarial study of the MMPI utilizing an Anglo and Mexican-American sample.* Unpublished master's thesis, Trinity University, San Antonio, TX.

Fuller, C. G. (1984). Comparisons of unacculturated and acculturated Hispanics with Blacks and Whites on the Minnesota Multiphasic Personality Inventory (Doctoral dissertation, Fuller Theological Seminary, 1984). *Dissertation Abstracts International, 45,* 1283B.

Hibbs, B. J., Kobos, J. C., & Gonzales, J. (1979). Effects of ethnicity, sex, and age on MMPI profiles. *Psychological Reports, 45,* 591–597.

Hutton, H. E., Smith, R., & Langfeldt, V. (1989). *Ethnic differences on the MMPI-based overcontrolled hostility scale.* Paper presented at the annual meeting of the California Forensic Mental Health Association, Asilomar, CA.

Lawson, H. H. (1980). Psychopathology and attitude toward mental illness of Mexican-American and European-American patients (Doctoral dissertation, University of Arizona, 1979). *Dissertation Abstracts International, 40,* 3945–3946B.

Lawson, H. H., Kahn, M. W., & Heiman, E. M. (1982). Psychopathology, treatment outcome and attitudes toward mental illness in Mexican and European patients. *International Journal of Social Psychology, 28,* 20–26.

Ledwin, A. G. (1983a). A comparative study of the MMPI-Español and a culturally sensitive linguistic version (Doctoral dissertation, United States International University, 1982). *Dissertation Abstracts International, 43,* 3884A.

Ledwin, A. G. (1983b). *A comparison between the MMPI-Español and a culturally linguistic revision.* Paper presented at the 18th Annual Symposium on Recent Developments in the Use of the MMPI, Minneapolis.

McCormick, R. J. (1986). Personality concomitants of the Puerto Rican syndrome as reflected in the Minnesota Multiphasic Personality Inventory (Doctoral dissertation, Rutgers University, 1986). *Dissertation Abstracts International, 47,* 4691B.

Murphy, J. R. (1981). Mexican Americans' performance on the MMPI: As compared with Anglo Americans (Doctoral dissertation, United States International University, 1978). *Dissertation Abstracts International, 41,* 3582B.

Page, D. (1987). *Minnesota Multiphasic Personality Inventory differences among Chicano, Anglo, and Black schizophrenics.* Unpublished senior project, California Polytechnic State University, San Luis Obispo, San Luis Obispo, CA.

Pando, J. R. (1974). Appraisal of various clinical scales of the Spanish version of the Mini-Mult with Spanish Americans (Doctoral dissertation, Adelphi University, 1974). *Dissertation Abstracts International, 34,* 5688B.

Penk, W. E., Robinowitz, R., Black, J., Dolan, M., Bell, W., Dorsett, D., Ames, M., & Noriega, L. (1989). Ethnicity: Post-traumatic stress disorder (PTSD) differences among Black, White, and Hispanic veterans who differ in exposure to combat in Vietnam. *Journal of Clinical Psychology, 45,* 729–735.

Plemons, A. G. (1980). *The relationship of acculturation to MMPI scores of Mexican American psychiatric outpatients.* Unpublished doctoral dissertation, Palo Alto School of Professional Psychology, Palo Alto, CA.

Plemons, A. G. (1977). A comparison of Anglo- and Mexican-American psychiatric patients. *Journal of Consulting and Clinical Psychology, 45,* 149–150.

Quiroga, I. R. (1972). The use of a linear discriminant function on Minnesota Multiphasic Personality Inventory scores in the classification of psychotic and nonpsychotic Mexican-American psychiatric patients (Doctoral dissertation, University of Oklahoma, 1972). *Dissertation Abstracts International, 33,* 448–449B.

Roche Psychiatric Service Institute (1978). *Survey of summary statistics on basic MMPI scales of various ethnic groups of mental health clients.* Unpublished manuscript, Nutley, NJ.

Selters, R. R. (1974). An investigation of the relationship between ethnic origin and reactions to the MMPI (Doctoral dissertation, Baylor University, 1973). *Dissertation Abstracts International University, 34,* 5210B.

Velásquez, R. J. (1987). Minnesota Multiphasic Personality Inventory differences among Chicano state hospital patients (Doctoral dissertation, Arizona State University, 1986). *Dissertation Abstracts International, 47,* 4668B.

Velásquez, R. J. (1991). *Hispanic-White differences on the MMPI as a function of profile validity.* Unpublished manuscript, San Diego State University, San Diego, CA.

Velásquez, R. J., & Callahan, W. J. (1990). MMPIs of Hispanic, Black, and White DSM-III schizophrenics. *Psychological Reports, 66,* 819–822.

Velásquez, R. J., Callahan, W. J., & Carrillo, R. (1991). MMPI differences among Mexican-American male and female psychiatric inpatients. *Psychological Reports*, 68, 123–127.

Velásquez, R. J., Callahan, W. J., & Young, R. (1993). Hispanic-White MMPI comparisons: Does psychiatric diagnosis make a difference? *Journal of Clinical Psychology*, 49, 528–534.

Velásquez, R. J., Gimenez, L. (1987). MMPI differences among three groups of Mexican-American state hospital patients. *Psychological Reports*, 60, 1071–1074.

MMPI Research in Rehabilitation/Disability Settings

Clark, S. A. (1991). A descriptive study of the MMPI and industrially-injured immigrant Hispanic workers (Doctoral dissertation, United States International University, 1991). *Dissertation Abstracts International*, 52, 2290B.

Clark, S. A., Velásquez, R. J., & Callahan, W. J. (1992). *MMPI performance of Hispanics by country of origin.* Unpublished manuscript, San Diego State University, San Diego, CA.

Clark, S. A., Velásquez, R. J., & Callahan, W. J. (1992). MMPI-ER two-point codes of industrially injured Hispanic workers by DSM-III-R diagnosis. *Psychological Reports*, 71, 107–112.

Clark, S. A., Velásquez, R. J., Callahan, W. J., & Lopez, C. (1993). MMPI-ER differences among Hispanic worker's compensation applicants by psychiatric diagnosis. *Journal of Applied Rehabilitation Counseling*, 24, 15–18.

Du Alba, L., & Scott, R. L. (1993). Somatization and malingering for workers' compensation applicants: A cross-cultural MMPI study. *Journal of Clinical Psychology*, 49, 913–917.

Fierro, R. J. (1986). The psychological effects of early referral to vocational rehabilitation among Mexican-American industrially injured workers (Doctoral dissertation, United States International University, 1986). *Dissertation Abstracts International*, 47, 1657A.

Fierro, R. J., & Leal, A. (1988). Psychological effects of early versus late referral to the vocational rehabilitation process: The case of Mexican origin industrially injured workers. *Journal of Applied Rehabilitation Counseling*, 19, 35–39.

Goldberg, S. D. (1981). The use of the MMPI psychopathic deviate scale in evaluation of Mexican American patients: A symbolic interactionist perspective (Doctoral dissertation, United States International University, 1980). *Dissertation Abstracts International*, 41, 4663B.

McGill, J. C. (1980). MMPI score differences among Anglo, Black, and Mexican-American welfare recipients. *Journal of Clinical Psychology*, 36, 147–151.

North, R. C. (1991). *Item analysis of MMPI scale 8 in a Spanish translation.* Unpublished doctoral dissertation, Cambridge Graduate School of Psychology, Los Angeles, CA.

Vega, S. (1984). The cultural effects upon MMPI responses of industrially-injured Mexican and Anglo American males (Doctoral dissertation, University of Southern California, 1983). *Dissertation Abstracts International*, 44, 2278B.

MMPI Research in Nonclinical Settings

Altus, W. D., & Clark, J. H. (1949). The effect of adjustment patterns upon the intercorrelation of intelligence subtest variables. *Journal of Social Psychology*, 30, 39–48.

Azan, A. A. (1989). The MMPI Version Hispana: A standardization and cross-cultural personality study with a population of Cuban refugees (Doctoral dissertation, University of Minnesota, 1989). *Dissertation Abstracts International*, 50, 2144–2145B.

Butcher, J. N., Dahlstrom, W. G., Graham, J. R., Tellegen, A., & Kaemmer, B. (1989). *Manual for the restandardized Minnesota Multiphasic Personality Inventory: MMPI-2. An administrative and interpretive guide.* Minneapolis: University of Minnesota Press.

Callahan, W. J., & Velásquez, J. R. (1993). *MMPI-2 performance of Hispanic, Asians, and white college students.* Unpublished manuscript, San Diego State University, San Diego, CA.

Fitch, R. S. (1973). Examination of selected MMPI profiles of four groups of Spanish-American and Anglo-American adolescent females (Doctoral dissertation, Baylor University, 1972). *Dissertation Abstracts International*, 38, 2360B.

Francis, B. S. (1964). *Culture and sex role determinants of personality profiles.* Unpublished master's thesis, Trinity University, San Antonio, TX.

Fuller, C. G., & Malony, H. N. (1984). A comparison of English and Spanish (Nuñez) translations of the MMPI. *Journal of Personality Assessment*, 48, 130–131.

Guzman, D. S. (1979). *Analysis of Mexican-American and Anglo-American differences on the MMPI.* Unpublished master's thesis, San Jose State University, San Jose, CA.

Hargrave, G. E., & Berner, J. G. (1984). *POST psy-*

chological screening manual. Sacramento: California Commission on Peace Officer Standards and Training.

Inwald, R. E. (1980). *Effect of two-parent background on race differences in psychological testing.* Paper presented at the 88th annual meeting of the American Psychological Association, Quebec, Canada.

Karle, H., & Velázquez, R. J. *Comparability of the English and Spanish versions of the MMPI-2: A study of bilingual Latino college students.* Unpublished manuscript, San Diego State University, San Diego, CA.

Knatz, H. F., Inwald, R. E., Brickwell, A. L., & Tran, L. N. (1987). *Predictions of job performance using the IPI and MMPI for White, Black, and Hispanic public safety officers.* Unpublished manuscript.

Leung, R. (1986). MMPI scoring as a function of ethnicity and acculturation: A comparison of Asian, Hispanic, and Caucasian gifted high school students (Doctoral dissertation, Rosemead School of Psychology, Biola University, 1986). *Dissertation Abstracts International, 47,* 2622B.

Lopez-Ramirez, N. I. (1987). The impact of changing environment on six behavioral and psychological traits in Puerto Rican adults (Doctoral dissertation, Pennsylvania State University, 1986). *Dissertation Abstracts International, 47,* 2622B.

Loya, F., & Munoz, A. (1981). *A comparison of the MMPI scales among Anglo, Black, and Hispanic individuals.* Paper presented at the 7th International Conference on Personality Assessment, Honolulu.

Meadow, A., Stoker, D. H., & Zurcher, L. A. (1967). Sex role and schizophrenia: A cross-cultural study. *British Journal of Social Psychology, 1,* 250–259.

Montgomery, G. T., Arnold, B. R., & Orozco, S. (1990). MMPI supplemental scale performance of Mexican Americans. *Journal of Personality Assessment, 54,* 328–342.

Montgomery, G. T., & Orozco, S. (1985). Mexican Americans' performance on the MMPI as a function of acculturation. *Journal of Clinical Psychology, 41,* 203–212.

Morris, R. B. (1983). *A comparison of the Minnesota Multiphasic Personality Inventory and the Inventario Multifasico de la Personalidad with bilingual subjects.* Paper presented at the 18th Annual Symposium on Recent Developments in the Use of the MMPI, Minneapolis, MN.

Nogueras, J. A. (1983). The standardization of the Minnesota Multiphasic Personality Inventory (MMPI) on a selected group of migrant and non-migrant Puerto Rican students (Doctoral dissertation, Pennsylvania State University, 1983). *Dissertation Abstracts International, 44,* 119A.

Padilla, E. R., Olmedo, E. L., & Loya, F. (1982). Acculturation and the MMPI performance of Chicano and Anglo college students. *Hispanic Journal of Behavioral Sciences, 4,* 451–466.

Penn, M. P. (1963). *A cross-cultural comparison using MMPI profiles from college students.* Unpublished master's thesis, University of Arizona, Tucson.

Pina, G. (1978). An investigation into the effects of language and acculturation in the assessment of psychopathology of Chicano males using the TAT (Doctoral dissertation, American University, 1978). *Dissertation Abstracts International, 39,* 1495B.

Polishuk, P. (1980). Personality characteristics and role preferences among Hispanic protestant ministers (Doctoral dissertation, Fuller Theological Seminary, 1980). *Dissertation Abstracts International, 41,* 2342B.

Prewitt-Diaz, J. O., Norcross, J. A., & Draguns, J. (1984). MMPI (Spanish translation) in Puerto Rican adolescents: Preliminary data on reliability and validity. *Hispanic Journal of Behavioral Sciences, 6,* 179–190.

Reilley, R. R., & Knight, G. E. (1970). MMPI scores of Mexican-American college students. *Journal of College Student Personnel, 11,* 419–422.

Velásquez, R. J. (1993a). *Reliability of the MMPI-2 with Mexican American college students.* Unpublished manuscript, San Diego State University, San Diego, CA.

Velásquez, R. J. (1993b). *Mexican students' performance on the Spanish version of the MMPI-2.* Unpublished manuscript, San Diego State University, San Diego, CA.

Whitworth, R. H. (1988). Anglo- and Mexican-American performance on the MMPI administered in Spanish or English. *Journal of Clinical Psychology, 44,* 891–899.

Whitworth, R. H., & McBlaine, D. D. (1993). Comparison of the MMPI and MMPI-2 administered to Anglo- and Hispanic-American university students. *Journal of Personality Assessment, 61,* 19–27.

Relevant MMPI Reviews on Hispanics

Campos, L. P. (1989). Adverse impact, unfairness, and bias in the psychological screening of Hispanic peace officers. *Hispanic Journal of Behavioral Sciences, 11,* 122–135.

Dahlstrom, L. E. (1986). MMPI findings on other American minority groups. In W. G. Dahlstrom, D. Lachar, & L. E. Dahlstrom, *MMPI patterns of American minorities* (pp. 50–86). Minneapolis: University of Minnesota Press.

Dana, R. H. (1988). Culturally diverse groups and MMPI interpretation. *Professional Psychology: Research and Practice, 19,* 490–495.

Graham, J. R. (1993). Use with special groups. In J. R. Graham, *MMPI-2: Assessing personality and psychopathology* (2nd ed., pp. 193–217). New York: Oxford University Press.

Greene, R. L. (1987). Ethnicity and MMPI performance: A review. *Journal of Consulting and Clinical Psychology, 55,* 497–512.

Greene, R. L. (1991). Specific groups: Adolescents, the aged, Blacks, and other ethnic groups. In R. L. Greene, *The MMPI-2/MMPI: An interpretive manual* (pp. 331–354). Needham Heights, MA: Allyn & Bacon.

Velásquez, R. J. (1984). *An atlas of MMPI group profiles on Mexican Americans* (Occasional Paper No. 19). Los Angeles: Spanish Speaking Mental Health Research Center, University of California, Los Angeles.

Velásquez, R. J. (1992). Hispanic American MMPI research (1949–1992): A comprehensive bibliography. *Psychological Reports, 70,* 743–754.

Velásquez, R. J. (1993). *Use of the MMPI on Hispanic Americans: A review of research.* Unpublished manuscript, San Diego State University, San Diego, CA.

Velásquez, R. J. (1993). *Use of Spanish versions of the MMPI on Hispanic Americans: A review of research.* In review.

Studies Utilizing the Rorschach

Brown, F. (1960). Intelligence test patterns of Puerto Rican psychiatric patients. *Journal of Social Psychology, 52,* 225–230.

Ceccoli, V. C. (1987). Relationship between cognitive functioning as measured by WISC-R and Rorschach data of referred Hispanic children (Doctoral dissertation, Texas A & M University, 1987). *Dissertation Abstracts International, 48,* 3073A.

Crain, W. C., & Smoke, L. (1981). Rorschach aggressive content in normal and problematic children. *Journal of Personality Assessment, 45,* 2–4.

Espino-Navarrete, C. (1975). Characteristics of Hispanic patients reporting spiritualism phenomena (Doctoral dissertation, New York University,

1975). *Dissertation Abstracts International, 43,* 1975B.

Gomez, M. V. (1988). A projective study of the affective expression of bilinguals (Doctoral dissertation, Northwestern University, 1988). *Dissertation Abstracts International, 49,* 2854B.

Johnson, D. L., & Spikes, M. P. (1965). Rorschach and TAT responses of Negro, Mexican-American, and Anglo psychiatric patients. *Journal of Projective Techniques, 29,* 183–188.

Kaplan, B. (1955). Reflections of the acculturation process in the Rorschach test. *Journal of Projective Techniques, 19,* 30–35.

Kaplan, B., Rickers-Ovsiankina, M. A., & Joseph, A. (1956). An attempt to sort Rorschach records from four cultures. *Journal of Projective Techniques, 20,* 172–180.

Kranau, E. J. (1983). Level of acculturation/biculturation and Rorschach protocols of Hispanic Americans and Anglo Americans (Doctoral dissertation, Oklahoma State University, 1983). *Dissertation Abstracts International, 44,* 3200B.

Tori, C. D. (1989). Homosexuality and illegal residency status in relation to substance abuse and personality traits among Mexican nationals. *Journal of Clinical Psychology, 45,* 814–821.

Tulchin, S. H., & Levy, D. M. (1945). Rorschach test differences in a group of Spanish and English refugee children. *American Journal of Orthopsychiatry, 15,* 361–368.

Relevant Rorschach Reviews on Hispanics

Frank, G. (1993). The use of the Rorschach with Hispanic Americans. *Psychological Reports, 72,* 276–278.

Studies Utilizing the TAT

Bracero, W. (1990). Bilingualism and biculturalism in the TAT responses of normal Puerto Rican women (Doctoral dissertation, New York University, 1990). *Dissertation Abstracts International, 51,* 5565B.

Constantino, G., & Malgady, R. G. (1983). Verbal fluency of Hispanic, Black, and White children on TAT and TEMAS, a new thematic apperception test. *Hispanic Journal of Behavioral Sciences, 5,* 199–206.

Constantino, G., Malgady, R. G., & Vasquez, C. (1981). A comparison of the Murray-TAT and a new Thematic Apperception Test for urban Hispanic children. *Hispanic Journal of Behavioral Sciences, 3,* 291–300.

Crespo-Gonzalez, E. I. (1989). It loses something in the translation: The communication of emotion among Puerto Ricans living in the U.S. (Doctoral dissertation, Adelphi University, 1989). *Dissertation Abstracts International, 50,* 5376B.

Field, P. B., Maldonado-Sierra, E. D., & Coelho, G. V. (1963). A student-TAT measure of competence: A cross-cultural replication in Puerto Rico. *Perceptual and Motor Skills, 16,* 195–198.

Gomez, M. V. (1988). A projective study of the affective expression of bilinguals (Doctoral dissertation, Northwestern University, 1988). *Dissertation Abstracts International, 49,* 2854B.

Johnson, D. L., & Sikes, M. P. (1965). Rorschach and TAT responses of Negro, Mexican-American, and Anglo psychiatric patients. *Journal of Projective Techniques, 29,* 183–188.

Leman, J. F. (1966). *Aggression in Mexican-American and Anglo-American delinquent and non-delinquent males as revealed in dreams and Thematic Apperception Test responses.* Unpublished doctoral dissertation, University of Arizona, Tucson.

Pina, G. (1978). An investigation into the effects of language and acculturation in the assessment of psychopathology of Chicano males using the TAT (Doctoral dissertation, American University, 1978). *Dissertation Abstracts International, 39,* 1495B.

Urrabazo, R. (1986). Mexican American male self-concept: An interpretation and reflection on Thematic Apperception Test and Kinetic Family Drawing results of Mexican American teenagers (Doctoral dissertation, Graduate Theological Union, 1986). *Dissertation Abstracts International, 47,* 435B.

Vasquez, C. I. (1981). Fantasies of bilingual children: An exploration into relationship of bilingualism, self-concept, and parental interaction (Doctoral dissertation, City University of New York, 1981). *Dissertation Abstracts International, 42,* 3837B.

Warren, M. (1988). Achievement and power motivation of inmates on the Thematic Apperception Test (Doctoral dissertation, Hofstra University, 1988). *Dissertation Abstracts International, 49,* 2980A.

11

The Assessment of Psychopathology in Racial and Ethnic Minorities

Bernadette Gray-Little

In the United States ethnicity and race provide a basis for an immediate form of status differentiation. It was perhaps inevitable that ethnicity, like gender, would become a strategic point for the analysis of a wide variety of individual and social behaviors. Comparison of racial and ethnic groups has been of interest to psychologists since the introduction of psychological tests at the end of the last century. Even before that time America's founders and social philosophers of the late eighteenth and early nineteenth centuries offered theories of race differences in an effort to rationalize the contradiction between democracy for whites and the treatment of blacks and native Americans (see Gosset, 1965, for a discussion of early race theories). The thrust of most of these theories was that nonwhites belong to different species from whites, and consequently there was no compelling reason that they should be afforded the same treatment. Later in the nineteenth century the work of Darwin undermined the scientific respectability of such arguments, but offered a new rationale in the form of natural selection and hereditary determinism. Social Darwinists construed the conflict between classes and races as the natural struggle among subgroups of the species with inevitable domi-

nation by the superior group. Social Darwinism was endorsed by many psychologists and social scientists of the day who were convinced that the methods of social science offered proof of the inequality of racial and ethnic groups (Galton, 1891; Hall & Sander, 1900). Experiments aimed at identifying race differences were among the first to be conducted when rudimentary mental tests were introduced in the 1890s, and the advent of modern intelligence tests during the first decade of the twentieth century strengthened the conviction that psychological tests would be pivotal in assessing racial and ethnic differences (Cook & Reynolds, 1933; Garth, 1931). Some of the most respected psychologists of that time—Yerkes, Terman, Thorndike—considered IQ tests to be capable of proving the inferior genetic potential of blacks, native Americans, Mexicans, and groups from Eastern and Southern Europe (Gosset, 1965; Kamin, 1974; Gould, 1981).

The success of the intelligence test movement was followed by attempts to devise instruments to measure character and personality traits. In 1922 a cross-cultural study of personality was conducted using the Downey Will Temperament Test (McFadden & Dashiell, 1922). The results were interpreted as showing

Mexicans, Indians, blacks, and Chinese and Japanese immigrants were inferior to whites in personality traits such as kindliness, integrity, and refinement. In one of the earliest uses of psychological tests to assess psychopathology, Hollingsworth (1920) administered the Woodworth Personal Data Sheet of neurotic tendencies to a large number of World War I recruits and reported that blacks were less emotionally fit than whites. A review of psychiatric assessment reveals a similar history: the practice of psychiatry, including its ways of diagnosis, has been influenced by the social ethos and political systems as much as by scientific investigation (Fernando, 1991; Wilkinson, 1986; Thomas & Sillen, 1972).

During the past two decades substantial effort has been devoted to eliminating racial and ethnic bias in the assessment of psychopathology, with some observers concluding that there is no evidence of such bias in major psychological tests or in the application of diagnostic systems. Despite efforts to overcome ethnocentricity in psychological assessment and in the psychiatric interview, evidence to be reviewed below indicates that a client's race and ethnicity still influence clinical assessment.

RACE, ETHNICITY, AND SOCIAL CLASS

The primary purpose of this volume is to present practical applications in the assessment of psychopathology. Before turning to a discussion of assessment processes, however, a few caveats are in order regarding the use of the terms race and ethnicity. The terms race and ethnicity are often used interchangeably and may refer to the same demographic characteristics, but often they do not. The primary distinction is that *race* refers to a major biological subgroup of interbreeding persons with similar physical characteristics, whereas *ethnicity* refers primarily to cultural features, the nonmaterial aspects or conceptual structures that determine patterns of living such as language, customs, religion, and values. Fernando (1991) argues that ethnicity is primarily a psychological matter, a shared sense of belonging together arising from similarities among persons within a group, but that also may arise when external pressures lead to the formation of an alliance against a common enemy or threat. Obviously persons who differ in race can belong to the same ethnic group, and those differing in ethnicity may belong to the same race. Complicating this distinction further is socioeconomic class, which refers to the rank an individual has with regard to the distribution of resources, and which in a stratified society may develop some of the same features as ethnicity. Thus it is common in sociological literature to refer to the culture of lower-class society or to middle-class values. Current research in several areas suggests that social class has a more profound effect than ethnicity in such areas as childrearing, aspirations and academic achievement, the outcome of child behavior disorders, and psychiatric symptomatology (Dohrenwend & Dohrenwend, 1974; Eaton, 1980). Because of the history of social and economic discrimination against ethnic and racial minorities in the United States, many such groups are also socially and educationally disadvantaged, and as a result, all of these distinctions—race, ethnicity, and recognizable class—may be applied to one group. African-Americans thus constitute a racial group with loosely clustered cultural elements, whose members are disproportionately represented among lower socioeconomic classes; the same can be said of native Americans. The term Asian-American also refers to racial and ethnic distinctions, whereas the designation Hispanic is based largely on common language, and may include persons of African, European, and native American descent.

The history and treatment of racial and ethnic groups has varied substantially within American society. In this discussion there is no assumption that racial and ethnic minorities are inherently similar to one another or that the study of one minority provides information on all. Indeed it might be argued that in the United States each group shares elements of the national culture as well as distinctive cultural features. Only when the distinctive cultural features also overlap is there a basis for assuming greater similarity among ethnic groups than between an ethnic group and the majority. Within the four ethnic racial groups referred to below, African-Americans, Asian-Americans, Hispanics, and native Americans, there are many variations. Native Americans, for example, represent over three hundred tribes with different cultures and languages, while Asian-Americans and Pacific Islanders represent as many as thirty national and cultural groups (Dana, 1993). Thus in the content of their beliefs and values, and in particular behavior patterns, racial and ethnic groups may be more similar to the dominant culture than to one another. This point is illustrated by differences in utilization of hospital-based psychiatric services: there are higher utilization rates for blacks and native Americans than for whites, but Japanese-, Chinese-, and Mexican-Americans have lower rates (Snowden & Cheung, 1990). These patterns are not accounted for by socioeconomic factors or by variations in rates of psychopathology.

RACE, ETHNICITY, AND PSYCHOPATHOLOGY

A legitimate question can be raised about what constitutes membership in a particular ethnic group. We have said that ethnicity is primarily a psychological matter, a sense of belonging together. And yet persons designated as Hispanic or Chinese American, for example, may differ widely in how fully they identify with their respective ethnic groups. Without knowledge of ethnic identification, assignment of a person to one group or another is based largely on self-identified racial membership, and this too provides little assistance in understanding psychopathology. Several authors have attempted to develop race-sensitive scales for the assessment of psychopathology (Costello, 1977; Galper, 1973) or more general ethnic identification (Cross, 1978; Cuellar, Harris, & Jasso, 1980; Thomas, 1971), but these scales have either not been fully developed or have not found widespread use in clinical practice. As a result there are no commonly accepted instruments to indicate whether ethnic identification is central

to understanding psychopathology in a given patient.

There is at present no theory that adequately elucidates the significance of race and ethnicity for psychopathology. When racial and ethnic groups are thought of as distinct cultural groups, there is little reason to believe that particular levels of distress and psychopathology are inherent to the cultural features themselves. There is no basis for assuming, for example, that Chinese culture inherently causes psychopathology to a greater extent than German culture, or that Asians are more prone to disorder in any absolute sense than are Caucasians. When members of a racial or ethnic group are differentiated from others in the same society, however, and occupy a subordinate position, they are considered minorities, and to the extent that minorities are thought of as having disadvantaged status in the social structure, they might be expected to have higher levels of distress (Eaton, 1980; Mirowsky & Ross, 1980). Thus when we examine racial and ethnic factors in the assessment of psychopathology, we are considering the effects of a complex network of racial, cultural, and socioeconomic features, as well as the effects of diverse experiences of racism and discrimination.

Additionally, current diagnostic systems fail to set forth a plan by which the rules of diagnosis might incorporate race, ethnicity, or social class. For example, in a recent examination of eleven diagnostic and interview schedules, including DSM-III, Lopez and Nunez (1987) found only meager consideration of ethnic factors.

In the absence of well-developed theories and lacking specific rules of practice, diagnosticians are left to their own discretion regarding the role of ethnicity in the assessment of psychopathology. In practical assessment situations the effects of the client's race, ethnicity, and social class are difficult if not impossible to disentangle from one another, as well as from biases of the assessor or assessment instruments and procedures. A given diagnostician may overemphasize ethnicity to the point that clinical symptoms are partially discounted (Lopez & Hernandez, 1986), dismiss race and ethnicity as irrelevant, overpathologize symptoms in some racial or social-class groups (Loring & Powell, 1988; Umbenhauer & DeWitte, 1978), or strive for a sensitive integration of cultural and clinical features.

The present discussion is relevant to several questions that have frequently been raised about ethnicity and psychopathology. First, are there racial or ethnic differences in the rates or manifestations of psychopathology? Do educational and socialization practices or other biases, such as the formation of stereotypes or expectations of finding a particular pattern of traits or symptoms, lead psychologists to interpret the same behavior differently depending on the ethnicity of the client? Does a similar bias influence tests used to assess psychopathology in racial and ethnic minorities, that is, do psychological test results show comparable relevance to behavior when used with racial and ethnic minorities? The answers to these questions are complex and interdependent, and they all involve measurement. There are two prominent measurement traditions in the assessment of psychopathology (Blashfield & Livesley, 1991). In psychiatry the standard medium of assessment has been the clinical interview, which is used to assess past and present problems with the goal of assignment to a diagnostic category. In psychology much more attention has been given to the use of psychological tests to assess psychopathology dimensionally. Here, the emphasis has been on severity of symptoms or traits, and to a lesser extent, the assignment of diagnoses. The traditional clinical interview allows more flexibility, whereas the use of psychological tests permits more objective and standardized measurement; the standardized psychiatric interview is seen as having features of both approaches. Although the distinction between dimensional and categorical approaches to assessment may be partly illusory (Robins, 1985), research on the two types of measurement occurs in relatively distinct bodies of literature. Both traditions, however, are represented in research on race and psychopathology, and both are essential to a discussion of the assessment of psychopathology because psychiatric interviews and observations

often constitute the criterion to which psychological tests predict. In the sections to follow, discussion of the interview will precede discussion of psychological tests, as almost all of the interpersonal features that affect the assessment interview are also relevant to the testing situation.

PSYCHIATRIC ASSESSMENT OF PSYCHOPATHOLOGY

The bulk of research on the diagnosis of ethnic and racial minorities has concerned the incidence of schizophrenia and affective disorders in African-Americans, and to a lesser extent, Hispanics. Consideration of diagnostic bias in the assessment of native Americans and Asian-Americans is virtually nonexistent (Snowden & Cheung, 1990). The preponderance of studies indicate that blacks are diagnosed as schizophrenic more frequently than are Caucasians. In addition, affective or mood disorders, which are typically seen as having a less dire prognosis, are diagnosed at a disproportionately low rate. Explanations of these findings fall into two classes. The first, a social causation explanation, postulates that the most severe disorders, the schizophrenias, are more common among blacks and Hispanics due to their status as disadvantaged minorities and their lower social class. The second class of explanations attributes the finding to bias in diagnosticians or to their lack of familiarity with manifestations of distress and coping among ethnic and racial minorities.

Social Causation

According to this theory, there is a higher rate of serious mental disorder among blacks and Hispanics due to their status as minorities. Because membership in a racial or ethnic minority is a basis for differentiation in power, prestige, and resources, minority status might reasonably be seen as contributing to distress and psychopathology in much the same way as low socioeconomic status (Eaton, 1980). In 1974

Dohrenwend and Dohrenwend reviewed community studies of psychiatric epidemiology and found an inverse relationship between social class and mental disorder in 85 percent of the studies that provided social-class data. This finding was most consistent for schizophrenia, with a less clear-cut pattern for neurotic level disorders. For many years the effects of race and social class were considered additive, but numerous studies conducted over the past two decades reported a dissipation of the apparently higher levels of distress among racial minorities when social class was controlled. Kessler and Neighbors's (1986) reanalysis of several studies of this type indicates an interaction of race and social class, with the effect of race greatest among the lowest social classes and almost nonexistent, with an occasional reversal, at the highest income levels. Thus they caution against the conclusion that minority status makes no independent contribution to understanding psychopathology.[1] Given the evidence of bias in diagnosis to be presented below, however, statements regarding the interaction of ethnicity and social class with psychopathology can only be provisional.

Distortions in Diagnosis

The second class of explanations centers on distortions in diagnoses assigned to ethnic minorities. The prototypical explanation attributes the distortion to ethnocentrism or racism in the diagnostician, but there are several variants. These include social distance between diagnostician and patient, information-processing errors, and ethnic-specific manifestation of psychopathology. Each of these approaches will be discussed below. The methods used to address these problems are varied but consist largely of comparisons of diagnosis based on a traditional clinical interview with a more objective standardized psychiatric interview; analogue studies in which groups of judges are asked to evaluate case materials with identical clinical features but with race varied; and studies comparing treatment responses to members of different ethnic groups who have similar symptoms or diagnosis.

Bias and Social Distance

Bias in the diagnostician and social distance or status discrepancy between ethnic patients and mental health professionals may lead to error in assessing ethnic minority clients. Because these two sources of error are often indistinguishable in practice, they will be discussed together. A social-distance explanation posits that bias occurs when the patient and diagnostician hold very different positions in society. The diagnostician needs to be able to take the role or perspective of the other, but different social positions make that difficult to do. If the behavior of the other is unintelligible or foreign, it is more likely to be labeled insane or abnormal (Rosenberg, 1984). A very compatible labeling-theory perspective holds that social distance between an agent of control (diagnostician) and a rule breaker (patient) will lead to harsher evaluation of the rule breaker (Scheff, 1966; Rosenfield, 1984). The predominant normative interpretation of mental health professionals who are mostly white and middle-class can work to the detriment of lower-class patients and members of racial minorities (Umbenhauer & Dewitte, 1978). Among mental health professionals who are themselves members of a minority group, social-class differences may exist, and more important, their training, which is done mostly by whites, may lead them to view patients of their own ethnic or racial group as "the other."

There is some evidence in support of social distance; for example, DeHoyos and DeHoyos (1975) found consistent underrecording of symptoms for black and low-income clients. The average length of the admission note for black patients was 12.9 lines, but 18.4 lines for whites. The longest entry, 49 lines, was for a young, middle-class, male college student, with whom the authors speculate it was easier for the psychiatrists to get involved and to understand. Rosenfield (1984) also presented results indicating that the greater the status difference between the diagnostician and patient, the greater the likelihood of involuntary hospitalization. Ironically, although black patients receive more serious diagnoses and are more likely to be hospitalized involuntarily, they receive, on the average, only two-thirds the duration of treatment offered to whites (Manderscheid & Barrett, 1987).

Perhaps the most notable recent investigation of the effect of bias and social distance is a study by Loring and Powell (1989), who conducted an analogue study in which male and female, white and nonwhite psychiatrists were asked to diagnose case materials developed to represent a set of disorders. The race and gender were varied for four of the presentations, and a fifth case presented no information on race and gender. Loring and Powell reported results that can be interpreted as support for both social distance and racial bias in diagnosing black patients. Consistent with a social-distance explanation, diagnosticians were more accurate in diagnosing the case of the same gender and race than when gender or race was different. They were most accurate, however, when neither race nor gender was identified, suggesting that these bits of information led them to entertain faulty hypotheses associated with race and gender or to initiate a faulty processing of base rate information associated with race and gender groups.[2] The modal response across all groups of psychiatrists was the correct response; however, because this diagnosis was selected less than 50 percent of the time, a review of the pattern of errors is very instructive. First, there was no consistent pattern of misdiagnosis in the unidentified case material. Second, among the gender- and race-identified cases, the erroneous diagnosis given to black males was more severe than the correct diagnosis, and the most frequent erroneous diagnosis given to the black male patient, paranoid schizophrenia, fits a stereotype of black males. It is of interest to note that this misdiagnosis was not assigned to the white male patient by even one male psychiatrist. Thus, consistent with a racial-bias hypothesis, there was overestimation of pathology in the black male patient. In general, misdiagnoses assigned to white males and to females were consistent with a pattern of underestimation of pathology.

Loring and Powell (1989) speculate that psychiatrists and other mental health professionals internalize standards provided in their training, for example, that black male psychiatric patients

are dangerous, violent, and suspicious. When gender and race information accompany the case, the stage is set for a hypothesis confirming bias (Darley & Gross, 1983) in that the diagnostician begins to develop hypotheses stemming not only from the symptoms, but also from gender and ethnicity. The case information is then used to confirm these hypotheses. Thus, contrary to indications that race, ethnic, and cultural factors are ignored, this research suggests that such information is used in a way that leads to error. Research by Loring and Powell is just a recent example of a series of studies indicating overdiagnosis of severe pathology or recommendations of more restrictive treatment for black and Hispanic patients. Similar results have been found in several studies (Blake, 1973; Flaherty & Meagher, 1980; Lawson, Yesavage, & Werner, 1984; Raskin, Crook, & Herman, 1975; Simon, Fleiss, Gurland, Stiller, & Sharpe, 1973; Mukherjee, Shukla, Woodle, Rosen, & Olarte, 1983; Pakov, Lewis, & Lyons, 1989; Soloff & Turner, 1981). A number of these researchers and others have also found that the association between race and diagnosis is present when the diagnosis is obtained through a traditional interview conducted by a hospital physician, but that the association is attenuated when the diagnosis is derived from structured interviews or other objective criteria (Craig, Goodman, & Haugland, 1982; Mukherjee et al., 1983; Pakov et al.; Raskin et al., 1975). The clinical interview may be an erratic criterion. Training for awareness of bias and ethnocentrism is an important part of addressing this problem. Greater use of standardized interviews, which provide more consistent and more accurate information, should also be encouraged (Robins, 1985).

The Information-Processing Perspective

It has also been argued that inaccuracies in the diagnosis of minority patients constitute a specific example of error in processing information, not racial bias. The information-processing approach to diagnostic error has been articulated by Lopez (1989), who argues that error in diagnosing minorities is just a particular case of the more general problem of systematic errors made by clinical judges. According to Lopez, a clients's race, gender, age, and socioeconomic status influence the way clinicians form judgments. Because not all possible information can be gathered, clinical judgments are influenced not only by presenting symptoms, but also by knowledge about the base rates in the reference population (e.g., native American, older females, etc.), by social distance between the patient and therapist, and by the ability of the diagnostician to understand the meaning of the patient's symptoms. Consistent with Lopez's view is cross-cultural research by Tseng and McDermott (1981), who found that Japanese psychiatrists were more likely than Caucasian psychiatrists to rate videotapes of Caucasian Americans as indicating emotional lability. These ratings presumably reflect different norms for affect expression and may be the reverse of the common tendency to see Asian-American patients as passive and emotionally stilted. In a similar vein, Caucasian American and Chinese-American therapists gave diametrically different ratings to videotapes of clients from their respective groups; in both instances therapists gave more adaptive ratings to clients of their own cultural group and more pathological, stereotypical ratings to the racial outgroup (Li-Repac, 1980). Portions of Loring and Powell's research are also consistent with an information-processing explanation.

The advantage of the information-processing approach to diagnostic bias is that it takes advantage of existing theory and research regarding errors in judgment and the selective use of information. Its weakness, however, is that it fails to account for the consistent direction of bias in the assessment of pathology in black and low-income clients. Lopez's review of the literature revealed an overpathologizing bias in the assessment of lower-class individuals and of blacks relative to whites, and a minimizing bias toward whites and females for some disorders. There are few studies showing whites or persons of middle- or upper-income level to be diagnosed more severely than case information warrants, even when diagnosticians are themselves racial minorities (Loring & Powell, 1989). The

weight of the processing error is to maintain negative views of racial minorities and lower-income patients. Thus, to account adequately for the overpathologizing of minority patients, some amount of negative bias must be considered. The effect of negative bias can be far-reaching, affecting not only present assessment, but also memory. Park and Rothbart (1982) demonstrated that memory structures are more complex for in-group than for out-group members; we form more categories for storage of information regarding in-group members. (See DeHoyos & DeHoyos, 1975, described above, for an illustration of the effect of social distance on diagnosis.) It is conceivable that when recalling information about an ethnic minority patient, mental health professionals are prone to fill in with stereotypical information (due to impoverished information storage), leading to a diagnosis that confirms the stereotype and ultimately contributes to the development of false statistical data on rates of psychopathology in ethnic minority groups. Clinicians are actively engaged in a variety of cognitive processes during assessment. Training programs should include instruction on the processes of decision making and clinical judgment in order to inoculate clinicians against cognitive processing errors (Turk & Salovey, 1988).

Racial and Ethnic Variations in Symptoms of Distress

Finally, there is the possibility that racial and ethnic minorities manifest symptoms of distress in distinctive ways that can lead to misdiagnosis. Mental health and mental illness have to do with emotions felt by people within themselves, but the expression of emotions is influenced by cultural and social factors (Coulter, 1979; Mesquita & Frijda, 1992, Nichter, 1981). Feelings may be expressed in idioms, including poems and stories. In situations where the professional and client share similar understandings of the idioms of expression, communication is eased and idioms natural to both can be used. In the absence of shared understanding there is potentially a gulf, just as when diagnostician and patient speak different languages. Current diagnostic categories may not have universal integrity, so that the combination of symptoms that constitute "depression" or "somatization," for example, may vary from one group to another. The existence of cross-national or cross-cultural variations in the expression of disorder and the occurrence of culture-specific syndromes are well documented in anthropological literature (Westermeyer, 1987). Although several authors have pointed to variations in symptom patterns among American ethnic groups, relatively little systematic attention has been devoted to this topic.

Liss, Welner, Robins, and Richardson (1973) reported a better fit between symptoms and diagnosis for white than black patients in a review of symptoms in 256 patients. They also found a greater frequency of delusions and hallucinations in black patients who were schizophrenic as well as those who were not. In general, blacks had a higher frequency of symptoms unrelated to the diagnosis they received. Tonks, Paykel, and Klerman (1970), Raskin et al. (1975), and Helzer (1975) found no remarkable difference in symptoms of depression for black and white patients. By contrast, Simon et al., 1973, reported more tension, headaches, and somatic complaints among black patients, but they did not control for social class. More frequent somatic symptoms in depression have been reported for Hispanics (Fabrega, Rubel, & Wallace, 1967; Maduro, 1983; Smith Kline, 1978; Weaver & Sklar, 1980) and Asian-Americans (Sue & Morishima, 1982; Marsella, Kinzie, & Gordon, 1973), but again these findings may be confounded with socioeconomic or educational factors. Several authors have also described ethnic minority persons as more restrained in the expression of emotion. This last observation is difficult to evaluate, however, since it may be attributable to differences in the expression of distress, to reserve shown by ethnic minorities who are wary of the mental health system, or to stereotyping on the part of the mental health professional (Scott & Gaitz, 1975). Nonetheless, when taken together the body of research on ethnic variation in the expression of distress indicates that diagnostic categories may not be an equally "good fit" for all groups.

PSYCHOLOGICAL TESTING

The psychological assessment of ethnic minority persons will often present a predicament for the clinician who may suspect that current assessment practices are discriminatory but have little in the way of an empirically based alternative. Psychological tests were developed to provide objective and standardized appraisals that would support inferences about behavior or psychological processes. With any psychological test used to measure psychopathology in ethnic groups, there is an implicit assumption that an underlying disorder is expressed in the same way in each population and that the test in question adequately represents these various symptoms. If the disorder is manifest in different symptoms in different groups (see above), however, this assumption is violated and the scale is not equally appropriate for all groups. A second assumption is that the scores obtained represent true scores, whereas in fact each score measures the target construct with a certain level of error, and the amount of error may differ from one group to another (Walters, Greene, Jeffrey, Kruzich, & Haskins, 1983; Choca, Shanley, & Van Denburg, 1992) Furthermore, the psychological assessment of psychopathology often consists not only of test administration, but also of interview and observation, and thus many of the issues raised regarding the psychiatric interview are equally germane to the testing situation. Insofar as many psychological tests require interpretation, the use of the tests themselves may also be subject to distortions arising from bias, social distance, and the application of false base rates.

In a recent comprehensive discussion of multicultural assessment, Dana (1993) divided assessment instruments into those representing emic and etic perspectives. An emic perspective attempts to evaluate behavior from within a culture, using rules derived from that culture. By contrast, an etic perspective attempts to apply a single, universal standard across all groups. Obviously the use of truly etic measures would facilitate the development of a universal science of human behavior and psychopathology. The problem with most etic measurement, as it is currently practiced, is that the instruments are not universal but are instead developed on one particular group, e.g. white middle-class American adults, and then imposed on other groups as though they were universal. Ironically, the tests Dana identifies as fostering emic assessment of psychopathology—picture-story techniques, inkblots, drawings—require extensive training, and as they rely on subjective interpretation, are among the ones most susceptible to assessor bias. Besides, among the etic techniques listed by Dana are included some of the measures for which extensive efforts have been made to insure cultural sensitivity—for example, the MMPI and several alcoholism and depression measures. Obviously it is beyond the scope of this chapter to review all major psychological tests for use with different ethnic groups. It seems obvious, however, that a particular test is not inherently culturally sensitive or biased; this depends on its application and on the skill and the politics of its user. Brief discussions of two types of psychological tests, objective and projective measures, will illustrate this point.

Objective Assessment of Psychopathology

Among objective tests used to assess psychopathology, the MMPI is most prominent, and there is extensive research on its use with American ethnic groups (Dahlstrom, Lachar, & Dahlstrom, 1986). Greene (1987) summarized research published through 1985 that had reported performance on MMPI as a function of ethnic group membership and that had found meaningful scale differences (T score of 5 points or more).[3] As a preface to a review of Greene's finding, it should be noted that ethnic and racial differences can occur at the item, scale, or profile level. In clinical situations, however, scale elevation and profile interpretation are most common. Greene's review focuses exclusively on scale (clinical, validity, and special) comparisons, and it is difficult to extrapolate from this level of analysis to the impact of race and ethnicity on configurational analysis. The substantial majority of the reviewed studies pre-

sented black-white comparisons, but eleven compared Hispanics with whites, seven concerned native Americans, and three involved Asian groups; most studies presented multiple scale comparisons. The results were presented separately by ethnic group, and within each ethnic group they were clustered into sets using normal, psychiatric, prison, and substance-abuse samples. With regard to black-white differences, Greene concluded that there was no consistent pattern across all clusters of samples. This statement seems like an overgeneralization, however, in view of the fact that among the normal and psychiatric samples, which constitute the majority of the comparisons, 70 percent of the comparisons showed blacks to have higher or more pathological scores; only among substance abusers were whites typically found to have higher scale scores. Greene does note that the greater the attention given to profile validity and the more stringent the controls for economic and educational levels, the less likely there are to be differences found between blacks and whites. The Hispanic-white comparisons yielded no consistent differences. By contrast, there was a consistent pattern of higher scores for native Americans and Asian-Americans than for whites. The small number of studies involved in the latter groups should be borne in mind, but these findings may have significant practical implications; for example, the MMPI is widely used by the Indian Health Service (Dana, 1993). Few of the studies comparing native Americans or Asian-Americans with whites provided controls for educational or economic level, and the differences may be partially attributable to these factors.

Because of the large number of similarities among the groups and the failure of most studies to eliminate the confounding effects of educational and economic levels, Greene infers that it is premature to conclude that new norms are needed for specific ethnic groups. It is equally premature to conclude that existing norms are universally applicable to all American ethnic groups, however, since the critical question about ethnic differences is not addressed in most comparisons: What do the differences mean? The opposite question also needs to be addressed: What are the implications of similar scores? Does the failure to find differences between Hispanics and whites, for example, mean that a given score has the same interpretation? Obviously, more research must be addressed to these questions. Of the few studies examining empirical correlates of MMPI scores for whites and blacks, some report similar behavioral correlates, whereas others do not (Greene, 1987). In the absence of conclusive information regarding the predictive validity of the MMPI scores for ethnic minorities, there will be differences of opinion about how to proceed in clinical situations. For example, Dahlstrom, Lachar, and Dahlstrom (1986) caution against the use of a culture-specific correction of MMPI profiles obtained with black samples since such corrections may result in less accurate diagnosis when compared with available criteria (judgments and ratings of mental health professionals). On the other hand, following a synthesis of six summaries of black-white MMPI studies published from 1960 to 1987, Gynther (1989) argued for a correction, suggesting that for black patients scales F, 8, and 9 should be played down in order to avoid overdiagnosis of psychosis. The only resolution to these divergent views lies in accumulating information on the accuracy of predictions for each group. Care must also be taken to avoid the use of biased criteria. The inclusion of ethnic minorities in the standardization sample for the recently developed MMPI-2 may be helpful in addressing some of the problems identified above, but too little research has been conducted with the MMPI-2 to draw firm conclusions thus far. For example, Shondrick, Ben-Porath, and Stafford's (1992) comparison of court-ordered evaluations of black and white offenders showed only one significant difference (scale 9) among the clinical and validity scales. By contrast, a recent study by Timbrook and Graham (1993) found no validity scale differences among matched samples of blacks and whites, but for the clinical scales black men scored significantly higher than whites on scales 8 and 9 and, among women, blacks had higher scores on scales 4, 5, and 9. Their comparison of unmatched samples revealed significant racial differences for men

and women on the validity scales. Furthermore, due to the small percentage of the population represented by some ethnic groups, for example native Americans, it is unlikely that including a representative number in the standardization sample will address the problems alluded to above.

In addition to concerns regarding the meaning of scale elevations, there are related but more subtle issues that arise in the use of the MMPI with ethnic groups. *Sensitivity* (the proportion of true positives) refers to the capacity of scales to identify pathology when it is present and *specificity* (the proportion of true negatives) to the probability that scores will be appropriately low when no psychopathology is present. Although MMPI scales are generally found to be sensitive to pathology in ethnic minority groups, several studies have indicated that several clinical and special scales may be less able to distinguish psychiatric from nonpsychiatric samples in ethnic minority groups. For example, Walters et al. (1983) found that the McAndrews Alcoholism scale for the MMPI was equally able to identify black and white alcoholics and to distinguish white alcoholics from nonalcoholics, but it was not able to discriminate blacks who were alcoholic from those who were not. Pollack and Shore suggest a similar problem for several MMPI clinical scales with native American populations, a failure to differentiate severe pathology from moderate to normal reactions, as well as problems in distinguishing among clinical groups.

The Millon Clinical Multiaxial Inventory-I (MCMI-I)[4] is a more recently developed inventory designed to assesses psychopathology. There are some important differences between the MCMI-I and the MMPI in both theoretical underpinnings and construction (see Choca et al., 1992). Unlike the original MMPI, the standardization sample for the MCMI-I did include representative percentages of minority groups (a total of 19 percent, comprising African-Americans and Asian-Americans, and mixed ethnics). In addition, the procedures for converting raw scores into standard scores include separate conversion tables for men and women, African-Americans, Hispanics, and the general population. Despite these efforts and evidence of similar factor structure for blacks and whites, however, several recent studies indicate that significant racial (black-white) differences occur not only at the level of item endorsement, but also in the standardized scale scores, as well as in the way the MCMI-I predicts DSM-III diagnoses for a range of disorders including anxiety, affective, substance abuse, psychotic, and personality disorders (Choca et al., 1992). Choca implies that until the exact nature of these differences is understood, Gynther's admonition to underinterpret MMPI scale scores for blacks may be applicable to the MCMI-I as well.

Subjective Assessment of Psychopathology

As indicated above, projective tests have been considered more culturally sensitive than objective tests because of their ambiguous stimuli, which are assumed not to be culture-bound, and also because the use of language in the presentation of test materials may be minimal (Dana, 1993; Sundberg & Gonzales, 1981). Holtzman (1980) notes that this belief rests on three assumptions: first, that the responses to projective stimuli provide an adequate sample on which to make judgments about personality and psychopathology; second, that the determinants of the responses are basic and the same for all groups; and third, that projectives provide an equally adequate assessment for all groups. With regard to the first assumption, there is agreement about what constitutes an adequate sample of responses for some projective tests. For example, with the Exner Rorschach scoring system, a minimum of fifteen to twenty responses is considered scorable. Response production is an important element in using such a test with ethnic minority patients, who often give fewer responses than Caucasians and who may thus less often give valid or interpretable protocols (Howes & DeBlassie, 1989). The second assumption, that the determinants of responses are basic and universal, is difficult to verify. It is known, however, that situational factors such as the examiner's sex and the quality of rapport can affect both the productivity of the patient and also the type of projection (Abel, 1973; Pedersen, 1987). There is virtually no information directly bearing on the third assumption, that projectives provide an equally adequate assessment for all groups. As with the MMPI, confirmation of this assumption hinges on demonstrating the predictive validity of projectives with all groups.

Among the projective techniques used to assess psychopathology, the Rorschach is probably still number one despite rumors of its imminent demise a decade ago. The Rorschach has also been used extensively in anthropological studies, and there is perhaps more research focusing on cross-cultural comparisons than on its use with American ethnic groups. The first black-white comparison on the Rorschach was conducted over fifty years ago (described by Abel, 1973); a study involving Puerto Rican children was done in 1966 (Ruse and Berkowitz, cited in Abel, 1973); and a number of studies were completed by Boyer and Klopfer and their associates with Apache children and adults (1963; 1964; 1968). Only a small number of recent studies have addressed the performance of ethnic groups on the Rorschach (Howes & DeBlassie, 1989; Scott, 1981), and a cursory examination of Exner's (1986) comprehensive scoring and interpretive guide revealed no reference to considerations of race and ethnicity in use of the Rorschach. (The Holtzman Inkblot Test has had considerable application in cross-cultural investigations, and some research using this instrument has been conducted with American ethnic groups, but the Holtzman is not primarily a clinical instrument and has found limited application in clinical settings.) In the use of inkblots with ethnic minorities, the assessor must be aware that there are few empirical data to provide a guide, and although the use of the Rorschach or other inkblot techniques offers flexibility, the interpretation of such tests can also provide a screen for the assessor's projections.[5]

In contrast to the Rorschach, picture-story tests have been extensively researched with American minority populations (Dana, 1993; Henry, 1987; Snowden & Todman, 1982;

Sundberg & Gonzales, 1981). The prototype of the picture-story test is Murray's Thematic Apperception Test, or TAT. The scoring of the TAT with any population is problematic. In most clinical situations patients' stories are examined for themes and conflicts, and the scoring may be entirely impressionistic; few clinicians seem to adhere to a standard system. Thus the scoring, and possibly the interpretation, of the TAT is more variable than the Rorschach, for which there are standard scoring systems (Erdberg & Exner, 1984). Ethnic-specific versions of the TAT have been developed for African-Americans, several native American tribes and Hispanics.

The TAT was first adapted for use with blacks by Thompson (T-TAT, 1949), who modified facial features and darkened the skin color of characters on the cards in order to enhance identification with the stimulus figures. These modifications seemed to result in greater response production, but that finding is often disputed because word count was used as a measure of responsiveness. Another version of the TAT, the Black Thematic Apperception Test (B-TAT) was developed for use with black persons by Bailey and Green (1977), who also changed the hair style and clothing of the figures to enhance identification. Again there was a suggestion of increased response production (see Snowden & Todman, 1982, for a detailed critique of these TAT modifications). Even with the modifications mentioned above, however, black respondents remained relatively reserved in their response to TAT cards, raising the possibility that it is not the level of physical similarity with the stimulus that is critical, but the psychological meaning of the stimuli and the projective assessment process. The most recent development in this progression is a test developed by Williams (Williams & Johnson, 1981). The Themes Concerning Blacks or TCB goes further than its predecessors in trying to depict not only black characters but also features of black life in different settings. There is also a scoring system, but comparisons with the TAT indicate that the TCB is essentially a different test and its empirical correlates have not been fully tested (Dana, 1993). Each of these tests —

T-TAT, B-TAT, and TCB, seems to facilitate responsiveness and can be considered an alternative to the original TAT, but none has yet found general use in clinical situations, and further psychometric development is needed.

Apparently numerous modifications of the TAT characters have been made to depict features closer to a variety of native American tribes, but there are no systematic scoring systems for use with these pictures and thus interpretation is dependent on clinical inference. Some guidelines for use of the original TAT have been provided Henry (1987) for use with the Lakota people and by Monopoli (1984) for use with the Navajo, Hopi, and Zuñi. Dana (1985, 1993) recommends that interpretation of TAT with native Americans must be predicated not only on expertise with the TAT, but also extensive tribe-specific knowledge, often including tribal language. Reticence or low responding has also been found to be of concern in using the TAT with native American groups. Whether this reticence is due to economic or educational factors, to cultural differences in the meaningfulness of the task or stimuli, or to reservations about the assessment process is undetermined.

By far the most fully developed adaptation of the TAT is TEMAS (Spanish for themes), originally developed for use with Hispanic children and adolescents (Malgady, Rogler, & Constantino, 1987). Differences from the original TAT include ethnicity of the characters and the use of color rather than achromatic pictures. The authors indicate that the TEMAS, compared with traditional projective tests, enhances self-disclosure in Hispanic clients. They have also presented rudimentary evidence of criterion-related validity, a scoring system, and group-specific norms for blacks, Hispanics, and whites, and the test is now available for general use in clinical situations (Constantino, Malgady, & Rogler, 1988). With continued enhancement of its psychometric qualities, TEMAS may prove to be highly useful in the assessment of psychopathology and already seems to offer some technical improvements over the original TAT.

Given the difficulty of establishing validity and reliability for projective techniques, and that even the basic assumption that projectives provide access to the depths of the unconscious is not empirically tested, prudence should characterize their use with ethnic minorities (Snowden & Todman, 1982).

CONCLUSIONS AND RECOMMENDATIONS

The appropriate assessment of psychopathology in racial and ethnic minorities cannot be dealt with simply by issuing a list of culturally sensitive instruments. Nor can this issue be resolved by cataloguing a series of abnormal behaviors that the clinician should interpret in a culturally sensitive and nonpathological manner. Such approaches would be appealing because of their conceptual simplicity and the seeming ease with which various formulas might be learned. Practically, however, the burden would be substantial: each behavior and symptom might be viewed differently in each ethnic group; and although development of promising culture-specific tests is under way, new tests must undergo extensive development just to achieve the quality of our currently flawed instruments (Constantino et al., 1988; Jones, in press; Williams & Johnson, 1981). Furthermore, communication among clinicians and scholars would be greatly complicated by a proliferation of culture-specific instruments or diagnostic systems (Jones & Thorne, 1987). Thus, obvious solutions have substantial limitations and must await further research. In practical assessment situations, however, some compromise is necessary between what might ideally be possible in the future and what can reasonably be accomplished in the present. Where do these observations lead us? There are many specific recommendations that might be made regarding individual tests and symptom interpretation, but there are three issues that cut across all the problems discussed above and that deserve immediate attention: assessor bias, education and training for diversity, and a better understanding of the role of moderator variables.

First on the list is the need to attend to assessor bias and misuse of information. Psycho-

logical tests and other assessment procedures are no better than the person who uses them. The assessor is a product not only of formal training but also of beliefs, family experiences, and social-group memberships. Westermeyer (1987) notes that the attitudes, values, and behavior constituting the culture of the clinician are often unobserved and to a great extent exist outside of conscious awareness. Examination of the attitudes toward ethnic or racial minorities that result from one's upbringing can be threatening and for that reason may be resisted. Psychologists must seek opportunities to examine sources of personal and social bias and the ways these affect the assessment of psychopathology. Self-scrutiny, directed group discussions, and reading can be beneficial both to the trainee and to the experienced clinician in the process of examining assessor bias.

Self-scrutiny is not enough. The clinician must develop expertise regarding psychopathology and diagnosis in minority groups and greater sophistication in making clinical judgments. Assessors need to be aware of the varied manifestations of distress and coping in the populations they serve. It is critical that practitioners know enough about the cultural and social-class background of their patients to distinguish coping strategies from symptoms of psychopathology. For example, are the characteristics of emotional reserve and suspiciousness, attributed respectively to Asian and African-American patients, symptoms or coping strategies? Although we have at times discussed general minority status in assessment situations and in research, the effects of specific cultural arrangements rather than general minority status must be considered. Thus, familiarity with the literature on the assessment of psychopathology in particular target populations is required; information about one group does not apply to all. For example, if one is to make interpretive adjustments in use of the MMPI with black patients, relevant information is needed about the scales requiring adjustment, the amount of adjustment needed, and potential pitfalls in making such corrections. It would also be important to know that corrections that are warranted in the use of the MMPI with blacks may differ from those that are justifiable with various native American groups. Expanded training to process clinical information more accurately should also be included here.

At several points in this discussion the statement has been made that economic and educational factors may be more important than race or ethnicity in accounting for differences found between groups. The frequency of this claim points to the importance of moderator variables in research on psychopathology and underscores the importance of context in understanding behavior. Despite the frequent association between psychopathology and socioeconomic status, very little attention has been devoted to understanding what SES means for the development of psychopathology. Thus, when the statement is made that the differences are not racial but are due to social class, we may absolve ourselves of racism (Adebimpe, 1979), but we are no closer to understanding how psychopathology is affected by SES than how it is affected by ethnicity. In clinical practice and in research the psychological meaning of social class, just as of ethnicity, must receive serious consideration.

The most frequently mentioned alternatives to standard assessment procedures are the development of ethnic-specific norms and ethnic-specific tests. The argument in favor of these alternatives is that they offer more accurate assessment of psychopathology in specific ethnic groups and provide a kind of sensitivity already available to the majority. Opponents of these alternatives typically argue that such steps are premature and imply that continuing with business as usual is the best strategy because use of standard measures enhances communication. Jones and Thorne (1987) suggest assessment approaches that include standardized instruments and that can be adapted for use with individuals from different ethnic groups. These include the use of *narrative accounts* that become the basis for interviews and a collaborative relationship between patient and assessor, and *postassessment narratives*, which follow the administration of standard instruments and which allow the clinician to gather personal information that will be used in interpreting the patient's re-

sponses. Postassessment narratives provide information about the meaning of the assessment tasks and materials to the patient and can be a useful adjunct to either psychological tests or standardized psychiatric interviews. The postassessment narrative might also be a step in a research program aimed at determining the equivalence of standard psychological tests across groups.

The critical element in both the accounts method and postassessment narratives is reliance on the meaningfulness and primacy of subjective information. This feature makes the ability to establish rapport and a collaborative relationship between patient and clinician pivotal. Thus these approaches offer an alternative to the psychologist who is already acquainted with the values, attitudes, and behavior characteristics of the culture of the patient; their use hinges on the assessor's being both open to other groups and well-informed. These procedures draw needed attention to an important point that underlies much of our discussion. Whether problems in the assessment of psychopathology in minority patients are attributed to bias, faulty information processing, or misuse of psychological tests, one thing seems clear: to correct these problems clinicians must become engaged in understanding individual and cultural processes in their patients and in themselves.

NOTES

1. Support for their position can also be found in research with a variety of psychological tests. For example, Davis, Hoffman, and Nelson (1990) found that differences between native Americans and whites on the California Psychological Inventory remained after education and economic level were controlled.

2. Loring and Powell presented data on both an AXIS I and an AXIS II case, but only the AXIS I case is discussed here.

3. The number of studies reporting statistically significant differences was larger than the number reviewed by Greene, who argued that small score differences (less than a T score of 5 or half a standard deviation) are not clinically meaningful.

4. A second version of the MCMI-II is also being developed. Because the percentage of ethnic minority persons in the standardization sample of the MCMI-II is substantially smaller percentages than included in the MCMI-I, it is possible that racial/ethnic differences will be even greater.

5. One of the most famous uses of the Rorschach with black populations is featured in Kardiner and Ovesey's work *The Mark of Oppression* (1951). The authors' interpretations of their patients' test and interview responses provide a striking example of how vulnerable projective interpretation is to stereotypes and prejudgments.

REFERENCES

Abel, T. M. (1973). *Psychological testing in cultural contexts*. New Haven, CT: College and University Press.

Adebimpe, V. R. (1979). Overview: White norms and psychiatric diagnosis of Black patients. *American Journal of Psychiatry, 138*, 279–285.

Bailey, B. E., & Green, J. (1977). Black Thematic Apperception Test stimulus material. *Journal of Personality Assessment, 41*, 25–30.

Blake, W. (1973). The influence of race on diagnosis. *Studies in Social Work, 43*, 184–192.

Blashfield, R. K., & Livesly, W. J. (1991). Metaphorical analysis of psychiatric classification as a psychological test. *Psychological Bulletin, 100*, 262–270.

Boyer, L., Klopfer, B., Brawer, F. B., & Kawai, H. (1963). Comparisons of shamans and pseudoshamans of the Apaches of the Mescalero Indian Reservation. *Journal of Personality Assessment, 28*, 173–180.

Boyer, L., Boyer, R. M., Brawer, F. B., Kawai, H., & Klopfer, B. (1964). Apache age groups. *Journal of Projective Techniques and Personality Assessment, 28*, 397–402.

Boyer, L., Boyer, R. M., Kawai, H., Scheiner, S. B., & Klopfer, B. (1968). Apache "learners" and "non-learners". *Journal of Projective Techniques and Personality Assessment, 32*, 147–159.

Choca, J. P., Shanley, L. A., & Van Denburg, E. (1992). *Interpretive guide to the Millon Clinical Multiaxial Inventory*. Washington, DC: American Psychological Association.

Constantino, G., Malgady, R. G., & Rogler, L. H. (1988). *TEMAS (Tell-Me-A-Story) Manual*. Los Angeles: Western Psychological Services.

Cook, K. M., & Reynolds, F. E. (1933). *The education of native and minority groups: A Bibliography 1923–1932*. U.S. Office of Education Bulletin, No. 12.

Costello, R. M. (1977). Construction and cross-validation of an MMPI black-white scale. *Journal of Personality Assessment, 41*, 514–519.

Coulter, J. (1979). *The social construction of mind. Studies in ethnomethodology and linguistic philosophy*. London: Macmillan.

Craig, T., Goodman, A. B., & Hauglaund, G. (1982). Impact of DSM-III on clinical practice. *American Journal of Psychiatry, 139*, 922–925.

Cross, W. E. (1978). The Thomas and Cross models of psychological Nigrescence: A review. *Journal of Black Psychology, 5*, 13–31.

Cuellar, I., Harris, I. C., & Jasso, R. (1990). An acculturation scale for Mexican American normal and clinical populations. *Hispanic Journal of Behavioral Science, 2*, 199–217.

Dahlstrom, W. G., Lachar, D., & Dahlstrom, L. E. (Eds.). (1986). *MMPI patterns of American minorities*. Minneapolis: University of Minnesota Press.

Dana, R. H. (1993). *Multicultural assessment perspectives for professional psychology*. Boston: Allyn & Bacon.

Dana, R. H. (1988). Culturally diverse groups and MMPI interpretation. *Professional Psychology: Research and Practice, 19*, 490–495.

Darley, J. M., & Gross, P. H. (1983). A hypotheses-confirming bias in labelling effects. *Journal of Personality and Social Psychology, 44*, 20–33.

Davis, G. L., Hoffman, R. G., & Nelson, K. S. (1990). Differences between Native Americans and Whites on the California Psychological Inventory. *Psychological Assessment: A Journal of Consulting and Clinical Psychology, 2*, 238–242.

DeHoyos, A., & DeHoyos, G. (1965). Symptomatology differentials between Negro and White schizophrenics. *International Journal of Social Psychology, 11*, 245–255.

Dohrenwend, B. P., & Dohrenwend, B. S. (1974). Social and cultural influences on psychopathology. *Annual Review of Psychology, 25*, 417–452.

Eaton, W. W. (1980). *The sociology of mental disorders*. New York: Praeger.

Erdberg, P., & Exner, J. E. (1984). Rorschach Assessment. In G. Goldstein & M. Hersen (Eds.), *Handbook of psychological assessment*. New York: Pergamon.

Exner, J., Jr. (1986). *The Rorschach: A comprehensive system: Vol. 1. Basic Foundations* (2nd ed.). New York: Wiley.

Fabrega, H., Rubel, A. J., & Wallace, C. A. (1967). Some social and cultural features of working class

Mexican psychiatric outpatients. *Archives of General Psychiatry, 16,* 704–712.

Fernando, S. (1991). *Mental health, race, and culture.* Hampshire, England: Macmillan Education Ltd.

Galper, R. E. (1973). Functional race membership and recognition of faces. *Perceptual and Motor Skills, 37,* 455–462.

Galton, F. (1891). *Hereditary genius* (Rev. ed.). New York: Macmillan.

Garth, T. R. (1931). *Race psychology: A study of racial mental differences.* New York: McGraw-Hill, 1981.

Gosset, S. (1965). *Race: The history of an idea in America.* New York: Schocken.

Gould, S. J. (1981). *The mismeasure of man.* New York: Norton.

Greene, R. L. (1987). Ethnicity and MMPI performance: A review. *Journal of Consulting and Clinical Psychology, 55,* 497–512.

Gynther, M. D. (1972). White norms and Black MMPIs: A prescription for discrimination? *Psychological Bulletin, 78,* 386–402.

Hall, G. S., & Sander, F. H. (1980). Pity. *American Journal of Psychology, 11,* 534–591.

Henry, W. E. (1987). *The analysis of fantasy.* Malabar, FL: Krieger.

Hollingsworth, H. L. (1920). *The psychology of functional neuroses.* New York: Appleton, 1920.

Holtzman, W. H. (1980). Projective techniques. In H. C. Triandis & J. W. Berry (Eds.), *Handbook of cross-cultural psychology* (Vol. 2). Boston: Allyn & Bacon.

Howes, R. D., & DeBlassie, R. R. (1989). Modal errors in the cross cultural use of the Rorschach. *Journal of Multicultural Counseling and Development, 17,* 79–84.

Jones, E. E., & Thorne, A. (1987). Rediscovery of the subject: Intercultural approaches to clinical assessment. *Journal of Consulting and Clinical Psychology, 55,* 488–495.

Jones, E., & Korchin, S. (Eds.). (1982). *Minority issues in mental health.* New York: Holt, Rinehart & Winston.

Jones, R. L. (In press). *Handbook of tests and measurements for black populations.* Richmond, CA. Cobb & Henry.

Kamin, L. (1974). *The science and politics of IQ.* New York: Wiley.

Kardiner, A., & Ovesey, L. (1951). *The mark of oppression: A psychosocial study of the American Negro.* New York: Norton.

Kessler, R. C., & Neighbors, H. W. (1986). A new perspective on the relationships among race, social class, and psychological stress. *Journal of Health and Social Behavior, 27,* 107–115.

Lawson, W. B., Yesavage, J. A., & Werner, P. D. (1984). Race, violence, and psychopathology. *Journal of Clinical Psychiatry, 45,* 294–297.

Li-Repac, D. (1980). Cultural influences on clinical perception. A comparison between Caucasian and Chinese-American therapists. *Journal of Cross-Cultural Psychology, 11,* 327–342.

Liss, J. L., Welner, A., Robins, E., & Richardson, M. (1973). Psychiatric symptoms in White and Black inpatients. I: Record study. *Comprehensive Psychiatry, 14,* 475–481.

Lopez, S. R. (1989). Patient variable biases in clinical judgment: Conceptual overview and methodological considerations. *Psychological Bulletin, 106,* 184–203.

Lopez, S., & Hernandez, P. (1986). How culture is considered in evaluations of psychopathology. *Journal of Nervous and Mental Disease, 176,* 598–609.

Lopez, S., & Nunez, J. A. (1987). Cultural factors considered in selected diagnostic criteria and interview schedules. *Journal of Abnormal Psychology, 96,* 270–272.

Loring, M., & Powell, B. (1988). Gender, race, and DSM-III: A study of the objectivity of psychiatric diagnostic behavior. *Journal of Health and Social Behavior, 29,* 1–22.

Maduro, R. (1983). Curanderismo and Latino views of diseases and curing. *Western Journal of Medicine, 139,* 868–874.

Malgady, R. G., Rogler, L. H., & Constantino, G. (1987). Ethnocultural and linguistic bias in mental health evaluation of Hispanics. *American Psychologist, 42,* 228–234.

Manderscheid, R., & Barrett, S. (Eds.) (1987). *Mental health in the United States.* DHHS Pub. No. ADM 87–1518. Washington, DC: U.S. Government Printing Office.

Marsella, A. J., Kinsie, D., & Gordon, P. (1973). Ethnic variations in the expression of depression. *Journal of Cross-Cultural Psychology, 4,* 435–458.

McFadden, S. J., & Dashiel, J. F. (1992). Racial differences as measured by the Downey Well-Temperament Individual Tests. *Journal of Applied Psychology, 7,* 30–53.

McGill, J. (1980). MMPI score differences among Anglo, Black, and Mexican-American welfare recipients. *Journal of Clinical Psychology, 36,* 147–151.

Mesquita, B., & Frijda, N. H. (1992). Cultural variations in emotions: A review. *Psychological Bulletin, 112,* 179–204.

Mirowsky, J., II, & Ross, C. E. (1980). Minority status, ethnic culture, and distress: A comparison of Blacks, Whites, Mexicans, and Mexican Americans. *American Journal of Sociology, 86,* 479–495.

Mukherjee, S., Shukla, S., Woodle, J., Rosen, A., & Olarte, S. (1983). Misdiagnosis of schizophrenia in bipolar patients: A multiethnic comparison. *American Journal of Psychiatry, 140,* 1571–1574.

Nichter, M. (1981). Idioms of distress: Alternatives in the expression of psychosocial distress. A case study from South India. *Culture, Medicine, and Psychiatry, 5,* 379–408.

Park, B., & Rothbart, M. (1982). Perception of outgroup homogeneity and levels of social categorization: Memory for the subordinate attributes of in-group and out-group members. *Journal of Personality and Social Psychology, 42,* 1051–1068.

Pedersen, P. (1987). Ten frequent assumptions of cultural bias in counseling. *Journal of Multicultural Counseling and Development, 5,* 17–25.

Pollack, D., & Shore, J. H. (1980). Validity of the MMPI with Native Americans. *American Journal of Psychiatry, 137,* 946–950.

Raskin, A., Crook, T. H., & Herman, K. D. (1975). Psychiatric history and symptom differences in Black and White depressed inpatients. *Journal of Consulting and Clinical Psychology, 43,* 73–80.

Robins, L. (1985). Epidemiology: Reflections on testing the validity of psychiatric interviews. *Archives of General Psychiatry, 42,* 918–924.

Rosenberg, M. (1984). A symbolic interactionist view of psychosis. *Journal of Health and Social Behavior, 25,* 289–302.

Rosenfield, S. (1984). Race differences in involuntary hospitalization: Psychiatric vs. labeling perspectives. *Journal of Health and Social Behavior, 25,* 14–23.

Scheff, T. (1966). *Being mentally ill: A sociological theory.* Chicago: Aldine.

Scott, J., & Gaitz, C. M. (1975). Ethnic and age differences in mental health measurements. *Disorders of the Nervous System, 35,* 389–393.

Scott, R. (1981). FM: Clinically meaningful Rorschach index with minority children? *Psychology in the Schools, 18,* 429–433.

Shondrick, D. D., Ben-Porath, Y. S., & Stafford, K. (1992, May). *Forensic assessment with the MMPI-2: Characteristics of individuals undergoing court-ordered evaluations.* Paper presented at the 27th Annual Symposium on Recent Developments of the MMPI (MMPI-2), Minneapolis.

Simon, R. J., Fleiss, J. L., Gurland, B. J., Stiller, P.

R., & Sharpe, L. (1973). Depression and schizophrenia in hospitalized Black and White mental patients. *Archives of General Psychiatry, 28,* 509–512.

Smith Kline Corp. (1978). *Cultural issues in contemporary psychiatry: The Hispanic American.* Philadelphia: Author. (Continuing Education series, audiotape)

Snowden, L. R., & Cheung, F. K. (1990). Use of inpatient mental health services by members of ethnic minority groups. *American Psychologist, 45,* 347–355.

Snowden, L., & Todman, P. (1982). The psychological assessment of Blacks: New and needed developments. In E. Jones & S. Korchin (Eds.), *Minority mental health.* New York: Holt, Rinehart, & Winston.

Soloff, P. H., & Turner, S. M. (1981). Patterns of seclusion: A prospective study. *Nervous and Mental Disease, 169,* 37–44.

Sue, D., & Sue, S. (1987). Cultural factors in the clinical assessment of Asian Americans. *Journal of Consulting and Clinical Psychology, 55,* 479–487.

Sue, S., & Morishima, J. K. (1982). *The mental health of Asian Americans.* San Francisco: Jossey-Bass.

Sundberg, N. D., & Gonzales, L. R. (1981). Cross-cultural and cross-ethnic assessment: Overview and issues. In P. McReynolds (Ed.), *Advances in Psychological Assessment* (Vol. 5).

Thomas, A., & Sillen, S. (1972). *Racism and psychiatry.* New York: Brunner/Mazel.

Thomas, C. S. (1971). *Boys no more.* Beverly Hills, CA: Glencoe.

Thompson, C. E. (1949). The Thompson modification of the Thematic Apperception Test. *Rorschach Research Exchange and Journal of Projective Techniques, 13,* 469–478.

Timbrook, R. E., & Graham, J. R. (1993, March). *Ethnic differences on the MMPI?* Paper presented at the 28th Annual Symposium on Recent Developments in the Use of the MMPI (MMPI-2 and MMPI-A), St. Petersburg Beach, FL.

Tseng, W. S., & McDermott, J. F. (1981). *Culture, mind, and therapy: An introduction to cultural psychiatry.* New York: Brunner/Mazel.

Tonks, C. M., Paykel, E. S., & Klerman, G. L. (1970). Clinical depression among Negroes. *American Journal of Psychiatry, 127,* 329–335.

Turk, D. C., & Salovey, P. (Eds.). (1988). *Reasoning, inference, and judgment in clinical psychology.* New York: Free Press.

Umbenhauer, S. L., & DeWitte, L. L. (1978). Patient race and social class: Attitudes and decisions among three groups of mental health professionals. *Comprehensive Psychiatry, 19,* 509–515.

Walters, G. D., Greene, R. L., Jeffrey, T. B., Kruzich, D. J., & Haskin, J. J. (1983). Racial variations on the MacAndrew Alcoholism Scale of the MMPI. *Journal of Consulting and Clinical Psychology, 51,* 947–948.

Warheit, G. J., Holzer, C. E., III., & Arey, S. A. (1975). Race and mental illness: An epidemiologic update. *Journal of Health and Social Behavior, 16,* 243–256.

Weaver, C., & Sklar, D. (1980). Diagnostic dilemmas and cultural diversity in emergency rooms. *Western Journal of Medicine, 133,* 356–366.

Welner, A., Liss, J. L., & Robins, E. (1973). Psychiatric symptoms in White and Black inpatients. II: Follow-up study. *Comprehensive Psychiatry, 14,* 483–488.

Westermeyer, J. (1987). Cultural factors in clinical assessment. *Journal of Consulting and Clinical Psychology, 55,* 471–478.

Williams, R. L., & Johnson, R. C. (1981). Progress in developing Afrocentric measuring instruments. *Journal of Non-White Concerns, 9,* 3–18.

Wilkinson, C. D. (Ed.). (1986). *Ethnic psychiatry.* New York: Plenum.

12

Issues in Clinical Assessment with Women

Judith Worell
Damon Robinson

The purpose of this chapter is to provide a framework for integrating issues related to gender into procedures for the assessment of women in clinical practice. Specifically, we consider some of the historical and current approaches to gender issues in the assessment process, and we provide suggestions for information-collection strategies that acknowledge the influence of gender-related variables on women's well-being. We discuss some of the issues and research related to gender bias in assessment, and we consider evidence for the influence of bias in the diagnostic process. We then review the impact of women's gendered experiences on subsequent psychological functioning and the relationships of these variables to diagnostic labeling. Finally, the role of gender in selected clinically relevant topics is discussed. Throughout, clinicians are cautioned to examine their own knowledge base, attitudes, and beliefs in the process of clinical assessment with women.

PURPOSES OF ASSESSMENT

Strategies and decisions in the assessment of clients in clinical settings are governed by a num-

ber of considerations, among which are the cultural assumptions, values, attitudes, and theoretical orientation of the clinician (Arkes, 1981; Butcher, 1987; Lopez, 1989; McReynolds, 1989; MacDonald, 1984; O'Leary & Murphy, 1992; Sherman, 1980). In this chapter, we consider assessment strategies in clinical practice with women within the context of a woman-centered approach. This view takes into consideration the disadvantages and injustices to women that accrue from societal gender stratification and the effects of these gender inequities on women's lives and experiences. In the context of gender, we caution the clinician to be aware that assessment issues may also be related to other group identity characteristics for each woman, including ethnicity, social class, and sexual orientation. Simple comparisons between women and men in most of the extant research fail to capture the complexities that should be considered when clients other than white middle-class women are being evaluated. Thus, we approach the task of assessment from a contextual view that considers the external conditions of a woman's life that may influence her interpretation of experience, her well-being, and the personal expression and effectiveness of her coping strategies.

Of the many purposes of clinical assessment, we will focus on those that are designed to inform an effective intervention process with adolescent and adult women: Identification of current problems, exploration of background/ history variables, evaluation for treatment suitability, appraisal of resources including appropriate therapist/client match and adjunct community services, negotiated treatment planning and goals, increased client understanding of self, and effectiveness of the interventions in terms of both process and outcome (Hansen, Stevic, & Warner, 1986; Jehu, 1992; Orlinsky & Howard, 1980; Worell & Remer, 1992). For some clinical settings, formal diagnosis and classification may be indicated, but these are not seen here as the major purpose of assessment with women. We also recognize that clinicians are currently called upon to evaluate women in the context of certain situations in which gender may be relevant, such as child abuse, child custody decisions, or homicide of an abusive partner; however, assessment for these critical decisions is beyond the scope of this chapter.

The range of assessment strategies appropriate to the goals listed above reflects a multimodal approach and embraces any of the following: systematic observation, interviews, self-report inventories, self-monitoring, life histories, diaries, analysis of person-environment interactions, information from relevant others including interview and rating scales, archival data, medical reports, and biopsychological assessment. Thus, information relevant to internalized behavior patterns as well as to situational/environmental circumstances is considered essential. Within any of these assessment approaches, possibilities for gender bias exist, and to this topic we turn our attention.

amined empirically in three contexts: "sociocultural etiological sex bias, sampling bias, and diagnostic sex bias" (p. 2). Since their analysis targeted mainly the DSM-III-R categories, it is only partly pertinent to the general issues regarding assessment bias. Lopez (1989) points out that research on assessment bias has typically implied a prejudgment based on prejudice toward women or minority groups, and he proposes four types of diagnostic errors: overpathologizing, in which women or minority groups are perceived as more disturbed than a comparison group; minimizing, in which "clinicians may have dismissed the woman's presenting problems as more normative than they actually were" (p. 186); and overdiagnosis or underdiagnosis, in terms of the probability of assigning a particular diagnostic category. In addition to these frameworks for conceptualizing gender bias, a number of biases in the assumptions underlying the DSM may disadvantage women, the most relevant here being the assumption that the dysfunction is located primarily within the person (McReynolds, 1989; Wakefield, 1991)

In the present context, we use the term *gender bias* to denote a systematic error of commission or omission in any aspect of the assessment process based on lack of knowledge and/or stereotyped attitudes or beliefs about women. Thus, clinicians' interpersonal behaviors with clients, choice and interpretation of assessment instruments, and diagnostic judgments are all potential targets for bias. There is no implication here that such bias, when it occurs, is intentional or within the individual's awareness. However, clinicians' appreciation of the possibilities for gender bias may enhance their sensitivity and consequent assessment strategies.

CONSIDERING GENDER BIAS

Concepts of gender bias in clinical assessment vary. Widiger and Spitzer (1989) refer to bias as "a systematic deviation from an expected value [and] sex bias . . . [as] a systematic deviation associated with the sex of the subject" (pp. 2–3). These authors contend that bias should be ex-

Some Questions About Gender Bias

The empirical attention to gender bias in psychological assessment was stimulated by the well-known study on "double standards" for clinical judgments of women's and men's mental health, based on comparative ratings of stereotypic gender-related traits (Broverman, Broverman, Clarkson, Rosenkrantz, & Vogel, 1970). The questions that drove subsequent research on gender bias typically focused on three issues:

1. Do clinicians differentially evaluate the same traits or behaviors for women and men according to culture-bound gender stereotypes that result in systematic bias (e.g., more pathological evaluations of women)? (e.g., Cowan, 1976; Fabricant, 1974; Hayes & Wolleat, 1978).
2. Do female and male clinicians arrive at different judgments as a function of gendered sociocultural expectations for women and men? (e.g., Harris & Lucas, 1976; Maslin & Davis, 1975; Nowacki & Poe, 1973).
3. Do clinicians of either sex arrive at different diagnoses and recommendations for treatment for female and male clients with the same presenting behaviors? (e.g., Ford & Widiger, 1989).

Research Approaches to Gender Bias

Trait Ratings

With respect to the first question on therapist evaluations, subsequent research on therapist gender bias has produced mixed results. A salient concern in summarizing these findings is the increasing awareness of the professional community about the possibilities of gender bias, such that social desirability factors may outweigh bias factors in the rating process (Hare-Mustin, 1983; Phillips & Gilroy, 1985). Indeed, some recent research has failed to document that women and men are rated differentially on scales that measure gender-related traits by clinicians (Poole & Tepley, 1988). It is still unclear, however, whether this outcome reflects reactivity to social desirability demands or a true change in social attitudes.

For example, some evidence of gender bias was found in several studies that employed measures of bias that are less reactive than trait ratings. Buczek (1981) used both incidental

memory of client information and counselor-formulated questions in a simulated client interview to assess bias. Both female and male psychologists tended to recall less total information from a female compared with a male "client," and information-seeking questions varied significantly according to topic, sex of therapist, and sex of client. These results suggest, among other things, that clinically relevant information obtained from women and men clients in an assessment interview may be solicited and processed differently. (See Lopez, 1989, for an information-processing view of gender bias in clinical judgment).

Evidence of both systematic bias and "bias of omission" was reported by Sesan (1988). In this study, bias was measured with a 70-item questionnaire representing content from the APA Task Force on Sex Bias and Sex-Role Stereotyping in Psychotherapy (APA, 1975, 1978). Responses from 192 former clients, representing 49 therapists, indicated that significantly more therapist bias was reported by women with less education and by those with children, compared with those without. The "error of omission" was reflected in subpopulations of clients who were survivors of either incest, rape, or battering. For these groups of women, many therapists failed to obtain critical items of information related to the trauma. Sesan's results suggest that clinical bias may selectively target subgroups of women, as a function of their educational level, parenthood status, or history of trauma and abuse. Taken together, these studies suggest that assessment of gender bias by means of stereotypical trait ratings is probably not a productive approach, and that nonreactive research methods may provide more useful information. For practicing clinicians, research suggesting that the assessment of some women may be biased by differential information-gathering strategies is well worth further attention.

Sex of Clinician

In response to the second question above regarding sex differences in bias among clinicians, some reviews have concluded that women and men clinicians do not differ consistently across measures in their ratings of personality traits or recommendations for treatment (Davidson & Abramowitz, 1980; Smith, 1980; Whitely, 1979). Sesan's (1988) study, despite finding some gender bias in reported clinician response, found no difference for sex of therapist. However, Buczek (1981) did find interactions among counselor sex, client sex, and topic in question-asking strategy, again pointing to the need for more nonreactive measures to explore this question further. At the practical level, it is suggested that both female and male clinicians may benefit from an examination of their own gender-related information and attitudes.

Differential Outcomes

With respect to the third research question on diagnostic categories, there is some support in analogue studies for gender bias that results in differential diagnostic outcomes for women and men clients (Ford & Widiger, 1989; Hamilton, Rothbart, & Dawes, 1986; Wrobel, 1993). This topic will be discussed further in the next section, along with other concerns related to application of the DSM diagnostic categories with women clients.

USING DIAGNOSTIC CATEGORIES FOR WOMEN

Probably the most heat in the gender-bias dialogue has been generated by the debate about the DSM diagnostic categories. The widely accepted psychiatric taxonomy in the United States, the DSM-III-R (APA, 1987) and its previous editions, have been criticized for numerous specific criteria and diagnoses judged to be biased toward women.[1] Clinicians' use of the DSM diagnostic categories for women clients has also been questioned for its fairness and accuracy. Some of the major criticisms have included the unreliability of many of the DSM categories, the lack of empirical support for the inclusion of such categories as "Self-Defeating Personality Disorder,"[2] the similarity between some of the DSM categories and accepted culturally based functioning for women (and men),

differential diagnosis based on gender, overpathologizing of "normal" functioning, and the location of pathology within the individual apart from her history and situation. (The following studies may be consulted for a more complete review of sex-role influences on mental health and diagnosis: Brown, 1987, 1990; Caplan, 1986; Kaplan, 1983; Landrine, 1989; Walker, 1986; Worell, 1987; Worell & Remer, 1992.) In response to these objections, the possibility of gender bias in the DSM criteria and their application has been acknowledged by many of its major proponents and authors (Spitzer, Williams, Kass, & Davies, 1989; Widiger, Frances, Spitzer, & Williams, 1988). In essence, the DSM may be considered a work in progress, and the ongoing reviews and critiques of its content reflect accumulating empirical and theoretical understandings about mental health and illness. Rather than explore the DSM dialogue in detail, we provide three examples that highlight some of the gender bias concerns: differential criteria, inappropriate diagnostic categories, and vulnerability to clinician bias.

Differential Criteria

Differential criteria for some "women's" and "men's" (according to prevalence) personality disorders were pointed out by Hamilton, Rothbart, and Dawes (1986). Certain "women's" disorders are constructed with criteria that contain global personality descriptions, while "men's" disorders are more likely to be defined in clear behavioral terms. Indeed, an examination of the personality disorders for which the DSM attributes higher rates among women than men yields a variety of subjective criteria that require clinicians' decisions about the degree to which they will consider that the client meets the criteria. For example, a criterion for histrionic personality disorder is "inappropriately sexually seductive in appearance or behavior" (APA, 1987, p. 349). This criterion clearly requires the clinician's judgment as to what may be inappropriate and is vulnerable to bias.

The call for more empirically based criteria to modify some of the subjective and consensus-based criteria might address the concerns about biased decisions on the part of the clinician (McReynolds, 1989; Widiger & Spitzer, 1991). Ford and Widiger (1989) suggest that the diagnostic criteria for personality disorders are not intrinsically gender-biased, but that such bias is embedded in the names of the disorders themselves. They further caution that "increasing the specificity of diagnostic criteria and removing sex-typed features from criteria sets may neither eliminate nor even substantially inhibit sex biases" (p. 304). From our viewpoint, gender-neutral labels and behaviorally based criteria might substantially reduce diagnostic bias. In the absence of such clarity, clinicians are cautioned to evaluate their subjective reactions to certain culturally gendered concepts and behaviors as they evaluate clients for DSM diagnosis.

Inappropriate Diagnostic Categories

The decision to include, omit, or revise particular diagnostic categories in the DSM is an ongoing dilemma (Widiger & Trull, 1991). Determination of what even constitutes a disorder is fraught with conflict (Wakefield, 1992). The conceptualizations of mental health and illness are profoundly affected by the cultural climate. Historical reviews of the nature of women's mental illness highlight the variability of both scientific and lay thought regarding the origin and course of diagnostic categories (see, e.g., Chessler, 1972/1989; Showalter, 1985; and Ussher, 1992). The recent politics of inclusion or exclusion of DSM-III-R categories are also well summarized elsewhere (Brown, 1990; McReynolds, 1989; Walker, 1986). We comment on two issues that have received sustained attention in the literature: the introduction of new categories that were believed to disadvantage women; and diagnosis with women who are survivors of trauma and abuse.

New Categories

For practicing clinicians, the relevance of two new diagnoses included in the appendix of the DSM are of particular concern. These are self-defeating personality disorder (SDPD)[2] and late luteal phase dysphoric disorder (to be included in the appendix of DSM-IV as premenstrual dysphoric disorder, or PDD), neither of which category has received substantive empirical support for reliability or validity. The disadvantage to women from the use of either diagnosis is to pathologize women's normal functioning and to put them at risk for discriminatory practices in the courtroom and in the workplace.

The characteristics listed for the SDPD have much in common with well-socialized traits for many American women (e.g., puts needs of others before her own), and are compatible with coping behaviors adopted by women in abusive or battering relationships (Franks, 1986; Walker, 1984). Thus, such behaviors may reflect situationally adaptive coping rather than a long-standing personality disorder. As such, diagnosing a personality disorder may serve more as victim blaming than as an appropriate treatment conceptualization.

Likewise, the second controversial category, late luteal phase dysphoric disorder (and similarly the proposed PDD), risks attributing anxiety or dysphoric moods to normal monthly functioning of all women. When women are asked to rate their moods on a daily prospective basis without reference to the menstrual cycle, the evidence for a stable correlation between mood swings and the menstrual cycle is questionable (Alagna & Hamilton, 1986; Parlee, 1982). Here, we advise that these diagnoses be carefully avoided by the gender-sensitive clinician.

Abuse Survivors

In addition to the inclusion of questionable new categories, the accumulation of research on survivors of abuse (e.g., incest, sexual assault, battering) has led to criticism of applying Axis II diagnostic labels to these populations. Examples here include borderline, histrionic, and dependent personality disorders. Indeed, evidence suggest that battered women, compared with nonbattered, are more likely to be diagnosed with a personality disorder (Back, Post, & D'Arcy, 1982). For most of these women, the abusive events tend to be repetitive, long-standing, and experienced within the context of an intimate relationship (parent, spouse, coworker, lover). The assignment of a personality disorder in such cases, with its implications of a characterological substrate, has been viewed by many clinicians as inappropriate (Douglass, 1987; Sato & Heiby, 1991; Walker, 1989).

Some professionals who work with survivors of abuse have suggested that these women's response syndromes are not pathological but represent a normally expected accommodation to the presence of continuing and unavoidable abuse (Brown, 1992; Finkelhor, 1990; Herman, 1992; Root, 1992; Walker, 1984). In such cases, it appears that posttraumatic stress disorder (PTSD) may be a more appropriate diagnosis for many of these women. Battered and sexually abused women, for example, reexperience the traumatic events in flashbacks, nightmares, and hypervigilance (Douglass, 1987), and may show heightened levels of arousal, anger, anxiety, and avoidance (Holmes & Lawrence, 1983; Walker, 1984). But even here, criticism of the diagnostic criteria for PTSD (Davidson & Foa, 1991; Finkelhor, 1990; Root, 1992) has led to the proposal of new diagnoses that are judged to reflect more adequately the victim's experience. Herman (1992) proposes a complex posttraumatic stress disorder that incorporates longer-term traumatic events and a wider range of symptomatology frequently experienced by such survivors. Similarly, Briere and Runtz (1987) advocate a post-abuse trauma label that would more effectively encompass the responses to childhood sexual abuse. Walker (1986) proposes the simple and inclusive term of abuse disorders, which would encompass both physical and sexual abuse. We suggest that clinicians working with physically, emotionally, or sexually abused women remain informed of advances in this important area.

And finally, the overlap or comorbidity rates of certain personality disorders with Axis I diagnoses in women with a history of abuse, particularly depression (Farmer & Nelson-Gray, 1990; Widiger, 1989) is of particular concern to those who work with women clients. For example, Pfohl, Stangle, and Zimmerman (1984) reported that the most frequently occurring personality disorders in a sample of depressed inpatients were, respectively, borderline, histrionic, and dependent. That these are categories with high incidence rates for women with a history of abuse raises important questions about treatment. That is, given alternative or dual diagnoses of depression and an assumed personality disorder, treatment strategies will vary with assumptions about which diagnosis takes precedence (Sate & Heify, 1991). Farmer and Nelson-Gray (1990) present a thoughtful discussion of this issue, which can be informative to clinicians who work with depressed women.

Clinician Bias

Questions about gender-biased diagnosis and assessment have also been asked with respect to clinicians' use of DSM categories and their own assessment practices. The evidence weighs toward a bias interpretation in many studies.

For example, psychologists presented with case histories using DSM criteria more frequently diagnosed women as histrionic, regardless of how closely the case material reflected the criteria for that disorder (Ford & Widiger, 1989). Mental health specialists more readily considered women to be depressed, even when the client did not meet the criteria for depression as defined by a diagnostic interview schedule (Potts, Burnam, & Wells, 1991). When presented with identical female and male stimulus persons, psychologists also diagnosed females more frequently than males as histrionic (Hamilton, Rothbart, & Dawes, 1986). When given a case example combining elements of several personality disorder criteria, clinicians most readily labeled females as histrionic (Adler, Drake, & Teague, 1990). These authors concluded that clinicians' use of the diagnostic criteria, rather than the content of the criteria, was the source of gender bias. In effect, clinicians may "make global judgments about personality disorders and be influenced by the patient's gender, even when it has no known relevance" (p. 125).

As noted previously, clinician bias in the use of the DSM can occur in a variety of ways. Such bias may result from overlooking specific areas of inquiry (e.g., an abuse history) or from more complicated factors such as diagnosing on the basis of the weight of a given criterion rather than the presence of criteria sufficient to meet the diagnostic threshold (Davis, Blashfield, & McElroy, 1993). Clinicians working with women clients are advised to be particularly sensitive to this range of potential for bias and to scrutinize their assessment approaches.

INTERPRETING INFORMATION ON WOMEN'S MENTAL HEALTH

Our concern for addressing issues of gender bias stems from our knowledge about the salience of gender in daily interactions (Pearson, 1985; Unger & Crawford, 1992) and the general lack of attention to gender issues in most professional training programs (Nutt & Gottlieb, 1993; Worell, 1992; Worell & Remer, 1992).

We know that the different life experiences of women and men play a large role in psychological distress. Cook (1990) suggests that "the sexes may develop the same psychological problems for different reasons, express psychological distress in different ways, and manifest different types of psychological problems in responses to life stresses" (p. 374). A woman's expression of feeling and symptomatology, for example, may influence the assessment of mental health concerns as well, particularly with the "strong gender-role prohibition against female anger, criticism, rebellion, or domination" (Bernardez, 1987, p. 28). Other well-socialized behaviors that are typical for many women include putting others before the self, desire to please (such as smiling a lot), concern with external appearance and body weight, depending on others to make decisions, over-attachment to relationships, etc. In the same vein, cross-gender behavior that violates cultural prescriptions may affect diagnosis as well. Psychologists evaluating personality disorder case-history descriptions attribute more pathology to cross-gender role behavior, suggesting an expectation for gender-role conformity (Waisberg & Page, 1988). Thus, it seems imperative for clinicians to remain open to the possibility of gender bias in their own approach to the assessment process at all levels, and in the instruments that they use to evaluate clients.

In response to these concerns, Laura Brown (1986, 1990) recommends "gender-role analysis" as an essential component of the assessment procedure. This analysis should include a personal preassessment of the clinician's gendered attitudes (differential expectations for women and men or for subgroups of women) and of deficits in knowledge about research on women's lives. Such an analysis is predicated on the assumption that we all hold some attitudes about what is "normal" with respect to gender, as well as about ethnicity, social class, and sexuality. As a result, some behaviors may be inappropriately pathologized, or relevant diagnostic information may remain untapped. Brown (1986) provides a useful format for conducting a gender-role analysis. In the following section, we consider areas of inquiry in the assessment process that address high base-rate events that are normative in the lives of women.

SCREENING FOR HIGH BASE-RATE EXPERIENCES

Clinical assessment with women must address the range of events, expectations, experiences, and understandings that have high probability for women in American culture. The purposes of this screening are to (1) uncover the influence of events that the client may neglect or withhold; (2) evaluate the importance of such information for understanding etiology; (3) assess the impact of such events and experiences on the client's present adjustment; and (4) determine the relevance of these experiences for intervention or referral.

Table 12.1 summarizes twelve areas of inquiry that should be routine in any assessment with women clients. For certain areas, such as physical and sexual abuse or eating disorders, some self-report instruments or interview schedules have been developed. For other areas, the clinician will need to be creative in exploring these important dimensions of the client's life.

TABLE 12.1 Suggested Areas for Assessment
with Women

1. *Abuse:* Current and past. Includes physical,
   sexual, and psychological, as well as
   employment discrimination and harassment.
2. *Caretaking responsibilities:* Role-strain issues. Is
   the client depressed because of "dysfunctional
   beliefs" or because she has the primary
   responsibility for two "jobs"—career and family
   care—that deplete her energy and preclude
   participation in relaxing activities?
3. *Health:* Includes reproductive and sexual
   history, weight-related concerns and eating-
   disordered behaviors, and overuse of
   prescription medications.
4. *Gender-role message:* How "traditional" are her
   beliefs about issues relevant to women? What
   are her concepts of the "good woman"? How
   do these messages affect her day-to-day
   functioning? In what ways do they limit her?
5. *Relationship beliefs:* Does she see herself as
   worthless without a romantic relationship? How
   does she view her present/past relationships?
   Do her relationships create stress through
   discrimination (e.g., being lesbian)?
6. *Previous therapy experiences:* Screen for
   messages retained and possibility of sexual
   abuse by prior therapist.
7. *Communication patterns:* Can she be assertive?
   How does she handle anger (e.g., does she
   appear depressed and passive when in fact she
   is angry)?
8. *Substance abuse:* Screen for alcohol,
   prescription medication, other substances. May
   reflect abuse experiences.
9. *Attributional style:* Does she make internal and
   global attributions of self-blame and have
   negative expectations?
10. *Ability to self-nurture:* Can she take care of her
    own needs or does she subordinate them to the
    caretaking of others?
11. *Career/employment concerns:* Is there conflict or
    stress at home or at work? Are there
    employment discrimination or harassment
    issues?
12. *Resource assessment:* Does the client have
    sufficient means? Is she receiving child
    support? Social and community support?

Although many of these topics may also be relevant for male clients, we emphasize their importance in particular for women because of the
high probability of their presence in women's
lives.

In the remainder of the chapter, we have selected assessment considerations for two clinical
issues with documented high base rates for
women: physical battering and sexual abuse.
These topics represent areas in which women's
prior experiences with assault, violence, and
personal violation may profoundly affect present
functioning. As well, these topics are at particular risk for being overlooked by clinicians in
both assessment and therapy procedures (see
e.g., Sesan, 1988).

ASSESSMENT FOR PHYSICAL AND SEXUAL ABUSE

Screening and evaluation for current and prior
abuse experiences is a particularly crucial part
of psychological assessment for women clients.
It has been estimated that over half of the clients
who seek treatment have experienced interpersonal violence in a close relationship (Ammerman & Hersen, 1992; Walker, 1989; Worell &
Remer, 1992). As with physical violence, estimates of rape and sexual abuse vary according
to the definitions used and the methods of gathering data. Research suggests that up to 27 percent of women have experienced childhood sexual abuse (Finkelhor, Hotaling, Lewis, &
Smith, 1990), and Russell and Howell (1983)
found that 46 percent of women in their prevalence study had experienced a rape or attempted rape during their adult lives. Further,
Russell (1986) found that 65 percent of incest
survivors in her survey study has been raped as
adults, whereas 35 percent of non-incest-survi-
vors had experienced adult rape. These data
suggest that any client who has been raped as
an adult should be assessed for possible childhood sexual abuse. Finally, with a nonclinical
college population, Koss (1985) reported that 62
percent of the women in her sample had experienced some type of sexual victimization.
These prevalence figures clearly highlight the

need for routine inquiry into experiences of physical and sexual abuse as part of any woman's psychological assessment.

Screening

Questioning a woman about current or previous abuse experiences may feel awkward, uncomfortable, and even intrusive to many clinicians. Indeed, such questions may never be asked (Craine, Hensen, Colliver, & MacLean, 1988; Pruitt & Kappius, 1992). Using a random sample of practicing psychologists, Pruitt and Kappius (1992) found that only 17 percent of the therapists surveyed routinely asked all clients about previous or current sexual abuse. It is clear, however, that when clinicians do ask their clients about physical and sexual abuse experiences, they are more likely to hear about such a history than when expecting clients to volunteer this information spontaneously (Briere & Zaidi, 1989).

For example, Jacobson, Koehler, and Jones-Brown (1987) compared the rates of reported assault experiences recorded in standard chart histories of a sample of one hundred psychiatric inpatients with rates obtained through structured interviews that directly inquired about prior abuse experiences. Overall, 91 percent of assault experiences reported in the interviews were not present in the charts, with 100 percent of childhood sexual abuse and adult sexual assault experiences not recorded. Thus, direct questioning may elicit more complete information regarding abuse history, although the authors caution that some of the observed discrepancy may also reflect the clinicians' hesitancy to record such information in a client's history. Similarly, routine psychiatric emergency-room charts of women were compared with similar charts from clinicians who directly screened patients for childhood sexual abuse (CSA) (Briere & Zaidi, 1989). The routine charts revealed a 6 percent CSA prevalence, while the charts reflecting a direct screening revealed a 70 percent prevalence.

The method of screening may affect a woman's reporting of abuse experiences as well. Dill,

Chu, Grob, and Eisen (1991) compared childhood sexual abuse prevalence reports obtained through routine intake interviews (which requested information about lifetime sexual abuse) with those obtained through a written self-report measure. A history of abuse was found in 35 percent of the intake interviews, compared with 52 percent of the self-report measures. Thus, some women who did report abuse in the written measure were not able or willing to report it in the interview.

There are many reasons for clients' failure to report current or past abuse—shame, guilt, self-blame, fear of retaliation by the abuser or rejection by family members, fear of breaking up the family, or believing that it is a private event. By not asking or assessing directly, therapists may unintentionally communicate that these are taboo topics, further reinforcing client reluctance to reveal abusive experiences. We have limited information about how these abuse experiences might differ among women from groups that vary in marital status, socioeconomic level, age, ethnicity, or sexual orientation, but we assume that no groups of women are invulnerable to physical or sexual abuse during their lifetimes. Regardless of whether clients reveal "signs" of abuse, assessment for a history of abuse (or current abusive living conditions) should be a routine part of assessment with any woman client. It should be noted that we are not advocating an approach that attempts to "prove" a history of abuse regardless of the evidence. Nor do we suggest that extensive attempts be initiated to reconstruct an abuse history based on a few symptoms. Rather, we are suggesting that routine screening for abusive experiences is warranted both by the high base rates for these events in women's lives and by the impact such a history may have on the conceptualization of appropriate treatment strategies.

Probing For Abuse Details

Having uncovered preliminary evidence of abuse in the client's life, the clinician will require further detailed information to make decisions relevant to an abuse history. Depending on the context of the assessment, a clinician may wish to evaluate the client further with formal interview schedules or scales or may elect to allow the information to be revealed within the context of the subsequent therapy. If the client discloses information implying current risk, we believe that further assessment is essential. What kinds of preliminary information signal current risk? Any of the following acts toward the client should serve as cues: physical coercion or violence to persons or property, verbal abuse (yelling, blaming, belittling, degradation, etc.), sexual debasement or coercion, threats (verbal or use of weapons), isolation from friends and family, excessive jealousy and checking behavior, and a variety of other interpersonal control behaviors. For each identified category, therapists also need to inquire about frequency, severity, duration, and degree of physical injury. If physical violence is a concern, therapists should assess for lethality (dangerousness to self or partner), and for the woman's safety.

Because of the oppressive effects of sexual trauma, continued violence, and coercion on their victims, such clients may deny and minimize their experiences and may be better served with structured scales that survey specific acts and events. There are a number of measures that are designed to elicit more detailed information about physical or sexual abuse. For evidence of physical abuse, readers are referred to reviews by O'Leary and Murphy (1992), Saunders (1992), Tolman (1992), and Walker (1984). For evidence of child or adult sexual abuse, reviews by Briere (1992), Courtois (1988), and Jehu (1992) provide discussions of useful scales and interview formats. Finally, we suggest specific scales such as those by Fitzgerald et al. (1988) and Koss (1985) that assess a range of unwelcome sexual experiences, from mild gender harassment through violent sexual assault. Experiences of repeated sexual harassment have been shown to have negative effects on victims that are similar to other forms of sexual coercion (Coles, 1986), and these should be regarded with equal concern for the well-being of the client.

SUMMARY AND CONCLUSIONS

We have taken the position here that assessment strategies with women clients should be designed with three themes in mind: (1) women as a group have had a subordinate status in American society that encourages and "normalizes" certain socialized gender-related behaviors; (2) societal expectations for women's behavior may frame and influence the assessment process; and (3) women as a group are at risk for repeated experiences of interpersonal violence and sexual abuse, which have significant and specific effects on their mental health. Consequently, we have reviewed research and practical applications that reflect the influences of these themes on the assessment process.

An integral part of the literature on the assessment and treatment of women clients has been concerned with questions of gender bias. Untangling the nature and sources of possible bias in assessment and diagnostic practice is a complex task. Existing research suggests that such bias comes from a variety of sources and may well include interaction effects. To some extent, all psychological assessment is contaminated with the subjectivity of diagnostic categories, diagnostic nomenclature, and clinicians' choice of, and blindness to, particular observations, questions, and their own understandings about mental health and illness. We suggest that clinicians examine their potential for overt and covert gender bias through (1) the examination of current research relative to understanding the interface between assessment and diagnosis with women's responses and expected behaviors following high-probability experiences (e.g., victimization); and (2) monitoring and challenging their own beliefs and expectations regarding women's behavior.

The existing research and focus on specific women's issues in therapeutic practice should shape our skills in working with this client population. From this focus we have gained an awareness of the importance of assessing a woman's presenting issues and symptoms within the context of her life, including both internal psychological functioning and the external sociocultural framework in which she lives. We have presented suggestions for target areas to be included in assessment with women clients. These areas reflect current knowledge regarding significant issues of inquiry with women but are certainly not an exhaustive list. It is our hope that future research on women's issues in therapeutic practice, particularly with regard to the impact of diversity among women (e.g., race, ethnicity, sexual orientation, etc.) will continue to contribute to the refinement of optimum assessment techniques and considerations.

NOTE

1. The DSM-IV was forthcoming at the time of writing of this chapter. Responses to this new edition in terms of the manner in which it addresses clinical issues with women have yet to be subjected to commentary and research.

2. The SDPD category is not included in the DSM-IV.

REFERENCES

Adler, D. A., Drake, R. E., & Teague, G. B. (1990). Clinicians' practices in personality assessment: Does gender influence the use of DSM-III Axis II? *Comprehensive Psychiatry, 31,* 125–133.

Alagna, S. W., & Hamilton, S. J. (1986). Social stimulus perception and self-evaluation effects of menstrual cycle phase. *Psychology of Women Quarterly, 10,* 327–338.

American Psychiatric Association (1987). *Diagnostic and statistical manual of mental disorders* (3rd ed. — revised). Washington, DC: Author.

American Psychological Association (1975). Report of the task force on sex bias and sex-role stereotyping in psychotherapeutic practice. *American Psychologist, 30,* 1169–1175.

American Psychological Association (1978). Guidelines for therapy with women. *American Psychologist, 33,* 1122–1133.

Ammerman, R. T., & Hersen, M. (1992). *Assessment of family violence: A clinical and legal sourcebook.* New York: Wiley.

Arkes, H. (1981). Impediments to accurate clinical judgments and possible ways to minimize their impact. *Journal of Consulting and Clinical Psychology, 49,* 323–333.

Back, S. M., Post, R. D., & D'Arcy, G. (1982). A study of battered women in a psychiatric setting. *Women and Therapy, 1,* 13–26.

Bernardez, T. (1987). Gender-based countertransference of female therapists in the psychotherapy of women. *Women and Therapy, 6,* 25–38.

Briere, J. N. (1992). *Child abuse trauma: Theory and treatment of the lasting effects.* Newbury Park, CA: Sage.

Brier, J. N., & Runtz, M. (1987). Post sexual abuse trauma: Data and implications for clinical practice. *Journal of Interpersonal Violence, 2,* 367–379.

Briere, J. N., & Zaidi, L. Y. (1989). Sexual abuse histories and sequelae in female psychiatric emergency room patients. *American Journal of Psychiatry, 146,* 1602–1606.

Broverman, I. K., Broverman, D., Clarkson, F. E., Rosenkrantz, P. S., & Vogel, S. R. (1970). Sex-role stereotypes and clinical judgments of mental health. *Journal of Consulting and Clinical Psychology, 34,* 1–7.

Brown, L. S. (1986). Gender-role analysis: A neglected component of psychological assessment. *Psychotherapy: Theory, Research, and Practice, 21,* 243–248.

Brown, L. S. (1987, August). *Toward a new conceptual paradigm for the Axis-II diagnoses.* In J. Worell (Chair), DSM-III-R. Symposium presented at the annual convention of the American Psychological Association, New York.

Brown, L. S. (1990). Taking account of gender in the clinical assessment interview. *Professional Psychology: Research and Practice, 21,* 12–17.

Brown, L. S. (1992). A feminist critique of the personality disorders. In L. S. Brown & M. Ballou (Eds.), *Personality and psychopathology: Feminist reappraisals* (pp. 207–228). New York: Guilford Press.

Buczek, T. A. (1981). Sex biases in counseling: Counselor retention of the concerns of a female and male client. *Journal of Counseling Psychology, 28,* 13–21.

Butcher, J. N. (Ed.) (1987). Special series: Cultural factors in understanding and assessing psychology. *Journal of Consulting and Clinical Psychology, 55,* 459–512.

Caplan, P. J. (1986). The myth of women's masochism. *American Psychologist, 39,* 130–139.

Chessler, P. (1972/1992). *Women and madness.* San Diego: Harcourt Brace Jovanovich.

Coles, F. S. (1986). Forced to quit: Sexual harassment complaints and agency response. *Sex Roles, 14,* 81–95.

Cook, E. P. (1990). Gender and psychological distress. *Journal of Counseling and Development, 68,* 371–375.

Courtois, C. A. (1988). *Healing the incest wound: Adult survivors in therapy.* New York: Norton.

Cowan, G. (1976). Therapist judgments of clients' sex-role problems. *Psychology of Women Quarterly, 1,* 15–24.

Craine, L. S., Hensen, C. E., Colliver, J. A., & MacLean, D. G. (1988). Prevalence of a history of sexual abuse among female psychiatric patients in a state hospital system. *Hospital and Community Psychiatry, 39,* 300–304.

Davidson, C., & Abramowitz, S. (1980). Sex bias in clinical judgments. Later returns. *Psychology of Women Quarterly, 4,* 377–395.

Davidson, J. R. T., & Foa, E. B. (1991). Diagnostic issues in posttraumatic stress disorder: Considerations for the DSM-IV. *Journal of Abnormal Psychology, 100,* 346–355.

Davis, R. T., Blashfield, R. K., & McElroy, R. A. (1993). Weighting criteria in the diagnosis of a personality disorder: A demonstration. *Journal of Abnormal Psychology, 102,* 319–322.

Dill, D. L., Chu, J. A., Grob, M. C., & Eisen, S. V. (1991). The reliability of abuse history reports: A comparison of two inquiry formats. *Comprehensive Psychiatry, 32,* 166–169.

Douglass, M. A. (1987). The battered woman syndrome. In D. J. Sonkin (Ed.), *Domestic violence on trial: Therapeutic and legal dimensions of family violence* (pp. 39–54). New York: Springer.

Fabrikant, B. (1974). The psychotherapist and the female patient: Perceptions and change. In V. Franks & V. Burtle (Eds.), *Women in therapy* (pp. 83–110). New York: Brunner/Mazel.

Farmer, R., & Nelson-Gray, R. O. (1990). Personality disorders and depression: Hypothetical relations, empirical findings, and methodological consideration. *Clinical Psychology Review, 19,* 453–476.

Finkelhor, D. (1990). Early and long-term effects of childhood sexual abuse: An update. *Professional Psychology: Research and Practice, 21,* 325–330.

Finkelhor, D., Hotaling, G., Lewis, I. A., & Smith, C. (1990). Sexual abuse in a national survey of adult men and women: Prevalence, characteristics, and risk factors. *Child Abuse and Neglect, 14,* 19–28.

Fitzgerald, L. F., Shullman, S. L., Bailey, M., Richards, N., Swecker, J., Gold, Y., Ormerod, A. J., & Weitzman, L. (1988). The incidence and dimensions of sexual harassment in academia and the workplace. *Journal of Vocational Behavior, 32,* 157–165.

Ford, M. R., & Widiger, T. A. (1989). Sex bias in the diagnosis of histrionic and antisocial personality disorders. *Journal of Consulting and Clinical Psychology, 57,* 301–305.

Franks, V. (1986). Sex-stereotyping and diagnosis of psychopathology. *Women and Therapy, 5,* 219–232.

Hamilton, S., Rothbart, M., & Dawes, R. B. (1986). Sex bias, diagnosis, and DSM III. *Sex Roles, 15,* 269–274.

Hansen, J. C., Stevic, R. R., & Warner, R. W. (1986). *Counseling theory and process.* Boston: Allyn & Bacon.

Hare-Mustin, R. T. (1983). An appraisal of the relationship between women and psychotherapy; 80 years after the case of Dora. *American Psychologist, 43,* 455–464.

Harris, L. H., & Lucas, M. E. (1976). Sex-role stereotyping. *Social Work, 21,* 390–395.

Hayes, K. E., & Wolleat, P. L. (1978). Effects of sex in judgment of a simulated counseling interview. *Journal of Counseling Psychology, 25,* 164–168.

Herman, J. L. (1992). *Trauma and recovery.* New York: Basic Books.

Holmes, M. R., & Lawrence, J. S. (1983). Treatment of rape-induced trauma: Proposed behavioral conceptualization and review of the literature. *Clinical Psychology Review, 3,* 417–433.

Jacobson, A., Koehler, J. E., & Jones-Brown, C. (1987). The failure of routine assessment to detect histories of assault experienced by psychiatric patients. *Hospital and Community Psychiatry, 38,* 786–792.

Jehu, D. (1992). Adult survivors of sexual abuse. In R. T. Ammerman & M. Hersen (Eds.), *Assessment of family violence: A clinical and legal sourcebook* (pp. 348–370). New York: Wiley.

Kaplan, M. (1983). A woman's view of the DSM-III. *American Psychologist, 38,* 786–792.

Koss, M. P. (1985). The hidden rape victim: Personality, attitudinal, and situational characteristics. *Psychology of Women Quarterly, 9,* 193–212.

Koss, M. P., & Gidycz, C. A. (1985). The sexual experiences survey: Reliability and validity. *Journal of Consulting and Clinical Psychology, 52,* 442–443.

Landrine, H. (1989). The politics of personality disorder. *Psychology of Women Quarterly, 13,* 325–240.

Lopez, S. R. (1989). Patient variable biases in clinical judgment: Conceptual overview and methodological considerations. *Psychological Bulletin, 106,* 184–203.

Loring, M., & Powell, B. (1988). Gender, race, and DSM-III: A study of the objectivity of psychiatric diagnostic behavior. *Journal of Health and Social Behavior, 29,* 1–22.

MacDonald, M. M. (1984). Behavioral assessment of women clients. In E. A. Blechman (Ed.), *Behavior modification with women* (pp. 60–93). New York: Guilford Press.

Maslin, A., & Davis, J. L. (1975). Sex-role stereotyping as a factor in mental health standards among counselors-in-training. *Journal of Counseling Psychology, 22,* 87–91.

McReynolds, P. (1989). Diagnosis and clinical assessment: Current status and major issues. In M. Rosenzweig & L. W. Porter (Eds.), *Annual Review of Psychology* (pp. 83–108). Palo Alto, CA: Annual Reviews.

Nowacki, C. M., & Poe, C. A. (1973). The concept of mental health as related to person perceived. *Journal of Consulting and Clinical Psychology, 40,* 160.

Nutt, R. L., & Gottlieb, M. C. (1993). Gender diversity in clinical psychology: Research, practice, and training. *The Clinical Psychologist, 46,* 64–73.

O'Leary, K. D., & Murphy, C. (1992). Clinical issues in the assessment of spouse abuse. In R. T. Ammerman & M. Hersen (Eds.), *Assessment of family violence: A clinical and legal sourcebook* (pp. 26–460). New York: Wiley

Orlinsky, D. E., & Howard, K. I. (1980). Gender and psychotherapeutic outcome. In A. M. Brodsky & R. T. Hare-Mustin (Eds.), *Women and psychotherapy: An assessment of research and practice* (pp. 3–34). New York: Guilford Press.

Parlee, M. (1982). Changes in moods and activation levels during the menstrual cycle in experimentally naive subjects. *Psychology of Women Quarterly, 7,* 119–131.

Pearson, J. C. (1985). *Gender and communication.* Dubuque: William C. Brown.

Pfohl, B., Stangl, D., & Zimmerman, M. (1984). The implications of DSM-III personality disorder in depressed patients. *Journal of Affective Disorders, 7,* 309–318.

Phillips, R. D., & Gilroy, F. D. (1985). Sex-role stereotypes and clinical judgments of mental health: The Brovermans' findings revisited. *Sex Roles, 12,* 179–183.

Poole, D. A., & Tepley, A. E. (1988). Sex roles, social roles, and clinical judgments of mental health. *Sex Roles, 19,* 265–272.

Potts, M. K., Burnam, M. A., & Wells, K. B. (1991).

Gender differences in depression detection: A comparison of clinician diagnosis and standardized assessment. *Psychological Assessment, 3,* 609–615.

Pruitt, J. A., & Kappius, R. E. (1992). Routine inquiry into sexual victimization: A survey of therapists' practices. *Professional Psychology: Research and Practice,* 474–479.

Root, M. P. P. (1992). Reconstructing the impact of trauma on personality. In L. S. Brown & M. Ballou (Eds.), *Personality and Psychopathology* (pp. 229–265). New York: Guilford.

Russell, D. E. H. (1986). *The secret trauma: Incest in the lives of girls and women.* New York: Basic Books.

Russell, D. E. H., & Howell, N. (1983). The prevalence of rape in the United States revisited. *Signs: Journal of Women in Culture and Society, 8,* 688–695.

Sato, R. A., & Heify, E. M. (1991). Depression and post-traumatic stress disorder in battered women: Consequences of victimization. *The Behavior Therapist, 14,* 131–136.

Saunders, D. G. (1992). Woman battering. In R. T. Ammerman & R. M. Hersen (Eds.), *Assessment of family violence: A clinical and legal handbook* (pp. 208–235). New York: Wiley.

Sesan, R. (1988). Sex bias and sex-role stereotyping in psychotherapy with women: Survey results. *Psychotherapy: Theory, Research, and Practice, 25,* 107–116.

Sherman, J. A. (1980). Therapist attitudes and sex-role stereotyping. In A. M. Brodsky & R. Hare-Mustin (Eds.), *Women and psychotherapy: An assessment of research and practice* (pp. 35–66). New York: Guilford Press.

Showalter, E. (1985). *The female malady.* New York: Pantheon Books.

Smith, M. (1980). Sex bias in counseling and psychotherapy. *Psychological Bulletin, 87,* 392–407.

Spitzer, R. L., Williams, J. B. W., Kass, F., & Davies, M. (1989). National field trial of the DSM-III-R diagnostic criteria for self-defeating personality disorder. *The American Journal of Psychiatry, 146,* 1561–1567.

Tolman, R. M. (1992). Psychological abuse of women. In R. T. Ammerman & M. Hersen (Eds.), *Assessment of family violence: A clinical and legal handbook* (pp. 291–312). New York: Wiley.

Unger, R. K., & Crawford, M. (1992). *Women and gender: A feminist psychology.* New York: McGraw-Hill.

Ussher, J. (1992). *Women's madness: Misogyny or*

mental illness? Amherst: University of Massachusetts Press.

Waisberg, J., & Page, S. (1988). Gender-role nonconformity and perception of mental illness. *Women and Health, 14*, 3–16.

Wakefield, J. C. (1992). Disorder as harmful dysfunction: A conceptual critique of DSM-III-R's definition of mental disorder. *Psychological Review, 99*, 232–247.

Walker, L. E. A. (1984). *The battered woman syndrome.* New York: Springer.

Walker, L. E. A (1986, August). Diagnosis and politics: Abuse disorders. In R. Garfinkel (Chair), *The politics of diagnosis, feminist psychology, and the DSM-III-R.* Symposium presented at the 94th annual convention of the American Psychological Association, Washington, DC.

Walker, L. E. (1989). Psychology and violence against women. *American Psychologist, 44*, 695–702.

Whitely, B. (1979). Sex roles and psychotherapy: A current appraisal. *Psychological Bulletin, 86*, 1309–1321.

Widiger, T. (1989). The categorical distinction between personality and affective disorders. *Journal of Personality Disorders, 3*, 77–91.

Widiger, T. A., Frances, A., Spitzer, R. L., & Williams, J. B. W. (1988). The DSM-III-R personality disorders: An overview. *The American Journal of Psychiatry, 135*, 786–795.

Widiger, T. A., & Spitzer, R. L. (1991). Sex bias in the diagnosis of personality disorders: Conceptual and methodological issues. *Clinical Psychology Review, 11*, 1–22.

Widiger, T. A., & Trull, T. J. (1991). Diagnosis and clinical assessment. *Annual Review of Psychology, 42*, 109–133.

Worell, J. (1987, November). *The DSM-III-R: Controversies in gender bias.* Invited paper presented at the annual meeting of the Association for the Advancement of Behavior Therapy, Chicago.

Worell, J. (1992, February). *Feminist frameworks in graduate education.* Paper presented at the annual meeting of the Association for Women in Psychology, Long Beach, CA.

Worell, J., & Remer, P. (1992). *Feminist perspectives in therapy: An empowerment model for women.* New York: Wiley.

Wrobel, N. H. (1993). Effect of patient age and gender on clinical decisions. *Professional Psychology, 24*, 206–212.

13

Psychological Assessment of Older Adults

Charles M. Morin
Cheryl A. Colecchi

Current demographic trends indicate that older adults represent the fastest-growing segment of the population. People aged sixty-five and older make up 12 to 13 percent of the current population and this proportion could reach 20 percent within the next twenty-five years (Atchley, 1985). As life expectancy increases, there is also an increasing need for mental-health services among the senior population. Epidemiological data suggest that 12.3 percent of community-dwelling elderly persons suffer from psychiatric disorders, including 4.9 percent who present with severe cognitive impairments (Myers et al., 1984; Regier et al., 1988). These estimates are much higher among the elderly living in nursing homes or other residential-care facilities. Although older adults are more likely than their younger counterparts to utilize health services, they are undertreated when it comes to mental-health problems (Lebowitz & Niederehe, 1992).

There is an increasing need for psychological assessment strategies specifically tailored to elderly individuals. While significant technological advances have improved the diagnosis and treatment of physical illness, the evaluation and diagnosis of psychological conditions in late life have lagged behind. Many psychological dysfunctions in older adults (e.g., depression) remain unrecognized or misattributed to the normal aging process (National Institute of Health, 1991). This problem is compounded by the high prevalence of coexisting medical and psychological disorders in late life. The need for assessment strategies becomes particularly salient as mental-health professionals are increasingly called upon to make decisions regarding an older person's retirement, nursing home placement, or the management of his or her day-to-day affairs.

This chapter reviews clinical issues and strategies in the psychological assessment of older adults. After discussing the rationale and objectives of psychological assessment in late life, a multidimensional evaluative framework is presented. Three assessment domains—cognitive, emotional, and behavioral—are reviewed, and a sample of disorders commonly seen in older adults is highlighted. Selected measures are discussed with reference to their psychometric properties, clinical usefulness, and limitations with an elderly population. Practical and conceptual issues in administering psychological tests and interpreting test data are reviewed. We conclude with recommendations for clinical practice and future research.

RATIONALE AND OBJECTIVES OF PSYCHOLOGICAL ASSESSMENT

The objectives of psychological assessment in older people, as for any age group, fall into three broad categories: diagnosis, treatment planning, and evaluation of treatment effects (Lawton & Storandt, 1984). The choice of assessment procedures will vary according to the referral question and the specific needs of a given situation. At the first level, psychological assessment may be clinically indicated for diagnostic purposes. For example, the most common referral question is to assist in the differential diagnosis of depression and dementia. In this context, evaluation of both cognitive and emotional functioning is required, and specialized neuropsychological measures are usually necessary. Additional information based on the observations of family or friends is typically used to complement these data. The second objective of assessment is to assist in decision making and in treatment planning. Psychologists and other mental-health practitioners are increasingly involved in determining whether the placement of elderly persons in nursing homes or other residential-care facilities is appropriate. In this context, assessment may need to have a broader focus, examining not only cognitive and emotional functioning but also specific behavioral and functional competencies (i.e., instrumental activities of daily living). The third objective of assessment is to establish a baseline and evaluate the therapeutic effects of psychosocial and pharmacological interventions. This type of evaluation involves more specialized measures, selected according to the nature of the target problems, and takes place in the context of either a clinical practice or outcome research.

ASSESSMENT DOMAINS AND STRATEGIES

Because of the various health, social, and economic changes that occur with aging, psychological assessment of the older adult must be multidimensional. Gerontology experts recommend that the following domains be covered: cognitive, emotional, behavioral, and physical (Gallagher, Thompson, & Levy, 1980; Lawton & Storandt, 1984). Increasing emphasis is also placed on environmental factors as well as on issues of stress, coping skills and social support networks, and life satisfaction. Because of this multidimensional framework and the limited resources available, it may be necessary to proceed in a sequential fashion, beginning with a multifocus screening measure and following up with more specialized instruments when clinically indicated.

Cognitive/Intellectual Assessment

Elderly patients are often brought in for psychological assessment by their loved ones because of cognitive complaints. These difficulties may be associated with depression, with misattributions of the normal aging process, or with organically based deficits related to dementia or other medical problems. Assessment of the elderly person with subjective cognitive deficits may pose several difficult tasks for the clinician. First, a differential diagnosis may need to be made between various dementing diseases or between dementia and an affective disorder. In many cases, patients may have concomitant disorders. The second task may involve going beyond diagnosis to describe the patient's cognitive strengths and weaknesses. The following section will attempt to elucidate how such differential diagnoses and descriptive assessments are made.

Normal Aging and Cognitive Functioning

In order to determine whether or not a patient is suffering from a dementing disease, the clinician must have some working knowledge of the effects of the normal aging process on intellectual functioning. Over the years, there has been much controversy regarding this relationship. Early cross-sectional studies indicated that there was a gradual decline in intellectual functioning across the adult lifespan beginning in the second to third decade. Longitudinal studies, on the other hand, revealed that individuals maintained (or in some cases increased) their intellectual abilities well into their sixties to eighties. In general, when age-appropriate norms are used, intellectual functioning tends to remain stable throughout life (see Schaie & Willis, 1986). The clinician must be cautious, however, when using scaled scores with the elderly, as their profile across subtests of intellectual functioning may reveal a pattern often associated with brain damage in younger persons (Lawton & Storandt, 1984). When assessing the relationship between aging and intellectual functioning, the focus must be on specific cognitive functions.

There is a consensus that there are some cognitive changes consistent with aging. Studies of the Weschler Adult Intelligence Scale (WAIS) have indicated that older adults do as well on the verbal subtests as younger adults, but that their scores on performance subtests tend to be lower than those of their younger counterparts (Botwinick, 1977, 1984; Hochanadel & Kaplan, 1984). Thus well-learned verbal skills, particularly those of reading, writing, vocabulary and word usage, arithmetic ability, and immediate memory tend to hold up with age. This phenomenon has become known as the "classic aging pattern" (Botwinick, 1977). It corresponds to Cattell's conceptualization of "fluid" and "crystalized" intelligence, the latter refering to previously overlearned knowledge and skills, while fluid intelligence is associated with abstract thinking, conceptualization, and novel problem solving.

Lezak (1983) summarizes the areas of cognitive functioning that are most affected by normal aging. These areas are memory, ability for abstraction, mental flexibility, and general behavioral slowing. While memory remains intact with older adults, there is a reduced capacity to remember information that exceeds the primary storage unit of six to seven items. Older adults may also be less efficient in acquiring and storing new information. Remote memory appears to be unaffected by age. Older persons have a diminished capacity for abstraction and complex conceptualization. They have more success with reasoning when the problem is meaningful and concrete. Decreased mental flexibility results in older adults having more difficulty adjusting to new situations or solving novel problems. One of the most consistent changes with aging is behavioral slowing, affecting visuospatial perceptual skills, memory, and psychomotor functioning in the elderly. Reduced speed rather than accuracy may account for, in part, their increased difficulty on timed performance tests.

Dementia

Dementia is a general term used to refer to a constellation of cognitive impairments resulting from organic brain disorders rather than the normal aging process. It is estimated that between 2.6 and 15.4 percent of the population over age sixty-five experience mild forms of dementia, and that 1.4 to 6.2 percent suffer from severe dementia (Mortimer, Schuman, & French, 1981). Dementia is not a single disease entity but may be caused by a variety of organic brain disorders, each having characteristic symptoms, etiology, and clinical course. To complicate matters, a host of medical disorders, drugs, toxic agents, and infectious states may mimic dementia. However, many of these conditions are reversible if diagnosed and corrected early. For a summary of reversible dementing agents, the reader is referred to Wedding (1986).

Primary degenerative dementia of the Alzheimer's type (Alzheimer's disease; AD) is the leading cause of dementia, accounting for approximately half of all persons with dementia (Terry, 1982). This disease involves an insidious onset caused by degeneration of brain tissue and brain atrophy. Patients with AD progress through several identifiable stages (Crook, 1987), with intellectual functioning progressively deteriorating with each stage. Forgetfulness is usually the first subjective complaint, but in the early phases there may be no objective memory deficits or interference with social, occupational, or daily life activities. In the more advanced stages, individuals may be disoriented to time and place and unable to recognize friends and relatives. The AD patient may also experience psychotic symptoms or become severely depressed or violent. Although the clinical course may vary, in most cases death results within five years of the onset of the disease.

Multi-infarct Dementia (MID) is the second most frequently occurring organic mental disorder in the aging population. An estimated 12 to 20 percent of patients presenting with symptoms of impaired cognitive functioning have MID (National Institutes of Health, 1981). It results from a variety of cerebrovascular conditions. The disorder is marked by such clinical features as abrupt onset, stepwise deterioration, a fluctuating course, focal neurological signs and symptoms, nocturnal confusion, depression, somatic complaints, emotional lability, and a history of hypertension and strokes (Poon et al., 1986). The nature and extent of cognitive impairment in the MID patient depends on the location and size of the lesion and on the availability of the collateral circulation (Marsden, 1976). Often impairment is evinced in short-term memory, concentration, abstract reasoning, speech functions, visuospatial functions, and apraxia. Since many of these impairments are also found in the AD patient, information about the history of the illness and laboratory findings are crucial in making a differential diagnosis (Thompson, Gong, Haskins, & Gallagher, 1987). Usually, the course of MID is characterized by "patchy" and rapidly deteriorating circumscribed symptoms rather than the slow, progressively uniform deterioration viewed in the AD patient.

Other common forms of dementia include alcohol dementia and subcortical dementia. According to Ryan and Butters (1984), deficits characteristic of the former include impairment in new learning, abstract reasoning, and perceptual organization. Degenerative disorders involving primarily subcortical structures (e.g., the basal ganglia) are Parkinson's and Huntington's diseases. In contrast to the widespread cognitive and personality disorganization that is characteristic of the diffuse dementias, cognitive impairment in the subcortical dementias involves difficulty with initiation, slowing of response rate, specific memory deficits, and

changes in verbal behaviors with decreased volume and output (Lezak, 1983). New learning is relatively preserved in subcortical dementia until advanced stages of the disease (Benson, 1983).

Depressed elderly patients may present with cognitive symptoms that mimic dementia. These impairments might include memory loss, decreased concentration, or even disorientation. However, in this case the major cause of the symptoms is not a degenerative brain disorder but rather a primary psychiatric disorder, usually depression. The term "pseudodementia" has been used to refer to such patients. It is important to rule out pseudodementia when conducting a cognitive assessment, as this condition is often reversible with treatment. It is very difficult to differentiate dementia from pseudodementia, and in some cases, depressive and dementing disorders may be concomitant. Additionally, depressive symptomatology often accompanies dementia. These symptoms may be due to the biological substrates of the disease or to patients' awareness of diminishing intellectual functioning and autonomy.

In general, factors differentiating the two disorders are psychiatric history and the onset of symptoms. The patient with pseudodementia tends to have a history of depression or psychiatric disorder. Cognitive impairments in pseudodementia, unlike dementia, are usually more subtle and selective, with an abrupt onset and rapid progression. Generally, symptoms are preceded by a disturbance in mood and other neurovegetative symptoms. Individuals with pseudodementia may emphasize cognitive deficits, particularly memory loss. Patients with dementia, on the other hand, tend to minimize cognitive impairments or even try to hide or compensate for them. Although memory complaints are common in those suffering from pseudodementia, testing does not always substantiate these complaints (O'Hara, Hinrichs, Kohout, Wallace, & Lemke, 1986). Patients with pseudodementia may also show inconsistent performance on neuropsychological tests (Wells, 1979). A number of screening instruments have also been shown to differentiate these two groups; these will be discussed later.

Assessment

Assessment of cognitive deficits should begin with a thorough clinical interview. It will be necessary to gather an in-depth history regarding onset, nature, and course of symptoms, as these factors are among the primary ones that differentiate these disorders. The patient's premorbid functioning can be assessed through his or her work and educational history. It is crucial to gather information on the patient's medical status and history, and medication and substance use in order to rule out reversible dementia. A family history of hypertension, strokes, or vascular problems may suggest a diagnosis of MID. In order to rule out cognitive impairment that is secondary to a psychopathology, the patient's current and past psychiatric status must be evaluated. Since many people with dementia are unable to describe their problems or the onset or course of their disorder accurately, the use of collaterals is essential. Family members' observations of everyday cognitive impairments are reliable sources of information (Williams, Klein, Little, & Haban, 1986).

Mental status examinations are a traditional part of a psychiatric evaluation. The following instruments are frequently used as screening measures of cognitive impairment: (1) the Mini-Mental Status Examination (MMS; Folstein, Folstein, & McHugh, 1975); (2) the Geriatric Mental Status Interview (Gurland, Copeland, Sharpe, & Kelleher, 1976); and (3) the Halifax Mental Status Scale (HMSS; Fisk, Braha, & Walker, 1991). The MMS and the HMSS are the briefest to administer, while the GMS, a semistructured interview technique, can typically be administered in one hour or less. These instruments have adequate reliability and tend to differentiate groups of healthy older adults from those with dementia and depression. While useful as brief screening instruments, their major limitation is their high rate of false negatives, especially for patients early in the course of dementia or with mild symptoms (Pfeffer et al., 1981). Therefore, the diagnosis of a particular dementia based on a mental status examination alone would be unwise.

Various rating scales have been developed specifically for detecting dementia and rating its severity. These instruments typically sample a more comprehensive range of cognitive functioning than do mental status examinations and use both interview techniques and direct performance measures (Kaszniak, 1986). The Alzheimer's Disease Assessment Scale (Rosen, Mohs, & Davis, 1984) and the Global Deterioration Scale (Reisberg, Ferris, & Crook, 1982) rate the severity of cognitive dysfunction and stages of deterioration of persons with progressive dementia. The Mattis Dementia Rating Scale (Mattis, 1976) is one of the most widely used dementia rating scales. In addition to assessing cognitive decline over time, this instrument has been shown to differentiate healthy elderly patients and those in the initial stages of AD. The "Ischemic Score" from the Dementia Score Scale (Hachinski et al., 1975) provides eight criteria of clinical features and course of symptoms that are useful in differentiating between AD and MID (Rosen, Terry, Fuld, Katzman, & Peck, 1980).

Mental status examinations and dementia-screening instruments serve a useful purpose when time is a major concern and a crude differentiation of disorders is the goal. However, such instruments do little to illuminate the overall pattern of cognitive dysfunction. When more in-depth assessment is requested, a multitude of neuropsychological tests and batteries are available for this purpose. Five areas of functioning that are typically assessed in a neuropsychological evaluation are: (1) attention and concentration; (2) memory; (3) language; (4) visuospatial skills; and (5) cognitive flexibility and abstraction (Albert, 1981). Additionally, premorbid functioning may be assessed through crystalized skills such as vocabulary and general fund of knowledge.

A great deal of research has focused on the use of neuropsychological tests to discriminate patients with AD from normal aged controls and patients with other dementias and depression. Although there is much variability between patients, in general, AD patients tend to score significantly lower than do normal subjects or patients with depression or MID on the WAIS (Butler, Dickinson, Katholi, & Halsey, 1983;

Perez, Stump, Gay, & Hart, 1976). The Luria-Nebraska Neuropsychological Battery has also been shown to discriminate between elderly patients with AD and major depression (McCue, Goldstein, & Shelly, 1989). On the Halstead-Reitan Battery, AD patients tend to have overall lower scores than do age- and education-matched controls with greater decrements on the Category and Trail-Making Tests (Bigler, Steinman, & Newton, 1980; Storrie & Doerr, 1979). There are specific areas of cognitive functioning that differentiate patients with AD from healthy elderly adults. Barth and Macciocchi (1986) summarize some of these areas as follows. Overall language deterioration in the AD patient appears to be related to substantially decreased cognitive performance and semantic processing. Speech initiation, articulation, repetition, and syntax are relatively unaffected until the later stage of the disease. There may be a decline in abstract reasoning and conceptual learning skills. Memory functions are most affected in patients with AD. During the initial stages of the disease immediate memory is not usually affected. During later stages, immediate, delayed, and remote retrieval processes are impaired. There are information processing problems and difficulty learning new information.

In the past, neuropsychological tests have come under attack due to the lack of age-appropriate norms that are based on a systematic distinction between healthy and organically impaired elderly (Klisz, 1978). Although this criticism is still a valid concern, there has been much progress in this area over the last decade. For example, the Wechsler Adult Intelligence Scale—Revised includes norms on adults through age seventy-five. A study conducted by Ryan and Paolo (1990) expanded these normative tables to include adults seventy-five and older. New findings on the Halstead-Reitan Neuropsychological Battery includes age-related interpretations (Heaton, Grant, & Matthews, 1986). The Luria-Nebraska Neuropsychological Battery includes age-adjusted interpretation of impairment (Golden, Hammeke, & Purisch, 1980). Ivnik and colleagues (1991) developed norms for the Wechsler Memory Scale for persons aged sixty-five to ninety-seven. La Rue, Yang, and Osato (1992) summarize some other standard neuropsychological instruments that now include old-age normative data. These tests include several of Benton's neuropsychological measures, such as the Visual Retention Test, Controlled Oral Word Associations, the Test of Line Orientation, the Selective Reminding Test, the California Verbal Learning Test (which adapts and extends the Rey Auditory Verbal Learning Test), the Continuous Visual Memory Test, Fuld's Object Memory Evaluation, and the Auditory-Verbal Learning Test.

Although there is no consensus among neuropsychologists regarding which tests should be selected for cognitive assessment of the elderly, La Rue (1986) outlines several important considerations to keep in mind. First, a broad range of cognitive functions should be assessed, as dementia is by definition a global impairment. Second, tests normed for this age group should be used. Third, measures of mood and personality should be included to assist in a differential diagnosis. Last, the battery should be brief and nonredundant to minimize frustration, fatigue, and expense.

Emotional/Affective Assessment

Cross-sectional studies indicate that personality is essentially stable in adulthood (Butcher et al., 1991; Costa et al., 1986). However, increased health problems and the many other changes associated with aging and retirement may increase the prevalence of certain disorders in late life. As affective and anxiety disorders are probably the most common ones, we have chosen to discuss their clinical features, assessment, and differential diagnosis.

Depression

Between 4 and 6 percent of community-residing older adults suffer from depressive syndromes, and about 15 percent report depressive symptoms (Blazer, 1989; Myers et al., 1984). Among the medically ill and persons living in long-term care facilities, 12 to 16 percent suffer from clinical depression and 20 to 30 percent present significant depressive symptomatology (Blazer, 1989, 1990). Dysthymia and major depression are the most common affective disorders, but the vast majority of older adults present with symptoms of depression secondary to physical illness. Dysphoria associated with changing life circumstances is also common in late life. Although longitudinal studies are lacking, cross-sectional data suggest a slight decrease in the prevalence of depression in late life (Gatz & Hurwicz, 1990; Newman, 1989). This apparent decline has been variously attributed to underreporting of depressed affect by older adults (Thompson, Futterman, & Gallagher, 1988), lack of recognition of symptoms by clinicians (Rapp, Parisi, Walsh, & Wallace, 1988), or greater immunity to depression in the current generation of older people (i.e., "cohort effect") (Blazer, 1989).

Although there has been little comparative empirical research on this issue, the clinical presentation of depression in late life may be different from that in younger patients (Addington & Fry, 1986; Raskin, 1979). For example, somatic symptoms are more common among the aged than in younger depressed patients. Concentration difficulty, memory impairments, and decreased energy are more frequent among the elderly, whereas low self-esteem and guilt are more common in younger patients. Older adults are more reluctant to acknowledge depressed affect and often exclusively emphasize the somatic symptoms. While this may reflect on the presence of concurrent medical disorders, a masked depression may be present when multiple somatic complaints are out of proportion to medical illness and there is lack of awareness or denial of affective symptoms (Thompson et al., 1988).

An important issue in late-life depression is the assessment of suicide potential. The suicide rate among older adults is 50 percent higher than the rate for adolescents or the national average. Elderly white males, particularly the "old old" (i.e., those over seventy-five), who are recently widowed and have a history of depression and alcoholism, are at significantly greater risk than other groups (Osgood, 1992). Older adults

provide less warning about intent, their means for committing suicide is often more lethal (the majority use a gun), and their completion rate is correspondingly higher than in younger adults. Although suicide potential should always be evaluated in any depressed patient, this need is even more imperative among the aging population.

The differential diagnosis of late-life depression is complicated by its high comorbidity with other psychiatric and medical conditions. First, depression is sometimes severe enough to produce cognitive symptoms similar in type and intensity to those in dementia—disorientation, memory loss, and concentration difficulty. Second, somatic symptoms such as sleep disturbances, decreased sexual desire, diminished energy, and aches and pains may not be as indicative of depression in the elderly as they are in young and middle-aged patients (Yesavage et al., 1983). Although the classic neurovegetative symptoms may reflect a true clinical depression, some of those symptoms may also be part of the normal aging process or secondary to physical illnesses. Finally, affective symptoms such as dysphoria or sadness may be indicative of reduced life satisfaction, given some normal changes in life circumstances, rather than clinical depression.

Assessment

The assessment of depression relies on standardized diagnostic interviews, clinician-rating scales, and self-report measures. The diagnostic interview schedules that include sections for affective disorders are the Structured Clinical Interview for DSM (SCID; Spitzer, Williams, & Gibbon, 1987); the Schedule for Affective Disorders and Schizophrenia (SADS; Endicott & Spitzer, 1978); and the Diagnostic Interview Schedule (DIS; Robins, Helzer, Croughan, & Ratcliff, 1981). Because these diagnostic interviews are based on DSM or Research Diagnostic Criteria (RDC), they are considered the "gold standards" against which other measures are validated. These assessment procedures, which must be administered by trained persons, represent the most reliable method for diagnosing and classifying psychopathology. However, older adults with cognitive impairments may not be able to tolerate such lengthy interviews. The Hamilton Rating Scale for Depression (HAM-D; Hamilton, 1960) is one of the most widely used clinician-rating scales in depression research. It is a twenty-one-item rating scale that is completed by a clinician based on an interview and observation of the patient. Geriatric data are available for medical (Norris, Gallagher, Wilson, & Winograd, 1987) and psychiatric populations. As depression often coexists with medical disorders and is frequently unrecognized by primary care physicians, the use of an interview-based assessment can significantly enhance its recognition among medical patients (Rapp, Smith, & Britt, 1990).

Self-report measures of depression include the Geriatric Depression Scale (GDS; Yesavage et al., 1983), the Beck Depression Inventory (BDI; Beck, Ward, Mendelson, Mock, & Erbaugh, 1961), the Zung Self-Rating Depression Scale (SDS; Zung, 1965), the Center for Epidemiological Studies Depression Scale (CES-D; Radloff, 1977), and the Depression Adjective Checklist (DACL; Lubin, 1967). Two scales frequently used to assess suicide potential are the Hopelessness Scale (Beck, Weisman, Lester, & Trexler, 1974) and the Scale for Suicidal Ideation (Beck, Kovacs, & Weisman, 1979). Several additional instruments contain subscales measuring depression, but except for the Brief Symptom Inventory (BSI; Derogatis & Melisaratos, 1983), other scales such as the MMPI-D, the Multiple Affect Adjective Checklist, and the Profile of Mood States have been used infrequently with the elderly.

Several studies have examined the reliability and validity of self-report measures of depression in older samples. Geriatric norms have also been reported for several of those scales (i.e., the BSI, BDI, SDS, GDS, and the CES-D). The BDI and GDS have been cross-validated in older samples against structured clinical interviews using DSM-III-R and RDC (Gallagher, Breckenridge, Steinmetz, & Thompson, 1983; Olin et al., 1992). As for most self-report measures, their sensitivity is generally adequate but their specificity is more problematic (Olin et al.,

1992). Because the BDI and the HAM-D are heavily loaded with somatic items, they may yield a high rate of false positives (Hyer & Blount, 1984; Thompson et al., 1988). The GDS is the only measure of depression that has been designed specifically for older adults. It is a thirty-item measure that is free from somatic items. Because of the simpler true-false response format of the GDS, its completion rate is higher than those of other scales with a multiple-choice response format, such as the SDS (Dunn & Sacco, 1989). Several scales, including the GDS, BDI, SDS, and HAM-D, have been found sensitive to treatment effects in outcome studies of late-life depression (Beutler et al., 1987; Steuer et al., 1984; Thompson, Gallagher, & Breckenridge, 1987).

In summary, self-report scales yield a global score of symptom severity. They are excellent for screening and for tracking changes in symptom severity over time. These measures do not provide information about symptom duration, onset, and course. The clinician should not rely exclusively on self-report measurement if the primary objective of assessment is to make a clinical diagnosis of depression. Self-report data should be complemented by observers' rating scales and structured diagnostic interviews.

Anxiety

Late-life anxiety has received very little attention compared with depression. The prevalence of anxiety disorders among community-dwelling elderly aged sixty-five or older is about 5.5 percent (Regier et al., 1988). Between 2 and 4 percent suffer from generalized anxiety disorders, whereas up to 10 percent report simple phobias (Blazer, George, & Hughes, 1991). Obsessive-compulsive disorders and true panic disorders are less frequent among the aged. There is an apparent decline in anxiety syndromes across the life span, with those aged sixty-five and older reporting less anxiety relative to the forty-five to sixty-four age group (Blazer et al., 1991). In one community survey, however, 17 percent of males and 21 percent of females over the age of fifty-five reported anxiety symptomatology that was judged to be of sufficient severity to warrant treatment (Himmelfarb & Murrell, 1984). Judging by the increased use of sedative-hypnotics with aging (Mellinger, Balter, & Uhlenhuth, 1984), symptoms of anxiety may be underreported by elderly individuals or confounded with the normal aging process and medical problems.

Presenting symptoms of anxiety in older patients involve primarily somatic concerns but also apprehension and behavioral agitation (Salzman, 1982). As for depressive disorders, the focus on somatic complaints may reflect greater hypochondriacal concerns or represent real symptoms of medical illness. Older adults also tend to verbalize their anxiety in terms of a general feeling of nervousness or apprehension (Gurian & Miner, 1991). Common themes for worries among the elderly include health, personal loss, the future, and economic security (Blazer, 1990; Wisocki, 1988). In contrast, younger people worry more about family and work or school-related matters (Borkovec, Shadick, & Hopkins, 1991). Because the elderly face a number of inevitable changes in late life (e.g., declining health, loss of social support networks), the issue of whether worry is necessarily pathological is particularly relevant in the aging population. Frail elderly persons with diminished economic resources who live alone in high-crime areas are likely to worry about those life circumstances.

As with affective and cognitive disorders, the differential diagnosis of geriatric anxiety is complicated by a high comorbidity with other medical and psychiatric disorders. The most difficult task is to determine the extent to which anxiety is primary or comorbid in nature, secondary to physical illness or medications, or a normal response to life events. Anxiety is highly correlated with health status (Himmelfarb & Murrell, 1984; Turnbull, 1989), and the exclusive endorsement of somatic symptoms may reflect an underlying yet undetected medical problem (Cohen, 1991; Sheikh, 1992). There is a significant overlap of symptoms between anxiety and depression (e.g., insomnia), so that these disorders may coexist and often become more blurred in late life. Behavioral symptoms of anxiety (e.g., agitation) may also be part of dementing illnesses.

Assessment

In addition to a clinical interview, more systematic assessment modalities for geriatric anxiety include self-report measures, clinician-rating scales, and diagnostic interview schedules. The three diagnostic interview schedules mentioned previously (i.e., SCID, SADS, DIS) also contain sections to evaluate anxiety disorders. One additional interview, the Anxiety Disorders Interview Schedule—Revised (Di Nardo & Barlow, 1988), was designed specifically for the assessment of anxiety disorders. Although there is no information on its use with older adults, administration of the ADIS-R is less time-consuming than the other interviews and also provides a differential diagnosis. It may be a promising instrument for clinical research on geriatric anxiety. Clinician-rating scales include the Hamilton Rating Scale for Anxiety (HAM-A; Hamilton, 1959) and the Anxiety Status Inventory (ASI; Zung, 1971). As with its depression counterpart, the HAM-A is heavily loaded with somatic items that tend to be overendorsed by older people (Sheikh, 1991). The ASI has adequate psychometric properties with younger adults, but no geriatric data are available.

Self-report measures of anxiety include the State-Trait Anxiety Inventory (STAI; Spielberger, Gorush, & Lushene, 1971), the Beck Anxiety Inventory (BAI; Beck, Epstein, Brown, & Steer, 1988), and the Zung Self-Rating Anxiety Scale (SAS; Zung 1971). Additional measures of psychological symptoms containing anxiety subscales are also available (e.g., SCL-90, POMS, MAACL), but only the BSI, an abbreviated form of the SCL-90, has been used with older adults (Hale, Cochran, & Hedgepeth, 1984). The STAI, a measure of state and trait anxiety, is the most widely used self-report instrument of anxiety in outcome research. Reliability and various indices of validity have been shown to be adequate with older adults, and normative data have also been reported (Nesselroade, Mitteness, & Thompson, 1984; Patterson, O'Sullivan, & Spielberger, 1980; Rankin, Gfeller, & Gilner, 1993). The STAI has been used to detect changes in anxiety in several outcome studies of late-life problems such as anxiety, insomnia, and memory impairments (DeBerry, Davis, & Reinhard, 1989; Morin, Kowatch, Barry, & Walton, 1993; Yesavage, 1982). The BAI covers somatic, cognitive, and behavioral manifestations of anxiety. The item content is more specific to anxiety symptomatology, and there is less overlap with measures of depression. It has been found effective in discriminating among anxiety disorders in younger adults (Beck et al., 1988). However, its content is heavily loaded with somatic items, limiting its usefulness when concomitant medical disorders are present. Geriatric data are not yet available. The SAS, like the clinician's version, measures somatic and affective dimensions of anxiety. Reliability, validity, and normative data for older adults have been reported (Zung, 1980).

Two important limitations of anxiety instruments are noteworthy. First, not a single instrument was designed specifically for older adults. Although their internal consistency and temporal stability may be adequate with older adults, the various indexes of validity (e.g., construct, ecological) are generally assumed rather than empirically based (Sheikh, 1991). This assumption is problematic given that anxiety manifestations may vary across age groups. A second and related issue concerns their poor discriminant validity, particularly with reference to the distinction between anxiety and depression. There is a substantial overlap in item content among measures of anxiety and depression. Not surprisingly, significant and positive correlations between these measures have been reported with both younger and older samples (Rankin et al., 1993). Although mixed anxiety-depression is increasingly recognized as a distinct syndrome, more refined measurement instruments are needed to evaluate the unique features of anxiety in late life (Hersen & Van Hasselt, 1992; Sheikh, 1991).

Functional/Behavioral Assessment

Assessment in the domains of cognitive and emotional functioning is typically geared toward answering referral questions regarding diagnosis and treatment planning. Nowadays, however, the clinician often is asked to make recommendations regarding the elderly individual's ability to function independently, continue to work, or benefit from particular support services. Diagnosis alone does not predict the ability to get along in one's environment or to care for oneself. These traditional areas of assessment, in and of themselves, are unable to answer such questions without some form of functional assessment.

Kemp and Mitchell (1992) have developed a hierarchical model of functional assessment based on the fact that all human functioning is multidetermined by an interaction of biological, psychosocial, and environmental components. At the lowest level of functioning are physical substrates, which include endurance, range of motion, strength, and coordination. The next level is the activities of daily living (ADLs), which involves such tasks as grooming, dressing, eating, toileting, and bathing. Instrumental activities of daily living (IADLs), the next highest level of the hierarchy, includes such skills as shopping, balancing a checkbook, paying bills, keeping appointments, using public transportation, preparing meals, communicating with others, and managing health and safety matters. Skilled performance refers to the individual's ability to drive, operate equipment, solve new everyday problems, relate to others, learn new tasks and procedures, and express thoughts articulately. The highest level of functional ability is that of social roles and includes the ability to relate to friends and others in a sensitive, rational, and mature manner, the ability to perform most paid jobs, and the ability to maintain an intimate relationship.

Lawton (1986) offers a slightly different conceptualization of functional assessment. Rather than focusing solely on the individual's skills or behavioral performance, his model assesses "the good life," indicated by positive qualities in four major sectors: behavioral competence, psychological well-being, perceived quality of life, and objective environment. The good life may be enhanced through increased functioning in any of the sectors. Well-being within a given sector may positively influence functioning in another sector.

Assessment

Assessment of the individual's everyday functioning ranges from unidimensional measures to multidimensional scales. Unidimensional measures typically assess ADLs and IADLs. In general, these measures have moderate to high reliability coefficients with more varied findings on validity. A review of numerous unidimensional instruments can be found in Kemp and Mitchell (1992).

Multidimensional procedures grew out of the fields of gerontology and rehabilitation. These measures combine major domains of a comprehensive evaluation into a single instrument or interview procedure. The best-known of these instruments is the Multidimensional Functional Assessment Questionnaire, also known as the OARS (Duke University Center for the Study of Aging, 1978). The OARS requires trained interviewers and has two parts. The first part assesses the individual's functioning in five domains: social resources, economic resources, mental health, physical health, and ADLs. The second part assesses services used. The OARS has norms derived from several large representative samples of older people. The Functional Assessment Inventory (FAI; Cairl, Pfeiffer, Keller, Burke, & Samis, 1983) is a shortened (thirty-item) version of the OARS and assesses the same five domains. The Comprehensive Assessment and Referral Evaluation (CARE; Gurland et al., 1977–78) yields information on psychiatric, medical, nutritional, economic, and social functioning. It utilizes trained interviewers, and the average administration time is ninety minutes. The SHORT-CARE (Gurland, Golden, Teresi, & Challop, 1984) is an abbreviated form of the CARE that assesses depression, dementia, and disability in the elderly. It also measures severity and change. The Multilevel Assessment Instrument (MAI; Lawton, 1982) is based on Lawton's conceptual model of the good life, mentioned above. The MAI contains scales assessing physical health, cognition, ADLs, time use, social interaction, personal adjustment, and perceived environment. It has three forms of alternate lengths of administration, allowing flexibility for hard-to-test individuals. All of the mentioned multidimensional instruments appear to have adequate psychometric properties.

PRACTICAL AND CONCEPTUAL ISSUES

Standardized administration of psychological tests to older adults is often compromised by fatigue and motivational factors and by declining physical functions with aging. The interpretation of test data can also be confounded by the presence of coexisting medical illnesses, the use of medication that can alter cognitive functioning, and the absence of age-appropriate norms. In this section, we examine potential sources of variance in the aging patient's cognitive, emotional, and behavioral functioning. Some of these are common to any age group, whereas others are unique to the older population.

As Plutchik (1979) cogently noted "psychological test performance is dependent on both functional and organic factors. If a patient does poorly on a block design test, this could reflect a cognitive deficit (i.e., not understanding the problem), a motivational deficit (i.e., not wanting to do the problem because of depression or apathy), a hearing or visual deficit (i.e., not being able to see the problem or hear the instructions), or a deficit in manipulative skills (i.e., not being able to do the problem)" (p. 23). The clinician needs to be cognizant of these sources of variance, as they could lead to misdiagnosis and in turn have severe implications for both the patient (unwarranted residential care placement) and the clinician (malpractice lawsuit).

Sensory and Physical Impairments

Hearing, visual, and physical impairments increase with age. Some of these impairments are secondary to an underlying illness, but others are fairly slow and progressive in nature and may only be detected long after their onset. Sensory deficits and physical impairments can interfere with cognitive and behavioral performance. For example, if the person cannot hear the instructions of a given test clearly or see the stimulus material properly, his or her test results will obviously be confounded. Likewise, the natural decline of fine motor coordination and behavioral slowing with aging may lead to spurious deficits on timed measures of visuomotor coordination.

Sensory deficits and physical impairments can also have adverse effects on the quality of life. Hearing loss can produce irritability, social isolation, and other depressive symptoms. Even mild to moderate degrees of hearing loss are often perceived as severe handicaps by older people (Mulrow et al., 1990). In the context of a clinical interview with an otherwise well-functioning elderly person, such deficits may be easily overlooked if the patient attempts to hide the problem in order to please the examiner. Visual defects can produce anxietylike symptoms such as apprehension and motor restlessness (Cohen, 1991). When cognitive functions are intact, a random response style on paper-and-pencil measures may suggest visual defects. Sensory deficits can also produce symptoms typically associated with psychotic disorders. In residential settings, for example, hearing loss and visual defects have been associated with functional psychiatric disorders, particularly paraphrenia (Eastwood & Corbin-Rifat, 1987). A sensory deprivation phenomenon often underlies psychological symptoms, and these may be reversible after correction of the sensory impairment.

It is imperative to inquire at the onset of assessment whether the lighting in the room is adequate and whether the patient can clearly see the printed materials and hear the examiner's questions and instructions. Auditory and visual attention should be evaluated first, as they are prerequisite functions to complete almost any test. Whenever deficits are suspected, a consultation from the appropriate subspecialty should be requested.

Fatigue, Practice Effects, and Motivational Factors

Deficits on measures of cognitive function may be due to patient/contextual variables rather than organic impairments. These include fatigue, lack of prior experience with stimulus materials, and motivation (Lawton & Storandt, 1984; Levy, 1981; Schaie & Schaie, 1977). Although fatigue is not a serious concern when testing is kept within a 2.5 hour duration (Grant, Storandt, & Botwinick, 1978), older adults in general and the more frail elderly with medical illness specifically are more susceptible to fatigue than healthy and highly functioning individuals (Levy, 1981). The timing of assessment is also important, as peak performance in older adults may be more subject to diurnal fluctuations.

Research on practice effects suggests that performance on the Digit Symbol subtest of the WAIS improved with practice (Grant et al., 1978). The current generation of older adults has had less exposure to testing situations than most younger individuals. The novelty of stimulus materials to older people and perhaps their different meaning may alter speed and response pattern. Motivation is another important factor to consider. Depression may be accompanied by significant motivational deficits that can be misinterpreted as performance deficits. Older adults are more cautious in reaching decisions and have lower expectations (Albert, 1981). In addition, considering that psychological evaluations are often requested by family members, or may even be court-ordered, there may be a greater level of cautiousness or even suspiciousness in older adults approaching a testing situation (Schaie & Shaie, 1977). The fear of losing autonomy/independence may lead to risk-avoiding behaviors, attempts to compensate for deficits, or withdrawal from a testing situation. In sum, it is important to keep in mind that deficits, particularly on performance-based measures, may be due to fatigue, limited exposure to stimulus materials, motivational deficits, or excessive cautiousness rather than true intellectual impairments.

Medical Illness

A variety of physical illnesses can alter cognitive performance and have a negative impact on emotional functioning. More than 80 percent of elderly people have one or more active medical illness. Because of declining health and increasing use of medications with aging, the interpretation of psychological test data from older adults is a more complex task than with younger adults. A most difficult issue in making a differential diagnosis is to distinguish true psychological symptoms, particularly those falling in the somatic cluster, from various illnesses producing similar clinical manifestations (Cohen, 1991; Thompson et al., 1988). For example, measures of depression/anxiety with items reflecting somatic complaints (e.g., sleep disturbances, fatigue) may be artifactually elevated in older people because of the normal declining physical functions associated with aging, the somatic effects of physical illness, or the side effects of medications. The various neurological diseases that can produce cognitive impairments and emotional symptoms similar to those seen in dementia/pseudodementia have been reviewed in the section on intellectual assessment.

Almost any life-threatening or terminal illness (e.g., cancer) will trigger various emotional reactions during the course of the illness. Other diseases may produce psychological symptoms because of the underlying metabolic or organic dysfunctions. For example, a variety of conditions such as Parkinson's disease, stroke, and brain tumor may present with depressive features, whereas other conditions such as thyroid dysfunctions or anemia may produce reversible depressionlike symptoms (e.g., cognitive impairments, psychomotor retardation, irritability) (see Saltzman & Shader, 1979; Koenig & Blazer, 1991). Anxiety is frequently associated with cardiovascular (e.g., congestive heart failure), pulmonary (e.g., chronic obstructive pulmonary), and gastrointestinal diseases (Cohen, 1991). Other medical conditions such as hypoglycemia, hyperthyroidism, and pheochromocytoma can cause symptoms of anxiety, especially those of autonomic arousal (e.g., hyperexcitability, tachycardia, shaking, etc.). Whether these manifestations of anxiety and depression represent emotional reactions to the illness, a biochemical by-product of the affected physical system, or an interaction of these is often unclear. When in doubt, the clinician must seek consultation with medical specialists to disentangle the causative factors.

Medications

The use of various drugs to treat medical conditions may complicate even further the clinical presentation of psychiatric disorders in late life. Several drugs can cause cognitive, behavioral, and emotional changes that may be misinterpreted. Older adults consume about 25 percent of prescription drugs. Because they metabolize drugs more slowly and require a lower dosage than younger adults, their response to medication is less predictable.

Depressive symptoms can be side effects of a variety of drugs, including some antihypertensives (e.g., reserpine, methyldopa, and propranolol), corticosteroids, and antiparkinsonian agents (Salzman, 1983; Salzman & Shader, 1979). Over 150 medications listed in the Physician's Desk Reference have anxiety or paradoxical anxiety as potential side effects, and about 90 medications also list agitation as a potential side effect (Cohen, 1991). Sedative-hypnotics, mostly benzodiazepines, are the most common class of psychotropic medication used by the elderly. These drugs are typically prescribed for anxiety and insomnia, and because of their CNS depressant properties, they may potentiate depressive symptomatology. Long-acting benzodiazepines (e.g., flurazepam) tend to accumulate in the body and may cause daytime psychomotor and cognitive impairments even though they may be used only at bedtime (Johnson & Chernik, 1982). Conversely, compounds with short half-lives or those used on an "as needed" basis can produce withdrawal symptoms similar to those of anxiety. Some benzodiazepines (e.g., triazolam) have also been shown to produce anterograde amnesia. Barbiturates may cause toxicity and produce confusion, lethargy, and even delirium. Excessive caffeine intake and sympathomimetic compounds in nonprescription drugs, as well as withdrawal from these substances and from alcohol, can also cause anxiety (Gurland & Meyers, 1988).

Delineation of the effects of medication on psychological functioning is often complicated by the nature, severity, and prognosis of the illness for which the medication is prescribed. The clinician needs to remain aware that some drugs can cause iatrogenic conditions, aggravate preexisting psychological dysfunctions, or produce symptoms similar to those seen in depression and/or anxiety.

Legal and Ethical Issues

At times, legal proceedings are initiated to evaluate an elderly person's competence related to management of personal estate, ability to care for self or personal liberty, or in health care decisions. If the person is found to be incompetent, the result could be loss of autonomy or even involuntary commitment. Typically, courts rarely require objective psychometric assessment of an elderly individual's functional capacity in making such decisions. More often, determination of competence or incompetence is based on a brief letter from a physician (Rosoff & Gottlieb, 1987). At times, however, the psychologist may be asked to assess the elderly person's functional capacities for legal purposes. When tests are used, it is crucial that they have age-appropriate norms and adequate psychometric properties for the elderly. They should have demonstrated ecological validity.

RECOMMENDATIONS FOR PRACTICE AND RESEARCH

"State-of-the-art" reviews on late-life psychological assessment concluded about a decade ago that there was a lack of adequate assessment methods specifically tailored for older adults (Gallagher et al., 1980; Lawton & Storandt, 1984). Significant advances have been made since then, and more research has focused on evaluating the psychometric properties of as-

sessment procedures with older adults and on developing age-appropriate norms. We conclude here by making some recommendations for clinical practice and future research.

Because of the multiple sources of variance in the aging patient's psychological functioning, a sequential approach is the most cost-effective approach when conducting a psychological assessment with older adults. A multidimensional screening measure may be used first, then followed up with more specialized assessment procedures. But even before undertaking formal testing, a clinical interview should be the first step. It should include a detailed history of the nature (cognitive, behavioral, somatic, affective), onset (insidious versus sudden), duration (state versus trait), and temporal course (fluctuating, persistent, progressive) of the patient's symptoms. A careful functional analysis will often provide clues as to the origin of the symptoms. Examination of their onset and temporal course in relation to other factors will help determine whether psychological symptoms are pathological, medically related, drug-induced, or a normal reaction to life events. The distinction between early and late onset is also useful, as late onset of anxiety/depressive disorders tends to be associated more frequently with medical illness and life events. As part of the clinical evaluation, it is essential to examine the effects of physical illnesses and medications on the elderly person's cognitive and emotional functioning. A complete listing of all prescribed and over-the-counter medications used should be obtained. Psychological and medical evaluations should be conducted in tandem and consultation from a pharmacist enlisted whenever possible.

Before selecting which instruments to use, the clinician and researcher must determine what the specific objectives of the assessment are, what type of information is needed, and what resources are available in terms of time and staff. If diagnosis is the primary goal of assessment, a structured clinical interview with standardized diagnostic criteria will be the most effective tool, even though it will be more costly. Specialized neuropsychological measures are usually needed in the differential diagnosis of dementia and depression. Administration of selected measures assessing specific functions are preferred to the administration of a full battery, as elderly individuals are more susceptible to fatigue.

Self-report measures of emotional states are excellent screening devices in otherwise well-functioning patients. They are economical and can be administered at repeated intervals to track changes over time. Their specificity, however, may be problematic, as some of these measures tap more than one affective dimension. Use of a total score from scales heavily loaded with somatic items can be misleading (i.e., can produce false positives) and can obscure differential diagnosis. A better strategy is to use scores from subscales tapping various dimensions of affect to more accurately reflect the nature of symptom clusters. Test data from self-report scales should not always be taken at face value, as they are subject to social desirability factors. The clinician needs to rely on his or her own observations and complement these with behavioral observations from nursing staff or the patient's family or friends. Use of collaterals is essential in the assessment of dementing illnesses.

Assessment instruments specifically designed for older adults are needed. It is time to move beyond the adaptation of measures developed with younger adults to the design and standardization of new instruments that are ecologically valid with older adults. Furthermore, norms for various age groups within the late-life span are also needed. Whereas previous studies have typically combined normative data for all older adults over fifty-five or sixty-five years of age, we need to clearly distinguish response patterns for the young, middle-aged, and old-old as the late-life period spans more than twenty-five years. There may be important differences in the presentation of cognitive impairments and emotional disorders between a sixty-five- and an eighty-five-year-old person. Clearly, we cannot expect the same findings from a fifty-five-year-old employed full-time with adequate economic, family, and health resources and an eighty-five-year-old widow living alone at the poverty level and with deteriorating health.

The psychological assessment of the elderly is a complex and challenging task. Changes in cognitive, emotional, and behavioral functioning can be a function of the normal aging process or of a variety of other factors. The greatest challenge in evaluating older adults is to remain aware of these multiple sources of variances, and at the same time to avoid over-normalizing genuine cognitive deficits and psychological dysfunctions.

ACKNOWLEDGMENT

Preparation of this chapter was partially supported by Grant MH47020 from the National Institute of Mental Health.

REFERENCES

Albert, M. S. (1981). Geriatric neuropsychology. *Journal of Consulting and Clinical Psychology, 49,* 835–850.

Atchley, R. C. (1985). *Social forces in aging.* Belmont, CA: Wadsworth.

Barth, J. T., & Macciocchi, S. N. (1986). Dementia: Implications for clinical practice and research. In S. B. Filskov & T. J. Boll (Eds.), *Handbook of clinical neuropsychology* (Vol. 2, pp. 398–425). New York: Wiley.

Beck, A. T., Epstein, N., Brown, G., & Steer, R. A. (1988). An inventory for measuring clinical anxiety: Psychometric properties. *Journal of Consulting and Clinical Psychology, 56,* 893–897.

Beck, A. T., Kovacs, M., & Weisman, A. (1979). Assessment of suicidal ideation: The Scale for Suicide Ideation. *Journal of Consulting and Clinical Psychology, 47,* 343–352.

Beck, A. T., Ward, C. H., Mendelson, M., Mock, J., & Erbaugh, J. (1961). An inventory for measuring depression. *Archives of General Psychiatry, 4,* 561–571.

Beck, A. T., Weisman, A., Lester, D., & Trexler, L. (1974). The measurement of pessimism: The Hopelessness Scale. *Journal of Consulting and Clinical Psychology, 42,* 861–865.

Benson, D. F. (1983). Subcortical dementia: A clinical approach. In R. Mayeux & W. G. Rosen (Eds.), *Advances in neurology: The dementias* (Vol. 38, pp. 185–194). New York: Raven Press.

Bigler, E. D., Steinman, D. R., & Newton, J. S.

(1980). Clinical assessment of cognitive deficits in neurologic disorder: I. Effects of age and degenerative disease. *Clinical Neuropsychology, 3,* 5–13.

Blazer, D. (1989). The epidemiology of depression in late life. *Journal of Geriatric Psychiatry, 22,* 35–51.

Blazer, D. (1990). *Emotional problems in later life: Intervention strategies for professional caregivers.* New York: Springer.

Blazer, D., George, L. K., & Hughes, D. (1991). The epidemiology of anxiety disorders: An age comparison. In C. Salzman & B. D. Lebowitz (Eds.), *Anxiety in the elderly: Treatment and research* (pp. 17–30). New York: Springer.

Botwinick, J. (1977). Intellectual abilities. In J. E. Birren & K. W. Schaie (Eds.), *Handbook of the psychology of aging* (pp. 580–605). New York: Van Nostrand Reinhold.

Botwinick, J. (1984). *Aging and behavior: A comprehensive integration of research findings* (3rd ed.). New York: Springer.

Butcher, J. N., Aldwin, C. M., Levenson, M. R., Ben-Porath, Y. S., Spiro, A., & Bosse, R. (1991). Personality and aging: A study of the MMPI-2 among older men. *Psychology and Aging, 6,* 361–370.

Butler, R. W., Dickinson, W. A., Katholi, C., & Halsey, J. H. (1983). The comparative effects of organic brain disease on cerebral blood flow and measured intelligence. *Annals of Neurology, 13,* 155–159.

Cairl, R., Pfeiffer, E., Keller, D. M., Burke, H., & Samis, H. V. (1983). An evaluation of the reliability and validity of the Functional Assessment Inventory. *Journal of the American Geriatrics Society, 31,* 607–612.

Chelune, G. J., & Moehle, K. A. (1986). Neuropsychological assessment and everyday functioning. In D. Wedding, A. M. Horton, Jr., & J. Webster (Eds.), *The neuropsychology handbook: Behavioral and clinical perspectives* (pp. 489–525). New York: Springer.

Cohen, G. D. (1991). Anxiety and general medical disorders. In C. Salzman & B. D. Lebowitz (Eds.), *Anxiety in the elderly: Treatment and research* (pp. 47–62). New York: Springer.

Crook, T. D. (1987). Dementia. In L. L. Carstensen & B. A. Edelstein (Eds), *Handbook of clinical gerontology* (pp. 96–111). New York: Pergamon Press.

DeBerry, S., Davis, S., & Reinhard, K. E. (1989). A comparison of meditation-relaxation and cognitive behavioral techniques for reducing anxiety

and depression in a geriatric population. *Journal of Geriatric Psychiatry, 22,* 231–247.

Derogatis, L. R., & Melisaratos, N. (1983). The Brief Symptom Inventory: An introductory report. *Psychological Medicine, 13,* 595–605.

Di Nardo, P. A., & Barlow, D. H. (1988). *Anxiety Disorders Interview Schedule—Revised* (ADIS-R). Albany, NY: Center for Stress and Anxiety Disorders.

Duke University Center for the Study of Aging (1978). *Multidimensional functional assessment: The OARS methodology* (2nd ed.). Durham, NC: Duke University Press.

Dunn, V. K., & Sacco, W. P. (1989). Psychometric evaluation of the geriatric depression scale and the Zung self-rating depression scale using an elderly community sample. *Psychology and Aging, 4,* 125–126.

Eastwood, R., & Corbin-Rifat, S. (1987). Hearing impairment, mental disorders, and the elderly. *Stress Medicine, 3,* 171–173.

Endicott, J., & Spitzer, R. L. (1978). A diagnostic interview: the Schedule for Affective Disorders and Schizophrenia. *Archives of General Psychiatry, 35,* 837–844.

Fisk, J. D., Braha, R. E., & Walker, A. (1991). The Halifax Mental Status Scale: Development of a new test of mental status and use with elderly clients. *Psychological Assessment: A Journal of Consulting and Clinical Psychology, 3,* 162–167.

Folstein, M. F., Folstein, S. E., & McHugh, P. R. (1975). "Mini-Mental State": A practical method for grading the cognitive state of patients for the clinician. *Journal of Psychiatric Research, 12,* 189–198.

Gallagher, D., Breckenridge, J., Steinmetz, J., & Thompson, L. (1983). The Beck Depression Inventory and research diagnostic criteria: Congruence in an older population. *Journal of Consulting and Clinical Psychology, 51,* 945–946.

Gallagher, D., Thompson, L. W., & Levy, S. M. (1980). Clinical psychological assessment of older adults. In L. Poon (Ed.), *Aging in the 1980's: Psychological issues.* Washington, DC: American Psychological Association.

Gatz, M., & Hurwicz, M. L. (1990). Are old people more depressed? Cross-sectional data on Center for Epidemiological Studies Depression scale factors. *Psychology and Aging, 5,* 284–290.

Golden, C. J., Hammeke, T. A., & Purisch, A. D. (1980). *The Luria-Nebraska Neuropsychological Battery Manual.* Los Angeles: Western Psychological Services.

Grant, E. A., Storandt, M., & Botwinick, J. (1978). Incentive and practice in the psychomotor performance of the elderly. *Journal of Gerontology, 33*, 413–415.

Gurian, B. S., & Miner, J. H. (1991). Clinical presentation of anxiety in the elderly. In C. Salzman & B. D. Lebowitz (Eds.), *Anxiety in the elderly: Treatment and research* (pp. 31–44). New York: Springer.

Gurland, B. J., Copeland, J., Sharpe, L, & Kelleher, M. (1976). The Geriatric Mental Status Interview (GMS). *International Journal of Aging and Human Development, 7*, 303–311.

Gurland, B. J., Golden, R., Teresi, J., & Challop, J. (1984). The SHORT-CARE: An efficient instrument for the assessment of depression, dementia and disability. *Journal of Gerontology, 39*, 166–169.

Gurland, B. J., Kuriansky, J., Sharpe, L., Simon, R., Stiller, P., & Birkett, P. (1977–78). CARE: Rationale, development, and reliability. *International Journal of Aging and Human Development, 8*, 9–42.

Gurland, B. J., & Meyers, B. S. (1988). Geriatric psychiatry. In J. A. Talbott, R. E. Hales, & S. C. Yudofsky (Eds.), *Textbook of psychiatry* (pp. 1117–1139). Washington, DC: American Psychiatric Press.

Hachinski, V. C., Iliff, L. D., Phil, M., Zihka, E., Du Boulay, G. H., McAllister, V. L., Marshall, J., Russell, R. W., & Symon, L. (1975). Cerebral blood flow in dementia. *Archives of Neurology, 32*, 632–637.

Hale, W. D., Cochran, C. D., & Hedgepeth, B. E. (1984). Norms for the elderly on the Brief Symptom Inventory. *Journal of Consulting and Clinical Psychology, 52*, 321–322.

Hamilton, M. (1959). The assessment of anxiety states by rating. *British Journal of Medical Psychology, 32*, 50–55.

Hamilton, M. (1960). A rating scale for depression. *Journal of Neurology, Neurosurgery, and Psychiatry, 23*, 56–61.

Heaton, R. K., Grant, I., & Matthews, C. G. (1986). Differences in neuropsychological test performance associated with age, education, and sex. In I. Grant & K. M. Adams (Eds.), *Neuropsychological assessment of neuropsychiatric disorders* (pp. 100–120). New York: Oxford University Press.

Hersen, M., & Van Hasselt, V. B. (1992). Behavioral assessment and treatment of anxiety in the elderly. *Clinical Psychology Review, 12*, 619–640.

Hertzog, C., Van Alstine, J., Usala, P. D., Hultsch, D. F., & Dixon, R. (1990). Measurement properties of the Center for Epidemiological Studies Depression Scale (CES-D) in older populations. *Psychological Assessment, 2*, 64–72.

Himmelfarb, S., & Murrell, S. A. (1984). The prevalence and correlates of anxiety symptoms in older adults. *Journal of Psychology, 116*, 159–167.

Hochanadel, G., & Kaplan, E. (1984). Neuropsychology of normal aging. In M. L. Albert (Ed.), *Clinical neurology of aging*, (pp. 231–244). New York: Oxford University Press.

Hyer, L., & Blount, J. (1984). Concurrent and discriminant validities of the geriatric depression scale with older psychiatric inpatients. *Psychological Reports, 54*, 611–616.

Ivnik, R. J., Smith, G. E., Tangalos, E. G., Petersen, R. C., Kokmen, E., & Kurland, L. T. (1991). Wechsler Memory Scale: IQ-dependent norms for persons ages 65 to 97. *Psychological Assessment: A Journal of Consulting and Clinical Psychology, 3*, 156–161.

Johnson, L. C., & Chernik, D. A. (1982). Sedative-hypnotics and human performance. *Psychopharmacology, 76*, 101–113.

Kaszniak, A. W. (1986). The neuropsychology of dementia. In I. Grant & K. M. Adams (Eds.), *Neuropsychological assessment of neuropsychiatric disorders* (pp. 171–220). New York: Oxford University Press.

Kemp, B. J., & Mitchell, J. M. (1992). Functional assessment in geriatric mental health. In J. E. Birren, R. B. Sloane & G. D. Cohen (Eds.) *Handbook of mental health and aging* (2nd ed., pp. 672–697). San Diego: Academic Press.

Klisz, S. (1978). Neuropsychological evaluation in older persons. In M. Storandt, I. Siegler, & M. R. Elias (Eds.), *The clinical psychology of aging* (pp. 71–96). New York: Plenum Press.

Koenig, H. G., & Blazer, D. (1992). Mood disorders and suicide. In J. E. Birren, R. B. Sloane, & G. D. Cohen (Eds.), *Handbook of mental health and aging* (2nd ed., pp. 379–407). New York: Academic Press.

La Rue, A. (1986, Fall). Neuropsychological assessment of older adults. *The Clinical Psychologist*, 96–98.

La Rue, A., Yang, J., & Osato, S. (1992). Neuropsychological assessment. In J. E. Birren, R. B. Sloane, & G. D. Cohen (Eds.), *Handbook of mental health and aging* (pp. 643–670). San Diego, CA: Academic Press.

Lawton, M. P. (1982). The well-being and mental health of the aged. In T. Field, A. Stein, H. Quay,

L. Troll, & G. E. Finley (Eds.), *Review of human development* (pp. 614–628). New York: Wiley.

Lawton, M. P. (1986). Functional assessment. In L. Teri & P. M. Lewinsohn (Eds.), *Geropsychological assessment and treatment* (pp. 39–84). New York: Springer.

Lawton, M. P., & Storandt, M. (1984). Clinical and functional approaches to the assessment of older people. In P. McReynolds & G. J. Chelune (Eds.), *Advances in psychological assessment* (Vol. 6, pp. 236–276). San Francisco: Jossey-Bass.

Lebowitz, B. D., & Niederehe, G. (1992). Concepts and issues in mental health and aging. In J. E. Birren, R. B. Sloane, & G. D. Cohen (Eds.), *Handbook of mental health and aging* (2nd ed., pp. 3–26). New York: Academic Press.

Levy, S. M. (1981). The psychosocial assessment of the chronically ill geriatric patient. In C. K. Prokop & L. A. Bradley (Eds.), *Medical psychology: Contributions to behavioral medicine* (pp. 119–137). New York: Academic Press.

Lezak, M. D. (1983). *Neuropsychological Assessment* (2nd ed.). New York: Oxford University Press.

Lubin, B. (1967). *Depression adjective checklists* (Manual). San Diego: EDITS.

Marsden, C. D. (1976). Cerebral atrophy. *Lancet, 2,* 10/9.

Mattis, S. (1976). Mental status examination for organic mental syndrome in the elderly patient. In R. Bellack & B. Karasu (Eds.), *Geriatric psychiatry* (pp. 77–121). New York: Grune & Stratton.

McCue, M., Goldstein, G., & Shelly, C. (1989). The application of a short form of the Luria-Nebraska Neuropsychological Battery to discrimination between dementia and depression in the elderly. *International Journal of Clinical Neuropsychology, 11,* 21–29.

Mellinger, G. D., Balter, M. B., & Uhlenhuth, E. H. (1984). Prevalence and correlates of the long-term regular use of anxiolytics. *Journal of the American Medical Association, 251,* 375–379.

Morin, C. M., Kowatch, R. A., Barry, T., & Walton, E. (1993). Cognitive-behavior therapy for late life insomnia. *Journal of Consulting and Clinical Psychology, 61,* 137–146.

Mortimer, J. A., Schuman, L. M., & French, L. R. (1981). Epidemiology of dementing illness. In J. A. Mortimer & L. M. Schuman (Eds.), *The epidemiology of dementia* (pp. 3–23). New York: Oxford University Press.

Mulrow, C. D., Aguilar, C., Endicott, J. E., Velez, R., Tuley, M. R., Charlip, W. S., & Hill, J. A. (1990). Association between hearing impairment and the quality of life of elderly individuals. *Journal of the American Geriatrics Society, 38,* 45–50.

Myers, J. K., Weissman, M. M., Tischler, G. L., Holzer, C. E., Leaf, P. J., Orvaschel, H., Anthony, J. C., Boyd, J. H., Burke, J. D., Kramer, M., & Stolzman, R. (1984). Six-month prevalence of psychiatric disorders in three communities. *Archives of General Psychiatry, 41,* 959–967.

National Institutes of Health. (1981). *The dementias: Hope through research* (NIH Publication No. 81–2252). Washington, DC: U.S. Government Printing Office.

National Institutes of Health. (1991). *Diagnosis and treatment of depression in late life: Consensus development conference statement.* Bethesda, MD: Author

Nesselroade, J. R., Mitteness, L. S., & Thompson, L. K. (1984). Older adulthood: short-term changes in anxiety, fatigue, and other psychological states. *Research on Aging, 6,* 3–23.

Newman, J. P. (1989). Aging and depression. *Psychology and Aging, 4,* 150–165.

Nolan, B. S. (1984). Functional evaluation of the elderly in guardianship proceedings. *Law, Medicine & Health Care, 127,* 210–218.

Norris, J. T., Gallagher, D., Wilson, A., & Winograd, C. H. (1987). Assessment of depression in geriatric medical outpatients: The validity of two screening measures. *Journal of the American Geriatrics Society, 35,* 989–995.

O'Hara, M. W., Hinrichs, J. V., Kohout, F. J., Wallace, R. B., & Lemke, J. H. (1986). Memory complaint and memory performance in the depressed elderly. *Psychology and Aging, 1,* 208–214.

Osgood, N. J. (1992). Suicide in the elderly: Etiology and assessment. *International Review of Psychiatry, 4,* 217–223.

Patterson, R. L. (1988). Anxiety in the elderly. In C. G. Last & M. Hersen (Eds.), *Handbook of anxiety disorders* (pp. 541–551). Elmsford, NY: Pergamon.

Patterson, R. L., O'Sullivan, M. J., & Spielberger, C. D. (1980). Measurement of state and trait anxiety in elderly mental health clients. *Journal of Behavioral Assessment, 2,* 89–97.

Perez, F. I., Stump, D., Gay, J. R., & Hart, V. R. (1976). Intellectual performance in multi-infarct dementia and Alzheimer's disease: A replication study. *Canadian Journal of Neurological Sciences, 3,* 181–187.

Pfeffer, R. I., Kurosaki, T. T., Harrah, C. H., Chance, J. M., Bates, D., Detels, R., Filos, S., & Butzke, C. (1981). A survey diagnostic tool for senile dementia. *American Journal of Epidemiology, 114,* 515–527.

Plutchik, R. (1979). Conceptual and practical issues in the assessment of the elderly. In A. Raskin & L. F. Jarvik (Eds.), *Psychiatric symptoms and cognitive loss in the elderly* (pp. 19–38): *Evaluation and assessment techniques.* Washington, DC: Hemisphere.

Poon, L., Crook, T., Gurland, B. J., Davis, K. L., Kaszniak, A. W., Eisdorfer, C., & Thompson, L. W. (1986). *Handbook for clinical memory assessment of older adults.* Washington, DC: American Psychological Association.

Radloff, L. S. (1977). The Center for Epidemiological Studies Depression Scale: A self-report scale for research in the general population. *Applied Psychological Measurement, 1,* 385–401.

Rankin, E. J., Gfeller, J. D., & Gilner, F. H. (1993). Measuring anxiety states in the elderly using the state-trait anxiety inventory for children. *Journal of Psychiatric Research, 27,* 111–117.

Rapp, S. R., Parisi, S. A., Walsh, D. A., & Wallace, C. E. (1988). Detecting depression in elderly medical inpatients. *Journal of Consulting and Clinical Psychology, 56,* 509–513.

Rapp, S. R., Smith, S. S., & Britt, M. (1990). Identifying comorbid depression in elderly medical patients: Use of the extracted Hamilton Depression Rating Scale. *Psychological Assessment, 2,* 243–247.

Raskin, A. (1979). Signs and symptoms of psychopathology in the elderly. In A. Raskin & L. F. Jarvik (Eds.), *Psychiatric symptoms and cognitive loss in the elderly* (pp. 3–18): *Evaluation and assessment techniques.* Washington, DC: Hemisphere.

Raskin, A., & Jarvik, L. (Eds.) (1979). *Psychiatric symptoms and cognitive loss in the elderly: Evaluation and assessment techniques.* Washington, DC: Hemisphere.

Regier, D. A., Boyd, J. H., Burke, J. D., Rae, D. S., Myers, J. K., Kramer, M., Robins, L. N., George, L. K., Karno, M., & Locke, B. Z. (1988). One-month prevalence of mental disorders in the United States. *Archives of General Psychiatry, 45,* 977–986.

Reisberg, B., Ferris, S. H., & Crook, T. (1982). Signs, symptoms, and course of age-associated cognitive decline. In S. Corkin, K. L. Davis, J. H. Growdon, E. Usdin, & R. L. Wurtman, (Eds.), *Alzheimer's disease: A report of progress* (Aging, Vol. 19, pp. 177–181). New York: Raven Press.

Robins, L. N., Helzer, J. E., Croughan, J., & Ratcliff,

K. S. (1981). National Institute of Mental Health Diagnostic Interview Schedule: Its history, characteristics, and validity. *Archives of General Psychiatry, 38,* 381–389.

Rosen, W. G., Mohs, R. C., & Davis, K. L. (1984). A new rating scale for Alzheimer's disease. *American Journal of Psychiatry, 14,* 1356–1364.

Rosen, W. G., Terry, R. D., Fuld, P. A., Katzman, R., & Peck, A. (1980). Pathological verification of ischemic score in differentiation of dementias. *Annals of Neurology, 7,* 486–488.

Rosoff, A. J., & Gottlieb, G. L. (1987). Preserving personal autonomy for the elderly. *The Journal of Legal Medicine, 8,* 1–47.

Ryan, C., & Butters, N. (1984). Alcohol consumption and premature aging: A critical review. In M. Galanter (Ed.), *Recent developments in alcoholism* (Vol. 2, pp. 223–250). New York: Plenum Press.

Ryan, J. J., & Paolo, A. M. (1990). Standardization of the Wechsler Adult Intelligence Scale—Revised for persons 75 years and older. *Psychological Assessment: A Journal of Consulting and Clinical Psychology, 2,* 404–411.

Salzman, C. (1982). A primer on geriatric psychopharmacology. *American Journal of Psychiatry, 139,* 67–74.

Salzman, C. (1983). Depression and physical cause. In T. Crook & G. D. Cohen (Eds.), *Physicians' guide to the diagnosis and treatment of depression in the elderly* (pp. 9–18). New Canaan, CT: Mark Powley Associates.

Salzman, C., & Shader, R. I. (1979). Clinical evaluation of depression in the elderly. In A. Raskin & L. F. Jarvik (Eds.), *Psychiatric symptoms and cognitive loss in the elderly* (pp. 39–72): *Evaluation and assessment techniques.* Washington, DC: Hemisphere.

Schaie, K. W., & Schaie, J. P. (1977). Clinical assessment and aging. In J. E. Birren and K. W. Schaie (Eds.), *Handbook of the psychology of aging* (pp. 692–723). New York: Van Nostrand Reinhold.

Schaie, K. W., & Willis, S. L. (1986). *Adult development and aging* (2nd ed.). Boston: Little, Brown.

Sheikh, J. I. (1991). Anxiety rating scales for the elderly. In C. Salzman & B. D. Lebowitz (Eds.), *Anxiety in the elderly: Treatment and research* (pp. 251–265). New York: Springer.

Sheikh, J. I. (1992). Anxiety and its disorders in old age. In J. E. Birren, R. B. Sloane, and G. D. Cohen (Eds.), *Handbook of mental health and aging*

(2nd ed., pp. 409–432). New York: Academic Press.

Spielberger, C. D., Gorush, R. L., & Lushene, R. E. (1971). *Manual for the State-Trait Anxiety Inventory*. Palo Alto, CA: Consulting Psychologists Press.

Spitzer, R. L., Williams, J. B., & Gibbon, M. (1987). *Instruction manual for the Structured Interview for the DSM-III-R (SCID-OP)*. New York: Biometrics Research Department, New York Psychiatric Institute.

Steuer, J., Mintz, J., Hammen, C., Hill, M. A., Jarvik, L. F., McCarley, T., Motoike, P., & Rosen, R. (1984). Cognitive-behavioral and psychodynamic group psychotherapy in treatment of geriatric depression. *Journal of Consulting and Clinical Psychology, 52*, 180–189.

Storrie, M., & Doerr, H. O. (1979). Characterization of Alzheimer type dementia utilizing an abbreviated Halstead-Reitan Battery. *Clinical Neuropsychology, 2*, 78–81.

Terry, R. (1982). Brain disease in aging, especially senile dementia. In R. Terry, C. Bolis, & G. Toffano (Eds.), *Neural aging and its implications in human neurological pathology* (Vol. 18, pp. 43–52). New York: Raven Press.

Thompson, L. W., Futterman, A., & Gallagher, D. (1988). Assessment of late-life depression. *Psychopharmacology Bulletin, 24*, 577–586.

Thompson, L. W., Gallagher, D., & Breckenridge, J. S. (1987). Comparative effectiveness of psychotherapies for depressed elders. *Journal of Consulting and Clinical Psychology, 55*, 385–390.

Thompson, L. W., Gong, V., Haskins, E., & Gallagher, D. (1987). Assessment of depression and dementia during the late years. In K. W. Schaie (Ed.), *Annual review of gerontology and geriatrics* (Vol. 7, pp. 295–324). New York: Springer.

Turnbull, J. M. (1989). Anxiety and physical illness in the elderly. *Journal of Clinical Psychiatry, 40*, 40–45.

Wedding, D. (1986). Neurological disorders. In D. Wedding, A. Horton, & J. Webster (Eds.), *The neuropsychology handbook: Behavioral and clinical perspectives* (pp. 59–79). New York: Springer.

Wells, C. E. (1979). Pseudodementia. *American Journal of Psychiatry, 136*, 895–900.

Wells, C. E., & Duncan, G. W. (1980). *Neurology for psychiatrists*. Philadelphia: F. A. Davis.

Whanger, A. D., & Myers, A. C. (1984). *Mental health intervention and therapeutic assessment with older persons*. Rockville, MD: Aspen.

Williams, J. M., Klein, K., Little, M., & Haban, G. (1986). Family observations of everyday cognitive impairment in dementia. *Archives of Clinical Neuropsychology, 1*, 103–109.

Wisocki, P. A. (1988). Worry as a phenomenon relevant to the elderly. *Behavior Therapy, 19*, 369–379.

Yesavage, J. A., Brink, T. I., Rose, T. L., Lum, O., Huang, V., Adey, M., & Leirer, V. O. (1983). Development and validation of a geriatric depression screening scale: A preliminary report. *Journal of Psychiatric Research, 17*, 37–49.

Yesavage, J. A., Rose, T. I., & Spiegel, D. (1984). Relaxation training and memory improvement in elderly normals: Correlation of anxiety ratings and recall improvement. *Experimental Aging Research, 8*, 195–198.

Zung, W. W. K. (1965). A self-rating depression scale. *Archives of General Psychiatry, 12*, 63–70.

Zung, W. W. K. (1971). A rating instrument for anxiety disorders. *Psychomatics, 12*, 371–379.

14
Personality Assessment of Neurologically Impaired Patients

Carlton S. Gass
Jane Ansley

Personality assessment plays a critical role in the evaluation and treatment of neurologically impaired (NI) individuals. Although neuropsychology's main interest has been in cognitive and perceptual-motor abilities, alterations in personality and emotional behavior have long been recognized to be common sequelae of brain damage (Harlow, 1868). In traumatic brain injury, for example, substantial personality change is estimated to occur with an incidence as high as 50 to 70 percent, with the changes commonly lasting well over ten years (Grant & Alves, 1987). Personality assessment data address important areas of competency that are beyond the scope of cognitive testing, including stress-coping efficacy, self-acceptance, personal responsibility, social interest and sensitivity, and the ability to initiate and sustain satisfactory interpersonal relationships. Inasmuch as personality factors (more than cognitive variables) affect psychosocial adjustment and eventual rehabilitative outcome (Fordyce, Roueche, & Prigatano, 1983; Oddy, Humphrey, & Uttley, 1978), assessment data can be a critical component in feedback to the patient and relatives, treatment planning, rehabilitation, and after-care. From a nosological standpoint, disturbances of personality and emotional functioning are fundamental to many of the organically based diagnoses described in the Diagnostic and Statistical Manual (American Psychiatric Association, 1987). In addition, the documentation of specific personality changes and emotional disturbances sometimes contributes to the diagnosis of a number of neuropathologic conditions. In the context of neuropsychological assessment, some personality measures may help identify psychological variables that adversely affect cognitive test performance as well as daily functioning (Gass, 1991a; Heaton & Crowley, 1981).

This chapter reviews some of the major issues and practical considerations involved in assessing the personality and emotional behavior of NI patients. In the first section, we discuss the importance of examinee preparation, specific content areas, estimation of premorbid personality, measurement of personality change, and patient test-taking limitations. This is followed by a review of the practical considerations involved in using each of the major assessment methods with NI patients.

GENERAL ASSESSMENT CONSIDERATIONS

Preparation of the Examinee

As a preliminary matter, many NI patients approach the psychological assessment situation without fully understanding the purpose of the evaluation. More concerned, perhaps, with their physical and cognitive difficulties, they may be inclined to view these evaluative procedures as both unnecessary and intrusive. It is therefore important for the clinician to invest a few moments preparing the examinee by discussing the purpose of the personality evaluation. In most cases, it is sufficient to inform the patient that the clinical information is obtained routinely as an important part of the overall evaluation; such data provides a more complete understanding of how she or he is functioning. Without this preparation, there is a greater risk of noncompliance and/or defensiveness.

Neurologically Relevant Content Areas

The personality changes associated with brain disease vary considerably across individuals, yet there are a number of widely reported affective and behavioral correlates of brain damage that have particular relevance for clinical assessment. These include depression, anxiety, emotional lability, irritability, suspiciousness, and aggression. Behaviors that represent the opposite end of the spectrum also occur, including euphoria, indifference, emotional flatness, naïveté, and placidity (Prigatano, 1987a). Frontal-lobe damage, in particular, has been associated with limited self-reflective insight, poor social awareness, impulsivity, and concreteness (Stuss, Gow, & Hetherington, 1992). Some of these problems are inadequately assessed by available test instruments (Nelson, Satz, Mitrushina, Van Gorp, Cicchetti, Lewis & Van Lancker, 1989; Prigatano, 1987b). This may be one reason why many clinicians rely primarily or exclusively on observation and interview data. One solution has been to develop specialized instruments that address personality content areas linked with specific types of brain pathology, such as epilepsy (Bear & Fedio, 1977; Warner, Dodrill, & Batzel, 1989), Alzheimer's disease (Alexopoulos, Abrams, Young & Shamoian, 1988; Devanand et al., 1992; Sinha et al., 1992), and closed-head injury (Levin et al., 1987). Another approach has been to construct a test that assesses areas of importance in a heterogeneous NI population, including denial and communication difficulties (Nelson et al., 1989). Finally, although it is a matter of debate, many clinicians believe that the Minnesota Multiphasic Personality Inventory (MMPI; Hathaway & McKinley, 1942) or its updated version (MMPI-2; Butcher, Dahlstrom, Graham, Tellegen, & Kaemmer, 1989), when used in conjunction with other clinical data, is ideally suited for assessing the multifaceted aspects of personality and psychopathology in neuropsychological settings.

Another important aspect of personality assessment is its role in differential diagnosis of psychiatric conditions that may mimic neurologic disease. Included here are psychological disturbances characterized by symptoms such as bizarre behavior, memory disturbances, transient amnestic episodes, or sensorimotor abnormality. To address this common referral question, an ideal test includes content areas that assist in the diagnosis of somatoform disorders (e.g., conversion, dissociative, and somatization disorders), as well as conditions that in some persons have a neuropathological substrate, such as bipolar disorder, depression, and schizophrenia. Although personality test findings indicative of psychopathology cannot be used to rule out the presence of brain disease, the results, when examined within the larger context of other clinical information, sometimes provide the best explanation for a patient's symptom presentation.

Estimating Premorbid Personality and Assessing Personality Change

Personality assessment of the NI individual is problematic in that the central substrate for personality and emotion (i.e., the brain) is itself dysfunctional; changes in personality functioning are therefore not unusual. The estimation of premorbid personality characteristics is important for several reasons. First, evidence suggests that premorbid personality traits correlate with features of postinjury emotional behavior and personality (Chatterjee, Strauss, Symth, & Whitehouse, 1992; Rutter, 1981). Premorbid behavior is therefore useful in predicting difficulties during the rehabilitation process. For example, premorbid problems involving substance abuse, aggressive behavior, difficulties with authority figures, noncompliance, and poor motivation all have important implications for rehabilitation and aftercare potential (Prigatano, 1987b). Second, knowledge of premorbid functioning provides a partial basis for estimating potential strengths as well as realistic parameters for behavioral improvement during periods of recovery and rehabilitation from head injury, stroke, and other nonprogressive forms of brain dysfunction. Third, premorbid estimation is important because the degree of personality change has a major impact on the patient's new role within the family as well as the family's ability to make the necessary adaptations (Klonoff & Prigatano, 1987; Lezak, 1978).

Changes in emotional and behavioral functioning are expected with many types of brain dysfunction. This is not surprising when one considers that the physical status of the brain itself is variable following the onset of a neurologic disease process (degenerative condition or tumor) or with the occurrence of a brain insult (e.g., traumatic injury or stroke). Not only do environmental contingencies change as a result of diminished brain function (e.g., activities such as reading lose their reward value), behavioral change in the patient may transform the surrounding environment, effectively reorganizing it and forcing it to adapt to his or her limitations. As a result of bidirectional (person-environment) influences, certain patterns of behavior and emotion may show a gradual shift, and psychologically descriptive information may have time-limited validity (Fordyce et al., 1983; Prigatano, 1987b). For example, someone with a damaged right hemisphere (RHD) may initially display a normal level of social activity,

but this may eventually give way to interpersonal withdrawal and avoidance as others react to the patient's inability to appropriately decipher and respond to their facial, gestural, and prosodic (voice tone) expressions of emotion (Etcoff, 1989).

Interview and observational data obtained from relatives are often essential for estimating premorbid personality and measuring subsequent changes. Behavior rating scales, for example, can be applied retrospectively and endorsed by relatives or peers in order to provide a baseline estimate of an individual's premorbid personality functioning (Nelson et al., 1989). Changes in behavior and emotional functioning often require repeated assessments and necessitate the use of measurement instruments that are reliable yet sensitive to change. Perhaps the most useful test information is provided by instruments that combine measures of stable trait characteristics with measures of more changeable features. For example, the MMPI-2 provides information on fairly stable characteristics related to shyness and social nonconformity (scales Si and Pd, respectively), while assessing more changeable features such as depression and anxiety (scales D and Pt, respectively).

Limitations in Test-Taking Ability

Some NI patients are unable to manage the administrative requirements of self-report and projective tests. Problems that may interfere with valid test administration include fatigue, confusion, diminished attentiveness and concentration, perseveration, aphasia, deficient reading skill, and visuoperceptual deficits. Unfortunately, patients do not always alert the examiner to these difficulties, and they sometimes "complete" tests in an invalid manner. For example, the examinee may not report losing track of the appropriate item numbers on an answer sheet, or may be unaware of hemispatial neglect and complete inattention for one side of visual stimuli (e.g., Rorschach or TAT cards). It is therefore imperative that the clinician consider the patient's perceptual and cognitive limitations and make every effort to circumvent any adverse effects these deficits may have on the testing process. Specific suggestions are presented in the sections concerning self-report and projective techniques. Unfortunately, some patients are too impaired to provide valid test responses, and the clinician must rely solely on information derived from interview, observation, and the behavior ratings made by those most familiar with the patient.

INTERVIEW AND OBSERVATIONAL METHODS

Clinical Interview

The clinical interview often provides a wealth of information regarding personality functioning, both premorbidly and following the onset of brain dysfunction. The interview offers several advantages over other commonly used assessment techniques. First, because it is open-ended, the patient or the patient's relatives can raise particular issues or problems that are not directly addressed by psychological test instruments or rating scales. Highly specific behaviors, in addition to more general behavior patterns, are typically identified. For example, the interview may expose the general problem of social inappropriateness with a number of specific examples, such as frequent interrupting, loudness, cursing, or making sexual remarks. In many cases, functional relationships between behavior and environmental stimuli can be identified and subsequently addressed using a direct behavioral intervention. Second, the interview can often help determine the patient's level of insight by contrasting self-reported information with that obtained concurrently from friends or relatives of the patient (Prigatano, 1992; Prigatano, Pepping, & Klonoff, 1986). This has important implications for patient care, as self-insight and appreciation of the environment are required in order to function effectively in the interpersonal and vocational spheres of life (Lezak, 1987). Finally, interview data assist in clarifying the patient's premorbid personality and behavior style, in addition to

providing information about changes that occurred following the onset of brain pathology.

Causal factors in the patient's current behavior and emotions can sometimes be identified with the help of historical information obtained in the interview. Although numerous and often complex, these factors and their interrelationships have important implications for treatment, rehabilitative planning, and aftercare. Premorbid personality often serves as the context for understanding changes, such as those that appear to represent a psychological reaction to the effects of brain damage. Reactive changes occasionally occur in response to diminished cognitive and sensorimotor abilities, though more important are the forced changes in life-style and reduction in the number and potency of reinforcers in the environment (e.g., losses in the social, vocational, and recreational spheres of life). Altered sexual functioning is another common source of adjustment problems following brain damage (Lezak, 1978). In addition to premorbid personality factors and reactions to losses, psychological trauma is a third factor that is sometimes precipitated by the situational context in which the brain injury occurred, and can be an important source of personality disturbance. For example, a subset of motor-vehicle accident and assault victims who present without any evidence of residual brain lesions or cognitive sequelae exhibit behavioral symptoms of posttraumatic stress disorder and/or hysteria following the injury (Adams & Victor, 1989).

A fourth factor that can be addressed by interview is the quality of the patient's social and emotional support system. In many cases, aberrant behavior appears to emerge out of a context of chronic and negative transactions with family members who, correctly or incorrectly, are perceived as being nonsupportive (Lezak, 1988). Additional considerations include physical alterations of the limbic system or corticolimbic pathways at the structural, neurochemical, or metabolic level, some of which can produce significant changes in behavior and emotion. In addition, cognitive-perceptual impairments resulting from brain dysfunction may predispose individuals to display certain personality characteristics, such as concreteness, behavioral rigidity, limited self-awareness, insensitivity, inappropriateness, diminished empathy, and self-centeredness. The etiology of some of these symptoms can be partially clarified by considering neurodiagnostic findings in conjunction with other data.

Direct Observation

Direct observation may reveal personality characteristics that are less evident on formal testing, including disturbances in affective expression, silliness and immature or "regressed" behavior, egocentricity, diminished sensitivity, lack of empathy, and behavioral signs of impaired social perception and awareness, such as unusual remarks or inappropriate actions. The cognitive testing context provides an opportunity to observe behavior samples that may have some generalizability to daily life settings. For example, the examinee's response to difficult tasks often yields information related to frustration tolerance, stamina, and impulse control. Response to failed performance may reveal evidence of appropriate concern and insight, or denial, apathy, indifference, lack of drive, and limited self-awareness. At the other extreme, patients who are perfectionistic sometimes respond to their own successful performance by making highly self-critical remarks. Dependency issues may be manifested in a constant request for feedback and reassurance during testing. Clues regarding stress-coping style may be present, as the examinee may withdraw from the tasks, rationalize failure, displace anger toward the examiner with aggressive remarks, criticize the tests themselves, become confused and overwhelmed, or suddenly break into tears in a catastrophic display of frustration. Further investigation may determine whether such behaviors are representative of a more general style of responding to stressors in daily living.

Behavior Rating Scales

Observational ratings of a patient's behavior and social competency by others (e.g., family members, friends and loved ones, treatment personnel) provide a systematic source of unique and often very detailed information that may be essential for obtaining a comprehensive understanding of the NI patient (Brooks & McKinlay, 1983; McSweeny, 1990; Nelson et al., 1989). Such information has uses that are similar to those that apply to clinical interview data. First, it provides semiobjective data that complement the phenomenologically based material obtained by means of patient self-report. It can be used to gauge the reporting accuracy and insightfulness of the patient; discrepant information commonly occurs when patients underestimate their own problems and limitations (Prigatano, Altman, & O'Brien, 1990). In some cases, however, the discrepancy between patient report and observer ratings exists because the observers are unaware of the actual subjective state of the patient. This occurs because in NI patients, particularly those with RHD, internal mood is sometimes incongruous with the outward display of affect (Ruckdeschel-Hibbard, Gordon, & Diller, 1986). Viewed in this light, observational ratings can be used to gauge the sensitivity of observers to the subjective emotional experience and mood of the patient.

Behavior ratings provided by family and friends are often used to estimate premorbid functioning and changes that occur postonset. Instruments that have been used in this manner include the Katz Adjustment Scale (KAS; Hogarty & Katz, 1971; Katz & Lyerly, 1963), the Neurobehavioral Rating Scale (NRS; Levin et al., 1987), and, more recently, the Neuropsychology Behavior and Affect Profile (NBAP; Nelson et al., 1989). The KAS is a 127-item descriptive rating form that has been used in many neuropsychological settings to measure changes in psychological status and social functioning following brain impairment (Fordyce et al., 1983; Posthuma & Wild, 1988; Stambrook, Moore, & Peters, 1990). It can be completed by the patient or by an informant and has the advantage of addressing positive as well as negative patterns of behavior. The Neurobehavioral Rating Scale (NRS) is used in many rehabilitation settings to assess behavioral changes following traumatic brain injury. This instrument is a modified version of the Brief Psychiatric Rating Scale (Overall and Gorham, 1962). Ratings are made using a structured interview format at several points in the patient's recovery process. The NRS has also been used to monitor changes in dementia patients (Sultzer, Levin, Mahler, High, & Cummings, 1992). More recently, the NBAP (Nelson et al., 1989) was created specifically to measure pre- to postonset changes in personality and affect in a heterogeneous neurologic population. This is accomplished by having the rater respond twice to each of the 106 items, first in reference to premorbid status and again in reference to the patient's present functioning.

Rating scales can be customized to address problem areas that are particularly common in certain types of brain disorders. For example, blunted affect, emotional withdrawal, distractibility, forgetfulness, conceptual disorganization, diminished self-insight, and disinhibition are common sequelae of closed-head injury, perhaps due to frequent involvement of the prefrontal and anterior temporal areas of the brain. These problem areas are addressed by the NRS (Levin et al., 1987). Some scales assess behavioral correlates of particular problems such as epilepsy (Bear & Fedio, 1977; Warner et al., 1989) and Alzheimer's disease (Alexopoulos, Abrams, Young, & Shamoian, 1988; Devanand et al., 1992; Sinha et al., 1992). The Sickness Impact Profile (SIP) assesses behavioral problems associated with nonspecific illness (Bergner, Bobbit, Carter, & Gilson, 1981), though it is often used with neurologic patients (Grant & Alves, 1987; Temkin, Dikmen, Machamer, & McLean, 1989). In contrast to these measures, the NBAP was specifically designed to be used with a variety of neurologic conditions, measuring five content areas with clear relevance to personality functioning: indifference, mania, depression, behavioral inappropriateness, and communication problems (pragnosia). Although construct validation is needed, the NBAP represents the most systematic effort to date to devise a content-relevant rating scale for use with neurologic patients.

Conclusions

Interview and observational methods provide rich and essential information for assessing personality. For those patients who are too impaired or uninsightful to provide valid psychological test results, these methods may be the sole source of personality assessment data. They offer the advantage of providing information that is idiographic (individualized), highly detailed and specific, and free of the distortions that can result from uninsightful patient self-report. Historical observations made by those who are most familiar with the patient may help in identifying contributing factors in the patient's current behavior and symptomatic presentation. Observation can also assist in treatment by identifying current functional relationships between environmental stimuli and specific behaviors. Behavior rating scales, which have shown increasing popularity, tend to be quick and efficient, requiring little clinician time. Such scales appear to be particularly useful as measures of change, using a repeated administration format. In addition, they can provide an empirical estimate of premorbid personality functioning that may be useful in identifying patient strengths, potential problem areas, and realistic parameters for functional improvement. Finally, ratings by family members and others who know the patient reflect their own perceptions of the patient, the patient's problems, and the degree of progress (or decline) in functioning. Highly unfavorable ratings are likely to be accompanied by significant family problems and should alert the clinician to the possibility that the family needs therapeutic assistance.

These methods also have a number of limitations. Interview data provide limited and unreliable information for making generalizations about personality traits (Nunnally, 1978). Although observers can be trained to form accurate personality judgments (Funder & Sneed, 1993), in clinical settings, family members or friends are not always thorough or objective; in some cases, they apply a halo effect retroactively in describing the premorbid status of the patient. The apparent need to convey a favorable image often leads to selective disclosure of historical information and a benign omission of problem areas. Nor are clinicians completely objective; they rely on an even more limited sample of behavior than do relatives, and at times they selectively attend to certain types of behaviors while neglecting others. In addition, clinical observations are usually made in rather artificial settings; inferences regarding personality characteristics may have limited applicability to many relevant daily life situations. Finally, observers show individual differences in leniency—the tendency to characterize people in a positive or negative manner—introducing another source of bias in personality description (Nunnally, 1978). Problems of selective bias, overgeneralization, and misinterpretation are common pitfalls of observational approaches (Cronbach, 1970).

Behavior rating scales typically have an appearance of face validity, but they usually lack supportive reliability and validity data to ensure that they are, in fact, measuring the personality constructs they are purported to measure. The clinician must not be lulled into assuming that a rating inventory provides comprehensive or multidimensional coverage of anything meaningful when the constructs that it purports to measure (e.g., "depressive mood," "anxiety," and "emotional withdrawal") are represented in toto by single-item scales. Furthermore, distortional response styles are as much a concern with observer ratings as they are in using self-ratings. Scales could be improved by including validity indicators that detect distortional response tendencies (e.g., leniency). Retrospective ratings of premorbid functioning, in particular, may tend to be overly optimistic. To minimize this bias, the clinician is advised to obtain such ratings from relatives as early as possible postonset (Grant & Alves, 1992). Some bias may be fostered by the procedure of having relatives make simultaneous ratings of pre- and postmorbid behaviors. This method may produce an implicit demand to embellish differences resulting from the neurologic impairment. Further research is needed to address these issues.

In addition to validity concerns, behavior rating scales typically provide rather limited (albeit useful) information concerning personality functioning and lack the comprehensive scope of the multidimensional self-report inventories. Even those scales that show promise in accurately measuring problem areas of special relevance to NI samples do not assess the wide variety of psychological disturbances that occur in neurologic samples. Nor do they address the broader range of psychopathologic variables that are germane to differential diagnosis (e.g., somatoform disorders, schizophrenia). Finally, none of the observational methods assess the phenomenological perspective or inner subjective experience of the patient. This limitation is particularly important with NI patients because many show a disparity between outward affect and internal subjective state. For example, problems such as aspontaneity, abulia, and emotional lability are commonly mistaken for depression, whereas bland affect is often misinterpreted by observers as emotional indifference and apathy. In most cases, such aspects of personality are more effectively measured by obtaining information directly from the patient.

SELF-REPORT INSTRUMENTS

Self-report measures continue to be the most widely used type of instrument for assessing personality and psychopathology in neurologic patients. Among these are the MMPI-2, the Beck Depression Inventory (Beck, Ward, Mendelsohn, Mock, & Erbaugh, 1961), the Millon Clinical Multiaxial Inventory-II (MCMI-II; Millon, 1987), and the Symptom Checklist 90—Revised (Derogatis, 1977). Many of the widely used self-report instruments have established validity and offer several advantages over other methods of assessment. They typically require only a limited amount of clinician time for test administration. Scoring and interpretation are often performed by a computer, which is an additional source of time savings for the clinician. Compared with other assessment methods, some of these instruments (e.g., MMPI-2, MCMI-II) provide a more comprehensive overview of problem areas and are therefore especially useful in addressing a wide range of diagnostic and treatment issues. Finally, because much of the information derived from self-report measures represents direct communication from the examinee, test results and their implications for patient care are more easily discussed with the patient and his or her family (Butcher, 1990; Gass & Brown, 1992).

Administrative Considerations

Although problems such as fatigue, poor concentration, and deficient reading skill are very common in NI patients, these difficulties can be identified and in many cases addressed in a manner that enables patients to provide valid self-report information. As a general guideline, the patient should be monitored to ensure that the test instructions are being followed. When a patient's ability to follow instructions is initially in question, the examiner should check this by having the patient read and answer the first several test items aloud, with the patient recording each response on the answer sheet. Periodic rechecking and breaks may be required, particularly if there are signs of fatigue and lapses in concentration. Probably the most common limiting factor in the use of self-inventories involves visual and/or reading difficulties. As a general rule, an audiotaped format, if available, is the preferred method of test administration with impaired patients (Butcher & Williams, 1992).[1] The clinician may also need to determine whether an enlarged or redesigned answer sheet format is required for patients who have visuomotor or fine motor deficits.

Interpretive Considerations

The most common criticism of self-report instruments as applied to neurologic patients is that patients' cognitive and perceptual deficits too often preclude them from completing such tests in a valid manner. This is particularly true in settings in which many of the patients are confused, lethargic, or have moderately severe cognitive impairment. Regardless of the setting, clinicians who do use self-inventories can be more confident in their interpretations if their instruments include a measure of response consistency, which can be used to rule out semirandom, careless, or "confused" responding.

A second objection to using self-report measures is that neurologic patients often lack the capacity to provide an accurate self-assessment (Nelson et al., 1989; Prigatano, 1987b). This objection, like the first one, would appear to apply more specifically to more severely impaired (e.g., demented) individuals. However, it has sometimes been assumed that even many of the less impaired individuals with RHD are unable to provide an accurate self-report because of limited awareness of their condition (Gainotti, 1989). This is the exception rather than the rule, since it appears that most RHD individuals exhibit generally good awareness for a variety of deficits (Ranseen, Campbell, & Blonder, 1993). Although it is true that in some cases RHD patients are unaware of their deficits (anosognosia), indifferent toward them (anosodiaphoria), or lack a normal outward expression of emotionality (aprosodia), there is little evidence to suggest that they are incapable of providing an accurate account of their personality functioning and emotional condition. Indeed, a considerable body of empirical literature exists indicating that RHD patients as a group describe themselves as at least as distressed, if not more so, than individuals with left hemisphere damage (LHD) (Gass & Lawhorn, 1992; Gass & Russell, 1986; Johnson & Hartlage, 1993; Lishman, 1968). RHD patients who are labeled indifferent by observers often report considerable distress and unhappiness (Ross & Rush, 1981; Ruckdeschel-Hibbard et al., 1986). In these cases, the self-report instrument has the advantage of "seeing through" the appearance of indifference and identifying the subjective experience of the patient.

The interpretation of self-report instruments is often problematic because of item-content transparency and the examinee's ability either to feign, exaggerate, minimize, or deny problems that exist. The tendency toward denial, which can have both a psychogenic and an organic etiology, is commonly observed in closed-head injury, epilepsy, and perhaps to a lesser extent, in other types of brain pathology. Many self-inventories, therefore, underestimate psychological disturbance in a significant number of NI patients. For this reason, instruments that incorporate a measure of test-taking attitude, such as the MMPI-2 or MCMI-II, offer an important advantage. Furthermore, validity scales themselves have important behavioral correlates that are relevant to compromised brain functioning. The MMPI-2 Lie scale, for example, has direct relevance for assessing self-reflective insight, social awareness, and flexibility of coping behavior. Individuals with elevated scores on the Lie scale often overestimate their abilities, make unrealistic plans for themselves, and resist corrective feedback from their environment.

The appropriateness of using traditional self-report measures with neurologic samples has sometimes been questioned on the grounds that none of these instruments were designed using brain-damaged individuals as the normative base (Cripe, 1989; Lezak, 1983; Nelson et al., 1989). However, in view of the relatively high incidence of psychological disturbance in neurologic patients, one would expect that the use of such norms, if they were available, would tend to underestimate (or "normalize") problems that exist in this population. Problems such as depression, irritability, dependency, or poor impulse control, for example, would be judged as less severe solely because they exist with greater frequency in the NI population. It is questionable, therefore, whether test norms specific to this population are necessary or even desirable.

A related issue concerns item content on self-report measures that may have an idiosyncratic meaning for individuals with organic brain dysfunction. Specifically, items that could potentially represent bona fide cognitive and sensorimotor symptoms of brain dysfunction (e.g., paralysis, weakness, fatigue, unusual or diminished sensation, distractibility, forgetfulness) are often included in measures that are intended to assess symptoms of psychopathology. To the degree that such items exist, interpretive caution is warranted. Clinicians commonly attempt to resolve this interpretive difficulty by performing mental adjustments, lowering scores on test scales that are thought to be artificially elevated by valid medical complaints. The accuracy of this approach hinges on the clinician's awareness of (1) the neurologically related item content on each scale; (2) the frequency with which the patient endorsed those items; and (3) the impact of that endorsement on the score obtained for each scale. These are empirical issues; the guesswork involved in an impressionistic approach is unlikely to yield accurate conclusions.

The question of item-content bias applies to many psychiatric instruments used in medical settings, including the Beck Depression Inventory (Levin, Llabre, & Weiner, 1988), and the MMPI and MMPI-2 (Alfano, Finlayson, Stearns, & Neilson, 1990; Bornstein & Kozora, 1990; Cripe, 1989; Gass & Russell, 1991; Meyerink, Reitan, & Selz, 1988). On the MMPI-2, scales Hs, D, Hy, Pt, and Sc are the most commonly elevated scales in neurologic samples, and all contain a number of items of a cognitive, physical, or sensorimotor nature. As an alternative to the practice of making mental adjustments, a systematic method of profile correction has recently appeared in the literature. This involves rescoring the MMPI (or MMPI-2) after eliminating key items that may represent neurologic symptoms. Alfano, Finlayson, Stearns, & Neilson (1990) proposed forty-four items that experts had identified as "potentially tapping valid symptoms or manifestations of neurologic disease or dysfunction." Concerned with the potential problem of "over-correction," Gass (1991b) used discriminative and factor analytic procedures to identify sixteen MMPI-2 items that have a strong statistical relationship with closed-head injury and reflect face valid neurologic-symptom content. These empirical procedures were subsequently used to extract a twenty-one-item correction factor for use with patients who have cerebrovascular disease (Gass, 1992).[2] Although some item overlap exists on these two factors, differences in composition suggest that no single correction index is appropriate for application across the spectrum of brain pathologies.

Conclusions

Self-report measures are a mainstay in the assessment of personality and psychological disturbance. In contrast with other methods of assessment, many self-report instruments have a substantial amount of psychometric and research support. Furthermore, measures such as the MMPI-2 offer the kind of comprehensive description of personality functioning that is often necessary for addressing diagnostic and patient care issues. The major drawbacks of using self-report measures occur in the subset of patients who are either too impaired to manage the testing requirements (e.g., reading) or who lack the requisite insight for accurate self-description. In many cases, the clinician can alter the administrative format to suit the particular needs of the handicapped patient. The problem of impaired self-insight, which compromises the validity of self-report, reinforces the need for other sources of assessment data. In addition, it underscores the value of including measures of test-taking attitude that themselves might eventually turn out to be useful predictors of insightfulness and related personality characteristics. Although it is questionable whether personality tests should have special norms based on neurologic samples, the presence of neurologically sensitive item content needs to be considered when using any self-report instrument to measure aspects of personality or psychological disturbance in NI patients.

PROJECTIVE TECHNIQUES

Projective techniques are commonly used with NI individuals, though there is surprisingly little literature addressing their application with this population. The limited literature that does exist tends to focus exclusively on response characteristics that discriminate brain-damaged from neurologically intact individuals. The major example of this is the identification of "organic signs" in Rorschach responses (see Goldfried, Stricker, & Weiner, 1971, for a review). More recently, with the availability of better procedures for detecting brain dysfunction, this particular application of personality tests is rarely considered except as a matter of historical interest. Unfortunately, the more general application, i.e., for clinically descriptive purposes, has received very limited attention with respect to neurologic samples. In view of the fact that neuropsychologists sometimes use the Rorschach, Thematic Apperception Test (TAT), or a Sentence Completion Test to assist in personality assessment, the paucity of research relating these measures to the extratest behavior of NI subjects is unfortunate and somewhat surprising.

The Rorschach Inkblot Technique

Techniques of Rorschach assessment vary significantly across existing Systems, with some emphasizing the blot's value as a stimulus to fantasy and others as a stimulus to perceptual-cognitive operations that are representative of those involved in processing analogous situations in daily life (Erdberg, 1990). The latter approach, which is embraced by the Comprehensive System (CS: Exner, 1978, 1986), appears to be ideally suited for assessing the manner in which personality functioning is affected by and interacts with cognitive and perceptual impairments. The structural aspect of the CS is made up of empirically sound elements that were included on the basis of demonstrated reliability and validity. These elements constitute a variety of areas of basic importance to understanding personality, including preferred style and efficacy of stress-coping, tendency to function logically and objectively versus being influenced by emotional factors, extent and quality of personal self-focus, quality of reality testing, efficacy in perceptually organizing complex stimulus situations, and responsiveness to affective experiences in daily life.

The Rorschach may be particularly advantageous with NI persons who have diminished verbal skills and are largely inaccessible using methods that rely more heavily on verbal processing and reasoning. It may be especially useful with individuals who are nondisclosive and defensive on self-report. Perhaps the major contribution of the Rorschach is its potential for bridging the perceptual-cognitive aspect of human functioning with other aspects of personality and behavior. It assists in describing the manner in which NI persons structure and organize their world, given the limitations of their perceptual and cognitive functioning. The structuring process behind blot responses includes visual scanning, encoding, labeling, rank-ordering potential responses, censoring, discarding, and selecting (Exner, 1989). Inasmuch as all of these processes are to some degree involved in the way people structure their experiences in daily life, unique and important information can be gleaned from the Rorschach. Although a significant amount of the clinician's time is required for its use, the amount of information gained may be well worth the investment.

Two closely related validity issues should be considered in using the Rorschach with NI patients. First, content interpretation, in particular, may be problematic as applied to persons with visuoperceptual deficits. It would be inappropriate to equate responses that reflect frank distortion of the blot caused by perceptual impairment with material that has direct projective and psychological significance. Neurologically intact perceptual processes must be assumed, for the most part, before projective material is interpreted (Exner, 1989). Second, although a large body of validity studies link Rorschach structural variables with extratest behavior in neurologically intact individuals, it is unclear whether in some cases the presence of organically based cognitive deficits vitiates this linkage. For example, the patient's verbal output is sometimes affected by speech comprehension deficits, expressive language problems including word substitutions and paraphasias, and impaired immediate and retentive (recent) memory. Just as caution should be applied to content-symbolic interpretation, so, too, clinicians should not automatically assume that the structural process of the examinee, which is ultimately analyzed on the basis of verbal output, carries the usual psychological implications when that process has been disrupted by neuropathologic factors.

Other Projective Instruments

The Thematic Apperception Test (TAT; Murray, 1938) uses story telling as a medium for assessing a broad range of personality attributes, including psychological needs or concerns, internal conflicts, and other problem areas. Transient states also influence TAT responses (Cronbach, 1970). As is the case with the Rorschach, the task yields the clearest data when the examinee has fairly intact visuoperceptual processes and is relatively effective with verbal communication. Unfortunately, NI patients tend to use fewer words, communicate fewer ideas, show fewer consistent themes, and adopt an approach that is overly simplistic and descriptive rather than creative (Lezak, 1983). To the extent that there is frontal lobe compromise, they are more apt to show problems of initiation (requiring prompting), lose the instructional set (requiring redirection), and produce material that is fragmented and disorganized. As a result, more time and effort are required of the examiner and the richness of the projective material is often compromised. Nevertheless, important themes are sometimes communicated, particularly by higher-functioning patients, and observed areas of neurobehavioral deficiency (e.g., perseveration, confusion, concreteness, ideational impoverishment) can be appropriately viewed as reflecting personality. Similarly, there is some evidence that as applied to NI individuals, the TAT may be particularly sensitive to problems related to dependency, social isolation, and poor impulse control (Bellak, 1986).

Sentence completion tests, having a semistructured format, can provide detailed information related to personality functioning, including the quality of adjustment to disability, effectiveness in coping with loss, and self-concept. Because of the relative simplicity of this task, many neurologic patients can complete it sufficiently to provide useful data. However, as a last resort, the examiner can read the items and record the responses for those patients who are unable to read and/or write. Figure drawings, which are often used to assess visuospatial and graphomotor skill, may also constitute a medium through which patients express certain aspects of personality or psychological conflict. However, in view of the association between drawing characteristics and intellectual factors—as well as their general sensitivity to brain dysfunction—the clinician must exercise extreme caution in using detailed aspects of drawing to make inferences regarding personality and psychological functioning.

CONCLUSIONS

Projective methods are commonly used with NI patients, particularly those in whom self-report data are of limited value. The Rorschach (CS), which is conceptualized primarily as a perceptual-cognitive problem-solving task, is the most widely used and perhaps most promising projective technique for assessing personality in this patient population. It uniquely addresses the manner in which perceptual and cognitive operations reflect broader aspects of personality functioning. To some degree, neurobehavioral impairments that show up on these tests can be legitimately viewed as personality attributes (e.g., concrete versus abstract, disinhibited versus self-controlled). In fact, the most common problems that emerge across projective tasks have implications for personality functioning, including response constriction and rigidity, stimulus-boundedness, structure-seeking, fragmentation, simplification, conceptual confusion, spatial disorientation, confabulation, and hesitancy and doubt (Lezak, 1983). Although these may be included as aspects of personality, their delineation may not require the use of projectives; such information can often be derived from a combination of neuropsychological test findings and observational data.

Projectives are not without disadvantages. Techniques involving the Rorschach and the TAT require a significant amount of the clinician's time. In many cases, brain dysfunction is associated with responses that are limited in quantity and qualitatively impoverished to the point of providing limited descriptive information. Furthermore, their assessment validity with NI persons has received inadequate attention. Although classes of responses to relatively unstructured stimuli correlate with personality variables in neurologically intact samples, it remains to be seen whether such responses, when directly affected by impaired brain functioning, still maintain their correlations with extratest behavior or more broadly defined traits. As a conservative measure, one may consider response patterns to have a greater probability of assessment validity to the extent that they stand apart from or are unrelated to areas of brain-related deficit. For example, unusual responses to visual stimuli are in general more likely to reflect a form of severe personality disturbance in individuals who have structurally intact visuoperceptual processes. Distortions, omissions, and extraneous detail on projective figure drawings are to be expected even in psychologically normal persons who have nondominant hemisphere impairment. Finally, unusual verbal output is more likely to be correlated with serious psychological disturbance when speech and language skills are intact. In general, all of these tests are likely to provide the clearest and most useful information when applied to individuals who have a milder degree of impairment.

SUMMARY

The role of psychological assessment in understanding and treating NI patients necessitates a thorough consideration of personality and emotional factors, as well as other aspects of neurobehavioral functioning. Although cognitive factors are important, personality variables have a major role in determining the patient's adaptation to brain injury and its effects, and more generally, the patient's quality of life. With many NI patients, the assessment of personality can be performed effectively using traditional test instruments and observational methods to assess specific problem areas. Clearly, constructive steps are now being taken in addressing the need for new techniques and instruments that are specifically tailored for the more severely impaired patient population (e.g., Nelson et al., 1989).

This chapter reviewed some of the unique challenges that confront clinicians who are involved in assessing the personality of persons with neurologic impairment. Some of these challenges vary across clinical settings; setting-specific priorities may partially influence the selection of a particular approach. For example, monitoring personality change is often a priority in acute head-injury settings, and for this purpose behavior ratings are commonly used. In contrast, for the task of differential diagnosis, which is often a priority in psychiatric settings, clinicians typically rely more heavily on self-report measures and projective techniques. Regardless of clinical setting, when one considers the sheer variation in the severity and types of problems presented by NI individuals, it is immediately apparent that no single technique, instrument, or method of assessment is optimally suited for all neurologic patients. Each method has its own distinct set of advantages and limitations, determined in part by the particular needs and circumstances of the patient. In conclusion, the clinician may be most effective using a pragmatic and flexible approach that accomplishes the assessment task using the optimal combination of instruments and procedures suitable for each patient. In this manner, the clinician can gain a better understanding of the patient and provide more helpful information to assist in clinical care.

NOTES

1. Exceptions to this are self-report measures that consist of items that require greater cognitive processing than is the case with dichotomous true-false items. Aurally presented items in which the examinee must select one option from among several or more alternatives, for example, usually require relatively intact immediate working memory. Another exception to the effective use of an audiotaped format occurs in patients who are severely impaired or have a receptive aphasia. An audiocassette version of the MMPI-2 is available through University of Minnesota Press.

2. Alfano, Paniak, and Finlayson (1993) have recently employed similar empirical procedures to devise a new MMPI corrective approach (thirteen items) specifically for closed-head-injury patients.

REFERENCES

Adams, R. D., & Victor, M. (1989). *Principles of neurology* (4th ed.). New York: McGraw-Hill.

Alexopoulos, G. S., Abrams, R. C., Young, R. C., & Shamoian, C. A. (1988). Cornell Scale for Depression in Dementia. *Biological Psychiatry, 23,* 271–284.

Alfano, D. P., Finlayson, A. J., Stearns, G. M., & Neilson, P. M. (1990). The MMPI and neurobehavioral dysfunction: Profile configuration and analysis. *Clinical Neuropsychology, 4,* 69–79.

Alfano, D. P., Paniak, C. E., & Finlayson, A. J. (1993). The MMPI and closed head injury: A neurocorrective approach. *Neuropsychiatry, Neuropsychology, and Behavioral Neurology, 6,* 111–116.

American Psychiatric Association (1987). *Diagnostic and statistical manual of mental disorders* (3rd ed.—revised) (DSM-III-R). Washington, DC: American Psychiatric Association.

Bear, D. M., & Fedio, P. (1977). Quantitative analysis of interictal behavior in temporal lobe epilepsy. *Archives of Neurology, 34,* 454–467.

Beck, A. T., Ward, C., Mendelsohn, M., Mock, J., & Erbaugh, J. (1961). An inventory for measuring depression. *Archives of General Psychiatry, 4,* 561–571.

Bellak, J. (1986). *The T.A.T., C.A.T., and S.A.T. in clinical use* (4th ed.). Orlando, FL: Grune & Stratton.

Bergner, M., Bobbit, R. A., Carter, W. B., & Gilson, B. S. (1981). The Sickness Impact Profile: Development and final revision of a health status measure. *Medical Care, 14,* 57–67.

Bornstein, R. A., & Kozora, E. (1990). Content bias of the MMPI Sc scale in neurological patients. *Neuropsychiatry, Neuropsychology, and Behavioral Neurology, 3,* 200–205.

Brooks, D. N., & McKinlay, W. (1983). Personality and behavioral change after severe blunt head injury—a relative's view. *Journal of Neurology, Neurosurgery, and Psychiatry, 46,* 336–344.

Butcher, J. N. (1990). *The MMPI-2 in psychological treatment.* New York: Oxford University Press.

Butcher, J. N., Dahlstrom, W. G., Graham, J. R., Tellegen, A., & Kaemmer, B. (1989). *MMPI-2 (Minnesota Multiphasic Personality Inventory-2): Manual for administration and scoring.* Minneapolis: University of Minnesota Press.

Butcher, J. N., & Williams, C. L. (1992). *Essentials of MMPI-2 and MMPI-A interpretation.* Minneapolis: University of Minnesota Press.

Chatterjee, A., Strauss, M. E., Smyth, K. A., & Whitehouse, P. J. (1992). Personality changes in Alzheimer's disease. *Archives of Neurology, 49*, 486–491.

Cripe, L. I. (1989). Neuropsychological and psychosocial assessment of the brain-injured patient: Clinical concepts and guidelines. *Rehabilitation Psychology, 34*, 93–100.

Cronbach, L. J. (1970). *Essentials of psychological testing* (3rd edition). New York: Harper & Row.

Derogatis, L. R. (1977). *SCL-R administration, scoring, and procedures manual.* Baltimore, MD: Clinical Psychometrics Research Unit, Johns Hopkins University School of Medicine.

Devanand, D. P., Miller, L., Richards, M., Marder, K. Bell, K., Mayuex, R., & Stern, Y. (1992). The Columbia University Scale for Psychopathology in Alzheimer's Disease. *Archives of Neurology, 49*, 371–376.

Erdberg, P. (1990). Rorschach assessment. In G. Goldstein & M. Hersen (Eds.), *Handbook of psychological assessment* (2nd ed., pp. 387–402). New York: Pergamon Press.

Etcoff, N. L. (1989). Asymmetries in recognition of emotion. In F. Boller & J. Grafman (Eds.), *Handbook of neuropsychology* (Vol. 3, pp. 363–383). New York: Elsevier.

Exner, J. E. (1978). *The Rorschach: A comprehensive system: Volume 2. Current research and advanced interpretation.* New York: Wiley.

Exner, J. E. (1986). *The Rorschach: A comprehensive system: Volume 1. Basic foundations* (2nd ed.). New York: Wiley.

Exner, J. E. (1989). Searching for projection in the Rorschach. *Journal of Personality Assessment, 53*, 520–536.

Fordyce, D. J., Roueche, J. R., & Prigatano, G. P. (1983). Enhanced emotional reactions in chronic head trauma patients. *Journal of Neurology, Neurosurgery, and Psychiatry, 46*, 620–624.

Funder, D. C., & Sneed, C. D. (1993). Behavioral manifestations of personality: An ecological approach to judgmental accuracy. *Journal of Personality and Social Psychology, 64*, 479–490.

Gainotti, G. (1989). Disorders of emotional and affect in patients with unilateral brain damage. In F. Boller & J. Grafman (Eds.), *Handbook of Neuropsychology* (Vol. 3, pp. 345–361). New York: Elsevier.

Gass, C. S. (1991a). Emotional variables in neuropsychological test performance. *Journal of Clinical Psychology, 47*, 100–104.

Gass, C. S. (1991b). MMPI-2 interpretation and closed-head injury: A correction factor. *Psychological Assessment, 3*, 27–31.

Gass, C. S. (1992). MMPI-2 interpretation of patients with cerebrovascular disease: A correction factor. *Archives of Clinical Neuropsychology, 7*, 17–27.

Gass, C. S., & Brown, M. C. (1992). Neuropsychological test feedback to patients with brain dysfunction. *Psychological Assessment, 4*, 272–277.

Gass, C. S., & Lawhorn, L. (1991). Psychological adjustment following stroke: An MMPI study. *Psychological Assessment, 3*, 628–633.

Gass, C. S., & Russell, E. W. (1986). MMPI correlates of lateralized cerebral lesions and aphasic deficits. *Journal of Consulting & Clinical Psychology, 54*, 359–363.

Gass, C. S., & Russell, E. W. (1991). MMPI profiles of closed-head-trauma patients: Impact of neurologic complaints. *Journal of Clinical Psychology, 47*, 253–260.

Goldfried, M. R., Stricker, G., & Weiner, I. B. (1971). *Rorschach handbook of clinical and research applications.* Englewood Cliffs, NJ: Prentice-Hall.

Grant, I., & Alves, W. (1987). Psychiatric and psychosocial disturbances in head injury. In H. S. Levin, J. Grafman, & H. M. Eisenberg (Eds.), *Neurobehavioral recovery from head injury* (pp. 232–261). New York: Oxford University Press.

Harlow, J. M. (1868). Recovery after severe injury to the head. *Publication of the Massachusetts Medical Society, 2*, 327–346.

Hathaway, S. R., & McKinley, J. C. (1942). *The Minnesota Multiphasic Personality Schedule.* Minneapolis: University of Minnesota Press.

Heaton, R. K., & Crowley, T. J. (1981). Effects of psychiatric disorders and their somatic treatments on neuropsychological test results. In S. B. Filskov & T. J. Boll (Eds.), *Handbook of clinical neuropsychology* (pp. 481–525). New York: Wiley.

Hogarty, G. E., & Katz, M. M. (1971). Norms of adjustment and social behavior. *Archives of General Psychiatry, 25*, 470–480.

Johnson, D. J., & Hartlage, L. C. (1993). Behavioral sequelae of unilateral cerebral vascular accidents. *Archives of Clinical Neuropsychology, 8*, 237.

Katz, M. M., & Lyerly, S. B. (1963). Methods of measuring adjustment and behavior in the community: I. Rationale, description, discriminative validity, and scale development. *Psychological Reports, 13*, 503–535.

Klonoff, P., & Prigatano, G. P. (1987). Reactions of family members and clinical intervention after traumatic brain injury. In M. Ylvisaker & E. Gobble (Eds.), *Community reentry for head-injured adults* (pp. 381–402). Boston: College Hill Press.

Levin, B. E., Llabre, M. M., & Weiner, W. J. (1988). Parkinson's disease and depression: Psychometric properties of the Beck Depression Inventory. *Journal of Neurology, Neurosurgery, and Psychiatry, 51,* 1401–1404.

Levin, H. S., High, W. M., Goethe, K. E., Sisson, R. A., Overall, J. E., Rhoades, H. M., Eisenberg, H. M., Kalisky, Z., & Gary, H. E. (1987). The Neurobehavioral Rating Scale: Assessment of the behavioral sequelae of head injury by the clinician. *Journal of Neurology, Neurosurgery, and Psychiatry, 50,* 183–193.

Lezak, M. D. (1978). Living with the characterologically altered brain injured patient. *Journal of Clinical Psychiatry, 39,* 592–598.

Lezak, M. D. (1983). *Neuropsychological assessment* (2nd ed.). New York: Oxford University Press.

Lezak, M. D. (1987). Assessment for rehabilitation planning. In M. Meier, A. Benton, & L. Diller (Eds.), *Neuropsychological rehabilitation* (pp. 41–58). New York: Plenum Press.

Lezak, M. D. (1988). Brain damage is a family affair. *Journal of Clinical and Experimental Neuropsychology, 10,* 111–123.

Lishman, W. A. (1968). Brain damage in relation to psychiatric disability after head injury. *British Journal of Psychiatry, 114,* 373–410.

McSweeny, A. J. (1990). Quality-of-life assessment in neuropsychology. In D. E. Tupper & K. D. Cicerone (Eds.), *The neuropsychology of everyday life: Assessment and basic competencies* (pp. 185–218). Boston: Kluwer.

Meyerink, L. H., Reitan, R. M., & Selz, M. (1988). The validity of the MMPI with multiple sclerosis. *Journal of Clinical Psychology, 44,* 764–769.

Millon, T. (1987). *Millon Clinical Multiaxial Inventory-II* (2nd ed.). Minneapolis, MN: National Computer Systems.

Murray, H. A. (1938). *Explorations in personality.* New York: Oxford University Press.

Nelson, L. D., Satz, P., Mitrushina, M., Van Gorp, W., Cicchetti, D., Lewis, R., & Van Lancker, D. (1989). Development and validation of the Neuropsychology Behavior and Affect Profile. *Psychological Assessment, 1,* 266–272.

Nunnally, J. C. (1978). *Psychometric theory* (2nd ed.). New York: McGraw-Hill.

Oddy, M., Humphrey, M., & Uttley, D. (1978). Stresses upon the relatives of head-injured patients. *British Journal of Psychiatry, 133,* 507–513.

Overall, J. E., & Gorham, D. R. (1962). The brief psychiatric rating scale. *Psychological Reports, 10,* 799–812.

Posthuma, A., & Wild, U. (1988). Use of neuropsychological testing in mild traumatic head injuries. *Cognitive Rehabilitation, 6,* 22–24.

Prigatano, G. P. (1987a). Personality and psychosocial consequences after brain injury. In M. Meier, A. Benton, & L. Diller (Eds.), *Neuropsychological rehabilitation* (pp. 355–378). New York: Plenum Press.

Prigatano, G. P. (1987b). Psychiatric aspects of head injury: Problem areas and suggested guidelines for research. In H. S. Levin, J. Grafman, & H. M. Eisenberg (Eds.), *Neurobehavioral recovery from head injury* (pp. 215–231). New York: Oxford University Press.

Prigatano, G. P. (1992). Personality disturbances associated with traumatic brain injury. *Journal of Consulting and Clinical Psychology, 60,* 360–368.

Prigatano, G. P., Altman, I. M., & O'Brien, K. P. (1990). Behavioral limitations that traumatic-brain-injured patients tend to underestimate. *The Clinical Neuropsychologist, 4,* 163–176.

Prigatano, G. P., Pepping, M., & Klonoff, P. (1986). Cognitive, personality, and psychosocial factors in the neuropsychological assessment of brain-injured patients. In B. P. Uzzell & Y. Gross (Eds.), *Clinical neuropsychology of intervention* (pp. 135–166). Boston: Martinus Nijhoff.

Ranseen, J. D., Campbell, D., & Blonder, L. X. (1993). Awareness of deficit in chronic unilateral stroke. *Archives of Clinical Neuropsychology, 8,* 260–261.

Ross, E. D., & Rush, A. J. (1981). Diagnosis and neuroanatomic correlates of depression in brain-damaged patients. *Archives of General Psychiatry, 38,* 1344–1354.

Ruckdeschel-Hibbard, M., Gordon, W. A., & Diller, L. (1986). Affective disturbances associated with brain damage. In S. B. Filskov & T. J. Boll (Eds.), *Handbook of clinical neuropsychology* (Vol. 2, pp. 305–337). New York: Wiley Interscience.

Rutter, M. (1981). Psychological sequelae of brain damage in children. *American Journal of Psychiatry, 138,* 12, 1533–1544.

Sinha, D., Zemlan, F. P., Nelson, S., Bienenfeld, D., Thienhaus, O., Ramaswamy, G., & Hamilton, S. (1992). A new scale for assessing behavioral agitation in dementia. *Psychiatry Research, 41,* 73–88.

Stambrook, M., Moore, A. D., & Peters, L. C. (1990). Social behavior and adjustment to moderate and severe traumatic brain injury: Comparison to normative and psychiatric samples. *Cognitive Rehabilitation*, 8, 26–30.

Stuss, D. T., Gow, C. A., & Hetherington, C. R. (1992). "No longer Gage": Frontal lobe dysfunction and emotional changes. *Journal of Consulting & Clinical Psychology*, 60, 349–359.

Sultzer, D. L., Levin, H. S., Mahler, M. E., High, W. M., & Cummings, J. L. (1992). Assessment of cognitive, psychiatric, and behavioral disturbances in patients with dementia: The Neurobehavioral Rating Scale. *Journal of the American Geriatrics Society*, 40, 549–555.

Temkin, N. R., Dikmen, S., Machamer, J., & McLean, A. (1989). General versus disease-specific measures: Further work on the Sickness Impact Profile for head injury. *Medical Care*, 27, Supplement, 44–53.

Warner, M. H., Dodrill, C. B., & Batzel, L. W. (1989). Economical screening for emotional disturbance in epilepsy: Anticipating MMPI profile elevations by means of the Washington Psychosocial Seizure Inventory. *Journal of Epilepsy*, 2, 83–89.

III
THE MEANING OF PERSONALITY TEST RESULTS

15
Standards and Standardization

Kurt F. Geisinger
Janet F. Carlson

We would like to begin this chapter with a fictionalized court case that draws heavily upon reality—as experienced by many psychometricians and others concerned with assessment. The case is that of *Jenna C.* v. *Unified School District.*

JENNA C. V. UNIFIED SCHOOL DISTRICT

It was a blustery day outside, but the temperature in the courtroom was at least 78 degrees. The various parties were nervously adjusting their seated positions and looking around the courtroom as though trying to memorize the scene. The court clerk called, "All rise; this court is now in session." A formal-looking judge entered the room and was seated. Her hair was a variety of shades of gray and tied sternly in a bun at the back of her head. Papers were shuffled. The judge fixed her stare on the attorney for the prosecution, who rose. "We call Dr. Glaubenweiss to the stand." The short, but distinguished-looking psychologist rose slowly, leaning heavily on his cane. He wore a gray tweed jacket, and gray flannel slacks. He began a slow trek to the front of the courtroom. The man reached the witness stand and turned slowly and stiffly.

As he took the oath, his heavy German accent was evident. He settled into the witness chair and in response to questions from the attorney began tracing his background—his education among masters in Vienna and Zurich, his many years of practice in New York, awards that he had received from various educational and civic groups, and the popular books that he had written on raising children with learning disabilities. He grunted and scowled in response to a query that *Newsweek* and other popular publications had referred to him as "the Benjamin Spock of the learning disabled." The questioning attorney asked the court to qualify the witness as an expert. The judge shifted her line of vision toward the opposing attorney, who began to rise. This second attorney was silent for a moment after he stood, then he stated slowly, "The people are not convinced that Dr. Glaubenweiss meets current standards as an expert in this area." He paused momentarily, but before he was able to continue, the first attorney retorted, "Your Honor, he has already been qualified as an expert in this district and six other federal districts as well as in Canada and several European countries. He has given invited talks at the annual meetings of the American Bar Association on the legal nature of learning disabilities; if he is not an expert, who is?"

The judge shrugged slightly, frowned momentarily, and stated, "The court recognizes him as an expert. Objections to and limitations on that qualification can be discussed in cross-examination."

The first attorney returned to his questioning. "Are you familiar with a student in the Unified School District who is being referred to in these proceedings as Jenna C.?"

"I am," Dr. Glaubenweiss responded.

"Did you make an appraisal of her educational status at the request of her parents and her counsel?"

"I did." Dr. Glaubenweiss took off his thick glasses as he responded and peered at them as if they troubled him.

"So Dr. Glaubenweiss, please tell the court what measures you used to assess Jenna C."

Dr. Glaubenweiss began reciting his procedures as he began to clean his glasses against his sweater vest. "I first met with Jenna C. along with her parents. Her parents told me that Jenna had not been performing as well as school officials thought that she should. They told me that they had tried both working with her themselves and tutoring, but that nothing worked. Then I met with Jenna on several occasions. During the first meeting, I conducted an interview with her to determine what activities she enjoyed and to establish rapport. On the second and third visits, I administered, of course," he paused for effect and then returned to his description, "I administered the Glaubenweiss Test of Learning Disabilities and the Glaubenweiss Survey of Instructional Deficits. Administration of these measures was quite straightforward and the results, as usual, were quite informative . . . definitive, really."

"And what were those results, Doctor?"

"That Jenna C. is experiencing significant learning disabilities of unknown origin and that her school district needs to provide additional instruction, one-on-one. They have been unwilling to do so, quite unwilling, and she is being harmed each and every day that they refuse. Indeed, the results show that she is learning disabled."

The attorney confirmed, "So your opinion is that she is learning disabled."

"Indeed correct," was the response.

"And how certain are you of your diagnosis, Doctor?"

"Oh. Quite certain, quite certain. I have never used the Glaubenweiss instruments and been incorrect. No, never. It's a certainty." After he finished speaking, he made a quiet "Humph" sound to no one in particular, as if he had been surprised by such a naive question.

"And you're scientifically convinced of the remediation that is needed?" the attorney asked.

"Ja, yes, quite certain. I detailed what is needed in my report. You have that, no? You want me to discuss my report?"

"No, Doctor, we have already entered your report as evidence; that is not necessary. Thank you, Doctor, thank you." The attorney looked at the judge and said, "That concludes our direct testimony then, your Honor, but we reserve the right to redirect after cross."

The judge stated, "So noted," and shifted her gaze to the defense attorney, who rose slowly, still intently reviewing a thick, dog-eared legal-sized pad of notes and questions. "Doctor, you have never published an article in a refereed journal, now have you?"

"A journal? No, not a journal. It's the wrong place to reach the people. The wrong place."

"And you've never engaged in empirical research, is that correct?"

"Wrong," he retorted, "I have indeed. I do research all the time, all the time. Silly question, silly."

"Let me rephrase my question, then, Doctor. You have never validated either your Glaubenweiss Test of Learning Disabilities or the Glaubenweiss Survey of Instructional Deficits, is that not correct?"

"No need to validate. They are valid measures. I know it."

"But there's a difference, isn't there, Doctor,

between validation and validity? Isn't it true that you believe that your measures are valid, but you have not validated them?"

"Ja. Validation is the process of proving that a measure is valid. These measures are valid, however, so there's no need to perform a validation study."

"Have there been any published studies by others documenting that your measures are valid, Doctor?"

"Not that I know of. Since only I use my measures, that would be difficult, no?"

"Have you developed norms for your measures, Doctor, norms against which to evaluate the meaning of scores?"

"No, there are no norms, but I know what scores mean."

The defense attorney managed to roll his eyes at the judge while informing the judge that he had completed his cross-examination. The prosecuting attorney had no additional questions and the judge called a recess in the trial.

A day later the prosecution rested and the defense, representing the Unified School District, began its case. Their first witness was Dr. Al Bookman. He was tall and lean and appeared only about twenty-five years old. His hair was blond and tidily cut. As he walked to the stand, his posture was athletic. He was wearing an expensive Italian suit, with a pin representing the American Psychological Association's Centennial Celebration on the lapel of his jacket.

As with Dr. Glaubenweiss, the initial questions to the defense witness concerned his background. He described his education at one of the large midwestern state universities; his seminal dissertation under the nationally prominent psychologist, Dr. Jack Baker, author of the Tennessee Three-factor Personality Indicator or TTPI; his brief ten-year record at the local state university, where he had quickly been tenured and promoted to the rank of professor; his two books entitled *Statistics in School Psychology* and *Measurement in School Psychology: Theoretical Perspectives*; his several dozen publications in academic journals; and his service on the consulting boards of several journals in the field. He taught courses at the state university in testing, statistics, and school psychology.

Once during the questioning, he was asked his age and responded forty-three. So young did he look that several people in the audience gasped and exchanged murmurs. The judge pounded her gavel but looked surprised herself. He was quickly recognized as an expert without reservation. Then the questioning related to his opinions and his basis for these opinions began.

"Dr. Bookman, have you reviewed the reports prepared by Dr. Glaubenweiss regarding Jenna C.?"

"Yes, I have."

"And, Professor, do you have an opinion about these reports?"

"Yes, I do." Unlike Glaubenweiss, whose voice rose and fell as he spoke, Bookman's voice was a monotone, without any discernable modulation.

"Please tell the court what your expert opinion is regarding Dr. Glaubenweiss's assessment of Jenna C."

"It is totally without foundation. The instruments that he used to make his assessments have never been validated and therefore are not useful in any manner. It is unacceptable for psychologists to make such baseless and utterly preposterous diagnoses. The numbers that his instruments yield are virtually random numbers."

"And, do you have problems with the manner in which Dr. Glaubenweiss administered his own tests, Professor Bookman?"

"Yes, indeed I do. In his deposition prior to the trial, Dr. Glaubenweiss stated that he administered the test differently to different children. In psychological testing, we work with standardized tests. Standardization means that tests are always administered under constant and precisely articulated conditions. Only then can the scores that emerge from them be meaningful. Standardization of test administration procedures is accomplished by the test developer. Before a test is published and used by other professionals, the test developer must make the test administration procedures uniform so that all administrators will give the test the same way. These test administration procedures are carefully described in the test manual. All psychologists know that one gives a test strictly in accordance with the procedures provided in the test manual. Dr. Glaubenweiss generated two instruments but he failed to develop constant methods for administering them. That is an unacceptable practice and would render the scores meaningless even if the measures were valid, which they are not."

The lawyer queried, "You don't like these tests much, do you, Professor Bookman?"

"I would not use the word, like. These instruments fail to meet the most minimal standards for use in a professional setting as provided in the *Standards for Educational and Psychological Testing* published by the American Educational Research Association, American Psychological Association, and the National Council for Measurement in Education in 1985."

"Let's move on to a different topic, Professor Bookman. Are you familiar with the assessment of learning disabilities?"

"I certainly hope so. That area has been the primary field of my research."

"Can you define for the court what is meant by learning disabilities?" The lawyer nodded toward the judge.

The witness turned toward the judge and said, "The consensus among experts in the field is that learning disabilities are diagnosed when discrepancies emerge between what one expects a child to learn in school and what that child actually learns. When a child is consistently below the level expected of him or her, and no other condition such as visual, hearing, or motor handicaps, mental retardation, emotional disturbance, or environmental, cultural, or economic disadvantage is present, then the diagnosis of learning disability is made. So we must first rule out explanations such as visual, hearing, or motor handicaps, mental retardation, emotional disturbance, or environmental, cultural, or economic disadvantage. These we do through various psychometrically sound measures and through interviews with parents and teachers, observations of the children, and interviews with the children themselves. Then we look for the most common learning disabilities: perceptual handicaps, brain injuries, dyslexia, and developmental aphasia. Many psychologists

have had good success with a variety of psychometrically sound measures. The Kaufman Assessment Battery for Children, the Stanford-Binet Fourth Edition, and the Third Edition of the Wechsler Intelligence Scale for Children are all appropriate. The reason that I prefer using the formulas that I calculated for identifying and assessing the extent of learning disabilities is that they recognize the underlying regression model that must be involved in assessing learning disabilities. In my research, I have established a multiple regression formula—essentially the formula for a straight line—that permits us to evaluate whether a child's academic performance is within the normal levels expected for a child based on his or her tested intellectual ability. When a child is no more than two standard errors of estimate below the predicted achievement level—using the regression formula—then he or she is not learning disabled."

Bookman, who had been looking at the judge as he spoke, paused and looked at his attorney, who had been trying to get his attention while rolling his eyes perceptively. Dr. Bookman became still.

The lawyer asked, "So it is a discrepancy between expected performance and actual performance that indicates a learning disability; is that correct, Doctor?"

"Yes. There are some exceptions, as in the case with children with other disabilities. But, in general, yes."

"And psychologists estimate expected performance with the use of tests such as intelligence tests, is that correct, Professor?"

"Yes, it is."

"And having tested Jenna C., do you believe that she is learning disabled?"

"No, I do not."

"And on what basis do you make this judgment?" the lawyer asked.

"Her tested achievement is within the range expected given her level of tested intelligence. Perhaps her achievement level is slightly below that which I might have expected, but not by much, and she is certainly not in the learning-disabled range. Therefore, she is not learning disabled."

"And you stake your professional reputation on it?"

"I do."

"Your honor, the defense rests."

The defense attorney sat down and the attorney for Jenna C. rose. "Dr. Bookman, you are a professor, is that correct?"

"Yes."

"And do you have a private practice, Professor?"

"No."

"And isn't it also true that you do not practice at all? That is, that you do not see any patients therapeutically?

"No, I supervise graduate students at the university clinic. These graduate students see clients, who are ultimately my clients, because I am the licensed psychologist who supervises these students and their clinical work," Bookman responded.

"But your graduate students actually meet with these patients, isn't that correct?"

"Yes, it is."

"And you do not see these patients yourself, isn't that also correct?"

"It's generally correct, although I listen to tapes of their therapy sessions and sometimes I have the occasion to meet some of these clients."

"How many assessments of learning disabilities have you made in your career, Professor Bookman?"

"Oh, I do not know. Dozens."

"Now, Professor let's see if I understand your assertion. You have been working in the field of psychology for over fifteen years and you consider yourself an expert in the assessment of learning disabilities, but you believe that you have made only a few dozen assessments?"

"That's not a fair statement. I am an expert because I have conducted research on assessments and have identified the ways in which we can make assessments of learning disabilities most effectively."

"Isn't it true, Professor, that you would not know a learning-disabled student if you saw one?" As the defense attorney rose, calling out, "Your Honor," the questioning attorney stated, "Withdrawn."

The attorney for Jenna C. asked again, "Professor, you stated that the standardization of tests is critical, did you not?"

"Yes," came the reply.

"And you stated that you disapproved of the fact that Dr. Glaubenweiss did not administer his instruments to Jenna C. in the same manner that he would to all other children, isn't that correct?"

"Yes, indeed." Bookman had a proud look about him, as if he believed that he had either stumped or actually educated the attorney for Jenna C.

"And you, who have assessed dozens of children, believe that Dr. Glaubenweiss should test every child the same way?" The attorney looked at Bookman quizzically.

"Yes, I do, with the possible exception of age differences. Of course, the administration of many tests differs depending on how old the child is when he or she is examined."

"So, age is the only variable that would lead you to administer a test differently, is that correct, Doctor?

"Yes, I believe so," affirmed Dr. Bookman.

"Well then, Professor, what about handicapped children, would you test them differently?"

"Yes . . . well, maybe, depending upon the nature of their disability."

"So now, Professor, you are saying that you would test children differently depending upon their age and upon whether or not they have a disability. All the others would be tested the same, is that now correct, Professor?"

"I don't think that your summarization is fair. All children would receive the same test. Just the administration would change. And of course if you administered the test in a manner which differed from the procedures provided in the test manual, you would have to 'flag' the score to show that the test administration was not performed in the prescribed manner. It's called a 'nonstandard score.'"

"But, Professor, you still appear to be saying that you would administer a test in the same manner to all children, but that you might administer it differently if a child were of a different age or had a disability. Is that now correct?"

"I guess that I could accept that, yes."

"Okay, Professor, let me try a different question. How would you test a young Hispanic child?"

The professor was silent for a few seconds, then, with one eyebrow beginning to twitch up and down somewhat nervously, in a quiet voice he asked, "Does he or she speak English?"

"Does it matter, Professor?"

"Well, yes. You see, Hispanics who speak English are included in the norm group of most major tests in relation to their proportion in the population. Therefore, one can use the standard tests with those Hispanics who speak English."

"What about those Hispanics who do not speak any English, could you use the same test with them, Professor?"

"No, but I could make a referral to a Spanish-speaking psychologist who would be able to test the child using a test in Spanish. That would be the proper procedure." Bookman sat up straight and smiled wanly as though he hoped that others would see him as confident in his response.

"And what about a Hispanic child who has lived in this country for several years. His English is not perfect, but neither is his Spanish. What would you do then, Professor?"

"First, I would give the child a test of language dominance — a test that assesses language skills in both languages. Alternatively, I could give tests of language proficiency in both English and Spanish. In either case, first I would make a determination of whether the child should be tested in English or Spanish. Depending on that answer, I would either test him in English myself or refer him to a Spanish psychologist."

"So, Professor, you are saying that you now believe that you would test all children alike, except if they differed by age, by having a disability of some sort, or if they did not speak English very well. Is that now a complete and correct list?"

Bookman stared downward toward the front wall of the witness box. His voice was soft now and somewhat wavering. "Yes, I believe that is correct. But you have to remember, the vast majority of children are normal. They can be tested using standardized tests without a problem."

The questioning attorney looked at Bookman gleefully. "But why would you need to test a normal child?" he exclaimed to a flustered Dr. Bookman. "That will be all," he informed the court.

The judge looked sad and as though she had eaten something too spicy for lunch and it had not agreed with her.

How would you decide the case of Jenna C.? What factors would you consider in your opinion? Many cases, especially cases of individual diagnosis, present real testing dilemmas. We can either test individuals using the procedures developed and refined carefully that were employed during the test's standardization or we can adapt testing procedures to meet the apparent needs of individual test takers.

Through Dr. Glaubenweiss's testimony, the foregoing case illustrates the importance of maintaining test standards in as uniform a manner as possible. And — courtesy of Dr. Bookman — it also highlights some of the problems inherent in retaining strict standards of test administration and scoring, problems that are especially apparent when one tests those who differ from the majority of the test-taking population. The litigious atmosphere surrounding cognitive assessment has been recognized for many years and has produced a rich legal history. It should be noted, however, that these same illustrative principles apply in the case of clinical personality assessment, family functioning, vocational assessment, or any form of assessment that depends on making score comparisons in order to evaluate an individual's standing. Projective techniques, too, may make some of the same sorts of comparisons, as scorers consider such things as whether or not a particular Rorschach percept constitutes a popular response and whether the response makes use of "common" or "rare" details of the blot.

Intelligence measures and personality measures certainly are not unrelated. In particular, individually administered measures of cognitive ability have a notable impact on the assessment of personality. This is partly because a test administrator spends a fair amount of time with a test taker and cannot help observing important characteristics of his or her functioning. Historically, clinical interpretations of intelligence test scores have been attempted (e.g., Glasser & Zimmerman, 1967; Zimmerman & Woo-Sam, 1973) although validation evidence for doing so is generally lacking. More recently, Kaufman (1979) has developed an elegant system for integrating psychometric data and qualitative observations to improve the clinical use of intelligence tests, a system that is described in his book entitled *Intelligent Testing with the WISC-R*. Thus, we believe that the history of legal challenges involving largely cognitive/ability testing has a direct bearing on standards and standardization of measures used to assess personality.

Consider the dilemma about adherence to standards versus adapting test administration to the needs of individuals by focusing on two of the examples provided in *Jenna C. v. Unified School District*: the assessment of minority, especially non-English-speaking, test takers and of those with disabilities. Before taking up these issues, however, we need to consider the relationship between test standardization and test administration procedures.

TEST STANDARDIZATION AND TEST ADMINISTRATION

"The standardization of a test is the establishment of uniform procedures for the (1) administration and (2) scoring of that instrument. . . . Without standardization, measurement is only an informal process that varies from one examiner to another" (Geisinger, 1984, p. 414). The *Standards for Educational and Psychological Testing* (American Educational Research Association et al., 1985) reveal that test administration procedures are controlled primarily through detailed instructions in test manuals. Standard 3.21 states, for example, that in test manuals "the directions for test administration should be presented with sufficient clarity and emphasis so that it is possible to approximate for others the administrative conditions under which the norms and the data on reliability and

validity were obtained" (American Educational Research Association et al., 1985, p. 29).

Test authors must develop manuals for their tests that clearly describe the administrative procedures that were followed when the norming, reliability, and validation data were collected as well as how the tests should be scored. In short, all information regarding both normal and atypical administration procedures must be provided in the test manual. Test administrators are expected under normal conditions to follow the standardized procedures carefully as described in the manual. Test norms—by which the meaning of individual test scores can be interpreted in conjunction with reliability and validity information—are developed by administering a test under standardized conditions to a large and representative group of test takers (Geisinger, 1984).

Some of the test standards appear on their face to conflict with one another regarding the modification of the procedures of test administration. For example, Standard 15.1 states that

> in typical applications, test administrators should follow carefully the standardized procedures for administration and scoring specified by the test publisher. Specifications regarding instructions to test takers, time limits, the form of item presentation or response, and test materials or equipment should be strictly observed. Exceptions should be made only on the basis of carefully considered professional judgment, primarily in clinical applications. (p. 83)

Standard 6.10 (American Educational Research Association et al., 1985) places limits on who can make these exceptions; it states that

> in educational, clinical, and counseling applications, test administrators and users should not attempt to evaluate test takers whose special characteristics—ages, handicapping conditions, or linguistic, generational, or cultural backgrounds—are outside the range of their academic training and supervised experience. A test user faced with a request to evaluate a test taker whose special characteristics are not within his or her range of professional experience should seek consultation regarding test selection, necessary modifications of testing procedures,

and score interpretation from a professional who has had relevant experience. (p. 43)

THE TESTING OF MINORITIES

The Larry P. case is a well-known trial that led to the banning of the use of intelligence tests for the placement of African-American students into classes for the educable mentally retarded or EMR in California (*Larry P.* v. *Wilson Riles*, 1972). It has been argued (e.g., Elliott, 1987; Lambert, 1981) that the amount of evidence provided at the trial was rather meager. Yet the evidence was sufficient to bring about a ban on the use of intelligence tests throughout the state of California. From across that state, five African-American children were chosen as individuals most likely to have been misplaced into EMR classes and were then retested by representatives of the Bay Area Association of Black Psychologists on behalf of the plaintiffs. These five children had been tested frequently in their years in the educational system. Four different psychologists tested these five children; three psychologists tested one child each and one tested two of them. Two of these psychologists testified in court about their test administrations. They believed that they needed to modify the test administration procedures. One psychologist stated, "If the purpose of psychological testing is to tap psychological function and if by asking a child a question different than the way it is posed in the manual affords me to tap that function, then that appears to be much more important to me than to be somewhat compulsive and concretistic in mentioning every word that is listed in the manual" (RT 1003; also cited in Elliott, 1987, p. 33). The second psychologist went a step further in openly criticizing psychologists who followed the standardized administration procedures for their "strict, almost pathological adherence to the manual" (RT 3102; also cited in Elliott, 1987, p. 33).

Some of the variations in test administration and scoring may help elucidate the nature of these adaptations. They accepted answers as correct that were not listed as such in the manual; they waived time limits; they rephrased questions; they went past discontinuation limits; and they even wrote new questions that were substituted for those actually on the test. One child responded to how scissors and a copper pan are alike with "they are both iron," which was accepted as correct. When one psychologist asked one of the children why criminals should be locked up, the psychologist also defined what criminals are so that the child could provide an answer. As a final example, when one of the children was asked "How are a yard and a pound alike?" the psychologist credited the following answer, "A yard has leaves, and a dog pound has dirt" (RT 3102; also cited in Elliott, 1987, p. 33).

On the one hand, adaptations of the uniform administration procedures may provide useful information about a test taker to a clinician working with that individual. On the other hand, it is also clear that violations of the standardization procedures to this extent make the scores that result from this test administration rather meaningless. Except with inexperienced or untrained test administrators, it is probable that departures from standardized testing procedures seldom follow from a willful disregard for test publishers' recommendations regarding test administration. Rather, failure to adhere strictly to these guidelines may result from what has been termed clinical intuition—a euphemism for common sense based on experience. For example, if a test giver realizes that a test taker has misunderstood instructions even after the standard set of directions has been provided, he or she is likely to intervene rather than to end up with an invalid set of responses. Similarly, when an invalid MMPI or MMPI-2 profile is obtained, test takers are sometimes retested with modified instructions, such as to respond quickly without thinking the statement over at length or to be less literal in interpreting statements. Test givers who stretch the limits of standard procedures in these ways probably believe that they are retaining a considerable measure of standardization—considerable enough that interpretations based on the test results are valid. The problem is that in attempting to ameliorate one source of invalidity, they have probably introduced another.

It is important to realize that departing from standardized testing procedures is not an all-or-nothing phenomenon. Essentially the question that confronts us is how much is too much movement away from the established standards of test administration. It is likely that at the time a test is standardized, some minor variations in the administration procedures occur naturally. Thus, when the test is given later, departures from standard procedures that go beyond the magnitude of those that have occurred during the test standardization process make scores less meaningful. Similarly, when the administration of a test differs from that used in its validation, the information carried by a specific score is, at least in part, lost.

Wherever one positions oneself on the continuum of adherence to standardized test procedures there are important ramifications. On one extreme of the continuum are zealots who believe that departures from standardized procedures are not permissible under any circumstances. Dr. Bookman's position appears to be fairly close to this extreme. Individuals at this end of the spectrum may question the probity of procedural modifications as well as test interpretations that take into account educational, cultural, linguistic, sociologic, or physical factors. They might advocate computer-generated reports, such as those available for objective tests of personality, despite the mixed evidence of validity and the sometimes contradictory content of these reports. Many experts suggest that computer-based interpretation "should always be used as only one element in the assessment process and especially not as a substitute for informed professional judgment" (Moreland, 1985, p. 230). In a similar vein, the American Psychological Association's guidelines for the use of computer-based tests and interpretations cast the reports generated as amounting to consultation from one professional to another. Thus the human professional receiving the report is the final gatekeeper of information so generated and bears the responsibility of evaluating the report and integrating its content with other information about the individual case (American Psychological Association, 1986; Butcher, 1987).

On the other end of the continuum are those who agree with Dr. Glaubenweiss and who have an abiding faith in the powers of clinical intuition. They would support Glaubenweiss's statements that he does not administer tests in the same manner to every test taker and that he knows what the scores mean without benefit of norms or validation research.

THE TESTING OF INDIVIDUALS WITH DISABILITIES

It is clear that disabilities of various types affect and in many cases hinder performance on tests of all types. These differences are clearest when we consider cognitive tests. Someone unable to move his or her hands and arms will have difficulty on nearly all of the performance-based subtests of the major tests of cognitive ability, such as the Stanford-Binet, Kaufman, and Wechsler series. A disability, of course, may affect performance in many ways in addition to the inability to actually perform the task in question. A disability affects the experiences that shape and in part determine an individual's life experience, which in turn influences both an individual's cognitive and personality development in myriad ways. Performance on personality tests, too, is affected by disabilities. Those with visual disabilities would have difficulty with many projective measures both directly (in their inability to view the stimuli themselves) and indirectly (in their differential and reduced history of dealing with visual stimuli). More generally, persons with disabilities may be more susceptible to fatigue than persons without disabilities. Certainly, visual, physical, and emotional handicaps might negatively affect one's tolerance for completing lengthy personality inventories, such as the MMPI-2.

Most large standardized testing programs have modifications of typical test administration procedures for those with disabilities. In fact, under the Americans with Disabilities Act (Equal Employment Opportunity Commission, 1991), tests and testing programs are required to make reasonable accommodations for test takers with disabilities. The testing literature has tended to address four types of disability: visual impairment, hearing impairment, learning disability, and physical handicap (Willingham, 1988). In addition, others can also be listed: emotional disturbance, mental retardation, neurological impairment, autism, speech disorders, and so on. Most paper-and-pencil cognitive testing programs, for example, offer a variety of modifications for different disabilities, depending on the particular needs of the disabled test taker. For any of these groups, tests may be administered with normal time limits, extended time limits, or in an untimed fashion. For example, tests administered to persons with visual impairments may present the regular test, a large-type version of the test, a Braille version, or the test may be provided on an audio cassette or with a reader. Time limits may be strictly applied, relaxed somewhat, or waived entirely. Test scores earned under any of the atypical test administrations are generally "flagged" or marked so that someone viewing the score immediately knows that the score was earned under conditions of a nonstandard test administration. There is extraordinarily little research in most testing programs to help a user of test scores to know how comparable the meaning of nonstandard scores is to those earned under standard conditions. The research needed to provide proper interpretability includes collection of normative data on the different test administration modifications, reliability data and validation studies of various types, as well as studies of how these test data are actually used by professionals in the field.

For the first time, the most recent edition of the test standards (American Educational Research Association et al., 1985) devotes a chapter to the testing of those with disabilities. Standard 14.4 states that "interpretive information that accompanies modified tests should include a careful statement of the steps taken to modify tests in order to alert users to changes that are likely to alter the validity of the measure" (p. 79). Standard 14.5 states that "empirical procedures should be used whenever possible to establish time limits for modified forms of timed tests rather than simply allowing handicapped test takers a multiple of the standard time. Fa-

tigue should be investigated as a potentially important factor when time limits are extended (p. 79)." The standards also caution professionals against interpreting test scores that emerge from nonstandard testing as if they were from standard testing; they report, "Strictly speaking, unless it has been demonstrated that the psychometric properties of a test, or type of test, are not altered significantly by some modification, the claims made for the test by its author or publisher cannot be generalized to the modified version" (p. 78). Standard 14.2 even stresses that test manuals need to remind test users to be cautious in using scores achieved via nonstandard test administrations. Such statements may leave us in the situation in which we simply cannot validly interpret the nonstandard test scores earned by those with disabilities. Only the largest testing programs have the resources to research the norms and validity of scores achieved under nonstandard administrations. Indeed, in even those cases, only the most common nonstandard test administrations will face scrutiny. There are not enough test takers earning scores with each kind of test modification to facilitate proper empirical research. Moreover, the criteria that would be used in such validation research are not likely to be widely available across many of the individuals in the research sample, and if any such criteria do exist, they are generally likely to lack meaningfulness.

As a profession, we need to begin training testing professionals who are also experts in various kinds of disabilities so that we can best modify our tests and interpret the scores that result from them to meet the needs of those individuals with disabilities. A good starting point would be lists of recommended testing accommodations and test-score interpretive rules of thumb written by those expert in both standardized testing and a particular disability.

One particularly thorny issue relates to the actual "flagging" of test scores that emerge from nonstandard testings. As noted above, the technical standards for testing professionals call for the explicit marking of such scores so that test users can easily identify the fact that the score emerged from an atypical administration. Advocates for persons with disabilities, on the other hand, argue that identifying scores in this way invades the privacy of those with disabilities by identifying them as having a disability without their prior authorization.

CONCLUSIONS

If we want meaning to be conveyed with the test scores that we use—and there is no other reason to use test scores other than as a short-cut communication device among and between professionals—then we need to administer our tests in accordance with the procedures that are called for in a test manual and that were used in conjunction with the norm, reliability, and validation research studies. Simply put, we must follow procedures.

There are situations, however, where it is apparent that following these set procedures makes little or no sense. Imagine administering the Picture Completion subtest from a Wechsler test or a Bead Memory subtest from the Stanford-Binet to a person who is blind. Is it possible for such a result to be meaningful? Of course not. To give other examples, test takers from varied cultures or subcultures, who use or prefer languages other than English—such as the so-called Limited-English Proficient (LEP) students—or who have experienced deprivations of various types may require somewhat different tests, test administrations, and test interpretations. At present, we are not able to answer what appear to be the most basic of questions.

If psychology does not take steps to remedy these deficiencies in our knowledge base, others will take them. Worse, however, is that individuals will take steps that are not based on knowledge. Judge Grady was the judge who tried the PASE v. Hannon (1980) case in Chicago, a case that reached a decision opposite to Larry P. v. Wilson Riles. Intelligence tests were permitted for making educational decisions about minority-group children in the Chicago city schools. Judge Grady, exasperated over the diversity of opinions issued by expert-witness psychologists, took the matter into his own hands. He read every item of both the Stanford-Binet Intelligence Scale and the Wechsler Intelligence Scale for Children into the court record for all readers to see and decided that the vast majority of these questions were not biased test items. He expressed his disappointment with psychologists in general and especially the expert witnesses in the case. The following two quotations on the court record reveal his opinion.

First, he said:

> None of the witnesses in this case has so impressed me with his or her credibility or expertise that I would feel secure in basing a decision simply on his or her opinion. In some instances, I am satisfied that the opinions expressed are more the result of doctrinaire commitment to a pre-conceived idea than they are the result of scientific inquiry. I need something more than the conclusions of witnesses in order to arrive at my own conclusions. . . . I have not disregarded the expert testimony in this case but neither do I feel bound by it. (p. 836; also cited in part by Bersoff, 1984, p. 104 and in part by Elliott, 1987, p. 193).

Furthermore, "at one point in the trial plaintiffs' attorney objected to a defense witness answering a question about the cultural bias of intelligence tests, on the ground that the witness, a school official, was not a qualified psychologist. Judge Grady overruled, saying, 'The fact that someone wears a hat that says 'psychologist' should not overly impress anyone who has sat through two weeks of this trial'" (Elliott, 1987, p. 193).

With all due respect for Drs. Glaubenweiss and Bookman, it is time to move beyond both purely judgmental, speculative interpretations of test results as well as extrapolations from the general population to specific cases that do not much resemble the remainder of the population. Especially in the personality assessment of individuals from a clinical population, validity issues loom large. Many personality inventories standardized on normal volunteer subjects are used regularly in clinical settings. Validation evidence for such uses of these instruments typically follows—rather than precedes—their publication. In this spirit, Ben-Porath and Waller (1992) caution against using "normal" personality tests to substitute for "clinical" ones and suggest that the former be used only to augment, rather than to replace, the latter. We agree, and we would add that this caveat is more poignant when the test taker hails from a clinical population that itself is demographically distinct, because of language dominance, ethnicity, handicapping condition, cultural differences, and so on. In these areas there is a striking paucity of research. "A ubiquitous issue in psychological testing is the questionable practice of assessing ethnic, socioeconomic, or linguistic minorities with instruments that have been conceived, standardized, and validated from a nonminority, middle-class English-speaking perspective" (Malgady, Rogler, & Costantino, 1987, p. 229). Twenty years ago, Padilla and Ruiz (1973) "maintained that psychometric research had yet to offer valid testing procedures (particularly projective techniques) for personality assessment of Hispanics, and it is safe to say that neglect of this topic persists today" (Malgady et al., 1987, p. 230). Some reliable Spanish translations of paper-and-pencil tests are available, but evidence of the scales' validities for Hispanic test takers generally has not been established, and most of these tests have been used for research purposes rather than as components of clinical assessment batteries. Along similar lines, Velasquez and Callahan (1992) note that between 1949 and 1992 the numbers of studies on Hispanics in clinical settings using the Rorschach and the Thematic Apperception Test were three and one, respectively. Only the MMPI was used in a sizable number of studies (i.e., sixty-one). According to these authors, several other personality measures, including the California Personality Inventory, 16PF, Beck Depression Inventory, and Comrey Personality Scales apparently were not used at all in research assessing personality among Hispanic clinical populations.

We are faced with a significant dilemma in all forms of assessment. Psychology holds the promise of answering such questions, but to date, these questions have been raised all too infrequently. When they are raised, perfunctory, "canned" responses—like those of Dr. Bookman—are commonly given. These questions need to be raised; they need to be thoroughly discussed; and they need to be an-

swered. At present, we have only fragments of answers, and our answers will undoubtedly evolve and change over time. With regard to special administration of tests for the disabled, we need to validate the scores that emerge from these assessments (American Psychological Association, Division of Evaluation, Measurement, and Statistics, 1993). As further interpretive guides, norms studies and reliability checks are needed as well as similar research for members of linguistic minorities. The time for answers to these questions is now, and the answers must come from research.

ACKNOWLEDGMENT

Portions of this chapter were presented in Kurt F. Geisinger's keynote address at the 1993 Spring Seminar "Assessment in the Helping Professions," sponsored by the Counseling and Psychological Services Department at the State University of New York, College at Oswego.

REFERENCES

American Educational Research Association, American Psychological Association, and National Council on Measurement in Education (1985). *Standards for educational and psychological testing.* Washington, DC: American Psychological Association.

American Psychological Association (1986). *Guidelines for computer-based tests and interpretations.* Washington, DC: Author.

American Psychological Association Division of Evaluation, Measurement, and Statistics (1993). Psychometric and assessment issues raised by the Americans with Disabilities Act (ADA). *The Score,* 15(4), 1–2, 7–15.

Anastasi, A. (1988). *Psychological testing* (6th ed.). New York: Macmillan.

Ben-Porath, Y. S., & Waller, N. G. (1992). "Normal" personality inventories in clinical assessment: General requirements and the potential for using the NEO Personality Inventory. *Psychological Assessment, 4,* 14–19.

Bersoff, D. N. (1984). Social and legal influences on test development and usage. In B. S. Plake (Ed.),

Social and technical issues in testing: Implications for test construction and use (pp. 87–109). Hillsdale, NJ: Erlbaum.

Butcher, J. N. (1987). The use of computers and psychological assessment: An overview of practices and issues. In J. N. Butcher (Ed.), Computerized psychological assessment: A practitioner's guide (pp. 3–14). New York: Basic Books.

Donlon, T. F. (1992). Legal issues in the educational testing of Hispanics. In K. F. Geisinger (Ed.), The psychological testing of Hispanics (pp. 55–78). Washington, DC: American Psychological Association.

Elliott, R. (1987). Litigating intelligence: IQ tests, special education, and social sciences in the courtroom. Dover, MA: Auburn House.

Equal Employment Opportunity Commission. (1991). Americans with Disabilities Act: A technical assistance manual on the employment provisions (Title 1). Washington, DC: Author.

Geisinger, K. F. (1984). Test standardization. In R. J. Corsini (Ed.) Encyclopedia of Psychology (vol. 3, p. 414). New York: Wiley.

Glasser, A. J., & Zimmerman, I. L. (1967). Clinical interpretation of the Wechsler Intelligence Scale for Children. New York: Grune & Stratton.

Kaufman, A. S. (1979). Intelligent testing with the WISC-R. New York: Wiley.

Lambert, N. M. (1981). Psychological evidence in Larry P. v. Wilson Riles: An evaluation by a witness for the defense. American Psychologist, 36, 937–952.

Larry P. v. Riles. 343 F. Supp. 306 (N.D. Cal. 1972), aff'd. 502 F. 2d (9th Cir. 1974); 495 F. Supp. 926 (N.D. Cal. 1979), aff'd. in part and rev'd in part, 793 F. 2d 969 (9th Cir. 1984).

Malgady, R. G., Rogler, L. H., & Costantino, G. (1987). Ethnocultural and linguistic bias in mental health evaluation of Hispanics. American Psychologist, 42, 228–234.

Moreland, K. L. (1985). Computer-assisted psychological assessment in 1986: A practical guide. Computers in Human Behavior, 1, 221–233.

Padilla. A. M., & Ruiz, R. A. (1973). Latino mental health: A review of the literature (DHEW Publication No. HSM 73-9143). Washington, DC: U.S. Government Printing Office.

PASE v. Hannon, 506 F. Supp. 931 (N.D. Ill. 1980).

Reynolds, C. (1985). Critical measurement issues in learning disabilities. Journal of Special Education, 18(4).

Velasquez, R. J., & Callahan, W. L. (1992). Psychological testing of Hispanic Americans in clinical settings: Overview and issues. In K. F. Geisinger (Ed.), Psychological testing of Hispanics (pp. 253–265). Washington, DC: American Psychological Association.

Willingham, W. W. (1988). Testing handicapped people—The validity issue. In H. Wainer & H. I. Braun (Eds.), Test validity (pp. 89–103). Hillsdale, NJ: Erlbaum.

Zimmerman, I. L., & Woo-Sam, J. M. (1973). Clinical interpretation of the Wechsler Adult Intelligence Scale. New York: Grune & Stratton.

16
What a Clinician Needs to Know About Base Rates

Stephen E. Finn
Jan H. Kamphuis

WHAT ARE BASE RATES?

What are your chances of being hit by lightning? Of winning a lottery? Of developing schizophrenia? The probabilities of these events, usually expressed in a percentage, are called base rates. Base rates are often calculated in clinical settings. Thus, if five out of every one hundred of your clients try to commit suicide, the base rate of suicide attempts in your practice is 5 percent. If you work in an inpatient hospital where three out of every five clients has schizophrenia, the base rate of schizophrenia is 60 percent.

Base rates are defined for specified populations and are restricted to them. For example, the base rate of schizophrenia in some inpatient settings may be 60 percent, but the base rate of schizophrenia in the general population is about 1 percent. Thus, if we know nothing else about a group of one hundred people than that they are alive, we would predict that one person in that group has schizophrenia. However, if we consider people who have one biological parent with schizophrenia, we would predict a much higher probability of schizophrenia, for the base rate of schizophrenia in this group of individuals is 5.6 percent (Gottesman & Shields, 1982).

To give another example, the base rate of suicide attempts for inpatients with major depression may be as high as 25 percent, but it's generally much lower in outpatient settings (e.g., in ours, it is around 5 percent). Thus, a base rate is the a priori chance or prior odds that a member of a specified population will have a certain characteristic, if we know nothing else about this person other than that he or she is a member of the population we are examining.

Base rates have important implications for a wide variety of issues in clinical practice. Although rarely acknowledged, base rates affect the prediction of behaviors (e.g., suicide), the interpretation of test data (e.g., MMPI scores), and the making of diagnostic decisions.

BASE RATES AND PREDICTIVE POWER

Suppose that from previous records you know that 5 percent of the inpatient population of your clinic will assault a staff person at some point in time. You could randomly predict that one of every twenty clients will commit assault and that all others will not. This would lead to the estimates depicted in Table 16.1. The column percentages show the base rates of actual assault and no assault (5 percent and 95 percent, respectively). In making your predictions you would match these base rates, as the row percentages indicate. To calculate the probability of the different cells in the table, cross-multiply the column and row percentages, since your predictions will be made randomly and are consistent with the axiom of independent probabilities.[1] Cell A shows the probability of your predicting assault for a client who will actually assault a staff person (.25 percent). Cell D shows the probability of your predicting no assault for a client who will not make an assault (90.25 percent). Thus, your predictions of assault, made with base rates alone, would be right 90.5 percent of the time (Cell A + Cell D = total accuracy).

Now suppose a colleague, unfamiliar with the concept of base rates, claims that he can identify future assaulters by having a five-minute conversation with each patient. Suppose further that he is able to successfully identify all assaulters (Cell A is 100 percent of 5 percent), but that he incorrectly classifies one out of every eight (12.5 percent) of nonassaulters as assaulters (Cell B is 12.5 percent of 95 percent). As can be seen in Table 16.2, his overall predictive accuracy, despite hours of interviews, will be lower than yours (88.1 percent, obtained by summing true positives or Cell A, and true negatives, or Cell D).

This is a counterintuitive point: Decisions based on more information may actually be less accurate than those based on less information. A procedure that has predictive power beyond the base rate accuracy is called *efficient*. Clearly, in the above example, the colleague's interview would not be considered efficient relative to the base rates. However, if we were exclusively interested in predicting true positives, he would be considered efficient, for by his method 100 percent of the assaulters were successfully identified versus only 5 percent of the assaulters successfully identified by base rates alone. In other words, efficiency depends on the purpose of the test or procedure; we will return to this issue when we discuss utilities. Let us assume for now that we are interested in the overall accuracy of our classifications: When is it useful (efficient)

TABLE 16.1. Predicting Assault by Base Rates Alone

	Assault	No assault	Row %
Predicted Assault	.25% True positive Cell A	4.75% False positive Cell B	5%
Predicted No assault	4.75% False negative Cell C	90.25% True negative Cell D	95%
Column %	5%	95%	100%

Notes:
True positive = cases for which assault was predicted and occurred
False positive = cases for which assault was predicted and none occurred.
True negative = cases for which no assault was predicted and no assault occurred.
False negative = cases for which no assault was predicted and assault did occur.

to use a test? When does it increase the number of correct decisions?[2]

IMPLICATIONS OF BASE RATES FOR CLINICAL PRACTICE

It is Difficult to Predict Phenomena with Low Base Rates

In general, it is easier to increase predictive accuracy when the events to be predicted are moderately likely to occur (i.e., occur with a probability close to 50 percent) than when the events are unlikely to occur (i.e., occur with a probability closer to 0 percent). This is easy to see from the example in the previous section. It is very difficult to design a test that will improve upon the overall accuracy of base rate predictions (such as those in Table 16.1) when the base rate is very low. As shown in the table, simply predicting "no assault" all the time will result in 95 percent predictive accuracy.

Meehl and Rosen (1955), in their paper on antecedent probabilities, derived a helpful rule from Bayes' theorem to help decide whether or not a test adds to predictive accuracy. In statis

TABLE 16.2. Using Interview Data to Predict Assault

	Assault	No assault	Row %
Predicted Assault	5% True positive **Cell A**	11.9% False positive **Cell B**	16.9%
Predicted No assault	0% False negative **Cell C**	83.1% True negative **Cell D**	83.1%
Column %	5%	95%	100%

Notes:

True positive = cases for which assault was predicted and occurred.

False positive = cases for which assault was predicted and none occurred.

True negative = cases for which no assault was predicted and no assault occurred.

False negative = cases for which no assault was predicted and assault did occur.

tical terms, a test or procedure increases the overall number of correct decisions when:

$$\frac{\text{Base rate of event}}{\text{Base rate of no event}} > \frac{\text{False positives, using the procedure}}{\text{True positives, using the procedure}} \quad (1)$$

In other words, a test or procedure predicts better than the base rate when the fraction of the base rate of occurrence to the base rate of nonoccurrence exceeds the fraction of the rates of false positives to the rates of true positives. In our example we would like to know whether:

$$\frac{\text{Base rate of assault}}{\text{Base rate of no assault}} > \frac{\text{False positives, using the interview}}{\text{True positives, using the interview}} \quad (2)$$

This would mean that the fraction of false positives (i.e., erroneously predicted assaulters) to true positives (i.e., successfully predicted assaulters) should be lower than 5 percent/95 percent = 0.05 percent. Let us verify this for the colleague. His false positive rate (Cell B) is 11.9 percent, his true positive rate is 5 percent (Cell A), which when divided results in 2.4 percent. This is greater than 0.05 percent; thus, the col-

league's predictions are not consistent with the rule for efficient tests. It is again demonstrated that his interviews lead to fewer correct decisions than merely following base rate predictions.

One way of dealing with the problem of predicting rare events is to increase the base rate—closer to a probability of 50 percent—by formulating a more restrictive definition of the population for which you are trying to predict the behavior. In our example, the colleague might get better results if he limits his predictions to patients who already have a history of assault. By thus making the definition more restrictive, he is likely to find more positive cases in his population, i.e., obtain a higher base rate. There would be a cost to this restriction—his interview could only be used with a subset of the entire psychiatric population—but it most likely would result in greater predictive accuracy.

Optimal Test Cutting Scores Vary by Base Rates

Very commonly, psychological tests that produce a range of numerical scores are used to classify patients into dichotomous categories. When this is done, one must set a "cutting score" and place people who obtain a score equal to or higher than the cutting score in one category and all other people in the other category. For example, in one school district in our area, students are eligible for classes for the "gifted" only if their IQ test scores are equal to or above 130.

For reasons similar to those outlined earlier, optimal cutting scores for psychological tests depend on the base rate of occurrence of the behavior or trait you are trying to predict with the test. To explain this, we will examine what happens when one overlooks the effects of base rates upon making predictions. Exner and Wylie (1977) attempted to predict suicide using multiple indictors from the Rorschach. They compared Rorschach protocols of successful suicides ($n1 = 59$) with the protocols of patients who made suicide attempts that failed ($n2 =$

TABLE 16.3. Exner and Wylie's Predictive Accuracy for Different Base Rates

Score on S-CON	Base rate = 24.6%			Base rate = 5%			Base rate = 1%		
	% True Positives	% True Negatives	% Total Accuracy	% True Positives	% True Negatives	% Total Accuracy	% True Positives	% True Negatives	% Total Accuracy
6	23	35	58	05	44	48	01	45	46
7	20	48	68	04	60	64	01	63	64
8	18	63	81	04	79	83	01	83	83
9	16	69	85*	03	87	90	01	90	91
10	13	72	85*	03	90	93	01	95	95
11	06	73	79	01	92	94*	00	96	96*

Note: *Denotes highest overall accuracy (hit rate).
The total percentages are not always equal to the sum of the true positives and true negatives because of rounding errors.

31), the protocols of depressed patients (n3 = 50), the protocols of schizophrenic patients (n4 = 50), and the protocols of normals (n5 = 50) to identify an optimal set of predictors of suicide (which later came to be known as the suicide constellation, or S-CON).

Based on the above groups, Exner and Wylie proposed a cutting score of eight on the S-CON for identifying a person as being at risk for a serious suicide attempt. Their sample had a base rate of 24.6 percent of suicide (59 out of 240). How can we determine overall predictive accuracy, taking base rates into account? First, let's make a table that crosses prediction of suicide with actual suicide, just as we did with assault in Tables 16.1 and 16.2. The overall accuracy can be calculated by multiplying the correctly predicted percentage of suicide cases with the base rate of suicide and adding to this the product of the percentage of correct "no suicide" predictions with the base rate of "no suicide." Table 16.3 shows the results for three different base rates.

As you can see in the table, a cutting score of nine or ten appears to maximize the overall hit rate in Exner and Wylie's sample, but at the cost of fewer true positive predictions than their proposed cutting score of 8.[3] More important, for settings in which the base rate of suicide is lower than 24.6 percent—and we assume that there (fortunately) are many such settings—a different cutting score should be used. For example, in a setting with a base rate of 5 percent or 1 percent, a cutting score of eleven signs maximizes the overall predictive accuracy. Clearly,

base rates are essential in deciding on optimal cutting scores for test predictions. Awareness of this issue can greatly improve our clinical decision making.

Where do we encounter base rate effects in clinical practice? As clinicians, we are often faced with situations in which the same numbers have different meanings in different settings (because different settings are likely to have different base rates). Two everyday examples will suffice: MMPI scores and clinical diagnoses. It has long been known that MMPI elevations should be interpreted differently across settings. This is reflected in statements in MMPI code books like "in inpatient settings, it is likely that the patient has . . ." or "in women, this score tends to be associated with. . . ." Why this type of qualification? Because the claims made are only valid for the patient population under study; with different base rates, different cutting scores or interpretations are necessary.

Although it is not yet widely recognized, the DSM-III-R diagnostic rules are also (in the best of cases) dependent on minimizing error for a certain base rate. For example, a client must meet five or more of nine criteria in order to be given the diagnosis of Passive-Aggressive Personality Disorder (PAPD). It is unclear from DSM-III-R for what setting or base rate this cutting score was chosen. However, as is clear from the S-CON example, this decision rule may not apply equally well across clinical settings if they have significantly different base rates of PAPD (Finn, 1982; Widiger, Hurt, Frances, Clarkin, & Gilmore, 1984). In a clinical setting that sees very few clients with PAPD, the best diagnostic rule may be eight or more criteria. In a setting that sees a great number of clients with PAPD, a cutting score of four or three criteria may maximize diagnostic accuracy.

Utilities

Back to the Exner and Wylie study: Our earlier discussion assumed that we strive to optimize the overall rate of correct diagnostic decisions. However, overall predictive accuracy may not be the appropriate criterion for evaluating the usefulness of a psychological test. Surely, failing to predict a suicide is of much more consequence than overpredicting suicide. Conversely, some might argue that underdiagnosing schizophrenia is less of a problem than overdiagnosing the disorder, in view of the societal "labeling costs" of being diagnosed schizophrenic. Hence, the usefulness of a certain test or procedure depends not only on base rates but on the relative seriousness of the types of error it produces. If a researcher designs a test to rule out a certain disorder, he or she should pay more attention to the rate of false negatives than to the rate of false positives.

The issues outlined above refer to the asymmetry of utilities (i.e., costs and benefits) of Type I (false negative) and Type II (false positive) errors. If you do not specify a decision about the weights that you attach to the two types of error, a default decision of equal weighing will result: the so-called utility-balanced diagnostic rule (Finn, 1983).

Salient Personal Experience Tends to Be Weighed More Than Base Rates

A great deal of research now shows that human decision makers are quite poor in using base rates to reach informed decisions. For example, in one of a series of classic studies, Kahneman and Tversky (1972, 1973) asked subjects to estimate the base rate of students in various graduate school programs, such as law, social work,

computer science, and engineering. Subjects then read the following short biography:

> "Tom W. is of high intelligence, although lacking in true creativity. He has a need for order and clarity, and for neat and tidy systems in which every detail finds its appropriate place. His writing is rather dull and mechanical, occasionally enlivened by somewhat corny puns and by flashes of imagination of the sci-fi type. . . ." (Kahneman & Tversky, 1973, p. 238)

After this, subjects made two ratings: (1) the degree to which Tom W. was similar to their experience of students in the different graduate programs; and (2) the likelihood that Tom W. was a graduate student in law, social work, computer science, etc. As you might anticipate, subjects weighed their personal experience more heavily than the estimated base rates in judging the likelihood of Tom W. pursuing various areas of study. For example, Tom W. was given the highest likelihood of studying computer science, although subjects estimated that only 7 percent of graduate students were in that area. Subjects considered him least likely to be studying social work or humanities, although they judged the base rates in these areas to be 17 percent and 20 percent, respectively. The overall correlation between base rates and likelihood ratings was $r = -.65$, while the correlation between similarity and likelihood ratings was $r = .97$.

The implications of this type of error for clinical practice are clear and have been expounded upon by others (e.g., Arkes, 1981). Let us return to the Exner and Wylie suicide constellation index for an example. You may tell fellow clinicians that in their outpatient setting (with a base rate of suicide of 5 percent) only 4 percent of clients with an S-CON score of eight are likely to be make serious suicide attempts. (See Table 16.3.) However, clinicians who have dealt with a suicide attempt from a past client with an S-CON score of eight may still claim that the suicide risk with such clients is extremely high and urge that they be hospitalized immediately. Past suicide attempts are very salient for clinicians and tend to override any information about base rates.[4]

Subjective Base Rate Estimates Are Difficult to Shift

Subjective base rates are probability estimates we develop and hold internally, based on our experience with a certain population. Thus, a clinician will probably have a subjective estimate of the base rate of psychosis in his or her clinical setting from accumulated experience working with clients. One well-known problem in clinical decision making occurs when practitioners develop relatively accurate subjective base rates in one setting but fail to shift their base rate estimates when making decisions in a different setting.

As an example, imagine that two different clinicians, Dr. Smith and Dr. Jones, are shown a videotape of diagnostic interviews of five clients who have mixed symptomatology of psychosis and severe dissociation. Dr. Smith specializes in the treatment of psychosis and primarily has seen psychotic clients for the last ten years of her professional life. Dr. Jones heads an inpatient program for the treatment of dissociative disorders, and most patients referred to the program have been previously diagnosed as having a dissociative disorder. Research has shown that Dr. Smith is more likely to diagnose the five clients as psychotic and Dr. Jones is more likely to diagnose them as dissociative (e.g., Katz, Cole, & Lowery, 1969). These biases probably do not reflect Dr. Smith's or Dr. Jones's salient experience with one or two clients, nor do they indicate that Dr. Jones and Dr. Smith are ignoring base rate information altogether. Rather, the two clinicians' diagnoses are likely to reflect their tendency to use their subjective base rate estimates from their own settings when making diagnostic decisions in a new setting. To make the most accurate diagnoses, each clinician would have to inquire about the relative frequency of psychotic and dissociative clients in the population from which the research sample was drawn, and then hold this information in mind when making a diagnosis. Although we tend to think of diagnoses as real and immutable, in fact their accuracy is influenced by base rates just as much as the Exner and Wylie (1977) S-CON index.

Base Rates Can Influence Perceptions and Information-Collection Strategies

An even more disturbing bias exists than base rates influencing diagnoses: subjective base rates also influence clinicians' information-collection strategies and their perception of signs and symptoms. The familiar adage need be modified only slightly to capture this problem: "We see what we *expect* to see."

To illustrate, let us return to the previous example. We already know that Drs. Smith and Jones are likely to differ on their diagnostic decisions. What is less evident is that Dr. Smith and Dr. Jones are likely to base their different diagnoses on different *symptom* ratings; Dr. Smith will actually "observe" more psychotic symptoms and fewer dissociative symptoms, while Dr. Jones is likely to perceive the opposite (Katz, Cole, & Lowery, 1969; Arkes & Harkness, 1980).

These biases are further complicated by another well-demonstrated factor: if Dr. Jones and Dr. Smith are allowed to interview these same patients independently (rather than viewing taped diagnostic interviews), their internalized base rates are likely to guide their symptom search. That is, Drs. Smith and Jones may further buttress their diagnostic biases by asking about symptoms that fit their internal expectations and failing to inquire about symptoms that are inconsistent with their diagnoses (e.g., Gauron & Dickinson, 1969). Thus, our original adage can be extended again: "We expect to see what we're used to seeing, we see what we expect to see, and we inquire about what we expect to see rather than about what we don't expect to see."

Davis (1976) used the phenomenon of subjective base rate bias to ingeniously explain the events of the controversial Rosenhan (1973) pseudopatient study. To review, Rosenhan and seven of his colleagues presented themselves at the admissions offices of twelve mental hospitals complaining of hearing a voice that said "empty," "hollow," and "thud." Apart from describing this symptom and falsifying their name, vocation, and employment, no other symptoms or history were simulated. Rosenhan reported that he and the other pseudopatients were hospitalized at all twelve hospitals and in eleven cases were given a diagnosis of schizophrenia.

Davis (1976) argued that the diagnosis and treatment of the pseudopatients was largely determined by the hospital psychiatrists' (perhaps subconscious) knowledge of the base rates of disorder and symptomatology in their settings. Given the low probability of normal persons presenting themselves at mental hospitals and asking for admission and the high base rate of auditory hallucinations among schizophrenics, Davis showed mathematically that psychiatrists' diagnoses may have been statistically justifiable. Furthermore, these base rates and the diagnoses they subsequently engendered seemed to keep the hospital staff from accurately perceiving features of patients that were inconsistent with schizophrenia or from inquiring about symptoms that would have pointed towards other diagnoses. Hospital records suggested that non-schizophrenic features were either ignored, inaccurately perceived, or not properly weighted when diagnoses were assigned and patients were observed in the hospitals. For example, a behavior that would have been perceived as innocuous in another setting (writing notes) was described in the nursing notes as pathologic ("Patient engaged in writing behavior").

High Cooccurring Base Rates Can Lead to the Erroneous Perception of Correlations and Causal Relationships

Suppose you are doing intakes in an inpatient hospital where for geographic or other reasons most of the clients are Hispanic, with a base rate of .90. Let's also imagine that because of the way different hospitals in the area share resources, your setting handles most of the severe psychoses, giving a base rate of .90 in your hospital for schizophrenia. We know from the clinical research literature that there is no association in the general psychiatric population between being schizophrenic and being Hispanic. Therefore, the fourfold table between Hispanic heritage and schizophrenia for 100 random admissions in your setting would prob-

TABLE 16.4 Co-occurrence of Schizophrenia and Hispanic Heritage in One Inpatient Setting

| | | Diagnosis of schizophrenia | | |
		Yes	No	Row %
Hispanic Heritage	Yes	81% Cell A	9% Cell B	90%
	No	9% Cell C	1% Cell D	10%
	Column %	90%	10%	100%

Note: $X^2 = 0$, phi $= 0$.

ably look like that shown in Table 16.4. As shown in the table, there is no significant association between Hispanic heritage and schizophrenia. Although there are a large number of cases in Cell A (Hispanic and schizophrenic), this is due simply to the co-occurrence of the two high base rates for Hispanic heritage and for schizophrenia. If a significant association existed, there would also be an over-representation of cases in Cell D, non-Hispanic, not schizophrenic. These figures and the resulting lack of association are exactly as expected given our previously mentioned knowledge about schizophrenia.

What most clinicians may not know is that if they were intake workers in such an inpatient setting, it would be very easy to perceive a correlation between Hispanic heritage and schizophrenia, even though none exists. Smedslund (1963), Nisbett and Ross (1980), Arkes (1981), and others have shown that high cooccurring base rates give observers the impression of a substantial association, because of the high number of cases in Cell A. Apparently, most of us have difficulty realizing that Cells B, C, and D are as important for estimating an association as is Cell A. You, as an intake worker, might be protected from overestimating an association if you already knew that the large number of clients you saw in Cell A was due to the peculiarities of geography and how your hospital shares resources with others. You might also be helped if you knew the research literature on schizophrenia and the general lack of association between schizophrenia and Hispanic heritage.

Suppose, however, that you were faced with variables that were not as well researched or understood?

This is the situation that one of us (Finn) faced several years ago as part of the Eating Disorders Research Group at the University of Minnesota. The research group was contacted over several years by a number of clinicians in Minneapolis who said they noted a strong association between a history of sexual abuse and eating disorders in women they were treating in psychotherapy. These clinicians were intrigued by the association they perceived and had begun musing about a causal relationship between sexual abuse of women and subsequent eating disorders. When the eating disorders research team assessed abnormal eating patterns and sexual abuse in the very clinical settings from which the reports came, the results were as follows. There was a high base rate of past sexual abuse among the eighty-five women in the sample (70 percent) as well as a high rate of abnormal eating patterns (82 percent). There was no significant statistical association at all between eating disorders and sexual abuse ($X^2 = 0$, $phi = 0$), and the cell frequencies of the fourfold table were exactly equal to those that would be derived from the cross-multiplication of cell and column frequencies: Cell A = 57 percent, Cell B = 25 percent, Cell C = 13 percent, and Cell D = 5 percent (Finn, Hartman, Leon, & Lawson, 1986). Although post-hoc hypotheses are questionable, it seems likely that the clinicians who gave the initial reports of an association between eating disorders and sexual abuse had been influenced by the large number of women in their settings who had both of these problems (i.e., the large number of cases in Cell A). In effect, the clinicians had no "control group" (women without sexual abuse or eating disorders) to help shape their perceptions.

HOW TO USE BASE RATES FOR YOU AND YOUR CLIENTS' BENEFIT

Should we clinicians give up entirely the task of making diagnostic and treatment decisions or use Ouija boards to guide our actions? We don't think so. A few simple guidelines can greatly help all of us to intelligently incorporate base rates in clinical decision making.

Investigate the Base Rates in Your Setting

If you want base rates to work for you, use the tests and decision rules that minimize overall error for your particular clients. This will require you to have at least some knowledge of the base rates of certain client characteristics in your setting. Pertinent information can be collected through examining previous records or perhaps through comparison with data from related settings. If you collect information about the base rates of phenomena of interest in your setting, you are likely to improve your clinical decision making in the long run.

Be Suspicious of Simple Interpretations of Test Scores

Error is a fact. Especially with low-base-rate phenomena, errors in prediction are a given. Be aware of this and avoid claiming more than you can substantiate, especially if you work in the area of forensic psychology. For example, clinicians are often asked to make predictions of dangerousness, suicide potential, and other low-base-rate characteristics in court. Consistent with the current ethical code of psychologists, you should appropriately qualify any opinions you express about a particular client showing such characteristics (APA, 1992; Principles 2.05, 2.08, and 7.04).

Tests are most useful if the base rate is close to 50 percent. We have seen in the hypothetical example of predicting assault in your clinic that it is difficult for a test to improve upon the base rate predictions if the base rates are extreme; i.e., close to 0 percent. It follows from Meehl's and Rosen's (1955) optimizing rule that tests are more likely to positively contribute to the quality of decision making when the base rate of the behavior to be predicted is closer to 50 percent.

Don't use fixed cutting scores. As shown earlier, statements like "an MMPI-2 T-score equal to or above 65 means . . ." should be critically examined. If you adopt simple rules of thumb such as the above, it may well lead to false decisions that can be avoided if base rates are respected. Remember, cutting scores for tests are based on minimizing errors given certain base rates. Therefore, a T-score of 65 may not be the optimal cutting score in your setting. It depends on whether the base rate in your setting equals the base rate on which the test cutting score was normed.

Look for cross-validated tests. As mentioned, cutting scores for tests are based on minimizing errors given certain base rates. Thus, limited trust is appropriate when cutting scores were based on one sample alone. More confidence can be placed on test predictions when the same results have been generated from multiple samples, especially if those samples have different base rates of the characteristic being predicted. In other words, look for tests that have been cross-validated in different settings and samples.

Use tests that were designed for your setting: There is a related recommendation: investigate the base rates in samples that were used to derive and standardize tests, in order to assess whether the test is appropriate in your setting. By studying the test manual you can determine what the base rates were in the standardization sample. You can then compare these base rates to those in your own setting. If base rate information is not explicitly given in the manual, you may still be on firm ground with the test if it was developed in a setting similar to yours.

If necessary, intelligently modify the recommended cutting score. You can intelligently modify your use of a test that was not designed for your setting by adjusting decision rules according to your own base rates. For example, as shown in Table 16.3, if the base rate of suicide in your setting is 5 percent or less, you should probably use a cutoff score on the S-CON that is higher than eight. To their credit, Exner and Wylie provided the figures that make such calculations possible. When no such data are available and you still want to use a test, you can at least specify the direction in which the cutoff score must be changed and moderate your con-

fidence in the test findings. As shown in Table 16.3, lower base rates generally go with more restrictive cutoff scores.

Ask Yourself: *What Are the Alternatives?*

Much improvement in clinical decision making could be accomplished if each of us remembered to think about base rates every time we made a clinical hypothesis. Unfortunately, research has resoundingly shown that simply resolving to think about base rates and the particular biases they produce rarely aids decision making (Fischoff, 1977; Kurtz & Garfield, 1978, Wood, 1978).

One debiasing strategy that does seem to produce improvement (Ross, Lepper, Strack, & Steinmutz, 1977) is to make yourself think about alternatives (test interpretations, diagnoses, hypotheses, etc.) after you have generated an initial impression. In our clinical work, we have found this strategy to be especially easy to implement with extreme base rate phenomena. For example, Finn saw a five-year-old girl in outpatient practice who appeared to be psychotically depressed. Part of this initial impression was based on a salient personal experience: the client strongly resembled a client Finn had worked with closely in an inpatient setting during his training. Finn stopped to question his initial impression, however, because he had never before run across a psychotic child in his particular outpatient setting. (His estimate of the local base rate of childhood psychosis was 0 percent.) Thinking about alternatives led to consults with other colleagues, which later revealed that the child's psychotic symptoms were due to the overdose and interaction of certain allergy medications.

As a general rule, when faced with what appear to be low base rate phenomena, we should all probably pause, take a second look, and carefully ask, "what are the alternatives?" If we find ourselves unable to generate other alternatives, it is time to seek the consultation of colleagues who work in different settings with different base rates. In the end, we may still decide to make a low base rate prediction or diagnosis; however, when going against the base rates, we should require more facts to support our conclusion.

Hunt for Disconfirming Information

Because base rates tend to influence both our information-gathering procedures and what we actually perceive, another good strategy is to hunt for information that will disprove our initial impressions. This goes against our natural tendency to look for information that confirms our internalized base rates. Thus, in the previous example, Finn should have rigorously sought all information that might prove his client *was* psychotically depressed, as well as information that was in accord with his internalized base rates. This would have helped him make an accurate diagnosis.

Delay Clinical Decisions while Information Is Collected

Consistent with the above strategies, research has generally shown that the most accurate clinical decision makers tend to arrive at their conclusions later than do less accurate clinicians (Sandifer, Hordern, & Green, 1970; Elstein, Shulman, & Sprafka, 1978). We may all be tempted to impress students and colleagues by showing how quickly we can diagnose a client or how few responses we need to interpret a Rorschach protocol. In such instances, however, we appear to be most susceptible to bias from internalized base rates.

When You Think There is an Association, Look for the Control Group

The Minneapolis clinicians who thought they perceived an association between eating disorders and sexual abuse are to be commended; they asked researchers to test this hypothesis among the women the clinicians were treating.

Unfortunately, many of us in clinical practice do not have research teams at our immediate disposal. In such a situation, a good strategy is to look for the control group that will test the association we think we perceive (i.e., clients who do not possess the characteristic of interest). To return to our example in Table 16.4, should clinicians perceive an association between Hispanic heritage and schizophrenia (because of the large number of cases in Cell A) they need only ask themselves, "Are non-Hispanic clients more likely than Hispanic clients to receive a diagnosis other than schizophrenia?" (a comparison of Cell B with Cell D). As one quickly sees, they are not, which proves that there is no association between Hispanic heritage and schizophrenia.

Don't Confuse Statistically Based Decisions with a Lack of Caring for Clients

When we urge clinicians to incorporate base rates into their clinical decision making, we find that many are reluctant to do so because they feel it involves "treating clients like numbers" or "not caring about the individual." Meehl (1977) bemoaned this same phenomenon in his classic paper "Why I Do Not Attend Case Conferences," reporting that when he spoke about base rates in case conferences some clinicians would respond, "We aren't dealing with groups, we are dealing with an individual case." Meehl responded pointedly in his paper to this reasoning: "if you depart in your clinical decision making from a well-established (or even moderately well-supported) empirical frequency . . . [this] will result in the misclassifying of other cases that would have been correctly classified had such nonactuarial departures have been forbidden" (p. 234). As clinicians, we may believe that we are caring more about clients when we avoid using statistics to make decisions that affect them. In fact, however, the costs of such decisions are likely to far outweigh their benefits. We show our greatest caring when we use all the information available to make the most accurate decisions possible about our clients.

ACKNOWLEDGMENT

We are grateful to Arnold H. Buss for his comments on an earlier draft of this chapter.

NOTES

1. The probability of two independent events cooccuring is equal to the probability of one event times the probability of the other event.

2. Many indices assess the psychometric quality of tests used for clinical decision making. *Sensitivity* is the probability of a person with a certain trait or condition being picked up by a test [a/(a + c)]; *specificity* is the probability that a person without a certain trait or condition being identified by the test as not having that trait or condition [d/(b + d)]. *Positive predictive power* is the likelihood of a person identified by the test as having a certain trait or condition actually possessing that characteristic [a/(a + b)]; *negative predictive power* indicates the probability of a person identified by the test as not having a certain trait or condition actually not having that characteristic [d/(c + d)]. All of these indices, including the rate of correct decisions we use in Tables 16.1–16.3, are helpful in clinical decision making, depending on the specific goal of the clinician. See Baldessarini, Finklestein, and Arana (1983) for a more in-depth discussion of these various indicators.

3. Exner and Wylie's (1977) cutting score of 8 is entirely reasonable; apparently they opted to increase the number of true-positive decisions at the cost of a slight decrease in the overall number of accurate decisions.

4. Hospitalization of such clients could be based on clinicians' decision to weigh false negative errors much more than false positive errors. However, if this is true, the clinicians should appropriately argue that even though their clients appear to have only a 4 percent probability of a serious suicide attempt, the negative utilities of not intervening are so high that some steps must be taken.

REFERENCES

American Psychological Association. (1992). Ethical principles of psychologists and code of conduct. *American Psychologist, 47,* 1597–1628.

Arkes, H. R. (1981). Impediments to accurate clinical judgment and possible ways to minimize their impact. *Journal of Consulting and Clinical Psychology, 49,* 323–330.

Arkes, H. R., & Harkness, A. R. (1980). Effect of making a diagnosis on subsequent recognition of symptoms. *Journal of Experimental Psychology: Human Learning and Memory, 6,* 568–575.

Baldessarini, R. J., Finklestein, S., & Arana, G. W. (1983). The predictive power of diagnostic tests and the effect of prevalence of illness. *Archives of General Psychiatry, 40,* 569–573.

Davis, D. A. (1976). On being *detectably* sane in insane places: Base rates and psychodiagnosis. *Journal of Abnormal Psychology, 85,* 416–422.

Elstein, A. S., Shulman, A. S., & Sprafka, S. A. (1978). *Medical problem solving: An analysis of clinical reasoning.* Cambridge, MA: Harvard University Press.

Exner, J. E., Jr., & Wylie, J. (1977). Some Rorschach data concerning suicide. *Journal of Personality Assessment, 41,* 339–348.

Finn, S. (1982). Base rates, utilities, and DSM-III: Shortcomings of fixed-rule systems of psychodiagnosis. *Journal of Abnormal Psychology, 91,* 294–302.

Finn, S. E. (1983). Utility-balanced and utility-imbalanced rules: Reply to Widiger. *Journal of Abnormal Psychology, 92,* 499–501.

Finn, S. E., Hartman, M., Leon. G. R., & Lawson, L. (1986). Eating disorders and sexual abuse: Lack of confirmation for a clinical hypothesis. *International Journal of Eating Disorders. 5,* 1051–1060.

Fischoff, B. (1977). Perceived informativeness of facts. *Journal of Experimental Psychology: Human Perception and Performance, 3,* 349–358.

Gauron, E. F., & Dickinson, J. K. (1969). The influence of seeing the patient first on diagnostic decision making in psychiatry. *American Journal of Psychiatry, 126,* 199–205.

Gottesman, I. I., & Shields, J. (1982). *Schizophrenia: The epigenetic puzzle.* Cambridge: Cambridge University Press.

Kahneman, D., & Tversky, A. (1972). Subjective probability: A judgment of representativeness. *Cognitive Psychology, 3,* 430–454.

Kahneman, D., & Tversky, A. (1973). On the psychology of prediction. *Psychological Review, 80,* 237–251.

Katz, M. M., Cole, J. O., & Lowery, H. A. (1969). Studies of the diagnostic process: The influence of symptom perception, past experience, and ethnic background on diagnostic decisions. *American Journal of Psychiatry, 125,* 937–947.

Kurtz, R. M., & Garfield, S. L. (1978). Illusory correlation: A further explanation of Chapman's paradigm. *Journal of Consulting and Clinical Psychology, 46,* 1009–1015.

Meehl, P. E. (1977). Why I do not attend case conferences. In *Psychodiagnosis: Selected papers* (pp. 225–302). New York: Norton.

Meehl, P. E., & Rosen, A. (1955). Antecedent probability and the efficiency of psychometric signs, patterns, or cutting scores. *Psychological Bulletin, 52,* 194–216.

Nisbett, R. E., & Ross, L. (1980). *Human inference: Strategies and shortcomings of social judgment.* Englewood Cliffs, NJ: Prentice Hall.

Rosenhan, D. L. (1973). On being sane in insane places. *Science, 179,* 250–258.

Ross, L., Lepper, M. R., Strack, F., & Steinmutz, J.

(1977). Social explanation and social expectation: Effects of real and hypothetical explanations on subjective likelihood. *Journal of Personality and Social Psychology, 35,* 817–829.

Sandifer, M. G., Hordern, A., & Green, L. M. (1970). The psychiatric interview: The impact of the first three minutes. *American Journal of Psychiatry, 126,* 968–973.

Smedslund, J. (1963). The concept of correlation in adults. *Scandinavian Journal of Psychology, 4,* 165–173.

Widiger, T. A., Hurt, S. W., Frances, A., Clarkin, J. F., & Gilmore, M. (1984). Diagnostic efficiency and the DSM-III. *Archives of General Psychiatry, 41,* 1005–1012.

Wood, G. (1978). The knew it all effect. *Journal of Experimental Psychology: Human Perception and Performance, 4,* 345–353.

17

Assessment of Malingering

David T. R. Berry
Martha W. Wetter
Ruth A. Baer

Nonveridical self-reports can be an important problem in psychological assessment. Sometimes termed response sets, these deliberately inaccurate self-appraisals seriously distort test results. Nichols, Greene, and Schmolck (1989) classify inaccurate self-reports into two major categories, content nonresponsivity (CNR) and content-responsive faking (CRF). CNR involves responding without reference to the content of the question, as in random responding, "yea saying," or "nay saying" (Tellegen, 1988). CRF involves responding in a way that either minimizes or maximizes problems. Thus, CRF may involve "faking good," in which a person attempts to deny or downplay difficulties, or "faking bad," which occurs when someone who is undergoing psychological testing overreports symptoms so that he or she appears to be in worse condition than is actually the case. Recent evidence suggests that these may be independent dimensions as opposed to two ends of a single continuum. Thus, individuals may "fake good" on some aspects of their testing but "fake bad" on others (Lanyon, Dannenbaum, Wolf, & Brown, 1989; Lees-Haley, English & Glenn, 1991). The focus of this chapter, however, is on the "fake bad" or "malingering" approach to testing.

Unfortunately, malingering of symptoms must be considered with increasing frequency as psychologists contribute to decision making in adversarial settings such as the courtroom (Grossman, Haywood, & Wasyliw, 1992), the prison system (Benedict & Lanyon, 1992), and in professional fitness evaluations (Grossman, Haywood, Ostrov, Wasyliw, & Cavanaugh, 1990). *In fact, we contend that the possibility of malingering of symptoms must be carefully considered in any assessment for which findings of psychopathology carry important contingencies for the patient.* This chapter seeks to contribute to the quality of professional practice in these situations by highlighting the need for considering the overreporting of symptoms in certain situations; reviewing selected practical and theoretical issues; briefly summarizing current information on detecting overreporting of symptoms on the more commonly used objective clinical personality tests that feature validity scales; and presenting tests and procedures specifically designed to detect malingering.

CONCEPTUAL AND PRACTICAL ISSUES

As noted earlier, malingering of symptoms involves responding in such a way that a more negative picture of psychological health is presented than is consistent with reality. A number of practical and theoretical issues arise in the assessment of malingering of symptoms, including etiology of symptoms, exaggeration versus fabrication of symptoms, global versus specific overreporting, socially acceptable versus unacceptable goals, and the costs of misdiagnosis of malingering. Regarding the etiology issue, DSM-IV (APA, 1994) distinguishes malingering from other nonveridical presentations with reference to two dimensions: the extent to which the symptoms are under conscious control and the extent to which the symptoms appear to be motivated to achieve internal versus external goals. Symptoms produced by conscious/volitional mechanisms to gain an external goal are classified as malingering, symptoms produced by unconscious mechanisms for intrapsychic goals are classified as somatoform disorders (conversion disorder, somatoform pain disorder, etc.), and symptoms produced consciously for apparently internal/intrapsychic goals are classified as factitious disorders (see Rogers, Bagby, & Dickens, 1992, for a more complete consideration of these issues). Currently, a final determination of volition underlying symptom production is impossible except in rare instances (e.g., confession, demonstration of preservation of a supposedly defective function such as moving an allegedly paralyzed limb), suggesting that this is a difficult or perhaps impossible differentiation to make. In fact, the practical and conceptual utility of the distinction remain to be demonstrated, making its clinical application problematic (Cunnien, 1988).

Another thorny issue involves the relative contribution to the symptom picture of accurate symptom reports, exaggeration of actual problems, and fabrication of symptoms. Some portion of malingerer's complaints might reflect an actual disorder, another subset might be secondary to exaggeration of actual disorder, and a final group might be completely fabricated. Clearly, sorting out these components is a challenge to any assessment, and unfortunately, cases of this type are not uncommon in forensic practices. An important unresolved issue in these situations is whether to dismiss the case as a "malingerer" once exaggeration and/or fabrication are noted, or to report the response set as a caution and attempt to sort the picture out on the basis of available evidence (Rogers, 1988).

A third issue involves the "strategy" adopted by the overreporter. Clinically, some malingerers appear to attempt to simulate a specific condition, perhaps one they are familiar with from past personal exposure or have learned of from the media or other sources. In contrast, other malingerers appear to adopt a strategy of endorsing any apparently pathological item that they encounter. This dimension of specificity of simulation is a potentially important one, because analogue research suggests that "global" fakers are more easily detected than "specific" fakers (Berry, Baer, & Harris, 1991). The increased availability of knowledge regarding mental disorders suggests that the incidence of "specific" malingerers is at least potentially on the rise, and this may need to be addressed in formulating detection strategies. A related issue involves the client's level of knowledge regarding assessment procedures and validity scales intended to detect overreporting. "Coaching" or "cramming" by unscrupulous individuals or organizations may further increase the difficulty of detection (Lamb, 1992; Rogers, Babgy, & Chakraborty, 1993).

Another issue presented here is that of socially unacceptable versus acceptable goals. Although most would condemn the litigant fabricating problems to obtain a large damage award, the distressed applicant for mental health services who exaggerates actual problems to gain a higher priority for access to therapy might be more difficult to criticize. Dahlstrom, Welsh, and Dahlstrom (1972) refer to this situation as a "cry for help or pleading for special attention. This is particularly likely in a screening situation in which the patient may come to feel that unless he dramatizes his condition he will not be given appropriate attention" (p. 118). This voluntary "dramatization" of one's condition for a more socially acceptable purpose (obtaining access to needed care) clearly constitutes overreporting of symptoms. However, it would probably not be described as "malingering" by most practitioners, who routinely provide "cry-for-help" interpretations of exaggerated self-reports in nonforensic clinical settings. Further research is needed to determine if this distinction is a conceptually viable one or simply a reflection of the same phenomenon seen in different contexts.

The final issue discussed here is that of the costs of false positive errors in identification of malingering. *Labeling a patient as a malingerer has enormous consequences practically and psychologically and should not be done without thorough consideration of available evidence.* We recommend caution and a healthy respect for the limits of available techniques. With rare exceptions, a patient should never be labeled a malingerer on the basis of a single finding. The greater the amount of converging evidence, the greater the confidence in the diagnosis of malingering. The clinician should bear in mind the serious impact that such a label has on the patient and make this diagnosis only in the face of strong and consistent findings. On the other hand, false negatives in the assessment of malingering also have associated costs, often running to the hundreds of thousands or even millions of dollars, which represent resources unavailable for the care of other patients, and these costs must also be taken into consideration.

A PROPOSED STRATEGY FOR CLINICAL PRACTICE

This brief and limited review of potential complications in identifying malingering of symptoms highlights the challenges inherent in this task. However, despite the intrinsic difficulties, clinicians are routinely asked to make these distinctions. To complicate the matter further, in most clinical settings the time available for assessment procedures is limited. The clinician may be reluctant or unable to devote major portions of precious assessment time to address an issue that might have a low base rate in his or her setting. A two-stage process is proposed to address this dilemma in any evaluation from which the patient has something to gain from a finding of psychopathology. In the first stage, the clinician carefully reviews historical data,

interview information, behavioral observations, and validity scales from routinely administered personality tests for evidence of overreporting. If no suspicious signs are identified, no further exploration of the issue need be undertaken. However, in the face of suggestive data from any of the available sources, additional time should be devoted to the question of malingering through use of more specialized procedures discussed below. Multiple and converging lines of evidence suggesting malingering will obviously constitute the strongest basis for identifying the response set.

OBJECTIVE PERSONALITY INVENTORIES

Until recently, most research into the detection of malingering utilized scales derived from objective personality tests. Thus, a survey of personality inventories with overreporting indices commonly used in clinical settings will be presented next. These tests are classified into three groups based on the extent of published research supporting their utility in detecting overreporting of symptoms.

Tests Adequately Validated for Sensitivity to Overreporting of Symptoms

MMPI/MMPI-2

According to Lubin, Larsen, & Matarazzo (1984), the 566-item MMPI was the most commonly used personality/psychopathology test through the early 1980s. Because of space limitations and widespread familiarity with this "classic," no further general background information on the MMPI will be given here, although interested readers are referred to Dahlstrom, Welsh, & Dahlstrom (1972) for a wealth of detail on the MMPI. Berry, Baer, & Harris (1991) meta-analytically reviewed the literature through 1989 on the detection of malingering on the MMPI. They concluded that available evidence supported the utility of MMPI-based malingering scales, with a strong overall effect size of 2.07 (A Z-score effect size of 1 is equal to a magnitude of difference of 1 pooled standard deviation). Among the indices examined, the F, F-K, and Ds scales had the most power to identify overreporting of symptoms (effect sizes of 2.3, 1.9, and 2.2 respectively). The F scale consists of 64 statistically rare items covering a variety of content areas and is elevated by random responding, psychosis, and/or overreporting of symptoms, giving it a wide band sensitivity that complicates its interpretation. The F-K index, proposed by Gough (1950) involves subtracting the raw K scale score from the raw F scale score. Since F is thought to measure the tendency to emphasize problems and K is thought to reflect minimization of symptoms, the larger the positive difference between the two, the greater the probability of an overreporting response set. Although the Lanyon et al. (1989) and Lees-Haley, English, and Glenn (1991) studies on the independence of the two response sets raise important theoretical concerns regarding the logic underlying the F-K scale, in practice this scale has often performed reasonably well as a rough index of the overreporting response set. The Ds scale, described by Gough (1954), apparently taps commonly held stereotypes regarding mental illness that do not, in fact, characterize psychiatric patients. The malingerer may thus erroneously endorse items on this scale in an effort to fabricate symptoms of mental illness. Although the meta-analysis indicated fairly strong utility of these MMPI overreporting indices, the authors suggested that future research should investigate cutting scores derived for specific subgroups such as prisoners, disability applicants, etc., and should focus on comparisons that included actual patient groups rather than exclusively analogue designs. Finally, noting the publication of the MMPI-2, the authors called for research on revised validity scales, stating "many of the conclusions drawn in this review of the MMPI may be applicable to the MMPI-2. However, further research is necessary to confirm this hypothesis" (p. 596).

The MMPI-2 (Butcher, Dahlstrom, Graham, Tellegen, & Kaemmer, 1989) is a revised version of the MMPI, altered by rewording or removing objectionable or otherwise problematic items, renorming on a nationally representative sample, adding new content scales, deriving uniform T-scores, and most important for present purposes, adding new validity scales. Validity scales introduced for the MMPI-2 include Fb, VRIN, and TRIN. The Fb scale, concentrated in the last 300 questions, complements and was constructed in a fashion similar to the F scale, which is found exclusively in the first 370 items. Fb's 40 rarely endorsed items are intended to be sensitive to random and/or overreporting response sets. The VRIN scale is intended to be sensitive exclusively to random responding, whereas the TRIN scale is designed to be responsive to "yea saying" or "nay saying." Elevations on the F and/or Fb scale may be clarified through reference to the VRIN scale, in that a combination of F/Fb and VRIN elevations is probably secondary to random responding, whereas an elevated F/Fb combination without a VRIN elevation may be due to overreporting or psychosis.

Although the MMPI-2 had been released for only a relatively short time at the time of this writing, a number of papers have already appeared evaluating its validity scales. Wetzler and Marlowe (1990) studied F-K scores in an inpatient psychiatric population and suggested that previously used cutting scores might need to be adjusted for the MMPI-2. Graham, Watts, and Timbrook (1991) evaluated MMPI-2 validity scales in analogue subjects answering as if they had a very serious psychological disorder and contrasted with psychiatric inpatients. They found that F, F-K, and Fb scales differentiated the two groups, although at higher cutting scores than traditionally used. Graham et al. (1991) also noted that gender-adjusted cutting scores might be necessary when employing these overreporting indices. Berry, Wetter, Baer, Widiger, Sumpter, Reynolds, and Hallam (1991) found that the F, Fb, and VRIN scales were sensitive to random responding, and Wetter, Baer, Berry, Smith, and Larsen (1992) found that although all three scales were again sensitive to random responding, VRIN was insensitive to overreporting of symptoms, supporting the interpretive combination of F, Fb, and

VRIN in clarifying the source of F and Fb elevations. Lees-Haley, in a series of investigations of overreporting on the MMPI-2 by personal injury litigants, found that low Ego Strength (Es) scores might be suggestive of the response set (Lees-Haley, 1991a), and that a rationally derived "Fake Bad Scale" (FBS) might have utility in identifying malingering in personal-injury litigants (Lees-Haley, English, & Glenn, 1991; Lees-Haley, 1992), although the more traditional validity scales had some success as well (Lees-Haley, 1991b). In an analogue study, Cassisi and Workman (1992) combined the MMPI-2 L, F, and K scales into a 102-item independent inventory for evaluation of response sets and obtained favorable results. In the related area of evaluation of mild closed-head-injury patients, Villanueva and Binder (1993) found that MMPI-2 F scale scores correlated negatively and reliably with indices of effort on a neuropsychological test of malingering (Portland Digit Recognition Test). Timbrook, Graham, Keiller, and Watts (1993) investigated the incremental validity of Subtle and Obvious scales relative to the F scale in the detection of malingering. In an analogue design, they found that the F scale was more powerful in prediction of this response set than the Subtle and Obvious scales. Wetter, Baer, Berry, Robison, and Sumpter (1993) compared MMPI-2 data from general population normals provided with information both on PTSD or paranoid schizophrenia and monetary incentives for simulating the disorder with matched psychiatric patients. They found that analogue subjects simulating the target disorders were readily detected by elevated scores on F, F-K, Ds, and Fb, despite the information and incentives provided to facilitate their task.

Overall, currently available evidence suggests that the MMPI-2 validity scales operate much as did those on the MMPI. Thus, F, Ds, and F-K, as well as the new Fb, appear useful for detecting overreporting of symptoms. Additionally, the VRIN and TRIN scales were designed to address the possibility of random responding or "yea saying/nay saying" as alternative explanations for elevations on these scales. Lees-Haley has suggested additional potential malingering scales that deserve further investigation. Thus, continuing clinical use of these MMPI-2 scales as indicators of malingering of symptoms is supported. Further research, particularly into the issue of appropriate cutting scores for specific populations, will be of further help in this regard.

MCMI-II

The MCMI-II (Millon, 1987) is a revision of the 175-item MCMI (Millon, 1982). The MCMI-II has 22 clinical scales and several validity scales. Intended to be used only in a clinical population, the MCMI-II includes several unique features, such as use of base rates instead of the popular norm-based T-score scaling, theoretical derivation based on Millon's theories of personality and psychopathology (Millon, 1969, 1981), and coordination with DSM-III-R diagnoses (APA, 1987). The MCMI-II addresses the issue of overreporting of symptoms through a complex variety of detection scales and corrections. The Validity Index includes four extremely low-frequency response items (e.g. "I have not seen a car in ten years") and is thought to be most sensitive to the presence of random responding. Random responding indicated by the Validity Index precludes further interpretation of test results and thus ideally screens out this response set as an explanation for elevations on "Fake Bad" scales. The Disclosure scale is intended to assess the extent to which the test taker was answering test questions openly and reflects differentially weighted raw scores from a number of diverse scales. The Debasement scale provides an index of the extent to which the respondent emphasized psychological problems, whereas the Desirability scale assesses minimizing of psychological problems. Interestingly, although the Disclosure scale was intended to be independent of under- or overreporting response sets, it has been found to be positively correlated with the Debasement scale as well as negatively correlated with the Desirability scale. Thus, a "Fake Bad" approach to the test should elevate Debasement and Disclosure, as well as lower Desirability scale scores.

In addition to these detection scales, the MCMI-II incorporates adjustments for response sets into its scoring. Thus, the observation that different personality styles have characteristic tendencies to under- or overreport (for example, Histrionic and Avoidant personality features, respectively) is reflected in adjustments to several personality scales based on the individual characteristics of the test taker (see manual for details). Additionally, influences of transient (state) conditions, such as elevated levels of anxiety and dysthymia that may contribute to overreporting, are offset through deflation of certain clinical personality disorder scales (see manual for details).

Thus, the MCMI-II includes a large number of scales and adjustments to detect and correct for overreporting of symptoms. Choca, Shanley, and Van Denburg (1992) suggest that the Disclosure index appears to function well at detecting "faking bad." Bagby, Gillis, and Dickens (1990) found elevations on both the Disclosure index and the Debasement scale in an analogue study of college students instructed to fake bad. Positive results for these scales were also reported in a similar analogue study by Retzlaff, Sheehan, and Fiel (1991). Bagby, Gillis, Toner, and Goldberg (1991) compared college students with a fake bad response set with psychiatric inpatients and found the expected differences on the Debasement and Disclosure indices. Lees-Haley (1992) also found these scales effective in identifying PTSD patients judged to have spurious claims.

Although the unique construction of the MCMI-II lends it many strengths, there are certain possible drawbacks vis-à-vis the detection of malingering. First, Millon states in the manual that "Deliberate misrepresentation . . . on clinical inventories is much less frequent than is commonly thought" (Millon, 1987, p. 195), suggesting an assumption of a low base rate of malingering, which is probably not true for all settings. Another major concern is that the test was developed to be used only in psychiatric patients and assumes this status. Thus, the test "overpathologizes" in normals, as any clinician self-administering the instrument will find. This raises the possibility of mislabeling as psychopathology the responses of a normal individual "faking bad." Other concerns center on the De-

basement scale. Developed from the responses of twelve graduate students asked to "fake bad," BR scores for the scale were then set to identify various fractions of the distribution of patient scores according to clinician estimates of the prevalence of various levels of overreporting. The small and highly selected derivation sample and the rational determination of BR scores suggest the need for careful cross-validation in clinically relevant samples. Additionally, it appears that even the highest possible scores on the Debasement scale do not result in rejection of the protocol as invalid; rather, the response set is described in the computer-generated reports as "corrected for" through adjustments to other scales. Finally, although the manual and computer interpretations mention the corrections for overreporting and other response sets, it is difficult if not impossible to determine the algorithms for these adjustments, which leaves the clinician unsure of how much faith to place in them.

In summary, the MCMI-II includes overreporting indices that have had some support from the research literature, suggesting that significant elevations on the Debasement or Disclosure scales should trigger further investigation of the question of malingering using the more specific techniques described below. Millon's use of an adjustment to offset differing levels of overreporting that appear characteristic of particular diagnostic groups is a potentially important point, because it implies that overreporting may actually be part of the symptom picture for certain disorders.

California Psychological Inventory

The California Psychological Inventory (Gough, 1957) recently published in a revised edition (Gough, 1987), is a self-report questionnaire aimed at assessing normal personality. It targets twenty basic features of personality, referred to as "folk-concepts," thirteen special-purpose scales such as "management potential," three structural scales of interpersonal functioning, and three validity scales. The validity scales are "good impression," "communality," and "well-being." The Good Impression (Gi) scale assesses "faking good." The Communality (Cm) scale is composed of items with extremely high or low endorsement frequencies. Elevations on this scale are probably due to random responding. The Well-being scale (Wb) is intended to be sensitive to a "fake bad" approach to the test. Interestingly, the Wb was derived from the original Ds scale on the MMPI (see above). For the original CPI, a forty-four-item subset of the original seventy-four MMPI items was chosen to shorten the scale and eliminate "declarations of rather extreme psychopathology" (Gough, 1987; p. 36). The Wb scale on the revised CPI has again been shortened, this time to thirty-eight items. The Wb items are keyed in the opposite direction from the Ds items. Thus, low scores on Wb suggest faking bad on the test. The Cm scale, noted earlier, can assist in interpretation of the Wb scale by assessing the possibility of random responding as an alternative explanation for deviations on Wb. The 1987 CPI manual describes analogue research in which the Wb scale was able to identify fake bad profiles from fifty male and fifty female subjects of otherwise unspecified demographic characteristics. Lanning (1989) evaluated the ability of the revised CPI to detect invalid approaches to the test. In general, the validity scales were able to discriminate fake-bad and random from valid protocols successfully, but differentiation between fake-bad and random responding was more difficult. Although not extensively tested in its CPI incarnation, the longer Ds scale has stood up repeatedly in its MMPI version. Thus, low Wb scores should signal attention to the possibility of a fake-bad approach to the test, and trigger further investigation of the topic and confirmation through use of other procedures. Additional empirical evaluations of this use of the Wb scale in the revised CPI would be helpful in supporting this application.

Promising Tests Requiring Additional Validation for Sensitivity to Overreporting

The Basic Personality Inventory

The Basic Personality Inventory (BPI), introduced by Jackson (1989), targets many of the same dimensions of psychopathology as the MMPI. The BPI was developed using a construct-oriented measurement strategy. The constructs were identified through a factor analytic approach based on the MMPI and the Differential Personality Inventory. Psychometric procedures used to select items and form scales on the BPI were chosen to maximize item-scale correlations and minimize interscale correlations.

The BPI consists of twelve scales, each containing twenty true/false items. Eleven scales are content-oriented and focus on three areas: neurotic tendencies (Hypochondriasis, Depression, Anxiety, Social Introversion, and Self-Depreciation); psychotic tendencies (Persecutory Ideas, Thinking Disorder); and antisocial tendencies (Denial, Interpersonal Problems, Alienation, Impulse Expression). A twelfth scale focuses on deviant items covering diverse aspects of psychopathology. Although not formally a validity scale, the diverse content of the Deviation scale may be comparable in some ways to the F scale on the MMPI, and hence lend some sensitivity to overreporting of symptoms. Two published studies describe the response of the Deviation scale to malingering. Helmes and Holden (1986) contrasted college student groups given three different response sets (fake good, fake bad, and honest) with a group of psychiatric patients. The fake-bad group had the highest scores on the Deviation scale, and a discriminant function including the Deviation scale, the Self-Depreciation scale, and the Denial scale succeeded in correctly classifying 87 to 90 percent of the subjects in the study. Bagby, Gillis, and Dickens (1990), in a totally analogue design, also contrasted financially motivated college students faking bad, faking good and answering honestly. Again the fake-bad group had the highest Deviation scale scores. Discriminant function analyses including the Deviation, Self-Depreciation, and Denial scales generated decision rules that correctly classified nearly 80 percent of the fake-bad subjects.

Although the results reported for the Deviation scale are very promising, the literature supporting this scale is significantly less than that on overreporting indices from more established tests. Based on this, the BPI is not recommended for use as the sole personality inventory in situations where malingering is an important consideration. Publication of additional evidence in support of the Deviation scale and the Basic Personality Inventory may rectify this situation. Until that time, however, elevations on the Deviation scale should still raise the possibility of overreporting of symptoms.

The Personality Assessment Inventory

The Personality Assessment Inventory (PAI: Morey, 1991) is the current "new kid" on the personality assessment block. "The PAI is a self-administered, objective inventory of adult personality designed to provide information on critical clinical variables. The PAI contains 344 items which comprise . . . 4 validity scales, 11 clinical scales, 5 treatment scales, and 2 interpersonal scales. . . . The development of the PAI . . . emphasized both rational and empirical methods of scale development . . ." (p. 1). The PAI appears to be generating a good deal of interest among clinicians, suggesting the need to address the issue of overreporting of symptoms on the test.

As noted above, the PAI features four validity scales: Inconsistency (ICN), Infrequency (INF), Negative Impression Management (NIM), and Positive Impression Management (PIM). ICN includes ten pairs of empirically derived items that reflect the consistency with which the individual approaches the test. Diverse content suggests that elevations due to discordant paired responses will be due primarily to inconsistent responding. The INF scale consists of eight items selected for low endorsement rates in all subjects and designed to be answered similarly regardless of clinical status (e.g., "My favorite poet is Raymond Kertezc"). These items are distributed evenly throughout the test and thus are sensitive to changes in attention or effort across the test. According to the manual, elevation of either of these scales is extremely likely to represent random responding (this rule correctly identifies 94 percent of totally random protocols, with about a 6 percent false positive rate in "real" protocols).

The ability of ICN and INF to identify random or careless responding is important because NIM, like most malingering scales based on low-response-frequency items, tends to elevate in the presence of random responding. Thus, ICN and INF serve to clarify NIM, much as VRIN and TRIN shed light on an elevated F scale from the MMPI-2. The nine NIM items include a subset intended to identify exaggeration of problems and another subset designed to detect fabrication of symptoms. Empirically derived cutting scores based on NIM correctly classified 96 percent of an analogue malingering group given a global "fake bad" response set, with a 19 percent false positive rate in a patient sample. Use of a "two-standard deviations above the clinical mean" rule for identifying overreporting decreased the false positive rate in patients to 6 percent but dropped the true positive rate in analogue malingerers to 87 percent. NIM scores correlated .54 with MMPI F scores, suggesting some overlap in the construct measured, and four "critical items" for identifying "potential malingering" are presented. The results on NIM reported in the manual are promising, and as independent cross-validation data are published, this scale should become a useful indicator for detection of overreporting of symptoms.

Tests Not Adequately Validated for Sensitivity to Overreporting

NEO-PI-R

One of the most popular personality inventories in recent years has been the NEO-PI-R (Costa & McCrae, 1991) which assesses the "Big Five" personality traits. Although apparently a robust index of normal personality, this instrument includes only a single validity item, which asks the test taker whether the test has been answered honestly and accurately. Obviously, a subject motivated to malinger for financial or forensic reasons would be sorely tempted to manipulate his or her response to this item to avoid raising questions about veracity of answers. For this reason, it seems prudent to include along with the

NEO-PI-R another inventory with more extensive validity scales in an evaluation in which the subject's veracity might be at issue (Ben-Porath & Waller, 1992a, 1992b; see Costa & McCrae, 1992, for another opinion).

16PF

The 16PF (Cattell, Eber, & Tatsuoka, 1970) included no validity scales in its original form. However, Winder, O'Dell, & Karson (1975) developed a Faking Bad scale for Form A of the test by selecting the fifteen items that showed the greatest shift when subjects responded under honest versus fake-bad conditions. Karson and O'Dell (1976) reported the average score on this scale to be two, and recommended that scores of six or above should be considered suspicious and twelve or more presumptive of malingering. Krug (1978), using a large nationally representative normal sample, found that 90 percent of all subjects scored below six on this scale. Based on correlations between the Fake Bad and primary trait scores, Krug proposed a series of adjustments to trait scores to correct for overreporting. No data on this scale have been published in the past fifteen years, nor has its sensitivity to overreporting been cross-validated in designs employing patient groups. Thus, although elevations of the Faking Bad scale should raise the possibility of overreporting of symptoms, this index is not as well developed as scales discussed above, and the 16PF should probably not be given alone in a situation where the possibility of overreporting must be seriously considered.

Specific Tests and Procedures for Detection of Malingering

In the last few years, significant progress has been made in the psychometric detection of malingering. At least three major tests or procedures have been developed specifically to detect simulation of psychopathology. These procedures are currently in various stages of validation as described below. At the present time, the SIRS (Rogers, Bagby, & Dickens, 1992) is clearly the best-validated procedure available. However, the other procedures may accumulate additional support over the next few years, and relevant literature should be monitored for refinements and/or the introduction of new assessment approaches. These procedures may be considered when a patient has important potential gains contingent on the finding of psychopathology, and suspicious findings emerge from historical data, interview information, test behavior, or overreporting indices from objective personality tests as noted above. Formal decision-making rules on combinations of different types of evidence on malingering have not been investigated at the time of this writing. However, the presence of strong potential gain from appearing mentally ill, significant elevations on overreporting scales from objective personality tests, and suspect scores from the specialized procedures described below argue strongly for the presence of malingering. Of course, further research is necessary to investigate the accuracy of various combinations of approaches to the detection of malingering.

The M Test

The M test is a thirty-three item true/false test incorporating three subscales: genuine symptoms of schizophrenia; atypical attitudes not characteristic of mental illness; and bizarre or unusual symptoms rarely found in mental illness (Beaber, Marston, Michelli, & Mills, 1985). In the initial validation study, analogue malingerers asked to simulate schizophrenia were distinguished from hospitalized patients at a fairly high level. However, Gillis, Rogers, and Bagby (1991) evaluated the test in a combination of simulation and naturalistic designs and found it only modestly accurate in its ability to identify a group of suspected forensic malingerers. Rogers, Babgy, and Gillis (1992) described a modified version of the M test with two new subscales that were more successful at detecting malingering of psychiatric disorder. These results are promising, and further consistent findings would raise the confidence level in this test. At present, however, the M Test should not be considered fully validated.

Psychological Test Battery to Detect Faked Insanity

Schretlen and Arkowitz (1990) described a test battery that included the MMPI, the Bender-Gestalt, and a four-subtest Malingering Scale. Validity scale data are used from the MMPI, the Bender is scored for errors suggestive of malingering using a manual developed by the authors, and the Malingering Scale consists of four WAIS-R-like subtests, each including items presented in random order of difficulty. In the initial report, the battery showed promise in detecting prisoners who simulated insanity for financial incentives. In a subsequent report Schretlen, Van Gorp, Wilkins, and Bobholz (1992) cross-validated the battery in a sample with enhanced ecological validity and found that it continued to perform well in identifying overreporters. Additionally, they found that each component of the battery provided an increment in predictive power relative to the remaining procedures, suggesting that multiple probes for malingering may be more effective than individual ones. Thus, presently available data on this battery are promising, although it has not yet been marketed or released for use as a fully validated test. Further supporting data and cross-validation by independent investigators may ultimately lead to its publication as a formal malingering battery.

Structured Interview of Reported Symptoms (SIRS)

Rogers, Bagby, and Dickens (1992) published the Structured Interview of Reported Symptoms (SIRS), an objective method for the identification of malingering. The SIRS includes 172 items organized into 13 scales and administered in an interview format. In a series of recent publications, Rogers and colleagues have documented the utility of the instrument for detection of malingering in a variety of populations, including prisoners, actual psychiatric patients, suspected malingerers, and analogue simulators from the general population (Rogers, Gillis, Bagby, & Monteiro, 1991; Rogers, Gillis, & Bagby, 1990; Rogers, Gillis, Dickens, & Bagby,

1991; Rogers, Kropp, & Bagby, 1992). Although publication of independent cross-validation studies is an important final hurdle for the battery, at the present time the SIRS appears to be the best available technique for the identification of malingering. However, given the time required to administer and score (reportedly thirty to forty-five minutes), it seems likely that clinicians will wish to administer the procedure only when suspicion of overreporting of symptoms is heightened by situational, historical, behavioral, or test data as noted above.

SUMMARY

Deliberate overreporting of symptoms is an important issue in clinical personality assessment, particularly in situations where patients have desirable outcomes contingent on findings of psychopathology. Many objective personality inventories include scales with some utility for detecting malingering. However, these indices are not, by and large, accurate enough to support their use as sole criteria for identifying malingering in a patient. The presence of consistent information from other domains such as historical data, interview information, or behavioral observations raises the confidence level regarding the presence of malingering. Finally, in situations where strong suspicions are raised regarding malingering it is recommended that additional data be sought through administration of one or more of the special procedures recently developed to identify malingering. Converging data from all domains would of course provide the strongest support for the diagnosis of malingering, and the level of certainty in the clinical data base should be carefully considered by the clinician contemplating such a diagnosis.

REFERENCES

American Psychiatric Association (1994). *Diagnostic and statistical manual of mental disorders* (4th ed.). Washington, DC: Author.

Bagby, R., Gillis, J., & Dickens, S. (1990). Detection

of dissimulation with the new generation of objective personality measures. *Behavioral Sciences and the Law, 8*, 93–102.

Bagby, R., Gillis, J., Toner, B., & Goldberg, J. (1991). Detecting fake good and fake bad responding on the MCMI-II. *Psychological Assessment, 3*, 496–498.

Beaber, J., Marston, A., Michelli, J., & Mills, M. (1985). A brief test for measuring malingering. *American Journal of Psychiatry, 142*, 1478–1481.

Benedict, L., & Lanyon, R. (1992). An analysis of deceptiveness: Incarcerated prisoners. *Journal of Addictions and Offender Counseling, 13*, 23–31.

Ben-Porath, Y., & Waller, N. (1992a). "Normal" personality inventories in clinical assessment: General requirements and the potential for using the NEO Personality Inventory. *Psychological Assessment, 4*, 14–19.

Ben-Porath, Y., & Waller, N. (1992b). Five big issues in clinical personality assessment: A rejoinder to Costa & McCrae. *Psychological Assessment, 4*, 23–25.

Berry, D., Baer, R., & Harris, M. (1991). Detection of malingering on the MMPI: A meta-analysis. *Clinical Psychology Review, 11*, 585–598.

Berry, D., Wetter, M., Baer, R., Widiger, T., Sumpter, J., Reynolds, S., & Hallam, R. (1991). Detection of random responding on the MMPI-2: Utility of F, Back F, & VRIN scales. *Psychological Assessment, 3*, 418–423.

Butcher, J., Dahlstrom, W., Graham, J., Tellegen, A., & Kaemmer, B. (1989). *MMPI-2: Manual for administration and scoring.* Minneapolis: University of Minnesota Press.

Cassisi, J., & Workman, D. (1992). The detection of malingering and deception with a short form of the MMPI-2 based on the L, F, and K scales. *Journal of Clinical Psychology, 48*, 54–58.

Cattell, R., Eber, H., & Tatsuoka, M. (1970). *Handbook for the 16 Personality Factor Questionnaire.* Champaign, IL: Institute for Personality and Ability Testing.

Choca, J., Shanley, L., & Van Denburg, E. (1992). *Interpretive guide to the Million Clinical Multiaxial Inventory.* Washington, DC: American Psychological Association.

Costa, P., & McCrae, R. (1991). *NEO PI-R manual.* Odessa, FL: Psychological Assessment Resources.

Costa, P., & McCrae, R. (1992). Reply to Ben-Porath and Waller. *Psychological Assessment, 4*, 20–22.

Cunnien, A. (1988). Psychiatric and medical syndromes associated with deception. In R. Rogers (Ed.), *Clinical assessment of malingering and deception,* New York: Guilford Press.

Dahlstrom, W., Welsh, G., & Dahlstrom, L. (1972). *An MMPI handbook,* Vol. I Minneapolis: University of Minnesota Press.

Gillis, J., Rogers, R., & Bagby, R. (1991). Validity of the M test: Simulation design and natural-group approaches. *Journal of Personality Assessment, 57*, 130–140.

Gough, H. (1950). The F and K dissimulation index for the MMPI. *Journal of Consulting Psychology, 14*, 408–413.

Gough, H. (1954). Some common misconceptions about neuroticism. *Journal of Consulting Psychology, 18*, 287–292.

Gough, H. (1957). *Manual for the California Psychological Inventory.* Palo Alto, CA: Consulting Psychologists Press.

Gough, H. (1987). *California Psychological Inventory administrator's guide,* Palo Alto, CA: Consulting Psychologists Press.

Graham, J., Watts, D., & Timbrook, R. (1991). Detecting fake-good and fake-bad MMPI-2 profiles. *Journal of Personality Assessment, 57*, 264–277.

Grossman, L., Haywood, T., Ostrov, E., Wasyliw, O., & Cavanaugh, J. (1990). Sensitivity of MMPI validity scales to motivational factors in evaluations of police officers. *Journal of Personality Assessment, 55*, 549–561.

Grossman, L., Haywood, T., & Wasyliw, O. (1992). The evaluation of truthfulness in alleged sex offenders' self-reports: 16PF and MMPI validity scales. *Journal of Personality Assessment, 59*, 264–275.

Helmes, E., & Holden, R. (1986). Response styles and faking on the Basic Personality Inventory. *Journal of Consulting and Clinical Psychology, 54*, 853–859.

Jackson, D. (1989). *Basic Personality Inventory Manual.* Port Huron, MI: Sigma Assessment Systems.

Karson, S., & O'Dell, J. (1976). *A guide to the clinical use of the 16PF.* Champaign, IL: Institute for Personality And Ability Testing.

Krug, S. (1978). Further evidence on 16PF distortion scales. *Journal of Personality Assessment, 42*, 513–518.

Lamb, D. (1992). *Malingering closed-head injury on the MMPI-2: Effect of information about symptoms and validity scales.* Unpublished doctoral dissertation, University of Kentucky, Lexington, Kentucky.

Lanning, K. (1989). Detection of invalid response patterns on the California Psychological Inventory. *Applied Psychological Measurement, 13*, 45–56.

Lanyon, R., Dannenbaum, S., Wolf, L., & Brown, A. (1989). Dimensions of deceptive responding in criminal offenders. *Psychological Assessment, 1,* 300–304.

Lees-Haley, P. (1991a). Ego strength denial on the MMPI-2 as a clue to simulation of personal injury in vocational neuropsychological and emotional distress evaluations. *Perceptual and Motor Skills, 72,* 815–819.

Lees-Haley, P. (1991b). MMPI-2 F and F-K scores of personal injury malingerers in vocational neuro psychological and emotional distress claims. *American Journal of Forensic Psychology, 9,* 5–14.

Lees-Haley, P. (1992). Efficacy of MMPI-2 validity scales and MCMI-II modifier scales for detecting spurious PTSD claims: F, F-K, Fake Bad Scale, Ego Strength, Subtle-Obvious scales, DIS, and DEB. *Journal of Clinical Psychology, 48,* 681–689.

Lees-Haley, P., English, L., & Glenn, W. (1991). A fake bad scale on the MMPI-2 for personal injury claimants. *Psychological Reports, 68,* 203–210.

Lubin, B., Larsen, R., & Matarazzo, J. (1984). Patterns of psychological test usage in the United States. 1935–1982. *American Psychologist, 39,* 451–454.

McMahon, R. (1993). The Millon Clinical Multiaxial Inventory: An introduction to theory, development, and intrepretation. In R. J. Craig (Ed.), *The Millon Clinical Multiaxial Inventory: A clinical research information synthesis* (pp. 3–22). Hillsdale, NJ: Erlbaum.

McNiel, K., & Meyer, R. (1990). Detection of deception on the Millon Clinical Multiaxial Inventory (MCMI). *Journal of Clinical Psychology, 46,* 755–763.

Millon, T. (1969). *Modern psychopathology.* Philadelphia: Saunders.

Millon, T. (1981). *Disorders of personality, DSM-III: Axis II.* New York: Wiley.

Millon, T. (1982). *Millon Clinical Multiaxial Inventory Manual* (2nd ed.). Minneapolis: National Computer Systems.

Millon, T. (1987). *Millon Clinical Multiaxial Inventory-II: Manual for the MCMI-II.* Minneapolis: National Computer Systems.

Morey, L. (1991). *Personality Assessment Inventory: Professional manual.* Odessa, FL: Psychological Assessment Resources.

Nichols, D., Greene, R., & Schmolck, P. (1989). Criteria for assessing inconsistent patterns of item en-dorsement on the MMPI: Rationale, development, and empirical trials. *Journal of Clinical Psychology, 45,* 239–250.

Retzlaff, P., Sheehan, E., & Fiel, A. (1991). MCMI-II report style and bias: Profiles and validity scale analyses. *Journal of Personality Assessment, 56,* 466–477.

Rogers, R. (1988). Introduction. In R. Rogers (Ed.), *Clinical assessment of malingering and deception.* New York: Guilford Press.

Rogers, R., Bagby, R., & Chakraborty, D. (1993). Feigning schizophrenic disorders on the MMPI-2: Detection of coached simulators. *Journal of Personality Assessment, 60,* 215–226.

Rogers, R., Bagby, R., & Dickens, S. (1992). *Structured Interview of Reported Symptoms (SIRS) and test manual.* Odessa, FL: Psychological Assessment Resources.

Rogers, R., Bagby, R., & Gillis, J. (1992). Improvements in the M test in assessment of malingering. *Bulletin of the American Academy of Psychiatry and the Law, 20,* 101–104.

Rogers, R., Gillis, J., & Bagby, R. (1990). The SIRS as a measure of malingering: A validation study with a correctional sample. *Behavioral Sciences and the Law, 8,* 85–92.

Rogers, R., Gillis, J., Bagby, R., & Monteiro, F. (1991). Detection of malingering on the SIRS: A study of coached and uncoached simulators. *Psychological Assessment, 3,* 673–677.

Rogers, R., Gillis, J., Dickens, S., & Bagby, R. (1991). Standardized assessment of malingering: Validation of the SIRS. *Psychological Assessment, 3,* 89–96.

Rogers, R., Kropp, P., & Bagby, R. (1992). Faking specific disorders: A study of the SIRS. *Journal of Clinical Psychology, 48,* 643–647.

Schretlen, D., & Arkowitz, H. (1990). A psychological test battery to detect prison inmates who fake insanity or mental retardation. *Behavioral Sciences and the Law, 8,* 75–84.

Schretlen, D., Van Gorp, W., Wilkins, S., & Bobholz, J. (1992). Cross-validation of a psychological test battery to detect faked insanity. *Psychological Assessment, 4,* 77–83.

Tellegen, A. (1988). The analysis of consistency in personality assessment. *Journal of Personality, 56,* 621–663.

Timbrook, R., Graham, J., Keiller, S., & Watts, D. (1993). Comparison of the Weiner-Harmon Subtle-Obvious scales and the standard validity scales in detecting valid and invalid MMPI-2 profiles. *Psychological Assessment, 5,* 53–61.

Van Gorp, W., & Meyer, R. (1986). The detection of faking on the Millon Clinical Multiaxial Inventory (MCMI). *Journal of Clinical Psychology*, 42, 742–747.

Villanueva, M., & Binder, L. (1993). Association between MMPI-2 validity indices and the Portland Digit Recognition Test. *Journal of Clinical and Experimental Neuropsychology*, 15, 106.

Wetter, M., Baer, R., Berry, D., Robison, L., & Sumpter, J. (1993). MMPI-2 profiles of motivated fakers given specific symptom information. *Psychological Assessment*, 5, 317–323.

Wetter, M., Baer, R., Berry, D., Smith, G., & Larsen, L. (1992). Sensitivity of MMPI-2 validity scales to random responding and malingering. *Psychological Assessment*, 4, 369–374.

Wetzler, S., & Marlowe, D. (1990). Faking bad on the MMPI, MMPI-2 and Millon-II. *Psychological Reports*, 67, 117–118.

Winder, P., O'Dell, J., & Karson, S. (1975). New motivational distortion scales for the 16PF. *Journal of Personality Assessment*, 39, 532–537.

IV
SOURCES OF PERSONALITY INFORMATION

18
"Behavioral Observations"

Martin Leichtman

THE TSAT

Over the past several years, I and a number of colleagues have developed a technique that is by conservative estimates among the most potent assessment instruments created in the last half century. Qualities that recommend the test to experienced clinicians include the remarkable ease with which it can be administered, the rapidity with which it can be mastered, the range of subjects with whom it can be used, and the fact that it can be employed by psychologists of widely differing theoretical persuasions. Moreover, when used in conjunction with other assessment instruments, it does not lengthen standard test batteries.

Similar to but more powerful than its namesake, the Test Situation Apperception Test (TSAT) is based on two dramatic alterations in TAT procedures. First, in place of dated 1930s illustrations, TSAT stimulus material consists of clients playing themselves in real-life situations. Second, instead of subjects making up a story, psychologists are required to do so.

Test procedures are simple. First, psychologists enlist the aid of a confederate, preferably a respected mental health professional, whose function is to send clients with the instruction that testing is needed because they may suffer from psychological problems requiring diagnosis and treatment. Second, after beginning sessions with a few minutes of discussion about why clients have come and the procedures to be used, psychologists administer a number of tests in a pleasant, businesslike way that does not interfere with subjects' ordinary propensities to act as they wish. The choice of tests is unimportant, although ideally they should contain both items subjects can do easily and ones with which they may experience failure; tasks whose purpose seems clear and others that are a bit odd; and some activities that are potentially interesting and others that are likely to be experienced as boring. Third, at the conclusion of the evaluation, psychologists write a paragraph they believe best describes the clients and their behavior during the test process. As with the TAT, authors are free to use their imagination if they choose, but with the stipulation that stories must be rooted in the actions they have observed. Finally, psychologists can then consider where the main characters described in these stories fit within the classificatory scheme of their choice. If they have no preference in the matter, they may wish to consider a system recently developed for the TSAT by the American Psychiatric Association (1987).

The operation of the test can be illustrated by its use with a fifteen-year-old troubled by morbid thoughts that so interfered with his schoolwork he was unable to finish the tenth grade. Asked by the referring psychiatrist whether the boy exhibited severe character pathology as well as an obsessive-compulsive disorder, a psychologist wrote the following paragraph on the basis of the TSAT:

A tall, slender, effeminate adolescent whose nervous mannerisms are reminiscent of the actor Anthony Perkins, Don approached the tests with considerable anxiety and a strong desire to be ingratiating. Yet he had little idea of how to interact in socially appropriate ways and, from the first, treated the examiner as an intimate admirer who would be fascinated by his every thought, no matter how strange. Thus, he began the first session by launching into a detailed lecture on his odd obsessions as if he were a case in a medical text. On the tests, he tried to be precise and meticulous, but had increasing difficulty doing so. So eager was he to impress that he was loath to give one answer to a question when three would do, but often was unable to decide which of the three were good and which poor. He had particular difficulty with mathematical tasks because he had forbidden himself to use certain numbers and he clutched his left side when they were mentioned. He worried constantly about making mistakes and, when encountering test items he could not do, he would begin to shake, noting nonchalantly that he often had such "violent spasms" when upset. As the testing progressed, his thinking became looser. Occasionally he used odd words of his own creation or spoke in Russian to demonstrate his proficiency in a language he had taught himself. Toward the end of the tests, tangential associations to a question led him to give an elaborate description of an imaginary kingdom he had invented and about which he spent many hours each day fantasizing over the last several years.

Classifying his TSAT story according to the DSM-III-R scheme favored by his colleague, the psychologist suggested that while there was evidence of the obsessive-compulsive problems noted by the psychiatrist, they were present in a boy with prominent schizotypal personality characteristics who was at high risk for decompensation.

In addition to the standard TSAT task, an optional variation may be undertaken as well. After completing the initial story, psychologists are encouraged to imagine that their clients will soon enter situations that bear some similarity to testing. For example, they may assume that a child who has just taken intelligence and academic achievement tests is about to enter a remediation program or an adult who has taken the Rorschach is soon to begin psychotherapy. A second story may then be written about how subjects are likely to behave in such situations and how teachers or therapists might most effectively respond to them.

Field tests of the TSAT indicate that it possesses some extraordinary characteristics. For example, the scope of its application extends far beyond that of any established assessment instrument. It may be utilized in unmodified form with subjects who range in age from neonates to the elderly and who display every known form of psychopathology. It is equally appropriate for the severely retarded and the gifted, and neither physical disabilities nor neurological impairments pose any restrictions on its use. Indeed, the TSAT can even be employed with other species, although how far down the phylogenetic scale we may proceed before it ceases to be fruitful is still a matter of contention.

As a means of studying character and predicting behavior, the TSAT has been found to have greater content validity than other projective tests. Early investigations suggest that concurrent validity is high. For example, there is an impressive correlation between diagnostic impressions formed by experienced psychologists on the basis of the TSAT and those advanced by experienced clinicians on the basis of interviews. In addition, studies of predictive validity have established that subjects described as reflective on the TSAT do well in expressive psychotherapy, subjects who are depicted as distractible, hyperactive, and emotionally labile will frequently display these characteristics at home and at school, and subjects who are describcd as assaulting the examiner on the TSAT not only have histories of violent behavior but are at high risk for aggressive acting out in the future.

To this point, only three problems have been noted with the test. First, reliability is a bit lower than many objective instruments, though higher than most projective tests. Second, the TSAT is subject to misuse. Misunderstanding the nature of the task, supervisors and colleagues at times do not focus on the subjects of the stories but instead analyze protocols from the standpoint of what they reveal about their authors. On occasion, this has exposed psychologists to rude comments about their clinical judgment, their literary style, and even their grammar and punctuation. Third, and most important, because the test does not require so much as a modestly priced manual or inexpensive scoring forms, let alone a costly kit, there is little likelihood of interesting a major publisher in it. In the absence of advertising and vigorous marketing, the TSAT may be destined for oblivion.

BEHAVIORAL OBSERVATIONS AND THEIR NEGLECT

There is, of course, no Test Situation Apperception Test. What has been described is a thinly disguised version of a section of test reports that typically follows an initial paragraph devoted to reasons for referral, background information, and questions the evaluation seeks to answer and precedes the body of the report in which findings are presented in one form or another (Huber, 1961; Klopfer, 1960; Ownby, 1987; Seagull, 1979; Tallent, 1976). These paragraphs may be labeled "Behavioral Observations," "General Observations," "Clinical Observations," or "Test Behavior," included in the report with no designation at all, or simply incorporated into the introduction or later sections of the report.

That a chapter on the topic in a handbook on assessment should begin in so curious a manner might be attributed simply to the immaturity of the author and a lapse of judgment on the part of the editors were it not for a more curious fact. "Behavioral Observations" possess the qualities ascribed to our hypothetical instrument, yet are among the most neglected and poorly handled aspects of psychological evaluations (Tallent, 1976).

Reasons for this neglect are not hard to find. To begin with, there is little that is unique about such observations. They are similar to those made by psychiatrists as part of a consultation, and for that matter, by teachers, nurses, and, indeed, anyone having contact with clients. In evaluations involving a variety of disciplines, the psychologist's "Behavioral Observations" may well seem redundant (Tallent, 1976).

More important, such observations appear mundane and plebeian to professionals whose identity, livelihood, and self-esteem rest on claims to a command of rigorous scientific techniques or an artistry with esoteric projective methods that enables them to penetrate surface appearances and reveal aspects of personality and behavior hidden from other disciplines and the lay public. If we must deal with observations of behavior, we would prefer to do it in our own way, using state-of-the-art recording equipment, coding systems and rating scales, and trained observers whose reliability can be monitored (Woody & Robertson, 1988).

A third strike against "Behavioral Observations" lies in their "subjectivity." As our hypothetical test suggests, reports of test behavior do resemble TAT stories. Given differences in personalities, skills, and theoretical orientations among psychologists and the selectivity necessary to describe hours of test behavior in a single paragraph, it is to be expected that a variety of accounts can be generated about the same situation, accounts that may reveal as much about their authors as their subjects. And it is to be expected that this fact alone renders these sections suspect in a discipline in which subjectivity is identified with a lack of reliability, undisciplined speculation, and unrecognized bias—and in which striking anecdotes and empirical studies can be offered to justify this view (Fogel & Nelson, 1983).

Given these attitudes, it is hardly surprising that, with a few notable exceptions (e.g., Knoff,

1986; Sattler, 1988; Tallent, 1976), the topic is touched upon only in a perfunctory manner in most of the literature on report writing and often addressed haphazardly, if at all, in the teaching and supervision of assessment. Nor is it surprising to find that "Behavioral Observations" are often among the most poorly written and least useful aspects of evaluations. Tallent (1976, p. 87), for example, observes: "It should be a matter of concern that there is no rationale or consensual basis for what should appear in this section; this becomes obvious when we consider how much irrelevant and unoriginal data are found here." Because of these problems, some psychologists suggest that this paragraph can often be omitted altogether (Ownby 1987) or treated in specialized ways in the body of the report (Appelbaum, 1972).

Yet most practicing clinicians are reluctant to dispense with "Behavioral Observations" in their traditional form because of a conviction that they can make important contributions to test reports. To clarify the nature of these contributions and provide a framework for presenting them, this chapter will examine the ways in which they are grounded in assumptions governing common clinical practice. In particular, it will consider three sets of issues: (1) ways of conceptualizing the behavior in the test situation to which this section of the report is devoted; (2) the role of behavioral observations in the inference process through which psychologists answer diagnostic questions; and (3) the function these paragraphs serve in the reports through which this information is conveyed.

THE "BEHAVIOR" OBSERVED

"Behavioral Observations" and Their Rationale

Of the problems encountered in "Behavioral Observations" paragraphs, two types are especially worthy of note because of what they reveal about how these accounts are conceived. Undoubtedly the most exasperating is the long, banal description of behavior that has little bearing on the psychological issues the report is in-

tended to address (Tallent, 1976). For example, clinicians who have had extensive contact with a child may be informed that he has blue eyes and blond hair, wore jeans and a T-shirt emblazoned with the word "Cougars" to the initial test session, smiled when meeting the examiner in the waiting room, but glanced apprehensively at his mother, walked down the hall holding the psychologist's hand, looked in the toy closet upon entering the office, but came to the desk when asked, and so forth. At the other extreme are "Behavioral Observations" that consist of little more than a terse statement such as: "The patient is a white, female Caucasian, age thirty-six, who exhibited constriction, dysphoric affect, and psychomotor retardation in the course of the testing." In contrast to rambling, unfocused accounts of subjects' behavior, such paragraphs are blessedly brief and move readers on quickly to the main test findings. At the same time, their impersonal, technical tone typically heralds a report written in the same fashion that will afford little sense of what subjects are like as people.

What is most significant about the first example is that it may be seen as a conscientious effort to act on a central tenet of the catechism that all psychologists, regardless of sect, learn at the beginning of their training: Everything a person thinks, feels, and does is behavior and merits careful observation. This tenet is hard to dispute. In fact, so much can be gleaned from careful observation of test behavior that psychologists can give remarkably good diagnostic pictures of profoundly disturbed children on the basis of how they act in the process of being "untestable" (Kaplan, 1975; Leichtman & Nathan, 1983). Yet the principle is difficult to translate into practice. Acting on it, inexperienced clinicians may produce the long, meandering narratives of test behavior that have the unintended consequence of suggesting that no test behavior is of particular significance. Skilled clinicians can use test behavior to gain insights into every aspect of psychological functioning, but the value of their observations does not derive chiefly from the assumption that all behavior is important. Hours of testing yield an enormous volume of material, and the precept provides no basis for deciding how observations are to be selected and organized into a paragraph of presumably moderate length.

The second example may be seen as an outgrowth of assumptions rooted in a purely psychometric approach to testing that takes laboratory procedures as its models (see Cronbach, 1960, pp. 59–60). Though willing to concede that everything that occurs in the test situation is behavior, adherents of such a perspective presuppose that there are two classes of behavior and a "class system" based on qualitative differences between them. On the one hand, there are test data, data gathered in standardized, delimited conditions, subject to rigorous observation and precise measurement, and analyzed in terms of established norms. On the other, there are those additional observations psychologists make while gathering these data, observations that center on more obvious, superficial behavior, that are less systematic and more subject to bias, and that are, in any case, only a limited sample of the kind of behavior that can be explored more fully in diagnostic interviews. The former data are viewed as the source of the unique, invaluable contributions psychologists make to diagnostic evaluations. The latter are relatively unimportant, and hence are best stated in as brief and objective a manner as possible.

For "Behavioral Observations" to play an effective role in test reports, a rationale is required that involves greater specificity than the view that all behavior is important and that recognizes that these accounts have a legitimate and even indispensable role to play in the report.

The Nature of the Test Process

The basis for such a rationale can be appreciated if we examine the process though which test data are gathered. Consider, for example, that process with John, a five-year-old referred for an evaluation eighteen months after he suffered organic damage that resulted in a variety of cognitive impairments, hyperactivity, attentional problems, and aggressive behavior. As would be anticipated, referral questions center

on assessment of his intellectual abilities and the impact of his injury on his psychological development. As would also be anticipated with the referral, the psychologist receives fair warning that the boy will not be easy to test.

This warning is repeated by the receptionist, who makes it clear that she wants the rambunctious child out of her waiting room quickly. Upon meeting John, the psychologist encounters a feisty youngster who, like his father, is dressed in cowboy boots, western attire, and a belt with a large silver buckle, and who walks with a swagger. Initially frightened, the boy alternates between hiding behind his parents and challenging the examiner with a large jackknife that is a gift from his father. When the examiner shows an interest in the knife, John is able to leave his parents and come to the office. There, after a few minutes of talk about his knife, his boots, and his interests, all occasions to boast about how masculine and daring he is, John agrees to take the tests.

Not surprisingly, testing is an arduous undertaking for both parties. John is highly impulsive, distractible, and labile. Though eager to show off what he can do, he has no tolerance for tasks he might fail or that prove mildly frustrating. Consequently, he races through many items carelessly and tries to avoid or refuse others; he changes tasks he thinks are too hard into ones he can do easily; he reverses roles, giving the examiner the tests instead of taking them himself; and, when all else fails, he attacks the test equipment, banging it angrily on the table or threatening to cut it with his knife. Working with John requires the examiner to make a number of decisions: when and how to provide the boy with support and reassurance and when and how to be firm and keep him at tasks he is ready to slough off; whether to accept an answer as a genuine response or repeat the item now or later; when to tolerate defensive efforts to avoid or change tasks and when and how to confront John about them; and so forth. Such decisions are seldom conscious or deliberate; rather, they are usually intuitive and only half recognized. Indeed, much of what the examiner does to enable the testing to flow smoothly consists of an expression, a posture, a tone of voice, or a way of establishing the rhythm of testing that are not recognized at all.

Yet even if such tactics are not consciously planned, as the testing progresses, the psychologist does develop a sense of particular patterns that govern his interaction with John and allow the evaluation to be conducted with a minimum of disruption. Sensing that John fatigues easily, the examiner quickly learns that a more accurate picture of his abilities can be obtained when breaks are allowed and test sessions shortened. Intuitively recognizing the youngster's attentional problems, the psychologist engages in a variety of actions to help him register tasks. For example, in giving a vocabulary test, the examiner finds himself lifting the book of pictures, turning the page, and replacing it with a flourish every few items, actions that he realizes on later reflection are efforts to refocus the boy's attention and offset his concentration problems. Aware of John's hypersensitivity to failure, the examiner finds subtle ways of being reassuring, is more tolerant of defensive strategies than he is with many other youngsters, reorders some test items, returns to easy items on occasion, and finds other opportunities for the boy to display skills.

Above all, almost from the first, the examiner senses the importance of maintaining a specific relationship. John works best when he experiences the man as a paternal mentor who is tough enough to control him, ready to help him master the tasks before him, and an appreciative audience for the skills he displays and his tales of masculine prowess. In contrast, when he feels that the examiner exposes his incompetence or when he feels threatened by anxieties stirred by projective materials, John either experiences the examiner as dangerous and responds by acting in a reckless, challenging manner or suddenly regresses, converses in baby talk, and acts like a two-year-old.

As John is tested in ways that make allowance for his problems and his need for a particular kind of working relationship, data are obtained that have an important bearing on planning treatment. John's level of intellectual functioning, although obscured by his behavioral problems, is substantially higher than a year earlier, but a marked discrepancy between verbal skills

and difficulties in visual-motor areas is now apparent. Both his behavior and the test results underline the centrality of a number of conflictual issues — those bearing on competence, maintenance of a masculine identity, and dealing with trauma around the injury he has sustained. They also suggest that his high activity level and impulsivity are not simply consequences of his brain injury, but also serve defensive functions as they enable him to deny, avoid, or escape threatening situations. Finally, not only the tests, but even more the interactions that make testing possible, offer a basis for recommendations about how teachers can help John with his learning problems and about transference themes that subsequently prove to be central to his therapy (Leichtman, 1992a; 1992b).

Though perhaps disagreeing with some decisions the examiner makes in handling this testing, most psychologists will recognize the test process as a familiar one that illustrates the two critical components of test administration stressed in almost every manual and text on the subject. First, the examiner strives to "establish rapport," and second, within the context of this relationship, tests are administered in a standardized form or at least as close to a standardized form as seems possible. Yet the case also illustrates a point of particular importance that is typically acknowledged in manuals and texts only to be quickly glossed over in the interests of emphasizing the standardization of test conditions: *Depending on differences in clients and examiners, there are, in fact, marked variations in how "rapport" is established and even what constitutes "standardized administration."*

Rapport, for example, is usually described in general, abstract ways as if it consists of little more than adopting a "positive, nonthreatening tone," "putting the child at ease," and "conveying interest and enthusiasm" to create a positive, relaxed atmosphere (Wechsler, 1991). However, in emphasizing the "importance of rapport" in the administration of the Stanford-Binet, Terman and Merrill (1960) write:

> To elicit the subject's best efforts and maintain both high motivation and optimal performance level throughout the test session are the *sine qua*

non of good testing, but the means by which these ends are accomplished are so varied as to defy specific formulation. The address which puts one child at ease with a strange adult may belittle or even antagonize another. The competent examiner, like the good clinician, must be able to sense the needs of the subject so that he can help him accept and adjust to the testing situation. Sympathetic, understanding relationships with children are achieved in the most diverse ways and no armory of technical skills is a satisfactory substitute for this kind of interpersonal know-how. (pp 50–51)

Stylistic and personality differences among examiners also affect this process. As Phares (1988, p. 163) observes, "There are many ways to achieve good rapport—perhaps as many as there are clinicians."

Similarly, there is considerable diversity in "standardized" test administration. Sattler (1988, p. 87) notes, "Countless variations preclude giving an examination that is always the same." Even with relatively simple evaluations, the pace of testing differs because some children react quickly and others slowly, and the number and types of follow-up questions vary with the ambiguity of responses and examiners' judgments of them. Moreover, with individuals referred because of serious emotional problems, evaluations are anything but simple. Clients come struggling desperately to hide their psychoses, fearful of failure, angry, frightened, elated, depressed, or oppositional. Obtaining an accurate diagnostic picture requires giving tests in ways that address clients' concerns and cope with the defensive maneuvers through which they seek to escape serious engagement with the tests (Palmer, 1983). While at times this necessitates explicit interpretations and modification of test procedures, in most cases it is done without going beyond the parameters of standard test administration. As with John, examiners may handle these problems in subtle, often nonverbal ways through their posture, expression, or tone of voice, through the timing of the tests, or through judgments about whether to accept responses, repeat them, or inquire further. In a sense, test instructions are like a play. Examiners are bound by the script, but there is wide latitude for how they and their clients interpret

their roles. This latitude is, in fact, the subject of an extensive literature on examiner effects on test performance and their implications for the validity of particular tests such as intelligence scales (see Jensen, 1980; Sattler, 1988) or the Rorschach (Exner, 1986).

These influences, it should be stressed, are not unfortunate intrusions of extraneous variables into the test process that can be minimized or fully controlled, but rather inescapable consequences of the fact that tests are given by one human being to another. If tests could be given to each subject in exactly the same way, the result would be less useful information rather than more. For example, were John tested in this manner, we might learn little more than that the boy's hyperactivity, distractibility, and defensiveness interfered with his performance on tests and with every other aspect of his life, a point already clear to the receptionist after a few minutes' contact with him.

Even more important, it is essential to realize that "rapport" and appropriate test administration are not simply general conditions to be met to assure valid testing. Rapport involves more than developing a positive, accepting relationship; it requires sensing roles clients strive to enact that are central to their identities and in natural, intuitive, often unrecognized ways enacting reciprocal roles. Administering tests effectively involves not only adhering to their instructions, but also attending to and helping compensate for the specific manner in which clients' problems may interfered with their responding to those instructions appropriately. With young and markedly disturbed clients, examiners function as what psychoanalysts describe as "auxiliary egos." Each testing has its own unique form determined by the relationships that make it possible.

To consider the nature of psychological testing, then, is to appreciate that it occurs within and is shaped by its interpersonal context. As Cronbach (1960) notes:

> The tester has been accustomed to think of himself as an unemotional, impartial task-setter. His traditions encourage the idea that he, like the physical scientist or engineer, is "measuring an object" with a technical tool. But the

"object" before him is a person, and the testing involves a complex psychological relationship. (p. 602)

"Behavioral Observations" may be viewed as ways of conceptualizing the test process that seek to do justice to these "real social-psychological complexities" and to report them in ways that not only allow for an assessment of the validity of test data, but also make use of valuable information learned in administering the tests.

Testing as a Standardized Interview

Historically, the group that has given the greatest attention to these complexities has been psychoanalytically oriented psychologists, many of whom have been followers of Rapaport (Schachtel, 1966; Schafer, 1954; Schlesinger, 1973; Shevrin and Shectman, 1973; Sugarman, 1978, 1981; Berg, 1986; Lerner, 1991). Like Rapaport (Rapaport, Gill, and Schafer, 1945–1946), they view testing as similar to a standardized clinical interview. In contrast to open-ended interviews, tests provide a common, invariant framework that confronts clients and examiners with distinct challenges. Yet like clinical interviews, the interpersonal context of the test situation or "the patient-examiner relationship" is seen to have a significant bearing on how those challenges are handled and the information derived from them. Schafer (1954), for example, notes:

> The clinical testing situation has a complex psychological structure. It is not an impersonal getting-together of two people in order that one, with the help of a little "rapport" may obtain some "objective" test responses from the other. The psychiatric patient is in some acute or chronic life crisis. He cannot but bring many hopes, fears, assumptions, demands and expectations into the test situation. He cannot but respond intensely to certain real as well as fantasied attributes of that situation. Being human and having to make a living—facts often ignored—the tester too brings hopes, fears, assumptions, demands and expectations into the test situation. He too responds personally and

often intensely to what goes on—in reality and in fantasy—in that situation, however well he may conceal his personal response from the patient, from himself, and from his colleagues. (p. 6)

Assimilating the test situation to a psychoanalytic model, these theorists argue that test productions and their interpretation need to be understood in the light of potent forces of transference and countertransference (Schafer, 1956; Sugarman, 1981).

Although many psychologists may question the specific psychoanalytic interpretations these theorists offer of the test situation, most accept their general assumptions. They accept that the test situation has three basic components—the client, the examiner, and the tests; that each of these components has certain more or less invariant features—the social prescriptions governing the roles of tester and test taker and the structure of the tests themselves; and that as a result of what both participants bring to the situation and their interaction, each of these components is given a distinctive form. "Behavioral Observations" may be viewed as descriptions of these forms in each individual case.

From this perspective, these sections of reports should answer three sets of questions. First, how do clients present themselves? What roles are they trying to enact, and what concerns do they bring to the test situation? Second, what is the nature of the relationship that emerges as examiners try to engage them in the test process in ways that balance the need to maintain rapport with the need to administer tests in appropriate ways? And third, what are clients' attitudes toward the tests, their general modes of approaching them, and reactions toward their productions? Psychologists may also wish to include observations of a host of other matters, but answers to these questions are germane in every case and a core around which to organize these paragraphs.

Conceiving of "Behavioral Observations" in this way has important implications for how they may be written. Insofar as they are understood as answers to a delimited set of questions, they need not be long. Although a psychologist has enough material to write pages on a client's dress, appearance, and manner during the testing, a few lines may be sufficient to give a reasonable view of the overriding impression they create. Indeed, the term "Behavioral Observations" is a misnomer in the sense that what is sought are generalizations. A multitude of observations may go into formulating an impression of a youngster's attitude toward and modes of approaching the tests, but only a good example or two are necessary to illustrate it.

BEHAVIORAL OBSERVATIONS AND THE INFERENCE PROCESS

Attitudes Toward Clinical Impressions

Psychologists typically are most comfortable with those questions about the test situation concerned with clients' modes of handling the tests, because answers can be based on observable behavior that lends itself to quantification (see Sattler, 1988). In contrast, many are uneasy with questions about the roles clients play, and even more about relationships with examiners, because these require greater reliance on subjective impressions and clinical judgment. Consequently, there are significant differences of opinion about how these answers should be given and what role they should play in the inference process through which diagnostic formulations are developed.

Articulating a position shared by many psychologists with psychometric and behavioral orientations, Knoff (1986) advocates caution in the use of observations of behavior. He asserts:

> To date, there is no empirically sound observational system available for completion by the practitioner during or immediately after the individual assessment session; nor are there procedures to control the potential bias when data (observed or recalled) are generalized into diagnostic hypotheses (p. 552).

Accordingly, he recommends: (1) recognizing that "assessment observations are based on a narrow, artificial situation and may not represent the child's behavior in 'real life' situations";

(2) emphasizing "observed and documented behavior over recollections and inferences"; (3) "utiliz[ing] observers behind one-way mirrors and determining interrater reliabilities for observations and interpretations"; and (4) stressing "consistencies across the entire assessment process" and "discounting inconsistencies that may be situation-specific and 'chance fluctuations'" (p. 552).

Most clinicians, however, are likely to find these recommendations excessively cautious and impractical. Though useful in training, one-way mirrors and checks on interrater reliability can play little role in a busy clinical practice. Too heavy an emphasis on documented behavior and a reluctance to generalize, while admirable from a scientific standpoint, may diminish the usefulness of reports to referral sources and leave the task of generalizing to others who are probably less skilled and certainly less familiar with the data. Most important, this approach underestimates the value of what Polanyi (1958) describes as "personal knowledge," the judgment and expertise that constitute the art of a profession.

The Interplay of Inferences from Different Sources of Data

An alternate approach to the problem is one that encourages the use of a disciplined subjectivity in the inference process. A useful exercise in teaching this kind of clinical skill consists of having trainees rate the degree of pathology exhibited by clients they have just tested on a five-point scale ranging from normality to psychosis and categorize the client's character style and type of pathology according to DSM-III-R or whatever nosological scheme is preferred in their setting. In approaching these tasks, they are asked to imagine that they will not be allowed to score and analyze tests or make use of individual test responses, but must rely solely on their impressions of clients in the test situation and articulate the bases for those impressions. Then they are asked to repeat the task assuming answers to the diagnostic questions must be based only on information gathered from each of the tests they have administered. Finally, they compare the answers they have offered.

The exercise has a number of benefits. First, subjective impressions are brought into the open where they can be examined rather than driven underground where they are less likely to disappear than influence diagnoses in unacknowledged ways. Second, insisting that distinct sets of inferences be made from different sources of data helps wean novice psychologists away from a covert overreliance on their behavioral observations and teaches them to how to use test data. Third, the exercise sharpens skills in forming clinical impressions since these impressions can be compared with those of supervisors, other members of clinical teams, teachers, and family. Finally, by encouraging comparison of inferences from a variety of sources of data, it teaches an approach to formulating diagnostic pictures that is invaluable in clinical work.

As clinicians gain increasing experience, there is a substantial degree of convergence in the diagnostic opinions they form on the basis of behavioral observations and test data. They find that the young woman who appears for testing in a tight skirt, behaves seductively with the examiner, and approaches tests in a flighty, impressionistic manner often produces test results that point to a histrionic character. The adolescent who wears a Harley-Davidson T-shirt and a surly expression and who makes it clear that he doesn't give a damn about the examiner and his "friggin' tests" often displays antisocial signs on many tests. The sad, lethargic man with the self-critical attitude usually scores high on depressive indices of the Rorschach and MMPI. This correspondence of inferences made from behavior in the test situation and particular tests contributes substantially to clinicians' conviction about the correctness of their formulations.

Even more can be learned when impressions based on observations diverge from those based on other sources of data. A youngster who seems bright may score poorly on intelligence tests; a man who appears well attuned to reality may exhibit thought disorder signs on the Rorschach; a seemingly cheerful, carefree woman may give TAT stories that suggest a significant suicidal potential. In such cases, it is essential not to discount the behavioral presentation or dismiss it as a "chance fluctuation." Rather, inquiring into the discrepancies is essential in understanding clients and growing as a clinician.

One explanation of these differences is, of course, that one set of inferences is wrong. Discovering that their opinions based on behavioral observations consistently fail to jibe with what tests reveal can be a powerful impetus for young clinicians to hone their clinical skills. In individual cases, even experienced clinicians find that analysis of tests helps them recognize mistaken impressions of a client. At the same time, tests are not infallible. If a child seems intelligent, yet does poorly on the WISC-III, a careful review of the test is in order.

The most interesting situations are those in which there are differences between behavioral impressions and test data and the examiner trusts both. Making sense of these discrepancies yields insights into individuals' personalities that can be critical in treatment planning because the ways in which skilled clinicians experience clients are seldom, in fact, idiosyncratic and purely subjective. Typically they are similar to the experiences of family, teachers, therapists, and others who enter into intimate relationships with clients. The boy with low scores on intelligence tests who looks much smarter is often a youngster who works hard to create that impression. He may come for help precisely because of the problems caused by the gulf between his abilities and the expectations he and others have for him. Similarly, the contrast between a client's seemingly normal self-presentation and a vulnerability to decompensation seen on the Rorschach or between a cheerful exterior and suicidal themes on projective tests are issues that should be highlighted in case formulations to assure that disastrous mistakes are avoided as treatment is undertaken.

The Value of Subjectivity

Behavioral observations offer more than simply an additional source of data; they provide a unique type of information. To establish rapport and conduct tests effectively with human beings with significant psychological problems requires that examiners intuitively sense and respond to their clients' emotional states, defensive styles, and modes of relating to others. In reflecting on their experience of the testing— on why they make the decisions they do in the course of testing, on the roles they assume, and on the feelings the encounter stirs in them— psychologists not only learn a great deal about clients but can also better understand the struggles of families, therapists, teachers, and hospital staff who live with and care for them.

By its very nature, much of the data collected about an assessment is personal and private. Yet its value lies in this subjectivity, which affords access to insights to which dispassionate, objective observers will be blind (Sugarman, 1981). For example, in testing a youngster with ADHD, the examiner experiences not only the usual fatigue and frustration that arise in coping with marked impulsivity and distractibility, but also an intense, disconcerting aversion to the boy. When, with some reluctance, he shares these feelings in his report, the boy's psychiatrist and teachers are relieved and reveal that they have similar reactions that have been hard to acknowledge. The family therapist adds that she suspects that the parents feel the same way and that their anger and guilt interfere with accepting the child and setting appropriate limits for him. Clearly dealing with the youngster's attentional problems, hyperactivity, and learning disability will not be enough. Effective treatment will require understanding and addressing why he is hated and needs to make himself hateful.

The value of subjective data is not confined to those cases in which unanticipated information about clients is uncovered. In every testing, the psychologists' personal experience of clients provides a means of translating objective, quantitative, often impersonal data from tests into full-bodied pictures of human beings. This experience also allows psychologists empathize with families and treaters to whom their reports are often addressed. It is this integration of objective and subjective data that enables psychologists to reconcile the "scientific" and "humanistic" aspects of the assessment process (Sugarman, 1978).

Perhaps the most significant contributions the examiner's experience of clients can make in formulating cases are to treatment recommendations. Although clinicians at times act as if diagnosis and treatment are separate processes, clients do not. For them, diagnosis is the first step in a treatment process. Even proponents of objective instruments recognize that when conducted properly, testing can have important therapeutic benefits (see Butcher & Finn, 1983). Psychodynamic psychologists who view testing as a clinical interview go further. Treating the test situation as paradigmatic of the therapy process, they argue that transference-countertransference patterns established in the former can predict those that will arise in the latter (Schlesinger, 1973; Sugarman, 1981). With John, the neurologically impaired youngster described above, the relationship established with the psychologist during the testing afforded a remarkably good basis for anticipating the ways in which he was to use his therapist and the issues that would disrupt the therapeutic relationship in the years that followed (Leichtman, 1992b). Appelbaum (1972) attaches such importance to this aspect of the testing that he advocates devoting a major section of the report to "How the Patient Responds to Various Interpersonal Approaches."

Although many psychologists would dispute so close an identification of testing and therapy, they will acknowledge important common features. Therapists, like testers, need to establish rapport and engage in explorations in which they seek to learn what clients are like, including secrets and vulnerabilities wished hidden. Also, as psychologists help children take intelligence or achievement tests, they grapple with many of the same problems with which teachers and tutors struggle in educational settings. Because of these similarities, examiners can draw on their experiences of what facilitated and disrupted testing to make the kinds of specific, individualized recommendations that are of particular help to those who will treat clients.

Appreciating the potential benefits of the use of subjective data helps place concerns about their liabilities in a proper perspective. Those liabilities are not quite as great as some fear. Though drawing on private, emotion-laden experience, psychologists can check their impressions against those of others and against test data. Even so, we can never be sure that our impressions are not biased or idiosyncratic. However, confining reports to objective data because of concerns about bias and unreliability will not keep our virtue unsullied. There are sins of omission as well as commission; Type I as well as Type II errors. To ignore subjective data may be to neglect vital information about clients, miss opportunities to offer richer pictures of them in reports, and diminish the utility of treatment recommendations. Clients may be better served when psychologists risk mistakes, trust their capacities to make empathic contact with their clients, and work to develop the kinds of skills that warrant such trust.

THE FUNCTIONS OF "BEHAVIORAL OBSERVATIONS" SECTIONS IN REPORTS

The importance of the phenomena about which "Behavioral Observations" are made and their significance in inference process are not sufficient to justify devoting a separate introductory section of test reports to them. Such information, after all, can be included in a variety of places. In fact, contending that the formats in which these observations are treated separately create an artificial distinction between internal and external aspects of personality, Sugarman (1981) argues that these data should be integrated throughout the body of the report. However, there are a number of reasons for accepting the traditional approach to report writing in which "Behavioral Observations" follow an introductory statement of presenting problems and questions to be answered and precede discussion of test findings and their implications.

Consumer Rights

One reason for this format is "truth in packaging." Because reports are based on information gathered in circumstances that may influence the nature of the data and their analysis, readers have a right to know about test conditions at their outset. These observations are especially important when clients' resistances or idiosyncratic approaches to testing raise questions about the validity of findings. Psychologists may be concerned that such revelations will undermine faith in their reports, but readers are entitled to this information and usually give greater credence to interpretations in which problematic aspects of testing are considered carefully.

A description of test conditions early in a report may be of particular help to psychologists who evaluate the individual later. Differences in findings, such as a sharp drop in IQ scores, can be understood quickly when it is clear that the belligerent youngster just tested was compliant and cooperative several years ago.

Humanizing Reports

Some authorities have implied that by focusing on how clients look, behave, and interact in social relationships, "Behavioral Observations" deal with more superficial aspects of personality than those revealed by tests. However, far from constituting a criticism of these sections, this point provides a second reason for opening reports with them. Beginning reports with vivid descriptions of how clients present themselves helps assure that readers will approach subsequent information and interpretations with images of recognizable human beings in mind.

Although it can be argued that "Behavioral Observations" are unnecessary because every paragraph of a report should serve this function, translating such a principle into practice is difficult. Much of what we pride ourselves upon as psychologists—our ability to quantify behavior, our analytic skills that enable us to attempt to isolate aspects of behavior, our technical language and often esoteric theories, our talents at fitting individuals into diagnostic categories—may interfere with readers' maintaining an image of the subjects our reports as real people. Most of us have had occasion to complain that other psychologists' reports are too riddled with jargon, too preoccupied with numbers, too mechanistic in their description of seemingly discrete functions, or too filled with convoluted theoretical formulations whether they are about psychosexual development or central processing dysfunctions. Yet all but the most talented or obtuse of us recognize that such problems are not easily avoided in our own reports.

It could hardly be otherwise. What distinguishes jargon from precise communication, useless tables from refined quantification, and sophisticated theories from empty abstractions is often how much the reader shares the language, sophistication, or theoretical framework of the writer. What may seem mechanical or confusing to one reader in one context may be quite useful to another in a different context. Even outright vices in report writing that cannot be rationalized in this manner, like other vices, are ones from which few of us are free. Writing reports is difficult, demanding work; the volume of this work is often heavy and time limited; and our skills and training as psychologists, not to mention as writers, are frequently less than we, and even more our readers, wish.

When reports start with good "Behavioral Observations," the failings of later sections in this regard are minimized. As in person perception experiments in which information presented first has a potent effect on how later information is organized and understood (Asch, 1946; Luchins, 1957), these paragraphs increase the likelihood that readers will view technical discussions of test findings, jargon, and even abstruse theorizing later in reports as efforts to describe attributes of human beings rather than ignore them or think of clients as collections of functions, traits, or psychic structures.

Persuasion

Appelbaum (1970) stresses that reports must not only be "right," but also convincing to those responsible for implementing their recommendations. Besides being scientists and experts, he suggests, psychologists should also be salesmen. "Behavioral Observations" have a good deal to contribute to the task of persuasion.

Referral sources have ambivalent attitudes to-ward psychologists (Shectman, 1979). For both realistic and unrealistic reasons, those with less clinical sophistication may defer to psychologists' authority too readily, accepting recommendations uncritically and applying them too rigidly. Yet these same individuals may suspect that our complex methodologies and seemingly arcane theories represent a pseudoscience that blinds us to what is obvious and practical in assisting clients. Such suspicions are likely to be especially high when conclusions about clients from testing differ from what their overt behavior or presenting symptoms lead others to believe. Similar problems occur even when there is a difference of opinion with sophisticated clinicians who share the same theoretical perspective, as for example when test findings suggest a markedly different view of a client than does a psychiatric interview.

Although it has been suggested that readers are put off by reports that tell them what they already know about clients (Tallent, 1976), the opposite may be the case. Well-observed accounts of how clients present themselves in the testing situation can reassure others that psychologists are seeing the same individuals they are. When reports start by establishing a common ground, readers are more inclined to accept test results that differ from surface impressions and to see differences of opinion as a product of the perspectives afforded by particular methods rather than of a misdiagnosis on someone's part.

Art and Style

Appelbaum (1970) also suggests that writing effective test reports involves art as well as science and salesmanship. He notes:

> Just as advertising people do, the writer of psychological reports may use techniques of art (again, with different motives as well as technical differences). As does the artist, the writer of a test report may arouse expectations, build, sustain and relieve tension, integrate and recapitulate. (p. 351)

By providing a transition from statements of symptoms and referral questions to the body of reports, "Behavioral Observations" can make important contributions in these respects as well. However, since few reports I have read, including my own, qualify as works of art, the issues Appelbaum raises are perhaps best discussed under the heading of "style."

Because behavioral and characterological problems manifest themselves so readily in the test situation, a description of how patients present themselves and act often provides readers with an experience of the clients' difficulties that goes far beyond what is often a generic list of symptoms in the introduction. What is meant by "hyperactivity," for example, can be brought home to the reader by a vignette describing trying to test this particular child while he is sitting on, under, and through his chair. Similarly, readers gain an appreciation of a referral problem stated as "problems managing aggression" when an examiner recounts walking on eggshells as she tries to cope with a client's simmering rage and subtle — and at times none too subtle — intimidation.

"Behavioral Observations" can stimulate an interest in learning more about clients by drawing attention to incongruous phenomena. For example, when an examiner experiences an adolescent as dependent and surprisingly cooperative in spite of the boy's effort to maintain a tough, antisocial facade, readers are likely to be curious about why. Or the contrast between presenting problems and the psychologist's observations may highlight central issues that reports need to address. Why is a child who is impulsive, hyperactive, and distractible at school capable of working diligently for extended periods of time in the test situation? Why does a client others describe as psychologically minded and insightful leave the examiner feeling frustrated and annoyed as he tries to use the testing to help explore and clarify the man's problems? What is one to make of the cheerful, relentlessly upbeat woman whose history has been one of repeated trauma and loss? Such questions capture the reader's attention and prepare the way for answers that may be critical in recommending particular forms of treatment.

Even where "Behavioral Observations" are consistent with both presenting symptoms and test findings, they can provide an initial statement of a theme that subsequent sections of reports will develop with increasing richness. For example, with Don, the adolescent described in the introduction, "Behavioral Observations" give readers a sense of his obsessional and schizotypal characteristics. Subsequent sections of his report use data from the tests to amplify the particular qualities of his thinking, his relationships with others, and his central conflicts and defensive structure.

The stylistic contributions of "Behavioral Observations" to reports can be as varied as the individuals tested, the goals of reports, and the talents and ingenuity of their writers. What is important for present purposes is a recognition of the diverse opportunities these sections afford for making their subjects come alive and transforming reports into something more than dry inventories of test findings.

CONCLUSION: THE TEST SITUATION AS A TEST

Although there is no TSAT, the test situation in fact resembles a projective test. Like a TAT card, it has an objective structure to which all clients must respond in some way. Tester and test-taker play more or less objective roles according to prescribed social conventions, and the tests are standardized tasks to which all subjects must respond. Yet like a TAT story, the meanings clients and examiners attribute to each aspect of the test situation may be extraordinarily varied allowing for an appreciation of individual differences.

Just as clients will ascribe a wide range of psychological characteristics to the boy looking at a violin in a TAT card, so too will they seek to define themselves in a multitude of ways in the test situation through how they dress, carry themselves, and interact. Just as the boy may have a host of attitudes toward the violin — an eagerness to learn, a desire to show off, a sense of helplessness and inadequacy, resentful compliance or open defiance with parental demands, or utter indifference — so to will clients exhibit a multiplicity of attitudes and behaviors toward the tests. And just as diverse relationships may be ascribed to two figures in a TAT card, so too will the interactions between client and examiner assume innumerable forms. Children, for example, may assimilate tests to their concept of school tests and treat examiners as teachers. Yet one will play the role of good, compliant student eager to win praise and approval from a benign and interested teacher; a second will feel like a hopeless failure forced to confront her inadequacies by a stern taskmaster; and a third will act like a truant kept after school, working halfheartedly on assignments while watched but ready to abandon the lesson altogether the moment the teacher's back is turned. Others experience the relationship like that of a delinquent before a judge or parole officer—one defiant and rebellious, another hiding such feelings to run a con game. Still others treat the relationship as a search for care and nurturance, a seduction, a performance before an audience, or a desperate attempt to conceal their craziness.

No additional test need be administered to obtain such rich data. It is there for the taking, and there to be used to improve diagnosis and enliven the reports through which they are communicated.

REFERENCES

American Psychiatric Association. (1987). *Diagnostic and statistical manual, mental disorders* (3rd ed., rev.) (DSM-III-R). Washington, DC: Author.

Appelbaum, S. A. (1970). Science and persuasion in the psychological test report. *Journal of Consulting and Clinical Psychology, 35*, 349–355.

Appelbaum, S. A. (1972). A method of reporting psychological test findings. *Bulletin of the Menninger Clinic, 36*, 535–545.

Asch, S. E. (1946). Forming impressions of personality. *Journal of Abnormal and Social Psychology, 41*, 258–290.

Berg, M. (1986). Diagnostic use of the Rorschach with adolescents. In A. I. Rabin (Ed.), *Projective techniques for adolescents and children* (pp. 111–141). New York: Springer.

Butcher, J. N., & Finn, S. (1983). Objective personality assessment in clinical settings. In M. Hersen,

A. Kazdin, & A. S. Bellack (Eds.), *The clinical psychology handbook* (pp. 329–344). New York: Pergamon.

Cronbach, L. J. (1960). *Essentials of psychological testing* (2nd ed.). New York: Harper.

Exner, J. E. (1986). *The Rorschach: A comprehensive system* (2nd ed.). New York: Wiley.

Fogel, L. S., & Nelson, R. O. (1983). The effects of special education labels on teachers' behavioral observations, checklist scores, and grading of academic work. *Journal of School Psychology, 21*, 241–252.

Huber, J. T. (1961). *Report writing in psychology and psychiatry.* New York: Harper & Row.

Jensen, A. R. (1980). *Bias in mental testing.* New York: Free Press.

Kaplan, L. J. (1975). Testing nontestable children. *Bulletin of the Menninger Clinic, 39*, 420–435.

Klopfer, W. G. (1960). *The psychological report: Use and communication of psychological findings.* New York: Grune & Stratton.

Knoff, H. M. (1986). The personality assessment report and the feedback and planning conference. In H. M. Knoff (Ed.), *The assessment of child and adolescent personality* (pp. 547–582). New York: Guilford Press.

Leichtman, M. (1992a). Psychotherapeutic interventions with brain-injured children and their families: I. Diagnosis and treatment planning. *Bulletin of the Menninger Clinic, 56*, 321–337.

Leichtman, M. (1992b). Psychotherapeutic interventions with brain-injured children and their families: II. Psychotherapy. *Bulletin of the Menninger Clinic, 56*, 338–360.

Leichtman, M., & Nathan, S. (1983). A clinical approach to the psychological testing of borderline children. In K. Robson (Ed.), *The borderline child: Approaches to etiology, diagnosis, and treatment* (pp. 121–170). New York: McGraw-Hill.

Lerner, P. (1991). *Psychoanalytic theory and the Rorschach.* Hillsdale, NJ: Analytic Press.

Luchins, A. S. (1957). Primacy-recency in impression formation. In C. I. Hovland, L. Mandell, E. H. Campbell, T. Brock, A. S. Luchins, A. R. Cohen, W. J. McGuire, I. L. Janis, R. L. Feierabend, & N. A. Anderson (Eds.), *The order of presentation in persuasion* (pp. 33–61). New Haven, CT: Yale University Press.

Ownby, R. L. (1987). *Psychological reports: A guide to report writing in professional psychology.* Brandon, VT: Clinical Psychology.

Palmer, J. O. (1983). *The psychological assessment of children* (2nd ed.). New York: Wiley.

Phares, E. J. (1988). *Clinical psychology: Concepts, methods, and profession* (3rd ed.). Chicago: Dorsey Press.

Polanyi, M. (1958). *Personal knowledge: Towards a post-critical philosophy.* Chicago: University of Chicago Press.

Rapaport, D., Gill, M. M., & Schafer, R. (1945–1946). *Diagnostic psychological testing* (2 vols.). Chicago: Year Book.

Sattler, J. M. (1988). *Assessment of children's intelligence and special abilities* (3rd ed.). San Diego, CA: Jerome M. Sattler.

Schachtel, E. (1966). *Experiential foundations of Rorschach's test.* New York: Basic Books.

Schafer, R. (1954). *Psychoanalytic interpretation in Rorschach testing.* New York: International Universities Press.

Schafer, R. (1956). Transference in the patient's reaction to the tester. *Journal of Projective Techniques, 20,* 26–32.

Schlesinger, H. (1973). Interaction of dynamic and reality factors in the diagnostic testing interview. *Bulletin of the Menninger Clinic, 37,* 495–517.

Seagull, E. A. W. (1979). Writing the report of a psychological assessment of a child. *Journal of Clinical Child Psychology, 8,* 39–42.

Shectman, F. (1979). Problems in communicating psychological understanding: Why won't they listen to me?! *American Psychologist, 34*(9), 781–790.

Shevrin, H., & Schectman, F. (1973). The diagnostic process in psychiatric evaluations. *Bulletin of the Menninger Clinic, 37,* 451–494.

Sugarman, A. (1978). Is psychodiagnostic assessment humanistic? *Journal of Personality Assessment, 42,* 11–21.

Sugarman, A. (1981). The diagnostic use of countertransference reactions in psychological testing. *Bulletin of the Menninger Clinic, 45,* 473–490.

Tallent, N. (1976). *Psychological report writing.* Englewood Cliffs, NJ: Prentice-Hall.

Terman, L., & Merrill, M. (1960). *Stanford-Binet intelligence scale.* Boston: Houghton-Mifflin.

Wechsler, D. (1991). *Wechsler intelligence scale for children—third edition: Manual.* San Antonio, TX: Psychological Corporation.

Woody, R. H., & Robertson, M. (1988). *Becoming a clinical psychologist.* Madison, CT: International Universities Press.

19

Idiothetic Assessment Experience Sampling and Motivational Analysis

Eric Klinger
Debi Kroll-Mensing

The client, despite continuing medication, suffered from what she experienced as unremitting depression. Her life was not perfect, but she could report no adverse events sufficient to account for her mood. Conventional tests merely confirmed her depression. Induced to carry a "beeper"—which emitted a signal at quasi-random intervals—she began to note down her thoughts, mood, and circumstances at each beep. She soon discovered that her mood in fact varied greatly and that its low points coincided with specific thoughts and events. These, related to her family relationships and temporary joblessness, constituted specific solvable problems for her to tackle—a much less amorphous and ominous state of affairs than an undifferentiated, uncontrollable pall of depression. Within a few weeks her mood had improved greatly, even as she phased out medication for the first time in years.

This client offers an example of what we might call the microdiagnostic and therapeutic roles of experience sampling. Others, too, have reported such benefits. Thus, a client suffering from intermittent anxiety was unable to provide clues as to instigators before a similar procedure of "cognition sampling" (Hurlburt & Sipprelle, 1978). The sampling revealed a pattern of increased anxiety after being annoyed by his children, annoyance that triggered self-doubts as to his capability as a parent. With this linkage revealed, he was able to work on the specific issues of parenting. His anxiety greatly decreased.

Experience sampling constitutes one of a growing family of methods that supplement traditional clinical assessment. They provide a fine grain of information about clients that aids in formulating diagnoses and treatment plans. They are able to do so by compensating for the weaknesses of more established assessment methods.

THE PROBLEM: THE SCYLLA AND CHARYBDIS OF CLINICAL ASSESSMENT

When clinicians seek to inform themselves about their clients, they most often use measures that (a) depend on somebody's long-term memory; and (b) require someone else to interpret the information retrieved (Fiske, 1971), such as the clients themselves or those who know them. That is, clients either describe specific past events ("I felt choking sensations") or generalize about themselves ("When I leave home I get terribly nervous"). But both memories and people's general formulations about themselves are notoriously subject to lapses and distortion. Furthermore, when clients respond to standard self-report measures, they may interpret the items in ways unanticipated by their diagnosticians, with confused communication as a result. Asked whether they "often have headaches," individual clients may have quite divergent experiences that they classify as headaches, and one person may interpret "often" quite differently from another. Thus, the quality of the individual experience is lost, which may also represent a significant clinical loss.

As applied to questions about conscious experience, self-statement endorsements may be unrepresentative of actual thought content. Using predetermined item inventories of cognitions runs the risk that subjects may report

> (a) the importance rather than the frequency of a cognition; (b) that subjects may base their responses on having similar but not identical thoughts, as suggested by questionnaire items; (c) that individuals may respond to items based on the relevancy of a cognition rather than its frequency; (d) that subjects may base their answers on an affective experience, which they then translate into a language-based self-statement format. (D. A. Clark, 1988, p. 3, in an apt summary of points made by Glass & Arnkoff, 1982)

Another kind of problem is that information from conventional measures is often in the form of psychodiagnosis or of rather broad characterizations. It is important to know that a client scores high on a depression scale, for example, but it may be of particular importance in a given case to understand the pattern of fluctuations in depression, the contingencies involved, and the nature of what the client means in describing a mood as depression. To obtain this kind of information, clinicians have typically conversed with patients, but in doing so they rely on their patients' memories, which are highly selective and not necessarily representative and which often distort what they portray. Thus, a memory of a conversation may include only a fraction of

what was actually said, and both the language and the emotional tone of the conversation may be different in memory than in actuality.

If that is a Scylla of clinical assessment, a Charybdis is to sample clients' behaviors systematically by asking them, upon some agreed-upon set of cues, to write down what they are currently doing or experiencing, perhaps along with the situational context. This produces information that is minimally dependent on memory, although it is still bound to be somewhat selective. If clients actually express their experiences in their own words, their reports are also likely to preserve some of the individual character of the experience. But this, too, exacts a cost. Overly idiographic assessment provides few ready means for comparing clients' responses to those of others. If it is primarily verbal, it becomes cumbersome to quantify it or to relate it to common dimensions that distinguish among individuals. Therefore, it becomes hard to say where or how a particular set of experiences compares with population norms—how, for instance, an individual client's anxiety experience differs in kind and degree from others in the population.

THE IDIOTHETIC STRATEGY

It is these dilemmas that the two kinds of methods to be described here—experience sampling and idiothetic motivational assessment—were intended to resolve. Experience sampling is designed to assess the content of conscious experience, including perception, thought, affect, and action. Idiothetic motivational assessment, at least in the form of the Motivational Structure Questionnaire, assesses respondents' goals and concerns. Both of these assessment approaches employ a two-stage procedure. At the first stage, the *idiographic* stage, subjects describe the objects of assessment in their own idiosyncratic ways. The identity of the thoughts or concerns listed and the narrative descriptions of them are idiographic in the sense that they convey individual peculiarities and are not directly comparable to anyone else's statements. This step is followed by a second, *nomothetic* stage: subjects now rate their thoughts or concerns on scales provided by the assessor. When these ratings are grouped and averaged or stated as proportions within subjects, they provide indices comparable across different subjects.

This strategy has a long history, but in 1981 it gained a label, *idiothetic* (Lamiell, 1981), that appears to be gaining acceptance. Idiothetic approaches have the advantage of fitting assessment to the subject's individuality while still permitting quantitative comparisons among different individuals. That is, each person produces descriptions and lists that differ qualitatively from those of others; but each person also rates his or her qualitatively unique content using the same rating scales used by other respondents, thereby yielding numbers that can be compared with those of others. Just what these numbers are and how they are aggregated varies with the measurement instrument and the purpose of the assessment.

ASSESSMENT OF CONSCIOUS CONTENT WITH EXPERIENCE-SAMPLING METHODS

"Experience sampling" generally refers to subjects' reporting the perceptions, thoughts, feelings, and actions they were experiencing just before a series of signals. While thought sampling developed in Minnesota (Klinger, 1978), other variants were being developed independently elsewhere by Hurlburt (1979) for assessing thoughts and by Csikszentmihalyi and his colleagues for assessing activities and affect, the latter giving it the label "experience sampling method" (ESM; Csikszentmihalyi, Larson, & Prescott, 1977).

Most such research focuses on thoughts and feelings. "Thoughts" here refers loosely to any mental content, whether covert verbal activity such as self-talk or mental images. These range from "wondering when the red light would change" to "imagining myself rafting down the Mississippi." The reports may be narrative descriptions, ratings, or, as in the Thought-Sam-

pling Questionnaire (TSQ; Klinger, 1978; Klinger & Cox, 1987–88), both. Hurlburt (1990) has added intense, probing postsampling interviews to the procedure.

Behavior sampling, of which experience sampling is an outgrowth, has a long history in work settings (e.g., Tippett, 1935) and dream investigations (Aserinsky & Kleitman, 1953). The immediate ancestor of the TSQ, in fact, was a 1971 dream-sampling questionnaire in use by Allen Rechtschaffen, from which the TSQ was heavily modified and expanded. The rating scales of the TSQ have varied somewhat from one investigation to another, but they have generally included scales to assess the sharpness, vividness, and detail of the imagery in a particular thought, its dominant modalities (visual, auditory), spontaneity (versus deliberateness), fancifulness, controllability, time orientation, and the subject's concurrent attentiveness to external stimulation (Klinger, 1978; Klinger & Cox, 1987–88; Kroll-Mensing, 1992). It has been applied in the laboratory (Klinger, 1978; Klinger & Murphy, 1994), at athletic contests (Klinger, Barta, & Glas, 1979), during films (Hurlburt & Melancon, 1987), at work (Roberson, 1989), and in free-living situations (Brunstein & Ganserer, 1989; Csikszentmihalyi & Larson, 1987; Hurlburt, 1979; Klinger & Cox, 1987–88). Methods used to generate signals have ranged over experimental tones, pagers, self-contained beepers, programmable wristwatches, hand-held computers, and taps on the shoulder. Schedules for signaling—that is, the timing of the beeps—take numerous forms. Some investigators schedule beeps at essentially random intervals within some range (for example, no less than five minutes between beeps nor more than ninety minutes, with an average of forty-five minutes). Random intervals offer the advantage that subjects are unable to predict occurrence. Other investigators have used fixed, constant intervals between beeps. Still others dispense with beeps altogether by instructing subjects to sample their thoughts whenever they become aware of experiencing a certain kind of thought, feeling, impulse, action, or situation—for example, a self-critical thought, an impulse to smoke a cigarette, or anger.

Reliability and Validity of Thought-Sampling Measures

Individual-subject scores based on the self-ratings have exhibited reasonable stability and internal consistency (Csikszentmihalyi & Larson, 1987). Factor analyses—based on intrasubject correlations among thought-sampling scales across a subject's different thought samples—have also yielded reasonable stability in factor structure (Hurlburt, 1987; Klinger & Cox, 1987–88). Data from investigations of adolescent and adult populations, comparing responses from the first half of a week's sampling to the second half, demonstrate adequate stability of activity estimates and psychological states, as well as consistency within individuals (Csikszentmihalyi & Larson, 1987). Freeman, Larson, and Csikszentmihalyi (1986; cited by Csikszentmihalyi & Larson, 1987) report stability coefficients ranging from .45 to .75 for activity and concentration variables in a sample of twenty-eight adolescents who participated in an ESM study at two time periods separated by two years, indicating adequate test-retest reliability.

Support for the validity of data derived from ESM comes from a variety of sources, including convergence between ESM data and physiological measures, convergence between data provided by ESM and responses to other self-report measures, and the ability of data derived from ESM to distinguish between divergent groups of respondents, such as various forms of psychopathology (Csikszentmihalyi & Larson, 1987). TSQ scales have recently been found related to measures of anxiety and depression (Kroll-Mensing, 1992) and to certain personality scales (Klinger & Murphy, 1994). For example, anxiety is significantly related to perceived inappropriateness of thoughts, and inversely to their perceived controllability and comfortableness, both intraindividually (as when anxiety and thought are correlated across occasions for the same individual) and across individuals (Kroll-Mensing, 1992).

One critical issue in the use of ESM is the proportion of signals to which respondents respond with appropriate reporting. One review of research using ESM (Csikszentmihalyi & Larson, 1987) indicates that response frequency varies in a range of about 70 to 86 percent of the possible sampling occasions. The most common reasons reported for missing signals were malfunction of the equipment or difficulty in receiving the sampling cue, followed by forgetting to carry the signaling device or inability to respond due to competing demands of other activities.

Delays in response to the ESM cues are reported to be typically fairly brief. Fifty percent of the adults in a study by Hormuth (1986) and 64 percent of the adolescents in a study by Csikszentmihalyi and Larson (1984) responded immediately to the sampling cue. Additionally, Hormuth (1986) reports response rates of 70 percent within three minutes, 80 percent within five minutes, and 90 percent within eighteen minutes of the ESM signal.

Judging from the results of debriefings, most respondents do not experience ESM as overly intrusive. Only 32 percent of a U.S. and 22 percent of a German adult sample complained regarding the disruptiveness of ESM (Hormuth, 1986). Also, 75 percent of the German adults stated that they would be willing to participate again in a similar investigation.

ESM is applicable in a wide variety of situations and populations. It is not a particularly difficult task: respondents' generally high confidence in their thought-sampling ratings indicates that they are not overwhelmed by its demands (Klinger, 1978a). ESM has been used to sample respondents' life experience over a variety of time periods ranging from several hours to several months. It has been used with respondents ranging in age from ten to eighty-five years and with a wide variety of populations, including those suffering from schizophrenia, eating disorders, chemical dependency, anxiety, and depressive disorders, as well as nonclinical, nonpathological populations of adults and adolescents (deVries, 1992b).

ESM research has found a number of interesting clinical group differences, although sample sizes tend to be small and controls weak. Thus, schizophrenics evinced less correlation between thought content and mood than did nonschizophrenic mental patients (deVries, 1992). Bulimic women reported more depression than a normal female control group (Larson & Asmussen, 1992). Contexts and effects of alcohol use are drastically different from those surrounding marijuana use (Larson, Csikszentmihalyi, & Freeman, 1992). DeVries (1992) presents many other applications and findings with ESM, including monitoring developments in patients' behaviors and experiences outside the therapy session and the circumstances surrounding various medical conditions.

Advantages of the Experience-Sampling Method (ESM)

There are a number of advantages inherent in ESM compared with endorsement techniques. First, subjects are asked to provide a description of the experience they had immediately preceding the stimulus cue. Thus, ESM does not rely on the retrospective report of such events, as is the case with endorsement methods. As a result of their spontaneity and immediacy, experience samples would appear to provide less biased estimates of respondents' actual experiences, relatively free from the unreliability and distortion introduced by the mood and memory biases that afflict retrospective methods (Hurlburt & Sipprelle, 1978). Thus, the immediacy of ESM reports may enhance their accuracy by accommodating people's processing limitations (Tellegen, 1985).

Second, ESM generally allows for a wider array of responses than do endorsement techniques (Davison, Robins, & Johnson, 1983). Most often respondents are simply asked to record their immediately preceding cognition or image in a narrative or free-response format without the constraints or demands of responding to experimenter-defined categories. Thus, sampling techniques give respondents the freedom to provide an account of their inner experience as it actually occurs in the course of a sampling period instead of responding in a generalized manner to the prestructured response format of endorsement methods.

Options for the Characterization of Sampled Experiences in ESM

A number of options exist for the characterization of subjects' experience samples. For example, respondents' experience samples can be rated by an external observer, the respondents themselves can rate their own experience samples at a later time period, and finally, respondents can be asked to rate the characteristics of their experience samples immediately following their narrative report. An example of this latter approach is provided by the Thought Sampling Questionnaire (TSQ; Klinger, 1978; 1987–88), which quantifies and hence allows standardization and comparison of respondents' inner experiences. The TSQ combines respondents' narrative reports of their inner experiences with their subsequent characterizations or ratings of the experiences on a number of dimensions, including vividness, directedness, controllability, and responsivity to the outside environment. Hurlburt (1990) has extended this method with intensive interviews after the thought-sampling period to ascertain in greater detail the character of the subject's experiences. Because ESM is such a flexible tool, the particular rating scales and related methods can be designed in accordance with the investigator's or clinician's particular purposes.

Research Investigating Anxiety and Depression from an Experience-Sampling Vantage Point

Early studies of mood that incorporated cognitive sampling techniques tended to focus on depression. These investigations provided a number of preliminary observations. For example, the cognitions of depressed patients sampled at twenty-six-second intervals were characterized by a greater preoccupation with an experimental task involving distraction—what they term "periods of fruitless rumination"—compared with their nondepressed sample, who were more focused on "real life preoccupations" (Fennel & Teasdale, 1984, p. 66). Working with a sample of gynecological patients, Dent and

Teasdale (1988) found a significant association between the number of depressive cognitions reported and the severity of self-reported depression two weeks later but not five months later.

Larson, Raffaelli, Richards, Ham, and Jewell (1990) report the results of an investigation of the cognitive and affective experience of 406 students from the fifth through the ninth grade using ESM. They compared the responses of students identified as depressed on a self-report inventory with the responses of nondepressed students. Pagers were used on a random schedule to cue students to sample their thoughts and mood seven times a day over a one-week period. They found that depressed students could be distinguished from nondepressed students on the basis of their cognitive content, affective experience, perceptions of others, and social isolation. The cognitive content of depressed students was focused significantly more often on family and less often on sports. With regard to affective experience, depressed students experienced significantly more variablity in affect, on the average more negative affect and less positive affect, and reported decreased energy compared with nondepressed students.

Surprisingly, these investigators found that depressive affect was not linked to a particular context. However, depressed students did report that they experienced more social isolation and spent more time in their bedrooms and less time in the company of others. Additionally, depressed students' social perceptions were significantly more negative; viewing those around them as less supportive, especially family, and expressing a desire to be alone more often, particularly when in the company of family. Gender differences were found only for time spent with same-gender friends. Male students spent significantly less time with friends of the same gender.

An emotion-actuated experience-sampling study in a college population by Wickless and Kirsch (1988) provides some evidence about the specificity of anxious and sad moods and their relationship to cognitive themes. Students trained to sample their cognitions and emotions were randomly assigned to report their experi-ences in response to one of three emotions: anxiety, anger, or sadness over a three-day period. Depressive, anxious, and angry cognitions were associated more strongly with their corresponding emotions than with noncorresponding affective states. However, there were also significant associations between loss-related cognitions and anxiety and between threat-related cognitions and depression. A stepwise multiple regression indicated that anxiety was uniquely predicted by threat-related cognitions, whereas sadness was predicted by both threat-related and loss-related cognitions. Loss-related cognitions also predicted anger.

Hurlburt (1990) has used intensive interviews to assess more closely the properties of previously collected thought samples in normals, schizophrenics, and depressed individuals. By using intrasubject statistical analyses and then inspecting these across subjects, he has arrived at results that in part pose problems for existing theory. For example, he finds that "when not decompensating," his schizophrenic patients may have "extremely clear emotional experiences"—i.e., unblunted ones (Hurlburt, 1990, p. 254). In fact, their inner experience may seem "*hyper*-clear" (p. 254). Furthermore, his schizophrenics appear to engage in more visual and concrete imagery, with even words appearing visually and sometimes in motion. Hurlburt concludes: "*Schizophrenia seems to be more a disorder of perception than of association*" (1990, p. 257).

In an investigation of four depressed individuals compared with nondepressed and schizophrenic subjects, Hurlburt noted that the cognitive processes of the depressed subjects may tentatively be characterized by (a) decreased symbolization of inner experience; (b) decreased perceptual clarity of mental imagery; (c) a tendency to report inner experiences in metaphorical terms rather than purely descriptive terms; and (d) what Hurlburt terms "unconstancy" of the inner speech or cognitive processes (e.g., inner speech or imagery perceived as occurring in different parts of the body). He notes that this conclusion contrasts with his interpretation of Beck's (1967, 1976) conceptualization that cognitive processes in affective disorders are intact and similar to those of normals except for abnormal content and/or focus (Hurlburt, personal communication).

An ESM investigation of test anxiety similarly produced results that contradict prevailing theory (Klinger, 1984). Students were sampled for thought content and anxiety during a course examination. Instead of the predicted finding that anxiety produces disruptive cognitions that interfere with performance, the pattern of results suggested that anxiety was more clearly an effect than a cause of poor performance.

Kroll-Mensing (1992) thought-sampled students varying in anxiety and depression scores over three days. Despite the strong correlations between these two dimensions of mood, the results indicate a number of significant cognitive differences between them, such as the time orientation of thoughts, their spontaneity, patterns of imagined interactions, and the functions attributed to them. The results also provided evidence regarding the validity of commonly used questionnaire measures of clinically relevant cognition and mood.

Conclusion

In conclusion, ESM is a highly flexible method. Although labor-intensive, it is relatively easy to use, is generally acceptable to clients and subjects, has acceptable stability and validity, and is capable of generating unique perspectives on inner experience. These perspectives can enrich clinicians' understanding of their clients, contribute to improved diagnosis and intervention, and generate data capable of challenging established theory.

IDIOTHETIC ASSESSMENT OF MOTIVATIONAL STRUCTURE

There is another prominent context in which endorsement methods of personality assessment need supplementation: in the assessment of individuals' motivational structure. Although measures of "drives" and "needs" yield some degree of valid prediction, their explanatory and presumably predictive power is for some purposes weaker than measures that assess people's *current concerns* (Klinger, 1971). This construct refers to the *latent state* of an organism between commitment to striving for a goal and either goal attainment or disengagement from the goal. The construct by itself does not refer to conscious content and posits a separate concern corresponding to each current goal pursuit.

Methods for assessing concerns initially employed intensive interviews. These were later replaced by questionnaires (Klinger, 1987), the most recent form of which is the Motivational Structure Questionnaire (MSQ; Cox & Klinger, 1988; Cox, Klinger, & Blount, 1992; Klinger & Cox, 1986), an adaptation of the Interview Questionnaire (IntQ; Klinger, 1987). The IntQ has also been adapted specifically for work settings under the title Work Concerns Inventory (Roberson, 1989).

Since the original publication of current concerns theory (Klinger, 1971, 1975, 1977), the concerns construct has been joined by a number of related constructs: the personal project (behavior sequences directed at a personal goal; e.g., Palys & Little, 1983); the personal striving (a typical goal for an individual; e.g., Emmons, 1986; Emmons & King, 1988); and the life task (a societally prescribed developmental task such as gaining independence or selecting a mate; e.g., Cantor et al., 1987). Each of these approaches has produced useful data through the use of idiothetic instruments, with varying degrees of similarity to the MSQ.

The MSQ asks respondents first simply to list their current concerns. For each concern listed, respondents then select an "action word" from a list of verb classes that describe what they want to do about the goal object or goal state of each concern (e.g., get, keep, do, restore, escape, avoid, etc.). Subsequently respondents rate each concern for the extent to which they (versus another) take an active part in striving for the respective goal; their commitment to achieving it; the amount of joy and of unhappiness (i.e., ambivalence) they imagine experiencing upon goal attainment; the amount of sorrow they imagine experiencing in the event of failure; the probability of success; the probability of success if they do nothing about it; the probable amount of time before goal attainment, and the amount of time before they must start doing something about the goal; and the facilitating or impeding effect of alcohol consumption on goal attainment.

These responses permit the calculation for each subject of numerous indices, such as mean commitment, proportion of concerns that entail aversive verbs, mean ambivalence, inappropriate commitment, pessimism, and vulnerability to depression (Cox et al., 1992; Klinger & Cox, 1986). Finally, subjects may be asked to complete a *goal matrix* in which they rate the extent to which each goal pursuit facilitates or interferes with each other goal pursuit (Emmons & King, 1988).

These written instruments are not only less labor-intensive than interviews, at least for the assessors; they are also more effective in extracting information regarding both the identity and the characterization of subjects' concerns. Whereas interviews with college students produced a mean of eighteen different concerns, the IntQ has produced mean numbers of concerns ranging from about fifteen (a poorly educated alcoholic group) to sixty-five (a well-motivated student group) in its various versions and populations (Klinger, Barta, & Maxeiner, 1981; Klinger, 1987).

For respondents, however, the time commitment continues to be considerable. The current version of the MSQ takes college students an average of about two hours to complete. A short form that requests all nontrivial concerns but eliminates some rating scales takes college students an average of about an hour. There are wide individual variations. Because of the time required, the validity of response is unusually dependent on subjects' motivation. If they are aware that the number of concerns they list bears on the time they will spend subsequently in rating them, poorly motivated subjects may restrict the number of concerns they write down. For subjects motivated by hourly pay, by time-based extra credit in courses, or by a desire for clinical improvement, this is less likely to be a significant problem.

Because of the unconventional form of such instruments, standard methods for assessing some aspects of reliability and validity are hard to apply. Thus, with concerns changing when goals are reached or abandoned and new ones taken on, stability measures are bound to underestimate reliability; and without multi-item assessments of the same construct, homogeneity measures are inapplicable. However, there are some compelling reasons to consider their reliability and validity sufficient for at least some practical purposes (Klinger, 1987). For example, with a one-month interval between administrations of the IntQ, and excluding concerns that were not listed at a given administration for plainly legitimate reasons (e.g., the goal had not yet been selected or had already been reached or abandoned), 82 percent of the concerns listed at one administration were also listed at the other one. Test-retest correlations for theoretically more stable indices are also respectable, even when the two administrations are separated by a one-month inpatient alcoholism treatment program that might be expected to make significant changes in motivational patterns: e.g., number of concerns listed (.66), proportion of goals that are appetitive (.42), mean probability of success (.47).

With regard to validity, when IntQ administrations have been followed by subjects keeping a log of their daily activities, 81 percent of the activities they engaged in a week later are relatable to one or another of the concerns originally listed on the IntQ, as are 60 percent of those activities engaged in four weeks later (Klinger, 1987). Similarly, subjects who took the Work Concerns Inventory (WCI) matched 76 percent of their activities sampled over the following week with one or another WCI goal (Roberson, 1989). Furthermore, the IntQ and WCI scales permit significant predictions of the frequency with which activities related to a particular concern will subsequently occur (Klinger, 1987; Roberson, 1989). Indices based on these ratings have been found related to subjects' satisfaction with their jobs (Roberson, 1989), subsequent response to inpatient treatment for alcoholism (Klinger & Cox, 1986), and clinical scales of the Minnesota Multiphasic Personality Inventory and self-reported patterns of alcohol use (unpublished data). Indices of personal strivings based on goal-matrix ratings, which reflect conflict, are related to measures of personal well-being, affectivity, and health (Emmons & King, 1988, 1989).

The IntQ and subsequently the MSQ have shown themselves to be useful tools in relation to substance use and abuse. A number of IntQ/MSQ indicators predict immediate outcome in inpatient treatment of alcoholism (Klinger & Cox, 1986) and are correlated with MMPI scales, measures of substance use, and a number of personality measures (articles in preparation). Data to examine motivational clustering among alcoholics, obtained with MSQ assessment and other measures, are under analysis. A counseling method built on current concerns theory and designed around the MSQ (Cox & Klinger, 1988; Cox, Klinger, & Blount, 1991) has shown promise in clinical pilot applications and is currently the subject of an outcome investigation (Cox, Klinger, & Blount, 1992).

Clinical Applications of the MSQ

The MSQ-based counseling method, systematic motivational counseling (SMC; Cox & Klinger, 1988; Cox, Klinger, & Blount, 1992), is the best developed of clinical MSQ applications, although its clinical trials have so far been restricted to substance abuse disorders. The specific method, which is used in the context of a therapeutic relationship, begins with an administration of the MSQ, followed by eleven treatment components. Five of these are "core components" applied to all SMC clients; the other six are applied flexibly according to the requirements of the particular case.

The first SMC component entails reviewing the client's MSQ responses and clinically assessing their validity and implications. This component sets in motion the therapeutic dialogue with respect to such issues as unrealistically over- or undervalued goals, undue optimism or pessimism about attaining them, and the completeness and sincerity of the goals listed. This also provides initial information regarding the goals that it may be desirable to change.

The second component is devoted to examining the interrelationships among the client's goals by administering a goal matrix, on which, for each pair of goals, the client indicates the extent to which one goal facilitates or hampers striving for the other. This then provides a view of the client's goal conflicts.

The remaining core components are (3) setting specific treatment goals; (4) constructing "goal ladders" (highly detailed sequences of subgoals that lead to attainment of longer-term goals); and (5) setting between-session goals. The subsequent components, applied as warranted, are (6) improving clients' abilities to meet goals, which may involve skill training or education (or referrals for such) or social work interventions; (7) resolving conflicts among goals; (8) helping clients disengage from goals for which conflicts cannot be resolved or that may be inappropriate or destructive; (9) identifying new positive incentives as potentially life-enhancing goals; (10) shifting from an aversive to an appetitive lifestyle by helping clients reconceptualize their goal striving and abandon unnecessary aversive goals; and (11) reexamining client's sources of self-esteem, to shift them toward sources that provide positive satisfaction rather than simply relief from negative emotions and self-doubt.

Although SMC has hitherto been developed for use with substance abuse disorders, it is potentially applicable to a wide variety of situations in counseling and psychotherapy, ranging from vocational and marital problems to student counseling to treatment for depression. The first systematic assessment of outcomes with SMC is still under way, with a population of substance abusing traumatic-brain-injury patients. However, informal feedback from counselors applying the method has been encouraging. This is supported by the numerous student subjects of MSQ and IntQ studies who have commented spontaneously on the value to them of the personal self-knowledge they gained through simply having completed the instrument. It is also supported by counselors' convictions that clients' MSQ responses laid out for them a view of their clients' lives, perspectives, and conflicts that it would be hard to obtain, certainly as efficiently, in the course of normal treatment.

There is no claim here that SMC components are unique or unprecedented. However, the method is theoretically based on a wide sweep of empirical general psychology (Klinger, 1975, 1977), is explicitly focused on motivational patterns, and is organized to work with those patterns more systematically than is likely to be the case without it. The information at the core of this systematic treatment procedure is provided initially by the MSQ.

ACKNOWLEDGMENT

Portions of this chapter appeared in Klinger, E. (in press). Effects of motivation and emotion on thought flow and cognition: assessment and findings. In P. E. Shrout & S. T. Fiske (Eds.), *Personality Research, Methods and Theory: Festschrift for Don Fiske*. Hillsdale, NJ: Erlbaum. Other portions were adapted from part of Kroll-Mensing (1992).

REFERENCES

Aserinsky, E., & Kleitman, N. (1953). Regularly occurring periods of eye mobility and concomitant phenomena during sleep. *Science, 118,* 273–274.

Beck, A. T. (1967). *Depression: Clinical, experimental and theoretical aspects.* New York: Harper & Row.

Beck, A. T. (1976). *Cognitive therapy and the emotional disorders.* New York: New American Library.

Cantor, N. N., Norem, J. K., Niedenthal, P. M., Langston, C. A., & Brower, A. M. (1987). Life tasks, self-concept ideals, and cognitive strategies in a life transition. *Journal of Personality and Social Psychology, 53,* 1178–1191.

Clark, D. A. (1988). The validity of measures of cognition: A review of the literature. *Cognitive Therapy and Research, 12* 1–20.

Cox, W. M., & Klinger, E. (1988). A motivational model of alcohol use. *Journal of Abnormal Psychology, 97,* 168–180.

Cox, W. M., Klinger, E., & Blount, J. P. (1991). Alcohol use and goal hierarchies: Systematic motivational counseling for alcoholics. In W. R. Miller & S. Rollnick (Eds.), *Motivational interviewing: Preparing people to change addictive behavior* (pp. 260–271). New York: Guilford Press.

Cox, W. M.., Klinger, E., & Blount, J. P. (1992). *Systematic motivational counseling: A treatment manual.* Unpublished manual.

Csikszentmihalyi, M., & Larson, R. (1984). *Being adolescent: Conflict and growth in the teenage years.* New York: Basic Books.

Csikszentmihalyi, M., & Larson, R. (1987). Validity and reliability of the experience-sampling method. *Journal of Nervous and Mental Disease, 175,* 526–536.

Csikszentmihalyi, M., Larson, R., & Prescott, S. (1977). The ecology of adolescent activity and experience. *Journal of Youth and Adolescence, 6,* 281–294.

Davison, G. C., Robins, C., & Johnson, M. K. (1983). Articulated thoughts during simulated situations: A paradigm for studying cognition and emotion. *Cognitive Therapy and Research, 7,* 17–40.

deVries, M. W. (1992a). The experience of psychopathology in natural settings: Introduction and illustration of variables. In M. W. deVries (Ed.), *The experience of psychopathology: Investigating mental disorders in their natural settings* (pp. 3–26). Cambridge: Cambridge University Press.

deVries, M. W. (Ed.). (1992b). *The experience of psychopathology: Investigating mental disorders in their natural settings.* Cambridge: Cambridge University Press.

Emmons, R. A. (1986). Personal strivings: An approach to personality and subjective well-being. *Journal of Personality and Social Psychology, 51,* 1058–1068.

Emmons, R. A., & King, L. A. (1988). Conflict among personal strivings: Immediate and long-term implications for psychological and physical well-being. *Journal of Personality and Social Psychology, 54,* 1040–48.

Emmons, R. A., & King, L. A. (1989). Personal striving differentiation and affective reactivity. *Journal of Personality and Social Psychology, 56,* 478–84.

Fennell, M. J. V., & Teasdale, J. D. (1984). Effects of distraction on thinking and affect in depressed patients. *Journal of Clinical Psychology, 23,* 65–66.

Fiske, D. W. (1971). *Measuring the concepts of personality.* Chicago: Aldine.

Glass, C. R., & Arnkoff, D. B. (1982). Think cognitively: Selected issues in cognitive assessment and therapy. In P. C. Kendall (Ed.), *Cognitive assessment*. New York: Guilford Press.

Hormuth, S. (1986). The sampling of experiences *in situ. Journal of Personality. 54*, 262–317.

Hurlburt, R. T. (1990). *Sampling normal and schizophrenic inner experience*. New York: Plenum.

Hurlburt, R. T., & Sipprelle, C. N. (1978). Random sampling of cognitions in alleviating anxiety attacks. *Cognitive Therapy and Research, 2*, 165–169.

Klinger, E. (1971). *Structure and functions of fantasy* New York: Wiley.

Klinger, E. (1975). Consequences of commitment to and disengagement from incentives. *Psychological Review, 82*, 1–25.

Klinger, E. (1977). *Meaning and void: Inner experience and the incentives in people's lives.* Minneapolis: University of Minnesota Press.

Klinger, E. (1978). Modes of normal conscious flow. In K. S. Pope & J. L. Singer (Eds.), *The stream of consciousness: Scientific investigations into the flow of human experience* (pp. 225–228). New York: Plenum.

Klinger, E. (1984). A consciousness-sampling analysis of test anxiety and performance. *Journal of Personality and Social Psychology, 47*, 1376–1390.

Klinger, E. (1987). The Interview Questionnaire technique: Reliability and validity of a mixed idiographic-nomothetic measure of motivation. In J. N. Butcher & C. D. Spielberger (Eds.), *Advances in personality assessment* (Vol. 6, pp. 31–48). Hillsdale, NJ: Erlbaum.

Klinger, E., Barta, S. G., & Glas, R. A. (1981). Thought content and gap time in basketball. *Cognitive Therapy and Research, 5*, 109–114.

Klinger, E., Barta, S. G., & Maxeiner, M. E. (1981). Current concerns: Assessing therapeutically relevant motivation. In P. C. Kendall & S. D. Hollon (Eds.), *Assessment strategies for cognitive-behavioral interventions* (pp. 161–196). New York: Academic Press.

Klinger, E., & Cox, W. M. (1987–1988). Dimensions of thought flow in everyday life. *Imagination, Cognition and Personality, 7*, 105–128.

Klinger, E., & Murphy, M. D. (1994). Action orientation and personality: Some evidence on the construct validity of the action control scale. In J.

Kuhl & J. Beckmann (Eds.), *Volition and personality: Action versus state orientation.* (pp. 79–92). Göttingen, Germany: Hogrefe.

Kroll-Mensing, D. (1992). *Differentiating anxiety and depression: An experience sampling analysis.* Unpublished Ph.D. dissertation, University of Minnesota.

Lamiell, J. R. (1981). Toward an idiothetic psychology of personality. *American Psychologist, 36*, 276–289.

Larson, R., & Asmussen, L. (1992). Bulimia in daily life: a context-bound syndrome. In M. W. deVries (Ed.) (1992). *The experience of psychopathology: Investigating mental disorders in their natural settings* (pp. 167–179). Cambridge, England: Cambridge University Press.

Larson, R., Csikszentmihalyi, M., & Freeman, M. (1992). Alcohol and marijuana use in adolescents' daily lives. In M. W. deVries (Ed.), *The experience of psychopathology: Investigating mental disorders in their natural settings* (pp. 180–192). Cambridge: Cambridge University Press.

Larson, R. W., Raffaelli, M., Richards, M. H., Ham, M., & Jewell, L. (1990). Ecology of depression in late childhood and early adolescence: A profile of daily states and activities. *Journal of Abnormal Psychology, 99*, 92–102.

Palys, T. S., & Little, B. R. (1983). Perceived life satisfaction and the organization of personal project systems. *Journal of Personality and Social Psychology, 44*, 1221–1230.

Roberson, L. (1989). Assessing personal work goals in the organizational setting: Development and evaluation of the Work Concerns Inventory. *Organizational Behavior and Human Decision Processes, 44*, 345–367.

Tellegen, A. (1985). Structures of mood and personality and their relevance to assessing anxiety, with an emphasis on self-report. In A. H. Tuma & J. D. Maser (Eds.), *Anxiety and the anxiety disorders* (pp. 681–706). Hillsdale, NJ: Erlbaum.

Tippett, L. H. C. (1935). A snap reading method of making time studies of machines and operatives in factory surveys. *Journal of the British Textile Institute Transactions, 26*, 51–55.

Wickless, C., & Kirsch, I. (1988). Cognitive correlates of anger, anxiety, and sadness. *Cognitive Therapy and Research, 12*, 367–377.

20

Early Memories in Personality Assessment

Arnold R. Bruhn

Long before other projective procedures emerged, early memories were. Munroe (1955) asserts that early childhood memories (EMs) were the first projective procedure, and I am unaware of a dissenting opinion. The professional literature dates at least to the Henris' work in the 1890s and Miles's (1893) paper around the same time. Although one would expect by now that the literature on EMs would be extensive, rich and, mature, paradoxically the opposite is true. Now one hundred years old, EMs as a projective technique were until recently hardly into adolescence.

It can be argued that EMs provide a foundation or point of grounding for every other projective technique. If this premise is accepted, it is puzzling why so little is known about an area that is critical to clinical assessments and psychotherapeutic interventions. For instance, might it not be useful—some might argue essential—to inquire routinely about an individual's most traumatic experience or inappropriate sexual experiences before a process of psychotherapy is undertaken? It is interesting that not a single publication, to my knowledge, has ever been reported on either subject. Nor was it even possible to study such material systematically using a standard methodology until

the arrival of the Early Memories Procedure (EMP) (Bruhn, 1989a). It can also be argued that it would be helpful to explore such clinically relevant experiences as an incestuous relationship, a traumatic loss, or sexual abuse before we interpret a 4–6 Minnesota Multiphasic Personality Inventory (MMPI) profile or a response involving a mutilated animal on Card 2 of the Rorschach. Early memories and autobiographical memories can help us anchor our interpretations of either test.

If we have received any training at all in what I call applied autobiographical memory, or recollections involving clinically relevant experiences, we have perhaps been taught something about EMs. Thus I will try to emphasize the familiar here while introducing the less familiar. Although a convincing case can be made for the special role of EMs in the spectrum of life experiences, such an argument does not warrant ignoring other memories or discounting their importance. Life continues after childhood. For adult clients, marriages, births, graduations, deaths, divorces, wars—all events of potentially major significance—are more likely to occur after age eight than before. Life experiences after age eight are important to consider when we undertake an evaluation. In fact, to

TABLE 20.1. Time Line of Autobiographical Memory Publications[a]

1890s	Several pioneering papers on EMs: Miles (1893); Henri & Henri (1898).
1899	Freud: "Screen Memories," a classic paper.
1900–1910	Several excellent survey ("normative") studies of EMs.
1917	Freud: Analysis of the first EM of Johann Goethe, German dramatist, poet, and scientist.
1912–1937	Adler: Classic contribution to EMs, including an excellent but little-known case study, *The Case of Miss R* (1929).
1932	Bartlett: *Remembering . . .*, a classic book that argued for the concept of memories as constructions versus veridical reproductions.
1948	Waldfogel: Monograph and first partial review of the literature.
1961	Langs & Reiser: A psychoanalytically based EM scoring system.
1968	Mayman: Presidential address to the Society for Personality Assessment on EMs. Papers in the early 1970s relating to an object-relations-based EM scoring system.
1978–present	Neisser: His work with autobiographical memory, especially *Memory Observed: Remembering in Natural Contexts* (1982).
1979	Olson (editor): The first book on EMs—a collection of classic EM papers and some new papers, mostly by Adlerians.
1982	Binder & Smokler: A discussion of how EMs can be used to focus psychotherapy.
1982	Bruhn & Last: A theoretical review of four EM models. The cognitive-perceptual (CP) model introduced.
1982	Bruhn & Schiffman: An analysis of attitudes about personal control/responsibility using EM data.
1983	Last: The Comprehensive Early Memories Scoring System (CEMSS) introduced.
1984	Bruhn: Review of EM field, the first since Waldfogel.
1984	Bruhn & Bellow: First memory of Dwight David Eisenhower. Introduces application of CP method to EMs and compares interpretations to those from other models.
1985	Bruhn: First illustration of process interpretation in a set of EMs.
1986	Rubin (editor): *Autobiographical Memory*, in the tradition of Neisser (generally not clinically oriented).
1987	Bruhn & Bellow: Early memories of Golda Meir interpreted using CP model.
1989	Bruhn: *Early Memories Procedure (EMP)* published. First procedure to assess EMs and the whole of autobiographical memory.
1989	Bruhn: *Romantic Relationships Procedure (RRP)* published. Assesses most important romantic relationships.
1990	Davidow & Bruhn: Replicates earlier results (1983), which demonstrated how delinquents and nondelinquents could be distinguished via EM data.
1990	Bruhn: The first book on applied autobiographical memory (Praeger).
1991	Bruhn & Last: The CEMSS revised (CEMSS-R) and expanded.
1991	Ross: *Remembering the Personal Past*, a compendium of material relevant to applied autobiographical memory.
1992	Tobey & Bruhn: Distinguish dangerous from nondangerous chronic psychiatric patients via EMs with a false-positive rate of 6 percent
1994	Bruhn & Feigenbaum: *The Interpretation of Autobiographical Memories*, a foundation book for clinical practice.

In the last 100 years, there have been perhaps 300 papers on EMs, many of these unpublished dissertations, or roughly three per year. Perhaps there are as many as a dozen papers, in total, on *later* memories.

[a]Copyright by Bruhn (1994) and used by permission of the author

argue the contrary is so absurd that it is amazing that we have excluded such experiences from our traditional assessment process until relatively recently.

Let us begin with a brief history of the field of EMs and autobiographical memories. A chronological listing of key dates appears as Table 20.1. The pioneering work of the Henris (1898) and of Miles (1893) caught the attention of Freud (1899), who was sufficiently stimulated by their work to undertake his paper, "Screen Memories." This classic paper included what Bernfeld (1946) argued was Freud's self-analysis, as opposed to what Freud represented as an analysis of one of his patients. A flurry of papers appeared around the same time, including a surprisingly fresh-sounding paper by G. Stanley Hall (1899), the first president of the American Psychological Association, on the process of recovering EMs. Several survey papers, or what would be the equivalent of normative studies in our day, appeared in rapid succession. Colegrove (1899) and Potwin (1901) reported intriguing studies of EMs of various nonclinical groups that have never been replicated using modern statistics and sampling procedures.

Although Freud wrote little about EMs in the years after "Screen Memories" was published, Adler (1912) began to emphasize their use as an assessment tool. His work, which continued through the mid 1930s, is summarized by Ansbacher and Ansbacher (1956). Adler's considerable skill as a diagnostician is perhaps best illustrated in what is now a relatively unknown book, *The Case of Miss R* (1929). Adler tended to emphasize the first EM, although others in his school (e.g., Mosak, 1958) have utilized the second EM as well. Adler emphasized the helpfulness of the first EM in discovering the individual's "style of life."

After Freud's second major paper on EMs appeared in 1917, a study of Goethe's first EM, publications on the subject declined dramatically outside Adlerian circles. Waldfogel's (1948) monograph, which included a partial review of the field, helped to survey work to that date. In 1961, Langs and Reisser devised an EMs scoring system, a detailed and extremely thorough procedure from a psychoanalytic perspective. Mayman's (1968) presidential address to the Society for Personality Assessment reflected his interest in developing an EMs-based system for assessing object relations. Mayman's work encouraged many clinicians to follow his lead, including such recent work as Ryan's (1974). Olson's (1979) edited book on EMs, more than eighty years after the first paper on early memories was published, was actually the first book-length publication on the subject.

Meanwhile, Neisser's pioneering work (1982) on autobiographical memory, a reaction to traditional laboratory memory studies, began in the late 1970s. The work of Rubin (1986) and his colleagues follows a similar tradition. Both continue the work of Bartlett (1932). This work, although conceptually fascinating, is not oriented to the practicing clinician.

Bruhn and Last (1982) identified four distinct models of EM interpretation, including the cognitive-perceptual (CP) model, which was introduced. The Comprehensive Early Memories Scoring System (CEMSS) followed shortly thereafter (Last, 1983). Bruhn's partial review of the literature (1984) was the first since Waldfogel (1948). Several illustrations of the CP model followed, including Eisenhower's first EM (Bruhn & Bellow, 1984) and Golda Meir's EMs (Bruhn & Bellow, 1987). The use of process interpretations in a set of EMs was introduced by Bruhn (1985) and later elaborated (1990b, 1992a, 1992b). The EMP, the first procedure to assess the whole of autobiographical memory, was published by Bruhn in 1989(a). Supplementary procedures (Romantic Relationships Procedure, 1989c; Memories of Father, 1993a; Memories of Mother, 1993b; and Memories of Spouse, 1993c) followed. The CEMSS was revised and expanded by Last and Bruhn in 1991. Pilot work on criminality and EMs by Bruhn and Davidow in 1983 preceded a 1990 main study by Davidow and Bruhn with an EMs scoring system designed to distinguish delinquents from nondelinquents. This work evolved to a new EMs scoring system designed to identify dangerousness potential (Tobey & Bruhn, 1992). Meanwhile, Ross's scholarly book (1991) gave researchers interested in applied autobiographical memory easy access to papers from several different theoretical and/or research traditions.

Although major advances in autobiographical memory research have taken place since the late 1970s, much work remains. We now have in place standardized techniques, such as the EMP, which permit comparable research to proceed. There are four relatively articulated EMs models from which to choose. There are several broad-gauged EMs scoring systems available, including a psychoanalytic system (Langs & Reisser, 1961) and the comprehensive system (CEMSS-R) (Last & Bruhn, 1991), which is oriented toward the CP model. Excellent specialty scoring systems are available, including methods for scoring object relations, attitudes toward personal responsibility, criminality, violence proneness, depression, etc. Several review-oriented publications are available, which simplify access to relevant research (Bruhn, 1984; Bruhn & Last, 1982; Ross, 1991; Waldfogel, 1948). The adolescent era in autobiographical memory research is over. I believe that a mature age of exploration and productive research lies ahead.

AUTOBIOGRAPHICAL MEMORY: AN OVERVIEW

The first major empirical study of autobiographical memory was reported by Frederick Bartlett (1932) in his classic work *Remembering*. Nearly fifty years passed before Neisser continued the thread of Bartlett's work, which had been inundated and pushed aside by a flood of laboratory research in the interim.

Autobiographical memory research has been done largely within a schema theory paradigm. Although memory researchers have traditionally sought to eliminate variables related to personality in studying the operation of memory, schema theory provides the ideal bridge between memory and personality. Ross (1991) has commented that "the major rationale of schema theories is that knowledge is not carried piecemeal but as an integrated set of related representations or actions" (p. 138). CP theory takes Ross's statement a bit further: recollections of one's early life are particularly susceptible to this process as each major lesson extracted from life's experiences can be processed and superimposed upon the corpus of one's EMs. These EMs can then become, just as Ross describes, an "integrated set of related representations or actions." At another level, if we grant that EMs can serve multiple functions, EMs become a vehicle to assess where individuals are in their current developmental process.

Why do we emphasize EMs in the recon-

structive process? Although EMs can reflect an "integrated set of representations or actions," they may also reflect the least sophisticated level of our schematic understanding of self, others, and the world. Why might this be? We tend, on balance, to be more confused by earlier experiences precisely because at the time we were less well equipped cognitively and experientially to understand what happened to us and why, compared with how we might now understand similar events as mature adults. Part of the "confusion" occurs because many early experiences are infused with powerful feelings—troubling feelings—that might not arise for us now if psychologically similar experiences occurred for the first time. However, these childhood feelings remain in their appropriate pristine state when their corresponding experiences are not reexamined and reprocessed in light of present understandings. From another perspective, our childhood understanding of events tends to continue to influence our current understandings if the childhood construction is not unearthed and challenged in light of present adult knowledge. We thus tend to experience life at present through what might be described as two personas: an adult persona with a contemporary adult's understanding of the world, and the persona of a child whose confusion and upset about various past events are often reflected in a selection of EMs. The preceding is especially likely to be true of the person who has suffered severe trauma in early life.

From another perspective entirely, EMs—rather than portray a vertical picture of childhood events—are often distorted and highly selective. Sometimes, in fact, EMs can be more accurately described as fantasies about the past with little fact to sustain them. This description of EMs is consistent with the premises of CP theory. A view of EMs as fantasies about the past is more likely to be accurate when the memory does not involve a serious trauma—for instance, recurring abuse of some kind or a death. In either case, spontaneously recalled EMs *are assumed to speak to present concerns* even when the past event is traumatic in nature.

What basis do we have for believing that EMs speak to present concerns, or what CP theory (Bruhn, 1984, 1985, 1990a, 1990b, 1992a, 1992b; Bruhn & Feigenbaum, in preparation) refers to as major unresolved issues? According to CP theory, memory does not serve as a warehouse for useless, antiquated attitudes or beliefs. EMs imbued with extremely negative affect are believed to be particularly important. This is especially true for very negative EMs that are also quite clear. CP theory holds that very clear EMs become so because they are infused with an extra jolt of psychic energy to "spotlight" them and make them stand out as a figure against the ground of other less significant events. Clarity thus becomes a signal of importance that, if put into words, might say: "there is something important about this recollection—notice it and work with it." However, it is not just the recollected event itself that is important. We can conceptualize an EM with extremely negative affect as representing a *category of psychologically similar experiences* that requires attention and reprocessing. Thus, a recollection that makes us uncomfortable compels us to notice it and *similar situations that are brought forth by association and likewise make us uncomfortable.*

As CP theory sees it, negative-affect EMs thus serve as schematic representations of major unresolved issues. These issues are dramatically acted out to alert us to similar patterns that are presently transacted in our lives. The negative affect in the memory on one hand signals its importance and on the other hints that a processing problem associated with earlier life events needs to be reevaluated in light of present understandings. The reader who seeks a more detailed explication of CP theory, the only theory of personality based on memory functioning, is referred to Bruhn and Feigenbaum (in preparation). Additional clinically oriented applications are available in Bruhn (1990b).

MODELS OF EARLY MEMORY INTERPRETATION

The four primary EM interpretive models (Table 20.2) are designed to assess issues specific to their respective theories of personality. For instance, the Adlerian model is concerned with

---

TABLE 20.2. Four EM Models

1. Freudian: Classical psychoanalysis
   Selected references: Freud (1899/1950, 1917/1955)
2. Adlerian: School of individual psychology
   Selected references: Adler (1912/1917, 1927, 1929, 1931, 1937)
   Ansbacher & Ansbacher (1956)
   Olson (1979)
3. Ego-psychology
   Selected references: Chess (1951)
   Hartmann (1958, 1964)
   Mayman (1968, 1984a, 1984b)
4. Cognitive-perceptual
   Selected references: Bruhn (1984, 1985, 1990a, 1990b, 1992a, 1992b)
   Bruhn & Bellow (1984, 1987)
   Bruhn & Feigenbaum (in preparation)
   Bruhn & Schiffman (1982c)
   Tobey & Bruhn (1992)

---

an individual's fictive final goal and the degree of social interest. Freud's classical id-oriented model is concerned about how instinctual drives are gratified. A critical element of the ego-psychological approach is a belief that the EM product represents a method of coping with conflicts through fantasy. The CP approach conceptualizes the universal set of readily recoverable spontaneous EMs via an EMP (Bruhn, 1989a) as a single episodic memory. The primary purpose of this episodic memory is to articulate the individual's current major unresolved life issue. For psychotherapy clients this issue is what, at a deeper level, precipitates their coming in to therapy. The "memory" is preconsciously organized to express the nature of the problem, how it arose, what keeps it from resolution, and, often, how it can be resolved (if positive affect EMs are given).

Each model is philosophically distinct and formulated with a specific goal in mind. Each is useful for its own purpose, and each is embedded to various degrees in its own treatment orientation. In other words, each treatment model has a different goal in mind, even though a hypothetical client, cloned into fours, might still be "cured" by all four methods according to DSM-III-R criteria.

Two papers treat this topic in the context of a selected review of the theoretical literature (Bruhn, 1990b; Bruhn & Last, 1982). Bruhn and Feigenbaum (in preparation) illustrate differences among three of the four models in a presentation of Freud's (1917), Rom's (1965) Adlerian, and Bruhn's CP interpretation of Goethe's EMs. This approach permits a cross-model comparison of interpretations of the same material, something that has not previously been undertaken in the literature.

SELECTING THE APPROPRIATE PROCEDURE

Before selecting an autobiographical memory procedure, the clinician will want to consider what role he or she will occupy in the treatment process. If we are functioning as assessment people or intake workers who will render an opinion or report findings but not interpret the results, our potential range of choices is broader. Often in such instances, we are not concerned with the fine points of assessment. Rather, we want to rule out a thought disorder, a severe personality disorder, some serious defects in "object relations," and so forth. We might also want to know whether the gender of a potential therapist might be problematic, whether the client is introspective and reflective, and so forth. Traditionally, only the earliest memory, or perhaps the first two or three memories in an oral format have been requested. Or, if we have been acculturated in that tradition, we might employ the Menninger Packet, which includes two EMs, the earliest memory of mother, and the earliest memory of father. In some intake situations, a thorough assessment of autobiographical memory is unnecessary.

On the other hand, if we must interpret the results to the client, or if we will be serving as therapist, I would recommend the EMP. This procedure enables us to obtain the detailed information necessary when a specific opinion is required—e.g., indications of posttraumatic stress disorder or a dysfunctional family background, or a history of substance abuse or sexual abuse. The EMP will be discussed in more detail in later sections.

DEFINITIONS

How can we define an EM or an autobiographical memory? Although such a matter is basic to a scientific process, simple it isn't. Bruhn (1984) examined the literature and found a variety of approaches. Some researchers defined an EM operationally, for instance. Whatever the subject said in response to the question "What is your earliest memory?" was considered the earliest memory.

In practice, we frequently encounter problems around the following issues:

1. When is a memory not an EM? Should the cut-off point be the eighth birthday, as suggested by many Adlerians? Should the age of the subject enter into our decision? For instance, for a seven-year-old child any memory would be "early" by this criterion. But what about eighteen-year-olds versus eighty-year-olds? Should the same cut-off age hold for both groups?

2. What if the event happened many times?—"I always used to go to picnics at my grandmother's after church in the summer." Do *pattern* memories, or memories of repeated events, have a different function than a single-event ("I remember one time . . .") recollection? If so, should a formal distinction be made between them?

3. What if the individual does not recall the event, but remembers someone describing it? Should such EMs be eliminated?

4. What if the individual remembers that something happened but can't picture it visually? Is this variable important?

5. What if the event turns out not to be true?

As a result of my literature review in 1984 and subsequent experience, I would offer the following definition of an EM. The preliminary definition offered below, adapted from Bruhn (1990b), takes into consideration the points raised above:

An EM is a recollection of a specific, one-time childhood event of the form, "I remember one time. . . ." EMs ordinarily describe events that occurred before the eighth birthday. This definition usually works best with individuals aged twelve to approximately sixty. Older or younger individuals may need a different age cut-off. In addition, the following are noted in relation to the questions raised above.
  —the individual should recall the event independent of someone else's reporting of it. If the individual only recalls someone's reporting of the event, it should not be considered an EM. The same principle holds for family pictures and videos.
  —the individual ordinarily will be able to reexperience the EMs visually. Sometimes, however, individuals who have trouble visualizing anything will not be able to visualize their EMs either.
  —whether the EM turns out to be true or false, distorted in some respect or accurate in every detail, is immaterial *for clinical purposes.* What is significant is that the individual has "owned" the experience and treats it as if were true.

The same definitional approach (Bruhn & Feigenbaum, in preparation) can be used with any autobiographical memory, except that the age of occurrence no longer becomes a consideration.

I recommend that EMs be limited, by definition, to recollections of specific events that happened one time because such memories are, in effect, stories.

Adler described an individual's EMs as:

the reminders he carries about with him of his own limits and of the meaning of circumstances. . . . [They serve as] a story he repeats to himself to warn him or comfort him, to keep him concentrated on his goal, to

prepare him, by means of past experiences, to meet the future with an already tested style of action. (Adler, 1931, p. 72)

My view is consistent with Adler's: EMs, as stories, have a beginning, middle, and end in addition to a main point or theme that can be derived and abstracted from the story through a precis technique. The latter will be discussed and illustrated in a later section. Most of us are acculturated to believe that life has a point, that we should have personal goals, that things happen for a reason or, minimally, that we can at least learn from them. Our EMs reflect what we have consciously learned or intuited preconsciously from our life experiences. These attitudes, understandings, expectations, and conclusions are schematically embedded in autobiographical memory as well as in our EMs and inevitably influence what we recall from our past and how we reconstruct these events.

I would therefore argue that while snapshot recollections, for lack of a better term, are interesting to ponder, they are difficult to interpret primarily because they are often fragments of an unknown event that falls beyond our current conscious remembrance. Examples of "snapshot" recollections are: "I remember how the sun used to play off the linoleum in the kitchen floor in the summer" and "the tall grass moving in waves in a summer breeze in the back field." Without a context of something happening in a time frame, it is difficult to assay the meaning of recollections like this.

For similar reasons, I exclude EMs of repeated events—"we always used to have a picnic at grandmother's in the summer after church." Such *pattern* memories, or memories of repeated events, often serve a different function than single-event EMs. In the preceding case, for example, the memory appears to operate as a mood stabilizer and a pleasant reminder of being loved, connected with family, nurtured, and cared for over a long period of time.

For research purposes, it is vital that we reach some degree of concordance about what an EM and an autobiographical memory are. Failing that, comparing research results will become virtually impossible. Bruhn and Feigenbaum (in preparation) present a more extensive discussion of the problems associated with definitions.

ORAL VERSUS WRITTEN MEMORIES: PROS AND CONS

Prior to 1984, methods for obtaining EMs and autobiographical memories were unsystematic and critically unexamined, as Bruhn's (1984) review points out. Some writers obtained EMs orally, some in writing. Some required only the earliest memory, others more. Some used an inquiry, some did not. Some requested a memory of a specific event, others held that any response to the probe qualified as an EM. Without consistency in methodology, it is difficult to interpret differences in research findings among investigators.

Bruhn (1984) first recommended a method for obtaining EMs orally in the context of a psychological test battery. This procedure was elaborated in Bruhn (1990b, especially pp. 66–69). Since this discussion is rather lengthy, the reader is directed to the preceding sources.

When an oral format is needed outside the context of a psychological assessment, I would recommend that the instructions from the EMP (Bruhn, 1989a) be read or closely paraphrased. There are times that a written format is contraindicated—for instance, with individuals who are thought disordered, severely depressed or anxious, blind, and so forth. Tobey and Bruhn (1992), for instance, in working with a mostly thought-disordered sample, read the EMP directions and tape-recorded responses. With this population, considerable refocusing was necessary, and many responses had to be excluded because of definitional restrictions.

Let's consider the more important pros and cons of oral versus written EMs and autobiographical memory procedures. The major advantages of an oral procedure are as follows:

1. The information is obtained immediately.
2. The client has less awareness as to the clinician's motive in requesting this information. Oral procedures, especially when undertaken without supplementary probes in the EMP (see, for instance, p. 11 as well as the recurring probe, "If you could change the memory in any way, what would that be?"), are not designed to foster reflection or insight.
3. The potential flexibility of an oral format can permit forays into areas opened up by spontaneous EMs. For instance, after a memory involving a painful loss, the clinician might wish to ask, "Have you experienced other such losses?" "Which was the worst one?" "How did it affect you?" and so forth.
4. Some clients cannot handle written formats. Two of the more obvious examples are thought-disordered clients and individuals who are blind.

On the other hand, there are many advantages to written formats. The most significant follow:

1. Less clinical time is required. Introducing the EMP, for example, commonly requires less than five minutes, versus fifteen to thirty minutes to solicit and transcribe a short set of spontaneous EMs.
2. Records written in a client's own hand are exact and not subject to clinical interpretation or transcription error ("I thought you said . . .").
3. Written formats provide clients time to reflect and introspect and the structured probes facilitate doing so. Novice clients have the opportunity to learn more about the process of insight-oriented psychotherapy.
4. For researchers, a procedure like the EMP offers a standardized form and reduces several potential sources of experimental "noise" or error variance. Examples of the latter include variance associated with who solicits the memories (gender, age, perceived status of experimenter, etc.).

5. Written assessments enable the clinician to proceed in more depth. The assessment can be more detailed and thorough. The EMP, for instance, requires at least twenty-one memories covering a wide range of clinically relevant topics of interest. Oral procedures rarely cover even 25 percent of the material probed by the EMP.

6. Written procedures are easier to interpret to clients, who have spent more time on the task and done more work. Similarly, it is easier to proceed from a written record in the client's handwriting and flip back and forth between memories as interpretive links are made among memories.

7. Written records provide proof in malpractice cases that clinically relevant areas were probed if the clinician is falsely accused of lack of diligence and failing to inquire.

8. Many individuals will reveal more to a computer than they will to someone in intake. The same principle holds for written procedures.

As is evident from the preceding, there are times when a clinician will definitely want to use a written and not an oral procedure, and vice versa. There are other occasions when both may be needed.

Some of the major differences between the EMP specifically and EMs obtained orally are summarized in Table 20.3.

SPONTANEOUS VERSUS DIRECTED MEMORIES

In 1982b, Bruhn and Schiffman raised the question of whether directed EM probes should be used in EM assessments. This question is just as relevant whenever any autobiographical memory assessment is undertaken.

How to structure an assessment of autobiographical memory should be determined by what we want to know. Assume that we begin with clients who present with an amorphous complaint: "I'm just not happy"; "my life is a mess"; "my relationships never seem to work out"; "my career is going nowhere, and I don't have a clue of what is wrong." Such complaints virtually require a broad-gauged autobiographical memory assessment approach. A set of *spontaneous* EMs will provide initial hypotheses to explore: "What is your earliest memory of a specific event, something that happened one time . . .?"; "What memory comes to mind next?"; and so forth. Spontaneous memories deliberately avoid specific schemas that might be relevant to later exploration with *directed* memory probes: "What is your clearest memory of your mother?"; ". . . the time you felt most ashamed?"; and so forth.

We can define *spontaneous* memories as those that are elicited solely or primarily by probes involving time ("your *earliest* memory of a specific event . . .?"; "your clearest or most important memory *lifetime?*") and associated probes ([after the earliest memory] "and what memory comes to mind *next?*"). On the other hand, *directed* memories probe a variety of schemas—the earliest memories of types of experiences (the first EMs of school, punishment), the clearest memory of a person/lifetime (mother, father), or the most affectively potent or strongest (most traumatic). Directed memory probes may explore a potentially huge array of categories having clinical relevance (mother, father, fighting, punishment, abuse) from many angles (earliest, clearest, strongest). Bruhn (1990b) discusses this topic in more detail. Historically, studies of directed memories probably began with Friedman's (1933) paper on first memories of school. This probe is useful in assessing attitudes with individuals who have school-related problems—e.g., achievement, school failure, concentration difficulties, and even separation issues. Other early papers on directed memory probes include first memories of spouse (Belove, 1980; Crandall, 1971) and first memories of punishment (Bruhn, 1976). The Menninger packet, which dates back to at least the 1950s, includes EMs of mother and father.

In most clinical circumstances, spontaneous memories should be solicited. Why? Because we can assume that any issue which arises in a

TABLE 20.3 Differences Between the EMP and EMs Obtained Orally[a]

	Oral EMs	EMP
Age/skills required	Must be 5 to 7 years or older. Some 5-, 6-, or 7-year-olds may not be testable if IQ or verbal ability is low.	Requires the equivalent of fourth-grade writing skills or dictating equipment if writing skills are poor.
Exclusionary criteria	Not appropriate for individuals who are actively psychotic or easily prone to psychotic episodes. Most individuals can produce at least a few EMs unless they are severely repressed or extremely unreflective. Some with poor verbal skills or low intellectual ability may also experience difficulty.	(Same as for oral EMs but in addition . . .) Some individuals with severe attention and concentration problems, certain organic difficulties, severe depression or anxiety, or very weak defenses (e.g., poorly functioning borderlines) may not be able to complete the EMP, especially in an acute episode. Generally speaking, individuals who can complete an MMPI can usually complete the EMP.
Time required	Obtaining a set of 5 to 10 EMs requires about 30 minutes of face-to-face time.	Orienting an individual requires about 5 minutes of face-to-face time at the end of the intake interview. Most individuals require 2½ to 4 hours on their own to complete the EMP.
Intensity of affective experience	The affective experience is predominantly positive and usually subdued relative to the EMP.	The affective experience is reported to be much more intense and negative by individuals who have shared their EMs orally and subsequently completed the EMP. Their explanations for the greater intensity include: (1) they had more time to complete the EMP; (2) they were not distracted by the examiner's reactions and were more involved with the task when they worked by themselves.
Reaction to the task	Most individuals enjoy talking about their EMs and respond positively to the task even when their EMs are moderately negative.	Most individuals report that they learn a great deal about themselves and comment that writing about their memories helps them to gain access to their feelings. Most experience the EMP as "inviting" although a significant minority experience it as "imposing" or "intimidating," primarily due to the length.
What individuals learn from the task	Most individuals evidence minimal understanding of what their EMs reveal about them.	A sample of 20 outpatients were asked to rate on a 5-point scale how much they learned about themselves from taking the EMP. The mean score was 2.9 (a "fair amount"), while the mode was 4 (a "moderate amount").

[a] Reproduced from Bruhn (1990b) and reprinted with permission of the author.

set of spontaneous EMs is important. CP theory posits (Bruhn & Feigenbaum, in preparation) that any spontaneous EMs in an EMP are directly related to an individual's major unresolved issue in process. The clearest and most negative in affective tone is likely to present the best statement of this issue, and the clearest and most positive in affective tone—if any—is likely to provide clues as to how the issue can be resolved. By contrast, many directed memories may not bear on the major unresolved issue (Bruhn & Schiffman, 1982b). For instance, the clearest memory of mother will tell us about salient aspects of the client's relationship with mother. But it may tell us little about what brought the individual into treatment. Some directed memories, however, are known to be important. The most traumatic memory/lifetime is important by definition as is a memory of an inappropriate sexual experience.

Until the advent of the EMP in 1989, it was not common practice for clinicians to inquire about such directed memories as the most traumatic memory/lifetime and an inappropriate sexual experience. The prevailing opinion among insight-oriented therapists was that when clients were ready to discuss such experiences they would naturally emerge in the course of a gradually unfolding psychotherapy process. We are beginning to discover that this assumption is often incorrect. For example, I have found in several outpatient samples that between roughly one-fourth and one-third of all psychotherapy clients tested with the EMP—even those who had been in therapy for ten years and more—revealed traumatic memories that they had not only never discussed in treatment but had never revealed to anybody. When asked why they had not told their therapists, the most common response was, "They never asked." This finding underscores the need to utilize directed memory probes, especially the more obvious ones included in the EMP.

THE EARLY MEMORIES PROCEDURE AS AN ASSESSMENT INSTRUMENT

The EMP (Bruhn, 1989a) was designed to help clinicians structure a standardized, psychody-

namically oriented assessment of autobiographical memory as well as to screen for such critical experiences as a family history of substance abuse, inappropriate sexual experiences, and abuse of various kinds. In addition, I structured the EMP to help prepare novice clients for insight-oriented psychotherapy by providing them with an experiential sampling of how a critical part of the psychotherapeutic process operates. To accomplish this goal, I requested that clients report various categories of memories likely to have clinical relevance, probe these recollections with a standard set of questions, rate their experiences for significance, and interpret a memory of their own choosing. A further requirement was made in consideration of the clinician's already busy schedule: the information-gathering process should not require more than five to ten minutes of one-to-one clinical time. Accordingly, the EMP was designed to be a largely self-administered, pencil-and-paper procedure.

The EMP is used in private practices, community mental health centers, university counseling departments, psychiatric hospitals, substance-abuse centers, and prisons, among other settings. The EMP can be used by almost any clinician who utilizes a psychodynamic, insight-oriented approach to therapy in which the personal history becomes an integral part of the treatment process. From the perspective of novice psychotherapy clients, the EMP helps them sort through a vast array of life events and reexperience those that are salient, for whatever reason.

The EMP has traditionally been used as part of an intake evaluation. Usually it is given to clients at the end of the initial visit for completion before the second visit. For experienced EMP clinicians, an interpretive session takes place in the second session. Bruhn (1990b, 1992a, 1992b) points out, however, that some clinical situations and symptoms contraindicate following this procedure—an acute crisis, profound depression, and so forth—so clinical judgment needs to be exercised as to when the EMP is administered. The EMP is also used as part of traditional psychological evaluations, often as part of a take-home package with the MMPI-2 or MCMI-2 in nonforensic situations.

In forensic cases, however, the client should be scheduled for a three-hour block of time to take the EMP on site in a testing room, just as one would schedule an MMPI-2 and other pencil-and-paper objective tests.

To maximize its potential utility, the EMP was constructed to assess the whole of autobiographical memory, not just EMs, and to sample categories of memories likely to have clinical relevance. Because the EMP was designed as a "hub" technique to ensure scope, ancillary "spoke techniques" were formulated to enable the clinician to explore in greater depth likely problem areas identified by the EMP. For instance, assume the EMP results pointed to difficulties in romantic relationships or the spousal relationship. The Romantic Relationships Procedure (RRP) (Bruhn, 1990c) and Memories of Spouse (MOS) (Bruhn, 1993c) were designed to assess such relationships. Or perhaps the most affective, negative memories on the EMP involve either mother or father. Memories of Mother (MOM) (Bruhn, 1993b) and Memories of Father (MOF) (Bruhn, 1993a) were devised to explore these relationships. Two other procedures—Business Relationships Procedure (BRP) and Memories of a Sib (MOAS)—are in prepublication.

The EMP is divided into two primary parts. Part I contains five EMs and a particularly clear or important memory/lifetime (spontaneous memories) together with rating scales for affective quality and memory clarity. Probes are also included that encourage clients to explore what made these recollections significant for them. Part II includes fifteen directed memories of various types, the subject's interpretation of a memory, and two pages of questionnaire data. The contents of the EMP and purposes of the probes can be found in Table 20.4.

The procedure was also intended to be sufficiently generic in format that any of the four EM interpretive models (Bruhn, 1990b; Bruhn & Last, 1982) could be used to assess the responses. In 1992, for example, in a Society for Personality Assessment (SPA) symposium in Washington, DC, individuals representing a CP, self psychology, and object relations perspective interpreted the same EMP protocol. Each perspective spoke to different facets of the

client's personality. The representatives of each model appeared equally comfortable working with the EMP as an assessment instrument.

How the EMP can be interpreted using a CP approach has been presented elsewhere (Bruhn, 1990b, 1992a, 1992b; Bruhn & Feigenbaum, in preparation). Because of space restrictions and the bulky nature of EMP protocols, it is not possible to present a full CP interpretation of an EMP here. However, I will reproduce Part I of a protocol from a man who previously had been in marital therapy with another therapist for approximately two years at the time the EMP was completed.

When the client was referred for treatment, his therapist commented that he had done as much as he could for the client in marital therapy, but the marriage appeared to have failed. He was therefore referring the client for individual work and parent counseling so that his role as marital therapist could be preserved if the couple later decided that they wanted to reconcile.

Because I was curious about what individual issues the client had brought to the marriage, I decided to begin with an EMP assessment. The results follow in Table 20.5. The reader who wishes to obtain more basic information about precis and process interpretations and how these are undertaken in an EMP is directed to Bruhn (1990b, 1992a, 1992b) and Bruhn and Feigenbaum (in preparation).

The results from the EMP are unusual in that recollections of explicit sexual abuse emerge in Part I of the EMP. In a clinical population, it is more common that such memories surface in Part II (see Bruhn, 1990b, p. 139). This result suggests that the client was already ready to talk about this issue if it came up in treatment. When I asked him if he had shared these experiences with his referring therapist, he said, "No." When I asked why he had not, he said, "He did not ask, and I did not know it was important."

Experiences like sexual abuse frequently exert a profound influence on the quality of the marital relationship. But without an appropriate assessment, such experiences are rarely volunteered, even when clinicians directly ask, "Have you ever been sexually abused?" Many clients

TABLE 20.4. Contents of the Early Memories Procedure[a]

Page	Contents	Purpose of probe
p. 1	Part I, Instructions.	—
p. 2	Earliest childhood memory	Determine earliest memory
p. 3	Next childhood memory	Assemble a set of spontaneous EMs
p. 4	Next childhood memory	Assemble a set of spontaneous EMs
p. 5	Next childhood memory	Assemble a set of spontaneous EMs
p. 6	Next childhood memory	Assemble a set of spontaneous EMs
p. 7	A particularly *clear* or *important* memory from one's entire life	Assesses unresolved issues, lifetime; "important" is deliberately ambiguous
p. 8	Additional autobiographical memories— *lifetime*	Assesses *motivation* for the task, among other things
p. 9–10	Rating scales for clarity and pleasantness for the first six memories	Pleasantness ratings should correlate with *present mood*—i.e., a high level of unpleasant affect in EMs should correlate with *present* affective disturbance. Memories that are particularly *vivid* draw extra psychic energy, which suggests that they should be especially important.
p. 11	Rank-order the three most significant EMs; explain why these memories are significant; explain why these particular memories were recalled	Assesses insight, ability to reflect and introspect, psychological mindedness
p. 13	Part II, instructions	—
p. 14	First school memory	Assesses attitudes toward achievement, mastery, independence
p. 15	First punishment memory	Assesses attitudes toward authority figures and fairness
p. 16	First sibling memory	Assesses sibling relationships, evidence of sibling rivalry
p. 17	First family memory	Assesses functioning in triadic or group situations
p. 18	Clearest memory of mother, lifetime	Assesses relationship with mother, attitudes toward women
p. 19	Clearest memory of father, lifetime	Assesses relationship with father, attitudes toward men
p. 20	A memory of someone you admire, lifetime	Assesses personal values and explores basis for potential role models
p. 21	Happiest memory, lifetime	Explores how strongest needs are best gratified
p. 22	Most traumatic memory, lifetime	Elicits psychic injuries
p. 23	A memory of your parents fighting, lifetime	Explores how conflict is likely to be processed
p. 24	A memory of a parent involving alcohol or drugs, lifetime	Probes whether individual has had to cope with a substance-abusing parent and issues related to same
p. 25	An incident that made you feel most ashamed, lifetime	Explores issues involving guilt
p. 26	A memory of being physically or emotionally abused, childhood	Probes whether individual has a history of being abused and, if so, how
p. 27	A memory of an inappropriate sexual experience, childhood or adolescence	Probes whether individual has a history of sexual traumas
p. 28	A fantasy memory	Assesses the individual's strongest needs and how he or she would ideally like to meet these needs. Compare this response with that on happiest memory for "actual vs. ideal" gratification

TABLE 20.4. (continued)

Page	Contents	Purpose of probe
p. 29	An interpretation of a memory—individual's choice	Assesses psychological mindedness, ability to reflect and introspect, and helps to establish how the individual understands cause and effect in his life
p. 30–31	Questionnaire—demographics, experience of and attitudes toward the EMP, time required to complete, the individual's beliefs about his EMs, and the individual's guess about the long-term reliability of his EMs	Provides basic research data about the individual, the EMP, and EMs

ᵃ Reproduced from Bruhn (1989b) with permission of the author.

don't think of *their* experiences as sexual abuse, or they are not connected with such experiences when the therapist asks the question; or, if they are, some are too embarrassed to acknowledge them in a face-to-face interview. In a structured *written* format like the EMP, however, many clients will disclose such experiences.

The EMP has several features or qualities that make it unique, or nearly so, among projective techniques. Several of the more noteworthy are listed below.

1. The EMP helps the clinician collect and organize especially salient parts of the client's personal history, such as a family history of substance abuse, physical or emotional abuse, neglect, sexual abuse, painful losses, and so forth. These experiences are packaged as "stories" so that clinicians are not just aware that these happened, but more important, of how clients construct them currently. Without the EMP, many of these experiences might never be mentioned in therapy.
2. The EMP educates clients about the process of insight-oriented psychotherapy. The procedure helps clients identify what is significant and important to them now. It encourages a reflective, introspective, historically oriented method of processing information. It helps clients appreciate that memories are not just history but

often vehicles that mirror maladaptive patterns and forms of acting and relating that will continue to be played out today without a firm commitment to change. No other projective technique, to my knowledge, is designed to help clients learn about themselves and to facilitate the process of psychotherapy.

3. I have pointed out earlier that the EMP and auxiliary spoke procedures can be used to anchor the results of other psychological procedures, such as the MMPI-2 and the Rorschach. This is accomplished by identifying the major unresolved issue from the EMP and articulating the schema contents that are associated with significant figures (mother, father) or classes of figures (teachers, authority figures) in the client's life. Once we know, for example, from the EMP that separation is the major unresolved issue, that mother is perceived as nonnurturing and rejecting, and that a favored aunt was shot to death while the client was present, it is much easier to interpret a clinically significant 7–2 profile on the MMPI and a Card 2 texture response on the Rorschach about an affectionate puppy that got hurt (blood). We have a clearer idea where the affect might derive. EMP data simplify the interpretive process and reduce the need

TABLE 20.5. Divorced White Male in His Forties[a]

Summary	Comments
EM 1	
Driving from R.I. to Massachusetts and going over a concrete bridge where a truck had plunged into a river and feeling sorry for the driver who had died under the water.	*Precis:* I feel bad when I experience losses/death.
	Perception of self: An observer.
	Perception of others: (Truck driver) vulnerable.
	Perception of world: Dangerous, unpredictable.
	Major issue: Attachment/loss.
Clearest: Driving over the bridge, sitting in the front seat of the car securely between my parents and looking down at the river.	*Comment:* This memory may be a disguised representation of suicidal impulses or a metaphoric statement of his present emotional state (devastated or "wrecked"). The CP method is superb at articulating the underlying form of a memory; however, metaphor often suggests an array of possible interpretations, which a process interpretation (see EM 2) may or may not support.
Feeling: Terribly sorry for the driver (who I did not know) who had lost his life.	
Change: Try to relate to or understand why a terrible thing like that would happen. I couldn't possibly have understood death at my young age so I doubt that I could have changed anything.	
Age: 3–5 years.	
EM 2	
Our scoutmaster used to invite us to work on merit badges at his house on Sunday and would molest me while his wife was at church singing in the choir.	*Precis:* (Pattern memory or report) Someone in a position of trust exploited me and sexually abused me.
	Perception of self: Too trusting, helpless, victim, unassertive (below, he wonders why he didn't tell his parents).
	Perception of others: (Male authority/scoutmaster) Devious, exploitative, abusive.
Clearest: Man much stronger than I, front of car or in his bedroom or scout tent.	*Perception of world:* Deceptive (things are not what they appear to be).
Feeling: Helpless—eventually turned me off [from] scout camp.	*Major issues:* (1) Trust; (2) adequacy; (3) assertiveness—responding more actively; (4) self-disclosure; (5) release of anger associated with being victimized and blaming the self.
Change: Try to understand why I didn't immediately go to my parents and tell. Eventually man was caught five years later when the police called me, then a high school football player, to confirm the scoutmaster had done that.	*Process interpretation:* (i.e., how are EM 1 and EM 2 linked?) Unexpected and terrible events occur (EM 1), which appear to be impossible to avoid. Similarly, in EM 2, the client was devastated and overpowered, much like the truck driver in EM 1. There is a tendency to depression with this perceptual set, especially when losses occur or disillusionment is experienced.
Age: 11 years.	*Comment:* This is a negative affect pattern memory, not a single event memory as requested. Negative affect pattern memories are nearly always extremely important, partly because of the repetitive nature of the experience.
EM 3	
The boys' initiation to group when 7 years old and moved to M. was to draw a girl's private. Easy—I had two sisters.	*Precis:* I want to be accepted as one of the guys.
	Perception of self: Adequate, accepted by peers.
	Perception of others: (Peers/boys) sexually preoccupied.
	Major issues: (1) Acceptance; (2) adequacy as a male.
Clearest: Surprised that [a] group that young could have such pictures and got them from older brothers and sisters who were married.	*Process interpretation:* This memory provides reassurance that he is "ok," not gay. It also indicates that he is concerned about being *accepted*, which helps us understand his passivity and unassertiveness in EM 2—he was probably

TABLE 20.5. Divorced White Male in His Forties[a] (continued)

Summary	Comments
Feeling: This sexual experience with same age boys was acceptable. *Change:* [not completed] *Age:* 7 years.	afraid that his scoutmaster wouldn't like him if he asserted himself and that his parents would be angry with him if he disclosed what had happened.
EM 4 Mrs. L. [his teacher] says aloof, independent . . . questions [my] remaining on safety patrol. "M. thought he was superior." *Clearest:* [not completed] *Feeling:* [not completed] *Change:* [not completed] *Age:* [not completed]	*Precis:* My teacher didn't like me because She believed that I thought myself better than others. *Perception of others:* (Female teacher) critical, rejecting. *Major issue:* Acceptance from others, inclusion in the group. *Process interpretation:* This memory, along with EM 3, emphasizes his need for acceptance, his sensitivity to criticism, and his fear of rejection. This pattern puts him at risk for abusive and exploitative relationships and makes assertiveness a particularly testy issue for him. At another level, he seems to be aware that he had withdrawn as a result of his having been molested.
EM 5 Parents left me overnight with W. (parents' friend) at camp site. I lived with M., liked because of water skiing with his daughters. *Clearest:* Reminded me of scout camp. *Feeling:* Scared. *Change:* Know difference between this and scout camp. This man was a friend but same church that sponsored that sponsored scout troop. *Age:* 12 years.	*Precis:* I become apprehensive and anxious in new situations. *Perception of self:* Untrusting of male authority figures (after sexual abuse by scoutmaster), likes being with girls, enjoys physical activity. *Perception of others:* (Male authority) nice, trustworthy. *Major issues:* None, because this is a positive-affect memory. But the client himself makes the connection to scout camp, which points to an issue with trust and a need to heal from this experience. *Process interpretation:* This memory resurrects his concerns from EM 2, in which he was sexually molested. He worries that it might happen again, which underscores his issues with trust. His experience in EM 2 appears to have exacerbated old separation issues.
Memory 6 I remember thinking J. (high school girl) pregnant in high school and couldn't understand how this could be possible but it was an issue. *Clearest:* Phone call from lobby of school to her home. *Feeling:* [not completed] *Change:* [not completed] *Age:* [not completed]	*Precis:* It was difficult to believe that a high school girl could become pregnant. *Perception of self:* Difficult understanding process in relationships—how certain events come to pass. *Perception of others:* Confusing. *Perception of world:* Surprising, unpredictable. *Major issues:* None, because this is a positive affect memory. But he seems to be confused about understanding relationships and processing cause and effect in relationships *Process interpretation:* In the last memory, he notes his attraction to some girls who are cute; here, he recalls a pregnant high school girl and remembers feeling confused about how something like this could have happened, presumably to someone this young. There seems to be an underlying confusion about relationships, probably connected with his being molested, in which he is trying to understand what makes certain events happen in relationships, particularly events associated with the expression of sexuality.

(continued)

TABLE 20.5. Divorced White Male in His Forties[a] (continued)

Summary of rating scale

	Pleasantness: 7-Point Scale	Clarity: 5-Point Scale
EM 1	2: moderately negative	1: very unclear
EM 2	1: very negative	5: exceptionally clear
EM 3	3: mildly negative	3: moderately clear
EM 4	2: moderately negative	1: very unclear
EM 5	5: mildly positive	3: moderately clear
Memory 6	5: mildly positive	5: exceptionally clear

Most significant memories

1. Most significant: 2
2. Next significant: 1
3. Next significant: 6

Q: Explain why these memories, especially your most significant early memory, are important to you.

A: EM 2—humiliation and put down—this was not supposed to happen to good boys; why was I the one; was I singled out or were others jeopardizing.

Q: Why do you think that you recall *these* from all your childhood experiences?

A: They were areas where I had fear from lack of control.

Interpretation of rating scales

Clearest EMs (5s on a 5-point scale) are usually the most significant memories. Particularly clear memories draw proportionately more psychic energy because the issue illustrated by the memory is currently focal. One can think of such EMs as being spotlighted.

If the clearest memory is also very positive (7 on a 7-point scale), this suggests that a strong need or wish has been gratified—likely a need that is primary in importance for the individual now. Such memories contain a self-message or reminder to the individual that takes the form, "This is what you need most, and here is how this need can be met." If the clearest memory is very negative (1), this suggests that a major issue is being played out, something that the individual is actively trying to work through now.

In this protocol, two memories are rated as 5s for clarity: EM 2 and memory 6 (see summary of rating scales). The client rates EM 2 as his most significant memory, thus providing independent evidence of its importance. The common denominator between the two memories involves sexuality. Due to the client's concerns about having been molested, there appear to be strong feelings about his own sexuality and his adequacy as a male. Such concerns are common among males who were sexually abused as youngsters.

Directed memories are requested to determine whether something important was omitted from the spontaneous memories in Part I. There are 15 directed memories in all.

Part II—Directed Memories

Summary	Comments

[In a full EMP, 15 directed memories would be reproduced and interpreted here. To save space, these are eliminated. I have included, however, "Your interpretation of a memory," which is part of this section. His "Memory of an inappropriate sexual experience" includes another memory in which an older boy tried to molest him sexually, but he resists his advances this time. This memory underscores his doubts about himself sexually—"Why *him?*" Readers who wish to see a full EMP protocol are directed to Bruhn (1990b, 1992b) and Bruhn and Feigenbaum (in preparation).]

Your interpretation of a memory

I think my early traumatic experience with control of the scoutmaster was one of the major causes of my lack of sensitivity toward people and especially women. The early sexual feelings were good but in the male environment

Comment: He is able to talk about the impact of EM 2—a key memory in his life. He raises questions about why he was picked out sexually, which causes him to doubt himself and to lose self-confidence. He recognizes that he tends to respond to women as he was responded to by the scoutmaster and also an older boy in a directed memory,

TABLE 20.5. (continued)

Summary	Comments
being forced upon me caused embarrassment and my sense of why am I being picked on like this. Self confidence, also. Took me a long time to realize women feel and can be friends rather than sexual objects. I still have problems understanding this and dealing with women. I look at good-looking women as bed partners. I don't particularly want to deal with fat or unkempt women. It has taken me many years to realize I can't be the person who wants to please everyone though I still try to do so.	other males who sexually abused him, or tried to do so. He is also aware of his need to please. All of the above reflect personal strengths and indicate areas that can be discussed with relative comfort. The focus of therapy will be directed toward accessing and expressing old feelings that are still locked up inside.

Synthesis of issues

This protocol illustrates a phenomenon common to experienced EMP interpreters—previously unidentified and untreated sexual abuse. Probably as a result of this experience, his sexual interest was awakened prematurely. His construction of relationships is that one is either predator or victim. He recognizes that other aspects of male/female relationships have been warped, at least partly because of this experience. His anger as a victim also appears to have been largely supressed, perhaps because he seeks approval so strongly.

Although we know that experiences of sexual abuse are extremely important, the client confirms that this experience was highly significant to him. He selects this memory as his most significant and chooses to interpret it from a field of 21 possible candidates (6 in Part I, 15 in Part II). And the CP method helps us to arrive at the same conclusion: EM 2 is the clearest (5) and most negative (1) memory as well as the only negative pattern memory. In retrospect, from a process perspective, EM 1 appears to tell us how devastated ('wrecked') he felt by this experience. EM 1 also suggests that suicidal ideation and impulses may be connected to this experience.

The experience of being sexually abused[b] by a respected and trusted member of the community left a nested set of related issues to process, beginning with trust and proceeding to becoming more active, self-disclosing painful feelings, and understanding cause and effect (or, from another perspective, human motivation) in relationships. Considerable anger associated with this experience was also suppressed. And it was vital to decide how—or whether—to confront the scoutmaster. Naturally, some of this work was directly associated with the experience of being sexually abused, and some was connected with the effects of that experience in subsequent and contemporary relationships, including his former martial relationship. The abuse experience had never been discussed in marital therapy in the context of what was happening in the marriage.

[a]Copyright by Bruhn (1994) and used by permission of the author.

[b]Since there has been so much written recently about the possibility of "suggested" memories of sexual abuse (e.g., Loftus, 1993), it is fair to raise the question here. Is it possible that sexual abuse memories in EMPs are fabricated? Certainly, it is possible. But I have never personally seen such an instance in more than 20 years of work with early memories. One variable that makes the EMP different as a procedure is that no "suggestion" takes place, as is common among some therapists: "What you have been telling me makes me wonder about whether you were ever sexually abused. . . ?" When therapists make these kinds of inquiries, I agree with Loftus: the possibility of suggested experiences among suggestible, and often imaginative, clients is increased. The risk is even greater with visualization techniques, which involve even more powerful uses of suggestion. However, the likelihood of such memories appearing on the EMP, given no prior suggestions, is minimal; not nil, but minimal.

for guesswork. Although the EMP does not provide a veridical history, it preserves the subject's highly selective current construction of that history.

The EMP offers other important advantages. First, it is inexpensive to administer and respectful of clinician time. Second, the interpretive process with the clinician helps clients feel understood as well as enabling them to apprehend their presenting problem in a broader historical context. Third, the EMP focuses the therapy process and enables change to take place more rapidly, if in fact it is possible for clients to make immediate structural changes in their lives. Fourth, the process of taking the EMP is itself therapeutic. Feelings are vented, and self-awareness is increased.

SCORING EARLY MEMORIES

How should an EM be scored? An illusion of historical truth, steeped into our conscious attitudes regarding EMs, has probably inhibited thinking in this domain. As one of my colleagues once put it, "Why do you want to score actual *memories?*" When Last took on this task for his dissertation, we decided, largely for reasons of expediency, to take the best of existing systems and largely be satisfied. The result was the CEMSS. Since one of the best systems at that time was the Manaster-Perryman (1974), the CEMSS bore more than an accidental resemblance to it. After Last completed his dissertation and I had time to use the CEMSS with clients, I decided to revise the CEMSS and adapt Klopfer's approach to the Rorschach. After all, both tasks required verbal responses and were relatively unstructured. The Rorschach, therefore, appeared to offer a potentially useful analogue.

Table 20.6 permits us to examine some of the similarities and differences between the two systems. The most obvious difference is that the CEMSS-R does not handle popular/original responses. Although I could have devised an analogue scale, I don't believe that researchers

TABLE 20.6 A Comparison of Klopfer/Rorschach Scoring System Variables with CEMSS-R/EMP Scoring Variables

Rorschach/Klopfer scoring variables	EM/CEMSS-R scoring variables
1. Location (of response)	Setting (II) of EM
2. Determinant	Characters (1); Sensory-motor aspect (III); Active vs. passive stance (VI); Affect (VIII); Type of affect (IX)
3. Content	Content and process themes (VII)
4. Popularity	—
5. Form level	Relation to reality (IV); Object relations (V); Damage aspect (X)
[Process interpretation]	[Process interpretation]

would be interested in "original" EMs for the same reason a Klopferian would want to recognize originality.

On the other hand, the CEMSS-R emphasizes two aspects of EMs that the Klopfer system does not treat prominently in Rorschach responses: object relations and damage aspects. Damage is scored to self, others, animals, and inanimate objects. Damage scores are believed to be related to narcissistic injuries or losses and to depression. Those who want to focus specifically on object relations in EMs are encouraged to consider other systems (Mayman, 1984a, 1984b; Ryan, 1974), as the CEMSS-R does not assess this area in the kind of detail that those with a special interest may prefer.

Returning to the question of how an EM should be scored, the short answer is, "I don't know." Ultimately, I believe that we have to regard an EM as we would any complex psychological phenomenon, create models that attempt to explain this phenomenon (or parts thereof), and construct scoring systems that derive from these models. The CEMSS-R (Last & Bruhn, 1991) derives from the CP model, while the Langs and Reiser (1961) flows from a psychoanalytic perspective, and Mayman's (1984a,

1984b) from the ego psychology school. In a similar vein, several Adlerians have experimented with social interest scales.

BOUTIQUE SCORING SYSTEMS

Our understanding of autobiographical memory is likely to be advanced through the development of custom or boutique scoring systems with highly specific functions. Such a process can be analogized to a gene-mapping procedure. Assume that you want to post-dictively predict a certain phenomenon through identifying relevant EM qualities or characteristics. These phenomena could be as diverse as scoring high or low on test X or demonstrating a target behavior in a particular context. We have a choice at this point. We could utilize a general-purpose or comprehensive system like the Manaster-Perryman (1974) or the CEMSS-R (Last & Bruhn, 1991), discussed previously, and hope that one or more EM variables are correlated with the test outcome or target behavior. We have here a shotgun approach: if we fire enough pellets, we should hit something. Sometimes there are advantages to a shotgun approach, but on balance, I would recommend a custom or boutique approach.

Boutique scoring systems almost require that we begin with a pilot sample. I ordinarily recommend that a pilot study be started with minimal preconceptions as to what EM aspects are likely to characterize a particular group. The stronger our preconceptions, the more we are likely to be blinded to other possibilities and relationships. I typically begin with a contextually oriented precis analysis ("when X occurs, I expect Y to follow") of each EM in the sample and ask myself how this particular perception bears upon the behavior or test score that interests me. For instance, with delinquent-proneness (Bruhn & Davidow, 1983; Davidow & Bruhn, 1990) Davidow and I undertook a precis analysis of the EMs of a set of delinquents and matched nondelinquents. From this analysis emerged a set of EM qualities and characteristics that distinguished the overwhelming majority of the delinquents from the nondelinquents. Some had to do with rule breaking, some had to do with failing, and so forth. With this information, we could begin to understand how delinquents constructed their past experiences and by extension how this constructive process might be related to a current delinquent lifestyle. When Tobey and I (1992) undertook a parallel process for a group of violence-prone psychiatric patients, we found—not surprisingly—that violence-prone individuals usually recalled violence, often by themselves or to themselves. The violence was sometimes physical, sometimes verbal, and other times psychological. I suspect, especially in the case of EMs, that if we wish to understand particular test outcomes or target behaviors, we must refine our skills in developing effective boutique approaches.

Examples of boutique approaches from my work and that of my students and colleagues include post-dictively predicting attitudes toward personal responsibility (Rotter Internal-External Locus of Control Scores, Bruhn, 1976; Bruhn & Schiffman, 1982c), delinquency proneness (Bruhn & Davidow, 1983; Davidow & Bruhn, 1990), and violence proneness (Tobey & Bruhn, 1992). Recently we have begun to test the power of our boutique systems against predictions made from the scores on the comprehensive system (CEMSS-R). This approach enables us to determine whether a boutique system provides us with any unique advantages over the comprehensive system.

Other groups have also utilized boutique approaches. For example, Achlin, Sauer, Alexander, and Dugoni (1989) identified a set of EM characteristics associated with depression. Roth (1977) predicted classroom behavior using an Adlerian-based system anchored with EM material. Early attempts to utilize boutique approaches date at least to Wolfman & Friedman's (1964) attempt to predict a presenting symptom of impotence from EM material and a brilliant dissertation by Malamud (1956), who identified differences in the EMs of authoritarian and nonauthoritarian personalities.

LEGAL AND MALPRACTICE CONSIDERATIONS

Historically, psychologists have been most vulnerable to legal actions when they have violated therapist/client boundaries and have acted inappropriately (for instance, engaged in sexual misconduct) or failed to take reasonable action (not warned individuals who have been targeted for harm by psychotherapy clients). Some of the most obvious problems have been debated and discussed extensively in the literature. A more subtle but still important potential malpractice consideration is failure to exercise due diligence. Assume, for example, that a marriage dissolves after the therapist fails to inquire as to whether either party was sexually abused. Suppose further that the history of sexual abuse was directly related to the marital difficulties. Is the therapist liable for failure to exercise due diligence? We have already alluded to a similar case in this chapter,[1] and I do not consider such circumstances rare. How we answer this question depends in part on whether we believe that marital problems are often caused by a history of sexual abuse. If we believe so, and if we believe that this variable becomes an important consideration, then we should make an appropriate inquiry. A similar relationship exists between depression and suicide, for example.

Consider an even more frequent circumstance. I administered EMPs to several clinical samples and asked clients, who were all in psychotherapy, whether they had described any memories in their protocols that they had never before told anybody, even their therapists. Many clients had been in psychotherapy for years, some for more than ten years. Approximately one-fourth to one-third of my samples reported one or more memories that they had never shared with anybody, including their present therapist. When asked why they had not done so, the most common response was, "They never asked." The next most common was that they were too embarrassed to do so.

As the number of insurance-reimbursed sessions continues to contract, I believe that the issue of due diligence will loom larger. When therapists treated clients in a leisurely manner over a period of years, traumatic memories were likely to surface "in due time." My research results suggest that at least two-thirds of clients were, in fact, able to share their experiences. As the number of psychotherapy sessions allowed by insurance companies declines, however, I believe that issues involving due diligence are more likely to become problematic, because there will be less time for traumatic experiences to emerge in the natural course of events.

CONCLUSION

The field of autobiographical memory is posed for rapid development. Procedures are available, solutions to prior methodological problems have been proposed, and a personality theory based on autobiographical memory has been articulated. I believe that the field of insight-oriented psychotherapy was founded—incorrectly—on the wrong cornerstone: dream work. Instead, we should have begun with autobiographical memory. More than any other psychological phenomenon, our memories of specific events tell us how we construct ourselves, others, and the world. They tell us about our strongest needs, our enduring interests, and our most troublesome problems. Once we understand autobiographical memory, we understand not only who we are but how we got to be where we are in our lives. Even better, our positive memories provide clues as to how our more troublesome problems can be resolved.

Often we can learn the most from what is obvious. At times, I have characterized applied autobiographical memory as the psychology of the obvious. I believe that we are at the gateway to a golden age in personality. What is obvious is now becoming transparently so to many of us. Let the new age begin.

ACKNOWLEDGMENT

Dr. Kenneth Feigenbaum and Dr. Bonnie Greenberg served as readers for this chapter. Their suggestions are deeply appreciated. Raquel Perry and Kathy Swanstrom collaborated in the preparation of the manuscript. Without their creativity, tolerance, and dedication the manuscript could not have been produced. Thank you!

NOTE

1. This case has been presented here for didactic purposes. For reasons that are unrelated to the client's history of sexual abuse, this marriage probably would have failed even if this condition had been disclosed and treated.

REFERENCES

Achlin, M., Sauer, A., Alexander, G., & Dugoni, B. (1989). Predicting depression using earliest childhood memories. *Journal of Personality Assessment*, 53, 51–59.

Adler, A. (1917). *The Neurotic Constitution*. New York: Moffat, Yard & Co. (Originally published in 1912 in German)

Adler, A. (1927). *Understanding human nature*. New York: Greenberg.

Adler, A. (1929). *The case of Miss R*. New York: Greenberg.

Adler, A. (1931). *What life should mean to you*. New York: Grosset and Dunlap.

Adler, A. (1937). The significance of early recollections. *International Journal of Individual Psychology*, 3, 283–287.

Ansbacher, H., & Ansbacher, R. (Eds.) (1956). *The individual psychology of Alfred Adler*. New York: Basic Books.

Bartlett, F. C. (1932). *Remembering: A study in experimental and social psychology*. Cambridge: Cambridge University Press.

Belove, L. (1980). First encounters of the close kind (FECK): The use of the story of the first interaction as an early recollection of a marriage. *Journal of Psychology*, 36, 191–208.

Bernfeld, S. (1946). An unknown autobiographical fragment by Freud. *American Imago*, 1, 3–19.

Bruhn, A. R. (1976). *Early memories of being punished as predictors of control stance*. Unpublished doctoral dissertation, Duke University, Durham, NC.

Bruhn, A. R. (1984). The use of early memories as a projective technique. In P. McReynolds & C. J. Chelume (Eds.), *Advances in psychological assessment* (Vol. 6, pp. 109–150). San Francisco: Jossey-Bass.

Bruhn, A. R. (1985). Using early memories as a projective technique: The cognitive-perceptual method. *Journal of Personality Assessment*, 49, 587–597.

Bruhn, A. R. (1989a). *The Early Memories Procedure*. 32 pages. Available from the author.

Bruhn, A. R. (1989b). *The Early Memories Procedure manual*. 12 pages. Available from the author.

Bruhn, A. R. (1989c). *The Romantic Relationships Procedure*. 28 pages. Available from the author.

Bruhn, A. R. (1990a). Cognitive-perceptual theory and the projective use of autobiographical memory. *Journal of Personality Assessment*, 55, 95–114.

Bruhn, A. R. (1990b). *Earliest childhood memories: Theory and application to clinical practice* (Vol. 1). New York: Praeger.

Bruhn, A. R. (1992a). The Early Memories Procedure: A projective test of autobiographical memory (Part I). *Journal of Personality Assessment*, 58, 1–15.

Bruhn, A. R. (1992b). The Early Memories Procedure: A projective test of autobiographical memory (Part II). *Journal of Personality Assessment*, 58, 326–346.

Bruhn, A. R. (1993a). *Memories of Father*, 38 pages. Available from the author.

Bruhn, A. R. (1993b). *Memories of Mother*, 38 pages. Available from the author.

Bruhn, A. R. (1993c). *Memories of Spouse*. 38 pages. Available from the author.

Bruhn, A. R., & Bellow, S. (1984). Warrior, general, and president: Dwight David Eisenhower and his earliest memories. *Journal of Personality Assessment*, 48, 371–377.

Bruhn, A. R., & Bellow, S. (1987). The cognitive-perceptual approach to the interpretation of early memories: The earliest memories of Golda Meir. In C. D. Spielberger & J. N. Butcher (Eds.), *Advances in personality assessment* (Vol. 6, pp. 69–87). Hillsdale, NJ: Erlbaum.

Bruhn, A. R., & Davidow, S. (1983). Earliest memories and the dynamics of delinquency. *Journal of Personality Assessment*, 47, 476–482.

Bruhn, A. R., & Feigenbaum, K. (In preparation). *The interpretation of autobiographical memories*.

Bruhn, A. R., & Last, J. (1982). Early memories: Four theoretical perspectives. *Journal of Personality Assessment*, 46, 119–127.

Bruhn, A. R., & Schiffman, H. (1982a). *Distinguishing Rotter internals from externals via themes from the earliest childhood memory*. 16 pages. Available from the first author.

Bruhn, A. R., & Schiffman, H. (1982b). Invalid assumptions and methodological difficulties in early memory research. *Journal of Personality Assessment, 46,* 265–267.

Bruhn, A. R., & Schiffman, H. (1982c). Prediction of locus of control stance from the earliest childhood memory. *Journal of Personality Assessment, 46,* 380–390.

Chess, S. (1951). Utilization of childhood memories in psychoanalytic theory. *Journal of Child Psychiatry, 2,* 187–193.

Colegrove, W. (1899). Individual memories. *American Journal of Psychology, 10,* 228–255.

Crandall, J. W. (1971). The early spouse memory as a diagnostic aid in marriage counseling. *Journal of Contemporary Psychotherapy, 3,* 82–88.

Davidow, S., & Bruhn, A. R. (1990). Earliest memories and the dynamics of delinquency: A replication study. *Journal of Personality Assessment, 54,* 601–616.

Freud, S. (1950). Screen memories. In J. Strachey (Ed. & Trans.), *The standard edition of the complete works of Sigmund Freud* (Vol. 3). London: Hogarth Press. (Originally published 1899)

Freud, S. (1955). A childhood recollection from "Dichtung and Wahrheit." In J. Strachey (Ed. & Trans.), *The standard edition of the complete works of Sigmund Freud* (Vol. 17). London: Hogarth Press. (Originally published 1917)

Friedman, A. (1933). First recollections of school. *International Journal of Individual Psychology, 1,* 111–116.

Hall, G. S. (1899). Note on early memories. *Pedagogical Seminary, 6,* 485–512.

Hartmann, H. (1958). *Ego psychology and the problem of adaptation.* New York: International Universities Press.

Hartmann, H. (1964). *Essays on ego psychology.* New York: International Universities Press.

Henri, V., & Henri, C. (1898). Earliest recollections. *Popular Science Monthly, 53,* 108–115.

Langs, R. J., & Reiser, M. F. (1961). *A manual for the scoring of the manifest content of the first memory and dreams.* Unpublished manuscript.

Last, J. (1983). *The Comprehensive Early Memories Scoring System Manual.* 14 pages. Available from the author at 17117 West Nine Mile Rd. #423, Southfield, MI 48075.

Last, J., & Bruhn, A. R. (1991). *The Comprehensive Early Memories Scoring System—Revised*

Manual. 17 pages. Available from the second author.

Loftus, E. F. (1993). The reality of repressed memories. *American Psychologist, 48,* 518–537.

Malamud, D. I. (1956). *Differences in the early childhood memories of authoritian and nonauthoritarian personalities.* Unpublished doctoral dissertation, New York University, New York.

Manaster, G. J., & Perryman, T. B. (1974). Early recollections and occupational choice. *Journal of Individual Psychology, 30,* 232–237.

Mayman, M. (1968). Early memories and character structure. *Journal of Projective Techniques and Personality Assessment, 32,* 303–316.

Mayman, M. (1984a). Early memories and character structure. In F. Schectman & W. H. Smith (Eds.), *Diagnostic understanding and treatment planning: The elusive connection* (pp. 122–140). New York: Wiley. (Reprinted from *Journal of Projective Techniques and Personality Assessment,* 1968, 32, 303–316.)

Mayman, M. (1984b). Psychoanalytic study of the self-organization with psychological tests. In F. Schectman & W. H. Smith (Eds.), *Diagnostic understanding and treatment planning: The elusive connection* (pp. 141–156). New York: Wiley. (Reprinted from *Proceedings of the Academic Assembly on Clinical Psychology.* Montreal: McGill University Press, 1963, pp. 97–117)

Miles, C. (1893). A study of individual psychology. *American Journal of Psychology, 6,* 534–558.

Mosak, H. H. (1958). Early recollections as a projective technique. *Journal of Projective Techniques, 22,* 302–311.

Munroe, R. L. (1955). *Schools of psychoanalytic thought.* New York: Dryden Press.

Neisser, U. (1982). *Memory observed: Remembering in natural contexts.* San Francisco: Freeman.

Olson, H. A. (1979). *Early recollections.* Springfield, IL: Thomas.

Potwin, E. B. (1901). Study of early memories. *Psychological Review, 8,* 596–601.

Rom, P. (1965). Goethe's earliest recollection. *Journal of Individual Psychology, 21,* 189–193.

Ross, B. M. (1991). *Remembering the personal past.* New York: Oxford University Press.

Roth, H. J. (1977). *The earliest recollection as one method of attempting to understand classroom behavior in school for male fifth and sixth grade students with reading problems.* Unpublished doctoral dissertation, Duke University, Durham, NC.

Rubin, D. C. (1986). *Autobiographical memory.* New York: Cambridge University Press.

Ryan, E. R. (1974). *Quality of object relations scale.* Available from the author at Department of Veterans Affairs, 950 Campbell Ave. #116B, West Haven, CT 06516.

Tobey, L. H., & Bruhn, A. R. (1992). Early memories and the criminally dangerous. *Journal of Personality Assessment, 59,* 137–152.

Waldfogel, S. (1948). The frequency and affective character of childhood memories. *Psychological Monographs, 62,* (4, Whole No. 291).

Wolfman, C., & Friedman, J. (1964). A symptom and its symbolic representation in earliest memories. *Journal of Clinical Psychology, 20,* 442–444.

21
Item Content in the Interpretation of the MMPI-2

James N. Butcher

Patients being assessed in a mental health setting usually expect that the psychologist or psychiatrist they are seeing will pay careful attention to the content of their communications about their symptoms. Moreover, when the mental health evaluation involves completing a self-report questionnaire, such as the MMPI-2, in which patients are asked to provide personal information about their symptoms and adjustment, there is an expectation that the information they share will be reviewed and synthesized by the clinician to understand their situation. However, this expectation is not always fulfilled. In fact, when objective interpretation by self-report assessment with the original MMPI emerged during the late 1930s and 1940s, there was a clear admonition against considering the self-report statements as personal communications. Rather, the traditional position developed by Hathaway and Meehl held that self-report of symptoms could not be trusted or accepted at face value (Meehl, 1945). Thus, the original MMPI (Hathaway & McKinley, 1940) was launched with the view that the content of the items was relatively unimportant and what actually mattered was whether the item was endorsed by a particular clinical group. This view led many clinicians, following the objective test approach, to ignore item content as a direct communication.

Psychologists today, even the empirically oriented MMPI-2 users, view the content of test item responses, at least when the persons being assessed are motivated to participate with the evaluation, as direct communications between the patient and the clinician (Butcher, Dahlstrom, Graham, Tellegen, & Kaemmer, 1989). As communications, item responses can provide direct reflections of how the patient views his or her problems. This view, referred to as the content approach to assessment, assumes, of course, that the patient *actually* has access to the information being requested. Patients will not be able to provide you with a clear idea of whether their feelings, beliefs, symptoms, and so forth, are common or rare. It is the task of the psychometric test to provide a framework to enable symptoms to be placed in a normative perspective. We would not expect clients to be able to diagnose themselves or provide accurate information about how others view them, but they could know and provide such things as whether they get headaches every day, whether they have been in jail, and whether they loved their mother.

As long as clients are willing to share personal information and have access to the information being requested, they are usually found to be excellent witnesses as to the presence or absence of mental health problems. After all, who could be a better witness to an individual's private events than the individual?

In order for clinicians to make maximal use of the information provided by patients, they must recognize that patients often hold the key to understanding their problems and can in fact provide accurate, useful information about themselves under appropriate conditions. When you want to know something about patients, ask them. When they do provide important information, we then need to determine if it is credible enough to accept at face value.

ASSESSING MOTIVATION TO PROVIDE ACCURATE SYMPTOMATIC AND BEHAVIORAL DESCRIPTION

Interpreting item response data on personality tests can be justified if the individual has access to the information in question and is willing to share it with the practitioner. The willingness to disclose personal information in a clinical situation is a key consideration. Research has shown that test defensiveness is associated with lower elevation on content scales (Lachar & Alexander, 1982; Faull & Meyer, 1993).

Several factors require careful consideration in determining if clients' responses to personality questions can be taken as accurate communications about themselves:

1. *Setting*. The setting in which the test was administered is an important consideration. Individuals being evaluated in a family custody case (see Pope, Butcher, & Seelen, 1993) or in an employment screening setting (Butcher, 1993) are not likely to be very open to endorsing problems and acknowledging faults. Rather, their test performance is likely to be characterized by elevated scores on measures of defensiveness on the MMPI-2, such as L, K, and S scales. Similarly, many individuals being

appraised in a personal injury lawsuit claim extreme and excessive problems in order to buttress their claims of injury or to gain attention for their symptoms. Therefore, protocols from such settings are often more a product of the desire to show disability rather than to reflect their own personality characteristics accurately.

2. *Instructions*. It is important to follow standard instructions when administering psychological tests. Deviant or destructive response attitudes can be imparted to clients by unintentional or misguided communications of the reasons for administering the test or unclear test administration instructions. For example, the staff in one pain clinic altered the instructions to the MMPI booklet in a way that had the effect of invalidating the tests administered. They eliminated the standard instruction page from the test booklet and substituted their own page, actually changing the name of the test to "Pain Experience Questionnaire." Their altered test instructions encouraged patients to respond to the items in the booklet "to record any pain or problems you were currently experiencing." The information gained through this process might have been useful and clinically interesting, but the resulting scale scores cannot be viewed as MMPI measures since the instructions deviated too much from the standard instructions on which the norms are based.

3. *Varying motivational sets*. Clients approach the test items from different perspectives. They define the test situation in their own terms and respond to the items in order to communicate their feelings, symptoms, and so forth. Their motivations and their understanding of test instructions require careful consideration in order to determine the utility of the test information provided. The MMPI-2

contains several measures that need to be evaluated in the determination of whether the response patterns are open and cooperative enough to provide useful information. Following are some different approaches to the MMPI-2, as reflected in the various validity indices. These validity patterns provide information as to the credibility of the individual's content themes. Content scales, being vulnerable to conscious distortion, require a higher standard of scrutiny to assure that information presented through the items is accurate (Lachar & Alexander, 1978).

a. *Accessible to the evaluation:* If the client has responded to the MMPI-2 validity indices with the following scale level performances, their item content is likely to reflect cooperative and frank presentation of problems through the item content. No deviant response sets are detected in the profile illustrated in Figure 21.1, and the information provided by the client is likely to be credible and clinically useful.

$$
\begin{aligned}
? &\quad = 0 \\
L &\quad \leq 54 \\
K &\quad \leq 54 \\
S &\quad \leq 54 \\
F &\quad \geq 55 < 89 \\
F\,(B) &\quad \geq 55 < 89
\end{aligned}
$$

b. *Inaccessible to the evaluation:* If the client has responded to the MMPI-2 validity indices with the following scale level performances, a high degree of test defensiveness is suggested. Caution in interpreting test item content as communications about problems should be exercised. A defensive profile is illustrated in Figure 21.2. (See also discussions by Baer, Wetter, & Berry, 1992.)

$$
\begin{aligned}
? &\quad \geq 1 \\
L &\quad \geq 61 \\
K &\quad \geq 61
\end{aligned}
$$

$$
\begin{aligned}
S &\quad \geq 61 \\
F &\quad \leq 54 \\
F\,(B) &\quad \leq 54
\end{aligned}
$$

c. *Overresponding to symptom:* If the client has responded to the MMPI-2 validity indices with any of the following scale level performances, caution should be exercised in interpreting test item content as communications about problems, because the individual has endorsed items in an exaggerated, nonbelievable manner. An exaggerated profile is illustrated in Figure 21.3. (See also discussions by Berry, Wetter, Baer, Larsen, Clark, & Monroe, 1992; Graham, Watts, & Timbrook, 1991; Rogers, Bagby, & Chakraborty, 1993; Schretlen, 1988; Wetter, Baer, Berry, D. T., Robison, L. H., & Sumpter, 1993; and Wetter, Baer, Berry, Smith, & Larsen, 1992.)

$$
\begin{aligned}
VRIN &> 80 \\
TRIN &> 80 \\
L &\leq 54 \\
K &\geq 54 \\
S &\geq 54 \\
F &\leq 90 \\
F\,(B) &\leq 90
\end{aligned}
$$

If the protocol is considered to be sufficiently valid for further interpretation according to the validity indices, there are several possible approaches to content interpretation in the MMPI-2. In the next section we will consider the three most frequently used content interpretation strategies: "critical items," Harris-Lingoes Content Subscales, and the MMPI-2 Content Scales. These different indices differ in several respects, primarily in terms of whether they can be used as psychometric indices as well as suggesting content themes. They are described here in terms of the increasing confidence that we can

MMPI-2 VALIDITY PATTERN

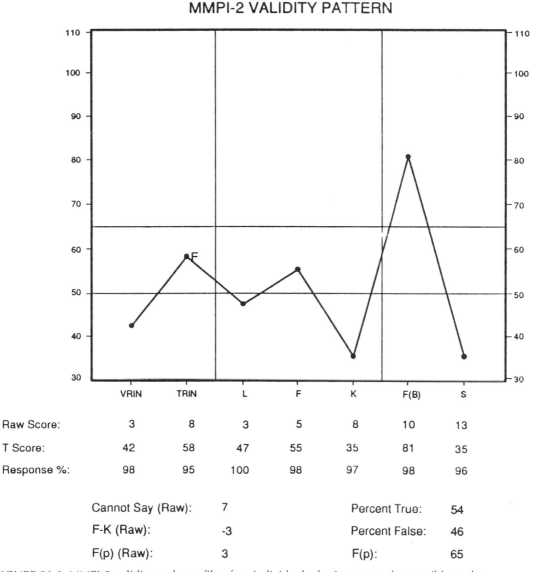

	VRIN	TRIN	L	F	K	F(B)	S
Raw Score:	3	8	3	5	8	10	13
T Score:	42	58	47	55	35	81	35
Response %:	98	95	100	98	97	98	96

Cannot Say (Raw):	7	Percent True:	54
F-K (Raw):	-3	Percent False:	46
F(p) (Raw):	3	F(p):	65

FIGURE 21.1 MMPI-2 validity scale profile of an individual who is open and accessible to the psychological evaluation.

have that they can serve as potentially valid psychometric scales as well as suggesting important content themes.

CRITICAL ITEM LISTS

The use of individual item responses on a questionnaire to reflect specific problems has a long history in personality assessment. Woodworth (1920), in the earliest formal personality questionnaire, the Personal Data Sheet, employed individual item responses as pathognomic signs of significant clinical problems. Over the past several decades, several sets of "critical items" have been developed out of the MMPI item pool for use as indicators of specific problems. One of the earliest approaches to use of single-

MMPI-2 VALIDITY PATTERN

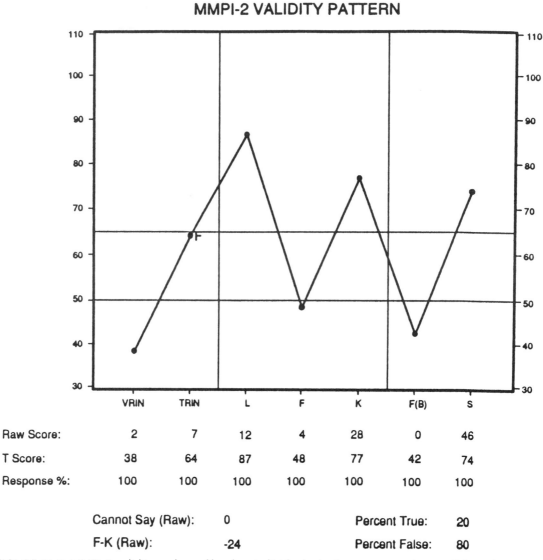

	VRIN	TRIN	L	F	K	F(B)	S
Raw Score:	2	7	12	4	28	0	46
T Score:	38	64	87	48	77	42	74
Response %:	100	100	100	100	100	100	100

Cannot Say (Raw):	0	Percent True:	20
F-K (Raw):	-24	Percent False:	80

FIGURE 21.2 MMPI-2 validity scale profile of an individual who is not open and accessible to the psychological evaluation.

item responses as behavioral data was introduced by Grayson (1955). He published a set of critical items for use in screening specific problems that came to be widely used in psychological screening for emotional problems. These items were rationally derived but not subjected to any empirical validation (Koss, Butcher, & Hoffman, 1976); they were simply used in an impressionistic manner as pathognomic indicators of problems. Two other sets of critical

items were developed for the original MMPI using more empirically based procedures: the Koss-Butcher Critical Items (Koss & Butcher, 1973) and the Lachar-Wrobel Critical Items (Lachar & Wrobel, 1979).

Koss & Butcher (1973) developed a set of six critical item lists following an empirical item selection procedure. In an initial empirical study, they found that groups of MMPI items (addressing Anxiety, Depressed—Suicidal,

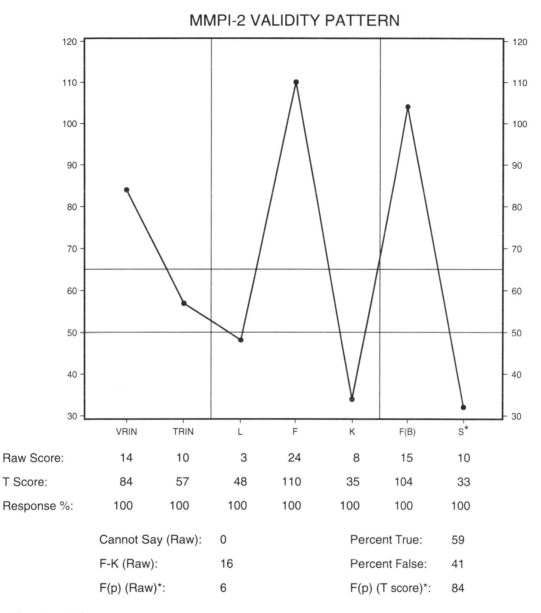

MMPI-2 VALIDITY PATTERN

	VRIN	TRIN	L	F	K	F(B)	S*
Raw Score:	14	10	3	24	8	15	10
T Score:	84	57	48	110	35	104	33
Response %:	100	100	100	100	100	100	100

Cannot Say (Raw):	0	Percent True:	59
F-K (Raw):	16	Percent False:	41
F(p) (Raw)*:	6	F(p) (T score)*:	84

*Experimental

FIGURE 21.3. Illustration of an MMPI-2 validity profile that is invalid due to symptom exaggeration and inconsistent responding.

Threatened Assault, Alcohol Problems, Para- noid, and Mental Confusion) empirically dif- ferentiated patients who were seeking admission to an inpatient psychiatric facility with different presenting problems. They concluded that in- dividuals tend to report through MMPI item content the problems they are experiencing. The Lachar-Wrobel critical item list cross-vali- dated several of the Koss-Butcher items and ex- tended the number of content categories by adding Characterological Adjustment (Antiso- cial Attitudes), Characterological Adjustment

(Family Problems), Somatic Symptoms, and Sexual Concern and Deviation.

Critical items can be effectively used in clinical assessment to highlight important problem areas that can be followed up in interview or in integrating test information from other sources. Critical item responses serve as possibly important clues to evaluate in developing clinical hypotheses. Caution should be exercised in the interpretation of single-item responses as indicators of significant problem areas. Single items are not reliable psychometric indicators. Sometimes momentary lapses or misreading/mismarking of items can result in items being endorsed inadvertently. In interpreting critical items, the meaning of a particular item response should be carefully appraised by confirming information obtained from other sources.

HARRIS-LINGOES CONTENT SUBGROUPS

The traditional empirical approach used in the construction of the MMPI clinical scales assumed that answers to test items are simply *signs* of problem types. The *way* in which an item is endorsed, not its content, is important in the prediction of behavior. An empirically derived scale has meaning only with respect to the empirical relationships that have been established for it, not with respect to the makeup of the constituent stimuli (items). Interpretation of the traditional clinical scales and code types thus requires that an extensive network of empirical correlates be established for each scale or index before meaning can be attached to particular scores.

Given the fact that items on the empirically derived clinical scales are heterogeneous in content, a particular scale elevation can result from different symptom patterns. Different patients with different problems can actually obtain similar scores on a particular scale. For example, a patient who is reporting a large number of physical complaints can obtain the same scale elevation on scale 2 as a patient who is reporting depressed mood but not claiming

physical symptoms. In an effort to solve this interpretive problem and refine the interpretation of MMPI clinical scales, Harris and Lingoes (1955) developed sets of content-homogeneous item subsets of the items making up several clinical scales that could be examined to provide a means of understanding the problems that contributed to scale elevation. They reasoned that MMPI scale elevations could be better understood if the actual problem themes contained in a particular scale could be evaluated.

Harris and Lingoes (1955) grouped the items making up several of the MMPI scales (D, Hy, Pd, Pa, Sc, and Ma) into several rational item groups to provide more meaningful understanding of the components of the parent scale (see Table 21.1). Only the factorially complex scales were subdivided. They did not consider it necessary to further subdivide the Hs and Pt scales, which were found to have more homogeneous items.

The Harris-Lingoes subscales can provide a very useful means of understanding obtained elevations on the clinical scales. For example, an elevation on the Pd scale of T = 75 following the empirical interpretation method would be interpreted by simply applying the personality descriptors in Table 21.2 as reflecting the individual's behavior and problems.

Of course, not all of the descriptors would apply for any given patient. These descriptors are simply the correlates that have been established for groups of individuals with prominent scale 4 elevations. If, however, we know that the individual has responded to items that fall predominantly on the Family Problems (Pd1) subscale and has relatively low scores on other subscales, then we can eliminate from consideration or at least place lower in our interpretive hierarchy the descriptors referring to the more antisocial aspect of Pd scorers. Our report might then focus primarily on the correlates that center on family relationship problems. Individuals with high Pd elevation deriving from family problems might respond to different treatment approaches than those with the more socially deviant components of Pd. An important interpretive consideration for the Harris-Lingoes subscales is that they should not be inter-

TABLE 21.1. Harris-Lingoes Subscales

Depression subscales
    Subjective Depression (D1)
    Psychomotor Retardation (D2)
    Physical Malfunctioning (D3)
    Mental Dullness (D4)
    Brooding (D5)

Hysteria subscales
    Denial of Social Anxiety (Hy1)
    Need for Affection (Hy2)
    Lassitude-Malaise (Hy3)
    Somatic Complaints (Hy4)
    Inhibition of Aggression (Hy5)

Psychopathic Deviate subscales
    Familial Discord (Pd1)
    Authority Problems (Pd2)
    Social Imperturbability (Pd3)
    Social Alienation (Pd4)
    Self-Alienation (Pd5)

Paranoia subscales
    Persecutory Ideas (Pa1)
    Poignancy (Pa2)
    Naivete (Pa3)

Schizophrenia subscales
    Social Alienation (Sc1)
    Emotional Alienation (Sc2)
    Lack of Ego Mastery, Cognitive (Sc3)
    Lack of Ego Mastery, Conative (Sc4)
    Lack of Ego Mastery, Def. Inhibition (Sc5)
    Bizarre Sensory Experiences (Sc6)

Hypomania subscales
    Amorality (Ma1)
    Psychomotor Acceleration (Ma2)
    Imperturbability (Ma3)
    Ego Inflation (Ma4)

preted out of the context of the parent scale. That is, Pd1 should not be considered to have interpretive meaning other than refining the elevation on the parent scale. Consequently, most practitioners do not interpret Harris-Lingoes scale elevations unless the parent scale is elevated in the significant range, above a T of 65.

As with the critical item approach to item content interpretation, caution needs to be exercised in the interpretation of content indica-

tors with relatively few items. Some of the Harris-Lingoes scales are quite short (six items) and thus are not considered sufficiently reliable for psychometric prediction. Elevations on Harris-Lingoes subscales provide the practitioner with clues to possible important content dimensions in the scale. Inferences based on the Harris-Lingoes scales should be carefully appraised and verified with information obtained from other sources.

MMPI-2 CONTENT SCALES

The MMPI-2 content scales were developed following a strategy that aimed at generating a set of homogeneous content scales that represent the major dimensions in a psychometric interpretive framework. The approach followed the scale construction strategy used by Wiggins (1966) in developing the Wiggins Content Scales for the original MMPI. Content themes were derived using a rational grouping of items from the experimental version of the MMPI-2. These item groups were then purified statistically using item-scale correlations on several normal and clinical samples. The MMPI-2 restandardization sample (N = 2600) was used for developing norms in the scales. See Butcher, Graham, Williams, and Ben-Porath, 1990, for a discussion of the scale development procedures.

The MMPI-2 content scales cover a broad range of symptoms, personality traits, and general problems. The scales are presented in a sequence on the profile sheet that facilitates their interpretation. In order to make scale interpretation easier, the scales have been grouped into four general symptom clusters: internal symptomatic behaviors, external aggressive tendencies, negative self-views, and general problem areas. The MMPI-2 content scales are briefly summarized below, following interpretive suggestions by Butcher et al. (1990). Readers interested in a more detailed description of interpretive strategies for the Content Scales are also referred to the discussion on clinical interpretation of the MMPI-2 content scales by Butcher and Williams (1992).

TABLE 21.2. Summary of Descriptors for Scale 4

High scores on scale 4 are indicative of persons who:
 1. have difficulty incorporating values and standards of society
 2. may engage in asocial and antisocial acts, including lying, cheating, stealing, sexual acting out, excessive use of alcohol and/or drugs (especially if $T > 75$)
 3. are rebellious toward authority figures
 4. have stormy relationships with families
 5. blame family members for difficulties
 6. have histories of underachievement
 7. tend to experience marital problems
 8. are impulsive and strive for immediate gratification of impulses
 9. do not plan their behavior well
10. tend to act without considering the consequences of their actions
11. are impatient; have limited frustration tolerance
12. show poor judgment; take risks
13. tend not to profit from experiences
14. are seen by others as immature and childish
15. are narcissistic, self-centered, selfish, and egocentric
16. are ostentatious and exhibitionistic
17. are insensitive to the needs and feelings of others
18. are interested in others in terms of how they can be used
19. are likable; create good first impressions
20. have shallow and superficial relationships
21. seem unable to form warm attachments with others
22. are extraverted and outgoing
23. are talkative, active, adventurous, energetic, and spontaneous
24. are judged by others to be intelligent and self-confident
25. have wide range of interests but lack clear direction
26. tend to be hostile, aggressive, resentful, rebellious, antagonistic, and refractory
27. have sarcastic and cynical attitudes
28. may act in aggressive ways
29. if female, may express aggression in more passive, indirect ways
30. may feign guilt and remorse when in trouble
31. are not seen as overwhelmed by emotional turmoil
32. may admit feeling sad, fearful, and worried about the future
33. experience absence of deep emotional response
34. feel empty and bored
35. if psychiatric patients, are likely to receive antisocial or passive-aggressive personality disorder diagnoses
36. have poor prognosis for psychotherapy or counseling
37. may agree to treatment to avoid something more unpleasant
38. tend to terminate treatment prematurely
39. in treatment tend to intellectualize excessively and to blame others for difficulties

Source: Graham (1993).

Internal Symptomatic Behaviors

This general cluster of scales contains measures that focus on symptoms of psychological distress. Each of the six scales grouped in this cluster reflects internal cognitive states or symptomatic behavior.

Anxiety. The ANX scale contains twenty-three items assessing symptoms of generalized anxiety. Individuals who score high on ANX acknowledge that they are experiencing symptoms of anxiety, including tension, somatic problems such as heart pounding and shortness of breath, sleep difficulties, excessive worries, and concentration problems. High scorers on ANX fear losing their minds, find life a strain, and have difficulties making even minor decisions. High scorers appear to be aware of these symptoms and are willing to admit to them freely.

Fears. The FRS scale contains twenty-three items assessing very specific fears or phobic behaviors. High scorers report an extreme number of specific fears or worries over many different situations or things. These fears include blood, high places, money, animals (such as snakes, mice, or spiders), leaving home, fire, storms and natural disasters, water, the dark, being indoors, and dirt. This scale does not include symptoms of general anxiety, only specific fears.

Obsessiveness. The OBS scale contains sixteen items focusing on maladaptive rumination and obsessive, unproductive thinking. Patients who score high on OBS have extreme difficulty making decisions and report that they tend to ruminate excessively about issues and problems, causing others to become impatient with them. They report that having to make changes distresses them. They also indicate that they experience compulsive behaviors like counting or saving unimportant things. High scorers are excessive worriers who frequently feel overwhelmed by their own thoughts. They feel that they are unable to function in a practical manner in daily activities.

Depression. The DEP scale contains thirty-three items focusing on clear symptoms of depression. Individuals who score high on DEP are considered to have significant depressive thoughts. They report feeling blue and uncertain about their future and seem uninterested in their lives. They are likely to brood, be unhappy, cry easily, and feel hopeless about the future. They feel empty and may have thoughts of suicide or wish that they were dead. High scorers may believe that they are condemned or have committed unpardonable sins. They often view their family and friends as unsupportive.

Health concerns. The HEA scale contains thirty-six items that address health symptoms and physical concerns. Individuals with high scores on HEA claim numerous physical symptoms across several body systems, including gastrointestinal symptoms (e.g., constipation, nausea and vomiting, stomach trouble); neurological problems (e.g., convulsions, dizzy and fainting spells, paralysis); sensory problems (e.g., poor hearing or eyesight); cardiovascular symptoms (e.g., heart or chest pains); skin problems; pain (e.g., headaches, neck pains); and respiratory troubles (e.g., coughs, hay fever or asthma). Patients who score high on HEA tend to worry about their health a great deal and tend to feel sicker more often than most people do.

Bizarre mentation. The BIZ scale is made up of twenty-four items that reflect severe symptoms of thought disorder. Individuals who score high on this scale are reporting many psychotic thoughts. They are claiming auditory, visual, or olfactory hallucinations. They report feeling that their thoughts are strange and peculiar. Paranoid ideation (e.g., the belief that they are being plotted against or that someone is trying to poison them) is reported. High scorers may also feel that they have a special mission or powers. High elevations on this scale (greater than 65) reflect severe and unusual thinking.

External Aggressive Tendencies

The four scales in this grouping center around aggressive, externalizing behaviors. They address four maladaptive approaches to other people, including cynical attitudes, loss of control when angry, antisocial practices, and Type A personality features.

Anger. The ANG scale, made up of sixteen items, focuses on loss of control while angry. High ANG scale scorers are likely to have problems controlling or modulating their anger. Individuals who score high on the scale report being irritable, grouchy, impatient, hotheaded, annoyed, and stubborn. They acknowledge feeling like swearing or smashing things at times. High scorers might lose self-control and become physically abusive toward people and objects.

Cynicism. The CYN scale contains twenty-three items that center around cynical beliefs and misanthropic attitudes toward others. Individuals who score high on the CYN scale report feeling negative toward others. They acknowledge feeling that other people harbor hidden, negative motives that they feel are directed toward them. They do not trust other people and believe that most people are honest simply through fear of being caught. High scorers report that other people use each other and are only friendly for selfish reasons. High scorers are likely to hold negative attitudes about people close to them.

Antisocial Practices. The twenty-two-item ASP scale centers on antisocial attitudes and behavioral characteristics. High scorers, in addition to holding misanthropic attitudes similar to high scorers on the CYN scale, are likely to report aberrant problem behaviors such as misbehavior during their school years. Antisocial practices such as being in trouble with the law, stealing, or shoplifting are also reflected in the item pool. High scorers admit to enjoying the antics of criminals and believe that it is all right for people to get around the law as long as it is not broken.

Type A. The TPA scale contains nineteen items that reflect a driven, competitive, and hostile personality style. High scorers on TPA endorse content suggesting that they view themselves as hard-driving, fast-moving, and work-oriented individuals. They also report that they frequently become impatient, irritable, and annoyed when they are interrupted. They do not like to wait or to be delayed in tasks they are working on. They indicate that there is never enough time in a day for them to complete their tasks. They tend to be direct, blunt, and overbearing in their relationships with others. Other people view them as aggressive, overbearing, and petty over minor details.

Negative Self-view

The measure contained in this cluster, the Low Self Esteem scale (LSE), was included as a means of assessing attitudes toward the self.

Low Self Esteem. The LSE scale contains twenty-four items and addresses negative self-views. High scorers on LSE tend to characterize themselves in negative terms and hold low opinions of themselves. They feel that they are not liked by other people and believe that they are

unimportant. They hold many negative attitudes about themselves including beliefs that they are unattractive, awkward and clumsy, useless, and a burden to others. High scorers report that they lack self-confidence and find it hard to accept compliments. They tend to feel overwhelmed by all the faults they see in themselves.

General Problem Areas: Social, Family, Work, and Treatment

Four content scales are grouped in this cluster. They address more general problems such as social maladjustment, family problems, symptoms and attitudes that reflect problems in engaging in productive work, and a group of behaviors and attitudes that reflect an unwillingness to commit to psychological treatment.

Social Discomfort. The SOD scale includes twenty-four items that reflect attitudes and beliefs involving uneasiness in social situations. Individuals who score high on the SOD scale tend to be very uncomfortable around others and express a preference for being by themselves. They are likely to avoid other people, sit alone rather than join in the group, and feel mistrustful of social relations. They tend to view themselves as shy and socially avoidant.

Family Problems. The FAM scale contains twenty-five items that focus on family relationship problems. High scorers report considerable family discord. Their families are described as lacking in love, quarrelsome, and generally unpleasant. High scorers may report hating members of their families. They tend to report that their childhood was marked by abusive relationships and that their past intimate relationships were troubled. The feel that their relationships have generally been unhappy and lacking in affection.

Work Interference. The WRK scale contains thirty-three items that address problems and negative attitudes related to work or achievement. High WRK scorers are likely to possess negative work attitudes or personal problems that contribute to poor work performance. High scorers report low self-confidence, concentration difficulties, obsessiveness, tension, and indecision. Some items reflect a lack of family support for the career choice, personal questioning of career choice, and negative attitudes towards coworkers.

Negative Treatment Indicators. The TRT scale contains twenty-six items that center around attitudes or problems in accepting help or in changing behavior. Individuals who score high on TRT possess negative attitudes toward doctors and mental health treatment. High-scoring individuals do not feel that others can understand or help them with their problems. They report that they have problems that they are not comfortable discussing with anyone. They tend not to want to change their behavior. They tend to give up rather than face crises or difficulties.

External Validity of Content Scales

Content scales, under appropriate conditions, perform as well as or better than scales developed by other scale construction approaches, such as empirically derived scales. A number of research studies have supported this interpretation. Ben-Porath, Butcher, and Graham (1991) found that MMPI-2 content scales actually outperformed the empirically derived clinical scales in discriminating schizophrenics from depressed inpatients. Hjemboe and Butcher (1991) found that the FAM scale significantly discriminated couples who were experiencing marital distress from normal couples. Egeland, Erickson, Butcher, and Ben-Porath (1991) reported that ASP scale scores were associated with women who had been identified as potential child abusers. Lilienfeld (1991) found that ASP scale scores were associated with the diagnosis of antisocial personality. Keller and Butcher (1991) found the HEA scale to be one of the most powerful discriminators between chronic pain patients and other clinical problem patients.

Three recent studies provided empirical verification for MMPI-2 content scales. In a recent study, Clark (1993) found that high-scoring patients in a Veterans Administration chronic pain program who had high scores on ANG showed frequent and intense anger, felt unfairly treated by others, felt frustrated, were oversensitive to criticism, quick tempered, tended to externalize anger, had tenuous anger control, were impulsive, and had anger control problems. Faull and Meyer (1993) found that the DEP content scale on MMPI-2 outperformed the MMPI-2 Depression scale in assessment of subjective depression in a group of primary medical patients. Ben-Porath and Stafford (1993) examined the predictive validity of the MMPI-2 content scales in a forensic setting. They reported that the WRK scale was associated with the inmate being unable to hold a job, sporadic work history, and unstable work history. They also found that the ANG scale was associated with marital problems, history of juvenile offending, history of violent behavior, history of property offenses, and drug abuse.

ADVANTAGES OF USING CONTENT-BASED SCALES IN CLINICAL ASSESSMENT

There are clear advantages to using homogeneous content scales in clinical assessment. First, the themes represented by the scale elevation can be viewed as direct communications between the patient and clinician about the patient's problems. A content scale score summarizes important messages from the patient as to how he or she views his or her current problems. Second, because the MMPI-2 content scales have strong psychometric properties, for example, they possess norms based on a large nationally based sample, the scale scores can serve as a useful means of comparing the relative prominence of a patient's reported problems with other patient groups. This means that the practitioner can have a better idea as to the *extent* of the individual's reported problems compared with others. Finally, an elevated score on a particular content scale represents the extent to which the client has shared extreme concerns about a particular problem with the practitioner. This information can be particularly valuable in clinical sessions in which test feedback is being provided to clients (see Butcher, 1990; Finn & Butcher, 1991; and Finn & Tonsager, 1992).

LIMITATIONS OF THE CONTENT INTERPRETATION APPROACH

There are important limitations to consider when using content-based measures in personality assessment. First, it is important for the practitioner to ensure that the client has responded to the test-taking situation with appropriate motivation to be understood by the clinician. Scores on personality inventories can be influenced by the motivation to deceive or distort the way they are viewed by the assessment staff. Careful evaluation of validity indicators, particularly the scales measuring test defensiveness, need to be conducted initially to determine the extent of the client's cooperation with the evaluation. Any content-based personality index, whether a content scale or critical item, can be manipulated by the client's desire to present himself or herself in a particular way.

A second important consideration in using a particular content measure is that the information available from it is limited by the range of item content contained in the measure. Appropriate limitations need to be placed on our interpretation when content is limited. For example, the information reported through the Harris-Lingoes subscale Pd1 does not contain all of the family problem items that are on the MMPI-2, only those that happen to be contained on the Pd scale. There are other family problem items in the MMPI-2 item pool that are not on the Pd1 subscale.

A third factor to consider in content interpretation is that the information we are obtaining from the client through MMPI-2 content is limited to what the client is able to provide. The subject may not know or have the capacity to recall accurately other important information needed for the assessment.

A fourth very important consideration is that content interpretation is limited by the information that the client is willing to provide in the assessment. Individuals may not provide some personal information—even in a help-seeking situation—because they fear the consequences of divulging information about themselves. Some people have "closed" areas that they will not discuss—even in therapeutic situations. Reluctance to share personal information in psychological assessment is particularly prominent in some assessment situations such as forensic evaluations or personnel screening where the motivation to present in a particular manner is high. Content interpretation of personality inventory responses assumes that the individual has a motivation to be understood and share personal information through the assessment process. The client could be prepared in pretesting instructions to respond to the items in a direct, open manner so that the information provided will be a clear reflection of his or her present mood and symptoms.

Another important factor in evaluating the adequacy of content-based information to the test interpretation process is that short content-based indices such as critical items may be unreliable and should not be used as psychometric indices. Momentary lapses of cognitive set or carelessness can result in mismarking items, thereby introducing irrelevant or incorrect information into the interpretive process. Critical items or short Harris-Lingoes subscales may not allow for the psychometric prediction of behavior. They should be used only for possible clues to important content themes. Support for their interpretation should be obtained from other sources of information in the MMPI-2 or from other clinical information available.

SUMMARY

In mental health settings, patients being assessed usually expect that the psychologist or psychiatrist they are seeing will pay careful attention to the content of their communications about their symptoms. Content interpretations of personality scales, like the MMPI-2, allow the practitioner to use patients' responses to questionnaire items as direct communications about their symptoms, attitudes, and behaviors. This, of course, assumes that the individual has the motivation to be understood and share personal information through the assessment process. The client should be prepared in pretesting instructions to respond to the items in a direct, open manner so that the information provided will be a clear reflection of his or her present mood and symptoms.

When motivation is appropriate MMPI-2 content measures provide an important and extensive amount of information about a patient's personality, attitudes, problems, and behavior. This information can be viewed as direct communication about problems and serves as a summary of the client's clinically relevant behavior. Three sources of content-based information were discussed in this chapter: the so-called "critical items," the Harris-Lingoes subscales contained on several clinical scales, and the MMPI-2 content scales. All three of these measures have utility in terms of providing information about the client's view of his or her problem situation. However, they differ in terms of reliability and the confidence we can have that they serve as predictive measures. Of the three content measures, only the MMPI-2 content scales have sufficient reliability and demonstrated external validity to serve as psychometric predictors.

This chapter also included an evaluation of content measures in which both the advantages and limitations of their use in clinical interpretation were highlighted. Content scales, in addition to providing a vehicle for the patient to express important problems directly, have external validities that exceed or equal empirically derived scales. Cautions in interpreting content measures were provided. Among these are the need to assure that the client has approached the content in a cooperative and frank manner.

REFERENCES

Baer, R. A., Wetter, M. W., & Berry, D. T. (1992). Detection of underreporting of psychopathology on the MMPI: A meta-analysis. *Clinical Psychology Review, 12,* 509–525.

Ben-Porath, Y. S., Butcher, J. N., & Graham, J. R. (1991). Contribution of the MMPI-2 content scales to the differential diagnosis of psychopathology. *Psychological Assessment, 3,* 634–640.

Ben-Porath, Y. S. & Stafford, K. P. (1993, August). *Empirical correlates of MMPI-2 scales in a forensic diagnostic sample: An interim report.* Paper given at the 101st Annual Meeting of the American Psychological Association, Toronto.

Berry, D. T., Wetter, M. W., Baer, R. A., Larsen, L., Clark, C., & Monroe, K. (1992). MMPI-2 random responding indices: Validation using a self-report methodology. *Psychological Assessment, 4,* 340–345.

Butcher, J. N. (1990). *Use of the MMPI-2 in treatment planning.* New York: Oxford University Press.

Butcher, J. N. (1993). *User's guide for the MMPI-2 Minnesota report: Adult clinical system* (rev. ed.). Minneapolis: National Computer Systems.

Butcher, J. N., Dahlstrom, W. G., Graham, J. R., Tellegen, A. M., & Kaemmer, B. (1989). *Minnesota Multiphasic Personality Inventory-2 (MMPI-2): Manual for administration and scoring.* Minneapolis: University of Minnesota Press.

Butcher, J. N., Graham, J. R., Williams, C. L., & Ben-Porath, Y. (1990). *Development and use of the MMPI-2 content scales.* Minneapolis: University of Minnesota Press.

Butcher, J. N., & Williams, C. L. (1992). *Essentials of MMPI-2 and MMPI-A interpretation.* Minneapolis: University of Minnesota Press.

Clark, M. E. (1993, March). *MMPI-2 anger and cynicism scales: Interpretive cautions.* Paper given at the 28th Annual Symposium on Recent Developments in the Use of the MMPI/MMPI-2. St. Petersburg, FL.

Egeland, B., Erickson, M., Butcher, J. N., & Ben-Porath, Y. S. (1991). MMPI-2 profiles of women at risk for child abuse. *Journal of Personality Assessment, 57,* 254–263.

Faull, R., & Meyer, G. J. (1993, March). *Assessment of depression with the MMPI-2: Distinctions between scales 2 and the DEP.* Paper given at the Midwinter Meeting of the Society for Personality Assessment, San Francisco.

Finn, S., & Butcher, J. N. (1990). Clinical objective personality assessment. In M. Hersen, A. E. Kazdin, & A. S. Bellack (Eds.). *The clinical psychology handbook* (2nd ed.). New York: Pergamon Press.

Finn, S. E. & Tonsager, M. E. (1992). Therapeutic effects of providing MMPI-2 test feedback to college students awaiting therapy. *Psychological Assessment, 1,* 278–286.

Graham, J. R. (1993). *MMPI-2: Assessing personality and psychopathology* (2nd ed.). New York: Oxford University Press.

Graham, J. R., Watts, D., & Timbrook, R. (1991). Detecting fake-good and fake-bad MMPI-2 profiles. *Journal of Personality Assessment, 57,* 264–277.

Grayson, H. M. (1951). *Psychological admission testing program and manual.* Los Angeles: Veterans Administration Center, Neuropsychiatric Hospital.

Harris, R. E., & Lingoes, J. C. (1955). Subscales for the MMPI: An aid to profile interpretation. Mimeographed materials. Department of Psychiatry, University of California.

Hathaway, S. R., & McKinley, J. C. (1940). A multiphasic personality schedule (Minnesota): I. Construction of the schedule. *Journal of Psychology, 10,* 249–254.

Hjemboe, S., & Butcher, J. N. (1991). Couples in marital distress: A study of demographic and personality factors as measured by the MMPI-2. *Journal of Personality Assessment, 57,* 216–237.

Keller, L. S., & Butcher, J. N. (1991). *Use of the MMPI-2 with chronic pain patients.* Minneapolis: University of Minnesota Press.

Koss, M. P., & Butcher, J. N. (1973). A comparison of psychiatric patients' self-report with other sources of clinical information. *Journal of Research in Personality, 7,* 225–236.

Koss, M. P., Butcher, J. N., & Hoffman, N. G. (1976). The MMPI critical items: How well do they work? *Journal of Consulting and Clinical Psychology, 44,* 921–928.

Lachar, D., & Alexander, R. S. (1978). Veridicality of self-report: Replicated correlates of the Wiggins MMPI content scales. *Journal of Consulting and Clinical Psychology, 42,* 267–273.

Lachar, D., & Wrobel, T. A. (1979). Validating clinicians' hunches: Construction of a new MMPI critical item set. *Journal of Consulting and Clinicial Psychology, 47,* 277–284.

Lilienfeld, S. (1991, March). *Assessment of psychopathy with MMPI and MMPI-2.* Paper presented at the 26th Annual Symposium on Recent Developments in the Use of the MMPI (MMPI-2), St. Petersburg, FL.

Meehl, P. E. (1945). The dynamics of "structured" personality tests. *Journal of Clinical Psychology, 1,* 296–303.

Pope, K. S., Butcher, J. N., & Seelen, J. (1993). *The MMPI/MMPI-2/MMPI-A in court: Assessment, testimony, and cross-examination.* Washington, DC: American Psychological Association.

Rogers, R., Bagby, R. M., & Chakraborty, D. (1993). Feigning schizophrenic disorders on the MMPI-2: Detection of coached simulators. *Journal of Personality Assessment, 60,* 215–226.

Schretlen, D. J. (1988). The use of psychological tests to identify malingered symptoms of mental disorder. *Clinical Psychology Review, 8,* 451–476.

Wetter, M. W., Baer, R. A., Berry, D. T., Robison, L. H., & Sumpter, J. (1993). MMPI-2 profiles of motivated fakers given specific symptom information. *Psychological Assessment, 5,* 317–323.

Wetter, M. W., Baer, R. A., Berry, D. T., Smith, G. T., & Larsen, L. (1992). Sensitivity of the MMPI-2 validity scales to random responding and malingering. *Psychological Assessment, 4,* 369–374.

Wiggins, J. S. (1966). Substantive dimensions of self-report in the MMPI item pool. *Psychological Monographs, 80* (22, Whole No. 630).

Woodworth, R. S. (1920). *The Personal Data Sheet.* Chicago: Stoelting.

22
Assessing Adaptive Capacities by Means of the Rorschach

Paul M. Lerner

Those of us who engage in assessment are increasingly recognizing the importance of a balanced assessment in which equal attention is accorded struggles and difficulties on the one hand and strengths and resources on the other. Test reports geared exclusively to psychopathology or diagnosis are one-sided and typically do not describe the individual in ways that are likely to lead to beneficial interventions.

For example, despite the anxiety stirred by his patient's suicidal potential, a therapist was reassured by the following comments from the testing report:

> To avoid experiencing depressive feelings this young man tends to resort to action. Given his current circumstances, one form of action to be alert to is suicide. He sees death as a way out, an escape, a viable alternative in situations in which he feels trapped and without options. Yet he is also in much pain and is accessible to therapeutic intervention. To judge from his willingness to discuss his fleeting suicidal thoughts with the examiner and his seeing cooperative relationships on the Rorschach, the risk of suicide could be appreciably reduced by providing him a containing therapeutic relationship.

In Rorschach parlance the human movement response has been looked to as a reliable indicator of an array of adaptive capacities ranging from creativity to ideational activity to interpersonal relatedness.

Rorschach himself, for instance, conceived of the movement response as reflecting an individual's capacity for "inner creation." By inner creation he is not referring to a capacity to create a work of art but rather to a creative factor in the act of experiencing itself by which one puts something of oneself into one's experience so as to bring that life in touch with the life around one (Schachtel, 1966).

Other theorists have attributed interpersonal meaning to the movement response. Piotrowski (1957) has suggested that from the human movement response one can infer an individual's conception of his or her "role in life." In a like way Schachtel (1966) conceives of the movement response as reflecting a person's basic orientation and attitudes toward himself or herself, others, and the surrounding world — that is, the individual's self-concept and his or her relational anticipations.

Dana (1968) concluded on the basis of an extensive review of the experimental literature that the human movement response expresses an interpersonal orientation. More specifically, he suggested that the movement response represents a "syndrome of potentials, capacities for reaching out into the environment in a variety of ways" (p. 144).

Based on the work of Mayman (1977), Schachtel (1966), and Lerner (1991), in this chapter I will review the Rorschach human movement response from the perspective of assessing adaptive capacities. More specifically, I will discuss the response in terms of the perceptual determinant of the response and its relationship to the capacity to take cognitive distance, the fantasy component of the response, kinesthesia and its relationship to creative experience, and the objective relational aspects of the response.

PERCEPTUAL DETERMINANT OF THE RESPONSE

Rapaport was the first theorist to point out the purely perceptual determinants of the movement response. Basing his ideas in part on Gestalt theory, he reserved the movement score for those responses in which the test taker saw and associated to "an actual, demonstrable, perceptual imbalance in the inkblot" (Mayman, 1977, p. 231). Rapaport suggested that at an unconscious level the subject saw the Gestalt and was perturbed by the imbalance. Accordingly, without conscious intent or awareness, the test taker then sets matters right by ascribing to the image direction that gives the configuration better balance and stability.

This sensitivity to imbalance, according to Mayman (1977), "is no mean achievement. If nothing else, it requires that one be able to transcend an atomistic survey of a blot area and pay attention, rather, to its dynamic composition" (p. 231). Mayman is suggesting here that at a purely perceptual level, in order to see imbalance one must have the capacity to take distance and to view the inkblots with perspective. People who have this capacity to take distance and gain perspective are able to examine life events critically and place them in context. They are attuned to the present, yet they also appreciate the significance of the past and the possibilities of the future. They stand in contrast to other individuals who take hold of an area in a piece-

meal manner, tend to see simple and static forms, view details too discretely, and are not prompted to see the more subtle perceptual properties, including the dynamic composition.

Also derived from Rapaport's notion of the actual perceptual basis of the movement response is the suggestion that to perceive movement requires a certain level of ideational activity. Rapaport himself put it more strongly; he suggested that movement responses indicated ideational potential and covaried with the intensity and range of ideational activity.

FANTASY COMPONENT OF THE RESPONSE

According to most theorists, requisite to the offering of the human movement response is the availability of a fantasy life one can dip into to help vivify the response. More than most other Rorschach responses, movement is distinguishable by its aliveness and vividness.

As on the Rorschach, access to fantasy enriches and safeguards one's day-to-day life. Fantasies, together with the capacity to fantasize, breath life into our lives. They play a role in reminding us who we are and help make us feel alive.

Fantasy is also, as Singer (1975) has demonstrated, a foundation of serenity and control. Life requires that each of us steer a middle course between the two extremes of external and internal stimulation. Excessive sensitivity to external stimulation has been found to play a pivotal role in overeating, alcoholism, and drug addiction. Unimaginative people also tend to be more vulnerable to boredom and impulsitivity. Often it is more sensible and realistic to think and fantasize about an activity than to actually do it. A well-developed fantasy life, then, serves as a containment for aggressive urges.

Movement responses invite and call for affective and associative elaboration. While such embellishments reflect the availability of fantasy, they indicate other capacities too. For many individuals they reflect an interest and investment in the task at hand, a willingness to go beyond merely what is called for and add something more. In addition, the tendency to embellish may also express an openness to different types of experiences, a capacity to relax tight controls and strict adherence to reality and indulge in what Freud (1900/1953) referred to as "primary process."

KINESTHESIA AND ITS RELATIONSHIP TO CREATIVE EXPERIENCE

Rorschach, as noted previously, considered the movement response indicative of one's capacity for "inner creation." Schachtel (1966) has both explicated and extended this notion. He put it this way:

> When one disregards specific attitudes and pays attention only to the general process of enlivening the percept by looking at it, not detachedly, but by putting oneself inside of it in imagination, by feeling from inside how it moves and lives, then one is concerned with those general qualities of the movement responses which make them representative of what Rorschach called the capacity for inner creation and what I believe to be a factor in man's capacity for creative experience. (Schachtel, 1966, pp. 230–231)

By creative experience, Schachtel is referring to a process whereby one puts something of oneself into one's own experience; a type of empathic projection, if you will. Accordingly, to make an experience creative one cannot be merely a mirror that reflects the image cast upon it; rather, one's own experiences must be aroused and then merge with the object of experience. Only at that point is something new experienced. Without this personal, subjective element, the object is reproduced, not experienced. For Schachtel, then, creative experience involves both an openness and sensitivity to the external world as well as the capacity to bring one's own attitudes and previous experiences to that which is perceived. In this way one is then able to understand and experience something in one's own unique manner and then integrate it into one's own life.

What is being described here is a way of understanding and relating to the world, including the world of interpersonal relationships. While the process involves both projection and empathy, it also comes close to imagination as well as to what certain psychoanalytic writers refer to as projective identification.

According to Schachtel, those attitudes that are available to the individual to use creatively in the act of experiencing are reflected in the kinesthetic aspect of the movement response. For example, a person's whose repertoire of kinesthesias, as reflected in Rorschach imagery, is limited to more passive activities such as resting, contemplating, reading, etc., will either selectively empathize with this aspect of others or will ascribe it to them. Conversely, those whose movement responses include a broad and complex array of kinesthesias would be more able to empathize projectively with a fuller range of experiences.

Rorschach and Schachtel explicitly note that while the movement response is related to "inner creation" or "creative experience," it is not necessarily related to the capacity for creative production. Nonetheless, Schachtel does acknowledge that creative experience is a prerequisite for creative production. Research evidence bearing on the relationship between the movement response and creativity supports Schachtel's contention.

Myden (1959) compared a group of creative individuals from the stage arts, visual arts, and literary arts who were renowned in their respective fields with a noncreative group and found that the creative group produced a significantly higher number of movement responses.

Dudek (1984) found that a group of highly creative architects not only offered significantly more movement responses than did a group of normal controls, but that the quality of their responses differed as well. Dudek noted:

> The inference to be drawn from the type of M perception that the architects as a group project is that they see themselves as active, energetic, socially aware persons who enjoy the "game" they are playing, but see it as that: the playing of a game. The emotional involvement is not one of depth or closeness. Both persons regard each other as they play their parts in an essentially

cooperative deal. The architect remains aloof and sees himself as different from others. He is, however, conscious of other people's reactions to him, oversensitive to emotional nuances, and although eager to please, somewhat resentful and cynical about the role he has chosen for himself. (p. 601)

OBJECT RELATIONAL ASPECTS OF THE MOVEMENT RESPONSE

Ever increasingly, clinical and nonclinical psychologists alike are appreciating the vital importance of an individual's interpersonal functioning and are being called upon to assess a person's capacity to make use of a relationship. Psychotherapists who refer their patients for testing are inevitably interested in the patient's treatability. From a psychoanalytic perspective, treatability includes a host of interpersonal capacities, including the capacity to establish a therapeutic alliance, the ability to envision a role for oneself in treatment, and the capacity to take distance from the transference and view it in an "as if" way.

Personnel psychologists engaged in selection and promotion are also asked to assess aspects of an individual's object relations. "Is this applicant capable of directing and supervising a sizable staff?" and "How might this employee's immediate boss be most helpful to him?" are questions often asked of the psychologist.

For example, in a report a potential employee was described as "bright, innovative, reliable, hard-working yet somewhat aloof and distant in her relationships." The report went on to suggest that "she would be most comfortable and would make best use of her supervisor were he or she to relate to her in a more professional, businesslike manner in which formality was maintained and one dealt with her directly, openly, matter-of-factly, but rather impersonally."

Finally, sports psychologists too are being requested to assist in evaluating certain interpersonal dimensions. In assessing young players eligible for the professional hockey draft, I am typically asked about the player's team orienta-

tion, his willingness to subordinate his own strivings to those of the team, and his openness to different styles of coaching.

Coincident with this growing interest among practitioners in the quality of an individual's object relations, parallel conceptual shifts are occurring within psychoanalytic theory. More specifically, from an earlier concern with wishes, urges, resistance, and the interplay between drive and defense, psychoanalytic interest has gradually shifted to a greater focus on the development and maintenance of the self and one's object relations.

Psychoanalytic theory not only has much to contribute to our ways of viewing and understanding the interpersonal realm but in addition can serve as a meaningful conceptual framework for assessing this domain in our patients and clients.

In this section I will discuss three major interpersonal concepts that are basic to psychoanalytic theory and then suggest ways one can assess each from a careful appraisal of the human movement response.

One especially useful concept is that of internal object relation. Theorists are emphasizing the distinction between internal object relations as opposed to relations between the self and others in the external world. As implied in the term, an internal object relation refers to the inner representation of a relationship that had existed in the outer world. While internal object relations derive from the internalization of early external relationships, they in turn exert considerable influence on present, ongoing object relations. An internal object relation is conceived of as consisting of three components, a self representation, an object representation (i.e., a representation of the other), and a representation of the relation, or interaction between the two.

Before turning to the movement response, it is important to note that in general and from this perspective, the Rorschach and other less structured tests are not viewed as assessing the individual's interpersonal functioning directly. Instead, it is argued that one is evaluating the test taker's representational world, and it is from a sampling of the representational world that one draws inferences regarding relational tendencies. By representational world, I am referring to the individual's internal reservoir of enduring internalized images of the self and of others around which the phenomenological world is structured and into which ongoing experiences of others are assimilated.

With respect to the movement response, Mayman (1977) in particular has drawn attention to the figure carrying out the action as that aspect of the response that provides a unique glimpse into the images that populate the person's inner life. Likening this specific Rorschach content to the manifest content of dreams and early memories, he suggests that such material has meaning in its own right and is much more than an embellished screen that conceals and hints at deeper levels of unconscious meanings.

Using the human figures themselves as a springboard for inferring the nature of an individual's self and object representations is no easy matter in practice. It requires a thorough understanding of the Rorschach and of personality theory as well as sufficient testing experience so as to be able to make sound clinical judgments.

For instance, understanding the nature of the interaction (i.e., antagonistic, competitive, cooperative, etc.) is usually straightforward and can be inferred directly from the response. Far more difficult and complex, however, is determining those characteristics referable to the self representation and those to the object representation.

The following example illustrates this. On Card III the individual saw "A fragile, bent-over woman who had just been slapped around by a male space creature with the head of a bird." The interaction here can be characterized as sadomasochistic. If in this percept, however, the test taker's self representation is the "woman," then one could conjecture that the individual's sense of self involves being vulnerable, abused, defenseless, and at the mercy of others who are seen as hurtful, alienated, and less than fully human. On the other hand, if the self is represented in the "male space creature," then one might suggest that the test taker sees himself or herself as estranged, hurtful, and monstrous, and others as weak, helpless, vulnerable victims.

By way of digression, a useful source of information for distinguishing self from object representations is the test taker's spontaneous comments offered throughout the testing, especially those remarks that express attitudes directly about the tests and indirectly about the examiner. The patient who gave the above response, in a variety of ways, let the examiner know that the tests made her feel stupid and inept. Recognizing in her spontaneous comments that the patient was presenting herself as a helpless victim and was placing the examiner in the role of the powerful victimizer, the examiner then inferred that in the Rorschach response the "woman" could be taken as a self representation and the "male space creature" as a representation of the other.

In addition to differentiating self from object representations, the examiner must push further and also attempt to place the representations in the context of the person's self system and object relational organization. The images considered referable to the self should be further evaluated in terms of whether they express what the test taker feels about himself or herself, or alternatively, reflect what he or she admires and would like to be.

In alerting us to the possible meanings involved in the precise figure depicted in the human movement response and in providing a test rationale to decode that meaning, Mayman (1977) has made a significant contribution. However, it is important to keep in mind that the inferential possibilities implied in these projected images are vast; yet only by carefully sifting through them and being able to identify their role in the individual's experience can these possibilities be realized.

A second useful interpersonal concept basic to psychoanalytic theory is that of narcissistic relatedness. Freud, in his article "On Narcissism," drew an important distinction between a "true object relation" and a "narcissistic object relation." In a true object relation the other is viewed as separate and distinct and as having motives and feelings distinct from one's own. By contrast, in a narcissistic object relation, the other is not regarded as separate and distinct, but instead as an extension of the self and as needed to fulfill functions one cannot manage intrapsychically.

Several aspects of the movement response can be used to distinguish these two modes of relating (Mayman, 1977, Lerner, 1991). Individuals who are able to enter into true object relations in which self-other boundaries are properly maintained produce human movement responses in which (1) there is a broad and complex array of images of others; (2) the response takes into account realistic properties of the blots themselves, that is, there is objectivity; and (3) from the description of the percept it is clear that the test taker is describing someone else and not himself or herself.

By contrast, individuals who relate themselves to others on a narcissistic basis and who blur self-other boundaries produce movement responses in which (1) the response is reported with undue vividness and conviction; (2) the action ascribed and the attributes expressed are largely fabulized rather than inherent in the percept itself; (3) there is an intense absorption and involvement in the behavior of the perceived figures; and (4) the test taker seems to infuse himself or herself into the described figure and thereby vicariously share in the other's experience.

In essence, implicit in these indices is the assumption that the nature of the relationship between the test taker and his or her movement responses, in terms of such dimensions as range, objectivity, and distance, reflects and parallels the quality of relationships the test taker establishes with others.

A third particularly helpful interpersonal concept that can be inferred from the movement response is projective identification. The term was originally coined by Melanie Klein to describe a process that is both developmental and defensive and involves projecting parts of the self and of an internal object representation into an external object. Herein, through projective identification one disowns and then gets rid of bad parts of the self.

I recently saw a forty-two-year-old, highly talented but incapacitated artist who was referred to me by her previous therapist of six months. During our first hour she spoke of being bewil-

dered, confused, perplexed, and lost. By the end of the hour I too felt confused and could make little sense of what she was telling me. From the perspective of projective identification, one could understand the confusion I felt as an expression of the patient's confusion, which she had "put into me."

While the process is defensive, it can be adaptive too. In the above example, in giving me her confusion, the patient relieved herself of her feelings. In this sense, I held or contained the confusion for her. This aspect of projective identification, the holding of another's feelings, has been described by Bion (1967) in terms of the metaphor of container and contained. Underlying the metaphor is the image of an infant emptying its bad contents into the mother, who accepts the unwanted projection, contains it, and alters it in such a way as to permit, in time, its reintrojection by the infant.

Projective identification is also adaptive in that it affords a special type of communication. That is, instead of using words, the individual communicates a feeling or a state or a desire by stirring that phenomenon in the other person. I have found this type of communicating most commonly in those individuals for whom words are dangerous and in individuals who tend to relate to others on a preverbal level.

Given that projective identification can be either defensive or adaptive, it may be concluded that there are various levels of projective identification depending on the aim (defense, control, communication) and the degree to which self-other boundaries are blurred and diffused.

Attempts to assess projective identification by means of the Rorschach have appeared rarely in the literature; however, involved in these efforts, in part, has been the use of the human movement response. Lerner and Lerner (1980), based on Kernberg's (1975) restrictive definition of the mechanism as a process in which parts of the self are split off and projected into an external object so as to control it, devised two scoring indices, one of which involved human movement.

The two scores were assumed to assess three subprocesses involved in projective identification: an externalization of parts of the self with a disregard to real characteristics of the external object; a capacity to blur boundaries between self and object; and a compelling need to control the object. In accord with theoretical and clinical expectations, the authors (Lerner and Lerner, 1980) found that the indices of projective identification appeared significantly more frequently in the test records of borderline patients than in those of neurotic and schizophrenic patients.

Cooper (1983) extended the work of Lerner and Lerner both conceptually and methodologically. Relying on Kernberg (1975), as well as the earlier writings of Klein (1949), he conceived of projective identification as involving the following three subprocesses: (1) fantasies of concretely putting a dangerous or endangered part of the self into another for the purpose of controlling the other; (2) fearful empathy with others; and (3) hyperalertness to external threat. Although Cooper adopted and extended several of the Rorschach indices used earlier by Lerner and Lerner, he also developed several new ones. Here again, use was made of the human movement response.

Listed below are those indices involving formal scores that have been developed for assessing projective identification. The list includes but is not restricted to those involving human movement.

Confabulatory responses involving human figures in which the form level is weak or minus (Fw− or F−). A confabulatory response is one in which a percept is overembellished with associative elaboration to the point that real properties of the blot are disregarded and replaced by fantasies and affects. Although the score has traditionally been regarded as a cardinal index of disturbed thinking (Rapaport, Gill, & Schafer, 1945), more recent authors (Athey, 1974; Blatt & Ritzler, 1974) have found the response to be indicative of regressed modes of object relations. More specifically, these authors have demonstrated that the quality of an individual's thought as organized on the Rorschach parallels the ways in which the person experiences and organizes object relations. For example, the tendency to lose the conceptual boundary between

one idea and another is paralled by a proclivity for losing the experiential boundary between self and other. In keeping with the conceptual stance being taken here, that is, that there are various levels of projective identification, this score is considered as indicating a lower level in which there is self-other blurring and the aim of the process involves defense and control of the other.

Human or human detail response in which the location is Dr (rare detail), the determinant is F(c) (the response is based on form and the nuances of shading are used to articulate and outline the response), and the figure is described as either aggressive or as the object of aggression. Involved in the (c) response is perceptual sensitivity coupled with a searching, penetrating, and articulating type of activity. Patients whose Rorschach records include this score present as hyperalert, overly sensitive, thin-skinned, and excessively vulnerable. Lerner and Lerner (1980), cognizant of the defensive aspects of the hyperalertness and heightened sensitivity, included this score as an indicator of projective identification based on the assumption that the high level of control implicit in the response reflects an insistent need to control the perceived dangerous other. Cooper (1983) included this index in his manual too; however, he conceived of the score as reflecting fearful empathy as well as a hypersensitivity to aggression in others.

In addition to the above, it is my experience that the response also indicates a tendency to rely heavily on preverbal communication. Individuals who offer this response are especially attuned to the visual, gestural, and emotional aspects of others. Their relationships, in this respect, may be likened to the infant's early experience with the mother.

From clinical experience, I have also found that individuals who offer the Dr, F(c), aggressive-content score but do not offer confabulatory responses often engage in higher-level forms of projective identification. While they do not blur self-other boundaries, they do see the environment as dangerous, defensively empathize with potential sources of danger, and communicate in preverbal ways such as putting parts of themselves (affects, fantasies, etc.) into others. For such individuals, projecting parts of the self into another is also defensive in that it serves to ward off threats of separation and abandonment.

Movement responses in which a human figure puts a substance or feeling into another human figure for the purpose of controlling, destroying, safeguarding, or repairing that figure. As an application of Klein's (1949) initial formulations, this score reflects the subprocesses of placing a disowned part of the self into another for the purpose of control or reparation. This index reflects either higher or lower levels of projective identification depending on the presence or absence of confabulatory responses in the test protocol.

Movement responses in which the subject is intensely absorbed in the behavior of the perceived figure, ascribes attributes and actions that are largely fabulized rather than inherent in the percept itself, and depicts with insistent regularity a narrow range of human interactions. Mayman (1977) has suggested that persons who offer these responses have difficulty maintaining self-other differences in interpersonal interactions. While I agree with Mayman that these percepts can reflect a tendency to blur self-other boundaries, I believe that such responses, with their insistent depiction of a narrow range of interactions, also reflect the presence of select, highly charged, insistent internal object relations, which when activated, as in treatment, result in a compelling need to pressure or coerce the other into experiencing and playing out a particular projected role.

SUMMARY

Basic to psychoanalytic theory is the concept of multidetermination. The concept holds, on the one hand, that any single piece of behavior can express various motives and can be observed from several points of view (i.e., dynamic, genetic, defensive, adaptive). On the other hand, the principle also suggests that any one motive can be expressed in a host of different behaviors.

Of the different points of view, typically, especially amongst clinical psychologists, short

shift has been accorded the adaptive. In our zeal to uncover signs of psychopathology and assign diagnostic labels, unfortunately, we have tended to overlook less obvious strengths and skills and deeper inner resources. As a consequence, testing has not always been as fully helpful as it could be.

To redress this imbalance, in this chapter I have emphasized the assessment of adaptive capacities. Specifically, I have reviewed and discussed the Rorschach human movement response as an indicator of various potentials including the capacity to take cognitive distance, the availability of fantasy, creative experience, and the quality of object relating.

Even though my focus here has been on the Rorschach, it should be kept in mind that the Rorschach or any so-called projective technique is neither the only nor necessarily the preferred way of assessing adaptive capacities. Instead, I would suggest a test battery including the Rorschach. Let me explain.

The importance of a test battery derives from Rapaport's notions regarding the concepts of projection and levels of structure. It has become commonplace among psychologists to distinguish between projective and nonprojective tests. Accordingly, in nonprojective tests the questions asked (such as "At what temperature does water boil?") have a single, verifiable answer. Likewise, the tasks set, such as copying a block design, have a confirmable solution. In projective tests, by contrast, there is no single, verifiable, correct response; rather, the person's answer will be based on intrapsychic determinants and not on an external criterion of validity.

In accord with Rapaport, however, I believe that such a sharp distinction does not exist. Projective tests also elicit responses that approach objective verifiability, such as the popular response on the Rorschach, while nonprojective tests may have some projective features.

On the issue of projective versus nonprojective responses, Rapaport (1950) has cogently argued, "any organization of the external world according to a principle of organization of the subject's private world is considered projection. From this vantage point then all the nonprojective tests, in so far as they reflect something about the personality, should be considered projective" (p. 348).

The distinction between projective and non-projective responses takes cognizance of the degree of structure in the test material and the task involved. From this perspective, "a hierarchy of structuring principles emerges; these principles not only organize unstructured material, but also bring structured material into an even more embracing organization. We are facing the issue of substructures. . . ." (Rapaport, 1950, p. 342).

Viewed in this context, a battery of tests permits the examiner to observe the individual in a variety of situations that differ in their relative degree of structure. In assessing adaptive capacities, noting the nature of the individual's reaction to differing levels of structure can have important implications.

REFERENCES

Athey, G. (1974). Schizophrenic thought organization, object relations and the Rorschach test. *Bulletin of the Menninger Clinic, 38*, 406–429.

Bion, W. (1967). *Second thoughts.* New York: Jason Aronson.

Blatt, S., & Ritzler, B. (1974). Thought disorder and boundary disturbances in psychosis. *Journal of Consulting and Clinical Psychology, 42*, 370–381.

Cooper, S. (1983). *An object relations view of the borderline defenses: A Rorschach analysis.* Unpublished manuscript.

Dana, R. (1968). Six constructs to define Rorschach M. *Journal of Projective Techniques and Personality Assessment, 32*, 138–145.

Dudek, S. (1984). The architect as person: A Rorschach image. *Journal of Personality Assessment, 48*, 597–605.

Freud, S. (1953). The interpretation of dreams. *Standard Edition,* Vols. 4 and 5. London: Hogarth Press. (Originally published 1900).

Freud, S. (1957). On narcissism: An introduction. *Standard edition* (Vol. 14, pp 73–102). London: Hogarth Press. (Originally published 1914).

Kernberg, O. (1975). *Borderline conditions and pathologic narcissism.* New York: Jason Aronson.

Klein, M. (1949). *Contributions to psychoanalysis.* London: Hogarth Press.

Lerner, P. (1991). *Psychoanalytic theory and the Rorschach.* Hillsdale, NJ: Analytic Press.

Lerner, P., & Lerner, H. (1980). Rorschach assessment of primitive defenses in borderline personality structure. In J. Kwawer, H. Lerner, P. Lerner, & A. Sugarman (Eds.), *Borderline phenomena and the Rorschach Test* (pp. 257–274). New York: International Universities Press.

Mayman, M. (1977). A multi-dimensional view of the Rorschach movement response. In M. Rickers-Ovsiankina (Ed.), *Rorschach psychology* (pp. 229–250). Huntington, NY: Krieger.

Myden, W. (1959). Interpretation and evaluation of certain personality characteristics involved in creative productions. *Perceptual and Motor Skills, 9*, 139–158.

Piotrowski, Z. (1957). *Perceptanalysis.* New York: Macmillan.

Rapaport, D. (1950). The theoretical implications of diagnostic testing procedures. *Congres International de Psychiatrie, 2*, 241–271.

Rapaport, D., Gill, M., & Schafer, R. (1945–1946). *Diagnostic psychological testing.* Chicago: Year Book.

Schachtel, E. (1966). *Experiential foundations of Rorschach's test.* New York: Basic Books.

Singer, J. D. (1975). *The inner world of daydreaming.* New York: Harper & Row.

V
PROBLEMS IN PERSONALITY ASSESSMENT

23
Assessing a Patient's Ability to Cope

Norman S. Endler
James D. A. Parker

Practical and research interest in the way individuals respond or react to stressful, upsetting, or painful situations has produced a large literature on the related concepts of defense, adaptation, and coping (for reviews of this diverse literature, see Cohen, 1987; Cramer, 1990; Haan, 1977, 1982; Lazarus & Folkman, 1984, 1987; Lazarus, Averill, & Opton, 1974; Parker & Endler, 1992; Stone, Greenberg, Kennedy-Moore, & Newman, 1991; Vaillant, 1986). A substantial part of this literature has focused on several basic research questions: identifying basic coping or defensive strategies for responding to stressful situations; assessing the impact of various person (dispositional) and situational variables on the use of particular coping strategies; and examining the association between specific coping strategies and various mental and physical health variables (Cox & Ferguson, 1991; Endler & Parker, 1990a, 1990b; Endler, Parker, & Summerfeldt, 1993a; Lazarus, Averill, & Opton, 1974; Lazarus & Folkman, 1984, 1987; Parker & Endler, 1992). To address these types of questions researchers have developed a vast array of methodologies to assess coping and defense strategies and reactions. This chapter provides an overview of some of the more widely used methodologies for assessing an individual's ability to cope with stressful situations.

DEFENSE MECHANISMS

The various tests and measures reviewed in this chapter have evolved from two relatively distinct research traditions. The oldest tradition has focused on the assessment of defense mechanisms—a core feature of psychodynamic theories. The idea that individuals sometimes make painful thoughts and feelings unavailable to consciousness was one of Freud's earliest discoveries. As Freud's ideas about psychoanalysis evolved, the concept of defense came to play an increasingly important role (for a discussion on this point, see Van der Leeuw, 1971). For example, before the early 1920s the concept of defense was important in Freud's theories because it acted as a counterforce against the push of the drives for discharge. With the development of Freud's structural model (i.e., id, ego, superego) in the 1920s, however, defense mechanisms were extended and reconceptualized as ego functions that protect the ego from instinctual demands (Freud, 1926/1959). The defenses, as Anna Freud noted in one of the first systematic works on the topic, are "the ways and means by which the ego wards off unpleasure and anxiety, and exercises control over impulsive behavior, affects and instinctive urges" (A. Freud, 1936/1946, p. 5).

Although early psychoanalytic theorists tended to conceptualize all defenses as pathological, later writers have modified this view. White (1948), for example, distinguished between primary defensive processes involving the *denial* of impulses, and secondary defensive adjustments involving the *disguise* or distortion of impulses. Both types of defensive processes were thought to have adaptive and maladaptive potential. A number of more recent theorists have distinguished between adaptive and nonadaptive defenses (see Haan, 1963, 1965, 1977; Kroeber, 1963; White, 1948), or organized defense mechanisms along a hierarchy of psychopathology (see Bond, Gardiner, Christian, & Sigel, 1983; Perry & Cooper, 1989; Semrad, Grinspoon, & Fienberg, 1973; Vaillant, 1971, 1976, 1986; Vaillant, Bond, & Vaillant, 1986). The consensus seems to be that individuals who utilize "mature" (and adaptive) mechanisms tend to have better mental health and have more gratifying personal relationships than individuals who utilize "immature" defenses (see Cramer, 1990; Morrissey, 1977; Schwartz, 1990; Snarely & Vaillant, 1985; Vaillant, Bond, and Vaillant, 1986; Vaillant & Drake, 1985). In addition, while the older psychoanalytic literature focused on the clinician's ability to recognize various defenses in their patients (see Fenichel, 1945; A. Freud, 1936/1946), much of the recent literature on defense mechanisms has focused on developing objective methodologies for assessing various defenses (for reviews see Cramer, 1990; Haan, 1982; Kline, 1991; Vaillant, 1986).[1] Many of the more widely used methods for assessing defense mechanisms are reviewed later in this chapter.

COPING PROCESSES

In addition to measures of defense mechanisms, the other group of measures evaluated in this chapter belongs to a second research tradition — the study of *coping* processes. Although not widely recognized, systematic interest in coping reactions and activities emerged out of the defense mechanism literature of the 1960s and early 1970s. Until this time, the concept of coping had been used informally in the psychological literature (for more discussion on the history of the coping construct, see Lazarus, 1993; Lazarus, Averill, & Opton, 1974; Lazarus & Launier, 1978; White, 1974). In the 1960s, however, a number of researchers began to refer to various "adaptive" defense mechanisms (like sublimation or humor) as "coping" activities (see Alker, 1968; Haan, 1963, 1969; Hunter & Goodstein, 1967; Kroeber, 1963; Margolis, 1970; Weinstock, 1967). According to Haan (1965): "coping behavior is distinguished from defensive behavior, since the latter by definition is rigid, compelled, reality distorting, and undifferentiated, whereas, the former is flexible, purposive, reality oriented, and differentiated" (Haan, 1965, p. 374). An increased emphasis on the study of adaptive strategies led many researchers to focus their attention on the *conscious* strategies available to individuals when faced with stressful or upsetting situations (for examples of early coping research, see Sidle, Moos, Adams, & Cady, 1969; Visotsky, Hamburg, Goss, & Lebovits, 1961). Although there is virtually an unlimited number of coping strategies available to an individual in a particular stressful situation, the first generation of coping researchers quickly began to identify a limited number of basic coping dimensions (see Averill & Rosenn, 1972; Cohen & Lazarus, 1973; Lazarus, Averill, & Opton, 1974; Pearlin & Schooler, 1978; Sidle, Moos, Adams, & Cady, 1969).

In the past two decades coping research has developed to the point that the concept figures prominently in many health psychology models (see Auerbach, 1989; Endler, 1988; Endler, Parker, & Summerfeldt, 1993a; Krohne, 1988; Lazarus & Folkman, 1984, 1987; Taylor, 1990, 1991; Thomae, 1987). Coping has come to be conceptualized in terms of an individual's behavioral, affective, and cognitive attempts to mediate a perceived discrepancy between situational demands and personal capacity or competence (Cox & Ferguson, 1991; Endler, 1988; Endler, Parker, & Summerfeldt, 1993a; Folkman & Lazarus, 1988; Lazarus & Folkman, 1984, 1987). In the health psychology area, coping is viewed as an important *moderator* or buffer variable in the interplay between physiological predispositions toward illness and the influences of psychosocial and environmental stimuli.

Although a great variety of coping tests and measures have appeared in the past two decades, there exists considerable agreement in the literature about what constitute some of the more important coping dimensions. If there is any consensus in the coping literature, it is primarily about the basic distinction between *emotion-focused* and *problem-focused* coping strategies. In general, this literature identifies problem-focused coping strategies as those that attempt to solve a problem, reconceptualize it, minimize its effects, or alter the situation. Emotion-focused coping strategies may include emotional responses, self-preoccupation, and fantasizing reactions. Most coping measures include scales that assess both of these basic coping dimensions (see Billings & Moos, 1984; Carver, Scheier, & Weintraub, 1989; Endler & Parker, 1990a, 1990b; Epstein & Meier, 1989; Folkman & Lazarus, 1980, 1985, 1988; Nowack, 1989; Patterson & McCubbin, 1987), or assess closely related constructs (see Amirkhan, 1990; Dise-Lewis, 1988; Feifel & Strack, 1989). The concept of *avoidance* coping is a third basic coping dimension frequently identified in the literature (see Amirkhan, 1990; Billings & Moos, 1981; Endler & Parker, 1990a, 1990b; Feifel & Strack, 1989; Nowack, 1989). Endler and Parker (1990a, 1990b) have suggested that avoidance coping strategies can be conceptualized to include *person-oriented* and *task-oriented* strategies. An individual can avoid a stressful situation by seeking out other people (social diversion) or by engaging in a substitute task (distraction).

The remainder of this chapter critically examines various coping and defense measures, paying close attention to the methodologies that have been used to develop and validate these measures. In the past few decades a vast collection of defense and coping measures have been developed; therefore we have focused our attention on some of the more widely used tests and measures.

ASSESSMENT OF DEFENSE MECHANISMS

Although a variety of methodologies exist for the assessment of various defense mechanisms, this area of research continues to be plagued by several basic problems (for more discussion about these problems, see Klein, 1991; Sjöbäck, 1991). There is little consensus in the literature about which defenses should be assessed and how these particular defenses might be defined. Researchers developing new measures usually select and define defense mechanisms in idiosyncratic ways (Skodol & Perry, 1993). To add to the confusion, some test developers have used the same names for particular defenses, even though the constructs have been defined quite differently.

Three methods have traditionally been used to assess defense mechanisms: (1) observer-rated measures; (2) self-report questionnaires; and (3) projective techniques. The following section examines defense measures related to the first two methods; projective measures of defense are not reviewed in this chapter. Table 23.1 presents a list of the defense mechanism measures examined in this chapter. Although there has been a long history of using projective techniques (e.g.,

TABLE 23.1. Summary of Defense Mechanism Measures Reviewed

Observer-rated measures	Self-report measures
Beardslee et al. (1985)	Andrews et al. (1993)
Haan (1963)	Bond et al. (1983)
Perry and Cooper (1986, 1989)	Byrne (1961)
	Gleser and Ihilevich (1969)
Semrad et al. (1973)	Haan (1965)
Vaillant (1971, 1974, 1975)	Joffe and Naditch (1977)
	Plutchik et al. (1979)
	Weinberger et al. (1979)

the Rorschach and Thematic Apperception Test) to assess various defense mechanisms (see Holt, 1956; Lerner, 1990; Schafer, 1954), most of the recent research on defense mechanisms has used observer-rated measures or self-report scales (for a recent review of projective techniques and the assessment of defense mechanisms, see Cramer, 1988, 1990).

Observer-Rated Measures

The most widely used method for assessing defense mechanisms has been rating procedures for clinical or interview material (e.g., case studies, transcripts of clinical interviews). Since the 1960s a variety of observer-rated systems have been proposed for the assessment of various defenses in psychiatric and normal populations (e.g., Haan, 1963; Jacobson, Beardslee, Hauser, Noam, & Powers, 1986; Perry & Cooper, 1986, 1989; Semrad, Grinspoon, & Fienberg, 1973; Vaillant, 1971, 1976, 1986; Weintraub & Aronson, 1963). Although many of the rating systems use identical names for some of the defenses that are assessed, it is important to note that there are frequently notable differences in the way these defenses are defined and conceptualized.

One of the first observer-rated systems for defense was developed by Haan (1963) from extensive interviews of subjects participating in the Oakland Growth Study (see Morrissey, 1977, for a detailed review of research using Haan's observer-rated measures). The sample consisted of ninety-nine normal adults (forty-nine men and fifty women) who were interviewed "in accordance with a schedule that covered their adolescent memories of self; social-family interaction; and present status of self, occupation, family etc." (Haan, 1963, p. 7). Before conducting the interviews, Haan (1963) developed specific definitions for twenty "ego mechanisms": ten *defense mechanisms* (isolation, intellectualizing, rationalization, doubt, denial, projection, regression, displacement, reaction formation, and repression) and ten *coping mechanisms* (objectivity, intellectuality,

logical analysis, tolerance of ambiguity, concentration, empathy, regression in service of ego, sublimation, substitution, and suppression). Using the definitions developed by Haan (1963), raters provide scores for the various defense and coping constructs using five-point scales.

The interrater reliability of Haan's system has been problematic, which has also been the case with a number of the observer-rated defense scales reviewed in this chapter. For the ten defense mechanism measures, Haan (1963) reported correlations between two independent sets of ratings that ranged from .20 to .79 (mean was .62) for male subjects, and from .19 to .75 (mean was .50) for female subjects. For the ten coping mechanism measures, correlations ranged from .51 to .83 (mean was .68) for male subjects, and from −.11 to .83 (mean was .41) for female subjects. Although Morrissey (1977) reviews several studies using Haan's rating scales that have found slightly higher correlations among raters, the modest size of these reliability coefficients is a serious limitation to this defense measure.

Vaillant (1971, 1974, 1975, 1976, 1977) has proposed a hierarchical model of defense mechanisms, extending from mature to immature defenses, that has had considerable impact on the defense mechanism literature (see Bond, Gardiner, Christian, & Sigel, 1983; Perry & Cooper, 1989; Skodol & Perry, 1993). In Vaillant's model, mature defenses are defined as activities like sublimation, humor, and suppression, while immature defenses are defined as activities like projection, hypochondriasis, and passive aggression. An intermediate class of defense is also identified—neurotic defenses—that includes activities like intellectualization, repression, and reaction formation. Vaillant (1971, 1974, 1975, 1976) has developed a rating system for assessing fifteen basic defenses that conforms to his defense model: five mature defenses (anticipation, suppression, altruism, sublimation, and humor), five neurotic defenses (intellectualization, repression, reaction formation, displacement, and dissociation), and five immature defenses (passive aggression, hypochondriasis, acting out, projection, and fantasy).

A positive feature of this rating system is that it was designed for use with various forms of clinical information (open-ended interviews, transcripts of interviews, etc.). Detailed definitions are provided (Vaillant, 1971) to rate the presence or absence of a particular defense.

Vaillant's rating system was originally validated using autobiographical data collected from a sample of ninety-five men (part of a longitudinal study) about how they had reacted to various stressful situations in their lives (Vaillant, 1971, 1974, 1975, 1976). The pattern of Vaillant's results suggests that mature defenses were related to good adult adjustment and immature defenses to poor adjustment, which is consistent with his hierarchical defense model. However, reliability data for several of the defense ratings have been less than satisfactory. For example, correlations between the defense ratings of two independent judges (Vaillant, 1976) ranged from $-.01$ to .95 (mean was .56). Although Vaillant and his colleagues have generated a vast amount of data on the relationships among psychopathology, adjustment, and defense, low reliabilities for various defense ratings limit the generalizability of this research. It is significant to note that reliability data for separate defense ratings are frequently not reported in research using this rating system (see Snarey & Vaillant, 1985; Vaillant & Drake, 1985; Vaillant, Bond, & Vaillant, 1986).

Semrad, Grinspoon, and Fienberg (1973) have developed a forty-five-item clinician-rated measure, the Ego Profile Scale (EPS), that conforms to a hierarchical model of defense mechanisms. Although the EPS was designed to be a brief and efficient measure of defense, little is known about this scale's psychometric properties. The EPS was rationally developed to assess nine basic defenses: three narcissistic behaviors (denial, projection, distortion); three affective behaviors (compulsive obsessive behavior, hypochondriacal behaviors, neurasthenic behaviors); and three neurotic behaviors (dissociation, somatization, anxiety). Each defense item is rated by the interviewer or trained observer on seven-point scales (five items for each defense).

Given the reliability problems that plague other researchers developing observer-rated scales for defense, it is unfortunate that Semrad et al. (1973) report no reliability data for the EPS. In a study of defense patterns in thirty-six depressed inpatients (Ablon, Carlson, & Goodwin, 1974), correlations between independent raters were nonsignificant for most of the EPS scales. A preliminary factor analytic study of the EPS (Semrad et al., 1973) also raises concerns about the scale's validity. Factor analysis of the forty-five EPS items in a sample of sixty-three patients (thirty-one "acute schizophrenics" and a cross-section of thirty-two psychiatric inpatients) failed to produce a nine-factor solution.

More recently, Perry and Cooper (1986, 1989) have developed the Defense Mechanism Rating Scales (DMRS) to assess various defense mechanisms from clinical interview or "life vignette" data. The DMRS consists of thirty defense mechanisms that can be classified into four basic defense clusters: "immature," "borderline" (also referred to as "image-distorting"), "neurotic," and "mature" defenses. Formal definitions for the various defenses are provided by Perry and Cooper (1986), and each defense has a three-point rating scale ("not present," "probably present," and "definitely present"). According to the test developers, "the scales are applicable to dynamically oriented interview data, such as might be obtained in an initial psychotherapy interview" (Perry & Cooper, 1989, p. 445). Although the developers of the DMRS have gone to considerable lengths to develop concise definitions for the various defense scales, interrater reliability has not been satisfactory (see Perry & Cooper, 1989). Interclass correlation coefficients for six raters who viewed forty-six videotaped clinical interviews ranged from a low of .11 (for "rationalization") to a high of .59 (for "acting out"), with a mean coefficient of .37. In addition, although the DMRS was developed to assess relatively stable personality variables, correlations between two sets of defense ratings (videotaped interviews at intake versus life vignette data collected three years later) ranged from a low of .17 to a high of .45 (with a mean correlation of .26).

Beardslee, Jacobson, Hauser, Noam, and Powers (1985), Jacobson, Beardslee, Hauser, Noam, and Powers (1986) and Jacobson, Beardslee, Hauser, Noam, Powers, Houlihan and Rider (1986) have developed an interviewer-rated system of defense mechanisms for use with various adolescent populations. Jacobson and colleagues developed their rating system to assess twelve basic defenses that they believed were pertinent to the study of defense mechanisms in adolescence. Although Jacobson et al. (1986) report some validity data that is consistent with their hierarchical model of defense, reliability data on the rating system is problematic. Interclass correlations for three judges who independently rated eighteen transcripts of a clinical interview ranged from .32 to .76 (with a mean of .57).

Self-Report Measures

In the past few decades a variety of self-report measures have been developed to assess a cross-section of defense constructs. Given the traditional view of defense mechanisms as unconscious processes, self-report questions might appear to be an inappropriate method for assessing defense. As noted by Brennan, Andrews, Morris-Yates, and Pollock (1990): "At first though the idea that one would be aware of habitually used unconscious defenses seems improbable, but given that they are habitual, one must eventually become familiar with much-used behaviors" (p. 592). Most self-report defense measures have been developed on the assumption that individuals are familiar enough with the way they react to stressful situations to provide information about habitual defense use (for more discussion on this point, see Bond, 1986; Kline, 1991). Thus, self-report measures are believed to assess "conscious derivatives of defense mechanisms" (Bond, Perry, Gautier, Goldenberg, Oppenheimer, & Simand, 1989, p. 102).

One of the first self-report measures of defense was a group of scales developed by Haan (1965) using items from the Minnesota Multi-phasic Personality Inventory (MMPI) and the California Personality Inventory (CPI; Gough, 1957). These scales were developed following a personality model (Haan, 1963; Kroeber, 1963) that distinguishes between coping mechanisms (adaptive activities) and defense mechanisms (nonadaptive activities). The criterion group for these self-report defense scales were subjects (forty-nine men and fifty women) rated high (top 25 percent) or low (bottom 25 percent) on specific defense mechanisms by judges who were using Haan's (1963) observer-rated defense scales. Using MMPI and CPI items that successfully distinguished between high- and low-defense groups, Haan (1965) developed nine coping mechanism scales (objectivity, intellectuality, logical analysis, concentration, tolerance of ambiguity, empathy, regression in service of the ego, suppression, and controlled coping) with internal reliability coefficients that ranged from .48 to .85 (with a mean of .69). Haan (1965) also developed seven defense mechanism scales (intellectualizing, doubt, denial, projection, regression, displacement, and repression) with internal reliability coefficients that ranged from .54 to .83 (with a mean of .70). Although Haan's (1965) self-report defense scales have never been cross-validated, the results of several construct validity studies have provided support for Haan's distinction between adaptive and nonadaptive defenses (for reviews on research with Haan's scales, see Cramer, 1990; Morrissey, 1977).

Joffe and Naditch (1977) expanded on Haan's work by using CPI items to develop a set of twenty self-report defense scales (ten coping mechanism scales and ten defense mechanism scales with labels identical to the twenty observer-rated scales developed by Haan, 1963, and discussed earlier in this chapter). They appear to have been successful in developing a set of defense scales with better psychometric properties than the measures developed by Haan (1965). Using a procedure similar to Haan (1965), Joffe and Naditch (1977) used interviewer-based defense ratings on a sample of 143 normal adults (the observer-rated scales developed by Haan, 1963) as the criterion for selecting CPI items. Unlike Haan (1965), however,

Joffe and Naditch (1977) cross-validated their results with an independent sample of 100 normal adults. Correlations between the twenty self-report scales and clinical ratings ranged from .20 to .57 (mean was .36) in male subjects, and from .21 to .57 (mean was .36) in female subjects. In addition, test-retest correlations (four weeks) in a sample of 203 college students ranged from .49 to .82 for male students (mean was .68), and from .46 to .81 (mean was .69) for female students. Joffe and Naditch (1977) also provide construct validity data consistent with an adaptive/nonadaptive defense model. For example, they found generally negative correlations between the ten defense mechanism scales and the standard CPI scales (which measure adaptive personality traits). A reverse pattern was found for the ten coping mechanism scales and the standard CPI scales.

One of the more widely used self-report measures of defense is the Defense Mechanism Inventory (DMI; Gleser and Ihilevich, 1969; Ihilevich & Gleser, 1986). The DMI was developed to assesses five defense mechanism clusters: "turning against the self," "turning against the object," "projection," "reversal," and "principalization" (for a more detailed review of the DMI, see Cramer, 1988, 1990; LaVoie, 1987). The definitions used to develop these defense clusters appear to have been drawn from the general psychoanalytic literature (see Gleser & Ihilevich, 1969); the scale is believed to assess relatively stable defense styles. The DMI consists of ten short stories that describe conflict situations (e.g., "You are waiting for the bus at the edge of the road. The streets are wet and muddy after the previous night's rain. A car sweeps through a puddle in front of you, splashing your clothing with mud"). After each story respondents are presented with four general questions: (1) actual behavior in the conflict situation; (2) possible impulsive fantasies; (3) possible thoughts; and (4) possible feelings. For each question respondents are asked to choose from five alternative statements their most likely and least likely response (each of the five statements corresponds to one of the five basic defense mechanism clusters). Normative data for the DMI is available on a variety of normative

groups (adolescents, adults, clinical patients; see Ihilevich & Gleser, 1986).

Various studies have examined the DMI's test-retest reliability using time-periods ranging from one week to two months (for a review, see Cramer, 1990; LaVoie, 1987). The results have consistently found DMI scores to be relatively stable, with test-retest correlations ranging from 0.48 to 0.93. Research on the validity of the DMI, however, has not been as consistent. The DMI was validated initially by asking psychologists and social workers to match the DMI items with a set of definitions on the defense mechanisms assessed by the DMI (Gleser & Ihilevich, 1969). Results showed satisfactory agreement with the DMI scales of "turning against self," "reversal of affect," and "principalization" (60 percent agreement), but not for the other scales. A second study asking raters familiar with the psychoanalytic literature to match DMI items with specific defense mechanisms produced similar results (Blacha & Fancher, 1977).

Although the DMI was developed to assess five distinct defense mechanisms, high intercorrelations have been reported among some of the scales. Gleser and Ihilevich (1969), for example, report intercorrelations among the DMI scales that ranged from 0.06 to 0.67 (with a mean correlation of 0.42) in a sample of college students, and from 0.00 to 0.79 (mean correlation was 0.46) in a sample of psychiatric outpatients. High intercorrelations among DMI scales have been reported by Vichers and Hervig (1981) and Frank, McLaughlin, and Crusco (1984). Factor analysis of the DMI in a sample of 174 college students produced a two-factor model that Frank et al. (1984) labeled "reflective/externalizing defenses" and "self-blaming defenses." High intercorrelations led Juni and Masling (1980) to propose that the DMI should be conceptualized as assessing a single aggression/inhibition continuum of defense.

Although a variety of studies have appeared examining the construct validity of the DMI (see Cramer, 1988, 1990; Ihilevich & Gleser, 1986), Kline (1991) has questioned the validity of using a self-report methodology to assess what by definition involves unconscious processes:

There is a basic flaw in the logic of the DMI, as there is in all tests of defenses where this questionnaire format is used. . . . In psychoanalytic theory defenses are utilised against conflicts that are unconscious. In the DMI the subject is supposed to identify with character [sic] in the vignette. However the conflict is at the conscious level. It is directly stated in the story. Thus no defense is necessary against it. Whatever response is chosen it cannot represent a defense, even if it did so for the character in the vignette. (Kline, 1991, p. 30).

Researchers who defend the use of self-report defense measures argue that these scales do not assess defense mechanisms directly but assess defense styles (Brennan, Andrews, Morris-Yates, and Pollock, 1990).

Bond, Gardner, Christian, and Sigal (1983) have developed the Defense Style Questionnaire (DSQ) to assess twenty-four separate defense mechanisms. The original scale consisted of eighty-one items (nine-point Likert scales) that were selected from a larger pool of items based on ratings of appropriateness by a group of clinicians (item-total correlations were also used in the final selection of items). A second-order factor analysis of the twenty-four defense scales in a sample of 209 subjects (the sample was a combination of forty-two psychiatric inpatients, fifty-six psychiatric outpatients, and 111 normal adults) produced a four-factor defense model: immature defenses, image-distorting defenses, self-sacrificing defenses, and adaptive defenses. Although Bond et al. (1983) report no reliability data for the DSQ, preliminary construct validity data are presented from the same group of subjects used in the factor analysis. The mature defense style was found to be related to higher levels of a measure of ego development (Loevinger, 1976); the reverse was found with the immature defense style.

The number of questions on the DSQ has recently been expanded from 81 to 88 items (Bond, 1986; Bond, Perry, Gautier, Goldenberg, Oppenheimer, & Simand, 1989), and Andrews, Pollock, and Stewart (1989) have used a group of clinicians to categorize the items into twenty defense subscales. Categorization of items was done in a way that was consistent with

the glossary of defense mechanisms developed for the DSM-III-R (for a copy of this glossary, see Vaillant, 1986). The DSQ was administered to 413 subjects (142 psychiatric outpatients, 67 adults consulting their family doctor, and 204 normal adults) and a second-order factor analysis was conducted with the twenty newly created defense subscales. The result was a three-factor model of defense style: mature defenses (e.g., sublimation or humor), neurotic defenses (e.g., reaction formation or undoing), and immature defenses (e.g., projection or somatization). Andrews et al. (1989) also conducted a factor analysis using the scoring system for the DSQ developed by Bond et al. (1983) and found a three-factor model (mature, neurotic, and immature defenses) to be more interpretable than the four-factor model proposed by Bond et al. (1983). Although internal reliability coefficients for many of the twenty defense subscales were less than satisfactory in a combined sample (n = 712) of normal adults and psychiatric patients (ranging from .07 to .82), coefficient alphas for the three higher-order factor scales were more satisfactory (Andrews, Singh, & Bond, 1993). Test-retest correlations (four weeks) in a sample of 89 normal adults (Andrews et al., 1993) for the three higher-order factor scales suggest that the three measures are highly reliable (.68 for mature defenses, .77 for neurotic defenses, and .86 for immature defenses).

Much of the recent research examining the construct validity of the DSQ has focused on the scoring system developed by Andrews, Pollock, & Stewart (1989). Pollock and Andrews (1989), for example, examined the defensive styles associated with various anxiety disorders (e.g., social phobic, panic, and obsessive-compulsive disorder) and found particular defense styles to discriminate between the diagnostic groups (see also Brennan et al., 1990). In addition, Andrews et al. (1993) have recently developed a forty-item version of the DSQ (items are a subset from the original scale) with three subscales: eight items assessing mature defense, eight items assessing neurotic defense, and twenty-four items assessing immature defense. Preliminary data suggest that the short version of the DSQ is more reliable than the original scale (Andrews et al., 1993).

Plutchik (1989), Plutchik and Conte (1989), and Plutchik, Kellerman, and Conte (1979) have developed the Life-Style Index (LSI), a 138-item measure that assesses eight defense mechanism clusters: "denial," "displacement," "projection," "reaction formation," "regression," "repression," "compensation," and "intellectualization." The LSI was developed following a series of face validity and factor analytic procedures with a small sample of undergraduates (n = 70). Although several validity studies have been conducted with the LSI using small samples of clinical and nonclinical samples, reliability data for the scale have not been encouraging. Split-half reliability coefficients for the eight LSI scales ranged from .16 to .75, with a mean of .55 (Plutchik et al., 1979).

In addition to creating tests that assess a cross-section of defense mechanisms, a number of researchers have focused on developing self-report measures for very specific defenses. MMPI items, for example, have been used to construct several different defense scales (see Little & Fisher, 1958; Sarason, 1958; Welsh, 1956). The concept of repression, however, appears to have received more attention than any other defense construct (Singer, 1990). Although there are disagreements about the concept (see Erdelyi, 1990), it is widely held that individuals who have a repressive style "are likely to use a variety of strategies to avoid awareness of affects and impulses that are incompatible with their self-images" (Weinberger, 1990, p. 343). A sizable body of literature has linked repressive style with a variety of health problems (for a review see Schwartz, 1990).

The Repression-Sensitization scale (R-S; Byrne, 1961; Byrne, Barry, & Nelson, 1963) has been the most common method for assessing repressive style. The R-S scale, which is made up of selected items from the MMPI that ask about the presence of symptoms, identifies individuals believed to use a variety of strategies to avoid awareness of impulses and affects. This scale was developed following the proposal that persons who do not acknowledge having many symptoms can be described as "repressors,"

while persons who do acknowledge symptoms can be described as "sensitizers."

Although a sizable literature on personality and health has developed using the R-S scale, this measure has several problems. Numerous researchers, for example, have found that the measure correlates very highly with measures of anxiety and social desirability (see Bell & Byrne, 1978, for a review of this research). As a consequence, it has been proposed that the R-S scale is primarily a measure of anxiety (Cramer, 1990; Slough, Kleinknecht, & Thorndike, 1984). Holmes (1990) has suggested that there is also a serious conceptual problem with the R-S scale: "there is no way to distinguish between individuals who actually have symptoms and do not report them ('repressors,' or more likely deniers) and individuals who do not have symptoms and therefore cannot report them (nonrepressors)" (Holmes, 1990, p. 94). The inability of the R-S scale to separate "repressors" from individuals who do not have any symptoms is a serious problem that all potential users of the scale should consider.

In response to some of the problems that have been reported with the R-S scale, Weinberger, Schwartz, and Davidson (1979) redefined the definition of repressors as individuals who score low on a measure of anxiety *and* high on a measure of social desirability like the Marlowe-Crowne Social Desirability Scale (Crowne & Marlowe, 1960). Low-anxious (or low-symptom) individuals were identified as those respondents low on the anxiety scale as well as low on the social desirability measure.

Davis (1990) and Weinberger (1990) review a variety of studies that tend, overall, to support the construct validity of using self-report measures of anxiety and social desirability (defensiveness) to assess repressive style. Holmes (1990), however, suggests that work conducted by Weinberger, Davis, and colleagues should be considered as empirical support for the concept of denial rather than repression. Referring to the original study by Weinberger et al. (1979), Holmes (1990) notes that "the problem is that individuals who are high on social desirability may be upset by and less willing to report undesirable events, but that does not mean that they are not aware of them. Indeed, the investigators reported that, although 'repressors' did not report undesirable events, they showed higher physiological arousal than other subjects" (Holmes, 1990, p. 95). If repressors had actually repressed the undesirable events and were now unaware of this material they should not have had higher arousal levels.

Summary

The study of defense mechanisms continues to generate interest from clinicians and researchers. A variety of observer-rated and self-report instruments have been developed to assess a cross-section of defense mechanisms. Potential users, however, should note that there is considerable variation in the psychometric properties of these measures. The published literature on many of the defense instruments reviewed in this chapter suggests that the measures have poor internal reliability (or inter-rater reliability), low or nonexistent test-retest reliability, and questionable validity. In addition, the normative data available for many of the defense measures are restricted to small samples with limited generalizability.

COPING ASSESSMENT

Unlike the assessment of defense, where a variety of methods have been utilized (e.g., self-report measures, observer-rated systems, projective tests), almost all recent coping research has involved the use of self-report measures. An important distinction is made in the coping literature between measures that assess basic coping styles and measures that assess coping responses used in particular situations. This distinction has been referred to as the *interindividual* versus *intraindividual* approach to coping assessment (Endler & Parker, 1990b, 1994; Endler, Parker, & Summerfeldt, 1993a; Parker & Endler, 1992; Folkman, Lazarus, Dunkel-Schetter, Delongis, & Gruen, 1986; Lazarus, 1993), and is analogous to the state/trait distinction frequently made in personality research (see Endler, 1983,

for an overview of the state/trait distinction). The *interindividual* approach to coping attempts to identify basic coping styles: habitual coping strategies used by particular individuals across different types of stressful situations. Self-report measures taking an interindividual approach typically ask the respondent how he or she *generally responds* to stressful situations.

The *intraindividual* approach to coping, on the other hand, attempts to identify basic coping behaviors or strategies used by individuals in particular types of stressful or upsetting situations. This approach "assumes that individuals have a repertoire of coping options available to them from which they can build what they believe to be the most effective strategy, depending on the nature of the situation" (Cox & Ferguson, 1991, p. 20). Although it is acknowledged that there is an almost unlimited number of potential coping strategies and reactions available to a person, it is assumed that these activities can be classified into a small number of basic coping dimensions. The goal for many researchers developing intraindividual measures is to study coping as a process. As noted by Lazarus (1993), "From a process perspective, coping changes over time and in accordance with the situational contexts in which it occurs" (p. 235). Self-report measures taking an intraindividual approach to coping assessment typically ask the respondent to report how he or she has reacted (or is reacting) to a *specific* stressful situation.

Table 23.2 presents a list of the coping measures examined in this chapter. Some intraindividual coping measures have been developed for use with different and diverse populations experiencing a wide variety of stressors, while other measures have been developed for use with populations experiencing very specific stressful situations (e.g., pain patients).

Interindividual Coping Measures

Miller (1980, 1987), and Miller and Mangan (1983) have created the Miller Behavioral Style Scale (MBSS). This thirty-two-item self-report scale was rationally developed to assess two basic coping styles: information-distractors (blunters)

TABLE 23.2. Summary of Coping Measures Reviewed

Interindividual measures	Intraindividual measures
Carver et al. (1989)	Amirkhan (1990)
Dise-Lewis (1988)	Billings and Moos
Endler and Parker	(1981, 1984)
(1990a)	Butler et al. (1989)
Epstein and Meier	Endler et al. (1993)
(1989)	Feifel et al. (1987)
Feifel and Strack (1989)	Folkman and Lazarus
Hammer and Marting	(1980, 1988)
(1988)	McCubbin et al. (1983)
Miller (1980, 1987)	Pearlin and Schooler
Nowack (1989)	(1978)
Patterson and	Stone and Neale (1984)
McCubbin (1987)	

and information-seekers (monitors). The MBSS asks respondents to imagine themselves in four different stress-evoking situations (e.g., "Imagine that you are afraid of flying and have to go somewhere by plane") and then to answer eight questions (yes/no response format) that ask about hypothetical responses. Four questions describe monitoring or information-seeking activities (e.g., "I would read and reread the safety instructions booklet"), and four questions describe blunting or information avoiding activities (e.g., "I would watch the in-flight film even if I had seen it before").

Although we could find no published study that reported internal reliability coefficients for the MBSS, test-retest reliabilities (Miller, 1987) for the monitoring and blunting scales were highly reliable over a four-month period (0.72 and 0.75, respectively). A variety of validity studies have been published on the MBSS. For example, the MBSS has been found to predict individuals likely to seek out or avoid information about electrical shock in a laboratory situation (Miller & Mischel, 1986; see also Miller, 1987), and to predict patient responses to either massive or minimal information about an upcoming medical procedure (Miller & Mangan, 1983).

Hammer and Marting (1988) have developed the sixty-item (four-point Likert scales) Coping Resources Inventory (CRI) to measure various "personal resources" available to individuals for coping with stress (for a review of this scale, see Friedman & Mulhern, 1991). The developers of the CRI view coping resources as traitlike variables that can influence the way an individual reacts to a stressful situation. The inventory has five coping scales (cognitive resources, social resources, emotional resources, spiritual/philosophical resources, and physical resources), plus a total resource score (based on the sum of the five scales). The CRI was developed from a pool of ninety-three coping items using rational (face validity) and empirical (item-total correlations) criteria with a sample of three hundred subjects (a combination of high school students, undergraduates, and normal adults). Internal reliability coefficients for the five coping resource scales ranged from .72 to .84, and six-week test-retest correlations for the scales in a sample of 155 high school students ranged from .60 to .78, suggesting that the CRI has acceptable reliability. Preliminary construct validity data, supporting the view that the CRI is a multidimensional measure, have also been published in the test manual (Hammer & Marting, 1988). As one reviewer has noted, however, "there is not enough information currently about its [CRI] psychometric properties to warrant its use in clinical settings with a high degree of confidence" (Friedman & Mulhern, 1991, p. 114).

The Life Situations Inventory (LSI), developed by Feifel and Strack (1989), is a self-report scale that assesses habitual coping behaviors for five conflict situations: decision-making situations, defeat in competition situations, frustration-producing situations, difficulty with an authority situations, and situations involving a disagreement with a peer. Respondents are asked to complete an identical set of twenty-one coping items for each of the five conflict situations (a total of 105 items). Each set of twenty-one items (four-point frequency Likert scales) assesses three basic coping strategies: problem solving (eight items), avoidance (eight items), and resignation (five items). To date, only preliminary psychometric information has been published on the LSI. Feifel and Strack (1989) began scale construction by creating a pool of seventy coping items that were generally related to problem solving, avoidance, and avoidance activities. The pool of items was reduced to twenty-eight items using rational considerations; item-total correlations in a sample of 182 middle-aged and elderly males were used to eliminate an additional seven items. Although we could find no published data on the scale's test-retest reliability, the LSI appears to be internally reliable (alphas ranged from 0.66 to 0.83 for the various scales). Intercorrelations of the scales among the five conflict situations have been presented as preliminary construct validity data for the LSI. For the problem-solving dimension, correlations among the five situations ranged from .37 to .65 (mean was .50); for the avoidance dimension, correlations ranged from .44 to .61 (mean was .48); and for the resignation dimension, correlations ranged from .21 to .48 (mean was .38).

Nowack (1989) has developed a brief self-report measure to assess four basic coping styles: intrusive positive thoughts, intrusive negative thoughts, avoidance, and problem-focused coping. The Coping Style Scale (CSS; Nowack, 1989) consists of twenty items (five-point frequency Likert scales), with five items on each of the four subscales. As with a number of recently developed coping scales, only preliminary psychometric data are available for the CSS. Nowack notes that "scale construction took place following a combination of factor analytic and rational procedures designed to eliminate weak or redundant items" (Nowack, 1989, p. 150). To date, however, little of this information has been published. Alpha reliability coefficients for the CSS scales were moderate, ranging from a low of 0.67 to a high of 0.72 (Nowack, 1989).

Epstein and Meier (1989) have developed the Constructive Thinking Inventory (CTI) to assess the coping strategies of constructive and destructive thinking. The sixty-four-item CTI consists of six scales: emotional coping (nine items), behavioral coping (twelve items), categorical thinking (twelve items), superstitious thinking (nine items), naive optimism subscale (seven items), and negative thinking (ten items). The CTI was derived from a factor analysis of

more than 100 items (the authors are vague about exactly how many items were used) with a sample of 124 undergraduate students. Given this small sample size, it is unfortunate that the factor structure of the CTI has not been cross-validated. Epstein and Meier (1989) report acceptable alpha reliability coefficients for the CTI scales with the derivation sample that range from a low of 0.67 to a high of 0.87.

Carver, Scheier, and Weintraub (1989) have developed a fifty-two-item measure called the COPE that assesses thirteen basic coping styles (four items per scale): five scales assess different problem-focused dimensions; five scales assess different emotion-focused dimensions; and there are scales that assess focusing on emotions, behavioral disengagement, and mental disengagement coping dimensions. The COPE was developed by Carver et al. (1989) using factor analysis with a sample of 978 undergraduate students. Internal reliabilities for the COPE scales in the derivation sample ranged from a low of 0.45 to a high of 0.92. Given the large number of factors (twelve) that Carver et al. (1989) derived from their initial factor analysis, and the low to moderate alpha coefficients of many of the scales, the factor structure of the COPE needs to be cross-validated. Six-week test-retest correlations for the COPE in a sample of eighty-nine undergraduates ranged from .46 to .86, suggesting that the scales have adequate reliability. Preliminary construct validity data have also been presented (Carver et al., 1989) that support the view that the COPE is a multidimensional measure of coping style. Carver et al. (1989) also administered the COPE to a group of 156 undergraduate students who were asked to report on their coping activities with a specific stressful situation. Correlations between scales on the situation-specific version of the COPE and the regular version of the COPE ranged from .07 to .76 (mean was .30).

The Coping Inventory for Stressful Situations (CISS) was developed by Endler and Parker (1990a, 1990b, 1990c, 1993, 1994) in a series of factor analytic studies with clinical and nonclinical populations. The forty-eight-item self-report measure assesses three basic coping styles (sixteen items on each scale): task-oriented coping, emotion-oriented coping, and avoidance-oriented coping. The sixteen items on the avoidance scale also have two subscales: an eight-item distraction measure and a five-item social diversion measure. The factor structure of the CISS has been cross-validated in samples of undergraduates, normal adults, and psychiatric inpatients using congruence coefficients (Endler & Parker, 1990a). Congruence coefficients across the diagonal were all above 0.90 and significant, while off-diagonal coefficients were low and nonsignificant, suggesting that the factor structure was virtually identical in all three groups. Factor structures for men and women were also compared in the various samples and found to be virtually identical (Endler & Parker, 1990a).

Unlike a number of coping scales reviewed in this chapter, extensive psychometric and normative data have been published on the CISS. For example, in a sample of 471 male and 771 female undergraduates, alpha reliability coefficients for the task, emotion, and avoidance scales were 0.90, 0.87, and 0.85 for males, respectively, and 0.90, 0.88, and 0.83 for females, respectively (Endler & Parker, 1990a). Test-retest correlations in a sample of 74 males and 164 female undergraduates (six weeks) found the task, emotion, and avoidance scales to be reliable (0.73, 0.68, and 0.55, respectively, for males; 0.72, 0.71, and 0.60, respectively, for females). T-score (standardized scores) and percentile information is available for male and female normal adults and male and female psychiatric patients.

A number of studies have examined the construct validity of the CISS (for a review, see Endler & Parker, 1994). For example, in a study examining the CISS and the MMPI-2 in a sample of 167 male airline pilots, Endler, Parker, & Butcher (1993) found that the CISS emotion scale was positively correlated with a variety of psychopathology indices from the MMPI-2. The CISS task scale, on the other hand, was unrelated to the various psychopathology measures. The relationship between basic coping styles, like task-oriented (or problem-focused) and emotion-oriented coping and indices of both mental and physical health is one of the

most extensively researched topics in the coping literature (see Auerbach, 1989; Clark & Hovanitz, 1989; Felton & Revenson, 1984; Fleischman, 1984; Miller, Brody, & Summerton, 1988; Suls & Fletcher, 1985).

Endler and Parker (1994) examined the concurrent validity of the CISS by asking subjects to provide retrospective reports about the coping responses they used when experiencing a specific stressful situation (studying for an upcoming examination). Since the CISS was developed to assess basic coping styles that are used by particular individuals across different types of stressful situations, it was predicted that there would be a strong association between specific coping styles (assessed by the CISS) and self-reports of congruent coping responses. Situation-specific coping responses were assessed using a twenty-one-item modified version of the CISS (CISS-Situation Specific Coping) that asked subjects to answer coping items with respect to how they had responded to the stress situation. Moderate to high correlations were found between specific coping styles (assessed by the CISS) and congruent coping responses (e.g., task-oriented coping style correlated strongly with task-oriented responses).

A special version of the CISS (also with forty-eight items and using identical scoring as the adult version) has also been developed for use with adolescent populations (CISS-Adolescent; Endler & Parker, 1990a). The CISS-Adolescent was developed using a sample of 313 thirteen-to fifteen-year-olds and 504 sixteen- to eighteen-year-olds. The results for each sample were factor analyzed producing factor structures virtually identical (using congruence coefficients) to the adult and clinical samples (Endler & Parker, 1990a). The factor structures for the male and female adolescent samples, when analyzed separately, were also virtually identical.

Several other researchers have also developed interindividual coping scales for use with adolescent populations. Dise-Lewis (1988) developed the Life Events and Coping Inventory (LECI) for use with twelve- to fourteen-year-old children. The LECI is a forty-nine-item (nine-point frequency Likert scales) coping inventory that assesses five basic coping strategies: aggression (seven items), stress-recognition (thirteen items), distraction (eleven items), self-destruction (eight items), and endurance (nine items). The five coping scales were derived from a factor analysis of the coping responses of 502 seventh- and eighth-grade students, although the factor structure has not been cross-validated. Internal reliability coefficients for the LECI coping scales have been reported to range from a low of 0.62 to a high of 0.86; test-retest reliability correlations (eleven weeks) in a sample of eighty-five children "ranged from $-.13$ to .61, with a median of .32" (Dise-Lewis, 1988).

Patterson and McCubbin (1987) have also developed a self-report coping measure for use with adolescent populations—the Adolescent Coping Orientation for Problem Experiences scale (A-COPE). Using an original pool of ninety-five coping items (five-point frequency Likert scale), Patterson and McCubbin (1987) administered the scale to 467 junior and senior male and female high school students. A series of factor analyses produced a final set of fifty-four coping items with factor loadings greater than 0.40 on twelve factors. Twelve scales were created from items loading on the twelve factors (the number of items on the various coping scales ranged from two to eight items). Alpha reliabilities of the A-COPE scales range from a low of 0.50 to a high of 0.76 in the derivation sample. Not surprisingly, given the large number of factors on the scale, the factor structure of the A-COPE has been difficult to cross-validate. Hanson, Cigrang, Harris, Carle, Relyea, and Burghen (1989) found a high degree of intercorrelation among the twelve scales in a sample of 135 adolescents. A second-order factor analysis of the twelve A-COPE scales produced two factors: a utilizing personal and interpersonal resources factor, and a ventilation and avoidance factor.

Intraindividual Coping Measures

Two types of intraindividual coping measures can be found in the coping literature. The first type—*situation-specific measures*—consists of intraindividual measures that assess basic cop-

ing strategies or responses for responding to a *specific* stressful situation (e.g., pain symptoms). The items used with these measures assess coping activities congruent with the particular situation. The second type—*multiple-situation measures*—consists of intraindividual measures that assess a number of basic coping strategies or responses (e.g., problem-focused or emotion-focused strategies) for responding to a *variety* of stressful situations. The items used with these measures assess a broad range of potential coping activities so that the scales can be used with individuals experiencing an array of different stressful situations. Respondents are usually asked to identify a recent stressful event and to respond to the coping items with reference to this specific event. Both types of measures (multiple- and specific-situation scales) can be used on multiple occasions with the same respondents to study coping responses over the course of a specific stressful episode or similar stressful situations—a process approach to coping (Lazarus, 1993).

Situation-Specific Measures

McCubbin, McCubbin, Patterson, Lauble, Wilson, and Warwick (1983) have developed a scale that measures the coping behaviors of parents who have a child with cystic fibrosis (Coping Health Inventory for Parents). From a pool of forty-five coping items (four-point intensity Likert scales), McCubbin et al. (1983) factor analyzed the coping responses of 185 parents who had a child with cystic fibrosis. These results produced a measure with three subscales: maintaining family integration, maintaining social support, and understanding the medical situation. Internal reliabilities for the three subscales were adequate, ranging from 0.71 to 0.79. Like many studies that report on the development of a new coping scale, McCubbin et al. (1983) present no evidence to support the construct and criterion validity of the scales, and test-retest reliabilities were not reported.

Butler, Damarin, Beaulieu, Schwebel, and Thorn (1989) have developed the Cognitive Coping Strategy Inventory (CCSI) to assess the coping strategies used by pain patients. Rational procedures were used (raters examined the face validity of items) to create seven coping scales: imaginative inattention, imaginative transformation/context, imagination transformation/sensation, attention diversion/external, attention diversion/internal, somatization, and catastrophizing. Butler et al. (1989) used internal reliabilities to reduce the number of items on each scale to ten. The internal reliabilities for the seven coping scales were satisfactory, ranging from 0.75 to 0.90. A second-order factor analysis of the seven scales found six of the seven scales loading on one factor (all loadings were above 0.72), which suggests that the CCSI assesses an overall cognitive coping factor.

Feifel, Strack, and Nagy (1987) have developed a nineteen-item self-report measure (the Health Coping Modes Questionnaire; HCMQ) that can be used to assess the coping responses of patients with life-threatening illnesses (e.g., cancer, myocardial infarction). A thirty-two-item pool of questions (four-point frequency Likert scales) was administered to 223 men with both life-threatening and non-life-threatening health problems. Using factor analysis and item-total correlations, Feifel et al. (1987) empirically derived an eight-item confrontation scale, a seven-item avoidance scale, and a four-item acceptance-resignation subscale. Internal alpha coefficients ranged from 0.66 to 0.70, and Feifel et al. (1987) presented construct validity supporting the separate coping dimensions measured by the MCMQ. Before one can advocate additional research with the MCMQ, however, the factor structure should be replicated. In particular, it is also essential that the MCMQ be validated (and factor analyzed) with females, since gender differences have been commonly reported in the coping literature (see Endler & Parker, 1990a, 1990b).

Multiple-Situation Measures

One of the first intraindividual coping measures to be developed is also one of the only systematic attempts to develop an interviewer-rated measure for coping strategies. Pearlin and Schooler (1978), in an early attempt to categorize and assess basic coping strategies, inter-

viewed approximately 2,300 adults about their activities for coping with stressful situations. The interview data were factor analyzed and produced seventeen different coping dimensions. Pearlin and Schooler (1978) classified the seventeen factors as related to one of three basic strategies for consciously responding to a stressful situation: responses that sought to change the situation; responses that sought to change the meaning or the appraisal of the situation; and responses that sought to control distressful emotions. Although the seventeen-factor model developed by Pearlin and Schooler has never been replicated, it is interesting to note that the three general coping dimensions are closely related to coping dimensions identified in a variety of studies using self-report measures (for a review, see Parker & Endler, 1992).

The Ways of Coping Checklist (WCC; Folkman & Lazarus, 1980) and the Ways of Coping Questionnaire (WCQ; Folkman & Lazarus, 1988) continue to be the most widely used self-report coping measures (for reviews of these scales, see Ben-Porath, Waller, & Butcher, 1991; Parker, Endler, & Bagby, 1993; Stone et al., 1990; Tennen & Herzberger, 1985). Although previous researchers have used the WCC and WCQ to assess coping responses in a variety of stressful situations, future researchers need to be cautious about perpetuating a widespread problem in the coping literature. Many researchers who have used the WCC or WCQ have added or dropped coping items depending on the population or research question under study (see Chataway & Berry, 1989; Felton & Revenson, 1984; Long, 1990; MacCarthy & Brown, 1989; Martin, 1990; Parkes, 1986; Revenson & Felton, 1989; Scheier, Weintraub, & Carver, 1986). These "customized" coping measures have dubious validity and reliability, thus limiting the generalizations that can be drawn from this work.

The WCC (Folkman & Lazarus, 1980) is a sixty-eight-item self-report measure (yes/no format) that assesses two basic coping strategies: problem-focused coping (twenty-four items) and emotion-focused coping (forty items; four items on the WCC are not scored). Respondents are asked to respond to the coping items with respect to how they have reacted to a particular stressful situation. Scoring for the WCC was developed from a factor analysis of the coping items in a sample of 100 middle-aged adults (Aldwin, Folkman, Shaefer, Coyne, & Lazarus, 1980). Although the sample size was probably too small to derive a stable factor structure, Aldwin et al. (1980) found seven interpretable factors: one problem-focused factor and six emotion-focused coping factors.

Attempts to cross-validate the WCC's factor structure have met with mixed results (for a review, see Tennen & Herzberger, 1985). For example, in a study with 425 medical students, Vitaliano, Russo, Carr, Maiuro, and Becker (1985) factor analyzed the WCC and found six factors. From these six factors, five interpretable coping scales were created. Problem-focused, seeking social support, blamed-self, and wishful-thinking scales were created using a pattern of items different from scales with these names identified by Folkman and Lazarus (1980) and Aldwin et al. (1980). Vitaliano et al. (1985) also found moderate to high correlations between the coping scales whether they used the scoring for the original coping scales (Folkman & Lazarus, 1980) (intercorrelations ranged from 0.24 to 0.95) or the revised coping scales (intercorrelations ranged from 0.31 to 0.87).

Folkman and Lazarus (1985) subsequently modified the WCC by dropping some items and adding new ones. The response format was changed from a yes/no format to four-point Likert frequency scales and the revised sixty-six-item scale (now known as the Ways of Coping questionnaire; WCQ) was administered to 198 undergraduates on three separate occasions. A factor analysis of the 324 completed questionnaires was used to develop eight coping scales: problem-focused (eleven items), wishful thinking (five items), distancing (six items), emphasizing the positive (four items), self-blame (three items), tension reduction (three items), self-isolation (three items), and seeking social support (seven items). Moderate internal consistency reliabilities for the subscales were reported by Folkman and Lazarus (1985), ranging from a low of 0.56 to a high of 0.85.

Folkman, Lazarus, Dunkel-Schetter, De-Longis, and Gruen (1986) administered the WCQ to eighty-five married couples on five different occasions over six months and selected fifty items to be factor analyzed from the pool of coping responses. This analysis produced an eight-factor solution that was used to construct eight scales: confrontive coping (six items), distancing (six items), self-controlling (seven items), seeking social support (six items), accepting responsibility (four items), escape avoidance (eight items), planful problem solving (six items), and positive reappraisal (seven items). This scoring system for the measure was eventually adopted by Folkman and Lazarus (1988) in the test manual for the WCQ. The eight coping scales had moderate alpha coefficients in the derivation sample (ranging from 0.61 to 0.79); however, test-retest reliability data for the WCQ has not been reported in the literature (see the test manual for the WCQ, Folkman & Lazarus, 1988). In addition, some researchers have had problems replicating the WCQ factor structure (see Parker, Endler, & Bagby, 1993). The lack of a stable scoring system for the WCQ limits the utility of this scale for longitudinal (process) coping research.

Folkman and Lazarus (1985) have suggested that the issue of test-retest reliability is difficult to apply to the WCQ because it assesses *situation-specific* coping activity. Thus, research on the reliability of the WCQ has been restricted to questions about internal reliability. The problem of whether test-retest data can be collected for situation-specific scales is similar to one encountered by researchers developing self-report measures for state anxiety (see Endler, Edwards, & Vitelli, 1991). State anxiety is influenced by the particular situation in which it is assessed. However, some researchers developing state anxiety measures have been able to demonstrate adequate test-retest reliability by collecting state anxiety data in two similar situations. A similar procedure could be followed by those developing situation-specific coping measures.

Billings and Moos (1981) have developed a brief measure for assessing situation-specific coping responses. On the basis of face validity, Billings and Moos (1981) classified nineteen coping items (yes/no format) into three categories very similar to those coping dimensions identified by Pearlin and Schooler (1978): active-behavioral coping (six items), avoidance coping (five items), and active-cognitive coping (six items). The three rationally derived coping scales had internal consistency reliabilities in a sample of 338 normal adults that ranged from a low of 0.44 to a high of 0.80 in the derivation sample (Billings & Moos, 1981). A study by Friedman, Nelson, Baer, Lane, Smith, and Dworkin (1992) with 143 cancer patients, however, found unacceptably low internal reliabilities for the three coping scales (ranging from .16 to .60). Billings and Moos (1984) have extended their research on coping behaviors by studying males and females who were entering treatment for depression. The authors expanded their scale from nineteen to thirty-one items and used a four-point Likert frequency scale rather than a yes/no format. They focused on studying three basic coping strategies: appraisal-focused, problem-focused, and emotion-focused coping. Preliminary internal reliability data for these three scales have not been encouraging, ranging from 0.41 to 0.66.

Stone and Neale (1984) have also attempted to develop a self-report measure that aimed to assess a broad range of coping responses. Their goal was to develop a scale that could be used in longitudinal (process-oriented) coping research. After creating a list of items that covered a broad range of coping responses, Stone and Neale (1984) classified these items into a number of broad coping strategies. In two separate studies, using slightly different rationally constructed coping scales, they found that the alpha reliabilities were low to moderate, ranging from 0.47 to 0.79 in the first study and from 0.36 to 0.78 in the second study.

Amirkhan (1990) has recently developed the *Coping Strategy Indicator* (CSI), a factor analytically derived measure of basic coping strategies and responses (using many items from the WCQ). On the bases of several factor analytic studies the CSI assesses three basic coping strategies: problem solving, seeking social support, and avoidance. Unlike many of the coping scales reviewed in this chapter, the factor structure of the CSI was cross-validated on several

different samples, and test-retest data have been provided. Alpha coefficients in a small sample of adults (n = 92) indicated high internal reliability for the CSI scales (ranging from 0.84 to 0.93). Convergent and discriminant validity data have also been presented suggesting that the CSI is a multidimensional measure of basic coping responses.

Parker and Endler (1991), Endler and Parker (1992), and Endler, Parker, and Summerfeldt (1993b) have developed a self-report measure for assessing basic coping reactions to a variety of health problems: the *Coping with Health, Injuries, and Problems* scale (CHIP). The CHIP is a thirty-two-item self-report measure tapping four basic coping reactions: distraction (eight items), palliative (eight items), instrumental (eight items), and negative emotion (eight items). Respondents are asked to indicate (using five-point Likert scales) how much they engaged in a specific activity when encountering a specific health problem. The CHIP's factor structure was established using a large sample of male and female adults (n = 598) reacting to a heterogeneous set of health problems (Endler & Parker, 1992; Endler et al., 1993b). The factor structure has been cross-validated for both men and women using confirmatory factor analysis with subjects making retrospective reports about coping behavior as well as subjects reporting on coping activities with respect to a current health problem. Internal alpha coefficients for the CHIP scales for men and women separately ranged from 0.78 to 0.84 in the adult derivation sample.

Preliminary construct validity data for the CHIP found the scale to converge and diverge in a theoretically meaningful manner with a variety of coping style and psychological distress measures (Endler & Parker, 1992; Endler et al., 1993b). The criterion validity of the CHIP has also been investigated by comparing the coping behaviors of adults with chronic and acute physical health problems (Endler et al., 1993b). As expected, patients in the chronic illness group reported using more negative-emotion coping behavior than the patients in the acute illness group. This result is consistent with research that has found people with chronic physical health problems to be more susceptible to emotional problems related to depression, anger, and anxiety (for reviews, see Taylor, 1990, 1991).

Summary

Researchers interested in the study of coping responses and reactions have developed a variety of self-report coping instruments (interindividual and intraindividual). Potential users of coping measures, like those interested in the assessment of defense mechanisms, however, should note that there is great variation in the psychometric properties of these measures. Many of the coping scales reviewed in this chapter have poor internal reliabilities, low or nonexistent test-retest reliabilities, and sparse validity data.

CONCLUSION

This chapter examines various measures that have been developed for assessing how individuals respond or react to stressful, upsetting, or painful situations. Two major types of measures are reviewed: scales assessing defense mechanisms (unconscious processes), and scales assessing coping reactions (conscious processes). Defense mechanisms have typically been assessed following three methods: (1) observer-rated measures; (2) self-report questionnaires; and (3) projective techniques. This chapter discusses and evaluates defense measures related to the first two methods and indicates that many of these measures have psychometric problems (e.g., poor reliability and validity data).

Almost all of the coping measures that have been developed are self-report questionnaires. These measures can be divided into those that measure basic coping styles (interindividual measures) and those that assess coping responses in particular situations (intraindividual measures). There is considerable diversity in the psychometric qualities of the various interindividual and intraindividual measures that have been developed. Prospective users of coping

and defense measures need to be careful that they select instruments or scales that are both reliable and valid.

ACKNOWLEDGMENT

The writing of this chapter was partially supported by a research grant (No. 410–91–1150) from the Social Sciences and Humanities Research Council of Canada (SSHRC) to Norman S. Endler and by a SSHRC Post-Doctoral Fellowship to James D. A. Parker.

NOTE

1. Regarding the persistent interest in defense mechanisms by researchers and clinicians, it is interesting to note that the Diagnostic and Statistical Manual of Mental Disorders (DSM-III-R; American Psychiatric Association, 1987) contains a list of defense mechanisms in its glossary of technical terms. A number of individuals have recently proposed that a separate axis for defense mechanisms should be included in future revisions to the DSM (Giovacchini, 1981; Vaillant, 1984; Skodol & Perry, 1993).

REFERENCES

Ablon, S. L., Carlson, G. A., & Goodwin, F. K. (1974). Ego defense patterns in manic-depressive illness. *American Journal of Psychiatry, 131,* 803–807.

Aldwin, C., Folkman, S., Shaefer, C., Coyne, J., & Lazarus, R. (1980, September). *Ways of Coping Checklist: A process measure.* Paper presented at the American Psychological Association Annual Convention, Montreal.

Alker, H. A. (1968). Coping, defense and socially desirable responses. *Psychological Reports, 22,* 985–988.

Amirkhan, J. H. (1990). A factor analytically derived measure of coping: The Coping Strategy Indicator. *Journal of Personality and Social Psychology, 59,* 1066–1074.

Andrews, G., Pollock, C., & Stewart, G. (1989). The determination of defense style by questionnaire. *Archives of general psychiatry, 46,* 455–460.

Andrews, G., Singh, M., & Bond, M. (1993). The

defense style questionnaire. *Journal of Nervous and Mental Disease, 181*, 246–256.

Auerbach, S. M. (1989). Stress management and coping research in the health care setting: An overview and methodological commentary. *Journal of Consulting and Clinical Psychology, 57*, 388–395.

Averill, J. R., & Rosenn, M. (1972). Vigilant and nonvigilant coping strategies and psychophysical stress reactions during anticipation of electric shock. *Journal of Personality and Social Psychology, 23*, 128–141.

Barnett, P. A., & Gotlib, I. H. (1988). Psychosocial functioning and depression: Distinguishing among antecedents, concomitants, and consequences. *Psychological Bulletin, 104*, 97–126.

Beardslee, W., Jacobson, A., Hauser, S., Noam, G., & Powers, S. (1985). An approach to evaluating adolescent adaptive processes: Scale development and reliability. *Journal of American Child Psychiatry, 24*, 637–642.

Bell, P. A., & Byrne, D. (1978). Repression-sensitization. In H. London & J. E. Exner (Eds.), *Dimensions of personality* (pp. 449–485). New York: Wiley.

Ben-Porath, Y. S., Waller, N. G., & Butcher, J. W. (1991). Assessment of coping: An empirical illustration of the problem of inapplicable items. *Journal of Personality Assessment, 57*, 162–176.

Billings, A. G., & Moos, R. H. (1981). The role of coping responses and social resources in attenuating the impact of stressful live events. *Journal of Behavioral Medicine, 4*, 139–157.

Blacha, M. S., & Fancher, R. E. (1977). A content validity study of the Defense Mechanism Inventory. *Journal of Personality Assessment, 41*, 402–404.

Bond, M. (1986). An empirical study of defense styles. In G. E. Vaillant (Ed.), *Empirical studies of ego mechanisms of defense* (pp. 1–29). Washington, DC: American Psychiatric Press.

Bond, M., Gardiner, S. T., Christian, J., & Sigel, J. J. (1983). An empirical examination of defense mechanisms. *Archives of General Psychiatry, 40*, 333–338.

Bond, M., Perry, J. C., Gautier, M., Goldenberg, M., Oppenheimer, J., & Simand, J. (1989). Validating the self-report of defense styles. *Journal of Personality Disorders, 3*, 101–112.

Brennan, J., Andrews, G., Morris-Yates, A., & Pollock, C. (1990). An examination of defense style in parents who abuse children. *Journal of Nervous and Mental Disease, 178*, 592–595.

Brown, G. K., Nicassio, P. M., & Wallston, K. A. (1989). Pain coping strategies and depression in rheumatoid arthritis. *Journal of Consulting and Clinical Psychology, 57*, 652–657.

Butler, R. W., Damarin, F. L., Beaulieu, C., Schwebel, A. I., & Thorn, B. E. (1989). Assessing cognitive coping strategies for acute postsurgical pain. *Psychological Assessment, 1*, 41–45.

Byrne, D. (1961). The Repression-Sensitization Scale: Rationale, reliability, and validity. *Journal of Personality, 29*, 334–349.

Byrne, D., Barry, J., & Nelson, D. (1963). The revised repression-sensitization scale and its relationship to measures of self-description. *Psychological Reports, 13*, 323–334.

Carver, C. S., Scheier, M. F., & Weintraub, J. K. (1989). Assessing coping strategies: A theoretically based approach. *Journal of Personality and Social Psychology, 56*, 267–283.

Chataway, C. J., & Berry, J. W. (1989). Acculturation experiences, appraisal, coping, and adaptation: A comparison of Hong Kong Chinese, French, and English students in Canada. *Canadian Journal of Behavioural Science, 21*, 295–309.

Clark, A. A., & Hovanitz, C. A. (1989). Dimensions of coping that contribute to psychopathology. *Journal of Clinical Psychology, 45*, 28–36.

Cohen, F. (1987). Measurement of coping. In S. V. Kasl & C. L. Cooper (Eds.), *Stress and health: Issues in research methodology* (pp. 283–305). Chichester, England: Wiley.

Cohen, F., & Lazarus, R. S. (1973). Active coping processes, coping dispositions, and recovery from surgery. *Psychosomatic Medicine, 35*, 375–389.

Coyne, J. C., Aldwin, C., & Lazarus, R. S. (1981). Depression and coping in stressful episodes. *Journal of Abnormal Psychology, 90*, 439–447.

Cox, T., & Ferguson, E. (1991). Individual differences, stress and coping. In C. L. Cooper & R. Payne (Eds.), *Personality and stress: Individual differences in the stress process* (pp. 7–30). Chichester, England: Wiley.

Cramer, P. (1988). The Defense Mechanism Inventory: A Review of research and discussion of the scales. *Journal of Personality Assessment, 52*, 142–164.

Cramer, P. (1990). *The development of defense mechanisms: Theory, research, and assessment*. New York: Springer-Verlag.

Crowne, D. P., & Marlowe, D. A. (1960). A new scale of social desirability independent of psychopathology. *Journal of Consulting Psychology, 24*, 349–354.

Davis, P. J. (1990). Repression and the inaccessibility

of emotional memories. In J. L. Singer (Ed.), *Repression and dissociation: Implications for personality theory, psychopathology, and health* (pp. 387–403). Chicago: University of Chicago Press.

Dise-Lewis, J. E. (1988). The Life Events and Coping Inventory: An assessment of stress in children. *Psychosomatic Medicine, 50,* 484–499.

Endler, N. S. (1983). Interactionism: A personality model, but not yet a theory. In M. M. Page (Ed.), *Nebraska Symposium on Motivation, 1982: Personality—Current theory and research* (pp. 155–200). Lincoln: University of Nebraska Press.

Endler, N. S. (1988). Hassles, health and happiness. In M. P. Janisse (Ed.), *Individual differences, stress and health psychology* (pp. 24–56). New York: Springer.

Endler, N. S., Edwards, J. M., & Vitelli, R. (1991). *Endler Multidimensional Anxiety Scales (EMAS): Manual.* Los Angeles: Western Psychological Services.

Endler, N. S., & Parker, J. D. A. (1989). Coping with frustrations to self-realization: Stress, anxiety, crises and adjustment. In E. Krau (Ed.), *Self-realization, success and adjustment* (pp. 153–164). New York: Praeger.

Endler, N. S., & Parker, J. D. A. (1990a). *Coping Inventory for Stressful Situations (CISS): Manual.* Toronto: Multi-Health Systems.

Endler, N. S., & Parker, J. D. A. (1990b). Multidimensional assessment of coping: A critical evaluation. *Journal of Personality and Social Psychology, 58,* 844–854.

Endler, N. S., & Parker, J. D. A. (1990c). State and trait anxiety, depression and coping styles. *Australian Journal of Psychology, 42,* 207–220.

Endler, N. S., & Parker, J. D. A. (1992, June). *Toward a reliable and valid method for multidimensional assessment of coping with health problems.* Paper presented at the annual meeting of the Canadian Psychological Association, Quebec City, Quebec.

Endler, N. S., & Parker, J. D. A. (1993). The multidimensional assessment of coping: Concepts, issues and measurement. In G. L. VanHeck, P. Bonaiuto, I. Deary, & W. Nowack (Eds.), *Personality psychology in Europe* (pp. 309–319). Tilburg, the Netherlands: Tilburg University Press.

Endler, N. S., & Parker, J. D. A. (1994). Assessment of multidimensional coping: Task, emotion, and avoidance strategies. *Psychological Assessment, 6,* 50–60.

Endler, N. S., Parker, J. D. A., & Butcher, J. N. (1993). A factor analytic study of coping styles and the MMPI-2 content scales. *Journal of Clinical Psychology, 49,* 523–527.

Endler, N. S., Parker, J. D. A., & Summerfeldt, L. J. (1993a). Coping with health problems: Conceptual and methodological issues. *Canadian Journal Behavioural Science, 25,* 384–399.

Endler, N. S., Parker, J. D. A., & Summerfeldt, L. J. (1993b). *Coping with health problems: Developing a reliable and valid multidimensional measure.* Manuscript submitted for publication.

Epstein, S., & Meier, P. (1989). Constructive thinking: A broad coping variable with specific components. *Journal of Personality and Social Psychology, 57,* 332–350.

Erdelyi, M. H. (1990). Repression, reconstruction, and defense: History and integration of the psychoanalytic and experimental frameworks. In J. L. Singer (Ed.), *Repression and dissociation: Implications for personality theory, psychopathology, and health* (pp. 1–31). Chicago: University of Chicago Press.

Feifel, H., & Strack, S. (1989). Coping with conflict situations: Middle-aged and elderly men. *Psychology and Aging, 4,* 26–33.

Feifel, H., Strack, S., & Nagy, V. T. (1987). Degree of life-threat and differential use of coping modes. *Journal of Psychosomatic Research, 31,* 91–99.

Felton, B. J., & Revenson, T. A. (1984). Coping with chronic illness: A study of illness controllability and the influence of coping strategies on psychological adjustment. *Journal of Consulting and Clinical Psychology, 52,* 343–353.

Fenichel, O. (1945). *The psychoanalytic theory of neurosis.* New York: Norton.

Fleischman, J. A. (1984). Personality characteristics and coping patterns. *Journal of Health and Social Behavior, 25,* 229–244.

Folkman, S. (1984). Personal control and stress and coping processes: A theoretical analysis. *Journal of Personality and Social Psychology, 46,* 839–852.

Folkman, S., & Lazarus, R. S. (1980). An analysis of coping in a middle-aged community sample. *Journal of Health and Social Behavior, 21,* 219–239.

Folkman, S., & Lazarus, R. S. (1985). If it changes it must be a process: A study of emotion and coping during three stages of a college examination. *Journal of Personality and Social Psychology, 48,* 150–170.

Folkman, S., & Lazarus, R. S. (1986). Stress processes and depressive symptomatology. *Journal of Abnormal Psychology, 95,* 107–113.

Folkman, S., & Lazarus, R. S. (1988). *Manual for the*

Ways of Coping Questionnaire. Palo Alto, CA: Consulting Psychologists Press.

Folkman, S., Lazarus, R. S., Dunkel-Schetter, C., DeLongis, A., & Gruen, R. (1986). The dynamics of a stressful encounter. *Journal of Personality and Social Psychology, 50,* 992–1003.

Frank, S. J., McLaughlin, A. M., & Crusco, A. (1984). Sex role attributes, symptom distress, and defensive style. *Journal of Personality and Social Psychology, 47,* 182–192.

Freud, A. (1946). *The ego and the mechanisms of defense.* New York: International Universities Press. (Originally published 1936)

Freud, S. (1959). *Inhibitions, symptoms, and anxiety. Standard edition* (Vol. XX, pp. 87–172). London: Hogarth Press. (Originally published 1926)

Friedman, A. G., & Mulhern, R. K. (1991). Coping resources inventory. In D. J. Keyser & R. C. Sweetland (Eds.), *Test critiques* (Vol. 8, pp. 111–114). Austin, TX: Pro-Ed.

Friedman, L. C., Nelson, D. V., Baer, P. E., Lane, M., Smith, F. E., & Dworkin, R. J. (1992). The relationship of dispositional optimism, daily life stress, and domestic environment to coping methods used by cancer patients. *Journal of Behavioral Medicine, 15,* 127–141.

Giovacchini, P. L. (1981). The axes of DSM-III. *American Journal of Psychiatry, 138,* 119–120.

Gleser, G. C., & Ihilevich, D. (1969). An objective instrument for measuring defense mechanisms. *Journal of Consulting and Clinical Psychology, 33,* 51–60.

Gleser, G. C., & Sacks, M. (1973). Ego defenses and reaction to stress: A validation study of the Defense Mechanisms Inventory. *Journal of Consulting and Clinical Psychology, 40,* 181–187.

Gough, H. G. (1957). *Manual for the California Personality Inventory.* Palo Alto, CA: Consulting Psychologists Press.

Haan, N. (1963). Proposed model of ego functioning: Coping and defense mechanisms in relationship to IQ change. *Psychological Monograph, 77* (No. 8), 1–27.

Haan, N. (1965). Coping and defense mechanisms related to personality inventories. *Journal of Consulting Psychology, 29,* 373–378.

Haan, N. (1969). A tripartite model of ego functioning: Values and clinical and research applications. *Journal of Nervous and Mental Disease, 148,* 14–30.

Haan, N. (1977). *Coping and defending: Processes of self-environment organization.* New York: Academic Press.

Haan, N. (1982). Assessment of coping, defense, and stress. In L. Goldberger & S. Breznitz (Eds.), *Handbook of stress: Theoretical and clinical aspects* (pp. 254–269). New York: Free Press.

Hammer, A. L., & Marting, M. S. (1988). *Manual for the Coping Resources Inventory.* Palo Alto, CA: Consulting Psychologists Press.

Hanson, C. L., Cigrang, J. A., Harris, M. A., Carle, D. L., Relyea, G., & Burghen, G. A. (1989). Coping styles in youths with insulin-dependent diabetes mellitus. *Journal of Consulting and Clinical Psychology, 57,* 644–651.

Holmes, D. S. (1990). The evidence for repression: An examination of sixty years of research. In J. L. Singer (Ed.), *Repression and dissociation: Implications for personality theory, psychopathology, and health* (pp. 85–102). Chicago: University of Chicago Press.

Holt, R. R. (1956). Gauging primary and secondary processes in Rorschach responses. *Journal of Projective Techniques, 5,* 14–25.

Hunter, C. G., & Goodstein, L. D. (1967). Ego strength and types of defensive and coping behavior. *Journal of Consulting Psychology, 31,* 432.

Ihilevich, D., & Gleser, G. C. (1986). *Defense mechanisms. Their classification, correlates, and measurement with the Defense Mechanism Inventory.* Owosso, MI: DMI Associates.

Jacobson, A. M., Beardslee, W., Hauser, S. T., Noam, G. G., & Powers, S. I. (1986). In G. E. Vaillant (Ed.), *Empirical studies of the ego mechanisms of defense* (pp. 47–59). Washington, DC: American Psychiatric Press.

Jacobson, A. M., Beardslee, W., Hauser, S. T., Noam, G. G., Powers, S. I., Houlihan, J., & Rider, E. (1986). Evaluating ego defense mechanisms using clinical interviews: An empirical study of adolescent diabetic and psychiatric patients. *Journal of Adolescence, 9,* 303–319.

Joffe, P. E., & Naditch, M. (1977). Paper and pencil measures of coping and defense processes. In N. Haan (Ed.), *Coping and defending: Processes of self environment organization* (pp. 280–297). New York: Academic Press.

Juni, S., & Masling, J. (1980). Reaction to aggression and the Defense Mechanism Inventory. *Journal of Personality Assessment, 44,* 484–486.

Kline, P. (1991). The relationship between objective measures of defences. In M. Olff, G. Godaert, & H. Ursin (Eds.), *Quantification of human defence mechanisms* (pp. 22–40). New York: Springer-Verlag.

Kroeber, T. C. (1963). The coping functions of the

ego mechanisms. In R. W. White (Ed.), *The study of lives: Essays on personality in honor of Henry A. Murray* (pp. 178–189). New York: Atherton Press.

Krohne, H. W. (1988). Coping research: Current theoretical and methodological developments. *German Journal of Psychology, 12,* 1–30.

LaVoie, A. L. (1987). Defense mechanisms Inventory. In D. Keyser & R. C. Sweetland (Eds.), *Test critiques* (Vol. 6, pp. 115–119). Kansas City, MI: Test Corporation of America.

Lazarus, R. S. (1993). Coping theory and research: Past, present, and future. *Psychosomatic Medicine, 55,* 234–247.

Lazarus, R. S., Averill, J. R., & Opton, E. M. (1974). The psychology of coping: Issues of research and assessment. In G. V. Coelho, D. A. Hamburg, & J. E. Adams (Eds.), *Coping and adaptation* (pp. 47–68). New York: Basic Books.

Lazarus, R. S., & Folkman, S. (1984). *Stress, appraisal, and coping.* New York: Springer.

Lazarus, R. S., & Folkman, S. (1987). Transactional theory and research on emotions and coping. *European Journal of Personality, 1,* 141–169.

Lazarus, R. S., & Launier, R. (1978). Stress-related transactions between person and environment. In L. A. Pervin & M. Lewis (Eds.), *Perspectives in interactional psychology* (pp. 287–327). New York: Plenum.

Lerner, P. M. (1990). Rorschach assessment of primitive defenses: A review. *Journal of Personality Assessment, 54,* 30–46.

Little, K. B., & Fisher, J. (1958). Two new experimental scales of the MMPI. *Journal of Consulting Psychology, 22,* 305–306.

Loevinger, J. (1976). *Ego development.* San Francisco: Jossey-Bass.

Long, B. C. (1990). Relation between coping strategies, sex-type traits, and environmental characteristics: A comparison of male and female managers. *Journal of Counselling Psychology, 37,* 185–194.

MacCarthy, B., & Brown, R. (1989). Psychosocial factors in Parkinson's disease. *British Journal of Clinical Psychology, 28,* 41–52.

Margolis, C. G. (1970). Coping and defensive responses in four role-playing situations. *Journal of Consulting and Clinical Psychology, 35,* 427.

Martin, P. (1990). Personality and coping in survivors of a myocardial infarction. *Journal of Social Behavior and Personality, 4,* 587–601.

McCubbin, H. I., McCubbin, M. A., Patterson, J. M., Lauble, A. E., Wilson, L. R., & Warwick, W. (1983). CHIP—Coping Health Inventory for Par-

ents: An assessment of parental coping patterns in the care of the chronically ill child. *Journal of Marriage and the Family, 45,* 359–370.

Miller, S. M. (1980). When is a little information a dangerous thing? Coping with stressful life-events by monitoring vs. blunting. In S. Levine & H. Ursin (Eds.), *Coping and health* (pp. 145–169). New York: Plenum Press.

Miller, S. M. (1987). Monitoring and blunting: Validation of a questionnaire to assess styles of information seeking under threat. *Journal of Personality and Social Psychology, 52,* 345–353.

Miller, S. M., Brody, D. S., & Summerton, S. (1988). Styles of coping with threat: Implications for health. *Journal of Personality and Social Psychology, 54,* 142–148.

Miller, S. M., & Mangan, C. E. (1983). Interacting effects of information and coping style in adapting to gynaecologic stress: Should the doctor tell all? *Journal of Personality and Social Psychology, 45,* 223–236.

Morrissey, R. F. (1977). The Haan model of ego functioning: An assessment of empirical research. In N. Haan (Ed.), *Coping and defending: Processes of self-environment organization* (pp. 250–279). New York: Academic Press.

Nowack, K. M. (1989). Coping style, cognitive hardiness, and health status. *Journal of Behavioral Medicine, 12,* 145–158.

Parker, J. D. A., & Endler, N. S. (1991, June). *Interaction of coping with health problems, personality, and psychological and physical distress.* Paper presented at the annual meeting of the Canadian Psychological Association, Calgary, Alberta, Canada.

Parker, J. D. A., & Endler, N. S. (1992). Coping with coping assessment: A critical review. *European Journal of Psychology, 6,* 321–344.

Parker, J. D. A., Endler, N. S., & Bagby, R. M. (1993). If it changes, it might be unstable: Examining the factor structure of the Ways of Coping Questionnaire. *Psychological Assessment, 5,* 361–368.

Parkes, K. R. (1986). Coping in stressful episodes: The role of individual differences, environmental factors, and situational characteristics. *Journal of Personality and Social Psychology, 51,* 1277–1292.

Patterson, J. M., & McCubbin, H. I. (1987). Adolescent coping style and behaviors: Conceptualization and measurement. *Journal of Adolescence, 10,* 163–186.

Pearlin, L. I., & Schooler, C. (1978). The structure of coping. *Journal of Health and Social Behavior, 19,* 2–21.

Perry, J. C., & Cooper, S. H. (1989a). An empirical study of defense mechanisms. I. Clinical interview and life vignette ratings. *Archives of General Psychiatry, 46*, 444–452.

Perry, J. C., & Cooper, S. H. (1989b). What do cross-sectional measures of defense mechanisms predict. In G. E. Vaillant (Ed.), *Empirical studies of ego mechanisms of defense* (pp. 47–59). Washington, DC: American Psychiatric Press.

Plutchik, R. (1989). Measuring emotions and their derivatives. In R. Plutchik & H. Kellerman (Eds.), *Emotion. Theory, research, and experience* (Vol. 4, pp. 1–35). New York: Academic Press.

Plutchik, R., & Conte, H. R. (1989). Measuring emotions and their derivatives: Personality traits, ego defenses, and coping styles. In S. Wetzler & M. M. Katz (Eds.), *Contemporary approaches to psychological measurement* (pp. 239–269). New York: Brunner/Mazel.

Plutchik, R., Kellerman, H., & Conte, H. R. (1979). A structural theory of ego defenses and emotions. In C. E. Izard (Ed.), *Emotions in personality and psychopathology* (pp. 229–257). New York: Plenum Press.

Pollock, C., & Andrews, G. (1989). Defense styles associated with specific anxiety disorders. *American Journal of Psychiatry, 146*, 1500–1502.

Revenson, T. A., & Felton, B. J. (1989). Disability and coping as predictors of psychological adjustment to rheumatoid arthritis. *Journal of Consulting and Clinical Psychology, 57*, 344–348.

Sarason, I. G. (1958). Interrelationships among individual difference variables, behavior in psychotherapy, and verbal conditioning. *Journal of Abnormal and Social Psychology, 56*, 339–344.

Schafer, R. (1954). *Psychoanalytic interpretation in Rorschach testing.* New York: Grune and Stratton.

Scheier, M. F., Weintraub, J. K., & Carver, C. S. (1986). Coping with stress: Divergent strategies of optimists and pessimists. *Journal of Personality and Social Psychology, 51*, 1257–1264.

Schwartz, G. E. (1990). Psychobiology of repression and health: A systems approach. In J. L. Singer (Ed.), *Repression and dissociation: Implications for personality theory, psychopathology, and health* (pp. 405–434). Chicago: University of Chicago Press.

Semrad, E., Grinspoon, L., Fienberg, S. E. (1973). Development of an Ego Profile Scale. *Archives of General Psychiatry, 28*, 70–77.

Sidle, A., Moos, R. H., Adams, J., & Cady, P. (1969). Development of a coping scale. *Archives of General Psychiatry, 20*, 225–232.

Singer, J. L. (1990). Preface: A fresh look at repression, dissociation, and the defenses as mechanisms and as personality styles. In J. L. Singer (Eds.), *Repression and dissociation: Implications for personality theory, psychopathology, and health* (pp. xi–xxi). Chicago: University of Chicago Press.

Sjöbäck, H. (1991). Defence, defence, and defence: How do we measure defence. In M Olff, G. Godaert, & H. Ursin (Eds.), *Quantification of human defence mechanisms* (pp. 4–21). New York: Springer-Verlag.

Skodol, A. E., & Perry, J. C. (1993). Should an axis for the defense mechanisms be included in DSM-IV? *Comprehensive Psychiatry, 34*, 108–119.

Slough, N., Kleinknecht, R. A., & Thorndike, R. M. (1984). Relationship of the Repression-Sensitization scales to anxiety. *Journal of Personality Assessment, 48*, 378–379.

Snarey, J. R., & Vaillant, G. E. (1985). How lower and working-class youth become middle-class adults: The association between ego defense mechanism and upward mobility. *Child Development, 56*, 889–910.

Stone, A. A., Greenberg, M. A., Kennedy-Moore, E., & Newman, M. G. (1991). Self-report, situation-specific coping questionnaires: What are they measuring? *Journal of Personality and Social Psychology, 61*, 648–658.

Stone, A. A., & Kennedy-Moore, E. (1992). Assessing situational coping: Conceptual and methodological considerations. In H. S. Friedman (Ed.), *Hostility, coping and health* (pp. 203–214). Washington, DC: American Psychological Association.

Stone, A. A., & Neale, J. M. (1984). New measure of daily coping: Development and preliminary results. *Journal of Personality and Social Psychology, 46*, 892–906.

Suls, J., & Fletcher, B. (1985). The relative efficacy of avoidant and nonavoidant coping strategies: A meta-analysis. *Health Psychology, 4*, 249–288.

Taylor, S. E. (1990). Health psychology: The science and the field. *American Psychology, 45*, 40–50.

Taylor, S. E. (1991). *Health psychology* (2nd ed). New York: Random House.

Tennen, H., & Herzberger, S. (1985). Ways of Coping scale. In D. J. Keyser & R. C. Sweetland (Eds.), *Test critiques* (Vol. 3, pp. 686–697). Kansas City, MO: Test Corporation of America.

Thomae, H. (1987). Conceptualizations of responses to stress. *European Journal of Personality, 1*, 171–192.

Vaillant, G. E. (1971). Theoretical hierarchy of adaptive ego mechanisms. *Archives of General Psychiatry, 24,* 107–118.

Vaillant, G. E. (1974). Natural history of male psychological health. II. Some antecedents of healthy adult adjustment. *Archives of General Psychiatry, 31,* 15–22.

Vaillant, G. E. (1975). Natural history of male psychological health. III. Empirical dimensions of mental health. *Archives of General Psychiatry, 32,* 420–426.

Vaillant, G. E. (1976). Natural history of male psychological health. V. The relation of choice of ego mechanisms of defense to adult adjustment. *Archives of General Psychiatry, 33,* 535–545.

Vaillant, G. E. (1977). *Adaptation to life.* Boston: Little, Brown.

Vaillant, G. E. (1984). The disadvantages of DSM-III outweigh its advantages. *American Journal of Psychiatry, 141,* 542–545.

Vaillant, G. E. (1986). *Empirical studies of ego mechanisms of defense.* Washington, DC: American Psychiatric Press.

Vaillant, G. E., Bond, M., & Vaillant, C. O. (1986). An empirically validated hierarchy of defense mechanisms. *Archives of General Psychiatry, 43,* 786–794.

Vaillant, G. E., & Drake, R. E. (1985). Maturity of ego defenses in relation to DSM-III Axis II personality disorder. *Archives of General Psychiatry, 42,* 597–601.

Van der Leeuw, P. J. (1971). On the development of the concept of defense. *International Journal of Psychoanalysis, 52,* 51–58.

Visotsky, H. M., Hamburg, D. A., Goss, M. E., & Lebovits, B. Z. (1961). Coping behavior under extreme stress: Observations of patients with severe poliomyelitis. *Archives of General Psychiatry, 5,* 423–448.

Vitaliano, P. P., Russo, J., Carr, J. E., Maiuro, R. D., & Becker, J. (1985). The Ways of Coping Checklist: Revision and psychometric properties. *Multivariate Behavioral Research, 20,* 3–26.

Waller, N. G. (1989). The effect of inapplicable item responses on the structure of behavioral checklist data: A cautionary note. *Multivariate Behavioral Research, 24,* 125–134.

Weinberger, D. A. (1990). The construct validity of the repressive coping style. In J. L. Singer (Ed.), *Repression and dissociation: Implications for personality theory, psychopathology, and health* (pp. 337–386). Chicago: University of Chicago Press.

Weinberger, D. A., Schwartz, G. E., & Davidson, R. J. (1979). Low-anxious, high-anxious, and repressive coping styles: Psychometric patterns and behavioral and physiological responses to stress. *Journal of Abnormal Psychology, 88,* 369–380.

Weinstock, A. R. (1967). Family environment and the development of defense and coping mechanisms. *Journal of Personality and Social Psychology, 5,* 67–75.

Weintraub, W., & Aronson, H. (1962). The application of verbal behavior analysis to the study of psychological defense mechanisms: Methodology and preliminary report. *Journal of Nervous and Mental Disease, 134,* 169–181.

Welsh, G. S. (1956). Factor dimensions A and R. In G. S. Welsh & W. G. Dahlstrom (Eds.), *Basic readings on the MMPI in psychology and medicine* (pp. 264–281). Minneapolis: University of Minnesota Press.

White, R. W. (1948). *The abnormal personality: A textbook.* New York: Ronald Press.

White, R. W. (1974). Strategies of adaptation: An attempt at systematic description. In G. V. Coelho, D. A. Hamburg, & J. E. Adams (Eds.), *Coping and adaptation* (pp. 47–68). New York: Basic Books.

24

Assessing the Severely Anxious Patient

Michele M. Carter
David H. Barlow

During the past two decades anxiety has been one of the most extensively investigated emotional states. From empirical investigations it is becoming increasingly clear that there is often considerable overlap in the clinical presentation of the various disorders. Indeed, it is generally held that anxiety, in various forms, is present and plays an important role in all of the emotional disorders (Hersov, 1985; Barlow, 1988). Considerable evidence exists that anxiety is present, for example, in clinical depression (Barlow, DiNardo, Vermilyea, Vermilyea, & Blanchard, 1986; Katon & Roy-Byrne, 1991; Clayton, 1990; Boyd, Burke, Gruenberg, Holzer, Rae, McEvoy, & Nestadt, 1984), schizophrenia (O'Connor, 1991; Winokur, 1988), and bipolar disorder (Winokur, 1988). Additionally, various levels of anxiety are present in several of the more severe personality disorders (Beck & Freeman, 1990; Benjamin, Silk, Lohr, & Westen, 1989; Snyder & Pitts, 1988; Kernberg, 1975).

In this chapter we will first present our conceptualization of anxiety as an emotional state. We will then discuss some of the psychometrically sound instruments, both self-report and clinician-administered, for measuring clinical levels of anxiety. That is, we will focus on instruments that have shown adequate reliability (via test-retest administration) and validity (both convergent and divergent), as well as several that have demonstrated some degree of specificity. Throughout we will attend to the specific problems inherent in the assessment of anxiety and discuss the necessity of a multitrait, multimethod approach.

WHAT IS ANXIETY?

As an emotional state, anxiety is perhaps the most universally experienced emotion. Anxiety is present in most living organisms and seems to serve an adaptive function at moderate levels of severity (Barlow, 1988). Until recently, despite the common occurrence of anxiety, researchers could not agree on a definition. Previous definitions viewed both anxiety and fear as uncontrolled expressions of emotions. More recently, fear and anxiety have been considered by most to be related emotions but with important divergent properties.

Fear is a primitive alarm triggered by present danger and is characterized by intense negative affect and arousal (Barlow, 1988; Beck & Emery, 1985). Anxiety, on the other hand, is oriented toward potential future threats and has been defined as a diffuse blend of intense emotional reactions that reflect anger, interest, excitement, and a primary component of fear (Barlow, 1988). A more accurate term for anxiety, then, might be "anxious apprehension." This term may better reflect the diffuse, subjectively distressing, future-oriented emotional state that sets the stage for a fear or alarm response (Barlow, 1988).

Anxiety is made up of three primary components: cognitive (e.g., "The next time I have an attack I will die," "If I speak in front of others I will make a complete fool of myself"), behavioral (e.g., avoidance of feared events or situations), and physiological (e.g., palpitations, sweating, trembling). These components are present to differing degrees in the anxious patient (Barlow, 1988) and are also reflected in several of the measures of anxiety presented in this chapter.

Since anxiety is a universal emotion, when does it become pathological? In our view anxiety becomes dysfunctional when it is self-defeating, overly intense, paralyzing, or occurs at inappropriate times (Barlow, 1988; Ingram & Kendall, 1987). In other words, when it produces sufficient distress and/or interferes with social or occupational functioning.

PREVALENCE OF ANXIETY

As distinct diagnostic categories, anxiety disorders are quite prevalent (Schatzberg, 1991). It has been estimated that more than 14 percent of adults in the United States will be affected by an anxiety disorder in their lifetime (Regier, Narrow, & Rae, 1990). The most common anxiety disorders are phobic disorders, with a lifetime prevalence rate of 12.5 percent, followed by obsessive-compulsive disorder and panic disorder, with lifetime prevalence rates of 2.5 percent and 1.6 percent, respectively (Regier, Narrow, & Rae, 1990). The pervasive nature of anxious symptomatology indicates that any thorough psychological assessment will necessarily incorporate at least a minimal exploration for various levels and types of anxiety.

ASSESSMENT OF ANXIETY

As is true with other psychopathological states, anxiety can be assessed from a variety of methods including self-report measures, clinical interviews, and psychophysiological techniques. Although psychophysiological assessment can provide valuable additional information, these procedures have been reviewed in detail elsewhere (see Turpin, 1991, for a review). Furthermore, psychophysiological measurement has generally been used as an outcome variable in numerous clinical trails but has yet to undergo the types of comparative investigations necessary to establish diagnostic or syndromal parameters for the various anxiety disorders. The focus of this chapter will therefore be on the former two categories of assessment. We will begin with descriptions of several self-report measures of anxiety, as they provide quick and useful information regarding anxious symptomatology. The measures described below are not intended to be an exhaustive list of self-report measures designed for the specific anxiety disorders. Additional questionnaires with acceptable psychometrics exist. Those presented below are a sampling of the more widely used and accepted self-report instruments used to measure anxiety.

SELF-REPORT SYMPTOM AND SYNDROMAL MEASURES OF ANXIETY

In its most basic form anxiety can be assessed at the level of the individual symptom, for example "heart palpitations" or "nervousness." Anxiety can also be assessed at the level of the syndrome, defined as a collection of symptoms or signs that co-occur with greater than chance frequency.

At the symptom level various affective checklists (Zuckerman & Lubin, 1965; Derogatis, Lipman, & Covi, 1973) are typically the instruments of choice. These measures generally consist of a list of items designed to assess the symptomatic behavior of psychiatric outpatients. The Symptom Distress Checklist (SCL-90), for example, consists of ninety items rated from zero (not at all) to four (extremely) and reflects nine primary symptom dimensions (Derogatis, Lipman, & Covi, 1973). The advantage of these measures is that they provide a comparatively quick assessment of anxious symptoms and can be used for measuring fluctuations in anxious symptoms over relatively short periods of time. The disadvantage of these instruments is that they often do not provide a method for measuring the frequency or severity of anxiety but only the presence or absence of anxious symptoms.

At the syndromal level, there are principally two psychometrically sound devices available: the Beck Anxiety Inventory and the State-Trait Anxiety Inventory, Form Y.

Beck Anxiety Inventory (BAI). The BAI is a twenty-one item self-report scale that measures the severity of anxiety in psychiatric populations (Beck & Steer, 1990; Beck, Epstein, Brown, & Steer, 1988). The items are primarily physiological and resemble DSM-III-R criteria for panic disorder. Each item is rated from zero (not at all) to three (severely) for how much the patient has been bothered by each over the past week. This inventory is relatively brief, taking about ten minutes to administer.

Fydrich, Dowdall, & Chambless (1992) conducted two studies to assess the psychometric properties of the BAI. In the first study they administered the BAI to a sample of forty anxious patients twice, once before the initial evaluation and once before the first treatment session (approximately eleven days). They reported that the BAI was highly internally consistent (alpha = .94) and evidenced a test-retest reliability of .67 (Fydrich, Dowdall, & Chambless, 1992).

In the second study Fydrich and colleagues (1992) conducted a multitrait-multimethod analysis to examine the convergent and divergent validity of the BAI. Their results indicated that the BAI is significantly correlated with other established measures of anxiety. They also reported that the BAI is significantly correlated with measures of depression but that the correlation between the BAI and measures of anxiety is significantly higher than the correlation between the BAI and measures of depression, thus suggesting discriminant validity (Fydrich, Dowdall, & Chambless, 1992).

State-Trait Anxiety Inventory, form Y (STAI-Y). The STAI-Y is a revised version of the earlier A-form (Spielberger, Gorsuch, & Lushene, 1970) and, like the original, consists of separate self-report scales for measuring state and trait anxiety (Spielberger, 1983). These measures are brief (approximately ten minutes each to complete), and are extensively used in both clinical and research settings. The state form (STAI-Y S-anxiety) consists of twenty items regarding feelings of apprehension, tension, nervousness, and worry. Each statement is rated from one (not at all) to four (very much so) for how the patient feels "at the moment" the questionnaire is completed. The trait form of this scale (STAI-Y T-anxiety) consists of twenty statements designed to assess how anxious one "generally" feels (Spielberger, 1983). The items are rated in a similar fashion to the state version, with scores ranging from one (almost never) to four (almost always). Scores for each scale can range from a minimum of twenty to a maximum of eighty.

Spielberger (1983) reported a mean alpha coefficient for both the state and trait version of the revised STAI to be greater than .90. The thirty-day test-retest reliability for the trait scale was .73. Spielberger (1983) also reported a median correlation between the state and trait version to be .65. As is the case with the BAI, the STAI-Y is also highly correlated with measures of depression (Fydrich et al., 1992). It should be noted that these analyses were performed with large samples of high school and college students and await similar analyses with clinical populations. Both the STAI and the BAI can be administered repeatedly to assess any changes in the severity of anxious symptomatology over a short period of time.

DISORDER-SPECIFIC SELF-REPORT MEASURES

While the above measures provide a quick assessment of the severity of the anxiety syndrome, neither has demonstrated an ability to discriminate between the various anxiety disorders. Several self-report measures have been designed to assess key features related to a particular anxiety disorder. Among such instruments are the Pen State Worry Questionnaire, the Social Interaction Anxiety Scale, the Maudsley Obsessional Compulsive Inventory, and the PTSD Symptom Scale.

Penn State Worry Questionnaire (PSWQ). The PSWQ is a sixteen-item questionnaire designed to measure the trait of worry, a central feature in generalized anxiety disorder (Meyer, Miller, Metzger, & Borkovec, 1990). Each statement is rated from one (not at all typical of me) to five (very typical of me) and takes approximately ten minutes to complete. Possible scores range from sixteen to eighty, with a mean of forty-eight for nonanxious subjects. In examining the psychometric properties of the PSWQ, Meyer and colleagues (1990) administered the device to large samples of college students and reported alpha coefficients of .93, indicating high internal consistency. Their results also indicated a high test-retest reliability (r = .92) over an eight-week period. In addition, the authors reported that the PSWQ is significantly more correlated with measures of trait anxiety than with measures of state anxiety or depression (Meyer et al., 1990).

In a separate clinical study, Meyer and colleagues (1990) reported that very high scores on the PSWQ were specifically sensitive to change over the course of cognitively oriented treatment. The PSWQ was administered to thirty-four GAD subjects in one of three treatment conditions: nondirective therapy, applied relaxation therapy, and coping desensitization plus cognitive therapy. Subjects in the cognitive therapy condition evidenced the greatest reduction in PSWQ scores (Meyer et al., 1990).

The content of the PSWQ suggests that it is capable of discriminating anxiety disorders characterized by worry, most notably generalized anxiety disorder (GAD), from other anxiety disorders. Brown, Antony, & Barlow (1992) examined the specificity of the questionnaire in a sample of 436 anxiety disorder patients and 32 normal controls. Their results provided additional evidence that the PSWQ is internally consistent and assesses a unidimensional construct (Brown et al., 1992). More important, it was indicated that the PSWQ was capable of discriminating between individuals with GAD, other anxiety disorders, and no-disorder controls (Brown, Antony, & Barlow, 1992).

Social Interaction Anxiety Scale (SIAS). The SIAS is a twenty-item scale that measures anxiety in social situations (Mattick & Clarke, 1989). The items are self-statements describing cognitive, affective, and behavioral reactions to a variety of situations involving social interactions. Mattick and Clarke (1989) administered the SIAS to samples of social phobics, college students, community volunteers, agoraphobics, and simple phobics and reported good discriminability between groups of subjects. They also reported alpha coefficients of .88 and test-retest correlations of .90 for intervals up to thirteen weeks (Mattick & Clarke, 1989).

Further examining the validity of the SIAS, Heimberg and colleagues (1992) administered the device to a sample of social phobics, community volunteers, and undergraduate psychology students. The results from this investigation provided additional validational support for the SIAS. The authors reported that the SIAS distinguished between social phobics and the comparison groups and that it was significantly correlated with other self-report measures of social anxiety. Furthermore, the SIAS discriminated between generalized social phobics (fear of more than one type of social situation) and nongeneralized social phobics (fear of one type of social situation). Subjects with multiple social fears scored significantly higher than subjects with one circumscribed social fear (Heimberg, Mueller, Holt, & Hope, 1992).

Maudsley Obsessional-Compulsive Inventory (MOCI). The MOCI, developed by Hodgson and Rachman (1977), measures the extent of different obsessive-compulsive (OC) symptoms. This scale contains thirty true-false items and can provide ratings for a total score as well as checking, washing, slowness, and doubting subscales (Hodgson & Rachman, 1977). This measure has been used widely to measure OC symptomatology in both clinical and research practice. Hodgson and Rachman (1977) administered this scale to one hundred obsessive-compulsive disorder patients and reported that the four subscales of the MOCI account for 43 percent of the scale's variance. The authors also reported that the scale exhibited one-month test-retest reliability of .80 and alpha coefficients greater than .70 for each of the four subscales (Hodgson & Rachman, 1977).

To further investigate the psychometric properties of the MOCI, Sternberger and Burns (1990) administered the questionnaire to a sample of 579 undergraduate students. Their results provided additional evidence that the MOCI is internally consistent (coefficient alpha = .75). These researchers also found that a principal component analysis extracted the original four subscales. Further, the MOCI was significantly correlated with other validated measures of OC symptomatology providing evidence of convergent validity. Finally, in an effort to assess the test-retest reliability, Sternberger and Burns (1990) mailed the MOCI to three hundred subjects approximately six to seven months later and reported correlations of .69 for the 59 percent of the subjects who responded (Sternberger & Burns, 1990).

PTSD Symptom Scale (PSS). The PSS is a brief seventeen-item questionnaire that contains three subscales designed to measure each of the major symptom areas including reexperiencing, avoidance and numbing, and hyperarousal (Foa, Riggs, Dancu, & Rothbaum, 1993). In examining the reliability and validity of this scale, Foa and colleagues administered the instrument to a sample of rape victims and reported a test-retest reliability of .74 and an internal consistency of .91. This scale also correctly identified PTSD status (measured by a validated structured clinical interview) in 86 percent of the sample (Foa, Riggs, Dancu, & Rothbaum, 1993).

Anxiety Sensitivity Index (ASI). The ASI is a sixteen-item questionnaire specifying possible adverse consequences to the experience of anxiety (Reiss, Peterson, Gursky, & McNally, 1986). Each item is rated from zero (very little) to four (very much). Examining the psychometric properties of this scale, Reiss and colleagues (1986) administered the ASI to a sample of 127 college students in two separate sessions held two weeks apart. They reported a test-retest reliability of .75 and Cronbach's alpha of .88.

In a second study, Reiss et al. (1986) administered the ASI to a sample of sixty-three patients with various anxiety disorders. Subjects diagnosed with panic disorder with agoraphobia scored significantly higher than the subjects with other anxiety disorders. All subjects with anxiety-disorder diagnoses were significantly elevated above a sample of college students (Reiss et al., 1986).

In a similar investigation, Taylor, Koch, and Crockett (1991) administered the ASI to a sample of thirty-eight subjects diagnosed with panic disorder (with or without agoraphobia) and thirty-nine subjects with anxiety disorders other than panic. Also administered were the Beck Depression Inventory (BDI) and the trait version of the STAI. Between-group comparisons indicated significant differences only on the ASI, with the panic disorder group being most elevated (Taylor, Koch, & Crockett, 1991). These results suggest that the ASI may assess the anxiety focused on somatic sensations believed to be characteristic of the panic disorders (Reiss, 1991).

Fear Survey Schedule-III (FSS-III). The FSS-III is a questionnaire that lists seventy-six fears that are common among phobic patients (Wolpe & Lang, 1964). Anxiety is rated on a Likert-type scale ranging from one (not at all disturbed) to five (very much disturbed).

Arrindell and van der Ende (1986) administered the FSS-III to a sample of 191 psychiatric inpatients one week after admission and again before the start of therapy. Using confirmatory factor analysis they revealed five interpretable factors: (a) social anxiety; (b) agoraphobia; (c) fears of bodily injury, death, and illness; (d) fears of sexual and aggressive scenes; and (e) fears of harmless animals. The reliability of each of the five factors ranged from .82 to .92. The reliability for the total score was also high (alpha = .96). The investigators, however, found that each of the subscales was more internally consistent than the total score and urged caution when utilizing the total score as a more general measure of fear (Arrindell & van der Ende, 1986; Arrindell, Emmelkamp, & van der Ende, 1984).

SUMMARY OF SELF-REPORT MEASURES

Each of the self-report measures described above possesses good reliability and validity. Several properties of such measures also make them useful in both clinically oriented and research-oriented settings. First, these scales are brief, taking less than thirty minutes to complete, and they thereby provide a comparatively quick assessment of anxiety and specific anxiety disorders. Second, such instruments are capable of being administered over a short period of time (e.g., weekly over the course of treatment), thereby allowing for the close examination of targeted symptomatology. Third, these measures are completed by the patient and require only minimal additional time from the clinician or researcher.

Although these measures have several useful properties, there are three primary difficulties with self-report measures in general that preclude sole reliance on them to assess anxious pathology. First, self-report measures are subject to bias. Some patients, for example, may exhibit a tendency to focus solely on one particular area and to minimize, ignore, or deny symptoms from other areas. The converse, endorsing virtually every symptom listed on a scale, also occurs.

Second, such measures are not intended to provide the crucial information regarding course, duration, or the functional relationship of symptoms necessary for diagnostic purposes (Hollon & Carter, 1994). For example, patients with excessive worry during the past month may exhibit elevated scores on the self-report measures specific to generalized anxiety disorder but would not meet criteria for a clinical diagnosis because the duration requirement of six months would not have been met. Patients who panic when in social situations may respond to the syndromal measures of panic in a manner characteristic of the disorder but would not be assigned the diagnosis of panic disorder since the attacks are triggered by situations when the person is the focus of others' attention (American Psychiatric Association, 1987). Either scenario presented above would result in a nosologic error and illustrate why self-report measures are not sufficient for diagnostic purposes.

Finally, these measures cannot incorporate clinical judgment. At the least, some clinical judgment is necessary to determine if anxiety is the primary problem or if it is instead a consequential manifestation of another disturbance. To allay some of these concerns, it would be prudent to include one or more of the psychometrically sound clinician-administered measures of anxiety as well.

CLINICIAN-ADMINISTERED SYNDROMAL MEASURES

There are several useful clinician-administered measures of the anxiety syndrome. The Hamilton Anxiety Rating Scale is perhaps the most extensively used device of this type.

Hamilton Anxiety Rating Scale (HARS). The HARS is a fourteen-item instrument originally designed to assess patients diagnosed with anxiety neuroses (Hamilton, 1959). Each item from this scale is rated from zero (not at all) to five (very severe), with total scores ranging from zero to seventy. The scale contains a psychic factor (e.g., anxious mood, tension) and a somatic factor (e.g., somatic-muscular, somatic-tension).

Maier, Buller, Philipp, and Heuser (1988) administered the HARS to a sample of patients with anxiety disorders and a sample patients with major depressive disorder. These investigators reported an interrater reliability of .74 for the total score. The authors also reported that the HARS was able to discriminate between subjects diagnosed as panic disorder with co-occurring major depressive disorder versus those with only a panic disorder diagnosis. The authors note that the validity of this scale may be limited, since they found that the HARS exhibited a high degree of overlap with features of depression as well as nonspecificity for the assessment of change from anxiolytics (Maier et al., 1988).

Several attempts have been made to revise this scale. Riskind and colleagues (1987) administered the original Hamilton scales for anxiety and depression to a sample of sixty patients diagnosed with generalized anxiety disorder (GAD) and sixty patients diagnosed with major depressive disorder (MDD). After conducting a factor analysis of the original scales, they recombined the items with the highest loading on the respective scales. Both the original and the revised scales discriminated between GAD and MDD patients, but the revised scale was correlated significantly higher with the anxiety diagnosis than were the original scales. The correlation between the two scales also dropped from .62 for the original scales to .15 for the revised scales (Riskind, Beck, Berchick, Brown, & Steer, 1987). The results from this investigation are tempered by the use of only GAD and MDD patients and await further validation with additional populations. The revised scales have thus not gained wide acceptance, and the original appears to remain the most frequently used version (Beck & Steer, 1991).

DISORDER-SPECIFIC CLINICIAN-ADMINISTERED MEASURES

There are also disorder-specific clinician-administered instruments that have proved useful and valid. These measures were designed to allow the clinician to cover information related to a specific diagnostic category. Examples of such instruments are the Yale-Brown Obsessive Compulsive Scale, the Multicenter Panic Anxiety Scale, and the Clinician Administered PTSD Scale.

Yale-Brown Obsessive Compulsive Scale (Y-BOCS). The Y-BOCS is a recently developed scale that allows the rater to assess the amount of time occupied by obsessions and compulsions during a typical day, the degree of functional impairment, the level of distress, attempts at resisting the symptoms, and the level of control over the symptoms (Goodman, Price, Rasmussen, Mazure, Fleischman, Hill, Heninger, & Charney, 1989a; Goodman, Price, Rasmussen, Mazure, Delgado, Heninger, & Charney, 1989b). This scale is made up of ten items, five to assess obsessions and five to assess compulsions, rated from zero (none) to four (extreme).

Goodman and colleagues (1989a) adminis-

tered the Y-BOCS to a sample of forty patients with obsessive-compulsive disorder and reported high interrater reliability, $r = .98$, and high internal consistency, alpha = .89 (Goodman et al., 1989a). To examine the validity of the Y-BOCS Goodman and colleagues (1989b) administered the device to a sample of eighty-one patients with obsessive-compulsive disorder. In this study they reported that the Y-BOCS was significantly correlated with two of three measures of obsessive-compulsive disorder and only weakly correlated with measures of depression and anxiety. Furthermore, they provided evidence that the Y-BOCS is sensitive to change in obsessive-compulsive symptoms, citing a strong correlation (.65) between pharmacologically treated patients and a reduction in the Y-BOCS (Goodman et al., 1989b).

Multicenter Panic Anxiety Scale (MC-PAS). The MC-PAS was developed by Shear and colleagues (1992). This scale was designed to resemble the Y-BOCS in its format and contains ratings for the frequency and distress of panic sensations, the severity of anticipatory anxiety, situational avoidance, and impairment in functioning. This scale also provides ratings for the phobic avoidance of physical sensations that may be reminiscent of the individual's panic sensations, or sensations that the patient fears may produce a panic attack (Shear, Sholomskas, Cloitre, Barlow, Gorman, & Woods, 1992). Examples include avoiding exercise or drinking coffee because of the physical sensations these activities produce. Each of the seven items is rated from zero (none) to four (extreme).

Analyses suggest that this measure has good psychometric properties. Sholomskas and colleagues (1992) administered the MC-PAS to a sample of thirty-four panic disorder subjects and reported significant correlations with a validated structured clinical interview ranging from .42 (panic-related impairment in social role) to .74 (frequency of full panic attacks). The authors also reported that the MC-PAS was sensitive to change over the course of treatment (Sholomskas, Shear, Cloitre, Brown, Barlow, Gorman, & Woods, 1992).

Clinician Administered PTSD Scale (CAPS).

The CAPS was developed by Blake and colleagues (1990) to assess the severity and frequency of PTSD symptoms. This instrument also gives guidelines for assessing behavior change following traumatic experiences. There are two forms of this scale: CAPS-1 assesses symptoms over a one-month period (current and lifetime version); and CAPS-2 assesses symptoms over the past week (one-week status version).

Based on a sample of twenty-five combat veterans, Blake and colleagues (1990) reported high internal consistency for each of the three PTSD symptom subgroups; reexperiencing (alpha = .77); numbing and avoidance (alpha = .85); and hyperarousal (alpha = .73). These investigators also reported significant correlations between the CAPS and established measures of PTSD, indicating convergent validity (Blake, Weathers, Nagy, Kaloupek, Klauminzer, Charney, & Keane, 1990).

Each of the above interviews is an effective tool that provides a total score marking the severity of the various signs and symptoms constituting a specific anxiety disorder. They are highly popular as measures of change in controlled outcome research in this area. The advantage to these measures is that they allow for some degree of clinical judgment. Like the self-report questionnaires, however, such measures cannot provide diagnostic information or distinguish between nosological entities or syndromal manifestations (Hollon & Carter, 1994). To accomplish this one must turn to one of the clinician-administered diagnostic instruments.

CLINICIAN-ADMINISTERED DIAGNOSTIC INSTRUMENTS

In determining the presence of diagnosable anxiety disorders, most investigators use one of the structured diagnostic interviews such as the Anxiety Disorders Interview Schedule—Revised, the Schedule for Affective Disorders and Schizophrenia, Lifetime Anxiety Version, or the Structured Clinical Interview for DSM-III-R. These instruments are structured in that they provide questions to be asked in a specific manner, but they also require clinical judgment to determine if further questioning is necessary and to evaluate the patient's responses (Page, 1991).

Anxiety Disorders Interview Schedule—Revised (ADIS-R). The ADIS-R is a structured clinical interview designed to assess the presence of DSM-III-R anxiety disorders and their accompanying mood disorders. The ADIS-R provides sufficient probes to extensively examine the presence, severity, and course of the anxious and mood disorders. This instrument also assesses a number of additional disorders that are related to and/or preclude the diagnosis of one of the anxiety disorders. These later sections serve as screens to rule out the presence of substance abuse, somatoform disorders, and psychosis (DiNardo & Barlow, 1988; Page, 1991).

DiNardo, Moras, Barlow, Rapee, and Brown (1993) evaluated the reliability of the ADIS-R in a sample of 267 outpatients. Sixty percent of the sample were randomly selected to undergo a second independent interview. Kappa coefficients calculated on principal diagnoses (defined as the disorder receiving the highest clinical severity rating) ranged from fair (.43 for panic disorder without agoraphobia) to excellent (greater than .79 for simple phobia, social phobia, and obsessive-compulsive disorder). Among the anxiety disorders, panic disorder without agoraphobia had the lowest kappa value. When all panic disorder categories were combined, the kappas were in the good to excellent range (.71 to .79) (Di Nardo et al., 1993). The primary disadvantage of this device is that it requires from two to three hours to complete.

Although the ADIS-R has been recommended as the most suitable clinician-rated structured interview for the reliable assessment of anxiety disorders (Page, 1991), there are two additional instruments that deserve mention as they are often used in research and clinical settings.

Schedule for Affective Disorders and Schizophrenia, Lifetime Anxiety Version (SADS-LA). The SADS-LA was developed by Fyer and colleagues (1985) to gather detailed lifetime information on the various anxiety disorders, symptoms, and traits (Mannuzza, Fyer, Klein, & Endicott, 1986). The SADS-LA also provides an overall psychiatric evaluation culminating in a DSM-III-R diagnosis and gathers extensive information regarding stressful life events. The SADS-LA also identifies three types of panic attacks (spontaneous, situationally predisposed, and stimulus-bound) and divides social phobia according to the presence of panic attacks, performance anxiety, and social anxiety (Page, 1991) The comprehensive format of this device results in a lengthy interview that can take more than four hours to complete and that may perhaps be problematic in general clinical settings.

The reliability of the SADS-LA was assessed in a sample of 104 patients with anxiety disorders. Each patient was assigned to either an "expert" rater (defined as members of the anxiety disorders clinic who had experience with anxious patients and who had demonstrated good reliability on a minimum of thirteen SADS-LA interviews) or a "field" rater (doctoral-level psychologists and psychiatric social workers who had completed a training program on the SADS-LA). The reliability of this instrument ranged from .60 to .90 for most DSM-III-R anxiety disorders except for simple phobia (Mannuzza et al., 1989). Diagnostic disagreements were determined to be largely (51 percent) due to variance in subject report. Good to excellent reliability was also found in examining the reliability of "subdisorder" irrational fears (Fyer et al., 1989).

Structured Clinical Interview for DSM-III-R (SCID). The SCID (Spitzer and Williams, 1988) is a semistructured interview designed to enable experienced clinicians to arrive at DSM-III-R diagnoses (Spitzer et al., 1990). The interview follows the DSM-III-R hierarchy and allows omission of categories that are preempted by the hierarchy. Furthermore, the SCID can be completed in a comparatively short time (sixty to ninety minutes) and generates current and lifetime diagnoses rather than the comprehensive description of psychopathology characteristic of the SADS-LA (Page, 1991).

Riskind and colleagues (1987) administered the SCID to seventy-five patients who presented for an intake evaluation. Each interview was videotaped and viewed by a second set of raters for reliability purposes. It was reported that the interrater reliability of the SCID for generalized anxiety disorder and major depressive disorder was .72 and .79, respectively, and .74 for the interview as a whole (Riskind et al., 1987). Further studies, however, are necessary to determine the validity of this device with respect to the other specific anxiety disorders (Page, 1991).

The clinical interviews described above have been designed for specific purposes. The task before the assessor is to understand the purpose for the interview and then to choose one that will fit the needs of the particular clinic or project. Issues to consider in the selection of a particular structured interview include adequate coverage of the relevant disorders, length of time to administer, amount of detail provided by the interview, and applicability to the targeted population (Page, 1991). If the primary purpose, for example, is to assess for the presence of anxiety disorders in detail, the ADIS-R may be the interview of choice. The coverage of other diagnostic areas, however, is not as detailed. If the primary purpose is a thorough assessment of all diagnostic categories, then the SADS-LA may be the interview of choice, although the length of time for administration is often prohibitive. If the purpose is to carefully follow the structure of the current diagnostic system, the SCID may be the instrument of choice. The potential user must also be aware of any limitations imposed by the setting, such as time and availability of qualified personnel. All of these issues must be addressed before selection of the appropriate interview for use in either clinical or research settings.

SUMMARY OF CLINICIAN-ADMINISTERED MEASURES

Clinician-administered instruments have proved extremely useful in assessing anxious symptomatology. They yield information from the level of the individual symptom, the syndrome, and the nosologic entity, and consequently provide a more complete assessment of anxiety than do the self-report measures. These measures also incorporate the judgment of the clinician and are not subject to the same biases as self-report measures. As such, they are clearly the most thorough method for assessing the anxious patient.

There are, however, several disadvantages to their use. As they are structured, proper administration requires extensive training to reach an acceptable level of proficiency. This generally involves viewing several videotapes, observing live interviews, and then conducting a number of interviews while being observed by, and matching with, experienced interviewers on specific criteria. Additionally, these instruments are lengthy, requiring from two to four hours to complete, depending on the level of pathology. The length of time to complete a structured interview in some settings is prohibitive. As they are generally too lengthy to administer over short periods of time (e.g., weekly or biweekly), they are primarily administered at pretreatment, posttreatment, and during follow-up assessment points.

Thus far we have described several measures of anxiety with excellent psychometric properties. Each of the described measures and the level of pathology each assesses is presented in Table 24.1. We turn now to a discussion of specific strategies for assessing the anxious patient, along with several common problems in accurate assessment.

STRATEGIES AND PROBLEMS IN ASSESSING ANXIOUS PATIENTS

The most basic form of assessment is, of course, behavioral observation. Much can be gleaned from simply paying attention to the patient's clinical presentation. Severely anxious patients will often appear restless and fidgety. They may also exhibit trembling, unsteady voice, hand-wringing, and an inability to maintain eye contact. Behavioral observations are captured in the clinician-administered instruments.

The form assessment takes following the behavioral observation can vary greatly. Some professionals may choose to have the patient com-

TABLE 24.1. Anxiety Measures as a Function of Pathological Classification

	Symptom	Syndrome	Nosologic disorder
Self-report			
SCL-90	x		
MMACL	x		
BAI	x	x	
STAI	x	x	
ASI	x	x	
FSS-III	x	x	
PSWQ*	x	x	
SIAS*	x	x	
MOCI*	x	x	
PSS*	x	x	
Clinician-administered			
HARS	x	x	
Y-BOCS*	x	x	
MC-PAS*	x	x	
CAPS*	x	x	
ADIS-R	x	x	x
SADS-LA	x	x	x
SCID	x	x	x

Note: * indicates measure assessing a specific anxiety disorder.

plete several self-report measures, followed by an unstructured clinical interview. Others may begin with an interview and follow it up with questionnaires. Still others may forego one or the other. We recommend incorporating all of these forms of assessment in a logical fashion starting with one of the structured clinical interviews such as the ADIS-R. This ensures a thorough assessment of the patient's concerns. Without such an interview, it is possible to neglect potentially important areas. Often anxious patients' primary complaints are not their sole complaints or even their most important presenting problems. There may be coprincipal or additional diagnoses present in the clinical picture (Barlow et al., 1986; Winokur, 1988). Missing a coprincipal or additional diagnosis can lead to inferential errors regarding potential treatment or the conclusions to be drawn from research results.

Following the diagnostic assessment it is advisable to have the patient complete several of the psychometrically sound self-report inventories that cover different areas. The most effective

TABLE 24.2. Anxiety Measures as a Function of Diagnostic Category

	Anxiety disorder					
	GAD*	Social	OCD	PTSD	PDA	Simple
Self-report						
BAI	x	x	x	x	x	x
STAI	x	x	x	x	x	x
ASI	–	–	–	–	x	–
FSS-III	–	–	–	–	–	x
PSWQ	x	–	–	–	–	–
SIAS	–	x	–	–	–	–
MOCI	–	–	x			–
PSS	–	–	–	x	–	–
Clinician-administered						
HARS	x	x	x	x	x	x
Y-BOCS	–	–	x	–	–	–
MC-PAS	–	–	–	–	x	–
CAPS	–	–	–	x	–	–
ADIS-R	x	x	x	x	x	x
SADS-LA	x	x	x	x	x	x
SCID	x	x	x	x	x	x

Note: GAD—generalized anxiety disorder; Social—social phobia; OCD—obsessive compulsive disorder; PTSD—post traumatic stress disorder; PDA panic disorder with agoraphobia; Simple—simple phobia.

method would be to include scales from each of the disorder-specific measures as well as one or two of the more general measures of the anxious syndrome (see Table 24.2). The inclusion of these measures is important in that they complement the diagnostic assessment and can often provide valuable additional validational information. Consider, for example, a patient diagnosed with panic disorder who at the end of treatment no longer meets the criteria for the disorder but remains elevated on measures of general anxiety (e.g., STAI) and anxiety sensitivity (ASI). Including these measures may provide additional insight into both the nature of the disorder and its treatment.

An alternative strategy might involve administering the battery of self-report measures before the structured interview. The rationale is that certain measures may be particularly state-dependent. Administration of the measures before the interview may therefore provide a different picture of the patient's pathology. That is, on occasion the interview itself can provide some temporary relief in symptomatology that may be reflected on the self-report measures. In either case, it is recommended that a thorough

assessment be guided by a general hypothesis-testing approach and include behavioral observations, self-report measures, and a structured clinical interview. In this manner one is employing a multitrait, multimethod approach to assessment in an effort to obtain convergent and discriminate diagnostic validity.

Finally, it is helpful to repeat the complete assessment package at the end of treatment at least. This provides necessary information regarding the effectiveness of any treatment and can form the basis for revising various aspects of treatment when needed.

Even when such a comprehensive approach has been employed, there are specific problems that may complicate the assessment of anxious patients. The first problem is the high incidence of comorbid diagnoses (Winokur, 1988). Most additional diagnoses for anxious patients are found among the other anxiety disorders (Barlow et al., 1986). The presence of two or more anxiety diagnoses (especially if they are coprincipal diagnoses) can impede accurate assessment due to symptomatic overlap in the patient's clinical presentation. For example, it may be difficult to accurately assess the patient who has coprincipal diagnoses of social phobia and panic disorder since the clinical picture of these two may overlap to a large degree. Furthermore, such a case may be elevated on all of the self-report measures designed to be specific to either disorder. There is often some level of depressive symptoms present in the anxious patient that can interfere with an accurate assessment (Clayton, 1990). It is prudent, therefore, to incorporate at least minimal exploration of depressive symptoms, perhaps with several self-report and/or clinician-rated instruments.

A related problem is that the behavioral presentation of severely anxious patients may mimic other DSM-III-R diagnostic entities. The apparently pressured speech, hyperactivity, and nervous energy occasionally seen among the severely anxious can at times mimic a hypomanic episode. With a history of depressive episodes the patient's clinical presentation can begin to resemble a subtype of bipolar disorder. These issues must be considered in attempting to conduct an accurate assessment of severely anxious patients.

FUTURE DIRECTIONS

There is no doubt that anxiety is a universally experienced emotional state that can at times become pathological. When anxiety does become dysfunctional, one must be concerned with accurate assessment as it is often the precursor to effective treatment planning. The current state of anxiety assessment has advanced considerably over the past two decades, but much remains to be done. In the future, the assessment of the severely anxious patient will need to be concerned with the accurate measurement of the manner in which anxiety disorders interact with other disorders. There is also a need for the continued development of other methods of assessment such as psychophysiological and in vivo assessment. Finally, the ultimate challenge in the area of anxiety assessment is the development of methods that can identify those who are at risk for one of the anxiety disorders before the development of the disorder. Strategic development in these direc-

tions will ensure that the assessment of the severely anxious patient continues to provide useful information for both clinical and research purposes.

REFERENCES

American Psychiatric Association. (1987). *Diagnostic and Statistical Manual of Mental Disorders* (3rd ed.—revi.). Washington DC: American Psychiatric Press.

Arrindell, W. A., Emmelkamp, P. M. G., & van der Ende, J. (1984). Phobic dimensions: I. Reliability and generalizability across samples, gender, and nations. *Advances in Behavior Research and Therapy, 6,* 207–254.

Arrindell, W. A., & Van Der Ende, J. (1986). Further evidence for cross-sample invariance of phobic factors: Psychiatric inpatient ratings on the Fear Survey Schedule-III. *Behavior Research and Therapy, 24,* 289–297.

Barlow, D. H. (1988). *Anxiety and its disorders: The nature and treatment of anxiety and panic.* New York: Guilford Press.

Barlow, D. H., DiNardo, P. A., Vermilyea, B. B., Vermilyea, J., & Blanchard, E. (1986). Co-morbidity and depression among the anxiety disorders. *Journal of Nervous and Mental Disease, 174,* 63–72.

Beck, A. T., & Emery, G. (1985). *Anxiety disorders and phobias: A cognitive perspective.* New York: Basic Books.

Beck, A. T., Epstein, N., Brown, G., & Steer, R. A. (1988). An inventory for measuring clinical anxiety. *Journal of Consulting and Clinical Psychology, 56,* 893–897.

Beck A. T., & Freeman, A. (1990). *Cognitive therapy of the personality disorders.* New York: Guilford Press.

Beck, A. T., & Steer, R. A. (1990). *Manual for the Beck Anxiety Inventory.* San Antonio, TX: Psychological Corporation.

Beck, A. T., & Steer, R. A. (1991). Relationship between the Beck Anxiety Inventory and the Hamilton Anxiety Rating Scale with anxious outpatients. *Journal of Anxiety Disorders, 5,* 213–223.

Benjamin, J., Silk, K. R., Lohr, N. E., & Westen, D. (1989). The relationship between borderline personality disorder and anxiety disorders. *American Journal of Orthopsychiatry, 59,* 461–467.

Blake, D. D., Weathers, F. W., Nagy, L. M., Kaloupek, D. G., Klauminzer, G., Charney, D., &

Keane, T. (1990). A clinician rating scale for assessing current and lifetime PTSD: The CAPS-1. *The Behavior Therapist, 13,* 187–188.

Boyd, J. H., Burke, J. D., Gruenberg, E., Holzer, C. E., Rae, D. S., McEvoy, L., & Nestadt, G. (1984). A study of co-occurrence of hierarchy-free syndromes. *Archives of General Psychiatry, 41,* 983–989.

Brown, T. A., Antony, M. M., & Barlow, D. H. (1992). Psychometric properties of the Penn State Worry Questionnaire in a clinical anxiety disorders sample. *Behavior Research and Therapy, 30,* 33–37.

Clayton, P. J. (1990). The comorbidity factor: Establishing the primary diagnosis in patients with mixed anxiety and depression. *Journal of Clinical Psychiatry, 51,* 35–39.

Derogatis, L. R., Lipman, R. S., & Covi, L. (1973). SCL-90: An outpatient psychiatric rating scale—preliminary report. *Psychopharmacology Bulletin, 9,* 13–27.

DiNardo, P. A., & Barlow, D. H. (1988). *Anxiety Disorders Interview Schedule—Revised (ADIS-R).* Albany, NY: Graywind Publications.

DiNardo, P. A., Moras, K., Barlow, D. H., Rapee R. M., & Brown, T. A. (1993). Reliability of DSM-III-R anxiety disorder categories using the Anxiety Disorders Interview Schedule—Revised (ADIS-R). *Archives of General Psychiatry, 50,* 251–256.

Foa, E. B., Riggs, D. S., Dancu, C. V., & Rothbaum, B. O. (1993). Reliability and validity of a brief instrument for assessing post-traumatic stress disorder. *Journal of Traumatic Stress, 6,* 459–473.

Fydrich, T., Dowdall, D., & Chambless, D. L. (1992). Reliability and validity of the Beck Anxiety Inventory. *Journal of Anxiety Disorders, 6,* 55–61.

Fyer, A. J., Endicott, J., Mannuzza, S., & Klein, D. F. (1985). *Schedule for Affective Disorders and Schizophrenia—Lifetime Version (modified for the study of anxiety disorders).* New York: Anxiety Disorders Clinic, New York State Psychiatric Institute.

Fyer, A. J., Mannuzza, S., Martin, L. Y., Gallops, M. S., Endicott, J., Schleyer, B., Gorman, J., Liebowitz, M. R., & Klein D. F. (1989). Reliability of anxiety assessment II. Symptom agreement. *Archives of General Psychiatry, 46,* 1102–1110.

Goodman, W. K., Price, L. H., Rasmussen, S. A., Mazure, C., Delgado, P., Heninger, G. R., & Charney, D. S. (1989b). The Yale-Brown Obsessive Compulsive Scale. II. Validity. *Archives of General Psychiatry, 46,* 1012–1016.

Goodman, W. K., Price, L. H., Rasmussen, S. A., Mazure, C., Fleischman, R. L., Hill, C. L., Heninger, G. R., & Charney, D. S. (1989a). The Yale-Brown Obsessive Compulsive Scale. I. Development, use, and reliability. *Archives of General Psychiatry, 46,* 1006–1011.

Hamilton, M. (1959). The assessment of anxiety states by rating. *Journal of Medical Psychology, 32,* 50–55.

Heimberg, R. G., Mueller, G. P., Holt, C. S., & Hope, D. A. (1992). Assessment of anxiety in social interaction and being observed by others: The Social Interaction Anxiety Scale and the Social Phobia Scale. *Behavior Therapy, 23,* 53–73.

Hersov, L. (1985). Emotional disorders. In M. Rutter & L Hersov (Eds.), *Child and adolescent psychiatry.* Oxford: Blackwell Scientific.

Hodgson R. J., & Rachman, S. (1977). Obsessional-compulsive complaints. *Behavior Research and Therapy, 15,* 389–395.

Hollon, S. D., & Carter, M. M. (1994). Treatment of depression in adults. In L. W. Craighead, W. E. Craighead, A. E. Kazdin, & M. J. Mahoney (Eds.), *Cognitive and behavioral interventions.* Needham, MA: Allyn & Bacon.

Ingram, R. E., & Kendall, P. C. (1987). The cognitive side of anxiety. *Cognitive Therapy and Research, 11,* 523–536.

Katon, W. & Roy-Byrne, P. (1991). Mixed anxiety and depression. *Journal of Abnormal Psychology, 100,* 337–345.

Kernberg, O. F. (1975). *Borderline conditions and pathological narcissism.* New York: Jason Aronson.

Lewis, Sir A. J. (1970). The ambiguous word "anxiety." *International Journal of Psychiatry, 9,* 62–79.

Maier, W., Buller, R., Philipp, M., & Heuser, I. (1988). The Hamilton anxiety scale: Reliability, validity and sensitivity to change in anxiety and depressive disorders. *Journal of Affective Disorders, 14,* 61–68.

Mannuzza, S., Fyer, A. J., Klein, D. F., & Endicott, J. (1986). Schedule for Affective Disorders and Schizophrenia—Lifetime Version modified for the study of anxiety disorders (SADS-LA): Rationale and conceptual development. *Journal of Psychiatric Research, 20,* 317–325.

Mannuzza, S., Fyer, A. J., Martin, L. Y., Gallops, M. S., Endicott, J., Gorman, J., Liebowitz, M. R., & Klein D. F. (1989). Reliability of anxiety assessment I. Diagnostic agreement. *Archives of General Psychiatry, 46,* 1093–1101.

Mattick, R. P., & Clarke, J. C. (1989). *Development and validation of measures of social phobia scrutiny fear and social interaction anxiety.* Unpublished manuscript.

Meyer, T. J., Miller, M. L., Metzger, R. L., & Borkovec, T. D. (1990). Development and validation of the Penn State Worry Questionnaire. *Behavior Research and Therapy, 28,* 487–495.

O'Connor, F. (1991). Symptom monitoring for relapse prevention in schizophrenia. *Archives of Psychiatric Nursing, 5,* 193–201.

Page, A. C. (1991). An assessment of structured diagnostic interview for adult anxiety disorders. *International Review of Psychiatry, 3,* 265–278.

Regier, D. A., Narrow, W. E., & Rae, D. S. (1990). The epidemiology of anxiety disorders: The epidemiological catchment area (ECA) experience. *Journal of Psychiatric Research, 24,* 3–14.

Reiss, S. (1991). Expectancy model of fear, anxiety, and panic. *Clinical Psychology Review, 11,* 141–153.

Reiss, S., Peterson, R. A., Gursky, D. M., & McNally, R. J. (1986). Anxiety sensitivity, anxiety frequency and the prediction of fearfulness. *Behavior Research and Therapy, 24,* 1–8.

Riskind, J. H., Beck, A. T., Berchick, R. J., Brown, G., & Steer, R. A. (1987). Reliability of DSM-III diagnoses for major depression and generalized anxiety disorder using the structured clinical interview for DSM-III. *Archives of General Psychiatry, 44,* 817–820.

Riskind, J. H., Beck, A. T., Brown, G., & Steer, R. A. (1987). Taking the measure of anxiety and depression. Validity of the reconstructed hamilton scales. *Journal of Nervous and Mental Disease, 175,* 474–479.

Schatzberg, A. F. (1991). Overview of anxiety disorders: Prevalence, biology, course, and treatment. *Journal of Clinical Psychiatry, 52,* 5–9.

Shear, M. K., Sholomskas, D., Cloitre, M., Barlow, D. H., Gorman, J., & Woods, S. (1992). *The Multicenter Panic Anxiety Scale (MC-PAS).* Unpublished manuscript.

Sholomskas, D., Shear M. K., Cloitre, M., Brown., T. A., Barlow, D. H., Gorman, J., & Woods, S. (1992). *Construct validity of the Multicenter Panic Anxiety Scale (MC-PAS).* Unpublished manuscript.

Snyder, S., & Pitts, W. M. (1988). Characterizing anxiety in the DSM-III borderline personality disorder. *Journal of Personality Disorders, 2,* 93–101.

Spielberger, C. D. (1983). *Manual for the State-Trait Anxiety Inventory (Form Y).* Palo Alto, CA: Consulting Psychologists Press.

Spielberger, C. D., Gorsuch, R. L., & Lushene, R. E. (1970). *Manual for the State-Trait Anxiety Inventory (Self-evaluation questionnaire).* Palo Alto, CA: Consulting Psychologists Press.

Spitzer R. L., & Williams, J. B. (1988). Revised diagnostic criteria and a new structured interview for diagnosing anxiety disorders. *Journal of Psychiatric Research, 22,* 55–85.

Spitzer, R. L., Williams, J. B., Gibbon, M., & First, M. B. (1990). *Structured Clinical Interview for DSM-III-R.* Washington, DC: American Psychiatric Press.

Sternberger, L. G., & Burns, G. L. (1990). Compulsive Activity Checklist and the Maudsley Obsessional-Compulsive Inventory: Psychometric properties of two measures of obsessive-compulsive disorder. *Behavior Therapy, 21,* 117–127.

Taylor, C. B., & Arnow, B. (1988). *The nature and treatment of anxiety disorders.* New York: Free Press.

Taylor, S., Koch, W. J., & Crockett, D. J. (1991). Anxiety sensitivity, trait anxiety, and the anxiety disorders. *Journal of Anxiety Disorders, 5,* 293–311.

Turpin, G. (1991). The psychophysiological assessment of anxiety disorders: Three systems measurement and beyond. *Psychological Assessment, 3,* 366–375.

Winokur, G. (1988). Anxiety disorders: Relationship to other psychiatric illness. *Psychiatric Clinics of North America, 11,* 287–293.

Wolpe, J., & Lang, P. (1964). Fear Survey Schedule for use in behavior therapy. *Behavior Research and Therapy, 2,* 27–30.

Zuckerman, M., & Lubin, B. (1965). *Manual for the Multiple Affective Adjective Check List.* San Diego, CA: Educational and Industrial Testing Service.

25
Assessing Suicidal Clients

Zigfrids T. Stelmachers

STANDARD OF CARE

All mental health professionals, sooner or later, are called on to evaluate a client who is known to be or may be suicidal. The ability to make such assessments is of particular significance since danger to self or others has become the major criterion for reimbursable hospitalization and involuntary commitment. Increasingly, mental health professionals are sued for malpractice because they did not properly evaluate a client's suicide potential. The courts feel that clinicians are obligated to predict the likelihood that a given client will commit suicide and typically apply the standard of "reasonable care and skill" ("the degree of learning, skill, and experience which ordinarily is possessed by others of the same profession"). Parenthetically, clinicians seem to impose a higher standard than the courts (Berman and Cohen-Sandler, 1982), which means that we may be held accountable to this higher standard when our colleagues are called to testify as expert witnesses.

Component 1, Assessment of Lethality, of the Certification Standards Manual for Crisis Intervention Programs, issued by the American Association of Suicidology, states, in part: "Assessment should represent a body of concepts and written procedures based on current research regarding lethality assessment as an integral part of . . . service. Lethality assessment should include an estimation of immediate as well as long range risk of self-destructive behavior." The highest level of such an assessment demands that it "should be done consistently according to current written principles and procedures."

The guidelines for such an evaluation would be likely to differ depending on the clinical setting (hospital, office, emergency room, suicide prevention center, etc.). Nevertheless, it is clearly no longer sufficient to ask clients if they are suicidal and record their answer as evidence that suicide risk has been evaluated. At the very minimum, any clinical setting needs a policy statement or guidelines addressing the issue of suicide risk assessment. Who can do it? What consultation/supervision needs to be obtained, by whom, under what circumstances? What instruments, if any, are to be used in the evaluation? What rescue action is proposed, given a certain level of risk?

Although a client's statements regarding suicidal intent are central in any evaluation, it is clear that one cannot rely on such statements alone, and that a more objective assessment, based on known risk factors, needs to be performed—and carefully documented, as any lawyer will readily advise you.

For more detailed discussion of legal issues and standards of care in outpatient settings, consult B. Bongar's "The Suicidal Patient: Clinical and Legal Standards of Care," 1991, American Psychological Association, Washington, DC.

INSTRUMENTS OF ASSESSMENT

Rating Scales

One of the most popular instruments for suicide risk assessment has been rating scales specifically developed for this purpose. Their popularity is partly based on the need for a quick assessment tool to be used by volunteers at suicide prevention centers. These rating scales show great variety: some rely on the subject as informant or are self-administered, others rely on second-party information; some are empirically constructed, others rationally derived; the items are weighted for some but not others, and the populations on which they are based show considerable heterogeneity. While most of them are indeed easy to administer and take little time to fill out, most of them also have major shortcomings.

Rothberg and Geer-Williams (1992), in their review of nineteen such scales, find that the application of these scales to selected clinical cases resulted in a "wide range of estimates for each case," and that one of the major findings of the study was "the relative absence of information on the psychometric properties of the suicide prediction scales." Their final conclusion was that "without such documentation, the proper application of the scales is limited." Because most rating scales are specific to certain populations and settings, their application to different groups reduces their validity (Brown & Sheran, 1972; Litman et al., 1974; Motto, 1985). This means that ideally one would have to develop different measuring instruments for schools, prisons, emergency services, or a medical-surgical hospital ward.

As mentioned before, most rating scales use unweighted items. To illustrate the problem: one of the early and rather frequently used scales contains the two following items, each receiving one point in the direction of elevated suicide risk: being "white" and having a "nervous or mental disorder, mood or behavioral symptoms, including alcoholism" (Tuckman and Youngman, 1968). Obviously being white contributes considerably less to suicide potential than suffering from a mental disorder. The only scale with an empirically derived weighting system is Motto's Suicide Risk Assessment Scale (1985). Items are scored from zero to one hundred depending on their contribution to suicide risk.

Rating scales also do not permit interaction among risk factors with possible potentiating effect, such as alcoholism with depression or dependent personality with divorce, etc.

Since scales emphasize communality and typically include only the most powerful risk factors, they by their very nature exclude idiosyncratic items and content critical for particular individuals. Thus, two persons can achieve the same overall risk score on the basis of very different sets of items and combinations of risk factors.

Finally, in addition to the already mentioned problem with reliability, there is the even more weighty problem of validity. The obvious criterion for a valid test of suicide potential is the occurrence of a suicidal event. But to use such an event as a criterion of antecedent risk is questionable because very high-risk individuals sometimes survive suicide attempts and low-risk persons end up committing suicide. Furthermore, those who eventually attempt or commit suicide may do so many years later, in a state of mind and under circumstances that may have little relationship to the situation at the time suicide risk was assessed (Stelmachers and Sherman, 1990).

Psychological Tests

In general, psychological tests are not very useful in emergency settings or any clinical situation that demands a quick appraisal of a client's suicidality. It simply takes too long to administer them. Therefore, psychological tests are rarely used in crisis intervention and suicide prevention centers.

There is also the ubiquitous base rate problem, carrying in its wake a huge number of false positive classifications. While most psychiatric clients who commit suicide and have taken an MMPI before the suicide show significant elevations on the depression scale, the vast majority of psychiatric patients with such elevations never commit suicide. Thus, using the depression scale as a predictor of future suicide would lack sufficient power to be of any practical use. More about this will be said in the discussion of specificity and sensitivity issues below.

Eyman and Eyman (1992) reviewed the literature of the usefulness of personality assessment in the evaluation of suicide risk. Although they claimed that "personality assessment can still be of aid in evaluating suicide risk," their basic conclusion is rather grim: "The Rorschach, TAT, and MMPI are not particularly useful instruments for the assessment of acute, immediate risk. Many components important in determining immediate lethality are not obtainable by psychological tests." On a more positive note, they feel that "Personality tests are best used in delineating the ego capacities and self-other representations that may predispose a person toward responding to major life crises with suicidal behavior." To do this best, they recommend the use of test batteries rather than individual tests. This, of course, makes the process even more impractical because of the time-consuming nature of such batteries.

Clinical Judgment

Most suicidologists agree that the best way to proceed is to use a subjective, global suicide risk assessment based on all available information, in addition to the already mentioned objective evaluation consisting of rating scales, psychological tests, standardized interviews, or other measuring instruments. Furthermore, if the instruments disagree with clinical judgment, the latter should prevail. Comparing the degree of concordance of an empirical suicide-risk scale and subjective clinical impression, one study found that 57 percent of the cases were rated the same and 32 percent were one category apart (e.g., high versus moderate or moderate versus low). Eleven percent were two categories apart (Motto, 1985). The author concluded that his rating scale "is intended as a supplement to, not a substitute for, clinical judgment," and that "when the scale is not consistent with clinical judgment, clinical judgment should be given precedence."

If, indeed, a subjective and intuitive clinical judgment is the preferred method for assessing suicide risk, let's have a closer look at this process.

Accepting the necessity for clinical judgment, one consequence immediately follows. Such a judgment requires highly trained and experienced professionals. There is, in fact, some evidence that highly qualified suicide experts can do spectacularly well in predicting—or, rather, postdicting—suicide (Shneidman, 1971). He postdicted with nearly perfect accuracy which five persons had committed suicide out of a sample of thirty, basing his judgment on lengthy case histories.

How well do less distinguished clinicians perform? One study (Stelmachers and Sherman, 1990) found that very experienced professional crisis-center staff showed surprisingly poor consistency in their suicide-risk ratings of thirty-three case histories. There were even instances when one staff member rated a case history one (minimum risk) while another gave a rating of seven (maximum risk). The intraclass correlation coefficient for the short-term risk ratings was found to be .49, indicating a substantial level of unreliability. However, there was a clinically acceptable level of agreement on the very high-risk cases.

In a later study, when asked to identify the content in each case history that mainly determined the rating, the staff selected a very small number of factors (a mean of 2.1 for "low" and 4.8 for "high" risk cases). The conclusion was that "we may base our judgments on a few items that, in a particular context, assume special significance. Such an approach would be more similar to a "critical item" methodology . . ." (Stelmachers and Sherman, 1992).

It was also found that the agreement among staff members was no better for crisis management procedures and clinical dispositions appropriate for the cases. The Kappa intraclass correlation coefficient did not exceed .24 for issuing legal holds, applying seclusion and restraint, or requesting psychiatric consultation or medications. The same was essentially true for such common clinical dispositions as hospitalization, referral to a Crisis Home Program or outpatient facility, or crisis intervention and release. Just as in the case of suicide-risk ratings, overall agreement on the clinical desirability of various crisis management procedures must be considered poor, although there were respectable correlations between suicide-risk ratings, on the one hand, and the restrictiveness of clinical dispositions on the other (.81).

The overall conclusion from the two studies was that "when good agreement among clinicians exists, it seems to be based mainly on general response tendencies, which, in turn, are generated by knowledge about base rates in a given population or by adherence to prevailing clinical philosophy, policies, and traditional practice. When clinicians attempt to be more differential in their judgments and to depart from these global response tendencies, they may gain a few points for *some* subjects, but lose accuracy for others."

PREDICTION VERSUS ASSESSMENT

Before suggesting remedies for this sad state of affairs, we need to consider perhaps the thorniest problem of them all, namely, the crucial difference between the prediction of a suicidal event and the assessment of suicide potential. To anticipate the conclusion, we know quite well how to do the latter but not the former. Why is the prediction of suicide so difficult?

First, there is the already-mentioned base rate problem, meaning that very few people end up committing suicide even within a correctly identified high-risk population. This issue is best addressed by Pokorny (1992). On the basis of several studies between 1960 and 1976, he concluded that "we do not possess any item of information or any combination of items that permit us to identify to a useful degree the particular persons who will commit suicide, in spite of the fact that we do have scores of items available, each of which is significantly related to suicide." The specificity and sensitivity of the available tools simply do not permit accurate enough prediction of such rare behaviors as suicide (sensitivity and specificity scores would have to be close to 99 percent to reach predictive values of about 80 percent).

Another reason for the poor predictability of suicide is the temporary fluctuation of risk over time. This is one reason why it is recommended to make at least two assessments for short-term and long-term risk (unspecified when one ends and the other begins). Naturally, even this two-part assessment strategy does not address the significant fluctuations over months, weeks, days, and sometimes hours. The outcome of suicide-risk assessment depends very much on the particular mental state of an individual at the particular time the assessment takes place. Motto (1992) states: "Uncomfortable as it is, we have no realistic choice but to deal in levels of risk that can vary from day-to-day or hour-to-hour, subject to the influence of numerous uncontrollable and unpredictable events."

This brings us to the next barrier to prediction. Chaos theory postulates that small differences in a microcosm at the point of impact are amplified as the process unfolds and eventually can lead to major macrocosmic changes that cannot be deduced from knowledge of the initial event. Tiny random events in the context of other relevant component parts of the system (such as general risk factors for suicide) can in time become critical events with the power to lead sequentially to very magnified outcomes (such as suicide). This has been referred to as "the butterfly effect": the butterfly flapping its wings in the Amazon creating a minute temperature change that eventually leads to a tornado in the United States (Lorenz, 1963). Furthermore, according to this theory, many processes in nature are chaotic, which imposes fundamental and absolute limits on prediction

(Gleick, 1987). If true, precise predictability cannot *in principle* be achieved by further gathering of information or reductionistic breaking down of a system into smaller and smaller parts.

Finally, the availability of an opportunity to commit suicide by means of the chosen method further limits our ability to accurately predict the temporal confluence of such an opportunity with a strong enough suicidal impulse. The probability of such a "coincidence" is quite small, considering the previously discussed fluctuation of suicide risk over time.

It should be added here that the known risk factors themselves change depending on the time interval between assessment and eventual suicide. Various longitudinal prospective studies have used a different follow-up period. Fawcett (1988) found a different set of predictors for early suicides (within one year) and long-term suicides (one to five years). Only one item, namely "hopelessness," was a significant predictor variable for both groups.

Since clinicians are mostly interested in the prediction of imminent suicide, the current knowledge does not permit any shortcuts to frequent and repeated evaluations of suicide risk to keep up with its ever-changing levels.

SUICIDE, PARASUICIDE, AND SELF-INJURIOUS BEHAVIOR

One of the questions most frequently asked of clinicians is: "Did he (or she) really mean to commit suicide?" This question implies an uncertainty on our part regarding the motives and intent of a person claiming or appearing to be suicidal. To somehow create a structure for a better understanding of suicidality, we have invented such terms as suicide ideation, impulse, threat, gesture, attempt, and completed suicide. To complicate matters, self-injurious and suicidal behaviors are often confused and can present similar patterns. Sometimes a hierarchy of suicide risk is implied from thought to threat to gesture to attempt and completion. Such a hierarchy is of questionable value because the categories overlap, coexist in the same individuals over time, and do not keep their assigned place

in the presumed rank ordering of risk (a certain kind of ideation, communicated in a particular way, may represent higher risk than an accidental completed suicide). Some individuals chronically threaten suicide while others, such as older white males, may complete suicide on their first try without having ever engaged in other suicidal behaviors beforehand.

Suicide attempters constitute a heterogeneous population whose risk may range from quite low to very high. Also, as has been pointed out, the antecedent suicide risk of suicide completers cannot be entirely judged simply by the outcome. This emphasizes the need to treat suicide risk as a continuous dimension, irrespective of the final result. Although suicide methods can be readily rank-ordered by their lethality, they cannot be relied on to provide a precise estimate of the seriousness of the attempt because the choice of method largely depends on its immediate availability and the suicidal person's knowledge about its effectiveness.

In the overall analysis, risk should be judged on the basis of the following components: (1) the degree of psychological disturbance, often referred to as "perturbation"; (2) suicidal intent by self-report and by objective evaluation; (3) the particular suicidal behavior exhibited; (4) lethality of plan/method selected or used; and (5) the final outcome (see Table 25.1).

From this proposed scheme various scenarios can be derived, and just about any combination is possible. For instance, the subject's perturbation may be low, the self-report may reveal an intent to die, but an objective evaluation of risk factors may indicate that the "real" purpose is a plea for help, the method chosen is of low lethality, but the outcome is death because of miscalculation. Or perturbation is judged to be high, self-report suggests that the intent is an attempt to communicate unhappiness and frustration, but the more objective evaluation indicates a more serious intent to die, the behavior exhibited is a suicide attempt, the lethality of the method is judged to be high, but successful intervention saves the subject with moderate injury. The point is that none of the components by itself is sufficient to make an adequate judgment of suicide risk. All of them have to be

TABLE 25.1. Relevant Components of Self-Destructive Behavior

Intent/Purpose		Plan/Action Method	Outcome
A. *Self-Report*	B. *Objective*	*Level of Lethality:*	*Death*
To Die	To Die	Low	
To Escape	To Escape	Moderate	*Injury:*
To Communicate	To Communicate	High	Light
To Reduce Tension	To Reduce Tension		Moderate
To Punish	To Punish		Severe
To Mutilate	To Mutilate		

Examples			
Self-Report Intent:	To Communicate	To Die	To Mutilate
Objective:	To Die	To Communicate	To Die
Plan:	Low Lethality	Low Lethality	High Lethality
Outcome:	Light Injury	Death	Severe Injury

taken together to do justice to the complexity of the process.

When we compare the different but overlapping populations of attempters and completers, we find that on average, over their lifetime, about 10 to 15 percent of individuals making nonfatal suicide attempts eventually go on to kill themselves (Roy and Linnoila, 1990). On the other hand, 30 to 40 percent of suicide completers have made at least one prior attempt (Maris, 1992). The implication is that most suicide attempters do not end up killing themselves (either because their life circumstances and mental state change or because of successful intervention), but their lifetime suicide risk is nevertheless significantly increased. Individuals with "suicidal careers" have learned to habitually respond to negative life changes by attempting suicide. The histories of such individuals may reveal a large number of suicide attempts, which because of the above considerations should not be taken as evidence for low long-term risk even though most of these attempts may be of low lethality. Evidently, a significant number of such chronic attempters *eventually* end up committing suicide (roughly about 1 percent per year, i.e., approximately 10 percent of today's attempters will commit suicide during the next ten years).

Suicide attempts and self-injurious behavior are even harder to distinguish. Kahan and Pat-

tison (1984) proposed a new diagnosis, "Deliberate Self-Harm Syndrome" (DSH), which they define as: "painful, destructive, injurious acts committed with willful intent upon one's own body without the apparent intent to kill oneself." They feel that suicidal behavior and DSH are related but clinically different phenomena. They find that the following features distinguish DSH from suicide attempts: (1) DSH is more frequent among young people; (2) it is equally frequent in both sexes (completed suicide is more frequent among males); (3) there is low lethality; (4) a sense of relief is experienced in most cases; (5) there is a chronic repetitious pattern; (6) different methods are used by the same individual; (7) self-harmers are seen by others as "manipulative" or "attention seeking"; and (8) death-oriented thoughts are rare.

Upon closer scrutiny, however, these distinguishing characteristics turn out not to be very helpful. Suicide attempts, compared with completions, are frequent among the young; many suicide attempts are of low lethality; suicide attempts often result in a significant decrease in perturbation following the attempt; many suicide attempts are also viewed as "manipulative" and "attention seeking." Furthermore, many persons who engage in self-injurious behavior add suicidal behavior to their repertoire, and some end up killing themselves. A good example of this can be seen in borderline personality disorders. At any given time, the same individual may engage in both types of behavior, and if the method is the same for both, such as cutting, it is indeed difficult to tell which is which. Persons who engage in these behaviors often claim that the purpose of their acts is quite clear to them and are sometimes willing to communicate this, but their self-report cannot be always trusted, because some of them may claim that a self-injurious act represented a suicide attempt if such a claim is perceived as being more advantageous to them.

In summary, DSH, suicide attempts, and completions represent different classes of self-destructive behavior, but in practice they are often hard to distinguish from one another. To the extent that each requires a different treatment approach, it makes our task more complicated—again illustrating the need for thorough training in this area.

IMMEDIATE INDICATORS

Risk factors for suicide can be conveniently grouped into the immediate indicators or proximate signs for impending suicide, on the one hand, and more general background factors, on the other. Maris (1992) found that "suicide attempts are not 'triggered,' that is, the immediate precursors of suicide attempts are not very different from their long-term causes. For the most part, the same factors seem to be operating in the week before the suicide attempt or death as are present as long-term causes of suicide attempts." This means that chronic and acute stressors that contribute to suicide are similar in content, except that acute negative life changes have a more powerful influence, probably because the individual has not yet had an opportunity to adjust himself or herself to them. One should note, however, that the similarity of chronic and acute stressors does not necessarily mean that suicidal behavior is not "triggered." As a matter of fact, it is not too difficult to elicit "critical" events that seem to have precipitated such behaviors. Of course, events can become "critical" because they activate dormant life-long conflicts or touch an area of particular vul-

nerability and sensitivity generated over many years.

One is advised to begin the assessment by concentrating on the more immediate signs, because they are most relevant for short-term prediction.

1. *Verbal communication.* One of the first and most easily observable signals may be verbal communications of intent, either reported directly by the individual or by people close to him or her.
2. *Plan.* Next, it is important to find out if an actual suicide plan has been formed—as distinct from a vague feeling of desire to "not be around any more." Has the plan been in existence for some time, and is it concrete, specific, and detailed?
3. *Method.* Has the method been selected, is the method available and lethal? In the United States, firearms accounted for more than half of all suicidal deaths for the period from 1985 to 1987. Hanging, strangulation, and suffocation rank a distant second, with solid and liquid poisons and gas poisoning close behind. These four categories account for all but 7 percent of suicide in this time period. In contrast to that, poisoning accounts for as much as 90 percent of all nonfatal suicide attempts, with self-cutting ranking next (McIntosh, 1992).
4. *Preparations.* Next, one needs to find out if the time and place for suicide are set and preparations made for death, such as writing a suicide note or a last will and testament, giving away possessions, and getting finances in order. Have provisions been made to avoid rescue—or facilitate it?
5. *Stressors.* Once the determination is made that an immediate intervention is not indicated, one would proceed to obtain information about recent acute stressors, critical events, and possible precipitants.
6. *Mental state.* Finally, a good mental

status evaluation will indicate whether the suicidal person exhibits some of the internal mental states associated with imminent suicide risk, such as despair, powerlessness, self-contempt, murderous rage, feeling alone, having death fantasies, lack of ambivalence, and inability to see alternatives to suicide.

7. *Hopelessness.* In most instances, a combination of these inner states eventually leads to the most powerful antecedent of suicide, namely, hopelessness. This factor emerges in study after study and should be evaluated separately from depression. To the extent that hopelessness and depression measure different mental states, the former seems to have a stronger relationship to suicide than the latter (Beck, Steer, Kovacs, & Garrison, 1985). Readily administered rating scales for measuring hopelessness may be employed (Beck, Weissman, Lester, & Trexler, 1974).

RISK FACTORS

Demographic

Sex has a known and significant relationship to suicide: rates are four to five times higher for men (the ratio is reversed for suicide attempts) (Garrison, 1992).

Age also has a substantial correlation with suicide rates: generally, the rates are higher for older people; this is especially true for white males. While there has been a recent relative increase in suicide rates among youth fifteen to twenty-four years of age (323 percent between 1957 and 1987), even the highest rate in this population barely surpassed the national rate of 12.7 per 100,000 in 1987 (Garrison, 1992).

Regarding *race*, blacks have consistently had lower suicide rates than whites (Garrison, 1992). White males constitute 72 percent of all reported suicides, compared with 1 percent for black females. Combining all three character-

istics, sex, age, and race, the extreme positions regarding suicide risk would be old, white males versus young, black females. There are also significant differences regarding the attempt/completion ratios depending on sex and age: while the typical rate in the general population is estimated to be approximately eight to one among young females, it may be as high as two hundred to one (McIntosh, 1993).

There are also relatively stable differences in suicide rates among various *ethnic and religious groups* as well as *geographic regions*. In addition to individual characteristics, the *cultural context* obviously has an influence on suicide rates. The problem for all demographic factors, including sex, age, and race, is that their contribution to the evaluation of suicide risk in individuals is relatively minor. Thus, to know that your patient is an old Hungarian (high-risk ethnic group) male, without further clinical data, would hardly make him a high-risk individual for suicide.

Personality Traits

Various traits have been identified, mostly anecdotally, as characteristic of suicidal individuals. The following is a list of such traits, but the degree of their association with suicide is largely unknown because their power is likely to depend on the context of other factors and life circumstances:

- inability to express emotions (persons who bottle up negative emotion may eventually show sudden and poorly controlled eruptions with unpredictable behavioral consequences)
- perfectionism and superresponsibility (persons who expect too much of themselves are therefore more vulnerable to feelings of failure)
- sensitivity and "tendermindedness" (sensitive persons are apt to be more reactive to negative life changes)
- pessimism (depressed individuals often show this characteristic)

- dependency (dependent persons are more vulnerable to experiences of rejection and interpersonal loss)
- rigidity (such persons are deficient in the ability to adapt to changing life circumstances, such as aging, retirement, or unemployment)
- impulsivity (such persons are by definition more unpredictable and hence less controllable)
- narcissism (narcissists are unwilling to accept undesirable developments that entail a lower quality of life, such as deterioration due to old age).

Family and Social Factors

It is well demonstrated that a family history of suicide significantly increases the risk of a suicide attempt in a wide variety of diagnostic groups (Roy, 1983). Twin studies demonstrate that monozygotic twin pairs show significantly greater concordance for suicide than do dizygotic twin pairs, but it may be that factors related to suicide represent a genetic predisposition to psychiatric disorders associated with suicide (Roy, 1992). The same review article by Roy concludes that "family, twin, Amish, and adoption studies reviewed here suggested that there may be family/genetic factors in suicide . . . adoption studies strongly suggest that there may be a genetic factor for suicide that is independent of, or additive to, to genetic transmission of affective disorder."

Suicide may also run in families because of role modeling, i.e., the adoption of the prevailing pattern in the family, including suicidal behavior, by other family members. Finally, a family suicide is obviously a significant stress factor resulting in an increased suicide risk among survivors (as a result, suicide survivors are recognized as a high-risk group, leading to such prevention efforts as the establishment of suicide survivor self-support groups).

While certain types of family characteristics seem to facilitate suicide, the absence of family relationships seems to do the same. Persons who are single, divorced, or widowed have a significantly higher suicide risk than do married people (Stack, 1992). Social isolation in general is rather typical of suicidal persons, who often feel alone, abandoned, and uncared for. They have fewer organizational memberships, fewer friends, and a lower quality of relationships, to the extent that they have them at all. Because of all this, preventing isolation is one of the cheapest and most effective intervention strategies.

Psychopathology

Of all the classes of risk factors, this is probably the most important one. The association of mental illness and suicide is well known and documented in numerous studies. A very comprehensive review by Tanney (1992) concludes that "mental disorders are more common in populations of persons completing suicide, and suicide and suicidal behaviors occur much more frequently than expected in populations of psychiatric patients." It is estimated that on the average, 38 percent of completed suicides had a known history of mental disorder and that eventually 4.75 percent of all psychiatric patients will die by suicide.

If one does not rely on the known psychiatric history of persons who have committed suicide, however, but instead digs into their backgrounds by way of clinical studies, a much higher percentage of these suicides can retrospectively receive psychiatric diagnoses. By using medical history through doctor and hospital records, family studies through psychiatric interviews designed to collect symptom information from primary informants, social service and police record searches to determine school and job performance, and employer interviews to determine socioeconomic status and behavior away from home, Robins (1981) was able to assign psychiatric diagnoses to 85 percent of the suicides in his study. This simply means that a significant number of individuals go through life with diagnosable psychiatric disorders that do not leave a paper trail of readily knowable psychiatric histories.

Of the different mental disorders, affective disorders are most often associated with suicide, especially major unipolar depressions with psychotic and melancholic features. Suicide rates are also relatively high among such mental illnesses as schizophrenia, anxiety disorders, and eating disorders, but relatively low among individuals with mental retardation, organic mental disorders, and personality disorders (the latter, as one can expect, have a relatively high nonfatal suicide attempt rate). A warning, though, about the suicide attempts associated with personality disorders. Individuals in this group by their very nature are often quite impulsive, tend to act out, use poor judgment, act irresponsibly, and are easily angered and frustrated. A suicide attempt by such an individual, even of low perturbation, can have an unintended result, namely completed suicide.

Substance-abuse disorders make up another relatively high-risk diagnostic group. The lifetime risk for suicide in this group, while not as high as once thought, is now estimated to be between 2 and 3.4 percent (Murphy & Wetzel, 1990). The earlier higher estimates probably resulted from the inclusion of individuals with concurrent depression. It seems probable that within this subgroup alcoholism is the primary and depression the secondary disorder.

The relationship of substance abuse to suicide very likely rests on three factors. First, intoxication itself has both a disinhibiting and depressant effect (about 20 percent of suicides are legally intoxicated at the time of their deaths; Brent, 1988). Second, substance abuse is felt by many authorities to represent a chronic self-destructive pattern because of its known eventual outcome (sometimes referred to as "subintentioned" suicide). Third, there is the already-discussed tendency of substance abusers to develop secondary depressions.

Stressors and Negative Life Changes

As mentioned earlier, this group of stressors can be either acute or chronic; if acute, they more properly belong under the proximate indicators of suicide.

1. *Loss.* The most important category of stress is probably loss of one kind or another, whether real, anticipated, or imagined: interpersonal and economic losses, loss of affection, loss of health, loss of freedom (such as arrest and incarceration), loss of dignity and self-respect. Some of the loss within the family structure has already been discussed. It has also been found that alcoholics in particular seem to be vulnerable to divorce and separation, which seems to be one of the main triggering factors for suicide in this group.

2. *Unemployment.* A statistical linkage between unemployment and suicide has been amply demonstrated, but from the data it is difficult to make individual-level interpretations regarding the suicide risk of unemployed *individuals.* It may be that unemployment does little more than trigger social processes that increase the probability of suicide for individuals who are already psychiatrically impaired (Wasserman, 1992).

3. *Physical Illness.* It makes ready sense to assume that serious physical illness may be one of the major stressors contributing to suicide. However, the relationship between the two seems more complicated than a simple linear causal link between illness and suicide. Mackenzie and Popkin (1983) in their review article conclude that "physical illness probably enhances the relative risk of death by suicide. This effect is more pronounced in men and seems to increase with age. Chronic incurable and painful conditions seem to exert the most significant effects. Cancer, peptic ulcer, spinal cord injury, multiple sclerosis, Huntington's chorea, and head injury are specifically associated with increased rates of death by suicide." The mechanism by which suicidality is initiated, however, seems to depend on depression precipitated by the loss of

function, and dependency and pain resulting from illness. Again, as in the case of alcoholism, depression turns out to be the ultimate culprit. The authors found that suicide in the absence of significant depression was relatively rare even among terminally ill patients. *Critical Period.* It has been found that psychiatric patients are particularly vulnerable to suicide during authorized and unauthorized passes from an inpatient psychiatric service and shortly following discharge from the hospital. In a study by Roy (1982), it was discovered that 81.3 percent of psychiatric patients who had committed suicide had recently changed from inpatient to outpatient care. Ten percent had committed suicide within four days of leaving the hospital, 29 percent within two weeks, and almost two-thirds by three months after leaving inpatient care. Most of these patients were socially quite isolated and thus did not have the benefit of social support. These data point to the need to provide aggressive follow-up care after hospital discharge.

MEDIATING OR PROTECTIVE VARIABLES

To make the evaluation complete, the clinician needs to address suicidal clients' strengths and positive aspects of their lives as well as the risk factors for suicide.

One obvious area of inquiry would be a person's lifelong ability to cope with stress, failure and loss, his or her previous success in resolving difficulties.

Another trait suggested as protective against suicide is "buoyancy," a resilience (Yufit, 1992), defined as the ability to bounce back and adapt to change.

And then there is the ubiquitous social support, which crops up as a powerful mediating variable in practically the entire psychosocial literature. Yufit (1992) mentions specifically the sense of belonging or connectedness and capac-

ity for intimacy, while Stack (1992) lists such factors as shared religious beliefs and practices, church attendance, and being married. Linehan, Goodstein, Nielsen, and Chiles (1983) developed a Reasons for Living Inventory that identifies six primary factors: survival and coping beliefs, responsibility to family, child-related concerns, fear of suicide, fear of social disapproval, and moral objections. Subsequent research demonstrated that the inventory differentiated suicidal from nonsuicidal subjects.

Finally, Yufit (1992) suggests that Erickson's (1982) developmental stages can serve as indicators of "basic strengths" antithetical to suicide: hope, will, purpose, competence, fidelity, love, care, and wisdom. Considering the above, the clinician's task is to discover and support the client's already-existing strengths and positive aspects of life and functioning.

SUMMARY AND RECOMMENDATIONS

1. Develop written guidelines for assessment of suicide potential.
2. Do not rely entirely on the client's statements regarding suicidal intent, but make an objective evaluation.
3. Use *some* measuring instrument, such as a rating scale, in addition to the interview, preferably one with empirically weighted items, but the ultimate decision should be based on your subjective-intuitive global judgment.
4. In the interview, give considerable weight to the mental status examination, and carefully evaluate such major constructs as hopelessness, cognitive restriction, and low psychic pain tolerance.
5. Pay attention to the primary and secondary psychiatric diagnoses, especially depression.
6. Be careful in your assessment of diagnostic groups that are generally considered at low risk for suicide, such as personality disorders; impulsivity

coupled with miscalculation can lead to death even in persons with low intent and perturbation.

7. Consider suicidality as a continuous dimension in terms of perturbation and lethality.

8. Be conscious at all times that you are making an assessment of suicide risk, not making a prediction of a suicidal event.

9. Involve the family to the extent possible and use collateral information to supplement the client's statements.

10. Obtain a history of family suicides and the client's previous suicide attempts.

11. Be familiar with all the major risk factors as well as with common precursors and triggering events of imminent suicide, including their interaction effects.

12. For highly suicidal individuals, make frequent risk assessments, realizing that risk fluctuates considerably and unpredictably over time.

13. Keep in mind that a history of many nonfatal suicide attempts increases the suicide risk.

14. Remember than there is no substitute for solid training and experience in suicidology.

15. Review each suicide, should one occur, for learning and corrective action. The input of an outside consultant or colleague is recommended in the process.

16. Remove opportunities to commit suicide, especially lethal ones, such as guns. Without an opportunity even an imminently suicidal person cannot commit suicide. This is one of the simplest and most effective methods of suicide prevention.

REFERENCES

Beck, A. T., Steer, R. A., Kovacs, M., & Garrison, B. (1985). Hopelessness and eventual suicide: A ten year prospective study of patients hospitalized with suicide ideation. *American Journal of Psychiatry, 142,* 559–563.

Beck, A. T., Weissman, A., Lester, D., & Trexler, L. (1974). The measurement of pessimism: The Hopelessness Scale. *Journal of Consulting and Clinical Psychology, 42,* 861–865.

Berman, A. L., & Cohen-Sandler, R. (1982, Summer). Suicide and the standard of care: Optimal vs. acceptable. *Suicide and Life-Threatening Behavior, 12*(2), 114–122.

Brent, D. A., Kupfer, D. J., Bromet, E. J., & Dew, M. A. (1988). The assessment and treatment of patients at risk for suicide. In A. J. Frances & R. E. Hales (Eds.), *Review of psychiatry,* (Vol. 7, pp. 353–385). Washington, DC: American Psychiatric Press.

Brown, T. R., & Sheran, T. J. (1972). Suicide prediction: A review. *Suicide and Life-Threatening Behavior, 2,* 67–98.

Erikson, E. H. (1982). *Life cycle completed.* New York: Norton.

Eyman, J. R., & Eyman, S. K. (1992). Personality assessment in suicide prediction. In R. W. Maris, A. L. Berman, J. T. Maltsberger, & R. I. Yufit (Eds.), *Assessment and prediction of suicide,* (pp. 183–201). New York: Guilford Press.

Fawcett, J. (1988). Predictors of early suicide: Identification and early prevention. *Journal of Clinical Psychiatry, 49* (10, Suppl.), 7–8.

Garrison, C. Z. (1992). Demographic predictors of suicide. In R. W. Maris, A. L. Berman, J. T. Maltsberger, & R. I. Yufit (Eds.), *Assessment and prediction of suicide* (pp. 484–498). New York: Guilford Press.

Gleick, J. (1987). *Chaos: Making a new science.* New York: Viking Penguin.

Kahan, J., & Pattison, M. (1984, spring). DSH: Deliberate self-harm syndrome. *Suicide and Life-Threatening Behavior, 14*(1).

Linehan, M. M., Goodstein, J. L., Neilsen, S. L., & Chiles, J. A. (1983). Reasons for staying alive when you are thinking of killing yourself: The Reasons for Living Inventory. *Journal of Consulting and Clinical Psychology, 51*(2), 276–286.

Litman, E. L., Farberow, N. L., Wold, C. I., & Brown, T. R. (1974). Prediction models of suicidal behaviors. In A. T. Beck, H. L. P. Resnik, & D. J. Lettieri (Eds.), *The prediction of suicide,* (pp. 141–159). Bowie, MD: Charles Press.

Lorenz, E. N. (1963). Deterministic nonperiodic flow. *Journal of Atmospheric Sciences, 20,* 130–141.

Mackenzie, T. B., & Popkin, M. K. (1987). Suicide

in the medical patient. *International Journal of Psychiatry in Medicine*, 17(1), 3–22.

Maris, Ronald W. (1992). The relationship of non-fatal suicide attempts to completed suicides. In R. W. Maris, A. L. Berman, J. T. Maltsberger, & R. I. Yufit (Eds.), *Assessment and prediction of suicide*, (pp. 362–380). New York: Guilford Press.

McIntosh, J. L. (1992). Methods of suicide. In R. W. Maris, A. L. Berman, J. T. Maltsberger, & R. I. Yufit (Eds.), *Assessment and prediction of suicide*, (pp. 381–397.). New York: Guilford Press.

McIntosh, J. L. (1993). Rate, number, and ranking of suicide for each U.S.A. state, 1990. National Center for Health Statistics. *NCHS Monthly Vital Statistics Report*, 41(7, Suppl.), 34–35, Table 15.

Motto, J. A. (1985, fall) Preliminary field-testing of a risk estimator for suicide. *Suicide and Life-Threatening Behavior*, 15, 139–150.

Murphy, G. E., & Wetzel, R. D. (1990). The lifetime risk of suicide in alcoholism. *Archives of General Psychiatry*, 47, 383–392.

Pokorny, A. D. (1983). Prediction of suicide in psychiatric patients; Report of a prospective study. *Archives of General Psychiatry*, 40, 249–257.

Robins, E. (1981). *The final months*. New York: Oxford University Press.

Rothberg, J. M., & Geer-Williams, C. (1992). A comparison and review of suicide prediction scales. In R. W. Maris, A. L. Berman, J. T. Maltsberger, & R. I. Yufit (Eds.), *Assessment and prediction of suicide*, (pp. 202–217). New York: Guilford Press.

Roy, A. (1982, September). Risk factors for suicide in psychiatric patients. *Archives of General Psychiatry*, 39, 1089–1095.

Roy, A. (1983). Family history of suicide. *Archives of General Psychiatry*, 40, 971–974.

Roy, A. (1992). Genetics, biology, and suicide in the family. In R. W. Maris, A. L. Berman, J. T. Maltsberger, & R. I. Yufit (Eds.), *Assessment and pre-diction of suicide* (pp. 574–588). New York: Guilford Press.

Roy, A., & Linnoila, M. (1990). Monoamines and suicidal behavior. In H. M. Van Praag, R. Plutchik, & A. Apter (Eds.), *Violence and suicidology: Perspectives in clinical and psychological research*, (pp. 141–183). New York: Brunner/Mazel.

Shneidman, E. S. (1971). Perturbation and lethality as precursors of suicide in a gifted group. *Suicide and Life-Threatening Behavior*, 1, 23–45.

Stack, S. (1992). Marriage, family, religion, and suicide. In R. W. Maris, A. L. Berman, J. T. Maltsberger, & R. I. Yufit (Eds.), *Assessment and prediction of suicide* (pp. 540–552). New York: Guilford Press.

Stelmachers, Z. T., & Sherman, R. E. (1990, Spring). Use of case vignettes in suicide risk assessment. *Suicide and Life Threatening Behavior*, 20(1), 255–274.

Tanney, B. L. (1992). Mental disorders, psychiatric patients and suicide. In R. W. Maris, A. L. Berman, J. T. Maltsberger, & R. I. Yufit (Eds.), *Assessment and prediction of suicide*, (pp. 277–320). New York: Guilford Press.

Tuckman, J., & Youngman, W. F. (1968). Assessment of suicide risk in attempted suicides. In H. L. P. Resnik (Ed.), *Suicidal Behaviors: Diagnosis and management* (pp. 190–197). Boston: Little, Brown.

Wasserman, I. M. (1992). Economy, work, occupation, and suicide. In R. W. Maris, A. L. Berman, J. T. Maltsberger, & R. I. Yufit (Eds.), *Assessment and prediction of suicide* (pp. 520–539). New York: Guilford Press.

Yufit, R. I., Bongar, B. (1992). Suicide, stress and coping with life cycle events. In R. W. Maris, A. L. Berman, J. T. Maltsberger, & R. I. Yufit (Eds.), *Assessment and prediction of suicide* (pp. 553–573). New York: Guilford Press.

26
Assessing Personality Disorders

Thomas A. Widiger
Cynthia J. Sanderson

Axis II is devoted to the diagnosis of personality (and developmental) disorders in DSM-III-R (APA, 1987). This special attention is in recognition of the importance of assessing for the presence of personality disorder symptomatology. Most patients will meet the criteria for at least one DSM-III-R personality disorder, and few (if any) will fail to have maladaptive personality traits. The personality of the patient can contribute to the occurrence, expression, and/or course of an Axis I mental disorder, can affect the treatment of these disorders, and can often itself be the focus of treatment. However, the assessment of personality disorders is controversial and problematic (Perry, 1992; Widiger & Frances, 1987). Our chapter will be concerned with issues that beset this domain of assessment and with various approaches for addressing these issues.

THE PROBLEM

Prior to DSM-III, mental disorder diagnoses were so unreliable that their validity was questionable. Some researchers essentially abandoned the DSM in favor of criteria sets that had a better potential for providing consistent, reliable diagnoses (e.g., Feighner et al., 1972). The authors of DSM-III followed their lead, providing specific and explicit criteria sets for each diagnosis. "The characteristic features consist of easily identifiable behavioral signs or symptoms . . . which require a minimal amount of inference on the part of the observer" (APA, 1987, p. xxiii). This approach, however, has been problematic for personality disorders. "For some disorders . . ., particularly the Personality Disorders, the criteria require much more inference on the part of the observer" (APA, 1987, p. xxiii). It is difficult, if not impossible, to provide specific, explicit criteria for the broad, complex behavior patterns that constitute a personality disorder (PD). As a result, the clinical diagnosis of a PD continues to be unreliable (Mellsop, Varghese, Joshua, & Hicks, 1982). The only PD to be diagnosed reliably in clinical practice has been the antisocial, and its validity has been controversial precisely because of the reliance on overt and specific acts of criminality, delinquency, and irresponsibility rather than more general and inferred traits of psychopathy (Hare, Hart, & Harpur, 1991).

The failure of the DSM-III-R PDs to be assessed reliably in clinical practice is also due in part to a failure to adhere closely to the criteria sets. Morey and Ochoa (1989) provided 291 clinicians with a list of the 166 DSM-III PD criteria (presented in a randomized order) and asked them to provide a DSM-III PD diagnosis for one of their patients and to indicate which of the criteria provided within the list were present or absent. Kappa for the agreement between the diagnoses provided by the clinicians and the diagnoses that would be given on the basis of their own assessments of the PD diagnostic criteria ranged from .11 to .58, indicating substantial disagreement. Seven times as many patients would receive a schizotypal PD diagnosis based on the clinicians' assessment of the schizotypal criteria than were given this diagnosis by the clinicians, and twice as many patients received a narcissistic PD diagnosis than would be given this diagnosis based on their assessment of the narcissistic criteria.

Sex bias in the diagnosis of personality disorders results in large part from a failure to adhere to the diagnostic criteria (Widiger & Spitzer, 1991), as demonstrated in studies by Adler, Drake, & Teague (1990), Ford and Widiger (1989), Hamilton, Rothbart, & Dawes (1986), and Warner (1978). Ford and Widiger, for example, provided clinicians with brief vignettes that varied with respect to the sex of the patient and the extent to which the patient met the DSM-III criteria for the antisocial and the histrionic personality disorders. Clinicians diagnosed the female patients with histrionic PD even when they met the DSM-III criteria for antisocial rather than histrionic PD. Adler et al., Hamilton et al., and Warner likewise demonstrated that sex bias occurred as a result of a tendency to be influenced as much by the sex of the patient as by the patient's symptomatology. Ford and Widiger demonstrated further that the sex of the patient did not influence the clinicians' assessments of the individual histrionic or antisocial criteria. They concluded that "sex biases may best be diminished by an increased emphasis in training programs and clinical settings on the systematic use and adherence to the criteria and diagnostic rules" (Ford & Widiger, 1989, p. 304).

Patients who meet the criteria for one personality disorder will often meet the criteria for another. The average number of personality disorders per inpatient is often three or four, with some patients meeting the criteria for as many as five, six, seven, and even more PD diagnoses (Skodol, Oldham, Rosnick, Kellman, & Hyler, 1991; Zanarini, Frankenburg, Chauncey, & Gunderson, 1987). Nevertheless, clinicians will usually provide just one and at most two personality disorder diagnoses per patient (Gunderson, 1992). Adler et al. (1990) provided forty-six clinicians with case histories that met the DSM III criteria for histrionic, narcissistic, borderline, and dependent PDs. "Despite the directive to consider each category separately . . . most clinicians assigned just one Axis II diagnosis" (Adler et al., 1990, p. 127): 65 percent provided only one, 28 percent provided two, 7 percent provided three, and none provided all four diagnoses.

SEMISTRUCTURED INTERVIEWS

One can obtain reliable assessments if one conducts a systematic interview that comprehensively assesses each of the PD criteria via a consistently applied set of questions, the responses to which are scored in a replicable fashion. A number of semistructured interviews for the assessment of personality disorders have been developed. The most commonly used in research are the Structured Interview for DSM-III-R Personality (SIDP-R; Pfohl, Blum, Zimmerman, & Stangl, 1989), the Structured Clinical Interview for DSM-III-R Personality Disorders (SCID-II; Spitzer, Williams, Gibbon, & First, 1990), the Personality Disorder Examination (PDE; Loranger, 1988), the Personality Interview Questions—II (Widiger, 1987), the Diagnostic Interview for Personality Disorders (DIPD; Zanarini et al., 1987), the Revised Diagnostic Interview for Borderlines (DIB-R; Zanarini, Gunderson, Frankenburg, & Chauncey, 1989), the Hare Psychopathy Checklist—Revised (PCL-R; Hare, 1992), and the Diagnostic Interview for Narcissism (DIN; Gunderson, Ronningstam, & Bodkin, 1990). An additional instrument is the Personality Assessment Form (PAF), but the PAF is not really a structured interview, as it does not provide any questions or a systematic assessment of each PD criterion. It simply presents a brief paragraph that describes the important features of each PD and a six-point scale with which to make a rating (Shea, Glass, Pilkonis, Watkins, & Docherty, 1987).

The DIPD, PAF, PDE, PIQ-II, SCID-II, and SIDP-R assess all of the DSM-III-R personality disorders, whereas the DIN, DIB-R and PCL-R are confined to just one personality disorder (narcissistic, borderline, and antisocial, respectively). As a result, the DIN, DIB-R, and PCL-R provide particularly thorough and informative assessments. However, they do not provide assessments of the DSM-III-R personality disorders. The DIB-R is based on the Gunderson and Zanarini (1987) formulation of borderline personality disorder, which contains a number of significant differences from the DSM-III-R, notably the inclusion of psychotic-like symptomatology (Widiger, Miele, & Tilly, 1992), but the DSM-IV revision of the borderline diagnosis will move somewhat closer to the DIB-R through the inclusion of the new criterion involving dissociative and paranoid symptomatology (Gunderson, Zanarini, & Kisiel, 1991). The PCL-R formulation of psychopathy is even more discrepant with the DSM-III-R formulation of the antisocial PD, but one may in fact prefer the PCL-R (Hare et al., 1991). The PCL-R places more emphasis on psychological traits of psychopathy, such as glib and superficial charm, egocentricity, and lack of empathy, whereas the DSM-III-R antisocial criteria were derived largely from Robins's (1966) more sociological and behavioral indicators of sociopathy.

There are also substantial differences among the interviews that assess all of the DSM-III-R personality disorders. The PDE, PIQ-II, and SIDP-R are organized with respect to thematic content areas (e.g., work, relationships, and emotions), whereas the DIPD and SCID-II are organized with respect to the DSM-III-R diagnostic categories. If it is one's intention to assess all of the criteria for all of the PDs, the reorganized format is preferable because it avoids the redundancy of repeatedly covering similar

ground and minimizes the halo effects that occur when each disorder is considered in turn. Once an interviewer has an opinion regarding a particular PD diagnosis, it is difficult to provide an objective, neutral assessment of the remaining diagnostic criteria.

Very few clinicians, however, will have the time to administer a complete PD semistructured interview. Loranger (1988) recommends that the PDE be administered in two sittings as it can take four hours to complete (most of the semistructured interviews require about two hours). Clinicians fail to provide a comprehensive assessment of personality disorder pathology in large part because it is impractical to do so in routine clinical practice. We therefore recommend that clinicians first administer and score a PD self-report inventory and then provide a thorough assessment of the five to seven PDs that obtained the highest elevations. The SCID-II is in fact constructed in this manner. The SCID-II includes a self-report screening questionnaire constructed to err in the direction of false positives. In addition, because the SCID-II is organized with respect to the PD criteria sets, the interviewer can easily skip the questions that concern the PDs obtaining the lowest scores.

One might be tempted to delete the use of a self-report inventory and simply confine an interview to those PDs that are most likely to be relevant based on one's initial impressions or referral information. However, a purpose for administering a systematic interview and inventory is to overcome inaccurate assumptions and misleading expectations. It is our presumptions and impressions that result in limited, unreliable, and gender-biased diagnoses. A self-report inventory will alert the clinician to areas of inquiry that might not have been anticipated or noticed during a clinical interview or prior assessment.

The SCID-II is particularly attractive because it was constructed to be used in conjunction with a self-report measure, but we would urge clinicians to become familiar with at least three different semistructured interviews. None is obviously better than another, and each will have its own advantages, attractions, and useful suggestions. The SCID-II is relatively expen-

TABLE 26.1. PDE, PIQ-II, SCID-II, and SIDP-R Questions for the DSM-III-R Histrionic Criterion: Constantly seeks or demands reassurance, approval, or praise.

PDE[a]:

29a. Some people are always turning to others for reassurance about themselves. Are you like that?

29b. Some people also have a great need to be appreciated and constantly praised. Are you like that?

PIQ-II[b]:

12a. Are you often unsure or concerned about how others feel about you? (If they have a boy/girlfriend), how about your boy/girlfriend?

12b. Do you ever (often) have to drop hints to get people to express their feelings about you or to reassure you?

12c. Is it important for you to be reminded of how others feel for you?

SCID-II[c]:

70a. Do you often go out of your way to get people to praise you?

70b. Do you do this a lot more than most people?

SIDP-R[d]:

L5. Is the praise and admiration of friends important to you? (If yes), what do you do to win their praise?

L6a. When someone gives you reassurance or compliments you, are you likely to go back to see if they still mean it?

L6b. Do you often seek out approval or reassurance?

[a]Loranger (1988); [b]Widiger (1987); [c]Spitzer et al. (1990); [d]Pfohl et al. (1989).

sive, the SIDP-R has been used in the most published studies (Pfohl et al., 1989), the PDE has a companion interview that was used in the World Health Organization's international epidemiologic study of personality disorders (Loranger, Hirschfeld, Sartorious, & Regier, 1991), videotape training material and workshops are available for the PDE, SCID-II, and SIDP-R, and the authors are currently developing a revision of the PIQ-II that will provide extensive discussion of and coordination with DSM-IV.

Most important, however, is that questions and scoring will vary across the interviews. Table 26.1 presents questions from the PDE, PIQ-II, SCID-II, and SIDP-R for the assessment of the histrionic criterion of constantly seeking or demanding reassurance, approval, or praise. It is evident that the interviews do not assess this criterion in an equivalent manner and could readily provide quite different results (Clark, 1992). For example, the SCID-II assessment is confined largely to praise. Demands for reassurance or approval are not assessed. The PDE requests the subjects to assess whether the trait is present in themselves, whereas the PIQ-II asks the person for examples of the trait.

Skodol et al. (1991) administered both the PDE and the SCID-II to one hundred personality disorder patients. Each interview was administered blind to the other. Agreement was surprisingly poor, with kappa ranging from .14 (schizoid) to .66 (dependent) and a mean kappa of only .45. SCID-II interviews yielded thirty-five PD diagnoses, whereas the PDE provided only fifteen. Skodol et al. (1991) concluded that "it is fair to say that, for a number of disorders (i.e., paranoid, schizoid, schizotypal, narcissistic, and passive-aggressive) the two [interviews] studied do not operationalize the diagnoses similarly and thus yield disparate results" (p. 22). Equally disappointing results were reported by O'Boyle and Self (1990) with respect to the PDE and SCID-II and by Pilkonis, Heape, Ruddy, and Serrao (1991) with respect to the PAF and PDE.

Variability among the interviews is perhaps unavoidable. The personality disorder criteria involve not only broad, complex behavior patterns that are interpreted differently across research sites, but also quite undesirable, embarrassing, and even reprehensible behaviors that are occurring in persons who may be characterized in part by grossly distorted (denigrated or inflated) perceptions of themselves. One cannot just ask persons if each PD criterion is present

(Widiger, Frances, & Trull, 1989). For example, narcissistic persons may not consider themselves to be narcissistic, or especially needy of attention and admiration. And even if they are aware of these needs, they may not want to admit to them in an interview. The semistructured interviews therefore vary in the extent to which they rely on the subject to simply rate themselves on each PD criterion. The SCID-II is perhaps the most straightforward. The PDE asks interviewees if others have told them that they have the trait (e.g., if anyone has ever told them that they lacked empathy). The PIQ-II often provides the person with a scenario or probe to elicit the trait (e.g., asking interviewees to describe how someone else feels in order to assess for a lack of empathy in the description).

All of the interviews emphasize that the subjects' self-assessments should not be taken at face value. Interviewers are encouraged to ask for examples after an affirmative response to assess for themselves whether the trait is indeed present. In other words, the PD interviews are truly *semi*structured. They allow and require considerable judgment and leeway on the part of the clinician. If they were fully structured they would essentially be self-report inventories that were administered orally.

The optimal degree of structure is frankly unclear. The administration of a PD semistructured interview can degenerate into a cursory, superficial symptom count. This may be acceptable and perhaps even desirable to researchers, but it can also provide a fragmented, piecemeal description of isolated behaviors, attitudes, and affects that lack an appreciation or even an awareness of their historical development, interrelationship, and social, environmental context.

> A good clinical assessment of personality begins with taking a history. The clinician asks the patient to tell important stories from across the life span, preserving the life context in which these occurred. Memorable events and important vignettes tell the story of the patient's relationships with family, loved ones, friends, authorities, and co-workers at home, at school, at work, and at leisure. (Perry, 1992, p. 1651)

Perry's relatively unstructured approach will offer a richer and more vivid description than a PDE, but it can also be unreliable, idiosyncratic, and misleading. However, we do recommend that clinicians and researchers precede the administration of a semistructured interview with an accounting of the major events, incidents, issues, and problems that the person has experienced across his or her lifetime. This request can lengthen some interviews considerably, but it does alert the interviewer to key events and issues that should be covered within the systematic questioning provided by a semistructured interview.

Table 26.2 presents interrater reliability data for the five interviews that assess all of the PDs. These findings demonstrate that each of the PDs can be assessed reliably, but equally clearly, each PD can be assessed unreliably even when a semistructured interview is used. Note the poor reliability obtained in the assessment of the paranoid (Zanarini et al., 1987), antisocial and paranoid (Standage & Ladha, 1988), schizotypal (Widiger, Freiman, & Bailey, 1990), histrionic (Brooks, Baltazar, McDowell, Munjack, & Bruns, 1991), dependent and paranoid (Hogg, Jackson, Rudd, & Edwards, 1990), and avoidant (Stangl, Pfohl, Zimmerman, Bowers, & Corenthal, 1985) personality disorders. The use of a semistructured interview does not ensure replicable, reliable assessments because there can be considerable variability in how the interview is administered and scored (e.g., some interviewers will take each question at face value, whereas others will apply substantial inquiry). A reliable and valid assessment of a PD diagnosis depends as much on the training, care, and dependability of the interviewers as it does on the interview. Given the poor reliability that is at times obtained even when a semistructured interview is used, it is surprising that many studies fail to obtain data on the reliability of their semistructured interview assessments. One cannot assume that one's assessments are reliable or replicable simply because one is using a semistructured interview that has been administered reliably in the past.

TABLE 26.2 Interrater Reliability Obtained for Various Semistructured Interviews

Study	Interview	PRN	SZD	SZT	ATS	BDL	HST	NCS	AVD	DPD	CPS	PAG
Zanarini et al. (1987)	DIPD	.52	—	.86	1.0	.94	.87	.87	1.0	.92	.92	.95
Loranger et al. (1987)	PDE	—	—	.80	.70	.96	.77	—	—	—	.88	—
Standage & Ladha (1988)	PDE	.43	—	.62	.38	.78	.77	.63	.69	.70	.62	—
Widiger et al. (1987)	PIQ	.71	.71	.64	.83	.75	.71	.77	.69	.52	.67	.63
Widiger et al. (1990)	PIQ-II	.69	.76	.45	.83	.58	.59	.70	.91	.82	—	.92
Arntz et al. (1992)	SCID-II	.77	—	.65	—	.79	.85	1.0	.82	1.0	.72	.66
Brooks et al. (1991)	SCID-II	.77	—	.89	—	.64	.43	.78	.56	.84	.66	.50
Hogg et al. (1990)	SIDP	.26	.65	.40	.89	.74	.53	.77	.75	.19	.54	.18
Jackson et al. (1991)	SIDP	.61	—	.67	—	.77	.70	—	—	.42	—	—
Stangl et al. (1985)	SIDP	—	—	.55	—	.95	.84	.85	.45	.88	.36	—
Trull (1992)	SIDP-R	.61	.95	.61	.91	.86	.78	.91	.83	.91	.70	.86

Note: Kappa values are provided, except for Hogg et al. (Pearson r correlations) and Trull (intraclass correlation). PRN = paranoid, SZD = schizoid, SZT = schizotypal, ATS = antisocial, BDL = borderline, HTS = histrionic, NCS = narcissist, AVD = avoidant, DPD = dependent, CPS = compulsive, PAG = passive-aggressive, DIPD = Diagnostic Interview for Personality Disorders, PDE = Personality Disorder Examination, PIQ-II = Personality Interview Questions—II, SCID-II = Structured Clinical Interview for DSM-III-R Personality Disorders, and SIDP-R = Structured Interview for DSM-III-R Personality.

SELF-REPORT INVENTORIES

A self-report inventory can be used in conjunction with a semistructured interview to screen out areas of functioning that need not be subjected to systematic scrutiny. The SCID-II provides such a questionnaire, but we would recommend that a clinician use an inventory constructed for the purpose of providing a comprehensive and independent assessment. If an inventory is going to be administered, it might as well be one that would be informative in its own right.

There are just as many self-report inventories to choose from as semistructured interviews. The three most commonly used in research are the Millon Clinical Multiaxial Inventory—II (MCMI-II; Millon, 1987), the Personality Diagnostic Questionnaire—Revised (PDQ-R; Hyler & Rieder, 1987), and the MMPI personality disorder scales developed by Morey, Waugh, and Blashfield (1985). Four more recently developed inventories are the Schedule for Normal and Abnormal Personality (SNAP; Clark, 1993, the Dimensional Assessment of Personality Pathology—Basic Questionnaire (DAPP-BQ; Livesley, 1990), the Wisconsin Personality Disorders Inventory (WISPI; Klein et al., 1993), and the Personality Assessment Inventory (PAI; Morey, 1991).

Again, each has its own advantages and disadvantages. The PDQ-R is popular in large part because it is inexpensive and relatively brief. Its original version (PDQ) was coauthored by the chair of the DSM-III and DSM-III-R Task Force (Robert Spitzer), and the items are linked directly to a DSM-III-R PD criterion. This approach, however, may be rather simplistic. Most of the PD criteria are represented by just one PDQ-R item, with a low threshold for their attribution. For example, the histrionic PD criterion of constantly seeking or demanding reassurance, approval, or praise is assessed by answering true or false to the single statement that "I need more reassurance, approval, or praise than most people" (Hyler & Rieder, 1987). Believing that one needs more reassurance than most people does not imply constantly seeking or demanding it.

The MCMI-II was constructed with more attention to psychometric principles, and it also offers a computerized report. A computerized report, however, can be very seductive (Matarazzo, 1986). There are too many reasons for obtaining an inaccurate assessment via a self-report inventory to rely exclusively on a computerized report. One specific limitation of the MCMI-II is that it attempts to represent both Millon's and the DSM's formulations of the personality disorders, which are at times not particularly congruent (Widiger & Corbitt, 1993). A clinician should always take the time to cross-validate self-report findings with a semistructured interview.

The Morey et al. MMPI PD scales have the advantage of being embedded within an already-popular self-report inventory. Readily interpretable cutoff points are not available, but Morey (1988) has provided norms for each scale. Bagby (1990) has also provided a translation to the MMPI-2. A limitation of the MMPI PD scales, however, is that Morey et al. and Bagby were confined to the existing MMPI(-2) items. They could not construct the optimal set of items to assess each personality disorder and had to use whatever items were available. Costa, Zonderman, Williams, and McCrae (1985) indicated that the MMPI item pool lacks a representation of the personality dimension of conscientiousness, which may be essential for assessing the compulsive personality disorder (Widiger & Trull, 1992).

The WISPI was constructed to assess the DSM-III-R PDs from the perspective of Benjamin's (1993) Structural Analysis of Social Behavior (SASB). The SASB is a complex model of personality that integrates interpersonal circumplex theory and psychoanalytic object relations theory. As such, it can be very intriguing and compelling. The WISPI will receive considerable research and clinical interest, as the SASB model has been hindered to date by the complexity of its assessment. A limitation of the WISPI, however, may be its close ties to the SASB. To the extent that some or most of the personality disorders are more than disorders of interpersonal style (Soldz, Budman, Demby, & Merry, 1993; Wiggins & Pincus, 1989) the WISPI may prove to be inadequate.

The SNAP and DAPP-BQ were constructed to assess dimensions of personality dysfunction identified through factor analyses of PD symptomatology (e.g., impulsivity, workaholism, aggression, entitlement, & aggression; Clark, 1990). An advantage of the SNAP and DAPP-BQ is that they assess relatively independent dimensions of dysfunction that have a concrete

relevance to treatment, rather than the overlapping and poorly differentiated PD diagnoses. A disadvantage is that many clinicians need or prefer to assess the DSM-III-R PDs.

The PAI does not provide a scale for each of the DSM-III-R personality disorders. Instead, it provides scales for borderline features, antisocial features, and for the interpersonal dimensions of dominance and warmth. One might be able to derive assessments for each of the personality disorders from these scales, but this has not yet been demonstrated.

Table 26.3 provides correlations of the MCMI(-II), PDQ(-R), and MMPI PD scales with interview-based assessments of the PDs and with each other. There is little to suggest from this research that one instrument is clearly preferable to another. The MCMI(-II) does appear to be weak with respect to the antisocial and compulsive PDs, but we in fact find the MCMI-II compulsive scale to provide a better representation of excessive, maladaptive conscientiousness than the PDQ-R or MMPI (Widiger & Corbitt, 1993). The choice among the alternatives will be likely to depend on their relative advantages with respect to the particular needs and interests of the clinician: whether one wants to assess the PDs from the perspective of the SASB (WISPI), Millon's model of personality disorders (MCMI-II), or normal personality functioning (SNAP); whether one already is administering the MMPI; whether one wants a relatively brief screening instrument (PDQ-R); or whether one wants a computerized report (MCMI-II).

ISSUES TO CONSIDER

The assessment of personality disorders is exceedingly difficult. It is not simply a matter of administering a semistructured interview and a self-report inventory. Three issues that are worth considering in particular are (a) the confusion of states with traits; (b) arbitrary and illusory categorical distinctions; and (c) adaptivity versus maladaptivity.

TABLE 26.3. Convergent Validity Coefficients for Various Self-Report Inventories[1]

Instruments	PRN	SZD	SZT	ATS	BDL	HST	NCS	AVD	DPD	CPS	PAG
MCMI/SIDP[a]	.29	.40	.31	.23	.32	.05	.04	.53	.51	−.29	.28
MCMI/SIDP[b]	.22	.39	.37	—	.32	.20	.18	.42	.38	−.05	.14
MCMI/SIDP[c]	.28	.20	.15	.30	.80	.22	.14	.31	.38	.15	.50
MCMI/SIDP[d]	.20	.31	.23	.14	.63	.07	.26	.56	.31	.02	.41
MCMI-II/PDE[e]	.38	.48	.39	.37	.60	.56	.41	.51	.38	−.05	.41
PDQ/SIDP[a]	.56	.33	.49	.78	.64	.47	.53	.51	.59	.52	.46
PDQ/SIDP[f]	.43	.24	.34	.55	.39	.42	.26	.30	.35	.47	.37
PDQ-R/PDE[1g]	.12	−.02	.54	.36	.46	.18	.42	.53	.52	.38	.21
PDQ-R/PDE[1h]	.10	.26	.00	—	.42	.22	.10	.37	.14	.37	.33
PDQ-R/SCID-II[1g]	.27	.43	.48	.42	.53	.24	.34	.63	.57	.30	.23
PDQ-R/SCID-II[1h]	.25	.00	−.03	—	.37	.32	.23	.46	.53	.42	.46
PDQ-R/SIDP-R[i]	.31	.60	.32	.44	.48	.40	.38	.35	.55	.47	.43
MMPI/SIDP-R[j]	.33	.47	.35	.53	.66	.31	.10	.47	.40	.24	.47
MCMI/PDQ[a]	.30	.28	.38	.15	.47	.15	.47	.68	.53	−.47	.59
MCMI/MMPI[j]	.33	.64	.41	.30	.55	.61	.66	.62	.52	−.38	.51
MCMI/MMPI[k]	.44	.35	.51	.14	.28	.66	.55	.65	.68	−.42	.50
MCMI/MMPI[l]	.69	.68	.78	.25	.54	.71	.55	.76	.68	−.31	.48
MCMI/MMPI[m]	.45	.61	.55	.14	.49	.71	.70	.77	.60	−.49	.70
MCMI/MMPI[m]	.19	.22	.57	.13	.49	.44	.49	.69	.59	−.50	.65
MCMI/MMPI[n]	.08	.67	.74	.15	.42	.68	.78	.82	.50	−.30	.57
MCMI-II/MMPI[o]	.50	.73	.86	.57	.68	.74	.65	.87	.56	−.04	.70
MMPI/PDQ-R[p]	.42	.26	.46	.51	.75	.32	−.04	.57	.60	.36	.62

Note: PRN = paranoid, SZD = schizoid, SZT = schizotypal, ATS = antisocial, BDL = borderline, HTS = histrionic, NCS = narcissist, AVD = avoidant, DPD = dependent, CPS = compulsive, PAG = passive-aggressive, MCMI(-II) = Millon Clinical Multiaxial Inventory(-II), SIDP(-R) = Structured Interview for DSM-III(-R) Personality Disorders; PDE = Personality Disorder Examination; PDQ(-R) = Personality Diagnostic Questionnaire (-Revised); SCID-II = Structured Clinical Interview for DSM-III-R Personality Disorders.

[1]All values are Pearson r correlations, with exception of kappa values from Hyler et al. (1990, 1992).

[a]Reich et al. (1987); [b]Torgersen & Alnaes (1990); [c]Nazikian et al. (1990); [d]Jackson et al. (1991); [e]Soldz et al. (1993); [f]Zimmerman & Coryell (1990); [g]Hyler et al. (1990); [h]Hyler et al. (1992); [i]Trull & Larsen (1991); [j]Streiner & Miller (1988); [k]Dubro & Wetzler (1989); [l]Morey & LeVine (1988); [m]Zarrelle et al. (1990); [n]McCann (1989); [o]McCann (1991); [p]Trull (1993).

States (Axis I) Versus Traits (Axis II)

Persons who are depressed will tend to describe themselves as being more dependent, introverted, self-conscious, vulnerable, and pessimistic than they would have before the onset of their depression. Hopelessness, low self-esteem, and negativism are typical manifestations of a depressed mood, and it is to be expected that depressed persons will provide inaccurate and distorted descriptions of their personality. This distortion will even continue after the remission of the more florid symptoms (Hirschfeld et al., 1989). It has been demonstrated in a multitude of studies that a self-report inventory will provide inflated or deflated (i.e., inaccurate) assessments of personality traits when the subject is

depressed, anxious, or psychotic (Widiger, 1993).

For example, Piersma (1987) observed substantial changes in MCMI scale elevations across a brief inpatient treatment. Twenty-five percent of his 151 patients were diagnosed with borderline PD by the MCMI at admission, and only 7.3 percent at discharge; 12 percent with schizotypal PD at admission and only 4 percent at discharge. Test-retest kappa was only .11 for the borderline diagnosis, .09 for compulsive, .01 for passive-aggressive, and .27 for schizotypal. The MCMI-II includes a variety of correction scales to control for the effects of depression and anxiety (Millon, 1987). However, Piersma (1989) reported comparable results for the MCMI-II. Significant decreases were found for the schizoid, avoidant, dependent, passive-aggressive, self-defeating, schizotypal, borderline, and paranoid scales. Significant increases were obtained with the histrionic and narcissistic scales (which include items that involve self-confidence, assertion, and gregariousness). Piersma (1989) concluded that "quite clearly . . . the MCMI-II is not able to measure long-term personality characteristics ('trait' characteristics) independent of symptomatology ('state' characteristics)" (p. 91).

We recommend that a self-report inventory not be administered within the first few days or in some cases within the first weeks of the initiation of treatment. This is a severe admonition because it is precisely during this time that such an assessment is usually desired, but the problem is equally severe.

Semistructured interviews have the potential to be more resilient to mood state distortions (Loranger et al., 1991; Widiger & Frances, 1987) but they are not immune to such effects (O'Boyle & Self, 1990; Stuart, Simons, Thase, & Pilkonis, 1992). An interviewer can easily fail to appreciate the extent to which the subjects' recent or current depressed mood is affecting their self-descriptions. In addition, because the results from a semistructured interview depend substantially on the training, care, and dependability of the interviewers, semistructured interviews can be very unreliable across time and across research sites. If the patient is not appreciably depressed or anxious, self-report inventories may provide more reliable assessments across long periods of time and across clinical and research sites.

An additional option is to administer an interview and/or an inventory to a close friend or relative of the patient (Ford & Landsman, 1992). This informant will (presumably) not be depressed or anxious and can have the advantage over a clinician in knowing the subject for some time before the onset of the Axis I disorder. Zimmerman et al. (1988), however, reported quite poor agreement between patient and informant interviews with the SIDP, with correlations ranging from .17 (compulsive) to .61 (antisocial). The informants identified sig-

nificantly more dependent, avoidant, narcissistic, paranoid, and schizotypal traits. Zimmerman et al. (1988) concluded that "patients were better able to distinguish between their normal personality and their illness" (p. 737), but it is also possible that the informants were more cognizant of the patients' maladaptive traits. Additional work is needed to determine whether close friends or relatives can indeed provide useful descriptions of the personalities of persons who are suffering from an Axis I mental disorder.

To differentiate between an Axis I and Axis II disorder the interviewer should confirm that the behavior pattern was evident since late childhood or early adulthood (APA, 1987). Curiously, no PD assessment instrument includes this requirement. Some do require that the symptoms be evident for a period of time (e.g., a few years) before the current moment. The PDE has perhaps the most explicit criteria, requiring that the symptom be evident in the past year and over a span of five years (but no indication of how often the symptom should be evident within the five years). However, nineteen of the PD symptoms (e.g., the borderline criterion of recurrent suicidal threats, gestures, or self-mutilating behavior) can be scored as present even if they have occurred just once over the five-year period. These exceptions are provided for "behaviors that may occur relatively infrequently, yet have considerable clinical significance, e.g., suicidal gestures, arrests, etc." (Loranger, 1988, p. 11). These exceptions are perhaps necessary results of assessing behavioral manifestations of a trait rather than the trait itself. Recurrent suicidality as a personality trait should be evident more than once over a five-year period, but particular manifestations of this trait will vary substantially in the frequency of their occurrence (Block, 1989). Self-mutilation is a prototypic borderline act, but some borderlines may never self-mutilate. On the other hand, just one occurrence of a suicidal gesture, no matter how intense or dramatic, could easily be attributable to a mood, psychotic, or anxiety disorder rather than to a borderline personality disorder.

Categorical Distinctions

It is "when personality traits are inflexible and maladaptive and cause either significant functional impairment or subjective distress that they constitute Personality Disorders" (APA, 1987, p. 335) but the thresholds for the DSM-III-R PD diagnoses do not themselves identify the point at which personality traits become maladaptive. For example, the decision to require four of seven features to make a diagnosis of avoidant PD was based simply on the rationale that three or fewer would not be sufficiently close to a prototypic case of avoidant PD to warrant a diagnosis. Persons with fewer than four features will have clinically significant maladaptive avoidant traits.

Because there is no clear or nonarbitrary boundary between the presence versus absence of a personality disorder, it is hardly surprising that clinicians disagree with respect to the threshold for a diagnosis. The poor reliability that has been obtained in clinical practice by Mellsop et al. (1982) and others is then understandable. Reliability with respect to the extent to which each PD is present tends to be much higher (Heumann & Morey, 1989). It is easier to agree on a decision that recognizes the shades of gray (e.g., the degree to which a maladaptive trait is present) than a decision that forces an arbitrary, black-white distinction somewhere along the shades of gray (e.g., presence versus absence of a borderline personality disorder). Pilkonis (1992) demonstrated that a change in the assessment of just one PD criterion could improve kappa with respect to the diagnosis of a personality disorder from .42 to .93, or reduce it from .42 to .18. The change in the assessment of a single PD criterion has no such effect on the assessment of the extent to which each PD is present.

The clinical practice of providing just one PD diagnosis per patient is also understandable. Patients will meet the criteria for five PDs, but it makes little sense within a categorical model to provide five PD diagnoses, as if the patient is suffering from five distinct and comorbid personality disorders, each with its own specific etiology and treatment implications. What makes more sense is to say that the patient has one personality disorder, characterized by a variety of maladaptive personality traits. Oldham et al. (1992) suggested that if a patient meets the criteria for two PDs, both should be given, but if the patient meets the criteria for three or more then a single diagnosis of "extensive" personality disorder be given with a dimensional description of the predominant characteristics.

Adaptivity Versus Maladaptivity

The adaptivity and maladaptivity of a personality trait will vary across time, roles, and situations. The same degree of tough-minded antagonism that is maladaptive within some situations (e.g., for success as a pastoral counselor or therapist) will be adaptive within others (e.g., for success as a police officer). Any particular personality disorder symptom can have adaptive as well as maladaptive consequences. Adaptive correlates of histrionic, compulsive, antisocial (psychopathic), narcissistic, and borderline traits have been noted by a variety of authors (e.g., Leaf et al., 1990; Sutker, Bugg, & West, 1993). This is not recognized by the black-white DSM-III-R PD taxonomy, with one notable exception. The DSM-III-R criteria for self-defeating personality disorder had an exclusion criterion that "the behaviors . . . do not occur exclusively in response to, or in anticipation of, being physically, sexually, or psychologically abused" (APA, 1987, p. 374) because submissive, deferential, and acquiescent behavior could very well be adaptive within the context of an ongoing abusive relationship (Walker, 1987). No PD self-report inventory, however, assesses for this exclusion criterion, nor do most of the semistructured interviews.

Rather than impose arbitrary, black-white distinctions of normality versus abnormality, one might consider an entirely different approach. An alternative classificatory system would be to describe a personality with respect to the five-factor dimensions of neuroticism, introversion versus extroversion, openness to experience, agreeableness versus antagonism, and conscientiousness, a dimensional model of normal personality that has substantial empirical support (Digman, 1990; Wiggins & Pincus, 1992). The personality of any person, whether or not they are a patient and whether or not they meet the DSM-III-R criteria for a personality disorder, can be described comprehensively within this model.

The DSM-III-R PDs can also be readily understood as maladaptive variants of the five factors, and one could provide a DSM-III-R PD diagnosis on the basis of a profile description along these five dimensions (Widiger, Trull, Clarkin, Sanderson, & Costa, 1994). For example, excessive neuroticism (particularly the facets of impulsivity, hostility, and depression) and antagonism would suggest a diagnosis of borderline personality disorder. However, rather than force persons into this categorical taxonomy, it is perhaps more informative to simply describe them along the five dimensions and then assess the maladaptivity and adaptivity of their traits within their social and occupational context and their personal goals, aspirations, and values.

A self-report inventory for the assessment of the five factors (and six facets within each factor) was developed by Costa and McCrae (1992; the Revised NEO Personality Inventory), with versions to be completed by the subject (Form S) or by an informant (Form R). Relatively inexpensive computer scoring and hand-scoring templates are also available. Regrettably, a semistructured interview for the five-factor model is not yet available.

CONCLUSIONS

We favor the use of a semistructured interview for the assessment of the personality disorders, particularly when the patient is appreciably depressed or anxious. Regrettably, however, few clinicians have been trained in the use of semistructured interviews. It is frankly surprising that clinical training programs will devote a whole semester to the use of projective techniques but not one minute to the use of semis-

tructured interviews. We would not recommend one semistructured interview over another, nor would we recommend that a clinician rely on any one of them. We would instead recommend that the clinician obtain a copy of all of them, gleaning from each useful questions, suggestions, and ideas. What is important is to have an explicit set of questions that are both systematic and comprehensive in their assessment and that are used consistently across patients.

We also advise an initial or joint administration of a self-report inventory. Given the complexity and difficulty of a personality disorder assessment, multiple methods should be the norm rather than the exception. Just as an interview is helpful in cross-validating the results of an inventory, an inventory can be helpful in checking the impressions from an interview and in identifying areas of inquiry for an interview. Self-report inventories may also provide better temporal and intersite reliability than a semistructured interview when subjects are not appreciably anxious or depressed. Administering an inventory or an interview to a close friend or relative of the patient will also be useful in identifying additional areas of personality dysfunction. In any case, we recommend that clinicians reinterview the patient after reviewing the results from an informant or a self-report inventory to resolve any inconsistencies or ambiguities.

We also advise that clinicians consider the social, occupational, and personal context in which the person must function, and ensure that the most significant social, personal, and occupational decisions, events, and incidents across the person's lifespan have been considered. A comprehensive assessment of the patient's entire personality, including adaptive as well as maladaptive traits, will also be more informative than simply a DSM-III-R personality disorder diagnosis.

REFERENCES

Adler, D. A., Drake, R. E., & Teague, G. B. (1990). Clinicians' practices in personality assessment:

Does gender influence the use of DSM-III Axis II? *Comprehensive Psychiatry, 31,* 125–133.

American Psychiatric Association. (1987). *Diagnostic and statistical manual of mental disorders* (3rd ed., rev. ed.). Washington, DC: Author.

Arntz, A., van Beijsterveldt, B., Hoekstra, R., Hofman, A., & Sallaerts, E. M. (1992). The interrater reliability of a Dutch version of the Structured Clinical Interview for DSM-III-R Personality Disorders. *Act Psychiatrica Scandanavica, 85,* 394–400.

Bagby, R. M. (1990). Status of the MMPI personality disorder scales on the MMPI-2. *MMPI-2 News and Profiles, 1*(2), 8.

Benjamin, L. S. (1993). *Interpersonal diagnosis and treatment of personality disorders* New York. Guilford Press.

Block, J. (1989). Critique of the act frequency approach to personality. *Journal of Personality and Social Psychology, 56,* 234–245.

Brooks, R. B., Baltazar, P. L., McDowell, D. E., Munjack, D. J., & Bruns, J. R. (1991). Personality disorders co-occurring with panic disorder with agoraphobia. *Journal of Personality Disorders, 5,* 328–336.

Clark, L. A. (1990). Toward a consensual set of symptom clusters for assessment of personality disorder. In J. Butcher & C. Spielberger (Eds.), *Advances in personality assessment* (Vol. 8, pp. 243–266). Hillsdale, NJ: Erlbaum.

Clark, L. A. (1992). Resolving taxonomic issues in personality disorders. *Journal of Personality Disorders, 6,* 360–376.

Clark, L. A. (1993). *Manual for the Schedule for Normal and Abnormal Personality (SNAP).* Minneapolis: University of Minnesota Press.

Costa, P. T., & McCrae, R. R. (1992). *Revised NEO Personality Inventory (NEO PI-R) and NEO Five-Factor Inventory (NEO-FFI) professional manual.* Odessa, FL: Psychological Assessment Resources.

Costa, P. T., Zonderman, A., Williams, R., & McCrae, R. (1985). Content and comprehensiveness of the MMPI: An item factor analysis in a normal adult sample. *Journal of Personality and Social Psychology, 48,* 925–933.

Digman, J. M. (1990). Personality structure: Emergence of the Five-Factor model. *Annual Review of Psychology, 41,* 417–440.

Dubro, A. F., & Wetzler, S. (1989). An external validity study of the MMPI personality disorder scales. *Journal of Clinical Psychology, 45,* 570–575.

Feighner, J. P., Robins, E., Guze, S. B., Woodruff, R. A., Winokur, G., & Munoz, R. (1972). Diagnostic criteria for use in psychiatric research. *Archives of General Psychiatry, 26,* 57–63.

Ford, M. R., & Widiger, T. A. (1989). Sex bias in the diagnosis of histrionic and antisocial personality disorders. *Journal of Consulting and Clinical Psychology, 57,* 301–305.

Ford, T. W., & Landsman, C. S. (1992). "What I could tell you:" The Chicago–New York study of intimate relationships. *Journal of Libidinal Drives, 7,* 37–40.

Gunderson, J. G. (1992). Diagnostic controversies. In A. Tasman & M. B. Riba (Eds.), *Review of psychiatry* (Vol. 11, pp. 9–24). Washington, DC: American Psychiatric Press.

Gunderson, J. G., Ronningstam, E., & Bodkin, A. (1990). The diagnostic interview for narcissistic patients. *Archives of General Psychiatry, 47,* 676–680.

Gunderson, J. G., & Zanarini, M. C. (1987). Current overview of the borderline diagnosis. *Journal of Clinical Psychiatry, 48* (Suppl.), 5–11.

Gunderson, J. G., Zanarini, M. C., & Kisiel, C. L. (1991). Borderline personality disorder: A review of data on DSM-III-R descriptions. *Journal of Personality Disorders, 5,* 340–352.

Hamilton, S., Rothbart, M., & Dawes, R. M. (1986). Sex bias, diagnosis, and DSM-III. *Sex Roles, 15,* 269–274.

Hare, R. D. (1992). *Hare Psychopathy Checklist—Revised.* Odessa, FL: Psychological Assessment Resources.

Hare, R. D., Hart, S. D., & Harpur, T. J. (1991). Psychopathy and the DSM-IV criteria for antisocial personality disorder. *Journal of Abnormal Psychology, 100,* 391–398.

Heumann, K., & Morey, L. C. (1990). Reliability and categorical and dimensional judgments of personality disorder. *American Journal of Psychiatry, 147,* 498–500.

Hirschfeld, R. M., Klerman, G. L., Lavori, P., Keller, M., Griffith, P., & Coryell, W. (1989). Premorbid personality assessments of first onset of major depression. *Archives of General Psychiatry, 46,* 345–350.

Hogg, B., Jackson, H. J., Rudd, R. P., & Edwards, J. (1990). Diagnosing personality disorders in recent-onset schizophrenia. *Journal of Nervous and Mental Disease, 178,* 194–199.

Hyler, S. E., & Rieder, R. O. (1987). *Personality Diagnostic Questionnaire—Revised (PDQ-R).* New York: Authors.

Hyler, S. E., Skodol, A. E., Kellman, H. D., Oldham,

J. M., & Rosnick, L. (1990). Validity of the Personality Diagnostic Questionnaire—Revised: Comparison with two structured interviews. *American Journal of Psychiatry, 147,* 1043–1048.

Hyler, S. E., Skodol, A. E., Oldham, J. M., Kellman, H. D., & Doidge, N. (1992). Validity of the Personality Diagnostic Questionnaire—Revised: A replication in an outpatient sample. *Comprehensive Psychiatry, 33,* 73–77.

Jackson, H. J., Gazis, J., Rudd, R. P., & Edwards, J. (1991). Concordance between two personality disorder instruments with psychiatric inpatients. *Comprehensive Psychiatry, 32,* 252–260.

Klein, M. H., Benjamin, L. S., Rosenfeld, R., Treece, C., Justed, J., & Greist, J. H. (1993). The Wisconsin Personality Disorders Inventory: I. Development, reliability, and validity. *Journal of Personality Disorders, 7,* 285–303.

Leaf, R. C., DiGiuseppe, R., Ellis, A., Mass, R., Backx, W., Wolfe, J., & Alington, D. E. (1987). "Healthy" correlates of MCMI scales 4, 5, 6, and 7. *Journal of Personality Disorders, 4,* 312–328.

Livesley, W. J. (1990). *Dimensions of Personality Pathology—Basic Questionnaire.* Unpublished manuscript, University of British Columbia.

Loranger, A. W. (1988). *Personality Disorder Examination (PDE) manual.* Yonkers, NY: DV Communications.

Loranger, A. W., Hirschfeld, R. M., Sartorius, N., & Regier, D. A. (1991). The International Pilot Study of Personality Disorders: Background and purpose. *Journal of Personality Disorders, 5,* 296–306.

Loranger, A. W., Lenzenweger, M. F., Gartner, A. F., Susman, V. L., Herzig, J., Zammit, G. K., Gartner, J. D., Abrams, R. C., & Young, R. C. (1991). Trait-state artifacts and the diagnosis of personality disorders. *Archives of General Psychiatry, 48,* 720–728.

Loranger, A. W., Susman, V. L., Oldham, J. M., & Russakoff, L. M. (1987). The Personality Disorder Examination: A preliminary report. *Journal of Personality Disorders, 1,* 1–13.

Matarazzo, J. (1986). Computerized clinical psychological test interpretations. *American Psychologist, 41,* 14–24.

McCann, J. T. (1989). MMPI personality disorder scales and the MCMI: Concurrent validity. *Journal of Clinical Psychology, 45,* 365–369.

McCann, J. T. (1991). Convergent and discriminant validity of the MCMI-II personality disorder scales. *Psychological Assessment: A Journal of Consulting and Clinical Psychology, 3,* 9–18.

Mellsop, G., Varghese, F. T. N., Joshua, S., & Hicks, A. (1982). The reliability of Axis II of DSM-III. *American Journal of Psychiatry, 139,* 1360–1361.

Millon, T. (1987). *Manual for the MCMI-II* (2nd ed.). Minneapolis, MN: National Computer Systems.

Morey, L. C. (1988). *The MMPI personality disorder scales: A manual and guide to interpretation.* Unpublished manuscript, Vanderbilt University, Nashville, TN.

Morey, L. C. (1991). *The Personality Assessment Inventory professional manual.* Odessa, FL: Psychological Assessment Resources.

Morey, L. C., & LeVine, D. J. (1988). A multitrait-multimethod examination of Minnesota Multiphasic Personality Inventory (MMPI) and Millon Clinical Multiaxial Inventory (MCMI). *Journal of Psychopathology and Behavioral Assessment, 10,* 333–344.

Morey, L. C., & Ochoa, E. S. (1989). An investigation of adherence to diagnostic criteria: Clinical diagnosis of the DSM-III personality disorders. *Journal of Personality Disorders, 3,* 180–192.

Morey, L. C., Waugh, M. H., & Blashfield, R. K. (1985). MMPI scales for DSM-III personality disorders: Their derivation and correlates. *Journal of Personality Assessment, 49,* 245–251.

Nazikian, H., Rudd, R. P., Edwards, J., & Jackson, H. J. (1990). Personality disorder assessments for psychiatric inpatients. *Australian and New Zealand Journal of Psychiatry, 24,* 37–46.

O'Boyle, M., & Self, D. (1990). A comparison of two interviews for DSM-III-R personality disorders. *Psychiatry Research, 32,* 85–92.

Oldham, J. M., Skodol, A. E., Kellman, H. D., Hyler, S. E., Rosnick, L., & Davies, M. (1992). Diagnosis of DSM-III-R personality disorders by two structured interviews: Patterns of comorbidity. *American Journal of Psychiatry, 149,* 213–220.

Perry, J. C. (1992). Problems and considerations in the valid assessment of personality disorders. *American Journal of Psychiatry, 149,* 1645–1653.

Pfohl, B., Blum, N., Zimmerman, M., & Stangl, D. (1989). *Structured Interview for DSM-III-R Personality. SIDP-R.* Iowa City: University of Iowa College of Medicine.

Piersma, H. L. (1987). The MCMI as a measure of DSM-III Axis II diagnoses: An empirical comparison. *Journal of Clinical Psychology, 43,* 478–483.

Piersma, H. L. (1989). The MCMI-II as a treatment outcome measure for psychiatric inpatients. *Journal of Clinical Psychology, 45,* 87–93.

Pilkonis, P. A. (1992, September). *Assessing person-*

ality disorders. Paper presented at Cornell University Medical Center—Westchester Division, White Plains, NY.

Pilkonis, P. A., Heape, C. L., Ruddy, J., & Serrao, P. (1991). Validity in the diagnosis of personality disorders: The use of the LEAD standard. *Psychological Assessment: A Journal of Consulting and Clinical Psychology, 3,* 46–54.

Reich, J., Noyes, R., & Troughton, E. (1987). Lack of agreement between instruments assessing DSM III personality disorders. In C. Green (Ed.), *Conference on the Millon clinical inventories* (pp. 223–234). Minnetonka, MN: National Computer Systems.

Robins, L. N. (1966). *Deviant children grown up.* Baltimore: Williams & Wilkins.

Shea, M. T., Glass, D. R., Pilkonis, P. A., Watkins, J., & Docherty, J. P. (1987). Frequency and implications of personality disorders in a sample of depressed outpatients. *Journal of Personality Disorders, 1,* 27–42.

Skodol, A. E., Oldham, J. M., Rosnick, L., Kellman, H. D., & Hyler, S. E. (1991). Diagnosis of DSM-III-R personality disorders: A comparison of two structured interviews. *International Journal of Methods in Psychiatric Research, 1,* 13–26.

Soldz, S., Budman, S., Demby, A., & Merry, J. (1993). Representation of personality disorders in circumplex and Five-Factor space: Explorations with a clinical sample. *Psychological Assessment, 5,* 41–52.

Soldz, S., Budman, S., Demby, A., & Merry, J. (1993). Diagnostic agreement between the Personality Disorder Examination and the MCMI-II. *Journal of Personality Assessment, 60,* 486–499.

Spitzer, R. L., Williams, J. B. W., Gibbon, M., & First, M. B. (1990). *User's guide for the Structured Clinical Interview for DSM-III-R. SCID.* Washington, DC: American Psychiatric Press.

Standage, K., & Ladha, N. (1988). An examination of the reliability of the Personality Disorder Examination and a comparison with other methods of identifying personality disorders in a clinical sample. *Journal of Personality Disorders, 2,* 267–271.

Stangl, D., Pfohl, B., Zimmerman, M., & Corenthal, C. (1985). A structured interview for the DSM-III personality disorders. A preliminary report. *Archives of General Psychiatry, 42,* 591–596.

Streiner, D. L., & Miller, H. R. (1988). Validity of the MMPI scales for DSM-III personality disorders: What are they measuring? *Journal of Personality Disorders, 2,* 238–242.

Stuart, S., Simons, A. D., Thase, M. E., & Pilkonis, P. (1992). Are personality disorders valid in acute major depression? *Journal of Affective Disorders, 24,* 281–290.

Sutker, P. B., Bugg, F., & West, J. A. (1993). Antisocial personality disorder. In P. B. Sutker and H. E. Adams (Eds.), *Comprehensive handbook of psychopathology* (2nd ed., pp. 337–370). New York: Plenum.

Torgersen, S., & Alnaes, R. (1990). The relationship between the MCMI personality scales and DSM-III, Axis II. *Journal of Personality Assessment, 55,* 698–707.

Trull, T. J. (1992). DSM-III-R personality disorders and the Five-Factor model of personality: An empirical comparison. *Journal of Abnormal Psychology, 101,* 553–560.

Trull, T. J. (1993). Temporal stability and validity of two personality disorder inventories. *Psychological Assessment, 5,* 11–18.

Trull, T. J., & Larsen, S. L. (1991, August). *External validity of two personality disorder inventories.* Paper presented at the 99th Annual Meeting of the American Psychological Association, San Francisco.

Walker, L. (1987). Inadequacies of the masochistic personality disorder diagnosis for women. *Journal of Personality Disorders, 1,* 183–189.

Warner, R. (1978). The diagnosis of antisocial and hysterical personality disorders. An example of sex bias. *Journal of Nervous and Mental Disease, 166,* 839–845.

Widiger, T. A. (1987). *Personality Interview Questions—II.* Lexington: University of Kentucky.

Widiger, T. A. (1993). Personality and depression: Assessment issues. In M. H. Klein, D. J. Kupfer, & M. T. Shea (Eds.), *Personality and depression. A current view* (pp. 77–118). New York: Guilford Press.

Widiger, T. A., & Corbitt, E. M. (1993). The MCMI-II personality disorder scales and their relationship to DSM-III-R diagnosis. In R. J. Craig (Ed.), *The Millon Clinical Multiaxial Inventory: A clinical research information synthesis* (pp. 181–202). Hillsdale, NJ: Erlbaum.

Widiger, T. A., & Frances, A. J. (1987). Interviews and inventories for the measurement of personality disorders. *Clinical Psychology Review, 7,* 49–74.

Widiger, T. A., Frances, A. J., & Trull, T. J. (1989). Personality disorders. In R. Craig (Ed.), *Clinical and diagnostic interviewing* (pp. 221–236). Northvale, NJ: Jason Aronson.

Widiger, T. A., Freiman, K., & Bailey, B. (1990). Convergent and discriminant validity of personality disorder prototypic acts. *Psychological Assessment: A Journal of Consulting and Clinical Psychology, 2,* 107–113.

Widiger, T. A., Miele, G. M., & Tilly, S. M. (1992). Alternative perspectives on the diagnosis of borderline personality disorder. In J. F. Clarkin, E. Marziali, & H. Munroe-Blum (Eds.), *Borderline personality disorder. Clinical and empirical perspectives* (pp. 89–115). New York: Guilford Press.

Widiger, T. A., & Spitzer, R. L. (1991). Sex bias in the diagnosis of personality disorders: Conceptual and methodological issues. *Clinical Psychology Review, 11,* 1–22.

Widiger, T. A., Trull, T. J. (1992). Personality and psychopathology: An application of the Five-Factor model. *Journal of Personality, 60,* 363–393.

Widiger, T. A., Trull, T. J., Clarkin, J. F., Sanderson, C. J., & Costa, P. T. (1994). A description of the DSM-III-R and DSM-IV personality disorders with the Five-Factor model of personality. In P. T. Costa & T. A. Widiger (Eds.), *Personality disorders and the Five-Factor model of personality* (pp. 41–56). Washington, DC: American Psychological Association.

Widiger, T. A., Trull, T. J., Hurt, S. W., Clarkin, J., & Frances, A. J. (1987). A multidimensional scaling of the DSM-III personality disorders. *Archives of General Psychiatry, 44,* 557–563.

Wiggins, J. S., & Pincus, A. L. (1989). Conceptions of personality disorders and dimensions of personality. *Psychological Assessment: A Journal of Consulting and Clinical Psychology, 1,* 305–316.

Wiggins, J. S., & Pincus, A. L. (1992). Personality: Structure and assessment. *Annual Review of Psychology, 43,* 473–504.

Zanarini, M. C., Frankenburg, F. R., Chauncey, D. L., & Gunderson, J. G. (1987). The Diagnostic Interview for Personality Disorders: Interrater and test-retest reliability. *Comprehensive Psychiatry, 28,* 467–480.

Zanarini, M. C., Gunderson, J. G., Frankenburg, F. R., & Chauncey, D. L. (1989). The Revised Diagnostic Interview for Borderlines: Discriminating BPD from other Axis II disorders. *Journal of Personality Disorders, 3,* 10–18.

Zarrella, K. L., Schuerger, J. M., & Ritz, G. H. (1990). Estimation of MCMI DSM-III Axis II constructs from MMPI scales and subscales. *Journal of Personality Assessment, 55,* 195–201.

Zimmerman, M., & Coryell, W. H. (1990). Diagnosing personality disorders in the community. A comparison of self-report and interview measures. *Archives of General Psychiatry, 47,* 527–531.

Zimmerman, M., Pfohl, B., Coryell, W., Stangl, D., & Corenthal, C. (1988). Diagnosing personality disorders in depressed patients. A comparison of patient and informant interviews. *Archives of General Psychiatry, 45,* 733–737.

27

Assessing and Understanding Aggressive and Violent Patients

Edwin I. Megargee

No clinical task is more challenging than the assessment or prediction of aggressive or violent behavior, and none can have more far-reaching consequences for all concerned. A person labeled "dangerous" can be served with a restraining order; lose parental rights in a custody dispute; be denied bail, probation or parole; and, in certain circumstances, even be subjected to indefinite preventive detention[1] (Stone, 1975). On the other hand, casualties can result from failure to predict future violence, as the writer discovered when he was pinned down for ninety minutes by Charles Whitman, a University of Texas student whose earlier confession of urges to go to the Texas Tower and shoot everyone in sight were not taken seriously by a Student Health Service psychiatrist; thirty-eight people were shot, fourteen fatally, before Whitman himself was slain.

As if such events were not enough to cause clinicians concern, lawsuits can result from the allegedly incorrect assessment of aggressive potential. In a series of cases beginning with *Tarasoff* v. *Regents of the University of California* in 1974, the courts have found that mental health workers who fail to appreciate the dangerousness of their clients and warn their potential victims may be liable for civil damages (Meyers,

1986; Stone, 1986). It is not surprising then that, according to Stone (1975, p. 25), "the generic concept of dangerousness has emerged as the paramount consideration in the law—mental health system."

It is not merely the gravity of the possible consequences that makes the assessment of aggression or violence so challenging. When appraising intelligence or diagnosing a thought disorder, clinicians can concentrate on the characteristics of their clients. However, by its very nature, aggressive behavior involves interpersonal interactions between two or more people, interactions that occur in a sociocultural context and that may involve constantly changing situational influences as the "scenario of violence" unfolds (Toch, 1969). Families, gangs, social groups or even, in certain specialized circumstances, governments may be the subjects of psychologists' assessments of aggressive proclivities. For those venturing to predict violence, the task is further complicated by the low base rate for violence in most settings, which inflates the effects of even modest false positive rates (Meehl & Rosen, 1955; Megargee, 1976; 1981, Monahan, 1981).

The primary purpose of this chapter is to provide a systematic procedure to assist clinicians in understanding and assessing the factors that lead to aggressive behavior. After presenting a brief working definition of aggression, it discusses the context and purposes of such assessments, how they influence procedures, and some of the ethical and legal pitfalls that may be encountered. The next section provides a broad overview of data that may be used in assessing aggressive behavior. This leads to a description of the "Algebra of aggression," a conceptual framework designed to help clinicians sort out and integrate relevant information and apply it to the problem of assessing dangerous behavior.

DEFINING AGGRESSION

Authorities often disagree on what constitutes aggression. Consequently, different theorists and researchers discussing "aggression" may be using incompatible semantic or operational definitions (Baron, 1977; Buss, 1961; Johnson, 1972). Is it aggression if a mosquito bites you on the arm? If you swat the mosquito? What if the mosquito you slap is on your spouse's cheek?

Recognizing that there are covert, indirect, unconscious, and passive forms of aggressive behavior, and that aggression occurs among other species, the focus of this chapter will be on overt, direct, intentional human aggression, i.e., *physical or verbal behavior that can cause people distress, pain, or injury, or damage their property or reputations.* Such behavior will be viewed as aggressive whether or not hurting the victim was the aggressor's primary intention and regardless of whether the behavior is classified as legal or illegal in the particular society in which it occurs.

DEFINING THE PURPOSE AND CONTEXT OF THE ASSESSMENT

The first step in any undertaking, whether it is building a birdhouse or planning an assessment, is to consider the purpose of the project and the setting or circumstances under which it will be carried out. Function dictates design, and, in the assessment of aggression, the context estab-

lishes the parameters within which an appraisal can be carried out.

Context of the Assessment

The physical setting and psychological context in which an assessment is conducted are always important, but this is especially so with regard to evaluations of aggressive or violent tendencies. It is not uncommon for such appraisals to be conducted in jails, prisons, or closed psychiatric wards; sometimes a third party, such as an attorney, police officer, or aide may be present. In some circumstances, the person being assessed is not even known to the assessor. As a consultant to the U.S. Secret Service, for example, the writer was occasionally asked to evaluate the threat posed by an anonymous, and hence unknown, letter writer.

In addition to the physical setting, the psychological and legal context may impose constraints on the assessment. The person being assessed often has a strong vested interest in the outcome; indeed in capital and death-row cases it may literally be a matter of life or death. This can place the psychologist and the subject in an adversarial relationship. Clinicians doing assessments that include an appraisal of people's potential for engaging in aggressive behavior or violence owe it to themselves to become fully informed of the general legal and ethical issues involved, as well as the specific laws and policies in their settings[2] (American Psychological Association, 1992; Bennett, Bryant, Vandenbos, & Greenwood, 1990; Brodsky, 1991; Monahan, 1980; Pope, Butcher, & Seelen, 1993; VandeCreek & Knapp, 1989). They must clearly understand "who is the client" (Monahan, 1972) and communicate this to the people being assessed at the outset so that subjects can make an informed decision regarding whether or not they will participate, and if so, how much they will communicate.

Because aggressive behavior may lead to some sort of litigation, psychologists doing such assessments should be meticulous about documenting their observations and keeping complete records. At the very least, they should be thoroughly familiar with their state or province's requirements about preserving clinical records and follow them to the letter. In some situations, it may be advisable to have written documentation that the person being appraised understands all the implications of the assessment and has given informed consent.

For your own protection, consider videotaping interviews in certain assessment situations. If you evaluate formerly·violent people being considered for release from secure settings, some of those you recommend for release will probably recidivate. When you are being sued by their victims or their estates, your erstwhile clients will be portrayed as raging beasts that any competent clinician would have kept caged for life. It may help if you can show a tape that demonstrates how well controlled, civilized, and reasonable these "monsters" were when you assessed them.

Purpose of the Appraisal

Most assessments of aggressive behavior fall into one of two general categories: "retrospective" and "prospective." In a *retrospective assessment*, psychologists are confronted with aggression that has already occurred and asked to explain it. For example, criminal liability might depend on whether the victim provoked the attack or if the perpetrator was legally sane at the time. Retrospective evaluation is especially important in treatment planning. Obviously it makes a difference whether a brain tumor, a change in medication, an abusive relationship, sadism, or altruism caused the aggression.

Some assessment techniques work much better in retrospective than they do in prospective assessments. For example, when administered to people who have committed assaultive crimes, the Overcontrolled Hostility (O-H) scale for the MMPI can help identify those whose violence paradoxically stems from excessive inhibitions against the overt expression of any sort of aggression (Megargee, Cook, & Mendelsohn, 1967). Apparently their inability to express anger causes their instigation to aggression to build up to the point that it over-

whelms even their massive defenses, resulting in an extremely violent act (Megargee, 1966). Their treatment needs differ greatly from those of other types of violent offenders. However, this syndrome is so rare that the O-H scale is of little use in predicting violent behavior.

In *prospective assessments*, clinicians are asked whether a person, group, or even a nation is likely to commit aggression in the future. If so, under what conditions will this happen? What form is the aggression likely to take? Against whom will it be directed? The answers to these questions might be used to help determine whether patients or prisoners are ready for release or if a child should be returned to the custody of a possibly abusive parent. As anyone who has ever bet on a sporting event knows, it is much more difficult to predict what will happen in the future than it is to explain what has happen in the past.

Risk assessment is complicated by the fact that for an act of aggression to occur, three basic elements are required:

1. An aggressor, that is, a person who is willing and able to carry out the aggressive act in question;
2. A target or suitable victim who will be the object of the aggressive behavior; and
3. Opportunity for the aggressor to attack the victim.

This goes considerably beyond personality assessment. It also requires assessing the potential perpetrator's ability to formulate and carry out a plan of attack, assessing his or her technical skills and access to weapons, predicting whether a suitable victim will be available, and finally, whether the would-be aggressor can obtain access to that victim (Cohen & Felson, 1979).

SOURCES OF INFORMATION

Psychological Tests

As a clinical psychologist for the Alameda County (California) Probation Department, the writer conducted a series of studies to determine which psychological tests or scales would best identify applicants for probation who were likely to assault citizens if released. It seemed then that it would be easy to compare the scores of offenders who had been convicted of extreme and moderately assaultive offenses with those of nonviolent criminals and normals. Once it was established which measure best *postdicted* criminal violence, it could be administered prospectively to determine its *predictive* validity. In the course of this research the Minnesota Multiphasic Personality Inventory (MMPI), the California Psychological Inventory (CPI), the Rorschach, the Holtzman Inkblot Technique (HIT), the Thematic Apperception Test (TAT), and the Rosenzweig Picture-Frustration Study (P-F) were all studied using samples of assaultive and nonassaultive juvenile or adult offenders. None, not even an MMPI scale we ourselves derived, was able to differentiate the assaultive from the nonviolent offenders (Megargee, 1964, 1965; Megargee & Cook, 1967; Megargee & Mendelsohn, 1962). The conclusion after reviewing the results of these and other studies in the literature was:

> Thus far no structured or projective test scale has been derived which, when used alone, will predict violence in the individual case in a satisfactory manner. Indeed, none has been developed which will adequately *post*dict, let alone *pre*dict, violent behavior (Megargee, 1970, p. 145).

This does not mean that these tests are useless; as we shall see, they can be very helpful in assessing some constructs relevant to aggression, such as hostility and inhibitions. But no test, by itself, can adequately differentiate aggressive from nonaggressive people. Aggression is simply too complex and multiply determined a phenomenon to be assessed adequately by any single test.

Recall the Texas Tower massacre. Not just one but three different individuals committed homicide in Austin that day. One was the sniper, Charles Whitman, a highly controlled person suffering from an undiagnosed brain tumor who had murdered his mother and his wife the night before (Johnson, 1972). The other two were an armed civilian and a police officer who managed to gain access to the tower and kill Whitman. How could a single measure have accurately identified three such diverse men with such differing motivations?

Other Sources of Assessment Data

Because aggressive behavior occurs in an interpersonal context and often offends people, it is noticed and documented more than most types of behavior. If it results in criminal charges or a civil suit, or if the aggressor is confined in a correctional or mental institution, there may be extensive records that can help the clinician determine where, when, and in what circumstances this individual is or is not likely to commit aggressive acts. In addition, medical charts showing the response to the administration, and especially the withdrawal, of medication and providing information on alcohol or substance abuse should be obtained.

Clinical interviews are useful not only for the content they elicit but also for the opportunity they provide to observe clients' emotional reactions. Are they quick-tempered? Do they have a sense of humor that helps them dissipate their anger?

Since aggressive behavior is interpersonal, friends, relatives, and coworkers who have observed a client's behavior in a variety of situations can provide a great deal of useful information. In institutional settings, psychologists should cultivate the people who actually spend a lot of time with the person being assessed. Nurses, aides, and fellow patients in mental health settings, and the correctional officers, teachers, work supervisors, and fellow inmates in correctional settings often know the clients' aggressive potential better than a therapist who sees them once a week. If people are feared by their peers, it should be taken seriously.

In outpatient or community settings, an interview in the residence can be enormously informative. There is no substitute for experiencing the sights, sounds, and smells of the person's home environment. Alcohol and substance abuse by the client or other family members are more evident in a dwelling where you may see or smell the residue. In a home visit you are also better able to ascertain if the person has access to weapons and is skilled in their use. Be alert for gun cabinets, hunting photographs, trophies, and shooting magazines, and inquire about recreational activities.

THE CONCEPTUAL FRAMEWORK

When all the data have been collected—the records, reports, test protocols, observations, and so on—the conceptual framework makes its contribution. By specifying the complex determinants of aggressive behavior, it helps clinicians sort out and interpret the meaning of their observations. A brief overview of this "algebra of aggression" will be presented, after which each of its components will be discussed.

The Algebra of Aggression

Because most human behavior, including aggression, is performed on a fairly routine basis, it is easy to lose sight of its complex determinants. However, each individual act is the result of the interaction of many factors and dozens of unconscious choices. In the "algebra of aggression," we stop the action for a moment and analyze the determinants of a single act occurring at a specific point in time and in a particular situation.

At any given time, a person is confronted with dozens of implicit or explicit choices about how to behave; some acts may be aggressive, others nonaggressive. The aggressive responses may be verbal or physical, mild or extreme, direct or indirect. How is this choice made?

According to the "algebra of aggression":

> Typically, a person selects the response that appears to offer the maximum satisfactions and the minimum dissatisfactions in that particular situation.

> This simple statement conceals a rapid but extremely complex internal bargaining process in which the capacity of a given response to fulfill many different drives and motives is weighed against the pain that might result from

that response, as well as from the postponement of the satisfaction of other competing drives. . . . By means of this "internal algebra," the net strength of each possible response is calculated and compared with all other responses, and the strongest one is selected.

What determines the net strength of a potential response? In the case of an aggressive or violent response, we can isolate several broad factors that interact to determine response strength. The first of these is *instigation to aggression*. Instigation to aggression is the sum of all the forces that motivate an individual to commit a violent or aggressive act. It includes both *intrinsic ("angry") instigation*, which is the conscious or unconscious wish to harm the victim in some fashion, and *extrinsic ("instrumental") instigation*, which is the yearning for other desirable outcomes which the aggressive act in question might accomplish, such as economic gain in the case of a robbery or perceived political benefits from an act of terrorism.

The second major variable is *habit strength*, the extent to which the response has been rewarded or punished in the past. Other things being equal (which they rarely are), the more often a given aggressive act directed at a particular target has been successful in the past, or the more one has observed people aggressing successfully, the more likely one is to aggress in the future. Habit strength is especially relevant in the case of extrinsic or instrumental aggression.

Instigation to aggression and habit strength both motivate people toward aggression. What stops them? Opposing the motivational factors is the third set of variables, namely *inhibitions against aggression*. They include all the reasons why a person would refrain from a particular aggressive act directed at a particular target. Included are both moral prohibitions which classify the particular act as wrong and practical considerations, such as fear of retaliation or the possibility the act may fail in its objective. Inhibitions can be general or specific and can vary as a function of the act, the target, and the circumstances.

Instigation, habit strength, and inhibitions are all personal characteristics, but behavior results from individuals interacting with their milieus. The fourth class of variables, *situational factors*, encompasses those external factors that may facilitate or impede aggressive behavior. These include *environments, settings, situations,* and *stimuli.* Among the external factors that might facilitate aggressive behavior are living under apartheid (environment), being in a war zone (setting), being present when a fight breaks out (situation), or a provocative gesture on the part of an antagonist (stimulus). Factors that might inhibit violence include living in a cloistered convent (environment), attending a symphony concert (setting), the presence of a police officer (situation), or having an opponent drop to his knees and raise his hands in supplication (stimulus). The common denominator of these events, according to Monahan and Klassen (1982), is that they all occur outside the skin.

Reaction potential, the fifth and last major construct, consists of the net strength of a given response after the inhibitory factors have been balanced against the excitatory ones. A response will be blocked and cannot occur whenever the inhibitions exceed the instigation. A response is possible (i.e., has a positive reaction potential) if the forces favoring the aggressive response exceed those opposing it. However, all the possible responses must first compete with one another; the one with the highest reaction potential—that is, the greatest capacity to satisfy the most needs at the least cost—should be chosen. (Megargee, 1993, pp. 620–621)

Symbolically then, if

$R_{j°k}$ = reaction potential for a particular act j directed at target k

$M_{j°k}$ = motivation for a particular act j directed at target k

H = habit strength

$I_{j°k}$ = inhibitions against act j directed at target k

S_f = situational factors favoring or conducive to aggressing

S_i = situational factors impeding or interfering with aggression

then the reaction potential for act "j" directed at target k is:

$$R_{j°k} = [M_{j°k} + H + S_f] - [I_{j°k} + S_i]$$

Of course other acts directed at the same or at other targets will each have their own reaction potentials. For some, the inhibitory factors $[I_{j°k} + S_i]$ will be stronger than the excitatory factors $[M_{j°k} + H + S_f]$. When this occurs, the reaction potential for those responses is zero, so they are blocked and cannot occur. Perhaps the person was not angry enough, or the act in question might have been too extreme or inappropriate for that target under those circumstances. However, there may be some responses for which the excitatory factors $[M_{j°k} + H + S_f]$ will exceed the inhibitions $[I_{j°k} + S_i]$. All of these responses are possible; they will compete with one another and with other nonaggressive responses that may also be possible.

Myers (1993) recently interviewed "Jusuf," a Bosnian sniper who had lost count of the number of people he had killed. Jusuf emphasized that he only shot Serbian soldiers he was specifically assigned to kill, and that he never fired at women, children, or old men. He performs this unpleasant task to defend his people against their enemies, but he much preferred his former job as an artist. In theory we could write equations showing that Jusuf's instigation is extrinsic, his habit strength high, and that although his inhibitions permit shooting Serbian soldiers at long range, they block him from shooting civilians or Serbian soldiers who are less than 500 meters away. If the situation changes and peace is restored, art would win out over sniping in the response competition. Given this brief overview of the conceptual framework, let us examine how it can be used in assessment and treatment.

ASSESSING THE PERSONAL FACTORS

The conceptual framework gives equal weight to personal and situational factors. The personal factors are instigation to aggression, habit strength, and inhibitions against aggression.

Intrinsic Instigation to Aggression

Depending on duration and intensity, intrinsic motives are referred to as *anger, hostility, rage,* or *hatred.* Obviously, the more intense and long-lasting the instigation, the easier it is to assess. Because anger and rage are transitory, they may not be observed in a particular session, so it is always advisable to see the client on two or more different occasions.

The primary questions clinicians must address are the amount and the direction of instigation to aggression. The secondary questions are the causes of this instigation and how the subject dissipates it. Or, more prosaically, "Is the client angry? At whom? Why? What does the client do about it?"

One of the best ways to assess anger and hostility is also the simplest: asking subjects, using a variety of synonyms, what makes them angry or annoyed, who aggravates them, what they would like to do when they are provoked, to whom they would like to do it, and what it is they actually do and why. Anger is a strong emotion; given the opportunity, many people will express it quite openly, even when it is not in their best interests to do so. Because anger is difficult to conceal, their friends and associates should also be able to comment on a client's temper.

Many self-report tests and scales have been constructed to assess anger and hostility.[4] One of the most widely used, at least in research, is The Buss-Durkee Hostility Guilt Inventory (Buss & Durkee, 1957), which features seven scales designed to assess various aspects of hostility and aggression, plus one for assessing guilt over its expression, a potential measure of inhibitions. More recently, since anger and hostility have been implicated as factors in cardiovascular and gastrointestinal disorders, a number of measures have been devised for use in behavioral medicine (Chesney & Rosenman, 1985). Spielberger and his colleagues (Spielberger, Jacobs, Russell, & Crane, 1983; Spielberger, Johnson, Russell, Crane, Jacobs, & Worden, 1985; Spielberger & Sydeman, 1994) have contributed a State/Trait anger measure, while Novaco's (1985) Anger scale focuses on the range of stimulus situations eliciting angry responses. Several special MMPI scales have focused on anger and its regulation; although they have proved unable to differentiate assaultive from nonassaultive criminals (Megargee & Mendelsohn, 1962). Cook and Medley's (1954) Hostility (Ho) scale has been found to relate to

atherosclerosis (Williams et al., 1980). It is not clear how many of these measures survived the recent revision of the MMPI, but MMPI-2 has an Anger content scale (Butcher, Graham, Williams, & Ben-Porath, 1989). Most of these scales are quite obvious and easily dissembled by clients motivated to conceal hostility. This is also true of the Rosenzweig Picture-Frustration Study, on which subjects indicate the responses cartoon figures would make to various frustrations (Rosenzweig, 1945; Rosenzweig, Fleming, & Clarke, 1947).

Less direct, and probably less valid, are those wide-band projective tests that include signs or indices purporting to reflect anger or hostility. These include symbolic content, such as anatomical responses or predatory animals, on the Rorschach (Phillips & Smith, 1953), and themes of fighting or conflict on apperceptive tests such as the TAT (Murstein, 1963). Situational factors such as the nature, tone, and purpose of the administration as well as the specific cards used strongly influence the responses obtained (Murstein, 1963). The less the TAT card suggests aggressive themes, the more weight one should give to their occurrence. Because the evidence for the validity of any single specific sign is weak (Megargee & Cook, 1967), clinicians assessing instigation to aggression should use projectives primarily to generate hypotheses to be tested with other data.

For both retrospective and prospective assessments it is important to determine the sources of clients' anger and hostility. Physiological sources include: (1) genetic factors that make some people more irritable than others; (2) certain diseases or conditions of the central nervous or endocrinological systems; (3) hormonal influences such as testosterone; (4) physical illness; (5) toxic factors and drugs, (6) fatigue; and (7) generalized arousal. Psychological sources include: (1) frustration; (2) physical or verbal attacks; and (3) territorial intrusions (Megargee, 1993). Motivation from all these different sources can add together.

The diagnosis of the source of the instigation can have direct implications for management and treatment. One of the best-established relationships in psychology is that frustration causes instigation to aggression (Dollard, Doob,

Miller, Mowrer, & Sears, 1939). Does a client's frustration, and hence anger, stem from unreasonable expectations? If so, cognitive therapy designed to correct these beliefs might be effective. On the other hand, if the grievance is genuine and the anger justified, a better solution might be to help the client find a more constructive way of coping with the situation, such as seeking redress in the courts.

How people deal with anger or hostility is also important to assess. According to "catharsis" theory, intrinsic instigation should be depleted by attacking the source of the provocation. If this is impossible, angry individuals may reduce instigation by attacking someone else (displacement), choosing an alternative response (response substitution), or observing someone else's aggressive behavior, either in real life or the media (vicarious aggression). The overcontrolled-assaultive type lacks such mechanisms so that instigation accumulates to the point that violence erupts. Assertion training could be helpful for such people (Megargee, 1966, 1993).

Extrinsic (Instrumental) Instigation to Aggression

People aggress not only because they are angry, but also because aggression may help them attain other goals. There is a vast array of possible motives both primary and secondary, for instrumental aggression.[5] A reformed bank robber reported to the writer that his primary motive had been the money he stole. He had found safer ways to obtain money, but he admitted that he missed the surge of power he had experienced holding a bank full of people at gunpoint and the excitement of escaping from the police after a high-speed car chase.

Although psychologists typically focus on intrinsic instigation, it seems likely that extrinsic motives lead to at least as much aggression, especially when we consider that for athletes, police officers, military personnel, and others occasional aggression is part of their job description. Not being a personality trait, extrinsic motivation is much more difficult to assess

than intrinsic. Lacking tests to assess instrumental motivation, clinicians must often rely on self-reports elicited in response to probing questions in an interview or infer how aggressive behavior is reinforced from case history data. Obviously this works better in retrospective than prospective assessments.

If the aggressive behavior is truly instrumental, the intervention most likely to work is to show the client a more effective nonaggressive strategy to attain the goal. While this would not eliminate the aggressive response from the person's repertoire, it should make the nonaggressive alternative more likely to be chosen in the response competition.

Habit Strength

Reinforcement of aggressive responses increases habit strength, the second major personal factor leading to aggression.[6] Angry instigation is reinforced by the pain or discomfort inflicted on the victim; instrumental by attaining goals by means of aggressive behavior. Reinforcement is strongest for the actual response and generalizes to others that are similar to it. The more a culture, society, or reference group approves of aggressive behavior, the more secondary reinforcement a person will receive.

Although habit strength is most readily acquired directly by reinforcement of an individual's own aggressive responses, people can also acquire habit strength indirectly by observing role models successfully engage in aggressive behavior. This may account in part for familial transmission of aggression, on the one hand, and how observing enactments of violence on television and other media can foster aggressive behavior, on the other (Bandura, 1983; Huesmann, 1988; Huesmann & Eron, 1984).

Extinction, that is, continued performance of unreinforced aggressive responses, is the only way to eliminate habit strength once it is required. This is virtually impossible given the rewards for aggression in our culture, especially for boys. Although punishment may temporarily suppress aggressive behavior, it does not eliminate such responses from one's repertoire.

Moreover, it may increase instigation. This is one reason why prisons are often ineffective.

Of all the constructs in the "algebra of aggression," habit strength should be the easiest to assess, based as it is on the individual's reinforcement history as documented in the case history. One can infer strong habit strength from a long history of aggressive behavior, especially if it appears to have been successful. Habit strength is also the variable that most strongly predicts aggression; the longer and stronger the history of aggression, the more likely an individual will behave similarly in the future.[7]

Inhibitions Against Aggression

Opposing instigation and habit strength are internal inhibitions, which can be general or specific and can vary as a function of the aggressive act, the target, and the circumstances. These include pragmatic concerns, such as fears that an attack will fail or that retribution will be forthcoming, as well as moral prohibitions (i.e. taboos, conscience, superego) that classify this act directed at this target at this time under these circumstances as "wrong."

Inhibitions are by far the most difficult of the personal constructs to assess (Megargee, in press). The mere absence of a history of aggressive behavior or failure to express animosity toward anyone does not necessarily indicate that people have strong inhibitions. A more parsimonious explanation would be that they lacked instigation.

To assess inhibitions directly, one must look for a circumstance in which a person is motivated to aggress and fails to do so. While such situations can be created in the laboratory, they are difficult to contrive in the clinic. Role playing, group therapy, and direct confrontations in an interview may afford opportunities to assess inhibitions directly. More often, clinicians have to ask people about what aggressive behaviors they find acceptable or unacceptable under various circumstances. Inhibitions are easier than anger to dissimulate, and potentially self-serving reports need to be cross-checked with the case history and reports by people who have had an opportunity to observe a client's behavior in provocative circumstances.

Often, however, clinicians must rely on indirect evidence such as personality test data. It is safest to use several possible sources and try to "triangulate" one's appraisal of inhibitions against aggression. Although Hartshorne and May's (1928; 1929) classic studies demonstrated the specificity of moral prohibitions, other things being equal, well-socialized people with strong values are more likely to have inhibitions against those forms of aggression that are censured by their culture than those who are poorly socialized. Among the best measures of socialization and values available are the California Psychological Inventory's (CPI) Socialization (So), Responsibility (Re) and Self Control (Sc) scales (Gough, 1987). These scales, which have been validated in many cultures, assess the degree to which individuals have assimilated (So) and understand (Re) their cultural values, and their ability to control their behavior and abide by these precepts (Sc) (Megargee, 1972).

Although the writer prefers using the CPI among "normal" populations, with more deviant or pathological groups the MMPI or MMPI-2 may be preferred (Butcher, Dahlstrom, Graham, Tellegen, & Kaemmer, 1989). Elevations on scales F, 4, 6, 8, and 9 suggest *deficient* inhibitions and controls; obviously, the more of these scales that are elevated, and assuming the profile is valid, the higher the elevations, the stronger the evidence. It is riskier to use the MMPI or MMPI-2 to assess positive characteristics, but a basically normal profile with the highest scores on scales L, K, 2, 0, and among men, 5, may be associated with inhibitions that may include some against aggression. A clinically elevated Overcontrolled Hostility (O H) scale score suggests a conflict between expression or suppression of hostility, but low scores are meaningless (Megargee, Cook, & Mendelsohn, 1967).

Projective tests can also be used to assess deficient controls and poor socialization. Consider a Rorschach or TAT administration as a structured interpersonal interaction between the client and the clinician for a mutually agreed-on purpose. In most instances in which aggression is being assessed, it is in the subject's best interest to cooperate, take the examination seriously, and produce a protocol that does not violate the implicit social norms governing the situation. One can therefore hypothesize that subjects who produce inappropriate or deviant responses may be lacking suitable inhibitions or controls. On the Rorschach, for example, uncontrolled color responses that disregard the form or shape of the blot, and blatant sexual, anatomical, gruesome, or gory content suggest that the respondent doesn't understand or disregards social conventions. On the other hand, a record with many well-differentiated responses with good form, using frequently interpreted blot areas and including a good number of Popular (P) responses indicates the respondent understands the proprieties and is willing and able to abide by them, at least in the context of the inkblot examination.

Compared with the Rorschach, there is much greater inter-examiner variability in the administration, scoring, and interpretation of the TAT and other apperceptive measures, making generalizations more difficult. If respondents *fail* to give aggressive themes in response to cards or scenes that strongly suggest aggression or conflict, then one might infer inhibitions against the expression of aggression, at least in the context of the examination (Megargee, 1967).

Another strategy is to examine the history to determine whether the person came from a home conducive to strong moral development. The conditions associated with socialization are well known, even if the actual mechanisms by which values are introjected may be poorly understood:

> A warm nurturing environment in which the children form a close bond of affection and respect with their caregivers combined with fair, consistent discipline is most conducive to developing internal controls. The more the agents of socialization, first the parents, and later the neighborhood, the church, and the school, share and enforce a strong common set of values, and the more they live up to and consistently exemplify these principles in their

everyday lives, the more likely it is that the children will incorporate them. . . . On the other hand. . . . parental absence and disharmony, inconsistency, rejection, abuse and poor role models are associated with problems in developing values and controlling behavior. . . . (Megargee, in press)

Although there are obviously many exceptions, the more the case history indicates that the client grew up in a milieu conducive to socialization, the more reasonable it is to hypothesize a normal set of values.

In addition to values stipulating that certain types of aggression are wrong, inhibitions are also fostered by empathy or compassion for the potential victim. Jusuf, the Bosnian sniper, distances himself from his victims emotionally as well as physically. Myers (1993, p. 7A) reported Jusuf does not "imagine who the men in his scope are, what they're like, if they have families. . . ." If he did, it would be more difficult to kill them.

The CPI Empathy (Em) scale, as well as its Sociability (Sy) and Social Presence (Sp) scales might be used to estimate this construct. Similarly, TAT themes emphasizing affiliation and warm, mutually satisfying interpersonal relations, along with an emphasis on Human Movement and controlled color on the Rorschach, would all suggest a capacity for relating to others that could strengthen inhibitions against aggression.

Unfortunately, it is much easier to decrease inhibitions than it is to foster them. Physiological factors that reduce inhibitions include: (1) injuries or diseases affecting the central nervous system; (2) certain endocrinological disorders; and (3) the chemical actions of disinhibiting substances such as alcohol. Psychological causes of inadequate inhibitions include: (1) failure to develop adequate inhibitions because of deficient socialization or abuse during childhood; and (2) being exposed to role models who approve of violence. Inhibitions against violence can also be temporarily overcome by conflicting values (i.e., it is wrong to attack someone but right to defend your honor), rationalizations, and peer pressure. An adequate assessment of inhibitions must explore whether people's inhibitions against aggression are easily overcome.

SITUATIONAL FACTORS AND EXTERNAL CONDITIONS

How Situational Factors Influence Aggression

Aggression results from the interaction of the personal factors discussed above with external conditions that can either facilitate or impede aggressive behavior or violence. These situational factors can be divided into *environments*, *settings*, *situations*, and *stimuli* to demarcate a rough continuum from widespread to focal influences. The boundaries between these terms are not significant; the point is that a wide range of external factors and events helps determine whether or not an aggressive act takes place. Situational influences involve times as well as places; much more violence occurs in New York City's Central Park between 2:00 and 4:00 A.M. on Sunday morning than from 2:00 to 4:00 P.M. on Sunday afternoon. Of course, personality and situational factors are not independent. Those peaceful people who flock to Central Park on a sunny afternoon generally shun it in the early morning hours, leaving it to the predators and police.

The circumstances and stimuli to which clients are exposed and the conditions in which they live are extremely important determinants of aggression. Cognitive expectancies interacting with situational realities can cause frustration, the major source of intrinsic instigation (Dollard et al., 1939). Environmental factors can moderate the relation of personality factors, such as empathy, to aggression (Rose & Feshbach, 1990). Given strong enough threat or provocation, almost anyone may become violent.

Since this book is about personality assessment, space does not permit a detailed discussion of all the external factors that influence aggression. Among those that have been emphasized in the literature are ambient temperature (Baron & Ransberger, 1978; Megar-

gee, 1977); architectural design (Newman, 1972); crowding (Megargee, 1977; Russell, 1983); the family, peer, and job environments; the availability of alcohol and of potential victims (Monahan & Klassen, 1982); and the behavior of antagonists, victims, associates, and bystanders (Megargee, 1993). Obviously the political climate is a major factor, as people from Baghdad, Beijing, Beirut, and Bosnia will attest. Probably the most widely discussed variable is the availability of weapons by either or both antagonists (Cook, 1982; MacDonald, 1975; Monahan & Klassen, 1982).

Assessing Situational Factors

In both prospective and retrospective assessments, clinicians must consider situational as well as personality factors. Monahan and Klassen (1982) suggest that we investigate the circumstances that led people to commit aggressive acts in the past and determine whether they correspond to the situations they are likely to encounter in the future. We might also ascertain the environmental and situational factors associated with peaceful periods to help guide recommendations for future treatment or environmental manipulation.

The less we know about the settings in which clients will find themselves or the situations and stimuli they will face, the more difficult it is to make accurate predictions. Only in institutional settings, such as prisons and inpatient mental health units, where the environmental factors are relatively constant for all subjects, does it appear possible to make reasonably accurate predictions based only on personality factors (McGuire & Megargee, 1976).

RESPONSE COMPETITION AND REACTION POTENTIAL

Any violent act will be blocked if inhibitory factors exceed motivating ones. However, if all the forces favoring a particular violent response exceed those opposing it, that act is *possible*, at least as long as those conditions prevail. Before it can be carried out, all the possible responses, both violent and nonviolent, must compete with one another; the one with the highest *reaction potential*—that is, the greatest capacity to satisfy the most needs at the least cost—should be chosen.

Assessing Reaction Potential

In a retrospective analysis of aggressive behavior, it is obvious that the act that was actually performed had the highest reaction potential. If that act was socially or personally undesirable, and the clinical goal is to decrease the likelihood of a recurrence, other more satisfactory alternatives should be investigated. Why were these acts not selected? Were the inhibitions too great? Their chance of success too low? Did cognitive beliefs suggest that the aggressive act was the more honorable alternative? Did friends or onlookers encourage the deviant behavior? The answers to such questions might indicate how the reaction potential of the objectionable behavior may be decreased and that of more acceptable responses increased.

In prospective assessments, the clinician's task is to try to determine the range of possible responses and estimate their relative reaction potential. Situational circumstances, such as whether or not certain interventions are attempted, may be critical. Instead of affixing a blanket label, such as "dangerous," these analyses should help clinicians make more sophisticated contingent predictions of the likelihood that clients will engage in specified aggressive behaviors under different sets of circumstances.

HIT RATES AND BASE RATES

The basic thesis of this chapter is that aggression is a complex, multiply determined, interpersonal interaction involving both personal and situational factors. To assess aggressive behavior, one must appreciate and consider its intricate determinants.

Because these elements are difficult to assess, it is inevitable that errors will occur. Although investigating the accuracy of predictions of aggressive behavior has inherent difficulties, the best studies seem to indicate that it is possible to achieve a hit rate of one in three; that is, for every three people clinicians identify as having a high likelihood of engaging in the type of aggressive behavior being studied, one will actually do so (Megargee, 1976, 1981; Monahan, 1981). This hit rate is quite adequate for some purposes, but not for others (Shah, 1977).

The effect of such errors can be magnified by the low base rates for the occurrence of aggressive behavior in many settings. The closer the base rate is to 50 percent, the higher the possible hit rate (Meehl & Rosen, 1954). As the frequency of the behavior decreases, the effects of even moderate false positive rates are greatly increased. Therefore, in addition to everything else, clinicians making prospective assessments must be aware of the base rates for aggressive behavior in their settings and their impact on the accuracy of their predictions (Meehl & Rosen, 1954; Megargee, 1976; Monahan, 1981).

NOTES

1. These are the possible consequences of being labeled "dangerous" in societies governed by laws and due process. Elsewhere being labeled "dangerous" can lead to simpler, more direct interventions, such as execution. In this century, the regimes of Joseph Stalin, Adolf Hitler, Idi Amin, and Pol Pot, to name a few, serve as examples.

2. For example, few psychologists are aware of the fact that threatening the life of the President of the United States is itself a crime (18 USC 871). Therefore, psychologists who fail to report such threats could themselves be accused of misprision of a felony.

3. Some scales were able to discriminate the criminals from the noncriminals, but this was of little use in an agency dealing exclusively with criminal offenders.

4. For comprehensive, but dated, reviews, see Megargee (1970) and Megargee and Menzies (1971).

5. See Megargee (1982, 1993) for lists of extrinsic motives.

6. Whereas the construct of intrinsic instigation originated in frustration/aggression theory (Dollard et al., 1939) and extrinsic instigation was suggested by

Buss's (1961) writings, the concept of habit strength comes from Hull's (1952) model of motivation. Habit strength is the major reason why the algebra of aggression postulates an additive rather than a multiplicative model. In theory, before a person has ever been reinforced for aggressing, his or her habit strength should be zero. In a multiplicative model, this would make it theoretically impossible for anyone to aggress for the first time.

7. Of course, such a history also suggests low inhibitions and high instigation.

REFERENCES

American Psychological Association. (1992). Ethical principles of psychologists and code of conduct. *American Psychologist, 47,* 1597–1628.

Baron, R. A. (1977). *Human aggression.* New York: Plenum.

Baron, R., & Ransberger, V. (1978). Ambient temperature and the occurrence of collective violence: The "long hot summer" revisited. *Journal of Personality and Social Psychology, 36,* 351–360.

Bennett, B. E., Bryant, B. K., Vandenbos, G. R., & Greenwood, A. (1990). *Professional liability and risk management.* Washington, DC: American Psychological Association.

Brodsky, S. L. (1991). *Testifying in court: Guidelines and maxims for the expert witness.* Washington, DC: American Psychological Association.

Buss, A. H. (1961). *The psychology of aggression.* New York: Wiley.

Butcher, J. N., Dahlstrom, W. G., Graham, J. R., Tellegen, A. M., & Kaemmer, B. (1989). *Minnesota Multiphasic Personality Inventory-2 (MMPI-2): Manual for administration and scoring.* Minneapolis: University of Minnesota Press.

Butcher, J. N., Graham, J. R., Williams, C., & Ben-Porath, Y. S. (1990). *Development and use of the MMPI-2 content scales.* Minneapolis: University of Minnesota Press.

Chesney, M. A., & Rosenman, R. H. (Eds.). (1985). *Anger and hostility in cardiovascular and behavior disorders.* Washington, DC: Hemisphere.

Clarke, J. W. (1982). *American assassins: The darker side of politics.* Princeton, NJ: Princeton University Press.

Cohen, L. E., & Felson, M. (1979). Social change and crime rate trends: A routine activity approach. *American Sociological Review, 44,* 588–608.

Cook, P. I. (1982). The role of firearms in violent crime: An interpretative review of the literature. In M. E. Wolfgang & N. A. Weiner (Eds.), *Criminal violence* (pp. 236–291). Beverly Hills, CA: Sage.

Cook, W. W., & Medley, D. M. (1954). Proposed hostility and pharisaic virtue scales for the MMPI. *Journal of Applied Psychology, 38,* 414–418.

Dollard, J., Doob, L. W., Miller, N. E., Mowrer, O. H., & Sears, R. R. (1939). *Frustration and aggression.* New Haven: Yale University Press.

Gough, H. G. (1987). *California Psychological Inventory: An administrator's guide.* Palo Alto, CA.: Consulting Psychologists Press.

Hartshorne, H. & May, M. A. (1928). *Studies in the nature of character: Volume 1. Studies in deceit.* New York: Macmillan.

Hartshorne, H. & May, M. A. (1929). *Studies in the nature of character: Volume 2. Studies in service and self control.* New York: Macmillan.

Hull, C. L. (1952). *A behavior system.* New Haven: Yale University Press.

Johnson, R. N. (1972). *Aggression in man and animals.* Philadelphia: W.B. Saunders.

MacDonald, J. (1975). *Armed robbery: Offenders and their victims.* Springfield, IL: Charles C. Thomas, 1975.

McGuire, J. S., & Megargee, E. I. (1976, September). Prediction of dangerous and disruptive behavior in a federal institution for youthful offenders. In C. S. Moss (Chair), *Objective studies on violence in correctional settings.* Symposium presented at the meeting of the American Psychological Association, Washington, DC.

Meehl, P. E., & Rosen, A. (1955). Antecedent probability and the efficiency of certain psychometric signs, patterns, and cutting scores. *Psychological Bulletin, 52,* 194–216.

Megargee, E. I. (1964, April). *The utility of the Rosenzweig Picture-Frustration Study in detecting assaultiveness among juvenile delinquents.* Paper presented at the meeting of the Southwestern Psychological Association, San Antonio, TX.

Megargee, E. I. (1965). Relation between Barrier scores and aggressive behavior. *Journal of Abnormal and Social Psychology, 70,* 307–311.

Megargee, E. I. (1966). Undercontrolled and overcontrolled personality types in extreme antisocial aggression. *Psychological Monographs, 80* (3, Whole No. 611).

Megargee, E. I. (1967). Hostility on the TAT as a function of defensive inhibition and stimulus situation. *Journal of Projective Techniques and Personality Assessment, 31* (4), 73–79.

Megargee, E. I. (1969). The psychology of violence: A critical review of theories of violence. In D. I. Mulvihill & M. M. Tumin (Eds.), *Crimes of violence: A staff report to the National Commission on the Causes and Prevention of Violence* (pp. 1037–1113). National Commission on the Causes and Prevention of Violence Staff Report Series, Vol. 13. Washington, DC: U.S. Government Printing Office.

Megargee, E. I. (1970). The prediction of violence with psychological tests. In C. D. Spielberger (Ed.), *Current topics in clinical and community psychology* (Vol. 2, pp. 97–156). New York: Academic Press.

Megargee, E. I. (1972). *The California Psychological Inventory handbook.* San Francisco: Jossey-Bass.

Megargee, E. I. (1976). The prediction of dangerous behavior. *Criminal Justice and Behavior, 3,* 3–21.

Megargee, E. I. (1977). The association of population density, reduced space and uncomfortable temperatures with misconduct in a prison community. *American Journal of Community Psychology, 5,* 289–298.

Megargee, E. I. (1981). Methodological problems in the prediction of violence. In J. R. Hays, T. K. Roberts, & K. S. Solway (Eds.), *Violence and the violent individual* (pp. 179–191). New York: S. P. Scientific and Medical Books.

Megargee, E. I. (1982). Psychological correlates and determinants of criminal violence. In M. Wolfgang & N. Weiner (Eds.), *Criminal violence* (pp. 81–170). Beverly Hills, CA: Sage.

Megargee, E. I. (1990, June). *Inhibitions against aggression as a personality construct: Theoretical, methodological and practical problems.* Plenary address to the IXth Biennial World Meeting of the International Society for Research on Aggression, Banff, Alberta, Canada.

Megargee, E. I. (1993). Aggression and violence. In H. Adams & P. Sutker (Eds.), *Comprehensive handbook of psychopathology* (2nd ed., pp. 617–644). New York: Plenum.

Megargee, E. I. (in press). Internal inhibitions and controls. In R. Hogan, J. Johnson, & S. Briggs (Eds.), *Handbook of personality psychology.* New York: Academic Press.

Megargee, E. I., & Cook, P. E. (1967). The relation of TAT and inkblot aggressive content scales with each other and with criteria of overt aggressiveness in juvenile delinquents. *Journal of Projective Techniques and Personality Assessment, 31* (1), 48–60.

Megargee, E. I., Cook, P. E., & Mendelsohn, G. A. (1967). Development and validation of an MMPI scale of assaultiveness in overcontrolled individuals. *Journal of Abnormal Psychology, 72,* 519–528.

Megargee, E. I., & Mendelsohn, G. A. (1962). A cross-validation of 12 MMPI indices of hostility and control. *Journal of Abnormal and Social Psychology, 65,* 431–438.

Megargee, E. I., & Menzies, E. S. (1971). The assessment and dynamics of aggression. In P. McReynolds (Ed.), *Advances in psychological assessment* (Vol. 2, pp. 133–156). Palo Alto, CA: Science and Behavior Books.

Meyers, C. J. (1986). The legal perils of psychotherapeutic practice: The farther reaches of the duty to warn. In L. Everstine & D. S. Everstine (Eds.), *Psychotherapy and the law.* New York: Grune & Stratton.

Monahan, J. (Ed.). *Who is the client? The ethics of psychological intervention in the criminal justice system.* Washington, DC: American Psychological Association.

Monahan, J. (1981). *The clinical prediction of violent behavior.* Rockville, MD: National Institute of Mental Health.

Monahan, J., & Klassen, D. (1982). Situational approaches to understanding and predicting violent behavior. In M. E. Wolfgang & N. A. Weiner (Eds.), *Criminal violence* (pp. 292–319). Beverly Hills, CA: Sage, 1982.

Murstein, B. I. (1963). *Theory and research on projective techniques (Emphasizing the TAT).* New York: Wiley.

Myers, L. (1993, July 13). Sniper in Bosnia has a wartime job nobody likes. *Tallahassee Democrat,* pp. 1A, 7A.

Newman, O. (1972). *Defensible space.* New York: Macmillan.

Novaco, R. W. (1985). Anger and its therapeutic regulation. In M. A. Chesney & R. H. Rosenman (Eds.). *Anger and hostility in cardiovascular and behavior disorders* (pp. 203–226). Washington, DC: Hemisphere.

Phillips, L. & Smith, J. (1953). *Rorschach interpretation: Advanced technique.* New York: Grune & Stratton.

Pope, K. S., Butcher, J. N., & Seelen, J. (1993). *MMPI/ MMPI-2/ MMPI-A in court: Assessment, testimony and cross-examination for expert witnesses and attorneys.* Washington, DC: American Psychological Association.

Rose, A., & Feshbach, N. (1990, June). *Empathy and aggression revisited: The effects of context.* Paper presented at the IXth Biennial World Meeting of the International Society for Research on Aggression, Banff, Alberta, Canada.

Rosenzweig, S. (1945). The picture-association method and its application in a study of reaction to frustrations. *Journal of Personality, 14,* 3–23.

Rosenzweig, S., Fleming, E. E., & Clarke, H. J. (1947). Revised scoring manual for the Rosenzweig Picture-Frustration Study. *Journal of Psychology, 24,* 165–208.

Russell, G. W. (1983). Crowd size and density in relation to athletic aggression and performance. *Social Behavior and Personality, 11,* 9–15.

Shah, S. (1977). Dangerousness: Some definitional, conceptual and public policy issues. In B. Sales (Ed.), *Perspectives in law and psychology.* New York: Plenum.

Spielberger, C. D., Jacobs, G. A., Russell, S. F., & Crane, R. S. (1983). Assessment of anger: The State-Trait Anger Scale. In J. N. Butcher & C. D. Spielberger (Eds.), *Advances in personality assessment* (Vol. 2, pp. 159–187). Hillsdale, NJ: Erlbaum.

Spielberger, C. D., Johnson, E. H., Russell, S. F., Crane, R. J., Jacobs, G. A., & Worden, T. J. (1985). The experience and expression of anger: Construction and validation of an anger expression scale. In M. A. Chesney & R. H. Rosenman (Eds.), *Anger and hostility in cardiovascular and behavior disorders* (pp. 5–30). Washington, DC: Hemisphere.

Spielberger, C. D., & Sydeman, S. J. (1994). State-Trait Anxiety Inventory and State-Trait Anger Expression Inventory. In M. E. Maruish (Ed.), *The use of psychological tests for treatment planning and outcome assessment* (pp. 292–331). Hillsdale, NJ: Laurence Erlbaum Associates.

Stone, A. A. (1975). *Mental health and the law: A system in transition.* Washington: U.S. Government Printing Office.

Stone, A. A. (1986). Vermont adopts *Tarasoff*: A real barn-burner. *American Journal of Psychiatry, 143,* 352–355.

Toch, H. (1969). *Violent men.* Chicago: Aldine.

VandenCreek, L., & Knapp, S. (1989). *Tarasoff and beyond: Legal and clinical considerations in the treatment of life-endangering patients.* Sarasota: Practitioner's Resource Series.

Williams, R. B., Haney, T. L., Lee, K. L., Kong, Y., Blumenthal, J. A., & Whalen, R. E. (1980). Type A behavior, hostility and coronary atherosclerosis. *Psychosomatic Medicine, 42,* 539–549.

28
Assessing the Psychopathic Personality

J. Reid Meloy
Carl B. Gacono

Hugo Münsterberg, one of the first forensic psychologists, wrote in his 1908 book *On the Witness Stand*, "we do not grasp for the poisonous fruit, because the danger holds us back" (p. 237).[1] We assume he was thinking about the nonpsychopathic individual who is, at times, inhibited and fearful, like many of the patients we see in our clinical practices.

On occasion, however, we are faced with the clinical assessment of the psychopathic personality, and if our work takes us into criminal forensic settings, psychopathy is a "specific constellation of deviant traits and behaviors" (Hare, 1991, p. 2) that cannot be ignored. This chapter is devoted to the practical assessment of psychopathic personality in clinical and forensic settings.

ASSESSMENT IN A CLINICAL OR FORENSIC SETTING

The purpose of assessing psychopathy varies with the nature of the setting and the functional outcome of the evaluation. It may involve questions of antisocial personality disorder, malingering, treatment amenability, sanity, violence potential, sadism, outpatient treatment, or classification (Gacono & Hutton, 1994). In clinical settings, the purpose is usually to determine the problem and the appropriate treatment to elicit change. The psychologist identifies with the *therapeutic* endeavor, even if his or her role is that of a diagnostician. In forensic settings, the purpose is usually to aid the trier of fact, the judge or jury, in answering a psycholegal question, such as dangerousness or sanity. The psychologist is performing an *investigation* to gather data and is not an agent of change. These two fundamentally different roles are often confused and may lead to misuse of information and unethical behavior (Meloy, 1989). It is central to sound clinical practice that the psychologist have a clear conception of his or her role before an assessment begins.

There is an additional problem in assessing psychopathy. Most psychopathic individuals are chronically deceptive and will lie to and mislead the assessor at every turn. The deceptive behaviors often involve projection of blame and malingering or exaggeration of psychiatric symptoms.[2] The goal of the psychopathic patient is usually to gain a more dominant or pleasurable position in relation to his objects, whether a person, an institution, or a legal proceeding.

This second concern is addressed by recognizing the need to gather data from three different sources: a clinical interview, independent historical information, and testing. The clinical interview means a face-to-face contact with the individual long enough to complete a mental status exam and gather self-reported problems and historical data that can be used to develop clinical hypotheses. It also allows for the emergence of transference and countertransference reactions that can be a potent source of psychodiagnostic information about the patient (Kernberg, 1984). Independent historical information refers to any data that are *not* self-reported by the patient and includes such things as other psychiatric and psychological records, medical records, school and military records, employment records, criminal records, and interviews with historical and contemporary observers of the patient (parents, siblings, legal and health care professionals). Testing refers to psychological, neuropsychological, and medical tests, historical or contemporary, that provide objective reference points to further understand the psychology or psychobiology of the patient. The elimination of any one of these three sources of knowledge about the patient will leave the psychologist vulnerable to gross manipulation in a treatment setting and may lead to impeachment as an expert witness in a forensic setting.

Although we are focusing in this chapter on the use of psychological testing to assess psychopathy, we cannot overstate the critical importance of both the clinical interview and the gathering of independent historical data to arrive at a reliable and valid understanding of psychopathy in an individual. Our subsequent discussion of tests and instruments assumes the competent and thorough completion of these other two clinical tasks.

PSYCHOPATHY AND ANTISOCIAL PERSONALITY DISORDER

The diagnosis of Antisocial Personality Disorder in DSM-III-R (American Psychiatric Association, 1987) is almost exclusively devoted to criminal and antisocial behaviors and remains so in DSM-IV (American Psychiatric Association, 1994). Although most psychopathic subjects will also meet the criteria for ASPD as defined by psychiatric nomenclature, only about one-third of ASPD samples will meet the criteria for psychopathic personality as defined by a reliable and valid measure (Hare, 1991). The clinical importance of this fact can be stated differently. Most antisocial-personality-disordered adults, both male and female, should not be considered severely psychopathic and will not meet the factor analytic definition of this construct—an individual whose behavior is characterized by a callous and remorseless disregard for the rights and feelings of others *and* a chronic antisocial lifestyle (Hare, 1991).

We integrate the construct psychopathy into Axis II by placing in parentheses the terms "mild, moderate, or severe psychopathy" after the DSM-III-R or DSM-IV recognized personality disorder, if one or several exist. For instance, "Axis II: Antisocial Personality Disorder (severe psychopathy)" might appear in a report. We then go on to explain in the next paragraph how *psychopathy* is defined and psychologically measured. The psychologist should recognize that the term, despite its one-hundred-year history (Meloy, 1988), is not currently accepted as a psychodiagnosis or as a personality disorder by the psychiatric or legal community; yet it can be effectively used as a discriminating clinical tool.

THE PSYCHOPATHY CHECKLIST— REVISED

The first and most important instrument for assessing psychopathy in both clinical and forensic settings is the Psychopathy Checklist Revised (Hare, 1991). This twenty-item, forty-point scale is completed following a structured clinical interview of the patient and a review of independent historical data. Further psychological testing is not necessary to complete this behavioral trait instrument. The items of the PCL-R, empirically derived from the original work of Cleckley (1941/1976), are listed in Table 28.1.

TABLE 28.1. The Hare Psychopathy Checklist—
Revised (PCL-R)

1. Glibness/superficial charm
2. Grandiose sense of self-worth
3. Need for stimulation/proneness to boredom
4. Pathological lying
5. Conning/manipulation
6. Lack of remorse or guilt
7. Shallow affect
8. Callous/lack of empathy
9. Parasitic life-style
10. Poor behavioral controls
11. Promiscuous sexual behavior
12. Early behavior problems
13. Lack of realistic, long-term goals
14. Impulsivity
15. Irresponsibility
16. Failure to accept responsibility for own actions
17. Many short-term marital relationships
18. Juvenile delinquency
19. Revocation of conditional release
20. Criminal versatility

A growing body of research has demonstrated the reliability and validity of the PCL-R for prison and forensic psychiatric populations (Hare, Harpur, Hakstian, Forth, Hart, & Newman, 1990; Hart & Hare, 1989; Hare, 1991). Interrater reliabilities range from .88 to .92, while test-retest reliabilities range from .85 to .90 (Schroeder, Schroeder, & Hare, 1983; Cacciola, Rutherford, & Alterman, 1990). The PCL-R is a homogeneous, unidimensional scale, with internal consistency varying between .85 and .87 (alpha coefficients). The mean standard error of measurement is 3.14, and the mean standard error of prediction is 4.26 (Hare, 1991) for prisoners and forensic psychiatric patients. Factor analysis yields two factors: aggressive narcissism (Meloy, 1992) and chronic antisocial behavior. Although a score of ≥ 30 has been used as the research convention for separating psychopathic from nonpsychopathic research subjects, we do not recommend the use of this cutoff for clinical purposes due to the standard error of the instrument. We recommend that the term "severe psychopathy" be reserved for individuals who score at least thirty-three points on the PCL-R, or one SEM unit

above the research cutoff. Individuals scoring below this level should be considered to have psychopathic traits, and discussion should avoid labeling them as psychopathic personalities. Traits can be described as mild to moderate, depending on the scale elevations (Gacono & Hutton, 1994).

A substantial validation literature has demonstrated that psychopathic prisoners, when compared with nonpsychopathic prisoners, commit a greater quantity and variety of offenses (Hare & Jutai, 1983); commit a greater frequency of violent offenses in which *predatory* violence (Meloy, 1988) is used against male strangers (Hare & McPherson, 1984; Williamson, Hare, & Wong, 1987); and have lengthier criminal careers (Hare, McPherson, & Forth, 1988). They also have a poorer response to therapeutic intervention (Ogloff, Wong, & Greenwood, 1990) which, in some cases, may be followed by an *increase* in their subsequent arrest rates for violent crimes (Rice, Harris, & Cormier, 1992). The psychophysiological research also indicates a pattern of chronic cortical underarousal (Meloy, 1992).

The PCL-R should only be used with populations where it has been validated.[3] This presently excludes its clinical use with adolescents, although research with this age group is proceeding (Forth, Hart, & Hare, 1990). Only licensed mental health professionals with forensic experience who are trained in the use of the PCL-R and familiar with current research should employ it for clinical assessments. Formal training is provided by Robert Hare, Ph.D., and his colleagues from the University of British Columbia. Alternatively, small clinician groups familiar with the test materials can practice rating a minimum of ten subjects and compare their interrater agreement before using it for clinical determinations. When problems arise, the study group should seek consultation with an expert on the PCL-R. Gacono & Hutton (1994) found that 75 percent of trainees' ratings (N = 110) were within one point of trainers' ratings in a reliability study at a large forensic hospital.

Each item is scored on a three-point scale: zero (the item does not apply); one (some elements apply); two (there is a reasonably good match). Items are not scored if there is no available information. When the examiner is uncertain about the scoring of several items, despite adequate data, half should be scored higher and half lower (Hare, 1991). If items are unscored, a prorated total score is eventually computed as outlined in the scoring manual (Hare, 1991).

Independent records review is absolutely necessary to use the PCL-R. If such information is not available, the PCL-R should not be used or should be postponed until such data are accessible. Gacono and Hutton (1994) found it helpful to develop a systematic method that clusters information relevant to certain items. For instance, item 18 (juvenile delinquency) and item 20 (criminal versatility) can be scored by recording offenses in the criminal record by chronological age. Trait-based items, such as 2 (grandiose sense of self-worth), may be found in hospital records that note the patient's attitudes of entitlement while on the inpatient ward. Record information also helps determine the degree, if any, of pathological lying (item 4) by comparing it with self-report during the clinical interview. The record review always occurs *before* the clinical interview, as it should in all forensic evaluations.

Following the record review, the clinician should obtain a chronological life history from the patient, and then assess, in order, items 20, 19, 18, 12, 17, 11, 3/14/15, 9, 10, 6/7/8/16, 1/2, 4/5, and 13. This sequence moves from more structured to less structured items. Data from earlier items contribute to scoring later items. For example, glibness and superficial charm (item 1) can often be scored by the end of the interview without further questions (Gacono & Hutton, 1994).

Items that can be scored by similar interview questions are grouped. For example, proneness to boredom (item 3), impulsivity (item 14), and irresponsibility (item 15) are related and can be scored on the basis of frequent address, job, and relationship changes, a lack of planning, substance abuse on the job, employment terminations, and job abandonment. Frequent speeding tickets and reckless driving also contribute to both proneness to boredom and irresponsi-

bility. The PCL-R interview is generally non-threatening and can build rapport with, and a sense of empathy for, the patient. Psychopathic subjects, however, may respond to such affectional overtures with indignation, indifference, or threats, affective defenses and behaviors that attenuate their unconscious feelings of envy (Meloy, 1988). In over 150 evaluations, subjects responding in this manner were determined on subsequent interview to be severely psychopathic (Gacono & Hutton, 1994).

Each item is scored separately, and the assessor should be careful to avoid introspection about etiology or preconceived notions of psychopathy when scoring the PCL-R, since this is one form of examiner bias. Ratings should be based on "lifelong patterns" and "typical functioning." Any male subject, in particular, will probably obtain a score of two points on some items but will not reach the clinical threshold for psychopathic personality (≥ 33). In fact, a subject could obtain a two-point score on sixteen items and still not reach this threshold, although he would be considered a psychopath for research purposes and would have clear-cut psychopathic traits for clinical decision making. The mean score for adult males in a forensic psychiatric hospital is 20 (SD = 8) and in a prison is 23 (SD = 8). The distribution is approximately normal with a slightly negative skew (Hare, 1991).

Evaluation of female or nonwhite individuals with the PCL-R should be done with caution. There are few published data on its use with women (Hare, 1991; Peaslee, 1992; Strachan, 1993). Black males show similar inter-judge reliability and validity findings on the PCL-R but do score significantly higher and show a less well-differentiated two-factor structure than white males do (Kosson, Smith, & Newman, 1990). There is no published research to date on its use with large samples of Hispanic, native American, or Asian males.

Assessment is strengthened when several independent measures are used. We recommend that several other tests be employed to further delineate the behavioral and intrapsychic characteristics of the psychopathic subject, within whom many individual differences will reside.

THE RORSCHACH

The Rorschach is ideally suited for contributing to the assessment of psychopathy. It avoids the face validity of self-report measures yet provides reliable and valid information about the personality structure and function of an individual (Exner, 1986). Although we hesitate to state that the Rorschach cannot be malingered,[4] we have found that the test is usually only "beaten" by the psychopathic patient if he sufficiently constricts his response frequency (Perry & Kinder, 1990).[5] Such a psychometrically invalid protocol (Exner, 1988), however, may still yield worthwhile psychodiagnostic information. We have found that ASPD males in general produce normative response frequencies (Gacono & Meloy, 1992), at least in research settings. Rorschachs taken for clinical purposes in pretrial criminal cases may be constricted, but the examiner should aggressively pursue a valid procotol (R ≥ 14) according to Exner's (1986) guidelines. Sexual homicide perpetrators, most of whom evidence moderate to severe psychopathic disturbance, do in fact produce grossly inflated response frequencies (Meloy, Gacono, & Kenney, 1994).

Although the clinician should administer and interpret the Rorschach according to the Comprehensive System (Exner, 1990), other psychoanalytically informed empirical measures of the Rorschach are also quite valuable. Two methods that we ordinarily use to complement the Comprehensive System include a measure of defenses (Cooper & Arnow, 1986) and an object relations measure (Kwawer, 1980). We have found both of these measures to have acceptable interjudge reliability (Gacono & Meloy, 1992). Kwawer (1979) found that his ten categories of "primitive interpersonal modes" (1980) were able to significantly differentiate between a borderline and an age and gender matched control sample of Rorschachs. Cooper, Perry, & Arnow (1988) reported interrater reliabilities for each of fifteen defenses ranging from .45 to .80, with a median of .62 (intraclass correlation coefficients). Interrater reliability for the borderline defenses as a group, most commonly seen in psychopathic

protocols, was .81. They did not find, however, any particular defense mechanism related to the presence of antisocial personality disorder (DSM-III-R) and speculated that the diagnosis of ASPD may be too psychodynamically heterogeneous. We agree.

Through a series of studies (Gacono, 1990; Gacono et al., 1990; Gacono & Meloy, 1991, 1992; Gacono & Meloy, 1994; Meloy & Gacono, 1992) we have validated the use of the Rorschach as a sensitive instrument to discriminate between psychopathic and nonpsychopathic subjects. Psychodynamic differences include more pathological narcissism and sadism, less anxiety, and less capacity for attachment. Personality organization (Kernberg, 1984) predominates at a borderline level. Commonly used defenses include devaluation, massive denial, projective identification, omnipotence, and splitting. Idealization and higher-level "neurotic" defenses are virtually absent. Psychopathic criminals produce significantly more narcissistic mirroring, boundary disturbance, and total primitive object relations than nonpsychopathic criminals (Gacono & Meloy, 1992).

The prototypical Rorschach protocol of the psychopathic subject will evidence the following select structural characteristics (Exner, 1990; see Table 28.2). The numbers represent mean scores or frequencies of the majority of the subjects in a sample of thirty-three male psychopaths in prison (Gacono & Meloy, 1994).

Deviations from these prototypical findings do not necessarily rule out a psychopathic disturbance and should deepen understanding of the individual differences within any one patient. For example, a psychopathic individual might also show histrionic features, structurally evident in some idealizing defenses; a color projection (CP) response; a low Lambda (L); and an elevated affective ratio (Afr). On the other hand, a paranoid psychopath might produce a constricted protocol; elevated Dd response; a low H + A:Hd + Ad ratio; and a positive hypervigilance index (HVI). A psychopathic subject scoring 36 on the PCL-R might also have the biochemical disorder of schizophrenia, evident on the Rorschach in a positive schizophrenia index (SCZI). What begins as a gross

TABLE 28.2. Select Comprehensive System (Exner, 1986) variables from a prototypical Rorschach of a psychopath

Responses		21
Core characteristics		
	Lambda	>.99
	D	0
	Adj D	0
Affects		
	FC:CF + C	1:4
	Afr	<.50
	Pure C	>0
	T	0
	Y	0
	Space	>2
Interpersonal relations		
	Pure H	2
	(H) + Hd + (Hd)	2.5
	COP	0
	Ag	0
	Sx	1
Self-perception		
	Rf	1
	Per	>2
	W:M	>3:1
Cognitions		
	X+%	54
	F+%	56
	X−%	22
	M−	1
	WSum6SpecSc	17

categorization of chronic antisocial behavior (DSM-IV) moves to the determination of the degree of psychopathic disturbance using the PCL-R and is further refined through the Rorschach to measure the internal structure and dynamics of the particular patient.

THE MMPI/MMPI-2

Our assessment of psychopathy next turns to the psychometric workhorse of the profession and of forensic psychology in particular. Although self-report measures in criminal populations are inherently unreliable (Hare, 1985), either the MMPI or the MMPI-2 should be used with other instruments in the assessment of psychopathy for the following reasons: to provide convergent validity for the other sources of data; to

measure self-report of psychopathology with a method that is sensitive to distortion; to measure domains of behavior that are not empirically abnormal; and to meet evidentiary standards for admissibility as a scientific method or procedure.[6]

The clinical scale most sensitive to "a variation in the direction of psychopathy" (McKinley & Hathaway, 1944, p. 172) is, of course, scale 4 (Pd). Most criminal populations will show remarkable homogeneity by elevating on this scale. McKinley and Hathaway (1944) developed this scale by contrasting two normative groups, married adults and college applicants, with a sample of female and male delinquents (ages seventeen to twenty-two) referred by the Minnesota courts to a psychiatric setting. These young adults had a long history of minor criminal behavior: stealing, lying, truancy, sexual promiscuity, alcohol abuse, and forgery. There were no homicide offenses in the histories of these subjects, of whom the majority were girls. Cross-validation indicated that a T score of ≥ 70 was achieved by 59 percent of a sample of one hundred male federal prisoners (McKinley & Hathaway, 1944). We note that the original criterion group was already incarcerated and had been selected for psychiatric study. Temporal reliability of this scale ranges from .49 to .61 for intervals up to a year (Dahlstrom et al., 1975) and was .71 in normals, according to McKinley and Hathaway (1944).

The MMPI scale 4 is composed of fifty items, of which half are answered true (twenty-four) and half answered false (twenty-six). Factor analysis has generally yielded five factors: shyness, hypersensitivity, delinquency, impulse control, and neuroticism (Greene, 1980). We recommend several texts to the clinician for validation and interpretation of scale 4 (Dahlstrom et al., 1972, 1975; Greene, 1980; Graham, 1978). Clinical interpretation should always address both elevation and configuration.

We also rely on the Harris and Lingoes (1955) Pd subscales for further understanding of scale 4. Originally derived from the MMPI through a rational analysis and not separately validated, they are composed of sixty-seven items, twelve of which are "off scale" and do not appear among the other scale 4 items. Five subscale items (64, 67, 94, 146, 368) appear in more than one of the subscales. Caldwell (1988) provided a very useful interpretation of these subscales for the MMPI.

The scale 4 items have undergone virtually no change in MMPI-2. The fifty items remain, and four have been reworded. Pd T scores, however, will be approximately ten T points lower for males and five T points lower for females across the range of the scale due to the new norms. The Pd scale, moreover, is not affected by educational level in either the MMPI-2 male or female normative samples (Butcher, 1990).

The Harris and Lingoes subscales have been substantially changed on the MMPI-2. Nichols (personal communication, April, 1993) determined that each subscale lost a certain number of items (see Table 28.3).

The MMPI-2 committee's justification for these deletions is that they were "off scale" items and did not contribute to clarification of elevation on the parent (Pd) scale. The Pd3 subscale, social imperturbability, was most heavily hit, losing 50 percent of its items. This measure of what Nichols (personal communication, April, 1993) calls "insouciance" has gotten consistently high negative loadings on anxiety and may best capture the social aggression of the psychopathic personality. The MMPI-2 deletions have decreased the subscales' reliability due to increased T score jumps for each remaining item, and may have affected the subscales' meanings and internal consistency. Further research is needed. Although these subscales have been compromised and may be less adequate than they were, we still think they can be used with confidence.

The major problem with the new antisocial practices (ASP) content scale (Butcher et al., 1989) is its face validity and the fact that it is suppressed with elevations on K. We view it as more of an attitude scale and await further research with psychopathic subjects. Lilienfeld (1991) found that it had relatively high loadings on two factors—negative emotionality and fearlessness—in a sample of college undergraduates, which is consistent with expected trait characteristics of adult male psychopathic personalities.

The most useful MMPI typology for classifying criminals was developed by Megargee and Bohn (1979). Of their sample of 1,214 federal inmates, 96 percent of the MMPI profiles could be assigned to one of their ten subtypes. Subsequent research has supported its concurrent validity (Booth & Howell, 1983; DiFrancesca & Meloy, 1989; Hutton, Miner, & Langfeldt, 1993) and questioned its predictive validity (Louscher, Hosford, & Moss, 1983). We recommend the typology be used to generate behavioral hypotheses concerning a particular subject's MMPI elevations and configuration, which can then be tested against other data sources. Unfortunately, the original study (Megargee & Bohn, 1979) remains out of print.

The application of the Megargee-Bohn typology to the MMPI-2 necessitated revision of their classification rules and procedures. Identical classifications were then achieved with 80 to 84 percent of subjects in samples of youthful male offenders and male prisoners. Validation of these typology revisions for MMPI-2 needs to be done (Megargee, 1993).

How does scale 4 and its subscales contribute to a clinical understanding of psychopathy? We

TABLE 28.3. Harris & Lingoes Pd subscale items and changes between MMPI and MMPI-2

Subscale			MMPI	deleted	MMPI-2
Pd1	Family discord		11	2	9
Pd2	Authority problems		11	3	8
Pd3	Social imperturbability		12	6	6
Pd4a (Pd4)	Social alienation		18	5	13
Pd4b (Pd5)	Self-alienation		15	3	12
		Total	67	19	48

Note: Courtesy of David Nichols, Ph.D.

TABLE 28.4. Pearson Product-Moment Correlations between PCL-R Scores and MMPI, MMPI-2 Pd Scores in samples of NGI acquittees

		N = 40 MMPI	N = 34 MMPI-2
Pd		.21	.20
Pd1	Family discord	.00	.10
Pd2	Authority problems	.34*	.31*
Pd3	Social imperturbability	.20	.23
Pd4	Social alienation	−.17	−.10
Pd5	Self-alienation	−.05	−.22

*Significance <.05 (one-directional test).

compared[7] the PCL-R, MMPI, and MMPI-2 Pd scores for two samples of male subjects who had been found not guilty by reason of insanity and were committed to an involuntary outpatient treatment program (Meloy, Haroun, & Schiller, 1990). Most of these subjects were Caucasian males diagnosed with paranoid schizophrenia who had committed a violent crime. The data are presented in Table 28.4.

The data suggest that although there is a positive relationship between elevations on MMPI and MMPI-2 Pd and the PCL-R, the product moment correlations are modest and nonsignificant. Our findings are consistent with those of Hare (1991), who found that correlations between the MMPI Pd Scale and the PCL-R ranged from .19 to .25. We think this is primarily due to the Pd scale's measurement of factor II of the PCL-R (chronic antisocial behavior) rather than factor I (aggressive narcissism). If the PCL-R factors are separately correlated with Pd, factor I ranges between .05 and .11 and factor II ranges between .28 and .31 (Hare, 1991).

The Harris and Lingoes subscales' correlations with the PCL-R indicate that Pd2, authority problems, are highest, and Pd1, family discord, is virtually nonexistent. Pd3, social imperturbability, is not significantly correlated but surprisingly *increases* between MMPI and MMPI-2. Most compelling is the negative correlation between the PCL-R and the MMPI-2 Pd5, self-alienation. This is, however, quite consistent with our psychodynamic findings concerning the psychopath that he does *not* feel

guilt, self-blame, or regretfulness concerning his antisocial history (Gacono & Meloy, 1992; Caldwell, 1988). In fact, his lack of superego constraint or sense of personal responsibility for his actions is a benchmark for his behavior (Meloy, 1988; Hare, 1991). Our findings also suggest that correlations between the PCL-R and Pd, although modest, do not change when a forensic psychiatric population is studied, rather than just a criminal population. The clinician should not hesitate to measure psychopathy despite the presence of a major mental disorder (Hart & Hare, 1989). A research question that we are beginning to investigate is whether elevations on scale 4 correlate with decreased effectiveness of psychotropic medications in a forensic psychiatric population.

Since distortion should be assumed in all forensic evaluations (Meloy, 1989), the MMPI/MMPI-2 validity scales take on special importance in evaluating for psychopathy. It appears that scales L and F remain the most useful in classifying fake-bad and fake-good profiles (Timbrook, Graham, Keiller, & Watts, 1993), and we refer the clinician to the extensive work of both Butcher et al. (1989) and Caldwell (1988) for their interpretive refinements concerning deviant responding to the MMPI-2 and MMPI, respectively.

MEASURES OF COGNITION AND INTELLIGENCE

Although not central to the assessment of personality, a standardized measure of intelligence, such as the Wechsler Adult Intelligence Scale—Revised (Wechsler, 1981), should be incorporated into the battery for assessing psychopathy. In the absence of time to complete a WAIS-R, we find that the Quick Test (Ammons & Ammons, 1977) gives a reliable estimate of intelligence, and it has been validated in forensic settings (Husband & DeCato, 1982; Randolph, Randolph, Ciula, Padget, & Cunco, 1980; Sweeney & Richards, 1988). An estimate of general intelligence provides a baseline for interpretive performance on other instruments, although IQ is independent of psychopathy (Hare, 1991).

Neuropsychological measures may provide useful information to the clinician, but differences between psychopathic and nonpsychopathic criminals have yet to be consistently demonstrated (Hare, 1991). Some neuropsychological tests are also useful in assessing malingering because of their face validity. Psychopathic malingerers will often perform worse than the expected norms of organically impaired patients. They will also evidence more impairment than observed behavioral functioning would suggest (Wylie, personal communication, May, 1993). We find two points most salient to the use of neuropsychological instruments in the assessment of psychopathy: first, any measures of performance are subject to motivational factors, and psychopathic patients may quickly realize that decrements in their performance on neuropsychological tests will contribute to their "disability" and perhaps avoidance of personal responsibility; and second, the genuine presence of neuropsychological impairment does not rule out psychopathy and may in fact be consistent with cognitive and emotional deficits already established in research with psychopaths (Hare, 1991).[8]

INTEGRATION OF FINDINGS

Perhaps the most difficult, and elegant, task of the clinician is to integrate the findings from various tests into an empirically accurate and theoretically consistent clinical picture of the patient. In the case of the psychopath in a criminal setting, findings may also need to withstand the rigors of cross-examination (Gacono & Hutton, 1994; Meloy, 1991; Pope, Butcher, & Seelen, 1993). Again, we cannot overstate the importance of the history and clinical interview and their usefulness to validate, or invalidate, test findings. Test results, moreover, provide contemporaneous and objective reference points for the support or refutation of developing clinical hypotheses, as well as data relevant to the management of psychopathic patients in an institution.

The tests we have emphasized—the Psychopathy Checklist—Revised, the Rorschach, and the MMPI/MMPI 2—provide main avenues to understanding the psychopathic patient. The PCL-R is based on observation of the individual and his or her history; the Rorschach accesses generally unconscious personality structure and psychodynamics; and the MMPI/MMPI-2 measures deliberate self-report of psychopathology and its distortion. Taken together, they will provide both discriminating and converging pieces of data.

For example, a patient is scored 2 on the PCL-R item 13, lack of realistic or long-term goals, partially arrived at on the basis of a series of frequent job changes in the subject's employment record. The MMPI-2 indicates a Pd2 (authority problems) T score of 75, providing insight into one of the reasons for frequent job changes, which is further confirmed through the subpoena of employer records. The Rorschach is scrutinized and yields S > 2 (H: characterological anger), Lambda >.99 (H: a simple, item-by-item approach to problem solving), and FC:CF + C of 1:4, with 2 Pure C responses (H: unmodulated affect with a marked propensity to emotional explosiveness). Further scrutiny of the employment records indicates several incidents of angry outbursts toward employers. A look at the long-sought-after military record also indicates a less than honorable discharge. The clinician then compares these findings with his clinical interview with the patient and recalls his countertransferential feelings of anxiety as the patient aggressively questioned his credentials before the interview began. Taken together, these approaches to understanding this hypothetical patient provide clinical understanding that is at once broader and more meaningful than the yield from any one test. It is the culmination of inference building (both convergent and divergent findings) across the three primary sources of data: the clinical interview, independent history gathering, and test results.

The clinical assessment of psychopathic personality is a complex task that involves both nomothetic comparison and idiographic delineation. It is most frequently needed in forensic settings but may present as an uninvited but crucial clinical obligation in any health care practice. The clinical psychologist, with his or her training in the appropriate use of tests, is most suited to the task. Clinical assessment helps us understand the internal world of psychopathy, one aspect of which was poetically captured by Edna St. Vincent Millay:

My candle burns at both ends;
It will not last the night;
But ah, my foes, and, oh, my friends—
It gives a lovely light.
                    "A Few Figs from Thistles"

NOTES

1. Münsterberg was a student of Wilhelm Wundt and arrived in the U.S. in 1892 at the invitation of William James to direct the psychology laboratory at Harvard. Although controversial and self-promoting, he made a seminal contribution to forensic psychology (Bartol and Bartol, 1987).

2. Malingering requires a separate evaluation with an instrument such as the Structured Interview of Reported Symptoms (SIRS) (Rogers, Bagby, & Dickens, 1992). Psychopathy becomes useful adjunctive information in this context.

3. The following portion of this chapter draws extensively from Gacono and Hutton (1994) with permission of Pergamon Press, Ltd., Headington Hill Hall, Oxford OX3 OBW, United Kingdom. See Gacono and Hutton (1994) for extensive training guidelines and clinical applications of the PCL-R (see also Serin, 1992).

4. John Cochran, Ph.D. (personal communication, April, 1993) administered the Rorschach to a subject in a criminal setting. When he studied the protocol, it sounded vaguely familiar. He found the same verbatim protocol in *The Rorschach: A Comprehensive System. Volume 2* (2nd edition)! The subject had memorized the responses to the entire protocol, one of many he could choose from in his Rorschach "library" that Dr. Cochran eventually observed in his prison cell.

5. Another psychopathic subject (PCL-R = 37.5), before an evaluation by Gacono, revealed that he had gone to the forensic hospital library and "researched" our Rorschach articles concerning psychopathy. Despite this knowledge, he produced a valid (R = 52) response protocol that revealed the psychodynamics of his personality and some of the motivations for his sexual murders.

6. The so-called Frye test (*Frye* v. *United States*, 293 F. 1013 [D.C. Circuit 1923]) was the case-law standard for determining whether a scientific principle or discovery was admissable as evidence. The court wrote, "the thing from which the deduction is made must be sufficiently established to have gained general acceptance in the particular field in which it belongs" (at 1013). It was usually applied to devices and processes, not to expert opinion (see *People* v. *Mendibles*, 245 Cal. Rptr. 553 [1988]). The "Frye" standard was rewritten by the U.S. Supreme Court during their 1992–1993 term in *Daubert* v. *Merrell Dow Pharmaceuticals* (113 Sup. Ct. 2786). The "Daubert" standard is now determined by case relevance and scientific validity, and not by general acceptance in the scientific community.

7. We thank Edmund Bienkowski, Ph.D., and Marilyn Clarke for their analysis of these data.

8. Neuropsychological impairments that appear genuine, moreover, may warrant further neurological workup with methods that eliminate motivational factors and measure brain structure or function. These procedures could include MRI, CAT, PET, EEG, or BEAM studies. One sexual murderer (PCL-R = 37) produced generally invalid psychological test results due to malingering, but also was found to have an abnormal visual evoked potential test using BEAM technology and an abnormal PET scan indicating decreased metabolic uptake in certain areas of his frontal cortex and midbrain. Based on these findings, and corollary behaviors, he received an additional diagnosis of organic personality syndrome, explosive type (DSM-III-R).

REFERENCES

American Psychiatric Association. (1987). *Diagnostic and statistical manual of mental disorders* (3rd ed.—rev.). Washington, DC: author.

American Psychiatric Association. (1994). *Diagnostic and statistical manual of mental disorders* (4th ed.). Washington, DC: author.

Ammons, R., & Ammons, C. (1977). The Quick Test: Provisional manual. *Psychological Reports Monograph Supplement 1–VII*, 11, 111–161. (Originally published 1962)

Bartol, C., & Bartol, A. (1987). History of forensic psychology. In I. Weiner & A. Hess (Eds.), *Handbook of forensic psychology* (pp. 3–21). New York: Wiley.

Booth, R., & Howell, R. (1983). Classification of prison inmates with the MMPI: An extension and validation of the typology. *Criminal Justice and Behavior, 7,* 407–422.

Butcher, J. (1990). Education level and MMPI-2 measured psychopathology: A case of negligible influence. *MMPI-2 News and Profiles, 1,* 3.

Butcher, J., Dahlstrom, G., Graham, J., Tellegen, A., & Kaemmer, B. (1989). *MMPI-2 manual for administration and scoring.* Minneapolis: University of Minnesota Press.

Cacciola, J., Rutherford, M., & Alterman, A. (1990, June). *Use of the psychopathy checklist with opiate addicts. Paper presented to the Committee on Problems in Drug Dependence.* National Drug Administration, Richmond, VA.

Caldwell, A. (1988). *MMPI supplemental scale manual.* Los Angeles: Caldwell Report.

Cleckley, H. (1976). *The mask of sanity.* (Originally published 1941) St. Louis: C. V. Mosby.

Cooper, S., & Arnow, D. (1986). An object relations view of the borderline defenses: A Rorschach analysis. In M. Kissen (Ed.), *Assessing object relations phenomena* (pp. 143–171). Madison, CT: International Universities Press.

Cooper, S., Perry, J., & Arnow, D. (1988). An empirical approach to the study of defense mechanisms: I. Reliability and preliminary validity of the Rorschach defense scales. *Journal of Personality Assessment, 52,* 187–203.

Dahlstrom, G., Welsh, G., & Dahlstrom, L. (1972). *An MMPI handbook: Volume I. Clinical interpretation* (rev. ed.) Minneapolis: University of Minnesota Press.

Dahlstrom, G., Welsh, G., & Dahlstrom, L. (1975). *An MMPI handbook: Volume II. Research applications* (rev. ed.) Minneapolis: University of Minnesota Press.

DiFrancesca, K., & Meloy, J. R. (1989). A comparative clinical investigation of the "how" and "charlie" MMPI subtypes. *Journal of Personality Assessment, 53,* 396–403.

Exner, J. (1986). *The Rorschach: A comprehensive system: Volume 1. Basic Foundations* (2nd ed.). New York: Wiley.

Exner, J. (1988). Problems with brief Rorschach protocols. *Journal of Personality Assessment, 52,* 640–647.

Exner, J. (1991). *The Rorschach: A Comprehensive System: Vol. 2. Interpretation* (2nd ed.). New York: Wiley.

Forth, A., Hart, S., & Hare, R. (1990). Assessment of psychopathy in male young offenders. *Psychological Assessment, 2,* 342–344.

Gacono, C. (1990). An empirical study of object relations and defensive operations in antisocial personality disorder. *Journal of Personality Assessment, 54,* 589–600.

Gacono, C., & Hutton, H. (1994). Suggestions for the clinical and forensic use of the Hare psychopathy checklist—revised (PCL-R). *International Journal of Law and Psychiatry, 17.*

Gacono, C., & Meloy, J. R. (1991). A Rorschach investigation of attachment and anxiety in antisocial personality disorder. *Journal of Nervous and Mental Disease, 179,* 546–552.

Gacono, C., & Meloy, J. R. (1992). The Rorschach and the DSM-III-R antisocial personality: A tribute to Robert Lindner. *Journal of Clinical Psychology, 48,* 393–405.

Gacono, C., & Meloy, J. R. (1994). *Rorschach assessment of aggressive and psychopathic personalities.* Hillsdale, NJ: Erlbaum.

Gacono, C., Meloy, J. R., & Heaven, T. (1990). A Rorschach investigation of narcissism and hysteria in antisocial personality disorder. *Journal of Personality Assessment, 55,* 270–279.

Graham, J. (1978). *The MMPI: A practical guide.* New York: Oxford University Press.

Greene, R. (1980). *The MMPI: An interpretive manual.* New York: Grune & Stratton.

Hare, R. (1985). Comparison of the procedures for the assessment of psychopathy. *Journal of Consulting and Clinical Psychology, 53,* 7–16.

Hare, R. (1991). *The Hare psychopathy checklist—revised manual.* Toronto: Multi-Health Systems.

Hare, R., Harpur, T., Hakstian, A., Forth, A., Hart, S., & Newman, J. (1990). The revised psychopathy checklist: Reliability and factor structure. *Psychological Assessment, 2,* 338–341.

Hare, R., & Jutai, J. (1983). Criminal history of the male psychopath: some preliminary data. In K. Van Dusen & S. Mednick (Eds.), *Prospective studies of crime and delinquency.* Boston: Kluner Mijhoff.

Hare, R., & McPherson, L. (1984). Violent and aggressive behavior by criminal psychopaths. *International Journal of Law and Psychiatry, 7,* 35–50.

Hare, R., McPherson, L., & Forth, A. (1988). Male psychopaths and their criminal careers. *Journal of Consulting and Clinical Psychology, 56,* 710–714.

Harris, R., & Lingoes, J. (1955). *Subscales for the MMPI: An aid to profile interpretation.* Unpublished manuscript, University of California.

Hart, S., & Hare, R. (1989). Discriminant validity of the psychopathy checklist in a forensic psychiatric population. *Psychological Assessment, 1,* 211–218.

Husband, S. & DeCato, C. (1982). The Quick Test

compared with Wechsler Adult Intelligence Scale as measures of intellectual functioning in a prison clinical setting. *Psychological Reports, 50*, 167–170.

Hutton, H., Miner, M., & Langfeldt, V. (1993). The utility of the Megargee-Bohn typology in a forensic psychiatric hospital. *Journal of Personality Assessment, 60*, 572–587.

Kernberg, O. (1984). *Severe personality disorders: Psychotherapeutic strategies.* New Haven: Yale University Press.

Kosson, D., Smith, S., & Newman, J. (1990). Evaluating the construct validity of psychopathy on black and white male inmates: three preliminary studies. *Journal of Abnormal Psychology, 99*, 250–259.

Kwawer, J. (1979). Borderline phenomena, interpersonal relations, and the Rorschach test. *Bulletin of the Menninger Clinic, 43*, 515–524.

Kwawer, J. (1980). Primitive interpersonal modes, borderline phenomena and Rorschach content. In J. Kwawer, A. Sugarman, P. Lerner, & H. Lerner (Eds.), *Borderline phenomena and the Rorschach test* (pp. 89–109). New York: International Universities Press.

Lilienfeld, S. (1991). Assessment of psychopathy with the MMPI and MMPI-2. *MMPI-2 News and Profiles, 2*, 2.

Louscher, P., Hosford, R., & Moss, C. (1983). Predicting dangerous behavior in a penitentiary using the Megargee typology. *Criminal Justice and Behavior, 10*, 269–284.

McKinley, C., & Hathaway, S. (1944). The Minnesota Multiphasic Personality Inventory V. Hysteria, hypomania and psychopathic deviate. *Journal of Applied Psychology, 28*, 153–174.

Megargee, E. (1993, March 28). *Using the Megargee offender classification system with MMPI-2: An update.* Paper presented at the MMPI-2/MMPI-A Symposium, St. Petersburg, FL.

Megargee, E., & Bohn, M. (1979). *Classifying criminal offenders.* Beverly Hills, CA: Sage.

Meloy, J. R. (1988). *The psychopathic mind: origins, dynamics, and treatment.* Northvale, NJ: Jason Aronson.

Meloy, J. R. (1989). The forensic interview. In R. Craig (Ed.), *Clinical and diagnostic interviewing* (pp. 323–344). Northvale, NJ: Jason Aronson.

Meloy, J. R. (1991). Rorschach testimony. *Journal of Psychiatry and Law, 19*, 221–235.

Meloy, J. R. (1992). *Violent attachments.* Northvale, NJ: Jason Aronson.

Meloy, J. R., & Gacono, C. (1992). The aggression response and the Rorschach. *Journal of Clinical Psychology, 48*, 104–114.

Meloy, J. R., Gacono, C., & Kenney, L. (1994). A Rorschach investigation of sexual homicide. *Journal of Personality Assessment, 62*, 58–67.

Meloy, J. R., Haroun, A., & Schiller, E. (1990). *Clinical guidelines for involuntary outpatient treatment.* Sarasota, FL: Professional Resource Exchange.

Munsterberg, H. (1933). *On the witness stand.* New York: Clark Boardman Co. (Originally published 1908)

Ogloff, J., Wong, S., & Greenwood, A. (1990). Treating criminal psychopaths in a therapeutic community program. *Behavioral Sciences and the Law, 8*, 81–90.

Peaslee, D. (1992). *A study of the female psychopath.* Unpublished doctoral dissertation, California School of Professional Psychology, Fresno.

Perry, G., & Kinder, B. (1990). The susceptibility of the Rorschach to malingering: A critical review. *Journal of Personality Assessment, 54*, 47–57.

Pope, K., Butcher, J., & Seelen, J. (1993). *The MMPI, MMPI-2 and MMPI-A in court.* Washington, DC: American Psychological Association

Randolph, G., Randolph, J., Ciula, B., Padget, J., & Cuneo, D. (1980). Retrospective comparison of Quick Test IQs of new admissions and a random sample of patients in a maximum security mental hospital. *Psychological Reports, 46*, 1175–1178.

Rice, M., Harris, T., & Cormier, C. (1992). An evaluation of a maximum security therapeutic community for psychopaths and other mentally disordered offenders. *Law and Human Behavior, 16*, 399–412.

Rogers, R., Bagby, M., & Dickens, S. (1992). *Structured interview of reported symptoms professional manual.* Odessa, FL: Psychological Assessment Resources.

Schroeder, M., Schroeder, K., & Hare, R. (1983). Generalizability of a checklist for the assessment of psychopathy. *Journal of Consulting and Clinical Psychology, 51*, 511–516.

Serin, R. (1992). The clinical application of the psychopathy checklist—revised (PCL-R) in a prison population. *Journal of Clinical Psychology, 48*, 637–642.

Strachan, C. (1993). *The assessment of psychopathy in female offenders.* Unpublished doctoral dissertation, University of British Columbia, Vancouver.

Sweeney, D., & Richards, H. (1988, March). *The Quick Test, the WAIS and the WAIS-R: Normative data, cultural bias, and psychometric properties in a forensic psychiatric population.* Paper presented at the midwinter meeting of the Society for Personality Assessment, New Orleans.

Timbrook, R., Graham, J., Keiller, S., & Watts, D. (1993). Comparison of the Wiener-Harmon subtle-obvious scales and the standard validity scales in detecting valid and invalid MMPI-2 profiles. *Psychological Assessment, 5,* 53–61.

Wechsler, D. (1981). *Wechsler Adult Intelligence Scale—Revised manual.* New York: Psychological Corporation.

Williamson, S., Hare, R., & Wong, S. (1987). Violence: Criminal psychopaths and their victims. *Canadian Journal of Behavioral Science, 19,* 454–462.

29
Assessing Criminal Responsibility

Kathleen P. Stafford
Yossef S. Ben-Porath

The not guilty by reason of insanity defense receives a share of publicity and legislative concern greatly disproportionate to its actual frequency of use and success. The frequency of insanity acquittals is greatly overestimated by attorneys, judges, legislators, and the general public (Burton & Steadman, 1978; Pasewark & Pantle, 1979). Callahan, Steadman, McGreevy, & Robbins (1991) reported data from eight states which indicated that the insanity plea was raised in less than 1 percent of felony indictments and that only 26 percent of these pleas resulted in acquittal by reason of insanity. Similarly, national data from 1978 indicate that only 1,625 defendants (one-tenth of 1 percent of the presumed offenders who stood trial) successfully pleaded not guilty by reason of insanity (Steadman, Monahan, Hartstone, Davis, & Robbins, 1982).

Despite the low frequency of insanity pleas, psychologists are regularly called on to perform evaluations of criminal responsibility. The sensitive, highly publicized nature of these cases, with their potential impact on the defendant and the community, demand a thorough understanding of the legal, ethical, scientific, and clinical issues involved. In this chapter, we ex-

plore each of these aspects of the assessment of criminal responsibility.

LEGAL ISSUES

The concept of not guilty by reason of insanity is based on the moral premise that it would be wrong to convict and punish a defendant for committing acts he or she did not appreciate were wrong or was unable to refrain from doing.

This moral premise has its roots in the English church or canon law concept of *mens rea*, which means guilty mind or evil intent. In the 1100s, canon law began to influence English common law, and the ecclesiastical notion of *mens rea* was merged with the civil concept of the *actus reas*, or the forbidden act, to form the common-law concept of criminality. The insanity defense is based on the presumption that there are persons who commit forbidden acts but who are not morally blameworthy because of a lack of *mens rea*, or capacity to knowingly choose to commit a wrongful act. Therefore, insanity is a legal and a moral concept, not a psychological construct.

The history of the insanity defense over the

last few centuries represents repeated attempts to develop a definitive legal test that ensures that the truly insane are not punished while those who are morally blameworthy receive their just deserts (Finkel 1988). These attempts to develop a definitive test usually occur in the wake of a celebrated case involving the death of an important figure that stirs deep public indignation.

The first of these celebrated cases was the English case of *Rex* v. *Arnold* in 1724. The judge in this case formulated the "wild beast test," by which a defendant would be considered criminally nonresponsible if he did not know what he was doing, "no more than an infant, a brute or a wild beast." This statement was qualified, in that not "every frantic and idle humor" was considered grounds for exculpation. This case is also significant because the judge overruled the prosecutor's objection to admission of evidence about the defendant's behavior subsequent to the crime. This ruling paved the way for experts to testify about examinations of the defendant performed after the crime, even though there was no expert testimony in Arnold's case.

In an 1843 English case, Daniel M'Naghten was acquitted by reason of insanity for shooting Prime Minister Peel's secretary in a failed attempt to assassinate the prime minister himself. In response, the House of Lords and Justices formulated the M'Naghten test, under which M'Naghten would have been convicted. Under the M'Naghten standard:

> [I]t must be clearly proved that, at the time of the committing of the act, the party accused was labouring under such a defect of reason, from disease of the mind, as not to know the nature and quality of the act he was doing; or if he did know it, that he did not know he was doing what was wrong.

The M'Naghten standard remains the sole test, or at least part of the standard, for insanity in approximately half of the jurisdictions in the United States today.

In this country, the sole emphasis on cognitive impairment of the M'Naghten test was balanced by formulation of the "irresistible impulse"

test in an 1887 Alabama court decision, *Parsons* v. *State*, and in an 1897 federal court case, *Davis* v. *United States*. The Davis case stated that a defendant would be considered insane if "though conscious and able to distinguish between right and wrong . . . his will . . . has been otherwise than voluntarily so completely destroyed that his actions are not subject to it but are beyond his control." The irresistible impulse test has been rejected by many jurisdictions and is used solely by none, but it is combined with the M'Naghten test as the legal standard for insanity in several states. The M'Naghten test or its derivatives is frequently referred to as the "cognitive" prong of these two-pronged insanity standards, and the irresistible impulse test or its derivatives is frequently referred to as the "volitional" prong.

The Durham or "product" test was proposed by Judge Bazelon of the U.S. Court of Appeals for the District of Columbia in 1954. This insanity standard provided that "an accused is not criminally responsible if his unlawful act was the product of mental disease or mental defect." By proposing a broader, more open-ended insanity standard, Judge Bazelon hoped to encourage psychologists and psychiatrists to testify more fully about their observations and findings so that the judge or jury would have more scientific information to consider in making the ultimate legal decision about criminal responsibility. Instead, experts continued to testify in a conclusory manner, giving opinions about whether or not a criminal act was "the product of a mental disease or defect," without presenting data and reasoning that would provide the judge or jury with scientific information to assist them in making this decision in a more informed manner. This problem with expert witnesses usurping the role of the fact finder by addressing the ultimate legal issue in a conclusory manner remains a concern today.

The Durham test was subsequently overturned by *U.S.* v. *Brawner* (1972) and replaced by the American Law Institute (ALI) test (1962) in the District of Columbia. A majority of jurisdictions in the country subsequently adopted at least the first paragraph of the ALI test:

1. A person is not responsible for criminal conduct if at the time of such conduct as a result of mental disease or defect he lacks substantial capacity either to appreciate the criminality of his conduct or to conform his conduct to the requirements of the law.
2. As noted in the Article, the terms "mental disease or defect" do not include an abnormality manifested only by repeated criminal or otherwise antisocial conduct.

In the wake of the acquittal by reason of insanity of John Hinckley in the attempted assassination of President Reagan, there was once again public clamor for the reformulation of the insanity standard or for abolition of the defense altogether. Congress responded with the Insanity Defense Reform Act of 1984, which is the current applicable standard in all federal jurisdictions (United States Code Section 20). The Insanity Defense Reform Act adopts the M'Naghten standard, eliminates the volitional prong of the test, adds the qualifier "severe" to "mental disease or defect," establishes that the defendant has the burden of proving the defense of insanity by clear and convincing evidence, and places the burden of proof on the defendant acquitted by reason of insanity to demonstrate that his release would not create substantial risk of bodily injury or serious property damage due to a present mental disease or defect.

In addition, a new rule, Rule 704(B), was added to the Federal Rules of Evidence, barring expert witnesses from stating "whether the defendant did or did not have the mental state or condition constituting an element of the crime or of a defense thereto." This change is designed to prevent expert witnesses from giving an opinion about the ultimate legal issue to be decided by the judge or jury—whether the defendant is sane or insane.

Several states also changed the insanity standard between 1982 and 1985 in the wake of Hinckley (Callahan, Mayer, & Steadman, 1987). Four jurisdictions eliminated the volitional prong by shifting from the ALI test or M'Naghten plus irresistible impulse tests to the simple M'Naghten test. Two states restricted the use of the insanity defense so that it could not be used to negate *mens rea* as a defense to certain types of offenses. Montana repealed the insanity defense altogether. But two jurisdictions actually expanded the insanity standard by repealing the M'Naghten test and adopting the ALI test. In addition, twenty-six states changed commitment/release provisions following an insanity acquittal, in response to the Hinckley verdict as well as to the 1983 U.S. Supreme Court case, *Jones* v. *United States*.

There are two other legal concepts, in addition to the insanity defense, that lead to an assessment bearing on criminal responsibility. These are the guilty but mentally ill plea, and the concept of diminished capacity.

The guilty but mentally ill (GMBI) plea developed as a legislative means to attempt to reduce insanity acquittals and to increase the length of confinement of mentally ill people charged with crimes. GBMI was first adopted in Michigan in 1975 in response to a Michigan Supreme Court ruling that struck down the automatic commitment provision for defendants acquitted by reason of insanity. It has since been adopted by at least eleven other states. In all of these states, defendants are required either to plead insanity or to indicate their intent to raise mental illness as a factor in their defense. The verdict of GBMI then becomes an option to the verdicts of guilty or not guilty by reason of insanity for the fact finder in the case.

The GBMI verdict has been criticized for leading to incarceration of mentally ill defendants without any mitigation or lessening of the penalty they would have received with a simple conviction, and without any guarantee of treatment. Instead, data suggest that the GBMI finding stigmatizes defendants, leads to harsher sentences, and delays granting of parole (Callahan, McGreevy, Cirincione, & Steadman, 1992.)

Diminished capacity is a legal doctrine that permits psychological testimony at trial regarding *mens rea* in the absence of an insanity defense. Approximately two-thirds of the states permit such testimony, usually with some limitations (Melton, Petrila, Poythress, & Slobogin, 1987). Testimony is often restricted to whether the defendant had the *capacity* to form the requisite *mens rea* at the time of the offense, barring expert testimony about the ultimate legal issue of whether he in fact had the necessary *mens rea*. Some courts require that a severe "mental disease or defect" caused the lack of capacity. And most states limit diminished capacity testimony to certain types of crimes. Diminished capacity is most often restricted to intentional homicides or to other specific-intent crimes that include a lesser offense requiring only general intent. (Specific-intent crimes require a purposeful or knowing state of mind, whereas general intent refers to recklessness or negligence in committing a criminal act.)

Clearly, the insanity standard, the option of GBMI, and the admissibility of diminished capacity testimony vary across jurisdictions. The clinician who undertakes an assessment of criminal responsibility must first become familiar with the relevant statutes and case law in the jurisdiction in which the case is being heard.

ETHICAL ISSUES

The Ethical Principles of Psychologists and Code of Conduct (APA, 1992) contains a section on Forensic Activities that is pertinent to assessment of criminal responsibility. The Ethical Principles also refer in a footnote to the Specialty Guidelines for Forensic Psychologists (1991), developed by APA Division 41. These guidelines are aspirational and not enforceable, but they provide detailed standards to consider in making informed decisions about difficult areas of forensic practice. Both the Ethical Principles and the Specialty Guidelines should be reviewed prior to undertaking a criminal responsibility evaluation.

As with any forensic assessment, one of the basic ethical concerns in the assessment of criminal responsibility involves the recognition that the ultimate decision is a legal, moral, or social policy issue to be determined by the trier of fact, not a psychological issue. Psychologists address only aspects of the ultimate legal issue to which some degree of scientific expertise can be applied. It is important to consider the limitations

in the applicability of our scientific knowledge to the assessment of mental state at the time of the offense and to ensure that personal values, interests, and attitudes do not intrude into the clinical evaluation process and opinion. Although preliminary jury simulation research (Rogers, Bagby, Crouch, & Cutler, 1990; Fulero & Finkel, 1991) indicates that testimony about the ultimate issue of sanity either does not affect, or does not unduly influence, jurors' verdicts, it is critical to remember the limited role of the psychologist in addressing criminal responsibility issues.

The assessment of mental state at the time of the offense is controversial. Morse (1978) stated, "(T)here is no scientific evidence to demonstrate that persons whose criminal behavior is affected by craziness are less able to obey the law than persons similarly affected by cultural influences or character traits" (p. 641). He pointed out that "crazy" individuals are capable of behaving rationally and normally when offered incentives to do so. Bonnie and Slobogin (1980) conceded that "a defendant's past psychological functioning cannot be reconstructed with scientific precision. The truth will remain very much in the shadows whether or not mental health professionals are permitted to offer their opinions" (p. 462). They pointed out that even though mental health professionals may be overly disposed toward pathological explanations of behavior, their training and experience lead them to consider explanations of behavior that do not proceed from common-sense analysis, and they therefore have a contribution to make beyond the judgment of laymen. Bonnie and Slobogin (1980) make a "case for informed speculation" in reconstructing the defendant's mental state at the time of the alleged offense.

In addition to the importance of basing assessments on professional expertise without usurping the role of the legal fact finder, the second major ethical issue to be considered in criminal responsibility evaluations is best described by the question *Who Is the Client?* (Monahan, 1980). Whether retained by the defense or prosecutor or appointed by the court, the psychologist is obligated to clarify his or her role for the defendant, to inform the defendant of the level of confidentiality that applies to the evaluation, and to explain any circumstances that would constitute an exception to that confidentiality.

The major question about the level of confidentiality of a criminal responsibility evaluation arises when a defense-retained expert is subpoenaed by the prosecution to testify at trial. One line of judicial thinking on this issue supports the notion that a defense-retained expert is covered by the attorney-client privilege and that the evaluation becomes part of the attorney's work product and is therefore privileged (*United States* v. *Alvarez*, 1975; *State* v. *Pratt*, 1979). Other courts (*Edney* v. *Smith*, 1976; *State* v. *Carter*, 1983) have ruled that raising an insanity defense constitutes a waiver of privilege regarding psychological records, just as raising the issue of emotional state as part of civil litigation constitutes a waiver of privilege of psychological records. Before evaluating a defendant at the request of defense counsel, it is important to clarify with the attorney the exceptions to confidentiality that may arise and to apprise the defendant of these limitations.

CLINICAL ASSESSMENT

There are a number of excellent detailed guides to the assessment of criminal responsibility (e.g., Rogers, 1986; Melton, Petrila, Poythress, & Slobogin, 1987; Shapiro, 1991). In addition, Rogers (1984) has developed the Rogers Criminal Responsibility Assessment Scales (R-CRAS) in an effort to standardize and organize the clinical data and inferences employed in conducting insanity evaluations. Although the R-CRAS is not a psychometric instrument, it can serve as a conceptual guide to assessment of criminal responsibility.

We have formulated a set of twelve questions to guide the clinician in conducting a criminal responsibility evaluation (Table 29.1).

The first question is essentially concerned with defining the referral issue by clarifying the relevant legal standard and the particular issue the clinician is being asked to address. The clinician needs to obtain a copy of the statute or case law that contains the applicable legal standard for the jurisdiction in which the defendant is being tried before beginning an evaluation of mental state at the time of the offense(s).

The second question involves identifying the client and clarifying the level of confidentiality, if any, that applies to the evaluation. Whether a report is to be prepared, to whom the report is to be distributed, and who is to pay for the evaluation must be clearly established before the evaluation is begun.

Third, once the clinical examiner has clarified these issues for himself or herself, the defendant must be apprised, verbally and in writing, of the examiner's relationship to the defendant, the level of confidentiality that applies to the relationship, and any circumstances that might constitute an exception to that confidentiality. It is incumbent upon the examiner to attempt to determine whether the defendant understands his or her legal situation and the purpose of the evaluation. If the defendant seems unaware that his or her mental state at the time of the offense may be the basis for the defense strategy, or if the defendant does not agree with this strategy or with the evaluation, the evaluation should proceed no further until he or she has had the opportunity to confer with defense counsel. Even if the defendant seems agreeable to participating in the evaluation, some assessment of his or her capacity to make an informed decision to participate should be made. Finally, a rough assessment of the defendant's ability to understand the nature of the criminal proceedings against him or her and to work with defense counsel should be made. If the examiner has reservations about the defendant's competency to stand trial, the referral source should be notified so that some consideration can be given to a full competency evaluation prior to proceeding further with the case. (Discussion of the evaluation of competency to stand trial is beyond the scope of this chapter.)

Fourth, before interviewing the defendant, the examiner should obtain as much information about the facts of the case as possible. Law enforcement reports of the investigation of the alleged offense(s), witness statements, transcripts from preliminary hearings or grand jury

TABLE 29.1. Questions for the Clinician Conducting a Criminal Responsibility Evaluation

---

1. What is the relevant legal standard for Not Guilty by Reason of Insanity, Guilty But Mentally Ill, and/or diminished capacity in the jurisdiction in which this case is being heard? Which issue(s) am I being asked to address?
2. Is the referral being made by the defense, the prosecution, or through court appointment? If a defense referral, what level of confidentiality applies to the evaluation results?
3. Does the defendant appear to understand his or her legal situation and the particular defense strategy suggested by the referral question? Does he or she appear to be competent to agree to participate in this evaluation? Do I have any reservations about his competency to stand trial?
4. What are the facts of the case against the defendant? Have I obtained law enforcement reports of the investigation of the alleged offense(s), witness statements, transcripts from preliminary hearings, lab reports, and any other available documents pertaining to the alleged offense(s)?
5. What is the defendant's account of the alleged offense(s)? His or her thoughts, feelings, mood, and behavior before, during, and after the crime, his or her reported motive, and his or her perception of the external events and the behavior of others at that time, are particularly relevant.
6. What is the defendant's level of functioning prior to and following the alleged offense(s)? Has he or she received mental health treatment in the past?
7. What sources of collateral information can be tapped to verify and expand upon the self-report data obtained from the defendant? School, military, employment, arrest, probation, and treatment records are common sources of third-party information. Family members, witnesses, and significant others may have relevant observations about mental state near the time of the offense.
8. What is the defendant's experience with the use and abuse of psychoactive substances? Is the defendant currently using alcohol or drugs? Was the defendant intoxicated at the time of the offense(s)? Are past or present symptoms attributable to a psychoactive substance-induced disorder?
9. What psychological tests can be administered to clarify diagnostic and psychological capacity issues and to assess the defendant's response set toward the evaluation?
10. Are there indications that the defendant may be malingering, or conversely, denying or minimizing, psychopathology?
11. What, if any, diagnoses of mental disorder apply to the defendant? Are these mental disorders of sufficient severity to potentially affect the capacity to know the wrongfulness of a criminal act, or if applicable, to form the requisite intent, or to refrain from committing the offense? If so, is there information to suggest that the mental disorder was active at the time of the offense?
12. Is there any indication of a relation between the severe mental disorder and the offense? If so, is there any information to suggest that symptoms of a severe mental disorder directly impaired the defendant's capacity to meet the relevant standard for criminal responsibility?

---

proceedings, laboratory reports, and tapes or transcripts of any statements made by the defendant to arresting officers provide useful data about the defendant's thinking and behavior at the time of the offenses.

With the background provided by official accounts of the alleged offense(s), the clinician is in a good position to begin to probe the defendant's account of events at the time. It is crucial to explore with the defendant more than once his or her thoughts, feelings, mood, and behavior before, during, and after the offense(s). The defendant's perceptions of external events, the behavior of others, and the precipitants and mo-

tives for his or her own behavior at the time need to be covered in as much detail as possible. Inconsistencies between the defendant's account and available third-party information, as well as variations in self-report data across time and situations, require mild confrontation and clarification.

It is also necessary to obtain a complete social history to assess the defendant's level of functioning prior to and following the alleged offense(s). To verify and expand on the information obtained from the defendant, it is critical to obtain collateral information from a variety of third-party sources. School, military, employment, arrest, probation, medical, and mental health records are fairly accessible sources of such information. Interviews with family members, witnesses, and significant others may yield observational data with direct bearing on mental state near the time of the offense(s).

A very important area of inquiry has to do with the defendant's use of psychoactive substances. Voluntary intoxication is generally not considered a mental disease or defect for purposes of the insanity defense, although intoxication may be considered a legitimate basis for a diminished capacity defense in some jurisdictions. Pathological intoxication, or alcohol idiosyncratic intoxication, is an uncommon disorder that may affect mental state at the time of the offense. Some states, such as Colorado and California, have developed case law on the notion of "settled insanity" (mental impairment that persists after the acute effects of a drug have worn off) that may qualify the defendant for the insanity defense. There is a well-documented statistical relation between alcohol abuse and violent behavior (e.g., Bushman & Cooper, 1990; Swanson, Holzer, Ganju, & Jono, 1990). Phencyclidine abuse and amphetamine delusional disorder have also been associated with high frequencies of unplanned, violent behavior (Rogers, 1986). Because of the association between substance abuse and criminal behavior, and because of the particular legal implications for symptoms and disorders related to the use of psychoactive substances, a detailed substance abuse history, particularly for the time period near the offense(s), is crucial to obtain from the defendant and from collateral sources. Serum or urine drug testing done near the time of the offense(s) can be very useful, although such testing is not entirely reliable. Medical and mental health records, arrest and probation records, and interviews with significant others may also yield information about a defendant's use of psychoactive substances.

Another important source of data for the criminal responsibility evaluation is psychological testing. Objections have been raised to the routine use of psychological tests for assessment of mental state at the time of the offense(s) because they have not been validated for this pur-

pose and because they measure the defendant's *present* level of functioning (Melton, Petrila, Poythress, & Slobogin, 1987). Nevertheless, selective use of psychological testing can be a useful tool in clarifying diagnosis, assessing long-standing psychopathology, measuring levels of functioning for cognitively impaired defendants, and providing data about the defendant's response set toward the evaluation itself. The Minnesota Multiphasic Personality Inventory—2 is particularly useful in providing actuarial information about response sets, diagnostic symptoms, and long-standing psychopathology (Pope, Butcher, & Seelen, 1993).

The assessment of the defendant's approach toward the evaluation is important because of the serious consequences the defendant charged with a crime faces and the incentive he or she therefore has to exaggerate or fabricate symptoms of psychopathology. It is always necessary to rule out malingering in conducting an evaluation of mental state at the time of the offense. Assessment of malingering is covered in detail in another chapter of this book by Berry, Wetter, and Baer. For purposes of this discussion, it is important to note that inconsistency is the hallmark of malingering. The most effective means of assessing malingering is therefore to gather data from multiple sources, to interview the defendant on more than one occasion, to administer the MMPI-2 and any other psychometric instruments that measure psychological impairments the defendant may be malingering, and to be very sensitive to inconsistencies across data sources and across time. Any discrepancies between the defendant's self-report and other sources of data should be probed carefully with the defendant to allow him or her to clarify his or her position, to explain possible inaccuracies in third-party information obtained, or to retract false claims he or she had previously made to the examiner. Unsophisticated defendants sometimes exaggerate symptoms due to anxiety about their legal situations, but with mild confrontation many of these defendants become more straightforward and are able to complete the evaluation process in a more fully disclosing manner. If the defendant continues to fabricate or exaggerate symptoms, the diagnostic impression of malingering and its implications for the assessment of criminal responsibility need to be conveyed to the referral source in the final report.

A less common but equally problematic approach to a criminal responsibility evaluation is the denial or minimization of psychopathology on the part of the defendant who may well have been significantly impaired at the time of the offense(s). This happens most frequently with defendants who have major mental disorders but who lack insight into their difficulties. Again, third-party information and psychometric data may be critical in documenting the extent and nature of the impairment and relating it to the defendant's capacity at the time of the offense(s). Denial of psychopathology also raises an ethical dilemma over whether the criminal responsibility evaluation should proceed if the defendant does not agree with a defense strategy based on mental state at the time of the offense(s). It is wise to notify the defense attorney if the defendant does not believe that the psychological evaluation should be part of his or her defense. There is case law that suggests that an insanity defense may be imposed over the objections of a defendant (*Whalem* v. *United States*), but there is also a line of judicial thought protecting the competent defendant's right to decide intelligently and voluntarily to forego the insanity defense (*Frendak* v. *United States*).

The eleventh question concerns a diagnostic formulation of the case, a determination of whether the mental disorders found are of sufficient severity to potentially impair the defendant's capacity to meet the applicable standard for criminal responsibility, and an assessment of whether the diagnosed mental disorder was active at the time of the offense. Mental disease or defect is not well defined by law for purposes of criminal responsibility. In some jurisdictions, attempts have been made to narrow the concept of mental disease or defect by requiring that the disorder be severe or that it cause substantial impairment, or by excluding voluntary intoxication or repeated criminal or antisocial conduct. There is some consensus among mental health professionals that overt psychotic conditions, severe organic disorders, and mental retardation are mental disorders that can affect criminal responsibility. Once a diagnosis has been carefully formulated, using current diagnostic criteria, information bearing on the severity of the disorder at the time of the offense(s) must be considered.

Finally, if there are indications that the defendant was suffering from a severe mental disorder when the offense(s) occurred, the examiner needs to consider whether there is a relationship between that disorder and the crime. Even if a chronic mental illness, such as schizophrenia, can be documented to have existed at several points in time before and after the crime, there may be no discernible relationship between symptoms of the disorder and the criminal behavior. To the contrary, there may be information suggesting that the defendant committed the act with a conventional, nonpsychopathological motive, or in a planful manner designed to avoid detection. Such information about his or her behavior at the time of the offense would suggest that despite a severe mental disorder, the defendant may have retained the capacity to meet the relevant legal standard for criminal responsibility.

COMMUNICATING THE RESULTS OF THE EVALUATION

In reporting the results of a criminal responsibility evaluation, the psychologist should start off by specifying the referral source and the referral question, using the appropriate statutory or case law citation. The specific sources of data on which the evaluation is based, including third-party information, the time, place, and duration of contacts with the defendant, and psychological tests administered, should be listed. The report should contain a statement about the information provided to the defendant in the course of obtaining his or her consent to participate in the evaluation, and a statement describing his or her understanding of the purpose of the evaluation and the limits of confidentiality.

The body of the report should contain a non-technical, understandable presentation of data directly relevant to the defendant's mental state at the time of the act. The results of psychological testing should contain an explanation of the tests administered and the relevance of the results. During the course of a comprehensive evaluation, extraneous information is inevitably obtained about sensitive areas, such as family problems, personal concerns or sexual functioning, which may not bear directly upon the legal purpose of the evaluation. Such information does not belong in the report.

A forensic evaluation should contain a separate section, clearly differentiated from the data base of the report, for interpretation and integration of the data and presentation of a clinical opinion. This part of the report is frequently given less time and consideration by the clinician than is warranted. The opinion section should contain a clear statement of whatever level of opinion or conclusions the clinician feels the data support. The reasoning that led the clinician to reach these conclusions and to discard alternative hypotheses or opinions should be clearly laid out so that the legal reader or trier of fact can follow the reasoning and form his or her own opinion about the issue. If the examiner cannot reach an opinion with reasonable scientific certainty, if he or she does not wish to address the ultimate legal issue, or if the law in a particular jurisdiction prohibits opinions about the ultimate legal issue, the examiner's assessment and formulation of the defendant's mental state at the time of the offense(s) must still be conveyed in a manner that will help the referral source understand the defendant's mental state. Statements regarding the defendant's "dangerousness" or rehabilitation potential, or recommendations for disposition of the case, are inappropriate and potentially prejudicial in a pretrial evaluation.

There are a number of valuable references designed to help the clinician present his or her data and findings in a responsible and clear manner on the witness stand (Melton, Petrila, Poythress, & Slobogin, 1987; Brodsky, 1991; Pope, Butcher, & Seelen, 1993). The clinician who receives a subpoena to testify regarding mental state at the time of the offense should contact the attorney who issued the subpoena to schedule a pretrial conference. Such a conference is important to ensure that the witness understands the issues that need to be introduced and clarified for the trier of fact, and that the attorney understands the limitations imposed on the witness by the data in the specific case as well as by the state of the field. On the witness stand, the clinician needs to be prepared to present information clearly, to avoid the use of technical terms when possible, to define technical terms when they must be used, to identify the source and limitations of the data, and to outline the scientific basis and reasoning for the findings of the evaluation. The expert witness cannot assume the role of advocate for either side of the case but is ethically required to present clinical information and opinions in an honest, nonmisleading manner.

RESEARCH ON ASSESSMENT OF CRIMINAL RESPONSIBLITY

Much of the research on mental state at the time of the offense focuses on variables that are correlated with insanity or GBMI verdicts in actuality or in simulated jury decision-making studies (e.g., Roberts, Golding, & Fincham, 1987; Finkel, 1988, 1990; Callahan, McGreevy, Cirincione, & Steadman, 1992). Attempts to explore the relationship between specific symptoms or disorders, such as command hallucinations, and criminal responsibility have been published (e.g., Thompson, Stuart, & Holden, 1992). There is also some literature on subsequent hospitalization and community follow-up and outcome for individuals found not guilty by reason of insanity (e.g., Golding, Eaves, & Kowaz, 1989; Norwood, Nicholson, Enyart, & Hickey, 1992). However, there is little systematic research on the reliability and validity of clinical judgments regarding criminal responsibility.

In terms of reliability of assessments of sanity, Melton, Petrila, Poythress, & Slobogin (1987) summarized the limited research then available on interrater agreement between clinicians' opinions regarding insanity. They found literature suggesting fairly high agreement (92 to 97 percent and coefficients between .82 and 1.00) among examiners who were trained to do forensic evaluations and who performed these evaluations for the court rather than the prosecution or the defense. However, agreement between pairs of examiners, in which one examiner was chosen by the defense and the other by the prosecution, was reported to be only 64 percent overall in another study they reviewed (Raifman, 1979). Melton et al. pointed out a number of problems with the comparability of these data, including the differences in forensic training, profession, and allegiance among the examiners, and differences in examination settings and legal sanity standards.

A subsequent study (Beckham, Annis, & Gustafson, 1989) in which Florida forensic evaluators were asked to assess symptomatology and sanity at the time of the act in a hypothetical, ambiguous case, found no significant differences in sanity opinions among examiners told they were appointed by the prosecution, the defense, or the judge. Overall reliability of ratings of the presence or absence of specific symptoms was reported to be .73. Sixty-four percent of the examiners rated the defendant as NGRI, but 5 percent of the examiners made no rating of sanity in this ambiguous case. This study also found differences between psychiatrists and psychologists in the way they appeared to weigh sources of information in reaching decisions about sanity, but not in their final outcomes.

Rogers, through development of the R-CRAS (1984) and subsequent research (e.g., Rogers and Ewing, 1992), has studied the process of reaching decisions about mental state at the time of the offense by attempting to standardize this procedure. The R-CRAS guides the clinician through the evaluation process by requiring ratings of a number of relevant variables, such as affect, delusions, observable bizarre behavior, and other symptoms at the time of the alleged crime, and preparation for, and level of activity during, the crime itself. The scale has been criticized for relying on ordinal ratings and failing to operationalize key variables such as self-control (Melton et al., 1987). However, Rogers has demonstrated adequate levels of interrater reliability on the clinical and decision variables of the scale.

Studies of validity of clinical opinions regarding insanity with both the R-CRAS and traditional methods have employed verdict as the criterion variable. Concordance rates of 88 to 97 percent between clinicians' opinions on the ultimate legal issue, and the actual verdict, have been reported (Melton et al., 1987; Rogers & Ewing, 1992). Confounding between clinical opinions and actual verdict is, of course, inevitable, since sanity evaluations and opinions are a major source of the evidence used to reach verdicts in these cases.

Finally, some systematic attempts to assess malingering in the context of criminal responsibility evaluations are being developed. The Structured Interview of Reported Symptoms (SIRS) (Rogers, Bagby, & Dickens, 1992) has been subjected to validation studies using both simulation and known-groups designs with suspected malingerers on an inpatient unit, correctional simulators, community simulators, correctional controls, community controls, psychiatric inpatients, and outpatient controls. Interrater reliabilities have been reported to average between .96 and .98. Classification rates for psychiatric patients and those feigning mental illness are reported to be 88 percent for the original cross-validation sample and in a subsequent study by Connell (1991). Rogers et al. reported false positive rates of 0 percent for definite feigning. They also reported correlations between .55 and .80 between scores on the various SIRS scales and on the F scale of the MMPI.

Schretlen, Wilkins, Van Gorp, & Bobholz (1992) reported the cross-validation of a psychological test battery to detect attempts to fake sanity among prison inmates, psychiatric inpatients, and substance abusers. The results of this simulation study were promising, with 97.6 percent correct classification of the cross-validation sample.

SUMMARY

We have examined a number of aspects of the assessment of criminal responsibility. We began by describing the legal background and the evolution of various standards of criminal responsibility. Next, we discussed ethical issues that are relevant to the psychological assessment of criminal responsibility. We then provided an outline for the practitioner assessing criminal responsibility in which we proposed procedures for the actual evaluation, the preparation of a report, and expert testimony. Finally, we reviewed the modest amount of literature published to date on the assessment of criminal responsibility. The brevity of this final section of our chapter points out the need for further scientific investigation in the area of assessing criminal responsibility. Research elucidating the ways in which experts develop their opinions on issues of criminal responsibility and identifying factors that predict agreement among experts, and between experts and triers of fact, could help provide additional guidance for practitioners assessing criminal responsibility.

REFERENCES

American Law Institute. (1962). *Model penal code, Section 4.01*. Philadelphia: Author.

Beckham, J. C., Annis, L. V., & Gustafson, D. J. (1989). Decision making and examiner bias in forensic expert recommendations for not guilty by reason of insanity. *Law and Human Behavior, 13*, 79–87.

Bonnie, R. J., & Slobogin, C. The role of mental health professionals in the criminal process: The case for informed speculation. *Virginia Law Review, 66*, 427–522.

Brodsky, S. L. (1991). *Testifying in court: Guidelines and maxims for the expert witness*. Washington, DC: American Psychological Association.

Burton, N., & Steadman, H. J. (1978). Legal professionals' perceptions of the insanity defense. *The Journal of Psychiatry and Law, 6*, 173–188.

Bushman, B. J., & Cooper, H. M. (1990). Effects of alcohol on human aggression: An integrative research review. *Psychological Bulletin, 107*, 341–354.

Callahan, L., Mayer, C., & Steadman, H. J. (1987). Insanity defense reform in the United States—Post-Hinckley. *Mental Disability Law Reporter, 11*, 54–59.

Callahan, L., McGreevy, M. A., Cirincione, C., & Steadman, H. J. (1992). Measuring the effects of the Guilty but Mentally Ill (GBMI) verdict: Geor-gia's 1982 GBMI reform. *Law and Human Behavior, 16*, 447–462.

Callahan, L., Steadman, H. J., McGreevy, M. A., & Robbins, P. C. (1991). The volume and characteristics of insanity defense pleas: An eight-state study. *Bulletin of the American Academy of Psychiatry and Law, 19*, 331–338.

Committee on Ethical Guidelines for Forensic Psychologists (1991). Specialty guidelines for forensic psychologists. *Law and Human Behavior, 15*, 655–665.

Connell, D. K. (1991). *The SIRS and the M test: The differential validity and utility of two instruments designed to detect malingered psychosis in a correctional sample*. Unpublished dissertation, University of Louisville.

Ethical principles of psychologists and code of conduct. (1992). *American Psychologist, 47*, 1597–1611.

Finkel, N. J. (1988). *Insanity on trial*. New York: Plenum Press.

Finkel, N. J. (1990). De facto departures from insanity instructions: Toward the remaking of common law. *Law and Human Behavior, 14*, 105–122.

Frendak v. United States 408 A.2d 364 (1979).

Fulero, S. M., & Finkel, N. J. (1991). Barring ultimate issue testimony: An "insane" rule? *Law and Human Behavior, 15*, 495–507.

Golding, S. L., Eaves, D., & Kowaz, A. M. (1989). The assessment, treatment and community outcome of insanity acquittees: Forensic history and response to treatment. *International Journal of Law and Psychiatry, 12*, 149–179.

Melton, G. B., Petrila, J., Poythress, N. G., & Slobogin, C. (1987). *Psychological evaluations for the courts—A handbook for mental health professionals and lawyers*. New York: Guilford Press.

Monahan, J. (Ed.). (1980). *Who is the client? The ethics of psychological intervention in the criminal justice system*. Washington, DC: American Psychological Association.

Morse, S. J. (1978). Crazy behavior, morals, and science: An analysis of mental health law. *Southern California Law Review, 51*, 527–654.

Pasewark, R. A., & Pantle, M. L. (1979). Insanity plea: Legislators' view. *American Journal of Psychiatry, 136*, 222–223.

Pope, K. S., Butcher, J. N., & Seelen, J. (1993). *The MMPI, MMPI-2 and MMPI-A in court: A practical guide for expert witnesses and attorneys*. Washington, DC: American Psychological Association.

Raifman, L. (1979, October). *Interjudge reliability of psychiatrists' evaluations of criminal defendants' competency to stand trial and legal sanity.* Paper presented at American Psychology-Law Society Convention, Baltimore, MD.

Roberts, C. F., Golding, S. L., & Fincham, F. D. (1987). Implicit theories of criminal responsibility: Decision making and the insanity defense. *Law and Human Behavior, 11,* 207–232.

Rogers, R. (1984). *Rogers criminal responsibility assessment scales (R-CRAS) and test manual.* Odessa, FL: Psychological Assessment Resources.

Rogers, R. (1986). *Conducting insanity evaluations.* New York: Van Nostrand Reinhold.

Rogers, R., Bagby, M. R., Crouch, M., & Cutler, B. (1990). Effects of ultimate opinions on juror perceptions of insanity. *International Journal of Law and Psychiatry, 13,* 225–232.

Rogers, R., Bagby, M. R., & Dickens, S. E. (1992). *Structured Interview of Reported Symptoms: Professional manual.* Odessa, FL: Psychological Assessment Resources.

Rogers, R., & Ewing, C. P. (1992). The measurement of insanity: Debating the merits of the R-CRAS and its alternatives. *International Journal of Law and Psychiatry, 15,* 113–123.

Schretlen, D., Wilkins, S. S., Van Gorp, W. G., & Bobholz, J. H. (1992). Cross-validation of a psy-chological test battery to detect faked insanity. *Psychological Assessment, 4,* 77–83.

Shapiro, D. L. (1991). *Forensic psychological assessment: An integrative approach.* Boston: Allyn & Bacon.

State v. Carter, 51 U.S.L.W., 2221.

State v. Pratt, 398 2d 421 (Md. Court of Appeals 1979).

Swanson, J. W., Holzer, C. E., Ganju, V., & Jono, R. (1990). Violence and psychiatric disorder in the community: Evidence from the Epidemiologic Catchment Area surveys. *Hospital and Community Psychiatry, 41,* 761–770.

Thompson, J. S., Stuart, G. L., & Holden, C. E. (1992). Command hallucinations and legal insanity. *Forensic Reports, 5,* 29–43.

United States v. Alvarez, 519 F.2d 1036 (3rd Cir. 1975).

United States ex.rel. Edney v. Smith, 425 F.Supp. 1038 (E.D.N.Y.1976), aff'd., 556 F.2d 556 (2d.Cir. 1977).

United States v. Brawner, 471 F.2d 969 (D.C.Cir. 1972).

Whalem v. United States, 346 F.2d. 812 (D.C. Cir. 1965).

30

Assessment in Inpatient and Residential Settings

Marco J. Mariotto
Gordon L. Paul
Mark H. Licht

Rational and decision-based operation of twenty four hour public or private inpatient/residential treatment programs for severely emotionally disabled and mentally retarded adults poses a formidable set of obstacles to the practicing clinician and/or administrator. The clients are the most disabled, the settings the most restrictive of client rights and thus the most vulnerable to abuse, the programs the most subject to outside political and administrative pressure and the most overwhelmed by regulations and paperwork of any service system (Paul, 1985, 1987b). Although there are deficiencies in our knowledge base regarding etiologies and effective treatment for many of the clients in such settings, a major obstacle to the efficient delivery of state-of-the-art services to the clients in these facilities has been the absence of objective, practical assessment technologies (Mariotto & Paul, 1984; Paul, 1987b).

The goals of this chapter are to present a practical, comprehensive assessment paradigm, one with maximum potential utility for serving the needs of decision makers (clinicians, administrators, or policy makers) in providing the most effective and cost-efficient treatment for our most severely disturbed and neediest clientele—those in inpatient and residential facili-

ties. We begin with a "typical" case scenario, outline the varieties of decisions and information needs within inpatient/residential settings, specify criteria for selecting assessment strategies to meet these needs, and end with a presentation of our comprehensive paradigm and its application to the case scenario.

ILLUSTRATIVE CASE SCENARIO

E. E. Jones, Ph.D., is the unit director of a twenty-four-bed adult treatment unit in a state hospital. This unit is primarily focused on treatment of the severely mentally ill with intermediate lengths of stay; it also contains a small three-bed intensive care subunit for short-term stabilization and diagnostic evaluations of recent psychiatric admissions to the hospital. The unit's treatment goal is social rehabilitation and the unitwide treatment program is based on a social-learning model. As unit director, beyond functioning as a staff psychologist, Dr. Jones is also responsible for the overall administration of the unit, including treatment programming, quality assurance, budgets, and supervision and training of the clinical staff. In addition, the hospital is a major training and research facility for a local university medical school. Dr. Jones coordinates several ongoing research protocols involving unit clientele as well as the training of clinical psychology interns. In fact, she has just finished the initial interview and orientation for a new psychology intern who is beginning a six-week rotation on the unit.

On Monday morning Dr. Jones is called by the hospital social service about possible placement for a client. The client, Ms. Smith, was found wandering the streets at 3:00 A.M. and brought to a community hospital emergency room by the police. She was combative, incoherent, and agitated upon admission to the emergency room. Dr. Jones collects information from a number of sources, including a hospital intake counselor who interviewed Ms. Smith at the community hospital. Dr. Jones decided to admit Ms. Smith to the hospital. Because Ms. Smith is incoherent, Dr. Jones must first get an emergency seventy-two-hour commitment order from the local magistrate. After admission, Dr. Jones collects more information from Ms. Smith and others, and based on this information, she assigns Ms. Smith to the intensive-care subunit.

During the first several days, the intensive-care treatment team collects information to identify problems, establish treatment goals, and formulate a treatment plan for Ms. Smith. Ms. Smith is a thirty-five-year-old divorced mother of two, currently unemployed and living in the streets. She has little contact with her family and has a police record of numerous arrests for prostitution and petty thievery. She is disoriented to time and place; exhibits myriad delusions and hallucinations, stereotypical movements, and incoherent speech; and spends most of her time alone and pacing in the hallway. Physiological data indicate a relatively healthy woman who had high blood levels of ETOH and cocaine on admission and is currently receiving high dosages of Haldol, Ativan, and carbamazepine. Based on this initial assessment, Dr. Jones and the treatment team decide that the initial treatment plan will be pharmacological, with the treatment goals focused on detoxification and the elimination and/or reduction of her florid symptomatology. Her admitting diagnosis is alcohol hallucinosis and cocaine withdrawal with "rule outs" for schizophrenia and bipolar disorders. Ms. Smith is judged competent enough to make her own decisions, and she is persuaded to admit herself for treatment voluntarily.

During the next two weeks, assessment information indicates that Ms. Smith's florid symptoms have generally decreased except when she is in large group settings that require social interaction. Dr. Jones decides to transfer her to the regular unitwide treatment program, where Ms. Smith evidences increases in social withdrawal, flat affect, and decreases in normal self-care activities. In addition, Dr. Jones receives further information that Ms. Smith has demonstrated a passive-dependent personality style and appears to be forgetful. Dr. Jones orders further assessment to determine any memory problems, and the treatment team changes her treatment goals to focus on increases in social interaction and learning affect regulation. Information is obtained that her memory problems are not severe, and she is assigned to a cognitive therapy treatment module. Ms. Smith is now given a new diagnostic label of major depression with psychotic features for her records.

Meanwhile, the new psychology intern is being trained in the social-learning program, and Dr. Jones must monitor her progress and assign her to specific treatment responsibilities. At the same time, Dr. Jones must change the night shift schedule; two staff members were involved in an automobile accident and will be absent from work for several weeks and there are no available replacements. She must decide how to change schedules and looks to past information on staff schedules that have worked the best in similar situations. While she is working on this problem, Dr. Jones receives a call from the research director at the hospital requesting immediate data on the effectiveness of the new cognitive therapy module to provide support for a grant application that is due in one week.

When Dr. Jones arrives home on Friday evening, she receives a call from the hospital notifying her that Ms. Smith was found attempting to hang herself with a clothesline in the showers. Dr. Jones immediately gathers clinical information on Ms. Smith to isolate any prodromal signs of the suicide attempt. She is able to ascertain that Ms. Smith was responding well to the treatment program, and the staff report complete surprise at the attempted suicide. However, other assessment information indicates that before the suicide attempt, Ms. Smith began to spend increasing amounts of free time on the unit off by herself crying in the dayroom, while she dramatically increased her social interactions during other planned activity periods. Dr. Jones points out this pattern to the new psychology intern, who monitors these data during the next week; the same pattern of social isolation and withdrawal occurs and the intern is able to prevent another attempt by Ms. Smith the following Friday. As a result of this information, Dr. Jones and the clinical staff change aspects of the cognitive therapy Ms. Smith is receiving to focus more directly on her feelings of isolation and hopelessness. Meanwhile, Dr. Jones is notified that the hospital administrator requires information on absolute and comparative unit effectiveness and staff utilization from unit directors for an emergency budget hearing in the state capital in two days.

During the next several weeks, Ms. Smith continues to improve in all areas of functioning, and Dr. Jones begins to collect information about Ms. Smith and her posthospital environment for discharge planning. This information enables Dr. Jones to decide that Ms. Smith should be released to a halfway house, and she provides information on Ms. Smith's treatment and response to the staff of that facility. Ms. Smith is discharged to the halfway house, and Dr. Jones gathers information to write the rotation evaluation for the psychology intern during a break in her scheduled meeting with an "evaluation" team from an accreditation agency that has been examining unit records and procedures. She also must decide on changes to the overall social-learning program in response to some procedural changes she has slowly and systematically implemented over the last six months. While she is examining the information necessary to make this unitwide change, she receives a call from an attorney. It seems that Ms. Smith's brother is accusing Dr. Jones

and the hospital of unlawful imprisonment of Ms. Smith and of malpractice as a result of her suicide attempt. Dr. Jones must now document for a judge her decisions and those of the hospital staff regarding Ms. Smith's treatment.

FORMAL ASSESSMENT PURPOSES, NEEDS, AND STRATEGIES

As exemplified in this case scenario, a multitude of administrative, clinical, and research decisions are involved in the daily operation of inpatient/residential treatment programs. Ideally, these decisions will be made to meet the primary goal of clinical work in general and these facilities in particular—i.e., to provide effective treatment within the context of legal, ethical, humane, and cost-efficient conditions. To meet this goal, the probable gains and losses of each alternative must be considered when decisions are made (see Paul, Mariotto, & Redfield, 1986a). Thus, some level of assessment is required to supply the information necessary for making the comparisons and predictions involved in evaluating these probable gains and losses.

While assessments for these purposes do occur in all facilities, they frequently involve the informal, subjective judgment of individual administrators or staff. However, to meet the primary goal, *formal* assessment should be employed whenever possible. This involves standardized procedures to provide information with known reliability and utility for making the necessary comparisons and predictions (see Wiggins, 1988).

In this section, the case scenario is used to highlight the varieties of decisions that must be made by the staff of inpatient/residential facilities. We also identify the domains and classes of variables on which information is required if these decisions are to be made on a rational basis. Next, we discuss the criteria for selecting assessment procedures that might be used to obtain this information. This section concludes with a description of the various sources and methods that constitute formal assessment strategies that might be practically used in inpatient/residential treatment settings.

Decision Problems and Information Needs

In 1969 Paul proposed that the primary goal of clinical work could be reduced to empirically derived answers to the following question: "*What* treatment, by *whom*, is most effective for *this* individual with *that* specific problem, under *which* set of circumstances, and *how* does it come about?" (p. 44). Embedded in this question are both the varieties of decisions facing administrative and clinical staff (summarized in Figure 30.1) and the domains and classes of variables that constitute the information necessary to support these decisions (summarized in Figure 30.2).

As indicated in Figures 30.1 and 30.2, decision problems and information needs involve both clients and staff (see Paul et al., 1986a, for elaboration). The following discussion is intended to facilitate understanding of the content of these figures by illustrating examples of each decision problem and information needed from the case scenario.

1. Placement and disposition decisions. In the case scenario, the first set of decisions that Dr. Jones had to make concerned the *placement and disposition* of the new client, Ms. Smith. The first of these decisions was whether to admit her and whether to get an emergency commitment order. Then, Dr. Jones had to decide to which program in the treatment unit Ms. Smith should be assigned. The information needed for these decisions includes all classes of variables within both the client and staff domains. Information is obviously required about Ms. Smith's problem behaviors, personal-social characteristics, and external life environments. In addition, to optimize the probability of placing Ms. Smith on the most appropriate treatment unit, it is also desirable to have global information on these same classes of variables for the aggregate client groups on the treatment units to which Ms. Smith might be assigned. Further, global information about each treatment unit's therapeutic techniques, staff personal-social characteristics,

and physical-social treatment environment is essential for making rational placement decisions.

Later, Dr. Jones had to make additional placement and disposition decisions concerning Ms. Smith. These resulted in Ms. Smith's being transferred from the intensive-care subunit to the regular unitwide program, and subsequently being discharged to the halfway house. These decisions require all the information for the initial placement decision, but the information can be more complete and detailed than is possible within the time constraints associated with initial placement decisions. Note that to rationally decide on transferring or discharging a client, information is also required on possible transfer or discharge settings. It is important to provide staff of the transfer or discharge setting with information on all classes of variables in both the client and staff domains from the pretransfer/discharge setting. This information assists in treatment continuity and in understanding the client, his or her problems, and the nature of treatments that have been both ineffective and effective with this individual.

Dr. Jones also had to make placement and disposition decisions concerning the staff of the treatment unit. At some point, Dr. Jones had to decide whether to hire each of the unit's staff members and to which of the unit's programs each would be assigned. Dr. Jones also had the continuous task of deciding whether any staff should be transferred to other programs or dismissed from employment. Obviously, these decisions require information on all variables within the staff domain for each staff member. However, to maximize the fit of individuals with treatment programs, such information is desirable for the aggregate staff group of each treatment unit or subunit to which an individual staff member might be assigned. In fact, to allow the best match of staff with client populations, global information on all classes of variables in the client domain is desirable for aggregate groups of clients from the treatment units or subunits involved.

2. Client problem identification and description. Once the initial placement was made to the intensive-care subunit, more thorough as-

DECISION PROBLEMS

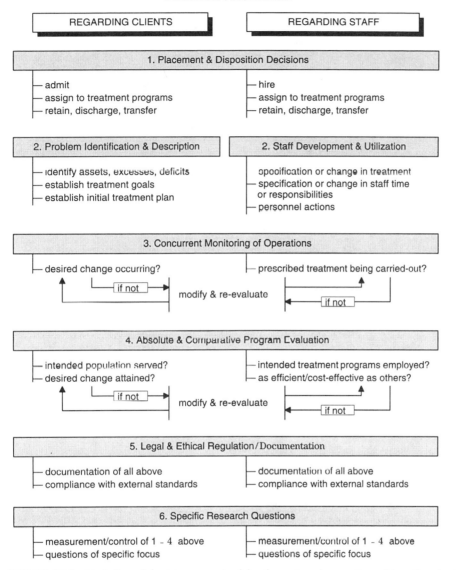

FIGURE 30.1. Varieties of decisions required for the rational operation of inpatient/residential facilities (adapted from Paul, 1994a).

sessments were conducted to obtain detailed information on all classes of variables within the client domain for Ms. Smith. This information, along with detailed information about the therapeutic techniques and treatment environments available at the facility, allowed Dr. Jones and the treatment team to make rational decisions concerning specific treatment goals and plans for Ms. Smith.

2. Staff development and utilization. Of course, treatment cannot be provided unless staff has been trained in appropriate procedures (i.e., staff development decisions). Further, in inpatient/residential settings, decision makers are responsible for many clients and may not be able to make decisions based solely on the needs of a single client. Thus, they must consider the most effective and efficient use of limited re-

CLASSES OF VARIABLES

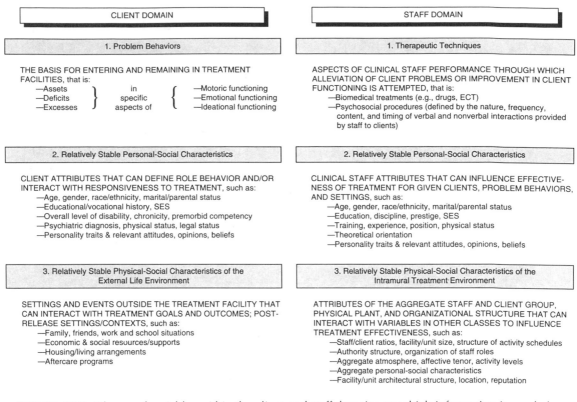

FIGURE 30.2. Classes of variables within the client and staff domains on which information is needed to support decisions in inpatient/residential settings (adapted from Paul, Mariotto, & Redfield, 1986a).

sources when deciding on treatment plans for individual clients (i.e., staff utilization decisions).

Dr. Jones had to decide on proper utilization of limited staff resources when the treatment unit temporarily lost two staff members. Also, certain changes to the overall treatment program were in progress, requiring staff training and adjustments to their utilization. Finally, decisions were necessary concerning the training and utilization of the psychology intern. Information needed for making all of these staff development/utilization decisions includes global levels of data on the problem behaviors of client groups to determine the targets for any staff development and utilization decisions, and detailed data on all classes of variables within the staff domain to determine the variables that might be impacted and/or manipulated by these decisions.

3. *Concurrent monitoring of operations.* Initial treatment plans are based on the original problem identification and description, as just described. Following this initial treatment decision, it is necessary to monitor the client's progress *and* the exact nature of the treatment that is being employed. Only in this way can rational decisions be made concerning the need to change or adjust the treatment program for individuals and for client groups.

Several adjustments were made to Ms. Smith's treatment plan based on ongoing assessments of her functioning and response to ongoing treatment (e.g., addition of socialization training and of cognitive therapy). These changes were based on new information about her initial problems and about new problems that became evident over time. For purposes of concurrent monitoring, it was important to monitor Ms. Smith's known problem behaviors.

It is equally important to monitor what initially may have appeared to be assets or at least non-problems; often these nonproblematic areas of functioning are later recognized as additional problems or become problematic as an undesired result (i.e., "side effect") of the procedures employed.

It is also important to have ongoing monitoring of what staff actually do with regard to clients (i.e., of the *actual* therapeutic techniques employed). Only in this way can one determine whether the prescribed procedures are being conducted properly. When concurrent monitoring of clients indicates treatment ineffectiveness, this information on therapeutic techniques is necessary to decide whether to change the prescribed treatment or to intervene with changes in staff training or utilization.

The information required for these decisions concerning concurrent monitoring of operations includes the same information described for initial problem identification and description and for staff development and utilization decisions. The primary difference is that for purposes of concurrent monitoring this information is necessary on an ongoing basis. Because some classes of variables are relatively stable (e.g., client and staff personal-social characteristics; physical-social characteristics of the external and intramural treatment environments), they need only be assessed periodically. However, the transitory nature of variables in the classes of problem behaviors and therapeutic techniques must be assessed frequently, if not continuously, for the purposes of concurrent monitoring.

4. *Absolute and comparative program evaluation.* Decision makers in inpatient/residential facilities are responsible for many clients and have limited resources. They must consider the most effective and efficient use of those resources in the long run. These decisions require absolute and comparative program evaluations. Dr. Jones had to provide information relevant to these decisions for the hospital administrator to use in an emergency budget hearing that would be likely to result in the continuation of some programs and the termination of others.

Program evaluation decisions require global information on all classes of variables in both the client and staff domains. This information is similar to the detailed information needed for concurrent monitoring and other decision problems described previously. However, for program evaluation purposes, only global information is needed on aggregate groups of clients and staff and over relatively lengthy periods of time.

5. *Legal and ethical regulation/documentation.* Clients of inpatient/residential treatment settings are often involuntarily confined and/or declared incompetent to make decisions concerning their own treatment. The nature of their problems frequently renders meaningless the notion of truly voluntary and "informed consent." Legal and ethical regulations are intended to safeguard these individuals against purposeful and/or unintentional abuses. Such regulations are important not only to protect clients against abusive actions (e.g., physically and/or emotionally abusive treatments; ineffective treatments), but also against nonactions (e.g., lack of active treatments or absence of known effective treatments). Ongoing assessments of all classes of variables in both the client and staff domains, for both individual clients and staff members and for aggregate groups of clients and staff, are necessary to provide the information needed for these legal and ethical decision problems. Note that this information is the *same* as that required to support all previous decision problems — it just *has* to be *documented*. Its use varies in that the information is compared with external standards established by legal and regulatory authorities. Such information is also necessary to protect the rights of staff by documenting the actions of individual staff members and aggregate staff groups. Dr. Jones needed this information to both meet accreditation standards and to defend the treatment staff's decisions and actions concerning the treatment of Ms. Smith.

6. *Specific research questions.* There are virtually unlimited research questions that are relevant to understanding the problems and appropriate treatments of people in inpatient/residential treatment settings. The specific information needs for making the de-

cisions involved in research in these settings vary depending on the particular basic or applied question being addressed. However, measurement and/or control of the same information required to support all clinical/operational decisions described earlier can provide more powerful designs and more valid and generalizable results, no matter what the specific research question. For example, Dr. Jones was asked for information on the effectiveness of a specific therapeutic procedure being tried on the treatment unit. This information was to be used in a new grant proposal for continued, more systematic investigations of the treatment's effectiveness. Thus, information on therapeutic techniques was necessary to document the independent variable. Also, information on staff personal-social characteristics and physical-social treatment environments was needed to further specify the independent variables, to document control variables, and to describe the "therapist" population. Information on all classes of variables within the client domain was necessary to provide measures of dependent variables, control variables, and to describe the subject population. The level of detail and whether information is needed at an individual or aggregate level varies based on the specific research question and design.

Criteria for Selecting Practical Procedures— the "Four Rs" of Assessment Procedure Utility

The sheer volume of information needed to support decisions in inpatient/residential facilities can easily overwhelm clinicians and administrators. A wide variety of sources and methods (assessment strategies) is available to gather this information. Before discussing the sources and methods, some criteria for selecting among practical procedures are necessary. Applying the logic of decision theory and generalizability theory to the operation of inpatient/residential treatment settings, Paul et al. (1986a) concluded that "the potential value of any information-gathering or assessment procedure in inpatient/residential settings will be determined by four considerations: Replicability, Representativeness, Relevance, and Relative cost" (p. 19)—the "Four Rs" of assessment procedure utility.

Replicability. This refers to the trustworthiness or dependability of the information obtained and is similar to traditional notions of reliability. However, replicability specifically refers to the equivalence of data across assessors— the degree to which assessors are interchangeable because they obtain the same information. Consistency across other dimensions that are frequently considered within the concept of reliability, yielding measures of stability (across the "time" dimension) or internal consistency (across the "items" dimension), does not necessarily indicate a dependable measure. The utility of these indices for the concept of reliability varies as a function of the variables being assessed. For example, stability is important when relatively stable characteristics are assessed, but it would not be expected with transitory phenomena. Similarly, greater internal consistency would be expected for unidimensional than for multidimensional scales. However, dependability across assessors is *always* essential for the information obtained to be a trustworthy basis for decision making (Cronbach, Gleser, Nanda, & Rajaratnam, 1972; Fiske, 1978, 1979). Thus, *replicability* specifically refers to the degree of data dependability across assessors; the greater the replicability of data, the greater the potential value of an assessment procedure.

Representativeness. This refers to the degree to which the people, content, and occasions of interest have been appropriately represented in the obtained information; that is, the degree to which obtained information is representative of *all* the information one would ideally have to make a particular decision. Since "appropriate" coverage of these dimensions, or facets, varies as a function of the decision problem for which it is to be used, information can have adequate representativeness for some decisions but not for others. Data indicating the degree of representativeness include those traditionally categorized under the concepts of content-, criterion-, and construct-related validity evidence for a particular purpose (Cronbach et al., 1972; Wiggins, 1988). The greater the representativeness of data for a particular decision, the greater the potential value of an assessment procedure.

Relevance. This refers to the degree to which representative information is obtained to support many different decision problems—i.e., its range of application. The overall utility of an assessment procedure is proportional to the number of separate decisions for which obtained information can be used (Cronbach & Gleser, 1965). The greater the relevance of data to overall decision making, the greater the value of an assessment procedure.

Relative cost. This refers to the expense of a specific assessment procedure compared with alternatives that could provide equally useful information. To evaluate relative costs, direct costs of materials and staff, offset costs of staff time and effort, and the value placed on decision outcomes must be considered (Cronbach & Gleser, 1965). Assessments that cost very little in terms of materials, time, and effort but produce data that are low in replicability, representativeness, and relevance can have very *high* relative costs because they result in poor decisions. Thus the "Four Rs" result in a relatively straightforward decision rule for selecting practical assessment procedures: "The lower the cost *and/or* the greater the replicability, representativeness, and relevance of the information obtained, the lower is the net relative cost, and the greater is the potential value of an assessment approach" (Paul et al., 1986a, p. 25).

Sources and Methods of Assessment in Inpatient/Residential Treatment Settings

The logic of decision and generalizability theory applied to the operation of decision-making requirements of inpatient/residential settings also reveals the importance of assessment procedures that can provide ongoing information in the general case—information of common relevance to the decision making for all clientele, staff, and treatment programs (Paul, Mariotto, & Redfield, 1986b). It is also noteworthy that assessments of functioning desired for the

general case are of "typical performance" in natural settings, rather than "maximum performance" in artificial (testing) situations (see Cronbach, 1984; Wiggins, 1988). Differences among decisions dictate the level of information required (i.e., global versus detailed) and whether information is needed on individuals or on aggregate groups of clients or staff. Both the levels of detail and of aggregation are important considerations in selecting the procedures for obtaining the needed information. Further considerations concerning the nature of the variables to be assessed include: (1) Are they stable or transitory? (2) Are they public or private events? and (3) Do they involve individuals' actions or interactions among individuals? All these considerations influence the practical selection of sources and methods for assessing specific classes of variables; they affect the replicability, representativeness, relevance, and relative costs of the information obtained.

Formal assessment consists of systematic procedures for observing phenomena and describing them with the aid of a numerical scale or category system (see Cronbach, 1984; Wiggins, 1988). Formal assessment procedures are defined and differentiated by the specific ways they answer the following questions: (1) *From whom* is information obtained? (2) *By whom,* (3) *when,* and (4) *how* is the information obtained, systematized, and recorded? The optimal answers to these questions vary across assessment purposes and situations and nearly always involve some tradeoffs among the "Four Rs." The issues and some of the tradeoffs are summarized here (see Paul et al., 1986b, for elaboration).

From whom is information obtained? An important consideration in selecting an appropriate assessment procedure is the source of the information—i.e., who is it that observed the phenomenon of interest? There are two broad categories of potential sources of information in inpatient/residential settings: indigenous sources and formal assessors.

Indigenous sources are those available to observe the phenomena of interest because they are already in the setting for purposes other than doing assessment. These include the subjects of assessment themselves (clients or staff members); significant others, such as relatives, friends, or associates; residential clients other than the subject of the assessment; and clinical staff other than the subject of assessment. Records and archives—observations that have been previously recorded—can serve as an additional indigenous sources for assessment of historical information. Such historical information could be useful for stable characteristics, such as some personal-social characteristics (e.g., demographics) and physical-social environments that do not change frequently.

Formal assessors are sources of information that are placed in the setting where the phenomena of interest occur for the specific purpose of observing and recording those phenomena. There are two categories of formal assessors. *Independent interactive assessors* are those that not only observe and record the phenomena of interest but also interact in the setting and thus are an integral part of the social situation in which the phenomena occur. *Independent noninteractive assessors* minimize their intrusion in the social setting, instead attempting to observe and record without affecting the natural situation.

Application of the "Four Rs" of assessment procedure utility helps to specify the optimal source of information for different phenomena. Private events, such as beliefs, opinions, and other cognitions, require that the source be the subject of the assessment because no other potential source has access to the phenomena of interest. However, for assessing public events, formal assessors are nearly always preferred because they are likely to provide the most trustworthy and useful information. Further, when the phenomena of interest allow for independent assessors, independent *noninteractive* assessors are typically the preferred sources because they can provide information that has greatest replicability, representativeness, and relevance. These advantages result because, of all potential sources, noninteractive assessors produce the least amount of disruption or change in the natural occurrence of the phenomena, can be thoroughly trained in the assessment task, and can focus their entire attention on this task during the assessment period. Of course, concerns of relative cost of assessments dictate that indigenous sources be employed for some purposes, particularly when assessing setting-dependent or low-frequency events. Independent interactive assessors are typically more practical for the assessment of unique information for single individuals, such as tests of maximum, rather than typical, performance (e.g., a medical exam, neuropsychological assessments, etc.).

By whom is the information obtained, systematized, and recorded? The information concerning the phenomena of interest can be obtained, systematized, and recorded either by the same person who observed the phenomena (*primary source*) or by someone else (*secondary source*). The most common use of secondary sources is when information is obtained via an interactive person-to-person interview, where the source of the information (i.e., the observer of the phenomena) is the person being interviewed while the person actually obtaining, systematizing, and recording the information is the interviewer. Another example of the use of secondary sources is when information is obtained via a search of records and archives. Most other forms of assessment employ primary sources for both observing and recording the information of interest.

Some types of information (e.g., stable characteristics) can be most efficiently obtained with secondary sources, particularly when record/archive searches are possible. The low level of cognitive and/or intellectual functioning in some inpatient/residential populations necessitates the use of secondary sources for historical information. However, for most other information needs, primary sources who are formal assessors provide the most replicable and representative data at the lowest relative cost.

When is information obtained, systematized, and recorded? The timing of observation occasions that serve as the basis for assessment is an essential consideration for developing or choosing a procedure. There are several variations in assessment procedures associated with differences in when information is obtained (i.e., in the occasions of observation). Some of these result from the degree to which the occasions of observation are programmed in advance to insure representative coverage of desired times and settings. Other variations result from the degree to which observations occur during short, discrete periods of observation as opposed to longer, more continuous observation periods.

Clearly, the greater the degree of prior programming, the greater the likelihood that the information will be representative for the desired purposes. Also, the more discrete the observation periods, the greater the replicability of the information. However, some phenomena (such as social interactions) typically require longer observation periods to obtain representative information on the phenomena of interest. In some assessment situations, particularly when assessing low-frequency events, the higher relative cost of many discrete, programmed observation periods would probably not provide an equivalent increase in replicability or representativeness.

In addition to when the observations of the phenomena occur, it is essential to consider when the observations are systematized (i.e., before or after observations) and recorded (i.e., immediately or delayed). Typical retrospective assessments involve long delays between observing and recording the information; the observers seldom know that they will be asked for the information until well after the phenomena have occurred. Such retrospective assessment procedures have low relative costs and can provide representative information for stable characteristics. However, for more transitory phenomena (such as problem behaviors and therapeutic techniques), the lower absolute cost would not be worth the reduced replicability and representativeness of retrospective assessments, thus arguing for use of more immediate recording and providing a priori knowledge of the specifics of the task.

How is the information obtained, systematized, and recorded? In addition to specifying from whom, by whom, and when information is obtained, formal assessment procedures must provide specific encoding devices for assigning numbers or categories to the phenomena observed and specific procedural rules for gathering and combining the information to be of use to decision makers (Wiggins, 1988). Although the encoding devices and procedural rules of the hundreds of formal assessment instruments designed for use in inpatient/residential settings differ, the low-cost availability of high-speed computers allows them to be categorized into two primary assessment approaches: direct observational coding (DOC) and questionnaires, inventories, checklists, and scales (QICS). For the purposes of our discussion, only the primary differences between DOC and QICS methods will be summarized here. Detailed descriptions of the difference between DOC and QICS approaches to assessment are presented in Paul (1986a).

QICS methods are the traditional approach to assessment in which a list of questions or items are presented in written or verbal form to the source of the information. Typically, the items refer to past events or interactions and the source is required to assign a judgment, rating, or category for each. Thus, QICS methods usually involve retrospective assessments of information observed over long-duration, continuous-observation periods; the information is typically systematized and recorded on a single occasion at a later point in time. The QICS approach frequently, but not always, requires the source to provide a judgmental interpretation of what was observed (e.g., ratings, rankings, or categorizations) rather than direct recordings of the units of observation. Variations of QICS instruments can be employed to obtain judgmental ratings of specific aspects of a client's functioning within a single-occasion examination, structured interview, or similar procedure as well.

In contrast, DOC methods require the source to record the information immediately at the time it occurs. Therefore, these methods involve multiple, discrete periods of observation, with minimal delays between observations and recordings. DOC methods also attempt to minimize judgmental interpretations by the source of the information by requiring duplicative, low-inference recordings (e.g., presence or absence). Further, the content and timing of observation periods are always systematized a priori. Variations of DOC methods can also be employed to obtain systematic observations of specific aspects of a client's functioning within a single-occasion examination, structured interview, or similar procedure.

Both QICS and DOC methods can be used to obtain information on transitory phenomena, stable phenomena, characteristics, interaction events, or individual's action events. Whereas QICS instruments can be used for assessing either private or public events, DOC methods are limited to the latter. QICS methods can also be used to obtain information on either individuals or groups directly. In contrast, DOC methods focus on individuals and provide information about groups by aggregating individual data. Similarly, DOC methods focus on obtaining detailed information and providing global information, when needed, by aggregating across appropriate detailed content units. In contrast, QICS methods typically collect information at either the detailed or global level, directly.

The tradeoffs between QICS and DOC assessment methods are many, but each has its place. Direct assessments of private events must employ QICS methods. Also, if the need for assessment is not determined until after the events have occurred, QICS methods become the only available alternative. QICS methods frequently have lower relative costs than DOC alternatives for assessing very stable public or private events and characteristics. However, when transitory, public events are to be assessed, the greater replicability, representativeness, and relevance of DOC methods render their net relative costs lower than those of QICS alternatives. It is with DOC assessments of ongoing client and staff functioning that the availability of low-cost computers have produced major changes in the nature and quality of practical assessment strategies for inpatient/residential settings. Standardized DOC approaches are now feasible, practical, and cost-effective for ongoing use rather than being limited to focal research studies.

THE MAXIMUM POTENTIAL UTILITY PARADIGM FOR FORMAL ASSESSMENT

The range of information required and the number of different sources and methods of assessment available to support the numerous ongoing decisions clearly dictate that multiple assessment strategies are needed for rational operation of inpatient/residential treatment facilities. Each practical assessment strategy (source-method combination) differs in the quality of data produced and each has limitations regarding representativeness of sampling of specific variables for particular decision problems. Consequently, we have recommended a comprehensive paradigm for the integrated application of formal assessment strategies to provide the necessary information for support of the ongoing decision functions outlined above and presented earlier in Figure 30.1 (see Paul & Mariotto, 1986). Joint consideration of the information needed from each class of variables (see Figure 30.2) and the relative strengths and weaknesses of practical assessment strategies from the perspective of the "Four Rs" results in a seven-strategy paradigm.

The paradigm consists of three *primary strategies* that provide the greatest quantity and most important common information in both the client and staff domains, and four *secondary strategies*. Secondary strategies provide information on variables that may interact with other variables to affect treatment effectiveness and for specific limited decisions where information is not available from the primary strategies. The secondary strategies also provide converging evidence for information needs that usually rely on relatively less trustworthy information. In this section, we briefly describe the primary and secondary strategies of the comprehensive paradigm. We also describe the prototypical instruments and systems. The chapter concludes with an illustration of the contribution of the primary strategies to the decision problems of the earlier case scenario.

PRIMARY ASSESSMENT STRATEGIES

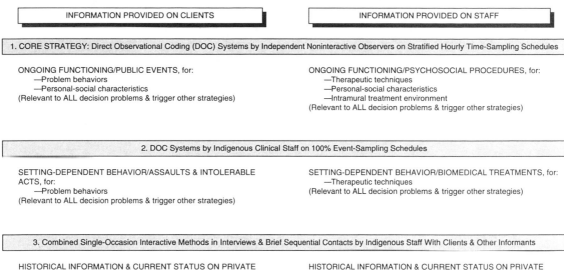

INFORMATION PROVIDED ON CLIENTS	INFORMATION PROVIDED ON STAFF
1. CORE STRATEGY: Direct Observational Coding (DOC) Systems by Independent Noninteractive Observers on Stratified Hourly Time-Sampling Schedules	
ONGOING FUNCTIONING/PUBLIC EVENTS, for: —Problem behaviors —Personal-social characteristics (Relevant to ALL decision problems & trigger other strategies)	ONGOING FUNCTIONING/PSYCHOSOCIAL PROCEDURES, for: —Therapeutic techniques —Personal-social characteristics —Intramural treatment environment (Relevant to ALL decision problems & trigger other strategies)
2. DOC Systems by Indigenous Clinical Staff on 100% Event-Sampling Schedules	
SETTING-DEPENDENT BEHAVIOR/ASSAULTS & INTOLERABLE ACTS, for: —Problem behaviors (Relevant to ALL decision problems & trigger other strategies)	SETTING-DEPENDENT BEHAVIOR/BIOMEDICAL TREATMENTS, for: —Therapeutic techniques (Relevant to ALL decision problems & trigger other strategies)
3. Combined Single-Occasion Interactive Methods in Interviews & Brief Sequential Contacts by Indigenous Staff With Clients & Other Informants	
HISTORICAL INFORMATION & CURRENT STATUS ON PRIVATE EVENTS & MULTIPLE-PERSPECTIVES, for: —Problem behaviors —Personal-social characteristics —External life environment (Relevant to ALL decision problems & trigger other strategies)	HISTORICAL INFORMATION & CURRENT STATUS ON PRIVATE EVENTS & MULTIPLE-PERSPECTIVES, for: —Therapeutic techniques (Relevant to ALL decision problems)

FIGURE 30.3. The primary strategies of a comprehensive paradigm for formal assessment to provide common information needed in inpatient/residential settings (adapted from Paul & Mariotto, 1986).

Primary Assessment Strategies

The primary strategies of the comprehensive paradigm are summarized in Figure 30.3. The target phenomena and class of variables within the client and staff domains as well as the decision problems to which data are applicable for each strategy also included in this figure.

The role of multiple-occasion DOC strategies. As shown in Figure 30.3, it is especially noteworthy that multiple-occasion direct observational coding (DOC) methods constitute two of the three primary strategies of the paradigm (Strategies 1 and 2). In addition to the fact that DOC methods, by design, have the potential for very high replicability (Fiske, 1979), DOC systems with broad content coverage applied with appropriate sampling schedules are the only practical assessment strategies for providing quality information on every client and staff member for *all* classes of decision problems in inpatient/residential settings. Desirable charac-

teristics of such DOC systems have been outlined elsewhere (Mariotto & Licht, 1986; Paul, 1986a), but their basic requirements are straightforward. Strategy 1 assessments (the Core Strategy) consist of direct-multivariate DOC systems employed by independent noninteractive observers on stratified hourly time-sampling schedules. These DOC systems should, minimally, provide information on how and where clients and staff spend their time, ongoing objective information on the assets, deficits, and excesses within the client problem-behavior class, and the psychosocial aspects of staff functioning within all three classes in the staff domain. This is the strategy that only becomes feasible and practical with the availability of low-cost computers. More detail on Strategy 1 is provided later in the description of the prototypical system.

Strategy 2 assessments consist of relatively noncomplex multiple-occasion DOC instruments employed by indigenous clinical staff on

100 percent event-recording schedules. The specific instruments of these DOC systems should be designed for integration with the regular clinical and administrative duties of clinical staff. Particular forms, or instruments, focus on client problem behaviors and staff therapeutic techniques that are not adequately covered by Strategy 1 assessments. These variables include low-frequency critical events (e.g., client assaults and consequent staff reactions), discrete biomedical treatments (e.g., drug administration), and other setting-dependent behavior (e.g., "on-time" attendance at activities). Although some segments of Strategy 2 systems, unlike Strategy 1, are program and population dependent, a prototypical Strategy 2 system is described later.

The role of single-occasion methods. As shown in Figure 30.3, the only more or less traditional single-occasion assessment methods to emerge as primary ones in the comprehensive paradigm are combined interactive procedures by indigenous clinical staff (Strategy 3). Strategy 3 assessments include a set of structured interviews conducted with clients and other informants at entry, when other events signal consideration of transfer, discharges, or other critical ("terminal") decisions, and a postdischarge followup in the community; brief sequential interactive assessments, integrated with ongoing services on a weekly/biweekly basis are also included. Strategy 3 provides the remaining critical information that is impossible or impractical to obtain with multiple-occasion DOC strategies (e.g., events that occur before admission and in the external life environment; thoughts, feelings and opinions, etc.) and the information for cost-effective concurrent monitoring of the physical health of clientele. Strategy 3 employs QICS methods and QICS and DOC variants to provide multiple-perspective assessments and most of the remaining information needed from all three classes of variables in the client domain as well as more limited information regarding staff therapeutic techniques. As with Strategy 2, many component instruments of Strategy 3 are dependent on specific programs and populations to be assessed, but some prototypic instruments are noted later.

Secondary Assessment Strategies

The secondary strategies of the comprehensive paradigm are summarized in Figure 30.4. All secondary strategies involve application of more or less traditional single-occasion procedures. As shown in Figure 30.4, Strategies 4, 5, 6, and 7 have narrower relevance than the primary strategies—none can contribute to concurrent monitoring decisions. Strategy 4 assessments, consisting of self-reports by indigenous clinical staff on standardized QICS instruments, provide most of the supplemental information on variables in the staff domain that is not provided by the primary strategies. These variables include historical and current information on individual staff for hiring/assignment decisions, other relatively stable personal-social characteristics of staff, and the judgmental attributes of the social characteristics of the intramural treatment environment (e.g., ward atmosphere). Since this strategy has the broadest relevance to decision problems of any of the secondary strategies, it is considered an important supplement to the primary strategies for rational operation of treatment programs.

The remaining secondary strategies summarized in Figure 30.4 provide only limited supplemental information that is applicable to a narrower range of decision problems than the previous strategies. Strategy 5 assessments are totally focused on physical characteristics of the internal and external environments that might interact with treatment goals and outcomes. Strategy 6 assessments are focused on formalizing information from archival records. This strategy is only critical for gathering information on physical and organizational variables in the intramural treatment environment (e.g., architectural and organizational structure), although such information is relevant to all but concurrent monitoring decision problems. Strategy 6 also provides converging and/or documentary evidence on historical information gathered with other strategies for both clients and staff (e.g., past work or treatment history and demographic information). Finally, Strategy 7 assessments are focused only on providing supplementary information relevant to a single

SECONDARY ASSESSMENT STRATEGIES

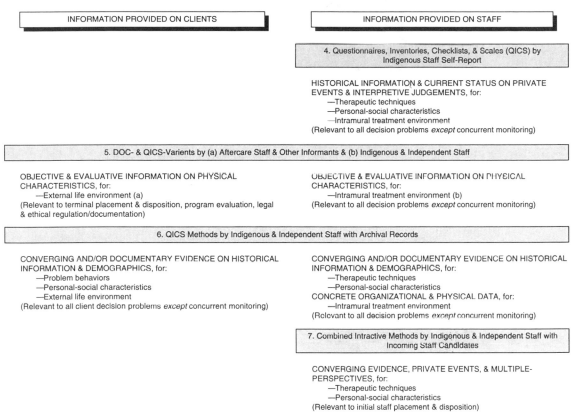

INFORMATION PROVIDED ON CLIENTS	INFORMATION PROVIDED ON STAFF

4. Questionnaires, Inventories, Checklists, & Scales (QICS) by Indigenous Staff Self-Report

HISTORICAL INFORMATION & CURRENT STATUS ON PRIVATE EVENTS & INTERPRETIVE JUDGEMENTS, for:
—Therapeutic techniques
—Personal-social characteristics
—Intramural treatment environment
(Relevant to all decision problems *except* concurrent monitoring)

5. DOC- & QICS-Varients by (a) Aftercare Staff & Other Informants & (b) Indigenous & Independent Staff

OBJECTIVE & EVALUATIVE INFORMATION ON PHYSICAL CHARACTERISTICS, for:
—External life environment (a)
(Relevant to terminal placement & disposition, program evaluation, legal & ethical regulation/documentation)

OBJECTIVE & EVALUATIVE INFORMATION ON PHYSICAL CHARACTERISTICS, for:
—Intramural treatment environment (b)
(Relevant to all decision problems *except* concurrent monitoring)

6. QICS Methods by Indigenous & Independent Staff with Archival Records

CONVERGING AND/OR DOCUMENTARY EVIDENCE ON HISTORICAL INFORMATION & DEMOGRAPHICS, for:
—Problem behaviors
—Personal-social characteristics
—External life environment
(Relevant to all client decision problems *except* concurrent monitoring)

CONVERGING AND/OR DOCUMENTARY EVIDENCE ON HISTORICAL INFORMATION & DEMOGRAPHICS, for:
—Therapeutic techniques
—Personal-social characteristics
CONCRETE ORGANIZATIONAL & PHYSICAL DATA, for:
—Intramural treatment environment
(Relevant to all decision problems *except* concurrent monitoring)

7. Combined Intractive Methods by Indigenous & Independent Staff with Incoming Staff Candidates

CONVERGING EVIDENCE, PRIVATE EVENTS, & MULTIPLE-PERSPECTIVES, for:
—Therapeutic techniques
—Personal-social characteristics
(Relevant to initial staff placement & disposition)

FIGURE 30.4. The secondary strategies of a comprehensive paradigm for formal assessment to provide common information needed in inpatient/residential settings (adapted from Paul & Mariotto, 1986).

decision problem—staff initial hiring and assignment.

Prototypic Instruments and Systems

The comprehensive paradigm is just what the name implies, comprehensive. We believe that implementation of the entire paradigm would provide *all* the common information needed with maximum potential utility for supporting *all* decision problems in inpatient/residential settings. The primary strategies also provide information to indicate when unique assessments are needed for specific individuals—i.e., they trigger other high-cost one-on-one strategies as well as providing the most important common

information themselves (see Figure 30.3). In fact, implementation of the Core Strategy with minimal supplements from Strategies 2 and 3, alone, would provide a rational basis for operation of inpatient/residential programs that far exceeds that which currently exists in the great majority of facilities (see Paul & Mariotto, 1986). Further, analysis of the costs and benefits of different modes of implementation of prototypic instruments demonstrates how the net relative cost of implementing and maintaining the comprehensive paradigm could be *less* than "free" (see Paul, 1986b). The following description of prototypic instruments and systems is intended to clarify those strategies that represent the greatest departure from current practices.

Primary Strategy 1. Licht, Paul, and Power

(1986) provide a review of standardized DOC systems with promise for Strategy 1 application. It should come as no surprise that the necessary research and development with DOC instruments to fulfill the requirements of the core strategy have been explicitly undertaken only by our own clinical-research group. The result of this effort is the Computerized TSBC/SRIC Planned-Access Observational Information System (Paul, 1995a). The TSBC/SRIC system and its component DOC instruments—the Time-Sample Behavioral Checklist (TSBC) (Paul, 1987a) and the Staff-Resident Interaction Chronograph (SRIC) (Paul, 1988)—are therefore the only ones ready for widespread standardized implementation to provide practical support of clinical services and research (Paul, 1995b) as well as being the Strategy 1 prototype.

The TSBC and SRIC are both employed by a cadre of full-time, technician-level, independent, noninteractive observers on hourly time-sampling schedules. The trained observers collect detailed time- and situation-specific continuous assessments of the functioning of every client and staff member within a treatment program, from the moment of entry to the moment of departure—time sampling all client waking hours, sixteen hours per day, seven days per week. This schedule usually requires two full-time-equivalent (FTE) observers per unit or ward of twenty to fifty beds, with the same cadre of observers serving two or more units. Daily entry of TSBC and SRIC data into computer files for storage and later production of summary scores and reports is typically accomplished by night-shift clinical staff using a desktop computer on each implementing unit. Because of the amount and quality of data provided by the TSBC/SRIC System, clinical staff time is freed to the extent that no marginal increase in costs is usually necessary to support observer positions (see Paul, 1986b).

The TSBC is the primary DOC instrument for providing information on the assets, deficits, and excesses of every client in impatient/residential settings and on how and where clients and staff spend their time. It also provides the most dependable information on less stable phenomena within the classes of client and staff personal-social characteristics and on some social aspects of the intramural treatment environment. TSBC observations cover every client and staff member on hourly time-samples. TSBC content codes used by observers are arranged into seven broad categories: location (where the client or staff member is during the observation); position (e.g., standing, lying down); awake-asleep (eyes open or closed); facial expression (e.g., smiling-laughing with apparent stimulus, grimacing-frowning with no apparent stimulus); social orientation (e.g., alone, with staff); appropriate concurrent activities (e.g., talking to others, reading); and crazy behavior (e.g., posturing, verbalized delusions, hallucinations, suicidal threats).

TSBC standard computer summaries and reports aggregate data across observations (typically fifty to one hundred per week for each client) to provide rate scores for each code and for higher-order composite scores. The higher-order scores include total appropriate and total inappropriate behavior as well as midlevel components of adaptive functioning (appropriate interpersonal interaction, instrumental activity, self-maintenance, individual entertainment) and of maladaptive functioning (bizarre motor behavior, bizarre facials and verbals, hostile belligerence). Stereotype/variability scores for specific classes of behavior and assault frequency (incorporated from Strategy 2 recordings) are also included in TSBC standard computer summaries and reports. TSBC standard weekly reports are generated on every client and staff member and on each unit's client and staff groups (means and standard deviations) every week; these reports provide information on "current status" (functioning in the previous seven days) as well as change scores from entry to the program and from the previous week. TSBC special reports can be generated to provide summary scores in the same formats; these may summarize data over any specific activity, time period, or variable in the TSBC or biographical data files for any specified individual or subgroup.

The documented quality and utility of TSBC data have been exceptional. For example, interobserver replicability coefficients

(Omega squares) obtained for one-day observations for individual codes of the TSBC have ranged from $r = .90$ to $r = 1.00$, with the median $r > .98$; the reliability of higher-order scores is even greater (Licht & Paul, 1987). Large-scale studies have also demonstrated substantial content-, criterion-, and construct-related validity evidence for TSBC higher-order scores. For example, weekly higher-order scores of client functioning account for nearly all the reliable variance in scores obtained from standardized QICS instruments during the same time period (Mariotto, Paul, & Licht, 1987). TSBC scores predict which clients achieve successful discharges (allowing objective "discharge readiness" guidelines) and their level of functioning in the community up to eighteen months postdischarge (rs in the .60s to .70s) (Paul & Mariotto, 1987). In essence, the TSBC has been documented to provide all of the decision-support functions expected of a Strategy 1 DOC system (see Paul, 1987a).

The SRIC is the primary DOC instrument for providing information on the psychosocial activities of clinical staff and treatment programs, including the nature, amount, content, and distribution of verbal and nonverbal interactions staff provide to clients. It also provides the most dependable information on some of the less stable phenomena related to social aspects of the intramural treatment environment. Unlike the brief observations used with the TSBC, SRIC observations employ ten-minute continuous observations of a single staff member and all client interactants. Typically one or two SRIC observations are collected per hour, with representative sampling of staff and activities over time. Each SRIC observation records the location, activity, residents (clients) present, residents shared with other staff, staff present, and group composition as well as staff-client interactions and noninteractive staff performance. SRIC content categories are arranged in a matrix format, with twenty-one staff categories crossed with five resident (client) categories. Observers record staff-client interactions and noninteractive staff behavior in the cells of the 5×21 matrix, with one matrix for each of ten successive minutes. The five resident categories

are: appropriate; inappropriate failure; inappropriate crazy; requests; and neutral. The twenty-one staff categories specify the nature of verbal and nonverbal response to client behavior and include: positive- and negative-verbal, -nonverbal, -nonsocial, -statement, -prompt, and -group reference; reflect/clarify; suggest alternatives; instruct/demonstrate; doing with; doing for; physical force; ignore/no response; announce; and attend/record/ observe. Staff initiations and noninteractive behavior are coded in the "neutral" resident category column.

SRIC standard computer summaries and reports aggregate data across observations (typically about one hundred per week for each treatment program) to provide mean rate scores (expressed as "average hourly rate") and standard deviations for each cell of the SRIC matrix and for sums over each staff and resident category. Mean rates and standard deviations are also provided for total interactions and total activity. Percentage scores are provided for codes and categories as well, to assist with profile interpretations. Standard computer summaries and reports further provide data on average clients present, average client/staff ratios, and the average number of contacts per hour, interactions per contact, and the total attention received by the average client. SRIC standard weekly reports are generated for the total program of implementing units every week; these reports provide information on overall psychosocial functioning of the aggregate staff group in the previous seven days. SRIC special reports can be generated to provide summary scores in the same format; these may summarize data over observations for a single staff member, for any group of staff identifiable as individuals or by common personal-social characteristics from biographical data files, for specified time periods, and/or for periods in which specified actions or interactions occurred.

As with the TSBC, the quality and utility of SRIC data have been exceptional. For example, the interobserver replicability coefficients (Omega squares) obtained for one-day observations for individual cells within the SRIC matrix have ranged from $r = .84$ to 1.00, with a median $r > .99$ (Licht, Paul, & Mariotto, 1988). Although traditional concurrent validity studies are impossible, because no other approach provides comparable data, discriminative and predictive SRIC evaluations have provided remarkable evidence of utility. Among these are correlations over time between specific classes of staff-client interactions and client improvement (*r*s in the .50s to .90s) and the ability of SRIC profiles to discriminate effective from ineffective treatment programs in ongoing operations (Paul, Mariotto, & Licht, 1988; Paul & Menditto, 1992). In essence, the SRIC has been documented to provide all of the decision-support functions expected of a staff-focused Strategy 1 DOC system (see Paul, 1988).

The complete Computerized TSBC/SRIC Planned Access Observational Information System contains computer programs and file-management procedures to efficiently retrieve standard computer summaries and reports from the ongoing TSBC and SRIC Strategy 1 data base to provide specific support for all of the decision problems presented in Figure 30.1. In addition to incorporating data on client assaults (Strategy 2), the total TSBC/SRIC System also incorporates biographical data forms for both clients and staff (from Strategy 3, 4, and 6 assessments) (Paul, 1995a, 1995b). These additional data are used as options for generating TSBC and SRIC special reports, as noted earlier. They also allow the generation of an additional set of quality assurance reports and the collection and retrieval of nearly all of the "minimal data sets" recommended for standard implementation by the NIMH Mental Health Statistics Improvement Program (Leginski et al., 1989).

The TSBC/SRIC System quality assurance reports provide ready access to client, staff, and program data that are directly targeted at absolute and comparative program evaluation and legal and ethical regulation/documentation. These three-page reports combine and sort higher-level functioning data from the TSBC and SRIC with information on client movement and length of stay, relatively stable personal-social characteristics, staff and client turnover, staffing levels, and costs as well as other variables for total treatment units. These reports can be readily generated to cover periods from

two weeks to a fiscal year or more for direct comparison of different time periods and/or different units.

In summary, the twenty-five-plus years of research and development on the TSBC/SRIC System has documented its utility, feasibility, and practicality with the full range of inpatient/residential treatment programs in mental hospitals and community facilities. The normative/feasibility data and interpretive user's manuals for the TSBC/SRIC System are based on more than one thousand and two-hundred clients and six hundred staff in thirty-six different treatment units located in seventeen different facilities. The normative client group ranges in age from eighteen to ninety-nine years, covering all diagnostic categories, including substance abusers, mentally retarded, and mentally ill with acute and chronic residential histories and lengths of stay ranging from three days to fifty-nine years. Staff in the feasibility/generalizability sample range from aide-level to doctoral-level personnel using individual, group, and unitwide treatment modalities with an exceptionally broad range of theoretical orientations, from psychodynamic to biological. Unit size ranges from eight to one hundred and twenty beds, both locked and open. In addition to the normative/feasibility samples, ongoing implementation of the TSBC/SRIC System for further development of staff training procedures, computer report formats, modes of data processing and distribution, and approaches to consulting on implementation have covered more than ten units in five different facilities.

The availability of staff user's manuals (Paul, 1995a) and an "implementation package" (Paul, 1995b), combined with previous publications (Paul, 1987a, 1988), provide everything needed to implement and use the TSBC/SRIC System; effectively this includes videotape observer training materials, computer programs, recording and processing forms, and training procedures for all levels of users. Although the size of the ongoing data base for the TSBC/SRIC System and the complexity of the computer programs used to retrieve and summarize these data were formerly an impediment to adoption, recent advances in computer technology have made such concerns moot. Version 3.1 of the TSBC/SRIC System is designed to run on commonly available desktop PCs at extremely low cost (see Paul, 1995a, 1995b).

Primary Strategy 2. Minimal Strategy 2 supplements to the information on client and staff transitory functioning provided by the time-sampling DOC instruments of Strategy 1 include event recording of every instance of client assaults and other intolerable acts and of each order and every administration of drugs or other biomedical treatment techniques. Most facilities already employ "incident reports" and other forms for this purpose. Paul and Mariotto (1986) recommend the best format for these minimal supplements. Laska, Siegel, and Simpson (1980) provide a prototypic approach for recording biomedical techniques. Paul and Shelite (in press a) provide a prototypic "incident report" form for recording client intolerable acts and the consequent staff response; "assault frequencies" from such recordings are incorporated within the TSBC/SRIC System, as described earlier.

Beyond the minimal supplements to Strategy 1, most of the component DOC instruments of a complete Strategy 2 system require parallel program structure across units to allow the information collected to be completely comparable over time and settings; consequently, the specific forms and focus will be both population- and program-dependent to fulfill all of the information functions of this strategy. We are aware of only one complete Strategy 2 DOC system that has been applied in a standardized manner across more than one type of adult inpatient/residential treatment program, the *Clinical Frequencies Recording System* (CFRS; Paul & Shelite, in press a); consequently, it serves as the prototype.

The CFRS includes a series of forms that are integrated with operation of treatment programs (see Paul & Shelite, in press a; Redfield, 1979). Beyond the minimal supplements just noted, these forms include three additional generic classes for ongoing recording of setting-dependent behavior: utilization of facilities and services (e.g., use of consumable items and other resources); "inappropriate time sheets," for

recording absence from scheduled activities and locations; and performance of adaptive behavior (e.g., appearance, "on-time" attendance). Specifically, the CFRS forms are designed to formalize, integrate, and simplify normal record-keeping, clinical treatment protocols, and critical events in such a way as to maximize information utility while minimizing staff time spent doing paperwork. Each of the CFRS forms focuses on a single class of performance. The CFRS becomes a "system" by compiling data across the multiple forms to provide higher-order weekly "rate per opportunity" scores for each client. Computer scoring provides such rate scores for each general class of performance as well as higher-order composites for total appropriate and total inappropriate behavior, self-care, interpersonal skills, and instrumental role performance. These are the scores that require parallel structures for comparability over time and units.

Psychometric characteristics of the CFRS indicate that with training, interobserver replicabilities of clinical staff have been uniformly excellent, with phi coefficients ranging from .94 to .97 for component instruments of the system. Studies show CFRS data to be free from drift, bias, and differential staff reactivity (Mariotto, 1979) and to be remarkably sensitive to intended and unintended change in individual clients as a result of psychosocial and biomedical interventions (Paul & Lentz, in press). Further, CFRS indices predict performance on a variety of tasks, including post-release level of functioning of clients (rs in the .50s and .60s).

Although the published CFRS is designed for use only with a specific social-learning program (Paul & Lentz, in press), it could be adapted with few modifications to most inpatient/residential applications if the accompanying program structure were also adopted. In lieu of adopting the program structure of the social-learning program, recommendations are provided elsewhere to assist in the development, selection, and application of Strategy 2 systems for other programs and/or populations (see Mariotto & Licht, 1986; Paul, 1986a; Paul & Mariotto, 1986; Redfield, 1979).

Primary Strategy 3. As noted earlier, the combined interactive assessments of Strategy 3 consist of two components: a set of structured interviews conducted with every client and other potential informant (e.g., a significant other, a knowledgeable staff member) and a set of brief sequential interactive assessments. The interviews are conducted at entry (and extending within a few days after entry), when other events signal the need for multiple-perspective assessment, or potential discharge, and at postdischarge follow-up (at least by telephone interview). The brief sequential interactive assessments are conducted weekly or biweekly as an integrated part of service delivery, with supplementary assessments of "satisfaction" when other events give reason for concern.

The procedures included in Strategy 3 are generally more traditional ones with which most readers are familiar. The formalization within the paradigm insures minimal coverage of the common information needed while reducing the costs, maximizing the relevance of data obtained, eliminating unnecessary redundances in coverage by different staff members, avoiding excessive collection of data that are better provided by other strategies, and removing needlessly frequent high-cost individual assessment sessions. Detailed recommendations for the means of structuring Strategy 3 assessments and for the development, selection, and application of a nuclear set of scales, or encoding devices, for any given population and program are provided by Paul and Mariotto (1986).

Although there are a number of available structured psychiatric interviews and self-report/informant-report instruments with excellent psychometric characteristics, most suffer from "overkill" from the Strategy 3 perspective; i.e., too many items and too much time and effort are devoted to gathering information that usually has low relevance and very high relative cost—the information is applicable only to limited decision problems, such as providing a psychiatric diagnosis or personality profile. The Structured Interview Schedules for Clients and Significant Others (SISCSO; Paul & Shelite, in press-b) are the closest approximation to a pro-

totypical set for this component of Strategy 3. These structured interviews gather information on present and historical level of functioning, psychiatric symptomotology, role functioning and expectations. The SISCSO has not yet been used extensively enough to provide the normative and psychometric data that are available from more established research interviews. However, these interviews do provide the parallel structure and content for administration to clients and other informants and allow the scoring of several standardized instruments to be derived from the item responses.

For generalized application in the comprehensive paradigm, the current SISCSO requires expansion to provide coverage of emergency conditions at intake, additional information for DSM-IV and future diagnostic systems, greater coverage of private events for less disabled populations, judgmental evaluation of client status by clinical staff, and the elicitation and documentation of satisfaction and assent/consent from each involved participant. This necessary expansion can be accomplished by the careful addition of a few nonredundant items from well-established research scales (e.g., Spitzer & Williams, 1986; Robins et al., 1985; Wing, Cooper, & Sartorius, 1974), from the SCL-90R (Derogatis, 1993), from the Life Skills Inventory (see Liberman, 1988), and from the interview measures discussed by Widiger in this volume (see Chapter 26). The addition of the Emergency Room/Admission Checklist and Physical Examination Checklist (Hedlund, 1977) to entry interviews, the Brief Psychiatric Rating Scale (Overall & Gorham, 1962) as expanded and descriptively anchored by the UCLA/NPI Mental Health Clinical Research Center (see Liberman, 1988) and the brief ratings of "expressed emotion" developed by the latter investigators would complete this component of Strategy 3.

The brief sequential interactive assessments of Strategy 3 require imposition of structure on treatment programs if data are to be comparable over time and facilities. These encoding devices are both program- and population-dependent and should follow earlier recommendations for selection or development (Paul, 1986a; Paul & Mariotto, 1986). However, readers should seriously consider the adaptation of a limited subset of forms for this component from among those discussed in Laska, Abbey, Geller, and Bank (1983); these forms have already been designed for use in computer-based information systems. The expanded BPRS, a short scale to measure clients' and significant others' satisfaction, the Mini-Mental Status Exam (Folstein, Folstein, & McHugh, 1975), and the Abnormal Involuntary Movement Scale, as modified by Lane et al. (1985), are also good candidates for inclusion in this component of Strategy 3.

We recommend the inclusion of a full-fledged set of Strategy 3 assessments to maximize the rationality of decision making, even though parallel program structures are required. However, minimal supplements to the TSBC/SRIC System and minimal Strategy 2 DOC coverage of assaultive behavior and biomedical treatment techniques can be implemented without much change in existing program structure. These minimal Strategy 3 assessments include full sets of entry and terminal-decision structured interviews, with at least telephone-interview follow-ups; initial standardized physical examinations and weekly monitoring of health status and drug side effects; and periodic collection of the subgroup of nuclear encoding devices on some standardized time schedule as well as when other data signal a change (see Paul & Mariotto, 1986).

Secondary Strategies 4, 5, 6, and 7. Because all instruments, or encoding devices, of the secondary strategies of the comprehensive paradigm consist of more traditional instruments, space limitations preclude presentation of a prototypic set. Paul and Mariotto (1986) provide recommendations for the development, selection, and application of these procedures as well as several recommendations for specific instruments. Note that the minimal data on client and staff biographical characteristics from Strategy 4 and 6 assessments (as well as from Strategy 3) are included in the TSBC/SRIC System, as are the minimal data on the intramural treatment environment from Strategy 6 assessments (see Paul, 1995b).

Illustrative Contribution of the Comprehensive Paradigm to the Case Scenario

Dr. Jones, as unit director, has installed the full-scale social-learning program from Paul & Lentz (in press), with the accompanying Strategy 2 CFRS. She has also implemented a complete system of Strategy 3 interactive assessments. In addition, all units of the hospital have installed the TSBC/SRIC System and full-week samples of client and staff TSBC and SRIC data are collected every three months from the various residential aftercare placements used by the hospital.

After Dr. Jones receives the call from the community hospital, the intake counselor collects information from the intake portion of the client entry form of the expanded SISCSO (Strategy 3). This information on Ms. Smith's physical and mental status enables Dr. Jones to decide that admission is appropriate and provides data for obtaining the court order from the magistrate. After admission, information on Ms. Smith's current and past level of functioning obtained from Ms. Smith and her brother on the client and significant-other entry forms of the SISCSO, combined with an examination of the most recent TSBC and SRIC standard weekly reports for client groups and available treatment programs, enables Dr. Jones to decide that the intensive care subunit is the appropriate initial placement. This information also allows assignment of a psychiatric diagnosis.

During the first several days on the intensive care subunit, information collected from a TSBC special report for Ms. Smith, from a CFRS summary report, and from brief sequential Strategy 3 interactive assessments enables the team to identify problems, establish initial treatment goals, and formulate the initial treatment plan. The information from these instruments also allows the team to closely monitor Ms. Smith's psychological and physical status. In addition, Dr. Jones is able to document Ms. Smith's competency and to share with Ms. Smith the obtained data, showing her relative status on the TSBC institutional norms, so as to jointly decide with her that voluntary admission is a prudent step.

Over the next two weeks, information from TSBC standard weekly reports provides detailed data on Ms. Smith's progress; examination of TSBC normative distributions enables Dr. Jones to decide to transfer Ms. Smith into the regular unitwide treatment program. Continued monitoring of the information from the TSBC standard weekly reports, supplemented by attendance data from the CFRS, triggers a decision by Dr. Jones to order several unique assessments. These assessments are focused on Ms. Smith's memory and her personality style. The information from these latter assessments triggers a decision for a neuropsychological consult to address the possible memory issues. The information obtained from the TSBC standard weekly report also results in the decision to change Ms. Smith's treatment goals, assign her to the cognitive therapy module, and communicate to her therapist in this treatment module Ms. Smith's passive-dependent interactional style.

Meanwhile, Dr. Jones uses a SRIC special report to monitor the intern's progress in training in the social-learning program. By comparing the intern's psychosocial interactions with the "ideal" social learning program criteria (requested as an option on the SRIC report), Dr. Jones is able to decide when the intern has progressed sufficiently to be assigned regular clinical duties. The ability of the TSBC/SRIC System to aggregate and store data over groups of clients and staff, at different times, and with time, place, circumstance specificity, enables Dr. Jones to respond rationally to the emergency staff shortage. Sitting at her office computer, Dr. Jones identifies the effects of past changes in staffing on the conduct of the treatment program and the program's effectiveness by examining sequential TSBC and SRIC special reports on the video monitor. She is similarly easily able to provide the research director with the necessary information on the potential effectiveness of the cognitive therapy module for the grant application by requesting TSBC/SRIC System quality assurance reports

for sequential periods before and after the module's introduction.

Because Dr. Jones also has a home computer with a modem that allows her to query the TSBC/SRIC System data base, she does not need to return to the hospital after she is notified of the suicide attempt. The computer programs that are an integral part of the TSBC/SRIC System enable her to request TSBC special reports on Ms. Smith from archival data, from which she identifies the pattern of social withdrawal and negative affect accompanied by "manic-like" increased activity that preceded the suicide attempt. She also checks the Strategy 3 brief interactive assessments of staff conducting cognitive therapy to identify the content focus of sessions. Monitoring of this pattern by the intern, using both TSBC special reports and CFRS information, results in the prevention of the second attempt and a change in focus of Ms. Smith's cognitive therapy. The data base from the TSBC/SRIC System, which includes the data from the other treatment units, also provides the necessary aggregate information on comparative unit effectiveness and staff utilization that the hospital administrator needs for the budget hearings. Dr. Jones simply requests quality assurance reports from all the units, covering the past six months, and forwards these reports to the administrator.

During the next several weeks, the TSBC and SRIC standard weekly reports and the CFRS weekly summaries provide the necessary detailed concurrent monitoring to track Ms. Smith's treatment. The normative data from the TSBC allow Dr. Jones to establish a level of functioning target for Ms. Smith's release. Since Ms. Smith's health insurance (despite her apparent indigent state, she had continued paying for an insurance policy!) will soon be exhausted, available norms for the TSBC suggest that she will need to be released to a halfway house rather than to fully independent living arrangements. TSBC and SRIC samples from the various halfway houses used by the hospital are examined to select an appropriate placement for Ms. Smith. When Ms. Smith's TSBC standard weekly report reaches criteria for "community placement readiness," a SISCSO assessment on the client "termination" form is undertaken with Ms. Smith to provide converging information, expectations for posthospital role behavior, and necessary data for a discharge diagnosis. Unfortunately, Ms. Smith's brother was unavailable for his scheduled SISCSO interview, but all other information converged to support release. Detailed reports of Ms. Smith's response to the inpatient treatment program and suggestions regarding staff therapeutic techniques gathered from the TSBC/SRIC System data base are provided to the staff of the halfway house to ensure continuity of effective procedures.

Meanwhile, the visitors from the accreditation agency report that their review is over and the unit "passed with distinction." The accreditation site visitors had been presented with quality assurance reports and several sample standard weekly reports on both the TSBC and SRIC; they commented that these summaries provided 80 percent of the necessary documentation. They also noted that the CFRS provided an additional 19 percent of the documentation, and all that was needed for the remaining 1 percent of needed documentation was information on Infection Control, which was handled by the supervisory nurse on the unit. One of the clinicians on the site-visit team commented that it was nice to see a unit where most of the staff time is spent providing therapeutic services rather than doing paperwork. Dr. Jones had not been concerned because concurrent monitoring of TSBC and SRIC standard weekly reports had shown her that the program was being appropriately implemented and that the client group was regularly improving. But compliments are always appreciated.

After the meeting with the site-visit team, Dr. Jones queries the data base and produces a SRIC special report, with the intern's first week's on the floor performance compared with the intern's last week's performance on one report. She uses this information to help her write the evaluation for the internship training director. In a similar manner, she spends some time examining the results of her procedural changes

on the unitwide treatment program with sequential TSBC/SRIC System quality assurance reports and by viewing selected SRIC and TSBC special reports on her computer monitor; she then begins to formulate a plan for future changes. The call from the attorney is met with a sigh and Dr. Jones returns to her computer to summarize the information from the primary strategies to document the reasons for the decisions made in the treatment of Ms. Smith— with knowledge that this will be simply a pain in the neck rather than a potential disaster.

REFERENCES

Cronbach, L. J. (1984). *Essentials of psychological testing* (4th ed.). New York: Harper & Row.

Cronbach, L. J., & Gleser, G. C. (1965). *Psychological tests and personnel decisions* (2nd ed.). Urbana: University of Illinois Press.

Cronbach, L. J., Gleser, G. C., Nanda, H., & Rajaratnam, N. (1972). *The dependability of behavioral measurements: Theory of generalizability for scores and profiles.* New York: Wiley.

Derogatis, L. R. (1993). *Symptoms Checklist-90-R.* Minneapolis: National Computer Systems.

Fiske, D. W. (1978). *Strategies for personality research.* San Francisco: Jossey-Bass.

Fiske, D. W. (1979). A demonstration of the value of interchangeable observers. *Journal of Behavioral Assessment, 1,* 251–258.

Folstein, M. F., Folstein, S. F., & McHugh, P. R. (1975). "Mini-Mental State": A practical method for grading the cognitive state of patients for the clinician. *Journal of the American Geriatrics Society, 12,* 189–198.

Hedlund, J. L. (1977). *Standard System of Psychiatry (SSOP): Applications summary.* St. Louis: Mental Health Systems Research Unit, Missouri Institute of Psychiatry.

Lane, R. D., Glazer, W. M., Hansen, T. E., Berman, W. H., & Kramer, S. I. (1985). The assessment of tardive dyskinesia using the abnormal involuntary movement scale. *Journal of Nervous and Mental Disease, 173,* 1–5.

Laska, E. M., Abbey, S., Geller, J., & Bank, R. (1983). Technology transfer: The Multi-State Information System. In E. M. Laska, W. H. Gulbinat, &

D. A. Regier (Eds.), *Information support to mental health programs*. New York: Human Sciences Press.

Laska, E. M., Siegal, C., & Simpson, G. (1980). Automated review system for orders of psychotropic drugs. *Archives of General Psychiatry, 37,* 824–827.

Leginsky, W. A., Croze, C., Driggers, J., Dumpman, S., Geersten, D., Kamis-Gould, E., Namerow, M. J., Patton, R. E., Wilson, N. Z., & Wurster, C. R. (1989). *Data standards for mental health decision support systems.* National Institute of Mental Health, Series FN No. 10, DHHS Pub. No. (ADM) 89–1589. Washington, DC: U.S. Government Printing Office.

Liberman, R. P. (Ed.). (1988). *Psychiatric rehabilitation of chronic mental patients.* Washington, DC: American Psychiatric Press.

Licht, M. H., & Paul, G. L. (1987). Replicability of TSBC codes and higher-order scores. In G. L. Paul (Ed.), *Observational assessment instrumentation for service and research—The Time-Sample Behavioral Checklist: Assessment in residential treatment settings (Part 2)* (pp. 69–94). Champaign, IL: Research Press.

Licht, M. H., Paul, G. L., & Mariotto, M. J. (1988). Replicability of SRIC codes, categories, indexes, and matrix profiles. In G. L. Paul (Ed.), *Observational assessment instrumentation for service and research—The Staff-Resident Interaction Chronograph: Assessment in residential treatment settings (Part 3)* (pp. 101–136). Champaign, IL: Research Press.

Licht, M. H., Paul, G. L., & Power, C. T. (1986). Standardized direct-multivariate DOC systems for service and research. In G. L. Paul (Ed.), *Principles and methods to support cost-effective quality operations: Assessment in residential treatment settings (Part 1)* (pp. 223–265). Champaign, IL: Research Press.

Mariotto, M. J. (1979). Observational system use in basic and applied research. *Journal of Behavioral Assessment, 1,* 239–250.

Mariotto, M. J., & Licht, M. H. (1986). Ongoing assessment of functioning with DOC systems: Practical and technical issues. In G. L. Paul (Ed.), *Principles and methods to support cost-effective quality operations: Assessment in residential treatment settings (Part 1)* (pp. 191–222). Champaign, IL: Research Press.

Mariotto, M. J., & Paul, G. L. (1984). The utility of assessment for different purposes. In M. Mirabi (Ed.), *The chronically mentally ill: Research and services* (pp. 73–82). New York: SP Medical and Scientific Books.

Mariotto, M. J., Paul, G. L., & Licht, M. H. (1987). Concurrent relationships of TSBC higher-order scores with information from other instruments. In G. L. Paul (Ed.), *Observational assessment instrumentation for service and research—The Time-Sample Behavioral Checklist: Assessment in residential treatment settings (Part 2)* (pp. 177–210). Champaign, IL: Research Press.

Overall, J. E., & Gorham, D. R. (1962). The Brief Psychiatric Rating Scale. *Psychological Reports, 10,* 799–812.

Paul, G. L. (1969). Behavior modification research: Design and tactics. In C. M. Franks (Ed.), *Behavior therapy: Appraisal and Status.* (pp. 29–62). New York: McGraw-Hill.

Paul, G. L. (1985). The impact of public policy and decision making on the dissemination of science-based practices in mental institutions: Playing poker with everything wild. In R. A. Kasschau, L. Rehm, & L. P. Ullmann (Eds.), *Psychological research, public policy, and practice: Towards a productive partnership.* New York: Praeger.

Paul, G. L. (1986a). The nature of DOC and QICS encoding devices. In G. L. Paul (Ed.), *Principles and methods to support cost-effective quality operations: Assessment in residential treatment settings (Part 1)* (pp. 63–112). Champaign, IL: Research Press.

Paul, G. L. (1986b). Net relative cost of the maximum potential utility assessment paradigm. In G. L. Paul (Ed.), *Principles and methods to support cost-effective quality operations: Assessment in residential treatment settings (Part 1)* (pp. 165–190). Champaign, IL: Research Press.

Paul, G. L. (Ed.). (1987a). *Observational assessment instrumentation for service and research—The Time-Sample Behavioral Checklist: Assessment in residential treatment settings (Part 2).* Champaign, IL: Research Press.

Paul, G. L. (1987b). Rational operations in residential treatment settings through ongoing assessment of client and staff functioning. In D. R. Peterson & D. B. Fishman (Eds.), *Assessment for decision* (pp. 145–203). New Brunswick, NJ: Rutgers University Press.

Paul, G. L. (Ed.). (1988). *Observational assessment instrumentation for service and research—The Staff–Resident Interaction Chronograph: Assessment in residential treatment settings (Part 3).* Champaign, IL: Research Press.

Paul, G. L. (Ed.). (1995a). *Observational assessment*

instrumentation for service and research — The Computerized TSBC/SRIC Planned-Access Observational Information System: Assessment in residential treatment settings (Part 4). Champaign, IL: Research Press.

Paul, G. L. (Ed.). (1995b). Observational assessment instrumentation for service and research — The TSBC/SRIC System implementation package: Assessment in residential treatment settings (Part 5). Champaign, IL: Research Press.

Paul, G. L., & Lentz, R. J. (in press). Psychosocial treatment of chronic mental patients (2nd ed.). Champaign, IL: Research Press

Paul, G. L., & Mariotto, M. J. (1986). Potential utility of the sources and methods: A comprehensive paradigm. In G. L. Paul (Ed.), Principles and methods to support cost-effective quality operations: Assessment in residential treatment settings (Part 1) (pp. 113–164). Champaign, IL: Research Press.

Paul, G. L., & Mariotto, M. J. (1987). Predictive relationships of TSBC higher-order scores to other measures of performance and outcomes. In G. L. Paul (Ed.), Observational assessment instrumentation for service and research — The Time-Sample Behavioral Checklist: Assessment in residential treatment settings (Part 2) (pp. 211–236). Champaign, IL: Research Press

Paul, G. L., Mariotto, M. J., & Licht, M. H. (1988). Discriminative relationships of SRIC scores and matrix profiles among staff and programs differing on independent criteria and effectiveness. In G. L. Paul (Ed.), Observational assessment instrumentation for service and research — The Staff–Resident Interaction Chronograph: Assessment in residential treatment settings (Part 3). (pp. 261–306). Champaign, IL: Research Press.

Paul, G. L., Mariotto, M. J., & Redfield, J. P. (1986a). Assessment purposes, domains, and utility for decision making. In G. L. Paul (Ed.), Principles and methods to support cost-effective quality operations: Assessment in residential treatment settings (Part 1) (pp. 1–26). Champaign, IL: Research Press

Paul, G. L., Mariotto, M. J., & Redfield, J. P. (1986b). Sources and methods for gathering information in formal assessment. In G. L. Paul (Ed.), Principles and methods to support cost-effective quality operations: Assessment in residential treatment settings (Part 1) (pp. 27–62). Champaign, IL: Research Press.

Paul, G. L., & Menditto, A. A. (1992). Effectiveness of inpatient treatment programs for mentally ill adults in public psychiatric facilities. Applied and Preventative Psychology, 1, 41–63.

Paul, G. L., & Shelite, I. (in press-a). The Clinical Frequency Recording System: Social-learning forms. Supplement to G. L. Paul & R. J. Lentz, Psychosocial treatment of chronic mental patients (2nd ed.). Champaign, IL: Research Press.

Paul, G. L., & Shelite, I. (in press-b). Structured Interview Schedules for Clients and Significant Others. Supplement to G. L. Paul & R. J. Lentz, Psychosocial treatment of chronic mental patients (2nd ed.). Champaign, IL: Research Press.

Redfield, J. P. (1979). Clinical Frequencies Recording Systems: Standardizing staff observations by event recording. Journal of Behavioral Assessment, 1, 211–219.

Robins, L. N., Helzer, E., Orvaschel, H., Anthony, J. C., Blazer, D., Burnam, M. A., Burke, J. D., Jr., & Eaton, W. W. (1985). The Diagnostic Interview Schedule. In W. W. Eaton & L. G. Kessler (Eds.), Epidemiological field methods in psychiatry. New York: Academic Press.

Spitzer, R. L., & Williams, J. (1986). The structured clinical interviews for DSM-III. New York: New York State Psychiatric Institute.

Wiggins, J. S. (1988). Personality and prediction: Principles of personality assessment. Malabar, FL: Krieger.

Wing, J. K., Cooper, J., & Sartorius, N. (1974). The measurement and classification of psychiatric symptoms. New York: Cambridge University Press.

31
Assessing Alcohol/Drug Abuse Problems

Roger L. Greene
Joseph A. Banken

The use of any form of psychological assessment in alcohol/drug abuse problems has been hampered by the traditional bias in this field against any form of assessment, which has stated more or less explicitly that once the person stops drinking/drugging the other problems will go away. It is only in the last few decades that progress has been made in the use of psychological assessment in this field with the recognition of the specific contributions that can be made by psychological assessment in planning interventions and treatment; the existence of persons with dual disorders that must be diagnosed and treated concurrently; and the need for screening for alcohol/drug problems in many areas of our society, which has increased public awareness of the role of assessment. This chapter will focus on the use of objective psychological procedures in several areas of assessing alcohol/drug abuse problems: (1) issues involved in screening for substance abuse problems; (2) traditional scales used to identify alcohol or drug problems; (3) the timing of psychological assessment within an alcohol/drug treatment program; (4) specific tests that have particular utility within the area; and (5) the identification of patients with dual disorders.

PRELIMINARY CONSIDERATIONS

A number of potential issues must be given explicit consideration in understanding research on alcohol or drug problems. The parameters of the person's use of substances need to be reported explicitly. These data can be as simple as whether the person uses substances constantly, only on weekends, or during binges. The type of substance(s) used is also important, at least as to generic class, e.g., sedative-hypnotics, stimulants, and so on, as well as whether the person uses only one substance or multiple substances. The work of Skinner and his colleagues (Morey & Skinner, 1986; Morey, Skinner, & Blashfield, 1984; Skinner, Jackson, & Hoffmann, 1974) may be very useful in this matter in terms of identifying patterns of use that then can be compared with psychological test performance.

The social and interpersonal aspects of the alcohol or drug use should be identified. Persons may use substances only alone, withdraw and isolate themselves as the result of the use of substances, only use in social contexts, or some combination of these behaviors.

The factors that have led the person to receive treatment need to be identified. Although persons enter treatment as a result of "hitting bottom," the factors that lead to that point are very different. Persons may be entering treatment because of the "encouragement" of the legal system, employers, spouses, and so on.

Any comparisons that are made between polydrug and alcoholic patients must consider the potential effects of age, since polydrug patients average fifteen to twenty years younger than alcoholics. The influence of socioeconomic class and education, which have significant effects on objective personality test performance, also must be considered. The general failure to even consider the role of such moderator variables, which is so characteristic of research in this area, must be corrected if meaningful data are to be obtained.

One of the most significant needs in this entire area is to focus on treatment process and outcome issues, i.e., whether subgroups of patients who use specific substances respond better to one type of treatment and whether they have differential recovery rates. The time is long past when delineating whether alcoholics or drug addicts are a unitary group is a viable question; the data are clear that substance users are very heterogeneous. Research questions need to be more sharply focused—such as, do alcoholics with both a 2–4/4–2 codetype and an elevated score on the MAC have better recovery rates in a confrontationally based AA program? Or are attrition rates across the course of treatment within this codetype higher or lower than in a 4–9/9–4 codetype, and if so, how can this problem be addressed? It would also be informative to determine whether patients within these specific subgroups have different histories of personal and familial substance use. Consequently, it is mandatory that researchers do more than simply report that the patients are in some unspecified treatment program. Detailed data bases that encompass both the individual's and his/her familial history of substance use as well as social and environmental factors that may be involved must be reported as well as the patient's MMPI performance. Substance use is a complex process; it is time that research designs start to appreciate this complexity and report data that can begin to provide some insight into the multitude of factors that are involved.

The point in time at which the data are collected is very important. If the data are collected too early in treatment, the patients may be too toxic to report accurately. This specific issue will be discussed below.

How the persons respond after they enter treatment must also be considered, particularly in any study that is evaluating treatment effectiveness or outcome. Some persons will continue to deny or minimize their use of substance(s) throughout treatment and/or leave treatment prematurely. Clinicians who collect their data early in treatment and do not consider that some patients may leave before completing treatment will have different results than those who collect data later or toward the end of treatment.

Finally, the basis on which the diagnosis is made must be given careful consideration. All too often it appears that the only criterion for the diagnosis is the person's presence in a treatment facility, with little regard for whether the diagnosis is appropriate or whether other psychiatric diagnoses are present. The assumption appears to be that false positive diagnoses do not occur in these facilities, which may be fairly safe given the denial and minimization that are characteristic of the misuse of substance(s). However, it is important to be aware of the variety of social, interpersonal, and legal factors that resulted in this person being identified as needing treatment. These issues/factors may be less important within a given facility since people may be referred for similar reasons, but they clearly are important when patients are compared across a variety of facilities. Individuals who receive treatment in a state or VA hospital may differ in a number of important ways from persons in a private hospital or who are maintained in an outpatient setting (see English & Curtin, 1975; Krauthamer, 1979; Pattison, Coe, & Doerr, 1973).

It should be apparent that until researchers start addressing the issues described above, it will be very difficult to reach any definitive conclusions about work in this area.

SCREENING FOR SUBSTANCE ABUSE PROBLEMS

There has been increasing concern over the last decade about identifying persons whose substance abuse may potentially interfere with their job functions, and screening for substance abuse is now required in a number of industries. The importance of such screening cannot be overestimated when it is considered that the lifetime prevalence rate for substance abuse disorders in adults approaches 16 percent (Regier et al., 1988), and at least 20 percent of adults who visit a physician have had an alcohol problem at one time (Cleary et al., 1988).

Similar concerns arise in clinical settings, where prevalence rates for substance abuse have been estimated to range from 12 to 30 percent (Moore et al., 1989). Clinicians frequently fail to recognize that the patient's symptoms may reflect substance abuse or dependence rather than, or in addition to, psychiatric symptomatology.

The critical need to identify individuals who may be abusing substances in the workplace and in clinical settings has resulted in the failure to consider the multitude of variables that may affect these assessments, particularly in disadvantaged groups. Investigators frequently overlook the relationship between sensitivity, specificity, and the prevalence of a given disorder, and the potential loss of predictive power when a test or procedure is used in a given setting (Baldessarini, Finkelstein, & Arana, 1983). Items 264 ("I have used alcohol excessively") and 489 ("I have a drug or alcohol problem") from the MMPI-2 (Butcher, Dahlstrom, Graham, Tellegen, & Kaemmer, 1989) can be used as examples of two different types of screening "tests" to illustrate these points.

Sensitivity, or how well the test identifies persons who abuse alcohol, is a critical variable in a screening instrument, since a test with low sensitivity will produce a large number of false negatives. In a sample of 291 inpatients at the Southwest Institute for Addictive Diseases in the Department of Psychiatry at Texas Tech University, item 264 on the MMPI-2 had a sensitivity of 77 percent in men (N = 174) and 59 percent in women (N = 117); item 489 had a sensitivity of 80 percent in men and 72 percent in women. Thus, these two screening "tests" missed about 20 percent of the male patients and 30 to 40 percent of the female patients who are already in a treatment program or have otherwise been identified as being substance dependent. The substantial effects of gender are not usually discussed in the use of these screening instruments, and the effects of ethnicity are even less well understood. It should be clear that the sensitivity of items 264 and 489 would decrease in settings such as the workplace where the person may be motivated not to report problems with alcohol. Unfortunately, it is in such settings where increased sensitivity is very desirable that the natural outcome is decreased sensitivity.

If both of these "tests" are used in conjunction with one another, there is a sensitivity of 59 percent in men and 32 percent in women in the above inpatient sample, while only 9 percent of the men and 15 percent of the women are classified as false negatives. This false negative rate, however, should be kept in mind when prevalence rates are discussed below.

Specificity, or how well the test identifies persons who do not abuse alcohol, is just important as sensitivity, since a test with low specificity will produce a large number of false positives. In the MMPI-2 normative sample (Butcher et al., 1989), item 264 has a specificity of 53 percent in white men (N = 933) and 76 percent in white women (N = 1184); item 489 has a specificity of 95 percent in white men and 97 percent in white women. Again, the substantial effects of gender are apparent on item 264. In the MMPI-2 normative sample, item 264 has a specificity of 73 percent in black men (N = 126) and 89 percent in black women (N = 188), and item 489 has a specificity of 93 percent in black men and 96 percent in black women. There also appear to be substantial gender difference in blacks on item 264. It should be readily apparent that depending on which of these two "tests" was used to screen individuals, a different sample would be identified.

It should be readily apparent that items 264 and 489 have much better specificity than sensitivity in white women and that the relationship between sensitivity and specificity varies among these two "tests" in white men. Only item 489 appears to have similar specificities across gender and ethnic groups in the MMPI-2 normative group, and it has reasonably good sensitivity.

As noted above, the lifetime *prevalence rate* for substance abuse disorders approaches 16 percent in men and 8 percent in women (Regier et al., 1988). Given these low prevalence rates for alcoholism in the general population, it is difficult for any screening instrument to improve on the base rate prediction that everyone is not alcoholic since it will be 84 percent accurate in men and 92 percent accurate in women. Gottesman and Prescott (1989) recently summarized the issues involved in the use of the MacAndrew Alcoholism scale (MAC: MacAndrew, 1965) in settings in which the prevalence rate is so low. Sensitivity and specificity also change as a function of prevalence rate, which is too complex to be explored here. Baldessarini et al. (1983) provide a thorough discussion of this issue.

The specific criteria that are used to define a substance-abuse disorder can vary widely and have substantial effects on the patients that are identified. Criteria that emphasize liver function, for example, will identify a different set of alcoholics than will criteria that emphasize social and occupational functioning. Researchers and clinicians frequently assume that an alcoholic is an alcoholic without considering how alcoholism is being defined in the development of a specific screening test. The specific criteria used to define alcoholism also place inherent limits on how well a screening test can identify such individuals. For example, a test that is designed to assess alcohol dependence in an inpatient setting will not perform in a similar manner in the workplace where the interest may be in the identification of persons who abuse substances. In addition, a critical hurdle for a screening test involves how well it can assess "wet" alcoholics, i.e., individuals who should be diagnosed as alcoholic by the specific criteria being employed but who for whatever reason are not being identified, rather than alcoholics in a treatment program.

Gender differences are rarely considered with standard screening instruments for substance-abuse problems such as the Michigan Alcohol Screening Test (MAST: Selzer, 1971) or the CAGE (Mayfield, McLeod, & Hall, 1974). It is obvious that women who have scores of ten or higher on the MAST or two or higher on the CAGE are reporting significant problems with alcohol. However, the few studies that have examined gender differences on the MAST routinely report that women have lower scores (Rivers, Rivers, & Newman, 1991), which clearly limits the utility of the MAST as a screening instrument in women. Even more serious are the findings of Babor, Kranzler, and Lauerman (1989), who found that women with high scores on the MAST differed from women with low scores only in their number of lifetime problems with alcohol, and that no screening scale worked well with women.

It is frequently conjectured that hidden or secretive drinking in women (Gearhart, Beebe, Milhorn, & Meeks, 1991) makes it more difficult to screen for their alcohol problems (Celentano, McQueen, & Chee, 1980). A number of potential explanations are provided for this hidden drinking: women are more likely to drink at home and by themselves; society (friends, law enforcement personnel) is more likely to "protect" women from the consequences of their drinking; and the role of the housewife makes it easier to conceal drinking. As Celentano et al. (1980) noted, however, most prevalence estimators of problem drinking have been developed in men, and the questions do not appear to be relevant to the areas of concern in women. Hence, "hidden" drinking in women may more accurately reflect the failure of screening instruments to ask the appropriate questions. Also, differences in prevalence rates for problem drinking for men and women need to be considered in evaluating "hidden" drinking. Osterling, Nilsson, Berglund, Moberg, and Kristenson (1992) found that unidentified problem drinking is proportional to problem drinking in men and women, which argues rather strongly against hidden drinking being exclusively a characteristic of women.

Gender differences also need to be examined when specific items are under consideration for use in a screening test. Two items are frequently recommended in this literature as being equally appropriate for men and women: (1) five or more drinks on a given day; and (2) getting into fights while drinking. These conclusions, however, do not take into consideration the differences in base rates with which these behaviors occur in men and women. For example, 49 percent of men and only 23 percent of women reported five or more drinks on any day in the last year (United States National Center for Health Statistics, 1985). The data on arrests and drug use among persons arrested also reveal substantial gender differences. Men are much more likely to be arrested (81.6 percent), yet drug use is nearly comparable for men and women if the person is arrested (Federal Bureau of Investigation, 1991).

Given the propensity for alcoholics to deny or minimize the seriousness of their disease, it could be argued that the identification of an individual via some screening instrument is of little practical value unless the person is willing to acknowledge that alcohol is a problem. It is important to understand whether screening is intended to identify individuals who need some type of intervention, which is the case in the clinical setting, or who need to be excluded from some high-risk occupation, which is more likely to be the case in the work setting. In the clinical setting, denying or minimizing alcohol problems has a different set of implications than in the workplace, and clinicians need to be aware of these issues.

TRADITIONAL SCALES USED TO IDENTIFY ALCOHOL OR DRUG PROBLEMS

A number of scales from objective psychological tests have been developed to identify individuals with alcohol or drug problems. Several scales have been developed specifically to screen persons who may abuse substances: the MAST (Selzer, 1971); the Self-Administered Alcoholism Screening Test (Swenson & Morse, 1975); and the Mortimer-Filkins Test (Mortimer, Filkins, Kerlan, & Lower, 1973), which have been reviewed rather frequently (see Jacobson, 1983, 1989; National Institute on Alcohol Abuse and Alcoholism, 1990). Because of the limitations of space, only a limited number of scales will be examined here: the MacAndrew Alcoholism Scale (MAC/MAC-R); the Addiction Admission Scale (AAS) and Addiction Potential scale (APS) from the MMPI-2 (Weed, Butcher, McKenna, & Ben-Porath, 1992); and scales B and T from the MCMI/MCMI-II. Each of these scales will be examined in turn.

The MacAndrew Alcoholism Scale (MAC/MAC-R)

A number of MMPI scales have been developed to identify persons who have alcohol and drug problems: Hampton's (1951) Al scale; Holmes's (1953) Am scale; Hoyt and Sedlacek's (1958) Ah scale; MacAndrew's (1965) MAC scale; Linden's (1969) ALX scale; Rosenberg's (1972) Composite Alcoholism Key [Cak]; Atsaides, Neuringer, and Davis's (1977) Institutionalized Chronic Alcoholism Scale [ICAS], and Davis, Offord, Colligan, and Morse's (1991) Common Alcoholism Logistic scale [CAL]. More recently, MacAndrew developed substance abuse scales to identify substance use in adolescents (1986) and women (1988). Two other MMPI scales have been developed to identify individuals who use drugs: Cavior, Kurtzberg, and Lipton's (1967) Heroin Addiction (He) scale and Panton and Brisson's (1971) Drug Abuse (DaS) scale. This review will be limited to those scales that are scored routinely on the MMPI/MMPI-2 (AAS; APS; and MAC/MAC-R). There are several extensive reviews of the MAC that can be consulted by the interested reader (Apfeldorf, 1978; Gottesman & Prescott, 1989; Greene & Garvin, 1988; MacAndrew, 1981; Megargee, 1985).

The MAC identifies white males who have a propensity to use substances with 70 to 75 percent hit rates and percentages of false negatives around 20 percent. Data on adolescents and white females who use substances are less reliable because of the limited research. When white males who use substances must be discriminated from other psychiatric patients, hit rates decrease and the percentage of false positives increases. When patients have dual disorders (a substance abuse/dependence diagnosis and some other DSM-III-R Axis I or II diagnosis), these discriminations become even more difficult, which will be explored in more detail below. Finally, the MAC should be used very cautiously with black males because of the extremely low hit rates and high percentages of false positives in psychiatric patients. It is unclear whether similar problems occur in other ethnic groups and with black females because there is no research on which to base any conclusions.

The research on the MAC with polydrug patients is clearly less complete than with alcoholic patients. Several conclusions can still be drawn, and a number of recommendations can be made for future research in this area. First, the elevated scores on the MAC in polydrug patients indicate that the MAC is sensitive to the misuse of all types of substances including alcohol. The MAC could be called more appropriately a "substance abuse" scale rather than an "alcoholism" scale. The "substances" that are misused do not have to be "street" drugs either, since legally prescribed medications are equally prone to such misuse. Second, there do not appear to be any ethnic differences between black and white male polydrug patients in terms of their mean performance on the MAC. Yet the finding that black male psychiatric patients score nearly in the same range as black polydrug and alcoholic patients suggests that the MAC is probably less effective with members of minority groups. Finally, data are needed on the performance on the MAC in other samples of polydrug patients such as women, adolescents, and so on. Until such information is available, the MAC should be used cautiously with these groups, too.

Addiction Admission and Addiction Potential Scales (MMPI-2)

Butcher and his colleagues (Butcher, 1991; Weed, Butcher, McKenna, & Ben-Porath, 1992) developed two new substance-abuse scales that are scored routinely with the MMPI-2. The Addiction Admission scale (AAS), a thirteen-item scale, differs significantly from the MAC in that it focuses on simple denial or acknowledgment of substance-abuse problems. The Addiction Potential scale (APS), a thirty-nine-item scale, was designed to identify personality features and lifestyle patterns that are related to alcohol and drug abuse. The APS was constructed by contrasting item responses of the MMPI-2 normative group (Butcher et al., 1989), psychiatric patients (Graham & Butcher, 1988), and alcoholics (McKenna & Butcher, 1987). Greene, Weed, Butcher, Arredondo, and Davis (1992) cross-validated AAS and APS in a sample of substance abusers and psychiatric inpatients, and they found nearly identical results to Weed et al. (1992).

Since AAS and APS are new MMPI-2 scales, there is little additional research on them. They appear to have utility in identifying individuals who have problems with alcohol or drugs. These scales do not show significant specificity in discriminating alcohol from drug abuse, but they are sensitive to the identification of substance abuse in general.

Scales B and T (MCMI/MCMI-II)

The Millon Multiaxial Clinical Inventory-II (MCMI-II), an updated version of the earlier Millon Multiaxial Clinical Inventory (MCMI), was developed from Millon's (1969) polythetic typology of personality and designed for use in clinical settings (Millon, 1987). The MCMI-II contains two substance-abuse scales: the Alcohol Dependence scale (scale B) was developed to assess the presence of alcoholism, and the Drug Dependence scale (scale T) was designed to assess recurrent or recent history of drug abuse. B, a forty-six-item scale, assesses a history of excessive drinking that has produced problems in the home and workplace. T, a fifty-eight-item scale, is associated with a history of drug use pronounced enough to cause difficulties in either home or the work situation. According to Millon (1987), both scales B and T contain numerous indirect items that may be useful in identifying psychiatric patients who are not eager to admit substance-abuse problems. However, there have been few studies using the MCMI with alcoholics (Bartch & Hoffman, 1985; Craig, Verinis, & Wexler, 1985). Only Millon's validation studies specifically assessed the relationship between the MAC and scales B and T using the MMPI and MCMI, with correlations of .44 and .51, respectively (Millon, 1983, p. 52).

The performance of the MCMI substance scales have been disappointing when used in substance-abusing populations (Gilbertini & Retzlaff, 1988; Miller & Streiner, 1990). Miller and Streiner (1990) reported that scale B is not as accurate as the MAC and that the scale should not be used.

THE TIMING OF PSYCHOLOGICAL ASSESSMENT

The primary dilemma regarding the timing of psychological assessment is that early assessment can provide information that is crucial for effective patient treatment planning, but psychological assessment conducted too soon after admission may be distorted by the consequences of toxicity or withdrawal. Many studies have demonstrated that when psychological testing is conducted during the first few days of treatment and later repeated, the second assessment reveals much less distress, agitation, and confusion (Beam & Karasievich, 1975; Craig, 1983; Graf, Baer, & Comstock, 1977; Libb & Taulbee, 1971).

Clinicians who treat alcoholics and other substance-dependent patients are well aware of the need to delay psychological assessment when the patient who enters the treatment program has withdrawal or brain-toxic effects. Despite the awareness of the need to delay assessment to allow for detoxification and withdrawal,

clear guidelines for the optimal time to administer the initial psychological assessment are lacking. Although Sherer, Haygood, and Alfano (1984) suggested that a ten-day delay after admission is sufficient for some psychological testing, other investigators have recommended longer delays. For example, Nathan (1991, p. 359) concluded that patients with depression, anxiety, or psychotic behavior need to be drug-free for four to six weeks "before they can be reliably diagnosed with a psychiatric disorder exclusive of the effects of their drug use." Recommendations regarding the optimal time for testing may vary depending on such factors as the drug abused by the patient, the severity and length of the abuse, and the type of psychological testing (neuropsychological versus personality).

OBJECTIVE PSYCHOLOGICAL TESTS TRADITIONALLY USED IN ALCOHOL OR DRUG TREATMENT PROGRAMS

Minnesota Multiphasic Personality Inventory (MMPI/MMPI-2)

There have been a number of reviews of the use of the MMPI in alcohol- and drug-abusing samples (Clopton, 1978; Graham & Strenger, 1988; Greene & Garvin, 1988; Morey & Blashfield, 1981), with most of the research focused on alcoholics. Several conclusions can be drawn from the performance of alcoholic patients on the standard MMPI validity and clinical scales. First, it is clear that there is not a unitary alcoholic personality. Instead there seems to be a number of smaller, more discrete subgroups of alcoholics, although the composition of these subgroups depends on the method used to identify them. The codetype research would suggest several subgroups (2–4/4–2, 2–7/7–2, 4–9/9–4) in both male and female alcoholics, and additional codetypes that are specific to males (1–2/2–1) and females (3–4/4–3, 4–6/6–4, and 4–8/8–4). Empirical methods such as cluster analysis also identify subgroups of alcoholic patients (2–7–8–4, 4–9, and 1–2–3–4) that have some degree of overlap with those identified by codetype research. These subgroups, however, only account for 25 to 35 percent of the alcoholic patients. Second, there has been only limited research examining whether these subgroups of alcoholics have different treatment outcomes/processes and/or drinking histories. It would be interesting to know whether specific subgroups of alcoholic patients are more successful in a particular type of treatment or that they have a particular history of substance use. Finally, more research is needed on groups other than the typical white male alcoholic, and it is important to include psychiatric and normal reference groups in order to better understand the actual role of alcohol and drug problems.

The research on the MMPI with polydrug patients has been very similar to the research on alcoholics, except that it has received limited attention until the last few years. One of the first questions examined was whether there was a polydrug "personality," and whether polydrug patients differed from alcoholics, i.e., did some personality types have a specific drug of choice? These initial studies usually involved a comparison of polydrug patients with alcoholics, and they demonstrated that groups of polydrug patients were experiencing more emotional distress than were alcoholic patients. There appear to be a number of conclusions that can be drawn from the MMPI performance of polydrug patients. First, it is clear that there is not a unitary polydrug personality, just as there is not a unitary alcoholic personality. Instead there seems to be a number of smaller, more discrete subgroups of polydrug patients, although the composition of these subgroups differs from those seen in alcoholic patients. The codetype research would suggest that several subgroups (4–8/8–4 and 4–9/9–4) are frequently seen in both male and female white polydrug patients, and that additional codetypes are specific to white males (6–8/8–6, 7–8/8–7, and 8–9/9–8). Second, black male polydrug patients appear to be less emotionally disturbed than white males. Third, and again similar to the alcoholic patients, there has been virtually no research examining whether these subgroups of polydrug patients have different treatment outcomes and/or histories of drug use. It would be interesting

to know whether specific subgroups of polydrug patients are more successful in a particular type of treatment or that they have a particular history of substance use. The influence of the multitude of moderator variables described above as they affect these subgroups of polydrug patients must be considered in any research in this area. Finally, more research is needed on groups other than the typical white or black male polydrug patient.

Millon Multiaxial Clinical Inventory (MCMI/MCMI-II)

There are no specific reviews of the MCMI or MCMI-II in substance-abuse samples as with the MMPI, nor are there studies that investigate its use in treatment planning. Choca, Shanley, and Van Denburg (1992) have provided a short section on substance abuse (pp. 122–125) in their *Interpretative Guide to the MCMI*. This lack of research is somewhat surprising given the high frequencies of psychiatric disorders that are generally found in substance-abuse settings (see the discussion of dual diagnosis, below).

A strength of the MCMI/MCMI-II is that it is designed specifically to assess personality disorders, although there is some debate over how closely the MCMI is aligned with DSM-III diagnoses (see Millon, 1985, 1986; Widiger & Sanderson, 1987; Widiger, Williams, Spitzer, & Frances, 1985; Widiger, Williams, Spitzer, & Frances, 1986). Clinicians also should keep in mind that the MCMI and MCMI-II use non-linear base rate cutoff scores to establish the presence of a personality disorder or clinical syndrome, and that the normative data are based on a patient sample.

The primary research with the MCMI has been to identify groups or clusters of alcoholic patients (Bartsch & Hoffman, 1985; Craig, Verinis, & Wexler, 1985; Gibertini & Retzlaff, 1988; Mayer & Scott, 1988). These studies typically identify groups of patients who show elevations on the following scales, although the exact percentage will vary across studies: antisocial and narcissistic, avoidant and dependent, passive-aggressive/negativistic; and compulsive. There has been little attempt to relate these groups of MCMI profiles to aspects of treatment other than the patient's style of drinking or using drugs. It should be apparent that there is plenty of opportunity to investigate the usefulness of the MCMI-II in substance-abuse settings.

Alcohol Use Inventory (AUI)

The Alcohol Use Inventory (AUI) was originally developed from research that analyzed the manner in which people described drinking problems (Horn & Wanberg, 1969). They identified common factors among these statements of individuals seeking assistance for alcoholism, which they used in developing the AUI.

The current version of the AUI (Horn, Wanberg, & Foster, 1987) consists of twenty-four heterogeneous scales that assess a variety of features associated with *alcohol* use. Since the AUI does not assess the use of other substances, it is limited to patients who only use alcohol or whose drug of choice is alcohol. Seventeen primary scales assess the benefits, styles, consequences, and concerns and acknowledgments related to alcohol use. Seven second-order scales were derived from factor analyses of the primary scales. These second-order scales assess enhanced functioning associated with alcohol use, degree of sustained drinking, life disruption, worry about drinking, and acknowledgment and awareness of drinking problems. One third-order scale assesses broad involvement with alcohol and is believed to reflect alcoholism.

The primary use of the AUI has been to describe the drinking patterns of patients who have been classified into groups or typologies based on the age of onset of drinking (Lee & DiClimente, 1985); diagnosis (Hyer, Leach, Boudewyns, & Davis, 1991); family history (Alterman, 1988; Jones-Saumty, Hochhaus, Dru, & Zeiner, 1983); gender (Olenick & Chalmers, 1991); level or amount of alcohol impairment (Rohsenow, 1982a, 1982b; Williams, Gutsch, Kazelskis, Verstegen, & Scanlon, 1980); locus of control (Donovan & O'Leary, 1978; O'Leary,

Donovan, & O'Leary, 1978); MCMI (Corbisiero & Reznikoff, 1991); MMPI (Donovan, Chaney, & O'Leary, 1978; Kline & Snyder, 1985; Robyak, Donham, Roy, & Ludenia, 1984); and reason for referral for treatment (Calsyn, Reynolds, O'Leary, & Walker, 1982). The diverse nature of the groupings that have been used in a variety of settings precludes any real generalizations about drinking patterns as assessed by the AUI.

No studies have used the AUI to assess treatment process or treatment outcome. Such research would seem to be the logical next step in the use of the AUI.

PRESENCE OF A DUAL DIAGNOSIS

The increased attention to dual disorders, some form of psychopathology in conjunction with substance abuse, also reflects an awareness of the comorbidity of these disorders. For example, Ross, Glaser, & Germanson (1988) reported that most patients (84 percent) in their substance-abuse treatment facility had a lifetime prevalence of psychiatric disorder with diagnoses of antisocial personality disorder, generalized anxiety disorder, and phobias being most frequent. It should be more difficult to screen for substance abuse in psychiatric patients, since they will share some symptoms with alcoholics as a result of their psychopathology and may have comorbid disorders.

When psychological assessments are conducted during the first few days of treatment, many patients may appear anxious, depressed, or psychotic, and it is difficult to determine whether those pathological patterns reflect the effects of toxicity or more enduring personality characteristics. Therefore, it is often difficult to use early assessment data to differentiate between those patients who have a dual diagnosis and those patients whose symptoms are residuals of substance abuse (Nathan, 1991). That uncertainty is a major roadblock because of the need to initiate specific treatments for those patients with dual disorders.

Substance-abuse patients frequently meet the DSM-III-R criteria for an additional mental disorder, such as anxiety disorder, mood disorder, or schizophrenia (Regier et al., 1990). Antisocial personality disorder is also a common additional diagnosis for substance-abuse patients, although substance-abuse patients have also been found to have a variety of other personality disorders (Hasselbrock, Meyer, & Keener, 1985; Kosten, Kosten, & Rounsaville, 1989; Kosten, Rounsaville, & Kleber, 1982; Kroll & Ryan, 1983; Nace, 1989; Nace, Saxon, & Shore, 1983; Poldrugo & Forti, 1988; Rounsaville, Dolinsky, Babor, & Meyer, 1987; Vaglum & Vaglum, 1985).

The presence of a dual diagnosis in a substance-abuse patient has important treatment implications, because the additional problems can affect the patient's responses to substance-abuse treatment as well as the length and outcome of treatment and can require that substance-abuse treatment be supplemented with additional treatment components designed to respond to the individual needs of the patient (Blume, 1989; Nace, Davis, & Gaspari, 1991; Osher & Kofoed, 1989). For example, substance-abuse patients with antisocial or borderline personality disorders have poorer treatment outcomes than other substance-abuse patients (Cadoret, Troughton, & Widmer, 1984; Kosten et al., 1989; Poldrugo & Forti, 1988; Rounsaville et al., 1987; Shuckit, 1985). An outcome study of alcoholics with schizotypal personality disorder found that even though their drinking had ceased after treatment, they were still impaired by anxiety, paranoia, and social problems (Kroll & Ryan, 1983).

Accurate psychological assessment in substance abuse programs is complicated by the neuropsychological deficits that result from prolonged drug and alcohol abuse (Grant, 1987; Kleinknecht & Goldstein, 1972; Ryan & Butters, 1982, 1984; Tarter & Edwards, 1985). Some deficits may be permanent, such as impairments in abstract thinking, problem solving, and complex motor skills. For other deficits, such as short term memory, concentration and attention, and visual memory, recovery begins soon after abstinence begins, and after two weeks of abstinence markedly improved functioning generally occurs (Allen, Faillace, &

Markley, 1971; Bean & Karasievich, 1975; Goldman, Williams, & Klisz, 1983; Parsons & Farr, 1981). However, alcoholics over the age of forty do not show the same recovery in neuropsychological functioning as younger alcoholics (Goldman et al., 1983; Grant, Adams, & Reed, 1984).

SUMMARY

Only recently has significant progress been made in the use of objective psychological procedures in assessing alcohol/drug abuse problems. This progress can be summarized within two major areas: screening and treatment planning and outcome.

Screening for substance use and abuse has become widespread in our society with the increased concern about the accurate identification of individuals whose substance use may interfere with job performance. However, the low prevalence of substance use and the need for appropriate diagnostic specificity makes meaningful research in this area difficult at best. Gender and ethnic differences in reporting substance abuse must be given careful consideration in designing and interpreting these screening instruments.

In order to enhance the contributions to treatment planning and outcome in substance-abuse settings, a number of practical considerations need to be addressed. First, the parameters of the person's use of substance(s) need to be reported explicitly. Social and interpersonal aspects of substance use and factors leading the person to enter treatment must be identified, and consideration needs to be given to moderating factors such as socioeconomic class and education. Second, objective psychological procedures need to be focused on treatment process and outcome rather than simply reporting a set of scores as being descriptive of a specific sample of patients. It should be evident that persons who use and abuse substances are a heterogeneous group, and research should examine for differences within specific MMPI-2 codetypes, MCMI-II profile patterns, or AUI profiles rather than reporting mean results for an entire group of patients. Third, the timing of psychological assessment following detoxification is a critical issue that needs empirical investigation. The development of guidelines for the optimal time for the administration of various types of objective psychological procedures is needed. Finally, the presence of dual psychiatric disorders in patients who abuse substances is only beginning to be recognized. The presence of dual diagnoses has important treatment implications that need to be examined explicitly.

REFERENCES

Allen, R. P., Faillace, L. A., & Markley, H. C. (1971). Recovery of memory functioning in alcoholics following prolonged intoxication. *Journal of Nervous and Mental Diseases, 153*, 417–423.

Alterman, A. I. (1988). Patterns of familial alcoholism, alcoholism severity, and psychopathology. *Journal of Nervous and Mental Disease, 176*, 167–175.

Apfeldorf, M. (1978). The MacAndrew Scale: A measure of the diagnosis of alcoholism. *Journal of Studies on Alcohol, 42*, 80–86.

Atsaides, J. P., Neuringer, C., & Davis, K. L. (1977). Development of an institutionalized chronic alcoholic scale. *Journal of Consulting and Clinical Psychology, 45*, 609–611.

Babor, T. F., Kranzler, H. R., & Lauerman, R. J. (1989). Early detection of harmful alcohol consumption: Comparison of clinical, laboratory, and self-report screening procedures. *Addictive Behaviors, 14*, 139–157.

Baldessarini, R. J., Finkelstein, S., & Arana, G. W. (1983). The predictive power of diagnostic tests and the effect of prevalence of illness. *Archives of General Psychiatry, 40*, 569–573.

Bartsch, T. W., & Hoffman, J. J. (1985). A cluster analysis of Millon Clinical Multiaxial Inventory (MCMI) profiles: More about a taxonomy of alcoholic subtypes. *Journal of Clinical Psychology, 41*, 707–713.

Bean, K. L., & Karasievich, G. O. (1975). Psychological test results at three stages of inpatient alcoholism treatment. *Journal of Studies on Alcohol, 36*, 838–852.

Blume, S. B. (1989). Dual diagnosis: Psychoactive substance dependence and the personality disorders. *Journal of Psychoactive Drugs, 21*, 139–144.

Butcher, J. N. (1991). *User's guide to the Minnesota report (MMPI-2): Alcohol and drug treatment system.* Minneapolis: National Computer Systems.

Butcher, J. N., Dahlstrom, W. G., Graham, J. R., Tellegen, A., & Kaemmer, B. (1989). *Minnesota Multiphasic Personality Inventory-2 (MMPI-2): Manual for administration and scoring.* Minneapolis: University of Minnesota Press.

Cadoret, R., Troughton, E., & Widmer, R. (1984). Clinical differences between antisocial and primary alcoholics. *Comprehensive Psychiatry, 25*, 1–8.

Calsyn, D. A., Reynolds, F. D., O'Leary, M. R., & Walker, R. D. (1982). Differential drinking patterns, personality characteristics, and field articulation of court-referred and non-court-referred male alcoholics in treatment. *International Journal of the Addictions, 17*, 249–257.

Cavior, N., Kurtzberg, R. L., & Lipton, D. S. (1967). The development and validation of a heroin addiction scale with the MMPI. *International Journal of the Addictions, 2*, 129–137.

Celentano, D. D., McQueen, D. V., & Chee, E. (1980). Substance abuse by women: A review of the epidemiologic literature. *Journal of Chronic Diseases, 33*, 383–394.

Choca, J. P., Shanley, L. A., & Van Denburg, E. (1992). *Interpretative guide to the Millon Clinical Multiaxial Inventory.* Washington, DC: American Psychological Association.

Cleary, P. D., Miller, M., Bush, B. T., Warburg, M. W., Delbanco, T. L., & Aronson, M. D. (1988). Prevalence and recognition of alcohol abuse in a primary care population. *American Journal of Medicine, 85*, 466–471.

Clopton, J. R. (1978). Alcoholism and the MMPI: A review. *Journal of Studies on Alcohol, 39*, 1540–1558.

Corbisiero, J. R., & Reznikoff, M. (1991). The relationship between personality type and style of alcohol use. *Journal of Clinical Psychology, 47*, 291–298.

Craig, R. J. (1983). Effects of opiate withdrawal on MMPI profile scores. *International Journal of the Addictions, 18*, 1187–1193.

Craig, R. J., Verinis, J. S., & Wexler, S. (1985). Personality characteristics of drug addicts and alcoholics on the Millon Clinical Multiaxial Inventory. *Journal of Personality Assessment, 49*, 156–160.

Davis, L. J., Jr., Offord, K. P., Colligan, R. C., & Morse, R. M. (1991). The CAL: An MMPI alcoholism scale for general medical patients. *Journal of Clinical Psychology, 47,* 632–646.

Donovan, D. M., Chaney, E. F., & O'Leary, M. R. (1978). Alcoholic MMPI subtypes: Relationship to drinking styles, benefits, and consequences. *Journal of Nervous and Mental Disease, 166,* 553–561.

Donovan, D. M., & O'Leary, M. R. (1978). The Drinking-Related Locus of Control Scale: Reliability, factor structure and validity. *Journal of Studies on Alcohol, 39,* 759–784.

English, G. E., & Curtin, M. E. (1975). Personality differences in patients at three alcoholism treatment agencies. *Journal of Studies on Alcohol, 36,* 52–61.

Federal Bureau of Investigation (1991). *Crime in the United States.* Washington, DC: Author.

Gearhart, J. G., Beebe, D. K., Milhorn, H. T., & Meeks, G. R. (1991). Alcoholism in women. *American Family Physician, 44,* 907–913.

Gilbertini, M. & Retzlaff (1988, August). *Personality and alcohol use patterns among inpatient alcoholics.* Paper presented at the 96th Annual Convention of the American Psychological Association, Atlanta.

Goldman, M. S., Williams, D. L., & Klisz, D. K. (1983). Recoverability of psychological functioning following alcohol abuse: Prolonged visual-spatial dysfunction in older alcoholics. *Journal of Consulting and Clinical Psychology, 51,* 310–324.

Gottesman, I. I., & Prescott, C. A. (1989). Abuses of the MacAndrew MMPI alcoholism scale: A critical review. *Clinical Psychology Review, 9,* 223–242.

Graf, K., Baer, P. E., & Comstock, B. S. (1977). MMPI changes in briefly-hospitalized non-narcotic drug users. *Journal of Nervous and Mental Diseases, 165,* 126–133.

Graham, J. R., & Butcher, J. N. (1988, March). *Differentiating schizophrenic and major affective disorders with the revised form of the MMPI.* Paper presented at the 23rd Annual Symposium on Recent Advances in the Use of the MMPI, St. Petersburg, FL.

Graham, J. R., & Strenger, V. E. (1988). MMPI characteristics of alcoholics: A review. *Journal of Consulting and Clinical Psychology, 56,* 197–205.

Grant, I. (1987). Alcohol and the brain: Neuropsychological correlates. *Journal of Consulting and Clinical Psychology, 55,* 310–324.

Grant, I., Adams, K. M., & Reed, R. (1984). Aging, abstinence, and medical risk factors in the prediction of neuropsychological deficit among long-term alcoholics. *Archives of General Psychiatry, 41,* 710–718.

Greene, R. L., & Garvin, R. D. (1988). Substance abuse/dependence. In R. L. Greene (Ed.), *The MMPI: Use in specific populations* (pp. 159–197). San Antonio, TX: Grune & Stratton.

Greene, R. L., Weed, N. C., Butcher, J. N., Arredondo, R., & Davis, H. G. (1992). A cross-validation of MMPI-2 abuse scales. *Journal of Personality Assessment, 58,* 405–410.

Hampton, P. J. (1951). A psychometric study of drinkers. *Journal of Consulting Psychology, 15,* 501–504.

Hasselbrock, M. N., Meyer, R. E., & Keener, J. J. (1985). Psychopathology in hospitalized alcoholics. *Archives of General Psychiatry, 42,* 1050–1055.

Holmes, W. O. (1953). *The development of an empirical MMPI scale for addiction.* Unpublished manuscript, San Jose (CA) State College.

Horn, J. L., & Wanberg, K. W. (1969). Symptom patterns related to excessive use of alcohol. *Quarterly Journal of Studies on Alcohol, 30,* 35–38.

Horn, J. L., Wanberg, K. W., & Foster, F. M. (1987). *Guide to the Alcohol Use Inventory.* Minneapolis: National Computer Systems.

Hoyt, D. P., & Sedlacek, G. M. (1958). Differentiating alcoholics from normals and abnormals with the MMPI. *Journal of Clinical Psychology, 14,* 69–74.

Hyer, L., Leach, P., Boudewyns, P. A., & Davis, H. (1991). Hidden PTSD in substance abuse patients among Vietnam veterans. *Journal of Substance Abuse Treatment, 8,* 213–219.

Jacobson, G. R. (1983). Detection, assessment, and diagnosis of alcoholism: Current techniques. In M. Galanter (Ed.), *Recent developments in alcoholism* (Vol 1, pp. 377–413). New York: Plenum.

Jacobson, G. R. (1989). A comprehensive approach to pretreatment evaluation: I. Detection, assessment, and diagnosis of alcoholism. In R. K. Hester & W. R. Miller (Eds.), *Handbook of alcoholism treatment approaches* (pp. 17–53). New York: Pergamon Press.

Jones-Saumty, D., Hochhaus, L., Dru, R., & Zeiner, A. (1983). Psychological factors of familial alcoholism in American Indians and caucasians. *Journal of Clinical Psychology, 39,* 783–790.

Kleinknecht, R. A., & Goldstein, S. G. (1972). Neuropsychological deficits associated with alcoholism. *Quarterly Journal of Studies on Alcohol, 137,* 928–931.

Kline, R. B., & Snyder, D. K. (1985). Replicated

MMPI subtypes for alcoholic men and women: Relationship to self-reported drinking behaviors. *Journal of Consulting and Clinical Psychology, 53,* 70–79.

Kosten, T. A., Kosten, T. R., & Rounsaville, B. J. (1989). Personality disorders in opiate addicts show prognostic specificity. *Journal of Substance Abuse Treatment, 6,* 163–168.

Kosten, T. A., Rounsaville, B. J., & Kleber, H. D. (1982). DSM-III personality disorders in opiate addicts. *Comprehensive Psychiatry, 23,* 572–581.

Krauthamer, C. (1979). The personality of alcoholic middle-class women: A comparative study with the MMPI. *Journal of Clinical Psychology, 35,* 442–448.

Kroll, P., & Ryan, C. (1983). The schizotypal personality on an alcohol treatment unit. *Comprehensive Psychiatry, 24,* 262–270.

Lee, G. P., & DiClimente, C. C. (1985). Age of onset versus duration of problem drinking on the Alcohol Use Inventory. *Journal of Studies on Alcohol, 46,* 398–402.

Libb, J. W., & Taulbee, E. S. (1971). Psychotic-appearing MMPI profiles among alcoholics. *Journal of Clinical Psychology, 27,* 101–102.

Linden, J. D. (1969). *The differential utility of a scale to identify alcoholics.* Paper presented at the annual meeting of the Midwestern Psychological Association.

MacAndrew, C. (1965). The differentiation of male alcoholic outpatients from nonalcoholic psychiatric outpatients by means of the MMPI. *Quarterly Journal of Studies on Alcohol, 26,* 238–246.

MacAndrew, C. (1981). What the *MAC* scale tells us about men alcoholics: An interpretive review. *Journal of Studies on Alcohol, 42,* 604–625.

MacAndrew, C. (1986). Toward the psychometric detection of substance abuse in young men: The SAP scale. *Journal of Studies on Alcohol, 47,* 161–166.

MacAndrew, C. (1988). Differences in the self-description of female alcoholics and psychiatric outpatients: Towards a depiction of the modal female alcoholic. *Journal of Studies on Alcohol, 49,* 71–77.

Mayer, G. S., & Scott, K. (1988). An exploration of heterogeneity in an inpatient male alcoholic population. *Journal of Personality Disorders, 2,* 243–255.

Mayfield, D. G., McLeod, G., & Hall, P. (1974). The CAGE questionnaire: Validation of a new alcoholism screening instrument. *American Journal of Psychiatry, 131,* 1121–1123.

McKenna, T., & Butcher, J. N. (1987, April). *Continuity of the MMPI with alcoholics.* Paper presented at the 22nd Annual Symposium on Recent Developments in the Use of the MMPI, Seattle.

Megargee, E. I. (1985). Assessing alcoholism and drug abuse with the MMPI: Implications for employment screening. In C. D. Spielberger & J. N. Butcher (Eds.), *Advances in personality assessment* (Vol. 5, pp. 1–39). Hillsdale, NJ: Erlbaum.

Miller, H. R., & Streiner, D. L. (1990). Using the Millon Clinical Multiaxial Inventory's Scale B and the MacAndrew Alcoholism Scale to identify alcoholics with concurrent psychiatric diagnoses. *Journal of Personality Assessment, 54,* 736–746.

Millon, T. (1969). *Modern psychopathology.* Prospect Heights, IL: Waveland.

Millon, T. (1983). *Millon Clinical Multiaxial Inventory manual* (3rd ed.). Minneapolis: National Computer Systems.

Millon, T. (1985). The MCMI provides a good assessment of DSM-III disorders: The MCMI-II will prove even better. *Journal of Personality Assessment, 49,* 379–391.

Millon, T. (1986). The MCMI and DSM-III: Further commentaries. *Journal of Personality Assessment, 50,* 205–207.

Millon, T. (1987). *Manual for the Millon Clinical Multiaxial Inventory-II* (2nd ed.). Minneapolis: National Computer Systems.

Moore, R. D., Bone, L. R., Geller, G., Mamon, J. A., Stokes, E. J., & Levine, D. M. (1989). Prevalence, detection, and treatment of alcoholism in hospitalized patients. *Journal of the American Medical Association, 261,* 403–407.

Morey, L. C., & Blashfield, R. K. (1981). Empirical classification of alcoholism: A review. *Journal of Studies on Alcohol, 42,* 925–937.

Morey, L. C., & Skinner, H. A. (1986). Empirically derived classifications of alcohol-related problems. In M. Galanter (Ed.), *Recent developments in alcoholism* (Vol. IV, pp. 145–168). New York: Plenum Press.

Morey, L. C., Skinner, H. A., & Blashfield, R. K. (1984). A typology of alcohol abusers: Correlates and implications. *Journal of Abnormal Psychology, 93,* 408–417.

Mortimer, R. G., Filkins, L. D., Kerlan, M. W., & Lower, J. S. (1973). Psychometric identification of problem drinkers. *Quarterly Journal of Studies on Alcohol, 34,* 1322–1335.

Nace, E. P. (1989). Personality disorder in the alcoholic patient. *Psychiatric Annals, 19,* 256–260.

Nace, E. P., Davis, C. W., & Gaspari, J. P. (1991).

Axis II comorbidity in substance abusers. *Archives of General Psychiatry, 48*, 118–120.

Nace, E. P., Saxon, J. J., & Shore N. (1983). A comparison of borderline and nonborderline alcoholic patients. *Archives of General Psychiatry, 40*, 54–56.

Nathan, P. E. (1991). Substance use disorders in the DSM-IV. *Journal of Abnormal Psychology, 100*, 356–361.

National Institute on Alcohol Abuse and Alcoholism (1990). Screening for alcoholism. *Alcohol Alert*, No. 8, PH285.

O'Leary, M. R., Donovan, D. M., & O'Leary, D. E. (1978). Drinking patterns of alcoholics differing in levels of perceived and experienced control. *Journal of Studies on Alcohol, 39*, 1499–1505.

Olenick, N. L., & Chalmers, D. K. (1991). Gender-specific drinking styles in alcoholics and nonalcoholics. *Journal of Studies on Alcohol, 52*, 325–330.

Osher, F. C., & Kofoed, L. L. (1989). Treatment of patients with psychiatric and psychoactive substance abuse disorders. *Hospital and Community Psychiatry, 40*, 1025–1030.

Osterling, A., Nilsson, L.-H., Berglund, M., Moberg, A.-L., & Kristenson, H. (1992). Sex differences in problem drinking among 42-year-old residents of Malmo, Sweden. *Acta Psychiatria Scandanavica, 85*, 435–439.

Panton, J. H., & Brisson, R. C. (1971). Characteristics associated with drug abuse within a state prison population. *Corrective Psychiatry and Journal of Social Therapy, 17*, 3–33.

Parsons, O. A., & Farr, S. P. (1981). The neuropsychology of alcohol and drug use. In S. B. Filskov & T. J. Boll (Eds.), *Handbook of Clinical neuropsychology* (pp. 320–365). New York: Wiley.

Pattison, E. M., Coe, R., & Doerr, H. O. (1973). Population variation among alcoholism treatment facilities. *International Journal of the Addictions, 8*, 199–229.

Poldrugo, R., & Forti, B. (1988) Personality and alcoholism treatment outcome. *Drug and Alcohol Dependence, 21*, 171–176.

Regier, D. A., Boyd, J. H., Burke, Jr., J. D., Rae, D. S., Myers, J. K., Kramer, M., Robins, L. N., George, L. K., Karno, M., & Locke, B. Z. (1988). One-month prevalence of mental disorders in the United States. *Archives of General Psychiatry, 45*, 977–986.

Regier, D. A., Farmer, M. E., Rae, D. S., Locke, B. Z., Keith, S. J., Judd, L. L., & Goodwin, F. K. (1990). Comorbidity of mental disorders with alcohol and other drug abuse: Results from the epidemiologic catchment area (ECA) study. *Journal of the American Medical Association, 264*, 2511–2518.

Rivers, P. C., Rivers, L. S., & Newman, D. L. (1991). Alcohol and aging: A cross-gender comparison. *Psychology of Addictive Behavior, 5*, 41–47.

Robyak, J. E., Donham, G. W., Roy, R., & Ludenia, K. (1984). Differential patterns of alcohol abuse among normal, neurotic, psychotic, and characterological types. *Journal of Personality Assessment, 48*, 132–136.

Rohsenow, D. J. (1982a). Social anxiety, daily moods, and alcohol use over time among heavy social drinking men. *Addictive Behaviors, 7*, 311–315.

Rohsenow, D. J. (1982b). The Alcohol Use Inventory as predictor of drinking by male heavy social drinkers. *Addictive Behaviors, 7*, 387–395.

Rosenberg, N. (1972). MMPI alcoholism scales. *Journal of Clinical Psychology, 28*, 515–522.

Ross, H. F., Glaser, F. B., & Germanson, T. (1988). The prevalence of psychiatric disorders in patients with alcohol and other drug problems. *Archives of General Psychiatry, 45*, 1023–1031.

Rounsaville, B. J., Dolinsky, Z. S., Babor, T. F., & Meyer, R. E. (1987). Psychopathology as a predictor of treatment outcome in alcoholics. *Archives of General Psychiatry, 44*, 505–513.

Ryan, C., & Butters, N. (1982). Cognitive effects in alcohol abuse. In B. Kissin & H. Begleiter (Eds.), *The biology of alcoholism* (Vol. 6, pp. 485–538). New York: Plenum Press.

Ryan C., & Butters, M. (1984). Alcohol consumption and premature aging: A critical review. In M. Galanter (Ed.), *Recent developments in alcoholism* (Vol. 1, pp. 223–250). New York: Plenum Press.

Selzer, M. L. (1971). The Michigan Alcoholism Screening Test: The quest for a new diagnostic instrument. *American Journal of Psychiatry, 127*, 89–94.

Sherer, M., Haygood, J. M., & Alfano, A. M. (1984). Stability of psychological test results in newly admitted alcoholics. *Journal of Clinical Psychology, 40*, 855–857.

Shuckit, M. A. (1985). The clinical implications of primary diagnostic groups among alcoholics. *Archives of General Psychiatry, 42*, 1043–1049.

Skinner, H. A., Jackson, D. N., & Hoffmann, H. (1974). Alcoholic personality types: Identification and correlates. *Journal of Abnormal Psychology, 83*, 658–666.

Swenson, W. M., & Morse, R. M. (1975). The use of a self-administered alcoholism screening test

(SAAST) in a medical center. *Mayo Clinic Proceedings, 50,* 204–208.

Tarter, R. E., & Edwards, K. L. (1985). Neuropsychology of alcoholism. In R. E. Tarter & D. H. Van Thiel (Eds.), *Alcohol and the brain: Chronic effects* (pp. 217–244). New York: Plenum Press.

United States National Center for Health Statistics (1985). *Health promotion and disease prevention, United States 1985, Vital and health statistics.* Washington, DC: Author.

Vaglum, S., & Vaglum, P. (1985). Borderline and other mental disorders in alcoholic female psychiatry patients: A case control study. *Psychopathology, 18,* 50–60.

Weed, N. C., Butcher, J. N., McKenna, T., & Ben-Porath, Y. S. (1992). New measures for assessing alcohol and drug abuse with the MMPI-2: The APS and AAS. *Journal of Personality Assessment, 58,* 389–404.

Widiger, T. A., & Sanderson, C. (1987). The convergent and discriminant validity of the MCMI as a measure of DSM-III. *Journal of Personality Assessment, 51,* 228–242.

Widiger, T. A., Williams, J. B. W., Spitzer, R. L., & Frances, A. (1985). The MCMI as a measure of DSM-III. *Journal of Personality Assessment, 49,* 366–378.

Widiger, T. A., Williams, J. B. W., Spitzer, R. L., & Frances, A. (1986). The MCMI and DSM-III: A brief rejoinder to Millon. *Journal of Personality Assessment, 50,* 198–204.

Williams, R. L., Gutsch, K. U., Kazelskis, R., Verstegen, J. P., & Scanlon, J. (1980). An investigation of relationships between level of alcohol use impairment and personality characteristics. *Addictive Behaviors, 5,* 107–112.

32

Assessing Patients and Therapists Who Have Been Involved in Therapist-Patient Sexual Intimacies: Evaluating Harm, Recovery, and Rehabilitation

Kenneth S. Pope

It is not unlikely that mental health professionals will encounter among their patients those who have been sexually involved with a previous therapist. Survey research, as shown in Table 32.1, has found that about 44 to 65 percent of psychologists and psychiatrists reported providing services to such patients (Bouhoutsos, Holroyd, Lerman, Forer, & Greenberg, 1983; Gartrell, Herman, Olarte, Feldstein, & Localio, 1987; Pope & Vetter, 1991; Stake & Oliver, 1991). The overwhelming majority of these patients (87 to 94 percent) are female.

Many clinicians may also encounter in their practice patients who are themselves therapists who have been involved, as therapists, in therapist-patient sexual intimacies. The research is less helpful in providing relevant estimates of the extent to which such therapists seek professional services. The research published in peer-reviewed scientific and professional journals has found that perhaps slightly over 12 percent of male therapists and 3 percent of female therapists have acknowledged, in anonymous self-report studies, engaging in therapist-patient sexual intimacies. Table 32.2, for example, presents a summary of the self-report studies of sex with

patients using national samples of psychologists. This research suggests that offenders are much more likely to be male, as does research concerning licensing disciplinary actions based on sexual misconduct (Pope, 1994).

Conducting an adequate psychological assessment of patients or therapists who have been involved in therapist-patient sexual intimacies poses some special challenges for clinicians. The purpose of this chapter is to highlight some of the fundamental issues in such assessments. Readers seeking additional information about patients and therapists who have become sexually involved and about assessment issues are referred to books by, for example, Bates and Brodsky (1989), Gabbard (1989), Noel and Watterson (1992), Pope (1994), Pope, Butcher, and Seelen (1993, particularly pp. 165–186), and Pope, Sonne, and Holroyd (1993, particularly pp. 237–267).

The chapter is organized into three major sections: (1) those issues relevant to the assessment of both patients and therapists, (2) those issues particularly relevant to the assessment of patients, and (3) those issues particularly relevant to the assessment of offenders.

TABLE 32.1 Percentages of Therapists Reporting Male and Female Patients Who Were Sexually Involved with a Previous Therapist

Ref. no.	Profession surveyed	Geographic area	Return rate[a]	% Reporting such patients[b]	Male patients[c]	Female patients[d]
1	Psychology	California	16%	45%	6%	94%
2	Psychiatry	national	26%	65%	9%	91%
3	Psychology	national	50%	50%	13%	87%
4[e]	Psychology	Missouri	31%	44%	—	—

Note: Adapted from Pope, 1993.

Reference key: (1) Bouhoutsos, Holroyd, Lerman, Forer, & Greenberg, 1983; (2) Gartrell, Herman, Olarte, Feldstein, & Localio, 1987 [see also 1986; Gartrell, Milliken, Goodson, Thiemann & Lo, 1992]; (3) Pope & Vetter, 1991; (4) Stake & Oliver, 1991.

[a]Percentage of psychologists or psychiatrists who returned survey forms
[b]Percentage of respondents who reported encountering at least one patient who had been sexually involved with a previous therapist
[c]Of all patients reported as having been sexually involved with a previous therapist, the percentage who were male
[d]Of all patients reported as having been sexually involved with a previous therapist, the percentage who were female
[e]This survey did not ask the gender of the patients who were reported as sexually involved with a previous therapist
Copyright © by American Psychological Association; used with permission.

TABLE 32.2. Self-Report Studies of Sex with Clients Using National Samples of Psychologists[a]

Ref. no.	Publication date	Sample size	Return rate	Male	Female
1[b]	1977	1,000	70%	12.1%	2.6%
2	1979	1,000	48%	12.0%	3.0%
3	1986	1,000	58.5%	9.4%	2.5%
4[c]	1987	1,000	46%	3.6%	0.4%
5[d]	1988	1,000	39.5%	3.5%	2.3%
6[e]	1989	1,600	56.5%	1.0%	0.4%

Note: Adapted from Pope, 1994.

Reference key: (1) Holroyd & Brodsky; (2) Pope, Levenson, & Schover; (3) Pope, Keith-Spiegel, & Tabachnick; (4) Pope, Tabachnick, & Keith-Spiegel; (5) Akamatsu; (6) Borys & Pope.

[a]Exceptional caution is warranted in comparing the data from these various surveys. For example, the frequently cited percentages of 12.1 and 2.6, reported by Holroyd and Brodsky (1977), exclude same-sex intimacies. Moreover, when surveys included separate items to assess post-termination sexual involvement, these data are reported in footnotes to this table. Finally, some published articles did not provide sufficiently detailed data for this table (e.g., return rate and frequencies for psychologists in an article reporting aggregate data for psychologists, social workers, and psychiatrists; percentages of male and female psychologists' responses to an item); the investigators supplied the data needed for the table.

[b]Although the gender percentages presented in the table for studies 2–6 represent responses to one basic survey item in each survey, the percentages presented for study 1 span several items. The study's senior author confirmed through personal communication that the study's findings were that 12.1% of the male and 2.6% of the female participants reported having engaged in erotic contact (whether or not it included intercourse) with at least one opposite-sex patient; that about 4% of the male and 1% of the female participants reported engaging in erotic contact with at least one same-sex patient; and that, in response to a separate survey item, 7.2% of the male and 0.6% of the female psychologists reported that they had "had intercourse with a patient within three months after terminating therapy" (p. 846).

[c]The survey also included a question about "becoming sexually involved with a former client" (p. 996). Gender percentages about sex with current or former clients did not appear in the article but were provided by an author. Fourteen percent of the male and 8% of the female respondents reported sex with a former client.

[d]The original article also noted that 14.2% of male and 4.7% of female psychologists reported that they had "been involved in an intimate relationship with a former client" (p. 454).

[e]The original article also asked if respondents had "engaged in sexual activity with a client after termination" (p. 288). Gender percentages for psychologists, which did not appear in the article but were supplied by an author, were 10.5% for male and 2.0% for female psychologists.

Copyright © by American Psychological Association; used with permission.

TABLE 32.3. Ten Common Scenarios in Therapist-Patient Sexual Involvement

Scenario	Criterion
1. Role trading	Therapist becomes the "patient" and the wants and needs of the therapist become the focus
2. Sex therapy	Therapist fraudulently presents therapist-patient sex as valid treatment for sexual or related difficulties
3. As if . . .	Therapist treats positive transference as if it were not the result of the therapeutic situation
4. Svengali	Therapist creates and exploits an exaggerated dependence on the part of the patient
5. Drugs	Therapist uses cocaine, alcohol, or other drugs as part of the seduction
6. Rape	Therapist uses physical force, threats, and/or intimidation
7. True love	Therapist uses rationalizations that attempt to discount the clinical/professional nature of the professional relationship and its duties (see also Twemlow & Gabbard, 1989)
8. It just got out of hand	Therapist fails to treat the emotional closeness that develops in therapy with sufficient attention, care, and respect
9. Time out	Therapist fails to acknowledge and take account of the fact that the therapeutic relationship does not cease to exist between scheduled sessions or outside the therapist's office
10. Hold me	Therapist exploits patient's desire for nonerotic physical contact and possible confusion between erotic and nonerotic contact

Note: Adapted from Pope & Bouhoutsos, 1986, p. 4.

ISSUES RELEVANT TO THE ASSESSMENT OF BOTH PATIENTS AND THERAPISTS

In this section, as in the two that follow, the list of issues is by no means comprehensive nor does it present original research not previously published. The relevant issues are probably well known by virtually all those who are skilled at psychological assessment and particularly by those who are knowledgeable about the topic of therapist-patient sexual involvement. The list attempts simply to highlight some of the fundamental issues that are so basic that they may easily be overlooked or obscured, and to present a useful review for clinicians who conduct such assessments, particularly if they are conducting assessments in this area for the first time.

Competence

Perhaps the most fundamental issue is the competence of the clinician conducting the evalu-
ation. Section 1.04(a) of the "Ethical Principles of Psychologists and Code of Conduct" (American Psychological Association [APA], 1992) states: "Psychologists provide services . . . only within the boundaries of their competence, based on their education, training, supervised experience, or appropriate professional experience" (p. 1600). Adequate competence to conduct assessments of those who have been involved in therapist-patient sexual intimacies involves at least two major aspects. First, the clinician must possess adequate competence in the general area of psychological assessment. Second, the clinician must possess adequate competence in working with those who have been involved, as patients or therapists, in therapist-patient sexual intimacies. This latter competence would include a broad and substantial knowledge of the forms that such intimacies tend to take (see Table 32.3), of the published research, and of the theoretical and clinical literature.

Multiple Relationships and (Apparent) Conflicts of Interest

When clinicians conduct assessments of patients or therapists who have been involved in extensive (i.e., sexual) boundary and role violations, it is particularly important that the clinician maintain clear boundaries and roles. If, for example, clinicians have previously shared a social, business, or similar relationship with an individual, it would be inappropriate to conduct a formal psychological assessment of that individual.

Personal Background

Clinicians must be alert to their own background to ensure that they are free from or take into account factors that may lead to bias in their evaluations of patients and therapists who have been involved in sexual intimacies. Holroyd and Bouhoutsos (1985), for example, found that therapists who had themselves been sexually intimate with patients tended to see less harm, if any, when assessing patients who had been sexually intimate with *other* therapists. Their finding makes intuitive sense: those who have found ways to rationalize placing their own patients at risk through therapist-patient sexual involvement are likely to have grown adept at minimizing—or failing to see at all—the harm that such involvement can cause. They may also tend to over-identify with other offenders and seek, either consciously or unconsciously, to find ways to exonerate them and allow them to return to practice as soon as possible.

What is less clear is how previous involvement with their own therapist may affect clinicians who conduct assessments of individuals who have been involved in therapist-patient sexual intimacy. The results of a national survey suggested that 2.19 percent of the male clinicians and 4.58 percent of the female clinicians reported engaging in sex, as adults, with their own therapist (Pope & Feldman-Summers, 1992). It is crucial that clinicians who have themselves been sexually exploited in therapy be certain that they have obtained adequate

help for any harm they suffered as a result, that they explore (either personally or with a supervisor or consultant) the ways in which their personal history may affect their clinical work, and that they—like all clinicians—remain alert to the appearance of any bias, countertransference, or other factors that might block or distort the assessment process (see, e.g., Pope, Sonne, & Holroyd, 1993).

Forensic Issues

As part of the initial information gathering, it is useful for the clinician to find out whether the individual was previously, is currently, or anticipates being involved in formal legal, administrative, or similar proceedings. Patients, for example, may have filed a malpractice suit, a complaint leading to criminal charges against the therapist (either in cases in which the patient was a minor, or if the patient was an adult, in those states that have enacted legislation criminalizing therapist-patient sex), a licensing action, and/or complaints with professional or institutional ethics committees.

Awareness of actual or potential forensic issues is necessary and useful in a variety of ways. First, understanding the degree to which forensic issues are or are likely to be present helps the clinician to clarify his or her own role and task. For example, is the requested assessment a clinical evaluation or a forensic evaluation?

Second, awareness of actual or potential forensic aspects can serve as a reminder for the clinician to clarify the question and implications of *who* is the client (see, e.g., Monahan, 1980; Pope, Butcher, & Seelen, 1993; Pope & Vasquez, 1991). For example, is the clinician being retained by the individual therapist or patient or by the therapist's or patient's attorney?

Third, if the assessment involves forensic aspects, the clinician can ensure that he or she practices in accordance with the appropriate professional guidelines for forensic services (see, e.g., APA, 1992, sections 7.01–7.06, p. 1610; Committee on Guidelines for Forensic Psychologists, 1991).

Fourth, awareness of actual or potential forensic aspects can help the clinician to be alert to factors (e.g., the desire to win a malpractice case) that *may* (or may not) influence patients and therapists to be less than completely candid when providing information or to distort their responses on standardized psychological tests.

Fifth, if the assessment is specifically requested as part of legal or other formal complaint proceedings, the clinician will need to clarify the scope of the issues to be considered by the tribunal, board, or committee. Sexual intimacies may be but one component of a malpractice suit. Especially when multiple components of a malpractice suit lead to a request for assessment, the clinician needs to ensure that the detailed history or narrative that the patient or therapist provides covers each component of the suit in the context of the interactions between therapist and patient (e.g., how the professional relationship began, how informed consent was addressed, how the therapist *and* patient assessed the patient's clinical condition and need for intervention, how each session was scheduled, how boundaries were addressed) but also how that history or narrative is reflected in, corroborated by, contradicted by, or ignored in the therapist's records and all other documents and sources of information that are available to the clinician (Pope, 1994).

Sixth, the clinician can ensure that the records of the assessment are adequately detailed and relevant for the purposes to which they may be put. They may, for example, be admitted as evidence in trials and formal hearings. The clinician can ensure that the records meet the relevant legal and professional standards for clinical and/or forensic services (see, e.g., APA, 1992, sections 5.03–5.04 & 5.09–5.11, pp. 1606–1607; Committee on Guidelines for Forensic Psychologists, 1991; Committee on Professional Practice and Standards, 1993).

Seventh, attending to actual or potential forensic aspects should serve as a reminder to the clinician to refrain from attempting to serve in the role of the patient's or therapist's attorney. Relatively few clinicians have adequate legal training and have been admitted to the bar; thus their attempts to provide legal counsel and ad-

vice are inappropriate, may violate state law, and may cause considerable damage to patients or therapists who view them as possessing legal knowledge and skills and who follow their "legal" counsel and advice. Furthermore, even if a clinician has legal training and has been admitted to the bar, to attempt to provide both legal advice or representation *and* to conduct a fair and disinterested psychological assessment constitutes a confusion of roles and relationships. For the patient or therapist who seems to have legal needs that are not currently being filled (e.g., a therapist who has been sued by a patient but who has not yet contacted an attorney) and who looks to the clinician for help, the clinician can make a clear statement about the clarity of roles and a recommendation that the individual promptly contact an attorney who is skilled and experienced in handling cases involving therapist-patient sexual intimacies.

Children and Adolescents

Although individuals who have been involved in therapist-patient sexual intimacies are most often portrayed in the literature as adults, it is important for the clinician planning an assessment to be aware that the patients are sometimes children or adolescents. In one case, for example, a therapist became sexually involved with both a mother and her daughter. One national study of 958 patients reported by their subsequent therapists to have been sexually involved with a previous therapist found that one out of every twenty of these patients was a minor at the time that the sexual involvement occurred (Pope & Vetter, 1991). Another national study found that the average age of minor male patients who had been sexually involved with a therapist was twelve years and six months, with the ages ranging from seven through sixteen (Bajt & Pope, 1989). The average age of minor female patients who had been sexually involved with a therapist was thirteen years and nine months, with the ages ranging from three through seventeen.

If the clinician discovers during the course

of the assessment that a child was involved in the sexual intimacies (e.g., a therapist who discloses that he or she was sexually involved with minor as well as adult patients), it is likely (depending on applicable state law, such circumstances as prior formal reports, etc.) that the clinician will be obligated to file a formal report of suspected child abuse with the appropriate legal authorities. It is important that the individual, either patient or therapist, who is to be evaluated be aware of the possibility of such mandatory reports as part of the informed consent to assessment, which is the next issue to be discussed.

Consent

Whether patient or therapist, the individual who is to be assessed has a right to understand the purpose(s), general methods, implications, and other important aspects of the assessment. Preparing to present this information provides the clinician planning an assessment with an opportunity to ensure that the clinician him- or herself clearly understands the purpose(s) and other vital aspects of the task. *Why* is the assessment being conducted? Is it to see if a patient has been harmed by sexual intimacies with a therapist and, if so, how? Is it to help identify the most promising treatment options for a patient or therapist? Is it to help develop a rehabilitation plan for a therapist? (Note: It is important that both clinician and therapist understand that a "treatment plan" is not identical to a "rehabilitation plan.") Is it to prepare the clinician to provide expert testimony in a legal case? Only by clarifying the task(s) and purpose(s) will the clinician be in a position to plan and conduct an assessment and to provide the individual who is to be assessed with adequate information, explanation, and discussion to allow him or her informed consent or informed refusal of the assessment.

Providing informed consent is *not* simply showering the individual with a large quantity of information in the form of jargon. Providing informed consent is probably better considered as a process of discussion in which the clinician

forms a professional opinion that the individual adequately understands the relevant information that he or she needs to make an informed decision (Pope & Vasquez, 1991). Because a variety of information may be relevant to the individual's decision (e.g., knowledge that there may be some circumstances—such as if the individual discloses child abuse or a homicidal threat against a specific individual—in which the clinician may make a discretionary or a mandated breech of confidentiality), it may be useful for the clinician to supplement the discussion with a written consent form (see, e.g., Pope, 1994; Pope, Butcher, & Seelen, 1993, appendix B: "Sample Informed Consent Form for Conducting Forensic Assessments," pp. 197–199). It is important for the clinician to be aware of any legislation, case law, administrative regulations, or professional standards that may mandate the use of written consent forms in certain jurisdictions or contexts.

Adequacy of the Assessment Sessions

One of the most difficult aspects of conducting an assessment is planning enough sessions to allow an adequate evaluation. When observation, testing, and clinical assessment are limited to an initial session, even if the session lasts several hours, the results and inferences rest on an extremely limited base. Conducting an adequate assessment involving a number of sessions that are spaced over several weeks can help enable both patients and therapists to develop (if possible) adequate trust and rapport with the clinician, allow the clinician to uncover more detailed information that may be crucial to understanding the individual and situation, provide an opportunity to evaluate the consistency of the individual's narrative account and memories as they are explored over time, and aid the clinician in overcoming any strong but misleading positive or negative impressions about the individual. Such misleading impressions may result from a variety of factors including (but not limited to) the individual's conscious or unconscious attempts to dissemble or present a "false front."

Feedback

In planning the assessment and informing the individual about the assessment process, the clinician will find it necessary to anticipate and plan for the form in which feedback will be given. Attending carefully to the feedback process is crucial in light of not only the confusion that can result from misunderstandings (e.g., if the individual finds that the clinician is reluctant to provide the individual with a copy of the formal assessment report and the raw data; if the individual initially learns of the results when listening to the clinician testify in court) but also the effects that feedback can have in such vital areas as, for example, the assessment process itself; thus, the assessment plan needs to include a "feedback plan" that is individualized to the person, the task, the circumstances, and the person's possible reactions to the feedback (see, e.g., Fischer, 1985; Finn & Tonsager, 1992; Gass & Brown, 1992; Pope, 1992; Schafer, 1954).

Exploring Assumptions

Finally, it is important for the clinician to refrain from accepting assumption as fact and to explore any assumptions that he or she may have formed. This chapter addresses the assessment of patients and therapists who have been involved in therapist-patient sexual intimacies. Unless there is clear and sufficient reason to believe that a patient has in fact been sexually involved with a therapist or that a therapist has in fact been sexually involved with a patient, it is crucial that the clinician avoid assuming that the individual's statements in this regard are necessarily accurate. As mentioned previously, clinicians must be aware of sources of bias and ensure that such factors do not distort the assessment process. Some clinicians may, for example, assume that all or virtually all patient claims of exploitation by a therapist are true, or that all or virtually all therapist denials of such involvement are true, or that the extent of harm suffered by a patient or the number of patients with whom a therapist has been involved is al-

ways or virtually always portrayed accurately by the individual. Assumptions reflecting such gross generalizations can prevent a careful and unbiased assessment of a particular individual, whether patient or therapist, and can lead to careless and biased "conclusions" masquerading as the persuasive findings of a scientifically based and professionally conducted formal assessment.

As noted elsewhere, the clinician must assure that there is adequate opportunity to conduct a comprehensive assessment (e.g., recognizing the severe limitations of a single-session evaluation) and that there are adequate sources of reliable information to justify any conclusions. If there is doubt that sexual intimacies actually occurred (e.g., in the absence of an acknowledgment by both therapist and patient that they engaged in sexual intimacies), clinicians are generally ill-equipped to "play detective." In all cases, clinicians must explicitly "indicate any significant reservations they have about the accuracy or limitations of their interpretations" (APA, 1992, p. 1603) in their oral or written reports of assessments.

ISSUES RELEVANT TO THE ASSESSMENT OF PATIENTS

Awareness of the research published in peer-reviewed scientific and professional journals will help clinicians remain alert to some of the more salient issues in evaluating patients who have been sexually involved with a previous therapist.

Patient Background and History

Table 32.4 describes the characteristics of 958 patients reported by their therapists to have been involved with a prior therapist. Such findings suggesting that almost one out of three had experienced child sexual abuse and one out of ten had experienced rape highlight the necessity of taking an extremely careful history and explicitly enquiring about such experiences. Research suggests that such experiences may not be vol-

TABLE 32.4. Characteristics of 958 Patients Who Had Engaged in Sexual Intimacies with a Therapist

	N	%
Patient was a minor at the time of the intimacies	47	5
Patient married the therapist	37	3
Patient had experienced incest or other child sex abuse	309	32
Patient had experienced rape prior to intimacies with therapist	92	10
Patient required hospitalization considered to be at least partially a result of the intimacies	105	11
Patient attempted suicide	134	14
Patient committed suicide	7	1
Patient achieved complete recovery from any harmful effects of intimacies	143	17*
Patient seen pro bono or for reduced fee	187	20
Patient filed formal (e.g., licensing, malpractice) complaint	112	12

Note: Adapted from Pope & Vetter, 1991, p. 431.

*17% of the 866 patients who experienced harm

Copyright © by Division 29 of the American Psychological Association; used with permission.

unteered by patients during routine screenings (Briere & Zaidi, 1989).

The presence of other traumatic events in the individual's history can create additional vulnerabilities that may magnify or aggravate the harm that can result from sexual involvement with a therapist. In such instances, the prior psychological fragility of the patient may in some ways be comparable to the fragile physical condition of someone who has been in one or more serious automobile accidents, suffered extensive trauma, perhaps made great progress in recovery, but still suffers from the sequelae of the previous injuries. Such a previously injured and physically fragile person might suffer much more harm when hit by a car going ten or twenty miles per hour compared with another person of similar age and weight but who is physically healthy and strong (i.e., lacking the physical vulnerability and lingering damages from the previous trauma). Again, knowledge of the research literature is not only an essential component of the clinician's competence but also a helpful resource in understanding potential patterns. One carefully controlled study (in which therapy patients who had engaged in sex with their therapists were compared with matched groups of individuals who had engaged in sex with their nontherapist-physicians and with therapy patients who had not engaged in sex with their therapists), for example, found that the greater prior levels of harm or pathology seemed to be associated with greater negative sequelae from sexual intimacies with a therapist (Feldman-Summers & Jones, 1984; see also Feldman-Summers, 1989). The study found other patterns as well; for example, the marital status of the therapist was systematically associated with the extent of harm.

It is crucial that the clinician read and evaluate such studies that have appeared in the peer-reviewed literature and maintain aware of new studies as they emerge. It is also crucial that the clinician distinguish between new distress or dysfunctions that emerge in regard to the sexual intimacies and the reemergence or exacerbation of previously existing distress or dysfunctions (Pope, 1994).

Patient Responses

As with any psychological assessment, the evaluation of a patient who has experienced sex with a therapist should *never* reflexively conclude that the patient fits a particular modal or common response pattern. However, certain responses appear to be common in such cases and to constitute a therapist-patient sex syndrome (Mann & Winer, 1991; Pope, 1985, 1986, 1988, 1989, 1994; Pope & Bouhoutsos, 1986; Pope, Keith-Spiegel, & Tabachnick, 1986; Pope, Sonne, & Holroyd, 1993; Sonne, 1989). The syndrome "appears to bear similarities to various aspects of borderline (and histrionic) personality disorder, posttraumatic stress disorder, rape response syndrome, reaction to incest, and reaction to child or spouse battering" (Pope, Keith-Spiegel, & Tabachnick, 1986, p. 148). It is, perhaps, unsurprising that responses to therapist-patient sex would be similar in some regards to responses to incest and rape in light of striking

TABLE 32.5 Therapist-Patient Sex Syndrome

Reaction	Comments
1. Ambivalence	Just as victims of incest abuse may experience contradictory impulses to cling to and flee from the abuser, victims of therapist-patient sex may experience contradictory impulses to cling to (and protect) and to flee from the offending therapist
2. Guilt	The irrational guilt is similar to that experienced by many rape and incest victims (who blame themselves and their own behavior); the guilt is irrational because it is always the therapist's responsibility to refrain from sexually exploiting a patient
3. Emptiness and isolation	Patients often feel empty and as if they can only be "filled up" by the offending therapist; even if they cognitively "know" that other patients have been exploited by therapists, they may feel as if they are the only one and as if the experience has separated them forever from the human race and from a normal life
4. Sexual confusion	Patients may come to feel as if their only worth or only way of relating to significant others is sexual
5. Impaired ability to trust	The therapist having violated and exploited a relationship that is founded on deep trust, the patient may find it difficult to trust anyone again
6. Boundary/role disturbance	The therapist having violated one of the most basic and important boundaries and roles, the patient may have difficulty recognizing and maintaining interpersonal boundaries and roles
7. Emotional lability	The patient's emotions may seem out of control; there may be large or frequent mood swings
8. Suppressed rage	Offending therapists are often skillful at directing patients to turn rage back on themselves; patients may become terrified of acknowledging or expressing their anger
9. Increased suicidal risk	Since patients may have suicidal feelings, an extremely careful assessment of suicidal risk should be a part of the assessment of any patient who has been sexually exploited by a therapist
10. Cognitive dysfunction	Dysfunctions may affect particularly the areas of attention and concentration, and may involve intrusive thoughts, unbidden images, flashbacks, and nightmares

Source: Pope, 1985.
Copyright © by American Psychological Association; used with permission.

and often-noted parallels of therapist-patient sex with incest or rape (e.g., Bailey, 1978; Barnhouse, 1978; Bates & Brodsky, 1989; Burgess, 1981; Chesler, 1972; Connel & Wilson, 1974; Dahlberg, 1970; Finkelhor, 1984; Gabbard, 1989; Gilbert & Scher, 1989; Herman, Gartrell, Olarte, Feldstein, & Localio, 1987; Kardener, 1974; Kavoussi & Becker, 1987; Maltz & Holman, 1984; Marmor, 1972; Masters & Johnson, 1976; Redlich, 1977; Russell, 1986; Saul, 1962; Siassi & Thomas, 1973; A. A. Stone, 1990; L. G. Stone; M. Stone, 1976).

The ten elements of therapist-patient sex syndrome (see Table 32.5) seem so frequently to appear in response to sexual involvement with a therapist that a comprehensive assessment needs to address carefully the degree to which each may or may not be present. Careful assessment in these ten areas may be helpful not only in providing a thorough evaluation of the consequences of therapist-patient sexual involvement but also in selecting modalities of treatment (e.g., individual therapy, group therapy) and in monitoring therapeutic outcome. The UCLA Post-Therapy Support Program, established in 1982 to provide group therapy and other services to patients who had been sexually involved with a previous therapist and to create a model for training therapists to work with this population, found, according to Dr. Janet Sonne—who helped establish the program and served as leader of its first therapy group—that the group experience appeared specifically helpful for all clients in alleviating 5 of the 10 major aspects of . . . therapist-patient sex syndrome . . . : emptiness and isolation, guilt, emotional lability or dyscontrol, increased suicidal risk, and cognitive dysfunction (i.e., flashbacks, intrusive thoughts, nightmares). Improvement in the other 5 aspects (impaired ability to trust, ambivalence, suppressed rage, sexual confusion, and identity and role reversal) tended to be more dependent on the specific dynamics of the individual client. (Sonne, 1989, p. 113; see also Sonne, 1987; Sonne, Meyer, Borys, & Marshall, 1985)

Clinician Responses

Finally, the clinician working with an individual who has had sexual intimacies with a therapist may experience a variety of sometimes powerful emotional reactions that, if unattended, may distort the assessment process. Table 32.6 notes some of the more common of these reactions.

ISSUES RELEVANT TO THE ASSESSMENT OF THERAPISTS

While sharing some similarities (which will not be repeated here) with evaluations of patients, assessments of therapists who have been sexually involved with patients also present the clinician with a different set of issues to be addressed.

Focus

As mentioned previously, one of the initial steps in planning an assessment is to clarify the task. It is important to avoid assuming that the psychological assessment of therapists who have sexually exploited their patients will necessarily focus on the offenses. Some offenders may seek therapy, of which a formal psychological assessment constitutes a first step in determining the mode (e.g., individual, group; behavioral, feminist, psychodynamic) as well as the treatment

goals and frequency of sessions, for issues unrelated to the offenses. A therapist, for example, may have exploited numerous patients, never faced a formal complaint, and feel that the violations do not constitute a problem or issue to be addressed in his or her own therapy; he or she may seek an assessment for any of the full range of reasons that anyone might seek such a service (e.g., as part of a general medical and psychological evaluation, a worker's compensation claim, an effort to determine whether counseling might be effective for "problems in living").

Even in instances in which a therapist seeks an evaluation that is to focus on sexual offenses, the focus may not be on rehabilitation. Some therapists, for example, may have found that violating the prohibition against sexually exploiting patients has caused them stress or other psychological difficulties or distress; they may seek assessment or therapeutic services to help them cope with such psychological events but view the services as unrelated to their desire or intention to continue offending. Other therapists may have been horrified at their engaging in sexual exploitation of a patient; they may decide that it is appropriate to discontinue providing therapeutic services and to practice in one or more of the other many areas of the discipline. Whatever the individual therapist's wants and expectations in regard to rehabilitation, it is important that the clinician avoid making reflexive assumptions. Only by careful discussion between the assessing clinician and therapist who seeks an assessment can the focus of the assessment be clarified. The sections that follow address assessments in which the sexual exploitation is a focus of the assessment.

The Attraction

In all aspects of the assessment, the clinician must work with the therapist to arrive at the most accurate understanding possible of why the therapist took each step leading up to, during, and after the sexual intimacies with the patient. What, for example, was the nature of the attraction that the therapist felt for the patient?

TABLE 32.6. Common Clinician Reactions to Victims of Therapist-Patient Sexual Intimacies

1. Disbelief and denial	The tendency to reject reflexively—without adequate data-gathering—allegations about therapist-patient sex (because, e.g., the activities described seem per se outlandish and improbable)
2. Minimization of harm	The tendency to assume reflexively—without adequate data-gathering—that harm did not occur, or that, if it did, the consequences were minimally, if at all, harmful
3. Making the patient fit the textbook	The tendency to assume reflexively—without adequate data gathering and examination—that the patient *must* inevitably fit a particular schema
4. Blaming the victim	The tendency to attempt to make the patient responsible for enforcing the therapist's professional responsibility to refrain from engaging in sex with a patient and holding the patient responsible for the therapist's offense
5. Sexual reaction to the victim	The clinician's sexual attraction to or feelings about the patient; such feelings are normal but must not become a source of distortion in the assessment process
6. Discomfort at the lack of privacy	The clinician's (and sometimes patient's) emotional response to the possibility that under certain conditions (e.g., malpractice, licensing, or similar formal actions against the offending therapist; a formal review of assessment and other services by the insurance company providing coverage for the services) the raw data and the result of the assessment may not remain private
7. Difficulty "keeping the secret"	The clinician's possible discomfort (and other emotional reactions) when he or she has knowledge that an offender continues to practice (and to victimize other patients) but due to confidentiality and/or other constraints, can take no steps to intervene
8. Intrusive advocacy	The tendency to want to guide, direct, or determine a patient's decisions about what steps to take or what steps not to take in regard to a perpetrator
9. Vicarious helplessness	The clinician's discomfort when a patient who has filed a formal complaint seems to encounter unjustifiable obstacles, indifference, lack of fair hearing, and other responses that seem to ignore or trivialize the complaint and fail to protect the public from offenders
10. Discomfort with strong feelings	The clinician's discomfort when experiencing strong feelings (e.g., rage, neediness, or ambivalence) expressed by the patient and focused on the clinician

Note: Adapted from Pope, Sonne, & Holroyd, 1993, pp. 241–261.
Copyright © by American Psychological Association; used with permission.

Table 32.7 presents the nineteen content categories of 997 descriptions provided in a national study of therapists' attraction to patients (Pope, Keith-Spiegel, & Tabachnick, 1986; see also Pope & Tabachnick, 1993). It is interesting to note that some of the descriptions (e.g., "hysterical," "low self-esteem," "paranoid," "narcissistic," "severely disturbed") probably do not fit the common stereotypes of characteristics to which people respond with sexual attraction.

Evaluations of a therapist's attraction to a patient are assessments of what the *therapist* feels and how the *therapist* responds to those feelings or impulses. In some cases the therapist's feelings and perceptions may seem to "fit" the patient, but this does not occur in all cases and perhaps not even in most cases. A therapist's ways of viewing and understanding a patient often involve considerable distortion and may, in extreme cases, seem to have no relationship

TABLE 32.7. Characteristics of Clients to Whom Psychotherapists Are Attracted

Characteristic	Frequency
Physical attractiveness (beautiful, healthy looking, athletic, nicely dressed, etc.)	296
Positive mental/cognitive traits or abilities (intelligent, articulate, insightful, creative, well-educated, etc.)	124
Sexual (sexy, sexual ideal, sexually active, sexual material discussed in therapy, etc.)	88
Vulnerabilities (needy, childlike, sensitive, fragile, etc.)	85
Positive overall character/personality (pleasant, good character, well-mannered, stylish, interesting, without significant pathology, positive outlook, etc.)	84
Kind (nice, warm, open, loving attitude toward children, etc.)	66
Fills therapist's needs (accepting, supportive, boosts therapist's image, touches therapist's vulnerabilities, fills needs for power, alleviates therapist's depression, pressures at home, loneliness, needs for intimacy, etc.)	46
Successful (accomplished, wealthy, from a good background, etc.)	33
"Good patient" (works well in or responds well to therapy, responsible, gratifying to work with, good therapeutic relationship, etc.)	31
Client's attraction (awareness of client being attracted to therapist and/or client's attraction to men or women generally)	30
Independence (self-sufficient, nonconforming, strong, confident, assertive, etc.)	23
Specific personality characteristics not falling into other categories (pleasure-oriented, honest, workaholic, funny, introverted, etc.)	14
Resemblance to someone in therapist's life (like mother, father, spouse, lover, someone from past, etc.)	12
Availability (client unattached)	9
Pathological characteristics (hysterical, low self-esteem, paranoid, narcissistic, severely disturbed, etc.)	8
Long-term client (attraction as part of the nature of long-term therapy)	7
Sociability (sociable, extraverted, etc.)	6
Miscellaneous (close to termination, intimate feelings, client is also a psychologist, age specification, etc.)	15

Source: Pope, Keith-Spiegel, & Tabachnick, 1986, p. 154.
Copyright © by American Psychological Association; used with permission.

whatsoever to the actual patient (see, e.g., Gabbard & Twemlow, 1989). Thus, a therapist may attribute his or her sexual attraction to the patient's exceptionally high IQ whereas the patient's IQ is in fact below average. A therapist may attribute his or her attraction to the patient's seductive behaviors whereas the patient was not engaging in behaviors that most people—including the patient and the evaluating clinician—would consider seductive (Pope, Sonne, & Holroyd, 1993). In all assessments of a therapist's attraction, it is important: (1) to avoid assuming that the therapist's perceptions, descriptions, and attributions about a patient are necessarily accurate; (2) to note—but only when adequate sources of information are available to justify such conclusions—actual or apparent consistencies or discrepancies between the therapist's view of the patient and the actual patient's characteristics and behaviors; and (3)

to seek a comprehensive understanding of the nature, occurrence, dynamics, and implications of the therapist's feelings of attraction regardless of the degree to which they do or do not seem to "fit" the actual patient.

Knowing and Acting

To the degree that the therapist's history of engaging in sex with one or more patients forms a focus of the assessment, it is important to explore the degree to which the therapist assumes responsibility for knowingly placing a patient at risk for serious harm. The prohibition against engaging in sex with a patient is long-standing and widely accepted by the mental health professions. It is not a trivial act. As noted in the previous section on therapist-patient sex syndrome, it is not uncommon for exploited paticnts to experience increased suicidal risk. Research suggests that as many as one out of one hundred such patients actually take their own life (Bouhoutsos et al., 1983; Pope & Vetter, 1991), 11 percent require hospitalization that is judged to be at least partly due to the sexual involvement (Pope & Vetter, 1991; see also Bouhoutsos et al., 1983), and perhaps far less than half seem to reach full recovery (Pope & Vetter, 1991).

What leads an individual who has been extensively trained and subsequently licensed by the state to place someone seeking help at risk for such serious and perhaps fatal consequences? Is it that the therapist did not know that engaging in sex with a patient was clinically, ethically, and legally (e.g., licensing regulations) prohibited? Or is it that the therapist knowingly chose to violate the prohibition and place the patient at risk for severe harm?

To the extent that the assessment process suggests that the therapist was unaware of any prohibition against engaging in sex with a patient, the therapist's graduate education, training, continuing education, professional memberships (which may require adherence to an ethics code that explicitly prohibits sexual involvement with patients), and other professional activities can be reviewed carefully to determine how the therapist remained unaware of the prohibition. It is worth noting that the prohibition against sexually exploiting patients is reflected so clearly and extensively in the professional and popular literature that instances in which a therapist was unaware of the prohibition are virtually nonexistent; however, a therapist's statement that he or she had never heard that therapist-patient sexual intimacies were prohibited should be carefully and fairly explored. A comprehensive assessment also addresses the therapist's understanding of the relationship between his or her lack of knowledge of the prohibition and his or her ethical obligation to be knowledgeable about such basic clinical and ethical principles. The ethics code of the American Psychological Association, for example, states that members "have an obligation to be familiar with this Ethics Code, and other applicable ethics codes, and their application to psy-

chologists' work" (APA, 1992, section 8.01, p. 1610).

To the extent that the assessment process suggests that the therapist, although aware that sexual intimacy with a patient is prohibited, was unable to control his or her behavior (i.e., did not make a choice to violate the prohibition and place the patient at risk for extensive harm), the factors that inhibited the therapist's ability to control his or her behavior can be carefully explored. If there were warning signs or events that might reasonably be construed as creating a condition in which the therapist would not be able to control his or her behavior, the therapist's responses to these signs or events can be carefully assessed. Therapists are trained to be alert to such signs and events and to take adequate steps to ensure that their patients are not placed at risk for harm. Section 1.13 of the "Ethical Principles of Psychologists and Code of Conduct" (APA, 1992), for example, states:

> (a) Psychologists recognize that their personal problems and conflicts may interfere with their effectiveness. Accordingly, they refrain from undertaking an activity when they know or should know that their personal problems are likely to lead to harm to a patient, client, colleague, students, research participant, or other person to whom they may owe a professional or scientific obligation.
> (b) In addition, psychologists have an obligation to be alert to signs of, and to obtain assistance for, their personal problems at an early stage, in order to prevent significantly impaired performance.
> (c) When psychologists become aware of personal problems that may interfere with their performing work-related duties adequately, they take appropriate measures, such as obtaining professional consultation or assistance, and determine whether they should limit, suspend, or terminate their work-related duties. (p. 1601)

Clinicians must be alert to the possibility that there may be instances in which therapists may lose, seemingly through no fault of their own, the ability to know that what they are doing is wrong and/or to control their behavior. A sudden-onset psychosis and certain forms of dementia may, for example, occur with little or no warning and may so significantly impair cognition and/or voluntary motor control that the therapist is essentially out of touch with reality and could not be reasonably held accountable for his or her actions. Such instances, however, must be carefully distinguished from those in which a therapist acts in such a way (e.g., injecting or inhaling cocaine before a therapy session; failing to take ethically required steps when the therapist experiences personal problems or stress) that would make it likely that the therapist would be unable to function adequately and would thereby place patients at risk for significant and perhaps fatal harm.

Finally, if the therapist was both aware of the prohibition and did not suffer some physical, psychotic, or similar disorder rendering him or her unable to control his or her actions, it is important for the clinician to obtain an adequate understanding of the therapist's cognitive functioning, personality, and other factors that enabled the therapist to choose to engage in voluntary behavior that placed the patient at risk for extremely serious harm.

Assessing Perceived Responsibilities to Victims

Again assuming that the violation of the prohibition is a focus of the assessment, it is important to explore the degree to which the therapist perceives any responsibility to those patients who have been sexually exploited and, if so, the degree to which the therapist has acted on that perception. Some therapists may feel no responsibility whatsoever; others may acknowledge some partial responsibility; still others may assume full responsibility for their own actions and take all possible steps to diminish any negative consequences to those affected by the sexual exploitation and to ensure that no future patients are placed at risk for future violations of the prohition.

> An essential part of any genuine rehabilitation is that the offending therapist must work through and come to terms with the specific offense and with the harm done to this particular patient.

Has the offending therapist acknowledged responsibility for sexually exploiting the patient? . . . Has the offending therapist formally apologized to the patient? [For many patients, the offending therapist's direct acknowledgment and apology is a significant factor in the patient's recovery. It addresses many aspects of the damage that the patient may be experiencing. . . .] Has the therapist done all that is reasonable and within his or her power to diminish the damage and promote the recovery of the exploited patient? For many offending therapists, authentic rehabilitation does not begin until this initial necessary step is taken. (Pope, 1989, pp. 133–134)

It is important to note that a therapist may seek rehabilitation even in the absence of any intention to resume practicing therapy. Rehabilitation may be viewed by such therapists as part of their assuming responsibility for the offense, of their working through their feelings about what they have done, and of their preparation for entering into other professional roles that do not involve providing therapy.

The clinician must be aware that any impulses the therapist has to assume responsibility vis-à-vis the victim (e.g., acknowledging responsibility, offering an apology, taking steps to minimize the victim's suffering and to promote the victim's recovery) may be in conflict with other impulses that the therapist is experiencing (e.g., fear, anger, denial) and with the advice of the therapist's attorney. In some instances, the defense strategy in malpractice trials and other formal actions may involve what are essentially attacks on the victim (see, e.g., Bates & Brodsky, 1989; Pope, 1990, 1994). Such competing impulses and influences may (or may not) cause exceptional distress for the therapist.

Exploring the ways in which the therapist experiences and responds to such diverse impulses is a necessary step in conducting a comprehensive assessment. For example, a therapist's choice to violate the prohibition against engaging in sex with a patient is likely to affect many people: not only the patient and the therapist, but also—should they become aware of the violation—the patient's family and friends, the therapist's other current and former patients, the therapist's family and friends, individuals who are considering therapy but who are uncertain whether they can and should trust therapists to help rather than exploit, policy makers who consider whether the current system is adequate to deter those who would exploit patients, the professionals who provide subsequent services to the victim and therapist, and the community of therapists more generally. An adequate assessment includes careful evaluation of the ways in which the therapist thinks and feels about those affected by his or her acts. In what ways, for example, has the therapist's sensitivity to and conceptualization of these various individuals and groups changed over the course of his or her career?

Assessing Perceived Professional Responsibilities

To the degree that the assessment focuses on the offense, it is also important to explore the degree to which the offending therapist feels any responsibility to acknowledge the offense to the appropriate professional or organizational bodies and, if so, to what degree the therapist has acted on that perceived responsibility. Adequate rehabilitation, whether or not the therapist seeks an eventual return to practice, may rest on the degree to which the therapist is able to discontinue efforts— which may include both actions and failures to act—to keep the unethical behavior "secret." For example, has the therapist voluntarily acknowledged the offense to the professional ethics committee and to the state licensing board and agreed to any sanctions or other steps that they might require? Just as a hit-and-run driver may begin to accept responsibility by notifying the police and someone who engages in tax fraud may begin to come to terms with the offense by notifying the government, the therapist who violates the prohibition against therapist-patient sex can begin to accept responsibility by ceasing to hide the fact of the offense. Whatever the therapist's perception of responsibilities in this regard, it is crucial that the clinician conduct a careful exploration and evaluation. It is also crucial that the clinician

conducting the evaluation be familiar with the relevant legal and ethical standards regarding maintaining confidentiality versus discretionary or mandatory disclosure of what the clinician learns from or about the therapist during the course of the evaluation.

As with the impulses noted in the previous section, the therapist may experience conflicting impulses or responsibilities and the therapist's feelings of responsibility may conflict with advice from the therapist's attorney. Again, it is important that the clinician adequately understand how the therapist experiences and responds to any such actual, potential, or apparent conflicts.

If Rehabilitation Is at Issue

As mentioned previously, therapists who have engaged in sex with a patient may seek assessment (and therapy) focusing on the sexual involvement for a variety of reasons other than seeking to return to practice as therapists. Some, however, may ask the clinician conducting the assessment to address issues related to rehabilitation and to participate in the process that may enable the therapist to resume treating patients. Clinicians may become part of this process by, for example, submitting written assessment reports, providing oral feedback to or consulting with a licensing board, or serving as expert witnesses in a administrative law hearing.

Rehabilitation of sexually exploitive therapists involves three distinct but interrelated questions: (1) whether (at least some) therapists who sexually exploit their patients can be rehabilitated; (2) if some sexually exploitive therapists can be rehabilitated, does the profession currently possess strategies for rehabilitation and for assessing rehabilitation that rest on clear, disinterested, and replicated evidence of effectiveness; and (3) if some sexually exploitive therapists can be rehabilitated and if there are adequately validated interventions and assessment methods, should policy support returning offenders to work with vulnerable patients?

The policy issue has not been extensively or conclusively addressed by the profession or the public. One central issue is the level of integrity and trust that the profession needs or wants to affirm and maintain.

> A judge might take a bribe to decide a major case, lose the judgeship, subsequently pay the debt to society through a prison term, and undergo extensive rehabilitation; yet the judge would obviously not resume the bench. A teacher running a preschool might sexually abuse the children, subsequently undergo extensive treatment and rehabilitation and satisfy legal requirements (i.e., jail or probation), and seem to present no threat of further abuse; yet the teacher would not subsequently be granted a license to operate a preschool (unless, of course, the teacher was able to conceal this history of child molesting, perhaps by moving to another state and providing false answers during the application process). If people found to have used their positions of trust to accept bribes for rendering certain legal decisions or to victimize students were allowed to resume the positions of trust that they had betrayed, the nature of those positions—what they mean to the society and to those whose lives they influence—would be profoundly changed. Violation of a clearly understood prohibition against such a grave abuse of power and trust precludes further opportunity to hold these special positions in the legal or educational professions, although numerous other opportunities in law or education (e.g., research, writing, and consultation) remain available to the rehabilitated perpetrator. (Pope, 1990, p. 234)

Clinicians must be aware of such policy issues and the context they create for any assessment of a therapist who seeks to return to practice.

If one assumes that at least some therapists can be rehabilitated and that professional policy should support the return of rehabilitated offenders to practice, then one of the most central questions for the clinician conducting an assessment that will be used as part of the process of returning the therapist to practice is: What evidence is there for the validity (or effectiveness) of the rehabilitation intervention that the therapist undertook and for the methods of assessing its effectiveness? Any serious approach to such issues must not rest upon simple claims

of effectiveness unsupported by evidence. Were simple claims of extensive experience in this area to be accepted as persuasive in regard to phenomena in the area of therapist-patient sex, then the profession might have accepted McCartney's impressive-sounding report of a forty-year study involving 1,500 patients in which McCartney found that therapist-patient sex tended to be beneficial for patients (McCartney, 1966; see Pope & Bouhoutsos, 1986, for a discussion of McCartney's data).

The evidence supporting methods of assessment and rehabilitation must meet minimal standards, such as being independently conducted (i.e., we tend to be less than disinterested evaluators of our own interventions) and replicated. Especially important is the criterion (or criteria) for success of the intervention. It is clear from the literature that a simple absence of formal complaints is a notoriously invalid indicator of whether a therapist has engaged in sex with a patient. A comparison of the estimates of actual therapist-patient sexual involvements as reported by therapists in anonymous surveys with the reported figures of malpractice suits, licensing complaints, and ethics sanctions based on therapist-patient sexual intimacies suggests that the complaints represent a minuscule percentage of the instances of actual involvements. Even the studies of exploited patients who return to therapy and thus have more information and support available to file complaints suggest that for this population of exploited patients, the percentage of those who file complaints is quite low. Furthermore, some of the complaints that *are* filed would never be made known to researchers seeking to investigate whether rehabilitation efforts are successful; for example, many potential or actual malpractice suits are settled in the preliminary stages and involve a secrecy clause in which the actual or potential plaintiff must agree never disclose the identity of the alleged perpetrator.

That only an extremely small percentage of exploited patients file formal complaints creates the notoriously misleading indicator of "success" for completely bogus rehabilitation interventions, as illustrated in the following passage.

A 5-year validation study might examine a seemingly promising but completely worthless rehabilitation method as applied to 10 offenders. Assume that each of the offenders, having completed a comprehensive but ineffective rehabilitation program, will offend again with another patient within the next 5 years of the study. If each of the 10 new victims has only a 5% chance of reporting the offense, then the binomial probabilities indicate that there is a 59.9% likelihood that *none* of them will report. Thus, an impressively presented but completely worthless rehabilitation program has more than a 50% likelihood of demonstrating complete effectiveness, even if *all* of the offenders reoffend with another patient. If the investigator does not take into account the base rate of reporting, he or she might report that the rehabilitation program was 100% successful (i.e., no evidence of any new offenses) when in fact there was 100% recidivism. . . . (Pope, Butcher, & Seelen, 1993, p. 185; see also Pope, 1990)

It is interesting to note that national survey research indicates that most clinicians do *not* believe that therapy mandated by a licensing board (e.g., for instances in which a therapist has violated the standards of practice) is clearly or even likely to be effective (Pope & Tabachnick, 1994).

CONCLUSION: ASSESSING THE ASSESSMENT

This chapter has highlighted a few of the important issues in assessing patients and therapists who have been sexually involved in therapist-patient sex. Although research suggests that only a small minority of exploited patients are knowledgeable about the complaint process and actually file formal complaints (Bouhoutsos et al., 1983; Pope & Vetter, 1991; Vinson, 1987), clinicians may find themselves offering expert testimony about their assessments of sexually involved therapists and patients and may face extensive cross-examination about their knowledge, competence, procedures, and conclusions. Pope, Butcher, and Seelen (1993, pp. 165–186) presented and discussed sixteen

TABLE 32.8. Issues in Assessing Assessments and Assessment Procedures

1. Adequate understanding of studies
2. Relevance
3. Internal consistency
4. Research foundations
5. Consistent application of evaluative criteria
6. Number of investigations
7. Sample size
8. Criteria for "success"
9. Duration
10. Questionable applications
11. Level of effectiveness
12. Reliability and validity
13. Independent verification
14. Ethically questionable practices
15. Peer-reviewed literature
16. Base rate issues

Note: Adapted from Pope, Butcher, & Seelen, 1993, pp. 165–186.

Copyright © by American Psychological Association; used with permission.

cross-examination questions (see Table 32.8 for focus of each question) focusing on assessments of harm for patients and on rehabilitation of offenders in therapist-patient sex cases (as well as an additional sixty-four cross-examination questions addressing more general assessment issues). Even if the assessment will not be part of legal proceedings, clinicians planning and reviewing assessments of patients and therapists who have been involved in therapist-patient sex may find it useful to assess critically their own plans and conclusions (as if they were conducting a cross-examination of themselves and their own work) in light of each of these sixteen issues. Such careful and critical evaluations may help identify potential weaknesses, unjustified assumptions, and subtle errors that might otherwise remain unnoticed.

REFERENCES

Akamatsu, T. J. (1988). Intimate relationships with former clients: National survey of attitudes and behavior among practitioners. *Professional Psychology: Research and Practice, 19,* 454–458.

American Psychological Association. (1992) Ethical principles of psychologists and code of conduct. *American Psychologist, 47,* 1597–1611.

Bailey, K. G. (1978). Psychotherapy or message parlor technology. *Journal of Consulting and Clinical Psychology, 46,* 1502–1506.

Bajt, T. R., & Pope, K. S. (1989). Therapist-patient sexual intimacy involving children and adolescents. *American Psychologist, 44,* 455.

Barnhouse, R. T. (1978). Sex between therapist and patient. *Journal of the American Academy of Psychoanalysis, 6,* 533–546.

Borys, D. S., & Pope, K. S. (1989). Dual relationships between therapist and client: A national study of psychologists, psychiatrists, and social workers. *Professional Psychology: Research and Practice, 20,* 283–293.

Bouhoutsos, J. C., Holroyd, J. C., Lerman, H., Forer, B., & Greenberg, M. (1983). Sexual intimacies between therapists and patients. *Professional Psychology, 14,* 185–196.

Briere, J. & Zaidi, L. Y. (1989). Sexual abuse histories and sequelae in female psychiatric emergency room patients. *American Journal of Psychiatry, 146,* 1602–1606.

Burgess, A. (1981). Physician sexual misconduct and patients' responses. *American Journal of Psychiatry, 136,* 1335–1342.

Butler, R. W., & Williams, D. A. (1985). Description of Ohio State Board of Psychology hearings on ethical violations: From 1972 to the present. *Professional Psychology: Research and Practice, 16,* 502–511.

Butler, S., & Zelen, S. L. (1977). Sexual intimacies between therapists and patients. *Psychotherapy, 14,* 139–145.

Chesler, P. (1972). *Women and madness.* New York: Avon.

Committee on Ethical Guidelines for Forensic Psychologists. (1991). Specialty guidelines for forensic psychologists. *Law and Human Behavior, 15,* 655–665.

Committee on Professional Practice and Standards, Board of Professional Affairs, American Psychological Association. (1993). *Record keeping guidelines.* Washington, DC: American Psychological Association.

Connel, N. & Wilson, C. (Eds.). (1974). *Rape: The first sourcebook for women.* New York: New American Library.

Cummings, N. A., & Sobel, S. B. (1985). Malpractice insurance: Update on sex claims. *Psychotherapy, 22,* 186–188.

Dahlberg, C. C. (1970). Sexual contact between patient and therapist. *Contemporary Psychoanalysis, 5,* 107–124.

Feldman-Summers, S. (1989). Sexual contact in fiduciary relationships. In G. O. Gabbard (Ed.), *Sexual exploitation in professional relationships* (pp. 193–209). Washington, DC: American Psychiatric Press.

Feldman-Summers, S., & Jones, G. (1984). Psychological impacts of sexual contact between therapists or other health care practitioners and their clients. *Journal of Consulting and Clinical Psychology, 52,* 1054–1061.

Finkelhor, D. (1984). *Child sexual abuse: New theory and research.* New York: Free Press.

Finn, S., & Tonsager, M. (1992). Therapeutic effects of providing MMPI-2 test feedback to college students awaiting therapy. *Psychological Assessment, 4,* 278–287.

Fischer, C. T. (1985). *Individualizing psychological assessment.* Monterey, CA: Brooks/Cole.

Gabbard, G. (Ed.) (1989). *Sexual exploitation in professional relationships.* Washington, DC: American Psychiatric Association.

Gartrell, N., Herman, J., Olarte, S., Feldstein, M., & Localio, R. (1986). Psychiatrist-patient sexual contact: Results of a national survey, I: Prevalence. *American Journal of Psychiatry, 143,* 1126–1131.

Gartrell, N., Herman, J., Olarte, S., Feldstein, M., & Localio, R. (1987). Reporting practices of psychiatrists who knew of sexual misconduct by colleagues. *American Journal of Orthopsychiatry, 57,* 287–295.

Gartrell, N. K., Milliken, N., Goodson, W. H., Thiemann, S., & Lo, B. (1992). Physician-patient sexual contact: Prevalence and problems. *Western Journal of Medicine, 157,* 139–143.

Gass, C. S., & Brown, M. C. (1992). Neuropsychological test feedback to patients with brain dysfunction. *Psychological Assessment, 4,* 272–277.

Gilbert, L. A., & Scher, M. (1989). The power of an unconscious belief. *Professional Practice of Psychology, 8,* 94–108.

Herman, J. L., Gartrell, N., Olarte, S., Feldstein, M., & Localio, R. (1987). Psychiatrist-patient sexual contact: Results of a national survey, II: Psychiatrists' Attitudes. *American Journal of Psychiatry, 144,* 164–169.

Holroyd, J. C., & Brodsky, A. M. (1977). Psychologists' attitudes and practices regarding erotic and nonerotic physical contact with patients. *American Psychologist, 32,* 843–849.

Kardener, S. H. (1974). Sex and the physician-patient

relationship. *American Journal of Psychiatry, 131*, 1134–1136.

Maltz, W., & Holman, B. (1984). *Incest and sexuality*. Lexington, MA: Lexington Books.

Mann, C. K., & Winer, J. D. (1991). Psychotherapist's sexual contact with client. *American Jurisprudence Proof of Facts*, 3rd series (Vol. 14, pp. 319–431). Rochester, NY: Lawyers Cooperative Publishing.

Marmor, J. (1972). Sexual acting out in psychotherapy. *American Journal of Psychoanalysis, 32*, 327–335.

Masters, W. H., & Johnson, V. E. (1976). Principles of the new sex therapy. *American Journal of Psychiatry, 110*, 3370–3373.

McCartney, J. (1966). Overt transference. *Journal of Sex Research, 2*, 227–237.

Monahan, J. (Ed.) (1980). *Who is the client? The ethics of psychological intervention in the criminal justice system*. Washington, DC: American Psychological Association.

Pope, K. S. (1985, August). *Diagnosis and treatment of Therapist-Patient Sex Syndrome*. Paper presented at the annual meeting of the American Psychological Association, Los Angeles.

Pope, K. S. (1986, May). *Therapist-Patient Sex Syndrome: Research findings*. Paper presented at the annual meeting of the American Psychiatric Association, Washington, DC.

Pope, K. S. (1988). How clients are harmed by sexual contact with mental health professionals. *Journal of Counseling and Development, 67*, 222–226.

Pope, K. S. (1989a). Rehabilitation of therapists who have been sexually intimate with a patient. In G. O.. Gabbard (Ed.), *Sexual exploitation in professional relationships* (pp. 129–136). Washington, DC: American Psychiatric Press.

Pope, K. S. (1989b). Therapist-Patient Sex Syndrome: A guide for attorneys and subsequent therapists to assessing damage. In G. O.. Gabbard (Ed.), *Sexual exploitation in professional relationships* (pp. 39–56). Washington, DC: American Psychiatric Press.

Pope, K. S. (1990). Therapist-patient sex as sex abuse: Six scientific, professional, and practical dilemmas in addressing victimization and rehabilitation. *Professional Psychology: Research and Practice, 21*, 227–239.

Pope, K. S. (1992). Responsibilities in providing psychological test feedback to clients. *Psychological Assessment, 4*, 268–271.

Pope, K. S. (1993). Licensing disciplinary actions for psychologists who have been sexually involved with a client: Some information about offenders. *Professional Psychology: Research and Practice, 24*, 374–377.

Pope, K. S. (1994). *Patients who have been sexually involved with a therapist: Assessment, therapy, forensics*. Washington, DC: American Psychological Association.

Pope, K. S., & Bouhoutsos, J. C. (1986). *Sexual intimacies between therapists and patients*. New York: Praeger/Greenwood.

Pope, K. S., Butcher, J. N., & Seelen, J. (1993). *The MMPI, MMPI-2, and MMPI-A in court: A practical guide for expert witnesses and attorneys*. Washington, DC: American Psychological Association.

Pope, K. S., & Feldman-Summers, S. (1992). National survey of psychologists' sexual and physical abuse history and their evaluation of training and competence in these areas. *Professional Psychology: Research and Practice, 23*, 353–361.

Pope, K. S., Keith-Spiegel, P., & Tabachnick, B. G. (1986). Sexual attraction to clients: The human therapist and the (sometimes) inhuman training system. *American Psychologist, 41*, 147–158.

Pope, K. S., Levenson, H., & Schover, L. R. (1979). Sexual intimacy in psychology training: Results and implications of a national survey. *American Psychologist, 34*, 682–689.

Pope, K. S., Sonne, J. L., & Holroyd, J. (1993). *Sexual feelings in psychotherapy: Explorations for therapists and therapists-in-training*. Washington, DC: American Psychological Association.

Pope, K. S., & Tabachnick, B. G. (1993). Therapists' anger, hate, fear, and sexual feelings: National survey of therapists responses, client characteristics, critical events, formal complaints, and training. *Professional Psychology: Research and Practice, 24*, 142–152.

Pope, K. S., & Tabachnick, B. G. (1994). Therapists as patients. A national survey of psychologists' experiences, problems, and beliefs. *Professional Psychology: Research and Practice, 25*, 247–258.

Pope, K. S., Tabachnick, B. G., & Keith-Spiegel, P. (1987). Ethics of practice: The beliefs and behaviors of psychologists as therapists. *American Psychologist, 12*, 993–1006.

Pope, K. S., & Vasquez, M. J. T. (1991). *Ethics in psychotherapy and counseling: A practical guide for psychologists*. San Francisco: Jossey-Bass.

Pope, K. S., & Vetter, V. A. (1991). Prior therapist-patient sexual involvement among patients seen by psychologists. *Psychotherapy, 28*, 429–438.

Redlich, F. C. (1977). The ethics of sex therapy. In

W. H. Masters, V. E. Johnson, & R. D. Kolodny (Eds.), *Ethical issues in sex therapy* (pp. 143–157). Boston: Little, Brown.

Russell, D. E. H. (1986). *The secret trauma: Incest in the lives of girls and women.* New York: Basic Books.

Saul, L. J. (1962). The erotic transference. *Psychoanalytic Quarterly, 31,* 54–61.

Shafer, R. (1954). *Psychoanalytic interpretation in Rorschach testing: Theory and application.* New York: Grune & Stratton.

Siassi, I., & Thomas, M. (1973). Physicians and the new sexual freedom. *American Journal of Psychiatry, 130,* 1256–1257.

Stone, A. A. (1990, March). No good deed goes unpunished. *The Psychiatric Times,* pp. 24–27.

Stone, L. G. (1980). *A study of the relationship among anxious attachment, ego functioning, and female patients' vulnerability to sexual involvement with their male psychotherapists.* Unpublished doctoral dissertation, California School of Professional Psychology, Los Angeles.

Stone, M. (1976). Boundary violations between therapist and patient. *Psychiatric Annals, 6,* 670–677.

Sonne, J. L. (1987). Proscribed sex: Counseling the patient subjected to sexual intimacy by a therapist. *Medical Aspects of Human Sexuality, 16,* 18–23.

Sonne, J. L. (1989). An example of group therapy for victims of therapist-client sexual intimacy. In G. O.. Gabbard (Ed.), *Sexual exploitation in professional relationships* (pp. 101–127). Washington, DC: American Psychiatric Press.

Sonne, J. L., Meyer, C. B., Borys, D., & Marshall, V. (1985). Clients' reaction to sexual intimacy in therapy. *American Journal of Orthopsychiatry, 55,* 183–189.

Stake, J. E., & Oliver, J. (1991). Sexual contact and touching between therapist and client: A survey of psychologists' attitudes and behavior. *Professional Psychology: Research and Practice, 22,* 297–307.

Vinson, J. S. (1987). Use of complaint procedures in cases of therapist-patient sexual contact. *Professional Psychology: Research and Practice, 18,* 159–164.

Appendix: Index of Psychological Tests and Procedures

ALCOHOL USE INVENTORY

Characteristics Assessed

The client's perceptions about four dimensions of alcohol use and abuse, including benefits derived from drinking; styles of drinking; consequences of drinking; and concerns associated with alcohol use.

Publisher

National Computer Systems
PO Box 1416
Minneapolis, MN 55440

The test is self-administered.

The test is computer-scorable and can be interpreted by computer.

Key References

National Computer Systems
PO Box 1416
Minneapolis, MN 55440

ALZHEIMERS'S DISEASE ASSESSMENT SCALE

Characteristics Assessed

Cognitive functions including memory, language and praxis; noncognitive functions including mood state and behavioral changes.

If Unpublished, where Test can be Obtained

Dr. Richard C. Mohs, Psychiatry Services (116A)
VA Medical Center
130 West Kingsbridge Road
Bronx, NY 10468

The test is not self-administered and usually takes about 45 minutes.
The administration cannot be delegated to clerical or nursing staff.

Key References

Rosen, W. G., Mohs, R. C., & Davis, K. L. (1984). A new rating scale for Alzheimer's Disease. *American Journal of Psychiatry, 141,* 1356–1364.

ANXIETY DISORDERS INTERVIEW SCHEDULE—REVISED

Characteristics Assessed

Assesses the severity of anxious syndromes and their accompanying mood states.

Publisher

Graywind Publications
1535 Western Ave.
Albany, NY 12203

The test is not self-administered and usually takes about 3 to 3/12 hours.
The administration procedure cannot be delegated to clerical or nursing staff.

The test is not computer-scorable and cannot be interpreted by computer.

Key References

DiNardo, P. A., & Barlow, D. H. (1988). Anxiety Disorders Interview Schedule—Revised (ADIS-R). Albany, NY: Graywind.

DiNardo, P. A., O'Brien, G. T., Barlow, D. H., Waddell, M. T., & Blanchard, E. B. (1983). Reliability of DSM-III anxiety disorder categories using a new structured interview. *Archives of General Psychiatry, 40,* 1070–1074

ANXIETY SENSITIVITY INDEX (ASI)

Characteristics Assessed

Assesses the negative consequences of the experience of anxiety.

If Unpublished, where Test can be Obtained

Steven Reiss
Department of Psychology
University of Illinois at Chicago
Chicago, IL 60064

The test is self-administered and usually takes about 10 minutes.
The administration procedure can be delegated to clerical or nursing staff.

The test is not computer-scorable and cannot be interpreted by computer.

Key References

Reiss, S., Peterson, R. A., Gursky, D. M., & McNally, R. J. (1986). Anxiety sensitivity, anxiety frequency and the prediction of fearfulness. *Behavior Research and Therapy, 24,* 1–8.

Taylor, S., Koch, W. J., & Crokett, D. J. (1991). Anxiety sensitivity, trait anxiety, and the anxiety disorders. *Journal of Anxiety Disorders, 5,* 293–311.

BASIC PERSONALITY INVENTORY (BPI)

Characteristics Assessed

Dimensions of psychopathology (e.g., Hypochondriasis, Anxiety, Depression, Thinking Disorder, etc.) divided into 11 clinical scales.

Publisher

Sigma Assessment Systems, Inc.
PO Box 610984
Port Huron, MI 48061-0984

The test is self-administered and usually takes about 35 to 40 minutes.
The administration can be delegated to clerical or nursing staff.

The test is computer-scorable and can be interpreted by computer.

The address of the official computer scoring and interpretation service is:

Sigma Assessment Systems, Inc.
PO Box 610984
Port Huron, MI 48061-0984

Key References

Jackson, D. N. (1988). *Basic Personality Inventory: BPI Manual.* Port Huron, MI: Sigma Assessment Systems, Inc.

BECK ANXIETY INVENTORY (BAI)

Characteristics Assessed

Self-report measure of anxiety symptomatology.

Publisher

Psychological Corporation
PO Box 9959
San Antonio, TX 78204-0959

The test is self-administered and usually takes about 10 minutes.
The administration can be delegated to clerical or nursing staff.

The test is not computer-scorable and cannot be interpreted by computer.

Key References

Beck, A. T., Epstein, N., Brown, G., & Steer, R. A. (1988). An inventory for measuring clinical anxiety: Psychometric properties. *Journal of Consulting and Clinical Psychology, 56,* 893–897.
Eydrich, T., Dowdall, D., & Chambless, D. L. (1992). Reliability and validity of the Beck Anxiety Inventory. *Journal of Anxiety Disorders, 6,* 55–61.

BECK DEPRESSION INVENTORY (BDI)

Characteristics Assessed

Depression.

Publisher

Psychological Corporation
PO Box 9959
San Antonio, TX 78204-0959

The test is self-administered and usually takes about 10 to 15 minutes.
The administration can be delegated to clerical or nursing staff.

The test is computer-scorable and can (a brief narrative) be interpreted by computer.

Other important features

21 four-choice statements

Key References

Beck, A. T., Ward, C. H., Mendelson, M., et al. (1961). An inventory for measuring depression. *Archives of General Psychiatry, 4,* 561–571.
Beck, A. T. (1987). *Beck Depression Inventory: Manual.* San Antonio, Texas: Psychological Corporation.

CLINICIAN ADMINISTERED PTSD SCALE (CAPS)

Characteristics Assessed

Assesses the severity and frequency of PTSD symptoms.

If Unpublished, where Test can be Obtained

Dr. Dudley David Blake
Psychology Services (116B)
Boston VAMC
150 South Huntington Ave.
Boston, MA 02130

The test is not computer-scorable and cannot be interpreted by computer.

Key References

Blake, D. D., Weathers, F. W., Nagy, L. M, Kaloupek, D. G., Klauminzer, G., Charney, D., & Keane, T. (1990). A clinician rating scale for as sessing current and lifetime PTSD: The CAPS-1. *The Behavior Therapist*, *13*, 137–188.

CLINICAL FREQUENCIES RECORDING SYSTEM (CFRS)

Characteristics Assessed

Low-frequency critical events and totally setting-dependent behavior of clients and staff in inpatient and residential treatment settings.

Publisher

Research Press
PO Box 9177
Champaign, IL 61826

The test is computer-scorable but cannot be interpreted by computer.

Other Important Features

A set of forms for completion by clinical staff as part of ongoing service delivery, specifically for a comprehensive social-learning program, but adaptable to other programs. Higher-order functioning scores are derived across forms to provide weekly "rate-per-opportunity."

Key References

Paul, G. L., & Shelite, I. (in press-a). *The Clinical Frequency Recording System (CFRS): Social-Learning Program Forms: Supplement to G. L. Paul & R. J. Lentz, Psychosocial Treatment of Chronic Mental Patients* (2nd Ed.). Champaign, IL: Research Press.
Redfield, J. P. (1979). Clinical Frequencies Recording Systems: Standardizing Staff Observations by Event Recording. *Journal of Behavioral Assessment*, *1*, 211–219.

COGNITIVE COPING STRATEGY INVENTORY (CCSI)

Characteristics Assessed

Seven scales assessing various reactions for coping with pain.

If Unpublished, where Test can be Obtained

See Butler et al. (1989).

The test is self-administered and usually takes about 10 to 12 minutes.
The administration can be delegated to clerical or nursing staff.

The test is not computer-scorable and cannot be interpreted by computer.

Key References

Butler, R. W., Damarin, F. L., Beaulieu, C., Schwebel, A. I., & Thorn, B. E. (1989). Assessing cognitive coping strategies for acute postsurgical pain. *Psychological Assessment*, *1*, 41–45.

COLUMBIA UNIVERSITY SCALE FOR PSYCHOPATHOLOGY

Characteristics Assessed

(Designed for Alzheimer patients): delusions, hallucinations, illusion, behavioral disturbance (aggression, wandering away, restlessness, confusion), vegetative symptoms of depression.

If Unpublished, where Test can be Obtained

Dr. D. P. Devarand
New York State Psychiatric Institute
722 West 168th Street
New York, NY 10032

The test is not self-administered and usually takes about 10 to 25 minutes.

The administration can be administered by a trained lay interviewer.

The test is not computer-scorable and cannot be interpreted by computer.

Other important features

This is a semistructured interview instrument that focuses on symptoms occurring during the past year.

Key References

Devarand, D. P., Miller, L., Richards, M., Marder, K., Bell, K., Mayeux, R., & Stern, Y. (1992). The Columbia University Scale for Psychopathology in Alzheimer's Disease. *Archives of Neurology, 49,* 371–376.

COMPREHENSIVE ASSESSMENT AND REFERRAL EVALUATION (CARE)

Characteristics Assessed

Psychiatric, medical, nutritional, economic, and social problems of the older person.

The test is not computer-scorable and cannot be interpreted by computer.

Other Important Features

Clinician rating scale

Key References

Gurland, B., Kuriansky, J., Sharpe, L., Simar, R., Stiller, P., & Birkett, P. (1977–1978). The Comprehensive Assessment and Referral Evaluation (CARE)—Rationale, development and reliability. *International Journal of Aging and Human Development, 8,* 9–42.

COMPUTERIZED TSBC/SRIC PLANNED-ACCESS OBSERVATIONAL INFORMATION SYSTEM

Characteristics Assessed

Incorporates all characteristics assessed by component Direct Observational Coding (DOC) instruments—the Time-Sample Behavioral Checklist (TSBC) and the Staff-Resident Interaction Chronograph (SRIC)—as well as biographical data for ongoing assessment of functioning and effectiveness of clients, staff, and treatment programs in inpatient/residential facilities.

Publisher

Research Press
PO Box 9177
Champaign, IL 61826

The test is not self-administered.
The administration can be delegated to clerical or nursing staff (see below).

The test is computer-scorable but cannot be interpreted by computer.

The address of the official computer scoring and interpretation service is:

Paul (1994b) contains all computer programs and file-management procedures for retrieving and scoring standard reports on an ongoing basis.

Other Important Features

Uses full-time technician-level observers and clerical staff for data collection. An ongoing system, with integrated training materials and procedures for all levels of staff to support collection, monitoring, processing, retrieval, distribution, and interpretation of information on clients, staff, and treatment programs in mental hospitals and community facilities.

Key References

Paul, G. L. (Ed.) (1994a). *Observational assessment instrumentation for service and research—The Computerized TSBC/SRIC Planned-Access Information System: Assessment in residential treatment settings* (Part 4). Champaign, IL: Research Press.

Paul, G. L. (Ed.) (1994b). *Observational assessment instrumentation for service and research—The TSBC/SRIC System implementation package: Assessment in residential treatment settings* (Part 5). Champaign, IL: Research Press.

CONSTRUCTIVE THINKING INVENTORY (CTI)

Characteristics Assessed

Six coping dimensions: emotional coping, behavioral coping, categorical thinking, superstitious thinking, naive optimism, and negative thinking.

If Unpublished, where Test can be Obtained

Dr. Seymour Epstein
Department of Psychology
University of Massachusetts
Amherst, MA 01003

The test is self-administered and usually takes about 15 minutes.
The administration can be delegated to clerical or nursing staff.

The test is not computer-scorable and cannot be interpreted by computer.

Key References

Epstein, S., & Meier, P. (1989). Constructive thinking: A broad coping variable with specific components. *Journal of Personality and Social Psychology, 57*, 332–350.

COPE SCALE

Characteristics Assessed

Thirteen basic coping styles.

If Unpublished, where Test can be Obtained

Dr. Charles S. Carver
PO Box 248185
University of Miami
Coral Gables, FL 33124

The test is self-administered and usually takes about 15 minutes.
The administration can be delegated to clerical or nursing staff.

The test is not computer-scorable and cannot be interpreted by computer.

Key References

Carver, C. S., Scheier, M. F., & Weintraub, J. K. (1989). Assessing coping strategies: A theoretically based approach. *Journal of Personality and Social Psychology, 56*, 267–283.

COPING WITH HEALTH, INJURIES, AND PROBLEMS SCALE (CHIP)

Characteristics Assessed

Four basic coping reactions or strategies that may be used in a cross-section of health problem situations (distraction coping, palliative coping, instrumental coping, and negative emotion coping).

If Unpublished, where Test can be Obtained

Dr. Norman S. Endler
Department of Psychology
4700 Keele Street
York University
North York, Ontario M3J 1P3 Canada

The test is self-administered and usually takes about 8 to 10 minutes.
The administration can be delegated to clerical or nursing staff.

The test is not computer-scorable and cannot be interpreted by computer.

Key References

Endler, N. S., & Parker, J. D. A. (1992). Toward a reliable and valid method for multidimensional assessment of coping with health problems. Paper presented at the annual meeting of the Canadian Psychological Association, Quebec City, Quebec, Canada, June.
Endler, N. S., Parker, J. D. A., & Summerfeldt, L. J. (1993b). Coping with health problems: Developing a reliable and valid multidimensional measure. Manuscript submitted for publication.

COPING INVENTORY FOR STRESSFUL SITUATIONS (CISS)

Characteristics Assessed

Task-oriented coping style, emotion-oriented coping style, and avoidance-oriented coping style

Publisher

Multi-Health Systems Inc.
908 Niagara Falls Blvd
North Tonawanda, NY 14120-2060

The test is self-administered and usually takes about 10 minutes.
The administration can be delegated to clerical or nursing staff.

The test is computer-scorable and can be interpreted by computer.

The address of the official computer scoring and interpretation service is:

Multi-Health Systems

Other Important Features

Adult and adolescent versions of the CISS are available

Key References

Endler, N. S., & Parker, J. D. A. (1990a). *Coping Inventory for Stressful Situations (CISS): Manual.* Toronto: Multi-Health Systems.

COPING RESOURCES INVENTORY (CRI)

Characteristics Assessed

Five "personal resources" variables: cognitive resources, social resources, emotional resources, spiritual/philosophical resources, and physical resources.

Publisher

Consulting Psychologists Press
3803 E. Bayshore Road
Palo Alto, CA 94303-9608

The test is self-administered and usually takes about 10 minutes.
The administration can be delegated to clerical or nursing staff.

The test is not computer scorable and cannot be interpreted by computer.

Key References

Hammer, A. L., & Marting, M. S. (1988). *Manual for the Coping Resources Inventory.* Palo Alto, CA: Consulting Psychologists Press.

COPING STRATEGY INDICATOR (CSI)

Characteristics Assessed

Three basic coping reactions or strategies that may be used in a cross-section of stressful situations (problem-solving coping, seeking social-support coping, and avoidance coping).

If Unpublished, where Test can be Obtained

Dr. James H. Amirkhan
Department of Psychology
California State University
Long Beach, CA 90840

The test is self-administered and usually takes about 8 to 10 minutes.
The administration can be delegated to clerical or nursing staff.

The test is not computer-scorable and cannot be interpreted by computer.

Key References

Amirkhan, J. H. (1990). A factor analytically derived measure of coping: The Coping Strategy Indicator. *Journal of Personality and Social Psychology*, 59, 1066–1074.

DEFENSE MECHANISM INVENTORY (DMI)

Characteristics Assessed

Five defense mechanism clusters ("turning against the self," "turning against the object," "projection," "reversal," and "principalization."

Publisher

PAR, Inc.
PO Box 998
Odessa, FL 33556

The test is self-administered and usually takes about 30 minutes.
The administration can be delegated to clerical or nursing staff.

The test is not computer-scorable and cannot be interpreted by computer.

Key References

Gleser, G. C., & Ihilevich, D. (1969). An objective instrument for measuring defense mechanisms. *Journal of Consulting and Clinical Psychology*, 33, 51–60.
Ihilevich, D., & Gleser, G. C. (1986). *Defense mechanisms. Their classification, correlates, and measurement with the Defense Mechanisms Inventory*. Owosso, MI: DMI Associates.

DEFENSE MECHANISM RATING SCALES (DMRS)

Characteristics Assessed

Thirty defense mechanisms that can be classified into four basic defense clusters: immature defenses, borderline defenses, neurotic defenses, and mature defenses.

If Unpublished, where Test can be Obtained

Dr. J. Christopher Perry
Department of Psychiatry
Cambridge Hospital
1493 Cambridge StreetCambridge, MA 02139

The test is not self-administered and usually takes several hours (depending on the type of clinical material used).
The administration cannot be delegated to clerical or nursing staff.

The test is not computer-scorable and cannot be interpreted by computer.

Other Important Features

The DMRS is an observer-rated defense mechanism measure.

Key References

Perry, J. C., & Cooper, S. H. (1989). An empirical study of defense mechanisms. I. Clinical interview and life vignette ratings. *Archives of General Psychiatry, 46,* 444–452.

DEFENSE STYLE QUESTIONNAIRE (DSQ)

Characteristics Assessed

Three defense mechanism clusters: "mature defenses," "immature defenses," and "neurotic defenses."

If Unpublished, where Test can be Obtained

Included as an appendix in Vaillant, G. E. (1986). *Empirical studies of ego mechanisms of defense.* Washington, DC: American Psychiatric Press.

The test is not self-administered and usually takes about 15 minutes.
The administration can be delegated to clerical or nursing staff.

The test is not computer-scorable and cannot be interpreted by computer.

Key References

Andrews, G., Singh, M., & Bond, M. (1993). The defense style questionnaire. *Journal of Nervous and Mental Disease, 181,* 246–256.
Bond, M. (1986). An empirical study of defense styles. In G. E. Vaillant (Ed.), *Empirical studies of ego mechanisms of defense* (pp. 1–29). Washington, DC: American Psychiatric Press.

DEMENTIA RATING SCALE

Characteristics Assessed

Attention, perseveration (both verbal and motor), drawing ability, verbal and nonverbal abstraction, and verbal and nonverbal short-term memory.

If Unpublished, where Test can be Obtained

Dr. Steven Mattirs
Department of Neurology
Montefiore Hospital and Medical Center
    and the Albert Einstein College of
    Medicine
Bronx, NY 10475

The test is not self-administered and usually takes about 10 to 15 minutes with normal elderly patients, 30 to 45 minutes with dementia patients.
The administration cannot be delegated to clerical or nursing staff.

Key References

Coblentz, J. M., Mattirs, S., Zingesser, L. H., Kasoff, S. S., Wisniewski, H. M., and Katzman, R. (1973). Pre-senile dementia: Clinical aspects and evaluations of cerebrospinal fluid dynamics. *Archives of Neurology, 29,* 299–308.
Montgomery, K. M. (1982). *A normative study of neuropsychological test performance of a normal elderly sample.* Unpublished Master's thesis. University of Victoria, British Columbia, Canada.

DIAGNOSTIC INTERVIEW FOR NARCISSISM

Characteristics Assessed

Narcissistic personality disorder

If Unpublished, where Test can be Obtained

Dr. John Gunderson
McLean Hospital
115 Mill Street
Belmont, MA 02178

The test is not self-administered and usually takes about 1 to 3 hours.

The administration cannot be delegated to clerical or nursing staff.

The test is not computer-scorable and cannot be interpreted by computer.

Other Important Features

Semistructured interview

Key References

Gunderson, J. G., Ronningstam, E., & Bodkin, A. (1990). The diagnostic interview for narcissistic patients. *Archives of General Psychiatry, 47,* 676–680.

DIAGNOSTIC INTERVIEW FOR PERSONALITY DISORDERS

Characteristics Assessed

Personality disorders.

If Unpublished, where Test can be Obtained

Dr. John Gunderson
McLean Hospital
115 Mill Street
Belmont, MA 02178

The test is not self-administered and usually takes about 1 to 3 hours.
The administration cannot be delegated to clerical or nursing staff.

The test is not computer scorable and cannot be interpreted by computer.

Other Important Features

Semistructured interview

Key References

Zanarini, M., Frankenburg, F. R., Chauncey, D. L., & Gunderson, J. G. (1987). The Diagnostic Interview for Personality Disorders: Interrater and test-retest reliability. *Comprehensive Psychiatry, 28,* 467–480.

DIMENSIONAL ASSESSMENT OF PERSONALITY PATHOLOGY—BASIC QUESTIONNAIRE

Characteristics Assessed

Maladaptive personality traits.

If Unpublished, where Test can be Obtained

Dr. John W. Livesley
Department of Psychiatry
University of British Columbia
2255 Wesbrook Mall
Vancouver, BC V6T 2A1 Canada

The test is self-administered and usually takes about 45 minutes.
The administration can be delegated to clerical or nursing staff.

The test is computer-scorable but cannot be interpreted by computer.

Key References

Schroeder, M. L., Wormworth, J. A., & Livesley, W. J. (1992). Dimensions of personality disorder and their relationship to the Big Five dimensions of personality. *Psychological Assessment, 4,* 47–53.

EARLY MEMORIES PROCEDURE

Characteristics Assessed

Contents: five spontaneous early memories; the clearest or most important memory lifetime; 15 directed memories (some early, some lifetime), including most traumatic memories. Assesses: major unresolved issue currently in process.

Publisher

Dr. Arnold R. Bruhn
7910 Woodmont Ave #1300
Bethesda, MD 20814

The test is self-administered and usually takes about 5 minutes for psychologists.

The test is not computer-scorable and cannot be interpreted by computer.

Other Important Features

Assesses clinically relevant aspects of autobiographical memory. Functions as a "hub" technique for other "spare" procedures, such as Memories of Spouse procedure.

Key References

Bruhn, A. R. (1990). *Earliest childhood memories: Theory and Application to Clinical Practice.* New York: Praeger

Bruhn, A. R. (1992a). The Early Memories Procedure: A projective test of autobiographical memory, Part 1. *Journal of Personality Assessment, 58,* 1–15.

Bruhn, A. R. (1992b). The Early Memories Procedure: A projective test of autobiographical memory, Part 2. *Journal of Personality Assessment, 58,* 326–346.

FEAR SURVEY SCHEDULE—III (FSS-III)

Characteristics Assessed

Self-report inventory of fears common among phobics.

The test is self-administered and usually takes about 20 minutes.
The administration can be delegated to clerical or nursing staff.

The test is not computer-scorable and cannot be interpreted by computer.

Key References

Wolpe, J., & Lang, P. J. A Fear Survey Schedule for use in behavior therapy. *Behavior Research and Therapy, 2,* 27–30.

Arrindell, W. A., & van der Ende, J. (1986). Further evidence for cross-sample invariance of phobic factors: Psychiatric inpatient ratings on the Fear Survey Schedule. *Behavior Research and Therapy, 24,* 289–297.

FUNCTIONAL ASSESSMENT INVENTORY (FAI)

Characteristics Assessed

Functional information in 5 domains (same as CARS)—social resources, economic resources, mental health, physical health, and ADL status.

The test is not self-administered and usually takes about 30 minutes.

Other Important Features

Abbreviated version of the OARS

Key References

Carl, R., Pfeiffer, E., Keller, D. M., Burke, H., & Samis, H. V. (1983). An evaluation of the reliability and validity of the Functional Assessment Inventory. *Journal of the American Geriatric Society, 31,* 607–612.

Pfeiffer, E., Johnson, T., & Chiofolo, R. (1981). Functional assessment of elderly subjects in four service settings. *Journal of American Geriatric Society, 10,* 433–437.

GENERAL TEMPERAMENT SURVEY (GTS)

Characteristics Assessed

Three broad dimensions of temperament: Negative Affectivity, Positive Affectivity, and Disinhibition.

Publisher

Available as part of the Schedule for Nonadaptive and Adaptive Personality (SNAP)
University of Minnesota Press
2037 University Avenue SE
Minneapolis, MN 55455

Where Test can be Obtained

Dr. L. A. Clark & Dr. D. Watson
Department of Psychology
Seashore Hall
University of Iowa
Iowa City, IA 52242-1407

The test is self-administered and usually takes about 20 minutes.
The administration can be delegated to clerical or nursing staff.

The test is (only as part of SNAP) computer-scorable but cannot be interpreted by computer.

Other Important Features

May be available through University Minnesota Press in the future

Key References

Watson, D., & Clark, L. A. (1993). Behavioral disinhibition versus constraint. A dispositional perspective. In D. M. Wegner & J. W. Pennebaker (Eds.). *Handbook of mental control* (pp. 506–527). New York: Prentice Hall.

Watson, D., & Clark, L. A. (1992). On traits and temperament: General and specific factors of emotional experience and their relations to the five-factor model. *Journal of Personality, 60,* 443–476.

GERIATRIC DEPRESSION SCALE

Characteristics Assessed

Measures depression in the elderly

If Unpublished, where Test can be Obtained

Dr. T. L. Brink, Clinical Gerontologist
1044 Sylvan Doctor
San Carlos, CA 94070
or
Dr. Jerome Yesavage
VA Medical Center
Palo Alto, CA 94305

The test is (both oral and written format) self-administered and is about 30 items long.
The administration can be delegated to clerical or nursing staff.

Other Important Features

Translation available in Spanish and French

Key References

Yesavage, J. A., Brink, T. L., Rose, T. L., & Leirer, V. O. (1983). Development and validation of a geriatric depression screening scale: A preliminary report. *Journal of Psychiatric Research, 17,* 37–49.

GERIATRIC MENTAL STATUS INTERVIEW

Characteristics Assessed

Contains almost 500 items considered relevant for assessing psychopathology in a geriatric psychiatric population.

The test is not self-administered and usually takes an average of 1½ hours.
The administration cannot be delegated to clerical or nursing staff.

Other Important Features

Semistructured interview guide — 1500 items

Key References

Gurland, B., Copeland, J., Sharpe, L., & Kelleher, M. (1976). The Geriatric Mental Status Interview (GMS). *International Journal of Aging and Human Development*, 7, 303–311.

HALIFAX MENTAL STATUS SCALE

Characteristics Assessed

Orientation, memory for a single phrase, concentration, comprehension of commands, naming objects, manual praxis, visual constructional ability.

If Unpublished, where Test can be Obtained

Dr. John Fisk, Coordinator
Neuropsychology Service
Department of Psychology
Camp Hill Medical Center
Halifax, Nova Scotia B3H 362 Canada

The test is not self-administered and usually takes less than 15 minutes.
The administration cannot be delegated to clerical or nursing staff.

Key References

Fisk, J. D., Braha, R. E., & Walker, A. (1991). The Halifax Mental Status Scale: Development of a new test of mental status for use with elderly clients. *Psychological Assessment: A Journal of Consulting and Clinical Psychology*, 3, 162–167.

HAMILTON ANXIETY RATING SCALE (HARS)

Characteristics Assessed

A clinician-administered scale designed to measure the severity of anxiety symptoms. Originally designed for use with patients diagnosed with anxiety neuroses.

The test is not self-administered and usually takes about 30 minutes.
The administration cannot be delegated to clerical or nursing staff.

The test is not computer-scorable and cannot be interpreted by computer.

Key References

Hamilton, M. (1959). The assessment of anxiety states by rating. *British Journal of Medical Psychology*, 32, 50–55.
Maier, W., Buller, R., Philipp, M., & Heuser, I. (1988). The Hamilton Anxiety Scale: Reliability, validity and sensitivity to change in anxiety and depressive disorders. *Journal of Affective Disorders*, 14, 61–68.

HARE PSYCHOPATHY CHECKLIST— REVISED

Characteristics Assessed

Rating scale for the assessment of psychopathy in male forensic populations. It yields dimensional scores concerning behavior and inferred personality traits.

Publisher

Multi-Health Systems, Inc.
908 Niagara Falls Boulevard
North Tonawanda, NY 14120-2060

The test is not self-administered and usually takes about 2 hours.
The administration cannot be delegated to clerical or nursing staff.

The test is not computer-scorable and cannot be interpreted by computer.

Other Important Features

Clinical interview and review of collateral information necessary; can also be used to classify and diagnose individuals for research and clinical purposes.

Key References

Hare, R. D., Hart, S. D., & Harpur, T. J. (1991). Psychopathy and the DSM-IV criteria for antisocial personality disorder. *Journal of Abnormal Psychology, 100,* 391–398.

HOPELESSNESS SCALE

Characteristics Assessed

Hopelessness

Publisher

American Psychological Association

The test is not self-administered but is based on self-report. It usually takes a few minutes.
The administration cannot be delegated to clerical or nursing staff.

Key References

Beck, A. T., Weissman, A., Lester, D., and Trexler, L. (1974). The Measurement of Pessimism: The Hopelessness Scale. *Journal of Consulting & Clinical Psychology, 42,* 861–865.

Beck, A. T., Steer, R. A., Kovacs, M., and Garrison, B. (1985). Hopelessness and Eventual Suicide: A Ten Year Prospective Study of Patients Hospitalized with Suicide Ideation. *American Journal of Psychiatry, 142,* 559–563.

INDIVIDUALISM-COLLECTIVISM (INDCOL) SCALE

Characteristics Assessed

Degree of individualism-collectivism (set of feelings, beliefs, behavioral intentions, and behaviors related to solidarity and concern for others).

If Unpublished, where Test can be Obtained

Dr. C. Harry Hui
Department of Psychology
University of Hong Kong
Pokfulam Road
Hong Kong

The test is self-administered and usually takes about 15 to 30 minutes.
The administration cannot be delegated to clerical or nursing staff.

The test is not computer-scorable and cannot be interpreted by computer.

Key References

Hui, C. H. (1988). Measurement of individualism-collectivism. *Journal of Research in Personality, 22,* 17–36

INTERVIEWER-RATED DEFENSE MECHANISM SCALES

Characteristics Assessed

Twelve basic defense mechanisms

If Unpublished, where Test can be Obtained

Dr. Alan Jacobson
Joslin Diabetes Center
1 Joslin Place
Boston, MA 02215

The test is not self-administered and takes several hours (depending on the type of clinical material used). The administration cannot be delegated to clerical or nursing staff.

The test is not computer-scorable and cannot be interpreted by computer.

Other Important Features

The Jacobson et al. measure is an observer-rated defense mechanism measure developed for use with adolescent populations.

Key References

Jacobson, A. M., Beardslee, W., Hauser, S. T., Noam, G. G., Powers, S. I., Houlihan, J., & Rider, E. (1986). Evaluating ego defense mechanisms using clinical interviews: An empirical study of adolescent diabetic and psychiatric patients. *Journal of Adolescence, 9*, 303–319.

Jacobson, A. M., Beardslee, W., Hauser, S. T., Noam, G. G., & Powers, S. I. (1986). In G. E. Vaillant (Ed.), *Empirical studies of the ego mechanisms of defense* (pp. 47–59). Washington, DC: American Psychiatric Press.

LOSS OF FACE MEASURE

Characteristics Assessed

Areas in which face-threatening concerns are salient.

If unpublished, where test can be obtained

Dr. Nolan Zane
Graduate School of Education
University of California, Santa Barbara
Santa Barbara, CA 93106

The test is self-administered and usually takes about 10 minutes.
The administration can be delegated to clerical or nursing staff.

The test is not computer-scorable and cannot be interpreted by computer.

Key References

Zane, N. W. S. (1991, August). *An empirical examination of Loss of Face among Asian Americans.* Paper presented at the 99th annual convention of the American Psychological Association, San Francisco, CA.

THE M TEST

Characteristics Assessed

Malingering of schizophrenia

If Unpublished, where Test can be Obtained

Dr. Rex Beaber
Division of Family Medicine
Room BH–134 CHS
UCLA Medical Center
Los Angeles, CA 90024

The test is self-administered and usually takes about 10 minutes.
The administration cannot be delegated to clerical or nursing staff.

The test is not computer-scorable and cannot be interpreted by computer.

Key References

Beaber R., Marston, A., Michelli, J., & Mills, M. (1985). A brief test for measuring malingering in schizophrenic individuals. *American Journal of Psychiatry, 142*, 1478–1481.

Gillis, J., Rogus, R., & Bagby, M. (1991). Validity of the M Test. *Journal of Personality Assessment, 57*, 130–140.

MAUDSLEY OBSESSIONAL-COMPULSIVE INVENTORY (MOCI)

Characteristics Assessed

Self-report measure to assess the existence and extent of different obsessive-compulsive complaints.

If Unpublished, where Test can be Obtained

Dr. R. J. Hodgson
Addition Research Unit
Institute of Psychiatry, 101
Denmark Hill, London, SE5 8AF England

The test is self-administered and usually takes about 10 to 15 minutes.
The administration can be delegated to clerical or nursing staff.

The test is not computer-scorable and cannot be interpreted by computer.

Key References

Hodgson, R. J., & Rachman, S. (1977). Obsessional-compulsive complaints. *Behavior Therapy, 15,* 389–395.

Sternberger, L. G., & Burns, G. L. (1990). Compulsive activity checklist and the Maudsley Obsessional-Compulsive Inventory: Psychometric properties of two measures of obsessive-compulsive disorder. *Behavior Therapy, 21,* 117–127.

MEMORIES OF SPOUSE

Characteristics Assessed

Contents: 15 spontaneous memories of spouse, beginning with first meeting, and several directed memories. Assesses: Problem areas in relationship. Provides an overview of the marriage, beginning with first meeting.

Publisher

Arnold R. Bruhn, Ph.D.
7910 Woodmont Ave #1300
Bethesda, MD 20814

The test is self-administered and usually takes about 5 minutes for psychologists.
The administration can be delegated to clerical or nursing staff.

The test is not computer-scorable and cannot be interpreted by computer.

Key References

Bruhn, A. R., & Feigenbaum, K. (1993). *The Interpretation of Autobiographical Memories.*

MILLER BEHAVIORAL STYLE SCALE (MBSS)

Characteristics Assessed

Two basic coping styles: Information-distractors (blunters) and information-seekers (monitors).

If Unpublished, where Test can be Obtained

Dr. Suzanne M. Miller
Department of Psychology, Weiss Hall
Temple University
13th and Columbia Streets
Philadelphia, PA 19122

The test is self-administered and usually takes about 10 to 15 minutes.
The administration can be delegated to clerical or nursing staff.

The test is not computer-scorable and cannot be interpreted by computer.

Key References

Miller, S. M. (1987). Monitoring and blunting: Validation of a questionnaire to assess styles of information seeking under threat. *Journal of Personality and Social Psychology, 52,* 345–353.

Miller, S. M., Brody, D. S., & Summerton, S. (1988). Styles of coping with threat: Implications for health. *Journal of Personality and Social Psychology, 54,* 142–148.

MILLON CLINICAL MULTIAXIAL INVENTORY—II

Characteristics Assessed

A measure of 22 personality disorders and clinical syndromes for adults undergoing psychological or psychiatric assessment or treatment.

Publisher

National Computer Systems
PO Box 1416
Minneapolis, MN 55440

The test is self-administered and usually takes about 45 to 60 minutes.
The administration procedure can be delegated to clerical or nursing staff.

The test is computer-scorable and is interpreted by computer.

The address of the official computer scoring and interpretation service is:

National Computer Systems
PO Box 1416
Minneapolis, MN 55440

Key References

Craig, R. J. (Ed.) (1993). The Millon Clinical Multiaxial Inventory: A clinical research information synthesis. Hillsdale, NJ: Lawrence Erlbaum.

Choca, J., Shanty, L., & Van Denburg, E. (1991). *Interpretive guide to the Millon Multiaxial Inventory.* Washington, DC: American Psychological Association.

Millon, T. (1987). Manual for the Millon Clinical Multiaxial Inventory—II. Minneapolis, MN: National Computer Systems.

MINI-MENTAL STATE (MMS)

Characteristics Assessed

Orientation; memory; attention; ability to name, follow verbal and written commands, and write a sentence spontaneously; and constructional ability.

If Unpublished, where Test can be Obtained

Dr. Marshal F. Folstein
Department of Psychiatry and Behavioral Science
Johns Hopkins Hospital
Baltimore, MD 21205

The test is not self administered and usually takes about 5 to 10 minutes.
The administration cannot be delegated to clerical or nursing staff.

The test is not computer-scorable and cannot be interpreted by computer.

Key References

Folstein, M. F., Folstein, S. E., and McHugh, P. (1975). "Mini-Mental State" A practical method for grading the cognitive state of patients for the clinician. *Journal of Psychiatric Research, 12,* 189–198.

Anthony, J. C., LeResche, L., Niaz, W., Von Korff, M. R., & Folstein, M. F. (1982). Limits of the mini-mental state as a screening test for dementia and delirium among hospital patients. *Psychological Medicine, 12,* 397–408.

MMPI PERSONALITY DISORDER SCALES

Characteristics Assessed

Personality disorders developed using original MMPI items.

Publisher

National Computer Systems
PO Box 1416
Minneapolis, MN 55440

The test is self-administered and usually takes about 1½ hours.
The administration can be delegated to clerical or nursing staff.

Key References

Morey, L. C., Waugh, M. H., & Blashfield, R. K. (1985). MMPI scales for DSM-III personality disorders: Their derivation and correlates. *Journal of Personality Assessment, 49,* 245–251.

THE MULTICENTER—PANIC ANXIETY SCALE (MC-PAS)

Characteristics Assessed

Clinician-rated composite symptom rating scale for panic disorder.

If Unpublished, where Test can be Obtained

Dr. Katherine Shear
Anxiety Disorders Clinic
Western Psychiatric Institute & Clinic
3811 O'Hara Street
Pittsburgh, PA 15213

The test is not self-administered and usually takes about 20 minutes.
The administration cannot be delegated to clerical or nursing staff.

The test is not computer-scorable and cannot be interpreted by computer.

Key References

Shear, M. K., Sholomskas, D., Cloitre, A., et al., (1992). The Multicenter—Panic Anxiety Scale. Unpublished manuscript.

Sholomskas, D., Shear, M. K., Cloitre, A., et al., (1992). Construct validity of the Multicenter Collaborative Panic Anxiety Scale (MC-PAS). Unpublished manuscript.

THE MULTIDIMENSIONAL FUNCTION ASSESSMENT QUESTIONNAIRE (OARS)

Characteristics Assessed

Individual functioning—provides functional information in five domains of social resources, economic resources, mental health, physical health, and ADL status.

If Unpublished, where Test can be Obtained

Older Americans Resources and Services Program
Duke University Center for Study of Aging and Human Development
Durham, NC 27710

The test is not self-administered and usually takes about 45 minutes to 1 hour.
The administration cannot be delegated to clerical or nursing staff.

The test is (computer-assigned ratings available in key reference) computer-scorable but cannot be interpreted by computer.

Key References

Duke University Center for the Study of Aging (1978). *Multi-dimensional functional assessment: The OARS methodology* (2nd ed.) Durham, NC: Duke University.

MPQ (MULTIDIMENSIONAL PERSONALITY QUESTIONNAIRE)

Characteristics Assessed

Primary scales: Well being, Social Potency, Achievement, Social Closeness, Stress Reaction, Alienation, Aggression, Control, Harm Avoidance, Traditionalism, Absorption. Higher-order scales: *Positive* Emotionality (Agentic and Communal); Negative Emotionality (Agentic and Alienated); and Constraint.

Publisher

University of Minnesota Press
2037 University Ave. SE
Minneapolis, MN 55455-3082

The test is self-administered and usually takes about 45 minutes.
The administration can be delegated to clerical or nursing staff.

The test is computer-scorable but cannot be interpreted by computer.

Key References

Tellegen, A. (1993). MPQ Manual. Minneapolis, MN: University of Minnesota Press.

MULTILEVEL ASSESSMENT INSTRUMENT (MAI)

Characteristics Assessed

Health, activities of daily living, cognition, time use, social interaction, psychological well-being (personal adjustment—moral and psychiatric symptoms), and perceived quality of life (perceived environment—housing quality, neighborhood quality, and personal security).

If Unpublished, where Test can be Obtained

Dr. M. Powell Lawton
Philadelphia Geriatric Center
5301 Old York Road
Philadelphia, PA 19141

The test is not self-administered and usually takes about 50 minutes (15 to 60 minutes). The administration cannot be delegated to clerical or nursing staff.

The test is not computer-scorable and cannot be interpreted by computer.

Other Important Features

interview format

Key References

Lawton, M. P., Moss, M., Fulcomer, M., & Kleban, M. (1982). A research and service oriented multilevel assessment instrument. *Journal of Gerontology, 37,* 91–99.

Lawton, M. P., Kleban, M. H., & Moss, M. (1980). *The Philadelphia Geriatric Center Multilevel Assessment Instrument.* Final report to the National Institute of Aging. Philadelphia: Philadelphia Geriatric Center.

MINNESOTA MULTIPHASIC PERSONALITY INVENTORY (MMPI)

Characteristics Assessed

The MMPI is an empirically derived personality inventory that was developed in the 1930s and 1940s to assist in the detection of mental health problems in medical and psychiatric settings. The MMPI has become the most widely used personality assessment instrument. A broad range of personality characteristics and clinical symptoms are addressed by the MMPI; for example, anxiety and somatization disorders, antisocial patterns, mood disorders, thought disorder, and potential problems with alcohol and drug abuse. There are four validity measures available to aid in the detection of invalidating conditions. The MMPI has been superseded by the MMPI-2 and MMPI-A.

Publisher

University of Minnesota Press
University of Minnesota
Minneapolis, MN 55455

Where Test can be Obtained

National Computer Systems
5605 Green Circle Drive
Minnetonka, MN 55343

The test is self-administered and usually takes about 1 1/2 hours.
The administration can be delegated to clerical or nursing staff.

The test is computer-scorable and can be interpreted by computer.

The address of the official computer scoring and interpretation service is:
National Computer Systems
5605 Green Circle Drive
Minnetonka, MN 55343

Key References

Dahlstrom, W. G., Welsh, G. S., and Dahlstrom, L. (1972). *An MMPI handbook. Volume 1*. Minneapolis, MN: University of Minnesota Press

Dahlstrom, W. G., Welsh, G. S., and Dahlstrom, L. (1975). *An MMPI handbook. Volume 2*. Minneapolis, MN: University of Minnesota Press.

MINNESOTA MULTIPHASIC PERSONALITY INVENTORY (MMPI-2)

Characteristics Assessed

The MMPI-2 is a revised version of the original MMPI and was published in 1989. A broad range of personality characteristics and clinical symptoms are addressed by the MMPI-2; for example, anxiety and somatization disorders, antisocial patterns, mood disorders, thought disorder, relationship problems, and potential problems with alcohol and drug abuse. There are eight validity measures available to aid in the detection of invalidating conditions. The traditional empirically based MMPI clinical scales are continuous with MMPI-2, and a number of new content and special scales to detect alcohol and drug abuse and marital problems have been published.

Publisher

University of Minnesota Press
University of Minnesota
Minneapolis, Minnesota 55455

Where Test can be Obtained

National Computer Systems
5605 Green Circle Drive
Minnetonka, MN 55343

The test is self-administered and usually takes about 1 1/2 hours.
The administration can be delegated to clerical or nursing staff.

The test is computer-scorable and can be interpreted by computer.

The address of the official computer scoring and interpretation service is:

National Computer Systems
5605 Green Circle Drive
Minnetonka, MN 55343

Key References

Butcher, J. N., & Williams, C. L. (1992). *Essentials of MMPI-2 and MMPI-A interpretation*. Minneapolis, MN: University of Minnesota Press.

Butcher, J. N., Dahlstrom, W. G., Graham, J. R., Tellegen. A., and Kaemmer, B. (1989). *MMPI-2 (Minnesota Multiphasic Personality Inventory—2): Manual for administration and scoring*. Minneapolis, MN: University of Minnesota Press.

MINNESOTA MULTIPHASIC PERSONALITY INVENTORY (MMPI-A)

Characteristics Assessed

The MMPI-A is a revised version of the original MMPI for adolescents and was published in 1992. A broad range of personality characteristics, clinical symptoms, and adolescent behavioral problems are addressed by the MMPI-A; for example, anxiety and somatization disorders, conduct problems, mood disorders, thought disorder, and potential problems with alcohol and drug abuse. There are seven validity measures available to aid in the detection of invalidating conditions. The traditional empirically based MMPI clinical scales are continuous with MMPI-A, and a number of new content have been developed to address adolescent problems. Special scales to detect alcohol and drug abuse have been published.

Publisher

University of Minnesota Press
University of Minnesota
Minneapolis, MN 55455

Where Test can be Obtained

National Computer Systems
5605 Green Circle Drive
Minnetonka, MN 55343

The test is self-administered and usually takes about 1 hour.
The administration can be delegated to clerical or nursing staff.

The test is computer-scorable and can be interpreted by computer.

The address of the official computer scoring and interpretation service is:
National Computer Systems
5605 Green Circle Drive
Minnetonka, MN 55343

Key References

Butcher, J. N., & Williams, C. L. (1992). *Essentials of MMPI-2 and MMPI-A interpretation.* Minneapolis, MN: University of Minnesota Press.

Butcher, J. N., Williams, C. L., Graham, J. R., Archer, R., Tellegen. A., Ben-Porath, Y. S., and Kaemmer, B. (1992). *MMPI-A (Minnesota Multiphasic Personality Inventory for Adolescents): Manual for administration and scoring.* Minneapolis, MN: University of Minnesota Press.

NEO PERSONALITY INVENTORY— REVISED (NEO PI-R)

Characteristics Assessed

Five major dimensions of personality: Neuroticism, Extraversion, Openness, Agreeableness, and Conscientiousness.

Publisher

Psychological Assessment Resources, Inc.
PO Box 998
Odessa, FL 33556

The test is self-administered and usually takes about 30 to 40 minutes.

The administration can be delegated to clerical or nursing staff.

The test is computer-scorable and can be interpreted by computer.

The address of the official computer scoring and interpretation service is:
Psychological Assessment Resources, Inc.
PO Box 998
Odessa, FL 33556

Other Important Features

Test has three forms: Form S for self-reports, Form R for observer ratings, and a shortened version of Form S, the NEO-FFI.

Key References

Costa, P., & McRae, R. (1990). Personality disorders and the five-factor model of personality. *Journal of Personality Disorders, 4,* 362–371.

Costa, P., & McRae, R. (1992). Normal personality assessment in clinical practice. *Psychological Assessment, 4,* 5–13, 20–22.

NEUROBEHAVIORAL RATING SCALE

Characteristics Assessed

Behavioral, emotional, and cognitive sequelae of head injury.

If Unpublished, where Test can be Obtained

Dr. Harvey Levin
Division of Neurosurgery
D 73
University of Texas Medical Branch
Galveston, TX 77550-2769

The test is not self-administered and usually takes about 10 minutes.
The administration cannot be delegated to clerical or nursing staff.

The test is not computer-scorable and cannot be interpreted by computer.

Other Important Features

Clinician ratings using 27 seven-point scales.

Key References

Levin, H. S., High, W. M., Goethe, K. E., Sisson, R. A., Overall, J. E., Rhoades, H. M., Eisenberg, H. M., Kalisky, Z., & Gary, H. E. (1987). The Neurobehavioral Rating Scale: Assessment of the behavioral sequelae of head injury by the clinician. *Journal of Neurology, Neurosurgery, and Psychiatry, 50*, 183–193.

Grant, I., & Alves, W. (1987). Psychiatric and psychosocial disturbances in head injury. In H. S. Levin, J. Grafman, & H. M. Eisenberg (Eds.), *Neurobehavioral recovery from head injury* (pp. 232–261). New York: Oxford University Press.

NEUROPSYCHOLOGY BEHAVIOR AND AFFECT PROFILE

Characteristics Assessed

Indifference, mania, depression, behavioral inappropriateness, and communication problems (pragnosia).

If Unpublished, where Test can be Obtained

Dr. Linda D. Nelson
Medical Center, Rt. 181, Bldg. 7
University of California, Irvine
Orange, CA 92668

The test is not self-administered.

The test is not computer-scorable and cannot be interpreted by computer.

Other Important Features

The instrument consists of 106 statements and five scales, and has self- and other-rater versions.

Key References

Nelson, L. D., Satz, P., Mitrushina, M., Van Gorp, W., Cicchetti, D., Lewis, R., & Van Lancker, D. (1989). Development and validation of the Neuropsychology Behavior and Affect Profile. *Psychological Assessment, 1*, 255–272.

PENN STATE WORRY QUESTIONNAIRE (PSWQ)

Characteristics Assessed

Brief self-report measure of trait worry.

If Unpublished, where Test can be Obtained

Dr. Thomas D. Borkovec
Penn State University
417 Bruce Moore Bldg
University Park, PA 16802

The test is self-administered and usually takes about 10 minutes.
The administration can be delegated to clerical or nursing staff.

The test is not computer-scorable and cannot be interpreted by computer.

Key References

Meyer, T. J., Miller, M. L., Metzger, M., & Borkovec, T. D. (1990). Development and validation of the Penn State Worry Questionnaire. *Behavior Research and Therapy, 28*, 487–495.

Brown, T. A., Antony, M. M., & Barlow, D. H. (1992). Psychometric properties of the Penn State Worry Questionnaire in a clinical anxiety disorders sample. *Behavior Research and Therapy, 30*, 33–37.

PERSONALITY ADJECTIVE CHECKLIST (PACL)

Characteristics Assessed

Assesses personality traits as conceptualized by Theodore Millon using a 153-word adjective checklist.

Publisher

21st Century Assessment
PO Box 608
South Pasadena, CA 91031

The test is self-administered and usually takes about 15 minutes.
The administration can be delegated to clerical or nursing staff.

Other Important Features

Easy to use; short; inexpensive

Key References

Strack, S. (1991). *Manual for the Personality Adjective Checklist* (PACL) Revised edition: South Pasadena, CA: Stephen Strack.
Strack, S. (1987). Development and validation of an adjective checklist to assess the Millon personality types in a normal population. *Journal of Personality Assessment, 51,* 572–587.

PERSONALITY ASSESSMENT FORM

Characteristics Assessed

Personality disorders.

If Unpublished, where Test can be Obtained

Dr. Paul Pilkonis
Western Psychiatric Institute & Clinic
3811 O'Hara Street
Pittsburgh, PA 15213

The test is not self-administered and usually takes about 1 to 2 hours.
The administration cannot be delegated to clerical or nursing staff.

The test is not computer-scorable and cannot be interpreted by computer.

Other Important Features:

Unstructured to semistructured interview

Key References

Pilkonis, P. A., Heape, C. L., Ruddy, J., & Serrao, P. (1991). Validity in the diagnosis of personality disorders: The use of the LEAD standard. *Psychological Assessment, 3,* 46–54.

PERSONALITY ASSESSMENT INVENTORY (PAI)

Characteristics Assessed

Dimensions of psychopathology, (e.g., Somatic Complaints, Anxiety, Paranoia, Alcohol Problems, Stress, Warmth, etc.) divided into eleven clinical scales, five treatment scales, and two interpersonal scales.

Publisher

PAR: Psychological Assessment Resources, Inc.
PO Box 998
Odessa, FL 33556

The test is self-administered and usually takes about 45 to 55 minutes.
The administration can be delegated to clerical or nursing staff.

The test is computer-scorable and can be interpreted by computer.

The address of the official computer scoring and interpretation service is:
Psychological Assessment Resources, Inc.

PO Box 998
Odessa, FL 33556

Key References

Morey, L. C. (1991). *The Personality Assessment Inventory: Professional Manual.* Odessa, FL: Psychological Assessment Resources.

PERSONALITY DIAGNOSTIC QUESTIONNAIRE—REVISED

Characteristics Assessed

Personality disorders

If Unpublished, where Test can be Obtained

Dr. Steve Hyler
New York State Psychiatric Institute
722 West 168th Street
New York, NY 10032

The test is self-administered and usually takes about 30 minutes.
The administration can be delegated to clerical or nursing staff.

The test is computer-scorable but cannot be interpreted by computer.

Key References

Hyler, S. E., Skodol, A. E., Kellman, H. D., Oldham, J. M., & Rosnick, L. (1990). Validity of the Personality Diagnostic Questionnaire—Revised: Comparison with two structured interviews. *American Journal of Psychiatry, 147,* 1043–1048.

PERSONALITY DISORDER EXAMINATION

Characteristics Assessed

Personality disorders

Publisher

Dr. A. W. Loranger
New York Hospital CMC
White Plains, NY 10605

The test is not self-administered and usually takes about 1 to 4 hours.
The administration cannot be delegated to clerical or nursing staff.

The test is not computer-scorable and cannot be interpreted by computer.

Other Important Features

Semistructured interview

Key References

Loranger, A. W., Susman, V. L., Oldham, J. M., & Russakoff, L. M. (1987). The Personality Disorder Examination: A preliminary report. *Journal of Personality Disorders, 1,* 1–13.

PERSONALITY INTERVIEW QUESTIONS—II

Characteristics Assessed

Personality disorders.

If Unpublished, where Test can be Obtained

Dr. Thomas A. Widiger
115 Kastle Hall—Psychology
University of Kentucky
Lexington, KY 40506-0044

The test is not self-administered and usually takes about 1 to 3 hours.
The administration cannot be delegated to clerical or nursing staff.

The test is not computer-scorable and cannot be interpreted by computer.

Other Important Features

Semistructured interview

Key References

Widiger, T. A., Frances, A. J., & Trull, T. J. (1989). Personality disorders. In R. Craig (Ed.), Clinical and diagnostic interviewing (pp. 221–236). Northvale, NJ: Jason Aronson.

Widiger, T. A., Freiman, K., & Bailey, B. (1990). Convergent and discriminant validity of personality disorder prototypic acts. *Psychological Assessment, 2,* 107–113.

PSYCHOLOGICAL TEST BATTERY TO DETECT FAKED INSANITY

Characteristics Assessed

Detection of simulated insanity

If Unpublished, where Test can be Obtained

Dr. David Schretlen
Department of Psychiatry
Johns Hopkins School of Medicine
Meyers 218
600 North Wolfe Street
Baltimore, MD 21205

The test is not self-administered and usually takes about 2 hours.
The administration cannot be delegated to clerical or nursing staff.

The test is not computer-scorable and cannot be interpreted by computer.

Key References

Schretlen, D., Wilkins, S., Van Gorp, W., & Bobholz, J. (1992). Cross-validation of a psychological test battery to detect faked insanity. *Psychological Assessment, 4,* 77–83.

Schretlen, D., & Arkowitz, H. (1990). A psychological test battery to detect prison inmates who fake

insanity or mental retardation. *Behavioral Sciences & the Law, 8,* 75–84.

PTSD SYMPTOM SCALE (PSS)

Characteristics Assessed

Self-report measure of the major symptom areas of PTSD including reexperiencing, avoidance and numbing, and hyperarousal.

If Unpublished, where Test can be Obtained

Dr. Edna Foa
Medical College of Pennsylvania at EPPI
1900 Henry Avenue
Philadelphia, PA 19129

The test is self-administered and usually takes about 15 minutes.
The administration can be delegated to clerical or nursing staff.

The test is not computer-scorable and cannot be interpreted by computer.

Key References

Foa, E. B., Riggs, D. S., Dancu, C. V., & Rothbaum, B. O. (1993). Reliability and validity of a brief instrument for assessing post-traumatic stress disorder. *Journal of Traumatic Stress, 6,* 459–473.

REVISED DIAGNOSTIC INTERVIEW FOR BORDERLINES

Characteristics Assessed

Borderline personality disorder.

If Unpublished, where Test can be Obtained

Dr. John Gunderson
McLean Hospital
115 Mill Street
Belmont, MA 02178

The test is not self-administered and usually takes about 1 to 3 hours.
The administration cannot be delegated to clerical or nursing staff.

The test is not computer-scorable and cannot be interpreted by computer.

Other Important Features

Semistructured interview

Key References

Zanarini, M. C., Gunderson, J. G., Frankenburg, F. R., & Chauncey, D. L. (1989). The Revised Diagnostic Interview for Borderlines: Discriminating BPD from other Axis-II disorders. *Journal of Personality Disorders*, 3, 10–18.

REVISED ISCHEMIC SCORE

Characteristics Assessed

Thirteen items that differentiate MID from AD.

If Unpublished, where Test can be Obtained

Dr. Gary W. Small
UCLA Neuropsychiatric Institute
760 Westwood Plaza
Los Angeles, CA 90024

The test is not self-administered and usually takes less than 1 hour.
The administration cannot be delegated to clerical or nursing staff.

Other Important Features

Semistructured interview procedure

Key References

Hachinski, V. C., Iliff, L. D., Phil, M., Zihka, E., DuBoulay, G. H., McAllister, V. L., Marshall, J.,

Russell, R. W., & Symon, L. (1975). Cerebral blood flow in dementia. *Archives of Neurology*, 32, 632–637.
Small, G. W. (1985). Revised Ischemic Score for diagnosing Multi-infarct Dementia. *Journal of Clinical Psychiatry*, 46, 514–517.

ROMANTIC RELATIONSHIP PROCEDURE

Characteristics Assessed

Contents: four longest-lasting or most important romantic relationships—three memories of each relationship.
Assesses: Problem areas and unresolved issues in romantic relationships.

Publisher

Dr. Arnold R. Bruhn
7910 Woodmont Ave. #1300
Bethesda, MD 20814

The test is self-administered and usually takes about 5 minutes for psychologists.
The administration can be delegated to clerical or nursing staff.

The test is not computer-scorable and cannot be interpreted by computer.

Key References

Bruhn, A. R., & Feigenbaum, K. (1993). *The Interpretation of Autobiographical Memories.* 7910 Woodmunt Ave. #1300 Bethesda, MD 20814

RORSCHACH

Characteristics Assessed

A perceptual-associative-judgmental task that infers certain current psychological states and traits; personality characteristics related to cognitive and perceptual functioning.

Publisher

Hans Huber
Länggasstrasse 76
POB CH–3000
Bern 9 Switzerland

The test is not self-administered and usually takes about 45 minutes to 1 hour.
The administration procedures cannot be delegated to clerical or nursing staff.

The test is not computer-scorable but can be interpreted by computer.

The address of the official computer interpretation service is:
RSP-2, RIAP-2
Rorschach Workshops
2149 Riceville Road
Asheville, NC 28805

Other Important Features

Extensive norms now available for various nonpatient and clinical populations if Comprehensive System used for scoring and interpretation.

Key References

Lerner, P. (1991). Psychoanalytic theory and the Rorschach, Hillsdale, NJ: Analytic Press.

Exner, J. (1993). The Rorschach: A Comprehensive System, Vol. 1 & 2, Third Edition. New York: John Wiley & Sons.

SCHEDULE FOR AFFECTIVE DISORDERS AND SCHIZOPHRENIA— LIFETIME VERSION

Characteristics Assessed

The SADS-LA provides a comprehensive assessment of anxiety and related disorders across the lifetime.

If Unpublished, where Test can be Obtained

Dr. Abby J. Fyer, Co-Director
Anxiety Disorders Clinics
New York State Psychiatric Institute
722 West 168th Street
New York, NY 10032

The test is not self-administered and usually takes about 3½ hours.
The administration cannot be delegated to clerical or nursing staff.

The test is not computer-scorable and cannot be interpreted by computer.

Key References

Mannuzza, S., Fyer, A. J., Martin, L. Y., et al., (1989). Reliability of anxiety assessment. I. Diagnostic agreement. *Archives of General Psychiatry, 46,* 1093–1101.

Fyer, A. J., Mannuzza, S., Martin, L. Y., et al., (1989). Reliability of anxiety assessment. II. Symptom agreement. *Archives of General Psychiatry, 46,* 1102–1110.

SCHEDULE FOR NONADAPTIVE AND ADAPTIVE PERSONALITY (SNAP)

Characteristics Assessed

Twelve primary traits (e.g., Aggression, Dependency) and three broad temperaments (e.g., Negative Affectivity) that are relevant to personality disorder. Also contains six validity indices and thirteen DSM-III-R Axis II PD diagnostic scales.

Publisher

University of Minnesota Press
2037 University Avenue SE
Minneapolis, MN 55455

The test is self-administered and usually takes about 1 hour.
The administration can be delegated to clerical or nursing staff.

The test is computer-scorable but cannot, at the present time, be interpreted by computer.

Other Important Features

Supplement for scoring the DSM-IV Axis II personality disorders will be available in the future; adolescent version is being tested.

Key References

Clark, L. A., Vorhies, L., & McEwen, J. L. (in press). Personality disorder symptomatology from the five-factor perspective. In P. T. Costa, Jr., & T. Widiger (Eds.). *Personality disorders and the five-factor model of personality.* Washington, DC: American Psychological Association.

Clark, L. A., McEwen, J. L., Collard, L. M., & Hickok, L. G. (1993). Symptoms and traits of personality disorder: Two new methods for their assessment. *Psychological Assessment,* 5, 81–91.

THE SHORT-CARE

Characteristics Assessed

Depression, dementia, and disability in elderly persons.

If Unpublished, where Test can be Obtained

Dr. Barry Gurland
Columbia University Center for Geriatrics and Gerontology
100 Haven Ave, Tower I III–297
New York, NY 10032

The test is not self-administered and usually takes about 30 minutes per session.
The administration cannot be delegated to clerical or nursing staff.

Other Important Features

Semistructured interview

Key References

Garland, B., Golden, R. R., Teresi, J., & Challop, J. (1984). The SHORT-CARE: An efficient instrument for the assessment of depression, dementia and disability. *Journal of Gerontology,* 39, 166–169.

SOCIAL INTERACTION ANXIETY SCALE (SIAS)

Characteristics Assessed

Measures cognitive, affective, and behavioral reactions to a variety of situations involving social interactions.

If Unpublished, where Test can be Obtained

Dr. Richard G. Heimberg
Center for Stress and Anxiety Disorders
1535 Western Avenue
Albany, NY 12203

The test is self-administered and usually takes about 10 minutes.
The administration can be delegated to clerical or nursing staff.

The test is not computer-scorable and cannot be interpreted by computer.

Key References

Heimberg, R. G., Mueller, G. P., Holt, C. S., & Hope, D. A. (1992). Assessment of anxiety in social interaction and being observed by others: The Social Interaction Anxiety Scale and the Social Phobia Scale. *Behavior Therapy,* 23, 53–73.

THE STAFF-RESIDENT INTERACTION CHRONOGRAPH (SRIC)

Characteristics Assessed

The nature, amount, content, and distribution of verbal/nonverbal interactions provided to clients by staff inpatient and residential settings (including context).

Publisher

Research Press
PO Box 9177
Champaign, IL 61826

The test is not self-administered and usually takes 10 minutes direct observational samples. The administration can be delegated to full-time technician-level observers for data collection.

The test is computer-scorable but cannot be interpreted by computer.

The address of the official computer scoring and interpretation service is:
Research Press
PO Box 9177
Champaign, IL 61826

Other Important Features

Key references provide videotape observer training materials and procedures and a summary of all technical development, reliability and validity evidence, and generalizability/feasibility data on 679 staff (aide-level to doctoral-level), 35 treatment programs (psychodynamic through biological) in adult treatment units (8 to 120 beds) covering mentally retarded, alcohol/substance abuse, and mentally ill populations in mental hospitals and community facilities.

Key References

Paul, G. L. (1988). *Observational Assessment Instrumentation for Service and Research-The Staff-Resident Interaction Chronograph: Assessment in Residential Treatment Settings* (Part 3). Champaign, IL: Research Press.
Paul, G. L. (1994b). *Observational Assessment Instrumentation for Service and Research-The TSBC/SRIC System Implementation Package: Assessment*

in Residential Treatment Settings (Part 5). Champaign, IL: Research Press.

STATE-TRAIT ANXIETY INVENTORY (STAI)

Characteristics Assessed

State form: measure of state anxiety; sensitive to changes in transitory anxiety.
Trait form: measure of relatively stable individual differences in anxiety proneness.

Publisher

Consulting Psychological Press
3803 East Bayshore Road
Palo Alto, CA 94303

The test is self-administered and usually takes about 20 minutes.
The administration can be delegated to clerical or nursing staff.

The test is not computer-scorable and cannot be interpreted by computer.

Key References

Spielberger, C. D. (1983). *Manual for the State-Trait Anxiety Inventory (Form Y)*. Palo Alto, CA: Consulting Psychological Press.

STRUCTURED CLINICAL INTERVIEW FOR DSM-III-R PERSONALITY DISORDERS

Characteristics Assessed

Personality disorders.

Publisher

American Psychiatric Press
1400 K Street, NW
Washington, DC 20005

The test is not self-administered and usually takes about 1 to 3 hours.
The administration cannot be delegated to clerical or nursing staff.

The test is not computer-scorable and cannot be interpreted by computer.

Other Important Features

Semistructured interview

Key References

Spitzer, R. L., Williams, J. B. W., Gibbon, M., & First, M. B. (1992). The Structured Clinical Interview for DSM-III-R (SCID): I. History, rationale, and description. *Archives of General Psychiatry, 49*, 624–629.

STRUCTURED CLINICAL INTERVIEW FOR DSM-III-R

Characteristics Assessed

Structured clinical interview designed to assess DSM-III-R diagnosable conditions.

Publisher

American Psychiatric Press
1400 K Street NW
Washington DC 20005

The test is not self-administered and usually takes about 3 hours.
The administration cannot be delegated to clerical or nursing staff.

The test is not computer-scorable and cannot be interpreted by computer.

Key References

Spitzer, R. L., & Williams, J. B. (1988). Revised diagnostic criteria and a new structured interview for diagnosing anxiety disorders. *Journal of Psychiatric Research, 22*, 55–85.

Riskind, J. H., Beck, A. T., Berchick, R. J., Brown, G., & Steer, R. A. (1987). Reliability of DSM-III diagnosis for major depression and generalized anxiety disorder using the structured clinical interview for DSM-III. *Archives of General Psychiatry, 44*, 817–820.

STRUCTURED INTERVIEW OF REPORTED SYMPTOMS

Characteristics Assessed

Malingering and deception.

Publisher

PAR, Inc.
PO Box 998
Odessa, FL 33556

The test is not self-administered and usually takes about 30 to 60 minutes.
The administration cannot be delegated to clerical or nursing staff.

The test is not computer-scorable and cannot be interpreted by computer.

Key References

Rogers, R., Gillis, R., & Bagby, R. (1990). The SIRS as a measure of malingering: A validation study with a correctional sample. *Behavioral Science and the Law, 8*, 85–92.
Rogers, R., Gillis, R., Bagby, R., & Monteiro, E. (1991). Detection of malingering on the SIRS: A study of coached and uncoached malingerers. *Psychological Assessment, 3*, 673–677.

STRUCTURED INTERVIEW SCHEDULES FOR CLIENTS AND SIGNIFICANT OTHERS (SISCSO)

Characteristics Assessed

Present and historical level of functioning, psychiatric symptomotology, role functioning, and expectations of adult mental patients at entry, predischarge, and follow-up for inpatient/residential facilities.

Publisher

Research Press
PO Box 9177
Champaign, IL 61826

The test is not self-administered and usually takes about 2 hours, each.
The administration cannot be delegated to clerical or nursing staff.

Selected instruments derived from the interview responses can be computer scored; users must write their own programs. Test cannot be interpreted by computer.

Other Important Features

A set of six structured interview protocols originally used with severely disabled chronic mental patients; Paul & Mariotto (1986) provide details and recommendations for expansion as a generic set for adult populations.

Key References

Paul, G. L. & Mariotto, M. J. (1986). Potential utility of the sources and Methods: A Comprehensive Paradigm. In G. L. Paul (Ed.), *Principles and Methods to Support Cost-Effective Quality Operations: Assessment in Residential Treatment Settings* (Part 1). Champaign, IL: Research Press.
Paul, G. L. & Shelite, I. (in press-b). Structured Interview Schedules for Clients and Significant Others: Supplement to G. L. Paul & R. J. Lentz, *Psychosocial Treatment of Chronic Mental Patients* (2nd Ed.). Champaign, IL: Research Press.

THE SUICIDE INTENT SCALE

Characteristics Assessed

Suicide intent.

Publisher

The Charles Press Publishers, Incorporated
Bowie, MD 20715

The test is not self-administered, but is based on self-report and usually takes a few minutes.
The administration cannot be delegated to clerical or nursing staff.

Key References

Beck, A. T., Schuyler, D., and Herman, I. (1974). Development of Suicidal Intent Scales. In A. T. Beck, H. L. P. Resnick, and D. J. Lettieri (Eds.) *The Prediction of Suicide* (pages 45–56).
Beck, R. W., Morris, J. B., and Beck, A. T. (1974). Cross Validation of the Suicide Intent Scale. *Psychological Reports, 34*, 445–446.

THE SUICIDE RISK ASSESSMENT SCALE

Characteristics Assessed

Suicide risk.

Publisher

American Journal of Psychiatry
American Psychiatric Association
1400 K Street NW
Washington, DC 20005

The test is not self-administered but is based on patient self-report. It takes about 30 minutes.
The administration cannot be delegated to clerical or nursing staff.

Other Important Features

This is one of the very few tests for estimating suicide risk with empirically weighted items

Key References

Motto, J. A. (1985). Preliminary Field Testing of a Risk Estimator for Suicide, Suicide and Life Threatening Behavior, *American Journal of Psychiatry*, 15.

SUINN-LEW ASIAN SELF-IDENTITY AND ACCULTURATION SCALE (SL-ASIA)

Characteristics Assessed

Level of acculturation among Asian-Americans.

If Unpublished, where Test can be Obtained

Dr. Richard M. Suinn
Department of Psychology
Colorado State University
Fort Collins, CO 80523

The test is self-administered and usually takes about 10 to 15 minutes.
The administration can be delegated to clerical or nursing staff.

The test is not computer-scorable and cannot be interpreted by computer.

Key References

Suinn, R. M., Ahuna, C., & Khoo, G. (1992). The Suinn-Lew Asian Self-Identity Acculturation Scale: Concurrent and factorial validation. *Educational and Psychological Measurement*, 52, 1–6.
Suinn, R. M., Rikard-Figueroa, K., Lew, S., & Virgil, P. (1987). The Suinn-Lew Asian Self-Identity Acculturation Scale: An initial report. Educational and Psychological Measurement, 47, 401–407.

SYMPTOM CHECKLIST—90—REVISED

Characteristics Assessed

Somatization, obsessive-compulsive behavior, interpersonal sensitivity, depression, anxiety, hostility, phobic anxiety, paranoid ideation, and psychoticism.

Publisher

National Computer System
PO Box 1416
Minneapolis, MN 55440

The test is self-administered and usually takes about 15 minutes.
The administration can be delegated to clerical or nursing staff.

The test is computer-scorable and can be interpreted by computer.

The address of the official computer scoring and interpretation service is:
NCS Assessments
Attn: Order Processing
PO Box 1416
Minneapolis, MN 55440

Other Important Features

Norms available for nonpatient adults and adolescents as well as psychiatric inpatients and outpatients.

Key References

Derogatis, L. R. (1977). *SCL-R administration, scoring, and procedures manual*. Baltimore, MD: Clinical Psychometrics Research Unit, Johns Hopkins University School of Medicine.

TEMAS (TELL-ME-A-STORY) THEMATIC APPERCEPTION TEST

Characteristics Assessed

Personality/psychopathology in Hispanics, blacks, and whites

Publisher

Technical Manual
Western Psychological Services
Los Angeles, CA

The test is not self-administered and usually takes a variable amount of time.
The administration cannot be delegated to clerical or nursing staff.

The test is not computer-scorable and cannot be interpreted by computer

Key References

Constantino, G., Malgady, R. G., & Rogler, L. H. (1988). TEMAS (Tell-Me-A-Story) manual. Los Angeles, CA: Western Psychological Services.

THEMES CONCERNING BLACKS (TCB)

Characteristics Assessed

Personality/psychopathology in blacks

Publisher

Williams & Associates
Department of Psychology
Washington University
St. Louis, MO

The test is not self-administered and usually takes a variable amount of time.
The administration cannot be delegated to clerical or nursing staff.

The test is not computer-scorable and cannot be interpreted by computer.

Key References

Williams, R. L. (1972). Themes Concerning Blacks. St. Louis, MO: Williams & Associates.
Williams, R. L. & Johnson, R. C. (1981). Progress in developing afrocentric measuring instruments. *Journal of Non-White Concerns*, 9, 3–18.

THE TIME-SAMPLE BEHAVIORAL CHECKLIST (TSBC)

Characteristics Assessed

Assets, deficits, and excesses in functioning of clients in inpatient and residential settings (including context); how and where clients and staff spend their time.

Publisher

Research Press
PO Box 9177
Champaign, IL 61826

The test is not self-administered and usually takes 1 hour for direct observational time samples.
The administration can be delegated to full-time technician-level observers for data collection.

The test is computer-scorable but cannot be interpreted by computer.

The address of the official computer scoring and interpretation service is:
Paul (1994b) contains all computer programs for scoring preplanned summary reports for clients, staff, and ward (or other) groups.

Other Important Features

Key references provide videotape observer training materials and procedures and a summary of all technical development, reliability and validity evidence, and normative data (N = 1205) for adult populations (ages 18– 99) in mental hospitals and community facilities (covering mentally retarded, alcohol/ substance abuse, acute and chronic mentally ill in all diagnostic categories).

Key References

Paul, G. L. (1987a). *Observational Assessment Instrumentation For Service and Research—The Time-*

Sample Behavioral Checklist: Assessment in Residential Treatment Settings (Part 2). Champaign, IL: Research Press.

Paul, G. L. (1987b). *Observational Assessment Instrumentation For Service and Research—The TSBC/SRIC System Implementation Package: Assessment in Residential Treatment Settings* (Part 5). Champaign, IL: Research Press.

WASHINGTON PSYCHOSOCIAL SEIZURE INVENTORY (WPSI)

Characteristics Assessed

Emotional and interpersonal adjustment and psychosocial functioning. (Also family background, financial status, medical management, intelligence.)

If Unpublished, where Test can be Obtained

Dr. Carl B. Dodrill
Epilepsy Center Za–50
325 Ninth Avenue
Harborview Hospital
Seattle, WA 98104

The test is self-administered.

The test is not computer-scorable and cannot be interpreted by computer.

Key References

Dodrill, C. B., Batzel, L. W., Queissel, H. R., & Temkin, N. R. (1980). An objective method for the assessment of psychological and social problems among epileptics. *Epilepsia, 21,* 123–135.

WAYS OF COPING QUESTIONNAIRE (WCQ)

Characteristics Assessed

Eight basic coping reactions or strategies that may be used in a cross-section of stressful situations.

Publisher

Consulting Psychologists Press
3803 E. Bayshore Road
Palo Alto, CA 94303-9608

The test is self-administered and usually takes about 10 to 12 minutes.
The administration can be delegated to clerical or nursing staff.

The test is not computer-scorable and cannot be interpreted by computer.

Key References

Folkman, S., & Lazarus, R. S. (1988). *Manual for the Ways of Coping questionnaire.* Palo Alto, CA: Consulting Psychologists Press.

Folkman, S., Lazarus, R. S., Dunkel-Schetter, C., DeLongis, A., & Gruen, R. (1986). The dynamics of a stressful encounter. *Journal of Personality and Social Psychology, 50,* 992–1003.

WISCONSIN PERSONALITY DISORDERS INVENTORY

Characteristics Assessed

Personality disorders

If Unpublished, where Test can be Obtained

Dr. Marjorie Klein
Department of Psychiatry
University of Wisconsin Medical School
1300 University Avenue
Madison, WI 53706

The test is self-administered and usually takes about 1 hour.
The administration can be delegated to clerical or nursing staff.

The test is computer-scorable but cannot be interpreted by computer.

Key References

Klein, M. H., Benjamin, L. S., Rosenfeld, R., Treece, L., Husted, J., & Greist, J. H. (1993). The Wisconsin Personality Disorders Inventory: I. Development, reliability, and validity. *Journal of Personality Disorders, 7* (4), 285–303

YALE-BROWN OBSESSIVE COMPULSIVE SCALE (Y-BOCS)

Characteristics Assessed

Clinician-rated measure of the severity of symptoms of obsessive-compulsive disorder. Contains separate subscales for obsessions and compulsions.

If Unpublished, where Test can be Obtained

Wayne K. Goodman
Department of Psychiatry
Yale University School of Medicine
The Connecticut Mental Health Center
34 Park Street
New Haven, CT 06508

The test is not self-administered and usually takes about 20 minutes.
The administration cannot be delegated to clerical or nursing staff.

The test is not computer-scorable and cannot be interpreted by computer.

Key References

Goodman et al. (1989a). The Yale-Brown Obsessive Compulsive Scale. I. Development, use, and reliability. *Archives of General Psychiatry, 46,* 1006–1011.
Goodman et al. (1989b). The Yale-Brown Obsessive Compulsive Scale. II. Validity. *Archives of General Psychiatry, 46,* 1012–1016.

Index